372.86 PAN

1846347

Dynamic Physical Education for Elementary School Children

Dynamic Physical Education for Elementary School Children

FOURTEENTH EDITION

ROBERT P. PANGRAZI
Arizona State University

San Francisco Boston New York
Cape Town Hong Kong London Madrid Mexico City
Montreal Munich Paris Singapore Sydney Tokyo Toronto

Publisher: Daryl Fox
Acquisitions Editor: Deirdre McGill
Development Manager: Claire Brassert
Project Editor: Susan Malloy
Assistant Editor: Christina Pierson
Marketing Manager: Sandy Lindelof
Cover Designer: Yvo Riezebos
Photo Researcher: Brian Donnelly, Cypress Integrated Systems
Manufacturing Buyer: Stacey Weinberger
Design and Project Coordination: Elm Street Publishing Services, Inc.
Production Editor: Steven Anderson
Composition: Thompson Type
Cover Printer: Coral Graphics
Printer and Binder: R.R. Donnelley, Willard

Cover Photo: © BananaStock Ltd.

Photo credits can be found on page 693.

ISBN 0-205-34438-0

Copyright © 2004 Pearson Education, Inc., publishing as Benjamin Cummings, San Francisco, CA 94111. All rights reserved. Printed in the United States of America. This publication is protected by Copyright and permission should be obtained from the publisher prior to any prohibited reproduction, storage in a retrieval system, or transmission in any form or by any means, electronic, mechanical, photocopying, recording, or likewise. For more information regarding permission(s), write to: Pearson Education, Inc., Permissions Department.

www.aw.com/bc

1 2 3 4 5 6 7—DOW—07 06 05 04 03

To my wife Debbie whom I love and respect.

She is not only a valued professional colleague,
but a special friend and companion who has enriched my life.

To my son and daughter, Charles and Connie, and their wonderful families.
I appreciate the joy and love they deliver on a regular basis.

Robert P. Pangrazi

Brief Contents

PART I
Instruction and Program Implementation

PART II
Teaching the Content of Physical Education

Contents

PART II

Teaching the Content of Physical Education 223

SECTION 4
Personal Health Skills 225

SECTION 5
Fundamental Motor Skills 299

Preface

The fourteenth edition of *Dynamic Physical Education for Elementary School Children (DPE)* represents a revision that adds to and updates much of the material in the text. I have worked diligently to keep the same chapter titles to help ease "revision stress." However, having said that, readers should know that there have been many changes based on the input of many reviewers and the evolving nature of the curriculum. The changes have been made to impact current issues in physical education such as inclusion, diversity, and subject matter integration. More information about that is provided in a section that follows.

GENERAL ORGANIZATION OF THE TEXT

The 29 chapters in *DPE* continue to be grouped into two major sections—*Instruction and Program Implementation* and *Teaching the Content of Physical Education.* Part I, *Instruction and Program Implementation,* contains the theory and requisite knowledge a teacher needs to develop a quality program. The chapters in Part I are separated into three sections that help students understand the need for quality physical education programs in schools, how to be a quality instructor, and the keys to program implementation. When combined with the Internet websites included at the end of each chapter, the *Instructor's Resource Manual,* the PowerPoint multimedia slides, and instructional videotapes, college and university instructors have a rich tool chest of ideas for helping pre-service and in-service teachers think, reflect, and improve the act of teaching.

Part I Instruction and Program Implementation

Section 1 Understanding the Need for Physical Education
- Chapter 1 Elementary School Physical Education
- Chapter 2 Teaching Children in the Physical Education Environment

Section 2 The Instructional Process
- Chapter 3 Planning for Quality Instruction
- Chapter 4 Improving Instructional Effectiveness
- Chapter 5 Management and Discipline
- Chapter 6 Evaluation
- Chapter 7 Children with Disabilities

Section 3 Program Implementation
- Chapter 8 Curriculum Development
- Chapter 9 Legal Liability, Supervision, and Safety
- Chapter 10 Facilities, Equipment, and Supplies
- Chapter 11 Interdisciplinary Instruction and Rainy Day Activities

Part II, *Teaching the Content of Physical Education,* is filled with instructional activities. No text on the market offers teachers a greater variety of teacher-tested activities, and the emphasis on this revision has been to add many new activities. This portion of the text is separated into four sections that are filled with activities and strategies designed to help teachers accomplish the content standards of a quality physical education program.

Part II Teaching the Content of Physical Education

Section 4 Personal Health Skills
- Chapter 12 Physical Activity and Fitness
- Chapter 13 Wellness: Developing a Healthy Lifestyle

Section 5 Fundamental Motor Skills
- Chapter 14 Movement Concepts and Themes
- Chapter 15 Fundamental Motor Skills
- Chapter 16 Introductory Activities: Applying Fundamental Motor Skills
- Chapter 17 Manipulative Skills

Section 6 Specialized Motor Skills
- Chapter 18 Body Management Skills
- Chapter 19 Rhythmic Movement Skills
- Chapter 20 Gymnastic Skills
- Chapter 21 Cooperative and Personal Challenge Skills
- Chapter 22 Game Skills

Section 7 Sport Skills
- Chapter 23 Basketball
- Chapter 24 Football
- Chapter 25 Hockey
- Chapter 26 Soccer
- Chapter 27 Softball
- Chapter 28 Track, Field, and Cross-Country Running
- Chapter 29 Volleyball

Section 4 contains many activities and techniques for teaching personal health skills, including methods for teaching students how to develop and maintain an active and healthy lifestyle. Section 5 brings together methods and activities for teaching fundamental motor skills. Movement concepts, fundamental motor skills, and body management skills encompass the majority of content in this section. Now pre-service and in-service teachers can identify activities and strategies that will improve student competencies in this important skill area. Section 6 is designed to improve specialized motor skills among students of diverse backgrounds. Chapters on manipulative skills, rhythmic movement skills, gymnastic skills, personal challenge skills, and game skills give in-depth coverage to the development of a personalized set of specialized skills. Finally, Section 7 focuses on developing sport skills. The chapters contain many skills, drills, and lead-up activities. These chapters use the paradigm of teach the skill properly, practice it in a drill, and apply in a lead-up game that assures success.

As an added organizational aid, each section is color-coded for ease of reference. Each chapter in a section contains a colored tab in the outside margin that corresponds with the color code for that section. This makes it easy to find a particular section quickly.

DPE is written for both classroom teachers and physical education teachers. Material is written and illustrated with many examples that make it easy to understand regardless of the degree of background in physical education. All activities in the text are listed in progression from the easiest activity to the most difficult. This enables teachers to plan a lesson that incorporates proper sequencing of skills. The accompanying text, *Lesson Plans for Dynamic Physical Education for Elementary School Children,* fourteenth edition, organizes the activities listed in *DPE* into a sequential set of lesson plans for an academic year. A new feature of the lesson plan book is the addition of a section that identifies what academic concepts can be taught within a physical education lesson. This makes it easy for the physical educator to show classroom teachers and administrators how physical activities contribute to academic outcomes of the school. Additionally, the content standards that are covered in each lesson plan have been added to the fourteenth edition. The lesson plan book offers three distinct sets of plans for students at differing developmental levels. *DPE* and *Lesson Plans* are used in a large number of schools as the foundation for a curriculum that is supplemented with local district materials and activities.

CONTENT STANDARDS AND COMPONENTS OF A QUALITY PROGRAM

With the age of accountability upon education, it has become vitally important to determine what should be taught and what youngsters should know when they leave the school environment. The American Alliance for Health, Physical Education, Recreation, and Dance (AAHPERD) and the National Association for Sport and Physical Education (NASPE) have done much to make physical educators aware of the need for content standards. Chapter 1 now contains content standards for the *Dynamic Physical Education* program. (A complete listing of the National Content Standards from NASPE are included in the Appendix.) The standards identified in Chapter 1 reflect the development of a program that stresses lifetime activity, competency in a wide variety of physical skills, the need for strong social and personal responsibility skills, and the knowledge needed to maintain personal wellness.

Chapter 1 also sets the tempo for identifying essential components of a quality program. Across the country, a wide variety of differing areas of instructional emphasis characterize physical education programs. Some view these differences as an outcome of diverse and differing points of view while others think all programs should follow one model. My own point of view is that difference is part of the American culture. However, even when large differences exist, similarities mark quality programs. I've outlined what I believe to be the key elements that characterize quality programs. This approach allows programs to have a unique element while maintaining essential components for success.

The inclusion and integration of content standards and essential components are an important feature in this text. A special box appears on the opening page of each chapter that highlights the standards and components relevant to the chapter material. For example, Chapter 12, *Physical Activity and Fitness,* offers activities that help students meet Standard 2. These features are designed to help pre-service and in-service teachers understand *why* they are teaching activities and to assist them in developing quality physical education programs that help children become active for life. Information and instructional activities are included only if they contribute to the standards or essential components found in Chapter 1.

NEW FEATURES

In addition to the information on the Content Standards and Essential Elements, the fourteenth edition of *DPE* reflects a number of other significant changes based on feedback from peer reviewers and users of *DPE* and changes in the field of physical education. This edition of *Dynamic Physical Education for Elementary School Children* provides new teachers with a sound foundation for establishing a well-rounded, comprehensive physical education program.

- Chapter 1 has a new section on justifying a physical education program. This section gives fodder for teachers who need to explain to others what a quality physical education program contributes to the total school program. A new section on content objectives has been added as well.
- Chapter 2 now includes new growth and development charts to reflect the most recent standards for growth. A new section on teaching specialized motor skills has been added along with an updated set of guidelines for safely exercising children.
- In Chapter 3, a new section has been added on reflective teaching. This section offers a strong rationale for reflection and a number of questions to start the process. Developmental levels and how they impact the selection of activities for instruction have been emphasized in this chapter. The *Lesson Plan* book has been more closely allied to the textbook for a seamless integration between the two resources.
- Chapter 5 has new sections on discipline and management. A new section on passive, aggressive, and assertive teachers sets the stage for communicating with students regardless of the style of management used. A new step-by-step approach for establishing a total management and discipline system is now in place in this chapter and makes it much easier for pre-service teachers to implement.
- Chapter 11 has taken a new look at interdisciplinary instruction and rainy day activities. Many new ideas for integrating academic concepts smoothly into a physical education lesson have been added. This chapter sets the stage for the academic integration concepts that have been added to the *Lesson Plan* book.
- A number of new fitness routines have been added to Chapter 12. This gives more variety of activity for children and assures interest in fitness-type activities. A new section has been written that clearly explains the relationship between physical activity and physical fitness. Chapter 13 (wellness) is closely related to the fitness outcomes, and a number of new learning activities have been added to teach wellness concepts. A new section on stress and relaxation has been added along with a new definition of wellness.
- Chapters 16–29 have been enriched with new activities and teaching suggestions. A new section in the rhythms chapter (19) has been added to help teachers modify activities to make them easier to learn and more appropriate for all students. Chapter 21 on relays and challenge skills has a new section on cooperative activities designed to foster teamwork and inclusion. The games chapter (22) contains many new games, and traditional games have been revised to make them more inclusive and cooperative in nature. The sport chapters (23–29) have many new lead-up games. Lead-up games in this text are designed to limit the number of skills youngsters have to apply to be successful. This ensures that, regardless of ability, all students play an important role in quality game play.

QUALITY CONTROL AND FIELD TESTING

A tradition that continues in this edition of *DPE* is to assure that all activities have been field-tested with children. I continue to teach elementary school children and evaluate new activities based in part on student reception and instructional effectiveness. A number of experts have been involved in evaluating and helping with this text to ensure the content is accurate and on the cutting edge. Chapter 19, *Rhythmic Movement Skills,* was enhanced by Jerry Poppen, an expert physical educator; Paul James, Wagon Wheel Records; Dr. Barbara Cusimano, Oregon State University, and Debbie Pangrazi, physical education resource teacher for the Mesa, Arizona, Public Schools. John Spini, current coach of the women's gymnastics team at Arizona State University, evaluated and contributed to Chapter 20, *Gymnastic Skills.* Dr. Carole Casten, CSU, Dominguez Hills, contributed the material for the section on rhythmic gymnastics. Dr. Virginia Atkins Chadwick, Fresno State University, and Dr. Julian Stein, George Mason University, evaluated and contributed to Chapter 7, *Children with Disabilities.* Jim Roberts, a Mesa, Arizona, physical education specialist, designed and field-tested the materials for developing responsible behavior. In addition, the authors are indebted to the Mesa School District elementary school physical education specialists in Mesa, Arizona, who have field-tested the activities and offered numerous suggestions and ideas for improvement. Dr. Steven Hogan, director of physical education and athletics, and Debbie Pangrazi, resource teacher, lead this stellar group of nearly 90 specialists. All of these individuals have unselfishly contributed their energies and insights to assure that quality activities and teaching strategies are part of this textbook. The result of this continued field testing is a book filled with activities, strategies, and techniques that "work."

SUPPLEMENTARY MATERIALS

Available with the fourteenth edition of *Dynamic Physical Education for Elementary School Children* is a complete package of supplements that offer students and instructors alike an integrated and comprehensive set of learning and instructional tools.

Lesson Plans for Dynamic Physical Education has been developed concurrently with the text and offers a broad range of activities and objectives. The lesson plans are presented in three developmental levels, allowing for a greater range of activity and ensuring that presentations are closely aligned to the maturity and experience of students. The plans are filled with activities and outcomes that enable teachers to plan and understand *why* various activities are being taught. Offering a framework for planning comprehensive lessons rather than serving to preempt teachers from planning duties is the major reason for utilizing the lesson plan book. As mentioned above, the lesson plans offer new sections on academic integration and content standards for each of the more than 110 individual lesson plans.

Lecture and Lesson Plan Videos: Two new 30-minute videotapes have been developed for this edition. In one, we discuss the value of a physical education program. In the second, a complete lesson is taught, modeling successful teaching techniques.

PowerPoint® Presentation CD-ROM: New PowerPoint® slides created by Dr. Brett Christie, Sonoma State University, feature lecture outlines, art from the book, and video clips demonstrating teaching techniques and students in action.

The **Instructor's Resource Manual,** by Dr. Carole Casten, CSU, Dominguez Hills, is closely correlated to the text. For each chapter, it provides a chapter summary, desired student outcomes, a discussion of the main concepts of the chapter, ideas for presenting the content, discussion topics, suggested written assignments, and a cooperative learning project.

The **Test Bank,** by Mike Ernst, CSU, Dominguez Hills, is available in printed and computerized format. It offers true/false, multiple-choice, matching, and essay questions for every chapter of the book. Answers and page references are provided for all but the essay questions. The 1500 test items are all included in the computerized test bank. Using this cross-platform CD-ROM, instructors can create tests, edit questions, and add their own material to the existing test bank.

Transparency Acetates: Important concepts and figures from the text are available in an easy-to-use format for lecture presentations.

Companion Website: A new website (www.aw.com/pangrazi) has been developed to complement the text. Features for instructors include PowerPoint® slides. Content for students includes learning objectives, quizzes, and Internet links. New video clips demonstrate actual classroom situations and allow students to observe effective teaching techniques.

Online Courses: In addition to offering Blackboard, we also offer Course Compass™—a nationally hosted online course management system. All CourseCompass™ and Blackboard courses offer pre-loaded content including testing and assessment, Web links, illustrations, and photos. To view a demonstration of any course, go to http://cms.awlonline.com. Visit www.coursecompass.com for a demonstration and more information about CourseCompass™.

ACKNOWLEDGMENTS

Useful textbooks are the result of cohesive teamwork among the publishing company, reviewers, and the author. I am indebted to the professional group at Benjamin Cummings for their major contributions to this text. Deirdre McGill, acquisitions editor, has given ongoing support and encouragement. I am particularly indebted to Susan Malloy, project editor, who coordinated the development and completion of this text with efficiency and thoughtfulness. I also appreciate the efficiency and competency of Brandi Nelson, project editor at Elm Street Publishing Services, who coordinated the production of the text. To these and many other individuals at Benjamin Cummings who go unnamed, please accept a hearty thank-you.

A sincere note of thanks goes to the following reviewers who provided valuable feedback that helped guide the author's efforts throughout the project:

Brett Christie, Sonoma State University; Jenelle N. Gilbert, California State University, Fresno; Rosemary Lassiter, Cleveland State University; John Lisk, University of South Carolina Aiken; Lynette Overby, Michigan State University; Mark A. Rivero, University of Nevada at Las Vegas; Deborah Smith, Clemson University; Eileen C. Sullivan, Boston University; Lucian Taylor, University of Kentucky; Doris L. Terrell, Clark Atlanta University; Jane Vallentyne, University of Alberta; and Louisa Webb, San Francisco State University.

PART I

Instruction and Program Implementation

SECTION 1 Understanding the Need for Physical Education

SECTION 2 The Instructional Process

SECTION 3 Program Implementation

SECTION 1

Understanding the Need for Physical Education

CHAPTER 1

Elementary School Physical Education

CHAPTER 2

Teaching Children in the Physical Education Environment

CHAPTER 1

Elementary School Physical Education

ESSENTIAL COMPONENTS

I	**Organized around content standards**
II	**Student-centered and developmentally appropriate**
III	**Physical activity and motor skill development form the core of the program**
IV	Teaches management skills and self-discipline
V	Promotes inclusion of all students
VI	Focuses on process over product
VII	Promotes lifetime personal health and wellness
VIII	Teaches cooperation and responsibility and promotes sensitivity to diversity

PHYSICAL EDUCATION STANDARDS

1	Students are able to move competently using a variety of fundamental and specialized motor skills.
2	Students can monitor and maintain a health-enhancing level of physical fitness.
3	Students are able to apply movement concepts and basic mechanics of skill performance when learning and refining motor skills.
4	Students comprehend the basic principles of wellness and are able to apply concepts that enable them to make meaningful decisions that positively impact their health and wellness.
5	Students participate in a wide variety of physical activities and learn how to maintain a personalized active lifestyle.
6	Students demonstrate empathy, understanding, and respect for the numerous differences exhibited by people in an activity setting.
7	Students exhibit responsible and self-directed behaviors that lead to positive social interactions in physical activity.

SUMMARY

Physical education is that phase of the general educational program that contributes to the total growth and development of each child, primarily through movement experiences. Program objectives provide the framework and direction for the physical education curriculum. Systematic and properly taught physical education can help achieve the major content standards, including movement competence, maintaining physical fitness, learning personal health and wellness skills, applying movement concepts and skill mechanics, developing lifetime activity skills, and demonstrating positive social skills. Modern programs of physical education have been influenced by cultural and educational factors related to games, sports, fitness, educational movement, perceptual-motor competency, federal mandates, value and attitude development, the Surgeon General's report, and the nationwide emphasis on physical activity.

OUTCOMES

- Justify the need for a quality physical education program in the elementary school setting based on the health benefits it can offer children.
- Cite the content standards of elementary physical education.
- List program objectives and recognize the distinctive contributions of physical education.
- Describe the educational reasons for including physical education as part of the elementary school experience.
- Define physical education and its role in the elementary school experience.
- Articulate how various pedagogical influences changed the course of elementary school physical education programs.
- Identify essential components of a quality physical education program.
- Verbally portray how a variety of societal influences and federal mandates impacted elementary school physical education.

WHAT IS PHYSICAL EDUCATION?

Physical education means many things to many people. Physical education professionals often describe it as essential subject matter dedicated to learning in the psychomotor domain and committed to developing lifetime physical activity patterns. However, some individuals mistakenly consider physical education to be the same as athletics or competitive sports. Some perceive physical education to be recess or free-time play. Suffice it to say that while some view it as a meaningful subject matter area, others report having less than satisfactory physical education experiences, if they had physical education at all.

So, what is physical education? It is part of the total educational program that contributes, primarily through movement experiences, to the total growth and development of all children. *Physical education* is defined as education through movement. It is an instructional program that gives attention to all learning domains: psychomotor, cognitive, and affective. No other area of the curriculum is designed to help children learn motor and lifetime activity skills. This makes physical education a necessary component of the total school curriculum. It is not enough to educate children academically; they must also be educated physically. Too often, physical educators try to do all things for their students including improving their academic skills. Certainly, whenever possible, it is important to do so. However, physical education programs should always place the majority of emphasis on learning physical skills. If students, particularly the unskilled, don't receive quality instruction in physical education, there is little opportunity for them to learn skills as adults. Unskilled youngsters often have little opportunity to learn new skills as compared to those who are skilled. For example, there are all types of opportunities for skilled youngsters to participate in little league, gymnastics clubs, and sport clubs. However, for the unskilled youngster, physical education may be the only place that offers an option to learn new skills. Therefore, a strong physical education program places emphasis on helping all youngsters succeed regardless of ability or skill level.

THE CURRENT STATUS OF PHYSICAL EDUCATION IN THE UNITED STATES

The differences in perceptions of physical education are no doubt a result of the wide variety of experiences offered under the physical education umbrella. Though professionals consider true physical education to be nothing less than a quality instructional program conducted by a physical education specialist, for many this is not the actual experience. Most states and districts require physical education in their schools. However, the SHPPS 2000 report shows that when physical education requirements by grade are analyzed carefully, each grade shows a decline from about 50 percent in grades 1–5 to about 5 percent in grade 12 (Burgeson et al., 2001). Many states and schools allow exemptions from physical education classes so that the actual percentage of kids receiving intruction is even less. Few children in America receive daily physical education instruction. Only about 8 percent of elementary schools provide daily physical education for their students. When physical education is taught in these grade levels, a "specialist" often teaches it, though many people having this designation do not hold valid credentials. In fact, only 17 percent of states require elementary level physical education teachers to be certified in physical education (U.S. Department of Health and Human Services, 1994). Classroom teachers often teach physical education and because these teachers have wide ranges of interests and qualifications, instruction often varies dramatically among schools.

A common picture of elementary school physical education might look something like this. Youngsters go to school and receive about 25 hours of overall instruction weekly. Out of the 25 hours, physical education may be scheduled for 30 to 60 minutes a week in a school that cares about physical education. This amounts to 2 to 4 percent of the total instructional time devoted to the health and wellness of students. Instruction may be carried out by a physical education specialist, classroom teacher, or paraprofessional. Often, up to 4 classes are sent to physical education at once so that the student to teacher ratio is 120 to 1 with one or two paraprofessionals sent to help. Small wonder that obesity and hypokinetic disease has become rampant throughout the United States. Many of America's schools do not value physical education and do little to ensure that all children receive daily physical education instruction as a minimum.

THE NEED FOR PHYSICAL EDUCATION

During the past decade, the interest in the benefits derived from an active lifestyle has spawned a wide assortment of health clubs, a vast array of books and magazines concerning exercise and fitness, a weekly smorgasbord of distance runs and triathlons, streamlined exercise equipment, and apparel for virtually any type of physical activity. Unfortunately, most of this interest and lifestyle change has occurred among middle- and upper-class Americans. Little change in activity patterns has occurred in lower-middle- and lower-class families.

The nation's enthusiasm for physical activity has not trickled down to elementary school youngsters. A statement issued by the American Academy of Pediatrics (1991) reported that children from the ages of 2 to 12 watch about 25 hours of television per week, more time than they spend in school receiving instruction. Health goals for the nation for the year 2010 (U.S. Department of Health and Human Services [USDHHS], 2000) are based on increasing daily levels of physical activity. Many of the goals directly target schools, or programs that can take place within the school setting. These goals place emphasis on reducing inactivity and increasing light to moderate physical activity. The need is clear: implement physical education programs to teach youngsters how to live an active and healthy lifestyle. What evidence is available that shows the benefits of a quality physical education program?

1. The percentage of youth who are overweight has more than tripled in the past 30 years (USDHHS, 2002). A recent study suggested that the prevalence of obesity is more strongly related to decreases in energy expenditure than to increases in energy intake (Jebb & Moore, 1999). The school environment discourages physical activity. Students are asked to move slowly, sit still, and walk everywhere they go, which results in a decrease in energy expenditure. A 30-minute physical education class can offer 1200 to 2000 steps of moderate to vigorous physical activity to counteract the effects of an inactive day (Beighle & Pangrazi, 2000). This would be a substantial contribution to the daily energy expenditure of students.
2. A positive experience in physical education classes will encourage youngsters to be active as adults. In a survey sponsored by the Sporting Goods Manufacturers Association (2000), 60 percent of respondents ages 18–34 reported that a positive experience in physical education classes encouraged them to be active in later life. On the other hand, of those respondents who said they were sedentary, only 10 percent said their physical education classes encouraged them to be active.
3. Overweight children grow into overweight adults. Studies (Guo et al., 1994; Must et al., 1992) show that adolescent weight is a good predictor of adult obesity. Since a quality program encourages active behavior, it makes sense that a program be in place to help youngsters understand the importance of proper weight management.
4. A quality physical education program educates youngsters physically but does not detract from the academic performance of the school. An argument often used is that spending time on physical education will lower the academic performance of students because they have less time to study and learn. To the contrary, studies have show that students who spend time in physical education classes do equally well or better in academic classes. Two major studies that looked at this issue are the Three Rivers Study (Trudeau et al., 1998) and a SPARK related activity program study (Sallis et al., 1999). In both cases, students received the health benefits of physical education without any negative impact on their academic performance.
5. Physical education gives students the skills they need to be active as adults. One commodity that youngsters have in contrast to adults is the time to practice and learn new skills. Few adults learn an entire new set of physical skills. More often than not, they practice and enhance skills they have learned earlier in childhood. Since many adults like to participate in activities that require a requisite skill level (i.e., golf, tennis, racquet ball, etc.), learning such skills during their school years makes it more likely they will feel able and competent to participate in later life.
6. Physical activity (which most often occurs in physical education classes) provides immediate and short-term health benefits for children (Bar-Or, 1995). For obese children, increased physical activity results in a reduction of the percentage of body fat. Additionally, increased activity reduces blood pressure and improves the blood lipid profile for high health-risk children. Finally, there is evidence to show that weight bearing activities performed during the school years offer bone mineral density benefits that carry over into adulthood (Bailey et al., 1996).
7. Active children become active adults. Telama et al. (1997) looked at retrospective and longitudinal tracking studies and concluded that the results "indicate that physical activity and sport participation in childhood and adolescence represent a significant prediction for physical activity in adulthood." The relationship is low but still indicates that activity during youth has an impact on adult activity levels. Another study (Raitakari et al., 1994) showed how strongly inactivity patterns track. In that study, the probability of an inactive 12-year-old remaining sedentary at age 18 years was 51–63 percent for girls and 54–61 percent for boys. This clearly delineates the legacy given to youth when we place them in an inactive school environment.

THE EVOLUTION OF ELEMENTARY SCHOOL PHYSICAL EDUCATION

A number of concerns, historical events, and pedagogical influences have significantly impacted elementary school physical education programs. Often these programs are created as responses to events that are publicized by the press and other interested parties. The many changes that have occurred in elementary school physical education programming clearly point out how the public's needs and concerns shape the direction of U.S. education.

The German and Swedish Influence

During the nineteenth century, in both Germany and Sweden, physical education systems that centered on body development were established in the schools. Around the middle of the century, German and Swedish immigrants to the United States introduced these concepts of physical education. The German system favored a gymnastic approach and required a good deal of equipment and special teachers. The Swedish system incorporated an exercise program in the activity presentations. The physical education program in many of the schools that adopted this system consisted of a series of structured exercises that children could perform in the classroom. The need for equipment and gymnasiums posed problems for the schools that followed these systems, and many economy-minded citizens questioned the programs. A combination of games and calisthenics evolved and became the first scheduled physical education activity offered in some U.S. schools. The Swedish system was structured and formal and often not suited to the needs of elementary school children.

The Emphasis on Games and Sports

When about one-third of the American men drafted in World War I were rejected as physically unfit for military service, the result was a new demand for physical education in the schools. State educational authorities legislated minimum weekly time requirements for physical activity in school programs. In many states, these laws established physical education as part of the school curriculum. The laws were, however, quantitative in nature, and little attention was given to program quality.

Training programs designed for soldiers during World War I placed an emphasis on games and sports and proved more effective than strict calisthenics. This shift to the use of games and sports for physical development spawned school programs with similar emphasis. John Dewey, professor of philosophy at Columbia University, had a profound impact on educational theory during the mid twentieth century. Since two of Dewey's cardinal aims of education stressed attention to physical activities, the teaching of games and sports in schools received impetus. These aims, the promotion of health and the worthy use of leisure time, became school curricular responsibilities. The school was deemed responsible for molding social change, and a high value was placed on games and sports.

Programs stressing sports and games primarily appeared in the secondary schools. Elementary school programs were merely diluted models of these secondary programs; they literally could have been described by answering the question, "What games are we going to play today?" During the Great Depression, equipment was difficult to secure, and physical education teachers were almost nonexistent. Physical education was relegated to a minor role, and in many schools was eliminated entirely.

During World War II, many new training programs for special groups appeared. Research proved the efficacy of physical fitness development, hospital reconditioning programs, and other innovative approaches. An improvement in the quality of physical education programs might have been expected after the war, but unfortunately, little positive effect trickled down to elementary school programs.

National Concern about Physical Fitness

A renewed emphasis on fitness occurred in the 1950s, following the publication of comparative studies of fitness levels of U.S. and European children, which were based on the Kraus-Weber tests. A study by Dr. Hans Kraus (1954), comparing strength and flexibility measurements of 4,000 New York–area schoolchildren with a comparable sample of Central European children, had far-reaching results. The press became concerned about the comparative weakness of U.S. children, and, as a consequence of this publicity, the fitness movement was born. One result of the uproar was the establishment of the President's Council on Physical Fitness and Sports, an agency established to promote physical fitness, not only among schoolchildren but also among citizens of all ages. Recently, the Council has begun to focus on increasing the activity of youngsters rather than just promoting fitness. This emphasis is manifested in a forthcoming award program for individuals who participate in regular physical activity and show the ability to maintain a physical activity regimen over an extended period of time.

Pedagogical Influences

Changes in physical education can be implemented from within the profession by teachers and professionals who see a need for different instructional methods and programs. The changes are often stimulated by dissatisfaction with the status quo and a desire to make physical education a more "needed" part of the school curriculum. The following are some of the major approaches that have influenced the course of elementary school physical education.

Movement Education

Movement education originated in England and was incorporated into U.S. programs during the late 1960s. To some degree, it was a revolt against structured fitness programs, which included calisthenics presented in a formal, command style. The demanding fitness standards advocated by the President's Council led some teachers to teach for fitness outcomes rather than to present a balanced physical education program that also taught skills and concepts. This practice created a backlash among some physical educators, who felt that creativity, exploration, and cognition should also be focal points of the profession.

Movement education programs shifted some of the responsibility for learning to children. The methodology featured problem solving and an exploratory approach. Adopting movement education led to the rejection of physical fitness–oriented activities, especially calisthenics, which were labeled as *training* and not education. Controversy arose regarding the application of movement principles to the teaching of specific skills, particularly athletic skills. There was a tendency to apply the exploration methodology to all phases of instruction without examining the effectiveness of such practices. Regardless of the questions raised, movement education resulted in better teaching methodology and increased emphasis on instruction focused on the individual. In addition, movement education offered an opportunity for diversity of movement through creative instructional methods and allowed students of all ability levels to find success.

Perceptual-Motor Programs

The focus of perceptual-motor programs was corrective in nature and attempted to remedy learning difficulties attributed to a breakdown in perceptual-motor development. Theorists held that children progressed through growth and developmental stages from head to foot (cephalocaudally) and from the center of the body outward (proximodistally) in an orderly fashion. When disruptions, lags, or omissions occurred in this process, certain underlying perceptual-motor bases failed to develop fully and impaired the child's ability to function correctly in both the physical and the academic setting.

Perceptual-motor programs flourished because of concern for slow academic learners, sometimes called *slow* or *delayed* learners. Some children identified as academically subpar demonstrated motor problems involving such movement factors as coordination, balance and postural control, image of the body and its parts, and relationships involving time and space. Perceptual-motor programs attempted to remediate these shortcomings and gave physical education teachers hope that their profession would be viewed as an integral part of a child's academic success. Unfortunately, when researchers examined the effectiveness of such programs, it was apparent that perceptual-motor activities did not improve academic achievement. Today, few perceptual-motor programs designed to replace physical education programs exist. However, the contribution of perceptual-motor programs in today's physical education programs is the integration of perceptual-motor principles into skill-learning sequences (such as using both sides of the body, practicing balance skills, and so forth).

Conceptual Learning

Conceptual understanding (that is, the application of abstract ideas drawn from experience) plays an important part in physical education. In the process of movement, children learn to distinguish between near and far, strong and weak, light and heavy, and high and low. Physical education gives children an opportunity to experiment with and establish an understanding of such movement concepts.

An example of a conceptual approach to physical education is the *Fitness for Life* program by Corbin and Lindsey (2002). Students spend time receiving information in a lecture situation and then utilize the information on themselves or on peers in a laboratory (physical education) setting. Emphasis is placed on information, appraisal procedures, and program planning. Students are expected to understand the "how, what, and why" of physical activity and exercise. They learn to use diagnostic tests in areas such as cardiovascular endurance, muscular strength and endurance, flexibility, body composition, and motor ability.

Conceptual learning is an important part of the physical education program. However, some teachers believe that solely using an academic approach focused on knowledge and cognitive growth instead of physical skills and activity will place physical education on a par with other academic areas. Others believe that when student knowledge is increased, attitudes and behaviors will change, causing physical activity to be incorporated into the student's lifestyle. Neither of these beliefs have been proven to date. Increasing a person's knowledge does not ensure a change in behavior any more than reading and gaining knowledge about how to play tennis will make a skilled tennis player. Students must experience and learn physical skills and understand the conceptual components. Physical activity is, and must remain, the core component of physical education because it is the only place in the school setting where physical skills are taught and learned.

Value and Attitude Development (Affective Domain Learning)

During the 1990s, the American public expressed concern about the lack of moral values among its youth. The political views of a number of U.S. leaders emphasizing law and order have created greater pressure on the schools to teach morals and values. In an annual Gallup Poll that reviews the public's attitudes toward schools, lack of discipline often heads the list of major problems. Discipline problems also rank as one of the major concerns of teachers. There is growing pressure on the schools to teach values, responsibility skills, and moral education.

Values, feelings, beliefs, and judgments have received more attention in the schools and in physical education classes in particular. Public concern about crime among professional athletes has also increased the demand from parents for help with responsibility training. Such issues as alcohol and substance abuse, sex education, and AIDS awareness are being presented in the elementary school years in an attempt to prevent students from developing problems later in life. Awareness programs are becoming more common in schools with physical educators who are often called on to conduct appropriate district-approved programs.

Federal Mandates

From time to time, concerns of citizens about their children have led to legislation that has impacted physical education curriculum and instruction. Two laws, in particular, continue to impact physical education programs throughout the United States.

Title IX: Equal Opportunity for the Sexes

Title IX of the Educational Amendments Act of 1972 has had a significant impact on most secondary school physical education programs. Title IX has had a lesser effect on elementary school physical education because the majority of programs at this level have long been coeducational. Title IX rules out separation of sexes and calls for all offerings to be coeducational. The law is based on the principle that school activities and programs are of equal value for both sexes and that students should not be denied access to participation on the basis of gender. Legal ramifications have forced schools to provide equal access to physical education activities for both boys and girls. Organizing separate competitions for the sexes is permissible, provided that mixed participation in an activity can be determined to be hazardous. In principle, the law also dictates that the most qualified teacher, regardless of gender, provides instruction.

Title IX also relates to the elimination of sexism and sex-role typing. Human needs and opportunities must be given precedence over traditional sexual stereotypes of masculinity and femininity. Appreciation for the physical abilities of the opposite sex is learned at an early age. Segregating children by sex in elementary school physical education classes is indefensible because it takes away the opportunity to learn that gender differences are small in the desire to perform well athletically.

PL 94-142: Equal Rights for Students with Disabilities

Public Law 94-142 has given hope for a full education to the 3.5 to 4 million youngsters in the United States with disabilities. This federal law mandates that all youngsters have the right to a free and public education and must be educated in the least restrictive educational environment possible. No longer can children with disabilities be assigned to segregated classes or schools unless a separate environment is determined by due process to be in the child's best interest. A 1990 amendment, Public Law 101-476 (also known as IDEA—Individuals with Disabilities Education Act), continues with the objective of providing handicapped individuals with the least restrictive environment in the school setting.

Mainstreaming is a term used to identify the practice of placing children with disabilities in classrooms with able children. These laws have resulted in degrees of mainstreaming (full or partial), allowing many children with disabilities to participate in regular physical education classes. The law, which is considered to be commendable and morally sound, often necessitates changing the structure and educational procedures of the school as well as the viewpoints and attitudes of school personnel. Many teachers do not have the educational background, the experience, or the inclination to handle children with disabilities in addition to children without disabilities. The answer is not to ignore the problem but to provide teachers with knowledge and constructive approaches that allow them to function successfully with children who have disabilities. If children with disabilities are to function in society when they become adults, they deserve and need the opportunity to participate with able youngsters.

In addition to the mainstreaming of students in regular education classes, the law mandates the preparation of a specific learning program for each disabled student, called an *individualized educational program* (IEP). Establishing the child's due process committee, developing the IEP, and monitoring that program in the best interest of the student is a process of considerable challenge and magnitude. IEPs can be used for able children as well, and help to make education more personal and individual.

Contemporary Social Influences

A Nationwide Concern for Health and Wellness

The Surgeon General's Report on Physical Activity and Health (1996) outlined clearly the health benefits of physical activity for all ages. The contributions of physical activity to health and wellness have been widely disseminated and efforts have been undertaken to promote physical activity among all segments of the population. Today's educators are centering increased attention on integrating physical activity into a healthful living style. This focus is pushing physical educators to develop programs that teach more than fitness and skill activities. Wellness is a broader concept than physical fitness. It is a dynamic state of well-being that implies living fully and deriving the most from life.

Eating wisely, controlling weight, dealing with tension, understanding body (muscular) movement, getting sufficient rest and sleep, controlling posture, keeping in shape, and dealing with forthcoming challenges (such as potential use of alcohol and drugs, and the danger of contracting AIDS or other infectious diseases) impact wellness. For example, the problem of weight control merits special attention in the elementary school. Unless lifestyle is changed at an early age, obese children usually become obese adults. Recent research shows that activity and inactivity track into adulthood, meaning that active children become active adults (Raitakari et al., 1994).

Human wellness is an area where physical education can have a lifelong impact on students. It is effectively presented when classroom teachers and physical education specialists work together. Identifying wellness as a common goal for all schoolchildren makes physical education an integral and vital part of the total school curriculum. Wellness instruction teaches concepts that help students develop and maintain an active lifestyle. Understanding the principles of fitness, the importance of daily physical activity, and the benefits of physical fitness increases the odds that students will stay active throughout their lives (Dale, Corbin, and Cuddihy, 1998).

A Demand for "Back-to-Basics" Schools

Basic schools were designed as a response to a perceived decline in academic performance. Basic schools stress discipline and cognitive learning, often at the expense of the arts and physical education. To increase academic rigor, the school day is lengthened and physical education and performing arts dropped to allow more time for "the 3 Rs." A demand for uninterrupted academic time often makes it impossible to schedule physical education time for youngsters. To combat this trend, physical education programs must demonstrate that they are instructional in nature, of high quality, and make unique contributions to the school curriculum. In 1983, the National Commission on Excellence in Education presented a critical review of the total process of U.S. education in *A Nation at Risk* (Gardner, 1983). In the report, physical education was not included as part of a basic education. Whether the omission was deliberate or happenstance is open to question. In the past, other deliberations and reports have included physical education as a part of basic instruction. Is it possible that the school experiences of commission members in the physical education area were largely of an unorganized fun-and-games approach, and that they perceived little need for such recreation? This attitude illustrates the importance of educating the public about the need for a quality physical education program in the quest to develop well-rounded students.

To conform to the concept of basic education, this text delineates fundamental content standards to be accomplished in physical education. Content standards are written in measurable terms so teachers and schools are held accountable for helping students reach a predetermined level of achievement. Even though accountability is a desirable concept, some abuse can occur when teachers are rewarded based solely on student achievement levels. Some teachers may turn to the use of memorization, drill, and rote learning and may encourage practice solely in areas in which students will be tested. In physical education, this often means teaching only fitness test activities so students score well on a mandated physical fitness test. This approach can result in an inferior and narrow program that satisfies the accountability concerns of the school, but does little to give students a well-rounded education.

A National Focus on Physical Activity

The document entitled *Healthy People 2000: National Health Promotion and Disease Objectives* (U.S. Public Health Service, 1990) focused on the role of physical activity in improving the health of all Americans. A majority of the 300 physical activity target goals are specifically directed toward improving the health status of U.S. children and youth. The goals focus on decreasing health risks and emphasizing preventative approaches to a healthy lifestyle. Several of the objectives in the physical activity area emphasize an increase in the amount of light to moderate activity (that is, activity that is similar in intensity to brisk walking) among children age 6 and older. For years, emphasis was placed on fitness goals and high-intensity activity. The *Healthy People* reports place more emphasis on moderate and regular physical activity. Much of the emphasis on improving the health status of youth is accomplished through a quality physical education program. The focus of the document is on the health benefits of exercise and activity for all students as contrasted to systems that only reward students who are physically gifted.

A successor to *Healthy People 2000* is *Healthy People 2010* (USDHHS, 2000). Two major goals addressed in this document are to: (1) increase the years of healthy life; and (2) eliminate health disparities. These major goals are supported with enabling goals concerned with promoting healthy behaviors, protecting health, achieving access to quality health care, and strengthening community prevention. The objectives are grouped into a number of focus areas similar to *Healthy People 2000*. New focus areas include disability, low income, race and ethnicity, chronic diseases, and public health infrastructure.

The release of the *Surgeon General's Report on Physical Activity and Health* (USDHHS, 1996) documented many health benefits achieved through moderate and regular activity. The report showed that people of all ages, both male and female, benefit from regular physical activity. Never before has a body of research been compiled to show the strong need for activity and fitness in the lives of youth. Activity programs are an absolute requisite for healthy youngsters.

THE CONTENT OF PHYSICAL EDUCATION

Whether speaking of academic class settings or physical education, a key to providing proper education includes following agreed-upon guidelines, or standards, that have been shown to ensure that children obtain the right kind of education. Content standards are the framework of a program; they determine the focus and direction of instruction. Standards specify the content of the program, what students should know and be able to perform. Standards express what knowledge students should possess and how they should demonstrate that knowledge when they exit a developmental level. The establishment of standards can make a significant contribution to the overall goal of school and U.S. society: the development of a well-rounded individual capable of contributing to a democratic society. Quality programs are driven by standards that move children toward high-level achievement.

Physical education content standards are taught nowhere else in the school curriculum. Should these standards not be accomplished in physical education classes, children will leave school without a well-developed set of physical skills. Over the past 10 years professionals have worked to identify a set of standards that give direction to physical education. One of the first works was a set of outcomes published in a booklet entitled *Outcomes of Quality Physical Education Programs* (1992b). A more recent publication by the National Association for Sport and Physical Education (NASPE), *Moving into the Future* (1995), moves beyond outcomes and delineates content standards for physical education. A positive result of efforts to identify standards is that there is general agreement among most professionals about what a physical education program should accomplish. NASPE identified seven major content standards for physical education that provide a basis for describing a physically educated person. Generally experts agree on the major content of the standards that constitute categories of emphasis for physical education instruction. Many school districts have developed similar sets of standards that allow room for program individuality.

The standards not only give direction to instruction but also form the framework for assessment and accountability in the program. A recent publication edited by Chepko and Arnold (2000) offers a wide range of strategies for assessing progress toward written standards. Some of the strategies recommended in the booklet are teacher observation, written tests, student logs, student projects, student journals, and class projects. The assessment strategies show teachers examples of many forms of assessment, with the expectation that individual teachers will modify and select assessment tools that are meaningful in their particular settings.

CONTENT STANDARDS FOR DYNAMIC PHYSICAL EDUCATION

In the following section, content standards for the *Dynamic Physical Education for Elementary School Children* program are delineated. The standards offer two levels of expected learning; a set of standards for children at developmental level I (see page 50 for an indepth discussion of developmental levels) and a set for youth at developmental levels II and III (grades 3–6). Following each standard is a detailed explanation and references to chapters in this text that offer instructional activities and strategies.

Standard 1: Students are able to move competently using a variety of fundamental and specialized motor skills.

Developmental Level I (grades K–2) students will be able to:

a. Apply movement concepts such as body and space awareness, relationships, and qualities of movement to a variety of locomotor and body management skills
b. Move efficiently using a variety of locomotor skills such as walking, running, skipping, and hopping
c. Combine locomotor and nonlocomotor skills into movement themes, for example, supporting body weight, bridges, and receiving and transferring weight
d. Perform body management skills on the floor and on apparatus including benches, balance beams, individual mats, and jumping boxes
e. Use a variety of manipulative skills such as tossing, throwing, catching, and kicking
f. Move rhythmically in a variety of settings including fundamental rhythms, creative rhythms, and simple folk dances

g. Perform simple gymnastic skills such as animal walks, body rolling, simple balances, and inverted balances
h. Use a variety of locomotor skills in low-organized game settings such as running, dodging, evading, and stopping

Developmental Levels II and III (grades 3–6) students will be able to:

a. Perform specialized sport skills with mature form such as throwing, catching, dribbling with foot and hand, kicking and striking, batting, punting, and passing
b. Use sport skills in a variety of activities such as volleyball pass, basketball dribble, and batting a softball
c. Perform a wide variety of gymnastic skills including tumbling, inverted balances, individual stunts, and partner stunts
d. Perform body management skills on a variety of apparatus including benches, balance beams, and climbing ropes
e. Move rhythmically in a variety of settings including folk, square, and line dances, rope jumping, and rhythmic gymnastics
f. Apply a wide variety of locomotor and manipulative game skills in low-organized game settings
g. Incorporate specialized sport skills in a variety of sport lead-up games

All people want to be skilled and competent performers. The elementary school years are an excellent time to teach motor skills because children have the time and predisposition to learn. The types and range of skills presented in physical education should be unlimited; youngsters need the opportunity to encounter and learn as many different physical skills as possible. Because youngsters vary in genetic endowment and interest, they should have the opportunity to learn about their personal abilities in many types of skills and settings. Major areas of movement competence and motor skill development are described next.

Movement Concepts Skills

Youngsters need to learn about the classification of movement concepts (Chapter 14), which includes body and space awareness, qualities of movement, and relationships. It is not enough to learn only skills; youngsters need to perform these skills in a variety of settings. This standard ensures children will be taught how movement concepts are classified. This standard is designed to give children an increased awareness and understanding of the body as a vehicle for movement, and for the acquisition of a personal vocabulary of movement skills.

Fundamental Motor Skills

Fundamental skills enhance the quality of life. This group of skills is sometimes labeled basic or functional skills. The designation *fundamental skills* is used because the skills are requisite for children to function fully in the environment. Fundamental skills are divided into three categories: locomotor, nonlocomotor, and manipulative skills.

Locomotor Skills. Locomotor skills (Chapter 15) are used to move the body from one place to another or to project the body upward, as in jumping and hopping. These skills also include walking, running, skipping, leaping, sliding, and galloping.

Nonlocomotor Skills. Nonlocomotor skills (Chapter 15) are performed in place, without appreciable spatial movement. These skills are not as well defined as locomotor skills. They include bending and stretching, pushing and pulling, balancing, rolling, curling, twisting, turning, and bouncing.

Manipulative Skills. Manipulative skills (Chapter 16) are developed through handling some type of object. Most of these skills involve the hands and feet, but other parts of the body can also be used. Manipulation of objects leads to better hand-eye and foot-eye coordination, which is particularly important for tracking items in space. Manipulative skills form the basis of many game skills. Propulsion (throwing, striking, striking with an implement, kicking) and reception (catching) of objects are important skills that can be taught by using beanbags and various balls. Rebounding or redirecting an object in flight (such as a volleyball) is another useful manipulative skill. Continuous control of an object, such as a wand or a hoop, is also a manipulative activity.

Specialized Motor Skills

Specialized skills are used in various sports and other areas of physical education, including apparatus activities, tumbling, dance, and specific games. Specialized skills receive increased emphasis beginning with developmental level II activities. In developing specialized skills, progression is attained through planned instruction and drills. Many of these skills have critical points of technique, and teaching emphasizes correct performance.

Body Management Skills. Efficient movement of the body (Chapter 18) demands integration of a number of physical traits, including agility, balance, flexibility, and coordination. In addition, youngsters need to develop an understanding of how to control their bodies while on large apparatus, such as beams, benches, and jumping boxes.

FIGURE 1.1 Developing manipulative skills.

Rhythmic Movement Skills. Individuals who excel in movement activities possess a strong sense of rhythmic ability. Rhythmic movement (Chapter 19) involves motion with a regular and predictable pattern. The aptitude to move rhythmically is basic to skill performance in all areas. A rhythmic program that includes dance, rope jumping, and rhythmic gymnastics offers a variety of activities to help attain this objective. Early experiences center on functional and creative movement forms. Instruction begins with and capitalizes on locomotor skills that children already possess: walking, running, hopping, and jumping. Rhythmic activities provide a vehicle for expressive movement.

Gymnastic Skills. Gymnastic activities (Chapter 20) make a significant contribution to the overall physical education experience for children in elementary schools. Gymnastic activities develop body management skills without the need for equipment and apparatus. Flexibility, agility, balance, strength, and body control are outcomes that are enhanced through participation in gymnastics. Basic gymnastic skills such as body rolling, balance skills, inverted balances, and tumbling skills are learned in a safe and progressive manner.

FIGURE 1.2 Learning body management skills.

Game Skills. Games (Chapter 22) are a laboratory where children can apply newly learned skills in a meaningful way. Many games develop large-muscle groups and enhance the ability to run, dodge, start, and stop under control while sharing space with others. Through games, children experience success and accomplishment. Social objectives touched through games are the development of interpersonal skills, acceptance of rule parameters, and a better understanding of oneself in a competitive and cooperative situation.

Sport Skills. Sport skills (Chapters 23–29) are learned in a context of application, using an approach of teaching skills, drills, and lead-up activities. Students learn the basic skills and then practice them doing different drills. After the skills have been learned and practiced, they are applied in lead-up activities. Lead-up activities reduce the number of skills youngsters have to use to be successful, therefore increasing their chance for successful participation. Sport skills involve proper techniques so the cognitive aspect of learning is important as well.

Standard 2: Students can monitor and maintain a health-enhancing level of physical fitness.

Developmental Level I (grades K–2) students will be able to:

a. Participate daily in at least 60 minutes of physical activity in and out of the school environment
b. Monitor the basic physiological changes that occur when being active (increased rate of breathing, increased heart rate, and perspiration)
c. Participate in activities that develop muscular strength and endurance (for example, climbing ropes, hanging activities, and supporting the body weight with arms and hands)
d. Perform a variety of flexibility activities
e. Identify how personal body composition and different body types impact physical performance

Developmental Levels II and III (grades 3–6) students will be able to:

a. Participate daily in at least 60 minutes of moderate to vigorous physical activity in and out of the school environment

b. Engage in a variety of activities that develop muscular strength ranging from exercises to climbing
c. Perform activities that increase and maintain flexibility
d. Know basic elements of safe participation in activity (including safe exercises, over training, muscle soreness, and inherent risk of activities)
e. Monitor the intensity of exercise by counting heart and breathing rates
f. Understand that all health related fitness components (body composition, muscular strength and endurance, flexibility, and cardiorespiratory endurance) need to be given attention for total physical fitness
g. Evaluate personal health related physical fitness and interpret the meaning of the results
h. Understand the basic principles of training such as frequency, intensity, and time

Physical fitness instruction (Chapter 12) concentrates on the process of participating in daily physical activity rather than being concerned about the product of fitness (how many repetitions, how fast, or how far). Giving students an opportunity to offer input about their fitness program and make personal activity choices prepares them for a lifetime of activity. When students accept responsibility for participating in regular activity, fitness is an authentic learning experience that may last a lifetime. Positive experiences in physical activity are a must. Meeting this standard means helping students develop positive attitudes that carry over into adulthood. What is gained if students develop high physical fitness levels in the elementary school years but leave school with a strong dislike of physical activity?

A portion of each class period should be allotted to learning and experiencing fitness. It is not enough to learn the facts of fitness; there must be a participatory experience in the elementary school years. This is not to say that knowledge is unimportant, but that it is not enough. Many people know the facts of fitness but do not stay active because they have not learned the activity habit. Students must participate in physical fitness activity; the best way to learn the amount of effort necessary to maintain personal fitness is to experience it. Too often, fitness has been seen solely as an aerobic experience. Today, it is clear that aerobics are important, but maintenance of strength and flexibility is equally vital. Fitness routines that incorporate interval training (alternating aerobic activities with strength and flexibility activities) show students that the best lifetime fitness experience is a balanced one. Teaching students how to correctly perform calisthenics gives them a series of activities they can perform in adulthood. In fact, after weight lifting, calisthenics are the most popular form of strength development for adults (Fitness Products Council, 1999).

Meeting this standard implies students will leave elementary school understanding the basic facts of fitness. Such concepts as the FIT principle (frequency, intensity, and time) can be taught in short question-and-answer episodes. Because each individual has unique needs and because programs must be developed according to these needs, an understanding of genetic diversity among peo-

FIGURE 1.3 Fitness is a participatory experience.

ple (such as differences in muscle type, cardiorespiratory endurance, and motor coordination) is requisite for helping students understand their physical capabilities. Understanding concepts such as proper exercise form, how much activity is enough, and how to safely participate in activity helps create a positive mindset in youngsters. Finally, students learn to personally evaluate their fitness levels in a semi-private setting. Doing self-testing on health-related fitness and charting physical activity offer students evidence about whether they are in the healthy fitness zone on the Fitnessgram and Activitygram evaluation (Cooper Institute, 2001).

Standard 3: Students are able to apply movement concepts and basic mechanics of skill performance when learning and refining motor skills.

Developmental Level I (grades K–2) students will be able to:

- **a.** Understand a vocabulary of basic movement concepts such as personal space, qualities of movement, body awareness, and the relationship of movements
- **b.** Understand words that describe a variety of relationships with objects, such as around, behind, over, through, and parallel
- **c.** Implement space awareness concepts and control of movements when performing locomotor movements in a group setting
- **d.** Understand basic mechanics of skill performance when performing specialized skills such as throwing, kicking, striking, and catching
- **e.** Appreciate the value of practice in learning motor skills

Developmental Levels II and III (grades 3–6) students will be able to:

- **a.** Find information regarding skill performance improvement including asking friends and coaches, self-evaluation, and learning to monitor personal accomplishments
- **b.** Know the importance of repetition and refinement for learning specialized motor skills
- **c.** Understand how warm-up and cool-down prevent injuries
- **d.** Incorporate the mechanics of skill performance in a variety of settings
- **e.** Use simple strategies when participating in a variety of lead-up games (modified rules, equipment, and number of participants)

The school years are the years of opportunity—the opportunity to experience and learn many different types of physical activities and skills. Related to this standard is the opportunity to learn basic concepts of movement (Chapter 14). Movement concepts help students understand what, where, and how the body can move. Again, emphasis is placed on experiencing the diversity of human movement. Allied to this experience is learning the correct mechanics of skill performance (Chapter 3). Students leave school knowing about stability, force, leverage, and other factors related to efficient movement.

Instruction is focused on teaching youngsters to be self-directed learners who can evaluate their performance and self-correct their skill technique. Accepting the premise that motor skills are only learned through repetition and refinement (the two Rs of physical education) is necessary if youngsters are to become competent performers. Much adult activity is done alone so students need to learn how to warm up for activity and cool down when finished. Understanding simple principles of motor learning (Chapter 3) such as practice, arousal, and refinement of skills will be knowledge that serves them in future experiences.

Standard 4: Students comprehend the basic principles of wellness and are able to apply concepts that enable them to make meaningful decisions that positively impact their health and wellness.

Developmental Level I (grades K–2) students will be able to:

- **a.** Explain why physical activity is important for good health
- **b.** Know basic muscle groups and bones related to movement
- **c.** Know that everybody should be active at least 30 minutes a day
- **d.** Understand the importance of eating a balanced diet

Developmental Levels II and III (grades 3–6) students will be able to:

- **a.** Make meaningful decisions about personal wellness by gathering information, considering the alternatives, and understanding the consequences that accompany such choices
- **b.** Know what types of physical activity are important for feeling good
- **c.** Understand factors that are detrimental to good health such as substance abuse and stress
- **d.** Understand how physical activity is important for weight control
- **e.** Understand the importance of safety, particularly in activity settings such as bicycling, swimming, sports, and as a pedestrian

f. Understand how proper nutrition is important for physical performance

This standard focuses on the knowledge necessary to make thoughtful decisions that impact an individual's health and wellness (Chapter 13). Meeting this standard does not have to turn physical education into a sedentary fact-learning experience. Instruction should be integrated into activity and skill development sessions. Simple principles about nutrition, stress, substance abuse, and safety can be woven into daily instruction so children have an opportunity to learn about healthy lifestyles.

Wellness implies developing a lifestyle that is balanced in all phases with *moderation* the keyword. Wellness is predicated on developing a clear understanding of choices and alternatives that lead to making wise choices. Students cannot make meaningful choices for wellness if they don't understand the consequences of their decisions. Wellness instruction involves studying the wisdom of past generations and integrating it into the lifestyles of current and future generations. In elementary school, basic wellness instruction covers how the skeletal, muscular, and cardiorespiratory systems function. In addition, students study lifestyle alternatives that impact wellness, including basic facts about nutrition, weight control, stress and relaxation, substance abuse, and safety.

Standard 5: Students participate in a wide variety of physical activities and learn how to maintain a personalized active lifestyle.

Developmental Level I (grades K–2) students will be able to:

a. Show willingness to try different physical activities
b. Understand how activities must be enjoyable for each individual if they are to be used throughout one's lifespan
c. Monitor the amount of time spent in short bouts of activity; for example, "I played tag for five minutes."
d. Set aside time for play each day

Developmental Levels II and III (grades 3–6) students will be able to:

a. Show a willingness to try many different activities and to identify those activities best suited to them
b. Demonstrate the ability to set physical activity goals in terms of time and type of activity
c. Know where opportunities are available for physical activity such as after school sports, intramurals, and private clubs and organizations
d. Identify physical activities that can be performed outside the school environment
e. Participate in activities in a variety of settings including with a friend, with parents, in the community, alone, or with a small group of friends

The basic premise of this content standard is that active children mature into active adults (Raitakari et al., 1994). Specifically, learning how to monitor personal activity levels, how to plan meaningful activity programs, and how to make informed decisions about physical activity are important outcomes. The PLAY program (Arizona Department of Health Services, 1999) and the Activitygram (Cooper Institute, 2001) are examples of programs designed to reward youngsters for monitoring and participating in daily physical activity. Youngsters need to learn where they can participate within their community and how to join clubs, YMCAs, and sport programs. Chapter 12 offers information on these programs and ways to increase physical activity levels of children.

The basic considerations for lifetime activity are several. Sallis (1994) classifies the factors that influence people to be active in four categories: psychological, social, physical environmental, and biological. A major role of physical education is to foster those factors that are often referred to as determinants of active living. Psychological determinants are among the most powerful. For example, students must derive enjoyment through physical activity if they are expected to participate as adults. Enjoyment increases when there is an adequate level of proficiency in a favored activity. Learning new motor skills demands time and an opportunity to practice, something that is difficult for most adults to find. Childhood is one of the few times in life when there is adequate free time to develop skill proficiency. Since most adults do not participate in activities unless they have an adequate level of perceived competence, learning skills becomes a priority of childhood. Another psychological factor is the rational basis for play. This can be established through activity orientations that are transferable to other situations. Such activities include a variety of games suitable for small groups, and sports activities adapted to local situations.

Social and environmental influences also affect lifetime activity patterns. These factors include having family and peer role models, receiving encouragement from significant others, and having opportunities to participate in activities with others in one's social group. Physical environmental factors include adequate programs and facilities, adequate equipment and supplies, safe outdoor environments, and available opportunities near home and at school. Included are adequate school opportunities such as recess, physical education, intramural games, recreation programs, and sports. Finally, biological factors include such factors as age, gender, and ethnic and/or socioeconomic status. For more details concerning determinants of physical activity, refer to Sallis' (1994) work.

A NASPE publication by Corbin and Pangrazi, *Physical Activity for Children: A Statement of Guidelines* (1998), outlines why youngsters need daily physical activity. It is the first document to offer a recommendation for how much activity youngsters need (minimum of 60 minutes per day). The publication discusses the physical activity pyramid and importance of participating in different types of physical activity including lifestyle activity, active aerobics, active sports and recreation, flexibility, and muscle fitness exercises. The document offers support and direction for teachers who need to offer justification for increasing the amount of daily physical activity for children.

Standard 6: Students demonstrate empathy, understanding, and respect for the numerous differences exhibited by people in an activity setting.

Developmental Level I (grades K–2) students will be able to:

a. Participate in a variety of multicultural activities
b. Understand how different individuals make a variety of contributions to the group
c. Explain simple differences and similarities among activities played in different cultural and ethnic backgrounds
d. Show empathy for the concerns and limitations of peers
e. Resolve conflicts in an acceptable nonviolent manner

Developmental Levels II and III (grades 3–6) students will be able to:

a. Understand how sport, games, and dance play a central role in modern day cultures
b. React in a positive manner toward individuals who have cultural or ethnic differences, or who have limitations
c. Demonstrate a willingness to participate with peers regardless of diversity or disability
d. Enjoy and interact with peers in a variety of physical activity settings
e. Resolve conflicts in an acceptable nonviolent manner

Physical education classes offer a unique environment for learning effective social skills. Children have the opportunity to internalize and practice the merits of participation, cooperation, competition, and tolerance. Some terms, such as *citizenship* and *fair play*, help define the desired social atmosphere. Through listening, empathy, and guidance, children learn to differentiate between acceptable and unacceptable ways of expressing feelings. Youngsters must develop an awareness of how they interact with others, and how the quality of their behavior influences others' responses to them.

Conflicts must be solved in a nonviolent manner (Chapter 5) that allows all parties to maintain self-esteem and dignity. Physical education offers an excellent opportunity to apply conflict resolution skills because misbehavior is easily observed. Students are taught to solve conflicts and disagreements in a peaceful and nonthreatening manner. Many diversity and gender issues (Chapter 4) arise in activity settings, and insightful and caring instruction can destroy negative stereotypes. Learning about the similarities and differences among cultures and how all people share common values and beliefs is an important outcome.

How the lesson is organized, the types of activities presented, how teachers view students who are less successful, and how children with disabilities are treated send implied messages to students (the hidden curriculum). When teachers and parents respond to children in a caring fashion, they teach youngsters they are loved, capable, and contributing people. If children believe they belong, are loved and respected, and that their successes outweigh their failures, they will be on the road to developing a desirable self-concept.

Standard 7: Students exhibit responsible and self-directed behaviors that lead to positive social interactions in physical activity.

Developmental Level I (grades K–2) students will be able to:

a. Follow rules and procedures in physical activity settings
b. Participate safely by observing safety procedures for equipment and apparatus
c. Understand and follow the rules of low-organized games
d. Cooperate in a group setting and be willing to take turns and help others
e. Show the ability to behave responsibly when differences of opinion occur
f. Play willingly with all students regardless of race, gender, or disability

Developmental Levels II and III (grades 3–6) students will be able to:

a. Reveal the ability to create and modify rules to better meet the needs of the group
b. Understand that cooperative skills must be developed before competitive games can be played

c. Understand how sports and games impact issues of gender and diversity
d. Recognize the benefits (social and physical) derived from participation in group games and activities
e. Show a willingness to follow rules, procedures, and safety guidelines in all physical activity settings
f. Behave in a caring and helping manner toward all peers

Responsible behavior (Chapter 5) implies behaving in a manner that doesn't negatively impact on others. Hellison (1995) and others have developed methodology for teaching responsible behavior. It is generally accepted that if responsible behavior is to be learned, it must be taught through experiences where such behavior is reinforced on a regular basis. Accepting consequences for one's behavior is learned and needs to be valued and reinforced by responsible adults. Responsible behavior occurs in a hierarchy of behavior from irresponsible to caring and behaving in a responsible manner. Physical education classes are an excellent setting for teaching responsibility because most behavior is highly visible. Youngsters in a competitive setting may react openly in an irresponsible fashion, offering instructors a "teachable moment" to discuss such unacceptable behavior. Additionally, youngsters have to learn to win and lose in an acceptable manner and to assume responsibility for their performances. Accepting the consequences of one's behavior is a lesson that arises regularly in a cooperative/competitive environment.

Cooperation precedes the development of competition, which makes it an important behavior to teach in elementary physical education settings. Without cooperation, competitive games cannot be played. The nature of competitive games demands cooperation, fair play, and sportsmanship, and when these are not present, the joy of participation is lost. Cooperative games teach children that all teammates are needed to reach group goals.

ESSENTIAL COMPONENTS OF A QUALITY PHYSICAL EDUCATION PROGRAM

Physical education teachers need to know the essential components of a quality physical education program. In other words, what are critical elements that should be included to ensure youngsters receive a quality physical education experience? The following components interlock to form a comprehensive physical education program that will be valued by parents, teachers, and students. Each of the components is described briefly in this section. In-depth coverage is offered in the referenced chapters under each point. Figure 1.5 identifies chapters in this book that provide more in-depth coverage of each component.

I. A quality physical education program is organized around content standards that offer direc-

FIGURE 1.4 Learning to cooperate with others.

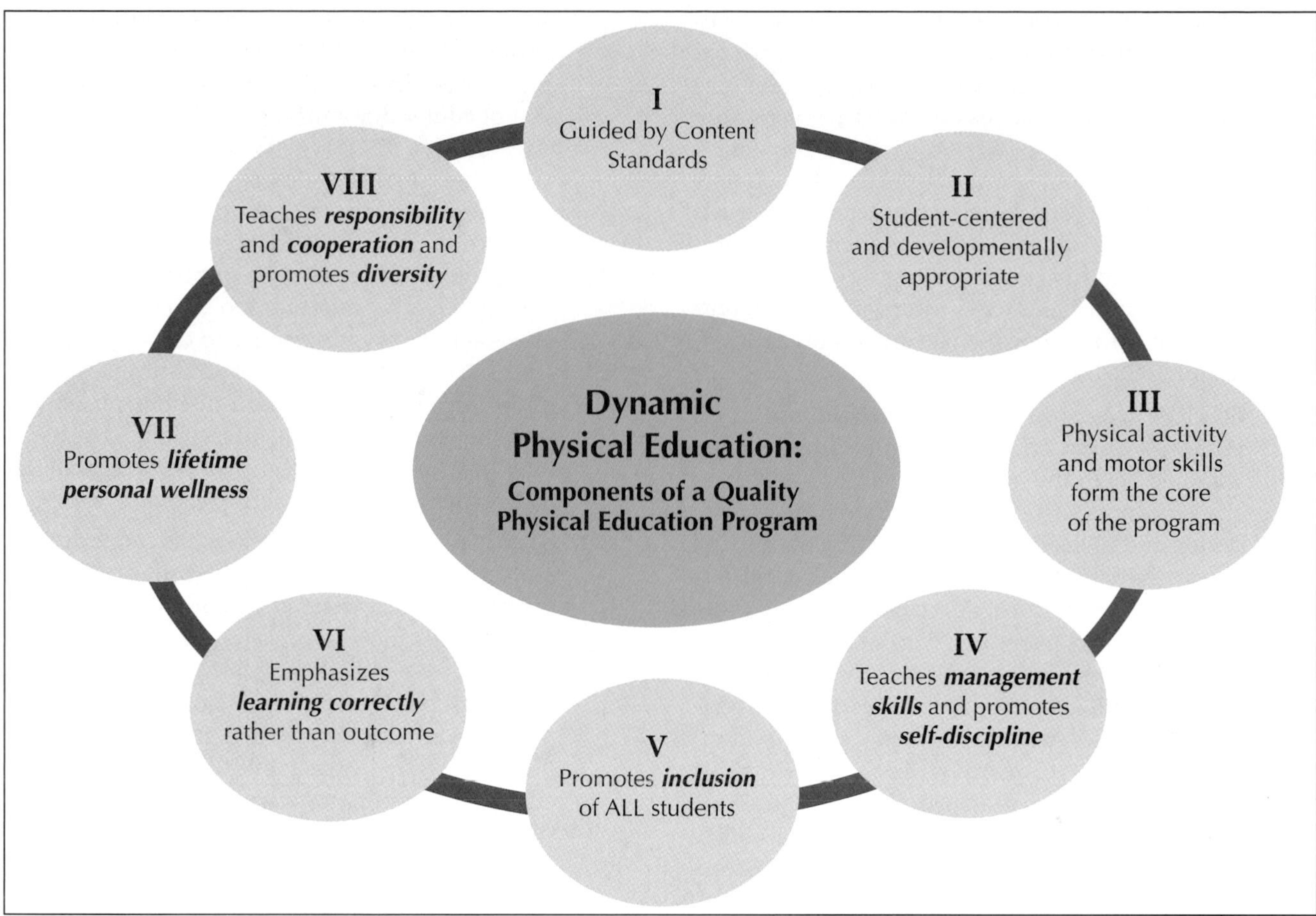

FIGURE 1.5 Essential components of a quality physical education program.

tion and continuity to instruction and evaluation. A quality program is driven by a set of content standards. These standards are defined by a number of competencies youngsters are expected to accomplish. Standards are measurable so both teachers and students know when progress has been made. Previously in this chapter you read about a comprehensive set of physical education content standards. Chapter 6 offers a number of evaluation strategies for checking to see if you and your students are meeting the standards.

II. **A quality program is student-centered and based on the developmental urges, characteristics, and interests of students.** Youngsters learn best when the skills and activities they must learn match their physical and emotional development. Including activities in the program because they match the competencies of the teacher is not a criterion. Teachers have to teach new activities outside their comfort zone if they are going to present a comprehensive program. See Chapter 8 to learn about the urges, characteristics, and interests of children and how they impact the creation of a quality physical education program. Chapter 4 offers many ideas for understanding and teaching to the personal needs of students. A quality program focuses on the successes of students so there is motivation to continue. Developing a positive set of behaviors toward physical activity is a key goal of physical education. Chapter 4 also discusses essential elements of teaching and how to positively reinforce youngsters during learning situations.

III. **Quality physical education makes physical activity and motor-skill development the core of the program.** Physical education is the only place in the total school curriculum where instruction is focused on teaching motor skills. Physical education is a unique discipline that focuses on physical activity to assure the physical development of students. It is mandatory that the program focus on skill development and quality physical activity. Chapters 2 and 12 explain the importance of physical activity for the optimal growth and development of youngsters.

IV. **Physical education programs teach management skills and self-discipline.** Physical education teachers are usually evaluated based on how students in their classes behave. Administrators and parents look to see that students are on task and receiving many opportunities to learn new skills. When a class is well-managed and students work with self-discipline, the experience compares to classroom instruction bringing credibility to the program. Chapter 5 offers many different methods for teaching management skills and promoting self-discipline.

V. **Quality programs emphasize inclusion of all students.** Instruction is designed for students who need help the most—less skilled youngsters and children with disabilities. Students who are skilled and blessed with innate ability have many opportunities to learn. They have the confidence to take private lessons, join clubs, and play in afterschool sport programs. Unskilled youngsters or children with disabilities lack confidence and often are unable to help themselves. Physical education is most likely the last opportunity youngsters will have to learn skills in a caring and positive environment. Instructional progressions designed to facilitate youngsters whose ability places them in the lower 70 percent of the class ensure a positive experience for all. Students who aren't naturally gifted must feel successful if they are expected to enjoy and value physical activity. See Chapter 7 for dealing with youngsters who have disabilities and modifying activities so all children can be successful.

VI. **In a quality physical education setting, instruction is focused on the process of learning skills rather than the product or outcome of the skill performance.** When youngsters are learning new motor skills, performing the skill correctly is more important than the outcome of the skill. Youngsters need to learn proper techniques first and then focus on the product of the skill performance. Translated, this means it is more important to teach a youngster to catch a beanbag properly than to worry about how many he catches or misses. Chapter 3 offers strategies for optimizing skill learning. Chapter 6 helps explain when to focus on the process or product evaluation of motor skills.

VII. **A quality physical education program teaches lifetime activities that students can use to promote their health and personal wellness.** Quality physical education programs prepare youngsters to participate in activities that they can perform when they become adults. If a program is restricted to team sports, the program will be of little value to the majority of adults. Participation in sports activities declines rapidly with age. Less than 5 percent of adults above the age of 30 report playing a team sport (USDHSS, 1996). By far, walking is the most often reported activity in adulthood. Other activities such as stretching exercises, bicycling, strength development exercises, jogging, swimming, and aerobics are also popular with adults. Quality physical education looks to the future and offers activities youngsters can enjoy and use as adults. Chapter 12 offers information about the importance of teaching lifetime physical activity skills in a physical education setting. Chapter 13 offers instructional strategies for teaching wellness and developing a healthy lifestyle.

VIII. **Quality physical education teaches cooperation and responsibility and helps students develop sensitivity to diversity and gender issues.** Cooperative skills have to precede competitive skills. Students have to agree to follow rules in order to enjoy group activities. The majority of fights and physical violence occur when youngsters are in a physical activity setting. Physical education is an effective laboratory for learning to behave responsibly because behavior is so observable to others. Situations in physical activity give rise to the need to resolve conflicts in a peaceful manner. Chapter 5 presents ways to teach youngsters responsible behavior and conflict-resolution techniques. Students need to learn about similarities and differences between cultures. Competitive activities such as the Olympics often bring cultures together and offer students the opportunity to see different cultures compete with respect and dignity. Coeducational activities help students understand how activities cut across gender and stereotypes. When gender differences occur in physical activities, it is an excellent time to point out that individuals differ regardless of race or gender. Chapter 4 offers a number of strategies for dealing with gender and diversity issues.

REFLECTION AND REVIEW QUESTIONS

How and Why

1. How have your perceptions of physical education changed based on your understanding of its evolution?
2. How does physical education fit into a school's curriculum?
3. How can the nationwide focus on health, wellness, and physical activity influence the lives of children?

4. How can content standards help teachers?
5. Why is it important to understand the essential components of physical education?

Content Review

1. Are physical education programs and physical education teachers necessary? Defend your answer.
2. Why is physical education a unique component of the total school curriculum?
3. Discuss the evolution of physical education.
4. What contributions have different pedagogical approaches made to the evolution of physical education?
5. How have federal mandates influenced physical education?
6. Discuss the content standards and explain the role they play in physical education.
7. State the essential components of a quality physical education program and discuss the significance of each.

FOR MORE INFORMATION

References and Suggested Readings

AAHPERD. (1986). *Physical activity and well being.* Waldorf, MD: American Alliance.

AAHPERD. (1990). *Professional preparation of the specialist teaching physical education to children.* Reston, VA: AAHPERD.

American Academy of Pediatrics. (1991). *Sports medicine: Health care for young athletes.* 2nd ed. Elk Grove Village, IL: American Academy of Pediatrics.

American Academy of Pediatrics. (1987). Physical fitness and the schools. *Pediatrics,* 80(3), 449–450.

Arizona Department of Health Services. (1999). *PLAY: Promoting lifetime activity for youth.* Phoenix, AZ: ADHS.

Bailey, D. A., Faulkner, R. A., & McKay, H. A. (1996). Growth, physical activity, and bone mineral acquisition. *Exercise and Sport Science Reviews,* 24, 233–266.

Bar-Or, O. (1995). Health benefits of physical activity during childhood and adolescence. *Physical Activity and Fitness Research Digest,* 2(4), 1–6.

Beighle, A. & Pangrazi, R. P. (2000). The validity of six pedometers for measuring the physical activity of children. Unpublished manuscript.

Burgeson, C. R., Wechsler, H., Brener, N. D., Young, J. C., & Spain, C. G. (2001). Physical education and activity: Results from the school health policies and programs study (SHPPS) 2000. *Journal of School Health,* 71(7), 279–293.

Chepko, S. & Arnold, R. K., Editors (2000). *Guidelines for physical education programs, K–12: Standards, objectives and assessments.* Boston: Allyn & Bacon.

Cooper Institute. (2001). *Fitnessgram test administration manual.* Champaign, IL: Human Kinetics.

Corbin, C., and Lindsey, R. 2002. *Fitness for Life.* 4th. ed. Champaign, IL: Human Kinetics.

Corbin, C. B. & Pangrazi, R. P. (1998). *Physical activity for children: A statement of guidelines* (AAHPERD National Guidelines). Reston, VA: NASPE Publications.

Dale, D., Corbin, C. B., & Cuddihy, T. F. (1998). Can conceptual physical education promote physically active lifestyles? *Pediatric Exercise Science,* 10, 97–109.

Fitness and Lifestyle in Canada. (1983, May). *Canada fitness survey.* Ottawa, Canada. (Report funded by Fitness Canada.)

Fitness Products Council. (1999). *U.S. Participation in Fitness Activities, 1987–1998.* North Palm Beach, FL: Sporting Goods Manufacturers Association.

Gardner, D. P. (Chair). (1983). *A nation at risk: The imperative for educational reform.* A report to the nation and the Secretary of Education, U.S. Department of Education. The National Commission on Excellence in Education. *Chronicle of Higher Education,* 26(10), 11–16.

Guo, S. S., Roche, A. F., Chumlea, W.C., Gardner, J. D., & Siervogel, R. M. (1994). The predictive value of childhood body mass index values for overweight at age 35 y. *American Journal of Clinical Nutrition,* 59, 810–819.

Hellison, D. (1995). *Teaching responsibility through physical activity.* Champaign, IL: Human Kinetics.

Jebb, S. A. & Moore, M. S. (1999). Contribution of a sedentary lifestyle and inactivity to the etiology of overweight and obesity: Current evidence and research issues. *Medicine and Science in Sports and Exercise,* 31, S534–S541.

Kraus, H. & Hirschland, R. P. (1954). Minimum muscular fitness tests in school children. *Research Quarterly,* 25, 178–187.

Must, A., Jacques, P. F., Dallal, G. E., Bajema, C. J., & Dietz, W. H. (1992). Long-term morbidity and mortality of overweight adolescents: A follow-up of the Harvard Growth Study of 1922 to 1935. *New England Journal of Medicine,* 327, 1350–1355.

National Association for Sport and Physical Education. (1988). *Guidelines for elementary school physical education.* Reston, VA: AAHPERD.

National Association for Sport and Physical Education. (1992a). *Developmentally appropriate physical education practices for children.* Reston, VA: AAHPERD.

National Association for Sport and Physical Education. (1992b). *Outcomes of quality physical education programs.* Reston, VA: AAHPERD.

National Association for Sport and Physical Education. (1995). *Moving into the future national physical education standards: A guide to content and assessment.* St. Louis: Mosby-Year Book.

Raitakari, O. T., Porkka, K. V. K., Taimela, S., Telama, R., Rasanen, L., & Viikari, J. S. A. (1994). Effects of persistent physical activity and inactivity on coronary risk factors in children and young adults. *American Journal of Epidemiology,* 140, 195–205.

Ross, J. G., Pate, R. P., Corbin, C. B., Delpy, L. A., & Gold, R. S. (1987). What's going on in the elementary physical education program? *JOPERD,* 58(9), 78–84.

Sallis, J. F. (1994). Influences on physical activity of children, adolescents, and adults or determinants of active living. *Physical Activity and Fitness Research Digest,* 1(7), 1–8.

Sallis, J. F., McKenzie, T. L., Kolody, B., Lewis, M., Marshall, S., & Rosengard, P. (1999). Effects of health-related physical education on academic achievement: Project SPARK. *Research Quarterly for Exercise and Sport,* 70, 127–134.

Sporting Goods Manufacturers Association. (2000). *Fitness and Sports Newletter.* (May/June issue).

Telama, R., Yang, X., Laakso, L., & Viikari, J. (1997). Physical activity in childhood and adolescence as predictors of physical activity in young adulthood. *American Journal of Preventative Medicine,* 13, 317–323.

Trudeau, F., Laurencelle, L., Tremblay, J., Rajic, M., & Shephard, R. J. (1998). A long-term follow-up of participants in the Trois-Rivieres semi-longitudinal study of growth and development. *Pediatric Exercise Science,* 10, 366–377.

U.S. Department of Health and Human Services. (1994). *School health policies and programs study.* Atlanta, GA: U.S. Department of Health and Human Services, Centers for Disease Control and Prevention, National Center for Chronic Disease Prevention and Health Promotion.

U.S. Department of Health and Human Services. (1996). *Physical activity and health: A report of the surgeon general.* Atlanta, GA: U.S. Department of Health and Human Services, Centers for Disease Control and Prevention, National Center for Chronic Disease Prevention and Health Promotion.

U.S. Department of Health and Human Services. (2000). *Healthy people 2010: National health promotion and disease objectives.* Washington, DC: U.S. Government Printing Office.

U.S. Department of Health and Human Services. (2002) *Prevalence of overweight among children and adolescents: United States, 1999.* Center for Disease Control and Prevention, National Center for Health Statistics.

U.S. Public Health Service. (1990). *Healthy people 2000: National health promotion and disease objectives.* Washington, DC: U.S. Government Printing Office.

Websites

American Alliance for Health, Physical Education, Recreation, and Dance
http://www.aahperd.org

American Heart Association
http://www.americanheart.org

Center for Disease Control and Prevention
http://www.cdc.gov

History of Physical Education
http://schools.eastnet.ecu.edu/pitt/ayden/hist/history.html

National Physical Education Standards
http://www.ed.gov/databases/ERIC_Digests/ed406361.html

Physical Education Articles on the Web
http://www.edweek.org/ew/vol-16/27physed.h16
http://www.edweek.org/ew/vol-16/27aldine.h16
http://www.edweek.org/ew/vol-16/25cdc.h16

Public Law 94-142
http://asclepius.com/angel/special.html

Title IX
http://www.ed.gov/pubs/TitleIX

	ESSENTIAL COMPONENTS
I	Organized around content standards
II	**Student-centered and developmentally appropriate**
III	**Physical activity and motor skill development form the core of the program**
IV	Teaches management skills and self-discipline
V	Promotes inclusion of all students
VI	Focuses on process over product
VII	Promotes lifetime personal health and wellness
VIII	Teaches cooperation and responsibility and promotes sensitivity to diversity

	PHYSICAL EDUCATION STANDARDS
1	Students are able to move competently using a variety of fundamental and specialized motor skills.
2	Students can monitor and maintain a health-enhancing level of physical fitness.
3	Students are able to apply movement concepts and basic mechanics of skill performance when learning and refining motor skills.
4	Students comprehend the basic principles of wellness and are able to apply concepts that enable them to make meaningful decisions that positively impact their health and wellness.
5	Students participate in a wide variety of physical activities and learn how to maintain a personalized active lifestyle.
6	Students demonstrate empathy, understanding, and respect for the numerous differences exhibited by people in an activity setting.
7	Students exhibit responsible and self-directed behaviors that lead to positive social interactions in physical activity.

C H A P T E R 2

Teaching Children in the Physical Education Environment

SUMMARY

Physical activity positively impacts the growth and development of children. Research supports the value of an active lifestyle for optimum growth and development. There is a positive correlation between the incidence of certain health disorders and a sedentary lifestyle. Lifetime involvement in physical activity often depends on early participation and gratification gained from such participation. Developing motor skills at an early age provides the tools needed to be physically active throughout life. Guidelines for safe participation in physical activity, including weight lifting, running, exercising in heat, and fitness testing, are delineated.

OUTCOMES

- Describe the need for physical activities.
- Cite stages of the growing child.
- Understand the relationship between physical activity and the development of muscular strength and endurance and skeletal growth.
- Define aerobic capacity and discuss its relationship to health and physical activity.
- Understand body composition and obesity and the relationship of each to the health and well-being of an individual.
- Discuss the role organized youth sports should play in the proper growth and development of children.
- Identify guidelines to follow for exercising children safely.
- Describe the proper approach to distance running and weight training for preadolescent children.

This chapter offers an overview of the impact of physical activity on the growing child. Many of the studies cited in this chapter offer excellent justification for including physical education in the total school curriculum. For example, the high levels of obesity in youth, the need for skill competency so children have tools to be active for a lifetime, and the long-term effects of physical activity are strong arguments for a well-taught, well-organized physical education program.

THE GROWING CHILD

Growth patterns are generally controlled by genetic makeup at birth. Although an unhealthy environment can have a negative impact on proper growth and development, this section examines maturation patterns that are common to the majority of youngsters. All youngsters follow a general growth pattern; however, each child's timing is unique. Some children are advanced physically for their chronological age, whereas others are slow maturers. Only when aberration from the norm is excessive is there cause for concern.

Growth Patterns

Teachers and parents should know if youngsters are maturing normally. When heights and weights are plotted on a graph from year to year, a distance curve can be developed. These curves (Figure 2.1) give an indication of how tall and heavy children are expected to be during a specific year of life. Another way to examine growth patterns is to look at a velocity curve. The velocity curve reveals how much a child grows on a year-to-year basis (Figure 2.2). Children go through a rapid period of growth from birth to age 5. From age 6 to the onset of adolescence, growth slows to a steady but increasing pattern. A general rule of thumb in regard to motor learning is that when growth is rapid, the ability to learn new skills decreases. Because the rate of growth slows during the elementary school years, this is an excellent window for learning motor skills.

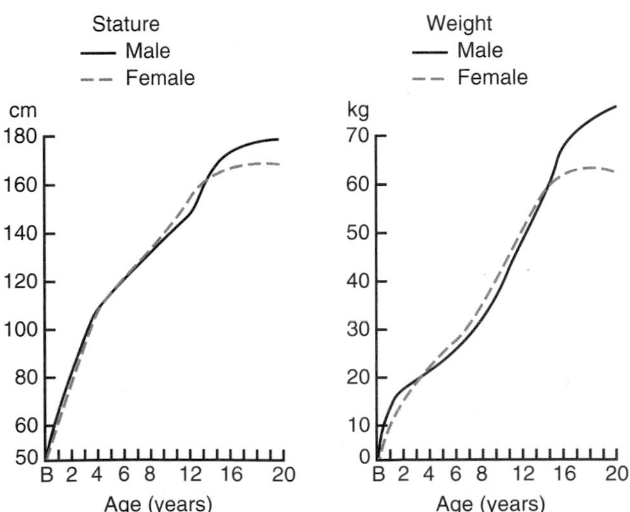

FIGURE 2.1 Distance curves for height and weight. (From Malina, R. 1975. *Growth and development: The first twenty years in man,* 19. Minneapolis: Burgess.)

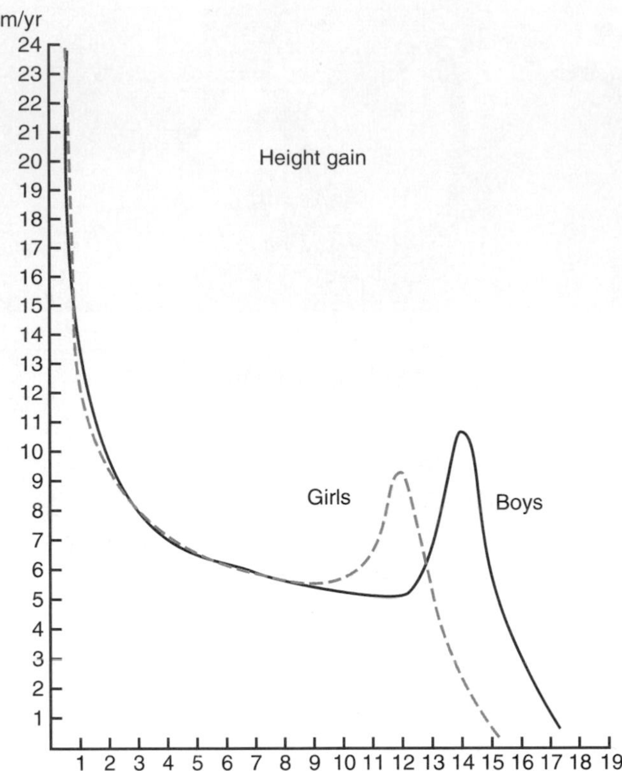

FIGURE 2.2 Growth velocity curve for height. (From Tanner, J. M., Whitehouse, R. H., & Takaishi, M. 1966. *Archives of Diseases in Childhood,* 41, 466.)

During adolescence, rapid growth occurs until adulthood is reached. During the elementary school years, boys are generally taller and heavier. Girls reach the adolescent growth spurt first, and grow taller and heavier during the sixth- and seventh-grade years. Boys quickly catch up and grow larger and stronger. Growth charts based on a large sample of children have been developed by the National Center for Health Statistics (Figures 2.3 and 2.4, pages 25 and 26). These tables can be consulted to identify both stature (height) and weight percentiles for children ages 2 through 20. The tables offer an opportunity to visualize marked differences between children in a so-called normal population.

Young children have relatively short legs for their overall height. The trunk is longer in relation to the legs during early childhood. The ratio of leg length (standing height) to trunk length (sitting height) is similar for boys and girls through age 11. The head makes up one-

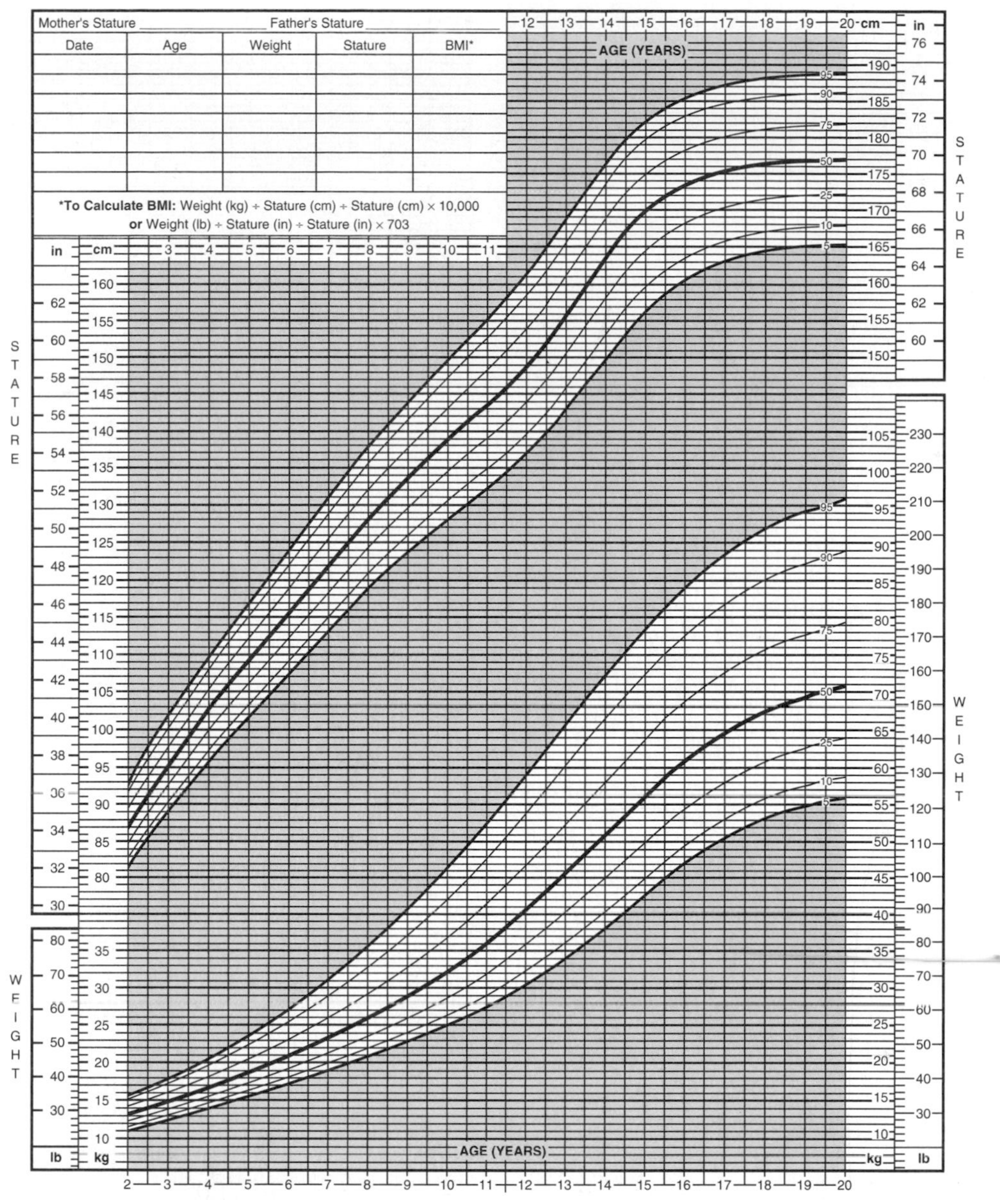

FIGURE 2.3 2 to 20 Years: Boys stature-for-age and weight-for-age percentiles. Developed by the National Center for Health Statistics in collaboration with the National Center for Chronic Disease Prevention and Health Promotion (2000).

fourth of the child's total length at birth and about one-sixth at age 6. Figure 2.5 (page 27) illustrates how body proportions change with growth. Because K–2 students have short legs in relation to their upper body, they are "top heavy" and fall more easily than adults do. This high center of gravity will gradually lower and give children increased stability and balance.

Body Physique

A child's physique (somatotype) affects the quality of his or her motor performance. Sheldon, Dupertuis, and McDermott (1954) developed the original scheme for somatotyping, identifying three major physiques, *endomorphy, mesomorphy,* and *ectomorphy.* Rating is assessed from standardized photographs on a 7-point scale, with 1 being the least expression and 7 the most expression of the specific component. The ratings of each component give a total score that results in identification of an individual's somatotype. A similar system of classification for children (Petersen, 1967) is available for teachers who are interested in understanding the body physiques of children.

In general, children who possess a mesomorphic body type perform best in activities requiring strength, speed, and agility. The *mesomorph* is characterized as having a predominance of muscle and bone and is often labeled "muscled." These children usually perform well

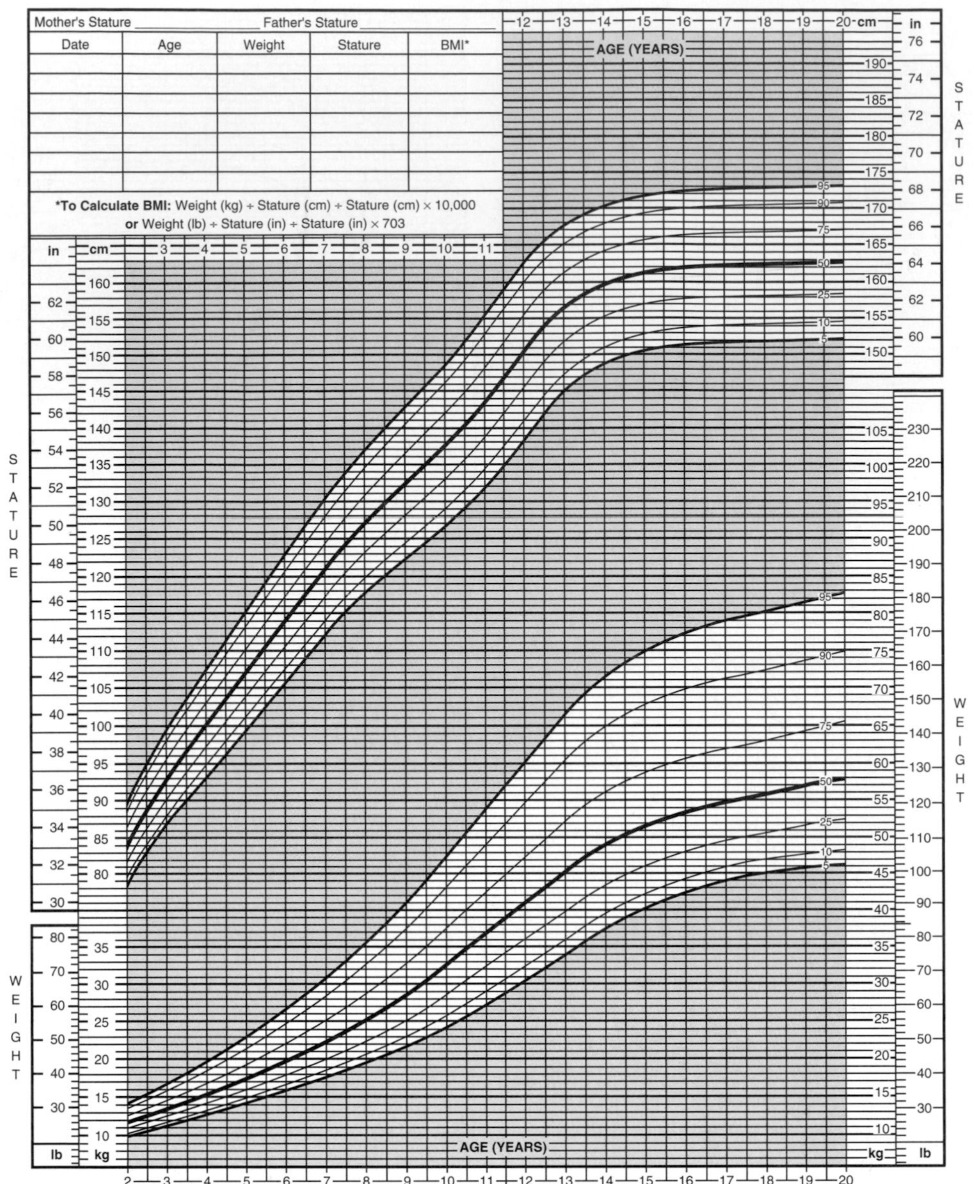

FIGURE 2.4 2 to 20 Years: Girls stature-for-age and weight-for-age percentiles. Developed by the National Center for Health Statistics in collaboration with the National Center for Chronic Disease Prevention and Health Promotion (2000).

in most team sports, because these activities require strength, speed, and agility. The *ectomorph* is identified as being extremely thin, with a minimum of muscle development, and is characterized as "skinny." These children may be less able in activities requiring strength and power, but able to perform well in aerobic endurance activities such as jogging, cross-country running, and track and field. The third classification is the *endomorph,* characterized as soft and round, with an excessively protruding abdomen. These children may perform poorly in many areas, including aerobic and anaerobic skill-oriented activities. The obese child is generally at a disadvantage in all phases of physical performance. Somatotype classification illustrates how dramatically children differ in body physique and necessitates that instruction accommodate individual differences.

Skeletal Maturity

Teachers often speak about the *maturity* of students. Physical maturity has a strong impact on the performance of children in physical education. Maturity is usually measured by comparing chronological age with skeletal age. Ossification (hardening) of the bones occurs in the center of the bone shaft and at the ends of the long bones (growth plates). The rate of ossification gives an accurate indication of a child's rate of matura-

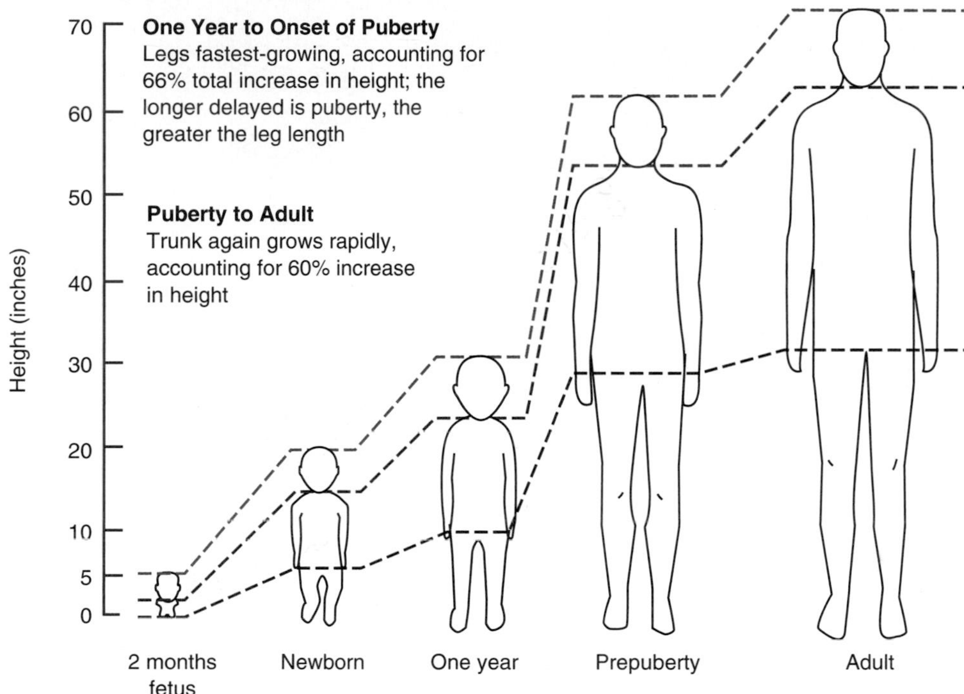

FIGURE 2.5 Changing body proportions from conception to adulthood. (From Whipple, D. 1966. *Dynamics of development: Euthenic pediatrics*, 122. New York: McGraw-Hill.)

tion. Maturation rate can be identified by X-raying the wrist bones and comparing the development of the subject's bones with a set of standardized X rays (Gruelich & Pyle, 1959; Roche, Chumlea, & Thissen, 1988). Children whose chronological age is beyond skeletal age are said to be late (or slow) maturers. If skeletal age is ahead of chronological age, children are labeled early (fast) maturers.

Studies examining skeletal age (Gruelich & Pyle, 1959; Krahenbuhl & Pangrazi, 1983) consistently show that a five- to six-year variation in skeletal maturity exists in a typical classroom of youngsters. For example, a class of third graders who are all 8 years old chronologically would range in skeletal age from 5 to 11 years. This means that some youngsters are actually 5-year-olds skeletally and are trying to compete with others who are as mature as 11-year-olds. Effective programs have to offer activities that are *developmentally appropriate* and suited to their level of maturity.

Early-maturing children of both sexes are generally heavier and taller for their age than are average- or late-maturing students. Obese children (endomorphs) are often more mature for their age than are normal-weight children and carry larger amounts of muscle and bone tissue. However, these obese children also carry a greater percentage of body weight as fat tissue (Malina, 1980), which decreases their motor performance. The motor performance of boys is related to skeletal maturity in that a more mature boy usually performs better on motor tasks (Clarke, 1971). For girls, however, motor performance appears not to be related to physiological maturity, and Malina (1978) found that late maturation is commonly associated with exceptional motor performance. Physical education programs often ask students to learn at the same rate, even though this practice may be detrimental to the development of students who are maturing at a faster or slower rate. Students do not mature at the same rate and are not at similar levels of readiness to learn (Figure 2.6, page 28). Offering a wide spectrum of developmentally appropriate activities helps ensure that youngsters will be successful regardless of the maturity factor.

FIGURE 2.6 Children the same age vary in size and maturity.

Muscular Development and Strength

In the elementary school years, muscular strength increases linearly with chronological age (Malina, 1980; Beunen, 1989). A similar yearly increase occurs until adolescence, at which time a rapid increase in strength occurs. When differences in strength between the sexes are adjusted for height, there is no difference in lower body strength from ages 7 through 17. When the same adjustment between the sexes is made for upper body strength, however, boys have more upper extremity and trunk strength (Malina, 1980). Boys and girls can participate on somewhat even terms in activities demanding leg strength, particularly if their size and mass are similar. On the other hand, in activities demanding arm or trunk strength, boys have an advantage, even if they are similar to the girls in height and mass. When pairing children for activities, students should not be paired with someone who is considerably taller and heavier (or more mature) and therefore stronger.

Muscle Fiber Type and Performance

The number of muscle fibers an individual possesses is genetically determined. An increase in muscle size is accomplished by an increase in the size of each muscle fiber. The size of the muscles is determined primarily by the number of fibers and secondarily by the size of the fibers. An individual is therefore somewhat muscularly limited by genetic restrictions.

Skeletal muscle tissue contains a ratio of fast contracting fibers (fast twitch [FT]) to slow contracting fibers (slow twitch [ST]) (Saltin, 1973). The percentage of fast- versus slow-contracting fibers varies from muscle to muscle and among individuals. The percentage of each type of muscle fiber is determined during the first weeks of postnatal life (Dubowitz, 1970). Most individuals possess a 50:50 split; that is, half of the muscle fibers are FT and half are ST. A small percentage of people have a ratio of 60:40 (in either direction), and researchers have verified that some people possess an even more extreme ratio.

What is the significance of variation in the ratio of muscle fiber type? ST fibers have a rich supply of blood and related energy mechanisms. This results in a slowly contracting, fatigue-resistant muscle fiber that is well suited to endurance-type (aerobic) activities. In contrast, FT fibers are capable of bursts of intense activity but are subject to rapid fatigue. These fibers are well-suited to activities demanding short-term speed and power (for example, pull-ups, standing long jump, and shuttle run). ST fibers facilitate performance in the mile run or other endurance-oriented activities.

Surprisingly, elementary-aged children who do best in activities requiring FT fibers also do best in distance running (Krahenbuhl & Pangrazi, 1983). Muscle fiber metabolic specialization does not occur until adolescence; this fact is a strong argument for keeping all youngsters involved in varied physical activity throughout the elementary years. A youngster who does poorly in elementary school may do quite well during and after adolescence, when a high percentage of ST fibers will aid in the performance of aerobic activity. On the other hand, the same child may do poorly in a physical education program dominated by team sports that demand quickness and strength. Designing a program that incorporates activities using a range of physical attributes (that is, endurance, balance, and flexibility) is essential.

Relative Strength and Motor Performance

Strength is an important factor in performing motor skills. A study by Rarick and Dobbins (1975) identified and weighted factors that contribute to the motor performance of children. The factor identified as most important was strength in relation to body size (*relative strength*). High levels of strength in relation to body size helped predict which students were most capable of performing motor skills. Deadweight (fat) was the fourth-ranked factor in the study and was weighted negatively. Obese children were less proficient at performing motor skills. Deadweight has a negative impact on motor performance because it reduces relative strength. Obese children may be stronger than normal-weight children in absolute terms, but are less strong when strength is adjusted for body weight. This lack of strength in relationship to body size causes obese children to find a strength-related task (such as a push-up or pull-up) much more difficult than the task would seem to normal-weight children. The need for varied and personalized workloads is important to ensure all youngsters the opportunity for success in strength-related activities. Strength is an important part of a balanced fitness program and offers youngsters a better opportunity to find success in a variety of motor development activities.

Aerobic Capacity: Children are not Little Adults

Maximal aerobic power is an individual's maximum ability to use oxygen in the body for metabolic purposes. The oxygen uptake of an individual, all other factors being equal, determines the quality of endurance-oriented performance. Maximal aerobic power is closely related to lean body mass, which explains differences in performance between boys and girls. When maximum oxygen uptake is adjusted per kilogram of body weight, it shows little change for boys (no increase) and a gradual decrease for girls (Bar-Or, 1983). This decrease in females is due to an increase in body fat and a decrease in lean body mass. When maximal oxygen uptake is not adjusted for body weight, it increases in similar amounts on a yearly basis for both boys and girls through age 12, even though boys have higher values as early as age 5.

Adults interested in increasing endurance-based athletic performance train extensively to increase aerobic power. A frequently asked question is whether similar training will increase the aerobic performance of children. A recent meta-analysis (Payne & Morrow, 1993) analyzed 28 studies dealing with the impact of exercise on aerobic performance in children. The results showed that training caused little, if any, increase in aerobic power in prepubescent children. If there is improvement in running performance in young children, Bar-Or (1983) postulates that it may occur because they become more efficient mechanically or improve in anaerobic metabolism. Another theory is that young children are active enough to make intergroup differences negligible (Corbin & Pangrazi, 1992).

Even though children demonstrate a relatively high oxygen uptake, they do not perform up to this level because they are not economical in running or walking activities. An 8-year-old child running at 180 m per minute is operating at 90 percent of maximal aerobic power, whereas a 16-year-old running at the same rate is operating at only 75 percent of maximum. This explains why young children are less capable than adolescents and adults at competing over long distances, even though they can maintain a slow speed for long distances (Bar-Or, 1983).

Children exercising at a certain workload perceive the activity to be easier than do adults working at a similar level. Youngsters were asked to rate their perceived exertion at different percentages of maximal heart rate (Bar-Or & Ward, 1989) and usually rated the exertion to be less stressful than did adults. Youngsters also demonstrate a rapid recovery rate after strenuous exercise. This implies that teachers should not judge workloads for children based on how they perceive the difficulty of an activity. Teachers also should use a child's rapid recovery rate to full advantage. Exercise bouts can be interspersed with restful episodes of stretching and nonlocomotor movements. This type of interval training is a particularly effective training method to use with children because it allows them to exercise aerobically and recover.

Obesity and Physical Performance

Obese children seldom perform physical activities on a par with leaner children (Bar-Or, 1983). In part, this is due to the greater metabolic cost of the obese child's exercise. Obese children require a higher oxygen uptake capacity to perform a given task. Obesity takes a great toll on a child's aerobic power because obese children must perform at a higher percentage of their maximal oxygen uptake (Figure 2.7). Usually, their maximal

FIGURE 2.7 Body composition impacts physical performance.

uptake values are lower than those of lean children. This gives obese children less reserve capacity and causes them to perceive higher exertion (Bar-Or & Ward, 1989) when performing a task. These reactions contribute to the common perception among teachers that "obese children don't like to run." Understand that asking obese children to run as far and as fast as normal-weight children is unrealistic. The task is more demanding for the obese child. Obese children have to work harder than normal-weight children to accomplish the same task and thus need adjusted workloads. There is no acceptable premise, physiological or psychological, for asking all children to run the same distance regardless of ability or body type.

Workloads should be based on time rather than distance. Lean and efficient runners should be expected to move farther than obese youngsters during a stipulated time period. All children *should not* have to do the same workload. Just as one would not expect kindergarten children to perform the same workload as that of fifth-graders, it is unreasonable to expect obese children to be capable of workloads similar to those of lean, ectomorphic youngsters. *Exercise programs for obese subjects should be designed to increase caloric expenditure rather than to improve cardiovascular fitness* (Rowland, 1991). The intensity of the activity should be secondary to the amount of time the student is involved in some type of moderate activity.

TEACHING SPECIALIZED MOTOR SKILLS

The majority of children will participate in some type of sport activity, if for no other reason than their parents want them to do so. Physical educators can offer expert advice to parents and community leaders. Since these programs may be administered by persons who have little understanding of young, immature children, it is important that teachers step forward and share their knowledge.

Allow Students to Learn All Skills and Play All Positions

Allow youngsters to play all positions when teaching sport skills. If the best athletes are always assigned to skilled positions, it becomes a situation of the rich getting richer and the poor getting poorer. Because all children deserve equal opportunity to learn sport skills, it should be a mandate to teachers that all children play all positions and receive similar amounts of practice time. In addition, reinforcement schedules need to be similar for children regardless of their current skill level. Children participate in activities that offer them reinforcement; it is easy to become discouraged if little encouragement and praise are given to participants trying to learn new skills and positions.

Understand that maturity plays an important role in dictating how youngsters learn motor skills. One of the reasons for helping children learn all skills and play all positions is that it will give them the opportunity to be successful when they reach maturity. For example, should the teacher identify a youngster as a pitcher or a right fielder; or as a lineman or quarterback? Often, these questions are answered for youngsters when teachers make judgments and force them to play a certain position. Often, such judgments are based on the maturity of the individual rather than the actual skill level. In a study by Hale (1956), skeletally mature athletes were found to be playing in the skilled positions in the Little League World Series. Chronologically, all players were 11 years old, with a skeletal age range similar to that described earlier. The most mature were pitchers and catchers, and the least mature played at less skilled positions. This study points out how skeletally mature children receive more opportunity to throw at an early age (through pitching and catching). These youngsters obviously have the chance to become better throwers due to the large number of opportunities they receive when throwing in games and practice. In contrast, children who are immature play right field and receive limited throwing or catching opportunities. Because these less mature children receive much less throwing practice, it is improbable that they will ever have the chance to close the skill gap and develop adequate skill competency.

Ensure Success for All Students

The willingness to try new experiences and participate in activities is driven by how people feel about their ability level—their *perceived competence.* Perceived competence becomes more specific as students mature. Young students think they are good and competent at everything. As they become older (third or fourth grade), they start to realize that other students are better in some areas. If these students are not given the chance to succeed in class, low perceived competence about their ability to perform physical skills is the result. This "learned helplessness" (Harter, 1978) eventually results in the students' disliking and dropping out of physical education. There is a strong possibility that they will leave school with negative feelings about developing an active lifestyle. Dropping out of physical education commonly occurs in junior high and high school, when students have the opportunity to make a choice. Unfortunately, it is quite possible that the process of feeling incompetent began in the elementary school years. Elementary school youngsters are often characterized as gifted (or not gifted) at a young age. This creates a self-fulfilling prophecy, with students identified as gifted receiving more feedback and being expected to reach higher levels of performance. Less able students receive less feedback and expectations remain low.

Assume all Youngsters have the Ability to Achieve

Even though teachers and parents make early judgments about the potential of students, it is difficult to identify outstanding athletes in the elementary school years. In a study by Clarke (1968), athletes identified as outstanding in elementary school were seldom outstanding in junior high school, and predictions based on elementary school performance were correct only 25 percent of the time. Most people would not risk discouraging a youngster if they knew they were going to be wrong 75 percent of the time. However, youngsters are often labeled at an early age, even though three out of four such predictions are incorrect. All children should be treated as if they have the potential to become successful. It is not the purpose of a physical education program to develop athletes, but rather to help *all* students develop physical skills within the limits of their potential. The program should not be presented in such a fashion that it allows the athletically gifted to excel and prosper at the expense of the less talented youngsters.

Understand that Starting Young Doesn't Ensure Excellence

There is no evidence to support the idea that starting a child's participation in sports at a young age ensures the child will become an outstanding athlete (Figure 2.8). In fact, many professional athletes did not even play their sport of excellence until the high school years. One reason that many parents and coaches push to have children start competing in a sport at an early age is that this competition offers the perception that a better athlete has been developed by the age of 8 or 9. The participating child may seem extremely gifted compared with the nonparticipant, because he or she has been practicing skills for four or five years. Naturally, the "early starter" looks advanced compared with a child who has not been in an organized program. In most cases, a child who is genetically gifted quickly catches up to and surpasses the "early superstar" in one to three years. As Shephard (1984a) states, "Any advantage that is gained from very prolonged training probably lies in the area of skill perfection rather than in a fuller realization of physical potential."

FIGURE 2.8 An early start does not guarantee success.

Children who have been in documented programs for many years may burn out at an early age. A *documented* program is one in which extrinsic rewards are offered. Examples of such rewards are trophies, published league standings, ribbons, and excessive parental involvement. Evidence shows that extrinsic motivation may ultimately decrease intrinsic motivation, particularly in children age 7 years and older. Researchers (Thomas & Tennant, 1978; Whitehead & Corbin, 1991) found that younger children (age 5) perceived a reward as a bonus, thus adding to the joy of performing a throwing motor task. This effect decreased with age, and by age 9 the reward was seen as a bribe; intrinsic motivation was undermined. There is no substitute for allowing young children to participate in physical activity for the sheer enjoyment and excitement involved in moving and interacting with peers.

If starting youngsters early can create early burnout, why do parents feel pressured to force their child into a sport program? One explanation is that they constantly compare their children to other children. Parents see other children participating and practicing sport skills in an organized setting. They worry that their children will be unable to "catch up" if they do not get them involved in a similar program immediately. Even though this is not true, parents need reassurance, and they need facts. Physical educators can help parents find programs that minimize pressure and focus on skill development. A key is to find programs that allow the child to participate regardless of ability, and to have fun while playing. Children consider having fun and improving their skills to be more important than winning (Athletic Footwear Association, 1990). Many children drop out of sport activities but would probably continue to participate if given the opportunity (Petlichkoff, 1992). Unfortunately, some programs become elitist and start eliminating and "cutting" less gifted players. It is difficult to justify this approach at the elementary school level. All children should be given the opportunity to participate if they choose to do so.

Another reason given for starting children at a young age is tied to the commodity that only children have—free time. Parents know they have little time in their lives to learn new skills. They feel their youngsters have an abundance of free time that can be devoted to practice. Unfortunately, if the child shows promise, greater emphasis is placed on increasing practice time since it becomes necessary "to ensure that all this talent is not lost." It is important to remind parents that life includes more than athletic development and that many youngsters have been maimed by an excessive emphasis on sports at the expense of intellectual and social development. Participation in activity should be self-selected. It should be student-driven rather than motivated by external factors. Similarly, students should have the opportunity to withdraw from participation in an activity if they choose. Withdrawal should be child-controlled rather than externally controlled (Gould, 1987). In other words, participants should not be forced out of the program due to cost, limitation of participants, or injury. On the other hand, if youngsters choose to withdraw, they should be allowed that opportunity without pressure.

GUIDELINES FOR EXERCISING CHILDREN SAFELY

As is usually the case with most things, moderation is a way to ensure that children are safe and grow up enjoying physical activity. Moderate exercise, coupled with opportunities to participate in recreational activity, helps develop a lasting desire to move. Some adults are concerned that a child may be harmed physiologically by too much activity. To date, there is no evidence that a healthy child is harmed through vigorous activity and exercise. Children can withstand a gradual increase in workload and are capable of workloads comparable to those of adults when the load is adjusted for height and size. Fatigue causes healthy children to stop exercising long before any danger to health occurs (Shephard, 1984a). In addition, the child's circulatory system is similar in proportion to that of an adult and thus is not at a disadvantage during exercise.

Exercising in the Heat

Caution should be used when exercising youngsters in hot weather. The arrival of summer does not mean that exercise must stop, but certain measures should be taken to avoid heat-related illness. Children are not little adults and do not adapt to extremes of temperature as effectively as adults do for the following physiological reasons (Bar-Or, 1983; American Academy of Pediatrics, 2000):

1. Children have higher surface area/mass ratios than those of adults. This allows a greater amount of heat to transfer between the environment and the body.
2. When walking or running, children produce more metabolic heat per unit mass than adults produce. Youngsters are not as efficient in executing movement patterns, so they generate more metabolic heat than do adults performing a similar task.
3. Sweating capacity is not as great in children as in adults, resulting in a lowered ability to cool the body.
4. The ability to convey heat by blood from the body core to the skin is reduced in children due to a lower cardiac output at a given oxygen uptake.

These physiological differences place children at a distinct disadvantage compared with adults when exercising in an ambient air temperature that is higher than the skin

TABLE 2.1 Weather guide: When the humidity and air temperature exceed the corresponding levels, intense activity should be curtailed.

Humidity Level (%)	Air Temperature (°F)
40	90
50	85
60	80
70	75
80	70
90	65
100	60

temperature. Individuals do acclimatize to warmer climates. However, children appear to adjust to heat more slowly (up to twice as long) than do adults (Bar-Or, 1983). Also, children do not instinctively drink enough liquids to replenish fluids lost during exercise. The American Academy of Pediatrics (2000) offers the following guidelines for exercising children during hot days:

1. The intensity of activities that last 15 minutes or more should be reduced whenever relative humidity and air temperature are above critical levels. Table 2.1 shows the relationship between humidity and air temperature and when activity should be moderated.
2. At the beginning of a strenuous exercise program or after traveling to a warmer climate, the intensity and duration of exercise should be restrained initially and then increased gradually over a period of 10 to 14 days to acclimatize to the effects of heat. When such a period is not available, the length of time for participation should be curtailed.
3. Children should be hydrated 20 to 30 minutes before strenuous activity (Figure 2.9). During the activity, periodic drinking (e.g., 150 ml of cold tap water every 20 minutes for a child weighing 40 kg) should be enforced.
4. Clothing should be lightweight and limited to one layer of absorbent material to facilitate evaporation of sweat and to expose as much skin as possible. Sweat-saturated garments should be replaced by dry ones. Rubberized sweat suits should never be used to produce weight loss.

The committee identifies children with the following conditions as being at a potentially high risk for heat stress: obesity, febrile (feverish) state, cystic fibrosis, gastrointestinal infection, diabetes insipidus, diabetes mellitus, chronic heart failure, caloric malnutrition, anorexia nervosa, sweating insufficiency syndrome, and mental retardation.

Distance Running

An often-asked question is how much and how far children should be allowed to run, particularly in a competitive or training setting. The answer is difficult because parents, teachers, and coaches seldom see the long-term effects of excessive running. The American Academy of Pediatrics Executive Committee (1990) identifies some of the concerns:

> Psychologic and social problems for the child runner can result from spending long hours in training

FIGURE 2.9 Water is mandatory for participation in strenuous activity in the heat.

> and setting unrealistic goals. This is similar to the effects of participation in other competitive sports, in which the child may be submitted to inappropriate pressures. A prepubertal child should be allowed to participate for the enjoyment of running without fear of parental or peer rejection or pressure. (p. 290)

A position taken by the International Athletics Association Federation (IAAF) Medical Committee was reprinted in 1983. In part, it states, "The danger certainly exists that with over-intensive training, separation of the growth plates may occur in the pelvic region, the knee, or the ankle. While this could heal with rest, nevertheless definitive information is lacking whether in years to come harmful effects may result." In view of these concerns, it is the opinion of the committee that training and competition for long-distance track and road-running events should not be encouraged. Up to the age of 12, it is suggested that not more than 800 m (one-half mile) should be run in competition. An increase in this distance should be introduced gradually—with, for example, a maximum of 3,000 m (nearly 2 miles) in competition for 14-year-olds.

Fitness Testing Considerations

Teachers often test children at the start of the school year in the one-mile run/walk. This practice should be discouraged, since many children may not have ample conditioning to participate safely in the activity. In addition, in many parts of the country, the start of the school year is hot and humid, adding to the stress placed on the cardiovascular system. A recommendation is to test only at the end of the school year after youngsters have had the opportunity to be conditioned. If this is not possible, at least allow youngsters 4 to 6 weeks to condition themselves. Rowland (1990) recommends starting with a one-eighth mile run/walk and gradually building to a one-mile run/walk over a 4-week period.

A strongly recommended alternative is to eliminate the mile run and substitute the PACER aerobic fitness test (see p. 237). The PACER can be administered indoors and does not require running to exhaustion. As a cardiovascular fitness measure, the PACER is as accurate as the mile run and produces much less emotional stress for participants.

Resistance Training

Resistance training for preadolescent children has generated concern among educators. Many worry about safety and stress-related injuries, while others question whether such training produces significant strength gains. Accepted thinking for years was that prepubescents are incapable of making significant strength gains because they lack adequate levels of circulating androgens. Evidence is continuing to build that contradicts this point of view. A study by Cahill (1986) demonstrated significant increases in strength among 18 prepubescent boys. A study by Servedio et al. (1985) showed significant strength gains in shoulder flexion. Weltman et al. (1986) conducted a 14-week, three-times-a-week program using hydraulic resistance training (circuit training using 10 different stations) in 6- to 11-year-old boys. Results showed an 18 to 37 percent gain in all major muscle groups. Strength can be increased through weight training in prepubescent youngsters; however, the way prepubescent children gain strength differs from adolescents and adults (Tanner, 1993). In preadolescent children, it appears that strength gains occur from motor learning rather than muscle hypertrophy. Youngsters develop more efficient motor patterns and recruit more muscle fibers, but show no increase in muscle size (Ozmun, Mikesky, & Surburg, 1991).

Note that the term *resistance training* is used here to denote the use of barbells, dumbbells, rubber bands, or machines as resistance. This is in sharp contrast to *weight lifting* or *power lifting,* which is a competitive sport for the purpose of determining maximum lifting ability. There is agreement among experts that weight training is acceptable for children, but weight lifting is highly undesirable and may be harmful. In a statement of strength training recommendations, the American Orthopaedic Society for Sports Medicine (AOSSM) (Duda, 1986) states, "(1) competition is prohibited, and (2) no maximum lift should ever be attempted." In addition, AOSSM recommends a physical exam, proper supervision by knowledgeable coaches, and emotional maturity on the part of the participating youngster. The American Academy of Pediatrics (2001) recommends that preadolescents and adolescents should avoid competitive weight lifting, power lifting, body building, and maximal lifts until they reach skeletal maturity.

Safety and prevention of injury are paramount considerations for those interested in weight training for children. It is questionable whether weight training is an appropriate activity for a typical group of children in a physical education class. When injuries were reported, most occurred due to inadequate supervision, lack of proper technique, or competitive lifting. The majority of weight lifting injuries were caused by the major lifts, the power clean, the clean and jerk, the squat lift, or the dead lift (Tanner, 1993). These lifts often are competitive and performed in an uncontrolled (ballistic) manner; they should not be used with preadolescent children. If knowledge and expertise are limited, weight training programs for children should be avoided. A knowledgeable instructor is required to provide an effective and safe program.

The long-term effects of strength training in children have not been studied. In addition, many experts worry about highly organized training programs that place emphasis on relative gains in strength. A weight training program should be one component of a comprehensive fitness program for children. The National Strength and Conditioning Association (NSCA) (1985) recommends that 50 to 80 percent of the prepubescent athlete's training must include a variety of different exercises such as agility exercises (basketball, volleyball, tennis, and tumbling) and endurance training (distance running, bicycling, and swimming).

When a variety of physical activities are experienced in elementary school physical education, there is little need for weight training within the school curriculum. However, weight training is acceptable on an individual basis with parental approval in a club setting. If a decision is made to develop a weight training program for children, it should be done in a thoughtful and studied manner. Proper supervision and technique are key ingredients in a successful program. Program prescription guidelines recommended by AOSSM and NSCA are as follows:

1. Training is recommended two or three times a week for 20- to 30-minute periods. High repetitions at low resistance appear to be most safe for elementary school–age children.
2. No resistance should be applied until proper form is demonstrated. Six to 15 repetitions equal one set; one to three sets per exercise should be done.
3. Weight or resistance is increased in 1- to 3-pound increments after the prepubescent does 15 repetitions in good form.
4. Maximal lifts should not be performed until youngsters are at least 16 to 17 years old.

REFLECTION AND REVIEW QUESTIONS

How and Why

1. How have your views of what is appropriate for children changed as a result of reading this chapter?
2. Why is it important for physical education teachers to understand "The Growing Child"?
3. How might physical education be different for an obese child as compared to a leaner peer?
4. Should children under 9 years old be permitted to play youth sports?
5. Is fitness testing in elementary physical education an appropriate practice? Defend your answer.

Content Review

1. What impact do growth patterns, body physique, and skeletal maturity have on skill acquisition and performance?
2. Explain the importance of physical activity for children.
3. Discuss the influence of muscular development and strength on physical activity for children.
4. Is training designed to improve aerobic capacity appropriate for children? Explain.
5. What can be done to maximize the youth sport experience for all children?
6. Describe the relationship between physical activity and intelligence.
7. How do adults and children differ with respect to exercising in the heat? Discuss guidelines for exercising students in the heat.

FOR MORE INFORMATION

References and Suggested Readings

American Academy of Pediatrics. (1990). Policy Statement: Risks in distance running for children. 86(5). (Reaffirmed January 1994).

American Academy of Pediatrics. (2001). Policy Statement: Strength training by children and adolescents. *Pediatrics,* 107(6), 1470–1472.

American Academy of Pediatrics. (2000). Policy Statement: Climatic heat stress and the exercising child and adolescent. *Pediatrics,* 106(01), 158–159.

Athletic Footwear Association. (1990). *American youth and sports participation.* North Palm Beach, FL: Athletic Footwear Association.

Bar-Or, O. (1983). *Pediatric sports medicine for the practitioner.* New York: Springer-Verlag.

Bar-Or, O., & Ward, D. S. (1989). Rating of perceived exertion in children. In O. Bar-Or (Ed.), *Advances in pediatric sport sciences.* Vol. III. Champaign, IL: Human Kinetics.

Beunen, G. (1989). Biological age in pediatric exercise research. In O. Bar-Or (Ed.), *Advances in pediatric sport sciences.* Vol. III. Champaign, IL: Human Kinetics.

Cahill, R. R. (1986). Prepubescent strength training gains support. *The Physician and Sportsmedicine,* 14(2), 157–161.

Clarke, H. H. (1968). Characteristics of the young athlete: A longitudinal look. *Kinesiology Review,* 3, 33–42.

Clarke, H. H. (1971). *Physical motor tests in the Medford boys' growth study.* Englewood Cliffs, NJ: Prentice-Hall.

Corbin, C. B., & Pangrazi, R. P. (1992). Are American children and youth fit? *Research Quarterly for Exercise and Sport,* 63(2), 96–106.

Dubowitz, V. (1970). Differentiation of fiber types in skeletal muscle. In E. J. Briskey, R. G. Cassens, & B. B. Marsh (Eds.), *Physiology and biochemistry of muscle as a food,* Vol. 2. Madison: University of Wisconsin Press.

Duda, M. (1986). Prepubescent strength training gains support. *The Physician and Sportsmedicine,* 14(2), 157–161.

Gould, D. (1987). Understanding attrition in children's sport. In *Advances in pediatric sport sciences.* Vol. 2. Behavioral issues. Champaign, IL: Human Kinetics.

Gruelich, W., & Pyle, S. (1959). *Radiographic atlas of skeletal development of the hand and wrist.* 2nd ed. Stanford, CA: Stanford University Press.

Hale, C. (1956). Physiological maturity of Little League baseball players. *Research Quarterly,* 27, 276–284.

Harter, S. (1978). Effectance motivation revisited. *Child Development,* 21, 34–64.

International Athletics Association Federation. (1983). Not kid's stuff. *Sports Medicine Bulletin,* 18(1), 11.

Krahenbuhl, G. S., & Pangrazi, R. P. (1983). Characteristics associated with running performance in young boys. *Medicine and Science in Sports,* 15(6), 486–490.

Malina, R. M. (1978). Physical growth and maturity characteristics of young athletes. In R. A. Magill, M. H. Ash, & F. L. Smoll (Eds.), *Children and youth in sport: A contemporary anthology.* Champaign, IL: Human Kinetics.

Malina, R. M. (1980). Growth, strength, and physical performance. In G. A. Stull & T. K. Cureton (Eds.), *Encyclopedia of physical education, fitness, and sports.* Salt Lake City, UT: Brighton.

Malina, R. M., & Bouchard, C. (1991). *Growth, maturation, and physical activity.* Champaign, IL: Human Kinetics.

National Strength and Conditioning Association. (1985). Position paper on prepubescent strength training. *National Strength and Conditioning Association Journal,* 7(4), 27–31.

Ozmun, J. C., Mikesky, A. E., & Surburg, P. R. (1991). Neuromuscular adaptations during prepubescent strength training (abstract). *Medicine and Science in Sports and Exercise,* 23(4), S31.

Pate, R. R., Dowda, M., & Ross, J. G. (1990). Associations between physical activity and physical fitness in American children. *American Journal of Diseases of Children,* 144, 1123–1129.

Payne, V. G., & Morrow, Jr., J. R. (1993). Exercise and VO_2max in children: A meta-analysis. *Research Quarterly for Exercise and Sport,* 64(3), 305–313.

Petersen, G. (1967). *Atlas for somatotyping children.* The Netherlands: Royal Vangorcum Ltd.

Petlichkoff, L. M. (1992). Youth sport participation and withdrawal: Is it simply a matter of fun? *Pediatric Exercise Science,* 4(2), 105–110.

Rarick, L. G., & Dobbins, D. A. (1975). Basic components in the motor performances of children six to nine years of age. *Medicine and Science in Sports,* 7(2), 105–110.

Roche, A. F., Chumlea, W. C., & Thissen, D. (1988). *Assessing the skeletal maturity of the hand-wrist: Fels method.* Springfield, IL: Thomas.

Rowland, T. W. (1990). *Exercise and children's health.* Champaign, IL: Human Kinetics.

Rowland, T. W. (1991). Effects of obesity on aerobic fitness in adolescent females. *American Journal of Disease in Children,* 145, 764–768.

Sallis, J. F., & McKenzie, T. L. (1991). Physical education's role in public health. *Research Quarterly of Exercise and Sport,* 62, 124–137.

Saltin, B. (1973). Metabolic fundamentals of exercise. *Medicine and Science of Sports,* 5, 137–146.

Servedio, F. J., Bartels, R. L., Hamlin, R. L., Teske, D., Shaffer, T., & Servedio, A. (1985). The effects of weight training, using Olympic style lifts, on various physiological variables in prepubescent boys. *Abstracted. Medicine and Science in Sports and Exercise,* 17, 288.

Sheldon, W. H., Dupertuis, C. W., & McDermott, E. (1954). *Atlas of men: A guide for somatotyping the adult male at all ages.* New York: Harper & Row.

Shephard, R. J. (1984a). Physical activity and child health. *Sports Medicine* 1, 205–233.

Smoll, F. L., & Smoll, R. E. (1996). *Children and youth in sport.* Dubuque, IA: Brown and Benchmark.

Tanner, S. M. (1993). Weighing the risks: Strength training for children and adolescents. *The Physician and Sportsmedicine,* 21(6), 105–116.

Thomas, J. R., & Tennant, L. K. (1978). Effects of rewards on changes in children's motivation for an athletic task. In F. L. Smoll & R. E. Smoll (Eds.), *Psychological perspectives in youth sports.* New York: Hemisphere.

Weltman, A., Janney, C., Rians, C. B., Strand, K., Berg, B., Tippitt, S., Wise, J., Cahill, B. R., & Katch, F. I. (1986). The effects of hydraulic resistance strength training in prepubertal males. *Medicine and Science in Sports and Exercise,* 18, 629–638.

Whitehead, J. R., & Corbin, C. B. (1991). Effects of fitness test type, teacher, and gender on exercise intrinsic motivation and physical self-worth. *Journal of School Health,* 61, 11–16.

Websites

Children and Physical Activity
http://www.cdc.gov/nccdphp/dash/presphysactrpt/index.htm
http://www.kidsource.com/kidsource/content4/promote.phyed.html
http://www.americanheart.org/presenter.jhtml?identifier=4596

Children's Health
http://www.aap.org/

Fitness Tests
http://www.cooperinst.org/ftgmain.asp
http://www.indiana.edu/~preschal

Obesity
http://www.cdc.gov/nccdphp/dnpa/obesity/index.htm
http://www.familyhaven.com/health/fitkids.html

Presidential Active Lifestyle Award
http://www.indiana.edu/~preschal/pala/pala/description.shtml

Strength Training and Children
http://www.acsm.org/pdf/YSTRNGTH.pdf

Youth Sports
http://www.nays.org/
http://kidshealth.org/parent/nutrition_fit/fitness/kid_sports_p3.html
http://www.betterbodz.com/kid/myth.html

SECTION 2

The Instructional Process

ESSENTIAL COMPONENTS	
I	Organized around content standards
II	**Student-centered and developmentally appropriate**
III	Physical activity and motor skill development form the core of the program
IV	**Teaches management skills and self-discipline**
V	Promotes inclusion of all students
VI	**Focuses on process over product**
VII	Promotes lifetime personal health and wellness
VIII	Teaches cooperation and responsibility and promotes sensitivity to diversity

PHYSICAL EDUCATION STANDARDS	
1	Students are able to move competently using a variety of fundamental and specialized motor skills.
2	Students can monitor and maintain a health-enhancing level of physical fitness.
3	**Students are able to apply movement concepts and basic mechanics of skill performance when learning and refining motor skills.**
4	Students comprehend the basic principles of wellness and are able to apply concepts that enable them to make meaningful decisions that positively impact their health and wellness.
5	Students participate in a wide variety of physical activities and learn how to maintain a personalized active lifestyle.
6	**Students demonstrate empathy, understanding, and respect for the numerous differences exhibited by people in an activity setting.**
7	Students exhibit responsible and self-directed behaviors that lead to positive social interactions in physical activity.

CHAPTER 3

Planning for Quality Instruction

SUMMARY

Effective teachers are able to use more than one style of teaching and may, in fact, use several styles during a particular lesson. In this chapter, planning strategies associated with quality instruction are described in detail. A number of preinstructional decisions must be made that influence the quality of the lesson. Quality teachers know how to regulate instructional space and how to use formations to maximize learning. Instructors need to understand the influence developmental patterns, arousal, feedback, and practice have on learning skills. A productive class environment demands consistent monitoring of student performance, an emphasis on safety, and a method for keeping students on-task. A comprehensive lesson plan format is offered to encourage effective planning.

OUTCOMES

- Describe various teaching styles and the best time to use each style to increase student learning.
- Describe the role of planning in preparing for quality instruction.
- Understand the relationships between instruction and the developmental and experiential level of the students.
- List preinstructional decisions that must be made before the actual delivery of the lesson.
- Know the basic mechanical principles required for efficient performance of motor skills.
- Cite effective ways to use equipment, time, space, and formations in the instructional process.
- Understand how to optimize skill learning. Include discussions of developmental patterns, arousal, feedback, practice sessions, and skill progression.
- Understand the rationale for the four components of a lesson and describe characteristics of each.
- Know how to improve the quality of instructional presentations through reflection and critique.

Planning is a critical part of teaching that ensures the implementation of a quality lesson. Preinstructional decisions, which determine how the lesson will be presented, are discussed here and in Chapter 4, "Improving Instructional Effectiveness." They include choosing a teaching style, using equipment effectively, utilizing class time, arranging for teaching space, and properly employing instructional formations. Planning also involves designing and implementing lesson plans that are both flexible and meaningful. On an average day, teachers must make many unexpected decisions. So, the job can be made much easier if as many decisions as possible are made prior to the actual lesson presentation. Preinstructional decisions are as important as the content of the lesson. If this phase of the lesson is not carefully planned, it can diminish the content presentation.

CHOOSE FROM A VARIETY OF TEACHING STYLES

One of the first steps to take when planning for instruction is to decide on the teaching styles that will be most effective for each skill. A teaching style provides direction for presenting information, organizing practice, providing feedback, keeping students engaged in appropriate behavior, and monitoring progress toward goals or objectives. Teaching styles are usually defined in terms of planning and setup of the environment, the instructional approach used, the students' responsibilities during the lesson, and expected student outcomes. Successful instructors are able to incorporate a variety of teaching styles (Harrison, Blakemore, Buck, & Pellet, 1996; Mosston & Ashworth, 1994; Rink, 1998; Siedentop & Tannehill, 2000).

There is no single "best" or universal teaching style. Even though some educators endorse their favorite approaches, evidence does not suggest that one style is more effective than another. A repertoire of styles that can be used with different objectives, students, activities, facilities, and equipment is the mark of a master teacher. Many variables have to be considered when selecting an appropriate teaching style including:

1. The objectives of the lesson such as skill development, activity promotion, knowledge, and social behaviors
2. The activities to be taught such as body management skills, manipulative skills, or rhythmic movement skills
3. The students, including individual characteristics, interests, developmental level, socioeconomic status, motivation, and background
4. The size of the class
5. The equipment and facilities available for instruction
6. The unique abilities, skills, and comfort of the teacher

The use of a different teaching style in an appropriate setting often improves the environment for students and teachers and increases the effectiveness of the program. A new or modified teaching style is not a panacea for all the ills of every school environment or setting and a teaching style cannot be selected without considering a number of variables. Teachers can use combinations of styles in a lesson or unit plan; they do not have to adopt just one style at a time. Figure 3.1 shows a continuum of teaching styles based on the degree of control and decision-making exercised by the teacher and students. At one end of the continuum (direct) the teacher makes instructional decisions exclusively. At the other end, children make the majority of decisions about their learning. Along the continuum there is a gradual shift in decision-making and responsibility for learning.

Direct Style

The direct style is the most teacher-controlled approach. The teacher provides instruction to either the entire class or small groups and guides the pace and direction of the class. Direct teaching often begins with an explanation and demonstration of skills to be developed. Students are organized into partners, small groups, or squads for practice. While students practice, the teacher actively moves around the area correcting errors, praising, encouraging, and asking questions. Independent practice follows and is supervised by an

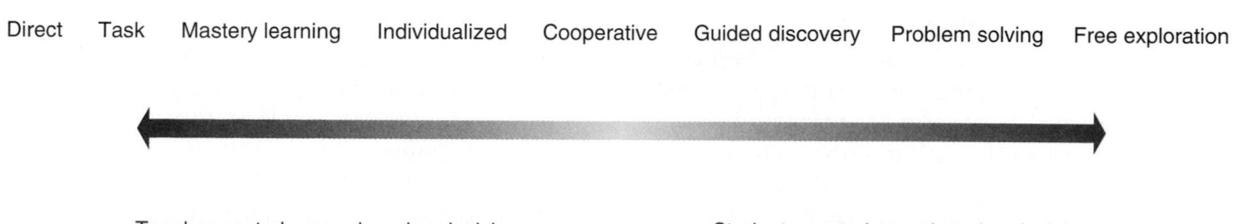

FIGURE 3.1 Continuum of teaching styles.

actively involved teacher. Throughout the class, students can be brought together for evaluative comments and instruction, or to focus on another skill. Students spend most of the class time engaged in predetermined subject matter aimed at reaching established goals. Direct instruction makes the teacher the major demonstrator, lecturer, motivator, organizer, disciplinarian, director, and corrector of errors.

The direct style, like any other type of instruction, can be effective or ineffective depending on how it is used and administered. The direct style is an effective strategy for teaching physical skills, especially when there is the possibility of an inherent hazard or accident with inexperienced students. The direct teaching format offers organization and close teacher supervision that is useful for activities, such as racquet skills, striking skills, and gymnastics. Students are offered little freedom to explore until they understand and demonstrate personal responsibility. The direct style is useful when discipline is a problem because it places more control in the hands of the teacher. The direct style is useful for beginning teachers with new students, new content preparations, large classes, or difficult-to-manage classes.

The direct teaching style places emphasis on creating a controlled class environment that is safe for students. Effective use of the direct style minimizes time spent passively watching, listening to a lecture-demonstration, or waiting in line. A challenge when using this style is offering activities that meet the needs of all students. Higher-skilled and lower-skilled students may be hindered when learning activities are too easy and unchallenging, or too difficult. This can be avoided, however, by offering learning tasks of varying difficulty.

Task (Station) Style

The task style of teaching involves arranging and presenting learning tasks at several learning areas or stations. Students rotate between learning stations and practice a variety of assigned tasks. Each station contains a number of tasks that students practice with a minimum of teacher direction. For example, students might spend 5 minutes at stations practicing four or five defined tasks. A cue or signal to rotate to a new station is given after time has elapsed. This style provides more freedom than does the direct approach because students make decisions to practice different tasks.

Using the task style allows teachers to move off center stage and away from being the central figure in the instructional process. Instruction focuses on visiting learning stations and interacting with students who need help. Less time is spent directing and managing the group as a whole. This approach requires more preparation time for planning and designing tasks. Adequate facilities, equipment, and instructional signs are necessary to keep students productive and working on appropriate tasks. The following guidelines are useful when selecting, writing, and presenting tasks:

1. Select tasks that cover the basic skills of an activity.
2. Select tasks that provide students with success and challenge. Create tasks that are developmentally appropriate. The most skilled student should be challenged, and the least skilled student should be successful.
3. Avoid tasks that carry a high safety risk.
4. Tape task cards on the wall, strap them to boundary cones, or place them on the floor. Another alternative is to provide a task sheet for each student that can be carried station to station and taken home for practice after school.
5. Write tasks so they are easy to comprehend. Use teaching cues or phrases that students have learned previously. Effective task descriptions explain what the skill is and how to do it (see the example in Figure 3.2). Periodically check to see if students understand and practice the tasks when unsupervised.
6. Incorporate a combination of instructional equipment that offers feedback and motivation such as targets, cones, hoops, ropes, and stopwatches.

The task style of instruction can utilize a variety of grouping patterns. Students work alone, with a partner, or in a small group. The partner or reciprocal grouping pattern is useful with large classes, limited amounts of equipment, and with skills where partners can time, count, record, or analyze each other. For example, one partner dribbles through a set of cones while the other is timing and recording. In a group of three students, one student bounces and catches a ball off the wall, another analyzes the form with a checklist, and the third counts and records the number of catches. The social aspect of being able to work on tasks with a partner or friend is a form of cooperative learning discussed later. Arrange learning tasks so students experience success frequently at first and become challenged by later objectives. Objectives can be modified daily or repeated, depending on the progress of the class.

Some teachers are uncomfortable when first using the task style because it implies less order and control compared to direct instruction. With proper planning, organization, and supervision, however, it offers an opportunity for students to practice a variety of tasks. Students often find the task style motivating because of the variety of learning tasks and self-paced learning. If students do not behave in a responsible manner, it may be necessary to practice self-management skills that focus on freedom, flexibility, and opportunities to make decisions.

Name______________________ Class______________ Grade______________

Your expected outcome is to master five of the following individual rope-jumping steps. You must be able to complete a minimum of 10 consecutive jumps when doing one of the steps. Please ask a friend to approve your performance before asking for instructor approval.

Approved by a friend	Approved by teacher	Skill to be completed
		Side Swing. Swing the rope, held with both hands to one side of the body. Switch and swing the rope on the other side of the body.
		Double Side Swing and Jump. Swing the rope once on each side of the body. Follow the second swing with a jump over the rope. The sequence should be swing, swing, jump.
		Running in Place. When the rope passes under the feet, the weight is shifted alternately from one foot to the other, raising the non-support foot in a running position.
		Spread Legs Forward and Backward. Start in a stride position with weight equally distributed on both feet. As the rope passes under the feet, jump into the air and reverse the position of the feet.
		Side Straddle Jump. Alternate a regular jump with a straddle jump. The straddle jump is performed with the feet spread to shoulder width.
		Cross Legs Sideward. When the rope passes under the feet, spread the legs in a straddle position (sideward) to take the rebound. As the rope passes under the feet on the next turn, jump into the air and cross the feet with the other foot forward. Then repeat with the other foot forward and continue this alternation.
		Toe-Touch Forward. Swing the right foot forward as the rope passes under the feet and touch the right toes on the next count. Then alternate, landing on the right foot and touching the left toes forward.
		Toe-Touch Backward. Same as the Toe-Touch Forward, except that the toes of the free foot touch to the back at the end of the swing.
		Shuffle Step. Push off with the right foot and sidestep to the left as the rope passes under the feet. Land with the weight on the left foot and touch the right toes beside the left heel. Repeat the step in the opposite direction.

FIGURE 3.2 Task card: Advanced individual rope-jumping steps.

Mastery Learning (Outcomes-Based) Style

Mastery learning is an instructional strategy that takes a general program outcome and breaks it into smaller parts, providing a progression of skills. These subskills are the focus of learning and are written as tasks that must be mastered before students are allowed to attempt more complex skills. The number of subskills depends on the complexity of the outcome. If mastery is not achieved, corrective activities are offered to help students learn in different ways, such as alternative instructional materials, peer tutoring, or any other learning activity that meets personal preferences. (For an in-depth discussion of mastery learning, see Guskey, 1985.) The following steps are used to implement the mastery style:

1. The outcome or movement competency is divided into sequenced, progressive units.
2. Necessary (prerequisite) competencies are evaluated.
3. Skill objectives for each of the successive learning units are established.
4. Students informally evaluate themselves to determine whether they are ready for formal testing by the teacher or a peer.
5. When a student is ready for formal evaluation, the teacher (or a peer) determines *pass* or *fail* for a particular outcome. If the performance of the outcome is satisfactory, the youngster moves to the next learning unit.
6. If the evaluation is not satisfactory, practice continues, incorporating alternatives or corrective measures.

The following outline demonstrates how a soccer lesson might be broken down to teach the target outcomes for dribbling, trapping, and kicking using the mastery learning style:

DRIBBLING OUTCOMES

1. Dribble the ball a distance of 10 yards, 3 consecutive times, making each kick travel no more than 5 yards.
2. Dribble the ball through obstacle course of 6 cones over a distance of 10 yards in 20 seconds or less.
3. With a partner, pass the ball back and forth 5 times while running for a distance of 20 yards, 2 consecutive times.

TRAPPING OUTCOMES

4. When the ball is rolled to you by a partner 5 yards away, trap it 4 of 5 times, using the instep method with the right and then the left foot.
5. Same as outcome 4 using the sole of the foot.
6. With a partner tossing the ball, trap 4 of 5 shots using the chest method.

KICKING OUTCOMES

7. Kick the ball to a partner, who is standing 5 yards away, 5 consecutive times with the right and left inside-of-the-foot push pass.
8. Same as outcome 7 using the instep kick. Loft the ball to your partner.
9. Kick 4 of 5 shots that enter the goal in the air from a distance of 10 yards.

Mastery learning is useful because students can move at an individualized pace and master preliminary skills needed to reach the outcomes. It offers a continuum of outcomes youngsters can practice in their spare time. For this reason, the style is well-suited for students with disabilities or those who are low-skilled. However, because the style requires self-direction on the part of the students, some students may take longer to acquire the discipline necessary to use this instructional format. Consider the amount of freedom, flexibility, and choice students can handle and yet be productive. When first introducing students to this style, use it sparingly and take time to teach the importance of self-management skills to students.

A rotational scheme utilizing small groups at learning stations can be implemented within this style. After an adequate amount of time, each group rotates to a new station. Another alternative is to allow students to rotate to any learning area they need to practice. A variety of grouping patterns (individually, with a partner, or with a small group) can be used depending on available facilities, equipment, objectives, and student choice. During the lesson, the teacher or peers can monitor successful completion of objectives. If class size is small, and the number of objectives also is small, it may be possible for a teacher to do all of the monitoring. Otherwise, a combination of procedures is recommended. Student involvement in the monitoring process enhances their understanding of the objectives and shares learning responsibility. Monitors can use a performance chart to check objectives at each learning station or carry a master list from station to station. Another approach is to develop a performance sheet for each student that combines teacher and peer monitoring (Figure 3.3). Peers monitor simple objectives while the teacher monitors more difficult ones. Students can also privately monitor themselves on the performance objectives. Try experimenting with several monitoring approaches depending on the activity, the number of objectives, the students' abilities, the size of the class, and the available equipment and facilities.

Name: ____________________

Instructor approved	Peer reviewed	Skill
______	______	1. Toss and catch with both hands
______	______	2. Toss and catch with right hand
______	______	3. Toss and catch with left hand
______	______	4. Toss and catch with the back of both hands (create soft home)
______	______	5. Toss, do a half turn and catch with both hands
______	______	6. Toss, do a heel click and catch with both hands
______	______	7. Place beanbag on foot, kick in the air, and catch
______	______	8. Place beanbag on foot, kick in the air, and catch behind back
______	______	9. Put beanbag between feet, jump up with beanbag, and catch
______	______	10. Toss overhead, move to another spot, and catch
______	______	11. Toss overhead, take 3 skipping steps, and catch
______	______	12. Toss overhead, lay down, and catch with hands

FIGURE 3.3 Performance objectives: manipulative skills using beanbags.

Individualized Style

The individualized style is based on the concept of student-centered learning through an individualized curriculum. This style uses a variety of teaching strategies designed to allow students to progress at an individual rate. Each student's needs are diagnosed and a program is prescribed to address those needs. Objectives are stated in behavioral terms. Students are required to learn cognitive factors before moving to psychomotor tasks.

Certain materials and hardware are necessary to establish the learning environment for individualized instruction, such as reference books, wall charts, and cards for recording student progress. Other useful equipment includes slide and overhead projectors, cassette tape recorders, videotape players, screens, and chalkboards. A learning center that includes materials, equipment, and software to direct the learning process can be established. An example of a learning center is shown in Figure 3.4. The individualized style of teaching basically follows five steps:

1. *Diagnosis.* Assessment is made to determine each student's level of cognitive and psychomotor knowledge.
2. *Prescription.* Each student is given a learning package based on his or her current level of knowledge.
3. *Development.* The student works on tasks in the learning package until he or she is able to perform them. Self-testing goals are offered, and the student decides whether to proceed to final evaluation.
4. *Evaluation.* The student goes to the teacher for final evaluation. Both psychomotor and cognitive progress are evaluated at this point.
5. *Reinforcement.* If a student completes the tasks successfully, the teacher gives positive reinforcement, records the data on the student's progress chart, and prescribes a new learning package based on the student's needs. If the student does not perform the task successfully, possible alternatives for reaching the objective are offered. The evaluation process offers an opportunity to counsel each student and reinforce critical points.

Learning packages form the core of the individualized style. The learning package is a student contract that provides an inventory of skills students need to accomplish in a meaningful sequence. The learning package consists of the following parts:

1. The content classification statement describes the task or concept to be learned. This could be a psychomotor task (such as the cartwheel) or a cognitive task (such as learning how to absorb force).
2. The purpose section explains what the package will do for the learner (for example, "This contract provides you with activities that will enable you to perform a cartwheel").
3. The learning objectives identify what is to be learned, under what conditions the learning will take place, and how the student will perform when learning has occurred.
4. The diagnostic test (pretest) determines the student's knowledge and skill level. The student is given a cognitive test as well as psychomotor tasks to perform for assessment.
5. The learning activities section offers different ways to learn a skill, concept, or activity. In each contract, different choices should be available. Students can

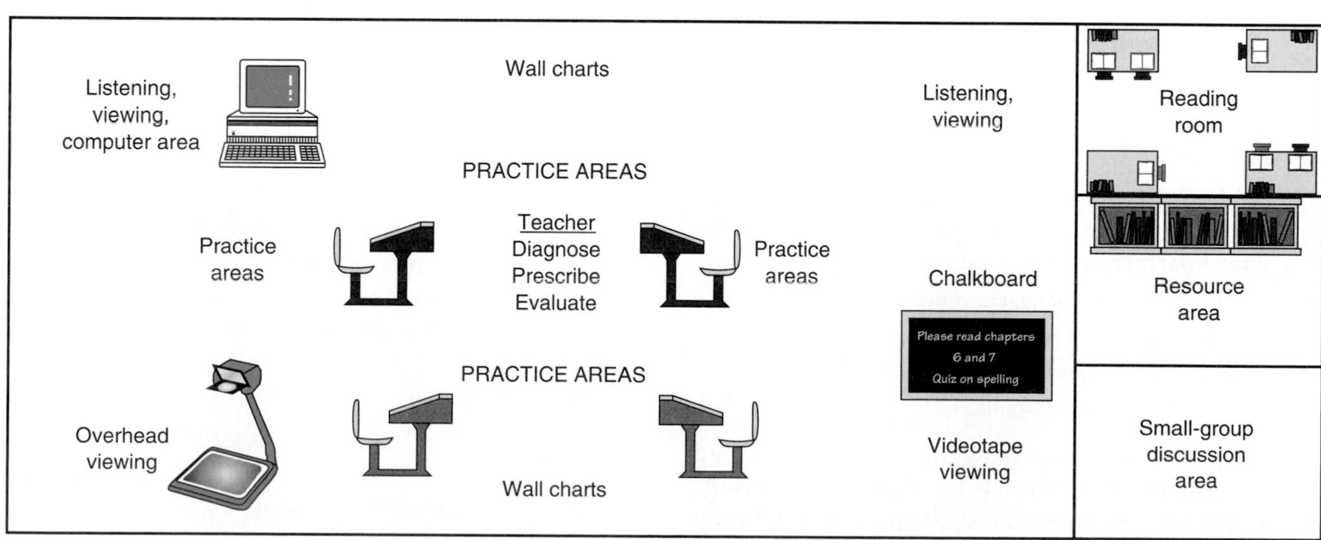

FIGURE 3.4 Organization of a learning center.

select any of the strategies to enhance learning. The following are examples of learning strategies: viewing and analyzing transparencies, listening to audiotapes for instruction in cognitive tasks, reading books that describe the task (referenced in advance by the instructor), viewing videotapes that offer demonstration and explanation of a skill to be performed, or studying charts that break down a skill into components. Students can ask other students who have successfully completed the activity to help them practice.

6. The self-test phase helps students decide whether they are ready for an evaluation to be given by the teacher. Students can ask their peers to evaluate whether they are ready for the final test.
7. The final evaluation is an observable measure of the student's achievement. The teacher judges psychomotor achievements, and cognitive learning is measured by a written exam.

The individualized style allows students to control the rate of learning and to receive personalized feedback about progress. Teacher control is dictated by the design of learning packages and the size of learning increments. Students are encouraged to investigate different approaches to learning through written material, various audiovisual media, and contacts with peers. To examine the learning process itself is a valuable experience that students can use later to learn new activities or skills. Individualized instruction is an effective style to use for some of the following reasons:

- Students, parents, and administrators know exactly what is expected and accomplished by students.
- Self-direction enhances the motivational level of most students.
- Students at most competency levels find success and challenge with objectives.
- Students progress through the objectives at their own rate.
- Students choose and sequence learning activities.
- Students have some choice concerning the grouping arrangement of skill practice (such as alone, with a partner, or in a small group).
- Students accept a greater degree of responsibility for learning.
- Teachers have greater freedom to give individual attention and offer feedback.

Despite its many advantages, the individualized style of instruction also has its problems. Most notably, the preparation for this style can be time-consuming; a teacher must develop performance objectives for each student and revise them accordingly over the course of the class. In addition, the teacher must develop an efficient system for monitoring student progress. Finally, incorporating the individualized style of instruction requires an adjustment period for teachers and students, who are usually more used to—and more comfortable with—the direct approach.

Cooperative Learning (Reciprocal) Style

When students compete against each other for a grade or another measure of success, they strive for a goal that only a few students can achieve. In competitive situations, students perceive they can reach their goals only if other students in the class fail (Johnson & Johnson, 2003). Cooperative learning is a style that focuses on the importance of people working together to accomplish common goals. In cooperative learning, students are assigned to groups where each member works to reach common goals. In cooperative activities, individuals seek outcomes that are beneficial to themselves and to the group. A resource for cooperative learning is the text by Johnson, Johnson, and Holubec, *Circles of Learning: Cooperation in the Classroom* (1990). Reciprocal teaching (Mosston and Ashworth, 1994) is another form of cooperative learning.

There is a strong research base (Slavin, 1990) that suggests cooperative learning helps foster constructive relationships among students. Emphasis is placed on joint rather than individual outcomes, and peers are given the opportunity to work with each other regularly. Because students are expected to foster the success of their peers rather than wishing for their failure, this style has the potential to enhance the social and psychological growth of students.

When using this style, learners are assigned a project or goal to complete as a team. Youngsters are grouped heterogeneously (that is, by mixing race, ability, or socioeconomic level) so there is diversity within the cooperative unit. Usually, there are two to five students in each group. They work through the assignment until all group members understand and complete it. The very nature of cooperative learning helps students realize that they cannot achieve the goal alone; that success occurs only when all members of the group reach the goal. The accomplishments of a group are successful if the outcomes are meaningful and cooperation and participation by all group members has occurred. A number of roles can be assigned to group members, including:

- A performer who does the skills or tasks
- A recorder who keeps track of statistics, trials, or key points made by the group
- A coach who provides skill feedback to the performer or times practice trials

- A presenter who communicates key points to the rest of the class
- A motivator who encourages and provides general and positive feedback to all group members

Cooperative learning is most successful when students switch roles often and stated group tasks proceed from simple to complex. Teachers need to monitor the groups to ensure all members contribute, but the responsibility for success truly lies with the students' ability to cooperate. Selected activities should require the knowledge and efforts of all members of the group. If students feel cooperation is not necessary to complete the task, the style is not effective. It must be clear that all members of the team are needed, even if in varying amounts of involvement. The tasks can be cognitive or psychomotor skills. The following are examples of class activities that could be used with the cooperative learning style:

- Design a fitness routine that requires each member of the group to design one or two exercises for inclusion. The overall routine must show balance (exercise all body parts) and be appropriate for the entire group.
- Modify a sport or game to make it more inclusive. The goal is to redesign the game so all students can play successfully.
- Each member of the group designs a drill that enhances skill learning and ensures that all members of the group improve. The drills must be cohesive and focus on a single skill to be learned (throwing, rope jumping, etc.).
- Break down a folk dance into various parts so it is easier to learn. Each member of the group is responsible for teaching one of the parts. The group must determine how the parts will be put together (taught) to the rest of the class.

Inquiry Style

The inquiry style of teaching is process-oriented rather than product-oriented, thereby placing greater importance on the learning process than on the final product or outcome. During this type of instruction, students are cognitively active as they experience learning situations that require them to inquire, speculate, reflect, analyze, and discover.

The teacher, on the other hand, plays the role of guiding and directing students, rather than commanding or telling. Students are challenged to discover their own answers and solutions. The teacher assumes responsibility for stimulating student curiosity about the subject matter. A combination of questions, problems, examples, and learning activities lead students toward one or more final solutions. This process follows a consistent and logical sequence so students can move from one step to the next after a certain amount of thinking. It may be necessary to modify questions and learning activities if students become frustrated or bored. The instructional environment is one of open communication where students feel comfortable experimenting and inquiring without fear of failure.

Advocates of inquiry methods of instruction feel this style should have a more prominent place in educational methodology—including in physical education—fearing that too many of today's approaches only emphasize listening, absorbing, and complying (Mosston and Ashworth, 1994). Proponents of this style believe it enhances students' ability to think, improves creativity, creates a better understanding of the subject matter, enhances individual self-concept, and develops lifelong learning patterns. Some educators argue that students who do not experience inquiry methods are dormant, unchallenged, and unused, but little evidence is available to support such claims.

Critics of the inquiry method, however, point out some problems with the approach: Too much time is spent on one subject or topic; a focus is on trivial or nonessential learning; most motor skills have one best solution that should be quickly explained; students already know the answers; and the instruction is difficult to plan because each class has a wide range of knowledge and ability.

Regardless of the pros and cons, there is little doubt that students need to be involved to a greater degree in the learning process. Guided discovery and problem solving are two types of inquiry that give the learner more control over the direction and content of the learning process. These styles are effective when the goal is to immerse students in the process of uncovering new and better methods for performing motor skills.

Guided Discovery (Convergent) Style

Guided discovery is used when there is a predetermined choice or result that the teacher wants students to discover. Consider teaching the concept of opposition (Example: a right-handed thrower should place the feet in a stride position with the left foot forward). Using guided discovery, students are given different foot patterns for experimentation, with the goal of selecting the best pattern. They practice right-handed throwing with the following limitations: feet together, feet in a straddle position, feet in a stride position with the left foot forward, and feet in a stride position with the right foot forward. After practicing the four different foot positions, students choose the position that seems best in terms of throwing potential.

Guided discovery is effective when the teacher is interested in having children discover the most suitable movement response when developing a new skill. This allows youngsters to try different ways of accomplishing the task and helps them learn why some solutions work better than others. The following are examples of skill techniques that can be explored and best solutions discovered:

1. Placement of the hands when catching
2. Angles of release for distance throwing with different implements such as the shot put, discus, football, and softball
3. Batting stance and foot pattern alterations for hitting the baseball or softball to various fields
4. Ready position for sport skills
5. How to stop and start quickly
6. The best place to enter in long rope-jumping skills
7. The role of a person's center of gravity and momentum in performing activities in gymnastics such as the forward roll

Problem-Solving (Divergent) Style

The problem-solving style involves input, reflection, choice, and response. The problem is structured so there is no one prescribed answer. When there is just one answer, problem solving becomes guided discovery. Problems selected vary from simple ones for primary-level children to more complex problems for intermediate-level children. A simple problem might be expressed as, "What are the different ways you can bounce a ball and stay in your personal space?" Emphasis may or may not be placed on a best way. A more complex problem involving deeper thought might be, "What is the most effective way to position and move your feet while guarding an opponent in basketball?" The solution could use an individual, partner, or group approach. The following are steps to problem solving:

- *Present the problem.* Present students with a problem in the form of a question or statement that provokes thought and reflection. No demonstration or explanation of appropriate responses is given, because students generate solutions.
- *Determine procedures.* Ask students to think about the procedures necessary for arriving at a solution. With younger children, problems are simple and this phase is minimal. It is important, however, because assessment of how to proceed toward a solution has cognitive value.
- *Experiment and explore.* In experimentation, students try different solutions, evaluate them, and make a choice. In exploration, the goal is to seek breadth of activity. Self-direction is important, and the teacher acts in an advisory role—answering questions, helping, commenting, and encouraging, but not providing solutions.
- *Observe, evaluate, and discuss.* All children have the opportunity to offer a solution and to observe what others have discovered. Various kinds of achievement demonstrations are used—by individuals, by small groups, by squads, or by part of the class. Discussion centers on justifying a particular solution.
- *Refine and expand.* After observing solutions that others have selected, and evaluating the reasoning behind the chosen solutions, all children are given the opportunity to rework their movement patterns, incorporating ideas from others.

Children learn that problems can be solved and they are able to find solutions. To do so, they must be equipped with techniques so they can proceed under self-direction toward a sound solution.

Problem solving works best when teaching concepts, relationships, strategies, and proper use of skills for specific solutions. One of the more difficult procedures, however, in the problem-solving style is designing problems that students have not previously solved. On the surface, this sounds simple, but a student who knows the answer or secures the solution ahead of time may pass it on to the rest of the class, and the process of exploring and solving is lost.

Free-Exploration Style

Free exploration is the most child-centered style of learning. Guidance by the teacher in the free-exploration style is limited to the selection of the instructional materials to be used and designation of the area to be explored. Two directives might be: "Today, for the first part of the period, you may select any piece of equipment and see what you can do with it," or "Get a jump rope and try creating a new activity." No limits are imposed on children except those dictated by safety. If necessary, forewarn or remind students how to use equipment safely. This style is used effectively to introduce new equipment, concepts, and ideas to children so they generate new ideas and responses. It often works best with young children who are experiencing activities and situations for the first time.

With free exploration, the teacher should avoid demonstrations and praising certain results too early because these can lead to imitative and noncreative behavior. This does not mean, however, that the teacher remains uninvolved. The teacher should move among students—encouraging, clarifying, and answering questions individually. Concentrate on motivating effort, since the student is responsible for being a self-directed learner. It is wise to offer students the opportunity for self-direction in small doses, increasing the time as they become more disciplined. Exploratory opportunities should be offered frequently because this phase of learning takes advantage of the child's love of movement experimentation and allows the free exercise of natural curiosity. Self-discovery is a necessary and important part of learning, and students should have this concept reinforced by experiencing the joy of creativity.

OPTIMIZE SKILL LEARNING

Helping students effectively learn motor skills requires that teachers understand a few basic principles of motor learning. Teaching motor skills is not a difficult task when teachers understand the basic tenets of proper performance techniques.

Understand Developmental Patterns

The learning and development of motor skills varies among children of similar chronological age. However, the *sequence* of skill development in youngsters is similar and progresses in an orderly fashion. Three development patterns typify the growth of primary-grade children:

1. Development, in general, proceeds from head to foot (cephalocaudal); that is, coordination and management of body parts occur in the upper body before they are observed in the lower. For example, children develop throwing skills before kicking competency.
2. Development occurs from inside to outside (proximodistal). Children control their arms before they control their hands. They can reach for objects before they can grasp them.
3. Development proceeds from general to specific. Gross motor movements are learned before fine motor coordination and refined movement patterns. As children learn motor skills, nonproductive movement is gradually eliminated. When learners begin to eliminate wasteful and tense movements and are able to concentrate on reproduction of a smooth and consistent performance, motor learning is occurring.

Know the Effect of Arousal

Arousal is the level of excitement stress produces (Schmidt, 2000). The level of arousal can have a positive or negative impact on motor performance. The key to proper arousal is to find the "just right" amount. With too little arousal, a youngster will be uninterested in learning. Too much arousal will fill a youngster with stress and anxiety resulting in a decrease in motor performance. The more complex a skill, the more likely it is that arousal may disrupt learning. On the other hand, if a skill is simple, such as skipping or running, a greater amount of arousal can be tolerated without causing a reduction in skill performance. Optimally, youngsters should be aroused to a level at which they are excited and confident about participation.

Competition affects the arousal level of children. When competition is introduced in the early stages of skill learning, stress and anxiety reduce a child's ability to learn. On the other hand, if competition is introduced after a skill has been overlearned, it can improve the level of performance. Since most elementary school youngsters have not overlearned skills, teachers should avoid competitive situations when teaching skills. For example, assume the objective is to practice basketball dribbling. The teacher places youngsters in squads and runs a relay requiring that they dribble to the opposite end of the gym and return. The first squad finished is the winner. The result: Instead of concentrating on dribbling form, students are more concerned about winning the relay. They are overaroused and determined to run as quickly as possible. Dribbling is done poorly (if at all), the balls fly out of control, and the teacher is dismayed by the result. Unfortunately, competitiveness overaroused the youngsters, who had not yet overlearned dribbling.

Offer Meaningful Skill Feedback

Feedback is important in the teaching process because it impacts what is to be learned, what should be avoided, and how the performance can be modified. Skill feedback is any kind of information about a movement performance. There are two types of skill feedback, intrinsic and extrinsic. *Intrinsic feedback* is internal, inherent to the performance of the skill, and travels through the senses, such as vision, hearing, touch, and smell. *Extrinsic feedback* is external and comes from an outside source, such as a teacher, a videotape, a stopwatch, and so on. Skill feedback should be encouraging (or constructive), given frequently, delivered publicly so all students benefit, and should be contingent on performance or (preferably) effort.

Knowledge of Results

Knowledge of results is extrinsic feedback given after a skill has been performed. Knowledge of results is a requisite for learning new motor skills. Knowledge of results is usually verbal information about performance; for example, telling players when they succeed or fail at a task. Knowledge of results provides information about an incorrect or unsuccessful performance. Learners need feedback about performance errors so they can adjust the practice trials that follow. This type of feedback need not be negative, but rather a statement of fact telling whether the skill performance resulted in a successful outcome.

Knowledge of results originates externally from a teacher, peer, or other source. It is an external variable most often controlled by the teacher to stimulate effective skill performance. Knowledge of results is critical in the early stages of learning motor skills. After performers start to master a skill, they can self-analyze their performance and develop a personal system of internal feedback rather than depend on knowledge of results.

Knowledge of Performance

This feedback is similar to knowledge of results in that it is verbal, extrinsic in nature, and occurs after the performance. Knowledge of results focuses on the outcome of a skill, whereas knowledge of performance relates to the process of the skill performance. When using this type of feedback, refer to specific components of the learner's performance. For example, "I like the way you kept your chin on your chest," or "That's the way to step toward the target with your left foot."

Knowledge of performance can increase a youngster's level of motivation because it provides feedback about improvement. Many youngsters become frustrated because they find it difficult to discern improvement. Feedback provides a lift and a rededication to continued practice. Knowledge of performance is a strong reinforcer, particularly when an instructor mentions something performed correctly. This feedback motivates youngsters to repeat the same pattern, ultimately resulting in improved performance. The most important aspect of this feedback is that it provides information for future patterns of action.

Make performance feedback short, content-filled, and concise. It should tell the youngster exactly what was correct or incorrect (for example, "That was excellent body rotation"). Concentrate on one key point to avoid confusing the youngster. Imagine a young student who is told: "Step with the left foot, rotate the trunk, lead with the elbow, and snap the wrist on your next throw!" Such excessive feedback would confuse anyone trying to learn a new skill.

If choosing between knowledge of results and knowledge of performance, focus on knowledge of performance. Knowledge of results relies solely on the performance outcome and doesn't' consider whether the skill was performed correctly. A youngster who manages to throw a ball into a basket might believe that the skill performance was performed correctly even though the technical points of the throw were performed incorrectly. The goal of elementary school physical education is to teach skills correctly, with less emphasis placed on the outcome of the skill performance. In contrast, strong emphasis is placed on product (performance) rather than process (technique) when youngsters choose to enter the competitive world of athletics.

A final point about knowledge of performance: Allow time for youngsters to internalize the feedback. Often, teachers tell a youngster something and at the same time ask them to "try it again." It is possible that the same mistake will be repeated because the youngster did not have time to concentrate on the feedback. Offer knowledge of performance feedback and move to another youngster. Follow up on your feedback at a later time. This allows the child a chance to relax, internalize the feedback, and modify future practice attempts.

Design Effective Practice Sessions

Practice is a key part of learning motor skills. It is not enough that students receive the opportunity to practice; they must practice with emphasis on quality of movement (practicing correctly). This section explains how to design practice sessions that optimize motor-skill learning.

Focus Practice on Process

The emphasis of practice often goes in two, sometimes conflicting, directions—product or process. Product- or performance-based practice has the teacher asking students to do the best they can and then reinforcing those who reach the desired outcome (product). Process-based practice, however, has the teacher encouraging students to learn the skill correctly without concern for the outcome. This leads to a product-process conflict. Students who think the teacher is interested in the product will be unwilling to concentrate on proper technique. Focus practice on learning a skill correctly by placing emphasis on technique and by encouraging experimentation. Emphasis on the outcome decreases a student's willingness to take risks and to learn new ways of performing a skill.

A way to minimize this conflict is to make sure students know the focus of the practice session. In most cases, it is best for elementary school children to focus on technique since they are learning new motor patterns. Excessive pressure to perform without mistakes can stifle students' willingness to try (especially less gifted children). If it is necessary to evaluate a skill outcome, the teacher should tell students why the outcome is important and that "we will practice doing our best today."

Use Mental Practice Techniques

Mental practice involves practicing a motor skill in a quiet, relaxed environment. The experience involves thinking about the activity and its related sounds, color, and other sensations. Students visualize themselves doing the activity successfully and at regular speed. Images of failure should be avoided (Schmidt, 2000). Mental practice stimulates children to think about and review the activity they are to perform. Some experience or familiarity with the motor task is requisite before the performer can derive value from mental practice. Mental practice is used in combination with regular practice, not in place of it. Before performing the task, prompt students to mentally review the critical factors and sequencing of the act.

Decide on Whole versus Part Practice

Skills can be taught by the whole or part method. The whole method refers to the process of learning the entire skill or activity in one dose. The part method breaks down a skill into a series of parts, then combines the parts into the whole skill. For example, in a rhythmic activity, each section of a dance is taught and then put together. A simple gymnastics routine might be broken into component parts and put back together for the performance.

Whether to use the whole or part method depends on the complexity and organization of the skills to be learned. Complexity refers to the number of serial skills or components there are in a task. Organization defines how the parts are related to each other. High organization means the parts of the skill are closely related to each other, making separation difficult. An example of a highly organized and complex skill is throwing, which would be difficult to practice without going through the complete motion. A low-organized skill is a simple folk dance, in which footwork and arm movements can be rehearsed separately. Generally, if the skills are high in complexity but low in organization, they can be taught in parts. If complexity is low but organization high, the skills must be taught as a whole. A final consideration is the duration of the skill. If the skill is of short duration, such as throwing, batting, or kicking, trying to teach the skill in parts is probably counterproductive. Imagine trying to slow down kicking while trying to teach it part by part. The performer would not develop proper pattern and timing.

When skill components are learned separately, students have to learn how to put the parts together. Practice time should be allowed for sequencing. For example, in a gymnastics routine, students might perform the activities separately, but find difficulty sequencing them because they have not learned how to modify each activity based on the previous one. Teaching a skill in parts is best used when it optimizes learning.

Determine the Length and Distribution of Practice Sessions

Short practice sessions usually produce more efficient learning than do longer sessions. This is due to both physical and mental fatigue (boredom). The challenge is to try to offer as many repetitions as possible within short practice sessions. Use varied approaches, challenges, and activities to develop the same skill in order to maintain motivational levels. For example, using many different types of beanbag activities helps maintain motivation but still focuses on tossing and catching skills.

Another way to determine the length of practice sessions is to examine the tasks being practiced. If a skill causes physical fatigue, demands intense concentration, or has the potential to become tedious, practice sessions should be short and frequent, with an adequate rest pause between intervals. Stop practice when youngsters become bored or tired, and play a game until they regain their enthusiasm to learn.

Practice sessions that are spread out over many days are usually more effective than sessions crowded into a short time span. The combination of practice and review is effective for youngsters because activities can be taught in a short unit and practiced in review sessions throughout the year. In the initial stages of skill learning, it is particularly important that practice sessions be distributed in this way. Later, when success in skill performance increases motivational levels, individual practice sessions can be lengthened.

Use Random Practice Techniques

There are two ways to organize the presentation of activities to be taught. The first is *blocked practice,* where all the trials of one task are completed before moving on to the next task. Since blocked practice is effective during the first stages of skill practice, learners find rapid improvement because they are practicing the same skill over and over. As a result, learners are often motivated to continue practicing. A drawback to blocked practice is that it makes learners believe they are more skilled than they actually are. When the skill is applied in a natural setting, performance level lowers, causing some youngsters to feel discouraged.

The other method is *random practice,* where the order of multiple task presentations is mixed and no task is practiced twice in succession. Goode and Magill (1986) showed that random practice was the most effective approach to use when learning skills. Blocked practice gave the best results during the acquisition phase of skill learning; however, students who learned a skill using random practice demonstrated a much higher level of retention.

Random practice results in better retention because the students are mentally generating solutions. When the same task is practiced over and over, youngsters not only become bored, but also don't think about how to solve the problem. Since the same motor program is used over and over to complete the task, little effort or thinking is required. In contrast, students using random practice forget the motor program used and have to consciously re-create the solution to be successful. Because youngsters become bored quickly when doing the same task over and over, random practice helps minimize this side effect.

Offer Variable Practice Experiences

Motor tasks are usually grouped into classes of tasks. For example, throwing is a collection of a class of movements. Throwing a ball in a sport can be performed in many different ways; the ball can travel at different speeds, different trajectories, and varying distances. Even though throwing tasks are all different, the variations have fundamental similarities. Movements in a class usually involve the same body parts and have similar rhythm but can be performed with many variations. These differences create the need for variable practice in a variable setting.

Practice sessions should include a variety of skills in a movement class with a variety of situations and parameters in which the skill is performed. If a skill to be learned involves one fixed way of performing it (a "closed" skill), such as place-kicking a football or striking a ball off a batting tee, variability is much less important. However, most skills are "open," and responses are somewhat unpredictable, which makes variability in practice the usual mode of operation (catching or batting a ball moving at different speeds and from different angles). Motor skills should be practiced under a variety of conditions so students can respond to a wide variety of novel situations.

Teach Skills in Proper Progression

Skill progression involves moving the learning process through ordered steps from the least challenging to the most challenging facets of an activity. Most motor skills can be ordered in an approximate hierarchy from simple to complex. Instructional progression includes reviewing previously learned steps before proceeding to new material and learning prerequisite skills before trying more difficult activities.

Developmental Levels and Progression

Children learn skills in a natural progression, but not at the same rate. Encourage youngsters to progress at a rate that is best suited for them. This usually means that all children will be learning a similar class of skills (throwing or striking, for instance) but will progress at different rates and practice different skills within the category. This premise forms the basis for presenting a "developmentally appropriate physical education program" (Barrett, Williams, & Whitall, 1992).

TABLE 3.1 Equating developmental levels to grades and ages

Developmental Level	Grades	Ages
II	K–2	5–7
III	3–4	8–9
IIII	5–6	10–11

Placing activities into developmental levels makes it easier to present activities that are appropriate to the maturity and developmental level of students. Understand that placing activities in levels serves as a general guideline for instruction. Some youngsters may be gifted or in need of special instruction. In that case, present activities that best suit the individual regardless of the recommended level. Since schools group children by chronological age and grade rather than by developmental level, Table 3.1 shows how developmental levels roughly equate with grades and ages. To help plan lessons in which skills are presented in proper sequence, activities in Chapters 16–29 have been placed in order of difficulty, from beginning to advanced. For instructional and lesson planning purposes, the accompanying lesson plan book, *Lesson Plans for Dynamic Physical Education* (Pangrazi, 2004) places the activities into developmental level lesson plans.

Developmental level I activities (used most often with kindergarten through second-grade children) are the least difficult and form the foundation for more complex skills. Most of these skills are performed individually or with a partner so as to increase the success of primary-grade children. Examples are tossing and catching, striking a stationary object, and playing games that simply incorporate fundamental locomotor movements. The number of complex decisions to make while performing the skill is minimized so youngsters can concentrate on the skill at hand. As youngsters mature and progress into *developmental level II* (usually grades 3–4), the tasks become more difficult and many are performed individually or within small groups. Environmental factors such as different speeds of objects, different sizes of objects, and games requiring locomotor movements and specialized skills (throwing, catching, and so on) are introduced at this level. In *developmental level III* (grades 5–6), students use skills in a number of sport and game situations. Simple skills previously learned are sequenced into more complex motor patterns. Cognitive decisions about when to use a skill and how to incorporate strategy into the game are integrated into the learning experiences at this level. See Table 3.2 for a quick comparison of typical activities for the three developmental levels. **The placement of activities into developmental levels is a general rule of**

TABLE 3.2 Characteristics of activities for developmental levels I, II, and III

Level	Typical Grades	Level of Difficulty	Individual or Group?	Examples and Characteristics
I	K–2	Least difficult; foundation for more complex skills; much concentration required to perform skills	Mostly individual; sometimes with a partner	Tossing and catching; striking a stationary object; games that incorporate basic locomotor skills
II	3–4	More difficult; skills are performed in a more consistent manner; less concentration required	Often individual or in small groups; groups and teams introduced	Specialized skills and variation in environmental factors (e.g., speeds and size of objects)
III	5–6	Advanced individual and specialized skills and activities; skills often performed automatically without thinking; able to perform well in group activities	Emphasis on playing with others and utilizing skills in cooperative and competitive settings	Sport and game situations; cognitive decisions and strategies are involved; more emphasis on manipulative activity, less on movement concept activities

thumb. There will always be exceptions. Expect to make exceptions to meet the developmental needs of students.

INTEGRATE MECHANICAL PRINCIPLES INTO INSTRUCTION

When planning for skill instruction, mechanical principles need to be considered an integral part of skill performance. It is best to teach young children the proper way to perform a skill so they won't have to unlearn it later. Many teachers have experienced the difficulty of changing a performer's motor patterns after a skill has been learned incorrectly. Stability, force, leverage, and motion are concepts that are best learned when they accompany a skill being taught. A discussion of each is covered in the following sections.

Stability

Stability reflects balance and equilibrium, which affect the performance of many sport skills. A stable base is necessary when one applies force to a projectile or absorbs force. Instability is useful in some activities, such as when a rapid start is desired. Introduce the following concepts:

1. The size of the base of support needs to be increased for greater stability. The base must be widened in the direction of the force being applied or absorbed.
2. The body's center of gravity must be moved lower, or closer to the base of support, when stopping quickly or applying/absorbing force (as in pushing/pulling). Lowering the center of gravity is accomplished by bending the knees and hips (Figure 3.5).
3. The center of gravity should be kept over the base of support (within the boundaries of the base) for stability and balance. When the center of gravity passes beyond the boundaries of the base of support, balance is lost. In most activities, keep the head up and eliminate excessive body lean. The ready position (Figure 3.6) is an example of a stable position used in many sport activities.
4. Use the "free" or non-weight-bearing limbs as counterbalances to aid stability. The ready position and fast starts are used in many physical activity settings and illustrate how stability and instability (used in fast starts) can enhance performance.

Force

Force is a measure of the push or pull that one object or body applies to another. Force is necessary to move objects of various types and sizes. The larger the object to be moved, the greater the amount of force required to cause the movement. Generating large forces usually requires the involvement of large muscle groups and a

FIGURE 3.5 Pulling.

FIGURE 3.6 Ready position.

greater number of muscles than does the generation of a smaller force. Torque is the twisting or turning effect that force produces when it acts eccentrically with respect to a body's axis of rotation. Concepts to remember when teaching children include the following:

1. When resisting or applying force, the bones on either side of the major joints should form a right angle to each other. A muscle is most effective at causing rotation when it pulls at a 90-degree angle.
2. To generate greater force, body parts are activated in a smooth, coordinated manner. For example, in throwing, the hips and trunk are rotated first and followed in sequence by the upper arm, lower arm, hand, and fingers.
3. More force is generated when more muscles are used. Muscles are capable of generating high levels of force when the contraction speed is low. For example, lifting a very heavy object rapidly is impossible.
4. Force should be absorbed over a large surface area and over as long a period of time as possible. An example of absorbing force over a large surface area is a softball player rolling after a dive through the air to catch a ball. The roll absorbs the force with the hands and the large surface area of the body.
5. The follow-through in striking and throwing activities is necessary to ensure maximum application of force and gradual reduction of momentum. An example is the continued swing of the baseball bat after striking the ball.

Leverage and Motion

Body levers amplify force into motion. Levers offer a mechanical advantage so that less effort is needed to accomplish tasks. Motion occurs after force has been applied or when force is absorbed. A simple lever is a bar or other rigid structure that can rotate about a fixed point to overcome a resistance when force is applied. Levers serve one of two functions: (a) They allow resistance greater than the applied force to be overcome, or (b) they serve to increase the distance or the speed at which resistance can be moved. The following are characteristics of levers and the effects they have on movement:

1. The three types of levers in the body are first-, second-, and third-class levers (Figure 3.7). Most of the body's levers are third-class levers; they have the point of force (produced by the muscles) between the fulcrum (the joint) and the point of resistance (produced by the weight of the object to be moved).
2. Most of the levers in the body are used to gain a mechanical advantage for speed, not to accomplish heavy tasks.

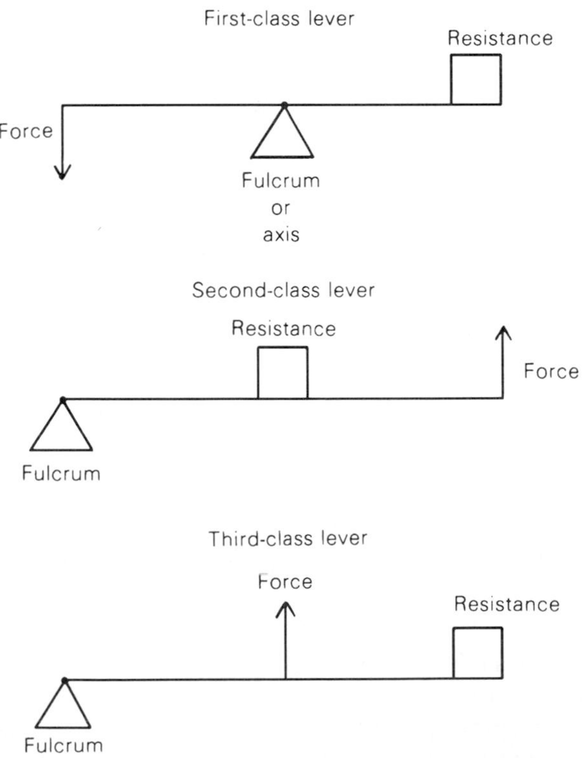

FIGURE 3.7 Types of levers.

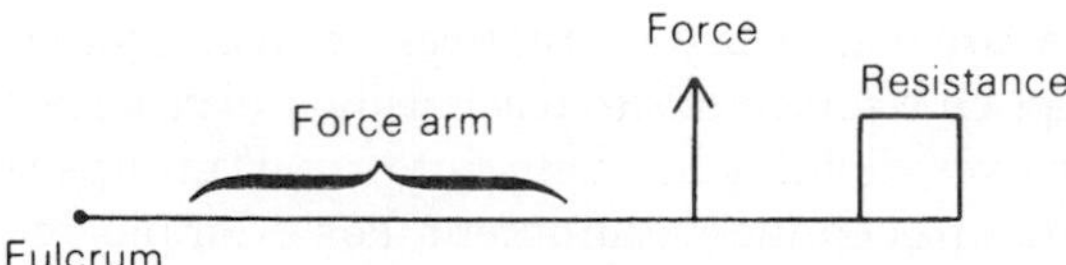

FIGURE 3.8 Longer arm force.

3. A longer force arm (distance from joint to point of force application) allows greater resistance to be overcome (Figure 3.8). This concept is useful when manipulating an external lever. For example, to pry open a paint can, force is applied to the screwdriver away from the rim rather than near the paint can. This allows the screwdriver to act as a longer lever.
4. A longer resistance arm (distance from joint to point of resistance) allows greater speed to be generated (Figure 3.9). Rackets and bats are extensions of the arm; that is, they offer longer resistance arms for applying greater speed. The longer the racket or bat, therefore, the greater the speed generated. Longer levers are more difficult to rotate, which is why young baseball players are encouraged to choke up to make the bat easier to swing and control. Even though the lever is shortened, bat velocity (at point of contact with the ball) is probably not much reduced. The important result is that performance improves through increased quality contacts.

Motion and Direction

The majority of skills in physical activities are associated with propelling an object. The following concepts of motion and direction are basic to throwing, striking, and kicking skills learned in physical education:

1. The angle of release determines how far an object will travel. Theoretically, the optimum angle of release is 45 degrees. The human body has various limitations, however, that cause the optimum angle of projection to be well below 45 degrees. For example, the angle of projection for the shot put is 40 to 41 degrees; for the running long jump, it is 20 to 22 degrees.
2. A ball rebounds from the floor or from the racket at the same angle at which it is hit. However, various factors, such as rotation applied to the ball, the type of ball, and the surface contacted by the ball, can modify the rebound angle.
3. In most throwing situations, the propelled object should be released at a point tangent to the target. During throwing, for example, the arm travels in an arc, and the ball must be released when the hand is in line with the target.

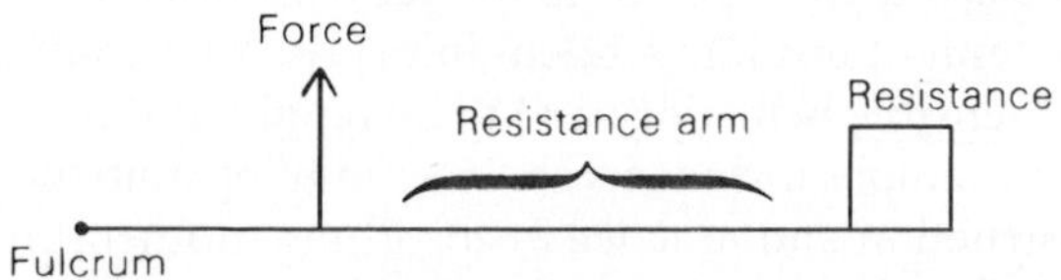

FIGURE 3.9 Longer resistance arm.

CONSIDER THE LEARNING ENVIRONMENT

The environment where youngsters experience physical education can have an impact on the effectiveness of instruction and learning. Factors such as space, equipment, and safety are important in the process of planning a quality experience. Environmental factors can be controlled entirely by the teacher, in contrast to student response and interest. There is little excuse for not considering and planning for these variables.

Predetermine Your Space Needs

A common error is to take a class to a large practice area, give students a task to accomplish, and fail to define or limit the space in which it should be performed. The class spreads out in an area so large it is impossible to communicate and manage the class. The skills being practiced and the ability of the teacher to control the class dictate the size of the space. Delineating a small area for participation makes it easier to control a class because students can see and hear better. As students become more responsive, the size of the area can be enlarged. Regardless of the size of the space, delineate the practice area. An easy way is to set up cones around the perimeter of the area. Chalk lines, evenly spaced equipment, or natural boundaries can also serve as restraining lines. A factor affecting the size of the practice area is the amount of instruction needed. When students are learning a closed skill and need constant feedback and redirection, it is important for them to stay near the instructor. Establish a smaller area where students can move in closer for instruction, and then return to the larger area for practice.

Available space is often divided into smaller areas to maximize student participation. An example is a volleyball game where only 10 students can play on one available court. In most cases, it is more effective to divide the area into two courts to facilitate a greater number of students. A related consideration when partitioning space is safety. If the playing areas are too close together, players from one area might run into players in the other area. A softball setting is unsafe if a player on one field can hit a ball into another play area.

Use Equipment Efficiently

Equipment can be a limiting factor. Before beginning the lesson, determine how much equipment is available since this will determine the structure of the lesson. For example, if there are only 16 paddles and balls for a class of 30, some type of sharing or station work will have to be organized. Know exactly what equipment is available and in working condition. It is an embarrassing experience to roll out a cart of playground balls only to find that half of them are not inflated.

How much equipment is enough? If it is individual-use equipment, such as rackets, bats, and balls, there should be one piece of equipment for each student (Figure 3.10). If it is group-oriented equipment, such as gymnastics apparatus, there should be enough to ensure waiting lines of no more than four students. Some teachers settle for less equipment because they teach as they have been taught. An often-observed example finds an instructor teaching volleyball with plenty of available equipment. Rather than have students practice individually (each with a volleyball) against the wall or with a partner, they divide the class into two long lines and use one or two balls. The majority of equipment remains on the sidelines leaving students to spend more time waiting in line than practicing skills.

If equipment is limited, it is necessary to adapt instruction for the time being. Be careful about accepting limited equipment without offering a voice of dissatisfaction. Some administrators characterize physical educators as being good people and always willing to "make do." Communicate with the educational leader regularly by explaining that instruction is much more effective when necessary equipment is available. Speak with parent-teacher groups about conducting fundraisers to purchase necessary equipment. Math teachers are not expected to teach math without a book for each student and physical educators cannot teach without adequate equipment. If you settle for less, you end up with less.

FIGURE 3.10 Each student must have a piece of equipment.

What are temporary alternatives when equipment is lacking? One solution is to teach using the task style. This involves dividing students into small groups so each group has enough equipment. For example, in a softball unit, have some students practice fielding, others batting, others pitching, and so on. Another approach is to divide the class in half and allow one group to work on one activity while another is involved in an unrelated activity. For example, due to a shortage of paddles and balls, one-half of the class is involved in racket skill practice while the other half is playing half-court basketball. This approach is less educationally sound and increases managerial and instructional demands. Another method is the peer review approach. While one student practices an activity, a peer is involved in offering feedback and evaluation. The peers share equipment and take turns being involved in practice and evaluation. A final method is to do what is most commonly done—design drills that involve standing in line and waiting for a turn. This is unacceptable from an educational standpoint.

Effectively distributing equipment is a key component of a quality lesson. Usually, the most effective method for distributing individual equipment is to place it around the perimeter of the area. It requires some set-up time prior to the lesson, but makes it easy for students to acquire a piece of equipment without confusion. Efficient equipment distribution reduces the time spent on a task that is not related to learning. Large apparatus should be arranged in the safest possible formation so all pieces are visible from all angles. The initial setup of equipment also depends on the focus of the lesson. For example, the height of the basket may be reduced to emphasize correct shooting form. The height of the volleyball net may be lowered to allow spiking. Nets may be placed at different heights to allow different types of practice. Equipment and apparatus should always be modified to best suit the needs of the learner. There is nothing sacred about a 10-foot basket or regulation-sized ball. If modifying the equipment improves the quality of learning, change it.

Ensure a Safe Environment

Do not underestimate the importance of a safe environment. Injuries are inevitable in physical education classes, but if they are due to poor planning and preparation, you may be found liable and responsible for such injuries (see Chapter 9). You are expected to foresee hazardous situations that might result in student injury. Rules dictating safe and sensible behavior need to be taught and practiced. For example, if students are in a tumbling unit, they need instruction and practice in absorbing momentum and force. Practice safety procedures, such as taking turns, spotting, and following directions.

Another component of a safe environment is a written curriculum that guides instructional presentations in proper progression. A written curriculum offers evidence to a safety committee or court of law that proper progression and sequencing of activities were used in the lesson presentation. In addition, proper progression of activities gives students confidence because they develop the skills needed to perform safely before moving on to the next level of difficulty.

Conduct safety inspections at regular intervals. If apparatus has not been used for some time, inspect it prior to the lesson to ensure that you will not have to stop a lesson to fix the equipment. Equipment such as tumbling mats, beanbags, and benches should be kept clean to prevent the spread of disease.

In spite of the foregoing precautions, accidents do happen. All activities in physical education have a certain degree of risk because students are moving. One of the most important outcomes of a physical education program is to offer students an opportunity to take risks and overcome fear. When students feel adequate safety precautions are in place, they are less hesitant to learn new activities that involve risk.

CHOOSE AN INSTRUCTIONAL FORMATION

Appropriate formations or arrangements facilitate learning experiences. Different formations are needed for activities done in place (nonlocomotor), activities where children move (locomotor), and activities in which balls, beanbags, or other objects are thrown, kicked, caught, or otherwise received (manipulative activities). Select a formation based on ensuring maximum activity for all students. When small groups are used, try to place no more than four students in a squad. This minimizes the amount of time spent standing and waiting for a turn.

Mass or Scattered Formation

Scatter youngsters throughout the area so each student has a personal space. This formation is useful for in-place activities and when individuals need to move in every direction. Place emphasis on not bumping into, colliding with, or interfering with classmates. Scattered formation is basic to such activities as wands, hoops, individual rope jumping, and individual ball skills.

Squad Formations

In squad formation, members stand about 3 feet apart in a column. In extended squad formation, the squad column is maintained with more distance (10 to 15 feet) between members. Figure 3.11 shows a regular and an extended squad formation.

Regular Ⓛ X X X X X X

Extended Ⓛ X X X X X X

FIGURE 3.11 Regular and extended squad formation.

Partner Formation

Partner formation is useful for reciprocal teaching, where partners help each other learn new skills. Catching and receiving activities can be practiced if each pair has a projectile. Keeping pairs aligned is necessary if space is limited or objects are being caught and thrown (Figure 3.12).

X X X X X X X X
↕ ↕ ↕ ↕ ↕ ↕ ↕ ↕
X X X X X X X X

FIGURE 3.12 Partner formation.

Lane or File

The lane, or file, formation is commonly used with locomotor activity (Figure 3.13). Students at the front of the lane move as prescribed and take their place at the rear of the lane.

X X X X
X X X X
X X X X
X X X X
X X X X
X X X X

FIGURE 3.13 Lane, or file, formation.

Line and Leader

Line-and-leader formation (Figure 3.14) is often used for throwing and catching skills. The leader passes back and forth to each line player in turn. Placing students in a semicircle-and-leader formation (Figure 3.15) can be used to make the distance from the leader equal for all players.

X X X X X X

Ⓛ

FIGURE 3.14 Line-and-leader formation.

FIGURE 3.15 Semicircle-and-leader formation.

Double Line

The double-line formation can be used for passing and kicking. Figure 3.16 shows a zigzag formation in which the ball is passed from one line to the next.

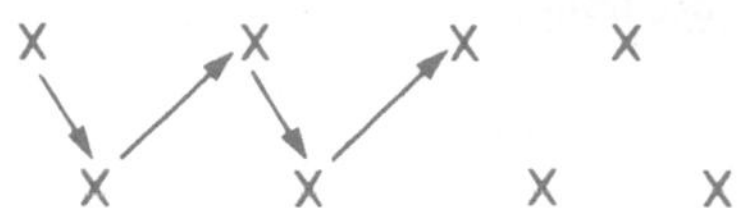

FIGURE 3.16 Double-line formation.

Regular Shuttle Formation

The regular shuttle formation (Figure 3.17) is used for practicing passing and dribbling skills on the move. It is often used for hockey, soccer, basketball, and football ball-carrying skills. The player at the head of one line dribbles toward, or passes to, the player at the head of the other line. Each player keeps moving forward and takes a place at the end of the other half of the shuttle.

FIGURE 3.17 Regular shuttle formation.

Shuttle Turn-Back Formation

Shuttle turn-back formation (Figure 3.18) is used for passing, kicking, and volleying for distance. The player at the head of one shuttle line passes to the player at the head of the other. After passing, players go to the back of their line.

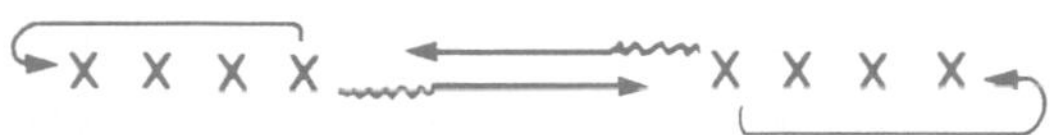

FIGURE 3.18 Shuttle turn-back formation.

Simultaneous Class Movement

There are times when certain activities require that the entire class move simultaneously. Without some structure and organization, this has the potential to become chaotic. For such activities, the following formations can be useful.

Children can start on opposite sides of the gym and exchange positions (Figure 3.19). On signal, they cross to the opposite side of the area, passing through the opposite line without contact.

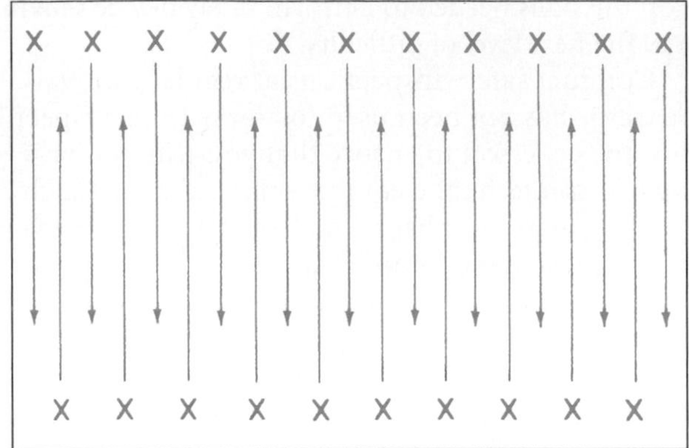

FIGURE 3.19 Exchanging positions on opposite sides.

You could also have children start on opposite sides of the gym, move toward the center and then back. A dividing line can be formed with ropes, wands, or cones to mark the center (Figure 3.20).

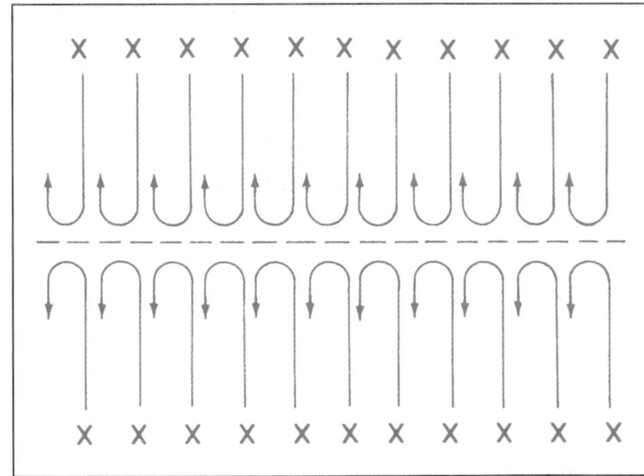

FIGURE 3.20 Moving to center and back on opposite sides.

Finally, children can start on each of four sides of the play area and alternately exchange sides (Figure 3.21). The children on one pair of opposite sides exchange first and then the others exchange. This formation is useful for class demonstrations—one half of the class demonstrates while the other half observes and evaluates.

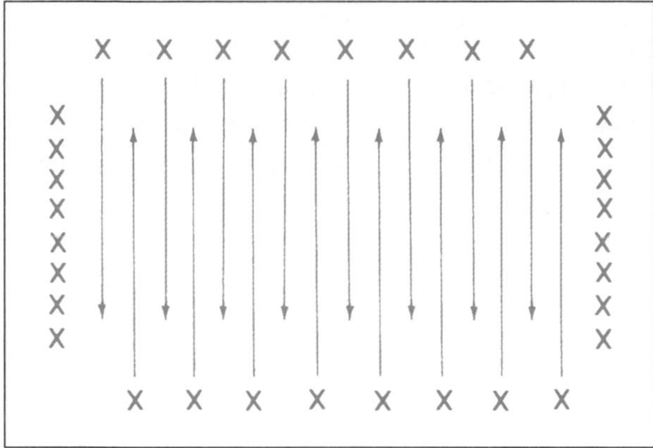

FIGURE 3.21 Exchanging on four sides.

DESIGN A LESSON PLAN FORMAT

Written lesson plans vary in form and length, depending on the activity and the background of the teacher. A written plan ensures that thought has been given to the lesson before children enter the activity area. It helps avoid spur-of-the-moment decisions that disrupt the unity and progression of instruction. Lesson plans can and should be modified when needed, but a written plan gives focus and direction to instruction. Progression is more apt to occur in a lesson when instruction is based on activities presented in previous lesson plans. Notes and changes can be written on the lesson plans to give direction for future modifications of the curriculum.

A standardized lesson plan format allows teachers and substitute teachers to interchange plans within a school district. Include the following basic information in your lesson plan.

1. *Objectives.* Instructional objectives are designed and listed for the purpose of accomplishing content standards. Writing effective objectives is discussed in the next chapter.
2. *Equipment required.* Identify amounts of materials and supplies required and how the equipment will be distributed.
3. *Instructional activities.* List actual movements and skill experiences to be taught. Place the activities in proper developmental sequence. Activities are not described in detail but give enough description so they can be easily recalled.
4. *Teaching hints.* Include organizational tips and important learning cues, including how equipment is arranged, how students are grouped, and proper teaching cues. If needed, list text and video references for in-depth information.

A common format is the four-part lesson plan. Figure 3.22 on pages 58–59 is an example of a lesson plan taken from the accompanying lesson plan book by Pangrazi (2004). This textbook contains a year's supply of lesson plans for each of the three developmental levels. Each lesson includes an introductory or warm-up activity, fitness activities, lesson focus, and closing activity. Using four parts prepares youngsters for the activity, ensures moderate to vigorous activity, teaches skills, and implements the skills in a game setting.

Lesson planning takes time. Comprehensive lesson plans are best written when you have time to plan and reflect. Lesson plans give direction to the day's lesson and may include many more activities than can be taught in a typical period. Many teachers use a 4″ by 6″ card to write down the actual activities they are teaching. The size of the card and brevity of information is much easier to refer to while teaching. The four major parts in a lesson plan consist of the following:

Introductory (Warm-Up) Activity

The introductory (warm-up) activity lasts 2 to 3 minutes and sets the tone for the rest of the lesson. If you are able to shape a class into a well-behaved group during the introductory activity, such behavior is easier to maintain throughout the remainder of the lesson. The first part of the lesson provides an opportunity to review class management skills, such as stopping on signal, running under control, and so on. Starting a lesson is a difficult phase of teaching that can be made easier by practicing management skills. An effective rule of thumb is to run and freeze your class three times. If all students are with you after three freezes, proceed to teach an introductory activity (Chapter 16). On the other hand, if students are not well managed at that point, skip the introductory activity and practice management skills. The premise for making this decision is that management skills take priority over physical development skills. It is impossible to teach if youngsters are not paying attention to you. Learning to respect others takes top billing in any educational setting and moves skill learning to a lesser priority.

Introductory activities serve several purposes in the lesson format including the following:

- Students receive immediate activity when they enter the activity area. Youngsters want to move immediately rather than having to sit down, be quiet, and listen to instructions. Offer vigorous activity first; then give instructions or discuss learning objectives while they recover from vigorous activity.
- They serve as a physiological warm-up, preparing students for physical activity.

Movement Skills and Concepts (7)
Twisting, Turning, Stretching and Relaxing Movements
Level I—Week 26

Objectives:

To apply movement concepts such as body and space awareness, relationships, and qualities of movement to a variety of locomotor and body management skills.

To combine locomotor and nonlocomotor skills into movement themes, e.g., supporting body weight, bridges, receiving and transferring weight.

DPE Content Standards:

Introductory Activity: 1, 5, 7
Fitness Activity: 2
Lesson Focus: 1, 4, 5
Game: 1, 6, 7

Equipment Required:

Music for Animal Movements
Teacher' s choice of equipment for introductory activity and manipulative skills in the lesson focus

Instructional Activities	Teaching Hints

Introductory Activity—Creative and Exploratory Opportunities

Put out enough equipment for all children to have a piece. Allow them to explore and create activities while moving. Another alternative is to have students work with a piece of equipment with a partner or small group.

Teaching Hints: Ask students to move and be active without being told what to do. Encourage independent thinking.

Fitness Development Activity—Animal Movements and Fitness Challenges

1. Puppy Dog Walk—30 seconds.
2. Freeze; perform stretching activities.
3. Measuring Worm Walk—30 seconds.
4. Freeze; perform abdominal development challenges.
5. Frog Jump—30 seconds.
6. Freeze; perform push-up position challenges.
7. Elephant Walk—30 seconds.
8. Freeze; perform stretching activities.
9. Bear Walk—30 seconds.
10. Freeze; perform abdominal challenges.
11. Crab Walk—30 seconds.
12. Freeze and perform stretching and relaxing activities.

Teaching Hints: Tape alternating segments (30 seconds in length) of silence and music to signal duration of exercise. Music segments indicate performing animal movements while intervals of silence announce doing the fitness challenges.

A variation is to place animal movement signs throughout the area and instruct students to move from sign to sign performing the appropriate animal movement each time they reach a new sign.

Lesson Focus Movement—Skills and Concepts (7)

Fundamental Skill: Twisting

1. Glue your feet to the floor. Can you twist your body to the right and to the left? Can you twist slowly, quickly? Can you bend and twist at the same time? How far can you twist your hands back and forth?
2. Twist two parts of the body at the same lime. Try three. More?
3. Can you twist one part of the body in one direction and another in a different direction?
4. Is it possible to twist the upper half of your body without twisting the lower part? How about the reverse?
5. Seated on the floor, what parts of the body can you twist?
6. Can you twist one part of the body around another? Why or why not?
7. Balance on one foot and twist your body. Can you bend and twist in this position?
8. Show different shapes that can be made using twisted body parts.

Teaching Hints: Select a few activities from each of the categories so students receive a variety of skills to practice. When possible, integrate the manipulative skill activities with fundamental skill activities. A common error is to teach all the activities from one category. The reason for multiple groups of activities is to provide variety and enhance motivation.

Teach youngsters the difference between a twist and turn. Twisting is rotating a selected body part around its own long axis. Twisting involves movement around the body part itself while turning focuses on the space in which the body turns. Turning here involves movement of the entire body.

FIGURE 3.22 Example of a lesson plan from *Lesson Plans for Dynamic Physical Education for Elementary School Children,* 14th ed. San Francisco: Benjamin Cummings.

Fundamental Skill: Turning

1. Turn your body left and right with quarter and hair turns. Turn clockwise and counterclockwise.
2. Post compass directions on the walls—north, south, east, and west. Have children face the correct direction on call. Introduce some in-between directions—northwest, southeast, etc.
3. Can you stand on one foot and turn around slowly, quickly, with a series of small hops?
4. Show me how you can cross your legs with a turn and then sit down. Can you get up without moving your feet too much?
5. When you hear the signal, turn completely around once. Next time turn the other way. Now try with two full turns; three.
6. Lie on your tummy and turn yourself around in an arc. Try seated position.

Emphasize maintaining balance while performing turning activities.

Perform twisting and turning movements in both directions. Also, try the movements in sitting position or on tummy.

Fundamental Skill: Rocking

1. How many different ways can you rock? Which part of the body is used to rock the highest?
2. Select a part of the body and show me how you can rock smoothly and slowly. How about quickly and smoothly?
3. Can you rock like a rocking chair?
4. Lie on your back and rock. Point both hands and feet toward the ceiling and rock on the back.
5. Lie on your tummy and rock. Rock as high as you can. Can you hold your ankles and make giant rocks?
6. Can you rock in a standing position? Try forward, sideways, and diagonal rocking directions.
7. Select a position where you can rock and twist at the same time.
8. Who can lie on his or her back, with knees up and rock side to side?

Make rocking a smooth and steady rhythm. It should be a controlled movement.

Rocking is usually best done when the body surface is rounded. Discuss how the body can be rounded to make rocking easier.

Manipulative Skill: Student's Choice

Select one or more manipulative activities that need additional developing with respect to the children's needs and progress. During the week's work, a different activity might be scheduled each individual day.

Since equipment was placed out for the introductory activity, use it for the manipulative skill.

Movement Concept: Stretching and Curling

1. While on your feet, show us a stretched position. A curled position.
2. Go very slowly from your stretched position to the curled one you select. Go rapidly.
3. Keeping one foot in place (on a spot), show how far you can stretch in different directions.
4. Show us a straight (regular) curled position. A twisted curled position. A tight curled position.
5. Select three different curled positions. On signal, go from one to the other rapidly. Repeat with stretch positions.
6. Explore and show the different ways that the body can support itself in curled positions.

Stretching and curling are somewhat opposite movements.

Encourage stretching through the full range of movement. The stretch is done slowly and smoothly.

Encourage holding the stretch for 6–10 seconds.

Movement Concept: Tension and Relaxation

1. Make yourself as tense as possible. Now relax.
2. Take a deep breath, hold it tight. Expel the air and relax.
3. Tense and reach as high as you can; slowly relax and drop to the floor.
4. Show how you can tense different parts of the body.
5. Tense one part of the body and relax another. Shift the tenseness to the relaxed part and vice-versa.
6. Press your fingers hard against your tensed abdominal muscles. Take your fists and beat lightly against the tensed position. Relax. Repeat.
7. Move forward, stop suddenly in a tensed position. Relax. Repeat.

Relaxation activities are an excellent way to finish the lesson. Help youngsters learn to recognize when a limb and muscles are relaxed.

A quiet atmosphere facilitates relaxing. Soft voices encourage students to "wind down."

FIGURE 3.22 (continued)

Game Activity

Midnight

Supplies: None
Skills: Running, dodging

A safety line is established about 40 ft from a den in which two or three players, the foxes, are standing. The others stand behind the safety line and ask, "What time is it, Mr. Fox?" One of the foxes is designated to answer in various fashions, such as "one o'clock," four o'clock," etc. When the fox says a certain time, the class walks forward that number of steps. For example, if the fox says, "six o'clock" the class has to move forward six steps. The fox continues to draw the players toward him. At some point, the fox answers the question by saying "Midnight," and chases the others back to the safety line. Any player who is caught becomes a fox in the den and helps to catch others.

Twins (Triplets)

Supplies: None
Skills: Body management

Youngsters are scattered throughout the area with a partner (twin). Commands are given such as "Take three hops and two leaps" or "Walk backward four steps and three skips." When the pairs are adequately separated, the leader calls out, "Find your twin!" Players find their twin and stand frozen toe to toe. The goal is to not be the last pair to find each other and assume the frozen position. Assure students move away from each other during the movements. One alternative is to find a new twin each time. Another variation is to separate twins in opposite ends of the playing area.

Variation: The game is more challenging when played in groups of three (triplets). When using this variation, new partners should be selected each time.

FIGURE 3.22 (continued)

- This part of the lesson can be used for anticipatory set (page 67) or to review previously learned skills. Anticipatory set pre-focuses on the skill and cognitive objectives of the lesson.

Fitness Activity

The second part of the lesson is designed to enhance health-related fitness and promote lifetime physical activity. A variety of exercises are used so students experience the wide range of options available for maintaining an active lifestyle. This portion of the lesson teaches youngsters the type and amount of activity necessary to maintain a healthy lifestyle. Talking about the importance of a healthy lifestyle is not enough; it must be experienced. Students are taught how to determine their personal workloads with an implied expectation that they will do their best. Forcing all students to do the same amount of activity fails to consider the genetic and personality differences inherent in a class of students. Physical fitness and activity are discussed in detail in Chapter 12.

Lesson Focus

For many adults, physical skills are the tools they use to participate in a physically active lifestyle. The lesson focus is designed to teach physical skills. It contains learning experiences designed to help students meet program content standards. Repetition and refinement of physical skills in a sequential and success-oriented setting characterize the lesson focus. This portion of the lesson (15 to 25 minutes) teaches students skills that are necessary to function comfortably in a lifestyle that features physical activity. Emphasis is placed on instruction that teaches the process of performing skills correctly. Chapters 14–29 are filled with many instructional units presented in the lesson focus.

Closing Activity

The closing activity brings closure to the lesson through evaluation of the day's accomplishments—stressing and reinforcing skills learned, revisiting performance techniques, and checking cognitive concepts. The closing activity may be a game that uses skills developed in the lesson focus or simply a low-organized game or activity children enjoy (see Chapter 22 for a variety of games). If a lesson is demanding or spirited, focus closing activities on relaxation and winding down so students return to the classroom in a calmer state of mind (Figure 3.23). See pages 295–296 for suggested relaxation activities. Taking a few minutes to relax may calm teachers and students and create goodwill between classroom teachers and specialists.

At times the closing activity is minimized or deleted entirely. For example, if a game or activity is the focus of the lesson, more time might be needed for instruction. Whether a game is played or not, avoid disciplining a class by suggesting, "We will not have a game if you don't quiet down." Closing activities are a useful part of the lesson and should not be used to bribe youngsters to behave. Doing so may cause youngsters to leave physical education classes with negative feelings.

REFLECTIVE TEACHING

Teaching is a full time job. Teachers who excel and impact the lives of their students put a great deal of time and energy into their teaching. Obviously, all who teach physical education work hard to accomplish goals. But, it is always easy to identify a truly outstanding teacher who seems to get students to perform at a high level. One of the elements that is obvious among great teachers is their level of caring and thinking. They spend a great deal of time thinking about the lessons they have presented in order to find new and better ways to get students to respond. This process is often referred to as reflection; the process of sitting back and asking the question, "How could I have done that better so students would learn more."

There are many things that make teaching difficult. For example, the weather, having to teach outside, having a limited amount of equipment, not knowing how certain youngsters will respond to your discipline techniques, etc. There are no simple answers to be found. What works one time may not work the next. There are teachers who like to put in an 8:00 to 3:00 day and you better not be in their way when the "clock strikes three." These teachers will teach the same way and the same thing year after year without change. It is often said that these teachers have been "teaching 20 years and have 1 year of experience." That approach is the opposite of reflection and trying to improve.

Quality teachers find time to reflect on all the factors related to their lessons. Most teachers admit that their first lesson of the week is not as polished and effective as one taught near the end of the week. A lesson taught during the first period of the week does not include all the finer points learned through trial and error. Instruction improves when teachers reflect on why some things worked and others didn't. Leave time at the end of the day to reflect and note ways the lesson can be improved. Try keeping a portfolio related to inspiration and insight you uncover during the reflection process. Write down personal growth indicators and situations that offer evidence you are growing professionally. Continue to reflect and see it as a dynamic and ongoing process. Examine Figure 3.24 for a list of questions that aid the reflection process. Add other questions that are specific and related to your professional growth.

REFLECTION AND REVIEW QUESTIONS

How and Why

1. Why is it important for teachers to understand and use a variety of teaching styles?

FIGURE 3.23 Relaxing during the closing activity.

Planning

- Did I prepare ahead of time? Mental preparation prior to a lesson ensures flow and continuity in a lesson.
- Did I understand the "whys" of my lesson? Knowing why you are teaching something will give you greater strength and conviction in your presentation.
- Did I state my instructional goals for the lesson? Students are more focused if they know what they are supposed to learn.
- Did I plan the lesson so students can participate safely, such as areas for running, no slippery spots, broken glass, objects to run into, adequate room for striking activities, etc.?

Equipment

- Was my equipment arranged prior to class? Proper equipment placement reduces management time and allows more time for instruction and practice.
- Did I use enough equipment to keep all students involved and assured of maximum practice opportunities?
- Did I notify the principal about equipment that needs to be repaired or replaced? On a regular basis, do I record areas where equipment is lacking or insufficient in quantity? Do I inform the principal of these shortcomings?
- Did I select equipment that is appropriate for the developmental of the students, i.e., proper size and types of balls, basketball hoop height, hand implements?

Methodology

- Did I constantly move and reposition myself during the lesson? Moving allows you to be close to more students so you can reinforce and help them. It usually reduces behavior problems.
- Did I teach with enthusiasm and energy? My energy and zest rubs off on my students.
- Did I try to show just as much energy for the last class of the day as I did for the first class of the day? Do I work just as hard on Friday as I did at the start of the week?
- Did I keep students moving during lesson transitions? Did I plan my transitions carefully so little time was needed to proceed to the next part of the lesson?

Instruction

- Was I alert for children who were having trouble performing the activities and needed some personal help? Youngsters want to receive relevant but subtle help.
- Did I praise youngsters who made an effort or improved? Saying something positive to children increases their desire to perform at a higher level.
- Did I give sufficient attention to the personalization and creativity of each student? Everybody feels unique and different and wants to deal with learning tasks in a personal manner.
- Did I teach for quality of movement or just offer a large quantity of activities in an attempt to keep students on task? Repetition is a necessary part of learning new skills.

Discipline/Management

- Did I teach students to be responsible for their learning and personal behavior? Students need to learn responsibility and self-direction skills.
- Did I evaluate how I handled discipline and management problems? Did I preserve the self-esteem of my students during behavior correction episodes? What are some ways I could have handled situations better?
- Did I make positive calls home to reinforce students who are really trying and working hard?

Assessment

- Did I bring closure to my lesson? This gives me feedback about the effectiveness of my instruction. It also allows students a chance to reflect on what they have learned. Did I ask for answers in a way that allows me to quickly check that all students understand?
- Did I evaluate the usefulness of activities I presented? Did I make changes as quickly as possible to ensure my lessons were improving and better meeting the needs of my students?
- Did I communicate with teachers and the principal about things that need to be improved or better understood? For example, did I say something about classes arriving late, teachers arriving late to pick up their class, schedule problems that cause excessive work, etc.?

FIGURE 3.24 Questions that aid the reflection process.

2. How can knowledge of motor learning help teachers maximize learning in physical education?
3. Why are mechanical principles taught in elementary physical education? How might these principles help teachers and students?
4. How does the college learning environment differ from an appropriate learning environment for elementary physical education?
5. How did your elementary physical education learning environment differ from that advocated in the chapter?

Content Review

1. What variables must be considered when choosing a teaching style?
2. Describe the teaching styles used in physical education. Include comments on the effective use of the different styles.
3. Discuss the basic tenets of motor learning required to "optimize skill learning."
4. Explain several mechanical principles and how they are used in elementary physical education.
5. Describe four instructional formations. How can these formations be used?
6. What are the four parts of a lesson? Discuss the characteristics of each part and its significance.
7. State several issues that physical education teachers must address when preparing to teach.

FOR MORE INFORMATION

References and Suggested Readings

Barrett, K. R., Williams, K., & Whitall, J. (1992). What does it mean to have a "developmentally appropriate physical education program"? *The Physical Educator,* 49 (3), 113–117.

Gabbard, C. (1994). *Physical education for children: Building the foundation.* 2nd ed. Boston: Allyn and Bacon.

Gallahue, D. L. (1995). *Developmental physical education for today's elementary school children.* 3rd ed. New York: McGraw-Hill.

Goode, S., & Magill, R. A. (1986). The contextual interference effects in learning three badminton serves. *Research Quarterly for Exercise and Sport,* 57, 308–314.

Graham, G., Holt/Hale, S. A., & Parker, M. (2001). *Children moving.* 5th ed. Mountain View, CA: Mayfield.

Guskey, T. R. (1985). *Implementing mastery learning.* Belmont, CA: Wadsworth.

Harrison, J. M., Blakemore, C. L., Buck, M. M., and Pellet, T. M. (1996). *Instructional strategies for secondary school physical education.* 4th ed. New York: McGraw-Hill.

Johnson, D. W. & Johnson, F. (2003). *Joining together: Group theory and group skills.* 8th ed. Boston: Allyn & Bacon.

Johnson, D. W., Johnson, R. T., & Holubec, E. J. (1990). *Circles of learning: Cooperation in the classroom.* 3rd ed. Edina, MN: Interaction.

Melograno, V. (1995). *Designing the physical education curriculum.* 3rd ed. Champaign, IL: Human Kinetics.

Metzler, M. W. (1999). *Instructional models for physical education.* Boston: Allyn and Bacon.

Mosston, M., & Ashworth, S. (1994). *Teaching physical education.* 4th ed. New York: Macmillan.

Nichols, B. (1994). Moving and learning: *The elementary school physical education experience.* 3rd ed. St. Louis: McGraw-Hill.

Pangrazi, R. P. (2004). *Lesson plans for dynamic physical education for elementary school students.* 14th ed. San Francisco: Benjamin Cummings.

Rink, J. E. (1998). *Teaching physical education for learning.* 3rd ed. Boston: WCB/McGraw-Hill.

Schmidt, R. A. & Wrisberg, C. (2000). *Motor learning and performance.* 2nd ed. Champaign, IL: Human Kinetics.

Slavin, R. 1990. Research on cooperative learning: Consensus and controversy. *Educational Leadership* 47(4): 52–55.

Siedentop, D. & Tannehill, D. (2000). *Developing teaching skills in physical education.* 4th ed. Mountain View, CA: Mayfield Publishing Co.

Websites

Lesson Planning
http://www.hcc.hawaii.edu/intranet/committees/FacDevCom/guidebk/teachtip/lesspln1.htm
http://www.hcc.hawaii.edu/intranet/committees/FacDevCom/guidebk/teachtip/lesspln2.htm
http://www.hcc.hawaii.edu/intranet/committees/FacDevCom/guidebk/teachtip/lesspln3.htm

Teaching Styles and Learning Styles
http://www2.ncsu.edu/unity/lockers/users/f/felder/public/Learning_Styles.html

ESSENTIAL COMPONENTS	
I	Organized around content standards
II	Student-centered and developmentally appropriate
III	Physical activity and motor skill development form the core of the program
IV	Teaches management skills and self-discipline
V	**Promotes inclusion of all students**
VI	**Focuses on process over product**
VII	Promotes lifetime personal health and wellness
VIII	**Teaches cooperation and responsibility and promotes sensitivity to diversity**

PHYSICAL EDUCATION STANDARDS	
1	Students are able to move competently using a variety of fundamental and specialized motor skills.
2	Students can monitor and maintain a health-enhancing level of physical fitness.
3	Students are able to apply movement concepts and basic mechanics of skill performance when learning and refining motor skills.
4	Students comprehend the basic principles of wellness and are able to apply concepts that enable them to make meaningful decisions that positively impact their health and wellness.
5	Students participate in a wide variety of physical activities and learn how to maintain a personalized active lifestyle.
6	**Students demonstrate empathy, understanding, and respect for the numerous differences exhibited by people in an activity setting.**
7	**Students exhibit responsible and self-directed behaviors that lead to positive social interactions in physical activity.**

CHAPTER 4

Improving Instructional Effectiveness

SUMMARY

There are instructional elements in quality lessons that cut across all presentations regardless of the students' age or grade, or lesson content. Diversity and gender are two areas that particularly impact instruction in physical education. A number of strategies for enhancing diversity and reducing gender stereotyping are outlined in this chapter. Instructional effectiveness can be improved by using instructional cues, demonstration, modeling, and feedback. Communication with students clearly increases by offering one or two key points while simultaneously demonstrating the desired behavior. Listening skills are as important as speaking skills when trying to establish meaningful relationships with students. Instructional cues—words or phrases—can be used as quick and efficient communication regarding proper technique in the performance of a particular skill or movement. Feedback to students can be delivered in various ways, including positive, negative, and corrective. Over time, positive feedback is the most effective for developing positive attitudes toward activity. Instruction is best when it is personalized and offers something of value to each individual.

OUTCOMES

- Know how to teach for the promotion of diversity in physical education classes.
- Understand how gender stereotypes can be minimized.
- Identify various ways to effectively communicate with youngsters in a physical education learning environment.
- Understand the procedures needed to develop effective instructional cues.
- Cite various ways to enhance the clarity of communication between the teacher and the learner.
- Identify essential elements of instruction and discuss the manner in which each relates to the learning environment.
- Describe the value of nonverbal behavior in the physical education setting.
- Describe various demonstration and modeling skills that facilitate an environment conducive to learning.
- Understand how instructional cues can be used to increase student performance.
- Articulate techniques that supply youngsters with meaningful feedback regarding performance.
- Describe various ways to personalize instruction within the physical education setting.

Quality instructors create a positive atmosphere for learning. They may not know more about skills and activities than less capable teachers, but they are able to apply a set of effective instructional skills. This chapter deals with instructional techniques all teachers can master. Becoming an effective teacher demands an inward look in order to see one's teaching personality and how it impacts learning. How teachers interact with students, in large part, influences how those students feel about themselves.

CHARACTERISTICS OF A QUALITY LESSON

Regardless of the teaching style used, an effective learning environment is characterized by a set of instructional behaviors that occur regularly. These behaviors do not describe a specific method or style and allow significant room for individual approaches to teaching content. The focus is less on what the teacher does and more on what students are doing. For example, any style of teaching that produces high rates of student-engaged time and positive attitudes toward the subject matter is considered an effective learning environment. Evidence from teacher effectiveness research (Brophy and Good, 1986; Evertson, 1989; and Siedentop and Tannehill, 2000) indicates that, regardless of the teacher's instructional style, an educational environment is most effective when the following elements are present:

1. **Students are engaged in appropriate learning activities for a large percentage of class time.** Effective teachers use class time wisely. They plan carefully and insist on appropriate learning activities that deal with the subject matter. Students need time to learn; effective teachers ensure that students use class time to receive information and practice skills. Developmental learning activities are matched to students' abilities and contribute to overall class objectives.
2. **The learning atmosphere is success oriented, with a positive, caring climate.** Evidence shows that teachers who develop a supportive atmosphere foster learning and positive student attitudes toward school. Appropriate social and organizational behavior needs to be supported by teachers. Students and teachers need to feel positive about working and learning in the physical education environment.
3. **Students are given clear objectives and receive high rates of information feedback from the teacher and the environment.** Students need to know what they are going to be held accountable for in the physical education class. Class activities are arranged so students spend large amounts of time on the required objectives. Instructional activities have a clear cut tie to the class objectives. Positive and corrective feedback are regularly offered. The environment is designed so students receive feedback on learning attempts even if the teacher is not available.
4. **Student progress is monitored regularly, and students are held accountable for learning in physical education.** Students are expected to make progress toward class objectives. Students are able to assess and record their progress toward objectives. Students know exactly what is expected of them and how the expectations are tied to the accountability system. Rewards are available for small steps of progress toward larger goals.
5. **Low rates of management time and smooth transitions from one activity to another characterize the environment.** Effective teachers are efficient managers of students. Students move from one learning activity to another smoothly and without wasting time. Timesaving procedures are planned and implemented efficiently. Students spend little time waiting during instructional activities. Equipment is organized to facilitate smooth transitions. Instructional procedures are all tightly organized with little wasted time.
6. **Students spend a limited amount of time waiting in line or in other unproductive behaviors.** Effective environments are characterized by high rates of time engaged in subject matter. In physical education, this means high rates of time spent practicing, drilling, and playing. Physical education is activity based and students learn by doing the activity, not waiting in line for an opportunity.
7. **Teachers are organized with high but realistic expectations for student achievement.** Structure learning activities to challenge students. Activities must not be too easy or too difficult. Students need success and challenge from learning activities. Expect students to learn, and hold them accountable for their progress.
8. **Teachers are enthusiastic about what they are doing and are actively involved in the instructional process.** Students need an enthusiastic model—someone who incorporates physical activity into his or her lifestyle. Active involvement means active supervision, enthusiasm, and high interaction rates with students. These characteristics enhance learning regardless of the teaching style used; they are important for ensuring student achievement and positive attitudes.

INCORPORATE ESSENTIAL ELEMENTS OF INSTRUCTION

Learning occurs when a well-planned curriculum is presented in a sound instructional manner. Education is effective when both a quality curriculum and able instruction are smoothly meshed. The curriculum is a critical component of the educational process; however, when the curriculum is poorly taught, student progress is limited. Hunter (1994) identified a set of essential elements for effective instruction, as shown in Figure 4.1. This section takes the theory of instruction and adapts it to physical education.

Write Measurable Student Outcomes

Educational outcomes give a lesson direction and meaning. Outcomes that are stated clearly let learners know what needs to be accomplished. Learning is enhanced when youngsters help select and set personal and group objectives. Discussions and teaching aids such as movies, videotapes, posters, and speakers can help teachers and students work toward desirable objectives. Learning outcomes are characterized as follows.

- *First, outcomes must define observable behavior.* Teachers and students must know when an outcome is reached. If an objective is not visible, neither party knows when it has been reached. Attainment in physical education is easier than in some other areas because most activities are overt and easy to observe.
- *Second, objectives must identify clearly and specifically the content to be learned.* Teachers and students will be comfortable when everyone clearly understands what is expected. Problems arise when students have to guess what the teacher wants them to learn. Students have a right to know what is expected and what they need to accomplish to reach the stated outcome. Stated outcomes help ensure that learning has occurred and that students know more than they did prior to reaching the desired outcomes. If outcomes are ambiguous or nonexistent, students have no way of knowing if they have improved or learned anything.

Outcomes can be written for the three learning domains—psychomotor, affective, and cognitive. Psychomotor domain outcomes are defined most commonly in physical education and cover areas such as learning physical skills and developing health-related physical fitness. Cognitive outcomes for physical education aim toward knowledge and comprehension of skill performance principles and precepts related to fitness and activity. Affective outcomes focus on attitudes and behaviors, such as learning to cooperate with peers on a team or behave in a responsible manner. Figure 4.2 provides examples of measurable student outcomes.

Determine the Instructional Entry Level

A challenge common to most teachers is the issue of, "At what skill level do I begin instructing my class?" Selecting the level of difficulty for skill instruction is challenging because students show a wide variation in ability and maturation level. An important step in determining a proper instructional entry level is to formulate a desired terminal outcome (one that is just beyond the grasp of the most skillful student in the class). Ask yourself, "When this lesson is over, where do I want the students to be?" Then, develop a progression of essential learning activities that lead to the terminal outcome.

Objectives

Set (hook)

Standards/expectations

Teaching

- Input
- Modeling/demo
- Direction giving (see below)
- Checking for understanding

Guided Practice

Closure

Independent Practice

(Hunter, M. C., 1994. *Mastery Teaching.* Thousand Oaks, CA: Sage Publications.)

FIGURE 4.1 Hunter's essential elements for effective instruction.

Psychomotor

"The student will demonstrate four ways to perform a forward roll."

"Using a jump rope, the student will be able to perform three consecutive forward crossover moves."

Cognitive

"The student will show an understanding of soccer rules by explaining when a corner kick is awarded."

"The student will demonstrate knowledge and understanding of rhythmic gymnastic routines by diagramming a sample floor routine for balls."

Psychomotor

"After participating in physical activity, the students will be able to express their personal satisfaction in their accomplishments."

"The students will be able to share how they feel about participating in physical activities with friends."

FIGURE 4.2 Examples of measurable outcomes.

A way to determine entry level is to move through a progression of activities until a majority of students have difficulty performing successfully. This accomplishes two things: it offers a review of skills (review makes students feel successful) and gives the instructor an estimate of the students' ability levels. Another approach is to let students self-determine a level of performance they feel is best suited for them. For example, when using balance beams, use task charts that list skills students are to perform on the beam. Students pick activities they feel competent in performing and progress at their own rate through the tasks. Instruction and learning is effective when students find an entry level that is appropriate for them.

Use Anticipatory Set

Anticipatory set refers to a technique designed to focus students on the instructional concept being presented. The opening instructional sequence in a lesson is one of the more difficult. Students typically enter the activity area socializing with friends rather than focusing on tasks to be learned. Use anticipatory set to "mentally warm up" a class. Anticipatory sets are most effective when they tie into students' past personal or learning experiences. For example, in a basketball unit, asking students to identify why they are missing so many shots encourages them to think about technique. Instructional focus might involve discussing hand placement, eyes on the basket, or keeping the shooting elbow in. Anticipatory set is also used to reveal the skill level of students in the class. For example, asking students, "What are three things we have to remember when tossing and catching beanbags?" reveals whether they know the basic tenets of catching skills. Identifying what students know is necessary for designing an effective lesson.

Another type of anticipatory set is to share with students the desired outcome. Tell students what they are going to learn and why it is important. Few people care about learning if the outcome is not stated or is thought to be unimportant. The more convinced students are about the importance of learning something, the more motivated they will be to participate.

It is not always necessary to use anticipatory set, but there should be a reason for the omission. If students already know the necessary information, there is little value in taking time for set. On the other hand, at the beginning of a lesson, after an interruption, or when choosing to move to a new objective, anticipatory set is effective. Examples of anticipatory sets are shown in Figure 4.3.

- "On Monday we practiced the skills of passing, dribbling, and shooting lay-ins. Yesterday we used those skills in a game of three-on-three. Take a few moments to think about the problems you had with dribbling or passing skills. (Allow time for thought and discussion.) Today we are going to use some drills that will help you improve in these areas."
- "Think of activities that require body strength and be ready to name some when called upon. (Allow time for thinking and discussion.) This week we are going to learn some activities that help us become stronger."
- "What is it called when we move quickly in different directions? Think of as many activities as you can that require agility, and be ready to share with the class. (Allow time for thinking and discussion.) This week we are going to learn how to do Tinikling. This rhythmic activity will improve your agility level."

FIGURE 4.3 Examples of anticipatory sets.

Deliver Meaningful Skill Instruction

Instruction is a cornerstone of learning because it is the way information is shared with students. Such information can include the definition of the skill; the elements or parts of the skill; and when, why, and how the skill should be used. The following are suggestions for effective instruction:

1. *Focus instruction on one or two key points.* It is difficult to remember a series of instructions. Telling students a number of points related to skill performance leaves them baffled and frustrated. In a series of points, most learners remember the first and the last point. Strong emphasis on one or two key points makes it easier for students to focus their concentration.
2. *Refrain from lengthy skill descriptions.* When instructions last longer than 30 to 60 seconds, students become listless because they can't comprehend and remember all of the input. Develop a pattern of short, concise presentations, alternated with practice sessions. Short practice sessions offer an opportunity to refocus on key points of a skill many times.
3. *Present information in its most basic, easy-to-understand form.* If a class does not understand the presentation, you have failed your students. Check for understanding (discussed further in the next section) to see if students comprehend the material.
4. *Separate management and instructional episodes.* Consider the following instructions during the presentation of a new game: "In this game, we will break into groups of five. Each group will get a ball and form a small circle. On the command 'Go,' the game will start. Here is how you play the game. . . ." A lengthy discussion of game rules and conduct follows.

Because the instructions are long, students forget what they were asked to do earlier. Or, they think about whom they want in their group rather than the game rules. Instead, move the class into game formation (management) and then discuss the activity to be learned (instruction). This serves two purposes: It reduces the length of the episode, and makes it easier to conceptualize how the game is played.

Monitor Student Performance

Monitoring class performance ensures that students stay on task and practice activities correctly. Effective monitoring involves being in a position where eye contact is made with all students. Students generally stay on task when they know someone is watching them. Try to be unpredictable when positioning yourself throughout the teaching area. If students know where you like to stand to teach and observe, some of them will move away from you. You will find students who enjoy being nearby and students who like to move as far away as possible. Random positioning assures contact and proximity with all students in the class.

A common but false assumption held by teachers is that you must move to the same area when giving instructions. The assumption is that students listen only when the teacher is on or near this "instructional spot." Not only is this incorrect, but it sometimes results in some rather negative consequences. Students who choose to exhibit deviant or off-task behaviors usually move as far away from the instructor as possible. If you always instruct from the same place, some of these students will try to move to a position that is difficult to observe. In addition, you may not move near certain students who need or want attention. Deliver instruction from the perimeter of the area and vary your location regularly.

Teacher movement coupled with effective observation keeps students on task. Moving into position to observe skill performance enhances your ability to improve student learning. For example, if you are observing kicking, stand to the side rather than behind the student. A judgment that needs to be made when observing performances is how long to stay with a single group of students. Spending too much time with one student may cause the rest of the class to move off task. Give a student one or two points on which to focus and then move to another student. Follow up later in the lesson to check student progress.

Because teacher movement affects observational effectiveness, it is a part of instruction that is best planned. To facilitate coverage, divide the instructional area into four (or more) equal areas and make an attempt to move into the far corner of each area a certain number of times. Try to give instructions and reinforcement from all four quadrants of the area. Ask a student to chart your movement if you are interested in reaching a personal goal. (See Figure 6.14, pages 123–125, for an example of a chart for recording different teacher behaviors.)

Use Instructional Cues

Instructional cues are keywords that quickly and efficiently communicate proper technique and performance of skills and movement tasks. Children learning new skills need a clear understanding of critical skill points because motor learning and cognitive understanding of the skill are developed simultaneously. Planning skill and movement activities without instructional cues can result in ineffective learning if students do not clearly understand proper technique and key points of performance. When using instructional cues, consider the following points.

Develop Precise Cues

Cues are short, descriptive phrases that call to the learner's attention key points of skill technique. Cues must be precise and accurate. They should guide learners and be part of instruction that enhances the quality of learning. Cues make it easier for learners to remember a sequence of new motor patterns. Study an activity and design cues that focus student learning on correct skill technique.

All teachers occasionally have to teach activities that they know little about. To develop cues in areas of less expertise, self-study must be conducted. Many textbooks and media aids delineate key points of skills. For example, *Teaching Cues for Basic Sport Skills* (Fronske and Wilson, 2002) offers teaching cues for a wide variety of physical activities. Other avenues of information are teachers who have strengths in different activities. Videotape an activity and analyze points of performance where students are having the most difficulty. It is unacceptable to teach without using cues just because you are unwilling to prepare for the skill presentation.

Use Short, Action-Oriented Cues

Effective cues are short and to the point. To avoid confusing and overwhelming the learner, choose a small number of cues to be presented during each lesson. The cues should contain key words and should be short. They should encourage the learner to focus on one phase of a skill during practice. For example, if learning to throw, offer a cue such as, "Begin with your throwing arm farthest from the target." This cue reminds the student not to face the target, which precludes trunk rotation in later phases of the throw. Other examples of throwing cues are:

"Step toward the target."

"Keep your eye on the target."

"Shift your weight from the rear to the front foot."

To examine the effectiveness of cues, see if they communicate the skill as a whole. Have all the critical points of throwing been covered, or is the skill incorrect in certain phases? With most skills, the performance can be broken into three parts: preparation, action, and recovery. Focus on one phase of a skill at a time, as most beginners can best concentrate on only one thing at a time. Action-oriented words are effective with children, particularly if they have an exciting sound. For example, "*Pop up* at the end of the forward roll," "*Twist* the body during the throw," or "*Explode* off the starting line." In other situations, let the voice influence the effectiveness of the cue. For example, if a skill is to be done smoothly and softly, speak in a soft tone and ask students to "let the movement *flooooow*" or to "move *smoooooothly* across the balance beam." The most effective cues use voice inflections, body language, and action words to signal the desired behavior.

Integrate Cues

Integration of cues involves putting the parts of a skill together so learners can focus on the skill as a whole. Integrated cues depend on prior cues used during the presentation of a skill, and assume the understanding of concepts from earlier phases of instruction. Examples of integrated cues are:

"Step, rotate, throw."

"Run, jump, and forward roll."

"Stride, swing, follow through."

The first integrated cue ("step, rotate, throw") reminds students to sequence parts of the skill. The second set of words ("run, jump, and forward roll") helps young children remember a sequence of movement activities. Integrated cues help learners to remember proper sequencing of skills and to form mental images of the performance.

Enhance Instruction by Demonstrating Skills

A quick and effective way to present a physical activity is to demonstrate (Figure 4.4). Effective demonstration accentuates critical points of performance. While demonstrating, simultaneously verbalize key focal points so students know what to observe. Both teachers and students can demonstrate instructional activities. Regardless of who does it, in the early stages of learning it is important that the demonstration be clear and unambiguous.

FIGURE 4.4 Effective teachers demonstrate skill techniques.

Teachers cannot be expected to demonstrate all physical activities well. Even skilled teachers need to devise substitutions for an instructor demonstration. Through reading, study, and analysis of movement it is possible to develop an understanding of how to present activities. If performing an activity is impossible, know what key points of the activity should be emphasized. Use visual aids and media to enhance instruction.

When possible, slow down the demonstration and present it step by step. Many skills can be videotaped and played back in slow motion. The replay can be stopped at critical instances so students can emulate a position or technique. For example, in a throwing unit, freeze at a point that illustrates the position of the arm. Have students imitate moving the arm into proper position based on the stop-action pose. Figure 4.5 offers examples for combining teaching cues and demonstration.

Use Students to Demonstrate Skills

If you can't demonstrate a skill, try to find a student who can help. Be sure students can correctly demonstrate the desired skill so they will not be embarrassed in front of the class. Usually, it is possible to find a capable student

- Students are in partners spread out about 20 yards apart, with one partner having a football. "When kicking the football, take a short step with your kicking foot, a long step with the other foot, and kick (*demonstrate*). Again, short step, long step, kick (*teaching cue*)."
- "Listen to the first verse of this schottische music. I'll do the part of the schottische step we just learned starting with the second verse (*demonstrate*). Ready, step, step, step, hop (*teaching cue*). When I hit the tambourine, begin doing the step."
- "Today we are going to work on developing fitness by moving through the Challenge Course. Move through the course as quickly as you can, but do your best at each challenge; quality is more important than speed. Travel through the course like this (*demonstrate*). Move under the bar, swing on the rope, and so forth (*teaching cue*). When I say go, start at the obstacle nearest you."

FIGURE 4.5 Combining demonstration and teaching cues.

FIGURE 4.6 Using a student to demonstrate a skill.

by verbally asking the class to perform the desired skill. Identify a student who is correctly performing the skill during the practice session and ask if he would be willing to demonstrate. Students usually will not volunteer to demonstrate unless they feel able. As the student demonstrates the skill, identify key points of the action.

Student demonstration interjects original ideas into the lesson sequence (Figure 4.6). It also helps to build self-esteem if youngsters can successfully demonstrate. If you are unsure about students' abilities to demonstrate, ask them to try the activity while all students are engaged. If they are successful, have them demonstrate. If not, let them know you will call on them at another time. At opportune times, stop the class and let children volunteer to show what they have done. Make your comments about demonstrations positive in nature. If a demonstration is unsatisfactory, go on to another child without comment or reprimand, saying only, "Thank you, Janet. Let's see what Carl can do." Or redirect the class to continue practicing. Ensure all students are selected at one time or another.

Check for Understanding

Checking to see if students comprehend instructional content is necessary to monitor student progress. Students are effective at displaying an exterior that says they understand even when they do not. Additionally, a common (but bad) habit of teachers is to ask periodically, "Does everybody understand?" It appears they are checking for understanding, however, this seldom is the case. More often than not, teachers do not even wait for a response. Additionally, it takes a brave and confident student to admit to a lack of understanding in front of the entire class. Therefore, it is important to find a quick and easy way to check for understanding without causing student embarrassment. The following are suggestions for monitoring student understanding:

1. *Use hand signals.* Examples might be: "Thumbs up if you understand," or "If you think this demonstration is correct, balance on one foot," or "Raise the number of fingers to signal which student you think did a correct forward roll." If the signals are given quickly and without comment, students will signal quickly and privately without embarrassment. Signaling with the head down and closed eyes can be used if the situation is touchy or embarrassing.
2. *Ask questions that can be answered in choral response.* Some students may mouth an answer even though they do not know the correct response. An indicator of the number of students who understand can be estimated by the intensity of the group response. A strong response by the class indicates the majority of youngsters understand.
3. *Direct a forthcoming check to the entire class rather than to a specified student.* For example, "Be ready to demonstrate the grapevine step." This encour-

ages all members of the class to focus on the activity, knowing they may be called on to demonstrate. Even though it does not ensure that everyone understands, it increases the possibility that students will think about the skill check.

4. *Use peer-checking methods.* Have students pair up and evaluate each other's performance using a checklist you have designed. More than one evaluation can be made by different students to help ensure the validity of the scoring.
5. *Use tests and written feedback to monitor cognitive concepts.* For example, written tests can be used to see if students can diagram and explain the options of an offense or defense. Asking students to list safety precautions for an activity ensures student understanding. Use some restraint when administering written instruments—an excess of written assessments will take a great deal of time away from skill practice. Use these instruments when the information cannot be gathered more efficiently with other methods.

Offer Guided Practice

Guided practice helps ensure that students are performing a skill correctly. Practice does not necessarily make perfect if it is incorrect practice. Correct practice develops correct skill patterns, whereas practicing skills with incorrect technique ingrains mistakes. Guided practice helps a class move through each step of a skill correctly. During the early phases of guided practice, small amounts of information are presented. New skills build on previously learned skills so students can see the importance of prerequisite learning.

Offer practice sessions as quickly as possible after students have been taught a skill. Allow them to get a "feel" for the skill as a whole before they work on parts. This opportunity to perform the skill before practicing smaller components enables the learner to see how the parts fit together. During guided practice sessions, monitor group responses and offer feedback to ease the pain of learning new activities. Make feedback specific, immediate, and focused on the skill being practiced. Make sure that drills and lead-up activities guarantee all students the same amount of practice. If anyone has to receive less practice, make it the skilled performer.

Bring Closure

Closure is a time to review learning that has taken place during the lesson. Closure helps increase retention because students review what they have learned. Focus closure discussions on what has been learned rather than just naming activities practiced. Closure is not simply a recall of activities that were completed, but a discussion of the application of skills and knowledge learned through practice.

Closure can be an opportunity to show how movement patterns in different skills are similar to each other. Often, students do not realize that a movement pattern is parallel to one learned earlier. Discussing what was learned focuses students on what they should be learning through practice. Use closure as a time to remind a class to tell their parents and others what they learned. How many times have parents asked, "What did you learn at school today?" only to hear the reply, "Nothing"? The following prompts are ways to initiate closure discussions:

> "Describe two or three key components of skill performance to your partner."
>
> "Demonstrate the proper skill when I (or a peer) give you a verbal cue."
>
> "Use a closing activity that requires implementation of learned skills."
>
> "Describe and demonstrate a key point for a new skill learned in the lesson."

PROVIDE INSTRUCTIONAL FEEDBACK

Delivering student feedback is an important part of instruction. Used properly, feedback enhances a student's self-concept, improves the focus of performance, increases the rate of on-task behavior, and improves student understanding. Consider the following points to enhance the quality of your instructional feedback.

Types of Feedback

Much of the feedback delivered by teachers is corrective with a focus on rectifying student performance. Outright negative feedback (such as, "That was a lousy throw") should always be avoided. Instead, corrective feedback should be offered with the intent of correcting a problem. Some corrective feedback is expected by students; however, when it is the only feedback offered, it creates a negative environment. A danger of overusing corrective feedback is that it will create a climate where students worry about making errors for fear the instructor may embarrass or belittle them. In addition, many youngsters surmise that no matter what they do correctly, they are never recognized for their effort.

Try to focus feedback on positive student performance. A positive atmosphere makes it easier for students to accept a challenge and to risk error or failure. Positive feedback also makes it easier to feel good about students because it focuses on their strengths. This is not to suggest that corrective feedback should never be used;

Siedentop and Tannehill (2000) suggest a 4:1 ratio of positive to corrective feedback is desirable. If your physical education experiences have been in a setting where most feedback is corrective, you may think it is the best way to teach even though it isn't. It is usually necessary for most teachers to consciously increase positive feedback and decrease negative feedback given to students.

Use Meaningful Feedback Statements

It is easy to develop patterns of interaction that are positive, yet habitual. For example, statements such as "Nice job," "Way to hustle," "Much better," "Right on," and "Great move" are used over and over. When used habitually, students may "tune out" and fail to feel the positive nature of the comments. These general comments also contain little specific information or value content, thus allowing for misinterpretation. For example, after a student performs a forward roll, a "nice job" reinforcement is delivered. You were pleased with the performance because the student's head was tucked. However, the student thought you were pleased because her legs were bent. Nonspecific feedback can easily result in an incorrect behavior being reinforced.

Adding specific information or value to feedback improves desired student behavior (Figure 4.7). The value content of a feedback statement tells students why it is important to perform a skill in a certain manner. Students clearly understand why their performance was positive and can build on the reinforced behavior. Examples of positive feedback with value content are:

"Good throw. When you look at your target, you are much more accurate."

"Excellent catch. You bent your elbows while catching, which created a soft home for the ball."

"That's the way to stop. When you bend your knees, you always stop under control."

Examples of feedback with specific content are as follows:

"That's the way to tuck your head on the forward roll."

"Wow! Everybody was dribbling the ball with their heads up."

"I'm impressed with the way you kept your arms straight."

Distribute Feedback Evenly

Feedback should be evenly distributed to all students by moving systematically from student to student, assuming there are no major discipline problems. This approach fosters contact with students a number of times during the lesson. In addition, it keeps students on task because they know the teacher is moving and "eyeballing" the class regularly. If skills are complex and refinement is a goal, it is better to take more time with individual students. This involves watching a student long enough to offer specific and information-loaded feedback. The end result is high-quality feedback to fewer students.

When offering instructional feedback to students, avoid close scrutiny of the student at the completion of the feedback. Many students become tense when you tell them how to do something and then watch to see if they do it exactly as they were instructed. Students will be more willing to try new ways of performing if allowed to practice without close observation. Observe carefully, offer feedback, move to another student, and recheck progress at a later time.

FIGURE 4.7 Delivering meaningful feedback.

Effective Feedback: Positive, Focused, and Immediate

Often feedback is group-oriented; that is, it is delivered to the entire class. This is an expedient method, but it also allows the most room for misinterpretation. Some students may not understand the feedback while others may not listen because it does not seem relevant. Sometimes feedback is directed to a youngster in a manner that other students are able to hear it. Negative or corrective feedback that "ripples" through the class can be a debilitating experience for youngsters. Direct negative or corrective feedback quietly to an individual in a way that only you and the involved student are privy to the discussion. This avoids resentment that might build due to embarrassment or humiliation in front of peers.

Focus feedback on the desired refinement of a task. For example, if you want students to "give" while catching a ball thrown by a partner, avoid giving feedback about the quality of the throw. If catching is the focus, feedback should be on catching, as in "Rachel is reaching out and giving with her hands when she catches the ball." It is not necessary to have students observe each other as they accomplish the desired outcome. Observing other students is effective only if the performer is capable of showing the skill correctly. If this approach is used exclusively, less skilled (or shy) performers will never have an opportunity to receive class feedback. It is just as effective to tell the class how well a student was doing and move on; for example, "Mike always keeps his head up when dribbling."

Offer feedback to students as soon as possible after a correct performance. When feedback is delayed, allow opportunity for immediate practice so students can apply the feedback information. Little is gained if students are told how to improve but are not allowed a chance to practice before leaving class. Few, if any, students remember points given in previous classes. If the end of class is approaching, it is probably best to limit feedback to situations that can be practiced immediately. Write down points of emphasis you want to teach at the next class meeting.

Nonverbal Feedback

Nonverbal behavior is another way to deliver feedback. Nonverbal feedback is effective because it is easily interpreted by students and often perceived as more meaningful than words. Beginning teachers often have a difficult time coordinating their feelings and words with body language. They may be pleased with student performance, yet carry themselves in a less-than-pleased manner (with a frown on their face and hands on their hips, for example). They may want to be assertive but take a submissive stance. For instance, when undesirable behavior occurs, an unsure teacher might place his hands in his pockets, stand in a slouched position, and back away from the class. These behaviors signal anything but assertiveness and send students mixed messages.

Many types of nonverbal feedback can be used to reinforce a class: the thrust of a finger into the air to signify "you're number 1," thumbs up, high fives, shaking hands, and so on (Figure 4.8). In contrast to the positive nonverbal behaviors, negative signals can be delivered, including hands on the hips, finger to the lips, frowning, and staring. Effective use of nonverbal feedback increases the validity and strength of verbal communication.

When using nonverbal feedback, find out how the customs and mores of different cultures impact the

FIGURE 4.8 Using nonverbal communication.

response of youngsters to different types of gestures. For example, Hmong and Laotian children may be touched on the head only by parents and close relatives. A teacher who pats the child on the head for approval is interfering with the child's spiritual nature. The okay sign, touching thumb and forefinger, is an indication of approval in the United States. However, in several Asian cultures it is a "zero," indicating the child is not performing properly. In many South American countries, the okay sign carries a derogatory sexual connotation. Ask for advice when using nonverbal gestures with youngsters from other cultures.

To make nonverbal feedback more convincing, practice it in front of a mirror and attempt to display different emotions. Another way is to display a variety of behaviors to someone who does not know you well. If this person can identify the emotions and see them as convincing, you are an effective nonverbal communicator.

Videotape recorders are effective tools for self-analysis. You can analyze how you look when under stress, when disciplining a student, when praising, and so on. It may be possible that you exhibit distracting or unassertive nonverbal behaviors, such as playing with the whistle, slumping, putting your hands in your pockets, or shuffling your feet. Just as verbal feedback must be practiced and critiqued, so must nonverbal behavior.

CONSIDER THE PERSONAL NEEDS OF STUDENTS

If teaching only involved presenting physical activities to students, it would be a rather simple endeavor. The uniqueness of each student in a large class is a factor that makes teaching complex and challenging. This section focuses on ways to make instruction meaningful and personal. Teachers who are able to make each student feel important impact the lives of their students. Understanding the diversity of classes, allowing students to make educational decisions, and encouraging student creativity are some of the ways to make a lesson feel as if it were specifically designed for each student.

Teach for Diversity

Multicultural education allows all students to reach their potential regardless of the diversity among learners. Four major variables of diversity influence how teachers and students think and learn: race/ethnicity, gender, social class, and ability. Multicultural education creates an educational environment in which students from a variety of backgrounds and experience come together to experience educational equality (Banks, 1999). Multicultural education assumes that children come from different backgrounds and helps them make sense of their everyday life. It emphasizes the contributions of various groups that make up our country, and focuses on how to learn rather than on what to learn.

Current trends in growth in the United States are causing changes in classrooms. Children who were previously excluded from classes because of language, race, economics, and abilities are now learning together. Teaching now requires a pluralistic mindset and the ability to communicate across cultures. It is our responsibility as educators to teach children to live comfortably and to prosper in this diverse and changing world. It is important that students celebrate their own culture while learning to integrate into the diversity of the world. For most students, classroom interaction between teachers and students is the major part of their multicultural education. There are a number of things teachers can do to teach students to value diversity.

1. Help students learn about the similarities and differences between cultures.
2. Encourage students to understand that people from similar cultures share common values, customs, and beliefs.
3. Make children aware of acts of discrimination and teach them ways to deal with inequity and prejudice.
4. Help youngsters develop pride in their family's culture.
5. Teach youngsters ways to communicate effectively with other cultures and races and with the other gender.
6. Instill respect for all people regardless of race/ethnicity, gender, social class, and ability.

How teachers perceive students strongly impacts their performance. Teachers who effectively teach for diversity hold high expectations for all students, including ethnic minority children and youth. Research shows that teachers tend to have lower expectations for ethnic minority youth (Vasquez, 1988). These low expectations occur in interpersonal interactions and in how students are placed in opportunities for enrichment and personal growth. At-risk youth need a rich curriculum that allows no room for failure and provides the necessary support for success.

One of the best ways to facilitate student diversity in group instruction is to vary teaching presentations. Some students learn easily via auditory methods while others learn better using visual means. Combining instructional methods by explaining and then demonstrating gives students the opportunity to learn through different modes. Diversity can also be increased through discussion sessions. The greater the number of students who participate, the better will be the chance for diverse points of view. When students are involved in discussions, they are usually attentive and participating in the learning process. Students are motivated by different approaches because they come from varied backgrounds. Getting to know students will increase the possibility of being able to effectively help them learn.

Some teaching tips that can help increase instructional effectiveness in a diverse setting follow:

- At the start of the school year (and at regular intervals thereafter) speak about the importance of encouraging and respecting diversity.
- When using group activities, insist that groups be diverse with regard to race, gender, and nationality.
- Be aware of how you speak about different groups of students. Do you refer to all students alike? Do you address boys and girls differently? Develop a consistent style for addressing all students regardless of their differences.
- Encourage all students to participate in discussions. Avoid allowing some students from certain groups to dominate interaction. Use a random method of picking students so all have an equal chance of contributing.
- Treat all students with respect and expect students to treat each other with dignity. Intervene if a student or group of students is dominating.
- When a difficult situation arises over an issue with undertones of diversity, take a time out and ask students to write down their thoughts and ideas. Allow all parties time to collect their thoughts and plan a response.
- Make sure evaluations and grades are written in gender-neutral or gender-inclusive terms.
- Encourage students to work with different partners every day. Students need to get to know other students in order to appreciate their differences.
- Invite guest speakers to class who represent diversity in gender, race, and ethnicity even if they are not speaking about multicultural or diverse issues.

- When students make comments that are sexist or racist, ask them to restate their ideas in a way that is inoffensive to others. Teach students that it is all right to express one's opinion but not in an inflammatory manner.
- Use rotating leaders when using groups. Give all students the opportunity to learn leadership skills.

Gender Differences

Teachers play a large role in how children learn to behave. Adults model gender-specific behaviors for children and youngsters who, in turn, copy the behavior. Research shows that teachers tend to treat boys and girls differently (Grossman & Grossman, 1994). For example, teachers pay more attention to boys and give boys more encouragement. Teachers give more praise for achievement to boys and call on girls less often than they call on boys. Teachers also respond to inappropriate behavior from boys and girls in different ways. Aggression is tolerated more in boys than in girls. However, disruptive talking is tolerated more in girls than in boys. Boys are reprimanded more than girls, and teachers use more "intense" means of disciplining boys.

The expectations teachers have for boys and girls strongly impacts how they interact in different ways with them. For example, teachers expect boys to be more active and more precocious than girls and not to be as good academically. As a result, they pay closer attention to them, and when they do well, boys are more likely to get positive attention. Girls, on the other hand, are expected to be more reserved and to do well academically, so they tend to be overlooked when they are doing "what they are supposed to do." When they misbehave, the teacher sees this as an aberration and is more negative to the female than she or he might be to the male. This is a common, yet unacceptable, pitfall among teachers. It takes a concerted effort to overcome these biases.

Some teachers believe that girls aren't able to perform at a level similar to boys even though research shows otherwise. Particularly in elementary school, differences in strength, endurance, and physical skills are minimal. An effective physical education environment helps all youngsters find success. Using the following teaching behaviors minimizes stereotyping by gender:

- Reinforce the performances of all students regardless of gender.
- Provide activities that are developmentally appropriate and allow all students to find success.
- Design programs that assure success in coeducational experiences. Boys and girls can challenge each other to higher levels if the atmosphere is positive.
- Don't use and don't accept student stereotypical comments, such as "you throw like a girl."
- Include activities in the curriculum that cut across typical gender stereotypes, such as rhythms are for girls, football is for boys.
- Arrange activities so the more aggressive and skilled students do not dominate. Little is learned if students are taught to be submissive or play down their ability.
- Arrange practice sessions so all students receive equal amounts of practice and/or opportunity to participate. Practice sessions should not give more practice opportunities to the skilled while the unskilled stand aside and observe.

- Expect all boys and girls to perform equally well. Teacher expectations communicate much about a student ability level. Students view themselves through the eyes of their teacher.

Encourage Creative Responses

An effective lesson includes more than planned experiences. Offering students an opportunity to create and modify new experiences is an important part of the total learning environment. Effective lessons include opportunities for creative expression and student input regarding lesson implementation.

By encouraging creativity in the classroom, a teacher helps students develop habits of discovery and reflective thinking, and to think abstractly. Self-discovered concepts are often better retained and retrieved for future use. To encourage creativity, set aside time for youngsters to explore (Figure 4.9). For example, offer a hoop with the challenge to "See how many movements can be done with it." Offer creative opportunities during appropriate segments of the instructional sequence. Ask children to add on to a movement progression just presented or to expand it in a new direction. Make the lesson plan flexible enough to allow for creativity at teachable moments. Stimulate creativity with a show-and-tell demonstration. After a period of exploration, allow youngsters to demonstrate movement patterns they have created.

Allow Students to Make Educational Decisions

Decision-making is a large part of behaving in a responsible manner, but responsibility is a learned skill that takes practice. Part of the decision-making process is learning consequences that are tied to decisions and the impact those decisions have on others. Cognitive development of students can be enhanced by allowing them to be an integral part of the lesson—choosing content, implementing the lesson, and assessing each other's techniques and development. When students are allowed to make decisions at a young age, incorrect decisions result in much less serious consequences and offer an opportunity to learn. If youngsters are always told how to behave when they are young, they may not know how to make serious decisions that impact their future as they age. Offer youngsters the opportunity to make decisions and choose from various alternatives, even if at times, they are poor choices. The following are strategies that can be used to help youngsters learn to make decisions in a safe environment.

FIGURE 4.9 Creating different movement variations.

1. *Limit the number of choices.* This strategy retains ultimate control for the teacher, but gives students a chance to decide, in part, how the outcome is reached. Use this technique when learners have had little opportunity to make decisions in the past. If you have a new class and know little about the students, limit their choices. For example, permit students the choice of practicing either a drive or a pass shot in a hockey unit. The desired outcome is that students practice striking skills, but they can decide which striking skill to practice.
2. *Let students modify activities.* Student modification of skills reduces pressure on you because it is no longer necessary to make exceptions and listen to student complaints that "it is too hard to do" or "I'm bored." Modification allows learners to change activities to suit their personal skill level. There are many modifications that can be made; some examples are:
   a. use a slower-moving family ball rather than a handball
   b. increase the number of fielders in a softball game
   c. lower the basket in a basketball unit
   d. decrease the length of a distance run or the height of hurdles
3. *Offer open-ended tasks.* This approach offers wide latitude for making decisions about the content of the lesson. Students get to decide how the task should be accomplished. You decide the educational outcome and students determine the means to reach it. For example:
   a. "Develop a game that requires four passes before a shot at the goal."
   b. "Plan a floor exercise routine that contains a forward roll, a backward roll, and a cartwheel."
   c. "Design a long-rope jumping routine that involves four people and two pieces of manipulative equipment."

This problem-solving approach has no predetermined answer. Students apply principles they have learned previously and transfer learned skills to new situations. Ultimately, the problem is solved through a movement response that has been guided by cognitive involvement.

Develop Positive Affective Skills

The performing arts (physical education, music, and drama) offer opportunities for affective domain development. They offer occasions to learn to share, express feelings, set personal goals, and function independently. Teamwork—learning to be subordinate to a leader, as well as being a leader—is learned. Effective instruction includes teaching the whole person rather than just physical skills. It is disappointing to hear a teacher say, "My job is just to teach skills. I'm not going to get involved in developing attitudes. That's someone else's job." Physical education offers an opportunity to develop positive attitudes and values. Much is lost when youngsters leave physical education with well-developed physical skills but negative attitudes toward physical activity and participation. Ponder the following situations:

1. A teacher asks everyone to run a mile knowing overweight students will run slowest. Many faster students who finish first will hurry the slower students to finish—an embarrassing situation. Obese students cannot change the outcome of the run even if they wanted to. Failure and belittlement for these students occurs every time they have to run. Small wonder such students hate physical activity.
2. Students are asked to perform skills in front of the class. Lesser skilled students feel unsure and perform more poorly because of the pressure. Many of them vow to never perform these skills again.
3. A student pitches in a softball game only to find herself unable to throw strikes. The teacher refuses to remove her from the situation and admonishes the student to "concentrate!" This student may never want to pitch again.

Few people have positive feelings about an activity if they are embarrassed or fail miserably. How youngsters feel about a subject affects their motivation to learn. Therefore, when planning, analyze whether the lesson will result in experiences that enhance the development of positive attitudes and values.

Students have to sense that you care about their feelings and want to avoid placing them in embarrassing situations. It is not a sign of weakness to care about students. Knowingly placing students in an embarrassing situation is never justified and results in negative student attitudes. It is not the content of the lesson plan but rather the attitude of the teacher that fosters positive feelings toward activity. The attitudes and values that students form are based in part on how they were treated by teachers and peers. To enhance the affective domain, how you teach is as important as what you teach. Students must be acknowledged as human beings with needs and concerns and should be treated in a courteous and nonderogatory manner. More often than not, the best way to discover how students feel is to ask them. If you ask, however, you must be ready to accept the feedback without taking it personally. The result will be an atmosphere that is conducive to the constructive development of positive attitudes and values.

Personalize Instruction

Even though most instruction is conducted as a group activity, it is obvious that the ability levels of students vary widely. As students mature, the range of ability increases because many students participate in extracurricular activities such as Little League baseball, YBA basketball, and private tutoring in gymnastics. This range of experiences demands that tasks be modified so all students find success. The following are some ways to personalize instruction to accommodate developmental differences among youngsters:

1. *Modify the conditions.* Modify tasks and activities to help all children experience success. For example, move partners closer together if they are learning to catch, use a slower-moving object such as a beach-ball or balloon, increase the size of the target, change the size of boundaries or goal areas, allow students to toss and catch individually, or increase the size of the striking implement. An optimum ratio of minimum error and maximum success is a goal. When students find little success they will exhibit off-task behavior in an attempt to draw attention away from their subpar performance. Such behavior is an indicator that the error rate is too high and learning is stymied.
2. *Use self-competition.* Surprising as it sounds, if the success rate is too high, students may become bored. When teaching individual activities, encourage students to set personal goals for themselves. For example, ask youngsters to see if they can beat their personal best performance. Challenges can be offered by asking students to accomplish higher levels of performance, use a faster-moving object, increase the distance to the goal or decrease its size. Students respond best to challenges that are personal and slightly above their current skill level.
3. *Offer different task challenges.* All students do not have to be working on the same tasks simultaneously. Offer a number of tasks of varying complexity

so students can find personal challenges. Task cards and station teaching allow students to learn at an optimum rate. When difficult skills are listed on task cards ensure that there is a balance of less demanding tasks as well. For example, students who have limited upper body strength might find inverted balances to be difficult, if not impossible. Include some activities using the legs so all students can work on balance skill challenges.

EMPLOY EFFECTIVE COMMUNICATION SKILLS

Communicating with a learner—indeed, with all learners—is critical, and communication skills can always be improved. For children to learn essential information, communication must occur in a manner that encourages students to listen. Quality instructors seem able to create a positive atmosphere for learning. They may not know more about skills and activities than less able teachers, but they often know how to communicate effectively. Meaningful feedback helps students learn when skills are performed correctly or need refinement.

Students want to communicate openly and honestly with adults. Behavior used when talking to students can help keep relationships strong. When talking with students, assume a physical pose that expresses interest and attention. Kneel at times so youngsters do not always have to look up. Check to see if facial and verbal cues reinforce your interest and concern. Some of the following suggestions can help to establish a positive bond with students and create a learning environment enjoyed by everyone.

1. *Speak about the behavior of students, not about their personal character.* The following is an example of speaking *about* a student's behavior: "Talking when I am talking is unacceptable behavior." Such feedback identifies behavior that can be improved upon and avoids questioning the self-worth of the student. This approach helps students feel you are interested in helping rather than belittling them. In contrast, saying something like "Why do you always have to act like a fool?" reflects on the child's character and undermines his or her self-esteem. It is also nonspecific, making it difficult to determine what behavior you are reprimanding. Focus on specific misbehavior followed by the type of behavior that should be displayed.
2. *Understand the child's point of view.* Imagine if someone embarrassed you in front of a class. How would you feel if you were inept and trying to learn a new skill with others watching? These and other emotions make listening difficult for youngsters. Unrestrained feedback can stress a youngster and increase behavior problems. When suggesting ways to improve performance, do so in a private manner (so other youngsters can't hear you) and allow them to practice without your scrutiny. Asking students to try something new and watching over them until they do it can be intimidating and cause resentment.
3. *Identify your feelings about the learner.* At times, mixed messages are sent to students. You may be unhappy with a student because of a previous incident, yet unwilling to confront that student. Instead, unkind feedback about a skill performance might be offered out of frustration with the student. This was not the intent but resulted due to pent-up feelings over a previous issue. Usually, when you have negative feelings toward a student, that student is able to perceive your unhappiness. Communicate how you feel (albeit negative), but make sure such communication is directed at correctable behavior.
4. *Accentuate the positive.* When teaching key instructional points of a skill, accent the positive. For example, stress that children "land lightly," rather than saying, "Don't land so hard." An easy way to emphasize key points positively is to say, "Do this because...." If there are several different and acceptable ways to perform movement patterns, be explicit with your points.
5. *Speak precisely.* Limit the use of open-ended directives and substitute those with precise goals. Instead of saying, "How many times can you ...?" or "See how many times you can ...," give children a definite target goal. Use directives such as "See if you can ... five times without missing," or "Show me five different ways to...." Encourage youngsters to set personal target goals.
6. *Optimize speech patterns.* Certain teacher mannerisms require attention and change. Avoid sermonizing at the least provocation. Excessive reliance on certain words and phrases—"Okay," "All right," and the irritating "and uh"—are unappealing to children. Acquire a broad vocabulary of effective phrases that indicate approval and good effort. A common list used by teachers shows 100 ways to say "good job." Also, a period of silence can be effective; it allows students time to internalize and digest the information.
7. *Conduct lengthy discussions in a classroom setting.* Whenever possible, hold lengthy discussions in the classroom. Students expect to physically move in the activity area, whereas they have learned to sit and interact cognitively in the classroom. Presenting time-consuming explanations in the classroom before students go to the activity area makes maxi-

mum use of activity time. Rules can be explained, procedures and responsibilities outlined, and formations illustrated on the chalkboard. Try to limit discussions in the activity area to 30 to 60 seconds.

8. *Respect student opinion.* Avoid humiliating a child who gives a wrong answer. There are a number of ways to deal with this issue. Pass over inappropriate answers by directing attention to more appropriate responses. Alternatively, suggest the student has offered a good answer, but that the question was not asked correctly. Ask the student to "save that answer" and then go back to that student when it is correct for another question. When injecting personal opinion into the question-answer process, label it as such and avoid overemphasizing its worth in comparison to student opinion. Try to not be stunned, show surprise, or take offense if children comment negatively in response to a query asking for candid opinions about an activity or procedure. When opinions are honest, some are bound to be negative.

Be a Good Listener

Listening skills are more difficult to learn than are speaking techniques. Teachers are trained to impart knowledge to students and have practiced speaking for years. Many students view teachers as people who speak but do not listen. Poor communication often occurs because of a breakdown in listening. There is truth in the adage, "You were given two ears and one mouth so you could listen twice as much as you speak." Each of the following promotes effective listening skills.

1. *Be an active listener.* Active listeners convince the speaker they are interested in what the speaker is saying. Much of this is done through nonverbal behavior, such as eye contact, nodding the head in agreement, facial expressions, and moving toward the speaker (Figure 4.10).
2. *Listen to the hidden message of the speaker.* Young children sometimes find it difficult to clearly express their feelings. The words expressed may not signal what the child is actually feeling. For example, a child may say, "I hate P.E." Most children do not hate all phases of physical education and most likely something more immediate (such as I don't like jumping rope) is the problem. Try acknowledging their feelings with a response such as, "You sound angry; are you having a problem you want to discuss?" This helps students realize their feelings are important and gives them an opportunity to clarify concerns. It prevents internalizing student anger (or frustration) and responding in an emotionally charged manner, such as "I don't want to hear that; now get back on task!"

FIGURE 4.10 Being an active listener.

3. *Paraphrase what the student said.* Paraphrasing is restating in your words what was said to you, including your interpretation of their feelings. For example, you might respond, "Do I hear you saying you are frustrated and bored with this activity?" If the paraphrasing is correct, it makes the student feel validated and understood. If the interpretation is incorrect, the student has an opportunity to restate his or her concern. It offers an indication of how students perceive various situations.
4. *Let students know you value listening.* Teachers who listen to students learn about their feelings. Let students know you will listen and then do something about it. If you are a good listener you will hear things that are not always positive. For example, students may state honestly which activities they enjoy and which they do not. They may express how they felt when they were criticized. This communication can be constructive if it is not taken personally. Even though it may not be valid criticism of the program or your procedures, it opens the door to good communication. A word of caution: If you find it difficult to accept such feedback, it is best to ask students to keep their comments to themselves. Avoiding such interactions is necessary if it affects your confidence.

REFLECTION AND REVIEW QUESTIONS

How and Why

1. Were the characteristics of a quality lesson present for all students in your elementary physical education classes as a child?

2. Using teacher talk, state five meaningful feedback statements. Use statements other than those presented in the chapter and discuss why your statements are meaningful.
3. How can you promote diversity in your classes? Why is this important?
4. What are your strengths and weaknesses with respect to communicating?

Content Review

1. What are the characteristics of a quality elementary physical education lesson? Explain each.
2. Explain the importance of several essential elements of instruction.
3. What are the key comonents of instructional feedback? Discuss each.
4. What methods can be used to make instruction personal and meaningful for students?
5. Discuss several important communication skills for teachers.

FOR MORE INFORMATION

References and Suggested Readings

Banks, J. A. (1999). *An introduction to multiethnic education.* 2nd ed. Boston: Allyn and Bacon.

Bennett, C. L. (1999). *Comprehensive multicultural education: Theory and practice.* 4th ed. Boston: Allyn and Bacon.

Brophy, J. & Good, T. (1986). Teacher behavior and student achievement. In M. Wittrock (Ed.). *Handbook of research on teaching.* New York: Macmillan.

Cushner, K., McClelland, A., & Safford, P. (1992). *Human diversity in education: An integrative approach.* New York: McGraw Hill.

Evertson, C. (1989). Classroom organization and management. In M. Reynolds (Ed.). *Knowledge base for the beginning teacher.* Washington, D.C.: American Association of Colleges for Teacher Education.

Fronske, H. & Wilson, R. (2002). *Teaching cues for basic sport skills.* San Francisco: Benjamin Cummings.

Gordon, A. & Browne, K. W. (1996). *Guiding young children in a diverse society.* Boston: Allyn and Bacon.

Grant, C. A. (Ed.). (1995). *Educating for diversity: An anthology of multicultural voices.* Boston: Allyn and Bacon.

Grossman, H. & Grossman, S. H. (1994). *Gender issues in education.* Boston: Allyn and Bacon.

Harrison, J. M., Blakemore, C. L., & Buck, M. M. (2001). *Instructional strategies for secondary physical education.* 5th ed. St. Louis: McGraw-Hill.

Hunter, M. C. (1995a). *Motivation theory for teachers.* Thousand Oaks, CA: Corwin Press.

Hunter, M. C. (1995b). *Teach for transfer.* Thousand Oaks, CA: Corwin Press.

Hunter, M. C. (1994). *Mastery teaching.* Thousand Oaks, CA: Sage Publications.

Melograno, V. J. (1996). *Designing the physical education curriculum.* 3rd ed. Champaign, IL: Human Kinetics.

Mosston, M. & Ashworth, S. (1994). *Teaching physical education.* 4th ed. New York: Macmillan.

Rink, J. E. (2002). *Teaching physical education for learning.* 3rd ed. Boston: WCB/McGraw-Hill.

Siedentop, D. & Tannehill, D. (2000). *Developing teaching skills in physical education.* 4th ed. Mountain View, CA: Mayfield Publishing Co.

Tiedt, P. L. & Tiedt, I. M. (1999). *Multicultural teaching: A handbook of activities, information, and resources.* 5th ed. Boston: Allyn and Bacon.

Vasquez, J. (1988). Contests of learning for minority children. *Educational Forum,* 52(3), 243–253.

Websites

Activity Cues
http://www.pecentral.org/climate/monicaparsonarticle.html

Communication
http://crs.uvm.edu/gopher/nerl/personal/comm/e.html
http://nonverbal.ucsc.edu/
http://www.pecentral.org/climate/monicaparsonarticle.html
http://www.bizmove.com/skills/m8g.htm

Elements of Instruction
http://www.humboldt.edu/~thal/hunter-eei.html
http://www.nycenet.edu/oit/news/EEI/Intro.htm

Enhancing Teacher Effectiveness
http://www.hcc.hawaii.edu/intranet/committees/FacDevCom/guidebk/teachtip/enhance.htm

Multicultural Education
http://www.ncrel.org/sdrs/areas/issues/educatrs/leadrshp/le4pppme.htm

CHAPTER 5

Management and Discipline

ESSENTIAL COMPONENTS

I	Organized around content standards
II	Student-centered and developmentally appropriate
III	Physical activity and motor skill development form the core of the program
IV	**Teaches management skills and self-discipline**
V	Promotes inclusion of all students
VI	Focuses on process over product
VII	Promotes lifetime personal health and wellness
VIII	**Teaches cooperation and responsibility and promotes sensitivity to diversity**

PHYSICAL EDUCATION STANDARDS

1	Students are able to move competently using a variety of fundamental and specialized motor skills.
2	Students can monitor and maintain a health-enhancing level of physical fitness.
3	Students are able to apply movement concepts and basic mechanics of skill performance when learning and refining motor skills.
4	Students comprehend the basic principles of wellness and are able to apply concepts that enable them to make meaningful decisions that positively impact their health and wellness.
5	Students participate in a wide variety of physical activities and learn how to maintain a personalized active lifestyle.
6	**Students demonstrate empathy, understanding, and respect for the numerous differences exhibited by people in an activity setting.**
7	**Students exhibit responsible and self-directed behaviors that lead to positive social interactions in physical activity.**

SUMMARY

Management and discipline are requisite parts of effective instruction. Management requires designing and implementing a preventive approach to discipline. This chapter presents effective class management skills that improve the efficiency and productivity of instruction. Dealing with behavior involves two major parts: The first part requires modifying and maintaining desirable behavior; the second phase is an approach to decrease undesirable behavior. Procedures such as time-out, reprimands, and removal of privileges are described. Ways to minimize the use of criticism and punishment are reviewed, and specific recommendations are listed.

OUTCOMES

- Describe the role of the teacher as it pertains to managing children in a physical education setting.
- Implement management and discipline skills that result in a positive and constructive learning environment.
- Identify techniques used to start and stop the class, organize the class into groups and formations, use squads, and prepare youngsters for activity.
- Cite acceptable and recommended procedures for dealing with inappropriate behavior.
- Describe techniques to increase or decrease specific behaviors.
- Explain the role of teacher reaction in shaping and controlling student behavior.
- Design or modify games that are effective in changing the behavior of children.
- Know the shortcomings of criticism and punishment when used to change and improve student behavior.
- Understand the legal ramifications associated with expelling a student from school.

Successful teachers effectively manage student behavior. Management skills may vary among teachers in emphasis and focus, but collectively they characterize quality teaching. Effective teachers make three assumptions: teaching is a profession, students are in school to learn, and the teacher's challenge is to promote learning. These assumptions imply a responsibility to teach a range of students, both those who accept instruction and those who do not. Competent teachers maintain faith in students who have not yet found success and expect them to do so eventually. The majority of children in a class are relatively easy to teach, but making appreciable gains among low-aptitude and indifferent students is the result of effective instruction.

A WELL-MANAGED CLASS

In a well-managed class, teacher and students assume dual responsibility for learning toward target goals. Presentations and instructional strategies used are appropriate for the capabilities of students and the nature of activity sequences. How teachers teach, more than the characteristics of a particular teaching style, determines what students learn. Effective class management and organizational skills create an environment that gives students freedom of choice in harmony with class order. Because a skillful instructor has the ability to prevent problems before they occur, less time is spent dealing with deviant behavior.

Be aware of the impact your behavior has on students. What students learn reflects your personality, outlook, ideals, and background. Recognize your personal habits and attitudes that affect youngsters negatively. A basic requisite is the ability to model behavior you desire from students. This means moving quickly if you demand that students hustle. It implies listening carefully to students or performing required fitness activities. Modeling desired behavior has a strong impact on students. The phrase, "Your actions speak louder than your words," has significant implications.

Effective instruction communicates to students that they are capable, important, and self-sufficient. Stressing a positive self-concept and offering experiences to promote success are invaluable aids to learning. Make clear what your expectations are for learning and behavior. Well-managed classes function with little wasted time and disruption. They run smoothly and are characterized by routines students expect and follow. The climate in a productive class setting is work oriented, yet relaxed and pleasant. The next section shows how to organize and move youngsters quickly and effectively.

DEVELOP EFFECTIVE CLASS MANAGEMENT SKILLS

Class management skills are prerequisites to effective instruction. Moving and organizing students quickly and efficiently requires comprehension of various techniques coupled with student acceptance of those techniques. If a class is unmanageable, it is unteachable. Most students enjoy a learning environment that is organized and efficient and allows a maximum amount of class time to be devoted to learning skills.

Teach class management skills in a manner similar to physical skill teaching. All skills need to be learned through practice and repetition until they become second nature. Viewing class management skills in this light makes it easier to have empathy for students who do not perform well. Just as students make mistakes when performing physical skills, some will perform management skills incorrectly. A simple statement to the point, such as, "It appears that you forgot how to freeze quickly. Let's practice," is much more constructive than indicting a class for its carelessness and disinterest.

Deliver Instruction Efficiently

If students are not listening when instructions are given, little learning will occur. Deliver instructions in small doses, focusing on one or two points at a time. Instructions should be specific and seldom last longer than 30 to 45 seconds. An effective approach is to alternate short instructional episodes with periods of activity. This contrasts with the common practice of delivering long and involved technical monologues on skill performance only to find many students have forgotten most of the information when practice begins. In a series of spoken items, people usually remember only the first and the last; thus, most students will be able to integrate and concentrate on only one or two points during skill practice. Minimizing the amount of content per instructional episode helps eliminate students' frustration and allows them to focus on stated goals. This is not to suggest that information should not be delivered to students, but that the "tell it all at the start" style should be replaced by the more effective "input, practice, feedback" model.

When giving instructions, tell students "when before what." Tell the class when to perform an activity before stating what the activity is. An effective way to implement "when before what" is to use a keyword, such as *Begin!* or *Start!* to start an activity. For example, "When I say *start,* I'd like you to . . ." or, "When I say *Go!* I want you to jog to a beanbag, move to your own space, and practice tossing and catching." Since the keyword is not given until all directions have been issued, students have to listen to all instructions before starting.

Stop and Start a Class Consistently

The most basic and important management skill is to be able to start and stop a class. Pick a consistent signal you want to use to stop a class. It does not matter what the signal is, as long as it always means the same thing. Using both an audio signal (such as a whistle blast) and a visual signal (such as raising the hand overhead) is useful because some youngsters may not hear the audio signal when engrossed in activity. Whereas a loud audio signal is used to stop a class, a voice command should be used to start the class. (See the previous discussion on keywords.) Regardless of the signal used to indicate a stop, it is best to select a different signal from the one used to start the class. If children do not respond to the signal to stop, take time to practice the procedure. Reinforce youngsters when they perform management behavior properly (Figure 5.1). Often, skill performance is reinforced but correct management behavior is not. Behavior that is not reinforced regularly will not be performed well.

Expect 100 percent compliance when students are asked to stop. If some students stop and listen to directions and others do not, class morale will degenerate. Students begin to wonder why they have to stop but other students don't. Scan the class to see if all students are stopped and ready to respond to the next set of directions. If you settle for less than full attention, students will fulfill those expectations.

Move Students into Groups and Formations Quickly

It is necessary to move students into small groups and instructional formations on a regular basis. Simple techniques can be used to accomplish this in an enjoyable and rapid fashion. For example, use the activity *Toe to Toe* (see page 555) to teach children to find partners quickly. The goal of the game is to get toe to toe with a partner as fast as possible. Other challenges are to get elbow to elbow or shoulder to shoulder or to look into the eyes of a partner. Students without a partner must go to the center of the teaching area (marked by a cone or spot) and find someone else without a partner. This gives students a designated spot to locate themselves, as opposed to feeling unwanted while running around the area looking for a partner. Place emphasis on rapid selection of the nearest person to keep children from looking for a favorite friend or telling someone that "he is not wanted" as a partner. If students insist on staying near a friend, tell the class to move throughout the area and find a different partner each time "toe to toe" is called.

To divide a class into two equal groups, have students get toe to toe with a partner. One partner sits down while the other remains standing. Those standing are asked to go to one area, after which those sitting are then moved to the desired space. Getting into groups is a skill that needs to be learned and practiced regularly.

Another activity for arranging students in groups of a selected size is *Whistle Mixer* (see page 567). When the whistle is blown a certain number of times, students form groups corresponding to the number of whistles

FIGURE 5.1 Class in freeze position.

and sit down to signify that they have the correct number in their group. Students left out go to the center of the area, find the needed number of members, and move to an open area. When this skill is mastered, students are able move quickly into properly sized groups. The use of hand signals to show the size of the desired group will make it easier for all students to recognize.

Other suggestions for finding partners are to ask students to find a partner wearing the same color, with a birthday during the same month, with a phone number that has two similar numbers in it, and so on. To arrange students in equal-sized groups, place an equal number of different-colored beanbags or hoops on the floor. Students are asked to move throughout the area. On signal, they sit on a beanbag. All students with a red beanbag are in the same group, green beanbags make up another group, and so on.

An effective technique for moving a class into a single-file line or circle is to have students run randomly throughout the area until a signal is given. On the signal to "fall in," students continue jogging, move toward the perimeter of the area, and fall in line behind someone until a circle is formed. This exercise can be done while students are running, jogging, skipping, or walking. As long as students continue to move behind another person, a circle will form automatically. Either you or a student leader can lead the line into a desired formation or position.

Another method of moving a class into formation is to ask students to get into various formations without talking. Youngsters can use visual signals but cannot ask someone verbally to move. Groups hustle to see how quickly they can form the desired formation. Another method is to hold up a shape drawn on a large card to signal the desired formation. Young students learn to visualize various shapes through this technique.

Use Squads to Expedite Class Organization

Some teachers find that placing students into squads helps them manage a class effectively. Squads offer a place for students to meet, keep certain students from being together, group students into prearranged teams of equal ability, and make it easier to learn students' names. The following are guidelines for using squad formation to maximize teaching effectiveness.

1. Don't select squads or groups in a manner that embarrasses a child who might be chosen last. In all cases, avoid using an "auction" approach, where student leaders look over the group and pick those whom they favor. A fast way to group youngsters into squads is to use the *Whistle Mixer* technique described previously.
2. A designated location should be used for assembling students into squad formation. On signal, children move to the designated area, with squad leaders in front and the rest of the squad behind.
3. Squads provide opportunities for leadership and following among peers. Use squad leaders so youngsters have an opportunity to learn leadership skills. Examples of leadership activities are moving squads to a specified location, leading squads through exercises or introductory activities, and appointing squad members to certain positions in sport activities.
4. The composition of squads can be predetermined. It may be important to have equal representation of the sexes on each squad. Squad makeup may be determined by ability level so you can quickly organize games with teams of similar ability. Squads can also be used to separate certain students so they don't have the opportunity to disrupt the class. So students get to work with all students in the class, change squad members on a regular basis.
5. In most cases, an even number of squads should be formed. This allows the class to be broken quickly into halves for games. Having a class of 30 students divided into six squads of five members each places a small number of students on each piece of apparatus and makes for less waiting in line in group activities.
6. Make the use of squads an exciting activity, not an approach that restricts movement and creativity. For example, place numbered cones in different locations around the activity area. When students enter the gym, instruct them to find their squad number and assemble. The numbers can be written in a different language or hidden in a mathematical equation or story problem. Another method is to distribute task cards specifying how the squads are arranged. The first squad to follow instructions correctly can be awarded a point or acknowledgment from the rest of the class. Examples of tasks for squads might be arranging the members in a circle, sitting with hands on head, or arranging themselves in crab position in a straight line facing northwest. Task cards can also be used to specify an introductory activity or to tell students where to move for the fitness development activity.

Know Students' Names

Effective class management requires learning the names of students. Praise, feedback, and correction go unheeded when students are addressed as "Hey, you!" Develop a system to expedite the task of learning names. One approach is to memorize three or four names per class period. Write the names on a note card, and identify those students at the start and throughout the period. At the end of the period, identify the students again. Once the first set of names has been memorized, a new set can be learned. The next time the class meets, those names learned previously can be reviewed and new students identified.

Tell students you are trying to learn their names. Asking students to say their name before performing a skill or answering a question can help you learn students' names. Once a name is learned, you may precede the question or skill performance with the student's name. For example, say, "Mary, it's your turn to jump."

Another effective way to learn names is to take a photograph of each class in squads and identify students by keying names to the picture. Identification is easier with students in squads, because they will be in the same location. Identify a few students whose names you know and a few you do not know before the start of the period. Set personal goals by calculating the percentage of students whose names you know after each period.

Establish Pre- and Post-teaching Routines

Children enjoy the sense of security that comes from knowing what to do from the time they enter the instructional area until they leave. There are a number of procedures that need to be routinely handled. The following are situations that occur before and after teaching and need to be planned for prior to the lesson.

Nonparticipation

An efficient system should be devised for identifying children who are not to participate in the lesson. This decision is best made before children arrive at the lesson area and is best made by someone (nurse or classroom teacher) other than the physical education teacher. This avoids a situation in which the physical education teacher encourages students to participate even though they are not supposed to do so. A note from the classroom teacher or school nurse, listing the names and health problems of those who are to sit out or to take part in modified activity, can be delivered as children enter the room. Accept the information at face value. This avoids the time-consuming procedure of questioning students on the sidelines to determine what the problem is and what the solution should be. A student with a note from home or from a physician should never be allowed to participate without parental permission.

Entering the Teaching Area

Nothing is more difficult than trying to start a class that has not entered the teaching area in a quiet, orderly fashion. Meet your class at the door before they enter the area. Explain how the class should enter the area and what they are supposed to do. Another successful approach is to have the class enter the area and begin jogging around the area. When told to freeze, the day's activities are described. Another less desirable method is to have youngsters enter the area and sit in squads behind their respective cones or floor markers. Instruction starts when all students are in position. Regardless of the method used, students should enter the area under control and know where they are supposed to meet.

When a classroom teacher allows students to "straggle" in late, or brings the entire class late, it disrupts the instructional process. Discuss the problem of tardiness with the teacher and try to find a solution. Try designating a couple of responsible students in each class to remind the classroom teacher that physical education begins in five minutes. Another solution is to have an area designated away from the teaching area where classes can assemble, and request that they line up at the gym door as soon as the entire group is ready. Allowing students to filter in one by one is disconcerting and a sure bet to irritate any physical education teacher. Resolve this problem quickly even if it requires asking the school's administrator to intervene.

Discussing the Lesson Content

Students enter the activity area expecting to move. Take advantage of this desire to move by having them participate in some activity before discussing the content of the lesson. Youngsters are more willing to listen after they have participated in vigorous activity. Allow students to try an activity before offering instruction on points of technique. Students listen to instruction better after they have tried an activity and found it difficult to perform correctly. Trying an activity before instructing allows an opportunity to assess the performance level of the students.

Closing a Lesson

A regular routine for closing the lesson is beneficial. It allows time for closure of the instructional content, and a procedure for leaving the teaching area. This may involve lining up at the door, returning to squads, or kneeling in a semicircle. Using a routine at the end of the lesson tends to calm and quiet youngsters, which is appreciated by classroom teachers picking up their class. Another way to calm students is to take a few minutes for relaxation activities (see pages 295–296).

Arranging Equipment

Make students responsible for securing equipment they use. Teach students how you want them to get the equipment and how to return it at the end of the lesson. This minimizes the amount of equipment rearrangement you will have to do. Place your equipment around the perimeter of the teaching area so it is easily accessible for all students. Using students to assist in distributing and gathering equipment before and after school allows an opportunity to work closely with students who need special attention.

Discussing Discipline Problems

Youngsters who misbehave during class need to be talked with after class. This makes it critical to schedule a minimum of 5 minutes passing time between classes. Scheduling classes back to back makes it impossible to talk with students, rearrange equipment, and take care of personal matters. If a student needs to be seen after school for an in-depth discussion, a "meeting appointment" form should be given to the classroom teacher and student. This reminds both parties of the student's obligation at the end of the school day.

Use Equipment Effectively

When using small equipment, such as balls, hoops, and jump ropes, be sure that every youngster has a piece for personal use. When large equipment or apparatus is used, establish as many stations or groups as possible. For a class of 30, a minimum of six benches, mats, or jumping boxes should be available so students have only a short wait in line. One way to avoid standing and waiting for a turn is to use return activities (see Chapter 18) where students are asked to perform a task or tasks on their return to their squad.

Teach students where the equipment is to be placed during instruction. Equipment should be placed in the same (home) position when the class is called to attention. For example, beanbags are placed on the floor, basketballs between the feet, and jump ropes folded and placed behind the neck. Placing the equipment in home position avoids the problem of youngsters striking one another with the equipment, dropping it, or practicing activities when they should be listening. To avoid playing with the equipment when it is placed on the floor, ask students to take a giant step away from it.

Distribute equipment to students as rapidly as possible. When students have to wait in line for a piece of equipment, time is wasted and behavior problems occur. For example, a common practice is to assign student leaders to get the equipment for their squad. This approach results in many students sitting and waiting. A better and faster method is to have the equipment placed around the perimeter of the area (Figure 5.2). On signal, youngsters move to acquire a piece of equipment, take it to their personal space, and begin practicing an assigned skill. This approach takes advantage of the natural urge to try the equipment and reinforces students who procure equipment quickly. The reverse procedure is used to put equipment away. Certainly, any method beats the often-used practice of placing the equipment in the middle of the area in a container and telling students to "run and get a ball." This approach raises the chances that youngsters will be aggravated or hurt.

Regardless of the method used to acquire equipment, clearly state what students are supposed to do with it once they have a piece of equipment. Waiting for all students to get a piece of equipment before allowing anybody to use it places control in the hands of the slowest and least cooperative student. The students who have hustled to get their equipment have to wait while the slowpokes take their time. Avoid this problem by allowing students to start practicing once they get their

FIGURE 5.2 Equipment around the perimeter.

equipment. Interact with those students who are slow and less cooperative while the others are practicing.

TEACH RESPONSIBLE STUDENT BEHAVIOR

Concern about student behavior and lack of discipline has increased emphasis on teaching responsible behavior to students. Don Hellison (1995) developed strategies and programs for teaching responsibility to older students. Elementary school teachers have adapted many of Hellison's concepts to elementary school programs. Much of the material that follows in this section has been implemented by Jim Roberts, a physical education specialist in the Mesa, Arizona, public schools.

A basic premise for learning responsible behavior is that it must be planned for, taught, and reinforced. Responsible behavior takes time and practice to learn, much like any other skill. Hellison (1995) suggests there is a hierarchy of responsible behavior. The ideas described in this section subscribe to the idea that there are different levels of responsible behavior that can be learned. Teaching responsible behavior as described here involves five levels of behavior. Each is defined below, followed by examples of typical student behavior at each level.

Level 0: Irresponsibility Level 0 students are unmotivated and undisciplined. Their behavior includes discrediting other students' involvement and interrupting, intimidating, manipulating, and verbally or physically abusing other students and perhaps the teacher.

Behavior examples:

- At home: Blaming brothers or sisters for problems; lying to parents
- On the playground: Calling other students names; laughing at others
- In physical education: Talking to friends when the teacher is giving instructions; pushing and shoving when selecting equipment

Level 1: Self-Control Students at this level do not participate in the day's activity or show much mastery or improvement. These students control their behavior enough so they do not interfere with other students' right to learn or the teacher's right to teach.

Behavior examples:

- At home: Refraining from hitting a brother or sister even though angry
- On the playground: Standing and watching others play; not getting angry at others because they did something to upset them
- In physical education: Waiting until an appropriate time to talk with friends; having control and not letting others' behavior bother them

Level 2: Involvement These students show self-control and are involved in the subject matter or activity.

Behavior examples:

- At home: Helping clean up the dishes after dinner; taking out the trash
- On the playground: Playing with others; participating in a game
- In physical education: Listening and performing activity; trying even when they don't like the activity; doing an activity without complaining or saying, "I can't."

Level 3: Self-Responsibility Level 3 students take responsibility for their choices and for linking these choices to their own identities. They are able to work without direct supervision, eventually taking responsibility for their intentions and actions.

Behavior examples:

- At home: Cleaning up without being asked
- On the playground: Returning equipment after recess
- In physical education: Following directions; practicing a skill without being told; trying new activities without encouragement

Level 4: Caring Students behaving at this level are motivated to extend their sense of responsible behavior by cooperating, giving support, showing concern, and helping.

Behavior examples:

- At home: Helping take care of a younger brother or sister or a pet
- On the playground: Asking others (not just friends) to join them in play
- In physical education: Helping someone who is having trouble; helping a new student feel welcome; working with all students; showing that all people are worthwhile

Responsible behavior is taught using a number of strategies. Post the levels of responsibility in the teaching area. Explain the different levels of behavior and identify acceptable behaviors at each level. After students have received an introduction to responsible behavior, implement the program by reinforcement of desired behavior and redirection of inappropriate behavior. The program is based on this two-pronged approach: (1) Catch students using responsible behavior and reinforce them; and (2) Redirect students behaving at level 0 by asking, "At what level are you performing and what level would be more acceptable?" An example is the following discussion between teacher and student:

> You see a student behaving at level 0 and open dialogue with the student in a nonconfrontational and nonadversarial manner:
>
> "Johnny, it appeared you were making fun of someone. . . ."
>
> "I wasn't making fun of anyone!"
>
> "Maybe not, but if you were, what level of behavior would it be?"
>
> "Zero!"
>
> "Is that the kind of person you want to be or the level of behavior you want to show?"
>
> "No!"
>
> "If you were at level 0, do you think you could make some changes? Perhaps you could move to level 1 and have self-control even if someone else makes you mad or even if you do not like that person."

Teacher feedback forms the core of the responsibility approach; however, there are many strategies for increasing responsible behavior in the instructional setting. The following are some strategies that can be used:

Model desirable behavior How you interact with your students encourages responsible behavior. Students do not care about how much you know until they know how much you care. Treat youngsters with dignity and respect and follow through with responsible action and words. In return, expect students to treat you and others with the same dignity and respect.

Use reinforcement Give students specific feedback about the quality of their behavior. If corrective feedback is given make sure it identifies the desired level of behavior. If reinforcing desirable behavior, be specific in identifying why the behavior is desirable and that you appreciate such acts. In some cases, it may be beneficial to identify a super citizen or give a "happygram" for special behavior.

Offer time for responsibility and reflection Allow time for students to think about the attitudes and behaviors associated with each of the levels. Ask the students to fill out a self-responsibility checklist at different times of the year. See Figure 5.3 for an example of a checklist.

Allow student sharing Offer students a chance to give their opinions about responsible behavior. Accept all students' feelings as important. Focus on ways to encourage higher levels of responsible behavior. Brainstorming to identify consequences of high and low behavior is an effective approach. Another practice is to ask different students to give examples of responsible behavior at different levels. Allow students time to share their feelings about how they feel when someone uses a high- or low-level behavior around them.

My Self-Responsibility Checklist

Name: ______________________________

Date: ____________________

Self-Control:

_______ I did not call others names.

_______ I had self-control when I became mad.

_______ I listened when others were talking.

_______ Other (describe) ____________________

Involvement:

_______ I listened to all directions before starting.

_______ I was willing to try all activities.

_______ I tried activities even when I didn't like them.

_______ Other (describe) ____________________

Self-Responsibility:

_______ I followed directions without being told more than once.

_______ I did not blame others.

_______ I worked on activities by myself.

_______ Other (describe) ____________________

Caring:

_______ I helped someone today.

_______ I said something nice to someone.

_______ I asked someone to do something with me.

_______ Other (describe) ____________________

FIGURE 5.3 Example of a responsibility checklist.

Encourage goal setting Help students set goals for responsible behavior they want to exhibit. This can be done at the start of the lesson by asking students to tell a partner the behavior they want to use today. At the end of the lesson, partners evaluate each other to see if the behavior was exhibited. Examples of behaviors are listening, hustling, following directions, being courteous, and complimenting others.

Offer opportunities for responsibility There are a number of times when students can be given responsibility in a class setting. Being a group leader, team captain, referee, scorekeeper, rule maker, or dispute resolver are roles that encourage students to exhibit high-level behavior. Since responsible positions affect other students, effective leaders have to behave responsibly.

Allow student choice Responsible behavior is best learned when students make choices. The natural consequences of self-selected choices are often the best teachers. Students can make choices about games they choose to play, fitness activities they select, and friends they choose. Discussion about how to make meaningful choices (see Chapter 13) is an important phase of learning to make responsible choices.

Conflict Resolution

Conflict between students often results in aggression and violence. About one in seven children is either a bully or victim (Beane, 1999). Nobody wants to create a world where the strong dominate and the weak live in fear and submission. Conflict is a part of daily life, and youngsters should understand that it is necessary to deal with conflict in an effective manner. Students can learn ways to respect others' opinions and feelings while maintaining their own worth and dignity.

There are a number of ways to solve conflicts, but the most common methods involve three types of behavior—dominating, appeasing, and cooperating. Students who use the dominating style are often unsure about their standing in the group. They want things to be done in their way but are afraid others will reject them. They often lack confidence and try hard to get others to accept their way of doing things. Youngsters who are appeasers lack confidence but want to be accepted by others. They do not like conflict and are willing to set aside their feelings in order to placate others.

Neither the dominating nor the appeasing approach for solving conflicts is effective in the long run. No one likes to be dominated or placed in the position of having to appease others. Conflict resolution can help students learn to solve conflicts in a peaceful manner with no apparent losers. This approach takes a cooperative approach to solving problems. Such an approach often builds positive feelings between students and leads to better group cohesiveness. The following are steps typically followed to resolve conflicts (Gordon & Browne, 1996). These steps are effective with younger children or children without experience in conflict resolution. If children are experienced at conflict resolution, they may be able to carry out the steps without instructor intervention.

1. *Stop the aggressive behavior immediately.* Students in conflict are separated immediately and given an opportunity to cool down. Time-out boxes are often an excellent place to send students to relax and unwind.
2. *Gather data about what happened and define the problem.* Find out what happened, who was involved, and how each youngster is feeling. Ask open-ended questions, such as "What happened?" "How did you feel about. . . ?" so youngsters can talk freely about the problem and what the problem was.
3. *Brainstorm possible solutions.* Keep in mind that brainstorming is a nonjudgmental process where all solutions are accepted regardless of their perceived value. Encourage youngsters to think of as many options as possible by asking open-ended questions, such as "How could we solve this problem?" "What other ways could we deal with this?"
4. *Test the solutions generated through brainstorming.* Ask a question such as "What solutions might work best?" Help students understand the implications of the solutions and how the solutions can be implemented. Accept solutions that may differ from your way of solving the problem.
5. *Help implement the plan.* Walk students through the solution so they develop a perception of the approach. Guide them through the steps by asking, "Who goes first?" "Who will take the next step?" As the solution is implemented, there may be a need to change it, which can be agreed on by the involved students.
6. *Evaluate the approach.* Observe to see that the plan is accomplishing the desired outcome. Encourage students to change the plan if necessary.

The conflict resolution process takes practice and time. It demands that you play certain roles and take an objective approach to resolution. The conflict resolution process demands certain behaviors from the instructor. Good listening to both parties is necessary. Both sides of the problem must be explored and students must feel as though the process was equitable. Blame is not assessed in this process. Placing blame only encourages self-defense behavior, such as appeasing or being aggressive. Students must trust that the process will be fair and objective and that they will receive a fair shake if they deal with the issue cooperatively.

PREVENT BEHAVIOR PROBLEMS

Many class management and discipline problems can be prevented through anticipation and planning. Anticipate the types of problems that might occur and have a plan for dealing with them when they do. Figure 5.4 offers a quick guide to suggestions for preventing behavior problems. Teachers often worry that a situation will

- Anticipate and explain the rules rather than waiting for them to be broken.
- Talk with students' parents and ask for suggestions for dealing with misbehavior.
- Avoid placing students in situations that give rise to misbehavior, such as pairing up with the "wrong students." Be aware of individual students' tolerance for failure. Some students are never willing to fail in front of peers.
- Call attention regularly to desirable behavior.
- Talk with students and try to better understand their feelings. For example, you may find that they feel that you, the teacher, don't like them.
- If feasible, give problem students added responsibility they are capable of handling. For example, make them student helpers or teacher's assistants.
- As a teacher, model behavior you expect students to emulate. For example, ask students to do things politely, and discuss problems in a caring manner.

FIGURE 5.4 Preventing discipline problems.

occur that they will not know how to handle. Developing a plan of attack for dealing with problems offers a sense of confidence and peace of mind. The first phase of an effective discipline plan is to begin the year on a proactive and positive note. Developing a comprehensive behavior management approach is a systematic way to deal with problems that affect all teachers and are generally ranked as the most serious concerns of teachers and parents.

Develop an Assertive Behavior Management Plan

The old adage, "know thyself," is never more important than when having to manage a class of students. How are you going to respond when misbehavior occurs? Are you going to be threatened, angry, sad, or unmoved? What types of behaviors are going to set you off and anger you quickly? How do you behave and respond to students when you are angry? These and many other questions arise when teachers assume the responsibility for a class. The one thing that can be assumed is that management and discipline skills will be needed regardless of what age or type of class is being taught. Generally, there are three ways a teacher communicates to students about misbehavior.

- **Passive communicator.** A passive teacher "hopes" to make all children happy in order to avoid being upset. Passive means trying to avoid all conflict and trying to please others. Directly or indirectly the passive teacher is constantly saying, "like me, appreciate what I do for you." Many passive teachers want to be perfect so everybody will like them and hope that students will behave perfectly. When students behave like students and go off-task, the Mr. Passive becomes upset and angry. A common pattern is for the passive teacher to let behavior slide until "he can't take it anymore." Then he loses composure and lashes out at the class in anger. When the anger subsides, Mr. Passive now wants to make up and again starts the cycle of letting things go and trying to be liked. This cycle is often repeated over and over.

  Passive teachers often turn over their power to students, particularly the least cooperative students. For example, they will say things like, "We are not going to start until everyone is listening!" Interpreted concretely, students may hear, "This is great. We don't have to start until we are finished with our conversation." Passive teachers also ignore unacceptable behavior and hope it will disappear. Ignoring seldom causes behavior to disappear; rather it becomes worse over time. Passive teachers often say things but never follow through. For example, "If you do that one more time, I am going to call your parents." When there is no follow through or it is impossible to follow through, the words are empty and meaningless and students soon learn disrespect for the teacher. Another common trait of a passive teacher is to ask questions that will result in information that is meaningless. For example, "What did you do that for? Or why are you doing this? Or don't you know better than that?" None of these questions will elicit useful information and the teacher will soon become frustrated and angry at all of the "I don't know" responses.
- **Aggressive communicator.** An aggressive responder wants to overpower others by coming on strong. Aggressive people feel it is a competition and they must win at all costs whenever communication occurs. A common trait with aggressive communicators is that they use the word "You" all the time. A number of statements keep students feeling defensive and attacked. Examples are, "You never listen to me; you are always the one in trouble; you are the problem here; you are always talking." Aggressive responders often think that they have all the answers and attempt to express others' viewpoints. For example, they may say to a student, "You think that because you did that last year, you can do it in my class." Obviously, no one knows what another is thinking and it serves no purpose to communicate this way.

  Aggressive communicators often use the words "always" and "never." These words are labeling words. They make students feel as if they are bad people who always behave in certain ways or never do anything right. Words that generalize and label create problems in communication and often result in alienation, rather than respect for a teacher. Aggressive communicators often see students as personally attacking them and focus on labeling the other person rather than dealing with the behavior. Often, they don't reveal how they feel about things and are unwilling to express their own thoughts and feelings. If students never know how a teacher feels, it is likely they will not develop much empathy for their instructor. A good rule of thumb is this: Any statement about the other person rather than your own feelings or thoughts will give your communication an attacking and aggressive flavor.

- **Assertive communicator.** An assertive responder does not beg, plead, or threaten. Rather, he or she uses a straightforward approach to express feelings and expectations. Assertive people are not afraid to say what they want and do not worry about what others will think of them. Teachers who want to be liked are quite concerned about what their students think. An assertive teacher wants what is best for students and doesn't worry about what they think. Assertiveness comes across to students as a "no-nonsense" approach that needs to be carried out. The approach is clear and direct and very concrete (requires little interpretation to be carried out). For example, an assertive teacher might say to a student who has been talking out of turn, "It upsets me when you talk while I am talking." This teacher is expressing feelings and making it clear what the unacceptable behavior is. Now follow that statement with an assertive statement that expresses the desired behavior, i.e., "That is your second warning; please go to time-out." Assertive communication places great emphasis on clarity without anger. High emotion is not part of assertive responding; rather it turns assertion into aggressiveness.

  An excellent way to make messages more assertive is to use the word "I" instead of "you." Talking about your own feelings and emotions will make the messages sound much more reasonable and firm. For example, "When you are playing with your equipment while I am talking, it bothers me and makes me forget what I planned on saying. Please leave your equipment alone when I talk." Such messages always identify the behavior that is disruptive or annoying, offer how you feel, and direct the student to behave in a proper manner. An excellent reference on discipline is *Conscious Discipline* by Bailey (2001). This is a valuable reference if you are unsure of how to become an assertive communicator.

Step 1. Determine Routines for Students

Being assertive is important. Students feel best when they know what your expectations are. Students expect to follow established routines. Explain your routines so students understand why the chosen procedures are used. Examples of routines that teachers often use are:

1. How students are supposed to enter the teaching area
2. Where and how they should meet—in sitting squads, moving and freezing on a spot, in a semicircle, and so on
3. What they should do if equipment is located in the area
4. What signal is used to freeze a class
5. How they procure and put away equipment
6. How will they be grouped for instruction

Once these routines are established and practiced, it is easier for both teacher and students to work together comfortably.

Step 2. Determine Rules and Procedures for the School Year

Rules are an expected part of the school environment. Most teachers want students to be respectful to them and to other students. It is not unreasonable to expect students to behave. If you can't manage students, you can't teach them anything. Most school administrators will judge your effectiveness by how well you manage students. Accept the fact that managing students is a necessary and important part of teaching; in fact, it is a requisite for the delivery of content. When creating your rules, select general categories rather than specific behavior. For example, "respect your neighbor" means many things, from not pushing to not swearing at another student. Post rules in the teaching area where all students can easily read them. The following are examples of general rules:

- *Stop, look, and listen.* This implies freezing on signal, looking at the instructor, and listening for instructions.
- *Take care of equipment.* This includes caring for equipment, distributing, gathering, and using it properly.
- *Respect the rights of others.* This includes behavior such as not pushing others, leaving their equipment alone, and not fighting or arguing.

The number of rules should be minimized. Try not to exceed three to five rules; more than this number makes it difficult for students to remember all the details and makes you appear overly strict. Numerous rules also make students rule-specific. A youngster may choose to chew gum in the multipurpose room because the rule is "no gum-chewing in the halls." When students become rule-specific, they do not learn to think about right and wrong and the spirit of the rule; rather they often look for exceptions to the rule. Rules are general guidelines for desired behavior rather than negative statements telling students what they can't do. Consider the following points when designing rules:

- Select major categories of behavior rather than a multitude of specific rules.
- Identify observable behavior. This makes it easy to determine whether a person is following a rule and does not involve subjective judgment.
- Make rules reasonable for the age level of students. Meaningful rules cut across all ages and can be used throughout the elementary school years.
- Limit yourself to three to five rules.
- State rules briefly and positively. It is impossible to write a rule that covers all situations and conditions. Make the rule brief, yet broad.

Step 3. Determine Consequences When Rules Are Not Followed

When rules are broken, students must learn to accept the consequences of their behavior. List and post consequences in a prominent place in the teaching area. Discuss the rules with students to make sure they understand and see the necessity of having behavior guidelines. Having agreed-on rules and consequences involves students in the development of an environment that, in part, they have designed. One of the best ways to earn students' respect is to treat them all in a fair and caring manner. Most students are willing to accept the consequences of their misbehavior if they think they will be treated in a manner consistent with and equal to how other students were treated. Animosity occurs when students sense that you play favorites. It is common for physical education teachers to favor gifted athletes and students who are physically attractive. Be aware of such behavior and prevent its occurrence. One reason for defining consequences prior to misbehavior is that it allows you to administer the consequences equitably. When a student chooses to break a rule, apply the consequences without judging the character or making a derogatory statement about the student. It is the student's misbehavior that has triggered the consequences.

Step 4. Have the Class Practice Rules Systematically

Rules stipulate expected class behavior. If a rule is in place for proper care of equipment, students need the opportunity to practice how the teacher wants equipment handled. If a rule requires students to stop and listen, practice such behavior and reinforce a proper response. Student behavior is not always correct, regardless of rules. It is common to hear teachers tell students, "I told you before not to do that." This assumes that telling students once will result in perfect adherence to rules. Obviously, this is not the case. Continue to allow time for students to practice desired behavior throughout the school year.

Implement Your Management Plan

There are a number of things that can be done the first week or two of teaching to ensure classes get off on the right foot. The first few days of school are a time to communicate your expectations in a manner that leaves students with a positive first impression. Students want to develop a positive relationship with you, and a meaningful start leaves them confident and excited about the experience. Consider the following points.

Create a Personal Behavior Plan

One of the key elements of a management approach is to understand and plan for how you will behave when disciplining students. Serious misbehavior can cause some teachers to become angry, others to feel threatened, and others to behave in a tyrannical manner. Part of your behavior plan will be to remind yourself how you should act when misbehavior occurs. Personal behavior plans usually include the following points:

1. *Maintain composure.* Students don't know your trigger points unless you reveal them. If you "lose it," students lose respect for you and believe you are an ineffective teacher.
2. *Acknowledge your feelings when student misbehavior occurs.* Do you feel angry, threatened, challenged, or fearful? How do you typically respond when a student defies you?
3. *Design a plan for yourself when such feelings occur.* For example, count to 10 before responding, or take 5 deep breaths. Avoid dealing with the student misbehavior until you are aware of how you feel.
4. *Know the options you have for dealing with the deviant behavior.* Talking with students is best done after class if it is going to take more than a few seconds. Limited time options are: quietly warn the student; quietly remove the student from class; or quietly send another student for help if the situation is severe.

Be a Leader, Not a Friend

Students want a teacher who is knowledgeable, personable, and a leader. They are not looking for a new friend; in fact, most students feel uncomfortable if they perceive that you want to be "one of them." Let students know what they will learn during the semester. Don't look to be a part of their personal discussions. There must be a comfortable distance between you and your students. This is not to say that you shouldn't be friendly and caring; it is important to be concerned about students as long as your concern is expressed in a professional manner. Being a leader means knowing where to direct a class. You are responsible for what is learned and how it is presented. Student input is important, but ultimately, it is your responsibility to lead a class to desired objectives.

Communicate High Standards

Students respond to your expectations. If you expect students to perform at high levels, the majority of them will strive to do so. A common but accurate expression is, "You get what you ask for." If you expect students to perform to the best of their abilities, they probably will do so. On the other hand, if you act as if you don't care whether they try, most students will do as little as possible.

Understand Why Students Misbehave

A number of situations cause students to misbehave. Some of these causes are listed in Figure 5.5. Understanding these reasons and being able to identify them when they occur will help you anticipate and prevent many behavior problems. There are times when students misbehave because they didn't understand the instructions. Give instructions and then proceed with the activity. If some students don't perform correctly, it may be that they didn't understand. Clarify the instructions and proceed. This two-tiered approach usually ensures directions were clear and that ample opportunity was given for all to understand.

- The student may be testing the teacher.
- The student may have some type of learning disability that causes the behavior problem.
- The student may be looking for reinforcement from the teacher.
- The student may have low self-esteem, which causes the student to misbehave while trying to become the center of attention.
- The student may not understand the directions given.
- The student may be bored and unchallenged by the activities.
- Performing the activities may result in continuous failure, so the student misbehaves to avoid revealing a lack of ability.
- Parents may deal with their children in a manner completely unlike the methods used in physical education.
- The teacher may not like the student, thus forcing the student to be combative and angry.
- Failure in other subjects may carry over to physical education.

FIGURE 5.5 Typical causes of misbehavior.

Discipline Individually and Avoid Group Negative Feedback

When negative feedback is delivered, it should be done privately and personally to individual students. Few people want to have negative comments delivered globally for others to hear. In addition, all students should not be punished for the behavior of a few misbehaving youngsters. Group negative feedback can have contrary results. If you criticize the entire group, there is a strong possibility that you will lose the respect and admiration of students who were behaving properly.

Avoid Feedback That Offers the Possibility for Backlash

Some verbal types of interactions may work in the short term but cause long-term negative consequences. The following types of feedback often work immediately but cause greater problems over the long haul. If students become resentful, they may have a tendency to be deviant when the teacher is not around. Some examples:

- *Preaching or moralizing.* The most common example of moralizing is telling students they "should know better than that!" Students make mistakes because they are young and learning. A part of learning is making mistakes. Correct mistakes in a quiet and caring manner.
- *Threatening.* Threats are ultimatums given in an attempt to terminate undesirable behavior even though you know the ultimatum will be impossible to carry out. For example, the threat, "If you do not stop that, I'm going to kick you out of class," sounds tough, but is usually impossible to enforce. You are not in a position to expel students, and some students are aware of your inability to carry out the threat. If students hear enough idle threats they start to tune out and respect gradually wanes.
- *Ordering and commanding.* If you are bossy, students begin to think they are nothing more than pawns to be moved around the area. Use patterns of communication that ask students to carry out tasks. Courtesy and politeness are requisites for effective teacher-student relationships.
- *Interrogating.* When there is a problem (such as a fight between students), an initial reaction is to figure out who started the fight rather than deal with

the feelings of the combatants. Little is gained by trying to solve "who started it." Students often shirk the blame and suggest it was not their fault. Try calmly saying, "You know fighting is not accepted in my class. You must have been very angry to place yourself in this situation." This encourages youngsters to talk about feelings rather than place blame. It also communicates a caring and concerned attitude toward youngsters even when they do something wrong.

- *Refusing to listen.* This commonly manifests itself as "Let's talk about it some other time." At times, during instruction, this response is necessary. However, if you always refuse to listen, students avoid interaction with the instructor and believe you don't care.
- *Labeling.* Labeling is characterized by telling children, "Stop acting like babies" or "You're behaving like a bunch of first graders." On an individual level, it might sound like, "You're always the troublemaker." This is degrading and dehumanizes youngsters. Often, labeling is done with the intent of improving performance. In actuality, it is usually destructive and leaves youngsters with negative feelings.

Give Positive Group Feedback

Positive feedback delivered to a class develops group morale. Classes should learn to view themselves as units that work together and are rewarded when they meet group goals. Students have to work within groups as adults, so learning about group cooperation and pride in accomplishment will help to ensure a smoothly running class, and benefit students in the long run.

MAINTAIN AND INCREASE DESIRABLE BEHAVIOR

Managing student behavior is a difficult task. Teachers often question themselves in terms of their ability to control and manage a classroom. A class of children is really a group of individuals, each of whom must be uniquely treated and understood. Some teachers question the importance of instructional discipline. The most basic of reasons is that it allows children to learn effectively without encroaching on the rights of others. U.S. society is based on freedom partnered with self-discipline. Americans have much personal freedom as long as they do not encroach on the rights of others. In similar fashion, children can enjoy freedom as long as their behavior is consistent with educational objectives and does not prevent other students from learning.

Most children choose to cooperate and participate in the educational setting. In fact, the learner is largely responsible for allowing the teacher to teach. No one can be taught who chooses not to cooperate. Effective management of behavior means maintaining an environment in which all children have the opportunity to learn. It is your responsibility to fashion a learning environment in which all children can learn and feel comfortable. Students who choose to be disruptive and off-task infringe on the rights of students who choose to cooperate. If a teacher has to spend a great deal of energy working with youngsters who are disorderly, students who want to learn are short-changed.

The purpose of this section is to present an action plan for modifying and maintaining desired behavior. There are three phases to such a program: (1) increasing desired behavior; (2) eliminating undesirable behavior; and (3) maintaining desirable behavior. The focus of a discipline program is on positive and constructive approaches designed to teach children responsible behavior. Figure 5.6 lists suggested strategies for modifying student behavior.

Increase Desired Behavior

Behavior that is followed by appropriate positive reinforcement occurs more often in the future. This principle is the key for increasing desired behavior. The strength of this simple principle is that it focuses on positive, desired educational outcomes. Key points for implementing the principle lie in deciding what to use

- Discuss with students the problem their behavior causes.
- Reinforce proper behavior exhibited by other students.
- Use time out from reinforcement.
- Use a behavior contract.
- Talk with the student and parents about the problem.
- Ask the student to perform activities that are failure-proof.
- Substitute one behavior for another: for example, ask a student who doesn't listen carefully to explain to others how to perform an activity, or make that student a leader.
- Use the Premack principle: If you stay on task for 10 minutes, you can have the last 5 minutes for free-time activity.
- Focus reinforcement on something the student does well.
- Use prompts to remind students when they are off task or misbehaving.
- If feasible and the behavior does not disrupt the class, ignore the behavior.

FIGURE 5.6 Strategies for modifying misbehavior.

as reinforcers, selecting those that effectively reinforce individuals, and properly using the reinforcers.

Social Reinforcers

Teachers most often use this class of reinforcers. Your positive behavior is the reinforcement given when students perform desired behavior. Most children have been involved in an environment filled with social reinforcers prior to attending school. Parents use praise, physical contact, and facial expressions to acknowledge desired behavior in their children. The following are examples of reinforcers that can be used with students in a physical education setting:

Words of Praise

Great job	Nice going
Exactly right	I really like that job
Perfect arm placement	That's the best one yet
Way to go	Nice hustle

Physical Expressions

Smiling	Winking
Nodding	Clenched fist overhead
Thumbs up	Clapping

Physical Contact

Handshake	High five

Find out what type of social reinforcers students are accustomed to responding to in the school setting. Certain reinforcers may embarrass students or make them feel uncomfortable. For example, some students may not want to be touched even to the point of receiving a "high five." Some students, particularly those of the opposite sex, may interpret a hug or pat on the back incorrectly. If unsure, ask the school administrator to define the acceptable social reinforcers to which students respond positively.

Activity Reinforcers

Various types of activities that children enjoy can be used as reinforcement. An effective way to determine activities that can be used as reinforcers is to observe children. Free time always ranks high among children's preferences. Some examples of activities that might be used to reinforce a class are free time to practice a skill, the opportunity to play a game, extra time in physical education class, the opportunity to help administer equipment, acting as a teacher's aide, being a teacher in a cross-aged tutoring situation, or being a team captain. Students might be given special privileges such as being "student of the day," getting to choose the game to play, or having lunch with the teacher.

Token Reinforcers

Many teachers feel a need to offer some type of token as a reinforcer. It may be points, gold stars, certificates, or trophies. Physical education is closely related to athletic competition, where awards are often given to winners. This causes some teachers to believe that tokens should be used to motivate children in physical education. The less favorable aspect of giving tokens (ribbons or certificates) is that when they are given only to winners, losers become less likely to be motivated to perform in the future. Some teachers give participation certificates or ribbons to all students; however, this gives the token little reinforcement value. In addition, there is evidence to show that extrinsic rewards may actually decrease a child's intrinsic desire to participate (Greene & Lepper, 1975; Whitehead & Corbin, 1991). Token reinforcers work best with primary-grade children. Young children are motivated by the tokens they receive. However, after the age of 9, students begin to see tokens as a form of bribery to behave in a certain manner. Generally, it is best to use token reinforcers only if it appears that social reinforcers are ineffective.

Selecting Reinforcers

A common question among teachers is, "How do I know what will be reinforcing to my students?" It is impossible to know what will reinforce a student until it is administered. Fortunately, there are a lot of things to which most children will respond, such as praise, attention, smiles, games, free time, and privileges. A practical way to identify effective reinforcers is to observe children during free time, analyzing the things they enjoy doing. Another simple solution is to ask them what they would like to do. Most youngsters will tell you that they would like more recess, free time, or other enjoyable activity.

Using Social Reinforcers

Effective use of social reinforcers requires praise and makes positive statements. You may feel uncomfortable when learning to administer positive reinforcement to youngsters because such behavior feels inauthentic. A common complaint from teachers learning how to reinforce is, "I do not feel real and children think I'm a fake." Any change in communication patterns feels uncomfortable at first. Trying new ways of communicating with a class requires a period of adjustment. New patterns of praise and reinforcement often feel contrived and insincere (fortunately, most students don't know the difference), and there is no way to avoid the discomfort. Teachers who are unwilling to experience the uneasiness of learning will usually remain unchanged. The assumption that patterns of speech learned as a child are effective in an instructional setting is false. Teachers are made, not born, and they find success through hard work and dedication. If practiced regularly, new behavioral patterns will become a natural part of your repertoire after a period of time.

Praise is effective when it refers to specific behavior exhibited by the youngster. This contrasts with general statements, such as, "Good job" or "You are an excellent performer." General and nonspecific statements do not tell the youngster what was done well. It leaves it to the student to try to identify what you had in mind. If the student's thoughts do not align with your intent, incorrect behavior is reinforced. To improve the specificity and effectiveness of feedback, describe the behavior to be reinforced rather than judge it. For example, compare the following:

Describing: "I saw your excellent forward roll, James; you tucked your head just right."

Judging: "That's a poor job. I do not see why you cannot do better."

In the first example, the youngster is identified and the specific behavior performed is reinforced. In the second situation, it is impossible to identify what is poor or to whom the feedback is directed. In most cases, if a question can be asked about delivered praise or criticism (such as what was good, or why was it a poor performance), the feedback is nonspecific and open to misinterpretation. To increase desired behavior, verbally or physically describe what makes the performance effective, good, or noteworthy. This reinforces the student and communicates to the rest of the class what behavior is expected by the instructor.

The Premack Principle

The Premack principle (Premack, 1965) is often used unknowingly to motivate students. This principle states that a highly desirable activity can be used to motivate students to learn an activity they enjoy to a lesser degree. In practice, this principle allows students to participate in a favorite activity if they perform a less enjoyable one. The Premack principle is often referred to as the "Eat your peas before you get dessert" rule. An activity that children enjoy is used to motivate youngsters to participate in activities they are reluctant to perform. The following are examples of the Premack principle:

- "You may shoot baskets [preferred] after you complete the passing drill [less desirable]."
- "When everybody is quiet [less desirable], we will begin the game [preferred]."
- "Those who raise their hand [less desirable] will be selected to answer the question [preferred]."

Prompt Desired Behavior

Prompts are used to remind students to perform desired behavior. They encourage the development of new patterns of behavior. There are a number of ways to prompt children in the physical education setting. The most common are the following:

1. *Modeling.* You or another student performs the behavior desired with the expectation that students respond in similar fashion. For example, placing your piece of equipment on the floor when stopping the class will remind the class to do likewise. Modeling is an effective prompt for desired behavior because young students emulate their teacher.
2. *Verbal cues.* This is a common method of prompting—using words such as "Hustle" and "Keep going." The purpose is to remind students of desired behavior. Usually, verbal cues are used to maintain the pace of the lesson, increase the intensity of the performance, or motivate youngsters to stay on task.
3. *Nonverbal cues.* Many physical cues are given through body language to communicate concepts such as "Hustle," "Move over here," "Great performance," "Quiet down," and so on. When teaching skills, nonverbal physical cues can prompt youngsters by moving them into proper position, helping them through the correct pattern, or placing body parts in proper alignment.

Prompts should not be used to the point at which students will not perform without them. The goal is to remove the prompt so that behavior is self-motivated. This process is called fading and involves gradual removal of the prompt. It is likely you will use prompts at opportune times; however, the major purposes of prompting are to implement new behavior patterns and to increase the occurrence of desired behavior. The weakest (least intrusive) prompt possible should be used to stimulate the behavior. For example, it is possible to give students a long lecture about the importance of staying on task. However, this approach is time-consuming and over-reactionary. It is not suited to multiple (repetitive) use and is ineffective in the long run. Select a cue that is closely identified with the desired skill and that is short and concise.

In addition to these points, be sure that the prompt identifies the task being prompted. For example, if you prompt the class to "hustle" and it is not tied to a desired behavior, there may be confusion. Some children may think your prompt means to perform the skill as fast as possible; others may think it means to stop what they are doing and hustle to the teacher. Tie the prompt to the desired behavior in a consistent manner and make sure that students clearly understand the meaning of your prompt.

Shape Desired Behavior

Shaping techniques can be used to build new and desired behavior. When desired behavior does not exist, *shaping*—using extinction and reinforcement—is used to create new behavior. Shaping is slow and inefficient, so it is used only if prompting is not possible. Two principles are followed when shaping behavior.

1. *Differential reinforcement is used to increase the incidence of desired behavior.* Reinforce responses that reach a predetermined criterion and ignore those that do not meet the criterion (extinction). An example of this principle involves asking a class to put their equipment down quickly. You decide that students should put the equipment on the floor within 5 seconds. Using differential reinforcement, reinforce the students whenever they meet the 5-second criterion and ignore their performance when it takes longer than 5 seconds.
2. *The criterion that must be reached for reinforcement to occur is increased.* In this step, you gradually shift the criterion standard toward the desired goal. For example, if the desired behavior is for the class to become quiet within 5 seconds after a signal has been given, it might be necessary to start with a 12-second interval. Why the longer interval? In all likelihood, it is not reasonable to expect that an inattentive class will quiet down quickly. If a 5-second interval is selected initially, there is a strong possibility that you and your students will be frustrated by the lack of success. In addition, this stringent standard of behavior will not be achieved very often, resulting in very few opportunities to reinforce the class. The result is a situation in which both you and the class feel they have failed. To avoid this possibility of failure, gradually move toward the desired behavior goal. In this case, start with 12 seconds until the class performs as desired. Next, shift to a 10-second interval and ask the class to perform to this new standard. The process is gradually repeated until the terminal behavior is reached.

DECREASE UNDESIRABLE BEHAVIOR

Most effective techniques for improving class behavior are designed to guide the student away from behavior that is disrupting the class. Corrective feedback and the use of consequences can be an effective means for decreasing undesirable behavior. Such consequences are actions that follow misbehavior and teach students that their behavior results in some action. Figure 5.7 outlines a specific plan for altering undesirable student behavior.

Use Corrective Feedback

As a first step, try using positive reinforcement to increase desired behavior with the hope that it will replace undesirable behavior. For example, if a skilled youngster is always criticizing less able youngsters, ask that student to help others and serve as a student assistant. The intent is to teach the youngster to deliver positive and constructive feedback rather than criticism. An

Changing behavior can be done if teachers are willing to experiment and be patient. Teachers want to change behavior quickly and on the spot and at times make incorrect decisions because they don't have time to think of an effective solution. In-class misbehavior can be temporarily stopped, but may often go unchanged for the future. Realize that change will require long-term action that must be planned ahead of time. The following steps can be used to develop a plan for changing behavior:

- Identify a single behavior that needs to be changed, improved, or strengthened. Don't pick more than one behavior as it will make it much more difficult to monitor change.
- Identify a behavior that will be substituted for the behavior to be changed.
- Determine what positively reinforces the student. Have a discussion with the student to see what is reinforcing.
- Decide whether a negative reinforcer is needed to give momentum to the change process.
- Develop a plan for getting the desired behavior to occur. This will generate a behavior that can be reinforced and used to replace the undesirable behavior.
- Put the plan into effect and set a time frame for evaluation of the plan. Decide what modifications are needed to make the plan more effective. This modification may demand a different set or schedule of reinforcers or negative consequences. If an entirely different plan is needed (because the behavior hasn't decreased or changed) make such changes and proceed.
- Continue evaluating and modifying the plan.

FIGURE 5.7 A plan for changing misbehavior.

effective rule of thumb before choosing to use corrective feedback is to reinforce the desired behavior twice. For example, assume a youngster is slow to stop on signal, but the majority of other students are stopping and listening properly. Ask the class to move and freeze again. Reinforce students who are on task. If the result is not acceptable, try it again. Many times, particularly with primary-grade children, the misbehaving students will emulate those who are being reinforced. If not, it may be necessary to use corrective feedback. Corrective feedback should be clear and specific. Students must know exactly what it is they are to stop and what desired behavior they are to start. Use corrective feedback as soon after the misbehavior as possible, just as positive reinforcement should be delivered immediately following the desired behavior.

When students are disciplined or corrected, they can respond in a negative manner causing class disruption if such feedback is not delivered correctly. The following steps will prevent teacher-student conflicts from occurring in front of other students. Whether delivering corrective feedback or consequences, use these steps to avoid embarrassing students and yourself.

1. *Do not address the student publicly.* Buy some time for talking with the student privately by giving the class a task to perform. It may be as simple as jogging around the area. This leaves you in control and allows time to discuss the situation with the misbehaving student.
2. *Isolate the student and yourself.* Don't correct a student where others can hear what you are saying. The problem is a private matter between you and the student.
3. *Deal with one student at a time.* Often, a couple of students are misbehaving together. Separate them and deal with their unacceptable behavior one on one.
4. *State your position once; repeat it once if you believe the student didn't understand.* Don't argue or try to prove your point. Take no more than 10–15 seconds to tell the student the unacceptable behavior and what acceptable behavior you would like to see.
5. *Deliver and move away.* Avoid eyeballing the behavior to completion; walk away after you have delivered the behavior you desire. Eyeballing a student after you have reprimanded him can appear to be confrontational. To get yourself back on track, positively reinforce one or two students who are performing the desired behavior.
6. *Don't threaten or bully the student.* It builds resentment in students and may cause greater problems at a later time.
7. *Avoid touching the student when correcting behavior.* Even if you have positive intentions, it can send mixed messages. Some students don't want to be touched and will aggressively pull away and make a scene in front of the class.
8. *Don't curse or raise your voice excessively.* Don't be sarcastic. Instead deliver clearly what you desire from the student in terms of acceptable behavior.

Use Consequences to Decrease Undesirable Behavior

When corrective feedback fails to cause the desired change in behavior, consequences must be used. Students need to understand that undesirable behavior will bring consequences. Becoming responsible for one's behavior may be one of the most, if not *the* most, important social learnings from the school experience. Consequences that can be used to decrease undesirable behavior include reprimands, removal of positive consequences, and time out.

Reprimands

This is a common approach used to decrease undesirable behavior. If done in a caring and constructive manner, reprimands can serve as effective reminders to behave.

- Identify the unacceptable behavior, state briefly why it is unacceptable, and communicate to students what behavior is desired. For example, "You were talking while I was speaking. It bothers other students, so please listen to me."
- Don't reprimand in front of other students. Not only does it embarrass students, it also can diminish their self-esteem. When students feel belittled, they may lash out and react in a manner more severe than the original behavior.
- Reprimands should speak about behavior, not the person. Ask the behavior to stop rather than telling a student that, "You are always causing problems in this class." Avoid general and negative statements related to the personality of the student.
- After reprimanding and asking for acceptable behavior, reinforce it when it occurs. Be vigilant in looking for the desired behavior since reinforcing such behavior will cause it to occur more often in the future.

Removal of Positive Consequences

This is a common approach used by parents, so many students are familiar with it. The basic approach is to remove something positive from the student when misbehavior occurs. For example, students give up some of their free time due to misbehavior. They lose points related to a grade. They are not allowed to participate in an activity that is exciting to them. For removal of positive consequences to be effective, make sure students really want to be a part of the removal activity. It doesn't work to keep a student out of a game if the student doesn't like the game. A few key principles should be followed when using this technique:

- Be sure that the magnitude of the removal fits the crime. In other words, children who commit a minor infraction shouldn't have to miss recess for a week.
- Be consistent in removal, treating all students and occurrences the same. Students believe teachers are unfair if they are more severe with one student than another. In addition, a student penalized for a specific misbehavior should receive the same penalty for a later repetition.
- Make sure students understand the consequences of their misbehavior before the penalties are implemented. This avoids applying penalties in an emotional, unthinking manner. If students know what the consequences will be, they are making the choice to accept the consequences when they choose to misbehave.
- It is helpful to chart a student's misbehavior to see if the frequency is decreasing. Regardless of the method used, if the behavior is not decreasing or is increasing, change methods until a decrease in frequency occurs.

Time Out

The time-out procedure is an equitable technique for dealing with youngsters in a manner that is consistent with society. Rules are clearly posted and consequences are clear and easy to comprehend. Time out is an effective approach for dealing with undesirable behavior that occurs randomly on an individual basis. The time-out approach moves youngsters out of the class setting and places them into a predesignated area when they misbehave (Figure 5.8). *Time out means time out from any reinforcement.* It does not imply that the student is a "bad person," but rather that unacceptable behavior has occurred and there is a need for time out to reconsider their misbehavior. When placing students in time out, communicate to children that they are acceptable individuals, but their misbehavior is unacceptable.

Being placed in time out communicates to youngsters that they have disrupted the class and must be removed so that the rest of the class can participate as desired. It is also acceptable for children to voluntarily use the time-out area as a "cooling-off" spot if they become angry, embarrassed, or frustrated. If youngsters have been placed in the time-out area for fighting or arguing, they should be placed at opposite ends of the area so that the behavior does not escalate. In addition, man-

FIGURE 5.8 Student assigned to time out.

date that they stay in their half (or quadrant) of the teaching area until the next meeting of the class. This prevents recurring agitation between the two combatants and the possibility of continued animosity.

The implementation of this plan should be discussed with students so they know exactly what is acceptable and unacceptable behavior and the actions that will be taken if they exhibit undesirable behavior. Post a list of desired behavior (rules) and consequences for unacceptable behavior, as discussed above, in the teaching area.

A key concept is that time out does not serve as a deterrent if the youngster receives reinforcement. Time out means receiving *no* reinforcement. If class is a negative experience for students, taking them out of class will be rewarding rather than a negative consequence. Caution must be used when placing students in the time-out area. Done incorrectly, time out is an opportunity to be highly reinforced. For example, a student who is sent to the office gets to avoid schoolwork while visiting with friends who come into the office. Notoriety can be achieved among peers for surviving the office experience and being able to tell others, "I was not scared at all." Another example: Being a spectator in our society is highly reinforcing. People are willing to pay high prices to watch others play sports or act. Sitting on the side of the teaching area and looking on as a spectator may be a more reinforcing experience than participating in class activities. If you put someone in time out, make sure they are not facing the class and interacting with peers. *Remember—If students don't enjoy being in class, time out will not work.*

As stated, establish a set of consequences and post it in the area. A possible set of consequences for unacceptable behavior follows.

First Misbehavior: The student is warned quietly on a personal basis to avoid embarrassment. At times, students are not aware that they are bothering others, and a gentle reminder will refocus the youngster.

Second Misbehavior: The student is told to go to a predesignated time-out spot and sit. Time-out stations are placed in the four corners of the instructional area. The student stays there until ready to reenter the activity and behave properly. It is acceptable for the student to sit in the time-out area and return immediately to the activity. The assumption is that the student has agreed to behave properly.

Third Misbehavior: The student goes to the time-out area for the remainder of the period. If the misbehavior continues each time the class meets, most schools have an in-school suspension program to deal with severe behavior. In-school suspension requires the student to leave his or her class of students and move into another room of students (different grade level). This ensures that the student will receive little, if any, reinforcement. The foregoing steps assume that you have communicated with the student about their misbehavior and how they are expected to behave.

If these consequences are ineffective, the next alternative is to discuss with the principal other more serious consequences. The last alternative is to call the parents in for a conference with the principal and teacher. Discretion must be used when deciding to call parents. There is a strong possibility that it will further alienate you and the student because of parental pressure and punishment at home. Another possibility is that parents will disagree with your assessment. If parents can't or won't support you, it may be a better option to not call the parents and to deal with the behavior in a school setting. Along the same lines, don't ask the principal to solve your problems with misbehaving students. The principal will soon come to believe that you cannot effectively manage students. Ultimately, this will erode the principal's confidence in your teaching ability.

Implement Behavior Contracts with Older Students

A behavior contract is a written statement specifying certain student behaviors that must occur to earn certain rewards or privileges. The contract is drawn up after a private conference to decide on the appropriate behaviors and rewards. It is agreed upon and signed by the student and teacher. This approach allows students to make decisions that will improve their own behavior.

The behavior contract may be a successful strategy for intermediate-grade students with severe behavior problems. Every attempt should be made to find rewards that occur naturally in physical education class (such as Frisbee play, jump rope games, aerobics, or basketball). If not possible, different types of rewards may have to be used. For example, a student who is interested in music could be allowed to spend some time selecting CDs or tapes to be used for class during the next week. As behavior improves and the student's attitude becomes more positive, rewards should be switched to physical education activities. The contract is gradually phased out over a period of time as the youngster gains control of the behavior and can participate in normal class environments.

Contracts can be written for a small group of students or for an entire class with similar problems, but teachers must be careful about setting up a reward system for too many students. The system can become too complex or time-consuming to supervise properly. The contract is best used with a limited number of students who have severe problems. Examples of behavior contracts are shown in Figures 5.9 and 5.10. The contract in Figure 5.9 can be used with an individual, a small group, or an entire class of students.

Incorporate Behavior Games for Overall Class Behavior

Behavior games are an effective strategy for changing class behavior in the areas of management, motivation, and discipline. These activities use the shaping technique and are useful in changing whole-class behavior

Date: ____________

I, ______________________________, agree to follow the rules as listed below:

1. Listen when the teacher is talking.
2. Do not touch others during class.

If all the rules are followed during physical education class, I will earn 10 minutes of basketball activity for myself and a friend after school on Thursday anytime between 3:00 and 3:45.

Signed: ______________________________, Student

Signed: ______________________________, Teacher

FIGURE 5.9 Individual behavior contract.

Group Behavior Contract

Our squad agrees to follow the rules listed below:

1. Listen when the teacher is talking.
2. Take care of the equipment.
3. Treat others as we would like to be treated.

One point is earned each time the music stops and every member of the squad is following the rules. No points are awarded if one or more members of the squad are not following the rules. Each point is worth 1 minute of free activity time to be awarded every other Friday.

Signed: Squad Number ____________________ ____________________

____________________ ____________________

____________________ ____________________

____________________ ____________________

FIGURE 5.10 Group behavior contract.

(as contrasted to individual student behavior). If you are having problems in any of these areas, a well-conceived behavior game may turn the situation around in a short period. These games can be packaged for a group of students to compete against each other or against an established criterion. The goal of the game is to use group contingencies to develop behaviors that enhance the learning environment and to eliminate behaviors that detract from the environment (Darst & Whitehead, 1975; Paese, 1982).

The list below provides an example of a behavior game used successfully with sixth-graders in an effort to improve management behaviors.

1. The class is divided into four to six squads. Each squad has a designated color for identification. Four boundary cones with appropriate colors are arranged to mark a starting area.
2. The rules of the game are as follows:
   a. Each squad member has to be ready for activity and in proper position at a designated starting time. *Reward:* 2 points.
   b. Each squad member has to move from one activity to another activity within the specified time (10, 20, or 30 seconds) and begin the appropriate behavior. *Reward:* 1 point for each instance.
   c. Each point earned is rewarded with 1 minute of free activity time on Friday. Free activity time includes basketball, Frisbee playing, rope jumping, or any other activity popular with students.
   d. The squad with the most points for the week earns a bonus of 5 points.
3. Explain the allotted time for each management episode (10, 20, or 30 seconds), and give a "go" signal. At the end of the allowed time, give the signal for "stop" and award points for appropriate behavior.
4. Squads that are successful are praised and points are recorded on a small card. The unsuccessful squads are not hassled or criticized, just reminded that they did not earn a point.
5. On Fridays, the appropriate squads are awarded the special free-time activities while the other squads continue with the regularly scheduled class activities.
6. The game is slowly phased out (faded) as students begin to manage themselves more quickly.

Research used to evaluate behavior games showed the following results:

- The use of group contingencies and free-time activities reduced overall class management time.
- The free-time activities were within the physical education curriculum objectives and served as a break from regular activities.
- The free-time activities gave the teacher an opportunity to interact with students on a personal level.
- Students enjoyed the competition and the feeling of success when they behaved appropriately.
- Students enjoyed the free time with novelty activities.
- The positive approach of the game seemed to improve the overall teaching-learning atmosphere. Students were more attentive and cooperative.
- Teachers estimated that more time was available for instruction because of the reduction in management time.

A key point to follow when designing behavior games is to structure them so that any student or squad is able to win the game. Each game need not generate one winner and many losers. All participants should be able to win. Be aware that one or two students may find it reinforcing to cause their team to lose the behavior game. They will try to break every game rule to make sure that their team loses consistently. In these cases, hold a special team discussion with a vote to eliminate those students from the team and the game. These students are sent to a time-out area or to in-school suspension. They can be asked to sit out for the duration of the behavior game.

Another effective behavior game can be used to help students persist at learning activities in a station-type approach. Often, four to six learning stations are used for instruction. Performance objectives or learning tasks are posted at each station for students to practice. However, it may be that some students are not motivated and do not use their time productively until you rotate to the station where they are working. Overall, the environment is not productive, and you quickly get tired of hassling unmotivated students. A possible solution to this situation is the following game:

1. Divide the class into four to six squads. Let the students pick a name for their squad.
2. Set up the learning stations with the activities to be practiced. An equal number of squads and learning stations is necessary.
3. Program a cassette tape with popular music. Intersperse short gaps of silence throughout the tape.
4. Inform students that if everyone in their squad is properly engaged in practicing the appropriate task, a point will be awarded to the squad at each gap in the music. If one or more persons are not engaged, the point will not be awarded.
5. The points can be exchanged for minutes of time in selected activities such as Frisbee play, juggling, or rope jumping. Fridays can be designated as reward day, when the accumulated time is used.
6. The music can be changed regularly, and the interval between gaps should be changed and slowly increased until the gaps are eliminated. The music then serves as a discriminative cue for future practice time.

Students enjoy exercising and practicing skills while listening to music. The music enhances the motivational level and productivity of the environment. Students can be allowed to bring their own music as a special reward for productive behavior. (Make sure the music is not offensive to others due to sexual, ethnic, or religious connotations.)

USE CRITICISM SPARINGLY

Use criticism and punishment with caution and good judgment. Criticism is sometimes used with the belief that it will improve the performance of students. Some teachers make scolding and criticism the behavior control tools of choice because these tools give the impression that the results are effective and immediate. Usually, misbehavior stops and the assumption is that the situation has been rectified. Unfortunately, this is not always the case. Criticism and punishment lend a negative air to the instructional environment and have a negative impact on both student and teacher. The old saying, "It hurts me more than you," is often the case. The majority of teachers feel uncomfortable when they must criticize or punish students. It makes them feel as though they cannot handle students and that the class is incorrigible. This feeling of incompetence leads to a destructive cycle where students feel negative about the instructor and the instructor feels negative about the class. In the long run, this is the debilitating impact of criticism and punishment.

As mentioned above, another negative aspect of criticism is that it does not offer a solution. In a study by Thomas, Becker, and Armstrong (1968), a teacher was asked to stop praising a class. Off-task behavior increased from 8.7 percent to nearly 26 percent. When the teacher was asked to increase criticism from 5 times in 20 minutes to 16 times in 20 minutes, more off-task behavior was demonstrated. On some days the percentage of off-task behavior increased to more than 50 percent. When attention is given to off-task behavior and no praise is offered for on-task accomplishment, off-task behavior increases dramatically. Using criticism makes teachers feel effective (students respond to the request of the criticism), but students do not actually change. In fact, the students are reinforced (they receive attention from the teacher) for their off-task behavior. In addition, since their on-task behavior is not praised, it decreases. The net result is exactly the opposite of what is desired.

MAKE PUNISHMENT A LAST RESORT

The question of whether punishment should be used in an educational setting is a difficult one. Punishment can have negative side effects because fear is the primary motivator. Consider the long-term need for punishment. If the long-term effects of using punishment are more beneficial than not using it, it is unethical not to use punishment. In other words, if a child is going to be in a worse situation because punishment was not used to deter self-destructive behavior, it is wrong not to use it. It may be necessary to punish a child for protection from self-inflicted harm (for example, using certain apparatus without supervision). It may be necessary to punish children so that they learn not to hurt others. Punishment in these situations will cause discomfort to teacher and child in the short run, but it may allow the student to participate successfully in society later.

Most situations in the educational setting do not require punishment because they are not as severe as those described above. A major reason for avoiding punishment is that it can have undesirable side effects. When children are punished, they learn to avoid the source of punishment. It forces them to be more covert in their actions. They spend time finding ways to be devious without being caught. Instead of encouraging students to discuss problems with teachers and parents, punishment teaches them to avoid these individuals for fear of being punished. Another side effect is that it teaches children to be aggressive toward others. Children who have been physically or emotionally punished by parents act in similar fashion to others. The result is a child who is secretive and aggressive with others—certainly less-than-desirable traits. Finally, if punishment is used to stop certain behavior, as soon as the punishment stops the behavior will return. Thus, little has been learned; the punishment has just led to short-term change.

If it is necessary to use punishment, remember the following points:

1. *Be consistent and make the "punishment fit the crime."* Students quickly lose respect for a teacher who treats others with favoritism. They view the teacher as unfair if punishment is extreme or unfair. Peers quickly side with the student who is treated unfairly, causing a class morale problem for the instructor.
2. *Offer a warning signal, as discussed previously.* This may prevent excessive use of punishment, as students often behave after receiving a warning. In addition, they probably view the teacher as caring and fair.
3. *Do not threaten students.* Offer only one warning. Threats have little impact on students and make them feel that you cannot handle the class. One warning gives students the feeling that you are not looking to punish them and are fair. Follow through; do not challenge or threaten students and then fail to deal with the behavior.
4. *The punishment should follow the misbehavior as soon as possible.* It is much less effective and more often viewed as unfair when it is delayed.
5. *Punish softly and calmly.* Do not seek revenge or be vindictive. If responsible behavior is expected from students, be sure you reprimand and punish in a responsible manner. Studies (O'Leary & Becker, 1968) show that soft reprimands are more effective than loud ones.

One more point related to punishment: Try to avoid having negative feelings about a student and internalizing student misbehavior. Being punitive when handling deviant behavior destroys any chance for a worthwhile relationship. Misbehavior should be handled in a manner that contributes to the development of responsible, confident students who understand that people who function effectively in society must adjust to certain limits. Forget about past bouts of deviant behavior and approach the student in a positive fashion at the start of each class. If this is not done, students are labeled, making behavioral change more difficult. Students may also learn to live up to the teacher's negative expectations.

If punishment is used, make sure that only those youngsters who misbehave are punished. Punishing an entire class for the deviant behavior of a few youngsters is unfair and may trigger undesirable side effects. Students become hostile toward those who caused the loss of privileges, and this peer hostility lowers the level of positive social interaction with the students who have misbehaved.

EXPULSION: LEGAL CONSIDERATIONS

If serious problems occur, discuss the problems with the classroom teacher and principal. Many times, deviant behavior is part of a larger, more severe problem that is troubling a child. A cooperative approach may provide an effective solution. A group meeting involving parents, classroom teacher, principal, counselor, and physical education specialist may open avenues that encourage understanding and increase productive behavior.

Legal concerns involving the student's rights in disciplinary areas are an essential consideration. While minor infractions may be handled routinely, expulsion and other substantial punishments can be imposed on students only after due process. The issue of student rights is complicated, and most school systems have established guidelines and procedures for dealing with students who have been removed from the class or school setting. Youngsters should be removed from class only if they are disruptive to the point of interfering with the learning experiences of other children and if all other means of altering behavior have not worked. Sending a child out of class is a last resort and means that both teacher and student have failed.

REFLECTION AND REVIEW QUESTIONS

How and Why

1. How would you respond to a child that consistently misbehaves?

2. How does it make you feel when a professor knows your name?
3. How might pre- and post-teaching routines change depending on the school?
4. Why is it important for teachers to know their own trigger points? What are your trigger points?
5. What rules would you have in your classes?
6. What types of emotions might you feel when placing a child in timeout?
7. As an adult, how does criticism make you feel?

Content Review

1. What class management skills are necessary to be an effective teacher?
2. Discuss the importance of using efficient instruction, a consistent stop signal, and moving students into formation quickly in an effective lesson.
3. How can knowing the names of students help teachers?
4. What types of routines do successful teachers establish?
5. Discuss the effective use of equipment.

FOR MORE INFORMATION

References and Suggested Readings

Bailey, B. A. (2001). *Conscious discipline.* Oviedo, FL: Loving Guidance, Inc.

Beane, A. (1999). *The bully free classroom.* Minneapolis: Free Spirit Publishing.

Canter, L., & Canter, M. (1997). *Assertive discipline: Positive behavior management for today's classroom.* Santa Monica, CA: Lee Canter and Associates.

Charles, C. M. (1989). *Building classroom discipline.* 3rd ed. New York: Longman.

Curwin, R. L., & Mendler, A. N. (1988). *Discipline with dignity.* Washington, DC: Association for Supervision and Curriculum Development.

Darst, P. W., & Whitehead, S. (1975). Developing a contingency management system for controlling student behavior. *Pennsylvania JOPER,* 46(3), 11–12.

Gordon, A., & Brown, K. W. (1996). *Guiding young children in a diverse society.* Boston: Allyn and Bacon.

Greene, D., & Lepper, M. R. (1975). Turning play into work: Effects of adult surveillance and extrinsic rewards on children's internal motivation. *Journal of Personality and Social Psychology,* 31, 479–486.

Hellison, D. (1995). *Teaching responsibility through physical activity.* Champaign, IL: Human Kinetics.

Nelson, J. (1996). *Positive discipline.* New York: Ballantine.

O'Leary, K. D., & Becker, W. C. (1968). The effects of intensity of a teacher's reprimands on children's behavior. *Journal of School Psychology,* 7, 8–11.

Paese, P. (1982). Effects of interdependent group contingencies in a secondary physical education setting. *Journal of Teaching in Physical Education,* 2(1), 29–37.

Premack, D. (1965). Reinforcement theory. In D. Levine (Ed.), *Nebraska symposium on motivation.* Lincoln: University of Nebraska Press.

Siedentop, D., & Tannehill, D. (2000). *Developing teaching skills in physical education.* 4th ed. Mountain View, CA: Mayfield Publishing Co.

Thomas, D. R., Becker, W. C., & Armstrong, M. (1968). Production and elimination of disruptive classroom behavior by systematically varying teachers' behavior. *Journal of Applied Behavior Analysis,* 1, 35–45.

Whitehead, J. R., & Corbin, C. B. (1991). Effects of fitness test type, teacher, and gender on exercise intrinsic motivation and physical self-worth. *Journal of School Health,* 61, 11–16.

Wolfgang, C. H. (1996). *The three faces of discipline for the elementary school teacher.* Boston: Allyn and Bacon.

Websites

Classroom Management
http://www.pecentral.org/climate/disciplinelinks.html#classroombehaviormanagementsites
http://www.honorlevel.com/techniques.html
http://www2.potsdam.edu/CRANE/campbemr/browsing/management_res,1.html
http://www.glencoe.com/sec/teachingtoday/tiparchive.phtml/4

Management Styles
http://education.indiana.edu/cas/tt/v1i2/what.html

Teaching Responsible Behavior
http://www.shea.sask.com/proceedings/jan2000/model1.htm
http://www.hellison.com/

CHAPTER 6

Evaluation

	ESSENTIAL COMPONENTS
I	Organized around content standards
II	Student-centered and developmentally appropriate
III	Physical activity and motor skill development form the core of the program
IV	Teaches management skills and self-discipline
V	**Promotes inclusion of all students**
VI	**Focuses on process over product**
VII	Promotes lifetime personal health and wellness
VIII	Teaches cooperation and responsibility and promotes sensitivity to diversity

	PHYSICAL EDUCATION STANDARDS
1	Students are able to move competently using a variety of fundamental and specialized motor skills.
2	Students can monitor and maintain a health-enhancing level of physical fitness.
3	Students are able to apply movement concepts and basic mechanics of skill performance when learning and refining motor skills.
4	Students comprehend the basic principles of wellness and are able to apply concepts that enable them to make meaningful decisions that positively impact their health and wellness.
5	Students participate in a wide variety of physical activities and learn how to maintain a personalized active lifestyle.
6	Students demonstrate empathy, understanding, and respect for the numerous differences exhibited by people in an activity setting.
7	Students exhibit responsible and self-directed behaviors that lead to positive social interactions in physical activity

SUMMARY

There are many types of evaluation, but all evaluation is done to improve instruction and increase learning. Ways to evaluate student learning include the use of checklists, logs, tests, and scoring rubrics. A grading system that communicates student progress to parents is difficult to design. There are many reasons for giving grades and just as many reasons for avoiding grading in elementary schools. A student progress report can be a useful approach for helping parents understand their child's progress in physical education. Growth in instructional effectiveness occurs when teachers choose to self-evaluate their instruction. A program checklist can be used to score the total physical education setting.

OUTCOMES

- Differentiate between formal and informal evaluation.
- Explain and understand the differences between process and product evaluation.
- Cite a number of ways to assess student learning.
- Know the advantages of a progress report for parents.
- Describe arguments for and against grading in physical education.
- Identify methods of instructional analysis of teacher behavior.
- Identify ways to self-evaluate instructional behavior.
- Recognize the key elements of an effective physical education evaluation form.

The purpose of evaluation is to determine whether progress is being made toward objectives. Evaluation should review all phases of education, including pupil progress, teacher performance, and program effectiveness. Student evaluation can be formal or informal and can focus on individual or group progress. Teacher evaluation can be used to improve the instructional process or to secure data for measuring teacher effectiveness. Program evaluation is used to examine the total program or selected program areas. Approaches and curricula that are effective need to be retained and enhanced, and what is deficient needs to be corrected.

EVALUATION: PROCESS OR PRODUCT?

Two types of evaluation pertain to students: process evaluation and product evaluation. *Process evaluation* relates to the performance of movement patterns with emphasis on correct technique. The form used to execute the movement is the point of focus rather than the outcome of the skill performed. In contrast, *product evaluation* focuses on performance outcomes in terms of measurable increments of what learners accomplish. For example, if product evaluation is applied to fundamental ball skills, the concern is with how many times the ball is caught without a miss. On the other hand, process evaluation focuses on the technical points of catching properly.

This leads to several questions: Should physical education focus on product outcomes or should it emphasize the process of learning skills correctly? Should physical education experiences be designed to develop high-quality athletes or should it focus on teaching all students the proper way to perform skills? Physical education has a unique role in the school curriculum. Nowhere else can students receive skill instruction and be provided the opportunity to learn the benefits of lifetime activity. Academics can teach character, knowledge, social skills, and the like, but only physical education can accomplish unique physical skill and activity outcomes. Physical education doesn't have to be like academics; in fact, it is important because it is different.

Physical education doesn't have an absolute and exact product. Cognitive knowledge is based on the building-block theory—that new learning is based on previously acquired facts. For example, math facts are necessary to perform higher math manipulations. Physical education differs in that the same set of skills is learned and refined throughout the school years. For instance, the skill of throwing is taught in elementary school and continues to be repeated and refined each year thereafter. After the basic skill is learned, little new is taught about throwing; emphasis is placed on repetition and refinement of the skill.

Perfection (of skill performance) does not occur in physical education, or sport for that matter. This contrasts with most academic areas that demand accuracy and correctness. New knowledge is based on previously learned information, which is based on a commonly accepted body of information. This contrasts with physical education, where correct performance is impossible to predict and errors are expected. Even the best athletes miss half of the baskets they shoot, or make an out in baseball about 70 percent of the time. Often, physical educators teach as though perfection were a realistic and reasonable goal. Youngsters may begin to believe that the product or outcome (such as making a basket) is more important than the process of performing the skill correctly. Teachers often encourage such thinking unknowingly by reinforcing skill attempts that are correct while failing to comment on a student's quality of performance.

Skill refinement is not synonymous with performance improvement. Teachers have been taught to evaluate their effectiveness based on how many students reach product benchmarks, such as the number of students who can make a number of baskets or jump a rope a certain number of times. Many teachers have written such outcomes with the intent of getting all students to reach them. Unfortunately, they promise a product that may not be achievable. For example, when adults hire a professional instructor to improve their golf swing, they do so without guarantees. Creditable golf pros will not guarantee a reduction in golf scores. Rather, they will assure their pupils that they can improve their swing, which, over time, *may* result in improved scores. They are unable to control the genetic makeup or the psychological willingness of individuals to change and improve. What can be guaranteed is that they will teach with enthusiasm, that they will be knowledgeable of the latest techniques, and that they will devote the time necessary to refine a skill. These expectations should be similar for teachers; other expectations may be unreasonable and unachievable.

The product of physical education is actually a process; it may be the process of learning skills properly, or the process of participation and performance. The ultimate goal of the physical education process is to graduate students who feel competent and willing to perform skills throughout a lifetime of activity. Leaving students a legacy of knowing how to live an active lifestyle is more important than their knowing that they could make 10 to 15 free throws or hit 20 successful tennis serves.

In addition, students benefit from being taught to value effort more highly than victory. Something is lost for many participants when winning dictates success. The process of doing one's best is the important issue in physical education. It is possible, but not common, to find students who participate in activity without worrying about winning and losing. In many areas in the school curriculum, emphasis is placed on cooperative learning. Physical education can benefit by such an approach. Evidence shows that cooperative learning improves self-esteem and attitude toward school and can temper the negative aspects of competition (Johnson, Johnson, & Holubec, 1990). Activity and participation can be enhanced by the joy of working together.

Consider the product-versus-process conflict and how it relates to a teacher's view of the instructional environment. A product-oriented teacher shows less concern for how students feel about learning, or about the technique and form used when performing skills. In a game of basketball, for example, the focus would be on the product or outcome of the game—winning or losing. The process-oriented teacher, on the other hand, is more concerned that students develop proper patterns of skill performance and positive attitudes toward the activity. The outcome of the game is secondary to the learning experience. Most teachers find themselves somewhere between the two viewpoints and place varying amounts of emphasis on process and product.

Three problems arise when trying to evaluate performance in physical education. The first is the need for a system of recording that is efficient, valid, and not excessively time-consuming. The second concerns the number of times a trait needs to be observed or measured before the evaluation can be considered reliable. The third problem pertains to the amount of in-class and out-of-class time needed for effective evaluation. Take the case of the physical education specialist who handles 300 to 600 students each day. How does the specialist evaluate this number of students adequately and record the items properly?

ASSESSING PERFORMANCE OUTCOMES

Assessment of student performance is an important issue that can be accomplished in many different ways. Informal assessment is often done on the spot when a teacher corrects or reinforces a student's performance. A number of more formal, yet alternative assessments are becoming popular because teachers are expected to assess and report student progress toward program standards (Chepko & Arnold, 2000).

Scoring Rubrics

A scoring rubric is a rating scale that lists multiple criteria related to a task or motor skill performance (Figure 6.1). The criteria are performance levels students are expected to achieve. A basic question common to most assessment is, "Can the child perform the stated motor pattern using correct technique?" To employ this type of assessment requires accurate knowledge of different learning stages so the child's pattern of development can be observed and categorized. Videotaping is useful for viewing the skill performance a number of times and in slow motion. For example, a 9-year-old youngster at the expected developmental level should be able to demonstrate stage-four catching form. If a child of this age tests at stage two, a developmental deficiency is indicated. Figure 6.1 is an example of a scoring rubric for catching skills. This rubric lists the four stages of catching. Evaluation involves judging the student's ability to catch, and matching the degree of skill with these stages.

Observation Checklists

Another means of process evaluation is to use an observation checklist. Criteria governing proper technique

Scoring Rubric for Catching Skills

	Stage 1—Arms held out and ball trapped against body	Stage 2—Anticipatory movement made to catch ball	Stage 3—Contact is made with the hands first	Stage 4—Catches with the hands and absorbs the force of the ball
Students				
Mike				
Mary				
John				
Lloyd				

FIGURE 6.1 Form showing rubric for scoring ball-catching skills.

Class______________ Grade______________ Date ______________

Scoring: 3 = above developmental level 2 = at developmental level 1 = below developmental level	Running			Jumping			Hopping			Skipping		
	Arm Action	Leg Action	Composite	Arm Action	Leg Action	Composite	Arm Action	Leg Action	Composite	Arm Action	Leg Action	Composite
Student's Name												

FIGURE 6.2 Observation checklist for locomotor skills.

for the movement pattern are listed, and the child's performance is checked against these points. Limiting coverage to two or three of the critical points of technique is usually best. Ratings for each point can be on a 3-point scale: above developmental level, at developmental level, and below developmental level. These can be numbered 3, 2, and 1, respectively, providing a point scale for ease of recording. The record sheet can also be organized so achievement levels are listed, and the evaluator circles the appropriate number. Figure 6.2 is an example of an observation checklist for some of the fundamental locomotor skills.

Skill Checklists

Checklists have long been used as a system for reporting progress to students and parents. A class roster with skills listed across the top of the sheet is a common method used for recording class progress. It can alert you to youngsters who are in need of special help. If grading is based on the number of activities students master, the checklist can deliver this information. Checklists are usually most effective when skills are listed in the sequence in which they should be learned. In this way, you can gear the teaching process to diagnosed needs. To avoid disrupting the learning process, it is best to record student progress informally while students are practicing. Figure 6.3 is a sample checklist for rope jumping.

Anecdotal Record Sheets

A record sheet that contains student names and has room for comments about student behavior can be used to assess student progress. Anecdotal records of student progress can be reinforcing to both student and teacher, as it is often difficult to remember how much progress has been made over a period of time. With anecdotal records, teachers can inform students of their initial skill level compared with their present performance.

A tape recorder is useful for recording anecdotal information. Comments can be recorded during observation and transcribed later. This process can help you learn the names and behavior patterns of students and can lead to an increased understanding of student performance. Observations should be recorded at the start of the unit and compared with observations made at a later date as instruction proceeds. A sample anecdotal record sheet is illustrated in Figure 6.4.

Student Self-Assessments

Students in the intermediate grades are capable of self-evaluation. They can be given lists of performance objectives and told to make judgments about their achievement. If more objectivity is desired, students can evaluate each other, or groups of two or three students can evaluate one another. Self-evaluation reduces the amount of teacher evaluation time and allows the teacher more time for instruction. The ability to evaluate

Rope-Jumping Checklist

Student	Jump in Place	Jump, Turn Both Ends	Jump, Pendulum Swing	Slow Time	Fast Time	Alternate-Foot Step	Swing Step Forward	Rocker Step	Spread Legs, Forward	Toe-and-Heel Touch	Shuffle Step	Cross Arms	Cross Arms, Backward	Double Jump	

FIGURE 6.3 Sample skill checklist.

Anecdotal Record Sheet

Class Ms. Massoney Date 2/14

Bob: Is making progress on the backward jump. Sent a jump rope home with him for practice.

Gene: Seems to be discouraged about rope jumping. Called parents to see if there is a problem outside of school.

Linda: Discussed the need for helping others. She is going to be a cross-aged tutor for next two weeks, as her performance in batting is excellent.

FIGURE 6.4 Sample anecdotal record sheet.

oneself and the desire to be evaluated are important outcomes of any effective program.

Student Logs

Intermediate-grade youngsters are capable of maintaining a log that indicates progress toward a goal over time. Assume students want to increase the amount of physical activity they accomplish each day. The teacher and students could discuss some goals that would help them become more active. Another approach is to ask students to develop behaviors they need to accomplish to reach their goals. The log should include goal behaviors they have accomplished over time—including decisions and choices made, time spent on goal behaviors, and a reflection area to record their perceptions of the experience.

Students can share their experiences and feelings about things they have tried. The logistics of activities each student has tried can be shared. Examining how well the stated outcomes were reached is the most common way to evaluate logs. For example, for students who wanted to increase their activity outside of school, a high score would go to youngsters who were active for 30 minutes five days a week. An acceptable score would go to students who were active three days a week. An unacceptable score would go to those who were active one day or less.

Written Tests

Written tests are administered to check the cognitive learning that has accompanied physical skill learning. The tests can be true–false or multiple choice for ease of correction. On the other hand, short answer or essay questions encourage students to apply knowledge to different situations. The reading level of students must be considered when writing tests or it will be difficult to tell whether it is a comprehension or knowledge test. Oral presentation of questions is often best for younger students. Even though it seems apparent, written tests give little, if any, indication of how a youngster will perform a motor skill. Be careful not to grade just on written tests that examine cognition since physical education is primarily based on becoming skilled physically.

Standardized Tests

Standardized tests are useful for evaluating measurable outcomes. These types of tests have been administered to large samples of youngsters, and the results are available for comparative purposes. Most of the tests require that exact testing procedures and protocol be followed. The disadvantages of standardized tests are their inflexibility and the need for specialized equipment. The Fitnessgram (Cooper Institute for Aerobics Research, 2002) is an example of a standardized test.

The test results, or at least an interpreted summary, can be included in a child's permanent health record and can be part of a periodic progress report to parents. The school report card should contain a section devoted to physical education. Test results for each class and for the school as a whole should be presented in a manner that is easily interpreted by students and parents. Testing is meaningless unless evaluators have a concern for raising student performance levels and upgrading the physical education program.

GRADING

There is wide variation in physical education grading policies in elementary schools, ranging from no grading to grading with letter grades similar to high school classes. Effective arguments can be made on each side of the issue, to grade or not to grade, and there is no clear-cut answer. If the decision is made to grade, a more difficult question arises: What type of grading approach should be used? For an in-depth review of grading systems and ideas for evaluation, the text by Lacy and Hastad (2003) is recommended.

Arguments against Using a Grading System

- Grades are difficult to interpret between teachers and schools. A grade means one thing to one teacher and another to a different teacher. When moving to a different school, the meaning of the grade does not transfer, and teachers at the new school may view the grade differently.
- Physical education does not place emphasis on content and product. Rather, it judges success by improvement on skills. Grades in academic areas reflect achievement and accomplishment; because grades in physical education reflect improvement and effort, they may be interpreted incorrectly.
- Often, physical education classes in elementary schools only meet once or twice a week. Testing for the purpose of assigning a grade is time consuming and takes away from learning opportunities. Physical educators in this setting are trying to squeeze as much learning as possible into a minimal amount of time, and grading reduces their instructional time.
- Physical education is diverse and broad in nature. Instruction covers all three learning domains, i.e., skill development, attitude formation, and content knowledge. Trying to grade all three of these areas is difficult and demands a great deal of time. In addition, which of these three domains is most important and can any of them be overlooked?
- Grading usually occurs in areas where standardized instruments have been developed. Fitness testing is the major area in elementary physical education where a variety of standardized tests have been developed. Due to the dearth of standardized tests in other areas, excessive attention is given to fitness testing.
- Physical education places emphasis on physical fitness and skill performance. Performance in these areas is strongly controlled by genetics, making it difficult for all children to achieve, even when they "give it their best effort." In addition, when grades are given for physical fitness performance, some youngsters feel discouraged because they trained and still did not reach standards of high performance (see Chapter 12).

Arguments for Using a Grading System

- Giving grades makes physical education similar to other academic areas in the school curriculum. This gives physical education credibility and gains respect from parents, teachers, and administrators.
- Grades communicate the performance of students to parents. Parents have a right to know how their youngsters perform in physical education. Grades are used by teachers in other areas and are easily understood and interpreted by parents; therefore, they should be used in physical education.
- When grades are not given, academic respect is lost. Physical education already suffers from the misguided perception that physical educators don't teach anything, they just "roll out the ball." Lack of a grading system may make it appear to others that little learning is occurring.
- A grading system provides accountability. When grades are given, administrators and parents often assume that teaching and student accomplishment have occurred.
- A grading system rewards skilled students. Students are rewarded in academic areas for their intelligence and performance and should be similarly rewarded for accomplishment in physical education settings.

Implementing a Grading System

If the decision is made to implement a grading system, more difficult issues follow. There are different ways to grade, and many issues have to be examined before developing a grading approach. Consider the following points when determining how you will assign grades.

Improvement or performance? Grades can be assigned on how youngsters perform in class or whether they improve. Because some youngsters are not gifted athletically, should you give them the opportunity to earn a high grade by showing improvement? If you feel physical education should grade in a manner similar to academics, will you assign high grades to students who demonstrate the highest level of physical skill?

Negative or positive? Grades can reward students for what they accomplish. For example, a grade may be earned by accumulating a number of points based on accomplishment of various skills and activities. In addition, extra points could be earned by doing well on knowledge tests and citizenship. The opposing point of view is to take away points when students don't behave or perform well. This approach can be negative, and students may lose their desire to participate in such an experience. The most common negative approach is to subtract points when students do not behave in an acceptable manner. This practice places a focus more on the negative aspects of student performance than on the positive constructs.

Teach for test results or for learning? When deciding how to grade students, consider how the grading system will affect your teaching. Some teachers may feel they have failed if students do not receive high marks. On the other hand, some teachers may feel that a certain number of students should fail. If fitness testing is a part of the grading package, some teachers may spend an excessive amount of time having students train for the test items rather than learning about fitness and discovering the many pathways to fitness.

Process or product? This issue is discussed in detail earlier in this chapter. Is the grade based on how well students learn skill patterns (such as throwing, kicking, or striking), or on the outcome (how many strikes are thrown or hits made)? The choice you make depends on whether you value correct skill technique or the outcome of the skill performance.

Broad or narrow perspective? Should the grade be based on a single factor, such as physical skill performance or written test performance? Should it be based on effort? Should it be based on attitude? Choosing only one or two areas would be grading from a narrow perspective. A broad-based approach would be to include all teaching areas and integrate them into a single grade.

Letter Grades or a Student Progress Report?

Letter grades tell parents very little about the performance of their youngsters in physical education. Many times the grade is a reflection of student behavior but the parent interprets it as an indicator of their student's physical skill level. A letter grade doesn't communicate progress or performance related to other students at a similar developmental level. A student progress report takes more time to compile, but gives parents much more information and helps to communicate the goals of the program.

Figure 6.5 is an example of a progress report that could be used to share information with parents. The seven areas of evaluation represent the seven major content standards of the program (See Chapter 1). If desired, some of the specific benchmarks under each standard could also be included. Note that program standards are divided into two major areas: (1) physical education skills; and (2) social skills and responsible behavior. Most teachers want an opportunity to separate behavior and skill performance when grading. This progress report allows students to be rewarded for effort and proper behavior regardless of their skill and physical ability. An advantage to evaluating a student based on developmental level is that it gives parents an idea of how their child is performing compared to others of similar development and maturity. This report helps parents understand that the skill performance of other children who are similar developmentally, are above, at, or below their child's skill level. This feedback may help temper unrealistic expectations of parents and coaches who do not have the perspective of seeing many children at similar developmental levels.

Since using a progress report takes more time than assigning letter grades, such a report can't be sent home as often as a simple letter grade. Most elementary school teachers are responsible for 350 to 600 students or more. Completing a progress report for each student four times a year would be an unrealistic expectation because of the inordinate amount of time it takes to complete. A solution is to offer a comprehensive and meaningful progress report once a year or once every second or third year. This approach alerts teachers to students they will have to grade for the forthcoming year and allows them time to review these youngsters in detail throughout the year.

SELF-EVALUATING INSTRUCTIONAL EFFECTIVENESS

A key to improving teaching ability is to be able to gather meaningful feedback about your own instructional behavior. It is often difficult to find someone capable of offering evaluative feedback. Principals and curriculum supervisors may be too busy to evaluate teaching regularly, or they may not possess the skills necessary for systematically evaluating teaching behavior. This accentuates the importance of finding ways for self-evaluating teaching as a primary avenue for improvement. Without regular and measurable means of evaluation, improving the quality of teaching becomes next to impossible. Teachers have long been told to talk less, move more, praise more, learn more names, and increase student practice time—all without documented methods of measurement. This section offers methods for evaluating teaching behavior that are observable and therefore measurable. If readers desire in-depth information on this subject, the texts *Developing Teaching Skills in Physical Education* (Siedentop & Tannehill, 2000) and *Analyzing Physical Education and Sport Instruction* (Darst, Zakrajsek, & Mancini, 1989) are excellent resources.

The do-it-yourself approach to evaluation is recommended because feedback that is reviewed in the privacy of one's office is easier to digest and less threatening. You can set personal goals and chart your performance privately. When you choose to evaluate your teaching procedures, you are making a commitment to change. This attitude is in contrast to the resistance that some

Progress Report for Physical Education

Student: ______________________ **Class:** ______________________

Students are expected to learn a wide variety of skills in physical education. The following areas reflect major program standards. Expectations are that your child will perform at or above developmental level (compared with other students the same age). If you are interested in discussing the progress of your child, please arrange a meeting with the physical education instructor.

Physical Education Assessment

Program Standards	Developmental Level Performance		
	Above	At	Below
Exhibits motor skills and movement competence			
Able to monitor and maintain physical fitness			
Understands human movement principles			
Uses lifestyle habits that foster wellness			
Possesses lifetime physical activity skills			

Social Skills and Responsible Behavior Assessment

Students are graded on social skills and responsible behavior in physical education classes. Rewards and consequences are recorded daily. Grades are based on how students perform in these areas.

O = Outstanding Exhibits effort and a positive attitude about participating in physical activities on a regular basis. Cooperates with classmates and receives no more than one behavior consequence during the nine-week grading period.

S = Satisfactory Willingly attempts activities. Puts forth average effort, displays a positive attitude, cooperates with classmates, and receives two to five behavior consequences during the nine-week grading period.

N = Needs Improvement Consistently exhibits off-task behavior and/or a negative attitude. Has difficulty cooperating with classmates. Parents are notified by mid-term of the grading period if their child is in jeopardy of receiving a grade of "N."

Program Standards	O	S	N
Develops quality social skills			
Exhibits responsible behavior			

Instructor's Comments

FIGURE 6.5 Sample progress report.

teachers feel when principals and supervisors evaluate them, and dictate change. Instructors often doubt the validity of the latter process and find reasons for *not* changing.

First steps to self-improvement are to decide what teaching behavior to evaluate and the best possible way to record and monitor the data. Evaluating a single teaching behavior when starting to evaluate your instructional effectiveness is preferable, since recording more than one variable at a time can be frustrating and confusing. After determining the behavior to change, design a coding form to facilitate recording the data.

Coding sheets are best designed for a specific teaching behavior. Areas on the sheet provide for the recording teacher's name, the date, focus and content of the lesson, grade level and competency of the students, duration of the lesson, and a short description of the evaluation procedure. Maintaining a consistent format for the coding sheets will make it easier to compare your performance throughout the year. Appropriate coding forms for gathering data on a number of teaching behaviors are offered in the next section. These forms are examples that can be modified to meet the specific needs of the instructor. Effective teachers usually make self-evaluation an ongoing, integral part of their teaching.

There are many ways to gather data about your teaching. For example, students who are not participating can gather the data; another teacher can gather the data easily; or the data can be gathered from an audiotape or a videotape. Most teachers feel comfortable evaluating their own teaching performance. Daily teaching behavior is least affected when outside observers are not present, making self-evaluation techniques more likely to reveal actual instructional patterns.

Instructional Time

It is important to know the amount of instruction you offer students. To analyze instructional time, the number of instructional episodes and the length of each episode are recorded. The average length of an instructional episode can be evaluated, as well as the percentage of the lesson that was used for instruction. Generally, episodes should be short and frequent, with an attempt made to limit each episode to 30 seconds or less.

How to Do It

1. Design a form for duration recording.
2. Have a colleague or a nonparticipating student turn on the stopwatch every time the instructor begins

Instructional Time

Teacher Charlene Darst Observer B. Pangrazi

Class 1st period Grade 5th Date and Time 3/22 - 9:05

Lesson focus Basketball Comments 1st class meeting of unit

Starting time 9:30 End time 10:00 Length of lesson 30 min

15	10	8	35	17	1:03	31	9	8
14	21	10	21	43	7			

Total instruction time 5 min 12 sec

Percentage of class time devoted to instruction 17%

Number of episodes 15 Average length of episodes 31.5 sec

FIGURE 6.6 Sample form for calculating instructional time.

an instructional episode; or record the lesson using an audiotape recorder and time the instructional episodes at the end of the day. Establish consistency in identifying the difference between instructional and management episodes.

3. Total the amount of time spent on instruction.
4. Convert the amount of time to a percentage of the total lesson time by dividing the total lesson time into the time spent on instruction. The average length of an instructional episode can be determined by dividing the amount of instructional time by the number of instructional episodes. Figure 6.6 is an example of a form that could be used.

Management Time

Management time is defined as episodes that occur when students are moved into various formations, when equipment is gathered or put away, and when directions are given relative to these areas. Disciplining a class is another example of time used for management. As a rule of thumb, if you are talking and not giving instructions, you are managing students. Figure 6.7 is an example of a form that can be used to record the amount of management time.

The length of each episode can be recorded by an observer. These data are useful for analyzing how much of the lesson time is devoted to management. You may be alerted to inefficient organizational schemes or realize that students are not responding quickly to explanations and requests.

How to Do It

1. Design a form to gather the desired data.
2. Record the lesson with an audiotape recorder. Time the episodes of management and note the length of each episode on the form.
3. Total the amount of management time and divide it by the length of the period to determine the percentage of management time in the lesson.
4. Total the number of episodes and divide this number into the amount of time devoted to management to find the average length of a management episode.

Management Time

Teacher Don Hicks

Observer Connie Orlowicz

Class 6th period

Grade 3rd

Date and Time 10/29 - 1:30

Lesson focus Manipulative skills

Comments

Starting time 1:30

End time 2:00

Length of lesson 30 min

55	10	21	20	35	18	29	10	10	21	9	19	21
11												

Total management time 4 min 49 sec

Percentage of class time devoted to management 16%

Number of episodes 14

Average length of episodes 20.6 sec

FIGURE 6.7 Sample form for calculating management time.

Practice Time (Time on Task) and Dead Time

To learn physical skills, students must have an opportunity for productive skill practice. Physical education programs have a finite amount of scheduled time per week. Practice time, or time on task, has also been referred to as ALT-PE. This is an acronym for Academic Learning Time in Physical Education. Practice time is the amount of time students spend practicing skills that result in accomplishment of program objectives. Gathering data to show the amount of time students are involved in productive, on-task activity can reveal whether there is adequate time to learn skills. In a well-regarded school district, the authors found that the average amount of activity time per 50-minute period was only 9 to 12 minutes. It is possible that more learning could occur if practice time were increased.

Duration recording is best for evaluating practice time. A student or fellow teacher observes the lesson and times when students are involved in practicing skills. Figure 6.8 shows the results of duration recording for practice time. Strive to increase the amount of time devoted to skill practice by using more equipment, implementing drills that demand a minimum of standing in line, or streamlining the amount of verbal instructions given.

The amount of dead time in a lesson also can be measured. Dead time occurs when students are off task or are doing something unrelated to practice, management, or instruction. Examples might be standing in line waiting for a turn, doing nothing because instructions were not understood, or playing a game and standing while waiting for the ball to come to them.

How to Do It

1. Design a form for collecting the data (Figure 6.9).

Teacher: Debbie Massoney
School: Whittier Elementary

Parts of the lesson	Practicing	Inactive, off task, listening
Introductory activity	1.5 min	0.5 min
Fitness development	6.5 min	1.5 min
Lesson focus	10.0 min	4.0 min
Game	5.0 min	1.0 min
Total	23.0 min	7.0 min

FIGURE 6.8 Results of a duration recording for practice time.

2. Identify a student who will be timed when practicing. This is a critical step. The student chosen should be neither exceptional nor below par and should give a realistic picture of the amount of practice time allotted. If evaluation of dead time is desired, then time when that student is not involved in on-task practice, management, or instructional activity. Another way to calculate dead time is to subtract the combined amounts of time used for practice, management, and instruction (assuming all have been timed) from the total length of the lesson.
3. Turn on the stopwatch when the student is involved in practice (or dead) activity. Stop the watch when the student stops (or starts) practicing. Record the amount of practice (or dead) time. Time all practice (or dead) episodes.
4. Total the amount of time devoted to student practice (in minutes) and divide it by the length of the lesson. This is the percentage of practice time in a lesson. Total the amount of dead time and divide it by the length of the lesson to compute the percentage of dead time.

Response Latency

Response latency is the amount of time it takes for students to respond when commands or signals are given. Response latency occurs when instructions are given to begin or stop an activity. An observer records the amount of time that elapses from the moment a command is given to start or stop an activity until the moment the students actually begin or stop. The amount of elapsed time is the response latency.

The average duration of response latency can be calculated. A certain amount of response latency should be expected. However, most instructors have a strong feeling about the amount of latency they are willing to tolerate. After more than a 5-second response latency, teachers usually become uneasy and expect the class to stop or start.

How to Do It

1. Develop a form for gathering the data (Figure 6.10 on page 118).
2. Have a nonparticipating student or colleague time the response latency that occurs when the class is asked to stop (start). The clock should run from the time the command to stop (start) is given until the next command is given or until the class is involved in productive behavior. Starting and stopping latency are two separate behaviors that must be recorded separately.

Practice Time

Teacher Eugene Petersen Observer P. W. Darst

Class 2nd period Grade 4th Date and Time 11/15 - 9:15

Lesson focus Gymnastics skills Comments week two

Starting time 9:25 End time 10:00 Length of lesson 35 min

35	10	2:04	25	29	1:39	17	55	34
43	1:55	1:01	33	10	10	18	1:17	4:50
24	39	31	34					

Total practice time 20 min 13 sec

Percentage of class time devoted to practice 57.8%

Number of episodes 22 Average length of episodes 55.1 sec

FIGURE 6.9 Sample form for collecting data on practice time.

3. Tally the number of response latency episodes and divide this number into the total amount of time devoted to response latency to calculate the average episode length.

Student Performance

Some classes have a greater percentage of students performing at optimum level than do others. The percentage of students performing the desired task is an excellent indicator of a well-managed class. The placheck (planned activity check) observation technique (Siedentop & Tannehill, 2000) is an excellent way to monitor the percentage of students who are on task.

Placheck (planned activity check) recording is a technique used to observe group behavior at different times during a lesson. At regular intervals, the observer scans the class from the left to the right side of the instructional area and records the number of students who were not performing the predefined behavior. (Recording the smaller number of students exhibiting a behavior is easiest. For example, if you are interested in identifying the percentage of students on task, generally it is easier to record the number of students *not* on task.) Each student in the class is observed one time only during a scan. The observer does not go back and change the decision, even if the student changes behavior during the interval. Intervals should last for 10 seconds and be randomly spaced throughout the lesson, with eight to ten observation intervals. Signals to scan the class should be recorded on a tape recorder at random intervals to cue the observer.

The placheck is used to monitor behavior that is "yes or no" in nature. In other words, students either are performing the desired behavior or are doing something else. Examples of areas that might be evaluated are on-task behavior, active behavior, or effort in performing an activity. Once the results are determined, a goal can be set to increase the percentage of students involved in the desired observable behavior.

How to Do It

1. Design a form for recording the desired data. Figure 6.11 is a sample form for placheck observation. The form can be used to identify three different types of student performance. The data gathered in Figure 6.11 evaluate on-task and off-task student behavior.

Response Latency

Teacher Jim Roberts Observer Bob Pangrazi

Class 2nd period Grade 2nd Date and Time 2/5 - 9:00

Lesson focus Movement concepts Comments

Starting time 9:05 End time 9:35 Length of lesson 30 min

Starting Response Latency

3	7	5	9	15	3	3	4	9	7	5	3	
2	4	10	7									

Stopping Response Latency

10	12	9	8	8	15	8	6	2	9	10	11	15
14	5	5	13									

Total amount of starting response latency 1 min 42 sec

Percentage of class time devoted to response latency 5.7%

Number of episodes 17 Average length of episodes 6 sec

Total amount of stopping response latency 2 min 41 sec

Percentage of class time devoted to stopping response latency 8.9%

Number of episodes 17 Average length of episodes 9.5 sec

FIGURE 6.10 Sample form for evaluating response latency.

2. Place 8 to 10 "beeps" at random intervals on a tape recording to signal when to conduct a placheck.
3. Have the observer scan the area in a specified and consistent direction from left to right each time the tape-recorded signal is heard. The class is scanned for 7 to 10 seconds while the observer records the number of students who are engaged in the desired behavior.
4. Convert the data to a percentage by dividing the total number of students into the number of unproductive students and then multiplying the result by 100. Four to six plachecks spaced throughout a class period will yield valid information about class conduct.

Instructional Feedback

Feedback given to students strongly affects the instructional presentation. It is possible to define and measure feedback so that meaningful goals for improvement can be established. The process of changing interaction patterns can create some discomfort, but ultimately it pays dividends. The following areas can be evaluated to give direction for implementing useful change.

Praise and Criticism

When students are involved in activity, feedback related to student performance should be administered. Feedback can be positive and constructive or negative and

Student Performance

Teacher Albert Santillan Observer Ms. Estfan

Class 8th period Grade 6th Date and Time 5/5 - 2:30

Lesson focus Rhythmic movement skills Comments

Starting time 2:30 End time 3:00 Length of lesson 30 min

Active/Inactive

On Task/Off Task

5	4	12	7	3	3	2	5	6	5
4	3								

Effort/Noneffort

Number of plachecks 12

Total number of students 30

Average number of students not on desired behavior 4.9

Average percentage of students not on desired behavior 16%

FIGURE 6.11 Sample form for placheck observation.

critical in nature. It is easy to ask a student or peer to record the occurrence of praise and criticism. The results can be tallied and evaluated at the end of the day. The number of instances and the ratio of positive to negative comments are calculated. With this information, goals can be set for increasing the number of comments per minute and modifying the ratio of positive to negative comments.

General versus Specific Feedback

Feedback to students can be general or specific. "Good job," "Way to go," and "Cut that out" are examples of general feedback. General feedback can be positive or negative; it does not specify the behavior being reinforced. In contrast, specific feedback identifies the student by name and reinforces an actual behavior; it also might be accompanied with a valuing statement. An example is, "Michelle, that's the way to keep your head tucked! I really like that forward roll!" To evaluate this area, general and specific feedback instances are tallied. Feedback can be positive or negative, and this distinction can also be made as part of the tallying process.

The use of first names is important in personalizing feedback and directing it to the proper individual. The number of times first names are used can be totaled. Valuing statements can also be evaluated. Data gathered in these categories are divided by the length of the lesson (in minutes) to render a rate per minute. Figure 6.12 is an example of a form that can be used to tally behaviors described in this section.

Instructional Feedback

Teacher ______ Observer ______

Class ______ Grade ______ Date and Time ______

Lesson focus ______ Comments ______

Starting time ______ End time ______ Length of lesson ______

Interactions unrelated to skill performance	+								
	–								
General instructional feedback	+								
	–								
Corrective instructional feedback									
First names									
Nonverbal feedback	+								
	–								

Ratio + to –/nonskill related ______

Ratio + to –/skill related ______

FIGURE 6.12 Sample form for feedback observation.

Corrective Instructional Feedback

Effective teachers inspire students to achieve higher levels of performance. Part of this process involves giving performers meaningful corrective feedback. Corrective feedback focuses on improving the performance of the participant. Corrective instructional feedback should be specific so performers know what they must correct. An example of corrective instructional feedback is, "You struck the soccer ball much too high. Try to strike it a little below center." This type of feedback tells the student what was incorrect about the skill attempt and how to perform the skill correctly.

Nonverbal Feedback

Much performance feedback is given nonverbally. Nonverbal communication is meaningful to students and may be equal to or more effective than verbal forms of communication. Examples of nonverbal feedback after a desired performance are a pat on the back, a wink, a smile, a nod of the head, the thumbs-up sign, and clapping the hands. Nonverbal feedback can also be negative: a frown, shaking the head in disapproval, walking away from a student, or laughing at a poor performance.

A student or another instructor can tally the number of positive and negative nonverbal behaviors exhibited by a teacher. Students are often better at evaluating the instructor in this domain, because they are keenly aware of the meaning of the instructor's nonverbal mannerisms.

How to Do It

1. Design a form to collect the data. Figure 6.12 is an example of such a form.
2. Audiotape a lesson for playback and evaluation at a later time.
3. Record the data to be analyzed. It is usually best to take one category at a time when beginning. For example, analyze the use of first names during the first playback, and then play the tape again to evaluate corrective feedback.
4. Convert the data to a form that can be generalized from lesson to lesson (i.e., rate per minute, rate per lesson, or ratio of positive to negative interactions).

Active Supervision and Student Contact

Effective instructors actively supervise students. Active supervision means moving among students and offering them personalized feedback. The number of times an instructor becomes personally involved with a student can be counted. One-on-one feedback differs from total class interaction and offers insight into each student's behavior and concerns.

Allied to this area is the relationship between teacher movement and active supervision. Many instructors establish a particular area in the gymnasium where they feel most comfortable teaching. Before instruction begins, they move to this area. This consistent movement pattern can cause students to drift to different areas, depending on their feeling about the activity or the instructor. Students who like the instructor will move closer, whereas students who dislike the teacher or are uneasy about the activity may move as far away as possible. This results in a configuration in which the better performers are near the instructor and the students who may be somewhat less able are farther away and more difficult to observe.

The teacher can avoid these problems by moving throughout the teaching area. A way to evaluate movement is to divide the area into quadrants and tally the number of times you move into each quadrant. A tally in the quadrant is made when you speak to a student or the class as a whole. Do not make a tally for just passing through a quadrant. The amount of time spent in each quadrant can also be evaluated. Try to spend similar amounts of time in each area. When students cannot predict where you will be next, they have a greater tendency to remain on task.

Teacher Movement

Teacher Alan Scarmazzo Observer Debbie Pangrazi

Class 5th period Grade 1st Date and Time 3/17 - 1:05

Lesson focus Movement concepts Comments

Starting time 1:15 End time 1:45 Length of lesson 30 min

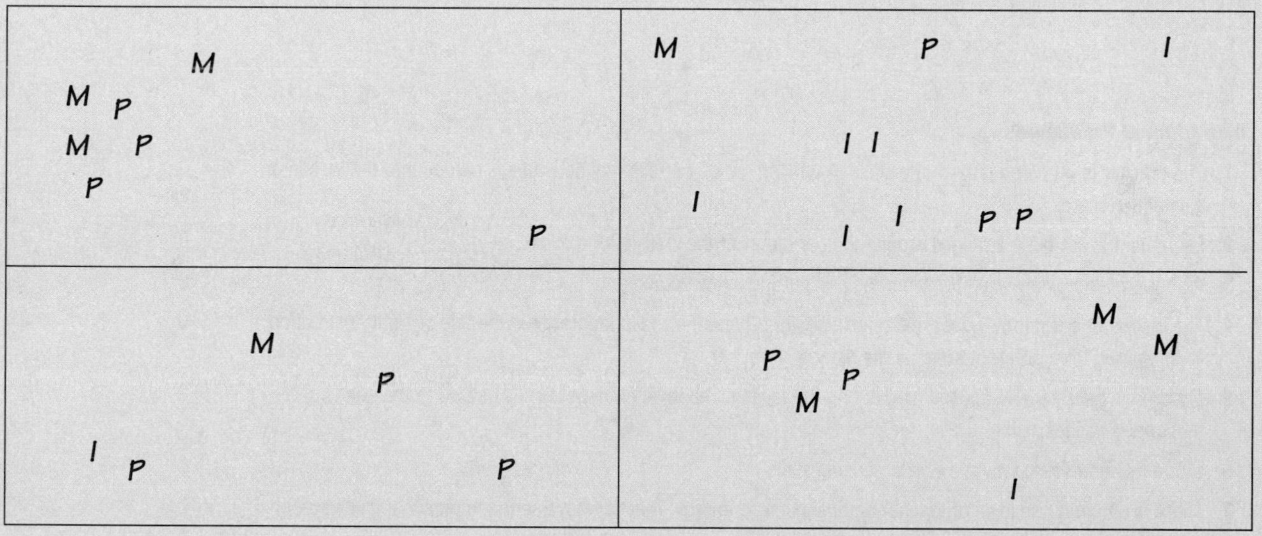

M M P M P P P	M P I I I I I P P I
M P I P P	M M P P M I

Total number of moves 28

Number of moves (I) 8 (M) 8 (P) 12

Average number of moves per minute .93

FIGURE 6.13 Sample form for evaluating active supervision and student contact (M = management activity, I = instructional activity, P = practice time).

Physical Education Program Evaluation

Program Philosophy

1. Physical education is regarded by the administration as an integral part of the total curriculum and is dedicated to the same curricular goal, the fullest possible development of each pupil for living in a democracy.	0	1	2
2. A written and up-to-date sequential curriculum is available and used by all instructors.	0	1	2
3. Lesson plans are developed from the course of study and are used as the basis for instruction.	0	1	2
4. A meaningful progression of activities is evident between developmental levels.	0	1	2
5. Students are scheduled in the physical education program on a regular basis.	0	1	2
6. Music, field trips, and extracurricular activities are not accepted as substitutes for physical education.	0	1	2
7. Students are excused from physical education on a long-term basis only when they can submit a physician's statement indicating the medical condition and the duration of the excuse.	0	1	2
8. Appropriate arrangements are made for students with medical, religious, or temporary health excuses.	0	1	2
9. A nurse, teacher, or staff member with suitable first aid training is available in case of accident.	0	1	2
10. The budget specified for equipment and supplies for physical education is adequate.	0	1	2
11. Physical education demonstration programs are offered regularly for purposes of public relations and general information.	0	1	2
12. The minimum amount per class of time allotted for physical education activity is 30 minutes.	0	1	2
13. Each class receives physical education instruction a minimum of three times per week, excluding recess and supervised play.	0	1	2
14. Class sizes are the same as those allotted to classroom teachers.	0	1	2
15. Program activities are coeducational in nature.	0	1	2
16. Classroom teachers do not keep students from physical education classes for disciplinary reasons.	0	1	2

Comments:

Instructional Procedures

1. The teacher is prepared prior to the class. A written set of instructional activities is carried into the lesson on a small notecard.	0	1	2
2. Equipment is correctly arranged around the perimeter of the class prior to class.	0	1	2
3. Proper procedures are used for acquiring and putting away equipment.	0	1	2
4. The instructor constantly moves and repositions him/herself so all students are in the line of sight. Instruction is conducted from different areas in the activity area.	0	1	2
5. Children in need receive special help during the lesson. The level of instruction is geared to the needs of students who lack skill.	0	1	2
6. Students understand why they are practicing skills.	0	1	2
7. There is an adequate level of teacher enthusiasm and energy. Teacher movement and personal involvement is evident.	0	1	2
8. Positive encouragement is given to all students. Youngsters are encouraged to do their best.	0	1	2
9. Students are directed to be responsible for their learning and personal behavior. Content instruction is stopped when there is a need to improve behavioral skills.	0	1	2

FIGURE 6.14 Sample evaluation form for physical education program (0 = no compliance; 1 = partial compliance; 2 = full compliance).

10. Instruction is focused on developing quality skills rather than changing activities often in an attempt to keep students on task. Adequate opportunity is given for repetition and refinement of skills.	0	1	2
11. Closure of the lesson is a positive experience. Students are encouraged to evaluate their level of responsibility. The pitfall of nagging students about their poor class performance is avoided.	0	1	2
12. Discipline and management problems are handled effectively. The self-esteem of students is preserved during behavior correction episodes.	0	1	2
13. Disciplinary measures in physical education instruction do not include punishment using physical activity.	0	1	2
14. Procedures for dealing with accidents, including administration of first aid, reporting, and follow-up, are in written form.	0	1	2
15. Knowledge of liability concerns related to physical education instruction and programming is evident.	0	1	2
16. Facilities, equipment, and activity areas that could be liabilities are reported in writing to appropriate administrators.	0	1	2
17. Bulletin boards, charts, pictures, and other visual materials are posted and used in the instructional process.	0	1	2
18. Teaching aids such as instructional signs, videotapes, and posters are used to enrich and supplement instruction.	0	1	2

Comments:

Curricular Offerings

1. The physical education program provides learning experiences to help each child attain the following:			
a. refinement of motor skills and movement competence	0	1	2
b. development of lifestyle habits that foster wellness	0	1	2
c. ability to monitor and maintain physical activity	0	1	2
d. understand and apply human movement principles	0	1	2
e. the enjoyment of a lifetime of physical activity	0	1	2
f. the acquisition of quality social skills	0	1	2
g. the ability to demonstrate responsible behavior	0	1	2
2. All children are considered important and the program is adjusted to suit the maturity and skill level of youngsters.	0	1	2
3. Each lesson has a portion of time (7 to 10 minutes) devoted to physical fitness activities.	0	1	2
4. The physical education program emphasizes and allocates enough time at the appropriate grade level for each of the following areas:			
a. Educational movement concepts	0	1	2
b. Fundamental skills, including locomotor, nonlocomotor, manipulative, and specialized skills	0	1	2
c. Rhythmic activities	0	1	2
d. Gymnastics activities	0	1	2
e. Games and relays	0	1	2
f. Sports and lead-up activities	0	1	2
5. Both indoor and outdoor teaching stations are available for physical education instruction.	0	1	2
6. Units of instruction last no longer than 3 weeks and include skill instruction.	0	1	2

Comments:

FIGURE 6.14 (continued)

Facilities, Equipment, and Supplies

1. Facilities include teaching stations that allow all students a minimum of three classes per week.	0	1	2
2. Outdoor facilities include the following:			
a. A physical education instructional area that is isolated from playground activities	0	1	2
b. Areas where different age groups can play without interference from each other	0	1	2
c. Areas for court games	0	1	2
d. Cement or asphalt spaces marked with a variety of game patterns	0	1	2
e. Backstops and goals for softball, soccer, and basketball	0	1	2
f. Suitable fencing for safety and control	0	1	2
g. Outdoor playground equipment, including climbing apparatus, turning bars, and tetherball areas	0	1	2
3. The outdoor area is free from rocks, sprinkler heads, and other hazards that might cause injury.	0	1	2
4. Indoor facilities meet the following standards:			
a. Clean, sanitary, and free from hazards	0	1	2
b. Well-lighted, well-ventilated, heated, cooled, and treated for proper acoustics	0	1	2
c. Surfaced with a nonslip finish and include painted game area lines	0	1	2
5. There is periodic inspection of all facilities and equipment, both indoor and outdoor, and a written report is filed with appropriate administrators.	0	1	2
6. Storage facilities are adequate for supplies and portable equipment.	0	1	2
7. An office that is located near the instruction area is provided for the physical education instructor.	0	1	2
8. Basic supplies are sufficient in the following areas:			
a. Manipulative equipment (one piece for each child): fleece balls, small balls, beanbags, wands, hoops, and jump ropes	0	1	2
b. Sport and game balls: softballs, footballs, volleyballs, basketballs, soccer balls, floor hockey sticks and pucks, tetherballs, and cageballs in sufficient numbers	0	1	2
c. Sport and game supplies: cones, pinnies, track-and-field standards, jumping pits, hurdles	0	1	2
d. Testing equipment: measuring tapes, stopwatches, calipers to measure skinfold thickness, and specialized apparatus	0	1	2
9. Sufficient materials are available for a varied rhythmic program: CD/tape player, tapes and CDs, tom-tom, and tambourine.	0	1	2
10. Capital-outlay items for the indoor facility include the following:			
a. Minimum of six tumbling mats (4 by 8 ft or larger)	0	1	2
b. Individual mats (one per student)	0	1	2
c. Sufficient climbing apparatus so that at least one-half of the class can be active at one time. Apparatus should include wall bars, chinning bars, horizontal bars, climbing ropes on tracks, and ladders.	0	1	2
d. Balance beam benches (at least 6)	0	1	2
e. Jumping boxes (at least 8)	0	1	2
f. Basketball goals, volleyball nets, hockey goals	0	1	2
g. Equipment carts (at least 2)	0	1	2

Comments:

FIGURE 6.14 (continued)

Movement related to the use of lesson time can be determined by the amount of time the teacher stays in a quadrant. The length of time a teacher stays in a quadrant can be recorded in a corresponding location on the form. At the end of the lesson, the amount of time the teacher has spent in each quadrant can then be analyzed. Another technique is to code the type of behavior that occurs each time the instructor moves into a new quadrant. For example, an "M" might signify management activity, an "I" instructional activity, and a "P" practice time. This approach reveals the location and amount of time spent on each behavior.

How to Do It

1. Develop a coding form similar to the one in Figure 6.13 on page 121.
2. Ask a nonparticipating student or a colleague to record the desired data on active supervision. An alternative is to videotape the lesson and evaluate it at a later time.
3. Evaluate the data by calculating the number of moves per lesson, and the number of moves during instruction, management, and practice.

EVALUATING YOUR PROGRAM

Your program should be evaluated regularly to ensure that it is achieving stated program goals. Evaluation instruments reflect program philosophy and objectives of individual districts. Figure 6.14 (pages 122–124) is a sample instrument that may be adapted for your use, depending on district needs and goals. This instrument can be used to expose serious program deficiencies and operational difficulties. The results, including program strengths and weaknesses, can be shared with administrators or used by teachers to evaluate a program they have developed. The instrument can also be used to compare programs or to identify effective programs.

In the sample instrument, evaluative statements are written as a set of standards that, when met, ensure an effective program. Four areas are listed for evaluation: (1) philosophy of the program; (2) instructional procedures; (3) curricular offerings; and (4) facilities, equipment, and supplies. The entire instrument can be used, or any of the four areas can be evaluated individually. Read each statement and determine the extent to which there is compliance with the accepted standard and circle the appropriate scale score. Comments can be made at the end of each section. Rate and assign points on the following basis: A rating of 2 represents full compliance (the program meets the standard fully without deficiencies), 1 represents partial compliance with room for improvement, and 0 represents no compliance (the deficiency is serious and a detriment to an effective program).

REFLECTION AND REVIEW QUESTIONS

How and Why

1. In a music or art class, would you want to be evaluated based on the product or the process? Why? How does this relate to your grading as a physical education teacher?
2. How is giving a child "on the spot" feedback regarding performance a form of evaluation?
3. How are you evaluated as a college student? Do you feel you are evaluated fairly? Explain your answer.
4. How can progress reports be more effective tools for communicating with parents?
5. Would you rather self-evaluate a lesson yourself using videotape or have a peer evaluate you during the lesson? Why?
6. Why might the ability to be self-critical be important for physical education teachers and physical education curriculum designers?

Content Review

1. What is the significance of focusing on the process in physical education? Include comments about how physical education and other academic areas differ with respect to evaluation.
2. Identify and describe several methods of assessing performance outcomes.
3. What are the advantages and disadvantages of a grading system?
4. State the steps to implementing a grading system.
5. How can teachers use self-evaluation of themselves?
6. Identify and explain 4 areas of teaching that can be evaluated. Within your comments, describe how to assess the specific areas.
7. What are the elements of a physical education program evaluation form?

FOR MORE INFORMATION

References and Suggested Readings

Chepko, S., & Arnold, R. K. (Eds.). (2000). *Guidelines for physical education programs: Grades K–12 standards, objectives, and assessments.* Boston: Allyn and Bacon.

Cooper Institute (2002). *Fitnessgram test administration manual.* 2nd ed. Champaign, IL: Human Kinetics.

Darst, P. W., Zakrajsek, D. B., & Mancini, V. H. (1989). *Analyzing physical education and sport instruction.* 2nd ed. Champaign, IL: Human Kinetics.

Johnson, D. W., Johnson, R. T., & Holubec, E. J. (1990). *Circles of learning: Cooperation in the classroom.* Edina, MN: Interaction.

Lacy, A., & Hastad, D. (2003). *Measurement and evaluation in physical education and exercise science.* 4th ed. San Francisco: Benjamin Cummings.

Lambert, L. T. (1999). *Standards-based assessment of student learning: A comprehensive approach.* Reston, VA: National Association for Sport and Physical Education.

Safrit, M. J. (1995). *Introduction to measurement in physical education and exercise science.* 3rd ed. St. Louis, MO: Times Mirror/Mosby.

Siedentop, D., & Tannehill, D. (2000). *Developing teaching skills in physical education.* 4th ed. Mountain View, CA: Mayfield Publishing Co.

Strand, B. N., & Wilson, R. (1993). *Assessing sport skills.* Champaign, IL: Human Kinetics.

Websites

Assessment Ideas
http://pe.central.vt.edu/assessment/assessment.html

Self-Assessment/Reflection
http://www.utexas.edu/academic/cte/getfeedback/selfref.html
http://www.coe.ufl.edu/school/proteach/pathwise/reflection.PDF

Video as an Assessment Tool
http://teaching.berkeley.edu/bgd/videotape.html

ESSENTIAL COMPONENTS	
I	**Organized around content standards**
II	**Student-centered and developmentally appropriate**
III	Physical activity and motor skill development form the core of the program
IV	Teaches management skills and self-discipline
V	**Promotes inclusion of all students**
VI	**Focuses on process over product**
VII	Promotes lifetime personal health and wellness
VIII	**Teaches cooperation and responsibility and promotes sensitivity to diversity**

PHYSICAL EDUCATION STANDARDS	
1	**Students are able to move competently using a variety of fundamental and specialized motor skills.**
2	Students can monitor and maintain a health-enhancing level of physical fitness.
3	Students are able to apply movement concepts and basic mechanics of skill performance when learning and refining motor skills.
4	Students comprehend the basic principles of wellness and are able to apply concepts that enable them to make meaningful decisions that positively impact their health and wellness.
5	Students participate in a wide variety of physical activities and learn how to maintain a personalized active lifestyle.
6	**Students demonstrate empathy, understanding, and respect for the numerous differences exhibited by people in an activity setting.**
7	Students exhibit responsible and self-directed behaviors that lead to positive social interactions in physical activity.

CHAPTER 7

Children with Disabilities

SUMMARY

Every state is required by federal law to develop a plan for identifying, locating, and evaluating all children with disabilities. Due process for students and parents is an important requisite when conducting formal assessment procedures. Mainstreaming involves the practice of placing children with disabilities into classes with able youngsters. Moving a child to a less restrictive learning environment is based on achievement of specified competencies that are required for moving into the new environment. The most common types of disabilities and ways to modify activities for successful participation are discussed. Programs for children with weight problems, motor deficiencies, and postural problems are detailed in a step-by-step manner.

OUTCOMES

- Understand the implications of PL 94-142 and IDEA for physical education.
- Explain due-process guidelines associated with assessment procedures.
- Develop a plan for identifying, locating, and evaluating all children with disabilities.
- Cite standards associated with assessment procedures for special children.
- Identify essential elements of a individualized educational program and list the stages of development.
- List guidelines for successful inclusion of students.
- Describe ways of modifying activities for inclusion.
- Describe characteristics of specific impairments and ways to modify learning experiences in physical education to accommodate children with disabilities.
- Locate nationally validated programs to assist in the screening, assessment, and curriculum development for children with special needs.
- Indicate a step-by-step approach used to develop a success profile for obese youngsters in the elementary school.
- Describe the attributes of good posture and explain its importance in successful physical performance.

The Education for All Handicapped Children Act (Public Law 94-142) was passed by the Congress of the United States in 1975. The purpose of the law is clear and concise:

> It is the purpose of this act to assure that all handicapped children have available to them . . . a free appropriate public education which emphasizes special education and related services designed to meet their unique needs, to assure that the rights of handicapped children and their parents or guardians are protected, to assist States and localities to provide for the education of all handicapped children, and to assess and assure the effectiveness of efforts to educate handicapped children.*

In short, the law requires that all children with disabilities, ages 3 to 21, receive a free and appropriate education in the least restrictive environment. The law includes youngsters in public and private care facilities and schools. Children with disabilities who can learn in regular classes with the use of supplementary aides and services must be educated with youngsters who are able. Physical education is the only specific area mentioned in PL 94-142. The law indicates that the term *special education* "means specially designed instruction, instruction in physical education, home instruction, and instruction in hospitals and institutions." A 1990 amendment, Public Law 101-476 (also known as *IDEA*—Individuals with Disabilities Education Act), continues with the objective of providing handicapped individuals with the Least Restrictive Environment in the school setting. Autism and traumatic brain injury have been added to the list of handicapping conditions that should receive the Least Restrictive Environment. IDEA provides that an individual transition plan be developed no later than age 16 as a component of the IEP process. Rehabilitation and social work services are included as related services.

To comply with PL 94-142, public schools must locate, identify, and evaluate all students who might have a disability. This is the screening process, and it must be followed by a formal assessment procedure. Assessment must be made, and an Individualized Education Program (IEP) must be developed for each youngster before placement into a special program can be made. The law states who will be responsible for developing the IEP and what the contents of the IEP will include. These are discussed later in the chapter.

*The term *handicapped* is used in PL 94-142 to include youngsters who are mentally retarded, hard of hearing, deaf, speech impaired, visually handicapped, seriously emotionally disturbed, orthopedically impaired, other health impaired, deaf-blind, multihandicapped, or specific learning disabled. Currently, the phrase *students with disabilities* is used throughout this chapter to identify youngsters with such conditions.

The passage of PL 94-142 offered a giant step forward in assuring equality and education for all Americans. The government also assured that funding would be made available to provide quality instruction. The law authorizes a payment to each state of 40 percent of the average per-pupil expenditure in U.S. elementary and secondary schools, multiplied by the number of children who are receiving special education and related services. The federal mandate reveals the concern of the public for comprehensive educational programs for all youngsters regardless of disability.

SCREENING AND ASSESSMENT

Important components of the IEP process are screening and assessment of students. Every state is required by PL 94-142 to develop a plan for locating, identifying, and evaluating all children with disabilities.

Screening

Screening is a process that involves all students in a school setting and is part of the "child find" process. It is often conducted at the start of the school year and is performed districtwide. The physical educator usually conducts screening tests, which may include commonly used test batteries (such as the Fitnessgram). In most situations, screening tests may be administered without parental permission and are used to make initial identification of students who may need special services.

Assessment

Assessment is conducted after screening evaluations have been made. Assessment is usually conducted after "child find" screening by referring identified students to special education directors. Assessment is performed by a team of experts, which may include the physical education specialist. Due process for students and parents is an important requisite when conducting formal assessment procedures. Due process assures parents and children that they will be informed of their rights and that they have the opportunity to challenge educational decisions they feel are unfair or incorrect.

Due Process Guidelines

To ensure that due process is offered parents and students, the guidelines discussed here must be followed:

Written Permission A written notice must be sent to parents stating that their child has been referred for assessment. The notice must explain that the district requests permission to conduct an evaluation to determine if special education services are required for their child. Also included in the permission letter must be the reasons for testing and the titles of the tests to be used. Before assessment can begin, the letter must be signed by the parents and returned to the district.

Interpretation of the Assessment The results of the assessment must be interpreted in a meeting with parents. Persons who are knowledgeable about the test procedures must be present to answer questions parents may ask. At the meeting, parents must be told whether their child has any disabilities and what services will be provided for the child.

External Evaluation If parents are not satisfied with the results of the assessment, they may request an evaluation outside the school setting. The district must provide a list of agencies that can perform such assessment. If the results differ from the school district evaluation, the district must pay for the external evaluation. However, if the results are similar, parents must pay for the external testing.

Negotiation and Hearings If parents and the school district disagree on the results of the assessment, the district is required to try to negotiate the differences. When negotiations fail, an impartial hearing officer listens to both parties and renders an official decision. This is usually the final review; however, both parties do have the right to appeal to the state department of education, which must render a binding and final decision. Civil action through the legal system can be pursued should the district or parents still disagree with this action. However, few cases ever reach this level of long-term disagreement, and educators should not be hesitant to serve the needs of children with disabilities based on this concern.

Confidentiality As is the case with other student records, only parents of the child or authorized school personnel can review the student's records. Review by other parties can be done only after written permission has been given by the parents of the child under review.

Procedures for Ensuring Assessment Standards

PL 94-142 requires that assessment is held to certain standards to ensure fair and objective results. The following areas are specifically delineated.

Selection of Test Instruments

Test instruments used must be valid examinations that measure what they purport to measure. Thus, when selecting instruments, it must be clear to all parties how the tests were developed and how they will measure correctly the area of possible disability. More than one test procedure must be used to determine the student's status. Both formal and informal assessment techniques should be used to ensure that the results measure the student's impairment rather than simply reflect the student's shortcomings.

It is an unfortunate situation that children must be labeled as disabled in order to reap the benefits of a special education program. The stigmatizing effect of labels and the fallibility of various means of testing students create a dilemma that must be faced. Although current pedagogical practices discourage labeling, it is double-talk, because school districts have to certify the disability (to receive funding) through which the child is classified.

Administration Procedures

Many disabilities interfere with standard test procedures. For example, many students have communication problems and thus must be tested in a manner that ensures that their motor ability is measured rather than their lack of communication skills. Many students have visual and hearing disabilities that prevent using tests that rely on these faculties.

A probability of misdiagnosis and incorrectly classifying children as mentally retarded can occur with certain ethnic groups, such as Native Americans, African Americans, and Spanish-speaking children. Some of these youngsters may be victims of a low standard of living and be only environmentally retarded and in need of cultural enrichment. This is subtle discrimination, but it must be replaced with understanding that children differ because of culture, poverty, migrancy, and language. Many of the tests are based on white, middle-class standards. Minority children should be carefully assessed to determine the validity of the testing procedure.

Team Evaluation

A number of experts should be used for assessment. Emphasis should be placed on a multidisciplinary team to help ensure that all facets of the child will be reviewed and evaluated. Evaluation professionals must be well trained and qualified to administer the various tests. It is the responsibility of the school district to ensure that this occurs.

DEVELOPING AN IEP

PL 94-142 requires that an IEP be developed for each child with a disability receiving special education and related services. The IEP must be developed by a committee as stipulated by the law. Included on the committee must be the following members: a local education association representative who is qualified to provide and supervise the administration of special education, the child's parents, the teachers who have direct responsibility for implementing the IEP, and, when appropriate, the student. Other individuals may be included at the discretion of the parents or the school district.

This program identifies the child's unique qualities and determines educationally relevant strengths and weaknesses. A plan is then devised based on the diagnosed strengths and weaknesses. Figure 7.1 is an example of a comprehensive IEP form. The IEP must contain the following material:

1. Current status of the child's level of educational performance.
2. A statement of long-term goals and short-term instructional objectives.
3. A statement of special education and related services that will be provided to the youngster. Also, a

☐ Initial Placement
☐ Re-evaluation
☐ Change of Placement
☐ Review

INDIVIDUALIZED EDUCATION PROGRAM

A. **STUDENT INFORMATION:**

Student Name ______ (Last, First, Middle) Student No. ______ Home School ______

Date of Birth ______ Chronological Age ___ (M___ or F___) Present Placement/Grade ______

Parent/Guardian Name(s) ______ Receiving School ______

Home Address ______ (Street, City/State, Zip) Program Recommended ______

Home Phone ______ Work Phone ______ Starting Date ______

Emergency Phone ______ Three (3) Year Re-evaluation Due Date ___/___/___

Primary Language (Home) ______ (Child) ______ Interpreter Needed: Yes ___ No ___

B. **VISION SCREENING RESULTS:** Pass ___ Fail ___
Date: ______ Comments: ______

HEARING SCREENING RESULTS: Pass ___ Fail ___
Date: ______ Comments: ______

C. **REQUIRED OBSERVATION(S):** (All categories other than regular teacher)

______ (Date(s)) By: ______ (Name(s)) ______ (Date(s)) By: ______ (Name(s)) ______ (Date(s)) By: ______ (Name(s))

D. **SUMMARY OF PRESENT LEVELS OF PERFORMANCE:**

Educational: ______

Behavioral: ______

E. Additional justification. See comments ______ (Initial) See addendum ______ (Initial)

F. **PLACEMENT RECOMMENDATION INDICATING LEAST RESTRICTIVE ENVIRONMENT:**

Related services needed: Yes ___ No ___ (*List below.)

Placement Recommendation		Person Responsible	Amount of Time (Range)	Entry Date On/About	Review Reports On/About	Projected Ending Date	IEP Review Date
Primary:							
*Related Services:							

Transportation Needed? Yes ___ No ___ (If Yes, submit MPS Special Education Transportation Request Form.)

Describe extent student will participate in regular program: ______

Page 1 of ___

FIGURE 7.1 Example of an individualized educational plan (IEP).

INDIVIDUALIZED EDUCATION PROGRAM

REPORT OF MULTIDISCIPLINARY CONFERENCE

Date Held ________

Student Name ________ Student No. ________

G. **PROGRAM PLANNING:**

Long-Term Goals: ________ Short-Term Objectives (Goals): ________

H. **EVALUATION:**

Evaluation criteria are described in the Individual Implementation Plan (IIP) which is available in the classroom file.

I. **PLACEMENT COMMITTEE:**

The following have been consulted or have participated in the placement and IEP decisions:

Names of Members	Position	Present (Initial)	Oral Report	Written Report	Signatures
	Parents/Guardian				
	Parents/Guardian				
	School Administrator				
	Special Ed Administrator				
	School Psychologist				
	Nurse				
	Teacher(s) Receiving				
	Teacher(s) Referring				
	Interpreter				

Dissenting Opinion: Yes ____ No ____ If Yes, see comments ____ (Initial) See addendum ____ (Initial).

J. **PARENT (OR GUARDIAN) STATEMENT:**

We agree to the placement recommended in this IEP. Yes ____ No ____

We give our permission to have our child counseled by the professional staff, if necessary. Yes ____ No ____

We understand that placement will be on a continuing trial basis and we will be contacted if any placement changes are contemplated. We are aware that such placement does not guarantee success; however, in order to help our child, we accept the responsibility to cooperate in every way with the school program. We acknowledge that we have been notified of and have received a copy of our due process rights pertaining to Special Education placement and have a basic understanding of these rights. We acknowledge that we have received a copy of the completed IEP Form.

Parent or Guardian Signature ________ Date ________

COMMENTS: ________

Page 2 of ____

FIGURE 7.1 (continued)

report as to the extent the youngster will be able to participate in regular educational programs.

4. The dates for initiation of services and anticipated duration of the services.
5. Appropriate objective criteria for determining on an annual basis whether the short-term objectives are being reached.

Developing and sequencing objectives for the student are the first steps in formulating the IEP. Short-range and long-range goals should be delineated, and data collection procedures and testing schedules established to monitor the child's progress. Materials and strategies to be used in implementing the IEP should also be established. Finally, methods of evaluation to be used are selected to monitor the student's progress and effectiveness of the program. Movement to a less restrictive environment is based on achievement of specified competencies that are necessary to function in the new environment.

The IEP must contain a section determining whether specially designed physical education is needed. If not, the child should be held to the same expectations as the peer group. A child who needs special physical education might have an IEP with specified goals and objectives and might be mainstreamed in regular physical education with goals that do not resemble those of classmates.

Continued and periodic follow-up of the child is necessary. Effective communication between special and regular teachers is essential, because the child's progress needs careful monitoring. At the completion of the designated time period or school year, a written progress report is filed along with recommendations for action during the coming year or time period. A program for the summer months can be an excellent prescription to ensure that improvement is maintained. Records should be complete so that information about the youngster's problem and the effects of long-term treatment are always available.

Criteria for Placement of Children

Several states have adopted criteria for determining eligibility of children for adapted physical education classes. State guidelines differ, but they should be followed closely when they are available. These standards are based on the administration of standardized tests for which norms or percentiles have been developed. This procedure helps ensure that objective guidelines are used and avoids subjective judgment that may be open to disagreement and controversy. For example, criteria used by the state of Alabama are as follows:

1. Perform below the 30th percentile on standardized tests of
   a. motor development
   b. motor proficiency
   c. fundamental motor skills and patterns
   d. physical fitness
   e. game/sport skills
   f. perceptual motor functioning
   g. posture screening.
2. Exhibit a developmental delay of 2 or more years based on appropriate assessment instruments.
3. Function within the severe or profound range as determined by special education eligibility standards.
4. Possess social/emotional or physical capabilities that would render it unlikely for the student to reach his or her physical education goals without significant modification or exclusion from the regular physical education class.

CREATING THE LEAST RESTRICTIVE ENVIRONMENT

PL 94-142 uses the term *least restrictive environment* to define placement of children with disabilities. Focus on placing a child into a setting that offers the most opportunity for educational advancement. It is inappropriate to place a youngster in an environment in which success is impossible. On the other hand, it is debilitating to put a child in a setting that is more restrictive than necessary. Special educators support a physical education program that offers a variety of experiences from participation in regular physical education classes to physical education in a full-time special school. Figure 7.2 shows a series of options that should be made available for physical education.

The least restrictive environment varies depending on the content of the instructional presentation. For example, for a student in a wheelchair, a soccer or football unit might be very restrictive, whereas in a swimming unit, the environment would not be restrictive. For an emotionally challenged student, the command style of presentation might be the least restrictive environment, while an exploration style of instruction would be more restrictive and invite failure. When curriculum content and teaching styles vary, the type of environment for the student may need to be modified. It is shortsighted to place students into a situation and then forget about them.

Inclusion and Mainstreaming

Inclusion is part of a much larger picture than just being mainstreamed in the regular physical education class. The larger picture demands that youngsters be taught to use their abilities to become active members of the school and community. Inclusion demands that the school and regular classes get ready to include students with disabilities. Too often, the youngster with a disability has to adapt to the class and school. Adaptations need to be made to teaching materials, equipment used, and expectations so youngsters can meaningfully achieve individual and academic goals. Through inclusive education, children with disabilities can mature into adults who are fully participating members of society. Meeting their needs helps them achieve academic and physical goals and enhances their overall quality of life. Inclusive education teaches all children to function together regardless of who or what they are. The focus is on valuing diversity, viewing the ability of others to contribute, and learning to become one with others regardless of differences.

Physical educators most often speak of inclusion in terms of mainstreaming. Mainstreaming involves the practice of placing children with disabilities into classes with able youngsters (Figure 7.3, page 134). Prudent

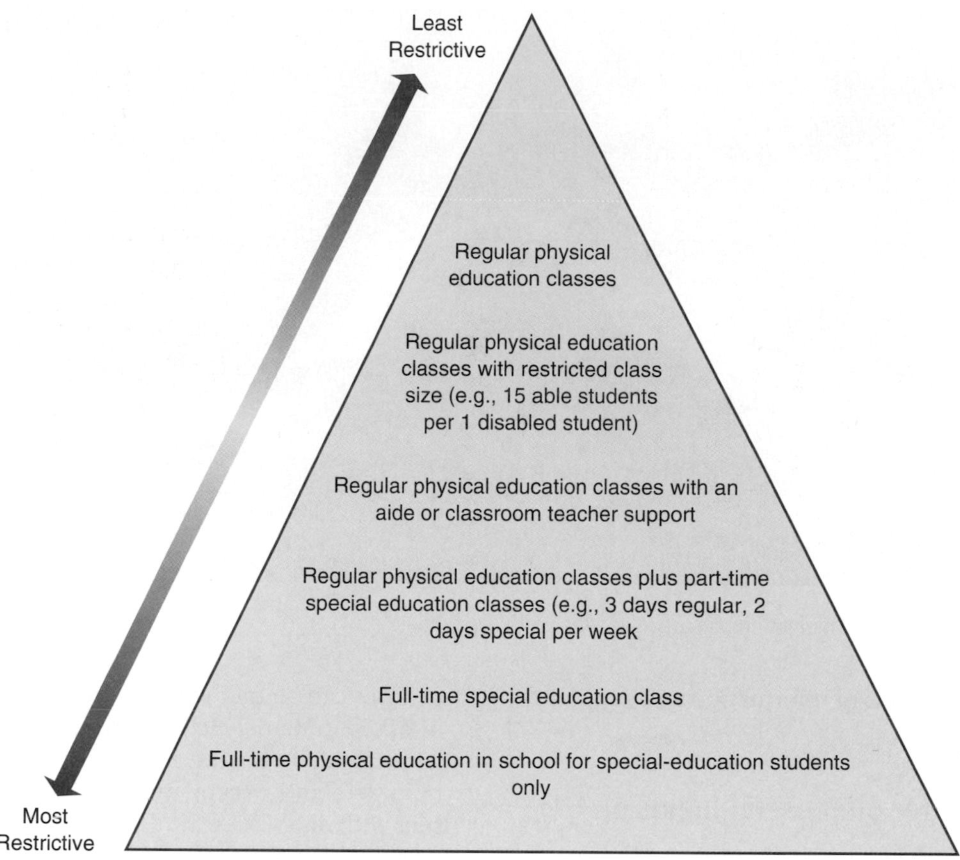

FIGURE 7.2 Physical education inclusion options, least to most restrictive environments.

placement in a least restricted educational environment means the setting is as normal as possible (normalization), yet ensures the child integrates and achieves success in that placement. The placement may be mainstreaming, but it is not confined to this approach. Several categories of student placement are relevant to physical education classes.

1. *Full mainstreaming.* Children with disabilities function as full-time members of a regular classroom group. Within the limitations of their challenge, they participate in physical education with able peers. An example is auditory-impaired students who with a minimal amount of assistance are able to participate fully.
2. *Mainstreaming for physical education only.* Children with disabilities are not members of the regular classroom groups but participate in physical education with regular classes. Students in this setting might have emotional disabilities and be grouped in a separate classroom but allowed to attend regular physical education classes.
3. *Partial mainstreaming.* Students take part in selected physical education experiences but do not attend on a full-time basis because they can only find success in some of the offerings. Their developmental needs are usually met in special classes.
4. *Special developmental classes.* Students with disabilities are in segregated special education classes.
5. *Reverse mainstreaming.* Able children are brought into a special physical education class to promote intergroup peer relationships.

Segregation is maintained only when it is in the best interests of the child. The thrust of segregated programs is to establish a level of skill and social proficiency that eventually enables youngsters to be transferred to a less restricted learning environment. Emphasis on placement in the least restrictive environment in which the child can profit most is the cornerstone of the educational process. Children with disabilities, working on their own, often are denied opportunities to interact with peers and become a part of the social and academic classroom network. Youngsters who are mainstreamed become the responsibility of the physical education specialist. However, they should maintain contact with support personnel such as the special education teacher, school psychologists, and speech therapists. Although the youngsters are the responsibility of the physical education specialist, support personnel

FIGURE 7.3 Successful mainstreaming of youngsters with disabilities.

should serve as a source of information and support for the teacher in charge.

Guidelines for Successful Inclusion

The concern is not whether to plan for inclusion, but how to do it effectively. Regardless of the setting, it is always necessary to teach a number of children with diverse impairments. Current learning strategies may not be appropriate for children with disabilities. Attitudinal change by the teacher is important—accept children as full-fledged participants and assume the responsibility to educate all students.

An important consideration when planning the IEP is whether the child is ready for inclusion. Some children with disabilities have developmental lags that can limit successful integration into normal classes. Both the class and the youngster with a disability must adapt. When children are deemed ready for placement, consultation between the physical education teacher and the special education supervisor is of prime importance. In a setting where emotions and feelings can run high, be sure that regular communication and planning occur. The reception and acceptance of the special child must not be left to chance. A scheduled plan should be instituted before the youngster is mainstreamed. Special and physical education specialists should discuss the needs of youngsters and develop realistic expected outcomes. Early in the inclusion process, the special education teacher may have to participate in physical education classes to ensure a smooth transition. Emphasize what children can do rather than what they cannot do.

All students need opportunities to make appropriate progress. The educational needs of children with disabilities can be met without jeopardizing the progress of other students. Help all students understand problems related to having a disability. Encourage students to understand, accept, and live comfortably with persons with disabilities. Students with disabilities are functional and worthwhile individuals who have innate abilities and can make significant contributions to society. The concepts of understanding and appreciating individual differences merit positive development and include three aspects:

1. Recognize the similarities among all people: their hopes, rights, aspirations, and goals.
2. Understand human differences and focus on the concept that all people have some type of disability. For some, disabilities are of such nature and severity that they interfere with normal living.
3. Explore ways to deal with individuals who differ and stress the acceptance of all children as worthwhile individuals. People with disabilities deserve consideration and understanding based on empathy, not sympathy.

Inclusion should allow children to make commendable educational progress, to achieve in those areas outlined in the IEP, to learn to accept limitations, to observe and model appropriate behavior, to become more socially accepted by others, and in general to become a part of the real world. Guidelines for successful integration of children with disabilities into physical education follow.

1. Beyond the regular program of activities, meet target goals as specified in the IEP. This involves resources beyond the physical education class, including special work and homework.

2. Build ego strength; stress abilities. Eliminate established practices that unwittingly contribute to embarrassment and failure.
3. Foster peer acceptance, which begins when the teacher accepts the child as a functioning, participating member of the class.
4. Concentrate on the child's physical education needs and not on the disability. Give strong attention to fundamental skills and physical fitness qualities.
5. Provide continual monitoring and assess periodically the child's target goals. Anecdotal and periodic recordkeeping are implicit in this guideline.
6. Be constantly aware of the child's feelings and anxiety concerning progress and integration. Provide positive feedback as a basic practice.
7. Modify the regular program to meet the unique capacities, physical needs, and social needs of youngsters with disabilities.
8. Provide individual assistance and keep youngsters active. Peer or paraprofessional help may be needed.
9. Consult regularly with the special education consultant.
10. Give consideration to more individualization within the program so youngsters with disabilities are smoothly integrated. Individual attention is based on the target goals of the IEP.

GENERATING PARENTAL SUPPORT

Placing parents on the school IEP committee establishes a line of communication between home and school and involves parents. Some kind of home training or homework can be recommended. If home training is indicated, two factors are important. First, parents must be committed in terms of time and effort. Their work need not be burdensome, but it must be done regularly in accordance with the sequenced lessons. Second, printed and sequenced learning activities must be given to parents if a systematic approach to the homework is expected. Materials should be understandable so that what is to be accomplished is not in doubt. Parents should see obvious progress in their child as assignments unfold.

Recruiting and Training Volunteer Aides

Recruiting and using aides can be an effective way to increase the amount of instruction and practice for youngsters. Volunteers are usually available among various community organizations, such as parent-teacher, foster grandparents, and community colleges. High school students can serve as volunteers and have been shown to work effectively with elementary school youngsters. An initial meeting with volunteer aides should explain the type of youngsters they will be working with and what responsibilities are required. Training should teach aides how to be most effective in assisting the instructor. Include learning how to work effectively with individuals, recording data, and developing special materials and instructional supplies. In addition, give potential aides an introductory experience in working with youngsters to see if they are capable and enjoy such work. Working with aides takes time and prior planning. The task of organizing and supervising aides can be burdensome if you have not learned to supervise and organize experiences.

Aides can assume many roles to increase the effectiveness of the instructional situation. They can gather and locate equipment and supplies prior to the lesson. They may officiate games and ensure that they run smoothly. Seasoned aides enjoy and are capable of offering one-on-one or small-group instruction to youngsters. Aides are not used to reduce the need for teacher involvement; rather they are there to implement instruction strategies that have been organized and developed by the professional educator.

EXAMPLES OF NATIONALLY VALIDATED PROGRAMS

For several years, nationally validated programs of proven practices in special education have been available for adoption. Portions of many of these programs are in or are related to physical education. These programs are funded and endorsed by the U.S. Office of Education. Some deal with screening, assessment, and curriculum for young children with special needs. Others feature management practices associated with special children. A number deal with early recognition and intervention so that the child can be fitted more successfully into the mainstreaming situation. Information pertaining to these programs can be secured from state departments of education or from the U.S. Office of Education. Programs that have been recognized for outstanding contributions and have been identified as demonstration projects are described below.

1. *Project Active.* This program provides direct service delivery to students with psychomotor problems through a competency-based teaching and individualized learning approach. A second component involves in-service training. Materials include a battery of tests and seven program manuals. Conditions addressed are low motor ability, low physical vitality, postural abnormalities, nutritional deficiencies, breathing problems, motor disabilities or limitations, and communication disorders.

2. *Project Unique.* This is a fitness assessment project designed to determine the best tests for measuring fitness in students with sensory (blind or deaf) or orthopedic impairments. Tests include AAHPERD items and others that can be administered in a mainstream setting.
3. *Project I Can.* This project consists of three separate programmatic systems, including preprimary skills; primary skills; and sport, leisure, and recreation skills. Each system includes an observational assessment approach, illustrative goals, objectives, instructional strategies, and program evaluation materials. Emphasis is placed on an achievement-based curriculum model.

MODIFYING ACTIVITIES FOR INCLUSION

Inclusion requires modifying activities to increase the opportunity for success. Children with disabilities are not the only students who need additional consideration; most youngsters benefit from modifications. Rules can be changed for everyone so that all youngsters have a chance to contribute to group success. When children learn to accept that everyone has a right to participate, physical education contributes to the development of quality citizens.

FIGURE 7.4 Modifying an activity for successful participation.

Be aware of situations that devalue a child socially. Never use the degrading method of having captains choose from a group of waiting children. Elimination games should be changed so that points are scored instead of players being eliminated. (This is an important consideration for all youngsters.) Determine the most desirable involvement for children with disabilities by analyzing participants' roles in game and sport activities (Figure 7.4). Assign a role or position that will make the experience as natural or normal as possible.

Offer a variety of individual and dual activities. Youngsters with disabilities may want to build confidence in their skills before they participate with others. Individual activities give children more practice time without the pressure of failing in front of peers. Try to arrange the environment so children with disabilities are not set apart from able classmates. Overprotectiveness benefits no one and prevents the special student from experiencing challenge and personal accomplishment. Avoid the tendency to underestimate abilities of students. The following sections offer ideas for modifying activities to facilitate integration of youngsters with disabilities.

Modifications for Youngsters Lacking Strength and Endurance

1. *Lower or enlarge the size of the goal.* In basketball, the goal can be lowered; in soccer the goal might be enlarged.
2. *Modify the tempo of the game.* For example, games might be performed using a brisk walk rather than running. Another way to modify tempo is to stop the game regularly for substitution. Autosubstitution is an excellent method for allowing students to determine when they are fatigued. They ask a predetermined substitute to take their place.
3. *Reduce the weight and/or modify the size of the projectile.* A lighter object moves more slowly and inflicts less damage on impact. A larger object is easier to track visually and to catch.
4. *Reduce the distance that a ball must be thrown or served.* Options are to reduce the dimensions of the playing area or add more players to the game. In serving, others can help make the serve playable. For example, in volleyball, other teammates can bat the serve over the net as long as it does not touch the floor.
5. *In games that are played to a certain number of points, reduce the number required for a win.* For example, play volleyball games to 7 or 11, depending on the skill and intensity of the players.
6. *Modify striking implements by shortening and reducing their weight.* Rackets are much easier to control

when they are shortened. Softball bats are easier to control when the player "chokes up" or selects a lighter bat.

7. *In some games it is possible to slow the ball down by letting some of the air out of it.* This reduces the speed of rebound and makes the ball easier to control in a restricted area. It also keeps the ball from rolling away from players when it is not under control.
8. *Play the games in a different position.* Some games may be played in a sitting or lying position, which is easier and less demanding than standing or running.
9. *Provide matching or substitution.* Match another child on borrowed crutches with a child on braces. Two players can be combined to play one position. A student in a desk chair with wheels can be matched against a child in a wheelchair.
10. *Youngsters can substitute skills for each other.* For example, a child may be able to strike an object but may lack the mobility to run. Permit substitute courtesy runners.

Modifications for Youngsters Lacking Coordination

1. *Increase the size of the goal or target.* Increasing the size of a basketball goal increases the opportunity for success. Another alternative is to offer points for hitting the backboard or getting near a goal. Since scoring is self-motivating, modification should occur until success is ensured.
2. *The lack of coordination will make the youngster more susceptible to injury from a projectile.* Offer protection by using various types of protectors (glasses, chest protectors, face masks, etc.).
3. *When teaching throwing, allow opportunity to throw at maximum velocity without concern for accuracy.* Use small balls that can be grasped easily. Fleece balls and beanbags are easy to hold and release.
4. *When learning to strike an object, begin with one that is held stationary.* The use of a batting tee or tennis ball fastened to a string offers children the opportunity for success. In addition, a larger racket or bat can be used and the youngster can choke up on the grip.
5. *If a great deal of time is spent on recovering the projectile, children receive only a few practice trials and feel frustrated.* Place them near a backstop or use a goal that rebounds the projectile to the shooter.
6. *When learning to catch, use soft, lightweight, and slow-moving objects.* Beach balls and balloons are excellent for beginning catching skills because they allow youngsters to track their movement visually. In addition, foam rubber balls eliminate the fear of being hurt by a thrown or batted projectile.

Modifications for Youngsters Lacking Balance and Agility

1. *Increase the width of rails, lines, and beam when practicing balance.* Carrying a long pole helps minimize rapid shifts of balance and is a useful lead-up activity.
2. *Increase the width of the base of support.* Teach youngsters to keep their feet spread at least to shoulder width.
3. *The more body parts in contact with the floor, the easier it is to balance the body.* When beginning balance practice, emphasize controlled movement using as many body parts as possible.
4. *Increase the surface area of the body parts in contact with the floor or beam.* For example, walking flat-footed is easier than walking on tiptoes.
5. *Lower the center of gravity.* This offers more stability and greater balance to the child. Place emphasis on bending the knees and leaning slightly forward.
6. *Ensure that surfaces offer good friction.* Floors and shoes should not be slick or children will fall. Carpets or tumbling mats increase a child's traction.
7. *Some children will require balance assistance.* A barre, cane, or chair can be used to keep the youngster from falling.
8. *Children with balance problems will inevitably fall.* Offer practice in learning how to fall so they gradually learn to absorb the force of the fall.

UNDERSTANDING SPECIFIC DISABILITIES

To assist a child with a challenge, an understanding of the disability and what it means to the child is essential. Basic information is provided here, and additional materials may be secured from special education consultants. National associations offer information about various disabilities and suggest ways of helping special children.

Mental Disabilities

The capacity of a child with a mental disability does not allow the child to be served by the standard program. Mental disabilities are a question of degree, usually measured in terms of intelligence quotient (IQ). Mildly impaired children (with IQs ranging roughly from 50 to 75 or 80) are most often mainstreamed in both physical education and the regular classroom. Children with IQs below 50 usually cannot function in a regular classroom environment; they need special classes. These children are generally not mainstreamed and so are excluded from the following discussion.

Academically, children with mild mental impairments are slower to understand directions, to follow directions, to complete tasks, and to make progress. Conceptually, they have difficulty pulling facts together and drawing conclusions. Their motivation to stay on task is generally lower. Academic success may have eluded them. These realities must be considered in the physical education setting. Improvement in these areas is a goal to be achieved.

Do these children differ physically from other students? In a study comparing 71 educable mentally challenged boys with 71 normal boys, aged 6 to 10 years, the following was noted. Differences between the impaired and the normal in respect to opportunities to be physically active tend to be substantial. Similarly, the motivation to be physically active may be less in children with mental impairments—a reflection of their general motor ineptness. The relatively large proportion of subcutaneous tissue in these youngsters is more than suggestive of a physically inactive life, resulting in a corresponding low level of motor performance (Dobbins, Garron, & Rarick, 1981).

In another study (Ulrich, 1983), a comparison was made between developmental levels of 117 disabled and 96 educable mentally challenged children using criterion-referenced testing of 12 fundamental motor skills and 4 physical fitness skills. The findings were similar to the previous study in that the educable mentally challenged students lagged three-and-a-half years behind normal children in motor skill development, as based on the researcher's selected criterion reference point. The investigator attributes this lag to a lack of opportunity for movement experiences at an early age. Subjects with disabilities were from special education classes, not from a mainstreaming situation.

Instructional Procedures

Studies of students with mild mental impairments show that they learn, but they do so at a slower rate and not to the depth of normal mentally functioning children. To help the mildly challenged develop their capacities so that they can become participating members of society, focus the learning process on fundamental skills and fitness qualities. Unless this base is established, the child with a mental disability faces considerable difficulty later in learning specialized skills. Minimizing skill and fitness lags can help ease the child into mainstream living.

A child with a mental impairment reacts well to goal setting, provided that the goals are challenging yet attainable. The pace of learning depends on the degree of impairment. Before such children can learn, they need to know what is expected and how it is to be accomplished. These should be challenging but within the performer's grasp. Often, past experiences have made children with mental impairments the victims of a failure syndrome. The satisfaction of accomplishment must supplant this poor self-image.

Place emphasis on gross motor movement that is progressive in nature. Teach activities that are presented through demonstration rather than verbalization. Many of the skills may have to be accompanied by manual assistance to help children get the "feel" of the skill. To avoid boredom and frustration, practice periods should be short. Allow ample opportunity for youngsters to show off skills they can perform so that they can enjoy the feeling of accomplishment. Shaping behavior by accepting approximation of the skill will encourage the child to keep trying. Progress arrives in small increments, and teachers must be sensitive to improvement and accomplishment, no matter how small. Trying should be rewarded. Many youngsters are reluctant to try a new activity. Instructions should be repeated a number of times. Adhere to safety rules since these youngsters may not understand the risk of injury involved.

Epilepsy

Epilepsy is a dysfunction of the electrical impulses emitted by the brain. It is not an organic disease. It can happen at any period of life but generally shows up during early childhood. With proper care and medication, many children overcome this condition and live normal lives. Epilepsy is a hidden problem. A child with epilepsy looks, acts, and is like other children except for unpredictable seizures. Unfortunately, epilepsy carries an unwarranted social stigma. A child with epilepsy meets with a lack of acceptance, even when adequate explanations are made to those sharing the child's environment. A major seizure can be frightening to others.

Gaining control of seizures is often a long procedure, involving experimentation with appropriate anticonvulsive medication in proper doses. Fortunately, most epilepsy can be controlled or minimized with proper medication. One factor in control is to be sure that the child is taking the medication as prescribed. Sometimes a child can recognize signs of seizure onset and should have the privilege of moving to the sideline without permission. A seizure may, however, occur without warning. Know the signs of a seizure and react accordingly.

Three kinds of seizures are identified. A petit mal seizure involves a brief period (a few seconds) of blackout. No one is aware of the problem, including the child. Sometimes it is labeled inattention and thus is difficult to identify. A psychomotor epileptic seizure is longer lasting (perhaps a few minutes) and is characterized by involuntary movements and twitching. The child acts like a sleepwalker and cannot be stopped or helped. The affected youngster does not respond when addressed and is unaware of the seizure. A grand mal seizure is a total seizure with complete neurological involvement. The child may become unconscious and lose control of the bladder or bowels, resulting in loss of urine, stool, or both. Rigidity and tremors can appear. The seizure must run its course.

Two points are important. First, throughout any seizure or incident, preserve a matter-of-fact attitude and try not to exhibit pity. Second, educate other children to understand and empathize with the problem. Stress what the condition is and, later, what it is not. Explain that the behavior during a seizure is a response to an unusual output of electrical discharges from the brain. Everyone needs these discharges to function in normal living, but the person with epilepsy is subject to an unusual amount of the discharges, which results in unusual activity. The condition involves a natural phenomenon that gets out of control.

Information about epilepsy should be a part of the standard health curriculum in the school, rather than a reaction to an epileptic seizure or to the presence of a student who may have seizures. Epilepsy can be discussed as a topic relevant to understanding the central nervous system. Certain risks are involved if the lessons have as their focus the problems of a particular child, because this may heighten the child's feelings of exclusion and place disproportionate attention on what might have been a relatively inconsequential aspect of the student's life. (This caution does not rule out helpful information being given to peers when a seizure has taken place.)

In the event of a grand mal seizure, some routine procedures should be followed. Have available a blanket, a pillow, and towels for clean up. Make the child comfortable if there is time. Do not try to restrain the child. Put nothing in the mouth. Support the child's head on the pillow, turning it to one side to allow the saliva to drain. Remove from the area any hard or sharp objects that might cause harm. Secure help from a doctor or nurse if the seizure continues more than 3 or 4 minutes or if seizures occur three or more times during a school day. Always notify the school nurse and the parents that a seizure has occurred. Assure the class that the seizure will pass and that the involved child will not be harmed or affected.

Instructional Procedures

Recommendations regarding special modes of conduct and guidelines governing participation in school activities must come from the child's physician, since most epileptic children are under medical supervision. The instructor should stay within these guidelines while avoiding being overprotective. Emphasize inclusion of the child rather than exclusion. If there is some doubt about control of the seizures, climbing and elevated activities should be eliminated.

Today's approach is to bring epilepsy into the open. A concerted effort should be made to educate today's children so that traditional attitudes toward the condition can be altered. Perhaps tomorrow's adults will possess a better understanding. The child with epilepsy is a normal, functioning person except at the time of a seizure. Epilepsy is not a form of mental illness, and most people with epilepsy are not mentally retarded.

Visual Impairment

Mainstreaming for the visually impaired must be handled carefully and with common sense. The *visually impaired* designation includes those who are partially sighted as well as those who are legally blind. One has only to move about in a dark room to realize the mobility problems faced by a visually impaired child. This disability poses movement problems and puts limits on participation in certain types of physical activity. Total mainstreaming may not be a feasible solution.

Bring children with visual impairment into contact with other children and focus on the child's unique qualities and strengths. Empathy for and acceptance of the visually impaired child are most important. The task of monitoring movement and helping this child should be considered a privilege to be rotated among class members. If participation in the class activity selected is contraindicated, the monitor can help provide an alternate activity.

Instructional Procedures

Visually impaired children have to develop confidence in their ability to move freely and surely within the limits of their disability. Since limited mobility often leads to reduced activity, this inclination can be countered with a personalized program where the lack of sight does not prove insurmountable. The child can take part in group fitness activities with assistance as needed. Exercises should pose few problems. Rope jumping is an excellent activity. Individual movement activities, stunts and tumbling, rhythms and dances (particularly partner dances), and selected apparatus activities can be appropriate. Even low balance beams, bench activities, climbing apparatus, and climbing ropes may be within the child's capacity. Manipulative activities, involving tactile senses, are not always appropriate. If the child has some vision, however, brightly colored balls against a contrasting background in good light can permit controlled throwing, tracking, and catching. Through the selection of activities, the sense of balance should be challenged regularly to contribute to sureness of movement. Because vision is limited, other balance controls also need to be developed.

The visually impaired child ordinarily cannot take visual cues from other children or the teacher, so explanations must be precise and clear. Use a whistle or loud verbal cue to signal the class. For some situations, an assigned peer can monitor activity, helping as needed or requested. In running situations, a helper can hold hands with the visually impaired child. Another method is to use physical guidance until the feel of a movement pattern is established. This should be a last choice, however, occurring only after the child has had a chance to interpret the verbal instructions and still cannot meet the challenge. Touching a part of the child's body to establish correct sequencing in a movement pattern may help.

Auditory Impairment

Children with auditory impairments are those who are deaf or who must wear hearing aids. In physical education classes, these children are capable of performing most, if not all, activities that able children can perform. Because most instruction is verbal, a deaf child is isolated and often frustrated in a mainstreaming situation unless other means of communication are established. Accomplishing this while keeping the class functioning normally constitutes a problem of considerable magnitude.

Some advocates for the deaf contend that implementing PL 94-142 with its emphasis on mainstreaming is not appropriate for deaf children and thwarts their development. Teaching the deaf is a challenging and specialized process, requiring different communication techniques. Many deaf children have poor or unintelligible speech and inevitably develop a language gap with the hearing world. Sign language, lip reading, and speech training are all important facets of communicative ability for the deaf (Figure 7.5). Integrating deaf children into a regular physical education class setting is a process that can be handled with common sense. The experience should be satisfying to the deaf child or it is a failure.

Instructional Procedures

Children with auditory impairments can perform physically and at the same level as children with normal hearing when given the opportunity. One successful approach when teaching both hearing-impaired and normal youngsters is to use contract or task card techniques. Written instructions can be read loudly by the teacher or monitor. Pairing children with severe hearing loss with others children can be a frustrating experience for both, but meaningful possibilities also exist. Such a pairing necessitates lip reading, the use of verbal cues, or strong amplification on a hearing aid. Visual cues, featuring a "do as I do" approach, can stimulate certain types of activity.

Keep the deaf child near you to increase the opportunities to read lips and receive facial cues. Avoid long delays for explanations or question and answer periods. This becomes a blank time for the hearing impaired and leads to frustration and aggressive action. For rhythmics, some devices can help. Keep record player speakers on

FIGURE 7.5 Using sign language with a student with an auditory-impairment.

the floor to provide vibration. Use a metronome or blinking light. For controlling movement patterns, use hand signals for starting, stopping, moving to an area, assembling near the teacher, sitting down, and so on.

Orthopedic Disabilities

Orthopedic disabilities in children encompass a range of physical ailments, some of which may involve external support items, such as splints, braces, crutches, and wheelchairs. A few postpolio cases may be encountered. Generalizing procedures for such a range of physical abnormalities is difficult. Children with orthopedic problems usually function on an academic level with other children and are regular members of a classroom. As such, they participate in regular physical education classes.

Instructional Procedures

Focus on what the child can do and on the physical needs that are to be met. Mobility is a problem for most, and modification is needed if the class activity demands running or agility. Individualized programs are made to order for this group, because the achievement goals can be set within the child's capacity to perform (Figure 7.6).

FIGURE 7.6 Youngsters with disabilities can find the joy of participation.

Although volleyball and basketball are popular team sports, there will be few leisure opportunities for individuals to participate in due to the difficulty of getting enough participants together for team play. Strong emphasis should be placed on individual and dual sports such as tennis, track and field, road racing, table tennis, badminton, and swimming. This allows the orthopedically impaired individual to play a dual sport with an opponent or to participate individually in activities such as road racing and swimming.

For wheelchair children, certain measures are implicit. Develop general musculature to improve conditions for coping with the disability and to prevent muscle atrophy. In particular, wheelchair children need strong arm and shoulder musculature to transfer in and out of the wheelchair without assistance. Flexibility training to prevent and relieve permanent muscle shortening (contracture) should be emphasized. Cardiorespiratory training is needed to maintain or improve aerobic capacity, as immobility in the chair decreases activity. From these experiences, the wheelchair child should derive a personal, functioning program of activity that can carry over into daily living.

Time devoted to special health care after class must be considered for children with braces or in wheelchairs. Children with braces should inspect skin contact areas to look for irritation. If they have perspired, a washcloth and towel will help them freshen up and remove irritants. Wheelchair children can transfer to a sturdy chair that is rigid and stabilized to allow the wheelchair to dry out. Adequate cushioning should be provided for any surface to which an orthopedically impaired person transfers, such as chairs, weight machines, and pool decks, for the prevention of pressure sores and skin abrasions. Schedules can be adjusted so that time for this care is available. Scheduling the class during the last period before lunch or recess or at the end of the day allows this time.

Emotionally Disturbed Children

PL 94-142 refers to behavior-disordered students as "severely emotionally disturbed." Emotionally disturbed children represent an enigma for mainstreaming. They have been removed from the regular classroom situation because they may cause a disruption and because they need psychological services. Physical education seems to be one area in which they can find success. Each case is different, however, and generalization is difficult.

Instructional Procedures

When working with emotionally disturbed youngsters, establish a learning environment that is fair and consistent. Clearly delineate what is expected and accepted in the instructional setting. In addition, rules must be defined, but nonpunitive in nature. Explanation of reasons for rules should be a regular topic of discussion as emotionally disturbed youngsters often feel that someone is making rules that are meant to punish them personally.

Youngsters must know who is in charge and what will be accepted. It may take a long period of time to develop confidence in the emotionally disturbed child, and vice versa. During this time it is important to build a sense of trust. A teacher who is patient and understanding can have a positive effect on children with this disability. Loving and forgiving teachers are most effective with the emotionally disturbed youngster.

Severely emotionally disturbed youngsters are in need of a stable and organized environment that focuses on individual progress. They will become easily frustrated and quit if the activities are too difficult or cause embarrassment. It is important to plan for unexpected outbursts, even when instructional procedures have been correct. If the unexpected is anticipated, you will not feel as threatened or hurt by the student's behavior. Take time to discuss and practice responsible behavior. These students need help building a positive self-concept, expressing their feelings appropriately, and learning to accept responsibility for their own behavior.

Learning Disabilities

Learning disabilities encompass a range of problems that lack a clear definition. Examples of terms used to describe various learning disabilities are *perceptual handicaps, brain injury, minimal brain dysfunction, dyslexia,* and *developmental aphasia.* This definition used by the federal government is so broad that over 40 percent of school-aged youngsters can qualify as being learning disabled. More boys than girls (a 2:1 ratio) are identified as having learning disabilities in today's schools. Additionally, many more elementary than secondary school children are identified. Characteristics of youngsters with learning disabilities can include one or more of the following: hyperactivity, short attention span, perceptual-motor problems, poor self-concept, clumsiness, poor short- or long-term memory, and an unwillingness to persevere when learning motor tasks.

The causes of learning disabilities are poorly understood. Two major theories are currently popular for explaining these problems (Horvath, 1990). The first theory supposes that learning disabilities are organically based, with one of the major causal factors being an injury to the brain. This brain-injured individual is unable to efficiently receive and integrate sensory impulses. The second hypothesis is that learning disabilities are biochemically based. This theory supposes that several biochemical factors such as allergies, mineral and vitamin deficiencies, and glandular disorders cause learning disabilities. Modify the physical education program on an individualized basis for these children, since their disabilities are unique.

Instructional Procedures

Teaching students with learning disabilities is similar to working with emotionally disturbed children. Structure the program and conduct it in similar fashion on a day-to-day basis. Youngsters should not be surprised with unexpected changes in the routines. Arrange the activity area so distractions are kept to a minimum. An unchanging structure allows the child to explore the environment with confidence. The teaching area should be restricted to the smallest possible size so that student-teacher distance is kept to a minimum. An environment without limits may cause some youngsters to feel threatened or out of control.

Youngsters with learning disabilities often find it difficult to learn independently or wait for a turn. Demand active participation and require students to be on task a large share of the lesson time. Introduce cross-aged tutoring or invite parent volunteers in to work individually with students. Attention based on firmness and concern will help these students learn motor skills and deal with extraneous distractions in their environment.

Asthma

About 1 of 15 children have asthma (U.S. Department of Health and Human Services, 1995). Asthmatic children have restricted breathing capacity. In the past, doctors were quick to excuse asthmatic children from participating in physical education classes. Recent research shows that physical activity is not contraindicated for children with asthma. A study by Varray, Mercier, Terral, and Prefaut (1991) showed that children with asthma could participate in high-intensity exercise without complications. Children who were 11 years old participated in a swimming program and reached an intensity level within 5 percent of their maximal heart rate. These youngsters showed a significant increase in cardiovascular fitness. Parents of the subjects reported their children showed a decrease in the intensity of wheezing attacks and the ability to control asthmatic attacks through relaxation and breathing exercises. The researchers concluded that when workloads are individualized for asthmatic children, their cardiovascular fitness can be enhanced through aerobic training.

Instructional Procedures

Check with the school nurse or other health professional to gather background information on students with asthma. Know how to recognize symptoms and deal with severe asthmatic bouts. Working with asthmatic children requires developing an awareness of the symptoms that require prompt action. If a student is coughing or wheezing, has difficulty breathing, or complains of chest tightness or pressure, immediate action should be taken. Recommended steps are to stop the student's current activity, follow the student's asthma management plan, help the student with medication, and then closely observe the effect. If the student fails to improve or is straining to breathe or speak without pausing for a breath, call for help immediately.

Talk with asthmatic children about their asthma and discuss their concerns about being active. Offer reassurance that you are aware of their limitations and understand the need to modify activity. The students are often the best judge of their own limitations if they don't feel pressured to push themselves excessively. Try to develop a shared understanding of what is an acceptable modification of the activity you are teaching. Include adequate warm-up activity with asthmatic youngsters. Ask children to suggest modifications. If an activity is too demanding and it cannot be modified, allow students to help with equipment, keep score, or referee.

Cerebral Palsy, Cardiac Problems, and Diabetes

Cerebral palsy, like epilepsy, has strong negative social implications. Peer education and guidance are necessary. The signs of cerebral palsy are quite visible and, in severe cases, result in odd, uncoordinated movements and a characteristic gait. Medical supervision indicates the limits of the child's activities. Children with cerebral palsy are usually of normal intelligence; their chief problem is control of movement. The excitability threshold is critical and must not be exceeded. Many need support services for special training in both neural and movement control.

Children with cardiac problems are generally under the guidance of a physician. Limitations and restrictions should be followed to the letter. The child should, however, be encouraged to work to the limits of the prescription.

Diabetes is an inability to metabolize carbohydrates that results from the body's failure to supply insulin. Insulin is taken either orally or by injection to control serious cases. If the child is overweight, a program of weight reduction and exercise prescription are partial solutions. Diabetics are usually under medical supervision. Knowing that a diabetic child is in the physical education class is important, because the child must be monitored to detect the possibility of hypoglycemia (abnormally low blood sugar level). The condition can be accompanied by trembling, weakness, hunger, incoherence, and even coma or convulsions. The solution is to raise the blood sugar level immediately through oral consumption of simple sugar (e.g., skim milk, orange juice) or some other easily converted carbohydrate. The diabetic usually carries carbohydrates, but a supply should be available to the instructor. Immediate action is needed because low blood sugar level can be dangerous, even leading to loss of life. The diabetic probably has enough control to participate in almost any activity. This is evidenced by the number of diabetic professional athletes who meet the demands of high activity without difficulty.

DESIGNING PROGRAMS FOR CHILDREN WITH SPECIAL NEEDS

The current emphasis on equal education has helped focus attention on children with special needs. Physical education can offer solutions to relevant problems through activity-oriented programs. Instruction has long been aimed at training the physically adept, with little concern or empathy shown for the less gifted. The programs presented in this section are for children with weight problems or posture aberrations.

Weight Problems

The prevalence of obesity has increased dramatically over the past 30 years (Wilmore, 1994). It is a difficult and sensitive issue. Each case is different, and the approach must fit the subject. Males with more than 25 percent body fat and females with more than 35 percent body fat are considered obese. The advantage of a percentage definition is that it is meaningful to parents. Skinfold measurement with calipers is used to identify obese individuals. Skinfold measurements can be converted to a percentage of body fat reading to make the measurement meaningful to parents and children. For research purposes, converting the readings to a percentage is not desirable, but for a student-oriented program, the procedure is acceptable. In most cases, the simplest test is the appearance of the child: A child who looks obese, is.

In any solution, the basic factors involved in obesity must be considered. These factors include genetics, emotional stability, hormonal functions, and intake-activity relationships. The overwhelming odds are that a fat child will stay fat. Heredity and environment are difficult to separate as causes for obesity, yet weight gain runs in families. A study at Laval University in Quebec, Canada, has provided strong evidence of a strong genetic component for obesity (Bouchard et al., 1990).

The assumption that obese children normally grow out of the condition is a fallacy. Some parents rationalize the problem, maintaining that their child "still has some baby fat but will grow out of it later." Unless active measures are taken, chances of solving the child's problem are small. Obese children often experience physical activities in ways different from children of normal weight. Success in physical activity is difficult for obese children to attain. When compared with their peers, heavy children are often physically inept. They may be the object of ridicule or the butt of jokes. Their peers sometimes call them names, such as Fatso, Tubby, and Lard Bucket. Children can be hurt deeply and driven even farther from active living, a direction opposite from the one they need to follow.

Not only does obesity impede the development of motor skills and limit the child's success in physical activities, but it also contributes to heart disease, because obese people are generally more inactive than their peers. The most common factor in obesity is an imbalance between caloric intake and energy expenditure. Many obese children fail to involve themselves in enough physical activity to burn up the calories they ingest. Excess calories are then stored in fat cells, and the child is pushed further into obesity.

A practical method for determining obesity uses calipers to measure skinfolds (Figure 7.7). Calipers are relatively inexpensive, and the measurement can be done quickly. Combining skinfold measurements over the triceps and calf muscles can be used to estimate the amount of body fat (Cooper Institute for Aerobics Research, 2002). To measure the skinfolds, the skin on the two sites is held with thumb and forefinger. The calipers are then applied to the skinfold, indicating a reading in millimeters. Three readings are taken and the median score used. If the sum of the triceps and calf skinfolds is more than 31 mm for boys and 40 mm for girls, youngsters are considered obese (Lohman, 1987).

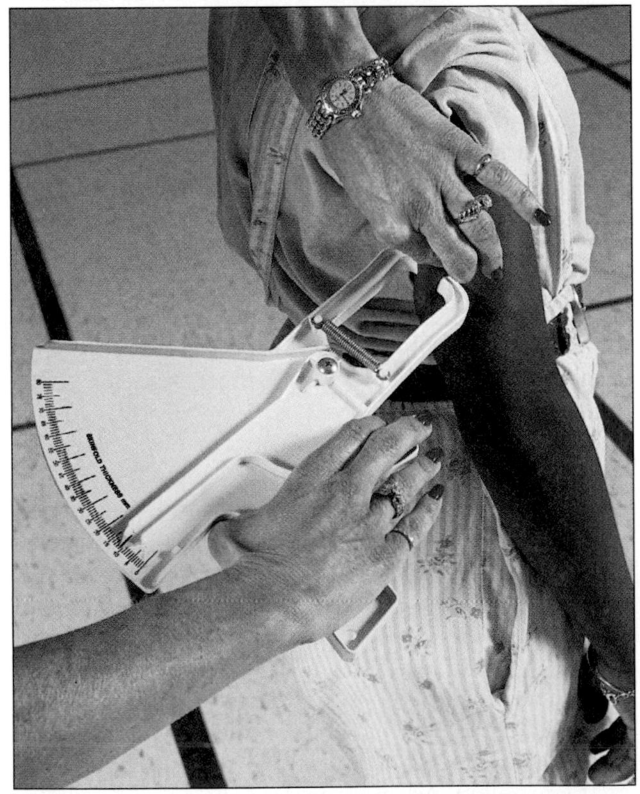

FIGURE 7.7 Measuring triceps skinfold with calipers.

One solution to obesity gives attention to both diet and activity. Unfortunately, this means that these children must alter their lifestyle, which requires adjustment not only in school life but also in home life. Without a genuine commitment from the child and without the cooperation of the child's parents, a remedial program can have little chance of success. For some children, commitment to the program is a relatively easy step, because they resent being fat and have wanted to do something about their obesity but have not known quite what to do. A protracted time commitment is important, because the remedial program must turn into a program for living or the child will revert to old habits. Getting parents to cooperate can be more difficult, especially if they themselves are obese. The parents may give lip service to cooperation but may in reality do nothing to change the home lifestyle that contributes to the child's obesity.

Counseling is an important part of the program for fighting obesity and should include both conferences with the child and support through printed instructions. Helping the child follow the activity prescription can be accomplished by the physical educator. Dealing with diet is extremely complex and involves changing the eating habits not only of the obese child but also of parents and siblings. This is complicated by the fact that in some cases, the obese child's diet is not substantially different from that of normal-weight classmates. It is also difficult for a child to change the food received at home, so diet control must be relegated to a minor role in the weight-control program.

Treating Obesity: Developing a Success Profile

Any weight-control program should include the entire school and involve the classroom teacher, because it is necessary to use some class time for conferences with the children in the program. The intermediate level is the most feasible time to deal directly with weight problems, since children at this level become more sensitive to their appearance and their relationships with peers. At the primary level, children usually have little motivation to deal with the problem.

Following is a step-by-step approach to developing a success profile for obese children in the elementary school setting. In many programs, youngsters are selected for treatment because someone feels uneasy about their physical predicament. More meaningful is a selection based on the youngsters' ability to deal successfully with the problem. This approach assumes that certain individuals are better suited to treatment than others. Not treating a child may be the better solution if the treatment outcome is likely to be failure, because failure only reinforces the child's belief that there is little hope, even when teachers want to help. The following approach selects children for treatment when they demonstrate a positive success profile.

Initial Screening of Potential Candidates

1. Explain the program to classroom teachers and emphasize the need for their support.
2. Ask classroom teachers to identify potential candidates.
3. Discuss with the classroom teacher the possibility of success for each candidate.
4. Hold a discussion with each of the students to explain the nature of the problem and the possibility of treatment and to determine if the student would like to participate.
5. Select students to be tested based on the comments of the classroom teachers, the students' comments, and the opinion of the physical education specialist.

Evaluation and Selection of Students This is the critical step in developing a successful program. Only students who appear able to follow program guidelines should be selected. The success profile identifies youngsters who have a reasonable opportunity to be successful. The following are areas included for evaluation:

1. *Fitnessgram data* (Cooper Institute, 2002). These include the following:
   a. *Skinfolds.* Children can be selected for inclusion in the program if they fall slightly below the minimum standard on the Fitnessgram. Some youngsters may be too obese for treatment in a physical education setting. Severe cases require medical attention and counseling beyond the scope of the physical education specialist.
   b. *Sit and reach for flexibility.*
   c. *Curl-ups to evaluate abdominal strength.*
   d. *PACER test to evaluate cardiovascular endurance.*
2. *Height and weight.* These data are collected only for the purpose of communicating with parents about where their child stands in relation to others (percentile ranking). Standard height and weight charts should be used (see Figures 2.3 and 2.4, pages 25–26).
3. *Children's Attraction to Physical Activity (CAPA)* (Brustad, 1993). The CAPA is a 15-item pencil and paper instrument, which assesses the extent of a child's interest in physical activity by giving him or her two opposing points of view from which to select. The score is then obtained by calculating the mean score for all 15 questions. This instrument is unique in that it focuses on dimensions that have been specifically identified as being important factors in their choices regarding physical activity behavior.

All of these factors are weighted in a relative fashion, with the exception of the skinfold measurement. It is usually wise to avoid including excessively obese children since the possibility of failure is high. All other factors are weighted, and children are selected when they demonstrate high perceived competence, a positive attitude toward physical activity, a reasonable fitness level, and support from the student, parents, and classroom teacher. The Success Profile Form (Figure 7.8 on page 146) can be used to chart the data.

Parental Involvement

1. Meet with the parents of selected students for a conference to explain the program. Topics covered in the meeting should be objectives of the program, operation and organization of the program, data gathered on the success profile, parent responsibilities, and need for follow-up conferences.
2. Give parents a handout explaining the program and the related responsibilities of the parents and child. This allows them to discuss the program at home.
3. Delineate to parents how the program is terminated if either the child or parent fails to perform his or her duties.
4. Give parents a "permission for my child to participate" form and ask them to return it within a stipulated time. Parents and child can discuss whether they really want to participate.

Implementation of the Program

After students have been selected, a weekly conference is arranged with each student.

1. The conference should last 10 to 20 minutes.
2. Create a student notebook, which is the property of the student. Allow students to personalize it and make it something of value. Included in the notebook are forms that define the student's workload and contain notes and information about exercise, nutrition, and weight control. Also include a form for communicating with parents about the child's progress and a parental check-off sheet stating that the youngster completed the weekly fitness assignment.

Name ____________________

Pre ____________ Post ____________

Success Profile

1. Height and weight
   - a. Height ________ inches
   - b. Height ________ percentile
   - c. Weight ________ pounds
   - d. Weight ________ percentile
2. Skinfold measurements
   - a. Triceps ________ mm
   - b. Calf ________ mm
3. Children's Attraction to Physical Activity (CAPA)
   - a. Score ________
4. Physical fitness test evaluation
   - a. Curl-Ups ________
   - b. Sit and Reach ________
   - c. PACER ________
5. Parent support ________
6. Classroom teacher support ________
7 Student interest ________
8. PE teacher interest ________

FIGURE 7.8 Success profile form for analyzing data relevant to weight-control program participation.

Assigning Fitness Activity Use the following guidelines when developing activity programs for obese children:

1. Assigned activity should be aerobic in nature to increase the caloric expenditure.
2. Record assigned activity in order to increase the amount of activity gradually and to ensure overload.
3. Find aerobic activities the child enjoys. The assignment should not be in lieu of activity already performed. Offer two or three choices for variety.
4. Make assignments in terms of minutes per day. Start with 10 minutes and increase 2 minutes per week, until a maximum of 30 to 40 minutes of exercise a day is reached.
5. Suggested activities are walking, skateboarding, roller skating or ice skating, bike riding, hiking, unorganized sport activities, orienteering, jogging, swimming, and rope jumping.

Follow-Up Activities

1. Every third week, send parents some type of communication that discusses the youngster's progress. This might be a note, phone call, computer printout, or personal visit.
2. Visit regularly with the classroom teacher and explain how the youngster is progressing, what treatment is being used, and those areas to be reinforced in the classroom.

Posture Aberrations

The physical education program should include vigorous physical activities that lead to fitness and strengthening of the muscle groups that maintain proper body alignment. Strengthening the abdominal wall and the musculature of the upper back and neck helps maintain proper body alignment. Enough flexibility of the various body segments must be attained so that children are able to move their body with ease and proper postural alignment.

The maintenance of correct posture contributes to physical attractiveness and wellness. *Posture* refers to the habitual or assumed alignment and balance of the body segments while the body is standing, walking, sitting, or lying. Posture is a reflection of the inner self. Appropriate posture radiates a positive self-image; improper posture (e.g., slouching) may reflect fatigue or a lack of confidence.

The association of posture with good health is justified. The antigravity muscles, those that help support the body against the forces of gravity, must be exercised regularly to accomplish body support with ease and without undue fatigue. From a mechanical standpoint, the musculature involved in correct posture must be balanced to hold the bones and joints properly. Faulty alignment can cause undue strain on supporting muscles and ligaments, which leads to early fatigue, muscle strain, and progressive displacement of postural support. In extreme cases, pain may result, and the position and function of vital organs, primarily those located in the abdomen, can be affected adversely.

What Is Correct Posture?

Posture varies with the individual's age, gender, and body type. Very young children often toe out while standing and walking to provide a wider, more stable base. Standing position exhibits an exaggerated lumbar curve and rounded shoulders, which are normal at this developmental stage. By age 6 or 7, however, the lumbar curve lessens and the prominent abdominal protrusion begins to disappear. At this stage, the feet and toes generally point ahead. The educational process should assist the child in making the transition from the normal exaggerated curves of young children to proper adult posture in adolescence.

The entire body posture is based on proper positioning of the feet. When the feet are positioned correctly, the rest of the body is more likely to line up properly. If weight is placed improperly on the heels with the knees in a locked position, the pelvis is tilted forward (down), with a compensating increased lumbar curvature and rounded shoulders. Toeing out during walking or standing is undesirable, because it leads to progressive arch trouble and other problems, such as less efficient walking and off-balance standing. Another undesirable adaptation occurs in the heel cord, which may curve outward where it joins the heel. Further change occurs as the bony structure of the foot slides toward the inside. This change culminates in a prominent inside malleolus. (The term malleolus refers to a bony protuberance.) The basic components of posture are illustrated in Figures 7.9 and 7.10 (page 148).

Lateral Deviations in Posture

Discussion to this point has reviewed the forward-backward plane of body movement, generally assessed from the side. The body also must be in balance in the lateral plane, as viewed from either front or back. The spinal column viewed from the back should show a straight, vertical line that divides the body into two symmetrical halves (Figure 7.11A, page 148).

A deviation occurs when this vertical line becomes either a single (C) curve (Figure 7.11B) or a multiple (S) curve (Figure 7.11C). Such deviations are coupled with one or more of the following body adjustments: (a) one shoulder higher than the other, (b) head tilts to one side, (c) hips not level, and (d) weight carried more on one leg than on the other. Marked deviations are noticeable, but moderate deviations are difficult to detect, especially when the body is clothed.

One way in which lateral curvature (scoliosis) can be detected is to have children bend forward and touch their toes. A serious curvature is indicated when the ribs protrude on one side. Early attention to lateral curvature is important because it generally gets worse with age. By the time youngsters reach high school, the curvature is probably well established and difficult to remedy.

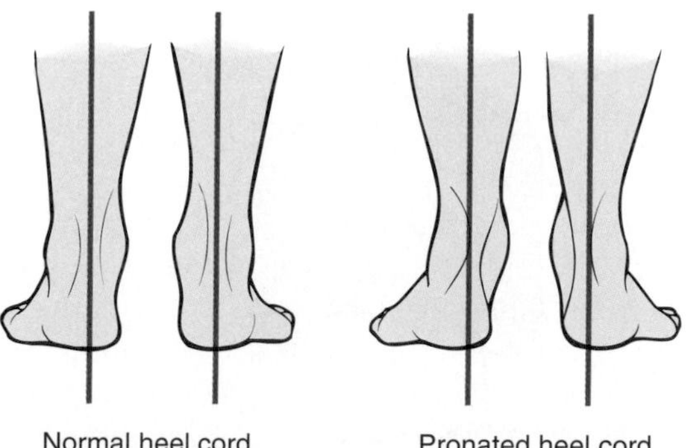

FIGURE 7.9 Normal and pronated heel cord.

Evaluating Posture

Because elementary school teachers are responsible for detecting and reporting physical problems of children, a program of posture evaluation can help identify posture problems. Evaluation can be done through observation, both formal and informal, and with measurement devices. A referral system should be established for individuals who exhibit marked posture deviations.

Posture Check Method For youngsters with posture problems, the application of the posture check can be an educational experience. Two methods of recording are presented: an individual form (Figure 7.12, page 149) and a class form (Figure 7.13, page 150). Teachers may prefer the single sheet, which includes all of the class, but the individual form is easier for parents and administrators to interpret. The class form is more adaptable to class analysis and comparisons. Each item is rated 1, 2, or 3 on an ascending scale. By averaging the rating numbers, a mean rating is obtained for each child.

Informal Observation Formal posture evaluation is an analysis of an assumed posture, which is not necessarily the posture used by children in daily living. To offset this testing effect, posture checks can be made informally when young people are participating in classroom and physical education activities. Teachers should notice how each child walks, stands, or sits when not conscious of an observer. The teacher can make notes and supplement the formal posture check.

Ear-Shoulder Method In normal posture, the lobe of the ear is directly above the point of the shoulder. Any

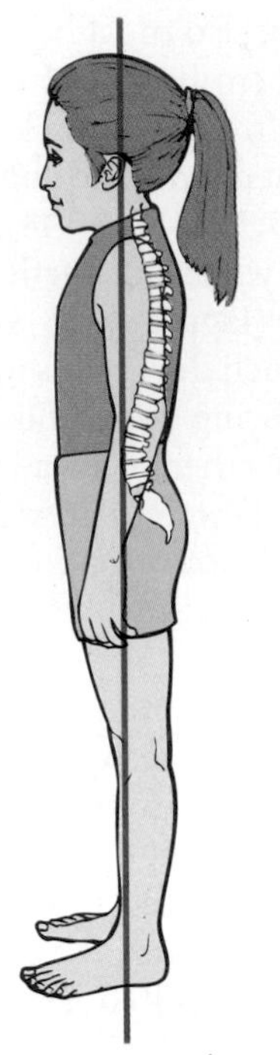

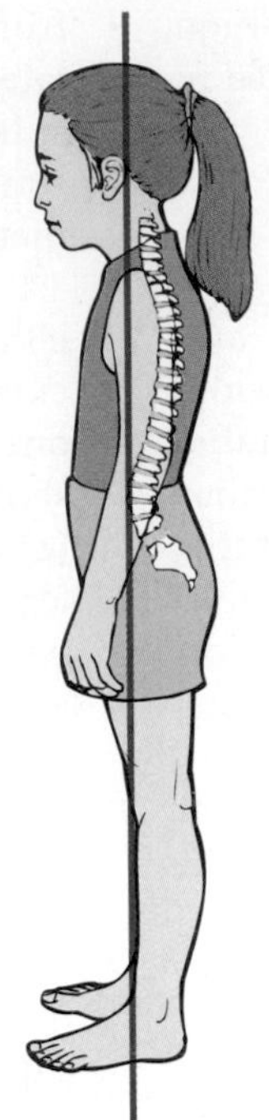

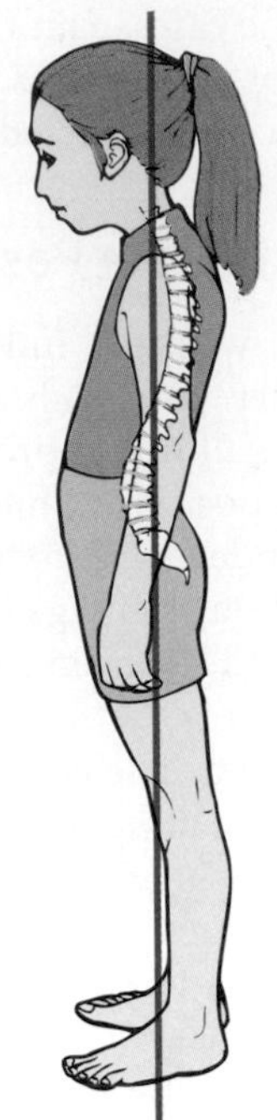

Correct posture	Fair posture	Poor posture
Head up, chin in, head balanced above the shoulders with the tip of the ear directly above the point of the shoulders, eyes ahead Shoulders back and easy, chest up Lower abdomen in and flat Slight and normal curves in the upper and lower back Knees easy Weight balanced with toes pointed forward	Head forward slightly Chest lowered slightly Lower abdomen in but not flat Back curves increased slightly Knees back slightly Weight a little too far back on the heels	Head noticeably forward, eyes generally down Chest flat or depressed Shoulder blades show winged effect Abdomen relaxed and prominent Back curves exaggerated Knees forced back in back-kneed position Pelvis noticeably tilted down Weight improperly distributed

FIGURE 7.10 Characteristics of correct, fair, and poor posture.

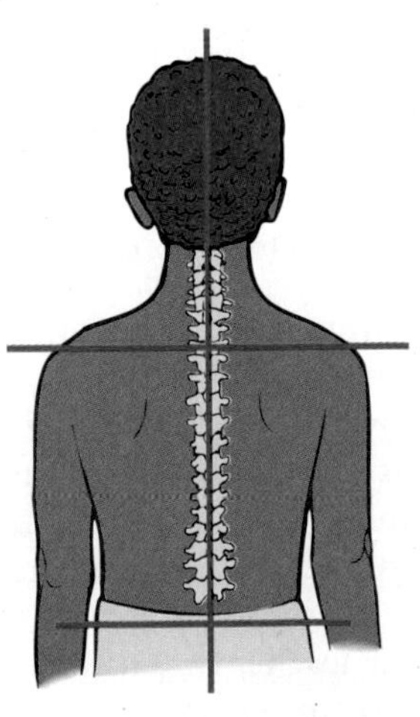

A. No deviation

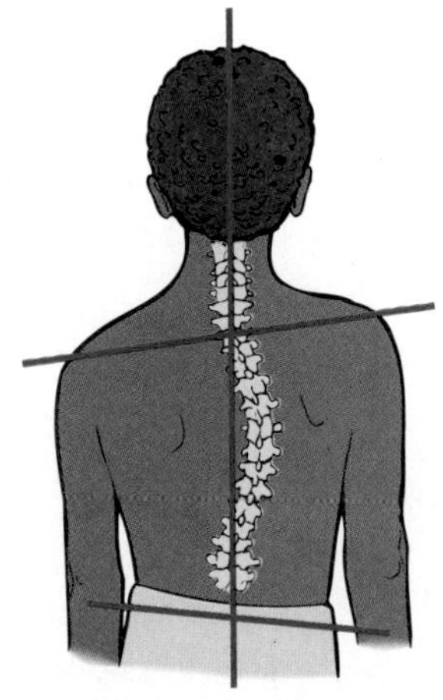

B. *C* curve

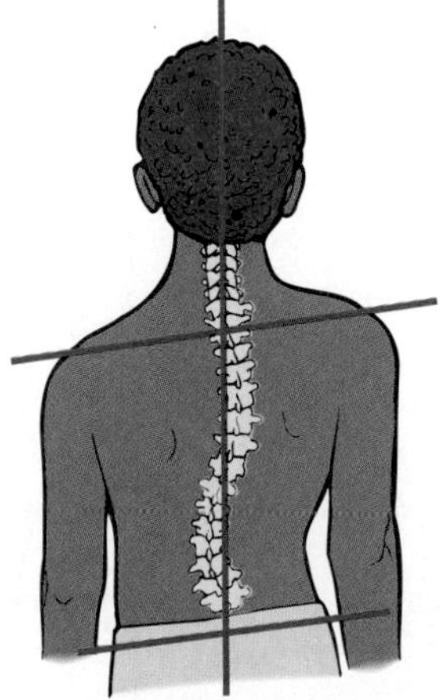

C. *S* curve

FIGURE 7.11 Lateral posture.

Posture Check Report

Name ______________________ Grade __________ School ______________________

Date ______________ Check made by ______________________________

Side View

Head		
Erect, chin in ________	Somewhat forward ________	Markedly forward ________
Upper Back		
Shoulders back ________	Slightly rounded ________	Rounded ________
Lower Back		
Slight natural curve ________	Moderately curved ______	Hollowed ________
Abdomen		
Flat ________	Slightly protruded ________	Protruding ________
Knees		
Relaxed ________	Slightly back ________	Hyperextended ________
Feet		
Pointed ahead ________	Pointed out somewhat ________	Pointed out ________

Front and Back View

Shoulders		
Level ________	Slightly uneven ________	Considerably uneven ________
Hips		
Level ________	Slightly uneven ________	Considerably uneven ________
Backs of Ankles and Feet		
Heels and ankles straight ________	Turned out somewhat ________	Pronated ________

Remarks

FIGURE 7.12 Individual posture check form.

departure from this relationship indicates a degree of back and shoulder roundness and can be used as a measure of general posture deviation. When one body area is out of alignment, other body segments compensate proportionally. For example, if the head is forward, other parts of the body would protrude to counterbalance the poor alignment. If one measures the degree by which the head is forward, then one has an estimate of general posture. Measurement can be made with a wand or pointer and can be expressed in terms of the number of inches the earlobe is positioned from the vertical line above the shoulder point. (In a deviated posture, the earlobe is usually forward, if anything.)

Videotaping and Self-Evaluation An effective way to identify obvious posture problems is to videotape and play back pictures of children standing, walking, and in other positions. In this way, they can observe themselves and make their assessments using the posture check report.

Referral A perceptive teacher observing children in study or play can screen children who need attention because of poor posture. Make referrals to the nurse,

Class Posture Check

Class ______________ School ______________

Date ______________ Teacher ______________

Code
Meets good postural standards 1
Slight but definite deviation 2
Marked deviation 3

	Side View						Front and Back Views			Remarks
Name	Hand and Neck	Upper Back	Lower Back	Abdomen	Knees	Feet	Level of Shoulders	Level of Hips	Feet and Ankles	
1.										
2.										
3.										

FIGURE 7.13 Class posture check form.

principal, or an appropriate agency for help. After a program has been established, the teacher can help by encouraging the child to fulfill the prescribed remedial exercises.

Posture and the Instructional Process

Posture is both a practice and a subject. The emphasis should be on hints, reminders, and encouragement during all phases of the program. Even the simplest movements present postural challenges that give opportunities for incidental teaching. Strong postural implications can be derived from exercises when the children understand the why of the movement. Values and advantages of correct posture should be stressed. Emphasis should be placed on helping children accept responsibility for their own posture. Nagging and overzealousness can have negative results. The following are examples of cues for correct posture:

Feet: "Feet forward. Weight on entire foot."

Lower back and abdomen: "Tuck the seat under. Flatten the tummy."

Upper body: "Shoulder blades flat. Chest high. Raise chest."

Neck and head: "Stand tall. Head high. Eyes ahead."

Walking: "Feet forward. Eyes ahead. Arms relaxed."

Sitting: "Seat back. Sit erect. Bend forward at the hips when working."

REFLECTION AND REVIEW QUESTIONS

How and Why

1. How do you feel about teaching individuals with disabilities?
2. Why is it important for children with disabilities to participate in physical education?
3. Do all children have disabilities? Explain your answer.
4. How can teachers generate parent and social support for children with disabilities?
5. How does our society look at obese children? Are these assumptions accurate?

Content Review

1. What implications do PL 94-142 and *IDEA* have for physical education teachers?
2. Discuss the screening and assessment procedures for evaluating students.

3. How are individual educational programs developed? Include comments on who is involved and what the IEP contains.
4. What are inclusion and mainstreaming? Discuss guidelines for successful inclusion.
5. Identify methods of modifying activities for inclusion.
6. Identify several disabilities and techniques for modifying activities to accommodate these disabilities.
7. Explain the process of designing programs for obese children with motor deficiencies.
8. Why is posture an important topic for physical education teachers?

FOR MORE INFORMATION

References and Suggested Readings

Auxter, D., Pyfer, J., & Huettig, C. (2001). *Principles and methods of adapted physical education and recreation with gross motor activities for small children with special needs.* Boston: McGraw-Hill.

Block, M. E. (1994). *A teacher's guide to including students with disabilities in regular physical education.* Baltimore: Brookes.

Bouchard, C., Tremblay, A., Despres, J. P., Nadeau, A., Lupien, P. J., Theriault, G., Dussault, J., Moorjani, S., Pinault, S., & Fourmier, G. (1990). The response to long-term overfeeding in identical twins. *New England Journal of Medicine,* 322, 1477–1482.

Brustad, R. J. (1993). Who will go out and play? Parental and psychological influences on children's attraction to physical activity. *Pediatric Exercise Science,* 5, 210–223.

Cooper Institute. (2002). *Fitnessgram 6.0 test administration manual.* Champaign, IL: Human Kinetics.

Dobbins, D. A., Garron, R., & Rarick, G. L. (1981). The motor performance of educable mentally retarded and intellectually normal boys after covariate control for differences in body size. *Research Quarterly,* 52(1), 6–7.

Dunn, J. M. (1997). *Special physical education: Adapted, individualized, developmental.* Madison: Brown & Benchmark.

Epstein, L. H., et al. (1984). The modification of activity patterns and energy expenditure in obese young girls. *Behavior Therapy,* 15(1), 101–108.

Foster, G. D., Wadden, T. A., & Brownell, K. D. (1985). Peer-led program for the treatment and prevention of obesity in the schools. *Journal of Consulting and Clinical Psychology,* 53(4), 538–540.

Horvat, M. (1990). *Physical education and sport for exceptional students.* Dubuque, IA: Wm. C. Brown.

Horvat, M., et al. (2003). *Developmental/adapted physical education: Making Ability Count.* 4th ed. San Francisco: Benjamin Cummings.

Jansma, P., & French, R. (1994). *Special physical education: Physical activity, sports, and recreation.* Englewood Cliffs: Prentice Hall.

Lohman, T. G. (1987). The use of skinfold to estimate body fatness on children and youth. *Journal of Physical Education, Recreation, and Dance,* 58(9), 98–102.

Sherrill, C. (1998). *Adapted physical activity, recreation and sport: Crossdisciplinary and lifespan.* Boston: WCB/McGraw-Hill.

Ulrich, D. A. (1983). A comparison of the qualitative motor performance of normal, educable, and trainable mentally retarded students. In R. L. Eason, T. L. Smith, & F. Caron (Eds.), *Adapted physical activity.* Champaign, IL: Human Kinetics.

U.S. Department of Health and Human Services. (1995). *Asthma & physical activity in the school.* (NIH Publication No. 95-3651). Washington, DC: National Institutes of Health.

Varray, A. L., Mercier, J. G., Terral, C. M., & Prefaut, C. G. (1991). Individualized aerobic and high intensity training for asthmatic children in an exercise readaption program. *Chest,* 99, 579–586.

Wilmore, J. H. (1994). Exercise, obesity, and weight control. *Physical Activity and Fitness Research Digest* 1(6), 1–8.

Yun, J., Shapiro, D., & Kennedy, J. (2000). Reaching IEP goals in the general physical education class. *Journal of Physical Education, Recreation, and Dance,* 71(8):33–37.

Websites

Adapted Physical Education
http://pe.central.vt.edu/adapted/adaptedmenu.html
http://www.palaestra.com/
http://www.pelinks4u.org/sections/adapted/adapted.htm

Adapted P.E. Assessment Tools
http://pe.central.vt.edu/adapted/adaptedinstruments.html

Adapted Physical Education National Standards
http://www.twu.edu/o/apens/

Children's Disabilities Information
http://www.childrensdisabilities.info/

Inclusion
http://www.palaestra.com/Inclusion.html

Legal Issues
http://asclepius.com/angel/special.html
http://www.ed.gov/offices/OSERS/Policy/IDEA/the_law.html

Programs
http://www.ed.gov/pubs/EPTW/eptw12/eptw12j.html

Obesity
http://www.niddk.nih.gov/health/nutrit/pubs/how%20can

SECTION 3

Program Implementation

CHAPTER 8

Curriculum Development

	ESSENTIAL COMPONENTS
I	**Organized around content standards**
II	**Student-centered and developmentally appropriate**
III	**Physical activity and motor skill development form the core of the program**
IV	Teaches management skills and self-discipline
V	**Promotes inclusion of all students**
VI	**Focuses on process over product**
VII	**Promotes lifetime personal health and wellness**
VIII	Teaches cooperation and responsibility and promotes sensitivity to diversity

	PHYSICAL EDUCATION STANDARDS
1	**Students are able to move competently using a variety of fundamental and specialized motor skills.**
2	Students can monitor and maintain a health-enhancing level of physical fitness.
3	Students are able to apply movement concepts and basic mechanics of skill performance when learning and refining motor skills.
4	Students comprehend the basic principles of wellness and are able to apply concepts that enable them to make meaningful decisions that positively impact their health and wellness.
5	Students participate in a wide variety of physical activities and learn how to maintain a personalized active lifestyle.
6	Students demonstrate empathy, understanding, and respect for the numerous differences exhibited by people in an activity setting.
7	Students exhibit responsible and self-directed behaviors that lead to positive social interactions in physical activity.

SUMMARY

This chapter offers a systematic approach for developing a curriculum and suggests formats for organization and evaluation. A written curriculum gives direction to the instructional program. A sequence of steps is offered for planning, designing, and implementing a comprehensive curriculum. The concepts of scope, sequence, and balance help ensure that the curriculum will meet the needs of all students.

OUTCOMES

- Define scope, sequence, and balance as each relates to curriculum development.
- List elements common to quality curriculum.
- Delineate your philosophy of physical education for children.
- List environmental factors that impact curriculum development.
- Specify the six-step approach in developing a quality curriculum.
- Specify the needs, characteristics, and interests of children and be able to explain how these age and maturity factors influence program development.
- Describe the difference between content standards and student-centered objectives.
- Cite the three learning domains and discuss characteristics of each.

Curriculum is a framework of child-centered physical activities that promote physical activity and skill development. A curriculum is a delivery system that gives sequence and direction to the learning experiences of students. The development of a curriculum includes a set of beliefs and goals that evolves from a theoretical framework or value orientation. *Value orientation* is a set of personal and professional beliefs that provides a basis for determining curricular decisions. Most often, physical educators have several value orientations, and physical education programs reflect a blend of different values. For example, a chosen model might include lifetime participation in physical activities, developing sport skills, acquiring fitness knowledge, improving social skills, acquiring disciplinary knowledge, or a combination of orientations.

When developing or revising an existing curriculum, the value orientation of the physical education staff toward the existing curriculum and toward proposed changes is a necessary consideration (Jewett, Bain, & Ennis, 1995). Determining the value orientation of the curriculum involves consideration of three major components: the subject matter to be learned, the students for whom the curriculum is being developed, and the society that has established the schools. Priorities in curriculum vary depending on the value orientations of the physical educators involved in the planning. Physical educators who place highest priority on subject matter mastery include an emphasis on sports, dance, outdoor adventure activities, physical fitness activities, and aquatic activities. This orientation places strong emphasis on learning skills and gaining knowledge so students have the opportunity to learn the subject matter and continue active participation for a lifetime. In contrast, instructors who favor a student-centered approach prize activities that develop the individual student. They emphasize helping students find activities that are personally meaningful. Other physical educators see student autonomy and self-direction as the most important goals. They focus instruction and curricula on lifetime sport skills and nontraditional activities, such as cooperative games and group activities, in an attempt to foster problem-solving and interpersonal skills.

The examples above illustrate a few of the different value orientations of physical educators. Usually, most curricula are put together by committee and therefore reflect a number of value orientations. Teachers need to know the value orientations that drive their curriculum so there is consistency in instructional goals. Finding common ground among value orientations makes it easier for a staff to present lessons that teach common goals and objectives. Before accepting a new teaching position, ask yourself the following questions about the school's curriculum. If you answer "no" to most of the questions below, it may be difficult for you to work comfortably in such a setting because it conflicts with your value orientation.

- Will the curriculum express a point of view about subject matter that is consistent with mine?
- Does the curriculum express a point of view about student learning that I believe?
- Does the curriculum express a point of view about the school's role in accomplishing social-cultural goals that is similar to my beliefs?
- Can I implement instructional strategies I value within this model?

DESIGNING A QUALITY CURRICULUM

The steps that follow offer a sequential approach for constructing a meaningful, well-planned curriculum guide. The first four steps are designed to establish the framework that guides selection of activities for the curriculum. These steps are often ignored because the focus is on activities that are easily implemented regardless of whether they contribute to content standards. The result is a curriculum with little direction, a situation similar to building a house or skyscraper without blueprints.

Step One: Develop a Guiding Philosophy

The initial step in curriculum design is to define a philosophy of physical education that reflects the educators' beliefs. This philosophy will guide the developmental process. A philosophical statement defines how physical education fits into the total school curriculum and what it will accomplish for each student. The following is an example of a philosophical platform for physical education.

> Physical education is that portion of the child's overall education that is accomplished through movement. It is education about and involving movement. Physical education must be largely an instructional program if it is to acquire a full partnership in the child's overall education. Only high-quality programs based on developmental goals with demonstrable and accountable outcomes achieve this respect. The overriding goal of U.S. education—to develop an individual who can live effectively in a democracy—guides the development of this program. Although physical education stresses psychomotor goals, it also contributes to cognitive and affective learning domains. Three major and unique contributions of physical education to the total school curriculum are:
>
> 1. *To develop personal activity and fitness habits.* The program teaches children the conceptual

framework under which personal fitness and lifetime activity habits are developed. This implies teaching the concept of human wellness (that is, teaching students how to maintain a vibrant and functional lifestyle throughout adulthood). Emphasis is placed on lifetime activity and personal habits that can be used in adulthood.

2. *To develop and enhance movement competency and motor skills.* Movement competency is rooted in developing a broad base of body management skills. The focus is on developing motor skills in a positive and nurturing environment. Personal competency in a wide variety of skills is an overriding theme of instruction.
3. *To gain a conceptual understanding of movement principles.* To move efficiently requires learning basic concepts of movement and understanding anatomical and mechanical principles. Physical education instruction integrates knowledge and skill performance to develop students who know how to move.

Step Two: Define a Conceptual Framework for the Curriculum

A conceptual framework is a series of statements that characterize the desired curriculum. These concepts establish the criteria that will be used to select activities and experiences included in the curriculum. The framework not only directs the activities but also reflects beliefs about education and the learner. Following are conceptual statements that define a child-centered, developmental curriculum.

- *Curriculum goals and objectives are appropriate for all youngsters.* This implies a balanced curriculum that covers fundamental skills, sport skills, games, rhythms and dance, gymnastics, and individual and dual activities. Emphasis is placed on developing a broad foundation of motor skills for all students.
- *Activities in the curriculum are selected based on their potential to help students reach content standards.* The elementary years are a time of experimentation, practice, and decision-making with all movement possibilities. The criterion for inclusion of activities is not based on whether teachers or students *prefer* certain activities. Activities are included in the curriculum because they contribute to student progress toward content standards.
- *The curriculum helps youngsters develop lifelong physical activity habits and understand basic fitness concepts.* Regardless of the philosophy of the curriculum, it should be designed so youngsters leave school with active lifestyle habits. Fitness is an important component of the curriculum and should be varied, positive, and educational. The fitness program is experiential, that is, students participate in fitness activities rather than just being told the facts of fitness. A meaningful curriculum helps students understand that physical activity and fitness are personal in nature, need to be maintained throughout life, and contribute to better health.
- *The curriculum includes activities that enhance cognitive and affective learning.* Children are whole beings and need to learn more than the physical performance of skills. They must understand skill performance principles and develop cognitive learning related to physical activity and wellness. Affective development, the learning of cooperative and social skills, is fostered through group activities that are inclusive of all children regardless of their widely varying skills and abilities.
- *The curriculum provides experiences that allow all children to succeed and feel satisfaction.* Quality programs focus on minimizing failure and emphasizing success. Activities that emphasize self-improvement, participation, and cooperation encourage the development of positive self-concepts. Physical education instruction focuses on learning, without being labeled a winner or loser.
- *The curriculum is planned and based on an educational environment that is consistent with other academic areas in the school.* Physical education teachers need the same working conditions as other teachers in the school setting. Class sizes similar to classroom teachers (20 to 35 students) and an assigned teaching area (such as a gym or multipurpose room) are needed for physical education instruction. Enough equipment for maximum activity and participation implies one piece of individual equipment for each youngster and ample apparatus to limit long lines while waiting a turn. A daily program ensures maximum opportunity for learning and retention.
- *Activities in the curriculum are presented in an educationally sound sequence.* Progression is the soul of learning and the curriculum should reflect progression vertically (between developmental levels) and horizontally (within each level and within each activity).
- *The curriculum includes an appropriate means of assessing student progress.* Student assessment includes health-related fitness, skill development, cognitive learning, and attitude development toward physical activity. Any assessment program should enhance the effectiveness of the program and should help teachers individualize instruction, communicate with parents, and identify youngsters with special needs.

Step Three: Consider Environmental Factors

Environmental factors are all those conditions within the community and school district that limit or extend the scope of the curriculum. Examples of environmental factors are the amount and type of equipment, budget size, and cultural makeup of the community. Other factors—such as the support of school administrators—can affect the type of scheduling or amount of required physical education in the school. Different communities may value certain types of activities or experiences for their children. Although environmental factors need to be examined carefully, they should not circumvent and limit curriculum scope and sequence. Rather, these factors should give direction to the curriculum development process. A well-designed curriculum is a goal, direction, and destination for the future, a high road to instructional success. Consider various environmental factors and try to use them to enhance the creativity and scope of the curriculum.

Following are examples of environmental factors that limit the development of a quality curriculum. Although these factors can sometimes be limiting, they can be handled creatively to ensure an effective curriculum. Think big; develop a comprehensive and ideal curriculum that is as varied, broad, and creative as possible. Seek to expand and develop the curriculum beyond these limiting factors.

School Administrators

The support of school administrators has a significant impact on the curriculum. It is important to communicate program goals to administrators. Like the general public, administrators may have misconceptions about physical education and its contribution to the overall education of students. In most cases, administrators will support physical education if they perceive that the program is built on sound educational principles that are documented and evaluated.

The Community: People and Climate

Occupations, religions, educational levels, cultural values, and physical activity habits within the community are factors that might affect curriculum development. Parents have a strong influence on the activity interests and habits of their children. The geographical location and the climate of the area are also important factors for consideration. The terrain (mountains, deserts, plains, and so on), combined with the weather conditions particular to each area, has an effect on people's activity interests. Extremely hot or cold climates influence markedly what activities are included in the curriculum and at what time of the year they should be scheduled.

Facilities and Equipment

Available teaching facilities dictate which activities can be offered. Facilities include on-campus as well as off-campus areas in the neighboring community. Off-campus facilities might be a community swimming pool or park. Equipment must be available in quality and quantity. One piece of equipment per child is necessary if students are to learn at an optimum rate. Equipment can be purchased with school funds or with special funds raised by students through demonstration programs. Some types of equipment can be constructed by school maintenance departments or as industrial arts projects. Another possibility is to ask students to bring equipment, such as jump ropes, soccer balls, and foam balls, from home.

Laws and Requirements

Laws, regulations, and requirements at the national, state, and local levels may restrict or direct a curriculum. Programs must conform to these laws. Examples of two national laws affecting physical education programs are Title IX of the Educational Amendments Act of 1972 and Public Law 94-142. Title IX enforces equal opportunities for both sexes, and PL 94-142 mandates equal access to educational services for students with disabilities. Individual states also may have various laws that affect physical education programming.

Scheduling

The schedule or organizational pattern of the school has an impact on curriculum development. How many times per week classes meet, the length of class periods, and who teaches the classes are factors to consider. Many scheduling alternatives exist: daily, two or three times per week, every other week, and other variations. Regardless of the various parameters, most elementary schools put together a scheduling committee that consists of a number of classroom teachers, specialists in other areas such as art and music, and the physical education teacher.

Consider several factors when developing schedules. Most often, 30 minutes is the amount of time scheduled for physical education classes. Some teachers prefer 40 minutes for upper-grade youngsters; however, such periods are long for primary-grade children. On the other end of the spectrum, periods can be too short. Some schools try to compress periods for primary-grade children to 20 minutes. A short period makes it difficult to present a balanced and complete lesson. Another important issue is how many periods a physical education teacher should teach per day. Physical education teachers should not be expected to have more contact time with students than classroom teachers do. Teaching physical education is demanding, and it is unfair to expect physical education specialists to teach all day without relief. An acceptable workload is eight or nine 30-minute periods per day with at least 5 minutes of passing time between classes so teachers can rearrange equipment, talk to students, and take care of personal matters. It is difficult to teach with classes scheduled back to back. Teachers need time to prepare for the next lesson. Passing time also avoids the situation where a class has to wait for the current class to finish.

Another important consideration is to schedule classes by developmental levels; for example, all developmental level I children should be scheduled within a particular block of time. Because physical education is equipment- and planning-intensive, scheduling by developmental level helps reduce the time needed for preparation and for placement or removal of equipment.

Budget and Funding

The amount of funding allocated for purchasing new equipment and replacing old supplies impacts the quality of the curriculum. Physical educators deserve parity in funding with other school program areas. Students are not expected to learn to read and write without materials and supplies. In similar fashion, they cannot learn physical skills without the necessary equipment and supplies.

Step Four: Determine Content Standards and Student Objectives

Content standards determine the direction of the program as dictated and desired by the state, district, or individual school. Such standards are fixed goals for learning. They determine what students should know and be able to do when they complete their schooling. Student progress is dictated by how students compare to the fixed standards rather than how they compare with other students. Content standards determine what criteria will be used to select instructional activities for the curriculum. The following are content standards for this textbook. See Chapter 1 for an in-depth discussion of each standard.

1. Students are able to move competently using a variety of fundamental and specialized motor skills.
2. Students can monitor and maintain a health-enhancing level of physical fitness.
3. Students are able to apply movement concepts and basic mechanics of skill performance when learning and refining motor skills.
4. Students comprehend the basic principles of wellness and are able to apply concepts that enable them to make meaningful decisions that positively impact their health and wellness.
5. Students participate in a wide variety of physical activities and learn how to maintain a personalized active lifestyle.
6. Students demonstrate empathy, understanding, and respect for the numerous differences exhibited by people in an activity setting.
7. Students exhibit responsible and self-directed behaviors that lead to positive social interactions that involve physical activity.

Write Student-Centered Objectives

After defining content standards, student-centered objectives are written. Objectives dictate the specific activities students will need to learn throughout the school year. Student-centered objectives are usually written in behavioral terms. Behavioral objectives contain three key characteristics: (a) a desired behavior that is observable; (b) a behavior that is measurable; and (c) a criterion for success that can be measured. Objectives are written for all three of the learning domains—psychomotor, cognitive, and affective. A description of each domain follows.

1. *Psychomotor domain.* This domain (Corbin, 1976) is the primary focus of instruction for physical educators. The seven levels in psychomotor domain taxonomy are movement vocabulary, movement of body parts, locomotor movements, moving implements and objects, patterns of movement, moving with others, and movement problem solving. This graduated list progresses in line with the developmental level of learners. Children learn the vocabulary of movement before proceeding to simple body-part movements. More complex movements are learned to enable youngsters to participate in activities with others and to solve personal movement dilemmas.
2. *Cognitive domain.* The cognitive domain was defined by Bloom (1956) and includes six major areas: knowledge, comprehension, application, analysis, synthesis, and evaluation. The focus of the cognitive domain for physical education is knowing rules, health information, safety procedures, and so on, and being able to understand and apply such knowledge. As students mature, they learn to analyze different activities, develop personalized exercise routines (synthesis), and evaluate their fitness levels.
3. *Affective domain.* The affective domain (Krathwohl, et al., 1964) deals with feelings, attitudes, and values. The major categories of learning in this area are receiving, responding, valuing, organization, and

characterization. The affective domain changes more slowly than do the psychomotor and cognitive domains. How teachers treat students and the feelings students develop toward physical education are ultimately more important than the knowledge and skill developed in physical education programs.

Behavioral objectives are time-consuming to write. Some teachers become bogged down and discouraged because the number of objectives appears overwhelming. A text edited by Chepko and Arnold (2000) offers a wide variety of behavioral objectives and sample assessment activities based on content standards. This text expedites the task of writing a standards-based curriculum. The following are examples of behavioral objectives related to content standards listed in Chapter 1:

Psychomotor Domain

1. Move efficiently using a variety of locomotor skills such as walking, running, skipping, and hopping
2. Perform body management skills on a variety of apparatus including climbing ropes, benches, and balance beams

Cognitive Domain

1. Understand words that describe a variety of relationships with objects such as around, behind, over, through, and parallel
2. Understand how warm-up and cool-down prevent injuries

Affective Domain

1. Show empathy for the concerns and limitations of peers
2. Demonstrate a willingness to participate with peers regardless of diversity or disability

Step Five: Select Child-Centered Activities

When selecting activities for a child-centered curriculum, a clear understanding of children is requisite. The task of designing a program that flows with children and doesn't run contrary to their urges, characteristics, and interests requires a clear view of their nature. It makes little sense to gather activities for instruction if they are not developmentally appropriate or do not appeal to children. The major criterion to follow when selecting activities for the curriculum is, "Do the activities contribute to content standards and student-centered objectives?" This approach contrasts with selecting activities because they are fun or because you enjoy them. Some teachers fail to include activities in the curriculum if they lack confidence or feel incompetent. This results in a curriculum that is designed for the teacher's benefit rather than students'. If an activity contributes to content standards, it is necessary to develop requisite instructional competency. Imagine a math teacher choosing not to teach fractions or multiplication tables to students because of feelings of incompetence. It is your responsibility to learn to teach new activities so students experience and learn all requisite physical skills.

As many activities as possible that contribute to content standards should be gathered in the planning stage. The greater the number of activities considered, the more varied and imaginative the final program. In this step, place emphasis on brainstorming, creating, and innovating without restriction. The finished curriculum will be deficient if it is limited at this step. Later steps will offer an opportunity to delete inappropriate activities.

Know the Basic Urges of Children

A basic urge is a desire to do or accomplish something. All children have similar urges, which are hereditary or environmentally influenced. Basic urges are linked closely to societal influences and are affected by teachers, parents, and peers. Usually, basic urges are similar among youngsters of all ages and not affected by developmental maturity. These urges provide direction for creating experiences that are child-centered.

The Urge for Movement

Children have an insatiable appetite for moving, performing, and being active. They run for the sheer joy of running. For them, activity is the essence of living. Design a physical education program that takes advantage of this craving for movement.

The Urge for Success and Approval

Children like to achieve and have their achievements recognized. They wilt under criticism and disapproval whereas encouragement and friendly support can promote growth and development. Failure can lead to frustration, lack of interest, and inefficient learning. Successes should far outweigh failures, and students should achieve a measure of success during each class meeting. Activities in the curriculum should be organized and presented in a manner that ensures that students will find an adequate amount of success.

The Urge for Peer Acceptance and Social Competence

Peer acceptance is a basic human need. Children want others to accept, respect, and like them. Teach and encourage peer acceptance in physical education and the overall school environment. Learning to cooperate with others, being a contributing team member, and sharing accomplishments with friends are important outcomes of the program.

The Urge to Cooperate and Compete

Children want to work and play with other children. They find satisfaction in being a needed part of a group and experience sadness when others reject them. Cooperation needs to be taught prior to competitive experiences since competition is impossible when people choose not to cooperate or follow the rules. Often, the joy of being part of a group far outweighs the gains from peer competition.

The Urge for Physical Fitness and Attractiveness

Boys and girls are eager to be fit, active, and attractive. Youngsters who have any type of disability suffer much humiliation. The opportunity to improve personal skills often helps students overcome subpar strength, lack of physical skill, inadequate physical fitness, and obesity.

The Urge for Adventure

The drive to participate in something different, adventurous, or unusual impels children to participate in interesting new activities. Youngsters are motivated by new and exciting activities and teaching methodologies. When youngsters want to know "what are we going to do today?" they are hopeful of something new and exciting. This urge is one of the reasons that physical education units in elementary schools should not be longer than 2 to 3 weeks in length.

The Urge for Creative Satisfaction

Children like to try different ways of doing things, to experiment with different implements, and find creative ways of accomplishing goals. Finding different ways to express themselves physically satisfies the urge for creative action.

The Urge for Rhythmic Expression

Physical education offers a variety of rhythmic activities that students can learn well enough to achieve satisfaction. Emphasize the natural rhythm involved in all physical activity, be it walking, running, or skipping. Many effective and beautiful sport movements can be done rhythmically, including shooting a lay-up, jumping a rope, and running hurdles.

The Urge to Know

Young people are naturally curious. They are interested not only in what they are doing but also in why they are doing it. Knowing why is a great motivator. It takes little time or effort to share with a class why an activity is performed and the contributions it makes to physical development.

Understand the Characteristics and Interests of Children

The urges of children represent broad traits that are typical of children regardless of age, sex, or race. In contrast, characteristics and interests are age- and maturity-specific attributes that influence learning objectives. The characteristics and interests chart (Table 8.1) provides information that influences appropriate selection and sequencing of curriculum activities. The information in the chart is broken out by the three learning domains—psychomotor, cognitive, and affective—and is grouped by developmental levels, which are discussed in the next section.

Step Six: Organize Selected Activities into Instructional Units

After appropriate activities that contribute to content standards have been selected, design a delivery system that assures all activities are taught. Activities are most often grouped by grade level or developmental level. Developmental levels are used to group activities and units of instruction in this textbook because it allows for greater variation of skill development among students. Figure 8.1 on page 164 illustrates the continuum of skill development through which most youngsters progress. Even though this developmental skill continuum is common to all youngsters, there are large variations among children. Placing activities in developmental levels offers activities that are appropriate for the maturity and developmental levels of all youngsters. On occasion, it may be necessary to move to a higher or lower developmental level to accommodate youngsters. Table 8.2 on page 164 shows how developmental levels roughly equate with grades and ages. The following section describes characteristics of learners at each level and identifies skills and competencies typical of children in each of the levels. Refer back to Table 3.2 in Chapter 3 for a summary of characteristics of activities at the three developmental levels.

Developmental Level I

For the majority of children, activities placed in developmental level I are appropriate for kindergarten through second-grade children. Most activities for younger children are individual in nature and center on learning movement concepts through theme development. Children learn about movement principles, and educational movement themes are used to teach body identification and body management skills. By stressing the joy and personal benefits of physical activity, positive behaviors can be developed that last a lifetime.

TABLE 8.1 Characteristics and interests of children

Characteristics and Interests	Program Guidelines
Developmental Level I	
Psychomotor Domain	
Noisy, constantly active, egocentric, exhibitionistic. Imitative and imaginative. Want attention.	Include vigorous games and stunts, games with individual roles (hunting, dramatic activities, story plays), and a few team games or relays.
Large muscles more developed; game skills not developed.	Challenge with varied movement. Develop specialized skills of throwing, catching, and bouncing balls.
Naturally rhythmic.	Use music and rhythm with skills. Provide creative rhythms, folk dances, and singing movement songs.
May become suddenly tired but soon recover.	Use activities of brief duration. Provide short rest periods or intersperse physically demanding activities with less vigorous ones.
Hand-eye coordination developing.	Give opportunity to handle different objects, such as balls, beanbags, and hoops.
Perceptual abilities maturing.	Give practice in balance—unilateral, bilateral, and cross-lateral movements.
Pelvic tilt can be pronounced.	Give attention to posture problems. Provide abdominal strengthening activities.
Cognitive Domain	
Short attention span	Change activity often. Give short explanations.
Interested in what the body can do. Curious.	Provide movement experiences. Pay attention to educational movement.
Want to know. Often ask *why* about movement.	Explain reasons for various activities and the basis of movement.
Express individual views and ideas.	Allow children time to be creative. Expect problems when children are lined up and asked to perform the same task.
Begin to understand the idea of teamwork.	Plan situations that require group cooperation. Discuss the importance of such.
Sense of humor expands.	Insert some humor in the teaching process.
Highly creative.	Allow students to try new and different ways of performing activities; sharing ideas with friends encourages creativity.
Affective Domain	
No gender differences in interests.	Set up same activities for boys and girls.
Sensitive and individualistic; self-concept very important.	Teach taking turns, sharing, and learning to win, lose, or be caught gracefully.
Accept defeat poorly. Like small-group activity.	Use entire class group sparingly. Break into smaller groups.
Sensitive to feelings of adults. Like to please teacher.	Give frequent praise and encouragement.
Can be reckless.	Stress safe approaches.
Enjoy rough-and-tumble activity.	Include rolling, dropping to the floor, and so on, in both introductory and program activities. Stress simple stunts and tumbling.
Seek personal attention.	Recognize individuals through both verbal and nonverbal means. See that all have a chance to be the center of attention.
Love to climb and explore play environments.	Provide play materials, games, and apparatus for strengthening large muscles (e.g., climbing towers, climbing ropes, jump ropes, miniature Challenge Courses, and turning bars).

(continued)

TABLE 8.1 Characteristics and interests of children *(continued)*

Characteristics and Interests	Program Guidelines
Developmental Level II	
Psychomotor Domain	
Capable of rhythmic movement.	Continue creative rhythms, singing movement songs, and folk dancing.
Improved hand-eye and perceptual-motor coordination.	Give opportunity for manipulating hand apparatus. Provide movement experience and practice in perceptual-motor skills (right and left, unilateral, bilateral, and cross-lateral movements).
More interest in sports.	Begin introductory sport and related skills and simple lead-up activities.
Sport-related skill patterns mature in some cases.	Emphasize practice in these skill areas through simple ball games, stunts, and rhythmic patterns.
Developing interest in fitness.	Introduce some of the specialized fitness activities to 3rd grade.
Reaction time slow.	Avoid highly organized ball games that require and place a premium on quickness and accuracy.
Cognitive Domain	
Still active but attention span longer. More interest in group play.	Include active big-muscle program and more group activity. Begin team concept in activity and relays.
Curious to see what they can do. Love to be challenged and will try anything.	Offer challenges involving movement problems and more critical demands in stunts, tumbling, and apparatus work. Emphasize safety and good judgment.
Interest in group activities; ability to plan with others developing.	Offer group activities and simple dances that involve cooperation with a partner or a team.
Affective Domain	
Like physical contact and belligerent games.	Include dodging games and other active games, as well as rolling stunts.
Developing more interest in skills. Want to excel.	Organize practice in a variety of throwing, catching, and moving skills, as well as others.
Becoming more conscious socially.	Teach need to abide by rules and play fairly. Teach social customs and courtesy in rhythmic areas.
Like to perform well and to be admired for accomplishments.	Begin to stress quality. Provide opportunity to achieve.
Essentially honest and truthful.	Accept children's word. Give opportunity for trust in game and relay situations.
Do not lose willingly.	Provide opportunity for children to learn to accept defeat gracefully and to win with humility.
Gender difference still of little importance.	Avoid separation of genders in any activity.

Developmental Level II

Developmental level II activities are usually appropriate for the majority of third- and fourth-grade children. In developmental level II activities, refinement of fundamental skills occurs and the ability to perform specialized skills begins to surface. Practicing manipulative skills enhances visual-tactile coordination. This is a time when children explore, experiment, and create activities without fear. While not stressing conformity, children learn the how and also the why of activity patterns. Cooperation with peers receives more emphasis through group and team play. Initial instruction in sport skills begins in developmental level II, and a number of lead-up activities allow youngsters to apply newly learned skills in a small-group setting.

TABLE 8.1 Characteristics and interests of children *(continued)*

Characteristics and Interests	Program Guidelines
Developmental Level III	
Psychomotor Domain	
Steady growth. Girls often grow more rapidly than boys.	Continue vigorous program to enhance physical development.
Muscular coordination and skills improving. Interested in learning detailed techniques.	Continue emphasis on teaching skills through drills, lead-up games, and free practice periods. Emphasize correct form.
Differences in physical capacity and skill development.	Offer flexible standards so all find success. In team activities, match teams evenly so individual skill levels are less apparent.
Posture problems may appear.	Include posture correction and special posture instruction; emphasize effect of body carriage on self-concept.
Sixth-grade girls may show signs of maturity; may not wish to participate in all activities.	Have consideration for their problems. Encourage participation on a limited basis, if necessary.
Sixth-grade boys are rougher and stronger.	Keep genders together for skill development but separate for competition in certain rougher activities.
Cognitive Domain	
Want to know rules of games.	Include instruction on rules, regulations, and traditions.
Knowledgeable about and interested in sport and game strategy.	Emphasize strategy, as opposed to merely performing a skill without concern for context.
Question the relevance and importance of various activities.	Explain regularly the reasons for performing activities and learning various skills.
Desire information about the importance of physical fitness and health-related topics.	Include in lesson plans brief explanations of how various activities enhance growth and development.
Affective Domain	
Enjoy team and group activity. Competitive urge strong.	Include many team games, relays, and combatives.
Much interest in sports and sport-related activities.	Offer a variety of sports in season, with emphasis on lead-up games.
Little interest in the opposite gender. Some antagonism may arise.	Offer coeducational activities with emphasis on individual differences of all participants, regardless of gender.
Acceptance of self-responsibility. Strong increase in drive toward independence.	Provide leadership and followership opportunities on a regular basis. Involve students in evaluation procedures.
Intensive desire to excel both in skill and in physical capacity.	Stress physical fitness. Include fitness and skill surveys both to motivate and to check progress.
Sportsmanship a concern for both teachers and students.	Establish and enforce fair rules. With enforcement include an explanation of the need for rules and cooperation if games are to exist.
Peer group important. Want to be part of the gang.	Stress group cooperation in play and among teams. Rotate team positions as well as squad makeup.

Developmental Level III

Developmental level III activities place more emphasis on specialized skills and sport activities. The majority of activities at this level are used with fifth- and sixth-grade students. Football, basketball, softball, track and field, volleyball, and hockey are added to sport offerings. Students learn and improve sport skills while participating in cooperative sport lead-up games. Less emphasis is placed on movement concept activities, and a larger percentage of instructional time is devoted to manipulative activity. Adequate time is set aside for the rhythmic program and for the program area involving apparatus, stunts, and tumbling.

After assigning activities to developmental levels, the activities in each unit are organized in order of difficulty,

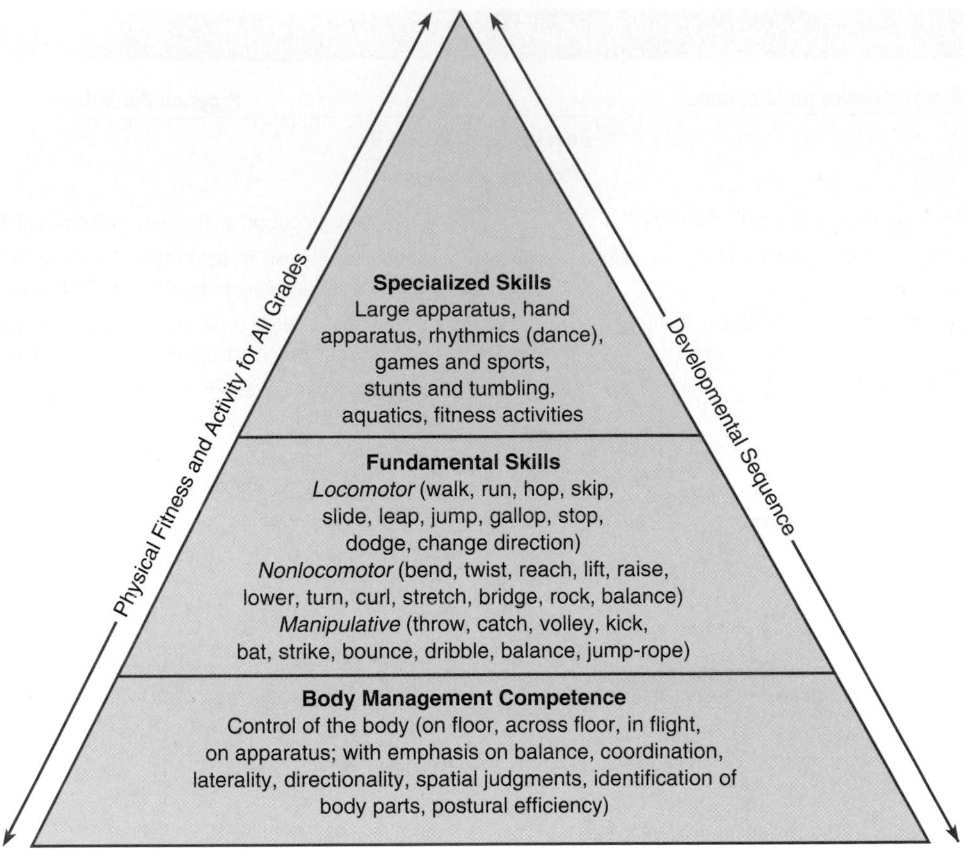

FIGURE 8.1 Continuum of skill development.

starting with the easiest to master and finishing with the most difficult. Organizing activities in progression (a) helps assure children will meet success because the easiest activities are taught first, (b) ensures that safety and liability factors are met, since the activities are presented in proper sequence, and (c) aids teachers in finding a starting point for sound instruction.

Another element that should be included in the unit of instruction is a list of teaching hints that encompass safety, teaching for quality, dispersing equipment properly, and instructional cues that enhance motor skill development. An accompanying lesson plan text by Pangrazi (2004) incorporates activities in this textbook and places them into lesson plans by developmental level. The lesson plans contain activity progressions, teaching hints, and learning objectives that help minimize the demands of planning. In addition to the weekly lesson plans, a yearlong curriculum plan is offered for each of the three developmental levels.

TABLE 8.2 Equating developmental levels to grades and ages

Developmental Level	Grades	Ages
I	K–2	5–7
II	3–4	8–9
III	5–6	10–11

Table 8.3 illustrates the parallel listing of the four parts of the lesson in the yearly plan. This plan ensures that youngsters learn many ways of warming up for activity and approximately 15 different types of fitness activity. In addition, they are exposed to 20 to 25 lesson activities that focus on skill development and 60 to 80 low-organized game activities.

Organizing the curriculum into weekly activity units is a common approach. When using this approach, instruction is focused on an activity over an entire week. The weekly plan has three major advantages. First, one comprehensive lesson plan will suffice for the week and keep planning duties manageable. The objective is to move children along the path of learning at an optimal rate. What cannot be covered one day is taught in the next lesson. Second, less orientation instruction is needed after the first day. Safety factors, teaching hints, and key points need only a brief review each day and equipment needs are similar from day to day. Third, progression and learning sequences are evident; both teacher and children can see progress.

TABLE 8.3 An example of a yearly plan: Developmental level II

Week	Introductory Activity	Fitness Development Activity	Lesson Focus Activity	Game Activity
1	Move and freeze on signal	Teacher leader movement challenges	Orientation	Back to Back Whistle Mixer
2	Fundamental movements and stopping	Teacher leader exercises	Manipulative skills using wands and hoops	Hand Hockey Cageball Kickover Home Base
3	Move and assume pose	Teacher leader exercises	Throwing skills (1)	Whistle Mixer Couple Tag Partner Stoop
4	Creative routines	Hexagon Hustle	Football-related activities	Football End Ball Five Passes
5	Four-corners movement	Hexagon Hustle	Manipulative skills using playground balls	Bounce Ball One Step
6	Run, stop, and pivot	Circuit training	Fundamental skills using tug-o-war ropes and relays	Nonda's Car Lot Indianapolis 500
7	European running	Circuit training	Stunts and tumbling skills (1)	Whistle Mixer Competitive Circle Contests Alaska Baseball
8	Magic number challenges	Astronaut drills	Soccer-related activities (1)	Circle Kickball Soccer Touch Ball Diagonal Soccer Soccer Take-Away
9	New leader	Astronaut drills	Soccer-related activities (2)	Soccer Touch Ball Diagonal Soccer Dribblerama Bull's Eye
10	Group over and under	Aerobic fitness	Fundamental skills using parachutes	Nine Lives Box Ball
11	Bend, stretch, and shake	Aerobic fitness	PE Games Recreational activities	Addition Tag Alaska Baseball Recreational Activities
12	Fastest tag in the West	Walk, trot, and jog	Walking and jogging skills	Recreational Activities
13	Jumping and hopping patterns	Challenge course fitness	Rhythms (l)	Whistle March Arches Home Base
14	Group tag	Walk, trot, and jog	Long rope-jumping skills	Fly Trap Trades Fox Hunt
15	Fleece ball fun	Challenge course	Stunts and tumbling skills (2)	Partner Stoop Crows and Cranes
16	Ball activities	Challenge course	Rhythms (2)	Fox Hunt Steal the Treasure Addition Tag
17	Partner leaping	Aerobic fitness and partner resistance	Basketball-related activities (1)	Birdie in the Cage Dribblerama Captain Ball Basketball Tag

(continued)

TABLE 8.3 An example of a yearly plan: Developmental level II *(continued)*

Week	Introductory Activity	Fitness Development Activity	Lesson Focus Activity	Game Activity
18	Bridges by three	Aerobic fitness and partner resistance	Basketball-related activities (2)	Captain Ball Five passes Around the Key
19	Locomotor and manipulative activity	Exercise to music	Throwing skills (2)	In the Prison Snowball Center Target Throw Target Ball Throw
20	Yarnball fun	Exercise to music	Fundamental skills using benches	Cageball Kickover Squad Tag
21	Low organizational games	Continuity drills	Hockey-related activities (1)	Circle Keepaway Star Wars Hockey Lane Hockey Circle Straddleball
22	Following activity	Continuity drills	Hockey-related activities (2)	Modified Hockey Lane Hockey
23	Moving to music	Aerobic fitness	Manipulative skills using paddle and balls	Steal the Treasure Trees
24	Stretching activities	Stretching activities	Track-and-field skills (1)	Potato Shuttle Relay Shuttle Relays
25	Stretching activities	Stretching activities	Track-and-field skills (2)	Circular Relays Shuttle Relays One-on-one contests
26	Move and perform task	Walk, trot, and jog	Manipulative skills using beanbags	Crows and Cranes Galloping Lizzie
27	Long rope routine	Parachute fitness	Rhythms (3)	Jump the Shot Beachball Batball Club Guard
28	Squad leader movement	Parachute fitness	Stunts and tumbling skills (3)	Trades Beachball Batball
29	European running with equipment	Exercise to music	Individual rope-jumping	Loose Caboose Wolfe's Beanbag Exchange Tag
30	Marking	Circuit training	Volleyball-related skills (1)	Beachball Volleyball Informal Volleyball
31	Tag games	Hexagon Hustle	Volleyball-related skills (2)	Beachball Volleyball Shower Service Ball
32	Combination movement patterns	Continuity drills	Rhythms (4)	Alaska Baseball Addition Tag
33	European running with variations	Aerobic fitness	Manipulative skills using frisbees	Frisbee Keepaway Frisbee Golf
34	Tortoise and hare	Aerobic fitness	Fundamental skills using balance beams	Hand Hockey Nonda's Car Lot
35	Move and perform task	Parachute exercises	Softball-related activities (1)	Throw It and Run Two-Pitch Softball Hit and Run
36	Walk, trot, and sprint	Teacher leader exercises	Softball-related activities (2)	Beat Ball Kick Softball In a Pickle

Each unit starts with basic skills and progresses to a point where further instruction and skill practice is necessary because students cannot perform adequately. Starting each unit with the easiest activity ensures success and review for all students. Instructional sequences for each day are built on the preceding lesson. An objection raised by some teachers is that a weekly unit program does not have enough variety, causing some children to tire of the same activities presented over a longer period. To remedy this, schedule units so the same type of activity is not presented for more than 2 weeks in succession. If more time is needed for a specific unit, add another week or two later in the year. Use a game activity to provide a change of pace when the motivational level of the class (and, in turn, the teacher) appears to be waning.

Another approach to yearly planning is to use a movement theme approach. This approach takes a set of skills or movements and offers a wide variety of activities for instruction related to the same skill. A wide variety of equipment is needed since the same skills are taught using different activities and equipment.

Check the Scope, Sequence, and Balance of the Curriculum

An important step in creating a quality program is to review and monitor the scope, sequence, and balance of the curriculum. These are important concepts that assure the curriculum is comprehensive and varied.

Scope is the yearly content of the curriculum. Scope is also referred to as the horizontal articulation of the curriculum. Monitoring the scope of the curriculum ensures that the entire content of the program will be covered in a systematic and accountable fashion. In elementary school physical education, the scope of the curriculum is broad; many activities are presented rather than in-depth coverage of a few activities. The reason for this is that student interest wanes if units are too long. Also, elementary school physical education is designed to help students learn about all the available types of physical activity.

Sequence, or vertical articulation, of the curriculum defines the skills and activities to be covered on a year-to-year basis. Sequence ensures that youngsters receive different instruction and activities at each developmental level. Of particular importance is the articulation of program material throughout elementary, junior, and senior high school programs.

Balance ensures that all objectives in the program receive adequate coverage. When reviewing the scope and sequence of the curriculum, checking for balance avoids a skewing toward one particular area. To assure balance, major areas of emphasis are determined based on program objectives. These areas can be allotted a percentage of program time based on the characteristics and interests of students. This determination reveals to administrators, teachers, and parents the direction and emphasis of the program. All areas have a proportionate share of instructional time, and the percentage of time allotted to each area reflects the needs and characteristics.

Another phase of balance is to alternate units based on the type of student interaction required, that is, individual, dual (partner), small group, or large group activities. Team sports require organization in a large group, whereas a movement concepts lesson is individual in nature. Learning to catch is a partner activity, whereas a lead-up game requires small groups. The yearly plans in *Dynamic Physical Education Lesson Plans* (2004) are balanced in this manner. Individual units are followed by a small or large group activity, etc. Balance ensures children do not have to stay with one type of activity too long. It gives them a chance to experience the type of organization they enjoy on a regular basis.

Step Seven: Evaluate and Modify the Curriculum

Evaluation schedules and suggested techniques for modifying the curriculum are an integral part of the curricular structure. A number of sources can supply evaluative data: pupils, teachers, consultants, parents, and administrators. The type of data desired can vary. Achievement test scores can supply hard data to compare preassessments and postassessments with those of other programs. Subjective assessments might include likes and dislikes, value judgments, problem areas, and needed adjustments. The evaluation schedule can select a limited area for assessment, or assessment can be broadened to cover the entire program. Collecting information is only the first step; the information must be translated into action. Modification of possible program deficiencies is based on sound educational philosophy. If the program has weak spots, identifying the weaknesses and determining the causes are important steps to take.

A pilot or trial project can be instituted if the new curriculum represents a radical change. One school in the district might be chosen to develop a pilot program. Site selection should offer the program a strong opportunity to succeed, for success depends in large part on the educational climate of the school. In some cases, the experimental program might be implemented with only one class in a school. Enthusiastic, skilled direction is necessary for such projects. Much information can be derived from this pilot process before an entire program is implemented throughout the school system.

REFLECTION AND REVIEW QUESTIONS

How and Why

1. What is your value orientation for physical education? How will this influence your teaching?
2. Why have a curriculum?
3. Who should be involved in the curriculum development?
4. What issues must be considered by curriculum designers?
5. Are the needs, interests, and characteristics of elementary students the same today as they were 30 years ago?

Content Review

1. List and discuss the six steps for designing a quality physical education curriculum.
2. What environmental factors can impact a curriculum? Discuss your answers.
3. Define and discuss the importance of standards and student objectives.
4. Explain the importance of student-centered objectives.
5. Explain the role of the scope, sequence, and balance of a curriculum.
6. What are the three learning domains? Explain each.
7. What components are common to quality physical education curricula?
8. What needs, characteristics, and interests of children must be considered when designing a physical education curriculum? Include comments regarding the impact of age and maturity on program development.

FOR MORE INFORMATION

References and Suggested Readings

Barrett, K. R., Williams, K., & Whitall, J. (1992). What does it mean to have a "developmentally appropriate physical education program"? *The Physical Educator,* 49(3), 113–117.

Bloom, B. S. (Ed.). (1956). *Taxonomy of educational objectives, the classification of educational goals, handbook I: The cognitive domain.* New York: David McKay.

Chepko, S., & Arnold, R. K. (Eds.). (2000). *Guidelines for physical education programs, K–12: Standards, objectives and assessments.* Boston: Allyn and Bacon.

Corbin, C. B. (1976). *Becoming physically educated in the elementary school.* Philadelphia: Lea & Febiger.

Gabbard, C. (1994). *Physical education for children: Building the foundation.* 2nd ed. Boston: Allyn and Bacon.

Gallahue, D. L. (1995). *Developmental physical education for today's elementary school children.* 3rd ed. New York: McGraw-Hill.

Graham, G., Holt/Hale, S. A., & Parker, M. (2001). *Children moving.* 5th ed. Mountain View, CA: Mayfield.

Jewett, A., Bain, L., & Ennis, K., 1995. *The curriculum process in physical education.* Dubuque, IA: Wm. C. Brown and Benchmark.

Kirchner, G., & Fishburne, G. J. (1998). *Physical education for elementary school children.* 10th ed. Boston: WCB/McGraw-Hill.

Krathwohl, D. R., Bloom, B. S., & Masia, B. B. (1964). *Taxonomy of educational objectives, handbook II: Affective domain.* New York: David McKay.

Lambert, L. T. (1999). *Standards-based assessment of student learning: A comprehensive approach.* Reston, VA: National Association for Sport and Physical Education.

Melograno, V. J. (1996). *Designing the physical education curriculum.* 3rd ed. Champaign, IL: Human Kinetics.

Mosston, M., & Ashworth, S. (1994). *Teaching physical education.* 4th ed. New York: Macmillan.

National Association for Sport and Physical Education. (1995). *Moving into the future national physical education standards: A guide to content and assessment.* St. Louis, MO: Mosby-Year Book.

Pangrazi, R. P. (2004). *Lesson plans for dynamic physical education for elementary school children.* 14th ed. San Francisco: Benjamin Cummings.

Rink, J. E. (1998). *Teaching physical education for learning.* 3rd ed. Boston: WCB/McGraw-Hill.

Siedentop, D., & Tannehill, D. (2000). *Developing teaching skills in physical education.* 4th ed. Mountain View, CA: Mayfield Publishing Co.

Wuest, D., & Lombardo, B. (1994). *Curriculum and instruction: The secondary school physical education experience.* St. Louis, MO: Mosby.

Websites

Learning Domains
http://coe.sdsu.edu/eet/Articles/BloomsLD/index.htm

Sample Curricula
http://www.sasked.gov.sk.ca/docs/physed/physed1-5/index.html
http://schools.eastnet.ecu.edu/pitt/ayden/pesites9.htm
http://www.republic.k12.mo.us/guide/pe.htm

CHAPTER 9

Legal Liability, Supervision, and Safety

	ESSENTIAL COMPONENTS
I	Organized around content standards
II	Student-centered and developmentally appropriate
III	Physical activity and motor skill development form the core of the program
IV	Teaches management skills and self-discipline
V	Promotes inclusion of all students
VI	Focuses on process over product
VII	Promotes lifetime personal health and wellness
VIII	Teaches cooperation and responsibility and promotes sensitivity to diversity

	PHYSICAL EDUCATION STANDARDS
1	Students are able to move competently using a variety of fundamental and specialized motor skills
2	Students can monitor and maintain a health-enhancing level of physical fitness.
3	Students are able to apply movement concepts and basic mechanics of skill performance when learning and refining motor skills.
4	Students comprehend the basic principles of wellness and are able to apply concepts that enable them to make meaningful decisions that positively impact their health and wellness.
5	Students participate in a wide variety of physical activities and learn how to maintain a personalized active lifestyle.
6	Students demonstrate empathy, understanding, and respect for the numerous differences exhibited by people in an activity setting.
7	**Students exhibit responsible and self-directed behaviors that lead to positive social interactions in physical activity.**

SUMMARY

This chapter explains the various legal terms and situations associated with physical education and describes instructional and administrative procedures common to the responsible and prudent conduct of the physical education program. It is a teacher's legal responsibility to create a safe environment in which risk and the opportunity for injury are minimized and to provide a standard of care that any reasonable and prudent professional with similar training would apply under the given circumstances. Safety instruction is designed to prevent accidents and should be included in lesson plans to ensure coverage. A comprehensive safety checklist is included to be sure that beginning teachers understand how to establish an accident-free environment.

OUTCOMES

- Define tort, negligence, liability, malfeasance, misfeasance, nonfeasance, and other terms common to legal suits brought against educators.
- List major points that must be established to determine negligence on the part of the teacher.
- Explain how to examine all activities, equipment, and facilities for possible hazards and sources of accidents.
- Identify common defenses against negligence.
- Describe supervisory responsibilities expected of all teachers.
- List guidelines for the proper supervision of instruction, equipment, and facilities.
- Describe aspects of sport programs that often give rise to lawsuits.
- Understand how to ensure safety, focusing on prevention.
- Outline an emergency care plan.

School district personnel, including teaching and nonteaching members, are obligated to exercise ordinary care for the safety of students. This duty is manifested as the ability to anticipate reasonably foreseeable dangers and the responsibility to take necessary precautions to prevent problems from occurring. Failure to do so may cause the district to be the target of lawsuits.

Compared with other subject matter areas, physical education is particularly vulnerable to accidents and resultant injuries. More than 50 percent of all accidents in the school setting occur on the playground and in the gymnasium. Even though schools cannot be held financially accountable for costs associated with treatment of injuries, they can be forced to pay these expenses if the injured party sues and wins judgment. Legal suits are conducted under respective state statutes. Principles underlying legal action are similar, but certain regulations and procedures vary among states. You should acquire a copy of the legal liability policy for your district. Districts usually have a written definition of situations in which teachers can be held liable.

All students have the right to freedom from injury caused by others or due to participation in a program. Courts have ruled that teachers owe their students a duty of care to protect them from harm. Teachers must offer a standard of care that any reasonable and prudent professional with similar training would apply under the given circumstances. A teacher is required to exercise the teaching skill, discretion, and knowledge that members of the profession in good standing normally possess in similar situations. Lawsuits usually occur when citizens believe that this standard of care was not exercised.

Liability is the responsibility to perform a duty to a particular group. It is an obligation to perform in a particular way that is required by law and enforced by court action. Teachers are bound by contract to carry out their duties in a reasonable and prudent manner. Liability is always a legal matter. It must be proved in a court of law that negligence occurred before one can be held liable.

TORTS

In education, a *tort* is concerned with the teacher–student relationship and is a legal wrong that results in direct or indirect injury to another individual or to property. *Black's Law Dictionary* (1996) defines a tort as

> a private or civil wrong or injury, other than breach of contract, for which the court will provide a remedy in the form of an action for damages. Three elements of every tort action are: existence of legal duty from defendant to plaintiff, breach of duty, and damage as proximate result.

As the result of a tort, the court can give a monetary reward for damages that occurred. The court can also give a monetary reward for punitive damages if a breach of duty can be established. Usually, the court rewards the offended individual for damages that occurred due to the negligence of the instructor or other responsible individual. Punitive damages are much less common.

NEGLIGENCE AND LIABILITY

Liability is usually concerned with a breach of duty through negligence. Lawyers examine the situation that gave rise to the injury to establish if liability can be determined. Four major points must be established to determine if a teacher is negligent.

1. *Duty.* The first point considered is that of duty owed to the participants. Did the school or teacher owe students a duty of care that implies conforming to certain standards of conduct? When examining duty or breach of duty, the court looks at reasonable care that a member of the profession in good standing would provide. In other words, to determine a reasonable standard, the court uses the conduct of other teachers as a standard for comparison.
2. *Breach of duty.* A teacher must commit a breach of duty by failing to conform to the required duty. After it is established that a duty was required, it must be proved that such duty was not performed. Two situations are possible: (a) the teacher did something that was not supposed to be done (for example, put boxing gloves on students to resolve their differences), or (b) the teacher did not do something that should have been done (for example, failed to teach an activity using proper progressions).
3. *Injury.* An injury must occur if liability is to be established. If no injury or harm occurs, there is no liability. Further, it must be proved that the injured party is entitled to compensatory damages for financial loss or physical discomfort.
4. *Proximate cause.* The failure to conform to the required standard must be the proximate cause of the resulting injury. It must be proved that the injury was caused by the teacher's breach of duty. It is not enough to prove simply that a breach of duty occurred. It must simultaneously be shown that the injury was a direct result of the teacher's failure to provide a reasonable standard of care.

Foreseeability

A key to the issue of negligence is foreseeability. Courts expect that a trained professional is able to foresee potentially harmful situations. Was it possible for the teacher to predict and anticipate the danger of the harmful act or situation and to take appropriate measures to prevent it from occurring? If the injured party can prove that the teacher should have foreseen the danger involved in an activity or situation (even in part), the teacher will be found negligent for failing to act in a reasonable and prudent manner.

This points out the necessity of examining all activities, equipment, and facilities for possible hazards and sources of accident. For example, a common game (unfortunately) in many school settings is bombardment, or dodge ball. Suppose that during the game, a student is hit in the eye by a ball and loses vision in that eye. Was this a foreseeable accident that could have been prevented? Were the balls being used capable of inflicting serious injury? Were students aware of rules that might have prevented this injury? Were the abilities of the students somewhat equal, or were some capable of throwing with such velocity that injury was predictable? Were all students forced to play the game? These questions would likely be considered in court in an attempt to prove that the teacher should have been able to predict the overly dangerous situation.

TYPES OF NEGLIGENCE

Negligence is defined by the courts as conduct that falls below a standard of care established to protect others from unreasonable risk or harm. Several types of negligence can be categorized.

Malfeasance

Malfeasance occurs when a teacher does something improper by committing an act that is unlawful and wrongful, with no legal basis (often referred to as an *act of commission*). Malfeasance can be illustrated by the following incident. A male student misbehaved on numerous occasions. In desperation, the teacher gave the student a choice of punishment—a severe spanking in front of the class or running many laps around the field. The student chose the former and suffered physical and emotional damage. Even though the student was given a choice whereby he could have avoided the paddling, the teacher is still liable for any physical or emotional harm caused.

Misfeasance

Misfeasance occurs when a teacher follows proper procedures but does not perform according to the required standard of conduct. Misfeasance is based on performance of the proper action, but not up to the required standard. It is usually the subpar performance of an act that might have been otherwise lawfully done. An example would be the teacher's offering to spot a student during a tumbling routine and then not doing the spotting properly. If the student is injured due to a faulty spot, the teacher can be held liable.

Nonfeasance

Nonfeasance is based on lack of action in carrying out a duty. This is usually an *act of omission*: The teacher knew the proper procedures but failed to follow them. Teachers can be found negligent if they act or fail to act. Understanding and carrying out proper procedures and duties in a manner befitting members of the profession are essential. In contrast to the misfeasance example, nonfeasance occurs when a teacher knows that it is necessary to spot certain gymnastic routines but fails to do so. Courts expect teachers to behave with more skill and insight than parents do (Strickland, Phillip, & Phillips, 1976). Teachers are expected to behave with greater competency because they have been educated to give students a higher standard of professional care than have parents.

Contributory Negligence

The situation is different when the injured student is partially or wholly at fault. Students are expected to exercise sensible care and to follow directions or regulations designed to protect them from injury. Improper behavior by the injured party that causes the accident is usually ruled to be *contributory negligence,* because the injured party contributed to the resulting harm. This responsibility is directly related to the maturity, ability, and experience of the child. For example, most states have laws specifying that a child under 7 years of age is incapable of contributory negligence (Baley & Matthews, 1984). To illustrate contributory negligence, assume that a teacher has thoroughly explained safety rules to be followed while hitting softballs. As students begin to practice, one of them runs through a restricted area that is well marked and is hit by a bat. Depending on the age and maturity of the child, the possibility is strong that the student will be held liable for such action.

Comparative or Shared Negligence

Under the doctrine of comparative negligence, the injured party can recover only if found to be less negligent than the defendant (the teacher). Where statutes apply, the amount of recovery is generally reduced in proportion to the injured party's participation in the circumstances leading to the injury.

COMMON DEFENSES AGAINST NEGLIGENCE

Negligence must be proved in a court of law. Many times, teachers are negligent in carrying out their duties, yet the injured party does not take the case to court. If a teacher is sued, some of the following defenses are used in an attempt to show that the teacher's action was not the primary cause of the accident.

Act of God

The act of God defense places the cause of injury on forces beyond the control of the teacher or the school. The defense is made that it was impossible to predict an unsafe condition, but through an act of God, the injury occurred. Typical acts would be a gust of wind that blew over a volleyball standard or a cloudburst of rain that made a surface slick. The act of God defense can be used only in cases in which the injury still would have occurred even though reasonable and prudent action had been taken.

Proximate Cause

This defense attempts to prove that the accident was not caused by the negligence of the teacher. There must be a close relationship between the breach of duty by the teacher and the injury. This is a common defense in cases dealing with proper supervision. Imagine a student is participating in an activity supervised by the teacher. When the teacher leaves the playing area to get a cup of coffee, the student is injured. The defense lawyer will try to show that the accident would have occurred regardless of whether the teacher was there.

Assumption of Risk

Clearly, physical education is a high-risk activity when compared with most other curriculum areas. The participant assumes the risk accompanying the activity when choosing to be part of that activity. The assumption of risk defense is seldom used by physical education teachers because students are not often allowed to choose to participate or not participate. An instructor for an elective program that allows students to choose desired units of instruction might find this a better defense than one who teaches a totally required program. Athletic and sport club participation is by choice, and players must assume a greater risk in activities such as football and gymnastics.

Contributory Negligence

Contributory negligence is often used by the defense in an attempt to convince the court that the injured party acted in a manner that was abnormal. In other words, the injured individual did not act in a manner that was typical of students of similar age and maturity. The defense attempts to demonstrate that the activity or equipment in question was used for years with no record of accident. A case is made based on the manner of presentation—how students were taught to act in a safe manner—and that the injured student acted outside the parameters of safe conduct. A key point in this defense is whether the activity was suitable for the age and maturity level of the participants.

AREAS OF RESPONSIBILITY

A two-tiered approach for analyzing injuries is useful for determining responsibility. The first tier includes duties the administration must assume in support of the program. The second tier defines duties of the instructor or staff member charged with teaching or supervising students. Each party has a role to fill, but some overlap occurs. The following example illustrates the differences.

A student is hurt while performing a tumbling stunt. A lawsuit ensues, charging the teacher with negligence for not following safe procedures. The administration could also be included in the suit, being charged with negligence for hiring an incompetent (not qualified) instructor. Two levels of responsibility should be considered when delegating responsibility because:

1. They identify different functions and responsibilities of the teaching staff and administration.
2. They provide a framework for reducing injuries and improving safety procedures.
3. They provide perspective for following legal precedents.
4. In the described responsibilities that follow, both administrative and instructional duties are presented.

Supervision

All activities in a school setting must be supervised, including recess, lunch times, and field trips. The responsibilities of the school are critical if supervision is to function properly.

Administration

Two levels are identified in supervision: general and specific. General supervision (for example, playground duty) refers to broad coverage, when students are not under direct control of a teacher or a designated individual. A plan of supervision should be made, designating the areas to be covered and including where and how the supervisor should rotate. This plan, kept in the principal's office, should cover rules of conduct governing student behavior. Rules should be posted prominently on bulletin boards, especially in classrooms. In addition to the plan, administrators must select qualified personnel, provide necessary training, and monitor the plan properly.

The general supervisor is concerned primarily with student behavior, focusing on the student's right to a relaxing recreational experience. Supervisors should observe the area, looking for breaches of discipline, particularly when an individual or group "picks on" another youngster. The supervisor needs to look for protruding sprinkler heads, broken glass, and debris on the play area. If it becomes necessary to leave the area, a qualified substitute must be found to prevent the area from going unsupervised.

Staff

General supervision is necessary during recess, before and after school, during lunch hour break, and during certain other sessions when instruction is not offered. The supervisor should know the school's plan for supervision as well as the emergency care procedures to follow in case of an accident. Supervision is a positive act that requires the supervisor to be actively involved and moving throughout the area. The number of supervisors should be determined by the type of activity, the size of the area, and the number and age of the students.

Specific supervision requires that the instructor be with a certain group of students (a class). An example is spotting students who are performing challenging gymnastic activities. If certain pieces of apparatus require special care and proper use, post rules and regulations near the apparatus (for upper-grade children). Students should be made aware of the rules and should receive appropriate instruction and guidance in applying the rules. When rules are modified, they should be rewritten in proper form. There is no substitute for documentation when the need to defend policies and approaches arises.

When teaching, arrange and teach the class so that all students are in view. This implies supervising from the perimeter of the area. If you are at the center of the student group with many students behind you, it will be impossible to supervise a class safely and effectively. Equipment and apparatus should not go unsupervised at any time when left accessible to students in the area. An example is leaving equipment on the playing field between classes. If other students in the area have easy access to the equipment, they may use it in an unsafe manner, and the teacher can be found liable if an injury occurs.

Do not agree to supervise activities in which you are unqualified to anticipate possible hazards. If this situation arises, send a written memo to the department head or principal stating such lack of insight and qualification. Maintain a copy for your files.

Merriman (1993) offers five recommendations to ensure that adequate supervision occurs:

1. The supervisor must be in the immediate vicinity (within sight and hearing).
2. If required to leave, the supervisor must have an adequate replacement in place before departing. Adequate replacements do not include paraprofessionals, student teachers, custodial help, or untrained teachers.
3. Supervision procedures must be preplanned and incorporated into daily lessons.
4. Supervision procedures should include what to observe and listen for, where to stand for the most effective view, and what to do if a problem arises.
5. Supervision requires that age, maturity, and skill ability of participants must always be considered, as must be the inherent risk of the activity.

Instruction

Instructional responsibility rests primarily with the teacher, but administrative personnel have certain defined functions.

Administration

The administration should review and approve the curricular plan. The curriculum should be reviewed regularly to ensure that it is current and updated. Be sure that activities included in the curriculum are based on contributions they make to the growth and development of youngsters. It makes little sense in a court of law to say that an activity was included "for the fun of it" or "because students liked it." Instead, make sure activities in the curriculum are included because they meet program objectives.

Administrators are obligated to support the program with adequate finances. The principal and higher administrators should visit the program periodically. Familiarity with program content and operation obviates the possibility that practices were occurring without adequate administrative supervision.

Instructional Staff

With regard to instruction, teachers have a duty to protect students from unreasonable physical or mental harm. This includes avoiding any acts or omissions that might cause such harm. Teachers are educated, experienced, and skilled in physical education and must be able to foresee situations that could be harmful.

The major area of concern involving instruction is whether the student received adequate instruction before or during activity participation. Adequate instruction means (a) teaching children how to perform activities correctly and use equipment and apparatus properly, and (b) teaching youngsters necessary safety precautions. If instructions are given, they must be correct, understandable, and include proper technique, or the instructor can be held liable. The risk involved in an activity must be communicated to the learner.

The age and maturity level of students play an important role in the selection of activities. Younger students require more care, instructions that are easy to comprehend, and clear restrictions in the name of safety. Some students have a lack of appropriate fear, and the teacher must be aware of this when discussing safety factors. A very young child may have little concern about performing a high-risk activity if an instructor is nearby. This places much responsibility on giving adequate instruction and supervision.

Careful planning is a necessity. Written curriculum guides and lesson plans can offer a well-prepared approach that withstands scrutiny and examination by other teachers and administrators. Written lesson plans should include proper sequence and progression of skill. Teachers are on defensible grounds if they can show that the progression of activities was based on presentations designed by experts and was followed carefully during the teaching act. District and state guidelines enforcing instructional sequences and restricted activities should be checked closely.

Proper instruction demands that students not be forced to participate. If a youngster is required to perform an activity unwillingly, you may be open to a lawsuit. In a lawsuit dealing with stunts and tumbling (Appenzeller, 1970), the court held the teacher liable when a student claimed that she was not given adequate instruction in how to perform a stunt called "roll over two." The teacher was held liable because the student claimed she was forced to try the stunt before adequate instruction was offered. Gymnastics and tumbling are areas in which lawsuits are prevalent due to a lack of adequate instruction. Posting the proper sequence of skills and lead-up activities may be useful to ensure they have been presented properly. Tread the line carefully between helpful encouragement and forcing students to try new activities.

For teachers who incorporate punishment as a part of the instructional process, the consequences of its use should be examined carefully before implementation. Physical punishment that brings about permanent or long-lasting damage is certainly indefensible. The punishment used must be in line with the physical maturity and health of the student involved. A teacher's practice of having students perform laps when they have misbehaved might go unchallenged for years. However, what if an asthmatic student or a student with congenital heart disease is asked to run and suffers injury or illness? What if the student is running unsupervised and is injured from a fall or suffers heat exhaustion? In these examples, defending such punitive practices would be difficult. Making students perform physical activity for misbehavior is indefensible under any circumstance. If a child is injured while performing physical punishment, teachers are usually found liable and held responsible for the injury.

The following points help ensure safe instruction:

1. Sequence all activities in units of instruction and develop written lesson plans. Problems occur when snap judgments are made under the daily pressure and strain of teaching.
2. Scrutinize high-risk activities to ensure that all safety procedures have been implemented. If in doubt, discuss the activities with experienced teachers and administrators.
3. Activities used in the curriculum must be within the developmental limits of the students. Since the range of maturity and development of youngsters in a class is usually wide, activities may be beyond the ability level of some students.
4. If students' grades are based on the number of activities in which they participate, some students may feel forced to try all activities. Teachers should make it clear to students that the choice to participate belongs to them. When they are afraid of getting hurt, they can elect not to perform an activity.
5. Include in written lesson plans necessary safety equipment. The lesson plan should detail how equipment should be arranged, the placement of mats, and where the instructor will carry out supervision.
6. If a student claims injury or brings a note from parents asking that the student not participate in physical activity, the request must be honored. Excuses are almost always given at the start of the period, when the teacher is busy with many other duties (such as getting equipment ready, taking roll, and opening lockers). It is difficult to make a thoughtful judgment during this time. The school nurse is qualified to make these judgments when they relate to health and should be expected to make such decisions. If the excuses continue over a long period of time, the teacher or nurse should schedule a conference with the parents to rectify the situation.
7. Make sure activities included in the instructional process are in line with the available equipment and facilities. An example is the amount of space available. If a soccer lead-up activity is brought indoors because of inclement weather, it may no longer be a safe and appropriate activity.

8. If spotting is required for safe completion of activities, it should always be done by the instructor or by trained students. Teaching students how to spot is as important as teaching them physical skills. Safe conduct is learned.
9. If students are working independently at stations, carefully constructed and written task cards can help eliminate unsafe practices.
10. Have a written emergency care plan posted in the gymnasium. This plan should be approved by health care professionals and should be followed to the letter when an injury occurs.

EQUIPMENT AND FACILITIES

School responsibility for equipment and facilities is required for both noninstructional and class use.

Administration

The principal and the custodian should oversee the fields and playground equipment that are used for recess and outside activities. Students should be instructed to report broken and unsafe equipment, as well as hazards (glass, cans, rocks), to the principal's office. If equipment is faulty, it should be removed from the area. A regular inspection of equipment and facilities, preferably by the physical education specialist, should be instituted, perhaps weekly. If a specialist is not employed, the inspection will have to be performed by the principal or the custodian. Results of the inspection should be filed with the school district safety committee. Replacement of sawdust, sand, or other shock-absorbing material should be done regularly.

Administrators should have a written checklist of equipment and apparatus for the purpose of recording scheduled safety inspections. Note the date of inspection to show that inspection occurs at regular intervals. If a potentially dangerous situation exists, post rules or warnings so students and teachers are made aware of the risk.

Proper installation of equipment is critical. Climbing equipment and other equipment that must be anchored should be installed by a reputable firm that guarantees its work. When examining apparatus, inspection of the installation is important. Maintenance of facilities is also important. Grass should be kept short, and the grounds inspected for debris. Holes in the ground should be filled, and loose gravel removed. Hazards found on playing fields need to be repaired and eliminated. A proper finish that prevents excessive slipping should be used on indoor floors. Shower rooms should have a roughened floor finish applied to prevent falls when the floors are wet.

Safe participation in an activity can be enhanced by the selection of equipment and facilities. Choice of apparatus and equipment should be based on the growth and developmental levels of students. For example, allowing elementary school children to use a horizontal ladder that was designed for high school students may result in a fall that causes injury. Understand the legal concept of an *attractive nuisance.* This implies that some piece of equipment or apparatus, usually left unsupervised, was so attractive to children that they could not be expected to avoid it. When an injury occurs, even though students may have been using the apparatus incorrectly, teachers and school administration are often held liable because the attractive nuisance should have been removed from the area when unsupervised.

Instructional Staff

Indoor facilities are of primary concern to physical education instructors. Even though the administration is charged with overall responsibility for facilities and equipment, including periodic inspection, the instructor should make a regular safety inspection of the instructional area. If corrective action is needed, the principal or other designated administrator should be notified in writing. Verbal notification is not enough, since it offers little legal protection to the instructor.

Arrange facilities in a safe manner. Often, the side and end lines of playing fields for sports such as football, soccer, and field hockey are placed too close to walls, curbings, or fences. The boundaries should be moved to allow adequate room for deceleration, even though the size of the playing area is reduced. In the gymnasium, students should not run to a line that is close to a wall. Another common hazard is placing basketball hoops too close to the playing area. The poles that support the baskets must be padded.

Proper use of equipment and apparatus is important. Regardless of the state of equipment repair, if it is misused, it may result in an injury. Give students instruction in the proper use of equipment and apparatus before they are issued to the students and used. All safety instruction should be included in the written lesson plan to ensure that all points are covered.

Equipment should be purchased on the basis of quality and safety as well as potential use. Many lawsuits occur because of unsafe equipment and apparatus. The liability for such equipment may rest with the manufacturer, but this has to be proved, which means that the teacher must state, in writing, the exact specifications of the desired equipment. The process of bidding for lower-priced items may result in the purchase of less safe equipment. If teachers have specified proper equipment in writing, however, the possibility of their being held liable for injury is reduced.

THE SPORTS PROGRAM

A common problem for school administrators with elementary school sports programs is providing qualified coaches. The administration should set minimum requirements for coaches and ensure that incompetent individuals are removed from coaching duties. When students are involved in extracurricular activities, teachers (coaches) are responsible for the safe conduct of activities. The following areas often give rise to lawsuits if they are not handled carefully.

Mismatching Opponents

A common error that gives rise to lawsuits is the mismatching of students on the bases of size and ability. Just because the competitors are the same gender and choose to participate does not absolve the instructor of liability if an injury occurs. The question that courts examine is whether an effort was made to match students according to height, weight, and ability. Courts are less understanding about mismatching in the physical education setting compared with an athletic contest, but mismatching is a factor that should be avoided in any situation.

Waiver Forms

Participants in extracurricular activities should be required to sign a responsibility waiver form. The form should explain the risks involved in voluntary participation and discuss briefly the types of injuries that have occurred in the past during practice and competition. Supervisors should remember that waiver slips do not waive the rights of participants, and that teachers and coaches still can be found liable if injuries occur. The waiver form does communicate clearly, however, the risks involved and may be a strong "assumption of risk" defense.

Medical Examinations

Participants must have a medical examination before participating. Records of the examination should be kept on file and should be identified prominently when physical restrictions or limitations exist. It is common to "red dot" the folders of students who have a history of medical problems. Students must not be allowed to participate unless they purchase medical insurance, and evidence of such coverage should be kept in the folders of athletic participants.

Preseason Conditioning

Preseason conditioning should be undertaken in a systematic and progressive fashion. Starting the season with a mile run for time makes little sense if students have not been preconditioned. Be aware of guidelines dealing with heat and humidity. For example, in Arizona, guidelines advise avoiding strenuous activity when the temperature exceeds 85°F and the humidity exceeds 40 percent. When these conditions are exceeded, running is curtailed to 10 minutes and active games to 30 minutes. Students should be hydrated prior to activity, with drinking water available on demand.

Transportation of Students

Whenever students are transported, teachers are responsible for their safety both en route and during the activity. Transportation liability can be avoided by not providing transportation, but instead requiring participants to meet at the site of the event (Pittman, 1993). If the school must provide transportation, licensed drivers and school-approved vehicles should always be used. Travel plans should include official approval from the appropriate school administrator. One special note: If the driver receives pay or reimbursement for the trip, the possibility of being held liable for injury increases dramatically. To make the matter worse, many insurance policies do not cover drivers who receive compensation for transporting students. When teachers transport students and receive reimbursement, a special insurance rider that provides liability coverage for this situation should be purchased.

SAFETY

The major thrust of safety is to prevent situations that cause accidents. It is estimated that over 70 percent of injuries in sport and related activities could be prevented through proper safety procedures. On the other hand, some accidents occur despite precautions, and proper emergency procedures should be established to cope with any situation. A comprehensive study of injuries received in sport and related activities was conducted by the U.S. Consumer Product Safety Commission (1997). This study involved a network of computers in 119 hospital emergency rooms that channeled injury data to a central point. The sports and activities that produced the most injuries were, in order, football, touch football, baseball, basketball, gymnastics, and skiing. The facility that produced the most disabling injuries was the swimming pool.

Learning to recognize potential high-risk situations is an important factor in preventing accidents. Teachers must possess a clear understanding of the hazards and potential dangers of an activity before they can establish controls. Instructors must not assume that participants are aware of the dangers and risks involved in various activities. Students must be told of all dangers and risks before participation.

Guidelines for Safety

1. In-service sessions in safety should be administered by experienced and knowledgeable teachers. Department heads may be responsible for the training, or outside experts can be employed to undertake the responsibility. Giving in-district credit to participating teachers offers strong evidence that the district is concerned about using proper safety techniques.
2. Medical records should be reviewed at the start of the school year. Students with disabilities should be identified and noted within each class listing before the first instructional day. If necessary, the teacher or school nurse can call the doctor of students with disabilities or activity-restricted students to inquire about the situation and discuss special needs. Physical education teachers should be notified by the classroom teacher or school nurse about youngsters who have special conditions such as epilepsy or temporary problems such as taking medication.
3. Throughout the school year, safety orientations should be conducted with students. Discussions should include potentially dangerous situations, class conduct, and rules for proper use of equipment and apparatus. Teachers should urge students to report any conditions that might cause an accident.
4. Safety rules for specific units of instruction should be discussed at the onset of each unit. Rules should be posted and brought to the attention of students regularly. Posters and bulletin boards can promote safety in an enjoyable and stimulating manner.
5. If students are to serve as instructional aides, they should be trained. Aides must understand the techniques of spotting, for example, and must receive proper instruction if they are to be a part of the educational process. Use caution with student aides because teachers are still responsible even if an aide performs a duty incorrectly.
6. Instructional practices need to be monitored for possible hazards. For example, students in competitive situations should be matched by size, maturity, and ability. Proper instruction necessary for safe participation should occur prior to activity. Instructors should receive a competence check to be sure that they are adequately trained to give instruction in various activities. The instructional area should be properly prepared for safe participation; if the area is lacking necessary apparatus and safety devices, instruction should be modified to meet safety standards.
7. An inventory of equipment and apparatus should include a safety checklist. Whenever necessary, send equipment in need of repair to proper agents. If the cost of repair is greater than 40 percent of the replacement cost, discarding the equipment or apparatus is usually a more economical choice.
8. When an injury occurs, it should be recorded and a report placed in the student's file. An injury report should also be filed by type, such as ankle sprain or broken arm. The report should list the activity and the conditions, to facilitate analysis at regular intervals. Analysis may show that injuries are occurring regularly during a specific activity or on a certain piece of equipment. This process can give direction for creating a safer environment or for defending the safety record of a sport, activity, or piece of equipment.
9. Teachers need up-to-date first-aid and CPR certification. Administrators should be sure that teachers meet these standards and should provide training sessions when necessary.

The Safety Committee

Safety should be publicized regularly throughout the school, and a mechanism should exist that allows students, parents, and teachers to voice concerns about unsafe conditions. A safety committee can meet at regular intervals to establish safety policies, rule on requests for allowing high-risk activities, and analyze serious injuries that have occurred in the school district. This committee should develop safety rules that apply districtwide to all teachers. It may determine that certain activities involve too high a risk for the return in student benefit. Acceptable criteria for sport equipment and apparatus may be established by the committee.

Include one or more high-level administrators, physical education teachers, health officers (nurse), parents, and students on the safety committee. School administrators are usually indicted when lawsuits occur; because they are held responsible for program content and curriculum, their representation on the safety committee is important. Students on the committee may be aware of possible hazards, and parents may often voice concerns overlooked by teachers.

The Emergency Care Plan

Before any emergency arises, teachers should prepare themselves by learning about special health and physical conditions of students (Gray, 1993). Most schools have a method for identifying students with special health problems. If a student has a problem that may require treatment, a consent-to-treat form should be on file in case the parent or guardian is unavailable. Necessary first-aid materials and supplies should be available in a kit and be readily accessible.

Establishing procedures for emergency care and notification of parents in case of injury is of utmost importance in providing a high standard of care for students. To plan properly for emergency care, all physical education teachers should have first-aid training. *First aid* is the immediate and temporary care given at an emergency before a physician is available. Its purposes are to save life, prevent aggravation of injuries, and alleviate severe suffering. If there is evidence of life-threatening bleeding or if the victim is unconscious or has stopped breathing, the teacher must administer first aid. When already injured persons may be further injured if they are not moved, then moving them is permissible. As a general rule, however, an injured person should not be moved unless absolutely necessary. If there is indication of back or neck injury, the head must be immobilized and should not be moved without the use of a spine board. Remember, the purpose of first aid is to save life. The emergency care plan should consist of the following steps:

1. *Administer first aid to the injured student as the first priority.* Treat only life-threatening injuries. The school nurse should be called to the scene of the accident immediately. Emergency care procedures should indicate whether the student can be moved and in what fashion. It is critical that the individual applying first aid avoid aggravating the injury.
2. *Notify parents as soon as possible when emergency care is required.* Each student's file should list home and emergency telephone numbers where parents can be reached. If possible, the school should have an arrangement with local emergency facilities so that a paramedic unit can be called immediately to the scene of a serious accident.
3. *Release the student to a parent or a designated representative.* Policies for transportation of injured students should be established and documented.
4. *Promptly complete a student accident report while the details of the accident are clear.* Figure 9.1 is an example of an accident form that covers the necessary details. The teacher and principal should both retain copies, and additional copies should be sent to the administrative office.

PERSONAL PROTECTION: MINIMIZING THE EFFECTS OF A LAWSUIT

In spite of proper care, injuries do occur, and lawsuits may be initiated. Two courses of action are necessary to counteract the effects of a suit.

Liability Insurance

Teachers may be protected by school district liability insurance. Usually, however, you must purchase your own policy. A common way many physical education professionals use to purchase liability insurance at a reasonable cost is to join AAHPERD. As a member, a group liability policy can be purchased for a modest amount. Most policies provide for legal services to contest a suit and will pay indemnity up to the limits of the policy (liability coverage of $500,000 is most common). Most policies give the insurance company the right to settle out of court. Unfortunately, when this occurs, some people may infer that the teacher was guilty even though the circumstances indicate otherwise. Insurance companies usually settle out of court to avoid the excessive legal fees required to try to win the case in court.

Recordkeeping

The second course of action is to keep complete records of accidents. Many lawsuits occur months or even years after the accident, when memory of the situation is fuzzy. Accident reports should be filled out immediately after an injury. Take care to provide no evidence, oral or written, that others could use in a court of law. Do not attempt to make a diagnosis or to specify the supposed cause of the accident in the report.

If newspaper reporters probe for details, avoid describing the accident beyond the basic facts. When discussing the accident with administrators, only the facts recorded on the accident report should be discussed. Remember that school records can be subpoenaed in court proceedings. The point here is not to dissemble, but to be cautious and avoid self-incrimination.

Safety and Liability Checklists

The following checklists can be used to monitor the physical education environment. Any situations that deviate from safe and legally sound practices should be rectified immediately.

Supervision and Instruction

1. Are teachers adequately trained in all of the activities that they are teaching?
2. Do all teachers have evidence of a necessary level of first-aid training?
3. When supervising, do personnel have access to a written plan of areas to be observed and responsibilities to be carried out?
4. Have students been warned of potential dangers and risks, and advised of rules and the reasons for the rules?
5. Are safety rules posted near areas of increased risk?
6. Are lesson plans written? Do they include provisions for proper instruction, sequence of activities, and safety? Are all activities taught listed in the district curriculum guide?

Student Accident Report

________________ **School**

In all cases, this form should be filed through the school nurse and signed by the principal of the school. The original will be forwarded to the superintendent's office, where it will be initialed and sent to the head nurse. The second copy will be retained by the principal or the school nurse. The third copy should be given to the physical education teacher if accident is related.

Name of injured ________________ Address ________________

Phone ________________ Grade ________ Home room ________ Age ________

Parents of injured ________________

Place of accident ________________ Date of accident ________________

Hour ________________ A.M. P.M. Date reported ________________ By whom ________________

Parent contact attempted at ________________ A.M. P.M. Parent contacted at ________________ A.M. P.M.

Describe accident, giving specific location and condition of premises ________________

____

Nature of injury ________________
(Describe in detail)

Care given or action taken by nurse or others ________________

____

Reason injured person was on premises ________________
(Activity at time—i.e., lunch, physical education, etc.)

Staff member responsible for student supervision at time of accident ________________

____

Is student covered by school-sponsored accident insurance? ________ Yes ________ No

Medical Care Recommended ________ Yes ________ No

Where taken after accident ________________
(Specify home, physician, or hospital, giving name and address)

By whom ________ **at what time** ________________ A.M. P.M.

Follow-up by nurse to be sent to central health office

Remediative measures taken ________________
(Attach individual remarks if necessary)

School ________________ Principal ________________

Date ________________ Nurse ________________

On the back of this sheet, list all persons familiar with the circumstances of the accident, giving name, address, telephone number, age, and location with respect to the accident.

FIGURE 9.1 Sample accident report form.

7. When a new activity is introduced, are safety precautions and instructions for correct skill performance always communicated to the class?
8. Are the activities taught in the program based on sound curriculum principles? Could the activities and units of instruction be defended on the basis of their educational contributions?
9. Do the methods of instruction recognize individual differences among students, and are the necessary steps taken to meet the needs of all students, regardless of gender, ability, or disability?
10. Are substitute teachers given clear and comprehensive lesson plans so that they can maintain the scope and sequence of instruction?
11. Is the student evaluation plan based on actual performance and objective data rather than on favoritism or arbitrary and capricious standards?
12. Is appropriate dress required for students? This does not imply uniforms, only dress (including shoes) that ensures the safety of the student.
13. When necessary for safety, are students grouped according to ability level, size, or age?
14. Is the class left unsupervised for teacher visits to the office, lounge, or bathroom? Is one teacher ever asked to supervise two or more classes at the same time?
15. If students are used as teacher aides or to spot others, are they given proper instruction and training?

Equipment and Facilities

1. Is all equipment inspected regularly and are the inspection results recorded on a form and sent to the proper administrators?
2. Is a log maintained recording the regular occurrence of inspections, the equipment in need of repair, and when repairs were made?
3. Are "attractive nuisances" eliminated from the gymnasium and playing field?
4. Are specific safety rules posted on facilities and near equipment?
5. Are the following inspected periodically?
   a. playing field for presence of glass, rocks, and metal objects
   b. fasteners holding equipment, such as climbing ropes, horizontal bars, or baskets
   c. goals for games, such as football, soccer, and field hockey, to be sure that they are fastened securely
   d. padded areas, such as goal supports
6. Are mats placed under apparatus from which a fall is possible?
7. Are playing fields arranged so participants will not run into each other or be hit by a ball from another game?
8. Are landing pits filled and maintained properly?

Emergency Care

1. Is there a written procedure for emergency care?
2. Is a person properly trained in first aid available immediately following an accident?
3. Are emergency telephone numbers readily accessible?
4. Are telephone numbers of parents available?
5. Is an up-to-date first-aid kit available? Is ice immediately available?
6. Are health folders maintained that list restrictions, allergies, and health problems of students?
7. Are health folders reviewed by instructors on a regular basis?
8. Are students participating in extracurricular activities required to have insurance? Is the policy number recorded?
9. Is there a plan for treating injuries that involves the local paramedics?
10. Are accident reports filed promptly and analyzed regularly?

Transportation of Students

1. Have parents been informed that their students will be transported off campus?
2. Are detailed travel plans approved by the site administrator and kept on file?
3. Are school vehicles used whenever possible?
4. Are drivers properly licensed and vehicles insured?
5. If teachers or parents use their vehicles to transport students, are the students, driver, and car owner covered by an insurance rider purchased by the school district?

REFLECTION AND REVIEW QUESTIONS

How and Why

1. Should teachers have professional insurance?
2. How can effective classroom management help teachers avoid legal issues?
3. How can teachers protect themselves from lawsuits?
4. Why is a safety and liability checklist important?

Content Review

1. What is a tort?
2. Identify four major points that must be established to determine if a teacher is negligent. Also, discuss the importance of foreseeability.
3. List and explain types of negligence.
4. Describe the common defenses against negligence.
5. Discuss the importance of supervision and instruction when examining responsibility.
6. Who is responsible for equipment and facilities? Explain your answer.
7. What are some issues related to sports programs that often result in lawsuits?
8. Briefly describe several guidelines for safety in physical education.
9. Explain the importance of an emergency care plan and discuss the steps in the plan.

FOR MORE INFORMATION

References and Suggested Readings

Appenzeller, H. (Ed.). (1998). *Risk management in sport: Issues and strategies.* Durham, NC: Carolina Academic Press.

Appenzeller, H. (1993). *Managing sports and risk management strategies.* Durham, NC: Carolina Academic Press.

Appenzeller, H. (1970). *From the gym to the jury.* Charlottesville, VA: Michie Company Law Publishing.

Baley, J. A., & Matthews, D. L. (1984). *Law and liability in athletics, physical education, and recreation.* Boston: Allyn and Bacon.

Black, H. C. (1996). *Black's Law Dictionary.* St. Paul, MN: West.

Blucker, J. A., & Pell, S. W. (1986). Legal and ethical issues. *Journal of Physical Education, Recreation, and Dance,* 57, 19–21.

Dougherty, N. J. (Ed.). (1987). *Principles of safety in physical education and sport.* Reston, VA: AAHPERD.

Dougherty, N. J., Auxter, D., Heinzmann, S., & Goldberger, A. S. (1994). *Sport, physical activity, and the law,* 2nd edition. Champaign, IL: Human Kinetics.

Gallup, E. M. (1995). *Law and the team physician.* Champaign, IL: Human Kinetics.

Gray, G. R. (1993). Providing adequate medical care to program participants. *Journal of Physical Education, Recreation, and Dance,* 64(2), 56–57.

Institute for the Study of Educational Policy, Law Division. (1986). *School athletics and the law.* Seattle: University of Washington Press.

Kaiser, R. A. (1984). *Liability and law in recreation, parks, and sports.* Englewood Cliffs, NJ: Prentice-Hall.

Merriman, J. (1993). Supervision in sport and physical activity. *Journal of Physical Education, Recreation, and Dance,* 64(2), 20–23.

Pittman, A. J. (1993). Safe transportation—A driving concern. *Journal of Physical Education, Recreation, and Dance,* 64(2), 53–55.

Strickland, R., Phillip, J. F., & Phillips, W. R. (1976). *Avoiding teacher malpractice.* New York: Hawthorn.

U.S. Consumer Product Safety Commission. (1992). *Handbook for public playground safety.* Washington, DC: U.S. Government Printing Office.

van der Smissen, B. (1990). *Legal liability and risk management of public and private entities.* Cincinnati, OH: Anderson.

Websites

Legal Issues and Physical Education
http://www.kin.sfasu.edu/finkenberg/kin511/Liability.html
http://library.cortland.edu/rguides/legal_issues_pe.html
http://www.nils.com/rupps/comparative-negligence.htm

Liability Insurance for Physical educators
http://www.aahperd.org/aahperd/template.cfm?template=membership.html

Playgrounds
http://www.cpsc.gov/CPSCPUB/PUBS/playpubs.html
http://www.parenthoodweb.com/articles/phw506.htm
http://www.playdesigns.com/

School Safety and Security
http://www.schoolsecurity.org/

CHAPTER 10

Facilities, Equipment, and Supplies

ESSENTIAL COMPONENTS	
I	Organized around content standards
II	**Student-centered and developmentally appropriate**
III	Physical activity and motor skill development form the core of the program
IV	Teaches management skills and self-discipline
V	Promotes inclusion of all students
VI	Focuses on process over product
VII	Promotes lifetime personal health and wellness
VIII	Teaches cooperation and responsibility and promotes sensitivity to diversity

PHYSICAL EDUCATION STANDARDS	
1	Students are able to move competently using a variety of fundamental and specialized motor skills.
2	Students can monitor and maintain a health-enhancing level of physical fitness.
3	Students are able to apply movement concepts and basic mechanics of skill performance when learning and refining motor skills.
4	Students comprehend the basic principles of wellness and are able to apply concepts that enable them to make meaningful decisions that positively impact their health and wellness.
5	Students participate in a wide variety of physical activities and learn how to maintain a personalized active lifestyle.
6	Students demonstrate empathy, understanding, and respect for the numerous differences exhibited by people in an activity setting.
7	**Students exhibit responsible and self-directed behaviors that lead to positive social interactions in physical activity.**

SUMMARY

Chapter 10 presents procedures associated with the design, purchase, maintenance, and construction of physical education facilities, equipment, and supplies. The term *equipment* refers to items that are more or less fixed in nature. Equipment has a relatively long lifespan, needs periodic safety checks, and requires planned purchasing. Supplies are nondurable items that have a limited period of use. When resources are limited, much equipment can be constructed. A comprehensive section on how to build equipment and supplies is offered.

OUTCOMES

- Identify standards to follow in the construction of outdoor and indoor physical education facilities.
- Understand that safety is an essential consideration in facility design.
- List recommended equipment for outdoor and indoor physical education areas.
- Outline a systematic plan for the storage of physical education equipment and supplies.
- Describe procedures for the care and repair of physical education equipment and supplies.
- Be able to construct selected physical education equipment and supplies.
- Illustrate floor lines and markings that enhance management potential and increase ease of instruction.
- List essential equipment and supplies for physical education in the elementary school.

The facilities for physical education are often classified in two categories: outdoor and indoor. Usually, outdoor space provides enough room for several classes to work simultaneously. When weather conditions require frequent use of indoor space, a minimum of one indoor teaching station for every eight classrooms is needed. In addition, to meet the needs of students with disabilities (as required by Public Law 94-142), another indoor play area, separate from but close to the regular indoor facility, is needed.

Physical education facilities should be planned in terms of maximum projected enrollment. Too often, planning is done in terms of the present situation. Later, when classrooms are added to the school, they are added without a change in physical education areas. What was previously an adequate arrangement now becomes a scheduling problem. Adding physical education facilities is difficult because of generally escalating costs and the relatively high cost of physical education facilities in comparison with the cost of adding regular classroom space.

OUTDOOR FACILITIES

Standards for outdoor play areas call for a minimum of 10 acres for the school, with an additional acre for each 100 pupils in the maximum projected enrollment. Parking areas, cycle racks, and entry roads are in addition to these standards. The outdoor areas should include field space for games, a track, hard-surfaced areas, apparatus areas, play courts, age-group–specific play areas, covered play space, and a jogging trail.

Fields should be leveled, drained, and turfed, because grass is the most usable field surface. An automatic sprinkler system is desirable, but sprinkler heads must not protrude to become safety hazards. Automatic installations permit sprinkling during the evening and night, so that the fields are not too soggy for play the next day.

A hard-top area should be marked for a variety of games, such as tetherball, volleyball, and basketball courts. Four-square courts, hopscotch layouts, and circles for games are examples of other markings that can be put on these surfaces. Simple movement pattern courses can also be marked. Some administrators prefer a hard surface for the entire play area, because this eliminates the mud problem and the need for sprinkling and in general lowers maintenance costs. Hard surfaces are used when play space is limited and when the number of students makes keeping a turf surface in adequate condition difficult.

As a minimum, space should be provided for a track, and it should be placed in an area where it will not interfere with other activities. For schools where a permanent installation is not practical, a temporary track can be laid out each spring (see page 674).

Separate play spaces for different age groups should be included in the planning. Such areas should contain apparatus designed for each age group. The play area for primary-level children should be well away from areas where footballs and softballs are used.

Small, hard-surfaced play courts can be located strategically near the edges of the outdoor area, thus spreading out the play groups. These courts, approximately 40 by 60 feet, can be equipped for basketball or volleyball or for both. A covered shed can be divided for use by different age groups. Climatic conditions would dictate the need for such facilities.

A jogging trail can stimulate interest in jogging. Small signs indicating the distances covered and markers outlining the trail are all that are needed. Stations with exercise tasks can be placed at intervals. For example, a station could have directions to accomplish a specified number of push-ups or sit-ups. Such a circuit is popularly called a *parcourse.*

An area set aside as a developmental playground is an important part of the total play space. The area should contain equipment and apparatus and should be landscaped to have small hills, valleys, and tunnels for children. A recommended approach is to divide the playground into various developmental areas so that children must use different body parts in different areas of the play space. For example, one area might contain a great deal of climbing equipment to reinforce arm-shoulder girdle development, and another area might challenge the leg and trunk regions. Equipment and apparatus should be abstract in nature; creation and imagination are left to the children. Apparatus can be manipulated and changed to suit the needs and desires of the youngsters.

SAFETY ON THE PLAYGROUND

Studies by the U.S. Consumer Product Safety Commission (1997) show that the majority of injuries (60 to 70 percent) are caused when children fall from apparatus and strike the underlying surface. The type of surface under the equipment is a major factor affecting the severity of injuries associated with falls from apparatus. Injuries range from minor bruises to skull fractures, concussions, and brain damage. Falls onto paved surfaces result in a disproportionately high number of severe injuries. Some deaths also have resulted from such falls.

Slides offer a high potential for accidents. The greatest number of injuries occur from falls over the side, from the platform, and from the ladder. Roughhousing, improper usage, and slipping are the most prominent causes of accidents. Rules should be established so that only one person is on the platform, with the next user waiting at the base of the ladder.

Concrete, asphalt, and other paved surfaces placed under apparatus require little or no maintenance, which is often the reason for their installation and use. However, hard surfaces do not provide injury protection from accidental fall impacts and therefore are unsuitable for use. Organic materials such as pine bark nuggets, pine bark mulch, shredded hardwood bark, and cocoa shell mulch are suggested. Other materials are wood chips, shredded tires, and sand. If hard surfaces are already in place, outdoor interlocking tiles or dense synthetic turf may be placed over the existing base.

If loose, organic materials are used, a 6-inch level of material to cushion the impact of falling should be a minimum. Frequent leveling, grading, and replacement of the material is necessary, as children will move the material away from the impact areas. The material should be screened to eliminate insects, animal excrement, and concealed sharp objects. Unfortunately, organic materials decompose, become pulverized and dusty, and mix with dirt, which causes a loss of their cushioning properties. In rainy or humid weather, they can absorb moisture and pack down, resulting in a loss of resiliency. Finally, materials must be selected that will not become firm during freezing temperatures.

The choice of materials needs to be based on local conditions and the availability of necessary funds. As important as the selection of the proper material is continuous and correct maintenance. Allied to proper maintenance is the need for a checklist of proper procedures to be followed. This form should be filled out and dated on a regular basis.

OUTDOOR APPARATUS AND EQUIPMENT

The continued emphasis on physical fitness should dictate the selection of outdoor equipment. Equipment that offers "sit and ride" experiences (swings, merry-go-rounds, and teeter-totters) does not meet this criterion. A second criterion is that of safety. Each piece of equipment should minimize the potential for injury. As a general rule, if equipment has moving parts, its potential for injury is increased. Suggestions for equipment are offered below based on their potential to develop various components of fitness. The categories can be useful if you want to establish a challenge course that develops all parts of the body. Outdoor equipment should stimulate children's creative drives and their desire to move.

Equipment for Upper Body Development

Most children do not receive enough activity that develops upper body strength. In order to develop arm-shoulder girdle strength on the playground, youngsters need the opportunity to climb and swing, and to elevate their bodies. Climbing is important for physical development and to help children learn to overcome the fear of new situations. The following are examples of equipment that could be used to develop arm-shoulder girdle strength:

- Large telephone cable spools that are fastened securely so they will not move or tip over. Youngsters can climb on and jump off the spools.
- Climbing poles placed next to platforms that children can reach by climbing the poles.
- Logs and clean railroad ties, positioned vertically, with handholds or handles placed in strategic locations for climbing.
- Climbing ropes attached to tracks (tracks can be locked up in a storage area when school is not in session).
- Tires attached to telephone poles or logs for climbing through and around.
- Jungle gyms that are attached securely.
- Horizontal ladders in a variety of combinations and forms. Arched ladders are quite popular and allow children to reach the rungs easily. Uniladders, consisting of a single beam with pegs on each side, offer a different ladder challenge to children.
- Logs anchored vertically with handholds provided for climbing.

Equipment for Lower Body Development

Equipment and apparatus for enhancing lower body development should encourage youngsters to use locomotor movements throughout the available space. Allow enough distance and area to ensure movement. Suggestions for lower body development are the following:

- Large spaces, which encourage free movement and running games.
- Railroad ties anchored vertically at varying heights and distances, which encourage children to walk, run, hop, and jump from one to the other.
- Used automobile tires fastened on the ground in different patterns to stimulate moving in and out, around and over the tires using different movements.
- Stairways and platforms for climbing on and jumping off.
- Stepping stones to encourage movement patterns. Stones can be placed so they encourage oppositional patterning while moving.
- Miniature challenge courses that contain tires to move over and through, sand pits to run or jump into, and poles or cones arranged for moving around and dodging.

Equipment for Balance Skills

Balance is improved through regular practice. A number of pieces of equipment can be used to challenge youngsters' balance skills. Youngsters should be encouraged to move under control while practicing balance. The following are suggestions for offering balance challenges:

- Balance beams made of 4-by-4-inch beams can be permanent installations. They can be arranged in various patterns but should not be more than 12 to 18 inches above the ground.
- Logs, anchored securely, can be used as balance beams.
- Include balance beams that start with a wide width of 6 inches and progress in difficulty to 1½ inches.
- Wooden ladders secured 6 inches above the ground offer opportunities to walk on the rungs and rails.

Equipment for Sport Skills

Basketball Goals

Outdoor basketball goals may or may not be combined with a court. Youngsters play a lot of one-goal basketball, and a regulation court is not needed for this game. The goals should be in a surfaced area, however. Outdoor baskets for elementary school use should be 8 to 9 feet above the ground. The lowered height sometimes poses a problem, because children can jump up and grasp the front of the rim, which may damage or tear the basket loose. Strong construction that withstands such abuse is one solution. Some schools have reverted to the 10-foot-high basket, thus putting it out of reach of most children.

Volleyball Standards

Volleyball standards should have flexible height adjustments, including a low height of 30 inches for use in paddleball.

Softball Backstops

Softball backstops can be either fixed or portable.

Tetherball Courts

Tetherball courts should have fastening devices for the cord and ball so that they can be removed from the post for safekeeping. The immediate playing area should be surfaced.

Track and Field Equipment

Jumping standards, bars, and pits should be available. These must be maintained properly.

INDOOR FACILITIES

The gymnasium must be well planned for maximum use. The combination gymnasium-auditorium-cafeteria facility leaves much to be desired and creates more problems than it solves. Although it may be labeled a "multipurpose room," a better description is probably "multiuseless." The cafeteria poses a particular problem. The gymnasium must be vacated before the lunch hour so that chairs and tables can be set up, and the facility is not available again for physical education activities until it has been cleaned, which usually involves mopping. This eliminates noontime recreational use, thus leaving little play area for the children during inclement weather. In extreme cases, a lack of help postpones gymnasium use for the early part of the afternoon, until the custodian has completed cleaning chores. Special programs, movies, and other events necessitating chairs and the use of the area also complicate the situation.

The gymnasium should be located in a separate wing connected to the classrooms by a covered corridor. It should provide ready access to play areas. Isolating the gym from the rest of the school minimizes the noise problem and allows afterschool and community groups to use the facilities without access to other parts of the school. The indoor facility should be planned in such a way that athletic contests can be scheduled there at times, but the primary purpose of the gymnasium is not as an athletic facility. Consideration for spectators should not be a major planning concern. Only after basic physical education needs have been met should the needs of spectators be considered.

In the gymnasium, markings and boundaries should be put on the floor to outline convenient areas for the more common activities. The markings should be painted on the floor after the first or second sealer coat has been applied. A finish coat should then be applied on top of the line markings. Figure 10.1 is an example of how floor markings can maximize the usefulness of a facility.

Temporary lines needed occasionally during the year can be applied with pressure-sensitive tape. These tapes are, however, difficult to remove completely and are likely to take off the finish when removed. A hardwood (preferably maple) floor is recommended for the gymnasium. Other surfaces limit community use and create both safety and maintenance problems.

For safety reasons and for rebound practice, walls should have a smooth surface for a distance of 8 to 10 feet up from the floor. Walls and ceilings should have acoustical treatment. In original construction, a recess for each set of ropes on tracks is an excellent feature. Insulation should conform to modern health standards, and older buildings should be scrutinized for unacceptable insulation materials, such as asbestos fibers and certain formaldehyde-based plastics.

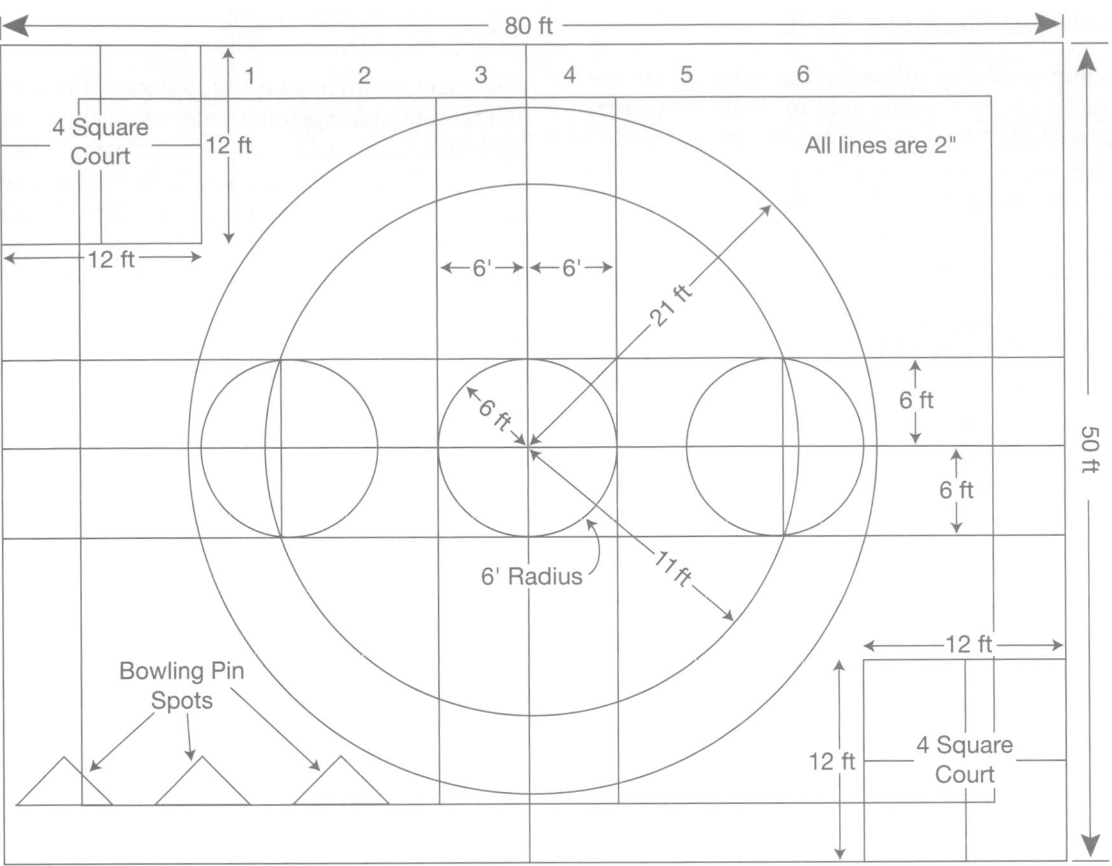

FIGURE 10.1 Floor markings to maximize gymnasium use.

The lighting should be of sufficient intensity, and fixtures should be recessed to prevent damage. Lights should be arranged so that they can be serviced from the floor. Exposed beams should be available for attaching apparatus, and all walls should have electrical outlets. A permanent overhead public address system is desirable, permitting permanent installation of a record, tape, or CD player for easy and quick access. In original construction, the player can be recessed.

Windows should be placed high on the long sides of the gymnasium. Protection from glare and direct sun should be provided.

If baskets and backboards need to be raised and lowered often, a motor-driven system eliminates laborious hand cranking. The system switch should be activated with a key.

Adequate storage space must be given careful thought. The storage space needed for the equipment and instructional supplies used in present-day physical education is considerable, and the area should be designed so that the materials are readily available.

One problem frequently associated with a combination auditorium-gymnasium facility is the use of the physical education storeroom for storage of bulky auditorium equipment, such as portable chairs on chair trucks, portable stages, lighting fixtures, and other paraphernalia for dramatic productions. Unless the storage facility is quite large—and most are not—an unworkable and cluttered facility is the result. The best solution is two separate storerooms for the dual-purpose facility, or at least one very large storeroom.

A separate storage area of cabinets is essential for outside groups that use the facility. These groups should not have access to the regular physical education supply room. If they are permitted to use school equipment, the equipment should be checked out to the group and later checked in again.

Many storage areas in European schools have doors on tracks, similar to U.S. overhead garage doors. This design has a number of advantages, the main one being that the overhead opening makes the handling of large apparatus much easier.

Most architects are unaware of the storage needs of a modern physical education program. Teachers can only hope that the architects designing new schools will be persuaded to allow for sufficient storage. For the physical education specialist, an office-dressing room is desirable. The office should contain a toilet and a shower.

If contract or task approaches are important in the instructional process, an area to house instructional materials is also desirable. This should be a place where the children can go to search through materials and view loop films and videotapes as they complete their learning packets.

EQUIPMENT AND SUPPLIES

Equipment refers to items of a more or less fixed nature. Supplies are those nondurable items that have a limited period of use. To illustrate the difference, a softball is listed under supplies, but the longer-lasting softball backstop comes under the category of equipment. Equipment needs periodic replacement, and budget planning must consider the lifespan of each piece of equipment. Supplies generally are purchased on a yearly basis. It is important to have adequate financing for equipment and supplies and to expend funds wisely.

If the objectives of the physical education program are to be fulfilled, instructional materials must be available in sufficient quantity. Enough equipment should be present so that the children do not waste practice time waiting for turns.

Policies covering the purchase, storage, issuance, care, maintenance, and inventory of supplies are necessary if maximum return on the allotted budget is to be realized. Program features should be decided first, and a purchasing plan should then be implemented based on these features. Having a minimal operational list of instructional supplies stabilizes the teaching process.

Equipment constructed by the school staff and homemade equipment should be considered. Quality must not, however, be sacrificed. Articles from home (including empty plastic jugs, milk cartons, old tires, and the like) should be regarded as supplementary materials. Care must be taken that the administration does not look for the cheap, no-cost route to securing supplies and thus sacrifice valuable learning experiences when the program needs require an appreciable investment.

Some articles can be constructed adequately at the school or in the home, and these merit consideration for the sake of economy. Such items as yarn balls, hoops, lummi sticks, balance beams, bounding boards, and others can be made satisfactorily by school staff, by parents, and in some instances by students. For other articles, the administration must be reminded that constructed equipment is usually a temporary solution only, undertaken in the early phases of a program when equipment costs are high and cannot all be met immediately.

PURCHASING POLICIES

The purchase of supplies and equipment involves careful study of need, price, quality, and material. The safety of the children who will use the equipment is of vital concern. Quantity buying by pooling the funds of an entire school district generally results in better use of the tax dollar. However, cooperative purchasing may require compromises on equipment type and brand to satisfy different users in the system. If bids are requested, careful specifications are necessary. Bids should be asked for only on specified items, and "just as good" merchandise should not be accepted as a substitute.

One individual within a school should be made responsible for the physical education supplies and for keeping records of equipment, supplies, and purchasing. Needs will vary from school to school, and it is practical for school district authorities to deal with a single individual at each school. Prompt attention to repair and replacement of supplies is possible under this system. The individual designated should also be responsible for testing various competing products to determine which will give the best service over time. Some kind of labeling or marking of materials is needed if this is to be accomplished.

An accurate inventory of equipment should be undertaken at the start and end of each school year. Through a sound inventory system, the durability of equipment and supplies and an accounting of supplies lost or misplaced can be established. The ordering of supplies and equipment should be done by the end of the school year or earlier, if possible. A delivery date in August should be specified so that orders can be checked and any necessary adjustments made before the school year begins.

Most equipment of good quality will last from 7 to 10 years, thus keeping replacement costs to a minimum. The policy of some purchasing agents of selecting low-cost items with little regard for quality is financially unsound. Budgetary practices should include an allotment for the yearly purchase of instructional supplies as well as major replacement and procurement costs for large items, which are usually staggered over a number of years. Once sufficient equipment and supplies have been procured, the budget considerations are for replacement and repair only.

INDOOR EQUIPMENT

Several principles should govern the choice of indoor equipment. First, a reasonable variety and amount of equipment should be available to keep children active. Included should be items to facilitate arm-shoulder girdle development (for example, climbing ropes, climbing frames, ladders, and similar apparatus). A criterion for selection is that most, if not all, indoor equipment should be of the type that the children themselves can carry, assemble, and disassemble. A regular trampoline, for example, would not meet this criterion.

Mats for Tumbling and Safety

Mats are basic to any physical education program. Enough mats must be available to provide a safe floor for climbing apparatus. At least eight should be present. The light, folding mats are preferable because they are easy to handle and store. They stack well and can be moved on carts. Mats should have fasteners so that two or more can be joined (Figure 10.2). The covers should be plastic for easy cleaning. (The one objection to plastic covers is that they are not as soft as the type of mat cover used for wrestling.) Mats should be 4 feet wide and 7 or 8 feet long. Heavy hand-me-down mats from the high school program may prove counterproductive, because they are difficult to handle and bulky to store.

Other mats that might be considered are thick, soft mats (somewhat similar to mattresses) and inclined mats. Soft mats are generally 4 inches or more thick and may entice the timid to try activities that they otherwise would avoid. Inclined mats are wedge-shaped and provide downhill momentum for rolls.

Individual Mats

A supply of 30 to 35 individual mats is used for the primary-level program. The mats, which can be 20 by 40 inches or 24 by 48 inches, are useful for practicing many movement experiences and introductory tumbling activities.

Tape/CD Player

A portable combination tape and CD player with remote control is the most affordable and versatile choice.

Balance-Beam Benches

Balance-beam benches have double use. They can serve as regular benches for many types of bench activity, and, when turned over, they can be used for balance-beam activities. Wooden horses or their supports can serve as inclined benches. Six benches are a minimum for class activity.

Balance Beams

A wide beam (4 inches) is recommended for kindergarten and first grade. Otherwise, a 2-inch beam can be used. Balance beams with alternate surfaces (2 and 4 inches) can be constructed from common building materials.

Chinning Bar

The chinning bar is especially useful for physical fitness testing and in body support activities. The portable chinning bar installed in the gymnasium doorway is an acceptable substitute.

FIGURE 10.2 Tumbling mats stored on wall with Velcro® fasteners.

Climbing Ropes

Climbing ropes are essential to the program. At least eight ropes should be present, but more than eight allow for better group instruction. Climbing rope sets on tracks are most efficient to handle (Figure 10.3). With little effort or loss of time, the ropes are ready for activity. Ropes on tracks are available in a variety of materials, but good-quality manila hemp seems to be the most practical. Ropes should be either 1¼ or 1½ inches in diameter.

Quality climbing ropes made of synthetic fibers are appearing on the market. The best are olefin fiber ropes, which are nonallergenic and have nonslip qualities, thus forestalling the problem of slickness, a characteristic of plastic ropes and even of older cotton ropes. Climbing ropes on tracks and other large apparatus can be purchased from Gopher Sport, 220 24th Avenue NW, P.O. Box 998, Owatonna, MN 55060-0998, Phone: 1-800-533-0446 or www.gophersport.com.

Volleyball Standards

Volleyball standards should adjust to various heights for different grade levels and games.

Supply Cart

A cart to hold supplies is desirable. Other carts can be used for the audio equipment and for regular and individual mats.

FIGURE 10.3 Climbing ropes on tracks.

Jumping Boxes

Small boxes used for jumping and for allied locomotor movements extend the opportunities to work on basic movement skills. Boxes should be 8 and 16 inches high (Figure 10.4). If the boxes are made about 16 by 16 inches with a rubber skid-proof surface on the bottom, they will be stable. Holes drilled through the sides provide fingerholds for ease of handling. Eight boxes, four of each size, are a minimum number for the average-sized class. Jumping boxes can be purchased from Gopher Sport, 220 24th Avenue NW, P.O. Box 998, Owatonna, MN 55060-0998, Phone: 1-800-533-0446 or www.gophersport.com.

Horizontal Ladder Sets

Horizontal ladders that fold against the wall make an excellent indoor equipment addition. The ladder may be combined with other pieces of apparatus in a folding set.

Other Indoor Items

A portable chalkboard is desirable, as is a wall screen for viewing visual aids. A large bulletin board and a wall chalkboard should be located near the main entrance to the gym. The wall chalkboard permits quick announcements or notes. An audiovisual cart or stand for projectors is helpful. It should contain sufficient electrical cord to reach wall outlets.

FIGURE 10.4 First graders using 16-inch jumping boxes.

Rebound nets for throwing and kicking have excellent utility. They do, however, pose storage problems. Substitute goals for basketball and related games can be designed. One suggested goal is 4 feet square, with the rim 5 feet above the ground. Beginners can find success with this goal design. The frame can be made of 1-inch pipe or plastic (PVC) tubing.

EQUIPMENT AND SUPPLIES FOR PHYSICAL EDUCATION

Knowing what equipment to obtain for your program and where to find it can be an obstacle, but it doesn't need to be a major obstacle. Figure 10.5 (pages 190–191) identifies the equipment, supplies and capital outlay items, needed to teach a quality physical education program. The items are listed by priority in two categories: materials and supplies, and capital outlay. Priority is based on cost, need, and versatility of the equipment. The first piece of equipment listed (playground balls) can be used to teach the most units, therefore making it the highest priority. The quantity of equipment is also listed to assure that the proper amount is ordered to facilitate a normal class size. Some of the equipment can be constructed, as described later in this chapter.

The majority of listed equipment is available from Gopher Sport, 220 24th Avenue NW, P.O. Box 998, Owatonna, MN 55060-0998, Phone: 1-800-533-0446 or www.gophersport.com. The author has worked closely with this company to develop a *Dynamic Physical Education* equipment list. This list offers all the equipment and teaching materials needed to implement a high-quality program. Equipment has been field tested and is

Priority	Material and Supplies	Quantity
1	8½″ inflatable rubber playground balls	36
1a	8″ foam balls (can be substituted for playground balls)	36
1b	8″ polyurethane coated foam balls (a substitute for playground balls; they are much more durable and give a true bounce. They can be used for all types of sport activities.)	36
2	6″ × 6″ beanbags, assorted colors	72
3	Jump Ropes (plastic segments for beginners and speed ropes for experienced jumpers)	
	7 ft length	36
	8 ft length	36
	9 ft length	18
	16 ft length (long rope jumping)	12
4	Hoops (solid or segmented)	
	30″ diameter	36
	36″ diameter	36
5	Wands (36″ length, ¾″ diameter hardwood)	36
6	Game Cones (12″ bright orange vinyl)	20
7	Tambourine, single head double ring	1
8	Plastic racquets (sized for elementary children)	36
9	Foam balls for racquet skills (2½″)	36
10	Fleece Balls (3–4″ diameter)	36
11	Floor Hockey Sticks and Pucks—36 of each	36
12	Whiffle Balls (use for throwing, hockey, softball, etc.)	36
13	Individual Mats (23″ × 48″ × ½″)	36
14	Partner Tug-of-War Ropes (handles on both ends made with nylon webbing or garden hose and ⅜″ nylon rope)	18
15	Juggling Scarves	108
16	Beachballs (18″ to 20″ diameter)	36
17	Soccer Balls (junior size or trainers)	18
18	Basketballs (junior size)	18
19	Footballs (junior size or foam rubber)	18
20	Volleyballs (lightweight trainer balls)	18
21	Softballs (extra soft)	18
22	Softball Bats (wood or aluminum)	3
23	Frisbees, 9″ to 10″ diameter	36
24	Magic Stretch Ropes	12
25	Cageball (24″)	1
26	Pinnies (four colors—12 each)	48
27	Ball Bags (nylon see-through mesh)	12
28	Team Tug-of-War Rope (¾″ × 50 ft nylon with sealed ends)	1
29	Stopwatches (digital)	6
30	Batons (for track & field relays)	12
31	Scooterboards, 12″ with handles	18
32	Bowling Pins	30
33	Lummi Sticks	72

FIGURE 10.5 Basic equipment, supplies and capital outlay items, needed for quality physical education.

Priority	Capital Outlay Items	Quantity
1	Tumbling Mats (4 ft × 8 ft × 1¼" thick; 4 sides of Velcro fasteners)	12
2	Cassette Tape Player	1
3	Parachute and Storage Bag (28 ft diameter)	1
4	Electric Ball Pump	1
5	Heavy Duty Equipment (Ball) Carts	4
6	Balance-Beam Benches (12 ft length)	6
7	Jumping Boxes (8" height)	6
8	Jumping Boxes (16" height)	6
9	Audiovisual Cart with Electrical Outlet (for tape player, etc.)	1
10	Sit-and-Reach Box (measure flexibility)	2
11	Utility Gym Standards (for volleyball nets, etc.)	2
12	Field Marker (for chalking lines)	1

FIGURE 10.5 (continued)

shipped quickly with an unconditional guarantee. If you are not satisfied with any Gopher purchase for any reason, at any time, contact Gopher and they will replace it, credit your account, or refund your money. For a current catalog or more information, call the number above or fax a request to (800) 451-4855.

STORAGE PLANS

When a class goes to the gymnasium for physical education, the teacher has a right to expect sufficient supplies to be available to conduct the class. A master list stipulating the kinds and quantities of supplies in storage should be established. A reasonable turnover is to be expected, and supply procedures should reflect this. Supplies in the storage facility should be available for physical education classes and for organized after-school activities. The supplies should not be used for games played during recess or for free play periods; each classroom should have its own supplies for such purposes. A system should be established for the storage of equipment and supplies. "A place for everything and everything in its place" is the key to good housekeeping. Bins, shelves, and other assigned areas where supplies and equipment are to be kept should be labeled.

Both teachers and students must accept responsibility for maintaining order in the storage facility. Squad leaders or student aides can assume major responsibility. At the end of the week, the teacher in charge of the storage area can assign older children to help tidy the area, put any stray items back in place, and repair or replace articles as needed. A principal will be more favorably inclined toward purchase requests when obvious care is taken of instructional materials.

Some schools use small supply carts of the type pictured in Figure 10.6. The carts hold those articles used most frequently. They take up some additional space but do save time in accessing needed items. The carts can be built inexpensively to meet specific needs, or commercially manufactured equipment carriers can be purchased. A cart that holds the audio equipment and carts that store and move mats and balls are helpful.

An off-season storage area, where articles not in present use can be kept, should be established. Equipment not in current use should be kept in this separate area, perhaps under lock and key.

FIGURE 10.6 Portable ball cart.

CARE, REPAIR, AND MARKING

A definite system should be developed for repairing supplies and equipment. A quick decision must be made about whether to repair an item locally or to send it out of the area for repair. If the repair process is lengthy and not cost efficient, using the article until it can no longer be salvaged may be preferable to being deprived of its use. An area should be established for equipment needing repair, so that all articles to be repaired are evident at a glance.

Balls must be inflated to proper pressures. This means using an accurate gauge and checking the pressures periodically. The inflation needle should be moistened before insertion into the valve. Children should kick only those balls made specifically for kicking (soccer balls, footballs, and playground balls).

Softball bats and wooden paddles should not be used to hit rocks, stones, or other hard materials. Neither should bats be knocked against fences, posts, or other objects that might cause damage. Broken bats should be discarded; they are unsafe, even when taped around the break. Children should learn to keep the trademark up when batting. Bats should be taped to prevent slippage.

Cuts, abrasions, and breaks in rubber balls should be repaired immediately. In some cases, repairs can be made with a vulcanized patch, such as those used for repair of tire tubes. In other cases, a hard-setting rubber preparation is of value. In some instances, repair may be beyond the scope of the school, and the ball should be sent away for repair.

For off-season storage, balls should be deflated somewhat, leaving just enough air in them to retain the shape. Leather balls should be cleaned with an approved conditioner.

Mats are expensive, and proper care is needed if they are to last. A place where they can be stacked properly must be provided, or if the mats have handles, they should be hung from those. A mat truck is another storage solution if there is space for storing the truck. The newer plastic or plastic-covered mats should be cleaned periodically with a damp, soapy cloth.

For small items, clean plastic ice-cream buckets make adequate storage receptacles. Most school cafeterias have these and other containers that can be used in the storage room to keep order. Small wire or plastic baskets also make good storage containers.

All equipment and supplies should be marked. This is particularly important for equipment issued to different classrooms. Marking can be done with indelible pencil, paint, or stencil ink. Few marking systems are permanent, however, and re-marking at regular intervals is necessary. Sporting goods establishments have marking sets. An electric burning pencil works well but must be used with caution so as not to damage the equipment being marked.

Rubber playground balls come in different colors, and assignment to classrooms can be made on the basis of color. A code scheme with different-colored paints can be used also. It is possible to devise a color system by which the year of issue is designated. This offers opportunity for documentation of equipment usage and care.

CONSTRUCTING EQUIPMENT AND SUPPLIES

This section is divided into two parts. The first part offers recommendations for sources and materials needed to construct equipment and supplies. The second part lists diagrams and specifications for building equipment in an economical manner. If the recommended equipment can be described adequately without an illustration, it is included in the first part.

Recommendations for Constructing Equipment and Supplies

The supply of balls can be augmented with tennis balls or sponge balls. Discarded tennis balls from the high school tennis team are useful. Holes can be poked in the tennis balls if they are too lively for young children to handle. Sponge balls are inexpensive and with care last indefinitely.

A good supply of ropes for jumping is essential. We are partial to the newer, plastic-link jump ropes; these ropes have good weight, come in attractive colors, can be shortened easily (by removing links), and can be purchased with color-coded handles. The handles provide good leverage for turning. However, ropes can also be made from cord. Heavy sash cord or hard-weave polyethylene rope is suitable. The ends should be whipped, heated, or dipped into some type of hardening solution to prevent unraveling. The lengths can be color coded with dye or stain. Kindergarten through grade 2 use mostly 7-foot ropes, with a few 6- and 8-foot lengths. Grades 3 through 6 use mostly 8-foot ropes, with a few 7- and 9-foot lengths. Instructors will require 9- or 10-foot ropes.

Enough ropes should be available in the suggested lengths to provide each child with a rope of the correct length. The supply of ropes should include eight to ten long ropes (14- to 16-foot) for long-rope jumping activities. A jump-the-shot rope can be made by tying an old, completely deflated volleyball on one end of a rope.

Beanbags are made easily. Good-quality, bright-colored muslin is suitable as a covering. Some teachers have asked parents to save the lower legs of worn-out denim jeans; this material wears extremely well and is free. Some instructors prefer a beanbag with an outer liner that snaps in place to allow for washing. Another idea is to sew three sides of the beanbag permanently. The fourth side is used for filling and has an independent stitch. The beans can be removed through this side when the bag is washed. Beanbags should be about 4 by 4 inches and 6 by 6 inches and can be filled with dried beans or peas, wheat, rice, or even building sand.

For games requiring boundary markers, pieces of rubber matting can be used; or small sticks or boards, painted white, are excellent. A board 1 by 2 inches across and 3 or 4 feet in length makes a satisfactory marker.

Tetherballs should have a snap-on fastener for easy removal.

Schools near ski areas may be able to get discarded tow ropes. These make excellent tug-of-war ropes.

Bowling pins or clubs can be turned in the school shop, or suitable substitutes can be made. For example, pieces of 2-by-2-inch lumber cut short (6 to 10 inches) stand satisfactorily. Lumber companies usually have dowels 1 to 1½ inches in diameter. Sections of these dowels make a reasonable substitute for clubs. Broken bats also can be made into good substitute clubs.

White shoe polish has numerous marking uses and can be removed from the floor with a little scrubbing.

Three-pound coffee cans can be used as targets. Empty half-gallon milk cartons also have a variety of uses.

Inner tubes can be cut in strips and used as resistance exercise equipment. The tube should be cut crossways in 1-inch-wide strips.

Old bowling pins can be obtained from most bowling alleys free of charge. Because the standard pins are too large for the children to handle easily, cutting 2 to 4 inches off the bottom is recommended. Parallel cuts through the body of the pin provide shuffleboard disks. For kindergarten and first-grade children, improvised balls can be made from crumpled newspaper bound with cellophane tape. Papier-mâché balls are also useful. Light foam rubber cubes can be trimmed to make interesting objects for throwing and catching.

Bamboo for making tinikling poles can sometimes be procured from carpet stores, which use the poles to give support to the center of a carpet roll. Plastic tinikling sticks are available commercially.

Good savings on rubber traffic cones can be realized if these are purchased from a highway department supply source, where they are usually less expensive than cones purchased from physical education equipment supply firms. Plastic jugs, half filled with sand, can be used in place of traffic cones.

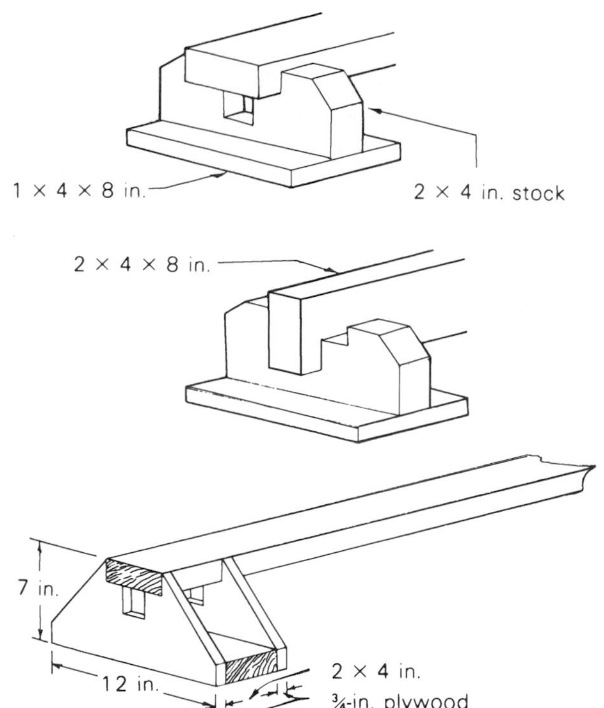

FIGURE 10.7 Balance beam with stand.

Diagrams and Specifications for Constructing Equipment and Supplies

Safety standards should apply to all school-constructed equipment; the construction and the materials used should not create any safety hazards. The design must be educationally sound and utilitarian.

Balance Beam

The balance beam is used for many kinds of activity. Two types of stand for a 2-by-4-inch beam are shown in Figure 10.7. The beam can be placed with the wide or the narrow side up, depending on the skill of the performer. If the beam is longer than 8 feet, a third stand should be placed in the middle. Care must be taken to sand and apply multiple coats of finish to the beam to prevent splintering and cracking.

Balance-Beam Bench

The balance-beam bench is a versatile piece of equipment. Its dimensions can be modified depending on the age of the users (Figure 10.8 on page 194). It should be made of hardwood or hardwood plywood and should be well-finished. Hooks can be fastened to the underside of the bench to provide even more uses for this important piece of apparatus.

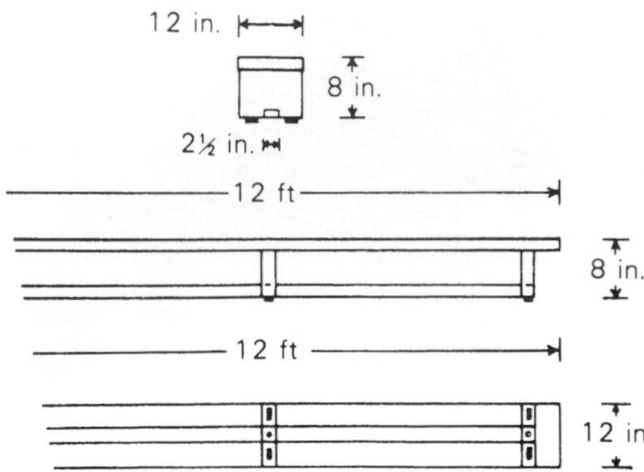

FIGURE 10.8 Balance beam bench.

Balance Boards

Many styles of balance board can be constructed, depending on the materials available and individual needs (Figure 10.9). Glue a piece of rubber matting to the top of the board to prevent slipping and place it on an individual mat or on a piece of heavy rubber matting. A square board is easier to balance than a round one, for its corners touch the floor and give more stability.

Batting Tee

Ideally, the batting tee should be adjustable to accommodate batters of various heights (Figure 10.10). Constructing an adjustable tee takes time, however, and the results are not always satisfactory. An alternative is to make several nonadjustable tees of different heights.

Materials:

One piece of 1-inch pipe, 24 to 28 inches long

One piece of radiator hose, 8 to 12 inches long, with an inside diameter of 1½ inches

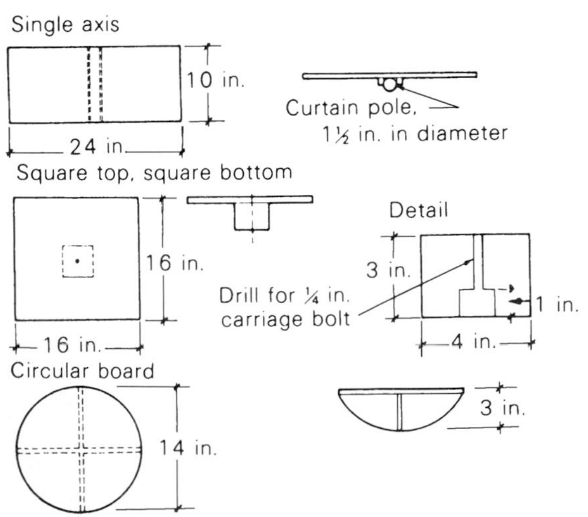

FIGURE 10.9 Styles of balance board.

One block of wood, 3 by 12 by 12 inches

One pipe flange for 1-inch pipe, to be mounted on the block

Screws and hose cement

Directions: Mount the flange on the block and screw the pipe into the flange. Place the radiator hose on the pipe. Paint as desired. To secure a good fit for the radiator hose, take the pipe to the supply source. If the hose is to remain fixed, then secure it with hose cement.

An alternative method is to drill a hole in the block and to mount the pipe directly in the hole with mastic or good-quality glue. Note that 1-inch pipe has an outside diameter of approximately 1 inch, allowing the hose to fit properly over it.

Blocks and Cones

Blocks with grooves on the top and on one of the sides are excellent for forming hurdles with wands. A 4-by-4-inch board, cut in lengths of 6, 12, and 18 inches, yields a variety of hurdle sizes. Cones can be notched and used in place of the blocks (Figure 10.11).

Bowling Pins

Bowling alleys give away old tenpins, which can be used for many purposes. Some suggested uses are as field and gymnasium markers, for bowling games, and for relays. The bottom 2 inches of the pin should be cut off, and the base sanded smooth (Figure 10.12). Pins can be numbered and decorated with decals, colored tape, or paint.

Conduit Hurdles

Conduit hurdles are lightweight and easy to store. Because they are not weighted and fall over easily, children have little fear about hitting them. The elastic bands can be moved up and down to create different heights and different challenges. Conduit can be purchased at most electrical supply houses.

Materials:

One piece of ½-inch electrical conduit pipe, 10 feet long

One piece of 1-inch stretch elastic tape

Wood doweling, ½ inch in diameter

Directions: Bend the piece of conduit to the following dimensions: Uprights should be 30 inches high, the base should be 30 inches wide, and the sides of the base should be 15 inches long. A special tool for bending the conduit usually can be purchased from the supply house where the conduit was bought. Sew loops on each end

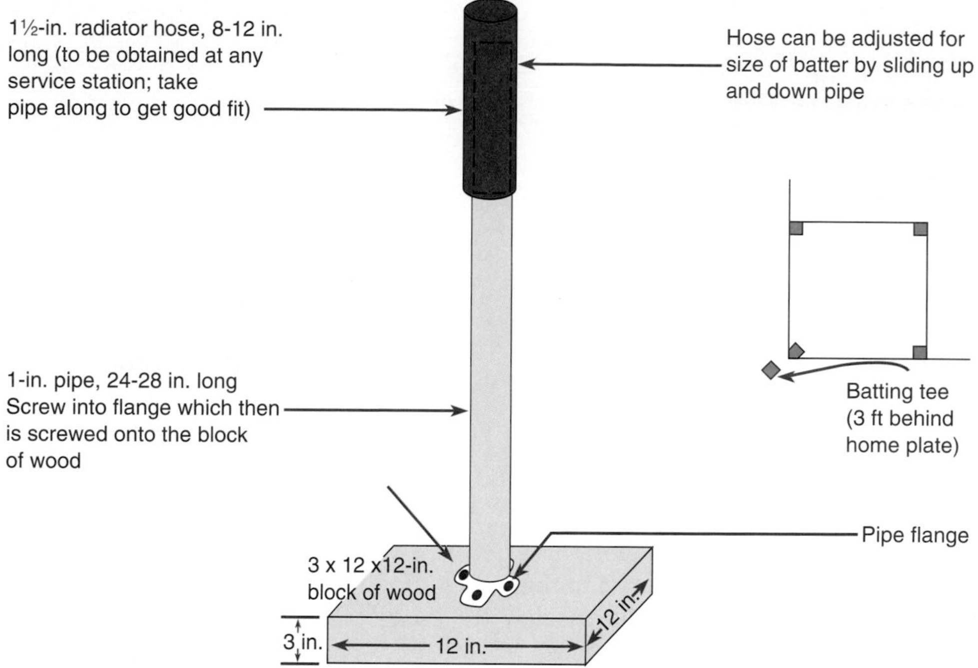

FIGURE 10.10 Batting tee construction.

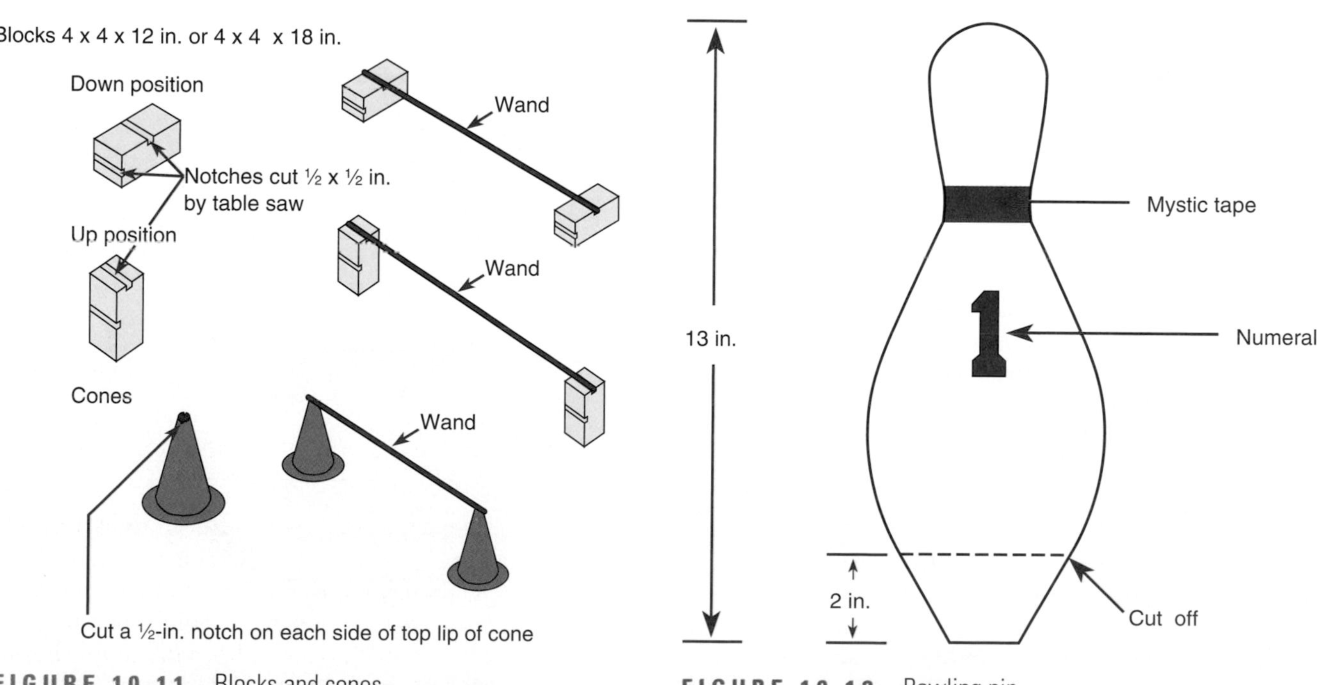

FIGURE 10.11 Blocks and cones.

FIGURE 10.12 Bowling pin.

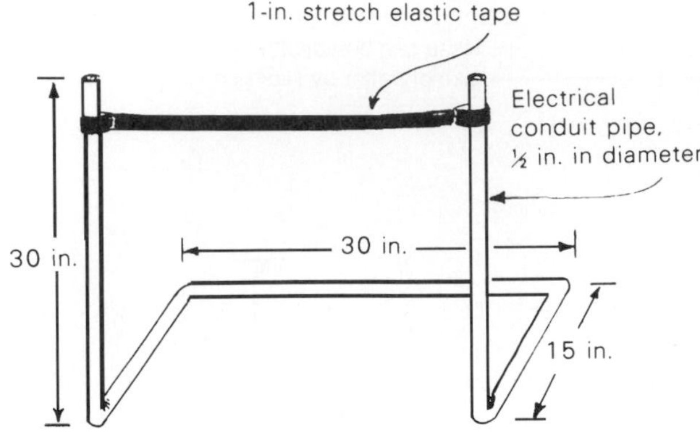

FIGURE 10.13 Conduit hurdle construction.

of the elastic tape, so that the tape will slide over the ends of the hurdles with a slight amount of tension. If necessary, short pieces of doweling can be put in the ends of the conduit to raise the height of the hurdle (Figure 10.13).

Footsies

Footsies can be made economically by the children. They provide an excellent movement challenge. The activity requires coordination of both feet to keep the footsie rotating properly.

Materials:

Plastic bleach bottle, half-gallon size

One piece of ⅛-inch clothesline-type rope

Old tennis ball

Large fishing swivel, preferably with ball bearings

Directions: Cut a circular strip about 2 inches wide out of the bottom of a bleach bottle. Cut two holes in the strip about 1 inch apart. Thread a 3-foot piece of clothesline through the holes, and tie a knot on the outside of the strip. Cut the clothesline in half and tie the swivel to each end of the cut cord. The swivel prevents the rope from becoming twisted.

Puncture the tennis ball with an ice pick, making two holes directly across from each other. Thread the line through the holes with a piece of wire or a large crochet hook. Tie a large knot near the outer hole so that the line cannot slip back through (Figure 10.14).

Gym Scooters

Scooters are easily constructed from readily available materials and can be made in many sizes and shapes. The casters should be checked to make sure that they do not mark the floor. Scooters have many activity applications and can also be used to move heavy equipment.

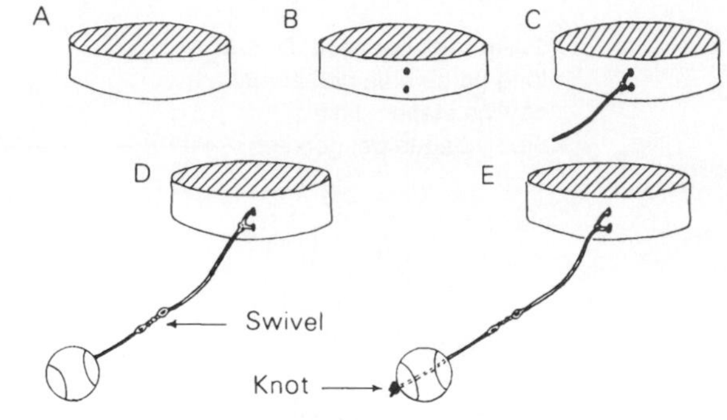

FIGURE 10.14 Footsie construction.

Materials:

One piece of 2-inch yellow pine board, 12 by 12 inches

Four ball-bearing casters with 2-inch wheels of hard rubber

Protective rubber stripping, 4 feet in length

Cement

Screws and paint

Directions: Actual dimensions of the board are around 1⅝ by 11⅝ inches. Two pieces of ¾-inch plywood glued together can be substituted. Cut and round the corners, smoothing them with a power sander. Sand all edges by hand, and apply two coats of paint. Fasten the four casters approximately 1½ inches diagonally in from the corners. A rubber strip fixed around the edges with staples and cement (Figure 10.15) will cushion the impact of the scooter on other objects.

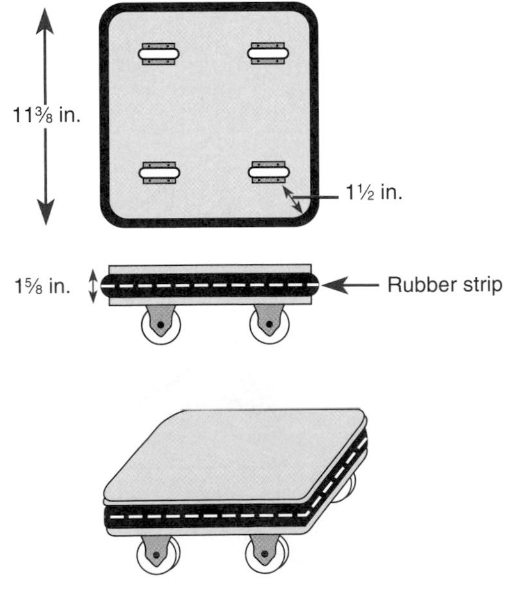

FIGURE 10.15 Gym scooter construction.

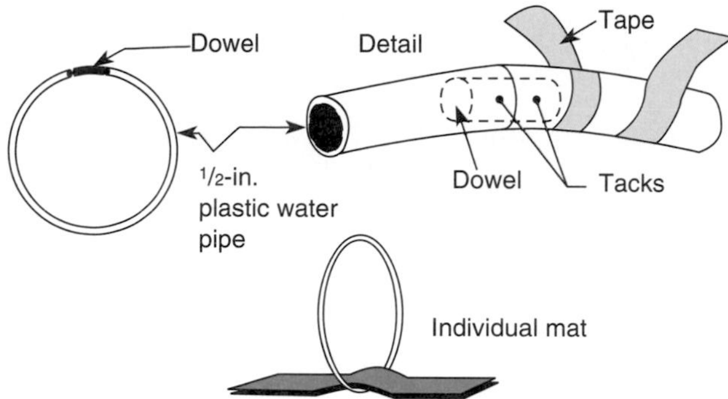

FIGURE 10.16 Hoop construction.

Hoops

Hoops can be constructed from ½-inch plastic water pipe (PVC), which unfortunately is available in drab colors only. The cost savings of using the pipe are, however, great. Hoops can be constructed in different sizes. A short piece of doweling, fixed with a power stapler or tacks, can be used to join the ends together (Figure 10.16). An alternative joining method is to use special pipe connectors. Weather-stripping cement helps make a more permanent joint.

Hurdle and High-Jump Rope

The weighted hurdle and high-jump rope is ideal for beginning hurdlers and high jumpers who may fear hitting the bar. The rope can be hung over the pins of the high-jump standards; the weights keep the rope fairly taut.

Materials:

One piece of ⅜-inch rope, 10 feet long

Two rubber crutch tips (no. 19)

Tacks (no. 14) and penny shingle nails

Sand

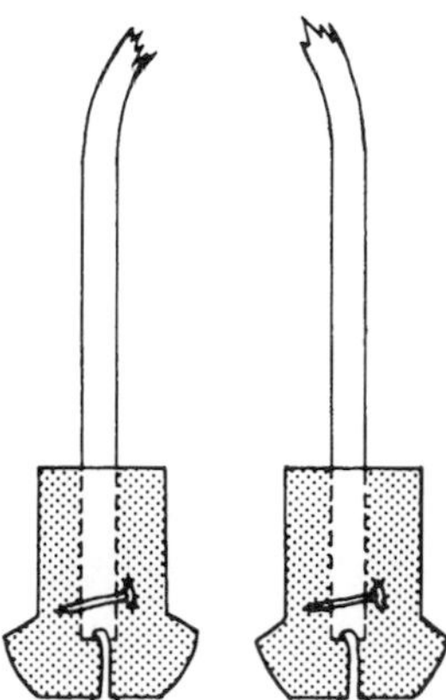

FIGURE 10.17 Weighted hurdle and high-jump rope construction.

Directions: Drive a carpet tack through the rope approximately ¾ inch from each end. Drive three nails into the bottom of each of the two rubber crutch tips. Place the rope ends inside the crutch tips and fill the tips with sand. Tape shut the top of the tips (Figure 10.17).

Individual Mats

Individual mats can be made from indoor-outdoor carpeting that has a rubber backing. This prevents the mat from sliding on the floor and offers some cushion. The mats also can be washed easily when they become soiled. Mats of different colors are preferable, because they can be used for games, for color tag, and for easy division of the class according to mat color. Carpet stores often have small pieces and remnants that they will sell cheaply or give away.

Another type of individual mat is designed to fold (Figure 10.18). These mats are useful for aerobic dance classes because they are lighter and easier to handle than the carpet mats. The major drawback is that the folding mats are more expensive.

FIGURE 10.18 Folding individual mat.

Jumping Boxes

Jumping boxes are used to develop a wide variety of body management skills. The dimensions can be varied to satisfy individual needs, but 8- and 16-inch boxes seem to be the most useful.

Materials:

¾-inch marine plywood

Wood screws, paint, and glue

Carpet pad remnants

Naugahyde or similar material to cover box top

Upholstery tacks

Directions: Cut the four sides to similar dimensions and then sand them together to make sure they are exactly the same size. Use a countersink and drill the screw holes, apply glue at the joints, and screw the sides together. When the box is assembled, sand all edges to remove any sharpness. Paint the boxes, preferably with a latex-based paint, because it does not chip as easily as oil-based enamel. If handholds are desired, drill holes and then cut them out with a saber saw (Figure 10.19). Covering is optional; if desired, cut a carpet pad remnant to match the size of the top of the box, and cover with a piece of Naugahyde. The Naugahyde should overlap about 4 inches on each side of the box so that it can be folded under a double thickness and then tacked down.

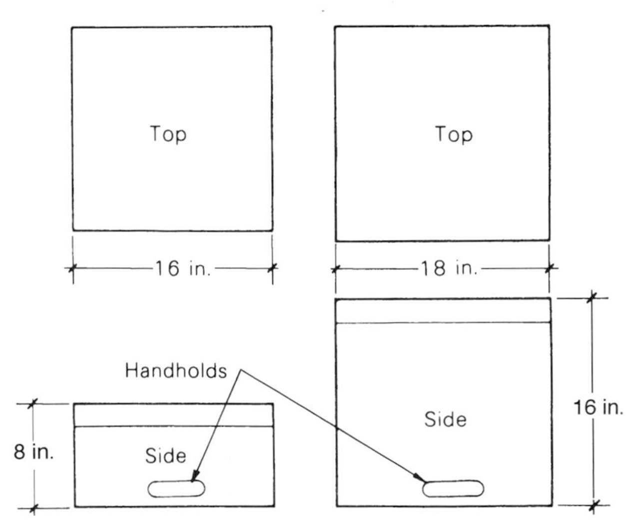

FIGURE 10.19 Jumping box construction.

Jumping Standards

Jumping standards are useful for hurdling, jumping, and over-and-under activities. Many shapes and sizes are possible (Figure 10.20).

Materials:

Two pieces of ¾-inch plywood 25 inches long, cut as shown

Two blocks of wood, 2 by 4 by 6 inches

Glue and paint

Broomstick, 48 inches long

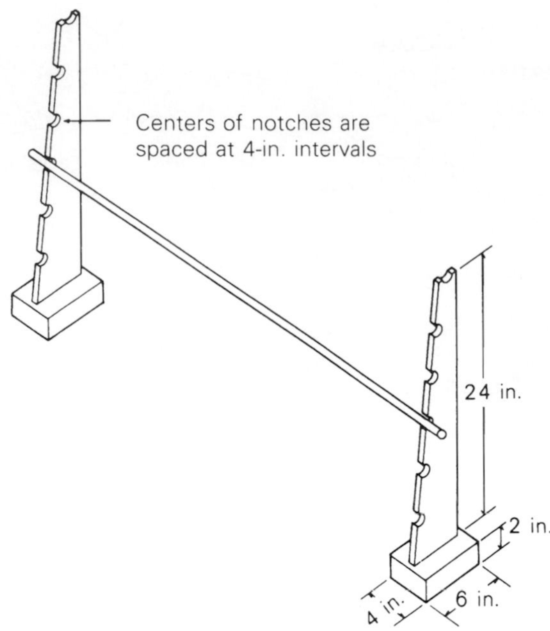

FIGURE 10.20 Jumping standard construction.

Directions: The wood blocks should be mortised lengthwise, about 1 inch deep. After the uprights have been cut to form, set them with glue into the blocks—making sure that the uprights are plumb. Paint as desired. Small circles of various colors can be placed at each of the corresponding notches of the uprights for quick positioning of the crosspiece.

Ladder

A ladder laid on the floor or on a mat provides a floor apparatus for varied movement experiences and has value in remedial programs and programs for exceptional children. Sizes may vary (Figure 10.21).

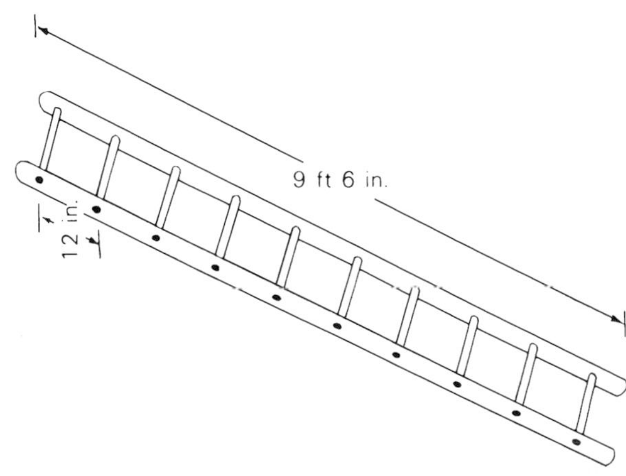

FIGURE 10.21 Ladder construction.

Materials:

Two straight-grained 2-by-4-inch timbers, 9½ feet long

Ten 1¼-inch or 1½-inch dowels, 20 inches long

Glue

Paint or varnish

Directions: Round the ends and sand the edges of the timbers. Center holes for the ladder rungs 12 inches apart, beginning 3 inches from one end. Cut the holes for the rungs 1/16 inch smaller than the diameter of the rungs. Put glue in all the holes on one timber, and drive in all the rungs. Next, glue the other timber in place. Varnish or paint the ladder.

Lummi Sticks

Lummi sticks are excellent tools for developing rhythmic skills. The sticks can also be used as relay batons.

Materials:

1-inch doweling, in 12-inch lengths

Paint and varnish

Directions: Notches and different colors are optional, but these decorations do make the sticks more attractive. If desired, use a table saw to cut notches ⅛ inch wide and ⅛ inch deep. Round off the ends and sand the entire stick. Paint and varnish the stick as shown in Figure 10.22.

Magic Ropes

Magic or stretch ropes can be made by stringing together 25 to 30 large rubber bands. Common clothing elastic also can be used to make the ropes (Figure 10.23).

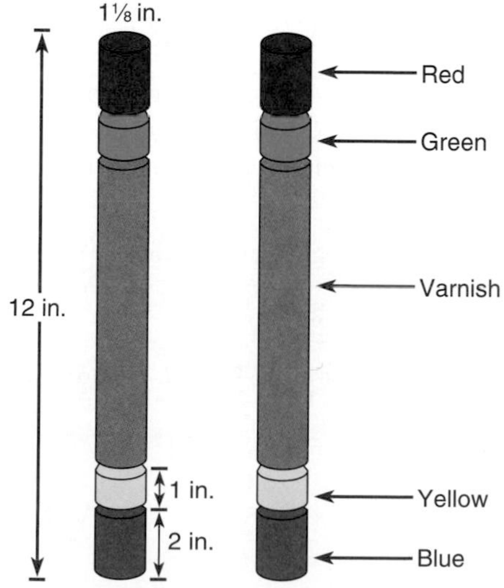

FIGURE 10.22 Lummi stick construction and decoration.

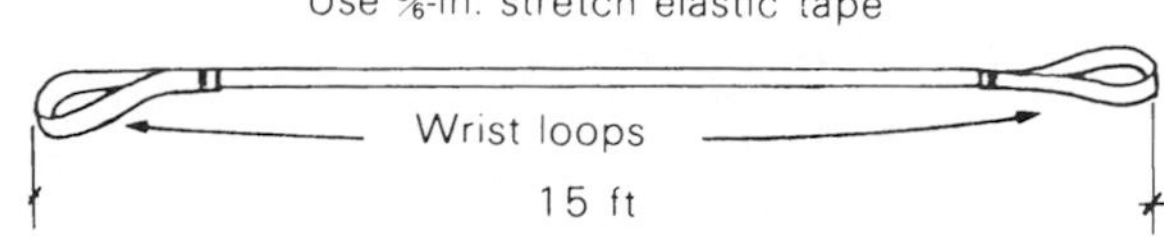

FIGURE 10.23 Magic rope construction.

Some teachers have had success with shock cord, which usually can be purchased at a boating marina or hardware store. Bungee cord of the proper length may also be used. Similar to shock cord, it may be purchased at many sports equipment outlets.

Outdoor Bases

There are many satisfactory methods for constructing bases. They can be made from heavy canvas by folding the canvas over three or four times and stitching it together. Heavy rubber matting can be cut to size. More permanent bases can be made from outdoor plywood and painted (Figure 10.24).

Materials:

Exterior ¾-inch plywood

Onc ½-inch carriagc bolt, 14 inchcs long

Paint

Directions: Cut the plywood into 12-by-12-inch squares. Bevel and sand the top edges. Drill a ½-inch hole in the center of the base and then paint the base. When the paint has dried, place the carriage bolt in the center hole and drive it into the ground. More holes can be used to make the base more secure. Large spikes can be substituted for the carriage bolt.

Paddles

Paddles can be made in many sizes and with different thicknesses of plywood (Figure 10.25 on page 200). Usually, ¼-inch plywood is recommended for kindergarten

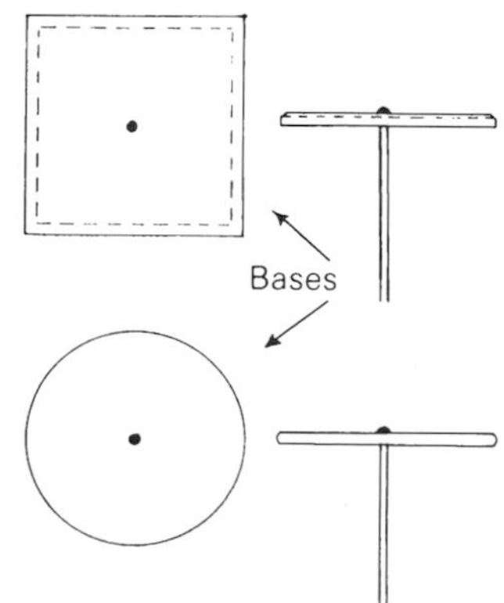

FIGURE 10.24 Outdoor base construction.

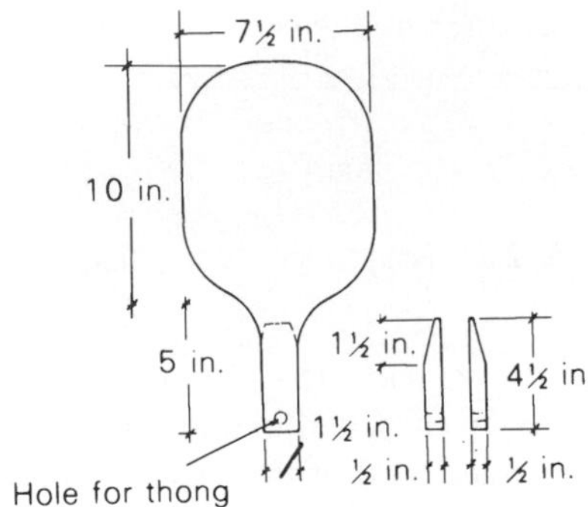

FIGURE 10.25 Paddle construction.

through grade 2, and ⅜-inch plywood for grades 3 through 6. Paddles can be painted or varnished, and the handles taped to give a better grip. Holes can be drilled in the paddle area to make it lighter and to decrease air resistance. Good-quality plywood, perhaps marine plywood, is essential.

For hitting a foam rubber ball or a newspaper ball, nylon-stocking paddles can substitute quite effectively for wooden paddles. Because of their light weight, they do not cause injuries. They are therefore excellent for primary-age children. A badminton bird can be used with the paddle for various activities, such as hitting over a net, and for many individual stunts.

Materials:

Old nylon stocking

Wire coat hanger

Masking tape or athletic tape

String or wire

Directions: Bend the hanger into a diamond shape. Bend the hook into a loop, which becomes the handle of the paddle (Figure 10.26). Pull the stocking over the hanger, beginning at the corner farthest from the handle, until the toe of the nylon is as tight as possible against the corner point of the hanger. Hold the nylon at the neck of the hanger and stretch it as tight as possible.

Tie the nylon securely with a piece of heavy string or light wire. Wrap the rest of the nylon around the handle to make a smooth, contoured surface. Complete the paddle by wrapping tape around the entire handle to prevent loosening.

Paddle Tennis Net Supports

The advantage of paddle tennis net supports is that they stand by themselves on the floor and still provide proper net tension. The stands come apart easily and quickly and can be stored in a small space. For lengths up to 8 feet or so, a single center board, with holes on each end, can be used, thus eliminating the need for bolting two pieces together (Figure 10.27).

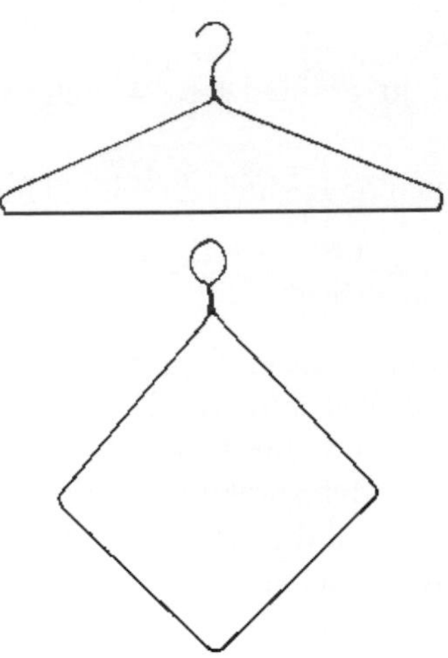

FIGURE 10.26 Frame for nylon-stocking paddle.

Materials:

Two broomsticks or ¾-inch dowels, 2 feet long

Two 1-by-4-inch boards, 2 feet long

One or more additional 1-by-4-inch boards

Glue

Directions: For the upright supports, drill a hole ¾ inch in diameter in the center of each 1-by-4 board. Drive the dowel into the hole, fixing it with glue. The dowels can be notched at intervals for different net heights.

The length of the crosspiece depends on how much court width is to be covered. If a single crosspiece is to be used, holes should be bored in each end. The holes should be big enough (⅞ in.) so that the dowel slides through easily. If the crosspiece is in two halves, ¼-inch bolts are needed to bolt the halves together, as indicated in the diagram.

Partner Tug-of-War Ropes

Partner tug-of-war ropes can be made from garden hose and ropes (Figure 10.28). The cheaper, plastic garden hose (⅝ inch in diameter) works much better than the

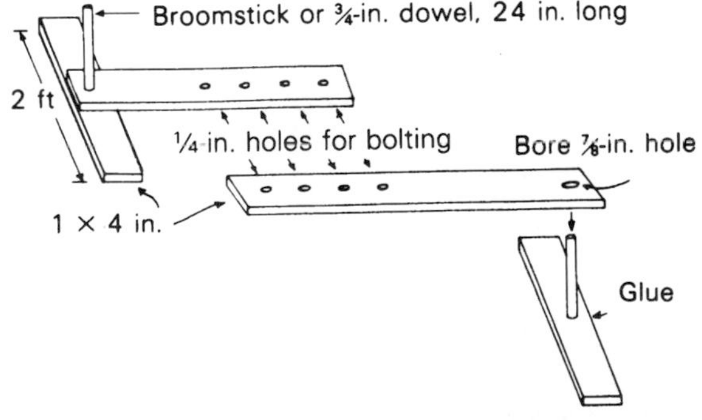

FIGURE 10.27 Paddle tennis net support construction.

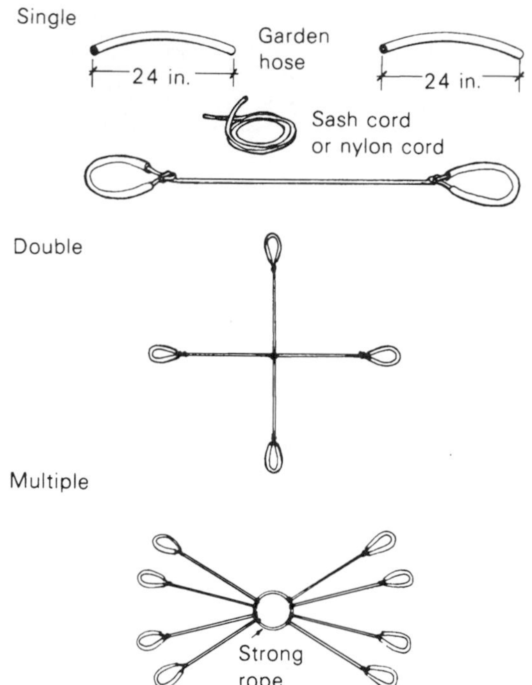

FIGURE 10.28 Partner tug-of-war construction.

more expensive rubber hose. The plastic hose then does not crease as easily and gives the hands more protection. The white, soft, braided nylon rope (⅜ inch in diameter) offers adequate strength and is much easier to handle than are other types of rope. A bowline knot should be used, because it does not slip and tighten around the hands. The ends of the nylon rope should be melted over a flame to prevent them from unraveling.

Plastic Markers and Scoops

One-gallon plastic jugs filled halfway with sand and recapped make fine boundary markers. The markers can be painted different colors to signify goals, boundaries, and division lines. The jugs also can be numbered and used to designate different teaching stations. Plastic bottles can be cut down to make scoops (Figure 10.29), which have many activity possibilities.

Rings, Deck Tennis (Quoits)

Deck tennis is a popular recreational net game that requires only a ring as basic equipment. The rings can be made easily by the students and are useful for playing catch and for target throwing. They can be fashioned from heavy rope by braiding the ends together, but the construction method illustrated in Figure 10.30 is easier. Weather-stripping cement helps strengthen the joints.

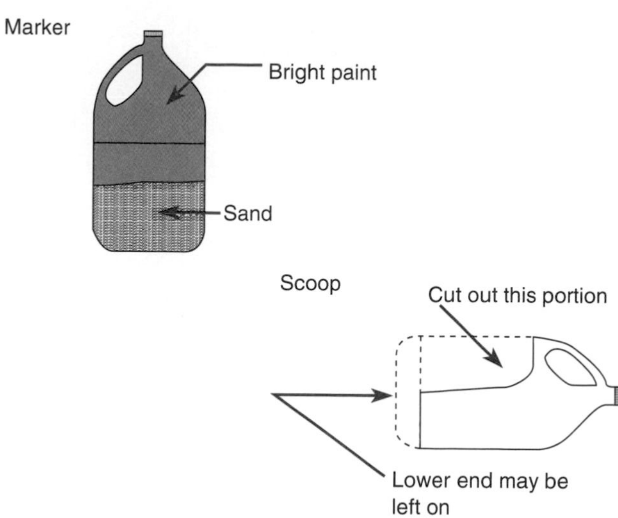

FIGURE 10.29 Plastic marker and scoop.

Ring Toss Target

Many ring toss targets can be made from 1-by-4-inch lumber and old broom or mop handles. They can be made to hang on the wall or to lie flat on the ground. The quoits constructed from garden hose are excellent for throwing at the targets. The target pegs can be painted different colors to signify different point values.

Materials:

Two 1-by-4-inch boards, 18 to 20 inches long

Five pegs, 6 inches long (old broom handles)

Screws and paint

Directions: Glue and screw the 1-by-4-inch boards together, as shown in Figure 10.31 on page 202. Bore the proper-sized holes in the boards with a brace and bit, and glue or screw the pegs into the holes. Note that two blocks must be screwed on the ends of the board placed on top so that the target stands level. Paint the base and the sticks, and, if desired, number the sticks according to point value.

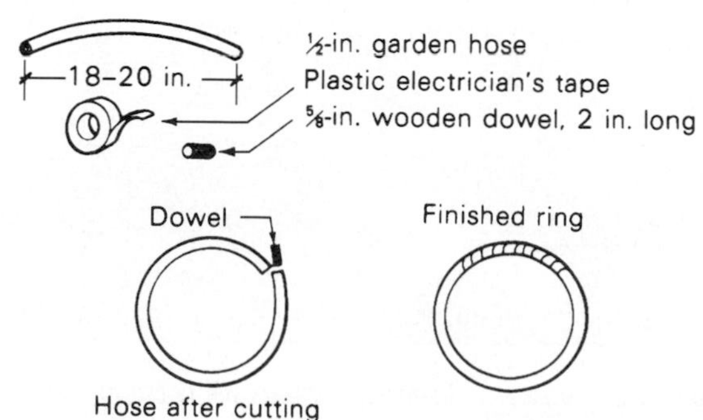

FIGURE 10.30 Ring construction.

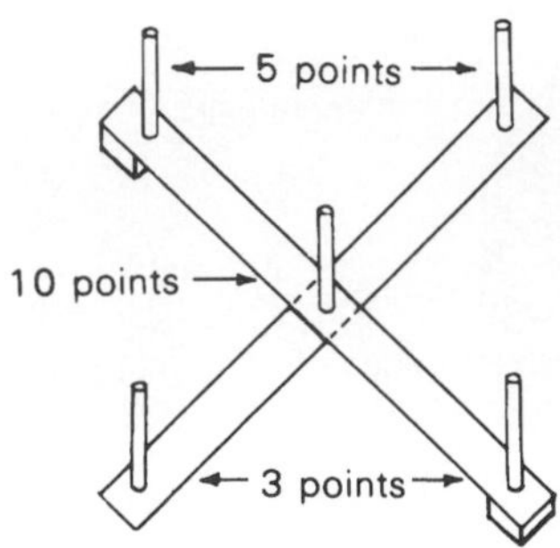

FIGURE 10.31 Ring toss target construction.

Sit-and-Reach Box

Sit-and-reach boxes are used for measuring flexibility in the Fitnessgram test. The basic sit-and-reach box is a 12-inch cube with a top that is 21 inches long. Sit-and-reach boxes for the Fitnessgram test require that the top of the box be calibrated in inches. The 9-inch mark is lined up with the side of the box where the feet are placed. Figure 10.32 shows a sit-and-reach box that is calibrated in both inches and centimeters.

Tire Stands

Tire stands keep tires in an upright position (Figure 10.33). The upright tires can be used for movement problems, over-and-through relays, and vaulting activities, and as targets. Tires are much cleaner and more attractive when they are painted both inside and out.

Materials:

Two 1-by-6-inch boards, 24 inches long, for side pieces

FIGURE 10.32 Sit-and-reach box with centimeters and inches scale.

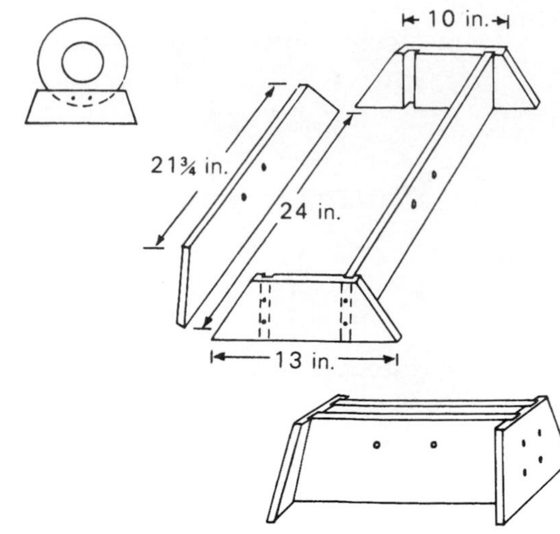

FIGURE 10.33 Tire stand construction.

Two 1-by-6-inch boards, 13 inches long, for end pieces

Four ⅜-inch carriage bolts, 2 inches long

Glue, screws, and paint

One used tire

Directions: Cut the ends of the side boards at a 70-degree angle. Dado each end piece with two grooves ¾ inch wide and ¼ inch deep. The distance between the grooves is determined by the width of the tire. Round off the corners and sand the edges. Glue and screw the stand together. Install the tire in the frame by drilling two ⅜-inch holes in each side of the frame and in the tire. Secure the tire inside the frame with the bolts. Paint both the tire and the frame a bright color. Note that the frame dimensions will vary according to the size of the tire, making it necessary to adjust the frame dimensions to the tire.

Track Starter

The track starter simulates a gun report. If many starters are made, the children can start their own races.

Materials:

Two 2-by-4-inch boards, 11 inches long

Two small strap hinges

Two small cabinet handles

Directions: Cut the boards to size, and sand off any rough edges. Place the two blocks together, and apply the two hinges with screws. Add the two handles on the outside of the boards. Open the boards and then slam them together quickly to obtain a loud bang (Figure 10.34).

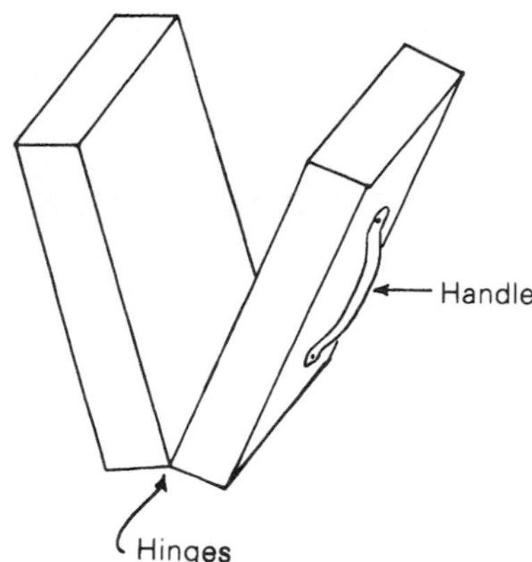

FIGURE 10.34 Track starter.

Wands

Handles from old brooms or mops make excellent wands (Figure 10.35). The handles may have different diameters, but this is not an important factor. The ends can be sanded, and the wands painted different colors. If noise is a concern, rubber crutch tips can be placed on the wand ends.

Yarn Balls

Yarn balls can be used to enhance throwing and catching skills and for many games. They have advantages over balls in that they do not hurt when they hit a child, and they can be used in the classroom or in other areas of limited space. Yarn balls can be made by the older children or by the PTA. Two construction methods are offered here; both work well. When possible, wool or cotton yarns should be used, because the balls will then shrink and become tight when soaked in hot water or steamed. Nylon and other synthetic yarns are impervious to water and so do not shrink and bond.

Materials for Method One:

One skein of yarn per ball

One piece of box cardboard, 5 inches wide and about 10 inches long

Strong, light cord for binding

Directions for Method One: Wrap the yarn 20 to 25 times around the 5-inch-wide dimension of the cardboard. Slide the yarn off the cardboard, and bind it in the middle with the cord to form a tied loop of yarn. Continue this procedure until all of the yarn is used up and tied in looped bunches. Next, take two of the tied loops and tie them together at the center, using several turns of the cord. This forms a bundle of two tied loops, as illustrated in Figure 10.36. Continue tying the bundles together until all are used. Now cut the loops and trim the formed ball. The cutting should be done carefully so that the yarn lengths are reasonably even, or considerable trimming will be needed.

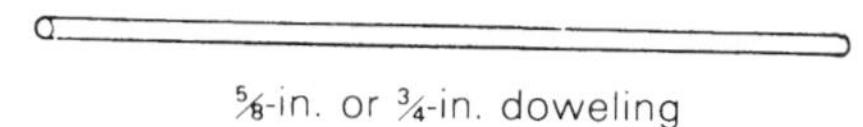

FIGURE 10.35 Wand dimensions.

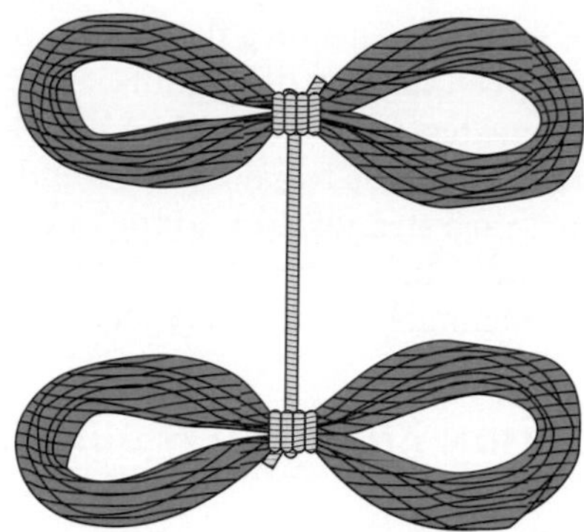

FIGURE 10.36 Yarn ball, method one.

Materials for Method Two:

Two skeins of yarn per ball

Two cardboard doughnuts, 5 or 6 inches in diameter

Strong, light cord for tying

Directions for Method Two: Make a slit in the doughnuts so that the yarn can be wrapped around the cardboard. Holding strands from both skeins, wrap the yarn around both doughnuts until the center hole is almost completely filled with yarn (Figure 10.37). Lay the

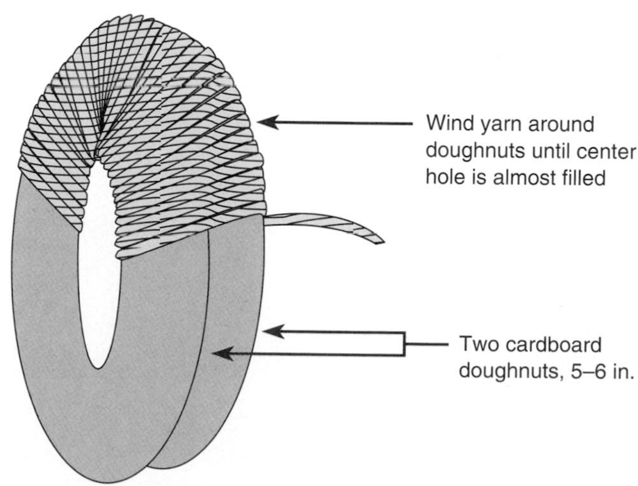

FIGURE 10.37 Yarn ball, method two.

doughnut of wrapped yarn on a flat surface, insert a pair of scissors between the two doughnuts, and cut around the entire outer edge. Carefully insert a double strand of the light cord between the two doughnuts and catch all of the individual yarn strands around the middle with the cord. Tie the cord as tightly as possible with a double knot. Remove the doughnuts, and trim the ball if necessary.

REFLECTION AND REVIEW QUESTIONS

How and Why

1. Do the school facilities in your area meet the standards of outdoor facilities?
2. How might teachers have to adapt because of the many "non-P.E." uses of the indoor physical education facilities?
3. Why would "homemade" equipment be necessary for some schools? Identify equipment that can be made by teachers.
4. How can teachers ensure appropriate maintenance of equipment?

Content Review

1. Present several standards for outdoor facilities. Include comments regarding playgrounds.
2. Identify 4 pieces each of outdoor equipment for upper body development, lower body development, and balance skills.
3. Discuss the standards for indoor facilities for physical education.
4. What is the difference between equipment and supplies? Provide examples of each.
5. List several pieces of equipment that are primarily used indoors.
6. Discuss the importance of purchasing policies, storage plans, and maintenance for equipment.

FOR MORE INFORMATION

References and Suggested Readings

McIntyre, S., & Goltsman, S. M. (1997). *Safety first checklist: Audit & inspection program for children's play areas.* Berkeley, CA: MIG Communications.

Morrison, M. L. (1993). *Evaluating and improving playground safety: A playground inventory and assessment system.* Pittsburgh: Injury Prevention Works.

Raatma, L. (1999). *Safety on the playground.* Mankato, MN: Bridgestone Books.

U.S. Consumer Product Safety Commission. (1997). *Handbook for public playground safety* (Publication No. 325). Washington, DC: Author.

Werner, P. H., & Simmons, R. A. (1990). *Homemade play equipment for children.* Reston, VA: American Alliance for Health, Physical Education, Recreation, and Dance.

Websites

Equipment
http://www.gophersport.com/Gopher/
http://pe.usf.edu/projects/fctpa/county/Pinellas/elorg-14.html

Guidelines for Facilities and Equipment
http://www.aahperd.org/naspe/pdf_files/pos_papers/instructional_mat.pdf

Making Physical Education Equipment
http://pe.central.vt.edu/preschool/prekhomemadeequipmentmenu.html
http://pe.usf.edu/projects/civitan/projects/equip/equip.html#directions

Playground Safety
http://www.cpsc.gov/CPSCPUB/PUBS/playpubs.html
http://www.uni.edu/playground/

CHAPTER 11

Interdisciplinary Instruction and Rainy Day Activities

ESSENTIAL COMPONENTS

I	**Organized around content standards**
II	Student-centered and developmentally appropriate
III	Physical activity and motor skill development form the core of the program
IV	Teaches management skills and self-discipline
V	**Promotes inclusion of all students**
VI	Focuses on process over product
VII	**Promotes lifetime personal health and wellness**
VIII	Teaches cooperation and responsibility and promotes sensitivity to diversity

PHYSICAL EDUCATION STANDARDS

1	Students are able to move competently using a variety of fundamental and specialized motor skills.
2	Students can monitor and maintain a health-enhancing level of physical fitness.
3	Students are able to apply movement concepts and basic mechanics of skill performance when learning and refining motor skills.
4	Students comprehend the basic principles of wellness and are able to apply concepts that enable them to make meaningful decisions that positively impact their health and wellness.
5	Students participate in a wide variety of physical activities and learn how to maintain a personalized active lifestyle.
6	**Students demonstrate empathy, understanding, and respect for the numerous differences exhibited by people in an activity setting.**
7	**Students exhibit responsible and self-directed behaviors that lead to positive social interactions in physical activity.**

SUMMARY

Children use knowledge learned in many settings. Interdisciplinary instruction integrates two or more subject matters and furthers the total development of children in each of the areas. Interdisciplinary instruction is thought to mirror life which crosses into many different areas on a regular basis. Rainy day activities can further the outcomes of physical education even though space is at a premium. Many situations arise in schools that restrict physical education to the classroom or other limited-space areas. The primary goal of rainy day activities is to offer students the possibility for movement even though space is limited.

OUTCOMES

- Understand how to deliver physical education in a limited-space area.
- List guidelines for presenting classroom and limited-space activities.
- Identify activities that offer physical development and skill improvement.
- Know how to integrate physical education content into the academic setting.
- Develop physical education content strategies for classroom teachers to teach with academic subjects.

It's raining today. An assembly is taking place in the gymnasium today. These two scenarios occur on a regular basis for physical educators. Teachers either have to move indoors to a small room or hallway or leave the multipurpose room for a classroom. Either way, it is stressful to take a classroom of youngsters expecting activity into a limited-space area. This chapter offers concepts and activities that can be used when such situations occur. The first part of the chapter deals with interdisciplinary instruction. Such instruction is often done in a classroom setting. Integration of content is a two-way street. Academic subjects can be integrated into physical education, and physical education content can be woven into the academic setting. The activities listed here are designed for in-depth learning of concepts that require discussion, study, and planning.

Much integration can be done during a physical education lesson by simply asking youngsters to add numbers, spell words, skip count, etc. These less comprehensive efforts to integrate academics into the everyday physical education lesson are listed in each of the lesson plans that accompany this textbook—*Lesson Plans for Dynamic Physical Education* (2004). The lesson plans contain many suggestions for integrating many academic concepts into the daily lesson plan.

The second part of the chapter offers many suggestions and specific activities for conducting a productive physical education lesson in a limited-space setting. It is possible to present activities that are both educational and active even though the environment is less than optimal. They are activity-based in nature and focus on fitness development, skill development, and cooperative games. Rainy day activities are meant to offer as much physical activity as possible in what is most likely a classroom space.

INTERDISCIPLINARY INSTRUCTION

What students learn can be applied in many settings. Learning is holistic; students use what they have learned in one area in many other areas. Interdisciplinary instruction focuses on integrating two or more subject areas in a way that enhances learning for students in each of the areas. Physical education offers many opportunities for integrating subject matter and activity. Integrating physical education activities with other subject matter areas is limited only by the ingenuity of the teacher and the interests of youngsters. Physical education teachers can enlist classroom teachers to integrate physical education concepts into academic presentations. Integrating physical education experiences with other areas of the curriculum not only demonstrates to children that the teacher values the program but also makes physical activity more meaningful to them. A caveat here: Teachers should only integrate subject matters when doing so allows them to do so more effectively or it aids the learning process. Choose opportune times to incorporate interdisciplinary techniques into physical education. The following sections give specific ideas for integrating academic content and physical education concepts.

Art

Posters, decorations, and costumes bring together art and physical education. Some ideas for integrating art and physical education follow:

1. Illustrate features of various games, such as ball toss targets, shuffleboard courts, hopscotch, and four-square playing areas.
2. Make bulletin boards and other displays for classrooms, halls, and gymnasium. Some themes might be proper diet, activity and physical fitness, examples of great athletes at work, lifetime sports and leisure activity, and basic skills needed for specific sports.
3. Select a skill (such as throwing) and illustrate the various phases of a successful throw. Illustrate and analyze the rules of opposition, proper arm position, body rotation, and the follow-through.
4. Watch another class participating in a sport and create some action figures that capture the flavor of the sport. Analyze basic movements in various sports and games for their similarities and differences.
5. Develop costumes for a mock Olympiad. Study insignias of various countries and place them on the uniforms. Teams of students may work together to research a country's flag and paint the flag on butcher paper. The flag can then be carried in by the team during an opening ceremony. A similar activity can be used for field day with each class creating and painting a flag.
6. Carry out a contest to develop a school insignia and slogan. Posters could be painted and entered in the competition. The winning insignia could be silk-screened onto T-shirts for school teams.
7. Design charts of athletic fields or game areas and illustrate where players should be placed for various game strategies.
8. Draw athletic fields and game areas to scale. Visit a ball park and attempt to draw the entire facility to scale, including bleachers, dugouts, dressing rooms, and showers.
9. Make programs for upcoming pageants, gymkhanas, and physical education demonstrations. The programs could be illustrated or contain a map of the school's location. Provide a description of the evening's program.

10. Posters of encouragement could be painted and put up to show support for intramural teams, classroom competitions, and afterschool sports programs.
11. Make progress charts for activities such as jogging, push-ups, curl-ups, and pedometer step counts. High achievers could be given an award for achievement, and other students could be rewarded for participating. Students could design and paint these awards.
12. Study sculpture, paintings, and other art forms that illustrate early physical activities. Greek friezes and Egyptian art are excellent sources for the study of sport, dance, and gymnastics.
13. Design a playground that is both artistic and functional. Discuss how the artistic design and function must be integrated for a successful playspace.
14. Make posters to promote physical education events such as field day, Olympiads, charity fund-raisers (e.g., Jump Rope for Heart or Hoops for Heart), or physical education night at the school. Posters can also be made in flier-size paper to be sent home with students to let parents know of the upcoming events.
15. Make a mural for a gym wall as a class project with the art teacher's assistance. Smaller paintings can also be made for bulletin boards in the gym or throughout the school.
16. Draw pictures of favorite physical activities done outside of school or during recess. Similarly, draw pictures of favorite physical education activities. Teachers can use this to determine which activities the students are enjoying and which activities need to be altered to enhance motivation.
17. Create fitness or skill teaching signs to be used during lessons.

Geography

Because the origins of physical education materials are diverse, geographical associations provide the classroom teacher with another source of learning experiences. It is possible to find clues about the play and sports habits of people in their location, terrain, and other geographical factors. Some areas of study could be the following:

1. Study the climate in different areas of the United States to ascertain how climate affects play habits. Factors such as altitude and weather could be studied.
2. Play and study games of different countries. Cultural factors such as dress, folklore, mores, and industries might be related to the games in which people participate.
3. During a rhythmic unit in which folk dances are being taught, discuss the origin of the dance and the characteristics of the country and its people. Make costumes to make the dances more authentic.
4. Have students or local cultural groups from other countries visit the class to explain their play habits and games.
5. Study the Olympics to see which countries dominate certain sports in the competition. This would give a clue to the emphasis certain countries place on various sports and might be traced to the type of physical education found in the schools and why they are successful in this sport. Also, this discussion could be tied into #1 since geography is a factor in determining success for many countries.
6. Study geographical and climatic factors of various areas to see how they affect athletic performance. For instance, discuss how altitude at the Mexico Olympic Games in 1968 seriously affected long-distance runners but aided long jumpers.
7. Language barriers during international competition often cause problems for officials and referees. Discuss attempts to remedy this problem.
8. Using pedometers, have students record their steps, convert steps to miles, and track a trip around the country, state, or city on a map. As they pass through different regions, cities, or streets, discuss the geography and the popular activities in the area. This activity is best accomplished by combining the steps of all class members to ensure everyone "stays together."

Health, Safety, and Wellness

It is difficult to separate health, safety, and wellness from physical education. Physical education should be carried on in a healthful and safe atmosphere. Many opportunities for cooperative teaching of related concepts arise between classroom teachers and various subject matter specialists. Safety considerations for each activity are important in the planning. Many more ideas for integrating the area of wellness can be found in Chapter 13.

1. Discuss physical fitness concepts. The basic steps in developing physical fitness and their relationship to the general health of the individual should be clearly understood.
2. Consider the importance of exercise in promoting physical and mental wellness. Carry out research to see what specific effects exercise has on the human body and mind. The effects of drugs, tobacco, and alcohol should be explored and discussed as a function of human wellness.
3. Declare a safety week for the school. Students could develop a list of safety standards for the school and make posters that illustrate proper safety techniques.

4. Relate activities and skills learned in physical education to leisure and recreation. Students should realize the value of learning skills at an early age so that they will be able to use the skills in lifetime activity.
5. When physical examinations are given to classes, discuss the reasons for periodic examinations. Cover congenital as well as acquired defects, conditions caused by disease, and the problems of contagious disease.
6. Discuss the value of exercise in promoting healing and improving certain conditions. Students with asthma, if their situation is faced openly, can learn to gauge how much activity they can handle. If a child's limb is broken, discuss the problem of muscle atrophy to demonstrate the need for exercise and use of muscles.
7. Conduct a posture checkup day. Discuss the mechanics of posture, with emphasis on methods of improving the posture of class members.
8. Analyze nutrition, rest, and body care to see the role they play in daily living and maintaining a healthy body.
9. Take a period to inspect equipment and facilities for safety. After the inspection, discuss existing conditions and new standards.
10. Develop simple experiments to show the immediate effects of exercise on the body. Try measuring pulse rate or breathing rate before and after exercise. Or, collect air exhaled at rest and after exercise in plastic bags. Consider reasons for the body adaptations demonstrated.
11. Explore the crucial balance between caloric intake and exercise. Children must understand that obesity is controlled through a combination of proper diet and adequate exercise. Discuss the activity pyramid and the food pyramid. Present the importance of balancing both pyramids for health.
12. Plan a daily and weekly schedule for work, rest, and play, and then compare the plan with recommended time allotments and with other students' schedules.
13. Prepare a unit on first aid to gain a basic understanding of proper procedures for treating injury.
14. Do a class project dealing with various physical and mental handicaps. This activity can foster a sensitivity to youngsters with handicaps in a physical education setting.
15. Analyze the fat content of foods by providing students with food labels (or nutritional information on their favorite foods), measuring utensils, and solid cooking oil. Students determine the amount of fat in each item and place that much solid cooking oil on a plate. For older students, have them record their diet for a day to find out how much fat they eat in one day.
16. Discuss the impact inactivity, smoking, substance abuse, and negative health behaviors have on muscles, bones, and organs.

History

Physical education is rich in historical background. Many present-day activities are based in tradition. Knowledge of the historical aspects of physical education should be developed. An appreciation of physical education could be furthered if children understood the background of an activity.

1. Study the origin of various activities. Events such as the discus throw, the shot put, and the pole vault are performed now only because of tradition.
2. Explore the origin and adaptation of present-day sports such as baseball, basketball, and U.S. football. Analyze the relationship between rule changes and the higher athletic achievements of modern athletes.
3. The history and development of sports equipment and facilities are often interesting and revealing to students. For example, compare the Roman Colosseum with present-day stadiums, or compare levels of performance with different types of poles used for vaulting.
4. Study a particular sport to bring out the records and achievements of outstanding players. Examples of questions to guide discussion might be the following: Who were big names and pioneers in sports? Who were the outstanding individuals who set records, and what were these records? What individuals achieved outstanding performances on an international level, including the Olympic performances? A sports quiz could be made up to include items from each of the categories. Be sure to include achievements of both women and men.
5. Study the ethnic background, historical context, and meaning of dances to make them more interesting.
6. Compare the fitness of different peoples. The ancient Greek, Persian, and Roman civilizations placed much emphasis on fitness, as do modern-day countries.
7. Study the fascinating history of the Olympics. The evolution from the ancient games to the present-day Olympics offers many insights into the values of different societies.
8. Study medieval knights and their jousting tournaments.
9. Study the games and activities of a specific historic era (i.e., the Civil War, the Depression, WWI) in the

United States. Have the popular games changed throughout the history of America?

Language Arts

Physical education materials make useful subjects for written and oral expression. The world of sports and games provides many examples of outstanding individuals who can serve as topics for presentations. Additional suggestions follow:

1. To increase motivation for reading, make use of game descriptions, rules of various sports, autobiographies of sports heroes, newspaper reports of game scores, and books oriented toward improvement in a given sport.
2. Use writing activities such as the following. Write a summary of a game program your school has conducted. Go to an intramural contest and report the results for the school newspaper. Find out as much as possible about your sports hero, and write a short story about that individual.
3. Practice oral expression by giving demonstrations and describing various points of performance, explaining rules of various activities to other students, reporting the results of a school contest to students who were unable to attend, or working in small groups to evaluate each other's performances.
4. To add some interest to spelling, learn words that will occur in the coming physical education lesson. A few different sports terms could be added to the weekly spelling list, and a spelling bee using only terms and words found in sports and physical education could be conducted.
5. Try writing plays about famous sports heroes, about the origin and development of games, or about imaginary athletes. Pantomime various sports and games activities, and let other members of the class attempt to guess the activity being pantomimed.
6. Study the origin of terminology used in physical education. Words such as *gymnasium, calisthenics,* and *exercise* have unique origins.
7. When playdays or demonstrations are to be organized, have the class write the script to be used by the announcers. Cover the basics of public speaking and the use of the public address system.
8. Dramatize stories about athletes, important people in the history of sports, and famous referees and officials. Work in small groups and then give presentations to the rest of the class.
9. Conduct choral readings of well-known poems about sports, such as "Casey at the Bat."
10. Listen to short story or poem and then act it out.
11. Write about physical activity done outside of school. To stimulate writing, have students write about their favorite activity, how they learned to swim, and so on.
12. After recording pedometer data and the lesson type (i.e., basketball, gymnastics) for several lessons, write a paragraph explaining why some activities may be more active than others.

Music

Rhythm is an integral part of physical education, and much of the program features both music and rhythm. Musical training should not be isolated from physical education. The two areas overlap and should blend in the children's experiences. Ideas for combining musical and physical education include the following:

1. Learn the characteristics of music and rhythm and interpret the rhythm through movement.
2. When action songs are presented, divide the learning of the song and the movement patterns between the music teacher and the physical education teacher.
3. To understand more about music, learn the names of different musical selections and become familiar with the heritage of music.
4. Create rope-jumping and ball-bouncing routines to a selected piece of music.
5. Do exercises to music in order to understand the different tempos found in music as well as learning to move to the tempo.
6. Use the tom-tom often in introductory activities. Learn the fundamental locomotor movements and do them to the beat of the drum.
7. In an activity such as European Rhythmic Running (pages 337–338), make your own rhythm by chanting, clapping hands, and stamping feet.
8. Make tapes for exercise to music.

Number Concepts (Mathematics)

Number concepts can be strengthened through physical education. Practical applications of the processes of addition, subtraction, division, multiplication, percentage computation, and measurement can be demonstrated through selected procedures. The following ideas can enhance numerical concepts:

1. Measure your own and other students' performances. Learn to read a tape measure and a stopwatch to evaluate performances in terms of distance, time, and height.
2. After a self-test or standardized fitness test, work out the class averages.

3. Learn percentages by working out batting averages, team standings, and field goal accuracy. This is an especially good task for the student who cannot participate because of an injury or illness.
4. For a study of geometric principles, analyze the layout of fields and game areas. Rectangles, diamonds, and circles are used often as playing areas.
5. To understand the metric system better, compare European and U.S. performances. Measurements at a track meet might be made with the metric system.
6. Enhance basic arithmetic skills by using equations instead of numbers as signals in games. For example, instead of calling out "Eight," say, "Thirty-six divided by three minus four."
7. Play number hopscotch to develop number recognition and memory. A large square containing 16 to 25 smaller squares is drawn on the playground, and a number is placed in each of the smaller squares. A leader calls out a sequence of numbers and a player hops into each of the squares containing the numbers called.
8. Measure and lay out a playing field. Laying out a track and areas for field events could be a class project.
9. Track the activities used during lessons. Calculate the frequency each activity is used and the percent of lessons that contain that activity or lesson focus. For example, Astronaut Drills were used in 15 lessons throughout the year or gymnastics was the lesson focus 11 percent of the time. Discuss why physical education involves a variety of activities.
10. Use recorded pedometer data and stride length to calculate miles traveled. Convert miles to kilometers.
11. Estimate the number of steps that will be taken in a year of physical education based on one week, three weeks, and nine weeks of pedometer data. Which was the closest? Why?

Science

1. Look at the area usually used to participate in a variety of activities (tennis, racquetball, football, soccer, walking, and hiking). Why do some activities use more space than others? Can the activities that use a lot of space be played in smaller areas? How?
2. Draw activities that require fast movement. Slow movement. Why are these types of movements necessary during the activity?
3. Draw a picture of students participating in a variety of activities at high, medium, and low levels. Can the activities be done at all three levels?
4. Diagram an obstacle course that would require classmates to move at different speeds and levels, but in their own personal space.
5. Demonstrate "light," "weak," and "gentle" movements. Do these movements require a lot of force or not much force? In personal space, demonstrate the opposite of light, weak, and gentle movements.
6. Discuss activities that require many different amounts of force. Similarly act out a book that involves a variety of forces being exerted.
7. Make each type of lever. Identify a joint in the body represented by the lever. For example, lifting a ball with the bicep is a third-class lever with the elbow as the fulcrum.
8. Determine the most stable body positions, or positions that are the easiest to stay balanced. Which position is easier to stay balanced in, on your tip toes, legs together, and reaching for the ceiling or with your feet flat on the floor, shoulder width apart, and knees bent? If being lower is more stable, in what position are you the most stable? Discuss why when walking on slick surfaces we usually bend our knees.
9. Create diagrams of the human body and label bones, muscles, and organs. For each muscle identified list one activity that uses that muscle. What activities use the most muscles?

Projects

Class projects in physical education and related areas form excellent educational opportunities. The teacher and children should plan together. Many ideas can be found for these projects. Playdays are an excellent one. A playday could be organized with one or more classes in the same school, with a class in another school, or among the children of the class itself. Demonstrations and exhibitions for parents are fruitful projects. A convocation program or demonstration in the gymnasium before other children merits consideration.

A schoolwide physical activity day can be planned by one grade. For example, the sixth grade class is in charge of organizing a physical activity day for the lower grades. Fliers are made, activities chosen and scheduled, as well as volunteers assigned for each activity. On the day of the event, with the help of an adult, the sixth graders monitor the activities and supervise the event.

A foreign country day can be planned, involving all specialists and teachers in the school. The physical education specialist could be responsible for preparing a show of games played in a certain country, the art teacher might assist in the preparation of native costumes, and the music teacher could teach a class to sing songs unique to the country. It might also be possible to cook a lunch that resembles food eaten in the selected country, and the foreign language teacher might help prepare a short play or skit in a foreign language.

Another suggestion is to invite another class to a rhythmic party. The program can be planned, invitations written, committees formed, and all the necessary details arranged. The enterprising teacher will think of many other project ideas. Projects could be done each season or once a year.

RAINY DAY ACTIVITIES

The basic premise of physical education is that it demands space and room for activity. At times, however, the need arises to conduct physical education in the classroom because of inclement weather. When weather is good, little need exists, because more than one class can use playground facilities. Adverse weather creates facility problems when indoor (gymnasium) space for a daily program is inadequate or nonexistent. This leaves the choice of conducting physical education in the classroom or having the children forgo their activity experiences for the day. Providing an instructional physical education program in the classroom setting requires the careful selection and teaching of appropriate activities in a challenging environment. Merely entertaining students with a variety of classroom games is less demanding but is not instructional. Games can be part of the offerings but should not be the only emphasis.

When an activity area is unavailable, teaching physical education in the classroom becomes necessary. Even though the effectiveness of the program is seriously hampered, it remains important that some physical activity be available to children. It is important that the sessions make a significant contribution to the fitness objective. In addition, sequenced skill presentations should be offered so that children have the opportunity to learn and enhance motor skills.

Minimize Noise

Children must recognize that activity is a privilege and that their cooperation is essential. They need to keep exuberance under control so that their activity does not interfere with other classes. (This can be a significant problem if one classroom is directly above or next to another.) If possible, an entire section of the school should have physical education periods at the same time. When all classes in the same part of the building are playing simultaneously, they will not disturb each other.

Prepare Facilities

When classroom desks and chairs are movable, a variety of activities are possible. Furniture can be pushed together to permit circle activities and rhythmic activities. Chairs and desks can be pushed to one side to form an open space. If mats, balance beams, or benches are to be used, several wider aisles can be made by pushing adjacent rows together. Rotating station groups offers excellent possibilities.

Instruction should be given in how to prepare desks for moving. All personal items must be put away, desktops cleared, and books and other objects stacked underneath in such a way that they will not fall out when the desks are moved. Place projecting items that might cause tripping in safe positions. If possible, open windows and lower the room temperature. If desks and chairs are fixed, space is more limited. Established aisles should be used, and as much space as possible cleared. Halls have a low priority for use. The noise permeates the entire building, and activity interferes with other students' passing.

Prepare Equipment and Supplies

If there is to be an appreciable amount of classroom physical education, a set of equipment and supplies separate from that used in the regular physical education program is needed. Having a supply cart that contains the items most used is an efficient system. The cart can be rolled directly into the classroom and saves sending monitors to a central point to carry items back to the classroom. Equipment carts that contain portable balance beams, light folding mats, balance boards, individual mats, and other equipment are also time-savers.

Each classroom should have a special collection of games, targets, manipulative objects, and other items for indoor play. Many of the items can be constructed by the children. Only supplies that will not damage the classroom should be used. Small sacks stuffed with excelsior, fleece balls, beanbags, yarn balls, rolled-up socks sewn together, balloons, and other articles of this nature can be used with little danger.

Maximize Activity

Plan judiciously to extract as much activity as possible from the experiences. As many children as possible should engage in activity at one time. Taking turns sometimes may be necessary, but standing around and waiting should be minimized. Safety must be a concern. Children should keep their feet well under their desks to avoid tripping players who are using the aisles.

Classrooms differ relative to the amount of usable space and the movable furniture, making it difficult to present a program that will fit most situations. Circuit training (pages 260–262) can be adapted for skill teaching. Use an instructional poster at each station for directions and cues. Another possibility is to combine circuit training with instruction. Assign one-half of the class to stations while the other half receives directed instruction from the instructor.

FITNESS DEVELOPMENT ACTIVITIES

Fitness activities can be adapted to limited space environments. A fitness corner permanently installed in the classroom can be used to supplement circuit training. This corner usually consists of a support beam mounted high on a wall or on the ceiling from which a variety of equipment—rings, hoops, trapezes, climbing poles and ladders, and climbing ropes—is hung. Several types are available from commercial sources. Equipment needs to be compact yet able to accommodate six or more children. Rubber bands made from inner tubes cut into two widths (1- and 2-inch) are useful for resistance exercises. A chart describing different resistance exercises can be posted. Some means of storage must be devised or the articles will be scattered around the classroom.

Aerobic Activities

Many of the fitness activities in Chapter 12 can be adapted for the classroom. For example, aerobic dancing can be performed alongside the youngsters' desks. Continuity drills can be performed by substituting running in place for jump roping. Astronaut drills can be performed up and down the aisles of the classroom. Circuit training can be effective in the classroom if there is enough room around the perimeter to create stations. The circuit could consist entirely of fitness activities or could combine fitness activities and other movement tasks. Fitness should not be eliminated from the program when youngsters have to enter the classroom. A little ingenuity will assure that fitness continues despite facility limitations.

Isometric Conditioning Exercises for Classroom Use

Isometric exercises are characterized by having virtually no movement of the body part, but a high degree of muscular tension. The muscles undergo a holding contraction of 8 to 12 slow counts. To prevent movement, the pulling, pushing, or twisting action is usually braced against some external force. This can be a desk, chair, wall, door frame, the floor, or a special isometric apparatus. Alternatively, one set of muscles can be worked against another, either individually or with a partner. Maximum or near-maximum tension of the muscle group must be reached and held for approximately 8 seconds. Repetition of an exercise at any one session is not needed, because maximum development is gained from one contraction at an exercise session. Contractions should be performed at different joint angles to ensure strength development throughout the full range of movement.

In the regular classroom, where narrow confines and furniture limit activity, isometrics have special value because they involve no movement. Many exercises can be done by children seated at their desks, with the desks used as braces. Isometric exercises are presented in five categories: (a) abdominal; (b) arms, chest, and shoulders; (c) back; (d) legs; and (e) neck. In each case, the arms provide the stabilizing force for the specified development, so in a sense, all of the exercises benefit the arms and shoulders.

Abdominal

1. Sit straight against a backrest. Hold the edges of the chair with the hands. Pull the stomach in hard against the backrest.
2. Sit with hands (palms down, fingers extended) on the lower portion of the top of the thighs. Press down with the hands and up with the legs. (This exercise can also be done by placing the hands on the knees and lifting the straightened legs.)
3. Stand about 4 feet behind a chair. Bend forward at the waist until the hands can be put on the back of the chair. (The elbows are straight.) With a strong downward pull from the abdominal wall and the arms, pull down against the chair.

Arms, Chest, and Shoulders

1. Stand or sit. Clasp the fingers together in front of the chest with forearms held parallel to the floor (elbows out). Pull against the fingers to force the elbows out. Be sure to keep the chest up, the shoulders back, and the head erect.
2. Stand or sit. Using a grip with the palms together and the fingers interlocked (knuckles upward), push the palms together. Be sure the elbows are up and out.
3. Sit. Drop the hands, straight down, to the sides. Curl the fingers under the seat. Pull up with the shoulders, keeping the body erect.
4. Sit. Rest the thumb and near part of the hands on top of the chair seat. Push to raise the seat completely off the chair. Hold.
5. Stand or sit. With the left palm up and the right palm down, clasp the hands in front of the body, chest high. Press down with the right hand, resisting with the left. Reverse.
6. Sit. Grasp two books (with a total thickness of about an inch) in an opposed thumb grip. Squeeze hard with both hands.

7. Sit or stand. Put both hands on top of the head. Slide the hands toward the elbows so that each grasps an elbow. Raise the arms high and attempt to pull them apart while resisting with the hands on the elbows.

Back

1. Sit. Bend forward and grasp the toes. Pull upward with the back while holding the toes.
2. Sit. Slide the hands forward to grasp the knees. From a slightly forward bend, pull back against the knee pressure. This exercise can also be done by placing the hands under the thighs near the knees.
3. Sit. Grasp the right hand under the chair. Apply pressure by leaning to the left. Reverse direction.

Legs

1. Sit with legs outstretched, the right ankle over the left. Press down with the right leg. Reverse position. Bend the knees and repeat right and left.
2. Sit, leaning forward. Cup the right hand around the outside of the left knee and vice versa. Force the knees outward against the inward pressure of the hands.
3. Sit, leaning forward. Place the cupped right hand against the inside of the left knee and vice versa. Force the knees together against the outward arm pressure.

Neck

1. Stand or sit. Clasp the hands behind the back of the head. Keeping the elbows well out, force the head back against the pressure of the hands.
2. Sit or stand. Place both hands flat against the forehead. Move the head forward against the pressure.
3. Sit or stand. Place the heel of the right hand against the head above the ear. Force the head to the right against the arm pressure. Repeat on the left side.

Isometric exercises using wands can be adapted for the classroom (see page 366). Instead of using a 36″ wand, consider the lummi stick or a 12-inch section of broom handle.

SKILL DEVELOPMENT ACTIVITIES

Rhythmics

Rhythmics are easily adapted to classroom activity, particularly when circle space can be arranged by moving the furniture to the center of the room. Rhythmic activities done in place are ideal, because children can be scattered in the available space. Selections featuring identification of body parts and individual movement are excellent for younger children. Lummi stick rhythms should be considered. If enough pathways in and around the furnishings can be arranged, fundamental movements guided by a drum or recorded music provide controlled activity. Chapter 19, on rhythmic activities, contains additional ideas.

Manipulative Activities

Selected manipulative activities can be used in the classroom. The major restriction is that many of the throwing, catching, kicking, rebounding, and batting activities do not suit the classroom situation. Prevention of facility damage is an overriding factor. Manipulative articles that cannot damage the facilities—balloons, yarn balls, paper balls, beanbags, and 8-inch foam rubber balls—are preferable. Target games in which the article is tossed or rolled at a target are recommended.

Individual activities in which a child handles an object are implemented easily. Children can balance beanbags on various body parts or toss and handle beanbags individually in a controlled situation. Juggling with scarves or small juggling balls is within the scope of classroom activities. Balloons, particularly for younger children, provide excellent challenges. A group of five or six children can be assigned two balloons. The children should try to keep the balloons aloft for a stipulated time period, while remaining glued to their chairs or the floor. A balloon that touches the floor is out of play.

Stunts and Tumbling

If there is room for six mats, a full-fledged tumbling program is feasible. With room for only one or two mats, tumbling is best used as a station in a teaching circuit. Individual stunt activities that demand little movement, especially in-place balance stunts, are examples of suitable activity.

Apparatus Activities

The difficulty of moving apparatus to the classroom, setting it up, and returning it is a serious limitation. Low, portable balance beams have value because these can be set up in aisles. A workable idea is to have apparatus set up at one or two stations. Balance boards, bounding boards, bongo boards, jumping boxes, and magic ropes are possible apparatus items for the stations.

Movement Experiences

Movement experiences that are done in personal space, either seated or standing, can be offered. For younger children, reinforcing the concept of laterality is an excellent activity. Commands that stimulate laterality are as follows:

"Point to the right, to the left, in front of you, behind you."

"Can you point your thumbs up, down, toward each other, away from each other? In the same direction to the right, to the left?"

"Put your arms out wide, forward, up high, down low."

"Turn your toes in, out. To the right, left."

"See if you can bend down, bend backward, to the right, to the left."

Identifying different body parts by touching provides similar experiences. Children can be asked to touch various body parts with the right hand, the left hand, and with both hands. Mirroring the movements of the teacher aids in visual recognition. The teacher makes various movements with the arms, and children mirror the movements. Later, they can try to copy the movements instead of mirroring them.

The Haida War Canoe Paddle is an interesting activity. (The Haidas were Indians who lived along the coast of British Columbia and traveled great distances in large canoes.) Each child uses a ruler as a paddle. The youngster at the head of the row is the bow paddler. All keep time with the bow paddler on the same side of the row. When the bow paddler shifts to the other side, all paddlers follow suit.

Other ideas, such as the following, can generate creative activity. Children can pretend to reel in a fish, catch fireflies, pound a hammer, pump up a tire, and so on. Poems also can elicit movement, particularly poems with specific movement commands. Two examples are provided. The first one starts with the children seated.

Two Little Hands

Two little hands go clap, clap, clap.
Two little feet go tap, tap, tap.
Two little knuckles go rap, rap, rap.
A quick jump from the chair.
Two little arms high in the air.
Two little fists grasp the hair.
Two little feet go jump, jump, jump.
Two little fists go thump, thump, thump.
Two little arms go pump, pump, pump.
One little body turns round and round.
One makes a face just like a clown.
One little body sits quietly down.

Exercise Time

I put my hands up high,
I put them way down low.
I put them way out wide,
And turn them up just so.
I jump with two feet fast,
I jump with two feet slow.
I turn round and round like a top,
Then I hold my head just so.
I move my hands like wings,
And then I try to swim.
I quickly sit way down,
And look around with a grin.

GAMES AND RELAYS

Games and relays selected for this section focus on activity for all children. Relays should be revolving in nature, where all team members are active throughout the activity.

Target Games

Target games can serve as one station in circuit training. They are high-interest activities and can offer challenge and variety to a fitness circuit.

BASKETBALL BOUNCE

Formation: Individual or by teams

Players: Two to six for each basket

Supplies: A basketball, volleyball, or other rubber ball; a wastepaper basket

Each player in turn stands behind a line that is 5 to 10 feet from a wastepaper basket. Five chances are allowed to bounce the ball on the floor and into the basket. Five points are scored for each successful basket.

BEANBAG PITCH

Formation: File—by rows

Players: Two to six for each target

Supplies: Beanbags; a small box for each team

A target box is placed at the head of each row. A pitch line is drawn 10 to 15 feet in front of the target. From behind the line, each player takes a specified number of pitches at the box. Scores are recorded for each player, and the team with the highest score wins. Many other targets are possible. The children can design them.

BOWLING

Formation: File—by rows

Players: Two to six for each target

Supplies: A bowling pin or pins; balls for rolling

Many bowling games are possible in the classroom, with the aisles used as the alleys. Various kinds of balls can be rolled. The target can be a single pin or a group of pins, and competition can be between individuals in a row or between rows. Children can design their own bowling games.

CHAIR QUOITS

Formation: File

Players: Two to six for each target

Supplies: A chair for each group; five deck tennis rings or rope rings

A line is established about 10 feet from a chair turned over so that the legs point toward the thrower. Each player throws the five rings. A ringer on the back legs scores 10 points, and one on the front legs scores 5 points. Score should be kept for several rounds.

TIC-TAC-TOE

Formation: None

Players: Two to four for each target

Supplies: A tic-tac-toe target board, six beanbags or yarn balls of one color and six of another

The tic-tac-toe target is constructed from 1-by-4-inch boards standing on end to make a throwing target a little less than 4 inches deep, with each of nine squares separated by a 1-inch wide border. The spaces themselves are 1 foot square. The target is mounted on a 4-by-4-foot piece of sturdy plywood. A prop should be placed behind the board so that it is tilted at about a 45-degree angle (Figure 11.1).

The object of the game is to get three squares covered in a line in any direction. Only one beanbag is permitted in a square. If a second beanbag lands inside a square, it is removed. The game can be played one against one or partners against partners. Alternate sides toss at the target.

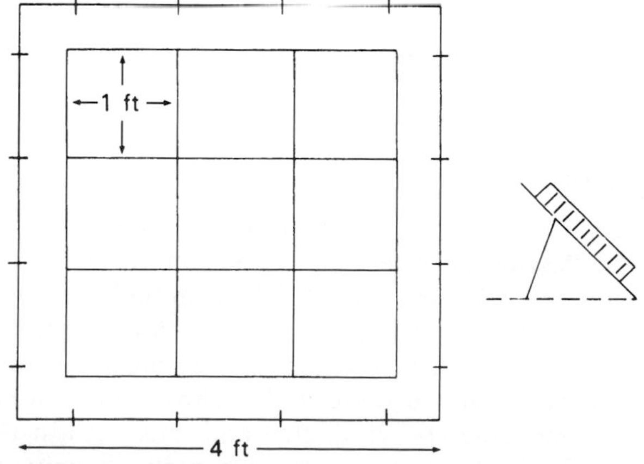

FIGURE 11.1 Tic-tac-toe target.

Games with Limited Movement

ANIMALS MOVE

Formation: Standing in the aisles between desks or scattered

Players: Entire class

Supplies: None

The player who is *it* stands at the front of the room and calls out the name of a mammal, bird, fish, or reptile, and a movement. For instance, the leader might call out, "Horses fly. Birds crawl. Salmon swim." When the leader states a correct relationship, the class must move accordingly. In this example, they would make a swimming movement. When an incorrect relationship is given, the children should not move. Those who move at the wrong time can sit down and wait until a new leader is selected. Games should be kept short so that all children have a chance to lead and no one has to sit out too long.

BICYCLE RACE

Formation: Rows

Players: Half the class

Supplies: Desks

The children stand in the aisle between two rows of desks. Alternate rows perform at a time. Children place one hand on their own desk and one on the desk next to them. On the signal "Go," the children, supported by their hands, imitate a bicycling motion with their legs. The child who rides the longest without touching the floor with the feet is the winner for the row. Winners can compete later for bicycle riding champion of the room.

DO IT AND GUESS IT

Formation: Small groups

Players: 3 to 5 per group

Supplies: Pencils, paper, pictures (active people or animals)

Each student has a pencil and piece of paper. One student is designated as the doer. This child chooses an activity to perform. If students are slow to pick an activity, use pictures of activities for them to select. The doer must actively perform the activity until the guessers have finished drawing what they think the doer is performing. The doers must draw the item based on the physical performance only; no questions or discussion are allowed. After 30 seconds of activity, the guessers reveal their drawing and see if they were correct. A new doer is then selected. To add a challenge for older children, terms such as jogging, throwing, or other standard physical activity terms may not be used.

DO THIS, DO THAT

Formation: Scattered

Players: Entire class

Supplies: None

One child is the leader and performs various movements, accompanied by commands of "Do this" or "Do that." All players execute the movements accompanied by "Do this." If the directions are "Do that," no one is to move. Those who move at the wrong time are eliminated and sit down in place. The game continues until some of the children have been eliminated. The game is then re-formed with another leader, who is selected from the children who were not caught.

IMITATION

Formation: Scattered

Players: Entire class

Supplies: CD player or tape recorder with musical selections

A leader stands in front of the class and performs for a musical phrase (eight counts) with any desired movement. For the next eight counts, the children imitate the same movements in the same sequence. The leader sets another round of movements, and the children again imitate. After a time, the leader selects another child to be the new leader.

O'GRADY SAYS

Formation: Scattered

Players: Entire class

Supplies: None

A leader stands in front and calls out various military commands, such as "Right face," "Left face," "About face," "Attention," and "At ease." The players are to follow only when the command is preceded by the words *O'Grady says.* Anyone moving at the wrong time is eliminated and must sit down. Additional commands involving other movements can be used. To be effective, the commands must be given rapidly.

PUT HANDS

Formation: Scattered—standing or seated

Players: Entire class

Supplies: None

One child is the leader and stands in front of the class. The leader gives certain directions verbally and then tries to confuse the class by doing something else. He might say, "Put your hands on top of your head" and put his own hands on top of his shoulders. Those who follow his actions instead of his words have a point scored against them. Possible directions are the following.

> "Put your hands on your shoulders [toes, knees, head, chest]."
>
> "Reach out to the side [to the front, to the back, up high]."
>
> "Put your right [left] hand on your shoulder [behind your back]."

After a short time, the leader should be changed.

Variation: Other movements can be introduced, such as "Right hand point west," "Left hand forward, right hand to the sky," and "Head right, jump left."

SHUFFLE FOOT

Formation: Scattered—by pairs

Players: Two

Supplies: None

One person is the "same"; the other is the "different." The two children stand facing each other about 3 feet apart. They clap three times, and on the third clap each puts a foot forward. If the feet are the same (right, right; left, left), the student designated the same wins. If the feet are different, the other child wins. The game goes on to a set number of points.

SIMON SAYS

Formation: Scattered—standing or seated

Players: Entire class

Supplies: None

One player is selected to be Simon and stands in front of the class. Simon gives a variety of commands, such as "Stand up," "Clap your hands," "Turn around," and others, and may or may not precede a command with the words *Simon says.* No one is to move unless the command is preceded by these words. Those who move at the wrong time are eliminated and must sit out the game. The leader gives commands rapidly, changing to different movements. Simon tries to confuse the class by doing all of the movements.

SNAP

Formation: Seated in a circle

Players: 10 to 15

Supplies: None

The game involves a three-count rhythm. The children must practice the rhythm well before the game can be successful. On count 1, the children slap their knees; on count 2, they clap their hands; and on count 3, they snap their fingers. Each child in the circle has a number. The leader calls a number on the third count. The player whose number was called then calls another number when snapping the fingers. The object of the game is to maintain a precise rhythm, calling the numbers back and forth across the circle.

The following are errors.

1. Breaking the rhythm
2. Not calling another number after yours has been called
3. Calling when your number has not been called
4. Calling the number of a player who has been eliminated

STICKY HANDS

Formation: Small circle

Players: 6 to 12

Supplies: None

Children stand close together in a circle. They extend their hands, which are "sticky like glue." A child who grasps a hand cannot let go. The children reach into the mass of hands and across the circle to find two hands (belonging to different people), which they grasp. The grips must not be released. By stepping over and around, twisting under and through, the group tries to unscramble itself.

WHO'S LEADING?

Formation: Circle—either sitting at desks or on the floor

Players: Entire class

Supplies: None

One child who is *it* steps away from the circle and covers the eyes. The teacher points to a child in the circle, who becomes the leader. The leader starts any desired motion with the hands, the feet, or any other body part. All of the children follow the movements. The child who is *it* uncovers the eyes and watches the group, as they change from one motion to another, to try to determine who is leading. Players should cover up for the leader, who also tries to confuse the guesser by looking at other players. The child who is *it* gets three guesses. If not successful, he or she chooses another child to be *it.* If the guess is correct, he or she gets another turn, but a limit of three turns should be imposed.

TEACHING TIP

The game seems to work best when the guesser is positioned in the center of the circle, where all of the children cannot be seen at once. The children can also be standing, but this gets tiring.

Games with Locomotor Movement

AROUND THE ROW

Formation: Rows

Players: As many as are in a row

Supplies: None

The game is played by rows, with an extra player for each row. On the command "March," children walk around the row. On signal, they stop marching and attempt to get a seat. One player is left out. The game continues to the next row, using the player left out as the extra. Walking only (no running) is permitted. Roughness should not be tolerated.

BALLOON FOOTBALL

Formation: Two lines facing each other 4 to 6 feet apart

Players: Entire class

Supplies: Balloon or light beach ball

The class is divided into two teams. Players sit in their chairs and keep one hand on the back of the chair throughout the game. The balloon or beach ball is tossed between the two teams. Both teams try to bat it over the heads of their opponents so that the ball touches the floor behind the opposing team. Each touchdown scores a point. A student should be placed behind each team to serve as scorekeeper and ball retriever. The balloon should be put into play at different places along the two lines to prevent action from being concentrated among a few players.

BALLOON VOLLEYBALL

Formation: Standing, sitting on the floor, or seated at desks

Players: Entire class

Supplies: Two balloons and a rope

Children are positioned on both sides of a rope stretched just above their reach. They try to bat a balloon back and forth across the rope. The balloon can be batted as often as necessary. Two balloons used at once provide good action. A system of rotation should be set up, so that all players have a chance to occupy a position near the rope. Scoring is accomplished when one side fails to control a balloon and allows it to touch the floor or a wall.

TEACHING TIP

A small marble or button placed inside the balloon causes it to take an erratic path, which adds interest to the game.

CLASSROOM MOUSETRAP

Formation: Circle

Players: Entire class

Supplies: None

Several pairs of children form arches around the circle. The arches remain up until the teacher says "Snap"; then they are brought down. The other children (the mice) scurry through the arches and try to avoid being caught. Anyone caught forms additional arches.

COLORS

Formation: Scattered—standing or seated

Players: Entire class

Supplies: A set of flash cards of different colors

The teacher flashes a color card. All children touch five different objects of that color and return to position. There is no scoring, just activity.

TEACHING TIP

Shapes can be the focus. The teacher holds up a shape (triangle, circle, square), and the children seek five articles of that same shape to touch.

HIDE THE BEANBAG

Formation: Scattered

Players: 15 to 20

Supplies: A small beanbag

One child, the searcher, stands to the side with eyes covered. The other children sit cross-legged. One child is given the beanbag and must hide it by sitting on it.

The searcher moves among the children, trying to locate the beanbag, as the children clap softly. They clap louder when the searcher nears the child with the beanbag. The searcher tries to identify the one with the beanbag. If the guess is correct, another child is selected to be the searcher. If the identification fails, the searcher tries again (up to three guesses), and then another child becomes the searcher.

HUNTER, GUN, RABBIT

Formation: Two lines facing each other

Players: Entire class

Supplies: None

The children are divided into two teams, which line up facing each other. They can sit or stand. Each team has a captain. The teams decide privately on one of the following three imitations.

1. *Hunter*—bring the hands up to the eyes and pretend to be looking through binoculars.
2. *Gun*—bring the hands and arms up to a shooting position and pretend to shoot.
3. *Rabbit*—put the hands in back of the head with fingers pointed up, and move the fingers back and forth like moving rabbit ears.

A signal is given, and each team pantomimes its choice. In scoring, the following priorities hold.

1. If one side is the hunter and the other the gun, the hunter wins because the hunter shoots the gun.
2. If one team selects the gun and the other imitates a rabbit, the gun wins because the gun can overcome the rabbit.
3. If one side is the rabbit and the other the hunter, the rabbit wins because it can outrun the hunter.
4. If both teams have the same selection, no point is scored.

The first team to score 10 points wins.

TEACHING TIP

The teacher should keep the game moving. One way to do this is to have the child on the right of each line go down the line and whisper the choice to the team members. The child then stands on the left, and a new child is at the right of each line, ready to select the next imitation.

ORIENTEERING

Formation: Standing

Players: Entire class

Supplies: Chart of a compass face (optional)

Students stand to the right of their desks. Either the teacher or a chosen student stands facing the class. This person calls out various directions: north, southwest, and so on. The rest of the class must quickly face in the proper direction. When students turn in the wrong direction, they can either sit down or have a point scored against them.

TEACHING TIP

1. To introduce children to a compass and to simple orienteering skills, a chart with the face and directional needle of a compass can be used. The leader turns away from the class, places the needle in a certain direction, and then shows the compass to the class. The class responds by turning toward the proper direction.
2. Regular orienteering can be done on a modified basis by setting up a course with the path to be followed described in terms of numbers of steps in a given compass direction. Inside some buildings, however, compasses are not accurate.

TEN, TEN, DOUBLE TEN

Formation: None

Players: Entire class

Supplies: A small object

All of the children except one leave the classroom. The child left in the room places the object in a spot that is visible but not too easily found. The children return to the room. As soon as a child sees the object, he or she pretends to search for another moment, so as not to give away the position. The child then calls out, "Ten, 10, double 10, 45, 15, buckskin 6," and sits down. The other children continue to search. The child who found the object first gets to place it for the next game.

WHO AM I?

Formation: Small circle or scattered

Players: 8 to 16

Supplies: None

The children recite this verse in unison:

> This morning as I walked down the street
> Whom do you think I chanced to meet?

One child is the demonstrator and proceeds to pantomime an action (e.g., firefighter, police officer, banker, baseball player). The children try to guess what the action represents. A successful guesser becomes the new demonstrator. If no one guesses, the present demonstrator gets another turn, after which another child takes over.

ZOO

Formation: Seated

Players: Entire class

Supplies: None

Children are in their regular seats. Seven children are chosen to stand in front of the class, and one of them is selected as the leader. The leader directs each of the other six children to choose a favorite animal and then places them in a line, saying the animal name as she does so.

On signal, the six children, performing in the order in which they were just announced by the leader, imitate the animal that they have chosen. (Ten to 15 seconds should be allowed for this.) On a second signal, the rest of the children stand, wave their arms, and jump or hop in place (turning around if they wish). They then sit down, close their eyes, cover them with their hands, and put their heads down on the desk.

The leader then arranges the six animals in a different order. When this has been done, the seated children raise their heads. Another signal is given, and the animals perform once again for a short period. Once this has been accomplished, any seated child can volunteer to place the six children in their original positions, naming the animal in each case. If the child succeeds in placing the animals in their original standing position and in calling them by their chosen animal name, the guesser becomes an animal in the zoo and chooses a name. The child then takes a place among the animals, and the game continues until 12 children (or some other designated number) are in the zoo. Other categories, such as flowers, Mother Goose characters, play characters, and so on, can be used.

Relays

Relays can be used occasionally in the classroom program. Most of the appropriate relays involve object handling or a task. Few classrooms have sufficient space for a variety of relays. Some relays can use the regular seating arrangement, but others may require special formations. Relays using the chalkboard for spelling, word formation, and arithmetic can be of value, but not as scheduled physical education activities.

FLAG CHASE

Formation: Hollow square—seated in chairs

Players: Entire class

Supplies: Four flags (or beanbags); chairs for all competitors; a marker centered 3 feet in front of each team

The class is divided into four even teams, facing center and seated on the sides of the square, with a marker in front of each team. The player on the left end of his or her team has a flag. On signal, this player runs to the marker, goes around it from the right (counterclockwise), and then runs to the seat on the right of the team. In the meantime, all players have moved one place to the left, vacating the right seat. The runner sits in the vacant chair, and the flag is passed down the line to the left. The player now in the leftmost seat becomes the new runner and runs the same course as the previous runner. The race ends when the flag has been returned to the lead-off runner in the original position in the left seat.

TEACHING TIP

1. An under-the-leg pass can be used, with the stipulation that the flag must go under all legs during transit.
2. The run around the marker can be omitted, with the runner going directly from the left to the right seat.

OVERHEAD RELAY

Formation: File—by rows

Players: Entire class

Supplies: A beanbag, eraser, or similar object for each team

Each row forms a team. The first person in each row faces the object that is to be passed to the desk behind. At the signal to pass, this child claps hands, picks up the object, and passes it overhead to the child behind. The next child places the object on the desk, claps hands, and then passes the object overhead. The last child in the row receives the object and runs forward to the head of the row, using the aisle to the right. After the runner has passed by, each child, using the same aisle, moves back one seat. The child who has come to the front then sits down in the first seat, places the object on the desk, claps hands, and passes the object overhead. This continues until the children are back in their original seats and the object is on the front desk. The first row finished wins.

REFLECTION AND REVIEW QUESTIONS

How and Why

1. Why should physical education teachers integrate academic content into their lessons?
2. Why might physical education teachers be apprehensive about teaching in limited spaces?
3. How can teachers make rainy day activities productive and enjoyable?
4. Can management skills in the gymnasium carry over during physical education in a classroom? Explain your answer.

Content Review

1. Discuss several ideas for integrating academic content into physical education lessons.
2. Identify guidelines for conducting physical education in limited indoor spaces.
3. What are some fitness development activities that can be used in limited space?
4. Discuss skill development activities that are easily adapted for confined areas.
5. Describe several games and relays appropriate for use in small spaces. Include target games, limited movement games, and games with locomotor movement.

FOR MORE INFORMATION

References and Suggested Readings

Beane, J. (Ed.). (1995). *Toward a coherent curriculum.* Alexandria, VA: Association for Supervision and Curriculum Development.

Christie, B. A. (2000). Topic Teamwork: A collaborative integrative model for increasing student-centered learning in grades K–12. *Journal of Physical Education, Recreation, and Dance,* 71(8), 28–32.

Cone, T. P., Werner, P., Cone, S. L., & Woods, A. M. (1998). *Interdisciplinary teaching through physical education.* Champaign, IL: Human Kinetics.

Cook, G. (1994). Topics and themes in interdisciplinary curriculum. *Middle School Journal,* 25(3), 40.

Cook, P. (1996). *Making connections: Helping teachers to implement an integrated approach to curriculum within their communities.* ERIC Digest #397003.

Davis, J.R. (1993). *Interdisciplinary courses and team teaching: new arrangements for learning.* Phoenix: Oryx Press.

Drake, S. (1995). Suggestions for teachers: Connecting learning outcomes and integrated curriculum. *Orbit: Ideas About Teaching and Learning,* 26(1), 28.

Fogarty, R. (1995). *Best practices for the learner-centered classroom.* Arlington Heights, IL: IRI/Skylight Training and Publishing, Inc.

Hange, J. (1995). Interdisciplinary curriculum and instruction: Teaming to improve learning and motivation. ERIC Digest #386433.

Pangrazi, R. P. (2004). *Lesson plans for dynamic physical education.* San Francisco: Benjamin Cummings.

Websites

Academic Standards
http://www.ade.state.az.us/standards/contentstandards. asp
http://www.cde.ca.gov/board/pdf/history.pdf
http://www.mcrel.org/compendium/browse.asp

Indoor Games
http://www.guidezone.skl.com/jm_games_sparks.htm#quiet

Learning through Movement
http://www.earlychildhood.com/Articles/index.cfm?FuseAction=Article&A=15
http://www.teachingvalues.com/whymovement.html

Rainy Day Ideas
http://outreach.missouri.edu/hesfn/bodywalk/classroom.htm

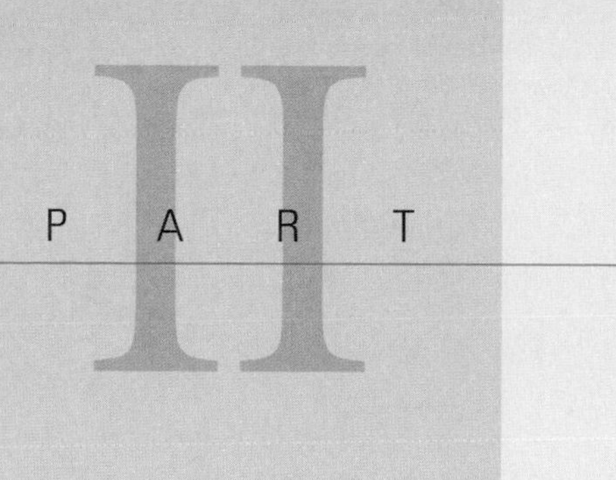

PART II

Teaching the Content of Physical Education

SECTION 4 Personal Health Skills

SECTION 5 Fundamental Motor Skills

SECTION 6 Specialized Motor Skills

SECTION 7 Sport Skills

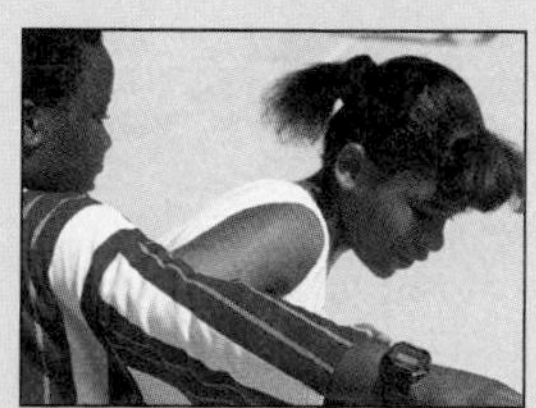

SECTION 4

Personal Health Skills

CHAPTER 12

Physical Activity and Fitness

ESSENTIAL COMPONENTS	
I	Organized around content standards
II	**Student-centered and developmentally appropriate**
III	Physical activity and motor skill development form the core of the program
IV	Teaches management skills and self-discipline
V	**Promotes inclusion of all students**
VI	Focuses on process over product
VII	**Promotes lifetime personal health and wellness**
VIII	Teaches cooperation and responsibility and promotes sensitivity to diversity

PHYSICAL EDUCATION STANDARDS	
1	Students are able to move competently using a variety of fundamental and specialized motor skills.
2	**Students can monitor and maintain a health-enhancing level of physical fitness.**
3	**Students are able to apply movement concepts and basic mechanics of skill performance when learning and refining motor skills.**
4	**Students comprehend the basic principles of wellness and are able to apply concepts that enable them to make meaningful decisions that positively impact their health and wellness.**
5	**Students participate in a wide variety of physical activities and learn how to maintain a personalized active lifestyle.**
6	Students demonstrate empathy, understanding, and respect for the numerous differences exhibited by people in an activity setting.
7	Students exhibit responsible and self-directed behaviors that lead to positive social interactions in physical activity.

SUMMARY

The value of a healthy lifestyle and the importance of teaching lifetime physical activity and fitness are discussed in this chapter. An understanding of the difference between health-related and skill-related fitness helps clarify the need for emphasizing lifetime activity. High-level fitness performance is no longer an objective for the majority of children. Instead, the goal is to increase the activity level of all students in order to improve their health status. Activity for children can be moderate in intensity and still offer many health benefits. Suggestions for developing a fitness module, motivating children to maintain fitness, and developing positive attitudes toward activities are included. A variety of exercises and proper performance techniques are described so a health-related program that meets the needs of all students can be offered.

OUTCOMES

- Differentiate between skill-related and health-related physical fitness.
- Describe the fitness status of youth in the United States.
- Explain the role that a broad program of physical fitness and activity plays in the elementary school curriculum.
- Identify the various components of health-related versus skill-related physical fitness.
- List guidelines for developing and maintaining physical fitness.
- Develop a fitness module.
- Cite strategies and techniques to motivate children to maintain physical fitness.
- Discuss the importance of fitness testing and cite several tests that could be used to measure fitness in children.
- Categorize various exercises by the muscle group involved.
- Characterize isotonic, isometric, and isokinetic exercises.
- Identify harmful physical activities and exercises.
- Plan and demonstrate numerous activities and exercises that can improve the physical fitness of children.

WHAT IS PHYSICAL ACTIVITY?

A body of research has been compiled to show the need for activity and fitness in the lives of youth. Activity programs are an absolute requisite for healthy youngsters. Physical education today has a clearer mandate than ever to play an important role in the total school curriculum. The fitness and activity program must produce an enjoyable and positive social experience so children develop a positive attitude toward activity.

This leads to the question as to how physical activity is defined. As a general definition, physical activity is bodily movement that is produced by the contraction of skeletal muscle and that substantially increases energy expenditure (adapted from USDHHS, 1996; Bouchard et al., 1990). Basically, physical activity is an all-encompassing term that includes exercise, sports, dance, and leisure activities. Whereas exercise is conducted with the intention of developing physical fitness, leisure activity is undertaken during discretionary time. Physical activity can be collected in long or short term bouts. Physical educators can play an important role in helping youth learn how to accumulate as much physical activity as possible throughout the day. By definition, the school day is filled with much sitting and inactivity, so the efforts of the teacher must be concentrated on helping students develop active patterns of living outside of the school environment. This leads to the next question: Is there an optimal amount of physical activity youth should be expected to accumulate on a daily basis?

HOW MUCH PHYSICAL ACTIVITY IS ENOUGH?

Corbin, Pangrazi, and Welk (1994) originated the Children's Lifetime Physical Activity Model (C-LPAM) to give teachers guidance in determining the volume of activity youngsters should expend in a day (Table 12.1).

Because young children are less inclined to voluntarily select continuous vigorous physical activity, the Children's Lifetime Physical Activity Model (C-LPAM) and its recommendations for the volume of activity as determined by calories expended over a period of time is best suited with children. The recommendations for 60 minutes or more of activity (total volume) for children and youth is higher than the caloric expenditure recommendations for adults. Adult recommendations are based primarily on the energy expenditure necessary to reduce risk of chronic disease associated with what is commonly called aerobic or cardiovascular fitness. It is important that children and youth gain experience in all areas of physical activity and for all parts of health-related physical fitness, not just aerobic or cardiovascular fitness. Such a recommendation requires an additional time commitment. For greater detail about physical activity for children, see the AAHPERD document authored by Corbin and Pangrazi (1998a). The following discussion offers guidelines for prescribing physical activity for children.

TABLE 12.1 Children's Lifetime Physical Activity Model (C-LPAM)

The Health Standard: A Minimum Activity Standard	
Frequency	Daily. Frequent activity sessions (3 or more) each day.
Intensity	Moderate. Alternating bouts of activity with rest periods as needed or moderate activity such as walking or riding a bike to school.
Time	Duration of activity necessary to expend at least 6 to 8 kcal/kg/day. Equal to calorie expenditure in 60 minutes or more of active play or moderate sustained activity which may be distributed over 3 or more activity sessions.
The Optimal Functioning Standard: A Goal for All Children	
Frequency	Daily. Frequent activity sessions (3 or more) each day.
Intensity	Moderate. Alternating bouts of activity with rest periods as needed or moderate activity such as walking or riding a bike to school.
Time	Duration of activity necessary to expend more than 6 to 8 kcal/kg/day. Equal to calorie expenditure in 60 minutes or more of active play or moderate sustained activity which may be distributed over 3 or more activity sessions.

1. Elementary school children should accumulate at least 60 minutes of age appropriate physical activity on all or most days. A minimum of 60 minutes of daily physical activity is recommended. Sixty minutes of daily activity is a preferred dosage because children become less active as they mature. Assuring that youngsters receive 60 minutes a day factors in their decreasing levels of activity. Figure 12.1 on page 228 shows the decrease in total daily activity of children as they age.
2. An accumulation of more than 60 minutes and up to several hours per day of appropriate activities is encouraged for school-age children. Even though 60 minutes or more of daily physical activity is recommended, this is a minimum criterion. Youngsters learn through movement, and physical activity should constitute a relatively large part of the child's day, including some periods that are more active than others. In a typical day the total amount of

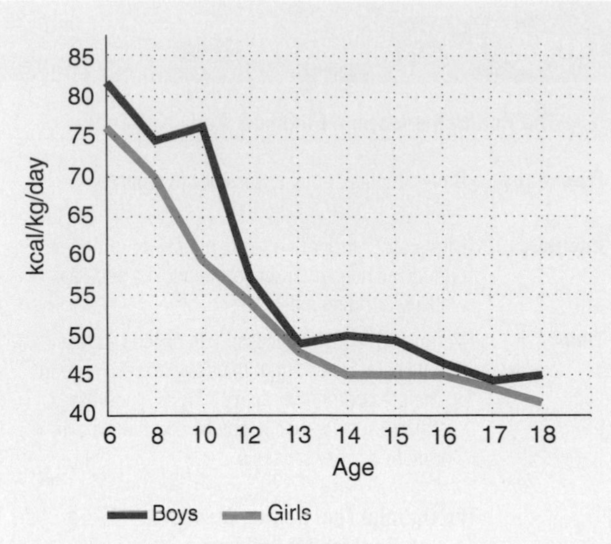

FIGURE 12.1 Total daily energy expenditure.

(Adapted from Rowland, T. W., 1990, *Exercise and Children's Health,* Champaign, IL: Human Kinetics.)

physical activity a child accumulates should exceed 60 minutes and total several hours. More than 60 minutes of activity is not only recommended, it should be mandated in the school setting.

3. Each day, youngsters should be involved in 10 to 15 minutes of moderate to vigorous activity. This activity should alternate with brief periods of rest and recovery. The natural movement pattern of children is an intermittent style of all-out activity that alternates with periods of rest and recovery. Continuous moderate to vigorous physical activity periods lasting more that 5 minutes without rest or recovery are rare among children prior to age 13. Because typical activities of children involve sporadic bursts of energy, a greater time involvement rather than a greater intensity of continuous involvement is recommended. Several (three to six or more) activity sessions spaced throughout the day are necessary to accumulate adequate activity time for elementary school children. Some of these periods should be 10 to 15 minutes or more in length, alternating intermittent activity and rest within this time period. Even though not recommended, if long periods of continuous activity are prescribed for children, the reasons for doing so should be well-established and made clear to the children performing them.

HOW MUCH AND WHAT TYPE OF PHYSICAL ACTIVITY?

Youngsters need to participate in a wide variety of physical activities. The Physical Activity Pyramid (Figure 12.2) is a model that is used to help teachers and students develop a balanced fitness approach.

The following discussion explains each level of the pyramid and recommends how such activity should be delivered to children. In general, the Physical Activity Pyramid encourages participation in activities from the lowest three levels of the pyramid with a greater emphasis on selections from activities lower in the pyramid. Developmental level, age level, and other factors such as hereditary predisposition ultimately determine the optimal amounts of activity required at the different levels of the pyramid.

Lifestyle Activities

Lifestyle activities are at the base of the pyramid because an accumulation of daily minutes of involvement in these activities has been shown to have positive health benefits. These activities are widely accessible and relatively easy to perform for people of all ages throughout their lifespan. These types of activities are often done as part of daily routine, and involve large muscles. Examples are walking to or from school, climbing the stairs rather than using the elevator, raking the leaves, and doing chores around the house that require more than a little calorie expenditure. For young children, active play involving large muscles is the most common type of lifestyle activity.

Recommendations for Developmental Level I Children

The greatest portion of accumulated minutes of physical activity for children of this age usually comes from lifestyle activities. Lifestyle activities for this age include active play and games involving the large muscles of the body. Climbing, tumbling, and other activities that require lifting the body or relocating the body in space are desirable activities when they can be performed safely. Activities are typically intermittent in nature rather than continuous (those done for long periods of time without stopping). These activities normally involve few rules and little formal organization. Lifestyle activities such as walking to school, when appropriate, and being involved in chores around the home are also appropriate.

Recommendations for Developmental Levels II & III Children

As with young children, a large portion of accumulated minutes of physical activity for children of this age will typically come from lifestyle activities. Lifestyle activities for this age include active play and games involving the large muscles of the body. Activities are typically intermittent in nature, though children at this age are

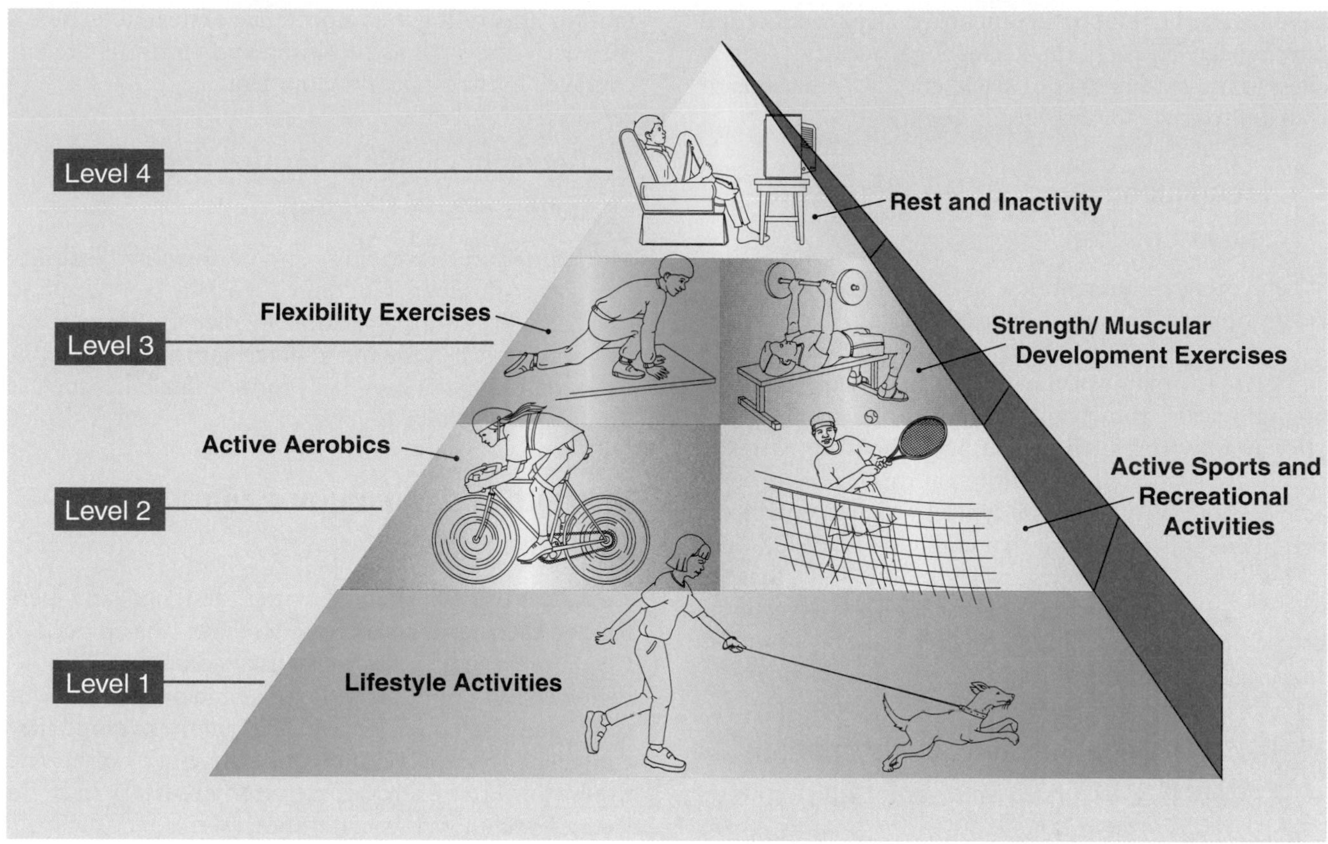

FIGURE 12.2 The Physical Activity Pyramid.
(Adapted from Corbin, C. B., and Lindsey, R., 1997, *Fitness for Life*, 4th ed., Glenview, IL: Scott, Foresman.)

more likely to be involved in continuous activities (those done for long periods of time without stopping). Lifestyle activities such as walking to school and being involved in chores around the home are appropriate.

Active Aerobics

Activities that are done for relatively long periods of time without stopping are considered to be aerobic in nature. Examples of active aerobics are brisk walking, jogging or running, biking, swimming, hiking, and other similar activities. For optimal health benefits some of these activities should be done at a moderate to vigorous intensity level.

Recommendations for Developmental Level I Children

Participation in some aerobic activities is appropriate if children are not expected to participate in them continuously for long duration. More appropriate are intermittent aerobic activities such as recreational swimming, family walking, or aerobic activities that are included in the lifestyle activity category such as walking or riding a bicycle to school or in the neighborhood. Participation in continuous aerobic activities of long duration are not recommended for this age group.

Recommendations for Developmental Levels II & III Children

Participation in aerobic activities of longer duration is appropriate for this age group, though participation in continuous aerobic activities for more than 10 or 15 minutes is not recommended. Most children do not voluntarily choose to participate in continuous activity so it is important to clearly discuss reasons for performing such activities (for example, fitness tests). Intermittent involvement in aerobic activities is appropriate (several short bouts of activity followed by rest intervals) and is preferred by children of this age.

Active Sports and Recreational Activities

Sports such as tennis, soccer, racquetball, and basketball and recreational activities such as canoeing and water skiing are included in this category. Some activities such as bowling and golf are also included because even activities that require relatively low energy expenditure have health benefits when included as part of a total physical activity program. Recreational activities such as chess and checkers are not active enough to be considered appropriate for this level.

Recommendations for Developmental Level I Children

When young children choose to be involved in sports it is appropriate that sports be modified to meet their developmental level. In general, active sports should not comprise the major proportion of activity for developmental levels I and II children. Age-appropriate recreational activities such as fishing or boating with the family are suggested for children at this level; however, activities of this type are not typically high in energy expenditure. It is important that children at developmental levels I and II have time to learn basic skills that are prerequisite to performing sports and other recreational activities such as catching, throwing, walking, jumping, running, and striking objects.

Recommendations for Developmental Levels II & III Children

At this developmental level youngsters start to become involved in active sports. For this reason a greater amount of time is dedicated to this type of activity. Lead-up games and emphasis on skill development are necessary to make the activities suitable for this age. An emphasis on conditioning for sport is unnecessary for this age group. More of the time spent in this type of activity will be dedicated to skill learning and playing games rather than conditioning. Age-appropriate recreational activities that have a lifetime emphasis or that can be done with family and friends are encouraged.

Flexibility Exercises

Exercises and physical activities designed and performed specifically to increase the length of muscles and connective tissues and to improve the range of joint motion are included in this category. Some activities at lower levels in the pyramid may contribute to the development of flexibility but specific exercises are often necessary to develop this part of fitness, even for the most active people.

Recommendations for Developmental Level I Children

In general, the amount of time spent on flexibility exercises for developmental levels I and II children is minimal. Children are more flexible than adults. For this reason this type of exercise is relatively easy for most children. Teaching some stretching exercises is important for illustrating the importance of flexibility. Active play activities such as tumbling and climbing are encouraged for flexibility development.

Recommendations for Developmental Levels II & III Children

More time is spent teaching and performing flexibility exercises at this level. Children, especially boys, begin to lose flexibility at this age. Some regular stretching is appropriate either in the form of age appropriate flexibility exercises or activities that promote flexibility such as tumbling and stunts.

Strength and Muscular Endurance Exercises

Exercises and physical activities designed and performed specifically to increase strength (the amount of weight one can lift) and muscular endurance (the ability to persist in muscular effort) are included in this category. Some activities at lower levels in the pyramid may contribute to the development of these parts of muscle fitness but extra exercises are often necessary to build strength and muscular endurance, even for the most active people.

Recommendations for Developmental Level I Children

Participation in some strength exercises as part of a physical education class or a regular family fitness program is appropriate. However, as long as children are accumulating adequate daily amounts of the activities from lower levels in the pyramid, it is not necessary for them to spend large amounts of time performing organized calisthenics on a regular basis. Modified fitness activities (see pages 244–247) are an excellent way to help youngsters learn about exercises in a positive, nonfailing manner. Formal resistance training is actually not recommended.

Recommendations for Developmental Levels II & III Children

Youngsters at developmental level III participate in strength development activities that require them to move and lift their body weight. Participation in active play and games and sports that require muscle overload are desirable for these youngsters. Exercises using body weight are appropriate when alternative exercises are offered to allow all children to be successful. It is important to show children the relevance of these exercises. Formal exercises and conditioning programs as part of youth sports or other activity programs should not typically constitute a major part of activity periods, though children who are highly motivated may benefit from greater exposure to these activities. Children of this age can develop modest gains in strength and muscular endurance using resistance training (see Chapter 2). However, other activities are generally better suited to the needs of most children, particularly in a class setting.

Rest and Inactivity

Total sedentary living (virtually no activity) as well as activities involving little large muscle activity—such as computer games—are included in this category. Involvement in reading, television watching, and relatively inactive recreational activities is beneficial to participants. Abstinence from these activities is not necessary if they do not limit involvement in other activities in the pyramid. They are recommended, however, primarily as a supplement to greater involvement in the activities in the first three levels of the pyramid.

Recommendations for Developmental Level I Children

Children at this level need some private time to be involved in play of types other than in activities using the large muscles. However, long periods of sedentary living (not typically a characteristic of young children) should be discouraged.

Recommendations for Developmental Levels II & III Children

Like younger children, children at this level need some private time to be involved in types of play other than large-muscle activities. However, long periods of sedentary living (not typically a characteristic of children of this age) should be discouraged. Time between activity periods can be less than for younger children.

WHAT IS PHYSICAL FITNESS?

Physical activity is a process that involves accumulating a wide variety of movement. Many experts believe that if there is enough physical activity accumulated, then physical fitness will take care of itself. Physical fitness is a product that is often measured to see if there is an adequate standard in place to ensure good health. The general definition of physical fitness is, "a set of attributes that people have or achieve relating to their ability to perform physical activity" (U.S. Department of Health & Human Services, 1996). An alternative definition of physical fitness is "a state of well-being with a low risk of premature health problems and energy to participate in a variety of physical activities" (Howley & Franks, 1997).

Two types of physical fitness most often identified are health-related physical fitness and skill-related physical fitness. The differentiation between *physical fitness related to functional health* and *physical performance related to athletic ability* makes it easier to develop proper fitness objectives and goals for youngsters. The components of health-related physical fitness are a subset of skill-related fitness components (Figure 12.3).

Health-related fitness is characterized by moderate and regular physical activity. It is designed for the masses who are generally unwilling to exercise at high intensities. Health-related fitness activities can be integrated into regular everyday activities that are often characterized as lifetime activities. In contrast, skill-related physical fitness includes the health-related components, but includes additional components that are somewhat related to genetic factors. Skill-related fitness is the right choice for people who want to perform at a high level, but is less acceptable for the majority of people because it requires training and exercising at high intensities. In addition, many individuals cannot reach high levels of skill-related fitness because of their genetic limitations. The following discussion describes and contrasts the differences between health-related and skill-related fitness.

Health-Related Physical Fitness

Health-related physical fitness includes aspects of physiological function that offer protection from diseases resulting from a sedentary lifestyle. Health-related fitness is often called *functional fitness* because it helps ensure a

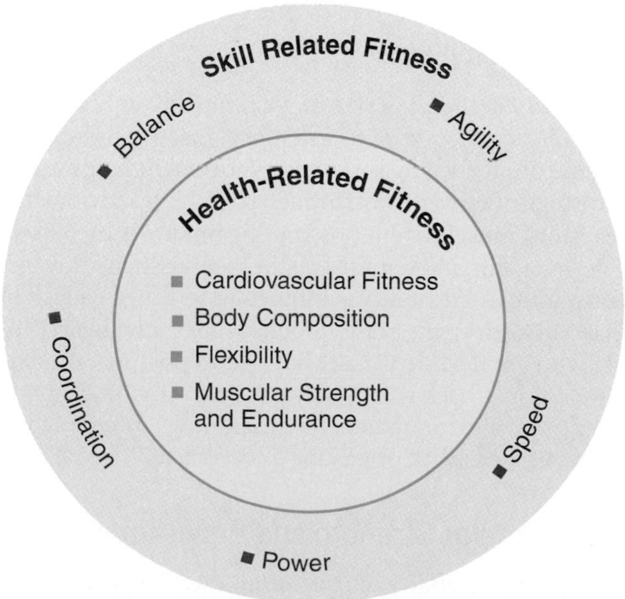

FIGURE 12.3 Components of physical fitness.

person will be able to function effectively in everyday tasks. Such fitness can be improved and/or maintained through regular and moderate physical activity. Specific components include cardiovascular fitness, body composition (ratio of leanness to fatness), abdominal strength and endurance, and flexibility. These components are all measured in the Fitnessgram test (Cooper Institute, 2002). The following are the major components of health-related fitness.

Cardiovascular Fitness

Aerobic fitness offers many health benefits and is often seen as the most important element of fitness. *Cardiovascular endurance* is the ability of the heart, the blood vessels, and the respiratory system to deliver oxygen efficiently over an extended period of time. To develop cardiovascular endurance, activity must be aerobic in nature. Activities that are continuous and rhythmic in nature require that a continuous supply of oxygen be delivered to the muscle cells. Activities that stimulate development in this area are paced walking, jogging, biking, rope jumping, aerobics, and swimming.

Body Composition

Body composition is an integral part of health-related fitness. Body composition is the proportion of body fat to lean body mass. After the thickness of selected skinfolds has been measured, the percentage of lean body mass can be calculated by using formulas that have been developed using other, more accurate methods of measuring body composition. The conversion of skinfold thickness to percent lean body mass is easier to communicate to parents than the more involved methods.

Flexibility

Flexibility is the range of movement through which a joint or sequence of joints can move. Inactive individuals lose flexibility, whereas frequent movement helps retain the range of movement. Through stretching activities, the length of muscles, tendons, and ligaments is increased. The ligaments and tendons retain their elasticity through constant use. Flexibility is important to fitness; a lack of flexibility can create health problems for individuals. People who are flexible usually have good posture and may have less low-back pain. Many physical activities demand a range of motion to generate maximum force, such as serving a tennis ball or kicking a soccer ball.

Muscular Strength and Endurance

Strength is the ability of muscles to exert force. Most activities do not build strength in areas where it is needed—the arm-shoulder girdle and the abdominal-trunk region. *Muscular endurance* is the ability to exert force over an extended period. Endurance postpones the onset of fatigue so that activity can be performed for lengthy periods. Sport activities require muscular endurance, because throwing, kicking, and striking skills have to be performed many times without fatigue.

Skill-Related Physical Fitness Components

Whereas health-related fitness is primarily sought for functional health, skill-related fitness is necessary for athletic accomplishment. It is strongly influenced by genetic factors. In addition to the health-related components, skill-related fitness components include agility, balance, coordination, power, and speed. Specific components of skill-related fitness are discussed below.

Agility

Agility is the ability of the body to change position rapidly and accurately while moving in space. Wrestling and football are examples of sports that require agility.

Balance

Balance refers to the body's ability to maintain a state of equilibrium while remaining stationary or moving. Maintaining balance is essential to all sports but is especially important in the performance of gymnastic activities.

Coordination

Coordination is the ability of the body to perform smoothly and successfully more than one motor task at the same time. Needed for football, baseball, tennis, soccer, and other sports that require hand-eye and foot-eye skills, coordination can be developed by practicing over and over the skill to be learned.

Power

Power is the ability to transfer energy explosively into force. To develop power, a person must practice activities that are required to improve strength, but at a faster rate involving sudden bursts of energy. Skills requiring power include high jumping, long jumping, shot putting, throwing, and kicking.

Speed

Speed is the ability of the body to perform movement in a short period of time. Usually associated with running forward, speed is essential for the successful performance of most sports and general locomotor movement skills.

ARE TODAY'S CHILDREN FIT?

A commonly held point of view among physical education teachers is that children today are less fit than children in previous generations. This opinion is used as a justification for more physical education time in the schools. Research (Corbin & Pangrazi, 1992) suggests, however, that the fitness of today's youngsters has not degenerated, showing they do quite well when compared to past students. When data from the last four national surveys of youth fitness conducted by AAHPERD and/or the President's Council on Physical Fitness and Sports were compared, children and youth today appeared to be as fit as they were in the past. It is difficult to compare youngsters from different eras because the only items that were used in all four surveys were pull-ups and the flexed arm hang. Youngsters, both boys and girls, showed an increase in performance when these two items were compared over four decades. The only area in which there has been a decline in performance is body composition (U.S. Department of Health and Human Services, 2002). Current data shows that the percentage of overweight children has tripled over the last 30 years.

Why Can't All Children Meet Established Standards of Fitness?

Is it realistic to expect all children to reach specified standards of fitness? What factors control fitness performance, and how much control do youngsters have over their fitness accomplishments? Payne and Morrow (1993) reviewed 28 studies examining training and aerobic performance in children and concluded that improvement is small to moderate in prepubescent children. They state that

> the relatively small-to-moderate increase in pre- to post-aerobic improvement and the weak relationship between type of training program and effect size lead to questions concerning traditional practices when dealing with children and their fitness. Are we expecting too much from traditional physical education or fitness programs? Have award structures, designed to motivate children within these programs or test batteries, been appropriately designed when children appear to elicit only small improvements in aerobic capacity? Clearly, curriculum planners, teachers, fitness directors, exercise physiologists, and physicians need to consider carefully the ramifications of these findings.

A significant amount of fitness test performance is explained by heredity (Bouchard, 1990; Bouchard, Dionne, Simoneau, & Boulay, 1992). Various factors such as environment, nutrition, heredity, and maturation affect fitness performance as reflected in physical fitness test scores. Research shows that heredity and maturation strongly impact fitness scores (Bouchard et al., 1992; Pangrazi & Corbin, 1990). These factors may have more to do with youth fitness scores than does activity level. Lifestyle and environmental factors also make a difference. For example, nutrition is a lifestyle factor that can influence test scores, and environmental conditions (heat, humidity, and pollution) strongly modify test performances. Some youngsters have a definite advantage on tests because of the types of muscle fibers they inherit (see Chapter 2). Even in an untrained state these children score better because of heredity.

Beyond heredity lies another factor that predisposes some youngsters to high (or low) performance. Recent research has shown that differences in "trainability" are strongly influenced by genetic predisposition (Bouchard et al., 1992). Trainability means that some individuals receive more benefit from training (regular physical activity) than do others. For example, assume two youngsters perform the same amount of activity throughout a semester. Child A shows dramatic improvement immediately while child B does not. Child A simply responds more favorably to training than does child B; child A inherited a system that is responsive to exercise. Child A not only gets fit and scores well on the test but also gets feedback that says, "the activity works—it makes me fit." Child B scores poorly, receives negative or no feedback, and concludes that, "activity doesn't improve my fitness, so why bother?" The truth is that child B may improve in fitness (to a lesser degree than child A) but it will take longer to show improvement. Child B will probably never achieve the fitness level attained by child A.

Another factor that impacts fitness performance is physical maturation. Teachers know that some youngsters mature faster than others. If two youngsters are the same age and sex, but one is physiologically older (advanced skeletal maturation), the more mature youngster usually performs better on tests than does the less mature child. Examining fitness norms shows that standards are raised as children grow older. Because age does not accurately reflect physical maturity, an immature active child might score lower than a more mature, less active youngster even though they are the same age. Maturation can override the effects of activity among young children. Age also plays a role in fitness performance (Pangrazi & Corbin, 1990). As little as three months difference in age helps youngsters perform better than younger children, regardless of training. Expect older students in the same class with younger children to perform better.

Many teachers and parents believe that fitness in youngsters is primarily a reflection of the amount of activity children perform on a regular basis. They assume youngsters who score high on fitness tests are active and those who don't score well are inactive. This assumption is often inaccurate. Physical activity is an important variable in fitness development for adults, but for children and youth other factors are of equal or greater importance. Studies have shown that the relationship between physical fitness and physical activity among children is low (Pate, Dowda, & Ross, 1990; Pate & Ross, 1987; Ross, Pate, Caspersen, Damberg, & Svilar, 1987). When teachers make the mistake of assuming that a child is inactive because of scores on a fitness test, this can create unforeseen problems.

Youngsters, particularly in elementary school, want to be successful. They try to behave in ways that please the teacher and impress their friends. When youngsters are encouraged to do regular exercise to improve their fitness scores, most take this challenge seriously. When fitness tests are given, students expect to do well on the tests if they have been exercising regularly and, of course, teachers also expect them to do well. If, however, they receive scores that are lower than expected, they become disappointed. They are especially discouraged if the teacher concludes that their low fitness scores are a reflection of inactivity. Such a conclusion as, "You weren't as fit as as some of your peers, therefore you must not have been active enough," can be a destructive and often untrue statement. It may cause a loss of self-esteem and a loss of respect between student and teacher. On the flip side, assuming that youngsters who make high scores on fitness tests are active can also be incorrect. Youngsters who are genetically gifted may be inactive, yet perform well on fitness tests. If teachers do not teach otherwise, these youngsters incorrectly develop the belief it is possible to be fit and healthy without being active.

Why the Continuing Belief that Children Are Unfit?

For years, the only available fitness test for teachers was the Youth Fitness Test (1976, 1987), which is currently available as *The President's Challenge* (President's Council on Physical Fitness and Sports, 2002). This test measures skill-related fitness and awards the Presidential fitness award to youngsters performing at the 85th percentile or better in all test items. Data from the National School Population Fitness Survey (Reiff et al., 1987), funded by the President's Council on Physical Fitness and Sports, showed that only one-tenth of 1 percent of boys and three-tenths of 1 percent of girls could pass a battery of six tests at the 85th percentile. Why are the standards so high? A probable explanation is that it compares with academic standards and test developers felt that physical education standards should be set at a similar level.

Because many physical educators and parents felt that the 85th percentile standard is unrealistically high, a second award was created—the National Fitness Award. To earn this award, youngsters must pass the same battery of test items at the 50th percentile or better. Unfortunately, when using a battery of tests, the overwhelming majority of students fail at least one item, causing them to lose the award and be identified as unfit. Only 15 percent of boys and 19 percent of girls were able to pass the 50th percentile standard. Using a battery of tests to define fitness is a sure way to fail the majority of children. Even at this lowered standard, over 80 percent of youngsters are failures. Common sense suggests that if youngsters pass 5 of 6 test items, they should be declared fit rather than unfit. As teachers, it is important to discuss the successes of children on fitness test items, rather than declare them unfit because they failed one item.

Another reason people continue to believe that youngsters are unfit is because the definition of physical fitness has changed over the years. Newer fitness tests are focusing on health-related fitness and its relationship to good health and feelings of well-being. High performance on fitness test items is not necessary for good health. Evidence shows that moderate amounts of health-related physical fitness are enough to contribute to good health (Blair et al., 1989; U.S. Department of Health and Human Services, 1996). When health-related fitness test items are used to evaluate fitness, today's children perform as well as (and better than) those in years past. Health-related fitness standards reveal that the majority of children are fit.

Finally, it is likely that many physical education teachers have chosen to believe that youngsters are unfit so that a strong case can be made for employing physical education teachers. This belief is counterproductive because the fitness of children has been measured for over 40 years and the fitness levels of youth have neither substantially improved nor declined over the last four decades (Corbin & Pangrazi, 1992). A better approach is to accept the fact that preadolescent youth are nonresponders to training and unlikely to show fitness improvement even with training regimens. The important issue is to teach youth about fitness, what type of effort it requires, the type of activity that will be needed in adulthood, and leave them with a positive feeling toward physical activity and fitness.

WHAT DO I NEED TO KNOW ABOUT FITNESS TESTING?

Consider the following question before implementing a testing program. The overriding consideration is to be sure the testing experience is positive and educational. Children can learn about their personal fitness and how to develop a lifestyle that maintains good health without being turned off by the testing experience. Imagine the number of children who have been embarrassed when their fitness test results are announced to the class.

Should I Use a Skill-Related or Health-Related Fitness Test?

Students should understand the difference between the types of fitness so they understand the purposes of each. Skill-related fitness helps improve performance in motor tasks related to sport and athletics. The ability to perform well on skill-related tests is influenced by predetermined genetic skills. If skill-related fitness is presented in elementary school, it should be accompanied with an explanation about why some people perform well with a minimum of effort whereas others, no matter how hard they try, never reach high levels of performance. Many obvious examples that are easily seen illustrate this, such as individual differences in speed, jumping ability, strength, and physical size.

In contrast, health-related physical fitness focuses on how much activity is required for good health. Emphasis is placed on the process of activity and participation rather than on the product of high-level physical skill performance. Health-related fitness batteries use criterion-referenced health standards (see page 237) in contrast to skill-related fitness tests that use percentile scores standards. Criterion-referenced standards relate to how much activity is required for good health. Performance in excess of the minimum is laudable, but not required for good health. This approach teaches students the importance of maintaining a personal level of fitness through regular activity rather than comparing one's fitness level with others.

What Are the Purposes of Fitness Testing?

Fitness tests are designed to evaluate and educate youngsters about the status of their physical fitness. Obviously, fitness tests have limitations, so the important thing is how the tests are used. The three major purposes of fitness tests are: (1) to offer personalized, informal self-testing, (2) to measure personal best fitness performance, and (3) to evaluate institutional accomplishment of fitness goals. A personalized self-testing approach is usually the best choice for the majority of students because it can be done in the least amount of time and it is administered as an educational process.

The *personalized self-testing approach* is student centered, concerned with the process of fitness testing, and places less emphasis on performance scores (product). When using this technique, students find a friend with whom they would like to work or can work alone if desired. Partners evaluate each other as they develop personal fitness profiles. The focus is on learning the process of fitness testing so they know how to evaluate their health status during adulthood. Students are asked to do their best, but the teacher supports rather than directs the process. Results are the property of the student and are not posted or shared with other students. The self-testing program is an educational endeavor; it allows for more frequent evaluation because it can be done quickly, privately, and informally.

Figure 12.4 on page 236 is an example of a self-testing form for the Fitnessgram test. It contains a column to check off whether students have met the minimum criterion-referenced health standard for each test item. The purpose of recording the data is to help students learn to self-evaluate without the stigma of others having to view or know about it. In addition, students may choose not to be tested on a certain item because they fear embarrassment (in the case of skinfold tests) or failure (in a mile run, for example).

The *personal best approach* is for gifted performers and students who want to measure their maximal performance. The objective is to achieve a personal best on each of the test items. This type of program has been used for years with most fitness tests. In addition, several awards (Presidential, National, and others) have been issued to elite-level performers. This is a formal testing program, as compared to the self-testing approach discussed previously. Test items are performed correctly, following test protocol to the letter. This program requires maximal performance that may not be motivating to less capable students. It requires a considerable amount of time to complete. If the personal best model were used with all students, it would embarrass many youngsters who fear they will perform poorly in front of peers. To avoid this situation, offer time outside of class when students can be tested. Students can choose to participate in a personal best testing session or decide to avoid such situations. Testing opportunities can be offered after or before school or on a weekend when school is not in session. Some city recreation departments are willing to offer fitness testing opportunities outside the physical education program.

The *institutional evaluation approach* is used to see if the institution (school) is reaching its desired fitness objectives. A common approach is to establish a percentage of the student body that must meet or exceed criterion-referenced health standards for a fitness test. If the percentage is below established institutional objective standards, the curriculum is then modified in an attempt to increase the percentage of students meeting the health standards. Because this type of testing impacts teachers and curriculum offerings, it must be done in a formal and standardized manner. A common approach is to train a team of parents to administer tests throughout the system. This ensures accuracy and consistency across

My Personal Fitness Record

Name ____________________ Age ________ Grade ________ Room ________

	Score		HFZ*
Body Composition			
Calf (leg) Skinfold			
Triceps (arm) Skinfold	+		
Total (leg and arm)	=		
Cardiovascular Endurance PACER			
Abdominal Strength Curl-ups			
Upper Body Strength Push-ups			
Back Strength Trunk Lift			
	L	R	
Lower Back Flexibility Sit and Reach			
	L	R	
Upper Body Flexibility Shoulder Stretch			

* HFZ means you have scored in the Healthy Fitness Zone.You have achieved or passed the minimum fitness standard required for good health and feeling good. Regardless of whether you scored in the HFZ for all the tests, you must maintain an active lifestyle for good health. Try to accumulate at least 60 minutes of activity everyday.

You do not have to share the results of your personal fitness record. It is for your information and should help you determine your health status. Ask your teacher if you need ideas for increasing your physical activity level. Students are learning the process of evaluating their fitness. The scores recorded may not be accurate.

FIGURE 12.4 My personal fitness record (Fitnessgram items).

all schools in the district. Each test item is reviewed separately, as it is quite possible that objectives are being reached for some but not all of the items. To avoid overtesting students, many districts evaluate students at regular intervals during their school career, such as in the fifth, eighth, and tenth grades. This practice minimizes the amount of formal testing youngsters have to endure during their school career.

What do I Need to Know About the Fitnessgram Health-Related Test?

The Fitnessgram (Cooper Institute, 2002) is a health-related fitness test that provides students, teachers, and parents with information about health. It is part of a comprehensive program promoted by the American Fitness Alliance (http//www.americanfitness.net) that includes Physical Best materials from AAHPERD and the Fitnessgram/Activitygram test software from the Aerobic Institute. The Fitnessgram system consists of a test battery and software for reporting health-related fitness results. In addition, a manual accompanies the software and covers test administration and software information. The test battery allows teachers to select test items if they choose to develop a customized test battery. The software also includes an Activitygram component that allows students to input information about their daily physical activity accomplishments. The Activitygram is a recall instrument that asks students to grade the intensity, level, and type of activity they participated in during the previous day.

What Are the Fitnessgram Test Items?

The test items in the Fitnessgram are briefly described. Where more than one item is offered, teachers have the choice of selecting the test they desire to use. A comprehensive test manual, related materials, and software can be ordered from The American Fitness Alliance, P.O. Box 5076, Champaign, IL 61825-5076.

Aerobic Capacity The PACER or one-mile run/walk is used to measure aerobic performance. The PACER is a more acceptable alternative to the mile, as it involves a 20-meter shuttle run and can be performed indoors. The test is progressive; it begins at a level that all youngsters can perform and gradually increases in difficulty. The objective of the PACER is to run back and forth over a 20-meter distance within a specified time. The pace starts slowly and gradually speeds up. The 20-meter distance is not intimidating to youngsters (compared to the mile) and avoids the problem of trying to teach young children to pace themselves rather than running all-out and fatiguing rapidly. Additionally, the least fit youngster drops out of the PACER first rather than being the last person left on the track.

Body Composition Body composition is evaluated using percent body fat, which is calculated by measuring the triceps and calf skinfolds or Body Mass Index (calculated using height and weight).

Abdominal Strength: Curl-up This item uses a cadence (one curl-up every three seconds). The maximum limit is 75. Students lie in a supine position with the knees bent at a 140-degree angle. The hands are placed flat on the mat alongside the hips. The objective is to gradually sit up and move the fingers down the mat a specified distance.

Upper Body Strength: Push-up This test is done to a cadence (one every 3 seconds) and is an excellent substitute for the pull-up. A successful push-up is counted when the arms are bent to a 90-degree angle. This item allows many more students to experience success as compared to the pull-up and flexed arm hang. Other alternative test items are the modified pull-up, the pull-up, and the flexed arm hang.

Trunk Extensor Strength and Flexibility: Trunk lift From a face-down position, this test involves lifting the upper body 6 to 12 inches off the floor using the muscles of the back. The position must be held until the measurement can be made.

Flexibility The back-saver sit-and-reach is similar to the traditional sit-and-reach test except that it is performed with one leg flexed to avoid encouraging students to hyperextend. Measurement is made on both the right and left legs.

What Are Fitnessgram Criterion-Referenced Health Standards?

The Fitnessgram uses criterion-referenced health standards instead of traditional percentile rankings. These standards represent a level of fitness that offers some degree of protection against diseases that result from sedentary living. The Fitnessgram uses an approach that classifies fitness performance into two areas: Needs Improvement and Healthy Fitness Zone (HFZ). All students are encouraged to score in the HFZ.

Criterion-referenced health standards for aerobic fitness are based on a study by Blair et al. (1989). This study reported a significant decrease in all-cause mortality when moderate activity lifted participants above the bottom 20 percent (least active segment) of the population. Risk level continues to decrease as activity levels increase but not as dramatically as simply getting out of the bottom 20 percent of the population. Aerobic capacity standards for the Fitnessgram HFZ correspond with achieving a fitness level above the lower 20 percent of the population. The upper end of the HFZ corresponds to a fitness level that excludes all but the top 20 percent (most active segment) of the population.

Criterion-referenced health standards for percent of fat are calculated from equations reported by Slaughter et al. (1988). Detailed information on the development of these equations and other issues related to the measurement and interpretation of body composition information is available in Lohman (1992). Williams et al. (1992) reported that children with body fat levels above 25 percent for boys and 30 to 35 percent for girls are more likely to exhibit elevated cholesterol levels and hypertension. The lower limit of the Fitnessgram HFZ corresponds to these levels of body fat.

Criterion-referenced health standards have not been established for abdominal strength, upper body strength, and flexibility. Instead, criterion-referenced training standards are used for these areas of fitness. The lower limit represents a performance level that youngsters should be able to accomplish if they are reasonably active. Stated another way, these standards reflect a reasonable expectation for students who are sufficiently active.

Should I Use Performance Recognition Awards?

For years, award systems have been designed to reward students who demonstrate high levels of fitness performance. The original intent of the award systems was to motivate youngsters to improve their level of fitness. However, recent research shows that performance awards usually only motivate youngsters who feel they have the ability to earn them (Corbin, Lovejoy, & Whitehead, 1988; Corbin, Lovejoy, Steingard, & Emerson, 1990). Many students find it impossible to earn such awards and often feel as though there is no use trying. Fitness awards focus on a single episode of accomplishment, making the act of participating in daily activity less important. Students learn that the only thing that counts with fitness is performance on the yearly test.

Reward systems that focus on improvement look at short-term changes. Fitness award systems ask students to look at their immediate health status. There is evidence to show that youngsters who achieve at an elite level do so because they are genetically gifted (Bouchard et al., 1992). If gifted students can pass the test without training, it leads them to believe they do not have to exercise regularly. If awards are used, it is best to reward participation in regular activity rather than fitness performance. Physical education should encourage behavior that lasts a lifetime. If the focus is on long-term behavior, discussions should emphasize participation in regular and moderate activity.

If used, an award system should incorporate the following points:

1. Base awards on achievement of goals that are challenging, yet attainable (Locke & Lathan, 1985). Goals that are difficult to attain fail to elicit effort from students (Harter, 1978). Students who are least likely to make an effort to earn an award are those with low self-esteem; these are probably the students who most need to achieve such goals.
2. If fitness goals do not seem attainable to youngsters, "learned helplessness" sets in (Harter, 1978). This phenomenon occurs when children believe there is no use trying to reach the goals and their efforts are in vain. "Learned helplessness" often occurs when performance rather than participation or effort is rewarded. Difficult-to-achieve goals teach youngsters who need to be motivated that there is no use in trying.
3. If an award system is used to motivate children's activity, the system should be phased out. Awards can motivate primary-grade children; however, by the age of 9 or 10 years, children start to see the rewards as bribery to do something (Whitehead & Corbin, 1991). Other children find achievement of the awards to be hopeless; they are not motivated but are discouraged by the rewards being given to others. Gradually removing awards helps students learn that participation is done for intrinsic and personal reasons.
4. An alternative and long-term approach to awards is to recognize students for regular participation in activity. This places the rewards in reach of all youngsters and helps establish activity habits that last a lifetime. In addition, this approach supports the research cited in the report of the Surgeon General on physical activity and health (U.S. Dept. of Health and Human Services, 1996).

CREATE POSITIVE ATTITUDES TOWARD ACTIVITY

Teachers can do a number of things to increase the possibility of students being "turned on" to activity. Fitness activity is neither good nor bad. Rather, how fitness activities are taught determines how youngsters will feel about making fitness a part of their lifestyle. The following strategies can help make activity a positive learning experience.

Personalize Fitness Activities

Students who find themselves unable to perform exercises are not likely to develop a positive attitude toward physical activity. Fitness experiences should allow children to determine their personal workloads. Use time as the workload variable and ask children to do the best they can within a time limit. People dislike and fear experiences they perceive to be forced on them from an external source. Voluntary long-term exercise is more probable when individuals are internally driven to do their best. Fitness experiences that allow children to control the intensity of their workouts offer better opportunities for development of positive attitudes toward activity.

Expose Youngsters to a Variety of Fitness Activities

Presenting a variety of fitness opportunities decreases the monotony of doing the same routines week after week and increases the likelihood that students will experience fitness activities that are personally enjoyable. Youngsters are willing to accept activities they dislike if they know there will be a chance to experience routines they enjoy in the near future. A year-long routine of "calisthenics and running a mile" forces children, regardless of ability and interest, to participate in the same routine whether they like it or not. Avoiding potential boredom by systematically changing fitness activities is a significant way to help students perceive fitness in a positive light.

Give Students Feedback about Their Performance

Teacher feedback contributes to the way children view fitness activities. Immediate, accurate, and specific feedback regarding performance encourages continued participation. Provided in a positive manner, this feedback can stimulate children to extend their participation habits outside the confines of the gymnasium. Reinforce all children, not just those who perform at high levels. All youngsters need feedback and reinforcement even if they are incapable of performing at an elite level.

Teach Physical Skills and Fitness

Physical education programs should concentrate on skill development as well as fitness. Some states mandate fitness testing, which causes teachers to worry that their students "will not pass." Unfortunately, the skill development portion of physical education is often sacrificed to allow for an increased emphasis on teaching fitness. Physical education has two major objectives: fitness *and* skill development. Skills are the tools that most adults use to attain fitness. The majority of individuals maintain fitness through various skill-based activities such as tennis, badminton, swimming, golf, basketball, aerobics, bicycling, and the like. People have a much greater propensity to participate as adults if they feel competent in an activity. School programs must graduate students with requisite entry skills in a variety of activities.

Be a Role Model

Appearance, attitude, and actions speak loudly about teachers and their values regarding fitness. Teachers who display physical vitality, take pride in being active, participate in fitness activities with children, and are physically fit will positively influence youngsters to maintain an active lifestyle. It is unreasonable to expect teachers to complete a fitness routine nine times a day and five days a week. However, teachers must exercise with a class periodically to assure students that they are willing to do what they ask others to do.

Care About the Attitudes of Children

Attitudes dictate how youngsters participate in activity. Too often, adults want to force fitness on children and "make them all fit." This results in insensitivity to the feelings of participants. Training does not equate to lifetime fitness. When youngsters are trained without concern for their feelings, the result will be fit children who may hate physical activity. Once a negative attitude is developed, it is difficult to change. This does not mean that youngsters should avoid fitness activity. It means that fitness participation must be a positive experience. Youngsters should not all be funneled into one type of fitness activity. For example, running may be detrimental to the health of obese children, and lean, uncoordinated students may not enjoy contact activities. The fitness experience works best when it is a challenge rather than a threat. A *challenge* is an experience that participants feel they can accomplish. In contrast, a *threat* appears to be an impossible undertaking, one in which there is no use trying. Keep fitness goals within the realm of challenge. A final note: whether an activity is a challenge or a threat depends on the perceptions of the learner, not the instructor. Listen carefully to students rather than telling them they should do it for their own good.

Start Easy and Progress Slowly

Fitness development is a journey, not a destination. No teacher wants students to become fit and then quit being active. A rule of thumb to follow is allow students to start at a level that they can *accomplish*. This usually means self-directed workloads within a specified time frame. Don't force students into heavy workloads too soon. It is impossible to start a fitness program at a level that is too easy. Start with success and gradually increase the workload. This avoids the discouragement of failure and excessive muscle soreness. When students successfully accomplish activities, they develop a system of self-talk that looks at their exercise behavior in a positive light. This minimizes the practice of self-criticism where students fail to live up to their own or others' standards.

Use Low-Intensity Activity

Make activity appropriate for the developmental level of the youngster. The amount of activity needed for good health is dictated by two variables—the intensity of the activity and the duration of the activity. Most children participate in high-volume–low-intensity activity as they exercise sporadically all day. This naturally occurring activity is consistent with the developmental level of children. In contrast, most adults are involved in high-intensity–low-volume activity because they have little time to be active for long periods. This contrast of activity styles leads adults to believe that children need to participate in high-intensity activities to receive health benefits. They view children as unfit because they often refuse to participate in high-intensity fitness activities. This focus on high-intensity activity causes some children to become discouraged and burned out at an early age. Youngsters are the most active segment of society (Rowland, 1990), and it is important to maintain and encourage this trait. When regular activity is reinforced, fitness follows to the extent possible for each child, given heredity and maturation level.

Encourage Lifetime Activity

A successful program would result in students exercising throughout their lifetimes. Certain activities may be more likely to stimulate exercise outside of school. There is some evidence (Glasser, 1976) that if the following activity conditions are met, exercise becomes positively addicting and a necessary part of one's life. These steps imply that many individual activities such as walking, jogging, hiking, biking, and the like are activities that students will use for fitness during adulthood.

1. The activity must be noncompetitive; the student chooses and wants to do it.
2. It must not require a great deal of mental effort.
3. The activity can be done alone, without a partner or teammates.
4. Students must believe in the value of the exercise for improving health and general welfare.
5. Participants must believe that the activity will become easier and more meaningful if they persist. To become addicting, the activity must be done for at least 6 months.
6. The activity should be accomplished in such a manner that the participant is not self-critical.

PROMOTE PHYSICAL FITNESS AND ACTIVITY

All children should have the opportunity to learn how to live an active lifestyle. When schools fail to teach children such skills, youngsters leave not knowing what it takes to become active and healthy adults. A recent statement issued by the American Academy of Pediatrics (1991) reported that children from the ages of 2 to 12 spend about 25 hours a week watching television. Even in school programs, children are fortunate to spend one hour a week in organized physical education lessons. Physical education instruction has to teach activity habits that carry over to out-of-school activities. Regardless of how often youngsters participate in physical education, time spent on physical fitness knowledge and activity is necessary. When youngsters are not taught fitness activities, they learn that such activities are unimportant or not valued by teachers and the school. Youngsters are experiential; that is, they learn from participation and develop perceptions based on those experiences. If physical activities are taught in school, youngsters begin to learn that daily activity is an important habit for a healthy lifestyle. Children are taught how to brush their teeth at a tender age so they learn the habit and protect their teeth for a lifetime. In similar fashion, it is just as important to teach children to be active so their physical health will not decay.

The purpose of fitness instruction at the elementary school level is to get youngsters in the habit of performing daily physical activity, not to develop high levels of fitness. Teaching different ways to develop and maintain fitness (even if only one day per week) tells students that the school values health and exercise as part of a balanced lifestyle. What better outcome than to teach youngsters to participate in some type of daily activity throughout life?

Consider the following for enriching and promoting the fitness and activity program.

1. Provide basic explanations of rudimentary anatomy and kinesiology. Children can learn the names and locations of major bones and muscle groups, including how they function in relation to selected joint action.
2. Provide an understanding of how fitness is developed. Explain the value of the procedures followed in class sessions so children understand the purpose of all fitness developmental tasks. In addition, teach children the basic components of a personal fitness program for life.
3. Knowledge of the values of physical fitness, how to apply the principles of exercise, and how fitness can become part of one's lifestyle can positively alter students' views of physical activity. Bringing the class together at the end of a lesson to discuss key fitness points promotes a clearer understanding of why fitness is important. To share cognitive information, establish a muscle of the week, construct educational bulletin boards to illustrate fitness concepts, or send home handouts explaining principles of fitness development.
4. Develop cognition of the importance of fitness for wellness. Help students understand how to perform fitness activities and why these activities should be performed. They need to know the values derived from maintaining a minimal fitness level.
5. Place bulletin boards in the teaching area to explain components of the physical education program to parents and students. Bulletin boards can explain skill techniques, motivational reminders, and fitness activities that will be upcoming in class. Classroom teachers are required to develop bulletin boards for their classes; when physical education teachers design visual aids for the gymnasium, credibility is enhanced.
6. Exploit the use of audiovisual aids. Audiotapes of fitness routines increase the motivation of youngsters. Exercise videotapes are an excellent medium for beginning a new fitness activity.
7. Help children understand the values of physical fitness and the physiology of its development and maintenance. Homework dealing with the cognitive aspects of fitness development communicates to parents that their children are gaining knowledge for a lifetime.

8. Emphasize self-testing programs that teach children to evaluate their personal fitness levels (see pages 109–110). In self-evaluation programs, children assess their fitness without concern about others judging them. Fitness and activity are personal for most adults and should be considered a personal matter for youngsters as well.
9. Cooperation at home is essential. Children are more likely to be involved in physical activity when their parents exercise regularly. Physical activities that are sent home for weekend and vacation participation help parents understand the importance of regular activity for them and for their children. An effective technique is to develop a fitness calendar that lists activities to be performed on various days. A monthly calendar outline listing various fitness activities can be sent home to parents.
10. Assign physical activity as homework for youngsters. Ask them to develop a notebook where they monitor the number of minutes and type of physical activity they accumulated outside of the school setting. The idea of maintaining an activity log is becoming much more popular. In fact, the President's Council on Physical Fitness and Sports is planning on offering an award to students who monitor and accumulate physical activity over a period of 6 to 12 weeks.
11. Physical education fitness exhibitions and school demonstrations for parents can feature a number of fitness routines and activities. Be sure that *all* students are allowed to participate and enjoy the activity. When parents see their youngsters vigorously exercising, support of the program is enhanced.

AVOID HARMFUL PRACTICES AND EXERCISES

The following points contraindicate certain exercise practices and should be considered when offering fitness instruction. For in-depth coverage of contraindicated exercises, see Lindsey and Corbin (1989) or Corbin, Lindsey, and Welk (2000).

1. The following techniques (Macfarlane, 1993) should be avoided when performing abdominal exercises that lift the head and trunk off the floor:
   - Avoid placing the hands behind the head or high on the neck. This may cause hyperflexion and injury to the discs when the elbows swing forward to help pull the body up.
   - Keep the knees bent. Straight legs cause the hip flexor muscles to be used earlier and more forcefully, making it difficult to maintain proper pelvic tilt.
   - Don't hold the feet on the floor. Having another student secure the feet places more force on the lumbar vertabrae and may lead to lumbar hyperextension.
   - Don't lift the buttocks and lumbar region off the floor. This also causes the hip flexor muscles to contract vigorously.
2. Two types of stretching activity have been used to develop flexibility. Ballistic stretching (strong bouncing movements) formerly was the most common stretching used, but this has been discouraged for many years because it was thought to increase delayed onset muscle soreness. The other flexibility activity, static stretching, involves increasing the stretch to the point of discomfort, backing off slightly to where the position can be held comfortably, and maintaining the stretch for an extended time. Static stretching has been advocated because it was thought to reduce muscle soreness and prevent injury. One study (Smith et al., 1993) disputed the muscle soreness and tissue damage theory with findings that showed ballistic and static stretching both produced increases in muscle soreness. In fact, the static stretching actually induced significantly more soreness than did ballistic stretching. Static stretching is an excellent choice, but ballistic stretching is probably not as harmful as once thought.
3. If forward flexion is done from a sitting position in an effort to touch the toes, the bend should be from the hips, not from the waist, and should be done with one leg flexed. To conform with this concern, the new Fitnessgram sit-and-reach test item is now performed with one leg flexed to reduce stress on the lower back.
4. Straight-leg raises from a supine position should be avoided because they may strain the lower back. The problem can be somewhat alleviated by placing the hands under the small of the back, but it is probably best to avoid such exercises.
5. Deep knee bends (full squats) and the duck walk should be avoided. They may cause damage to the knee joints and have little developmental value. Much more beneficial is flexing the knee joint to 90 degrees and returning to a standing position.
6. When doing stretching exercises from a standing position, the knees should not be hyperextended. The knee joint should be relaxed rather than locked. It is often effective to have students do their stretching with bent knees; this will remind them not to hyperextend the joint. In all stretching activities, participants should be allowed to judge their range of motion. Expecting all students to be able to touch

their toes is an unrealistic goal. If concerned about touching the toes from this position, do so from a sitting position with one leg flexed.

7. Activities that place stress on the neck should be avoided. Examples of activities in which caution should be used are the Inverted Bicycle, Wrestler's Bridge, and abdominal exercises with the hands behind the head.
8. Avoid the so-called hurdler's stretch. This activity is done in the sitting position with one leg forward and the other leg bent and to the rear. Using this stretch places undue pressure on the knee joint of the bent leg. Substitute a stretch using a similar position with one leg straight forward and the other leg bent with the foot placed in the crotch area.
9. Avoid stretches that demand excessive back arching. An example: While lying in prone position, the student reaches back and grabs the ankles. By pulling and arching, the exerciser can hyperextend the lower back. This places stress on the discs and stretches the abdominal muscles (not needed by most people).

IMPLEMENT A YEARLONG FITNESS PLAN

Developing a yearly plan of fitness instruction helps ensure that a variety of experiences is offered to learners. It also allows for progression and ensures that youngsters receive a well-rounded program of instruction. Plan physical fitness instruction in a manner similar to skill development sequences. Figure 12.5 is a sample yearly plan that might be used to distribute a variety of fitness activities throughout the school year.

When organizing a yearly plan for fitness instruction, consider the following. Units of fitness instruction should vary in length depending on the age of the youngster. Children at developmental level I need to experience a variety of routines to maintain a high level of motivation and to understand the different facets of fitness. During these years, exposure to many different types of activities is more important than is a progressive, demanding fitness routine. Make the first experiences of fitness instruction positive and enjoyable. As children mature, units can be extended to 2 weeks. In the upper grades, units of 3 weeks allow progression to occur within units. In spite of the varying length of units, adhere to one principle: *There are many methods for developing fitness, none of which is best for all children.* Offer a variety of routines and activities so youngsters learn that fitness is not lockstep and unbending. The yearly plan should offer activities that allow all types of youngsters to find success at one time or another during the school year.

The yearly plan reveals that routines become much more structured as youngsters grow older. Most of the activities listed for kindergarten through second-grade children are unstructured and allow for wide variation of performance. For older-grade children, emphasis on proper technique and performance increases. However, this is not to imply that every student must do every activity exactly the same. It is unrealistic to think that an obese youngster will be able to perform at a level similar to a lean child. Allow for variation in performance while emphasizing the importance of "doing your best."

DEVELOP QUALITY FITNESS ROUTINES

Fitness routines are exclusively dedicated to the presentation of a variety of fitness activities. The following are suggestions for successful implementation of the fitness routines.

1. Precede fitness instruction with a 2- to 3-minute warm-up period. Introductory activities are useful for this purpose because they allow youngsters an opportunity to "loosen up" and prepare for strenuous activity.
2. The fitness portion of the daily lesson, including warm-up, should not extend beyond 10 to 13 minutes. Some might argue that more time is needed to develop adequate fitness. However, the reality is that most teachers are only allowed a 20- to 30-minute period of instruction. Because skill instruction is part of a balanced physical education program, compromise is necessary to ensure that all phases of the program are covered.
3. Use activities that exercise all body parts and cover the major components of fitness. Children are capable performers when workloads are geared to their age, fitness level, and abilities.
4. A variety of fitness routines comprising sequential exercises for total body development is the recommended alternative to a yearlong program of regimented calisthenics. Use a diverse array of activities that appeal to the interest and fitness level of children to replace the traditional approach of doing the same routine day in and day out.
5. Exercises, in themselves, are not sufficient to develop cardiovascular endurance. Add aerobic activity, such as jogging, rope jumping, or walking, so youngsters learn the concept of a balanced approach to fitness.
6. Assume an active role in fitness instruction. Children respond positively to role modeling. If you actively exercise with children, hustle to assist those youngsters having difficulty performing selected exercises,

Developmental Level I

Week		Week	
1	Fitness Games and Challenges	19	Parachute Fitness
2	Four-Corners Movement	20	Jump Rope Exercises
3	Astronaut Drills	21	Walk, Trot, and Jog
4	Fitness Games and Challenges	22	Fitness Challenges
5	Fitness Challenges	23	Jump Rope Exercises
6	Circuit Training	24	Four-Corners Fitness
7	Animal Movements and Fitness Challenges	25	Fitness Games and Challenges
8	Astronaut Drills	26	Animal Movements and Fitness Challenges
9	Fitness Challenges	27	Jump Rope Exercises
10	Parachute Fitness	28	Parachute Fitness
11	Astronaut Drills	29	Four-Corners Movement
12	Walk, Trot, and Jog	30	Walk, Trot, and Jog
13	Parachute Fitness	31	Animal Movements and Fitness Challenges
14	Circuit Training	32	Parachute Fitness
15	Mini-Challenge Course	33	Fitness Challenges
16	Mini-Challenge Course	34	Astronaut Drills
17	Four-Corners Fitness	35	Circuit Training
18	Fitness Games and Challenges	36	Walk, Trot, and Jog

Developmental Level II

Week		Week	
1	Teacher Leader Movement Challenges	19	Exercises to Music
2	Teacher Leader Exercises	20	Exercises to Music
3	Teacher Leader Exercises	21	Continuity Drills
4	Hexagon Hustle	22	Continuity Drills
5	Hexagon Hustle	23	Aerobic Fitness
6	Circuit Training	24	Stretching and Jogging Activities
7	Circuit Training	25	Stretching and Jogging Activities
8	Astronaut Drills	26	Walk, Trot, and Jog
9	Astronaut Drills	27	Parachute Fitness
10	Aerobic Fitness	28	Parachute Fitness
11	Aerobic Fitness	29	Exercises to Music
12	Astronaut Drills	30	Circuit Training
13	Challenge Course Fitness	31	Hexagon Hustle
14	Walk, Trot, and Jog	32	Continuity Drills
15	Challenge Course	33	Aerobic Fitness
16	Challenge Course	34	Aerobic Fitness
17	Aerobic Fitness and Partner Resistance	35	Parachute Exercises
18	Aerobic Fitness and Partner Resistance	36	Teacher Leader Exercises

FIGURE 12.5 Yearly plan of fitness activities (figure continues on page 244).

Developmental Level III

Week		Week	
1	Teacher Leader Exercises	19	Exercises to Music
2	Teacher Leader Exercises	20	Exercises to Music
3	Teacher Leader Exercises	21	Continuity Drills
4	Hexagon Hustle	22	Continuity Drills
5	Hexagon Hustle	23	Aerobic Fitness
6	Circuit Training	24	Stretching Activities
7	Circuit Training	25	Stretching Activities
8	Astronaut Drills	26	Stretching Activities
9	Astronaut Drills	27	Parachute Fitness
10	Aerobic Fitness	28	Parachute Fitness
11	Aerobic Fitness	29	Exercises to Music
12	Astronaut Drills	30	Circuit Training
13	Challenge Course	31	Hexagon Hustle
14	Stretching Activities	32	Continuity Drills
15	Challenge Course	33	Squad Leader Exercises with Task Cards
16	Challenge Course	34	Squad Leader Exercises with Task Cards
17	Partner Aerobic Fitness and Resistance Exercises	35	Parachute Exercises
18	Partner Aerobic Fitness and Resistance Exercises	36	Squad Leader Exercises with Task Cards

FIGURE 12.5 (continued)

and are able to make exercise fun, your actions will instill in children the value of an active lifestyle.

7. When determining workloads for children, the available alternatives are time or repetitions. Base the workload on time rather than on a specified number of repetitions so youngsters can adjust their workload within personal limits. Beginning dosages for exercises should start at a level at which *all* children will succeed. The best way to ensure success is to allow students to adjust the workload to suit their capabilities. Using a specified amount of time per exercise allows less gifted children to perform successfully. All children should *not* be expected to perform exactly the same workload.
8. Use audiotapes to time fitness activity segments so you are free to move throughout the area and offer individualized instruction. Participation and instruction should be enthusiastic and should focus on positive outcomes. If you do not enjoy physical fitness participation, such an attitude will be apparent to students.
9. *Never* use fitness activities as punishment. Such a practice teaches students that "push-ups and running are things you do when you misbehave." The opportunity to exercise should be a privilege as well as an enjoyable experience. Think of the money adults spend to exercise. Take a positive approach and offer students a chance to jog with a friend when they do something well. This allows them the opportunity not only to visit, but also to exercise with a positive feeling. Be an effective salesperson; sell the joy of activity and the benefits of physical fitness to youngsters.

FITNESS ACTIVITIES FOR DEVELOPMENTAL LEVEL I

Fitness activities for young children have the potential to teach components of physical fitness and exercise the various body areas. All the fitness routines that follow alternate strength and flexibility activities with cardiovascular activity. For most routines, strength and flexibility activities are listed. Together, the introductory and fitness activity provide broad coverage by including activities for each of these five areas: arm-shoulder girdle, trunk, abdomen, legs and cardiorespiratory system, and flexibility.

Modified Fitness Activities

Many modified activities can be used to develop fitness routines for children at this level. Nonlocomotor activities should be alternated with locomotor activities to avoid excessively fatiguing youngsters. When youngsters are pushed too hard aerobically, they will express their fatigue in many different manners (by complaining, quitting, misbehaving, or sitting out). Know when to ease up. Instruction and activities should be sensitive to the capacities of youngsters.

ARM-SHOULDER GIRDLE DEVELOPMENT ACTIVITIES

The push-up (Figure 12.6) and crab (tummy toward the ceiling) positions are excellent for developing upper body strength. Allow students to rest with one knee on the floor in the up position rather than lying on the floor. Allow students to select a challenge they feel able to accomplish rather than being forced to fail trying to do push-ups. Many of the directives listed for the push-up position can be used for the crab position. One way to develop a sequence of push-up challenges is to begin with one knee on the floor while practicing a number of challenges. As youngsters develop strength, they can make a controlled descent to the floor from the up position. The following are examples of movement challenges that can be done with one knee down (beginning) or in the regular push-up (more challenging) position.

1. Hold your body off the floor (push-up position).
2. Wave at a friend. Wave with the other arm. Shake a leg at someone. Do these challenges in the crab position.
3. Lift one foot high. Now the other foot.
4. Bounce both feet up and down. Move the feet out from each other while bouncing.
5. Inch the feet up to the hands and go back again. Inch the feet up to the hands and then inch the hands out to return to the push-up position.
6. Reach up with one hand and touch the other shoulder behind the back.
7. Lift both hands from the floor. Try clapping the hands.

FIGURE 12.6 Push-up position.

8. Turn over so that your back is to the floor. Now complete the turn to push-up position.
9. Walk on your hands and feet. Try two hands and one foot. Walk in the crab position.
10. With one knee on the ground, touch your nose to the floor between your hands. As you get stronger, move your head forward a little and touch your nose to the floor. (The farther the nose touches the floor in front of the hands, the greater the strength demands.)
11. Lower the body an inch at a time until the chest touches the floor. Return to the up position any way possible.
12. Pretend you are a tire going flat. Gradually lower yourself to the floor as if you were a tire going flat.

TRUNK DEVELOPMENT ACTIVITIES

Trunk development movements include bending, stretching, swaying, twisting, reaching, and forming shapes. Examples of different trunk movements follow.

Bending

1. Bend in different ways.
2. Bend as many parts of the body as you can.
3. Make different shapes by bending two, three, and four parts of the body.
4. Bend the arms and knees in different ways and on different levels.
5. Try different ways of bending the fingers and wrist of one hand with the other. Use some resistance. (Explain resistance.) Add body bends.

Stretching

1. Keep one foot in place and stretch your arms in different directions; move with the free foot. Stretch at different levels.
2. Lie on the floor, stretch one leg different ways in space. Stretch one leg in one direction and the other in another direction.
3. Stretch as slowly as you can and then snap back to original position.
4. Stretch with different arm-leg combinations in several directions.
5. See how much space on the floor you can cover by stretching.
6. Combine bending and stretching movements.

Swaying and Twisting

1. Sway your body back and forth in different directions. Change the position of your arms.
2. Sway your body, bending over.

3. Sway your head from side to side.
4. Select a part of the body and twist it as far as you can in one direction and then in the opposite direction.
5. Twist your body at different levels.
6. Twist two or more parts of your body at the same time.
7. Twist one part of your body while untwisting another.
8. Twist your head to see as far back as you can.
9. Twist like a spring. Like a screwdriver.
10. Stand on one foot and twist your body. Untwist.
11. From a seated position, make different shapes by twisting.

ABDOMINAL DEVELOPMENT ACTIVITIES

The basic position for exercising the abdominal muscles is supine on the floor or on a mat. Movements should lift the upper and lower portions of the body from the floor, either singly or together. Since developmental level I children are top-heavy (large head, short legs), they find it difficult to perform most abdominal exercises. Early abdominal development should begin with youngsters lying on the floor and lifting the head. Follow by starting in a sitting position and gradually lowering the upper body (with head tucked) to the floor. The following activities stimulate children to develop abdominal and shoulder girdle strength. In addition, selected abdominal exercises (pages 253–257) can be modified to provide suitable challenges. Use directives like "Can you . . . ?" or "Show me how you can. . . ."

1. Lift your head from the floor and look at your toes. Wink your right eye and wiggle your left foot. Reverse.
2. In a supine position, "wave" a leg at a friend. Use the other leg. Use both legs.
3. Lift your knees up slowly, an inch at a time.
4. Pick your heels up about 6 inches off the floor and swing them back and forth. Cross them and twist them.
5. Sit up any way you can and touch both sets of toes with your hands.
6. Sit up any possible way and touch your right toes with your left hand. Do it the other way.
7. In a sitting position, lean the upper body backward without falling. How long can you hold this position?
8. From a sitting position, lower the body slowly to the floor. Vary the positions of the arms (across the tummy, the chest, and above the head).
9. From a supine position, curl up by pulling up on your legs.
10. From a supine position, hold your shoulders off the floor.
11. From a supine position, lift your legs and head off the floor.

LEG AND CARDIORESPIRATORY DEVELOPMENT ACTIVITIES

Leg and cardiorespiratory development activities include a range of movement challenges in general space or in place. Youngsters fatigue and recover quickly. Take advantage of this trait by alternating cardiorespiratory activities with arm, trunk, and abdominal exercises.

Running Patterns

Running in different directions

Running in place

Ponies in the Stable (page 338)

Tortoise and Hare (page 338)

European Rhythmic Running (pages 337–338)

Running and stopping

Running and changing direction on signal

Jumping and Hopping Patterns

Jumping in different directions back and forth over a spot

Jumping or hopping in, out, over, and around hoops, individual mats, or jump ropes laid on the floor

Jumping or hopping back and forth over lines, or hopping down the lines

Rope Jumping

Individual rope jumping—allow choice

Combinations

Many combinations of locomotor movements can be used to motivate youngsters. Following are possible challenges that might be used.

1. Run in place. Do some running steps in place without stopping.
2. Skip or gallop for 30 seconds.
3. Slide all the way around the gymnasium.
4. Alternate hopping or jumping for 30 seconds with 30 seconds of rest.
5. Jump in place while twisting the arms and upper body.
6. Do 10 skips, 10 gallops, and finish with 30 running steps.

7. Hold hands with a friend and do 100 jumps.
8. Jump rope as many times as possible without missing.
9. Hop back and forth over this line from one end of the gym to the other.
10. Try to run as fast as you can. How long can you keep going?

Animal Movements

Animal movements are enjoyable for primary-grade children because they can mimic the sounds and movements of the animals. Most of the animal movements are done with the body weight on all four limbs, which helps develop the arms and shoulders. Challenge youngsters to move randomly throughout the area, across the gymnasium, or between cones delineating a specific distance. Increase the distance or the amount of time each walk is performed to increase the workload. To avoid excessive fatigue, alternate the animal movements with stretching activities. The following are examples of animal movements that can be used. See Chapter 19 for descriptions of more animal movements.

Puppy Walk: Move on all fours (not the knees). Keep the head up and move lightly.

Lion Walk: Move on all fours while keeping the back arched. Move deliberately and lift the "paws" to simulate moving without sound.

Elephant Walk: Move heavily throughout the area, swinging the head back and forth like an elephant's trunk.

Seal Walk: Move using the arms to propel the body. Allow the legs to drag along the floor much as a seal would move.

Injured Coyote: Move using only three limbs. Hold the injured limb off the floor. Vary the walk by specifying which limb is injured.

Crab Walk: Move on all fours with the tummy facing the ceiling. Try to keep the back as straight as possible.

Rabbit Jump: Start in a squatting position with the hands on the floor. Reach forward with the hands and support the body weight. Jump both feet toward the hands. Repeat the sequence.

Fitness Games

Fitness games are excellent for cardiovascular endurance and create a high degree of motivation. Place emphasis on all students moving. One of the best ways to be sure this occurs is to play games that do not eliminate players. Players who tag someone are no longer it and the person tagged becomes it. This makes it difficult for players to tell who is it, which is desirable since it ensures that players cannot stop and stand when the it player is a significant distance from them. If various games stipulate a "safe" position, allow players to maintain this position for a maximum of 5 seconds. Because fitness games primarily focus on cardiovascular fitness, alternate the games with strength and flexibility activities. The following are examples of games that can be played.

Stoop tag: Players cannot be tagged when they stoop.

Back-to-back tag: Players are safe when they stand back to back with another. Other positions can be designated such as toe to toe, knee to knee, and so on.

Train tag: Form groups of three or four and make a train by holding the hips of the other players. Three or four players are designated as it and try to hook onto the rear of the train. If it is successful, the player at the front of the train becomes the new it.

Color tag: Players are safe when they stand on a specified color. The "safe" color may be changed by the leader at any time.

Elbow swing tag: Players cannot be tagged as long as they are performing an elbow swing with another player.

Balance tag: Players are safe when they are balanced on one body part.

Push-up tag: Players are safe when they are in push-up position. Other exercise positions, such as bent knee curl-up, V-up, and crab position, can be used.

Group tag: The only time a player is safe is when all are in a group (stipulated by the leader) holding hands. For example, the number might be "4," which means that students must be holding hands in groups of four to be safe.

Miniature Challenge Courses

Miniature Challenge Courses (Figure 12.7) can be set up indoors or outdoors. The distance between the start and finish lines depends on the type of activity. A good starting point is a distance of about 30 feet, but this can be adjusted. Mark the course boundaries with cones.

Each child performs the stipulated locomotor movement from the start to the finish line, then turns and jogs back to the start. Movement is continuous. Give directions in advance so that no delay occurs. The number of children on each course should be limited to normal squad size or fewer. The following movements can be stipulated:

All types of locomotor movements: running, jumping, hopping, sliding, and so on

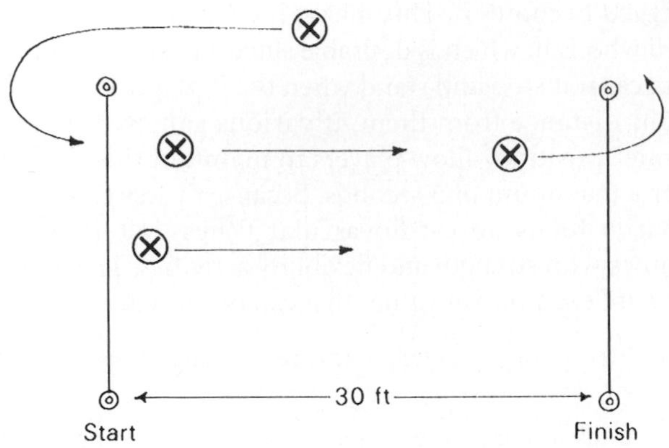

FIGURE 12.7 Miniature challenge course.

Movements on the floor: crawling, Bear Walk, Seal Crawl, and the like

Movements over and under obstacles or through tires or hoops

Sample Routine

1. Crawl under a wand set on two cones.
2. Roll down an inclined mat.
3. Log-roll up an inclined mat.
4. Move up and down on jumping boxes. Climb on the last box, jump, and roll.
5. Crawl through hoops or bicycle tires held by individual mats.
6. Walk a balance beam.
7. Pull the body down a bench in prone position.
8. Leap over five carpet squares.
9. Move through a tunnel created by four jumping boxes (or benches) covered with a tumbling mat.
10. Hang on a climbing rope for 10 seconds.
11. Crab walk from one cone to another and back.
12. Run and weave around a series of five cones.

Parachute Fitness Activities

The parachute has been a popular item in elementary physical education for many years. Usually used to promote teamwork, provide maximum participation, stimulate interest, or play games, the parachute can be used as a tool to develop physical fitness. By combining vigorous shaking movements, locomotor circular movement, and selected exercises while holding onto the chute, exciting fitness routines can be developed.

PARACHUTE FITNESS ACTIVITIES

1. Jog while holding the chute in the left hand. (music)
2. Shake the chute. (no music)
3. Slide while holding the chute with both hands. (music)
4. Sit and perform curl-ups. (no music)
5. Skip. (music)
6. Freeze, face the center, and stretch the chute tightly. Hold for 8–12 seconds. Repeat five to six times. (no music)
7. Run in place while holding the chute taut at different levels. (music)
8. Sit with legs under the chute. Do a seat walk toward the center. Return to the perimeter. Repeat four to six times. (no music)
9. Place the chute on the ground. Jog away from the chute and return on signal. Repeat. (music)
10. Move into push-up position holding the chute with one hand. Shake the chute. (no music)
11. Shake the chute and jump in place. (music)
12. Lie on back with feet under the chute. Shake the chute with the feet. (no music)
13. Hop to the center of the chute and return. Repeat. (music)
14. Sit with feet under the chute. Stretch by touching the toes with the chute. Relax with other stretches while sitting. (no music)

TEACHING TIP

Tape alternating segments (20 seconds in length) of silence and music to signal duration of exercise. Music segments indicate aerobic activity with the parachute while intervals of silence announce using the chute to enhance flexibility and strength development.

Space youngsters evenly around the chute.

Use different hand grips (palms up, down, mixed).

All movements should be done under control. Some of the faster and stronger students will have to moderate their performance.

Walk, Trot, and Jog

Four cones outline a square or rectangular area 30 to 40 yards on a side. (Indoors, the circumference of the gymnasium is used.) Children are scattered around the perimeter, all facing in the same direction. Signals are given with a whistle. On the first whistle, children begin to walk. On the next whistle, they change to a trot. On the third whistle, they jog faster, but still under control. Finally, on the fourth whistle, they walk again. The cycle is repeated with faster-moving youngsters passing on the outside of the area.

Another way to signal change is by drumbeat. One drumbeat signals walk, two beats signals trot, and three means run. The three movements can be presented in a random order. Different locomotor movements such as running, skipping, galloping, and sliding can be used for variation. At regular intervals, stop students and perform various stretching activities and strength development exercises. This allows short rest periods between bouts of activity. Examples of activities are one-leg balance, push-ups, curl-ups, touching the toes, and any other challenges.

WALK, TROT, AND JOG

Move to the following signals:

1. One drumbeat—walk.
2. Two drumbeats—trot.
3. Three drumbeats—jog.
4. Whistle—freeze and perform exercises.

Perform various strength and flexibility exercises between bouts of walk, trot, and jog. Examples of exercises are:

1. Bend and Twist
2. Sitting Stretch
3. Push-Up Challenges
4. Abdominal Challenges
5. Body Twist
6. Standing Hip Bend

TEACHING TIP

Tape alternating segments (30 seconds in length) of silence and music to signal duration of exercise. Music segments indicate walk, trot, and jog activity. Intervals of silence signal performance of the strength and flexibility exercises.

Any exercises can be substituted. Try to maintain the balance of exercising all body parts.

Jump Rope Exercises

Jump ropes are used in a number of exercises and aerobic activities. Playing music with taped intervals of silence is an excellent method for alternating periods of rope jumping and exercises. During the periods of silence, youngsters perform an exercise; during the music, children pick up their ropes and begin jumping.

JUMP ROPE ROUTINE

1. Jump rope—30 seconds. If not able to jump, practice swinging the rope to the side while jumping.
2. Place the rope on the floor and perform locomotor movements around and over the rope. Make different shapes and letters with the rope.
3. Hold the folded rope overhead. Sway from side to side. Twist right and left.
4. Jump rope—30 seconds.
5. Lie on back with rope held with outstretched arms toward ceiling. Bring up one leg at a time and touch the rope with toes. Lift both legs together. Sit up and try to hook the rope over the feet. Release and repeat.
6. Touch toes with the folded rope.
7. Jump rope—30 seconds.
8. Place rope on the floor and do various Animal Walks along or over the rope.
9. Do Push-up variations with the rope folded and held between the hands.
10. Jump rope—30 seconds.

TEACHING TIP

Tape alternating segments (30 seconds in length) of silence and music to signal duration of exercise. Music segments indicate aerobic activity with the jump ropes while intervals of silence announce using the jump ropes to enhance flexibility and strength development.

Teach youngsters to space themselves so they don't hit others with their rope.

Encourage nonjumpers. They will learn sooner or later. Give praise and keep them motivated.

Four-Corners Movement

Delineate a rectangle with four cones. Youngsters move around the perimeter of the rectangle. Each time they pass a corner, they change their movement pattern. On long sides, rapid movement such as running, skipping, or sliding are designated. Moving along short sides, students hop, jump, or do animal walks. Vary clockwise and counterclockwise directions. On signal, stop and perform flexibility and strength development challenges in place.

Using the four-corners ideas as a basis, other combinations can be devised. For example, the pattern in Figure 12.8 on page 250 requires running along one of the long sides and sliding along the other. One of the short sides has mats and requires three forward rolls, and the other short side requires an animal walk on all fours. Another variation that stimulates children is to place different equipment around the perimeter of the area. On signal, youngsters stop and pick up a piece of equipment and manipulate it for a specified time. By interspersing four-corners movement (aerobic movement) with equipment handling (resting), teachers implement interval training. Equipment that can be used might be beanbags, scooters, balance beams, benches, balls, and hoops.

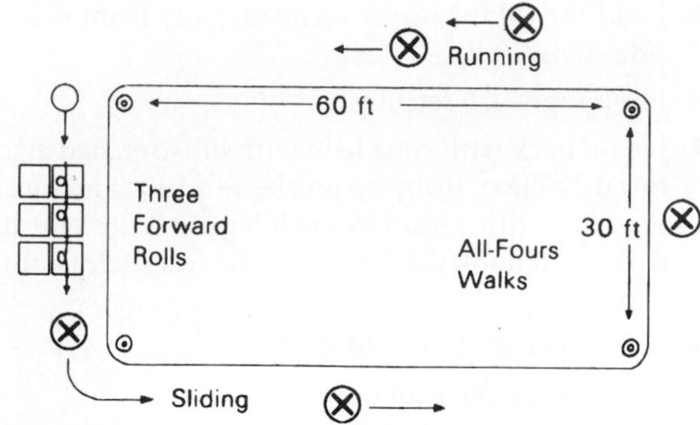

FIGURE 12.8 Four-corners movement formation.

FITNESS ACTIVITIES FOR DEVELOPMENTAL LEVELS II AND III

In contrast to the program of developmental level I activities, emphasis shifts to more structured exercises and routines. Starting off the year with teacher-leader exercises is suggested, as these are the basic exercises that can be used in other routines.

Exercises for Fitness Routines

Exercises selected fall into the following categories: (a) flexibility, (b) arm-shoulder girdle, (c) abdominal, (d) leg and agility, and (e) trunk-twisting and bending. Recommended exercises are presented under each of the five categories. Stress points, modifications, variations, and teaching suggestions are presented when appropriate. Include 6 to 10 exercises in a fitness routine, with two exercises from the arm-shoulder girdle group and at least one from each of the other categories.

Flexibility Exercises

BEND AND TWIST

Starting position: Stand with the arms crossed, hands on opposite shoulders, knees slightly flexed, and feet shoulder-width apart.

Movement: Bend forward at the waist (count 1). Twist the trunk and touch the right elbow to the left knee (count 2). Twist in the opposite direction and touch the left elbow to the right knee (count 3). Return to the starting position (count 4). Knees can be flexed.

SITTING STRETCH

Starting position: Sit on the floor with one leg extended forward and the other bent at the knee. The foot is placed in the area of the crotch. The toes of the extended foot are touched with the fingertips of both hands as the chest gradually moves forward (Figure 12.9).

FIGURE 12.9 Sitting stretch position.

Movement: Gradually bend forward, taking three counts to bend fully. Recover to sitting position on the fourth count.

Stress point: Bend from the hips.

PARTNER ROWING

Starting position: Partners sit facing each other, holding hands with palms touching and fingers locked. The legs are spread and extended to touch soles of partner's feet.

Movement: One partner bends forward, with the help of the other pulling backward, to try to bring the chest as close to the floor as possible (Figure 12.10). Reverse direction.

TEACHING TIP

Variation: Steam Engine. With both partners in the sitting position, alternate pulling hands back and forth like a pair of steam engine pistons. Do eight sets, right and left combined twists.

LOWER LEG STRETCH

Starting position: Stand facing a wall with the feet about shoulder width apart. Place the palms of the hands on the wall at eye level (Figure 12.11).

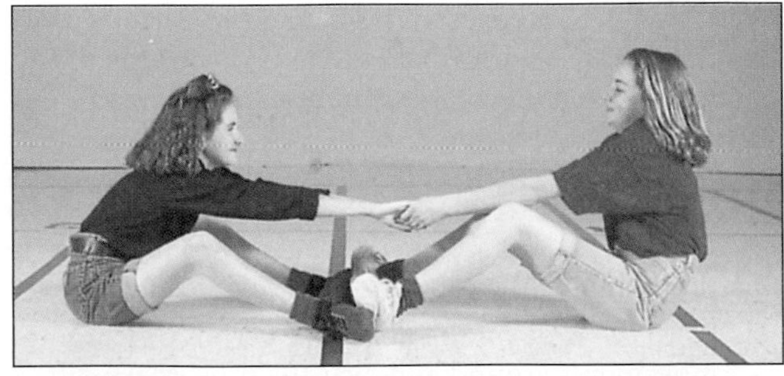

FIGURE 12.10 Partner rowing.

FIGURE 12.11 Lower leg stretch.

Movement: Slowly walk away from the wall, keeping the body straight, until the stretch is felt in the lower portion of the calf. The feet should remain flat on the floor during the stretch.

ACHILLES TENDON STRETCH

Starting position: Stand facing a wall with the forearms on it. Place the forehead on the back of the hands. Back 2 to 3 feet away from the wall, bend, and move one leg closer to the wall.

Movement: Flex the bent leg with the foot on the floor until the stretch is felt in the Achilles tendon area. The feet should remain flat on the floor as the leg closer to the wall is flexed. Repeat, flexing the other leg.

BODY TWIST

Starting position: Sit on the floor with the left leg straight. Lift the right leg over the left leg and place it on the floor outside the left knee (Figure 12.12). Move the left elbow outside the upper right thigh and use it to maintain pressure on the leg. Lean back and support the upper body with the right hand.

Movement: Rotate the upper body toward the right hand and arm. Reverse the position and stretch the other side of the body.

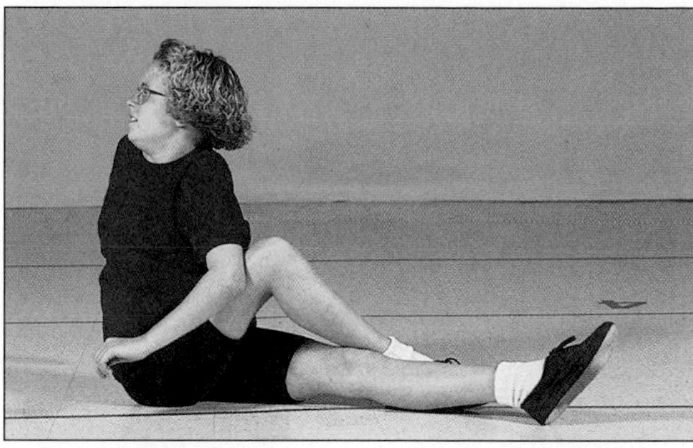

FIGURE 12.12 Body twist.

STANDING HIP BEND

Starting position: Stand with the knees slightly flexed, one hand on the hip and the other arm overhead.

Movement: Bend to the side with the hand resting on the hip. The arm overhead should point and move in the direction of the stretch with a slight bend at the elbow. Reverse and stretch the opposite side.

Arm-Shoulder Girdle Exercises

Arm-shoulder girdle exercises for this age group include both arm-support and free-arm types.

PUSH-UPS

Starting position: Assume the push-up position (see Figure 12.6), with the body straight from head to heels.

Movement: Keeping the body straight, bend the elbows and touch the chest to the ground; then straighten the elbows, raising the body in a straight line.

Stress points: The movement should be in the arms. The head is up, with the eyes looking ahead. The chest should touch the floor lightly, without receiving the weight of the body. The body remains in a straight line throughout, without sagging or humping.

TEACHING TIP

Variation: Some youngsters develop a dislike for push-ups because they are asked to perform them without any modification. Allow youngsters to judge their strength and choose a push-up challenge (page 245) they feel able to accomplish. Instead of asking an entire class to perform a specified number of push-ups, personalize the workload by allowing each youngster to accomplish as many repetitions as possible of a self-selected push-up challenge in a specified amount of time.

TEACHING TIP

Controlled movement is a goal; speed is not desirable. Push-ups should be done at will, allowing each child to achieve individually within a specified time limit.

RECLINING PULL-UPS

Starting position: One pupil lies in supine position. Partner is astride, with feet alongside the reclining partner's chest. Partners grasp hands with interlocking fingers, with some other suitable grip, or with an interlocked wrist grip.

Movement: The pupil on the floor pulls up with arms until the chest touches the partner's thighs. The body remains straight, with weight resting on the heels (Figure 12.13). Return to position.

Stress points: The supporting student should keep the center of gravity well over the feet by maintaining a lifted chest and proper head position. The lower student should maintain a straight body during the pull-up and move only the arms.

TEACHING TIP

Variation: Raise as directed (count 1), hold the high position isometrically (counts 2 and 3), return to position (count 4).

FIGURE 12.13 Reclining pull-ups.

TRICEPS PUSH-UP

Starting position: Assume the inverted push-up position with the arms and body held straight.

Movement: Keeping the body straight, bend the elbows and touch the seat to the ground, then straighten the elbows and raise the body.

Stress points: The fingers should point toward the toes or be turned in slightly. The body should be held firm with movement restricted to the arms.

ARM CIRCLES

Starting position: Stand erect, with feet apart and arms straight out to the side (Figure 12.14).

Movement: Do forward and backward circles with palms facing forward, moving arms simultaneously. The number of circles executed before changing can be varied.

Stress points: Avoid doing arm circles with palms down (particularly backward circles) as it stresses the shoulder joint. Correct posture should be maintained, with the abdominal wall flat and the head and shoulders held back.

CRAB KICK

Starting position: Crab position, with the body supported on the hands and feet and the back parallel to the floor. The knees are bent at right angles. On all crab positions, keep the seat up and avoid body sag.

FIGURE 12.14 Arm circles.

FIGURE 12.15 Crab kick.

Movement: Kick the right leg up and down (counts 1 and 2) (Figure 12.15). Repeat with the left leg (counts 3 and 4).

CRAB ALTERNATE-LEG EXTENSION

Starting position: Assume crab position.

Movement: On count 1, extend the right leg forward so that it rests on the heel. On count 2, extend the left leg forward and bring the right leg back. Continue alternating.

CRAB FULL-LEG EXTENSION

Starting position: Assume crab position.

Movement: On count 1, extend both legs forward so that the weight rests on the heels. On count 2, bring both feet back to crab position.

CRAB WALK

Starting position: Assume crab position.

Movement: Move forward, backward, sideward, and turn in a small circle right and left.

FLYING ANGEL

Starting position: Stand erect, with feet together and arms at sides.

Movement: In a smooth, slow, continuous motion, raise the arms forward with elbows extended and then upward, at the same time rising up on the toes and lifting the chest, with eyes following the hands (Figure 12.16). Lower the arms sideward in a flying motion and return to starting position.

FIGURE 12.16 Flying Angel.

Stress points: The abdominal wall must be kept flat throughout to minimize lower back curvature. The head should be back and well up. The exercise should be done slowly and smoothly, under control.

TEACHING TIP

Variation: Move the arms forward as if doing a breaststroke. The arms are then raised slowly, with hands in front of the chest and elbows out, to full overhead extension. Otherwise, the movement is the same as the Flying Angel.

Abdominal Exercises

For most exercises stressing abdominal development, start from the supine position on the floor or on a mat. When lifting the upper body, begin with a roll-up (curling) action, moving the head first so that the chin makes contact or near contact with the chest, thus flattening and stabilizing the lower back curve. The bent knee position better isolates the abdominal muscles and avoids stressing the lower back region. When doing abdominal exercises, avoid moving the trunk up to the sitting position (past 45 degrees) since it may cause pain and exacerbate back injury in susceptible individuals (Macfarlane, 1993).

Some youngsters develop a dislike for abdominal work in the early school years. This occurs because they are top heavy (large head, short legs) and unable to successfully lift their upper body off the floor. To ensure success, allow students to choose an abdominal challenge they feel able to accomplish. Instead of asking an entire class to perform a specified number of curl-ups, personalize the workload by allowing youngsters to accomplish as many repetitions as possible in a specified amount of time using a self-selected abdominal challenge.

REVERSE CURL

Starting position: Lie on back with the hands on the floor to the sides of the body.

Movement: Curl the knees to the chest. The upper body remains on the floor. As abdominal strength increases, the child should lift the buttocks and lower back off the floor.

Stress points: Roll the knees to the chest and return the feet to the floor after each repetition. The movement should be controlled, with emphasis on the abdominal contraction.

TEACHING TIP

Variations:

1. Hold the head off the floor and bring the knees to the chin.
2. Instead of returning the feet to the floor after each repetition, move them 1 or 2 inches off the floor. This activity requires greater abdominal strength as there is no resting period (feet on floor).

PELVIS TILTER

Starting position: Lie on the back with feet flat on the floor, knees bent, arms out in wing position, and palms up.

Movement: Flatten the lower back, bringing it closer to the floor by tensing the lower abdominals and lifting up on the pelvis. Hold for 8–12 counts. Tense slowly and release slowly.

KNEE TOUCH CURL-UP

Starting position: Lie on the back, with feet flat and knees bent, and with hands flat on top of thighs.

Movement: Leading with the chin, slide the hands forward until the fingers touch the kneecaps and gradually curl the head and shoulders until the shoulder blades are lifted off the floor (Figure 12.17). Hold for 8 counts and return to position. To avoid stress on the lower back, do not curl up to the sitting position.

FIGURE 12.17 Knee Touch Curl-up.

CURL-UP

Starting position: Lie on the back with feet flat, knees bent, and arms on the floor at the side of the body with palms down.

Movement: Lift the head and shoulders (Figure 12.18) to a 45-degree angle and then back in a two-count pattern. The hands should slide forward on the floor 3 to 4 inches. The curl-up can also be done as an 8-count exercise, moving up on count 1, holding for 6 counts, and moving down on the last count.

Stress points: Roll up, with the chin first. Do not lift the hands off the floor.

FIGURE 12.18 Curl-up.

CURL-UP WITH TWIST

Starting position: Lie on the back with feet flat and knees bent. Arms are folded and placed across the chest with hands on shoulders.

Movement: Do a partial curl-up and twist the chest to the left. Repeat, turning the chest to the right (Figure 12.19).

FIGURE 12.19 Curl-up with twist.

TEACHING TIP

Variations:

1. Touch the outside of the knee with the elbow.
2. Touch both knees in succession. The sequence is up, touch left, touch right, and down.

LEG EXTENSION

Starting position: Sit on the floor with legs extended and hands on hips.

Movement: With a quick, vigorous action, raise the knees and bring both heels as close to the seat as possible (Figure 12.20). The movement is a drag with the toes touching lightly. Return to position.

TEACHING TIP

Variation: Alternate bringing the knees to the right and left of the head.

FIGURE 12.20 Leg extension.

ABDOMINAL CRUNCHER

Starting position: Lie in supine position with feet flat, knees bent, and palms of hands cupped over the ears (not behind the head). An alternate position is to fold the arms across the chest and place the hands on the shoulders.

Movement: Tuck the chin and curl upward until the shoulder blades leave the floor. Return to the floor with a slow uncurling.

TEACHING TIP

Variation: Lift the feet off the floor and bring the knees to waist level. Try to touch the right elbow to the left knee and vice versa while in the crunch position.

Leg and Agility Exercises

RUNNING IN PLACE

Starting position: Stand with arms bent at the elbows.

Movement: Run in place. Begin slowly, counting only the left foot. Speed up somewhat, raising the knees to hip height. Then run at full speed, raising the knees hard. Finally, slow down. The run should be on the toes.

TEACHING TIP

Variations:

1. Tortoise and Hare. Jog slowly in place. On the command "Hare," double the speed. On the command "Tortoise," slow the tempo to original slow jogging pace.
2. March in place, lifting the knees high and swinging the arms up. Turn right and left on command while marching. Turn completely around to the right and then to the left while marching.
3. Fast Stepping. Step in place for 10 seconds as rapidly as possible. Rest for 10 seconds and repeat five or more times.

JUMPING JACK

Starting position: Stand at attention.

Movement: On count 1, jump to a straddle position with arms overhead. On count 2, recover to starting position.

TEACHING TIP

Variations:

1. Begin with the feet in a stride position (forward and back). Change feet with the overhead movement.
2. Instead of bringing the feet together when the arms come down, cross the feet each time, alternating the cross.

FIGURE 12.21 Treadmill.

3. On the completion of each set of 8 counts, do a quarter-turn right. (After four sets, the child is facing in the original direction.) Do the same to the left.
4. Modified Jumping Jack. On count 1, jump to a straddle position with arms out to the sides, parallel to the floor, and palms down. On count 2, return to position.

TREADMILL

Starting position: Assume push-up position, except that one leg is brought forward so that the knee is under the chest (Figure 12.21).

Movement: Reverse the position of the feet, bringing the extended leg forward. Change back again so that the original foot is forward. Continue rhythmically alternating feet.

Stress points: The head should be kept up. A full exchange of the legs should be made, with the forward knee coming well under the chest each time.

POWER JUMPER

Starting position: Begin in a semicrouched position, with knees flexed and arms extended backward.

Movement: Jump as high as possible and extend the arms upward and overhead.

TEACHING TIP

Variations:

1. Jump and perform different turns (quarter, half, and full).
2. Jump and perform different tasks (such as heel click, heel slap, clap hands, catch an imaginary pass, snare a rebound).

FIGURE 12.22 Trunk Twister.

Trunk-Twisting and Bending Exercises

TRUNK TWISTER

Starting position: Stand with feet shoulder width apart and pointed forward. The hands are cupped and placed loosely over the shoulders, with the elbows out and the chin tucked.

Movement: Bend downward, keeping the knees relaxed. Recover slightly. Bend downward again and simultaneously rotate the trunk to the left and then to the right (Figure 12.22). Return to original position, pulling the head back, with chin in.

BEAR HUG

Starting position: Stand with feet comfortably spread and hands on hips.

Movement: Take a long step diagonally right, keeping the left foot anchored in place. Tackle the right leg around the thigh by encircling the thigh with both arms. Squeeze and stretch (Figure 12.23). Return to position. Tackle the left leg. Return to position.

Stress Point: The bent leg should not exceed a right angle.

SIDE FLEX

Starting position: Lie on one side with lower arm extended overhead. The head rests on the lower arm. The legs are extended fully, one on top of the other.

FIGURE 12.23 Bear Hug.

Movement: Raise the upper arm and leg diagonally (Figure 12.24). Repeat for several counts and change to the other side.

FIGURE 12.24 Side Flex.

TEACHING TIP

Variation: Side Flex, supported. Similar to the regular Side Flex but more demanding. A side-leaning rest position is maintained throughout (Figure 12.25).

BODY CIRCLES

Starting position: Stand with feet shoulder width apart, hands on hips, and body bent forward.

Movement: Make a complete circle with the upper body. A specified number of circles should be made to the right and the same number to the left.

TEACHING TIP

Variations:

1. Circle in one direction until told to stop, then reverse direction.

FIGURE 12.25 Side Flex, supported.

2. Change to a position in which the hands are on the shoulders and the elbows are kept wide. Otherwise, the exercise is the same.

WINDMILL

Starting position: Stand with feet shoulder width apart and arms extended sideward with palms down.

Movement: Bend and twist at the trunk, bringing the right hand down to the left toes. Recover to starting position. Bend and twist again, but bring the left hand to the right toes. Recover to starting position.

Partner Resistance Exercises

Partner resistance exercises are used in conjunction with activities that demand considerable endurance, such as Aerobic Fitness Routines, jogging, or Astronaut Exercises. The exercises are simple and enjoyable; children can do them as homework with parents or friends. Partners should be roughly matched in size and strength so that they can challenge each other. The exercises are performed throughout the full range of motion at each joint and should take 8 to 12 seconds to complete. The partner providing the resistance counts the duration of the exercise; positions are then reversed.

ARM CURL-UP

The exerciser keeps the upper arms against the sides with the forearms and palms forward. The partner's fists are put in the exerciser's palms (Figure 12.26, page 258). The exerciser attempts to curl the forearms upward to the shoulders. To develop the opposite set of muscles, partners reverse hand positions. Push down in the opposite direction, starting at shoulder level.

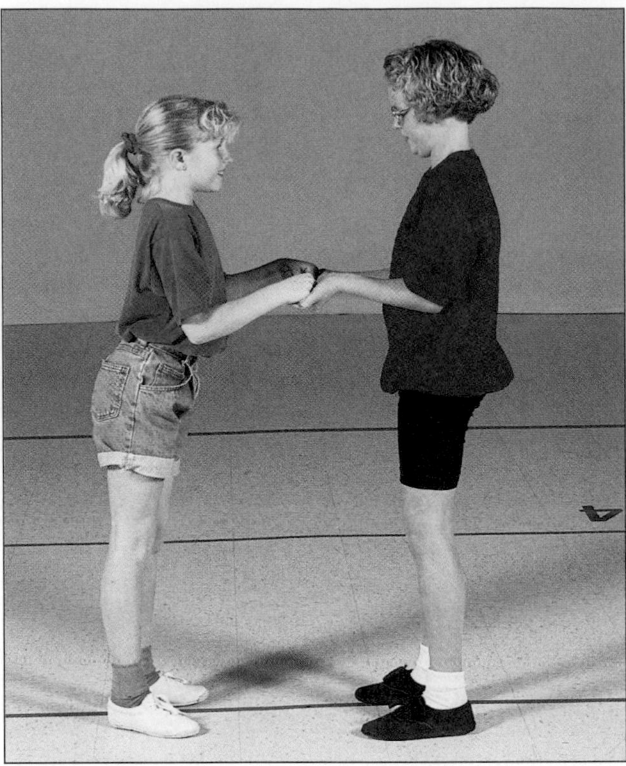

FIGURE 12.26 Arm Curl-up.

FIGURE 12.27 Back Builder.

FOREARM FLEX

The exerciser extends the arms and places the hands, palms down, on the partner's shoulders. The exerciser attempts to push the partner into the floor. The partner may slowly stoop lower to allow the exerciser movement through the range of motion. Try with the palms upward.

FIST PULL-APART

The exerciser places the fists together in front of the body at shoulder level. The exerciser attempts to pull the hands apart while the partner forces them together with pressure on the elbows. As a variation, with fists apart, the exerciser tries to push them together. The partner applies pressure by grasping the wrists and holding the exerciser's fists apart.

BUTTERFLY

The exerciser starts with arms straight and at the sides. The partner, from the back, attempts to hold the arms down while the exerciser lifts with straight arms to the sides. Try with arms above the head (partner holding) to move them down to the sides.

CAMELBACK

The exerciser is on all fours with head up. The partner pushes on the exerciser's back, while the exerciser attempts to hump the back like a camel.

BACK BUILDER

The exerciser spreads the legs and bends forward at the waist with head up. The partner faces the exerciser and places the hands on top the shoulders. The exerciser attempts to stand upright while the partner pushes downward (Figure 12.27).

SCISSORS

The exerciser lies on one side, while the partner straddles the exerciser and holds the upper leg down. The exerciser attempts to raise the top leg. Reverse sides and lift the other leg.

BEAR TRAP

Starting from a supine position on the floor, spread the legs and then attempt to move them together. Resistance is provided by the partner, who tries to keep the legs apart.

KNEE BENDER

The exerciser lies in prone position with legs straight and arms pointing ahead on the floor. The partner places the hands on the back of the exerciser's ankles. The exerciser attempts to flex the knees while the partner applies pressure (Figure 12.28). Try in the opposite direction, starting with the knee joint at a 90-degree angle.

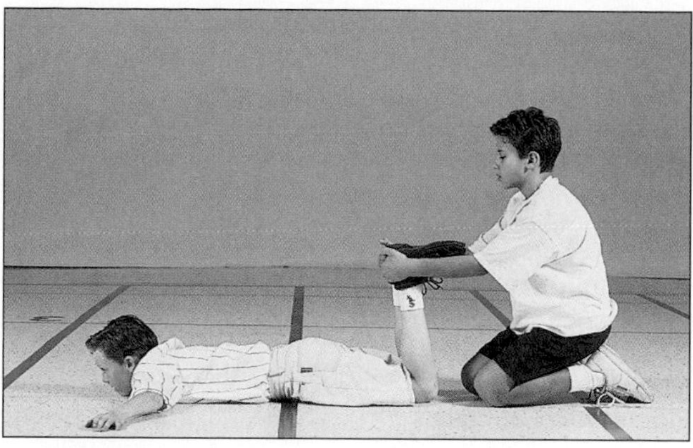

FIGURE 12.28 Knee Bender.

PUSH-UP WITH RESISTANCE

The exerciser is in push-up position with arms bent, so that the body is about halfway up from the floor. The partner straddles or stands alongside the exerciser's head and puts pressure on the top of the shoulders by pushing down (Figure 12.29). The amount of pressure takes judgment by the partner. Too much causes the exerciser to collapse.

Examples of Fitness Routines

When planning fitness routines, establish variety in activities and include different approaches. This minimizes the inherent weaknesses of any single routine. The routines should exercise all major parts of the body. Additionally, when sequencing fitness activities into a routine, try not to overload the same body part with two sequential exercises. For example, if push-ups are being performed, the next exercise should not be crab walking, as it also stresses the arm-shoulder girdle.

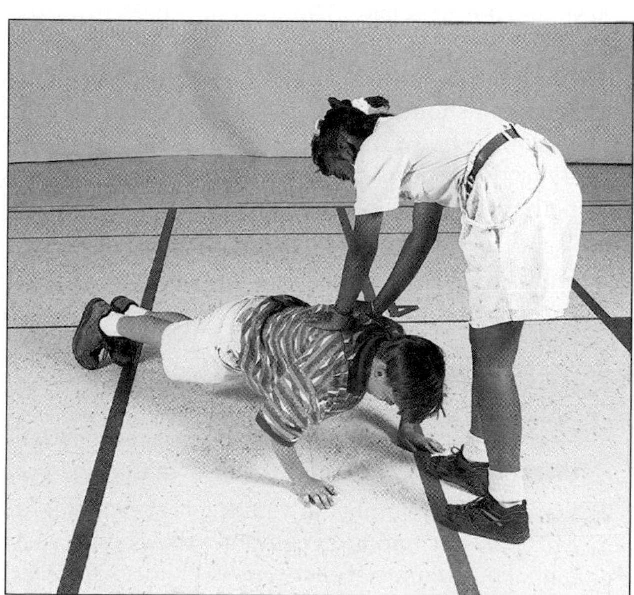

FIGURE 12.29 Push-up with resistance.

Measure exercise dosage for youngsters in time rather than repetitions. It is unreasonable to expect all youngsters to perform the same number of exercise repetitions. Fitness performance is controlled by a number of factors, including genetics and trainability, making it impossible for all children to do the same workload. When time is used to determine the workload, each child can personalize the amount of activity performed within the time constraints. It is reasonable to expect a gifted youngster to be able to perform more repetitions in a certain amount of time than a less genetically endowed child. An obese youngster may not be able to perform as many push-ups as a leaner peer. Develop positive attitudes toward activity by asking youngsters to do the best they can within the time allotted.

Student Leader Exercises

Students enjoy leading their peers in single exercises or an entire routine. Students need prior practice if they are to lead their peers effectively in a stimulating exercise session. Don't force children to lead because this can result in failure for both the child and the class. The following routine is an example of student leader exercises.

STUDENT LEADER EXERCISES

Encourage youngsters to do the best they can within the specified time limit.

Arm Circles	30 seconds
Push-Up Challenges	30 seconds
Bend and Twist	30 seconds
Treadmill	30 seconds
Sit-Up Challenges	30 seconds
Single-Leg Crab Kick	30 seconds
Knee to Chest Curl	30 seconds
Run in Place	30 seconds
Standing Hip Bend	30 seconds

Conclude the routine with 2–4 minutes of jogging, rope jumping, or other aerobic activity.

Squad Leader Exercises

Squad leader exercises give students an opportunity to lead exercises in a small group. This approach is an effective method for teaching students how to lead others and to help them learn to put together a well-balanced fitness routine. A student within each squad is given a task card that has exercises and activities grouped by how they impact different parts of the body (see the example below). After the first student has led the exercise for the desired amount of time, the card is passed to another member of the squad, who becomes the leader. To ensure a balanced routine, each new leader must select an exercise from a different group. The following is an example of how exercises and activities are grouped for the squad leader exercise routine.

Sample Task Card for Squad Leader Exercises

Aerobic Activities	**Abdominal Strength Exercises**
Running in Place	Reverse Curls
Jumping Jacks	Pelvis Tilters
Treadmill	Knee Touch Curl-ups
Power Jumper	Curl-ups
Rhythmic Jumping	Curl-ups with Twist
	Leg Extension
Flexibility Activities	**Upper Body Strength Exercises**
Bend & Twist	Push-up variations
Sitting Stretch	Reclining Pull-ups
Partner Rowing	Triceps Push-ups
Lower Leg Stretch	Arm Circles
Achilles Tendon Stretch	Crab Kicks
Body Twist	Crab Full-leg Extensions
Standing Hip Bend	Crab Walk

If there is a delay in starting an exercise, advise the squad to walk or jog rather than stand in place.

TEACHING TIP

The class is divided into groups of four to five students. Each group is given a task card that lists eight to ten exercises. One of the group members begins as the leader and leads the group through an exercise. Each time an exercise is completed, the card is passed to a new leader.

Use alternating intervals of music to signal exercising (30 seconds) with silence (5–8 seconds) to indicate passing the card.

Exercises to Music

Exercises to music add another dimension to developmental experiences. Many commercial CD sets with exercise programs are available. Using a homemade tape with alternating intervals of silence and music signals time for exercises and aerobic activity. For example, if doing Random Moving, students could run/walk as long as the music is playing and stretch when the silent interval occurs. Having the music pretaped frees you from having to keep an eye on a stopwatch. Many exercise modules work well with music, including Circuit Training, Aerobic Fitness Routines, Continuity Exercises, Astronaut Exercises, Squad Leader Exercises, and Rope-Jumping Exercises. Prerecorded music on CD is available from Human Kinetics, P.O. Box 5076, Champaign, IL 61825-5076 (800-747-4457) or www.humankinetics.com. A routine using music follows.

Sample Routine

Crab Kicks	25 seconds
Rope Jumping	30 seconds
Windmills	25 seconds
Walk and Do Arm Circles	30 seconds
Abdominal Crunchers	25 seconds
Jumping Jack variations	30 seconds
Side Flex	25 seconds
Two-Step or Gallop	30 seconds
Triceps Push-Ups	25 seconds
Aerobic Jumping	30 seconds
Push-Up Challenges	25 seconds
Leg Extensions	30 seconds
Walking to cool down	30 seconds

TEACHING TIP

Select music with a strong rhythm and easy-to-hear beat. When the music is on, students perform aerobic activities (for 30 seconds). When the silent interval is playing, students perform the strength development and flexibility exercises (25 seconds).

Use scatter formation.

Circuit Training

Circuit Training incorporates several stations, each with a designated fitness task. The student moves from station to station, generally in a prescribed order, completing the designated fitness task at each station. Exercises for the circuit should contribute to the development of all parts of the body. In addition, activities should contribute to the various components of physical fitness (strength, power, endurance, agility, and flexibility).

Instructional Procedures

1. Each station provides an exercise task to perform without the aid of another child. Exercises that directly follow each other should make demands on different parts of the body. This ensures that performance at any one station does not cause fatigue that could affect the ability to perform the next task.
2. Place an equal number of youngsters at each station. This keeps demands on equipment low and activity high. For example, if there are 30 children for a circuit of six stations, place 5 children at each spot.

Six-station course

1 Running in place	2 Curl-ups	3 Arm Circles
6 Crab Walk	5 Trunk Twister	4 Agility Run

Supplies and equipment: Mats for Curl-ups (to hook toes)
Time needed: 4 minutes—based on 30-second activity limit, 10 seconds to move between stations

FIGURE 12.30 Sample six-station circuit training course.

3. Music, whistle signals, and even verbal directions can be prerecorded to signal students to the next station. The tape provides time control and gives a measure of consistency to the circuit. Using tapes also allows you to help youngsters without worrying about timing each interval.
4. The number of stations can vary but probably should be no fewer than six and no more than nine. (Figures 12.30 and 12.31 show a six- and a nine-station course, respectively.)

Signs at the different stations can include the name of the activity and any necessary cautions or stress points for execution. When children move between lines as limits (as in the Agility Run), traffic cones or beanbags can be used to mark the designated boundaries.

Timing and Dosage

A fixed time limit at each station is the easiest way to administer Circuit Training. Children do their personal best during the time allotted at each station. A 10-second interval should be established to allow children to move from one station to the next. Later, this can be lowered to 5 seconds. Students start at any station, as designated, but follow the established station order. A second method of timing is to sound only one signal for the change to the next station. With this plan, the class ceases activity at their station, moves to the next, and immediately begins the task at that station without waiting for another signal.

The activity demands of the circuit can be increased by changing the exercises to more strenuous ones. For example, a station could specify knee or bench push-ups and later change to regular push-ups, a more demanding exercise. Another method of increasing intensity is to have each child run a lap around the circuit area between station changes. Cardiovascular endurance can be enhanced by dividing the class into halves. One half exercises on the circuit while the other is running lightly around the area. On signal to change, the runners go to the circuit and the others run.

Another method of organizing a circuit is to list several activities at each station. The circuit can be performed more than once so students do a different exercise each time they return to the same station. If the circuit is to be done only once, children can perform their favorite exercise. Exercises at each station should emphasize development of the same body part. An example of a circuit training routine follows.

Nine-station course

1 Rope jumping	2 Push-ups	3 Agility Run	4 Arm Circles
8 Windmill	7 Treadmill	6 Crab Walk	5 Reverse Curl
9 Hula-Hooping (or any relaxing "fun" activity)			

Supplies and equipment: Jumping ropes, mats for knee Push-ups (if used), hoops (if used)
Time needed: 6 minutes–based on 30-second activity limit, 10 seconds to move between stations

FIGURE 12.31 Sample nine-station circuit training course.

Sample Routine

Ask students to do the best they can for 30 seconds at each station. This implies that youngsters will not perform similar workloads. Fitness is a personal challenge.

Rope Jumping
Triceps Push-Ups
Agility Run
Body Circles
Hula Hoops
Reverse Curls
Crab Walk
Tortoise and Hare
Bend and Twist

Conclude circuit training with 2–4 minutes of walking, jogging, rope jumping, or other self-paced aerobic activity.

TEACHING TIP

Tape alternating segments of silence and music to signal duration of exercise. Music segments (begin at 30 seconds) indicate activity at each station; intervals of silence (10 seconds) announce it is time to stop and move forward to the next station.

Use signals such as start, stop, and move up to ensure rapid movement to the next station.

Ask students to do their personal best. Expect workloads to differ.

Alternate Toe Touching: Begin on the back with arms extended overhead. Alternate by touching the right toes with the left hand and vice versa. Bring the foot and the arm up at the same time and return to the flat position each time.

Continuity Exercises

Children are scattered, each with a jump rope. They alternate between rope jumping and exercises. A specified time period governs the length of the rope-jumping episode. At the signal to stop rope jumping, children drop the ropes and take the beginning position for the exercise selected. Many of the exercises use a 2-count rhythm. When children are positioned for the exercise, the leader says, "Ready!" The class completes one repetition of the exercise and responds "One, two!" This repeats for each repetition. To increase the enjoyment, the leader can say "P.E.!" and the class will perform the exercise and respond with "is fun!" A number of brief phrases can be used such as "Work hard; keep fit." To enable a successful experience for children, modify the push-up and abdominal challenges (pages 245–247). An example of a routine of continuity exercises follows.

Sample Routine

Rope jumping—forward	25 seconds
Double Crab Kick	30 seconds
Rope jumping—backward	25 seconds
Knee Touch Curl-Up	30 seconds
Jump and turn body	25 seconds
Push-Ups	30 seconds
Rocker Step	25 seconds
Bend and Twist	30 seconds
Swing-Step forward	25 seconds
Side Flex	30 seconds
Free jumping	25 seconds

Relax and stretch for a short time.

TEACHING TIP

Make a tape with music segments (25 seconds) alternated with silence segments (30 seconds). When the music is playing, students jump rope; when silence occurs, students do a flexibility and strength development exercise.

Exercises can be done in 2-count fashion. Exercises are done when the leader says "Ready." The class answers "One-two" and performs a repetition.

Allow students to adjust the workload to their level. This implies resting if the rope jumping is too strenuous.

HEXAGON HUSTLE

A large hexagon is formed using six cones. Students perform the "hustle" by moving around the hexagon, changing their movement patterns every time they reach one of the six points in the hexagon. On signal, the "hustle" stops and selected exercises are performed.

Instructional Procedures

1. To create a safer environment, children should move in the same direction around the hexagon.
2. Laminated posters with colorful illustrations should be placed by the cones to inform children of the new activity to be performed.
3. Faster children pass to the outside of slower children.
4. The direction of the "hustle" should be changed after every exercise segment.

Sample Routine

Tape alternating segments of silence and music to signal duration of exercise. Music segments (25 seconds) indicate moving around the hexagon; intervals of silence (30 seconds) announce flexibility and strength development activities.

Hustle	25 seconds
Push-Up from knees	30 seconds
Hustle	25 seconds
Bend and Twist (8 counts)	30 seconds
Hustle	25 seconds
Jumping Jacks (4 counts)	30 seconds
Hustle	25 seconds
Curl-Ups (2 counts)	30 seconds
Hustle	25 seconds
Crab Kick (2 counts)	30 seconds
Hustle	25 seconds
Sit and Stretch (8 counts)	30 seconds
Hustle	25 seconds
Power Jumper	30 seconds
Hustle	25 seconds
Squat Thrust (4 counts)	30 seconds

Conclude the Hexagon Hustle with a slow jog or walk.

TEACHING TIP

Outline a large hexagon with six cones. Place signs with locomotor movements on both sides of the cones. Locomotor movements to use include jogging, skipping, galloping, hopping, jumping, sliding, leaping, and animal movements. Sport movements such as defensive sliding, running backwards, and running and shooting jump shots can also be used. The signs identify the hustle activity students are to perform as they approach a cone.

During the hustle, faster moving students should pass on the outside of the hexagon.

Change directions at times to keep students properly spaced.

Astronaut Exercises

Astronaut Exercises are performed in circular or scatter formation. Routines are developed by moving using various locomotor movements, alternated with stopping and performing exercises in place. The following movements and tasks can be incorporated into the routine.

1. Various locomotor movements, such as hopping, jumping, running, sliding, skipping, giant steps, and walking high on the toes.
2. Movement on all fours—forward, backward, or sideward—with respect to the direction of walking. Repeat backward and forward using the Crab Walk.
3. Stunt movements, such as the Seal Walk, Gorilla Walk, and Rabbit Jump.
4. Upper torso movements and exercises that can be done while walking, such as Arm Circles, bending right and left, and body twists.
5. Various exercises are performed in place when the music stops. A balance of arm-shoulder girdle and abdominal exercises should be included.

Astronaut Exercises can be adapted successfully to any developmental level. The type of movements selected will determine the intensity of the routine. More active children pass on the outside. Enjoyment comes from being challenged by a variety of movements.

Sample Routine

Walk, do Arm Circles	35 seconds
Crab Full-Leg Extension	30 seconds
Skip sideways	35 seconds
Body Twist	30 seconds
Slide; change lead leg	35 seconds
Jumping Jack variations	30 seconds
Crab Walk	35 seconds
Curl-Ups with Twist	30 seconds
Hop to center and back	35 seconds
Four Count Push-Ups	30 seconds
Gallop Backwards	35 seconds
Bear Hugs	30 seconds
Grapevine Step (Carioca)	35 seconds
Trunk Twisters	30 seconds
Power Jumper	35 seconds

Cool down with stretching and walking or jogging for 1–2 minutes.

TEACHING TIP

Tape alternating segments of music and silence to signal duration of exercise. Music segments indicate aerobic activity; intervals of silence announce flexibility and strength development activities.

Use scatter formation; ask students to change directions from time to time in order to keep spacing.

Allow students to adjust the workload pace. They should be allowed to move at a pace that is consistent with their ability level.

Challenge Courses

Challenge Courses are popular as a tool for fitness development in the elementary schools. Students move through the course with proper form rather than run against a time standard. The course is designed to exercise all parts of the body through a variety of activities. Equipment such as mats, parallel bars, horizontal ladders, high-jump standards, benches, and vaulting boxes can make effective Challenge Courses. A variety of courses can be designed, depending on the length of the course and the tasks included. Some schools have established permanent courses. A sample indoor course, including a climbing rope, is illustrated in Figure 12.32.

The total equipment list for this course is as follows:

Three benches (16 to 18 in. high)

Four tumbling mats (4 by 8 ft.)

Four hoops

One pair of high-jump standards with magic rope

One climbing rope

One jumping box

Five chairs or cones

Aerobic Fitness Routines

Aerobics is a fitness activity for people of all ages that develops cardiorespiratory fitness plus strength and flexibility. A leader is designated who performs a series of movements that the other students follow. There are few limits to the range of activities a leader can present. The leader may integrate manipulative equipment (including balls, jump ropes, hoops, and wands) with the movement activities.

Instructional Procedures

1. Use movement patterns that are organized by units of 4, 8, or 16 counts.
2. Vary movements so stretching and flowing movements are alternated with the more strenuous aerobic activities.
3. Keep steps relatively simple. Focus on activity rather than becoming competent rhythmic performers.

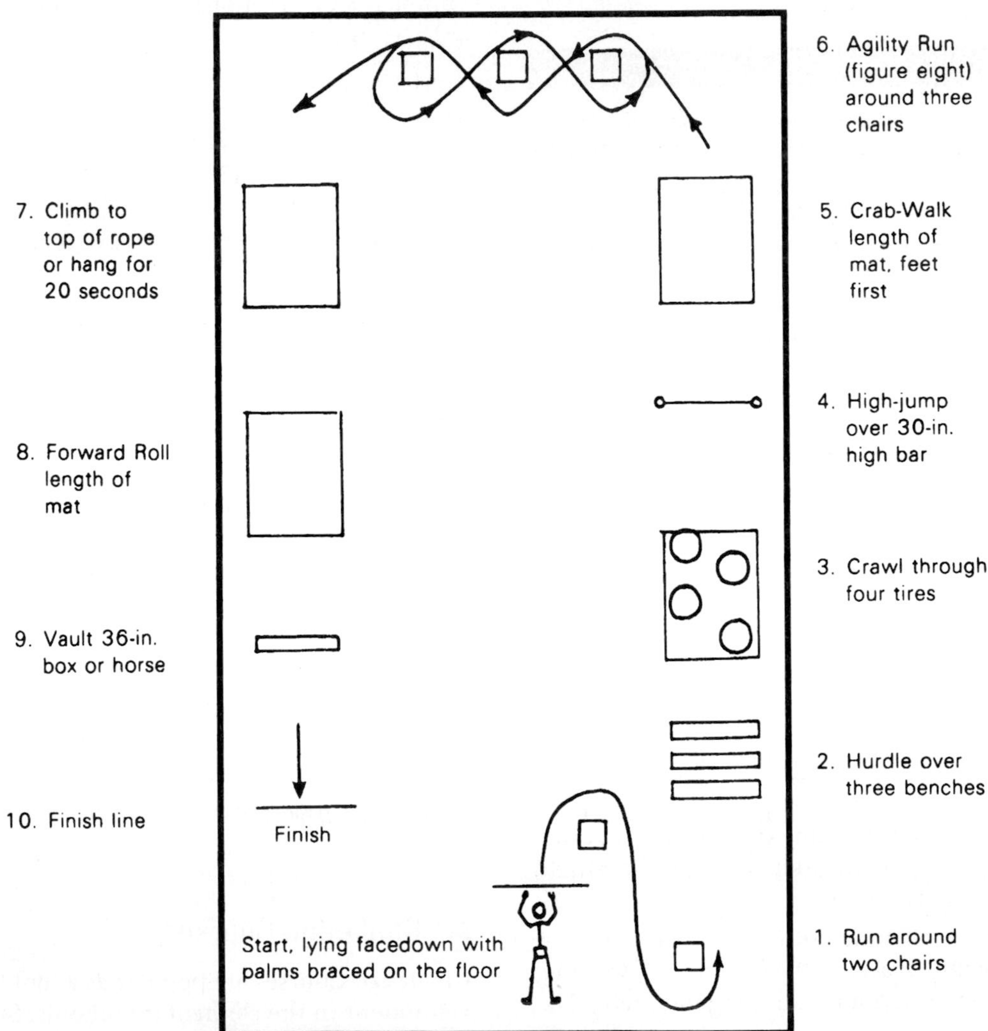

FIGURE 12.32 Indoor challenge course.

Stress continuous movement (moving with the flow) rather than perfection of routines. Running and bouncing steps are easily followed and motivating.

4. Routines are best when they are not rigid. Youngsters shouldn't have to worry about being out of step.
5. Establish cue words to aid youngsters in following routines. Examples are "Bounce," "Step," "Reach," and "Jump."

Basic Steps

The following are examples of basic steps and movements that can be used to develop a variety of routines. The majority are performed to 4 counts, although this can be varied.

RUNNING AND WALKING STEPS

1. *Directional runs*—forward, backward, diagonal, sideways, and turning.
2. *Rhythmic runs with a specific movement on the fourth beat.* Examples are knee lift, clap, jump, jump-turn, and hop.
3. *Runs with variations.* Run while lifting the knees, kicking up the heels, or slapping the thighs or heels; or run with legs extended as in the goose step.
4. *Runs with arms in various positions*—on the hips, in the air above the head, and straight down.

MOVEMENTS ON THE FLOOR

1. *Side leg raises.* Do these with a straight leg while lying on the side of the body.
2. *Alternate leg raises.* While on the back, raise one leg to meet the opposite hand. Repeat, using the opposite leg or both legs.
3. *Rhythmic push-ups.* Do these in 2- or 4-count movements. A 4 count would be as follows: halfway down (count 1), nose touched to the floor (count 2), halfway up (count 3), and arms fully extended (count 4).
4. *Crab kicks and treadmills.* Do these to 4 counts.

UPRIGHT RHYTHMIC MOVEMENTS

1. *Lunge variations.* Perform a lunge, stepping forward on the right foot while bending at the knee, and extending the arms forward and diagonally upward (counts 1 and 2). Return to starting position by bringing the right foot back and pulling the arms into a jogging position (counts 3 and 4). The lunge can be varied by changing the direction of the move and the depth and speed of the lunge.
2. *Side bends.* Begin with the feet apart. Reach overhead while bending to the side. This movement is usually done to four beats: bend (count 1), hold (counts 2 and 3), and return (count 4).
3. *Reaches.* Reach upward alternately with each arm. Reaches can be done sideways also and are usually 2-count movements. Fast alternating 1-count movements can be done, too.
4. *Arm and shoulder circles.* Make Arm Circles with either one or both arms. Vary the size and speed of the circles. Shoulder shrugs can be done in a similar fashion.

JUMPING JACK VARIATIONS

1. *Jump with arm movements.* Alternately extended upward and then pulled in toward the chest.
2. *Side jumping jacks.* Use regular arm action while the feet jump from side to side or forward and backward together.
3. *Feet variations.* Try different variations such as forward stride alternating, forward and side stride alternating, kicks or knee lifts added, feet crossed, or heel-toe movements (turning on every fourth or eighth count).

BOUNCE STEPS

1. *Bounce and clap.* This is similar to a slow-time jump-rope step. Clap on every other bounce.
2. *Bounce, turn, and clap.* Turn a quarter or half turn with each jump.
3. *Three bounces and clap.* Bounce three times and bounce and clap on the fourth beat. Turns can be performed.
4. *Bounce and rock side to side.* Transfer the weight from side to side, or forward and backward. Add clapping or arm swinging.
5. *Bounce with body twist.* Hold the arms at shoulder level and twist the lower body back and forth on each bounce.
6. *Bounce with floor patterns.* Bounce and make different floor patterns such as a box, diagonal, or triangle.
7. *Bounce with kick variations.* Perform different kicks, such as knee lift and kick; double kicks; knee lift and slap knees; and kick and clap under knees. Combine the kicks with 2- or 4-count turns.

ACTIVITIES WITH MANIPULATIVE EQUIPMENT

1. *Jump ropes.* Perform basic steps, such as forward and backward, and slow and fast time. Jump on one foot, cross the arms, and while jogging, swing the rope from side to side with the handles in one hand.
2. *Beanbags.* Toss and catch while performing various locomotor movements. Use different tosses for a challenge.

3. *Hula-hoops.* Rhythmically swing the hoop around different body parts. Perform different locomotor movements around and over hoops.
4. *Balls.* Bounce, toss, and dribble, and add locomotor movements while performing tasks.

Sample Routine

The following aerobic movements are suggestions only. When youngsters begin to fatigue, stop the aerobic fitness movements and perform flexibility and strength development. This allows students time to recover aerobically.

1. Rhythmic run with clap
2. Bounce turn and clap
3. Rhythmic 4-count Curl-Ups (knees, toes, knees, back)
4. Rhythmic Crab Kicks (slow time)
5. Jumping Jack combination
6. Double knee lifts
7. Lunges (right, left, forward) with single-arm circles (on the side lunges) and double-arm circles (on the forward lunge)
8. Rhythmic trunk twists
9. Directional run (forward, backward, side, turning)
10. Rock side-to-side with clap
11. Side leg raises (alternate legs)
12. Rhythmic 4-count push-ups (If these are too difficult for students, substitute single-arm circles in the push-up position.)

TEACHING TIP

Use music to stimulate effort. Any combination of movements can be used.

Keep the steps simple and easy to perform. Some students will become frustrated if the learning curve is steep.

Signs that explain the aerobic activities will help students remember performance cues.

Don't stress or expect perfection. Allow students to perform the activities as best they can.

Alternate bouncing and running movements with flexibility and strength development movements.

Partner Resistance and Aerobic Fitness Exercises

Partner resistance exercises combined with Aerobic Fitness Routines make an excellent fitness activity. Partner resistance exercises develop strength but offer little aerobic benefit. Combining them with Aerobic Fitness Routines offers a well-balanced program. The exercises listed below refer to partner resistance exercises (pages 257–259). Enough time is allotted so each partner has the opportunity to resist and exercise.

Sample Routine

Students find a partner and lead each other in aerobic activities. Partners switch leader and follower roles after each partner resistance exercise. See the aerobic fitness section for descriptions of activities.

Bounce and Clap	25 seconds
Arm Curl-Up	45 seconds
Jumping Jack variations	25 seconds
Camelback	45 seconds
Lunge variations	25 seconds
Fist Pull Apart	45 seconds
Directional Runs	25 seconds
Scissors	45 seconds
Rhythmic Running	25 seconds
Butterfly	45 seconds
Bounce with Body Twist	25 seconds
Resistance Push-Up	45 seconds

Walk, stretch and relax for a minute or two.

TEACHING TIP

Tape alternating segments of music and silence to signal duration of exercise. Music segments indicate aerobic activity (25 seconds); intervals of silence announce partner resistance exercises (45 seconds).

Teach the exercises first. A sign with aerobic activities on one side and partner resistance exercises on the other helps students remember the activities. The signs can be held upright by cones and shared by 2–4 students.

Take 6–10 seconds to complete a resistance exercise.

Sport-Related Fitness Activities

Many sport drills can be modified to place fitness demands on students. An advantage of sport-related fitness activities is that many children are highly motivated by sport activities. Thoughtful preplanning and creative thinking can result in drills that teach sport skills as well as provide fitness benefits. The following are some examples of fitness adaptations of sport skills.

BASEBALL/SOFTBALL

1. *Base running.* Set up several diamonds on a grass field. Space the class evenly around the base paths.

On signal, they run to the next base, round the base, take a lead, then run to the next base. Faster runners may pass on the outside.

2. *Most lead-up games.* Children waiting on deck to bat and those in the field perform selected activities (skill- or fitness-related) while waiting for the batter to hit.
3. *Position responsibility.* Start children at various positions on the field. On command, children are free to move quickly to any other position. Upon reaching that position, the child is to display the movement most frequently practiced at that position (for instance, shortstop fields ball and throws to first base). Continue until all players have moved to each position.

BASKETBALL

1. *Dribbling.* Each child has a basketball or playground ball. Assign one or more people to be *it.* On command, everyone begins dribbling the ball and avoids being tagged by those who are *it.* If tagged, that child becomes the new *it.* A variation would be for the *its* to begin the game without a ball. Their objective would be to steal a ball from classmates.
2. *Dribbling, passing, rebounding, shooting, and defense.* Using the concept of a circuit, assign selected basketball skills to be performed at each station. Be sure that there is ample equipment at each station to keep all youngsters active. Movement from one station to another should be vigorous and may include a stop for exercise.
3. *Game play.* Divide the class into four teams. Two teams take the court and play a game of basketball. The other teams assume a position along respective sidelines, and practice a series of exercises. The playing and exercising teams change positions at the conclusion of the exercise sequence.

FOOTBALL

1. *Ball carrying.* Divide the class into four to six squads. The first person in line carries the ball while zigzagging through preplaced boundary cones. The remainder of the squad performs a specific exercise. Upon completing the zigzag course, the first person hands off to the next person in line. This hand-off signifies a change in exercise for the remainder of the squad.
2. *Punting.* With partners, one child punts the ball to the other. After the receiver has the ball, the object is to see which child can get to the partner's starting position first. Repeat, with the receiver becoming the punter.
3. *Forward passing.* Divide the children into groups of no more than four. Children practice running pass patterns. Rotate the passing responsibility after every six throws.

VOLLEYBALL

1. *Rotating.* Place youngsters in the various court positions. Teach them the rotational sequence. As they reach a new court position, have them complete several repetitions of a specific exercise. On command, rotate to the next position. Select activities that exercise components of fitness to enhance volleyball skill development.
2. *Serving.* Divide the class evenly among available volleyball courts. Starting with an equal number of children and a number of balls on each side of the net, begin practicing the serve. At the conclusion of each successful serve, the children run around the net standard to the other side of the net and retrieve a ball and serve.
3. *Bumping and setting.* Using the concept of the circuit, establish several stations to practice the bump and set. Movement from station to station should be vigorous and may contain a special stop for exercise.

SOCCER

1. *Dribbling.* Working with a partner, have one child dribble the ball around the playground with the partner following close behind. On signal, reverse roles.
2. *Passing and trapping.* Working with partners or small groups, devise routines that cause the players to move continuously (e.g., jogging, running in place, performing selected exercises while waiting to trap and pass the soccer ball).
3. *Game play.* Divide the class into teams of three or four players per team. Organize the playground area to accommodate as many soccer fields as necessary to allow all teams to play. Make the fields as large as possible.

Sample Routine

Instructional Activities	Teaching Hints
Station 1: Soccer Lines Drill—Working with a beachball, dribble the ball back and forth between two lines as quickly as possible. Use only dribbling skills—long kicks not allowed.	Place even numbers of students at each station so they can partner up for the sport activities.
Station 2: Push-Up Challenges	

Instructional Activities	Teaching Hints
Station 3: Basketball Chest Pass—With a partner, practice the chest and bounce pass. If medicine balls are available, use them for strength development.	Use intervals of music and silence to signal changes to the next station. Begin this routine with 60 seconds at the sport related activities and 30 seconds at the strength and flexibility stations.
Station 4: Flexibility Activities	
Station 5: Volleyball Passing—Using a beachball, practice passing and setting with a partner(s). Keep the ball in the air as long as possible using two-handed passes and sets.	
Station 6: Abdominal Challenges	
Station 7: Hockey Circle Passing—One partner is stationary while the other circles around and passes to his partner. Change roles after 5 passes.	Ask students to replace the equipment where they found it.
Station 8: Trunk Challenges	

Walking and Jogging

Jogging and walking, fitness activities for all ages, can lead to regular activity habits and to a lifelong exercise program. *Jogging* is defined as easy, relaxed running at a pace that can be maintained for long distances without undue fatigue or strain. It is the first level of locomotion above walking. Jogging and walking are unique in that they require no special equipment, can be done almost anywhere, are individual activities, consume relatively little time, and are not geared to a particular time of day. For most people, this type of regular activity is an exercise in personal discipline that can enhance the self-image and raise the confidence level.

Instructional Procedures

1. Let youngsters find a friend with whom they want to jog or walk. This is usually a friend of similar ability level. A way to judge correct pace is to talk with a friend without undue stress. If students are too winded to talk, they are probably running too fast. The selected friend helps ensure that the experience is positive and within the student's aerobic capacity.
2. Jogging and walking should be done in any direction so children are unable to keep track of the distance covered. Doing laps on a track is one of the surest ways to discourage less able youngsters. They always finish last and are open to chiding by the rest of the class.
3. Jogging and walking should be done for a specified time rather than a specified distance. Why should all youngsters have to run the same distance? This goes against the philosophy of accommodating individual differences and varying aerobic capacities. Running or walking for a set amount of time will allow less able children to move without fear of ridicule.
4. Don't be concerned about foot action, since children select the most comfortable gait. Arm movement should be easy and natural, with elbows bent. The head and upper body should be held up and back. The eyes look ahead. The general body position in walking and jogging should be erect but relaxed. Jogging on the toes should be avoided.
5. Jogging and walking should not be a competitive, timed activity. Each youngster should move at a self-determined pace. Racing belongs in the track program. Another reason to avoid speed is that racing negates learning to pace during a run. For developing endurance and gaining health benefits, move for a longer time at a slower speed instead of running at top speed for a shorter distance.

Racetrack Fitness

Five or six fitness activities are arranged in the center (the Pit) of a large circle outlined with marking spots (the race track). If desired, tumbling mats can be placed in the center of the race track to delineate the pit stop area. Students work with a partner and alternate running (or doing other locomotor movements) around the race track and going to the pit to perform a strength or flexibility exercise. A different exercise should be performed each time so students assure variety in their workout. Intervals of 30 seconds of music with 10 seconds of silence are used to signal role changes. The student who was running the track now goes to the pit to exercise and vice versa.

Sample Routine

Instructional Activities	Teaching Hints
The following are some examples of exercises that can be used for Pit exercises. 1. Arm Circles 2. Bend and Twist 3. Abdominal Challenges 4. Knee to Chest Curl 5. Push-Up Challenges 6. Trunk Twister	Exercise descriptions should be placed on signs in the pit area so students easily see the sequence of activities and know how to perform the exercises. Different locomotor movements can be stipulated on a sign so students perform a variety of race track activities. For example, stipulate sliding, skipping, and grapevine movements.

Fitness Orienteering

Students work together as members of a team. Eight to ten stations are placed around the area in random fashion. Each squad is given a laminated "map" card of exercise stations. Each of the maps has the stations in different order so that there is only one squad at a "landmark." The team members exercise together (each member performing at their own pace) and "hunt" for the next exercise station listed on their map card when signaled. When they complete the station activity, one member of the squad picks up a letter from the "checkpoint" and the team moves to the next station. The goal is to complete the fitness orienteering stations, pick up a letter at each station, and return to the original starting point to unscramble "the secret word." Intervals of music (30 seconds) and silence (15 seconds) signal when to exercise and when to change to a new station.

Examples of checkpoint stations on the exercise map card are:

1. Run to the Northwest corner of the gym and pick up your letter now. When the music starts, continue to run to a different corner until the music stops.
2. Move to the individual mats and perform push-up challenges until the music stops.
3. Run to the benches and perform step-ups until the music stops. The count should be "up, up, down, down," with your steps.
4. Move to the red marking spots and perform two different stretches until the music stops.
5. Run and find the jump ropes. When the music starts, pick up the ropes and do some jump rope tricks you learned earlier.
6. Skip to the tumbling mats. When the music starts perform abdominal challenges.
7. As a group, jog to the three green marking spots and pick up your letter. Jog and try to touch at least 5 walls, 2 different red lines, and 3 different black lines. Stay together with your group.
8. Jog to the "jumping jacks" sign and perform jumping jacks with at least 4 different variations in arm or foot patterns.

Aerobic, Strength, and Flexibility Jackpot Fitness

Three different "jackpots" (boxes) are filled with fitness exercises and activities are placed around the teaching area. One jackpot is filled with a variety of strength development activities written on small index cards. A second jackpot is filled with flexibility activities. The third jackpot contains aerobic activities. Students can work individually or with a partner. They begin at one of the jackpots of choice and randomly pick out an activity to perform. If with a partner, they take turns selecting the card from the box. The only stipulations are that they must rotate to a different box each time and cannot select an activity they previously performed. If they pick an activity they performed on a previous stop, they return it to the jackpot and select another. A music interval of 30 seconds signals the duration of fitness activity followed by 10 to 15 second interval used for selecting a new activity from a different jackpot. Students are expected to perform as many repetitions as possible while the music is playing.

Examples of activities for the jackpot include the following:

Aerobic Jackpot

1. Carioca around the basketball court.
2. Perform a "mirror drill" with your partner for 30 seconds.
3. Jump rope using both slow and fast time.
4. Tortoise and Hare/Running in place.
5. Marching with high steps around the area.

Strength Jackpot

1. Perform Abdominal Challenges
2. Perform Push-Up Challenges
3. Do the Treadmill exercise
4. Do as many Power Jumpers as possible
5. Perform as many Crab Kicks as possible.

Flexibility Jackpot

1. Perform the Bend and Twist exercise.
2. Stretch using the Sitting Stretch.
3. Stretch using the Lower Leg Stretch.
4. Do the Standing Hip Bend.
5. Improve your flexibility performing the Body Twist.

Partner Interval Fitness

Students pair up with a partner and perform the activities below. The activities are designed so one partner performs aerobic activity while the other is stretching or doing strength development activities. Use timed intervals of 30 seconds of music and 10 seconds of silence to signal changing positions (or activity). All the activities below should be performed.

1. **High Fives.** One partner runs around the area and gives as many "high fives" as possible to others who are running. The other partner remains stationary and performs Push-Up Challenges. On signal, they switch roles. Various locomotor movements can be used as well as different styles of the "high five."

2. **Over and Around.** One partner makes a bridge on the floor while the other moves over and around the bridges of other students. This continues until a signal is given to "switch," which notifies them to change positions. This assures that one child is moving (working), while the other is resting. Try different types of bridges and movements to offer variety to the activity.
3. **Jump Rope and Exercise.** Each partner has a jump rope. One partner jumps the rope while the other partner folds the rope and performs strength or stretching activities. On signal, partners switch roles. An example of a stretching activity is to fold the rope in half and hold it overhead while stretching from side to side and to the toes. See pages 369–382 for other rope exercises.
4. **Stick and Stretch.** One partner tries to stick like glue to her partner who tries to move as far away as possible. All movement should be done under control. On signal, the other partner leads a stretching or strength development (resting) activity. On the next signal, the roles are reversed.
5. **Partner Swing and Exercise.** Partners swing each other under control while the first music interval is playing. On the next music interval, one partner leads the other in a stretching or strength development activity. The partners swing again followed by the other partner leading a stretching or strength development activity.

Interval Training

All fitness routines in this chapter take advantage of interval training principles. Interval training is effective with elementary school children because they fatigue and recover quickly. Interval training involves alternating work and recovery intervals. Intervals of work (large muscle movement dominated by locomotor movements) and recovery (dominated by nonlocomotor activity or walking) are alternated at regular timed intervals. The following are examples of motivating activities that can be alternated with recovery activities.

HIGH FIVES

Youngsters run around the area and, on signal, run to a partner, jump, and give a "high five." Various locomotor movements can be used as well as different styles of the "high five."

OVER AND UNDER

Students find a partner. One partner makes a bridge on the floor while the other moves over, under, and around the bridge. This continues until a signal is given to "switch," which notifies them to change positions. This assures that one child is moving (working), while the other is resting. Try different types of bridges and movements to offer variety to the activity.

ROPE JUMP AND STRETCH

Each student has a jump rope and is jumping it during the work interval. On signal, the student performs a stretch using the jump rope. For example, fold the rope in half and hold it overhead while stretching from side to side and to the toes.

STICK AND STRETCH

Working with a partner, one partner is *it* and tries to stick like glue to the partner, who attempts to escape. Students should move under control. Upon signal, *it* leads the other person in a stretching (resting) activity. On the next signal, the roles are reversed.

RUBBER BAND

Students move throughout the area. On signal, they time a move to the center of the area. Upon reaching the center simultaneously, they jump upward and let out a loud "yea!" or similar exhortation and resume running throughout the area. The key to the activity is to synchronize the move to the center. After a number of runs, take a rest and stretch, or walk.

Each of these activities is used for work intervals. Recovery intervals are characterized by strength development or stretching activities. Using timed intervals of music is an effective approach for motivating youngsters. For a start, tape 30 seconds of music followed by 30 seconds of silence, taping a series of these alternating music and silent intervals. The music sequence signals youngsters to perform the work interval, and the silent interval is time for performing stretching or strength development activities. As youngsters become more fit, the length of the music bouts can be increased by making a new recording.

Partner Fitness Challenges

Partner challenges are fitness activities that can be used with intermediate-grade youngsters. They can be used to develop aerobic endurance, strength, and flexibility. Another advantage of partner challenges is that they can be performed indoors as a rainy-day activity. It is best if youngsters are paired with someone of similar ability and size. Telling youngsters to pair up with a friend usually means they will select a partner who is caring and understanding. Emphasis should be placed on continuous movement and activity. The following are examples of partner activities that are both challenging and enjoyable.

CIRCLE FIVE

Partner 1 stands stationary in the center of the circle with one palm up. Partner 2 runs in a circle around 1 and "gives a high five" when passing the upturned palm. The size of the circle is gradually increased. Reverse roles on signal.

FOOT TAG

Partners stand facing each other. On signal, they try to touch each other's toes with their feet. Emphasize the importance of a touch, as contrasted to a stamp or kick.

KNEE TAG

Partners stand facing each other. On signal, they try to tag the other person's knees. Each time a tag is made, a point is scored. Play for a designated amount of time.

MINI MERRY-GO-ROUND

Partners face each other with the feet nearly touching and the hands grasped in a double wrist grip. Partners slowly lean backward while keeping the feet in place until the arms are straight. Spin around as quickly as possible. It is important that partners be of similar size.

AROUND AND UNDER

One partner stands with the feet spread shoulder width apart and hands held overhead. The other partner goes between the standing partner's legs, stands up, and slaps the partner's hands. Continue the pattern for a designated time.

BALL WRESTLE

Both partners grasp an 8-inch playground ball and try to wrestle it away from each other.

SITTING WRESTLE

Partners sit on the floor facing each other with the legs bent, feet flat on the floor, with toes touching and hands grasped. The goal of the activity is to pull the other's buttocks off the floor.

UPSET THE ALLIGATOR

One partner lays face down on the floor. On signal, the other opponent tries to turn the "alligator" over. The alligator tries to avoid being turned over.

SEAT BALANCE WRESTLE

Partners sit on the floor facing each other with the knees raised and feet off the floor. If desired, they place the hands under the thighs to help support the legs. Start with the toes touching. Each tries to tip the other person backward using the toes.

HEAD WRESTLE

Partners hold each other's left wrists with their right hands. On signal, they try to touch their partners' heads with their left hands, then switch the handhold and try to touch with the opposite hand.

PULL APART

One partner stands with the feet spread, arms bent at the elbows in front of the chest, with the fingertips touching. Partner 2 holds the wrists of the other and tries to pull the fingertips apart. Jerking is not allowed; the pull must be smooth and controlled.

PIN DANCE

Partners hold hands facing each other with a bowling pin (spot or cone) placed between them. On signal, each tries to cause the other person to touch the pin.

FINGER FENCING

Partners face each other with their feet one in front of the other in a straight line. The toes on the front foot of each partner should touch. Partners lock index fingers and attempt to cause the other to move either foot from the beginning position.

REFLECTION AND REVIEW QUESTIONS

How and Why

1. Why are America's youth perceived as being unfit and inactive?
2. Why must physical education teachers understand various concepts related to physical fitness and physical activity?
3. Should fitness testing awards be used?
4. Why do so many students fail fitness tests? Defend your answer.
5. How can teachers make fitness fun?
6. Should physical education teachers be physically fit? Explain.

Content Review

1. Discuss several major conclusions of the *Surgeon's General's Report on Physical Activity and Health.*
2. Differentiate between health-related fitness and skill-related fitness and identify the components of each.

3. How much activity and what type of activity should children participate in?
4. Are American children fit? Explain your answer.
5. Identify the purpose of physical fitness testing and the steps to implementing a fitness test battery. Include descriptions of several fitness tests and the fitness component each measures.
6. Describe methods for fostering positive attitudes towards physical activity.
7. Discuss guidelines for promoting fitness and physical activity for children.
8. Cite several harmful exercises.
9. Create a developmentally appropriate fitness routine. Be sure to identify the developmental level that will use the routine.
10. Describe or demonstrate numerous activities and exercises designed to improve the fitness of children.

FOR MORE INFORMATION

References and Suggested Readings

AAHPERD. (1987). *Youth fitness test manual.* Reston, VA: AAHPERD.

AAHPERD. (1999). *Physical best activity guide—Elementary level.* Champaign, IL: Human Kinetics.

AAHPERD. (1999). *Physical education for lifelong fitness: The physical best teacher's guide.* Champaign, IL: Human Kinetics.

AAHPER. (1976). *AAHPER youth fitness test manual.* Reston, VA: AAHPER.

American Academy of Pediatrics. (1991). *Sports medicine: Health care for young athletes.* Elk Grove Village, IL: AAP.

American College of Sports Medicine. (1995). *ACSM's guidelines for exercise testing and prescription.* 5th ed. Baltimore: Williams & Wilkins.

Bailey, R. C., Olson, J., Pepper, S. L., Porszaz, J., Barstow, T. J., & Cooper, D. M. (1995). The level and tempo of children's physical activities: An observational study. *Medicine and Science in Sport and Exercise,* 27(7), 1033–1041.

Bar-Or, O. (1983). *Pediatric sports medicine for the practitioner.* New York: Springer-Verlag.

Blair, S. N., Kohl, H. W., Paffenbarger, R. S., Clark, D. G., Cooper, K. H., & Gibbons, L. W. (1989). Physical fitness and all-cause mortality: A prospective study of healthy men and women. *Journal of the American Medical Association,* 17, 2395–2401.

Bouchard, C. (1990). Discussion: Heredity, fitness and health. In C. Bouchard, R. J. Shepard, T. Stephens, J. R. Sutton, & B. D. McPherson. (Eds.), *Exercise, fitness and health* (pp. 147–153). Champaign, IL: Human Kinetics.

Bouchard, C., Dionne, F. T., Simoneau, J., & Boulay, M. (1992). Genetics of aerobic and anaerobic performances. *Exercise and Sport Sciences Reviews,* 20, 27–58.

Cooper Institute. (2002). *Fitnessgram test administration manual.* 2nd ed. Champaign, IL: Human Kinetics.

Corbin, C. B., Lindsey, R., & Welk, G. (2000). *Concepts of physical fitness and wellness: A comprehensive lifestyle approach.* Boston: McGraw-Hill.

Corbin, C. B., & Lindsey, R. (1996). *Fitness for life teacher's resource manual.* 4th ed. Glenview, IL: Scott, Foresman.

Corbin, C. B., Lovejoy, P. Y., Steingard, P., & Emerson, R. (1990). Fitness awards: Do they accomplish their intended objectives? *American Journal of Health Promotion,* 4, 345–351.

Corbin, C. B., Lovejoy, P. Y., & Whitehead, J. R. (1988). Youth physical fitness awards. *Quest,* 40, 200–218.

Corbin, C. B., Pangrazi, R. P., & Welk, G. J. (1994). Toward an understanding of appropriate physical activity levels for youth. *Physical Activity and Fitness Research Digest,* 1(8): 1–8.

Corbin, C. B., & Pangrazi, R. P. (1992). Are American children and youth fit? *Research Quarterly for Exercise and Sport,* 63(2), 96–106.

Corbin, C. B., & Pangrazi, R. P. (1998a). *Physical activity for Children: A statement of guidelines.* Reston, VA: NASPE Publications. 21 pp. (AAHPERD National Guidelines)

Corbin, C. B., & Pangrazi, R. P. (1998b). Physical activity pyramid rebuffs peak experience. *ACSM's Health & Fitness Journal,* 2(1), 12–17.

Erickson, D. M. (1980). The effect of a random running program on cardiorespiratory endurance at the fourth, fifth, and sixth grade levels. Unpublished master's thesis, Department of Health and Physical Education, Arizona State University.

Glasser, W. (1976). *Positive addiction.* New York: Harper & Row.

Gortmaker, S. L., Dietz, W. H., Sobol, A. N., & Wehler, C. A. (1987). Increasing pediatric obesity in the U.S. *American Journal of Diseases in Children,* 14, 535–540.

Harter, S. (1978). Effectance motivation revisited. *Child Development,* 21, 34–64.

Howley, E. T., & Franks, B. D. (1997). *Health fitness instructor's handbook.* Champaign, IL: Human Kinetics.

Lindsey, R., & Corbin, C. (1989). Questionable exercises—Some safer alternatives. *Journal of Physical Education, Recreation, and Dance,* 60(8), 26–32.

Locke, E. A., & Lathan, G. P. (1985). The application of goal setting to sports. *Journal of Sport Psychology,* 7, 205–222.

Lohman, T. G. (1992). *Advances in body composition.* Champaign, IL: Human Kinetics.

Macfarlane, P. A. (1993). Out with the sit-up, in with the curl-up. *Journal of Physical Education, Recreation, and Dance,* 64(6), 62–66.

Pangrazi, R. P. (2004). *Lesson plans for dynamic physical education* (14th ed.). San Francisco: Benjamin Cummings.

Pangrazi, R. P., & Corbin, C. B. (1990). Age as a factor relating to physical fitness test performance. *Research Quarterly for Exercise and Sport,* 61(4), 410–414.

Pangrazi, R. P., & Hastad, D. N. (1989). *Fitness in the elementary schools.* 2nd ed. Reston, VA: AAHPERD.

Pate, R., Corbin, C. B., & Pangrazi, R. P. (1998). Physical activity for young people. *President's Council on Physical Fitness and Sports Research Digest,* 3(3), 1–8.

Pate, R. R., Dowda, M., & Ross, J. G. (1990). Association between physical activity and physical fitness in American children. *American Journal of Diseases of Children,* 144, 1123–1129.

Pate, R. R., & Ross, J. G. (1987). Factors associated with health-related fitness. *Journal of Physical Education, Recreation, and Dance,* 58(9), 93–96.

Payne, V. G., & Morrow, J. R., Jr. (1993). Exercise and VO_2 max in children: A meta-analysis. *Research Quarterly for Exercise and Sport,* 64(3), 305–313.

Plowman, S. A. (1993). Physical fitness and healthy low back function. *Physical Activity and Fitness Research Digest,* 1(3), 1–8.

President's Council on Physical Fitness and Sports. (2002). *The President's Challenge.* Washington, DC: President's Council on Physical Fitness and Sports.

Reiff, G. G., Dixon, W. R., Jacoby, D., Ye, X. Y., Spain, C. G., & Hunsicker, P. A. (1987). *The President's Council on Physical Fitness and Sports 1985 national school population fitness survey.* Washington, DC: U.S. Department of Health and Human Services.

Ross, J. G., & Gilbert, G. G. (1985). The national children and youth fitness study: A summary of findings. *Journal of Physical Education, Recreation, and Dance,* 56(1), 45–50.

Ross, J. G., Pate, R. R., Caspersen, C. J., Damberg, C. L., & Svilar, M. (1987). Home and community in children's exercise habits. *Journal of Physical Education, Recreation, and Dance,* 58(9), 85–92.

Rowland, T. W. (1990). *Exercise and children's health.* Champaign, IL: Human Kinetics.

Shaw, J. M., & Snow-Harter, C. (1995). Osteoporosis and physical activity. *Physical Activity and Fitness Research Digest,* 2(3), 1–8.

Slaughter, M. H., Lohman, T. G., Boileau, R. A., Horswill, C. A., Stillman, R. J., Van Loan, M. D., & Benben, D. A. (1988). Skinfold equations for estimation of body fatness in children and youth. *Human Biology,* 60, 709–723.

Smith, L. L., Brunetz, M. H., Chenier, T. C., McCammon, M. R., Hourmard, J. A., Franklin, M. E., & Israel, R. G. (1993). The effects of static and ballistic stretching on delayed onset muscle soreness and creatine kinase. *Research Quarterly for Exercise and Sport,* 64(1), 103–107.

U.S. Department of Health and Human Services. (1996). *Physical activity and health: A report of the Surgeon General.* Atlanta, GA: U.S. Department of Health and Human Services, Centers for Disease Control and Prevention, National Center for Chronic Disease Prevention and Health Promotion.

U.S. Department of Health and Human Services. (2002). Prevalence of overweight among children and adolescents: United States, 1999. Center for Disease Control and Prevention, National Center for Health Statistics.

Whitehead, J. R., & Corbin, C. B. (1991). Effects of fitness test type, teacher, and gender on exercise, intrinsic motivation, and physical self-worth. *Journal of School Health,* 61, 11–16.

Wilcox, R. R. (1980). RRP: An approach to cardiorespiratory fitness of primary school children, grades one, two, and three. Unpublished master's thesis, Department of Health and Physical Education, Arizona State University.

Williams, D. P., Going, S. B., Lohman, T. G., Harsha, D. W., Webber, L. S., & Bereson, G. S. (1992). Body fatness and the risk of elevated blood pressure, total cholesterol and serum lipoprotein ratios in children and youth. *American Journal of Public Health,* 82, 358–363.

Websites

Physical Activity and Fitness Assessment
http://www.cooperinst.org/ftgrefintro.aspment
http://www.indiana.edu/~preschal/pala/pala/description.shtml

Physical Activity, Fitness, and Children
http://www.americanheart.org/presenter.jhtml?identifier=4596
http://www.cdc.gov/nccdphp/dash/presphysactrpt/index.htm
http://www.cooperinst.org/ftgrefintro.asp
http://www.nlm.nih.gov/medlineplus/exercisephysicalfitness.html#children

Physical Activity Reports
http://www.cdc.gov.nccdphp/sgr/sgr.htm
http://www.health.gov/healthypeople/

Teaching Fitness Concepts
http://www.americanfitness.net/Physical_Best/
http://www.fi.edu/biosci/heart.html
http://www.jhbmc.jhu.edu/cardiology/partnership/kids/kids.html
http://www.usask.ca/education/ideas/tplan/pedlp/aerobics.htm

CHAPTER 13

Wellness: Developing a Healthy Lifestyle

ESSENTIAL COMPONENTS	
I	Organized around content standards
II	Student-centered and developmentally appropriate
III	Physical activity and motor skill development form the core of the program
IV	Teaches management skills and self-discipline
V	**Promotes inclusion of all students**
VI	Focuses on process over product
VII	**Promotes lifetime personal health and wellness**
VIII	Teaches cooperation and responsibility and promotes sensitivity to diversity

PHYSICAL EDUCATION STANDARDS	
1	Students are able to move competently using a variety of fundamental and specialized motor skills.
2	**Students can monitor and maintain a health-enhancing level of physical fitness.**
3	Students are able to apply movement concepts and basic mechanics of skill performance when learning and refining motor skills.
4	**Students comprehend the basic principles of wellness and are able to apply concepts that enable them to make meaningful decisions that positively impact their health and wellness.**
5	**Students participate in a wide variety of physical activities and learn how to maintain a personalized active lifestyle.**
6	Students demonstrate empathy, understanding, and respect for the numerous differences exhibited by people in an activity setting.
7	Students exhibit responsible and self-directed behaviors that lead to positive social interactions in physical activity.

SUMMARY

This chapter provides an overview of human wellness consisting of a number of interrelated areas that form a coordinated whole. The first phase of wellness is understanding how the body functions and needs to be maintained for good health. A number of roadblocks to wellness occur on the path to good health, and students need to develop the ability to avoid such deterrents. Effective teachers help students understand their feelings, values, and attitudes. Decision-making strategies need to be taught to students so they can make thoughtful and productive choices. This chapter offers many suggested learning experiences so youngsters can begin to comprehend and synthesize knowledge necessary for wellness.

OUTCOMES

- Describe how wellness instruction can be implemented in physical education.
- Identify various techniques used to help students develop awareness and decision-making skills.
- List teaching behaviors associated with the effective leadership of class discussions.
- Identify various roadblocks to wellness.
- Implement learning experiences related to wellness.
- Define health-related physical fitness and the relationship between total physical fitness and activity.
- Describe the value of proper nutrition.
- Understand the importance of dealing with stress and tension.
- Characterize the type and extent of substance abuse in elementary schools.
- Describe the importance of safety and first aid in physical education.

The need for teaching students how to maintain personal wellness for a lifetime is apparent when one examines the skyrocketing costs of minimal health care. Health insurance policies cost 5 to 10 percent of an individual's gross income. A short stay in the hospital may incur a bill for thousands of dollars, yet in spite of runaway costs, Americans continue to pay and put little or no effort into maintaining a healthy lifestyle.

Human wellness is defined as a state of positive health in the individual and comprises biological and psychological well-being as exemplified by quality of life as well as an overall sense of well-being (Corbin et al., 2000). Wellness allows an individual to participate fully in life. Having the energy and enthusiasm to undertake activities of all types after a full day's work is characteristic of people who are well. An individual who is well is not only free of sickness or other malady but is happy, vibrant, and able to solve personal problems.

Teaching students how to achieve a lasting state of wellness lends credibility to the physical education profession. For many years, physical educators were seen solely as teachers of physical skills who had little concern for the knowledge and comprehension involved in physical performance. The various personalities and unique needs of the student participants were often ignored by teachers who appeared to be concerned only about the product (that is, "Learn the skill or else!"). The age-old argument of product versus process can be moderated by teaching the process of developing physical wellness, for wellness is a process. There are no trophies or other extrinsic rewards for achieving it. Wellness is personal. When it is achieved, the individual is directly rewarded by an enhanced lifestyle. Teachers can no longer ignore the importance of teaching students the what, why, and how of maintaining a healthy profile. Maintaining wellness must be considered a primary objective of a quality physical education program.

Why teach wellness in the physical education setting? Teachers are often skeptical about teaching material other than physical skill activities, yet the ability to develop and maintain personal wellness will remain with an individual for a lifetime. This is one of the few long-lasting gifts teachers can offer to students. Achieving wellness is unique and personal. What is useful to one person may be superfluous to another. Teachers must therefore teach students how to search for wellness and then maintain it once found.

At present, the credibility of the physical education profession is strained. Teachers often offer students skills and activities they will never use again. For example, students may spend an inordinate amount of time in classes participating in activities they will not be able to play during adulthood, i.e., team sports. Small wonder that many adults believe that they learned little in physical education to help them after graduation. The point here is not to belittle team sports or similar activities but to suggest that the program offer equal or greater emphasis on activities that can be used in adulthood.

Teaching students how to maintain a state of wellness makes activity purposeful. Students begin to understand why certain activities and games are selected in place of others. Selection of activities for a lifetime of physical involvement can only occur after students have been exposed to a wide range of instructional units. A systematic approach to curriculum development is critical in ensuring that students know the many alternatives and pathways to personal fitness and health.

INTEGRATING WELLNESS INTO PHYSICAL EDUCATION INSTRUCTION

Paramount to all instruction dealing with wellness is an emphasis on self-responsibility for maintaining a healthy lifestyle. Regardless of what students are taught, if an emphasis is not placed on teaching students how to make personal decisions, little has been gained. Most students do what is asked of them when they are in school. However, the real issue is whether students will have the problem-solving skills that will enable them to make meaningful decisions throughout life, when teachers are no longer present.

Nowhere is it assumed that the achievement of wellness is the concern solely of physical education. Some aspects of wellness, such as development of a personalized level of physical fitness, are emphasized primarily in physical education. Other aspects can be developed cooperatively with classroom teachers. As a physical educator, you may justifiably raise the question: How can I develop physical fitness levels, teach skills, and accomplish all the topics listed under wellness? Once again, the question is one of priorities. What is gained if students leave school without a basic wellness understanding? Few schools offer health education programs, so if physical educators do not teach wellness, students will not learn about wellness.

There are different approaches used for teaching wellness in elementary school physical education classes. Physical activity is still the cornerstone of physical education, and the substitution of a knowledge-discussion program at the expense of activity is not recommended. On the other hand, a strong case can be made that activity without a knowledge base of how and why will be ineffective in the long run. If classroom time cannot be found for teaching wellness activities, discussions should be held to a 5-minute limit in physical education classes. Using some physical education class time for wellness instruction signals to students that wellness is an important part of the program. Examples of ideas that can be discussed in limited time without disrupting physical education are:

- learning how to measure the heart rate
- knowing what activities are aerobic and anaerobic
- identifying what muscles are strengthened by different exercises
- understanding why strength is important in skill performance
- knowing what foods should be avoided
- understanding how weight is maintained through caloric balance of exercise and eating

Each of these topics can be discussed quickly during a closure session at the end of the lesson. The intent of the discussions is to stimulate interaction and to promote rudimentary understanding of basic wellness principles.

School districts and parents are demanding that homework be assigned to raise academic standards. Physical education need not be an exception to the rule. Homework can encourage parental participation at home and help parents understand that physical education is more than just activity. In addition, meaningful homework experiences may enlighten teachers in other academic areas to view physical education in a more positive light.

Some districts have successfully designed programs that concentrate on wellness for a period of 2 to 4 weeks. Such wellness instruction is spaced out during the school year. During those weeks, physical education classes per se are canceled and moved to a classroom where the physical education specialist conducts wellness sessions. This results in concentrated instruction in a setting (the classroom) that is conducive to cognitive and affective development. Many variations of this approach have been developed to accommodate specific school parameters. At the least, wellness instruction gives children a better understanding of the body and its possibilities, which can mean higher achievement. At best, the wellness approach becomes the pursuit of excellence, inspiring children to make the most of their physical and movement potential.

INSTRUCTIONAL STRATEGIES FOR TEACHING WELLNESS

Physical education enhances the fitness and skill levels of students so they have a background that allows them to develop an active lifestyle. Another program goal is to help young people make responsible lifestyle decisions. People are faced with many decisions that positively or negatively impact their level of wellness. The ability to make responsible decisions depends on a wide range of factors: an understanding of one's feelings and clarification of personal values, an ability to cope with stress and personal problems, an ability to make decisions, and an understanding of the impact of various lifestyles on health.

Developing Awareness and Decision-Making Skills

The focus of wellness instruction should be on helping students to view themselves as total beings. Stability occurs when all parts fit together in a smooth and consistent fashion. When a problem occurs, the balance of physiology, thinking, and function is disrupted. Individuals must then use their knowledge, coping ability, and decision-making skills to restore the equilibrium associated with personal stability. Teachers can try to help students understand their feelings, values, and attitudes, and the impact that all of these have on coping and decision-making ability. A basis element to this process is helping students develop positive and strong self-concepts.

Helping Students Develop Positive Self-Concepts

A student who has a healthy self-image and positive self-concept will be better able to make a decision in the presence of peer pressure. Individuals who feel positive about themselves are less influenced by peer pressure than those with poor self-concepts. Through the process of education, each student should be made to feel important and worthwhile. Youngsters need to learn that they are not perfect and that change is desirable. The identification of personal strengths and weaknesses can offer direction for self-growth and for understanding personal limitations. **Self-concept** is defined as the total perception an individual has of self. Self-concept is enhanced when the individual has a strong, positive feeling of belonging and a sense of worth. These attitudes can be fostered by providing activities that help students:

1. Recognize that there are many individuals, yet each of us is unique.
2. Feel loved and able to love.
3. Be able to recognize and cope with feelings and emotions.
4. Function in a group, yet also be comfortable alone.
5. Like to and be able to do many things.
6. Relate successfully to others.

When dealing with areas of self-concept and personal worth, students should feel comfortable about expressing their feelings. They should feel free to ask questions without fear of ridicule or embarrassment. Discussions should be positive and criticism constructive. As students develop more positive feelings about themselves, their ability to make responsible decisions improves. They become able to make decisions in everyone's interests, including their own.

Coping Skills

Coping is the ability to deal with problems successfully. Learning to cope with life's problems is dependent on and interrelated with knowledge of self, decision-making skills, and the ability to relate to others. Specific strategies for coping include the following:

1. ***Admit that a problem exists and face it.*** Coping with a problem is impossible when the problem is not recognized.
2. ***Define the problem and decide who owns it.*** Individuals must identify what needs to be coped with and decide if the problem is theirs or belongs to others.
3. ***List alternative solutions to the problem.*** A basic step in decision making, problem solving, and coping is to identify what alternatives are open in a given situation.
4. ***Predict consequences for oneself and others.*** Once alternatives are identified, weighing the potential consequences of each, and then ranking them in order of preference, is an important process.
5. ***Identify and consult sources of help.*** All possible sources of help available to assist in carrying out alternatives should be considered. To do this, students need to have some knowledge of the available resources or know how to find resources.
6. ***Experiment with a solution and evaluate the results.*** If the decision did not produce satisfactory results, try another alternative. Evaluation of results also allows people to keep track of their abilities to come up with satisfying solutions.

Decision-Making Skills

Youngsters are faced with many life situations in which decisions must be made. Decision making is something that everyone does every day, often without thinking. Because it is a common act, it receives little attention until a person is faced with an important decision that has long-term consequences. Although schools attempt to help students learn how to make personally satisfying decisions, a major portion of teacher time is spent supplying information to students. Although this teacher function is extremely important, it is only one part of the decision-making process. Teachers should ask themselves the question, "If you are going to provide information to others, what do you want them to do with that information?" Opportunities should be provided that help students put the information to use.

Decision making is defined as a process in which a person selects from two or more possible choices. A decision cannot exist unless more than one course of action is available to consider. Decision making enables the individual to reason through life situations, to solve problems, and, to some extent, to direct behavior. There are no right answers for the decision made; rather, the decision is judged by a student's effective use of a process that results in satisfying consequences. This criterion distinguishes decision making from problem solving. Problem solving usually identifies one best or right solution for everyone involved. When making decisions, students should consider each of the following steps.

1. ***Gather information.*** If meaningful choices are to be made, gathering all available information is important. Information should be gathered from as many sources as possible. Students will generally consider information valid if they see that it comes from many different sources and that it allows them to view both sides of an issue. Too often, teachers present students with information that supports only the instructor's point of view.
2. ***Consider the available choices.*** The next step is to consider all of the available choices. It does not make sense to consider alternatives that, in reality, have no possibility of being selected. Considering the choices is an important step if students are to realize that they have many different possibilities from which to choose and that what they choose will influence the direction of their lives. In the school setting, many choices have been made for students. They sometimes come to believe that others make all decisions for them and that they, in turn, bear no responsibility for their successes or failures.
3. ***Analyze the consequences of choices.*** When the various choices are delineated, students must consider the consequences that accompany each choice. If the consequences are ignored, the choice made may be unwise and detrimental to good health. Making wise decisions about wellness demands that students be aware of the consequences. This means understanding why some people choose to smoke or drink, even when they understand the negative consequences. The most important role of the teacher is to help students identify both positive and negative consequences without moralizing or telling the students how to think.
4. ***Make a decision and implement it.*** When all the information has been gathered, students must make a decision and integrate it into their lifestyles. These

decisions are personal to each student and need not be revealed to others.

Skillful decision makers have more control over their lives because they can reduce the amount of uncertainty in their choices and limit the degree to which chance or their peers determine their future. Two individuals may face a similar decision and make different choices, because each person is different and places differing values on outcomes. The individual makes each decision unique. Learning decision-making skills therefore increases the possibility that students can achieve personal goals.

Decisions also have limits. Each decision is necessarily limited by what a person is capable of doing, by what a person is willing to do, and by the environment in which the decision is made. The environment in which decision-making skills are practiced is important for proper development of these skills. A nonjudgmental atmosphere is usually most appropriate. Since solutions differ for different people, the person making a decision should be free to select from any of the available choices and learn to accept the probable consequences and results of choices made.

FIGURE 13.1 Leading a wellness discussion.

LEADING DISCUSSION SESSIONS

The success of discussions depends on how effectively the teacher is able to establish and maintain the integrity and structure of the lesson and the students' psychological freedom (Figure 13.1). Integrity and structure mean that all students are dealing with the same issue in a thoughtful and responsible way. Psychological freedom means that individual students participate to the degree they want to by (a) commenting when they choose to do so or refraining from comment when they so desire, (b) responding to direct questions or choosing to "pass" for the time being, (c) agreeing or disagreeing with what others in the group have said, or (d) deciding what data they need, if any, and reaching out to ask for those data. This demands certain teacher behavior to establish a meaningful environment. A brief description of the necessary teaching behaviors follows.

Structuring

The purpose of structuring is to create a climate that is conducive to open communication by all parties. This is accomplished by outlining expectations and role relationships for both teacher and students. Structuring includes any of the following:

1. Establish the lesson climate at the beginning of the lesson by providing an explanation of what the students and teacher will be doing and how they will work together.
2. Maintain the established lesson structure by not allowing students to be pressured to respond and by seeing that no one's ideas are put down.
3. When necessary, add to or modify the lesson structure established at the beginning of the lesson. For example, this might involve changing to small-group sessions rather than continuing a total class discussion.

Focus Setting

The purpose of focus setting is to establish an explicit and common topic or issue for discussion. Because this teaching behavior is used in different circumstances, there are different ways it can be formulated:

1. A topic can be presented, usually in the form of a question, to the group for their discussion.
2. Focus setting can be used to restate the original question during the lesson or to shift to a new discussion topic when students indicate they have finished discussing the original question.
3. Focus setting can bring the discussion back to the original topic when a student unknowingly shifts to a new topic.
4. Focus setting can label a discussion question presented by a student as a new topic to allow discussion of that topic in place of a previous one.

Clarifying

The purpose of clarifying is to invite a student to help the teacher understand the substance or content of the student's comment. Whenever possible, the clarifying should give students an indication of what the teacher does not understand. In addition, the teacher's remarks should be formulated in such a way that the burden of understanding is placed on the teacher, rather than implying that the student is inarticulate, and therefore deficient. Clarifying is used by teachers only when they do not understand. The teacher does not assume the responsibility of clarifying for the students.

Acknowledging

Acknowledging informs a student that the teacher understands what the student has said and that the comments have made a contribution to the discussion. Unlike most teaching behaviors, this one can be implemented nonverbally as well as by verbal means. How acknowledging is worded and when it is used must be considered carefully. To use acknowledging only when the teacher understands and agrees, but to do something else when the teacher understands and disagrees, is a serious misunderstanding of the purpose and function of this teaching behavior. Acknowledging is intended to be a nonjudgmental way of saying "I understand."

Teacher Silence

Teacher silence is used is to communicate to students through nonverbal means that it is their responsibility to initiate and carry on the discussion. Teacher silence is used only in response to student silence. It protects the students' rights and responsibility to make their own decisions about the topic being discussed. In a sense, this teaching behavior is a nonbehavior.

UNDERSTANDING THE BODY AND HOW IT FUNCTIONS

The material in this section is couched in terms of the knowledge and understandings that elementary school students must develop. The areas presented are rudimentary and illustrate examples of knowledge, concepts, and experiences children must understand to develop a value set that enhances personal wellness. Because most children feel healthy and have little concern about health, this unit should focus on establishing a foundation for developing proper health attitudes for adolescent and adult life.

Students must understand two major categories of wellness concepts. The first is basic knowledge of how the body functions and how it can be maintained through proper care and activity. The second category centers on roadblocks that stand in the path of wellness. Some of these are stress, improper nutrition, obesity, anorexia, substance abuse, and personal safety problems. Basic concepts and suggested learning activities are listed for each area.

The Skeletal System

The skeletal system (Figure 13.2) is the framework of the body and consists of 208 separate bones. The bones act as a system of levers and are linked together by connections (*joints*) that allow movement. The bones are held together at the joints by ligaments and muscles. Ligaments are tough and incapable of stretching. They do not contract the way muscles do and are therefore subject to injury when the bones are moved beyond their natural range.

Joints that are freely movable are called *synovial joints.* Synovial fluid is secreted to lubricate the joint and reduce friction. A thin layer of cartilage also reduces friction at the ends of the bones. A disk, or meniscus, forms a pad between many of the weight-bearing joints for the purpose of absorbing shock. When a cartilage is damaged, joint dysfunction and pain can occur.

Muscular activity increases the weight-bearing stresses on bones. The bones respond to the added stress by increasing in mineral content and density, increasing in diameter, and reorganizing internal elements to cause an increase in bone strength. The bones serve as a mineral reserve for the body and can become deformed as a result of dietary deficiencies.

Within the human body bones, joints, and muscles establish levers. Three types of levers are identified and classified by the arrangements of the fulcrum, force, and resistance. The fulcrum is the turning point, or pivot point, of the lever and is synonymous with a joint when discussing levers in the human body. Force is generated by contracting muscles within the lever. The resistance is typically, but not always, outside of the body and "resists" the force from moving the bones or joints. Examples of resistance include gravity, a dumbbell, or a ball.

The forearm is an example of a first-class lever when it is extended at the elbow joint (fulcrum) by the triceps muscle (Figure 13.3A). A second-class lever exists where the gastrocnemius raises the weight of the body to the toes (Figure 13.3B). Examples of third-class lever actions are the movement of the biceps muscle to flex the forearm at the elbow joint (Figure 13.3C), the sideward movement of the upper arm at the shoulder joint by the deltoid muscle, and the flexion of the lower leg at the knee joint by the hamstring muscles.

Requisite Knowledge

1. The skeletal system consists of 208 bones and determines the external appearance of the body.

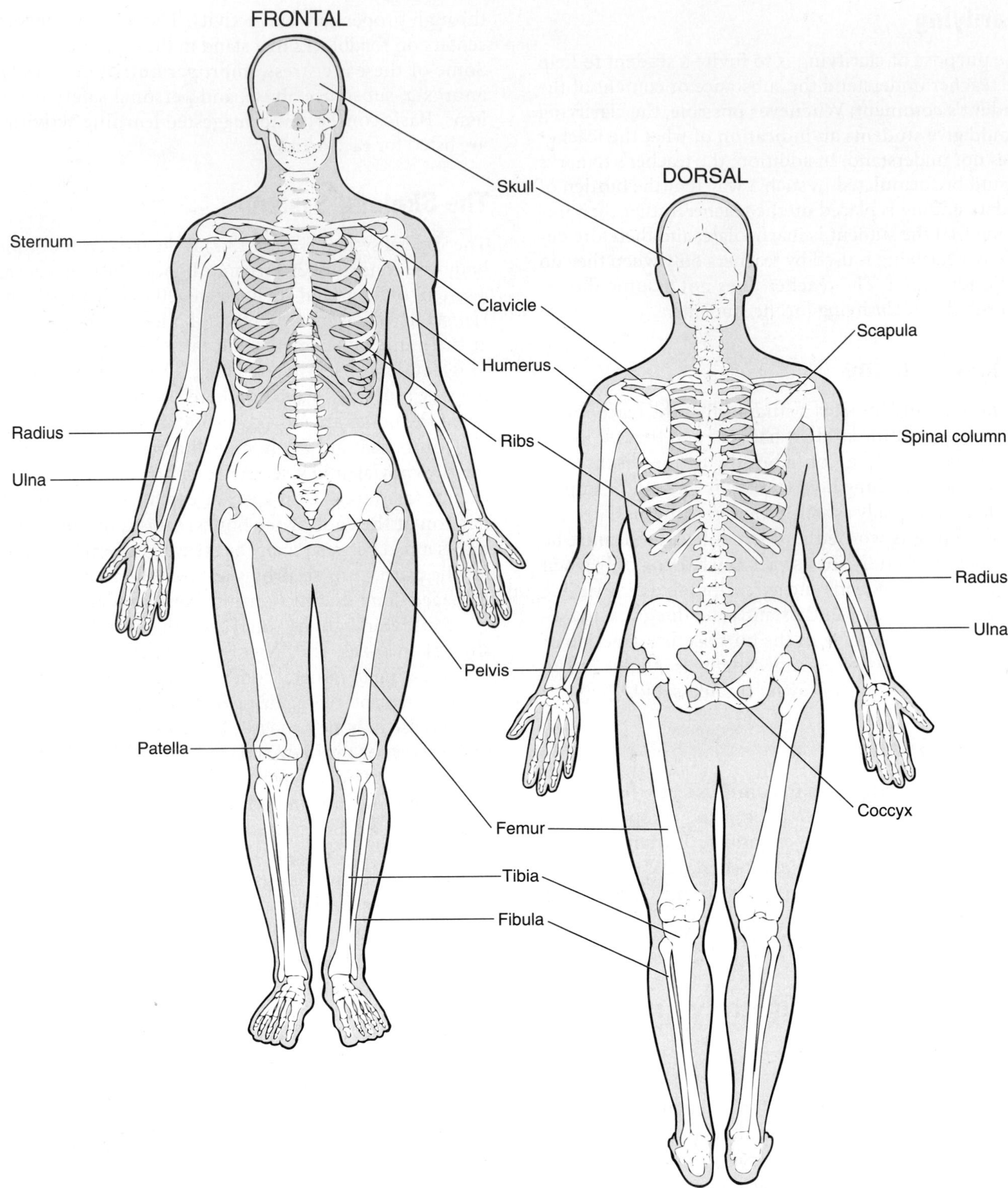

FIGURE 13.2 Skeletal system.

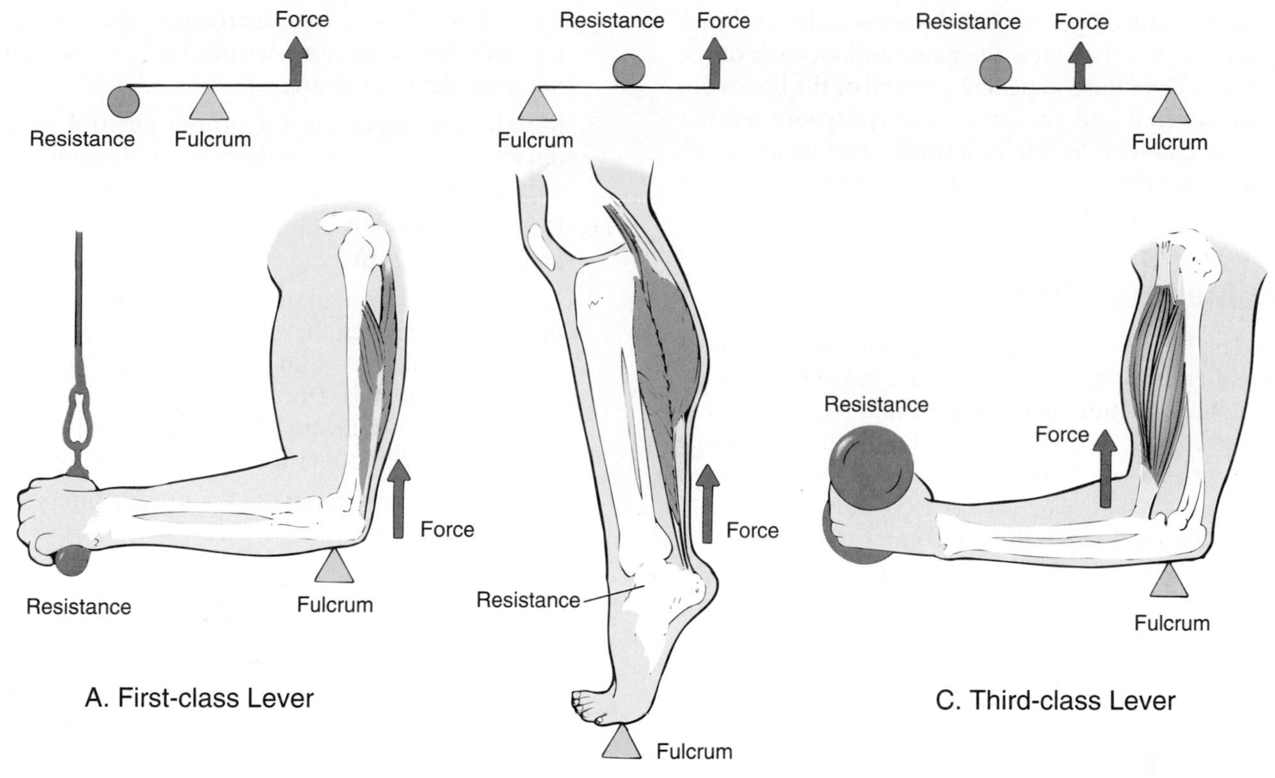

FIGURE 13.3 Types of levers in human joints.

2. Joints are places where two or more bones are fastened together to make a movable connection.
3. Bones are held together by ligaments and muscle tissue. The stronger the muscles surrounding the joint, the more resistant the joint is to injury.
4. Good posture results when the bones are in proper alignment. Alignment depends on the muscular system. When antigravity muscles are weak, greater stress is put on the joints, and poor posture results.
5. The bones and joints establish levers with muscles serving as the force.
6. The attachment of the muscle to the bone determines the mechanical advantage that can be gained at the joint. Generally, the farther from the joint the muscle attaches, the greater the force that can be generated.
7. The body has three types of levers. These are classified by the arrangement of the fulcrum, force, and resistance.

Suggested Learning Experiences

1. Identify and locate major bones significant in body movement. The following are suggested:
   a. head-skull
   b. arm-shoulder, girdle-radius, ulna, ribs, humerus, scapula (shoulder blade), clavicle (collarbone)
   c. chest-sternum (breastbone), ribs
   d. back-pelvis-spinal column, pelvis, coccyx
   e. thigh-leg-femur, tibia, fibula, patella (kneecap)
2. Identify the types of movement possible at selected joints. Study the neck, shoulder, elbow, wrist, spinal column, hip, knee, and ankle joints.
3. Catalog the types of levers found in the body. Illustrate the fulcrum, force, and resistance points.
4. Obtain animal bones from a grocery store and analyze their various components. Cartilage, muscle attachments, ligaments, and bone structure can be studied in this way.
5. Obtain outdated X-ray films from physicians. These are excellent sources for identifying differences in various bones and joints.
6. Discuss how levers in the body generate force for throwing, striking, and kicking.
7. Vary the size of the base of support and evaluate its effect on stability.
8. Develop a "Bone of the Month" bulletin board. Drawings similar to Figure 13.2 can be made and displayed in the gymnasium. Choose one bone to

be introduced per month. After each class, or once a week, briefly review the name and location of the bone. Over the course of 2 years all of the bones can be covered and reviewed. The classroom teacher may also wish to display a similar picture and work with the physical education teacher to reinforce the bones being learned during physical education.

The Muscular System

Muscles (Figure 13.4, page 283) apply force to the bones to create movement. Muscles create movement always through contraction, never by pushing. When one set of muscles contracts, another set that pulls in the opposite direction relaxes. This set is the *antagonistic muscle group.*

People are born with two distinct types of muscle fiber. These are often called slow-twitch and fast-twitch fibers. Slow-twitch fibers respond well to aerobic activities, whereas fast-twitch fibers are suited to anaerobic activities. This is one of the reasons people perform differently in different physical activities. For example, those born with a high percentage of slow-twitch fibers would be suited to distance running but might do poorly in sprint races.

Strength can be increased when muscles are overloaded. Overload occurs when a person does more than a normal amount of work. In young people, strength can be increased without a change in the muscle size. Exercises should overload as many muscle groups as possible to ensure total body development. Strength is an important factor in the development of motor skills.

Flexibility is the range of motion possible at a given joint. Exercises should apply resistance through the full range of motion to maintain flexibility. Extensor and flexor muscle groups are antagonists to each other, and both groups should be exercised equally.

Requisite Knowledge

1. Muscles can pull and shorten (contract); they never push.
2. Flexors cause a decrease in joint angle, and extensors cause an increase. There should be a balance of development between these antagonistic muscle groups.
3. The fixed portion of a muscle (origin) usually has muscle fibers attached directly to the bone or may be attached by a tendon to the bone. The moving portion of the muscle forms a tendon, which attaches to a bone (insertion).
4. Overload with proper progression is necessary for muscle development. Muscles become strong in both boys and girls through exercise. After adolescence, boys' muscles will increase in size owing to the male hormone testosterone. Girls' muscles do not show the same degree of increase.
5. Muscles are important for proper posture. Good muscle tone makes good posture comfortable and puts a minimum amount of strain on the joints.
6. Different types of training are necessary for aerobic and anaerobic activity.
7. Muscles are composed of many small fibers. When these fibers contract, they do so according to the all-or-none principle—that is, if they contract, they contract completely. Differences in the contraction strength of a muscle are a function of the percentage of muscle fibers recruited and asked to contract.
8. When muscles are fatigued, the muscle fibers will no longer contract.

Suggested Learning Experiences

1. Identify major muscles or muscle groups and their functions at the joint. Muscle groups suggested for elaboration are the following:
   a. head-neck-sternocleidomastoids
   b. arm-shoulder girdle-biceps, triceps, pectorals, deltoid, latissimus dorsi, trapezius
   c. body-abdominals (rectus abdominis and the obliques)
   d. thigh-leg-gluteus, hamstrings, rectus femoris (the quadriceps), gastrocnemius, soleus, sartorius
2. Learn the significance of the suffix -ceps in biceps, triceps, and quadriceps. The suffix refers to the points of origin (heads). The biceps has two points of origin (heads), the triceps has three, and the quadriceps has four.
3. The Achilles and patellar tendons should be identified. How the Achilles tendon got its name makes an interesting story. Achilles's mother dipped the infant Achilles in the River Styx to make him immune from arrows. Unfortunately, she held him by the heel cord, thus preventing that area from coming into contact with the magic water. Achilles was later killed by an arrow that hit his one vulnerable spot, hence the name Achilles tendon.
4. The sartorius muscle is called the tailor's muscle, because years ago, tailors sat cross-legged while sewing, thus causing the muscle to shorten. The tailors then had trouble making ordinary leg movements because of the shortened muscle.
5. Know approximately where each muscle originates and how it causes movement at the joint by attaching to a particular bone or bones. Recognize the muscles being developed by various exercises.

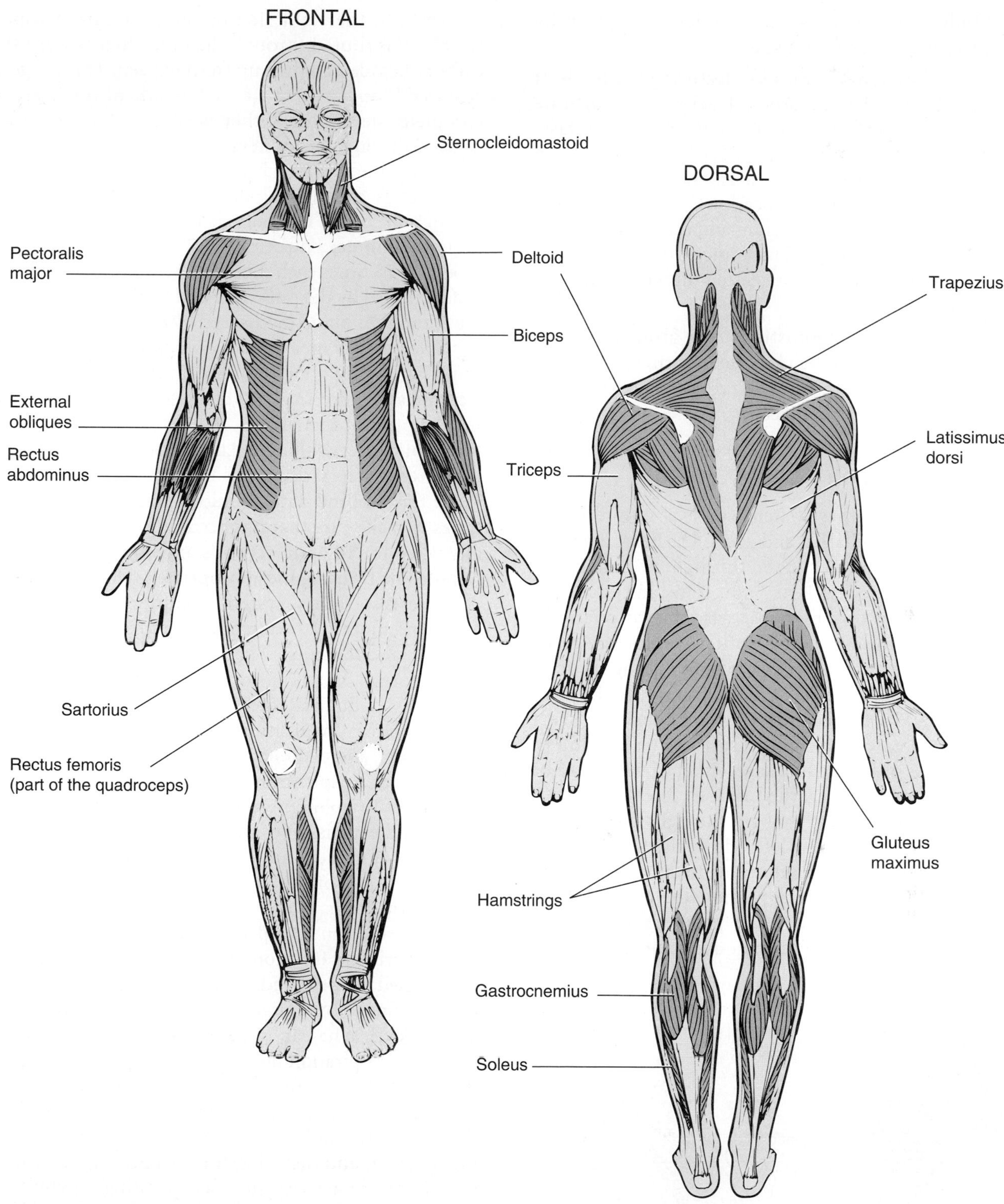

FIGURE 13.4 Muscular system.

6. Study animal muscle under a microscope. Identify various parts of the muscle.
7. Involve students in a project featuring a "Muscle of the Month." The classroom teacher can cooperate by presenting basic facts about the muscle in classroom work. The physical education teacher can make drawings showing the anatomy of the muscle (origin, insertion, and location) (Figure 13.5) and post these in the gymnasium and classroom. Pay attention to spelling and pronunciation. Over a two-year period, all of the suggested muscle groups can be studied.
8. Discuss how antagonistic muscle groups contract and relax alternately to cause movement. Identify which muscles are relaxed and which are contracting when movement occurs.

The Cardiorespiratory System

The cardiorespiratory system consists of the heart, lungs, arteries, capillaries, and veins. The heart is a muscular organ that pumps blood through the circulatory system—arteries, capillaries, and veins, in that order. The heart has its own blood vessels—the coronary arteries—that nourish it to keep it alive, for the heart draws no nourishment from the blood going through the chambers as it pumps. The blood supply to the heart is critical, and a decreased flow can damage the heart muscle. Decreased flow may result from a buildup of fatty deposits or from a blockage, either of which can be serious enough to be regarded as heart disease.

The heart has two chambers, the right and left ventricles (Figure 13.6). The left side of the heart pumps blood carrying nutrients and oxygen to the body through the arteries to the capillaries, where the nutrients and oxygen are exchanged for waste products and carbon dioxide. The waste-carrying blood is returned through the veins to the right side of the heart, from which the blood is routed through the lungs to discharge the carbon dioxide and pick up fresh oxygen. This oxygen-renewed blood returns to the left side of the heart to complete the circuit. Other waste products are discharged through the kidneys.

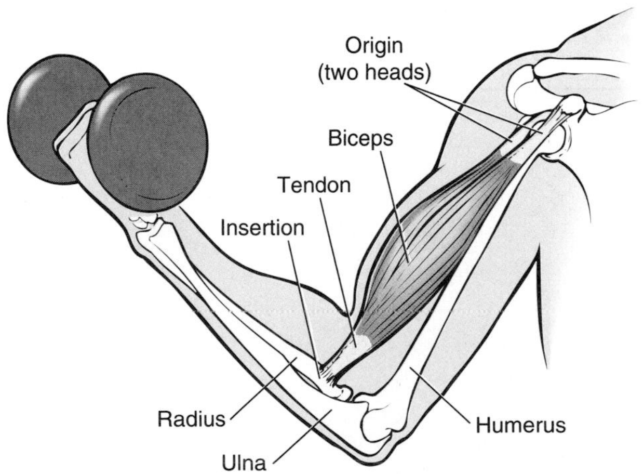

FIGURE 13.5 Anatomy of a muscle.

Each time the heart beats, it pumps both chambers. The beat is called the *pulse,* and its impact travels through the body. The pulse is measured in number of beats per minute: a pulse rate of 75 means that the heart is beating 75 times each minute. The output of the heart is determined by the pulse rate and by the *stroke volume,* the amount of blood discharged by each beat.

The pulse is measured by placing the two middle fingers of the right hand on the thumb side of the subject's wrist (Figure 13.7) while the subject is seated. Taking the pulse at the wrist is usually preferable to using the carotid artery (along the neck), because pressure on the carotid artery decreases blood flow to the brain. Pulse for baseline data should be taken two or three times to make sure that it is accurate. The pulse is usually taken for 10 or 15 seconds and converted to a per minute rate by using the appropriate multiplier.

The respiratory system includes the entryways (nose and mouth), the trachea (windpipe), the primary bronchi, and the lungs. Figure 13.8 shows components of the system. Breathing consists of inhaling and exhaling air. Air contains 21 percent oxygen, which is necessary for life. Inspiration is assisted by muscular contraction, and expiration is accomplished by relaxing the muscles. Inspiration occurs when the intercostal muscles and diaphragm contract. This enlarges the chest cavity, and expansion of the lungs causes air to flow in as a result of reduced air pressure. When the muscles are relaxed, the size of the chest cavity is reduced, the pressure on the lungs is increased, and air flows from the lungs. Air also can be expelled forcibly.

The primary function of the lungs is to provide oxygen, carried by the bloodstream, to the cells on demand. The amount of oxygen needed will vary depending on activity level. When an individual exercises strenuously, the rate of respiration increases to bring more oxygen to the tissues. If the amount of oxygen carried to the cells is adequate to maintain the level of activity, the activity is termed *aerobic* (endurance) exercise. Examples are walking, jogging, and bicycling for distance. If, because of high-intensity activity such as sprinting or climbing stairs, not enough oxygen can be brought to the cells, the body continues to operate for a short time without oxygen. This results in an oxygen debt, which must be repaid later. In this case, the activity is termed *anaerobic* exercise.

After exercise, the respiratory rate gradually returns to normal. The recovery rate is faster if the oxygen debt built up during exercise was a small one. An individual has recovered from an oxygen debt when blood pres-

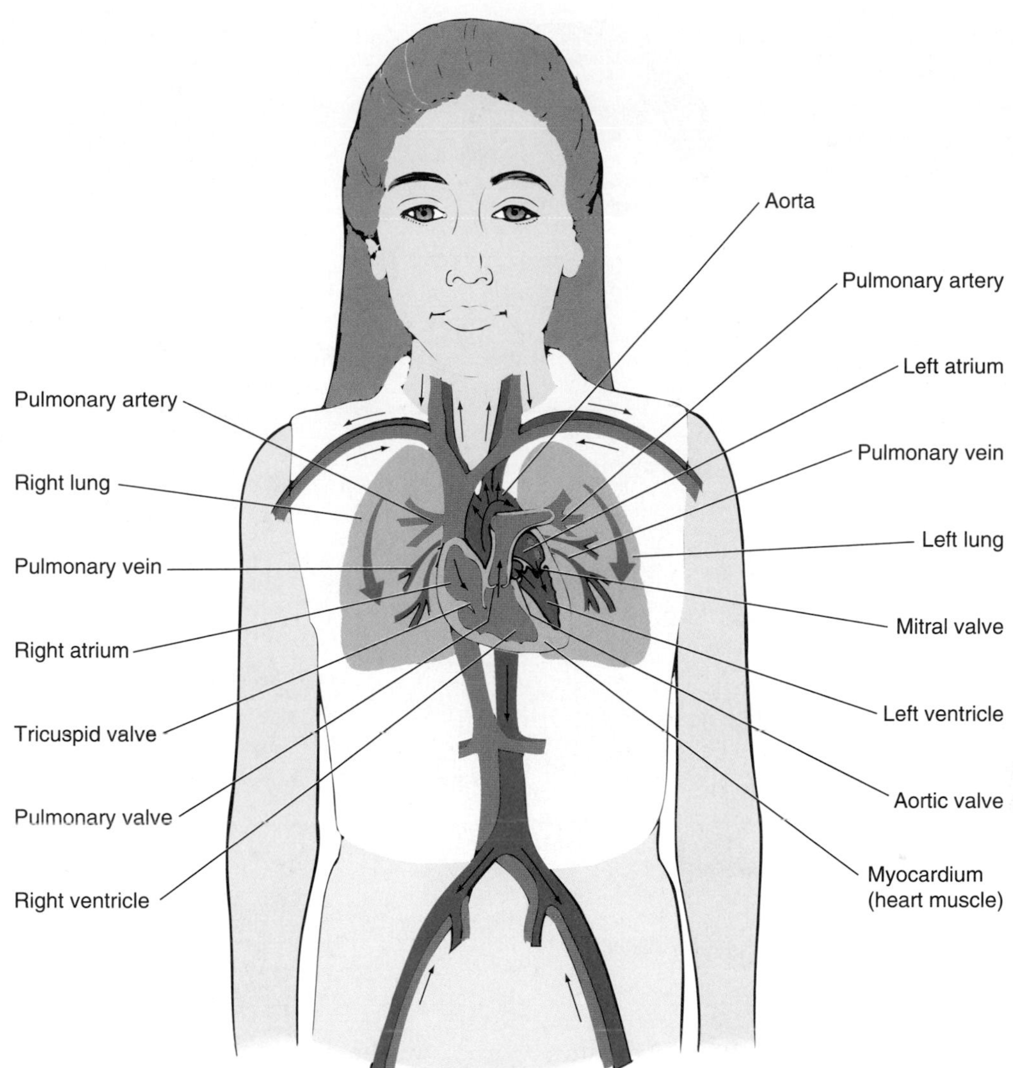

FIGURE 13.6 Structure of the heart (from the American Heart Association).

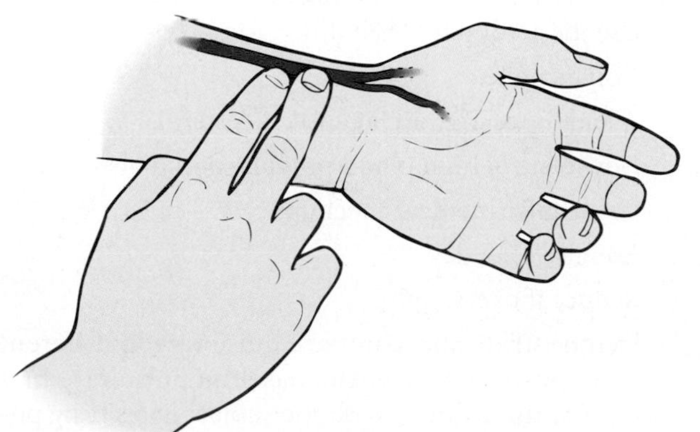

FIGURE 13.7 Taking the pulse at the wrist.

sure, heart rate, and respiration rate have returned to pre-exercise levels.

Requisite Knowledge

1. The heart is a muscular organ, and its development and maintenance are a function of the demands placed on it through exercise.
2. The heart beats faster when a person exercises.
3. An important factor in establishing cardiorespiratory conditioning is regular exercise. Regular exercise produces a training effect that results in a decreased resting heart rate and an increased stroke volume (the amount of blood the heart pumps each time it beats) due to hypertrophy of the heart muscle. If the training effect is to occur, the heart rate must be

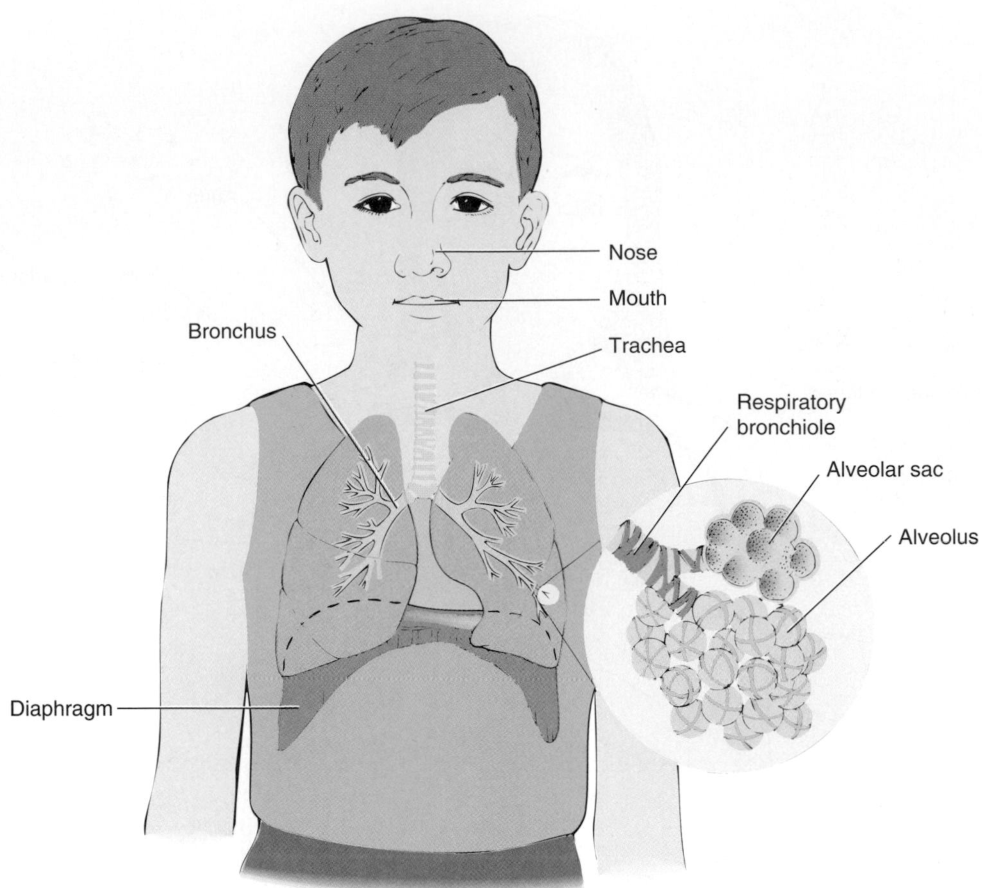

FIGURE 13.8 Components of the respiratory system.

elevated to the training zone for 10 to 20 minutes. (See suggested learning experience 7, following.)

4. Through exercise and training, the respiratory system is able to move more oxygen into the body because of an increase in the strength and endurance of the respiratory muscles.
5. The pulse rate varies depending on the level of fitness and other variables. Heart rate among girls usually averages 10 beats per minute more than among boys. As children grow older, their heart rate decreases. Fear, excitement, or a change in body position also affect the resting heart rate.
6. Cardiorespiratory conditioning is important for children. Many circulation and respiratory disorders in adults have a childhood origin.
7. Increased levels of cholesterol and other fats in the blood cause buildup of fatty deposits in the coronary arteries.
8. Some factors (such as heredity, sex, race, and age) affect the cardiorespiratory system, but are impossible to control. Risk can be minimized, however, by controlling other factors such as smoking, body weight, diet, blood pressure level, and amount of regular exercise.
9. The immediate effects of exercise are to increase the rate of breathing and the volume of air brought into the lungs.

Suggested Learning Experiences

1. Emphasize the risk factors of cardiovascular disease. Use the acronym DANGER.

   *D*on't smoke.

   *A*void foods high in fat and cholesterol.

   *N*ow control high blood pressure and diabetes.

   *G*et regular medical checkups.

   *E*xercise each day.

   *R*educe if overweight.
2. Demonstrate and compare pulse rate in different body positions. Take the baseline pulse rate first (two or three times) with the subject in a sitting position. Take the pulse rate with the subject standing and lying down (Figure 13.9).

FIGURE 13.9 Students checking their pulse rate.

3. Using a single subject, show the relationship between exercise and heart action. Take the resting pulse and record it on the chalkboard. Have the subject run in place for 1 minute. Take the pulse rate immediately for 10 seconds and record it. Continue taking the pulse at five 2-minute intervals to demonstrate recovery rate. (The pulse rate is approximately doubled after the stipulated exercise.) Discuss why pulse rate increases with exercise and how the heart is strengthened through regular exercise.
4. Take the blood pressure immediately after exercise and again after resting for 3 minutes. Compare the difference.
5. To show how excess weight affects an individual, use two subjects of the same sex who are similar in build. Take the baseline pulse rate for each and record it. Give one subject 15 pounds in added weight (use two 7½-pound weights) and have both subjects travel back and forth ten times across the width of the gym. Immediately take the pulse rates and record them. Compare the rates of the two subjects.
6. Compare pulse rate changes after different kinds of exercise—walking, running, rope jumping, and rope climbing. Standardize the exercise time factor at 1 or 2 minutes.
7. Calculate the heartbeat range that should be maintained to achieve the training effect and to ensure that the individual is not under- or overexercising. To do this, first determine the estimated maximum heart rate by taking 220 minus the student's age, then multiply the difference by 60 percent and by 80 percent. An example for a child of age 10 follows.

   220 minus 10 = 210

   60 percent of 210 = 126

   80 percent of 210 = 168

   The heart rate range for this student to maintain while exercising is 126 to 168. The pulse rate should be checked during exercise to see whether the training effect is occurring. Charts showing exercising heart rate ranges should be placed on bulletin boards in the gymnasium so that students can quickly translate the results.
8. Compare respiration rates before and after exercise.
9. Compare the volume of air moved before and after strenuous activity. Large plastic garbage bags can be used to collect expired air prior to exercise. After 2 minutes of exercise, expired air can be gathered in another bag. Compare the volume of air collected in the two bags.
10. Allow youngsters to listen to their heartbeats with a stethoscope. Have them exercise for a minute or two and listen to their heartbeats again.
11. Create an outline of the human body and appropriate size cutouts of major organs of the body. Each month a new organ is attached to the outline in the appropriate location and the organ is discussed. Comments regarding the organ's function and importance should be included. This discussion is then reviewed periodically throughout the month.

AVOID ROADBLOCKS TO WELLNESS

Wellness involves knowing what activities to avoid as well as what to do. Teaching about these activities should not be done by preaching and telling students what they should or should not do. Instead, place emphasis on showing students the pros and cons of various practices and the consequences of making certain decisions. The ultimate decision and responsibility rest with the student, not the teacher.

This section includes stress, nutrition and weight control, substance abuse, and personal safety. All are areas where behavior can be modified to enhance the quality of life. Students can make decisions in these areas that affect how they live and, sometimes, whether they will live.

Stress

Stress is the body's reaction to certain situations in life. Everyone experiences some stress. Stress, by itself, is probably not harmful, but handling stress is critical in determining the impact it will have on one's life. Many students are affected by stress. Often, students are seen as carefree and without worries. Quite the opposite is usually the case. Students live under the stress of parental and teacher expectations, peer pressure, and the necessity of becoming an independent being. If teachers appreciate that students are subject to stress, they can begin to deal with students in ways that alleviate possible stressors and allow for stress release. In this way, teachers can have an impact on the students' self-concept and their world view.

Psychologically, stress can take the form of excitement, fear, or anger. Physical changes also accompany psychological stress. For example, heart rate increases, blood pressure rises, ventilation rate increases, perspiration increases, body temperature may rise, and the pupils may dilate. This response to stress once aided human beings in survival and is labeled the "fight or flight" syndrome. When a situation arises that may cause one harm, the body's endocrine system prepares it to fight or to flee the situation. People often speak of the "adrenaline flowing" when they are scared or worried about upcoming situations.

Unfortunately, our society and schools offer few opportunities to relieve tension through activity, and few individuals find the motivation to do so. The resulting tension and stress that build up cause individuals to expend a great deal of energy in unproductive ways. People often feel fatigued when they are unable to release stress. Many nervous habits, such as constant movement while sitting, playing with an item in the hands, and various facial twitches, are the body's attempts to relieve tension.

The ultimate question when dealing with stress might be: "What does it matter if I'm under stress? All people are." It matters because excessive stress has many detrimental effects on the body. It increases the risk of heart disease and can lead to insomnia and hypertension. Indigestion is common in stressed individuals, as is constipation. Many backaches and general body aches originate through stress. Doctors are diagnosing more and more "psychosomatic" diseases that have no physical prognosis and appear to be caused by stress. Another serious problem associated with unrelieved stress is the tendency of individuals to try to cope by using substances such as alcohol, tobacco, and drugs.

Individuals who exhibit Type A behavior are much more likely to suffer from the ill effects of stress. Students need to learn to identify Type A behavior and to understand various methods of modifying it to achieve more productive patterns.

Type A behavior is characterized by some of the following patterns:

1. Moving everywhere rapidly, even when it is unnecessary.
2. Feeling bored and impatient with classes and how things are being done by others.
3. Trying to do 2 or more things simultaneously. (This is referred to as polyphasic thought or action.)
4. Having to always feel busy and feeling uneasy when time is taken to do nothing or to do something relaxing.
5. Needing to do everything faster and more efficiently than everyone else.
6. Exhibiting many strong gestures such as clenching the fists, banging a hand on the table, or dramatically waving the arms.

Learning to cope with stressful situations is important. The first step involves developing an awareness of what types of situations cause stress. Sharing situations with others often releases the tension and allows students to feel that they are "normal" and are maturing properly. In the physical education setting, emphasis should be placed on the role that activity can play in stress reduction. Involvement in enjoyable and success-oriented physical activities can decrease tension. This involvement has a side effect because the required concentration will provide a diversion from worries and stressors. Note, however, that if the activity is not enjoyable and if the student consistently fails to find success, the level of stress may actually increase.

Some experts believe that exercise applies stress to the body in a systematic fashion and thus prepares the individual to deal with other stressful situations. One goal of teachers should be to provide a variety of activities and to help students select activities that will be productive and meaningful ways of relieving tension.

Another beneficial strategy is to teach various relaxation techniques that help relieve general body stress. These are discussed in a later section in this chapter.

Requisite Knowledge

1. Stress affects all individuals to varying degrees. Some stress is necessary to stimulate performance and increase motivation.
2. The amount of stress one is able to cope with depends on how it is perceived. Positive self-concepts help people accept threatening situations in a less stressful manner.
3. When people have difficulty dealing with stress through productive methods, such as exercise, relaxation activities, and talking with friends, they often attempt to relieve stress through unhealthy and potentially dangerous means, such as alcohol, tobacco, and drug usage.
4. Stress causes changes in perceptible bodily functions. An awareness of these changes is necessary if students are to recognize when they are under stress and need to cope with its effects.
5. Stress appears to increase susceptibility to many diseases and causes psychosomatic illnesses.
6. Exercise is an excellent way to relieve stress and tension when the activity is perceived as enjoyable and success-oriented.
7. Stress is a critical risk factor that influences the onset of heart disease. Type A behavior is accompanied by an increased risk of heart disease.
8. There are different ways of relieving stress, among them are exercise, expressing feelings to friends, developing problem-solving skills, and performing accepted relaxation techniques.

Suggested Learning Experiences

1. Hold an isometric contraction at the elbow joint. With the other hand, feel the contraction in the biceps and triceps. Repeat the activity with other muscle groups. Discuss how stress causes generalized body tension that can result in tensed muscles and an increase in general body fatigue. Learning to recognize muscle tension is a desired outcome of this discussion.
2. Discuss the concept of "choking" under pressure. How does this relate to athletic performance? What happens when stress is greater than the individual's ability to cope with it? Discuss how some stress increases performance, while too much decreases it.
3. Discuss the importance of perception in stressful situations. How is stress perceived? Should students face up and admit it when they are worried or scared? Is it better to be "tough" and not tell anyone how they feel? Is it better to keep emotions inside or to share feelings with others?
4. Discuss the importance of finding activities in which students believe they are successful. How are positive self-concepts developed? Why are some people able to cope with failure and losing better than others?
5. Discuss situations in physical activity settings that give rise to increased stress, such as failing in front of others, not being selected for a team, being ridiculed for a poor performance, or losing a game that was personally important. How could these situations be handled differently?
6. Discuss the parameters of Type A behavior patterns. How can they be modified through activity and changes in behavior? Why do people develop Type A behavior? Are Type A behavior patterns productive?
7. Identify physical activities that seem to relieve tension and stress. Discuss the relationship between involvement in activity and the reduction of stress.
8. Identify and discuss unproductive attempts to relieve stress such as drinking, smoking, and drug abuse. Why are these methods chosen rather than exercise, discussions, or relaxation activities?
9. Discuss the many effects of stress on bodily health. Give students a stress inventory to see how much stress they are under and discuss ways of reducing this pressure.
10. Teach relaxation techniques such as deep breathing, progressive muscle relaxation, and personal meditation. Emphasize the importance of taking time for these activities daily. Just as brushing the teeth is necessary for healthy dentition, relaxation is necessary for a healthy body and mind.

Nutrition and Weight Control

Proper nutrition is necessary if students are to expect a high level of physical performance from their body. An important area of concern deals with the balance between caloric intake and expenditure in order to maintain proper weight control. Students should understand the reasons and methods for maintaining an optimum level of body weight. Discuss the impact of empty calories through excessive ingestion of junk foods. Explain the importance of a balanced diet to help the body grow and develop. Point out that the role of exercise in weight control and muscle development is as important as a balanced diet.

Students should learn about the elements of a balanced diet. A balanced diet draws from each of the basic

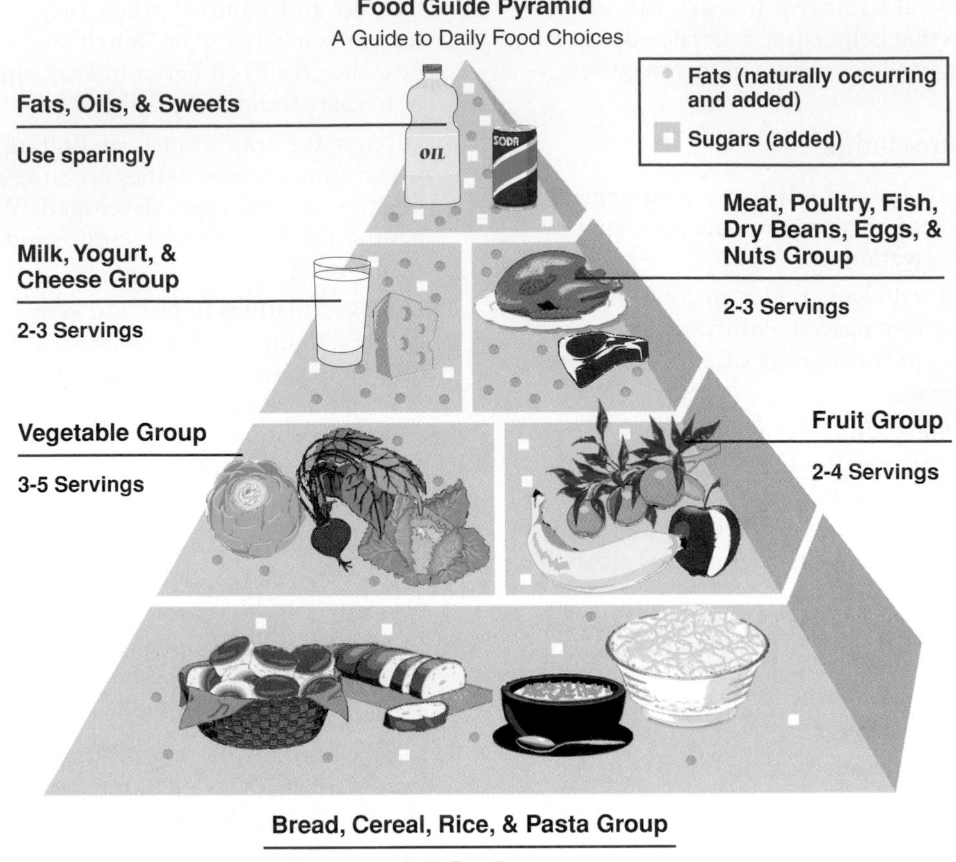

FIGURE 13.10 Food Guide Pyramid.
To order a copy of the Food Guide Pyramid or to download a copy, contact: Center for Nutrition Policy and Promotion, 1120 20th Street NW, Suite 200, North Lobby, Washington, DC 20036, (202) 606-8000, World Wide Web: http://www.usda.gov/cnpp/

food groups. Figure 13.10 is the food guide pyramid developed by the U.S. Department of Agriculture (1996). The pyramid illustrates how the most food should be eaten from the bread, cereal, rice, and pasta group. The smallest number of calories should be ingested from the fats, oils, and sweets group.

Foods high in cholesterol and fat should be consumed moderately. Some cholesterol and fat are necessary for proper body function. When too much fat is ingested, however, cholesterol and triglyceride levels in the blood plasma increase. This increase is probably detrimental to the body, for many studies have shown a relationship between high cholesterol and triglyceride levels and coronary heart disease. To travel in the bloodstream, fats must combine with water-soluble protein molecules called lipoproteins, which have an important effect on cholesterol and triglyceride levels. Some of these compound molecules are of a type called high-density lipoproteins (HDL), which are associated with a decreased risk of cardiovascular disease. Because polyunsaturated fats appear to increase HDL levels, the general recommendation is to include some polyunsaturates in the diet. Students should know which foods are high in saturated and unsaturated fats and should be encouraged to have their cholesterol levels monitored by a physician.

Depending on the criteria used, anywhere from 30 to 50 percent of students are overweight, meaning that their body weight is over the accepted limits for their age, sex, and body build. It is important for students to begin to develop an awareness of the caloric content of foods as well as the nutritional value. They can then begin to count calories and practice consistency in the amount of calories they ingest. Coupled with this awareness should be some comprehension of the number of calories expended through various types of physical activity (Figure 13.11). Students need to understand that when caloric intake exceeds caloric expenditure, obesity results. A well-documented and common cause of obesity is inactivity. Most experts believe that obese students do not eat more than normal weight students; rather, they exercise less.

Obesity is a roadblock to wellness. Life insurance companies view overweight people as poor risks because of their shorter life expectancy. Excessive body fat makes the heart work harder, increases the chance of having high blood pressure, and lowers the possibility of recovery from a heart attack. Even more detrimental to students is the psychological impact that obesity has on self-concept development. Students of normal weight find it much easier to perform physical tasks because strength in relationship to body weight is a critical performance factor. Overweight students are often punished more severely than normal weight students for the same type of deviance and may receive lower grades for a similar quality of work.

Activity	Calories per Hour
Moderate activity	*200–350*
Bicycling (5½ mph)	210
Walking (2½ mph)	210
Gardening	220
Canoeing (2½ mph)	230
Golf	250
Lawn mowing (power mower)	250
Lawn mowing (hand mower)	270
Bowling	270
Fencing	300
Rowboating (2½ mph)	300
Swimming (¼ mph)	300
Walking (3¾ mph)	300
Badminton	350
Horseback riding (trotting)	350
Square dancing	350
Volleyball	350
Roller skating	350
Vigorous activity	*Over 350*
Table Tennis	360
Ice skating (10 mph)	400
Tennis	420
Water skiing	480
Hill climbing (100 ft/hr)	490
Skiing (10 mph)	600
Squash and handball	600
Cycling (13 mph)	660
Scull rowing (race)	840
Running (10 mph)	900

FIGURE 13.11 Caloric expenditure.
Adapted from material from the President's Council on Physical Fitness and Sports, Washington, DC.

Requisite Knowledge

1. Diet should be balanced and contain foods from each of the 4 basic groups. This ensures that the body will receive essential nutrients.
2. Caloric expenditure (body functions plus exercise) and intake (eating) must be balanced to maintain a healthy weight. A weight-reducing program should include a reduction in caloric intake and an increase in daily exercise.
3. Activities vary in the energy they require. Individual needs must be considered in the selection of activities to promote weight control and physical fitness maintenance.
4. Junk foods add little if any nutritional value to the diet and are usually high in calories. Foods such as sugar, margarine and butter, oils, and alcohol are high in calories but make little or no contribution in terms of nutrition.
5. Excessive weight makes performing physical tasks difficult. This results in less success and in less motivation to be active, thus increasing the tendency toward obesity.
6. Obesity increases the risk of heart disease and other related diseases such as diabetes.
7. A majority of obesity cases are caused by inactivity or lack of sufficient activity. The majority of overweight students do not consume more calories than normal weight students; they are simply less active.
8. Vitamins are not nutrients but are catalysts that facilitate metabolic processes. Certain vitamin deficiencies can produce various diseases.
9. Various foods are excellent sources of specific nutrients. Students should be able to identify which foods to ingest to provide a balance of the needed nutrients, vitamins, and minerals.

Suggested Learning Experiences

1. Post a list of activities and their energy demands on the bulletin board. Discuss the need for selecting activities that will burn enough calories to balance caloric intake.
2. Maintain a food diary. Record all the foods eaten daily and the amount of calories in each. Compare the amount of calories ingested with the amount of calories expended.
3. Maintain a nutritious-food diary. Record all the foods eaten daily and categorize each by food group. Determine the percentage of carbohydrates, proteins, and fats in relation to all the food ingested during each day.
4. Develop a desirable and practical balanced diet that can be followed for 1 week. Arrange with parents to facilitate the diet within their budget restrictions.
5. Calculate the Recommended Daily Allowance (RDA) for various nutrients. Compare a daily intake with the recommendations for various minerals and vitamins.

6. Bring various foods to class that have labels offering nutrition information. Determine which foods are good buys for desired nutrients.
7. Develop an activity diary. For 1 week, record all activity over and above maintenance activities. Calculate the number of calories burned per day.
8. Discuss and analyze the ways in which society rewards physically fit individuals. Contrast these with the ways in which obese people are discriminated against in various situations.

Substance Abuse

Substance abuse is defined as the harmful use of alcohol, tobacco, or drugs. It is common in today's schools as students seek different ways to explore an expanding world. If students are expected to make wise and meaningful decisions in this area, they must understand the impact of various substances on their physical and psychological being. Facts, both pro and con, should be presented in a nonjudgmental environment, without moralizing and preaching. It is difficult for students to make personal decisions if most of the information they receive is from peers or moralizing adults.

Alcohol, tobacco, and drugs deter wellness and are usually detrimental to total health. The use and misuse of these substances should be discussed objectively with students because much of the information they receive is from biased sources, such as parents, peers, and various media formats. The physical education teacher can promote unbiased discussions and fact-seeking sessions that relate to wellness. Many times, the physical educator is the only person oriented to wellness promotion. As mentioned earlier, however, if the instructor feels strongly that an issue has only 1 acceptable point of view, then discussions should be avoided. Telling students only the reasons why not to do something can result in a strong polarization in the opposite direction.

Alcohol has both short-term and long-term effects. Short-term effects vary as a result of the depressant effect that alcohol has on the central nervous system. Some people become relaxed, others become aggressive, and some become active in differing degrees. Ultimately, a lack of coordination and confusion occur if a great deal of alcohol is ingested. The long-term effects of alcohol abuse may be liver damage, heart disease, and malnutrition. The greatest concern surrounding long-term drinking is the possibility of alcoholism. Most agree that alcoholism has the following components: loss of control of alcohol intake, presence of functional or structural damage (physical and psychological), and dependence on alcohol to maintain an acceptable level of functioning.

Students usually drink for any of the following reasons: curiosity, desire to celebrate with parents, peer pressure, to be like adults and appear more mature, to rebel against the adult world, because their models or admired adults drink, or because they are alcoholics. Students are often ambivalent about alcohol. They know its detrimental effects, and yet they see many of their friends and role models using it. The problem is a difficult one, and an understanding of both moderate use and abstinence is needed. An understanding of how to cope with peer pressure to drink alcohol is also needed and is discussed in the next section on basic concepts.

Tobacco use is common among junior and senior high students. Smoking increases significantly the possibility of heart attacks, strokes, and cancer. Chronic bronchitis and emphysema are diseases prevalent among smokers. A recent study revealed that the average life span of long-term smokers is seven years shorter than that of nonsmokers.

Students need to understand the impact of smoking on a healthy body. Along with this knowledge, they should examine why so many people choose to smoke. Today, the fastest growing segment of the smoking population is young girls and women. Students will make the final decision for their individual behavior, but before they do so, they need to understand thoroughly the ramifications of smoking.

The use of marijuana and of hard-core drugs should also be discussed. Outside agencies are often most helpful in discussing substance abuse in an objective manner with students. The use of steroids, "pep pills," and pain relievers in athletics should also be debated. In each case, the intent should be to enhance students' awareness so they know the alternatives and consequences. Substance abuse is contrary to the whole concept of physical wellness. Physical educators need to accept the challenge of increasing student understanding and knowledge in these areas.

Requisite Knowledge

1. The earlier one begins to smoke, the greater the risk to functional health.
2. People smoke for psychological reasons.
3. Young people may choose substance abuse out of curiosity, for status reasons, or from peer pressure.
4. Choosing a lifestyle independently of peers requires great courage.
5. Decisions about substance abuse are poor decisions if they are based on a dearth of knowledge. Wise and purposeful decisions can be made only when all of the alternatives and consequences are understood.

6. Substance abuse is often an attempt to cope with stress-related problems. Exercise and relaxation are much more productive, healthy methods of coping.
7. The use of alcohol, tobacco, and drugs always carries the risk of addiction. When people are addicted, they are no longer in charge of their lifestyles. All people, to some degree, are subject to addiction; no one is immune.
8. Spending time and effort on developing personal competencies is more productive than substance abuse. Personal competency in many areas reduces the need to "be like everyone else," and contributes to a positive self-concept.
9. The use of harmful substances frequently reduces the pleasure one can receive from experiencing the world. Physical performance is often reduced because of substance abuse.
10. A person can drink and smoke and still excel at athletics, but maximum performance levels may be reduced and the ultimate effect on the athlete will be harmful. Students see many professional athletes who smoke and drink. They need to be aware that this happens, but they should understand that the choice is undesirable from a wellness standpoint.

Suggested Learning Experiences

1. Identify and discuss the reasons why people choose or choose not to become involved in substance abuse.
2. Discuss the importance of making personal decisions based on what is best for you. Why do we follow others and allow them to influence our decisions, even when those decisions are not in our best interest?
3. Develop a bulletin board that illustrates the many ways used by the tobacco, alcohol, and drug industries to try to get young people to buy their products. Reserve a spot for advertisements (if any can be found) that admonish and encourage students to abstain or moderate the use of various substances.
4. Students often see professional and college athletes smoking and drinking on television while hearing from teachers and coaches that these habits impair performance. Discuss why these athletes can perform at a high level even though they may drink or smoke.
5. Students often choose to be part of a peer group at any cost. Discuss how our society often respects and honors individuals who have the courage to go their own way. Examples might be Columbus, Helen Keller, Braille, and so forth.
6. Identify and discuss the ways in which people in our society choose to relieve and dissipate stress. Discuss productive releases of tension such as recreation, hobbies, and sports.
7. Bring in speakers who are knowledgeable about the effects and uses of alcohol, tobacco, and drugs. If necessary, bring in a pair of speakers who might debate both sides of an issue.
8. Develop visual aids that identify the various effects that alcohol, tobacco, and drugs have on the body.

Safety and First Aid

Safety and first aid have often been part of the physical education program because more accidents occur in physical education than in any other area of the school curriculum. Safety is an attitude and a concern for one's welfare and health. An accident is an unplanned event or act that may result in injury or death. Often, accidents occur when they could have been prevented. The following are the most common causes of accidents: lack of knowledge and understanding of risks; lack of skill and competence to perform tasks safely, such as riding a bike or driving a car; false sense of security that leads people to think that accidents happen only to others; fatigue or illness that affect physical and mental performance; drugs and alcohol; and strong emotional states (such as anger, fear, or worry) that cause people to do things they might not otherwise do.

Traffic accidents are an area in which many deaths could be prevented. Wearing seat belts reduces the risk of dying by 50 percent. Drinking alcohol while driving increases the risk of an accident 20-fold compared to not drinking. Another factor that has reduced the number of traffic deaths is the 55-mph speed limit. Since students are going to drive, driver education and an awareness of the possibility of serious injury should be a part of the wellness program.

Bicycles are another source of numerous accidents. Automobile drivers have difficulty seeing bicycles, and the resulting accidents are often serious. Students need to learn bicycle safety. The physical education setting is often the only place where this training occurs. Classes in bicycling for safety and fitness are usually well received by middle school and high school students.

Swimming-related accidents are the second leading cause of accidental death among young adults. More than 50 percent of all drownings occur when people unexpectedly find themselves in the water. Another major cause of death from drowning is alcohol ingestion. Swimming and drinking do not mix well. Physical education programs should encourage all students to learn to swim and to learn water safety rules at sometime during their school career.

Physical education and sports are sources of injury in the school setting. Proper safety procedures should be taught, as well as first-aid techniques. Students should know how to stop bleeding, treat shock, and administer mouth-to-mouth respiration and cardiopulmonary resuscitation (CPR). Many physical education programs now include a required unit of instruction dealing with these topics. It is estimated that 100,000 to 200,000 lives could be saved by bystanders if they knew CPR.

Requisite Knowledge

1. Accidents are unplanned events or acts that may result in injury or death. The majority of accidents could be avoided if people were adequately prepared and understood the necessary competencies and risks involved.
2. Wearing seat belts and not drinking alcohol while driving will dramatically decrease the risk of death by automobile accident.
3. Bicycles are often not seen by car drivers. Bicycling safety classes can help lower the number of bicycle accidents.
4. Swimming-related accidents are the second leading cause of accidental death among young people. Water-safety programs and avoiding alcohol will dramatically decrease the risk of death by drowning.
5. Many thousands of lives could be saved if all people knew how to perform CPR.
6. All students should know how to stop bleeding and how to administer mouth-to-mouth respiration and CPR.
7. Basic first-aid procedures to prevent further injury to victims are competencies that all students should possess.

Suggested Learning Experiences

1. Discuss the causes of different types of accidents and how many accidents could be avoided.
2. Identify the types of accidents that happen to different age groups and why this appears to be the case.
3. Identify the role of alcohol and drugs in causing accidents. Why are these substances used in recreational settings?
4. Develop a bulletin board that illustrates how to care for shock victims. Practice the steps in a mock procedure.
5. Have an "accident day" when various types of accidents are staged that demand such treatments as stopping bleeding, mouth-to-mouth respiration, and CPR.
6. Outline the steps to follow in case of a home fire. Discuss how many fires could be prevented.
7. Conduct a bicycle safety fair. Have students design bulletin boards and displays that explain and emphasize bicycle safety.

ENHANCE STUDENT WELLNESS

It is apparent that the wellness of students can be seriously impaired when safety issues are dealt with incorrectly. However, proper nutrition, avoiding substance abuse, and practicing proper safety when bicycling or driving a car can enhance the wellness of participants. The purpose of this section is to help students further advance their wellness status through positive action rather than by simply avoiding various foods, substances, and situations. This section takes a 3-pronged approach: (1) physical fitness and activity, (2) stress reduction, and (3) self-evaluation. None of the areas will be covered in its entirety since many in-depth sources are available. A highly recommended source for helping students develop lifetime fitness is the text by Corbin and Lindsey (2002).

Physical Fitness and Activity

There are 2 types of physical fitness that are generally identified (pages 231–235). The first is skill-related physical fitness and the other is health-related fitness. See Chapter 12 for in-depth coverage about how to develop both types of fitness. A part of physical education should be used to teach students how to develop a health-related fitness plan they can use to monitor themselves throughout their lives. The basic steps for such a plan are as follows:

1. Identify present areas of fitness and weakness by pretesting. Many tests can be used to evaluate the 5 components of health-related fitness.
2. Identify the present activities that the students are performing by having them fill out a survey that lists a wide variety of activities. Post a chart that shows the components of health-related fitness enhanced by each activity. A good source for surveys and lists of activity benefits is *Fitness for Life* by Corbin and Lindsey (2002).
3. Select some activities that will build the health-related fitness components that each student needs, as identified in step 1. Each student will begin to have a personalized plan that is meaningful only to him or her.

4. Plan a week-long activity program that contains activities that are enjoyable and help alleviate weaknesses in various component areas. Evaluate the week-long program and develop a month-long program in order to provide longer range goals. In the program, delineate the frequency of exercise, the intensity, and the amount of time to be spent exercising.

Stress Reduction and Relaxation

Stress can be defined as a substantial imbalance between environmental demands and the individual's response capability. In situations that induce stress, the failure to meet the environmental demands usually has important consequences. For example, children can be pressured by parents' unrealistically high expectations, by their own desires to be accepted by peers, and by their desires to meet teacher expectations. Realistic, challenging, and attainable goals tend to eliminate many frustrating situations that could become stressful. Stress management is learning how to respond to situations that might cause tension. Both teacher and child must learn to recognize symptoms of stress before appropriate management techniques can be imposed. The emphasis in this discussion centers on what children should know about stress and what techniques they can adopt to prevent stressful situations.

First, children need to recognize that individuals react differently to stressful situations. Some learn to handle stress productively, so that it actually increases their effectiveness. Some may not sense that a situation is stressful and so may remain calm through a crisis. How an individual perceives a situation usually determines whether it is stressful. Teachers can aid youngsters in achieving a productive and healthy outlook on life that will minimize stress.

A second area of concern deals with the effects of stress on the body. Psychologically, stress can take the form of excitement, fear, or anger. Physical changes are also apparent when a person is under stress. The nervous system may respond to the stress through increased heart rate, increased blood pressure, increased respiration rate, increased muscle tension throughout the body, or decreased digestion (often accompanied by queasiness).

Unrelieved stress has detrimental effects on the body. It increases the risk of heart disease and can lead to insomnia and hypertension. Indigestion is common in stressed individuals, as is constipation. Backaches and general body aches often originate from stress. The inability to relieve stress through productive habits may lead to alcoholism, smoking, and drug abuse, usually among adults.

In the school setting, one antidote to stress is open communication between teacher and children. Teachers must be genuinely interested in helping children solve their problems and must ensure that the children know that they care. Teaching children to respect each other begins with the teacher's showing genuine respect for students. Children need to recognize that how they act influences how other children act toward them. A key for children is to make the most of their abilities: to do their best and allow the consequences to occur as they may. Comparison with others should be avoided. A healthy perspective for competition is a target goal. Place the significance of winning or being the top performer in proper perspective, and concentrate on high personal effort and doing one's best. Children should be made aware of the need for classroom and gymnasium expectations, standards, deadlines, and behavior control, without which schools could not operate effectively. Standards and rules should be realistic and administered fairly and consistently.

Studies have shown that sports and moderate physical activity decrease tension. A side effect of involvement in organized sport activities is that the concentration required provides a diversion from stress and worry. Some experts believe that exercise applies stress to the body in a systematic fashion and thus prepares the body to deal with other stressful situations. One goal of teachers should be to provide students with productive and meaningful ways to relieve tension. Coping skills should be taught to individuals who have characteristics that tend to attract attention. Stress management is learning how, in this situation, to respond to uncomplimentary remarks and teasing. Behavior control should receive attention. A good adage to emphasize is, "Stop to think before you act."

Relaxation is a skill that can be learned. Motor learning promotes patterned movement and inhibits unnecessary muscles from interfering. This results in an ability to relax muscles not specifically required for task performance. Children should learn that relaxation is necessary to achieve top performance in demanding skills, particularly those involving accuracy. A basketball player takes a deep breath, then exhales, to relax before shooting a free throw. Reduction of tension results in conservation of energy and allows the task to be done efficiently and smoothly.

Classroom teachers often feel that youngsters return from physical education classes "all psyched up" or "hyper." Relaxation activities are an important part of a balanced approach to a physical activity program. Taking a few minutes to relax at the end of the lesson can help students return to the classroom in a less stimulated state (Figure 13.12).

Many deep-breathing exercises are available. The relaxation response advocated by Benson (1990) replicates the effects of Transcendental Meditation™. Individuals sit comfortably and quietly and breathe deeply

FIGURE 13.12 Practicing relaxation activities.

through the nose. The word *one* is said each time the person exhales. Twenty-minute bouts, once or twice a day, are recommended.

A popular method is progressive muscle relaxation. In this technique, a muscle or muscle group is first tensed and then relaxed slowly and smoothly. All the major parts of the body are in turn relaxed as one works down from the head to the toes.

Deep breathing can be used to relax and can be done anywhere and anytime. It brings extra oxygen to the blood which causes the body to release endorphins that re-energize and promote relaxation. Slowly inhale through the nose and expand the abdomen before allowing air to fill the lungs. Reverse the process while exhaling. Continue for 3 to 5 minutes. A similar activity is called visualization. Slow, deep breathing is done while concentrating on each breath. Then focus concentration on one peaceful thought or create a picture in your mind of a beautiful place.

Regardless of the activity choice selected for relaxation, students should be taught the importance of taking time to relax. People are often told that they are wasting time if they are not busy scurrying here and there. It can be an important learning situation to take 4 or 5 minutes at the end of a class to sit down and relax. This communicates to students that relaxation is indeed important since the instructor allows time for the activity.

Self-Evaluation

The final step in maintaining wellness is being able to evaluate oneself on a regular basis. Individuals ultimately answer to themselves, and thus students need not share the results of their evaluations. Many surveys can help people evaluate their level of wellness.

Many other inventories, such as drinking and smoking scales, are available from various governmental agencies. Students can begin to see the extent of a problem and whether they have a problem or are improving.

Finally, teach students to evaluate their own levels of physical fitness. Each of the health-related fitness items can be evaluated easily. If students are not given time in the physical education program to evaluate their own fitness levels, they will probably not take the time for evaluation once they leave school. One of the best techniques is to give each student a self-testing card. Allow students to self-test themselves with a friend and record their performances. Instructors can file the cards and return them when it is time for another testing period. This system allows students to monitor their physical fitness gains or losses.

Behavior Self-Control

Students should be taught how to improve their self-control by altering their behavior. Attitudes can be changed by changing behavior patterns. Behavior self-control is a systematic approach to solving problems. It involves keeping records of behavior in order to understand the positive and negative variables that influence behavior. The following steps can be taught effectively to students to help them learn to manipulate their behavior.

1. **Maintain behavior records.** Students can learn to monitor their exercise patterns and record the performances on personal charts. They can then begin to observe their patterns of exercise, the duration of the exercise, and the intensity of effort. Such observation becomes self-reinforcing when, for example, students see clearly that they are exercising only 2 days per week and showing little gain, or when they observe rapid improvement after exercising 5 days per week for several weeks. Another advantage of recording behavior is that the routine act of recording reminds the performer that the behavior must be done. This routine reinforcement causes the behavior performance to improve.

2. **Develop a priority schedule.** If students want to exercise regularly, they must schedule the activity and make it a high-priority item. In other words, exercise must be done before other less important tasks are performed. Scheduling the activity for a certain number of days at a specified time is most effective.

3. **Analyze restrictive factors.** Even after behavior has been analyzed and priorities are set, students may find that desired behavior patterns are not being followed. The reasons for this must then be analyzed and other changes effected to increase the probability of carrying out the behavior. For example, the time of exercise may have to be changed or the length of the bout. Exercising for 2 shorter periods per day, instead of 1 long period, might be the answer. Exercising with a friend or changing the mode of exercise would be other possible solutions.

4. **Establish rewards.** To continue the activity over a long period of time, it can be helpful to establish personal contingencies that are available after performing the desired behavior. For example, students might relax and watch television immediately after exercise or take a long, hot shower. Regardless of the reward, it must be meaningful and worthwhile to the individual. Verbalizing internally after each exercise routine is also effective as a contingency. One might say to oneself, "I feel better and look stronger after every bout of exercise." In any case, if students can identify something positive that occurs because of or after the exercise bout, they will have a tendency to continue on the path of wellness.

REFLECTION AND REVIEW QUESTIONS

How and Why

1. Why is it important to teach wellness concepts to elementary students?
2. Is substance abuse a problem with elementary students? Defend your answer.
3. Why might physical education teachers be reluctant to include wellness in their lessons? Are these reasons warranted?
4. How can a teacher's behavior help when teaching wellness concepts?
5. Does your lifestyle reflect your value of personal wellness?

Content Review

1. Define wellness and discuss its integration into elementary physical education.
2. Describe several ideas for teaching wellness concepts in physical education.
3. What can teachers do to develop awareness and decision-making skills for students? Specifically, discuss the importance of coping and decision making skills.
4. Identify several teaching behaviors critical to leading effective class discussions.
5. What are the areas of understanding necessary for children to value personal wellness? Include several knowledge concepts and learning experiences for each area.
6. Discuss the importance of proper nutrition for children.
7. Describe various types of substance abuse as they apply to elementary students.
8. What concepts of safety and first aid are important for elementary students?

FOR MORE INFORMATION

References and Suggested Readings

Benson, H., & Klipper, M. Z. (1990). *The relaxation response.* New York: Avon.

Corbin, C. B., Lindsey, R., & Welk, G. (2000). *Concepts of physical fitness and wellness: A comprehensive lifestyle approach.* Boston: McGraw-Hill.

Corbin, C., and Lindsey, R. 2002. *Fitness for life.* Updated 4th ed. Champaign, IL: Human Kinetics.

Corbin, C., and Lindsey, R. 2002.. *Fitness for life teacher's resource manual.* Updated 4th ed. Champaign, IL: Human Kinetics.

Corbin, C.B., Pangrazi, R.P., & Franks, B.D. (2000). Definitions: Health, fitness, and physical activity. *President's Council on Physical Fitness and Sports Research Digest,* Series 3, No. 9.

Cottrell, R. R. 1992a. *Wellness: Stress management.* Dubuque, IA: Brown & Benchmark.

Cottrell, R. R. 1992b. *Wellness: Weight control.* Dubuque, IA: Brown & Benchmark.

Fahey, T. D., Insel, P. M. & Roth, W. T. (1999). *Fit and well: Core concepts and labs in physical fitness and wellness.* 3rd ed. Mountain View, CA: Mayfield.

Hafan, B. Q., & Hoeger, W. W. K. (1998). *Wellness: Guidelines for a healthy lifestyle.* 2nd ed. Englewood, CO: Morton.

Hoeger, W. W. K., & Hoeger, S. A. (1999). *Fitness and wellness.* 4th ed. Englewood, CO: Morton.

Jackson, A. W., Morrow, Jr., J. R., Hill, D. W., & Dishman, R. K. (1999). *Physical activity for health and fitness.* Champaign, IL: Human Kinetics.

Spindt, G. B., Weinberg, H., Hennessy, B., Holyoak, C., & Monti, W. H. (1993). *Moving with skill.* Dubuque, IA: Kendall/Hunt.

U.S. Department of Agriculture. (1996). *The food guide pyramid.* Pueblo, CO: Superintendent of Documents.

Websites

Body Systems
http://outreach.missouri.edu/hesfn/bodywalk/exhibitlessons.htm

Healthy Lifestyles for Children
http://www.ed.gov/databases/ERIC_Digests/ed416204.html
http://www.healthychild.com/database/a_wellness_approach_for_children.htm
http://www.healthpartners.com/Menu/0,1791,3013,00.html

Stress Management and Children
http://www.ed.gov/databases/ERIC_Digests/ed421480.html

Substance Abuse
http://www.kidsource.com/kidsource/pages/health.substance.html

SECTION 5

Fundamental Motor Skills

CHAPTER 14

Movement Concepts and Themes

ESSENTIAL COMPONENTS	
I	**Organized around content standards**
II	**Student-centered and developmentally appropriate**
III	Physical activity and motor skill development form the core of the program
IV	Teaches management skills and self-discipline
V	Promotes inclusion of all students
VI	Focuses on process over product
VII	Promotes lifetime personal health and wellness
VIII	Teaches cooperation and responsibility and promotes sensitivity to diversity

PHYSICAL EDUCATION STANDARDS	
1	**Students are able to move competently using a variety of fundamental and specialized motor skills.**
2	Students can monitor and maintain a health-enhancing level of physical fitness.
3	**Students are able to apply movement concepts and basic mechanics of skill performance when learning and refining motor skills.**
4	Students comprehend the basic principles of wellness and are able to apply concepts that enable them to make meaningful decisions that positively impact their health and wellness.
5	**Students participate in a wide variety of physical activities and learn how to maintain a personalized active lifestyle.**
6	Students demonstrate empathy, understanding, and respect for the numerous differences exhibited by people in an activity setting.
7	Students exhibit responsible and self-directed behaviors that lead to positive social interactions in physical activity.

SUMMARY

This chapter deals with movement concepts—understanding the classification and vocabulary of movement. Students learn the classification of movement concepts, including body awareness, space awareness, qualities of movement, and relationships. Emphasis at this level is placed on the process of moving rather than on the product of correct performance of a skill. Creativity is rewarded and ingenuity reinforced. Movement themes form the foundation of movement experiences necessary for developing fundamental and specialized skills.

OUTCOMES

- Explain how movement themes are used to develop an understanding of movement concepts.
- Define how human movement concepts are classified into four major categories.
- Explain the purpose of movement themes.
- Define the qualities of movement.
- Teach a variety of movement themes.
- Design a unique movement theme using the four-step approach.
- Specify individual cooperative partner activities and group activities to develop educational movement.

Physical education places emphasis on skill development in the elementary school years. It is important to learn fundamental skills in the early years because they are the building blocks for more sophisticated skills. There are two major parts of motor skill development: learning the various skills and learning the concepts of movement. It is helpful to treat each area separately for the purpose of instruction. This chapter deals with movement concepts—learning about the classification and vocabulary of movement. Chapter 15 covers motor skills and how to perform the skills correctly. The goals for a mature performer are to know both parts and to integrate knowledge and skill into successful performance. Figure 14.1 on page 302 shows the components in each major part.

With developmental level I children (ages 4 to 9), emphasis is placed on developing an understanding of movement concepts. Less emphasis is placed on skill technique and proper performance of skills. Children are taught skills correctly, but greater emphasis is placed on learning the vocabulary of movement. Students learn the classification of movement concepts, which includes body awareness, space awareness, qualities of movement, and relationships. The objectives are to show children how movements are classified and to take advantage of the motivation created by endless possibilities. Emphasis should be placed on the process of moving rather than on the product of correctly performing a skill. Creativity is to be rewarded and ingenuity reinforced.

Movement themes form the foundation of movement experiences necessary for developing more specific fundamental skills. Through this process, children develop an increased awareness and understanding of the body as a vehicle for movement, and acquire a personal vocabulary of movement skills. Movement themes are categorized according to the movement concept classifications of space awareness, body awareness, qualities of movement, and relationships.

CLASSIFICATION OF HUMAN MOVEMENT CONCEPTS

The movement concept categories of body awareness, space awareness, qualities of movement, and relationships offer structure and direction for planning new movement experiences. As youngsters experience movement, they also learn the vocabulary of movement in order to increase their understanding of the diversity and openness of movement possibilities.

Body Awareness

This category defines *what* the body can perform; the shapes it can make, how it can balance, and the transfer of weight to different body parts. Using these categories to develop challenges can add variety to movement.

1. Shapes the body makes: Many shapes can be formed with the body, such as long or short, wide or narrow, straight or twisted, stretched or curled, symmetrical or asymmetrical.
2. Balance or weight bearing: Balance demands that different parts of the body support the weight or receive the weight. Different numbers of body parts can be involved in the movements and used as body supports.
3. Transfer of body weight: Many skills demand moving the body weight from one body part to another, such as walking, leaping, rolling, and so on.
4. Flight: This category differs from transfer of body weight in that it is explosive movement and involves lifting the body weight from the floor or apparatus for an extended period of time. The amount of time off the floor distinguishes flight from transfer of weight. Examples include running, jumping onto a climbing rope, and hanging.

Space Awareness

Space awareness defines *where* the body can move. The spatial qualities of movement related to moving in different directions and at different levels are the focus. Teach youngsters to use space effectively when moving. The following elements determine how space can be modified and used in movement experiences.

1. *General or personal space.* Personal space is the limited area individual children can use around them, and in most cases is reserved for that individual only. General space is the total space that is used by all youngsters.
2. *Direction.* This refers to the desired route of movement, whether straight, zigzag, circular, curved, forward, backward, sideward, upward, or downward.
3. *Level.* This defines the relationship of the body to the floor or apparatus, whether low, high, or in between.
4. *Pathways.* This trait describes the path a movement takes through space. Examples are squares, diamonds, triangles, circles, figure eights, and others.
5. *Planes.* Planes are somewhat specific pathways defined as circular, vertical, and horizontal. The concept of planes is usually restricted in elementary school to performing simple activities in a specified plane.

Qualities of Movement

These constructs classify *how* the body moves. The qualities of movement relate closely to mechanical principles

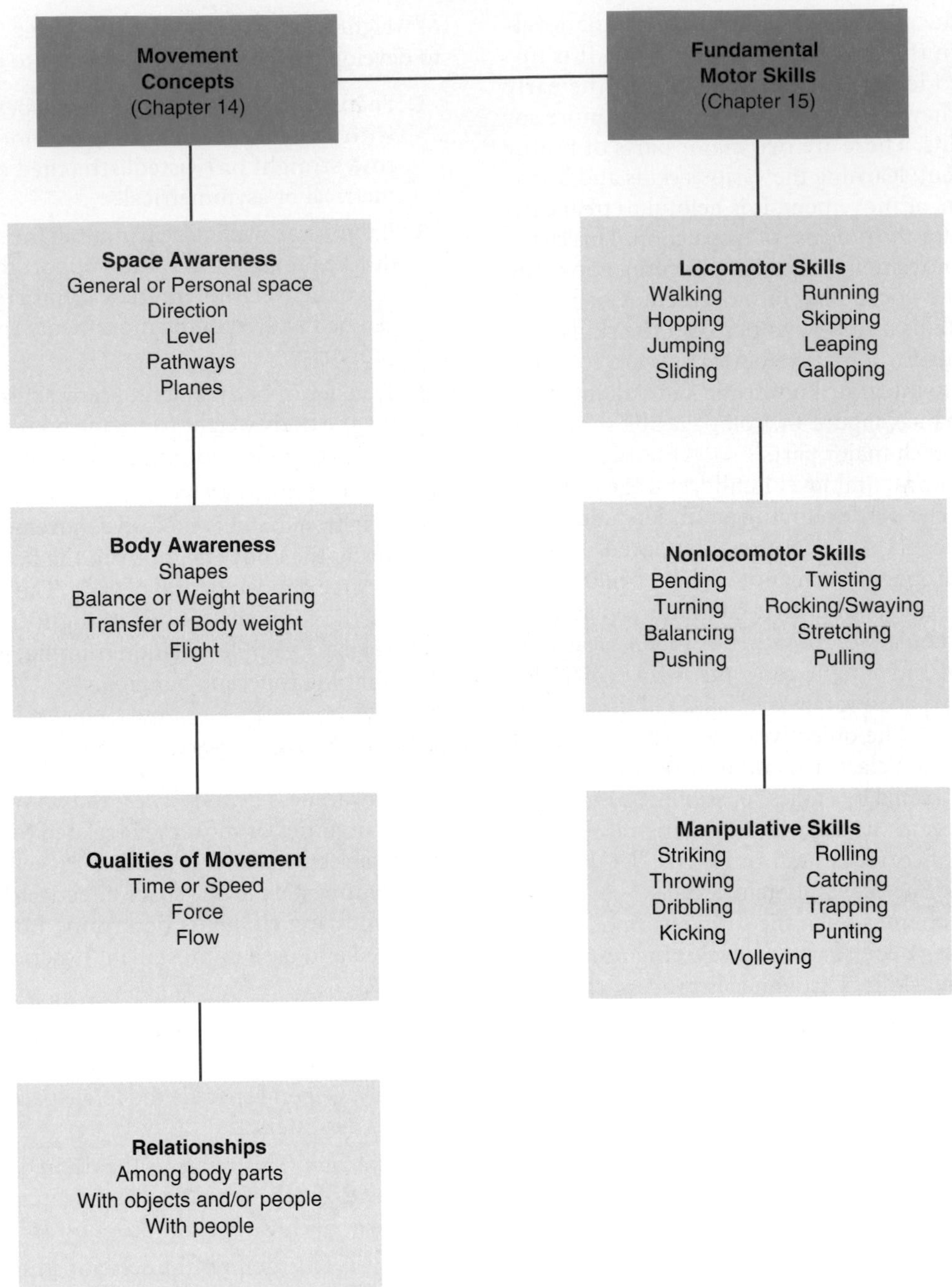

FIGURE 14.1 The components of movement concepts and fundamental motor skills.

used to move efficiently. In addition, they involve the following characteristics.

1. *Time or speed.* This quality deals with the speed and duration of movement. Children learn to move with varying speeds and to control speed throughout a variety of movements. They should learn the relationship between body shape and speed and be able to use body parts to generate speed. The time factor may be varied by using different speeds—moving to a constant rhythm, accelerating, and decelerating.
2. *Force.* Force is the effort or tension generated in movement. Force can be used effectively to aid in executing skills. Learning how to generate, absorb, and direct force is an important outcome. Force qualities may be explored by using words such as *light, heavy, strong, weak, rough,* and *gentle.*
3. *Flow.* This factor establishes how movements are purposefully sequenced to create continuity of movement. Most often this quality is discussed in terms of interrupted (bound) or sustained (free) flow. *Inter-*

rupted flow stops at the end of a movement or part of a movement. *Sustained flow* involves smoothly linking different movements or parts of a movement.

Relationships

This element defines with whom and/or what the body relates. A *relationship* is defined as the position of the performer to the apparatus or other performers. Examples of relationships are near–far, above–below, over–under, in front–behind, on–off, and together–apart. When done with other people, relationships such as leading–following, mirroring–matching, unison–opposites can be explored. Additionally, relationships can define the body parts of a single performer, such as arms together–apart or symmetrical–asymmetrical.

TEACHING MOVEMENT SKILLS AND CONCEPTS

Four steps are suggested for teaching movement skills and concepts using the problem-solving style. The problem-solving style is effective because it allows for multiple solutions to problems and encourages creativity among students. The following steps include many specific ideas for developing the problem and increasing the diversity of responses.

Step One: Set and Define the Problem

Define a problem for students so they know what to solve. The problem should include one or more of the the following definitions:

1. *What to do.* An action word directs the activity. Are children to move a certain way, go over and under, explore alternatives, or experiment with some non-locomotor movement? Direct them to run, jump, or use a fundamental skill.
2. *Where to move.* What space is to be used—personal or general? What directional factors are to be employed—path or level?
3. *How to move.* What are the force factors (light–heavy)? What elements of time are involved (even–uneven, acceleration–deceleration, sudden–sustained)? What are the relationships (over–under–across, in front of–behind)? What body parts are involved for support? For locomotion?
4. *With whom or what to move.* With whom are children to work—by themselves, with a partner, or as a member of a group? Is there a choice involved? With what equipment or on what apparatus are they to perform?

When initiating movement patterns, the challenge can be stated like this: "Let's see you move across the floor, changing direction as you wish, using a quick movement with one foot and a slow movement with the other."

Develop a Problem to Solve

1. Show me how a . . . moves. (Show me how an alligator moves.)
2. Have you seen a . . . ? (Have you seen a kangaroo jump?)
3. What ways can you . . . ? (What ways can you hop over the jump rope?)
4. How would you . . . ? How can you . . . ? (How would you dribble a ball, changing hands frequently?)
5. See how many different ways you can . . . . (See how many different ways you can hang from a ladder.)
6. What can you do with a . . . ? What kinds of things can you . . . ? (What can you do with a hoop?)
7. Can you portray a . . . ? (Can you portray an automobile with a flat tire?)
8. Discover different ways you can . . . . (Discover different ways you can volley a ball against a wall.)
9. Can you . . . ? (Can you keep one foot up while you bounce the ball?)
10. Who can . . . a . . . in such a way that . . . ? (Who can bounce a ball in such a way that it keeps time with the tom-tom?)
11. What does a . . . ? (What does a cat do when it is wet?)
12. Show . . . different ways to . . . . (Show four different ways to move across the floor.)

Step Two: Experiment and Explore

Encourage youngsters to enhance their movements and variety of responses. Variety can also be achieved by setting limitations and by asking youngsters to solve the problem in a different manner. Present problems in the form of questions or statements that elicit and encourage variety, depth, and extent of movement. Using contrasting terms can be an effective way to increase the depth and variety of movement. A number of examples follow:

Encourage Exploration and Variety

The following examples are useful for stimulating movement alternatives and/or imposing limitations:

1. Try it again another way. Try to . . . . (Try to jump higher.)
2. See how far (many times, high, close, low) . . . . (See how far you can reach with your arms.)

3. Find a way to . . . or find a new way to . . . . (Find a new way to jump over the bench.)
4. Apply . . . to . . . . (Apply a heavy movement to your run.)
5. How else can you . . . ? (How else can you roll your hoop?)
6. Make up a sequence . . . . (Make up a sequence of previous movements, changing smoothly from one movement to the next.)
7. Now try to combine a . . . with . . . . (Now try to combine a locomotor movement with your catching.)
8. Alternate . . . and . . . . (Alternate walking and hopping.)
9. Repeat the last movement and add . . . . (Repeat the last movement and add a body twist as you move.)
10. See if you can . . . . (See if you can do the movement with a partner.)
11. Trace (draw) a . . . with . . . . (Trace a circle with your hopping partner.)
12. Find another part of the body to . . . . Find other ways to . . . . (Find another part of the body to take the weight.)
13. Combine the . . . with . . . . (Combine the hopping with a body movement.)
14. In how many different positions can you . . .? (In how many different positions can you carry your arms while walking the balance beam?)
15. How do you think the . . . would change if . . .? (How do you think the balance exercise we are doing would change if our eyes were closed?)
16. On signal, . . . (On signal, speed up your movements.)

Increase Variety Using Contrasting Terms

Another way to increase the variety of movement responses is to employ terms that stress contrasts. Contrasting terms provide a way to stimulate variety of movement. Instead of challenging children to move quickly, for example, ask them to contrast a quick movement with a slow movement. The following list includes many common sets of contrasting terms that express relationships between movements or descriptions of ways to move.

Above–below, beneath, under
Across–around, under
Around clockwise–around counterclockwise
Before–after
Between–alongside of
Big–little, small
Close–far
Crooked–straight
Curved–flat, straight
Diagonal–straight
Fast–slow
Forward–back, backward
Front–back, behind
Graceful–awkward
Heavy–light
High–low
In–out
In front of–behind, in back of
Inside–outside
Into–out of
Large–small
Near–far
On–off
On top of–under, underneath
Over–under, through
Reach down–reach up
Right–left
Round–straight
Separate–together
Short–long, tall
Sideways–forward, backward
Smooth–rough
Standing upright–inverted
Sudden–sustained
Swift–slow
Tight–loose
Tiny–big, large
Top–bottom
To the right of–to the left of
Up–down
Upper–lower
Upside down–right side up
Upward–downward
Wide–narrow, thin
Zigzag–straight

Some of the terms may be grouped more logically in sets of three contrasts (such as forward–sideways–backward, up–down–in between, or over–under–through). Word meanings also can be emphasized according to rank or degree (as in near–nearer–nearest, or low–lower–lowest).

Step Three: Observe and Discuss Various Solutions

In this step, youngsters observe some of the patterns that others have created. Achievement demonstrations stimulate effort because children enjoy showing what they have put together. Discussions can focus on how to put together different movements into flow and continuity. Also, this can be a time to discuss that there are many ways to solve problems. Justifying and explaining solutions can help other students understand how to solve future problems.

Step Four: Refine and Expand Solutions to the Problem

This final step involves integrating various ideas students have observed and expanding their ideas. This step encourages integration of ideas and thoughts into new solutions. Students can work together to develop cooperative partner and small-group skills. Make problems realistic and allow opportunity for discussion and decision making between partners. The following are examples of activities that can be cooperatively developed:

1. One child is an obstacle, and the partner devises ways of going over, under, and around the positions the "obstacle" takes (Figure 14.2). Additional challenge can be added by having one partner hold a piece of equipment such as a wand or hoop to expand movements.
2. One partner supports the weight of the other, either wholly or in part (Figure 14.3), or the two work together to form different kinds of figures or shapes.
3. One child does a movement, and the other copies or provides a contrasting movement.
4. One child moves, and the other attempts to shadow (do the same movements). Do it slowly with uninterrupted flow predominating.

FIGURE 14.2 Going under a partner.

FIGURE 14.3 Supporting a partner's weight.

5. One partner does a movement. The other person repeats the movement and adds another. The first child repeats both movements and adds a third, and so on. Some limit on the number of movements can be set.
6. Children form letters or figures with their bodies on the floor or in erect positions.
7. Children practice copying activities. One child sets a movement pattern and the rest copy the actions.

MOVEMENT SKILLS AND CONCEPTS LESSON PLANS

The accompanying text, *Lesson Plans for Dynamic Physical Education,* 14th ed. (Pangrazi, 2004), contains lesson plans for teaching movement skills and concepts. Each of the lesson plans contains four or five parts that present a variety of experiences in movement concepts and skills. This variety of activities offers children a broad spectrum of challenges and ensures a balance of experiences. Each movement lesson plan contains the following sections:

1. *Movement themes.* Two or more themes are developed to focus on teaching the concepts of movements. Locomotor and nonlocomotor movements are used as the medium for developing a movement vocabulary. Movement themes focus on a movement quality around which children build patterns and sequences. Exploration is emphasized so children develop body awareness and an understanding of movement concepts.
2. *Fundamental skills.* This section presents a wide variety of experiences of fundamental skills. Locomotor skills covered include walking, running, galloping, skipping, sliding, leaping, hopping, and

jumping. Nonlocomotor movements covered are bending, rocking, swinging, turning, twisting, stretching, pushing, and pulling. Emphasis is placed on developing proper technique and using the skill in novel situations.

3. *Manipulative skills.* Manipulative skills are presented in each lesson using a variety of equipment. Skills practiced include throwing, kicking, striking, and catching.

TEACHING MOVEMENT THEMES

Movement themes are used to teach an understanding of movement concepts. Movement themes focus on a movement concept that children use to build movement patterns and sequences. The purposes are to explore and experiment with the theme, to gain a thorough understanding of the movement concept, and to develop skill in the movement area. Guide children toward the best response they can produce.

Movement themes help youngsters understand the concepts of movement. Some themes involve only a single principle or factor; while others involve two or more. Themes in this chapter focus on exploring different concepts of movement, but in actuality, isolating a particular factor is difficult. For example, in exploring balance, movement possibilities are expanded through the application of body shape, level, and time factors. The following themes are classified by four major concepts of human movement: body awareness, space awareness, qualities of movement, and relationships.

Body Awareness Themes

BODY SHAPES (FIGURE 14.4)

"Let's try making shapes and see whether we can name them. Make any shape you wish and hold it. What is the name of your shape, John? [Wide.] Try to make different kinds of wide shapes. Show me other shapes you can make. What is the name of your shape, Susie? [Crooked.] Show me different kinds of shapes that are crooked. Make yourself as crooked as possible."

FIGURE 14.4 Forming different shapes.

"Make yourself wide and then narrow. Now tall and then small. How about tall and wide, small and narrow, tall and narrow, and small and wide? Work out other combinations."

"Select three different kinds of shapes and move smoothly from one to another. This time I will clap my hands as a signal to change to a different shape."

"Select four different letters of the alphabet. On the floor, make your body shape successively like these letters. Try with numbers. Make up a movement sequence that spells a word of three letters. Show us a problem in addition or subtraction."

"Use your jump rope and make a shape on the floor. Make a shape with your body alongside the rope."

"Pretend to be as narrow as an arrow or telephone pole. Pretend to be as wide as a house, store, or hippopotamus."

"Squeeze into a tiny shape; now grow slowly into the biggest shape you can imagine. Travel to a different spot on the floor, maintaining the big shape. Quickly assume the tiny shape again."

"Move around the room in groups of three. On signal, form a shape with one standing, one kneeling, and one sitting."

"Pretend you are at a farm. Make a barn with your body."

"Jump upward, making a shape in the air. Land, holding that shape. Begin with a shape, jump upward with a half turn, and land in another shape."

"What body shapes can you assume standing on one foot?"

"Show me what body shapes can be made with your stomach in contact with the floor."

"Look to see where your personal space is in relation to general space. When I say 'Go,' run in general space. On the next signal, return to your space and sit down."

BALANCING: SUPPORTING BODY WEIGHT (FIGURE 14.5)

"Explore different ways you can balance on different surfaces of your body. Can you balance on three different parts of your body? On two? On one? Put together se-

FIGURE 14.5 Balancing on different body parts.

quences of three or four balance positions by using different body parts or different numbers of body parts."

"Can you balance on a flat body surface? What is the smallest part of the body you can balance on? Support the body on two dissimilar parts. On three dissimilar parts. Support the body on different combinations of body flats and body points."

"Use two parts of the body far away from each other to balance. Shift smoothly to another two parts."

"Who can balance on one foot with the arms stretched overhead? Out to the side?"

"Stand with feet together and eyes closed. Maintain balance while using different arm positions. Balance on one foot for ten counts."

"From a standing position, raise one leg, straighten the leg in front of you, swing the leg to side and back without losing your balance."

"Move from a narrow, unstable base to a wide, stable base."

"Balance on parts of the body forming a tripod." (Explain the term.)

"Show different balance positions with part of the weight supported by the head."

"In a hands-and-knees position, and later in a crab position, balance on the right arm and right leg, the left arm and left leg, the right arm and left leg, the left arm and right leg."

"Stand on your toes and balance, using different arm positions."

"Place a beanbag on the floor. How many different ways can you balance over it? Try with a hoop. How many different ways can you balance inside the hoop?"

"When I call out a body part or parts, you balance for 5 seconds on that part or part combination." (Use knees, hands, heels, flats, points, and a variety of combinations.)

"Keep your feet together and sway in different directions without losing your balance. Can you balance on one foot with your eyes closed? Bend forward while balancing on one foot? Lift both sets of toes from the floor and balance on your heels? Now sit on the floor. Can you lift your feet and balance on your seat without hand support? Can you balance on your tummy without your feet or hands touching the floor?"

"In a standing position, thrust one leg out sideways and balance on the other foot."

"Make a sequence by balancing on a narrow surface, change to a wide surface, and back again to a different narrow surface."

BRIDGES (FIGURE 14.6)

"Show me a bridge made by using your hands and feet. What other kinds of bridges can you make? Can you make a bridge using only three body parts? Only two?"

"Show me a wide bridge. A narrow one. A short bridge. A long one. How about a high bridge? A low one? Can you make a bridge that opens when a boat goes through? Get a partner to be the boat and you be the bridge. If you are the boat, choose three ways of traveling under a bridge. Each time the boat goes under the bridge, change the bridge to another means of support."

"As I touch you, go under a bridge and make another bridge."

"Show how you would make London Bridge fall down."

"With a partner, alternate going under a high bridge and going over a low bridge."

"Can you move one end of the bridge, keeping the other end still?"

"Make a bridge with one side of the body held upward. Change to the other side."

"Show me a twisted bridge. A curved bridge."

FIGURE 14.6 Making bridges.

"Be an inchworm and start with a long, low bridge. Walk the feet to the hands. Walk the hands forward while the feet are fixed."

"Make a bridge with three points of contact."

"Show me a bridge at a high level. At a low level. In between."

"Work up a sequence of bridge positions, going smoothly from one to the next."

FLIGHT

"Show me three different ways you can go through space. Try again, using different levels. Lead with different parts of your body."

"See how high you can go as you move through space. What helps you get height?"

"Practice various combinations for takeoff and landing. See if you can work out five different possibilities for taking off and landing, using one or both feet." (Possibilities are same to same [hop]; one foot to the opposite [leap]; one-foot takeoff, two-foot landing; two-foot takeoff, two-foot landing [jump]; two-foot takeoff, one-foot landing.)

"Run and jump or leap through the air with your legs bent. With your legs straight. With one leg bent and the other straight. Try it with your legs spread wide. With your whole body wide. With your whole body long and thin through the air."

"Project yourself upward beginning with the feet together and landing with the feet apart. Run, take off, and land in a forward stride position. Repeat, landing with the other foot forward."

"With a partner, find ways to jump over the partner as he or she changes shape."

"Using your arms to help you, run and project yourself as high as possible. Practice landing with bent knees."

MOVING WITH THE WEIGHT SUPPORTED ON THE HANDS AND FEET (FIGURE 14.7)

"Pick a spot away from your personal space and travel to and from that spot on your hands and feet. Try moving with your hands close to your feet. Far away from your feet. Show me bilateral, unilateral, and cross-lateral movements. Build up a sequence."

"Move from your personal space for 8 counts. Do a jump turn (180 degrees) and return to your space using a different movement."

"Lie on your stomach. Move using only your hands."

FIGURE 14.7 Taking the weight on hands and feet.

"Experiment with different hand–foot positions. Begin with a narrow shape and with hands and feet as close together as possible. Extend your hands from head to toe until they are as far apart as possible. Extend the hands and feet as wide as possible and move. Now try with the hands wide and the feet together. Reverse."

"Practice traveling so that both hands and feet are off the ground at the same time. Go forward, backward, sideward."

"With your body straight and supported on the hands and feet [push-up position], turn the body over smoothly and face the ceiling. The body should remain straight throughout. Turn to the right and left. Recover to your original position."

"What kinds of animal movements can you imitate? Move with springing types of jumps. What shapes can you assume while you move?"

RECEIVING AND TRANSFERRING WEIGHT

"Support the weight on two different body parts and then transfer the weight smoothly to another pair of parts. Add another pair of unlike parts if you can."

"Take a deep breath, let the air out, relax, and drop to the floor, transferring the weight from a standing position to a position on the floor. Can you reverse the process?"

"Show in walking how the weight transfers from the heel to the ball of the foot with a push-off from the toes. In a standing position, transfer the weight from the toes, to the outside of the foot, to the heel, and back to the toes. Reverse the order."

"Using three different parts, transfer weight from one to another in a sequence."

"Travel with a jump or a leap and then lower yourself gently to your back after landing. Repeat, only lower yourself smoothly to your seat."

"From a standing position, bend forward slowly and transfer the weight partially to both hands. Lift one foot into the air. Return it to the ground gently. Repeat with the other foot. Lift a hand and a foot at the same time and return them smoothly."

"Lower yourself in a controlled manner to take the weight on your tummy. Can you turn over and take the weight on your seat with your hands and feet touching the floor?"

"Move from a supine position (on your back) to a standing position without using your arms."

"Select a shape. See if you can lower yourself to the ground and return to your original position, retaining the shape."

"Try some jump turns, quarter and half. What is needed to maintain stability as you land?"

"Project yourself into the air and practice receiving your weight in different ways. Try landing without any noise. What do you have to do? See how high you can jump and still land lightly."

"See how many different ways you can transfer weight smoothly from one part of your body to another. Work up a sequence of three or four movements and go smoothly from one to another, returning to your original position."

STRETCHING AND CURLING

"In your own space, stretch out and curl. What different ways can you find to do this? Let's go slowly from a stretch to a curl and back to a stretch in a smooth, controlled movement. Curl your upper body and stretch your lower body. Now curl your lower body and stretch your upper body. Work out a smooth sequence between the two combinations."

"Show different curled and stretched positions on body points and on body flats. Go from a curled position on a flat surface to a stretched position supported on body points. Explore how many different ways you can support your body in a curled position."

"Stand in your personal space and stretch your arms at different levels. Lift one leg up and stretch it to the front, side, and back. Repeat with the other leg."

"Stretch with an arm and a leg until it pulls you over."

"In a sitting position, put your legs out in front. Bend your toes forward as far as possible. Bend them backward so that your heels are ahead of your toes. Turn both toes as far as you can inward. Turn them outward."

"Lie on the floor on your back. Stretch one leg at a time in different ways in space."

"Stand. Stretch to reach as far as you can with your hand. Try reaching as far as possible with your toe."

"Show how you can travel on different body parts, sometimes stretched, sometimes curled."

"Jump and stretch as high as possible. Now curl and roll on the floor." Repeat several times.

TAKING THE WEIGHT ON THE HANDS (FIGURE 14.8)

Establishing proper hand positioning for taking the weight on the hands (and later for the headstand) is important.

"Put your hands about shoulder width apart, with fingers spread and pointed forward. With knees bent, alternate lifting the feet silently into the air, one foot at a time. Pick a point ahead of your hands (2 feet or so), and watch it with your eyes. Keep from ducking your head between your arms."

"Place both hands on the floor. Kick up like a mule. Can you kick twice before coming down?"

"Take the weight on your hands. Make one foot go past the other while in the air."

"Do as many movements as you can while keeping your hands on the floor."

"See whether you can take the weight on your hands for a brief time. How do you get your body into the air? What different movements can you make with your feet while your weight is on your hands? See how long you can keep your feet off the ground. Repeat, trying to get your hips above your hands. Now add a twist at the waist to return your feet to the floor at a different spot."

"Try again, but shift the weight to one hand and land both feet at a different spot."

"Begin in a standing position and try to keep your feet over your head for as long as possible. Begin with the arms and hands stretched overhead, and repeat. Kick up one leg and then the other."

FIGURE 14.8 Taking the weight on the hands.

Space Awareness Themes (Where the Body Moves)

MOVING IN GENERAL SPACE

Goals in these movement experiences, in addition to developing movement competence, should enhance the ability to (a) share space with other children, (b) move through space without bumping anyone, and (c) develop consideration for the safety of others.

"Run lightly in the area, changing direction without bumping or touching anyone until I call 'Stop.' Raise your hand if you were able to do this without bumping into anyone."

"Let's try running zigzag fashion in the area without touching anyone. This time, when I blow the whistle, change direction abruptly and change the type of movement."

"Run lightly in general space and pretend you are dodging someone. Can you run toward another runner and change direction to dodge?"

"Get a beanbag and drop it to mark your personal space. See how lightly, while under control, you can run throughout the area. When the signal is given, run to your spot, pick up your beanbag, put it on your head, and sit down [or give some other challenge]. Try this skipping."

"We are going to practice orienteering. [Explain the term.] Point to a spot on the wall, and see whether you can run directly to it in a straight line. You may have to stop and wait for others to pass so as not to bump into anyone, but you cannot change direction. Stay in a straight line. When you get to your spot, pick another spot, and repeat."

"What happens when general space is decreased? You had no problem running without touching anyone in the large space. Now let's divide the area in half with cones. Run lightly within this area so as not to touch or bump anyone. Now it's going to get more difficult. I'm going to divide the space in half once more, but first let's try walking in the new area. Now, run lightly." (Decrease the area as feasible.)

"Get a beanbag and mark your personal space. Run around the beanbag until you hear a 'Bang,' and then explode in a straight direction until I call 'Stop.' Return to your personal space."

"From your beanbag, take five [or more] jumps [hops, skips, gallops, slides] and stop. Turn to face home, and return with the same number of movements. Take the longest steps you can away from home, and then return home with tiny steps."

"Show me how well you can move with these combinations in general space: run-jump-roll, skip-spin-collapse. Now you devise a series of any three movements and practice them."

"Today our magic number is five. Can you move in any direction with five repetitions of a movement? Change direction and pick another movement to do five times. Continue."

"Blow yourself up like a soap bubble. Can you huff and puff? Think of yourself as a big bubble that is floating around. When I touch you, the bubble breaks, and you collapse to the ground. This time, blow up your bubble and float around. When you are ready, say, 'Pop,' so the bubble bursts."

"I am going to challenge you on right and left movements. Show me how you can change to the correct direction when I say either 'Right' or 'Left.' Now begin running lightly."

"This time, see whether you can run rapidly toward another child, stop, and bow to each other. Instead of bowing, shake hands, and say, 'How do you do!'"

"From your personal space, pick a spot on a wall. See whether you can run to the spot, touch it, and return without bumping anyone. This time, it's more difficult. Pick spots on two different walls, touch these in turn, and return."

EXPLORING PERSONAL SPACE

Personal space is that space that can be reached from a fixed base. Youngsters can take this personal space with them when they are moving in general space. A graphic way to illustrate personal space is to have youngsters take an individual jump rope and double it. From a kneeling position, they swing it in a full arc along the floor. It should not touch another child or rope.

"Show us how big your space is. Keeping one foot in place, outline how much space you can occupy. Sit cross-legged and outline your space. Support your weight on different parts of your body and outline your space."

"Make yourself as wide [narrow, small, large, low, high] as possible. Try these from different positions—kneeling, balancing on the seat, and others. Show us what kinds of body positions you can assume while you stand on one foot. While you lie on your stomach. On your seat. Try the same with one foot and one hand touching the floor."

"Stand tall in your space. To the beat of a drum, move in increments to a squat position. Reverse."

"Move from a lying position to a standing position without using your arms or hands. Return to lying."

"Can you stay in one place and move your whole self but not your feet? Sway back and forth with your feet together and then with your feet apart. Which is better?"

"Sitting in your personal space, bend your toes forward; now backward. Bend your feet so that the heels move ahead of your toes."

"In a supine position (on your back) move your arms and legs from one position slowly and then move them back quickly to where you started. Explore other positions."

"Keeping one part of your body in place, make as big a circle as you can with the rest of your body."

"Explore different positions while you keep one leg [foot] higher than the rest of your body. Work out a smooth sequence of three different positions."

"Pump yourself up like a balloon, getting bigger and bigger. Hold until I say, 'Bang!'"

"In your personal space, show me how a top spins. Keep your feet together in place. With your arms wide to the sides, twist and make your feet turn."

CIRCLES AND THE BODY (FIGURE 14.9)

"Can you form full circles with your hands and arms at different joints—wrist, elbow, and shoulder? Now what circle can you make with your legs and feet? Try this lying on your back. Use other body joints to make circles."

"Travel in general space by skipping [running, hopping, sliding]. Stop on signal and make moving, horizontal [vertical, inclined] circles with an arm. Repeat, but on signal lie down immediately on your back and make the specified circle with one foot."

FIGURE 14.9 Forming circles.

"Show how a swimmer makes circles with the arms when doing the backstroke. Alternate arms and also move them together. Reverse the arm direction to make the crawl stroke. Make vertical circles with one arm and both arms across the body."

"Make a circle with one hand on your tummy and pat yourself on the top of the head with the other hand at the same time. Reverse hands."

"Keep one foot fixed and make a circle with the other foot by turning completely around."

"Select a partner. Match the arm circles the partner makes."

"Can you keep two different circles going at the same time? Make a circle turning one way, and another circle turning the other way. Repeat, using twisting actions of the body parts making the circles."

PLANES OF MOVEMENT

"Show me a variety of movements in a horizontal plane. In a vertical plane. In a diagonal plane. Put together combinations so that you go in sequence from one type of movement to another."

"Here is a challenge. When I call out a plane of movement, respond with one that is correct. Ready?" (Specify the plane of movement.)

"Using a jump rope doubled in one hand, make circles in the different planes. Try the same with a hula hoop."

"Crouch at a low level, spin upward toward the ceiling, then back to the floor. Spin in the other direction."

LEVELS

"Choose one way of traveling at a high level and another at a low level. Again, move at a high level and stop at a low level. Move at a low level and stop at a high level. Choose one way of traveling at a medium level and add this somewhere in your sequence—beginning, middle, or end."

"Select three different kinds of traveling movement with the arms at a high, medium, and low level. Link these movements together in a smooth sequence."

"Travel around the room raising your arms as high as possible. Travel on your tiptoes. Repeat with your arms as low as possible."

"Run at different levels. Run as high as you can. Run as low as possible. Run at a medium level."

"When I clap my hands, change direction and level."

"Move on all fours with your body at a high level, a medium level, and then as low as possible. Try these movements with your face turned to the ceiling."

"Use a jump rope or a line or board in the floor as your path to follow. Begin at the far end. Show me a slow, low-level movement down and back. What other ways can you go down and back slowly and at a low level? Change to a fast, high-level movement. On what other levels can you move?"

"Combine a low, fast movement down with a high, slow movement on the way back. Explore other combinations. Make different movements by leading with different parts of your body."

MOVING IN DIFFERENT WAYS

"Discover different ways you can make progress along the floor without using your hands and feet. See whether you can walk with your seat. Let your heels help you."

"What ways can you move sideward or backward? What rolling movements can you make? Look carefully before you move to make sure you have a clear space."

"Use large movements and travel through general space. Make your body into a straight line and move in straight lines, changing direction abruptly. With your body in a curved shape, move in a curved pathway."

"Each time you change direction, alternate a straight body and a straight path with a curved body shape and a curved path."

"Find ways of moving close to the floor with your legs stretched. Now move with your legs bent, keeping at a low level."

"As you travel forward, move up and down. As you travel backward, sway from side to side."

"Travel, keeping high in the air. Change direction and travel at a low level. Continue to alternate."

"Counting the four limbs [two arms, two legs], travel first on all four, then on three, next on an arm and a leg, and then on one leg. Now reverse the order."

"With your hands fixed on the floor, move your feet in different ways. Cover as much space as possible. With your feet fixed, move your hands around in different ways as far away from the body as you can. Move around general space the way a skater does. The way a person on a pogo stick does. Choose other ways. Change body direction as you move, but keep facing in the original direction."

Qualities of Movement Themes (How the Body Moves)

TIME (SPEED)

Speed involves the pace of action, which can be slow, fast, or any degree in between. Speed involves acceleration and deceleration; that is, the time factor either can be constant or can speed up or slow down. Time also can be even or uneven.

"With your arms, do a selected movement slowly and then quickly. Move your feet slowly and then as rapidly as you can. Change your support base and repeat."

"In turn, stretch a part of your body slowly and then return it to place quickly, like a rubber band snapping. Stretch the entire body as wide as possible and snap it back to a narrow shape."

"Travel through the area without touching anyone. Speed up when there is an open area and slow down when it is crowded."

"Choose a way of traveling across the floor quickly and then do the same movement slowly. Do a fast movement in one direction and, on signal, change to a slow movement in another direction."

"Select a magic number between 10 and 20. Do that many slow movements and repeat with fast movements of the same count."

"Choose a partner. With your partner a little bit away from you, begin moving rapidly toward your partner and decelerate as you draw close. Move away by beginning slowly and accelerate until you return to where you started. Repeat. Select the kinds of movement you wish to use together."

"Staying in your own personal space, begin with some kind of movement and accelerate until you are moving as fast as you can. Reverse by beginning with a fast movement and then slow down until you are barely moving. Put together a sequence of two movements by beginning with one and accelerating, then changing to another movement and decelerating. Try doing two different body movements at the same time—one that accelerates and one that decelerates."

CONTRASTING MOVEMENTS

Contrasting movements have wide and frequent application in the development of other themes. See page 304 for examples of contrasting words.

"Show me a fast movement. Now a slow one. Show me a smooth movement. Now a rough, jerky movement."

"Find three ways to rise from the floor and three ways to sink to the floor. Choose one way to rise and one way to sink. Try to do this three times very smoothly."

"Make yourself as tall as possible. Now, as short as you can."

"Move with a small and delicate skip. Change to a large skip."

"Show me a wide shape. Now, an opposite one. A crooked shape. Now, its opposite. Show me a high-level movement and its contrast. Can you do a balanced movement? What is its opposite?" (Use light–heavy and other contrasts as well.)

"Pick two contrasting movements. When I clap my hands, do one, and change to the other when I clap again. What are the movements you did?"

FORCE

"Show me different kinds of sudden movements. Do a sudden movement and repeat it slowly. Put together a series of sudden movements. Put together a series of sustained movements. Mix sudden and sustained movements."

"Pick a partner and do a quick, strong, movement followed by a quick, light movement."

"Take five strong, slow jumps, changing your body for each jump."

"When the drum beat is loud, walk heavily. When the drum beat is soft, walk lightly."

"Reach in different directions with a forceful movement. Crouch down as low as you can and explode upward. Try again, exploding forward. Move as if you were pushing something very heavy. Pretend you are punching a heavy punching bag."

"What kinds of movements can you do that are light movements? Can you make movements light and sustained? Light and sudden? Heavy and sustained? Heavy and sudden? Which is easier? Why?"

"Try making thunder [big noise with hands and feet] and then lightning [same movements without any noise], timing each with five slow counts."

"Can you combine heavy movements in a sequence of sudden and sustained movements? Can you make one part of your body move lightly and another part heavily?"

TENSION AND RELAXATION

"Make yourself as tense as possible. Now slowly relax. Take a deep breath and hold it tight. Expel the air and relax."

"Hug yourself hard! Now, harder. Follow this with the body relaxed. Shake the hands."

"Reach as high as possible with both hands, relax slowly, and drop to the floor. Tense one part of your body and relax another. Slowly shift the tension to the relaxed part, and vice versa."

"Run forward, stop suddenly in a tensed position, and then relax. Run in a tensed manner, change direction, and then run in a relaxed manner."

"Walk forward with tight, jerky movements. Change direction and walk with loose, floppy movements. Pretend that you are a boxer by using short, tense movements. Now move your arms like a floppy rag doll."

Relationship Themes (To Whom and What the Body Relates)

MOVING OVER, UNDER, AROUND, AND THROUGH THINGS

This theme is flexible and can use any available equipment as obstacles to go over, under, around, and through (Figure 14.10). It can be used effectively in a rotating station system. Equipment can be already arranged, or the children can set it up themselves.

"Using the equipment, explore different ways you can go over, under, around, or through what you have set up. Lead with different parts of the body."

"Three youngsters with jump ropes form a triangle, square, and rectangle, respectively, on the floor. Move in, out, and around the figures."

"Toss your beanbag in the air. When I call out a body part, sit down quickly, and put the beanbag on that part, or on one of the parts named."

SYMMETRICAL AND ASYMMETRICAL MOVEMENTS

Symmetrical movements are identical movements using similar body parts on opposite sides of the body. Asymmetrical movements are different movements using similar body parts on opposite sides of the body. Symmetry increases stability because of the counterbalance effect of the two body halves. Asymmetry, with its weight distributed unequally, leads to quick starts and easier sequential flow due to the unequal weight distribution throughout the body. An example of a symmetrical movement is balancing on a balance beam with both arms to the side. The arms are extended symmetrically

FIGURE 14.10 Moving over and under.

to increase stability and balance. An example of an asymmetrical movement is running where the legs are alternately flexed and extended.

"Show me different kinds of symmetrical movements. Now asymmetrical movements. Put together sequences of symmetrical and asymmetrical movements."

"Taking the weight on your hands, show symmetrical and asymmetrical movements of your legs."

"Run and jump high in the air, and place your limbs symmetrically in flight."

"Perform different movements like throwing, skipping, running, long jumping, and leaping and identify whether they are symmetrical or asymmetrical movements."

RELATIVE LOCATION OF BODY PARTS

"We are going to try some special ways of touching. Raise your right hand as high as you can—now down. Raise your left hand as high as you can—now down. Touch your left [or right] shoulder [elbow, knee, hip, ankle] with the right [or left] hand." (Try many combinations.)

"Now, point to a door [window, ceiling, basket] with an elbow [thumb, toe, knee, nose]. Let's see if you can remember right and left. Point your left [or right] elbow to the window." (Try different combinations.)

"When I name a body part, let's see if you can make this the highest part of your body without moving from your place."

"Now, the next task is a little more difficult. Move in a straight line for a short distance and keep the body part named above all the other body parts. What body parts would be difficult to keep above all the others?" (Possibilities are the eyes, both ears, both hips.)

"Touch the highest part of your body with your right hand. Touch the lowest part of your body with your left hand."

"Let's see if you can locate some of the bones in your body. When I name a bone, hold that bone, move and touch a wall, and return to your spot." (These challenges depend on bones that the children can identify. The same procedure can be used to identify selected muscles.)

"Now move around the room, traveling any way you wish." (The movement can also be limited.) "The signal to stop will be a word describing a body part. Can you stop and immediately put both hands on that part or parts?" (Or, "On 'Stop,' hide the body part.") "You are to move around the room again. When I call out a body part, find a partner and place the body parts together."

FIGURE 14.11 Leading with a foot.

"This time, when I call out a body part, you are to move around the room as you wish, while holding with one hand a named body part. When I call out another name, change the type of movement and hold the part with the other hand as you move. Now I will call out two body parts. Have the parts touch each other."

LEADING WITH DIFFERENT PARTS OF THE BODY (FIGURE 14.11)

"As you move between your beanbags [lines, markers], explore ways that different parts of your body can lead movements. Add different means of locomotion. Work at different levels."

"Have a partner make a bridge and you go under, leading with different parts of the body. Can you find five different ways to go under with different body parts leading? Now try finding five ways to go over or around."

"What body parts are difficult to lead with?"

FOR MORE INFORMATION

References and Suggested Readings

Gabbard, C. (1994). *Physical education for children: Building the foundation.* 2nd ed. Boston: Allyn and Bacon.

Gallahue, D. L. (1995). *Developmental physical education for today's elementary school children.* 3rd ed. New York: McGraw-Hill.

Gilbert, A. G. (1992). *Creative dance for all ages: A conceptual approach.* Reston, VA: AAHPERD.

Graham, G., Holt/Hale, S. A., & Parker, M. (2001). *Children moving,* 5th ed. Mountain View, CA: Mayfield.

Joyce, M. (1993). *First steps in teaching creative dance to children.* 3rd ed. Mountain View, CA: Mayfield.

Laban, R., & Lawrence, F. (1947). *Effort.* London: Union Brothers.

Logsdon, B. J., Barrett, K. R., Ammons, M., Broer, M. R., Halverson, L. E., McGee, R., & Robertson, M. A. (1984). *Physical education for children: A focus on the teaching process.* Philadelphia: Lea & Febiger.

Pangrazi, R. P. (2004). *Lesson plans for dynamic physical education.* 14th ed. San Francisco: Benjamin Cummings.

Thompson, M. A. (1993). *Jump for joy!: Over 375 creative movement activities for young children.* Englewood Cliffs, NJ: Prentice Hall.

Websites

Body Systems
http://outreach.missouri.edu/hesfn/bodywalk/exhibitlessons.htm

Healthy Lifestyles for Children
http://www.ed.gov/databases/ERIC_Digests/ed416204.html
http://www.healthychild.com/database/a_wellness_approach_for_children.htm
http://www.healthpartners.com/Menu/0,1791,3013,00.html

Stress Management and Children
http://www.ed.gov/databases/ERIC_Digests/ed421480.html

Substance Abuse
http://www.kidsource.com/kidsource/pages/health.substance.html

CHAPTER 15

Fundamental Motor Skills

ESSENTIAL COMPONENTS	
I	Organized around content standards
II	**Student-centered and developmentally appropriate**
III	**Physical activity and motor skill development form the core of the program**
IV	Teaches management skills and self-discipline
V	Promotes inclusion of all students
VI	**Focuses on process over product**
VII	Promotes lifetime personal health and wellness
VIII	Teaches cooperation and responsibility and promotes sensitivity to diversity

PHYSICAL EDUCATION STANDARDS	
1	**Students are able to move competently using a variety of fundamental and specialized motor skills.**
2	Students can monitor and maintain a health-enhancing level of physical fitness.
3	**Students are able to apply movement concepts and basic mechanics of skill performance when learning and refining motor skills.**
4	Students comprehend the basic principles of wellness and are able to apply concepts that enable them to make meaningful decisions that positively impact their health and wellness.
5	**Students participate in a wide variety of physical activities and learn how to maintain a personalized active lifestyle.**
6	Students demonstrate empathy, understanding, and respect for the numerous differences exhibited by people in an activity setting.
7	Students exhibit responsible and self-directed behaviors that lead to positive social interactions in physical activity.

SUMMARY

Fundamental skills embrace a broad spectrum of skills, from simple to complex. The more precise the motor skill, the more important the need is to establish proper technique. In teaching fundamental skills, correct technique prevails over experimentation. Students are hesitant to participate in various lifetime physical activities if they feel incompetent in performing various movement patterns. Fundamental skills are classified into three groups: locomotor, nonlocomotor, and manipulative.

OUTCOMES

- Understand that teaching fundamental movement is synonymous with providing instruction toward the acquisition of a specific skill.
- Identify basic fundamental and specialized motor skills.
- Describe the differences between locomotor, nonlocomotor, and manipulative skills.
- Cite stress points, instructional cues, and suggested movement patterns to enhance the learning of fundamental skills.
- Demonstrate the various stages of development associated with throwing, catching, kicking, and striking.
- Identify objects that can be used to help youngsters succeed in manipulative skills.
- Specify activities designed to develop fundamental and specialized motor skills.

Physical skills are the tools that most adults use to participate in leisure activities. Without a set of physical skills and a positive feeling about their ability to perform in activity settings, many people will relegate themselves to a lifetime of inactivity. *Fundamental skills* are skills that form the foundation of human movement, and are usually identified by a single verb, such as walking, batting, bouncing, jumping, or pitching. (Most of the fundamental skills end in the suffix *-ing*.)

Fundamental skills embrace a broad spectrum of skills, from simple to complex. Learning fundamental skills implies that proper technique is involved in skill performance. The more precise the skill, the more critical the need to establish proper technique. Teaching correct technique is necessary even when a child is more comfortable with a known departure from accepted form. A child who is right-handed and steps forward with the right foot while throwing should be taught to shift to a left-footed (opposite side) step to be sure the proper pattern is learned.

Learning fundamental skills requires an understanding of correct progressions and diligent practice. In contrast to learning movement concepts (Chapter 14), emphasis is placed on technique rather than on creating movement variations. After a skill has been learned, renewed emphasis is placed on practicing the skill under many varying conditions. Motor skills should be learned under a variety of conditions and practiced in as many situations as possible to ensure practice variability. Developing different experiences on which a response foundation is built allows youngsters to respond to the widest possible range of novel situations. Thus, motor learning moves through a complete cycle; from general to specific to general.

FUNDAMENTAL SKILLS

Fundamental skills are those utilitarian skills that children need for living and being. This group of skills is sometimes labeled *basic* or *functional*. The designation *fundamental skills* is used because the skills are necessary for children to function effectively in the environment. These skills set the foundation for adult activity and form the basis of competent movement. All individual, dual, and team sport activities use fundamental and specialized skills of one type or another. If children feel incompetent in performing movement patterns, they may be hesitant to participate in various leisure activities in adulthood. The following skills are grouped for ease of teaching and ease of comprehension by students. Although the skills are presented here individually, they are performed in a seemingly infinite number of combinations, depending on the sport or activity. Fundamental skills are divided into three categories—locomotor, nonlocomotor, and manipulative.

Locomotor Skills

Locomotor skills are used to move the body from one place to another or to project the body upward. They include walking, running, skipping, galloping, leaping, sliding, jumping, and hopping. They form the foundation of gross motor coordination and involve large muscle movement.

Nonlocomotor Skills

Nonlocomotor skills are performed without appreciable movement from place to place. These skills are not as well-defined as locomotor skills. They include bending and stretching, pushing and pulling, twisting and turning, rocking, swaying, and balancing, among others.

Manipulative Skills

Manipulative skills come into play when children handle an object. Most of these skills involve the hands and feet, but other parts of the body can also be used. The manipulation of objects leads to better hand-eye and foot-eye coordination, which are particularly important for tracking items in space. Manipulative skills form the foundation for many game skills. Propulsion (throwing, batting, kicking) and receipt (catching) of objects are important skills that can be taught by using beanbags and various balls. Rebounding or redirecting an object in flight (such as a volleyball) is another useful manipulative skill. Continuous control of an object, such as a wand or hoop, is also a manipulative activity.

LOCOMOTOR SKILLS

In the descriptions that follow, stress points emphasizing correct technique are listed for each of the locomotor skills. Instructional cues listed are short, concise phrases that remind students how to perform activities correctly. Suggested learning activities fall into two categories. The first, suggested movement patterns, consists of movement-oriented sequences that do not require rhythm. The second category, rhythmic activities, consists of sequences that use rhythmic background. A drum or appropriate recorded music is effective for reinforcing and expanding rhythmic possibilities.

Walking

When walking, each foot moves alternately, with one foot always in contact with the ground or floor. The stepping foot is placed on the ground before the other foot is lifted. The weight of the body is transferred from the heel to the ball of the foot and then to the toes for push-off. The toes are pointed straight ahead and the arms swing freely from the shoulders in opposition to the feet. The body is erect, with the eyes focused straight ahead and slightly below eye level. The legs swing smoothly from the hips, with knees bent enough to clear the feet from the ground. Marching is a precise type of walk, accompanied by lifted knees and swinging arms.

Stress Points

1. The toes should be pointed reasonably straight ahead.
2. The arm movement should feel natural. The arms should not swing too far.
3. The head should be kept up and the eyes focused ahead.
4. The stride length should not be excessive. Unnecessary up-and-down motion is to be avoided.

Instructional Cues

1. Head up, eyes forward.
2. Point toes straight ahead.
3. Nice, easy, relaxed arm swing.
4. Walk quietly.
5. Hold tummy in, chest up.
6. Push off from the floor with the toes.

Directives for Suggested Movement Patterns

1. Walk in different directions, changing direction on signal.
2. While walking, bring the knees up and slap with the hands on each step.
3. Walk on the heels, toes, and sides of feet.
4. Gradually lower the body while walking (going downstairs) and raise yourself again slowly (going upstairs).
5. Walk with a smooth, gliding step.
6. Walk with a wide base on the tiptoes, rocking from side to side.
7. Clap the hands alternately in front and behind. Clap the hands under the thighs while walking.
8. Walk slowly, and then increase the speed gradually. Reverse the process.
9. Take long strides. Take tiny steps.
10. On signal, change levels.
11. Walk quickly and quietly. Walk heavily and slowly.
12. Change direction on signal, but keep facing the same way.
13. Walk gaily, angrily, happily. Show other moods.
14. Hold the arms in different positions. Make an arm movement each time you step.
15. Walk in different patterns—circle, square, triangle, figure eight.
16. Walk through heavy mud. On ice or a slick floor. Walk on a rainy day. Walk in heavy snow.
17. Walk like a soldier on parade, a giant, a dwarf, a robot.
18. Duck under trees or railings while walking.
19. Point your toes in different directions—in, forward, and out.
20. Walk with high knees. Stiff knees. One stiff knee. A sore ankle.
21. Walk to a spot, turn in place while stepping, and take off in another direction.
22. Practice changing steps while walking.
23. Walk with a military goose step.
24. Walk and change direction after taking the magic number of steps. (One child picks a magic number.)
25. Tiptoe around the area and through puddles of water.
26. Walk as if you are on a balance beam. Walk across a tight rope.
27. Walk as if you are sneaking up on someone.
28. Walk with funny steps as if you were a clown.
29. Take heel-and-toe steps forward. Without turning around, walk heel-and-toe backwards.

Rhythmic Activities

When using recorded music, teach youngsters to hear the phrasing in the selection. Have children walk one way during a phrase and then change to another type of walk during the next phrase.

1. Walk forward one phrase (eight counts) and change direction. Continue to change at the end of each phrase.
2. Use high steps during one phrase and low steps during the next.
3. Walk forward for one phrase and sideward during the next. The side step can be a draw step, or it can be of the grapevine type. To do a grapevine step to the left, lead with the left foot, stepping directly to the side. Cross the right foot behind the left, and then in front of the left on the next step with that foot. The pattern is a step left, cross right (behind), step left, cross right (in front), and so on.
4. Find a partner. Face each other and join hands. Pull your partner by walking backward as your partner

resists somewhat (eight counts). Reverse roles. Now stand behind your partner and place the palms of your hands on your partner's shoulders. Push your partner by walking forward as your partner resists (eight counts). Reverse roles.

5. Walk slowly, then gradually increase the tempo. Now begin fast and decrease. (Use a drum for this activity.)
6. Walk in various directions while clapping your hands alternately in front and behind. Try clapping the hands under a thigh at each step, or clap the hands above the head in time with the beat.
7. Walk forward four steps, and turn completely around in four steps. Repeat, but turn the other way the next time.
8. While walking, bring the knees up and slap with the hands on each step in time with the beat.
9. On any one phrase, take four fast steps (one count to each step) and two slow steps (two counts to each step).
10. Walk on the heels or toes or with a heavy tramp. Change every four or eight beats.
11. Walk with a smooth, gliding step, or walk silently to the beat.
12. Walk to the music, accenting the first beat of each measure. Now sway your body to the first beat of the measure. (Use a waltz with a strong beat.)

Running

Running (Figure 15.1), in contrast to walking, is moving rapidly so that for a brief moment, both feet are off the ground. Running varies from trotting (a slow run) to sprinting (a fast run for speed). The heels can take some weight in distance running and jogging. Running should be done with a slight body lean. The knees are flexed and lifted while the arms swing back and forth from the shoulders with a bend at the elbows. Additional pointers for sprinting are found in the track, field, and cross-country running unit (Chapter 28).

FIGURE 15.1 Running.

Stress Points

1. The balls of the feet should be used for sprinting.
2. The faster one desires to run, the higher the knees must be lifted. For fast running, the knees also must be bent more.
3. For distance running, less arm swing is used compared with sprinting for speed. Less body lean is used in distance running, with comfort being the key. The weight is absorbed on the heels and transferred to the toes.

Instructional Cues

1. Run on the balls of the feet when sprinting.
2. Head up, eyes forward.
3. Bend your knees.
4. Relax your upper body.
5. Breathe naturally.
6. Swing the arms forward and backward, not sideways.

Directives for Suggested Movement Patterns

1. Run lightly throughout the area, changing direction as you wish. Avoid bumping anyone. Run zigzag throughout the area.
2. Run and stop on signal. Change direction on signal.
3. Run, turn around with running steps on signal, and continue in a new direction. Alternate turning direction.
4. Pick a spot away from you, run to it, and return without touching or bumping anyone.
5. Run low, gradually increasing the height. Reverse.
6. Run in patterns. Run between and around objects.
7. Run with high knee action. Slap the knees while running.
8. Run with different steps—tiny, long, light, heavy, crisscross, wide, and others.
9. Run with your arms in different positions—circling, overhead, stiff at your sides.
10. Run free, concentrating on good knee lift.
11. Run at different speeds.
12. Touch the ground at times with either hand while running.
13. Run backward, sideward.
14. Run with exaggerated arm movements. Run with a high bounce.
15. Run forward ten steps and backward five steps. Repeat in another direction. (Other tasks can be imposed after the ten steps.)

16. Run forward, then make a jump turn in the air to face in a new direction. Repeat. Be sure to use both right and left turns. Make a full reverse (180-degree) turn.
17. Run the *Tortoise and Hare* sequence (page 338) and *Ponies in the Stable* (page 338). These are interesting patterns.
18. Run with knees turned outward. Run high on your toes.
19. Show how quietly you can run. Pretend that you are running through high weeds.
20. Run to a wall and back to place. Run and touch two walls.
21. Run lightly twice around your spot. Then explode (run quickly) to another spot.

Rhythmic Activities

Many of the suggested movements for walking are equally applicable to running patterns. Some additional suggestions for running include the following.

1. Walk during a phrase of music and then run for an equal length of time.
2. Run in different directions, changing direction on the sound of a heavy beat (or on a signal).
3. Lift the knees as high as possible while running, keeping time to the beat.
4. Do *European Rhythmic Running* (pages 337–338) to supplement the running patterns described previously.

Hopping

Hopping involves propelling the body up and down on the same foot. The body lean, the other foot, and the arms serve to balance the movement. Hopping can be practiced in place or as a locomotor movement.

Stress Points

1. To increase the height of the hop, the arms must be swung rapidly upward.
2. Hopping should be performed on the ball of the foot.
3. Small hops should be used to start, with a gradual increase in height and distance of the hop.

Instructional Cues

1. Hop with good forward motion.
2. Stay on your toes.
3. Use your arms for balance.
4. Reach for the sky when you hop.
5. Land lightly.

Directives for Suggested Movement Patterns

1. Hop on one foot and then on the other, using numbered sequences such as 1–1, 2–2, 3–3, 4–4, 5–5, 2–1, 1–2, 3–2, 2–3, and so on. The first figure of a series indicates the number of hops on the right foot, and the second specifies the number of hops on the left foot. Combinations should be maintained for 10 to 20 seconds.
2. Hop, increasing height. Reverse.
3. See how much space you can cover in two, three, or four hops.
4. Hop on one foot and do a heel-and-toe pattern with the other. Now change to the other foot. See whether a consistent pattern can be set up.
5. Make a hopping sequence by combining hopping in place with hopping ahead.
6. Hop forward, backward, sideward.
7. Hop in different patterns on the floor.
8. Hop while holding the free foot in different hand positions.
9. Hold the free foot forward or sideward while hopping. Explore other positions.
10. Hop with the body in different positions—with a forward lean, a backward lean, a sideward balance.
11. Hop lightly. Heavily.
12. While hopping, touch the floor with the hands—first one and then both.
13. Hop back and forth over a line, moving down the line as you hop.
14. Trace out numbers or letters by hopping.
15. Turn around while hopping in place.
16. Hop forward and then backward according to a magic number (selected by a student). Repeat in another direction. Now add sideward hopping instead of going backward.
17. Hop softly so that no one can hear you.

Rhythmic Activities

Combining rhythm with hopping patterns is more difficult than walking, running, or skipping to rhythm because students fatigue rapidly. The suggested patterns combine other locomotor movements with hopping.

1. Walk four steps, hop three times, rest one count.
2. Walk four steps, then hop four times as you turn in place. Repeat in a new direction.
3. Hop eight times on one foot (eight counts) and then eight times on the other.
4. Hop forward and backward over a line to the rhythm, changing feet each phrase (eight counts).

5. Combine skipping, sliding, or galloping with hopping.
6. Practice the step-hop to music. (The child takes a step followed by a hop on the same foot. This is a two-count movement.)

Jumping

Jumping requires taking off with both feet and landing on both feet (Figure 15.2). The arms move forward with an upswing, and the movement of the body combined with the force of the feet helps lift the weight. A jumper lands lightly on the balls of the feet with the knees bent. Jumping can be done in place or as a locomotor activity to cover ground.

Stress Points

1. The knees and ankles should be bent before takeoff to achieve more force from muscle extension.
2. The landing should be on the balls of the feet, with the knees bent to absorb the impact.
3. The arms should swing forward and upward at takeoff to add momentum to the jump and to gain distance and height.
4. The legs must be bent after takeoff or the feet will touch the ground prematurely.

Instructional Cues

1. Swing your arms forward as fast as possible.
2. Bend your knees.
3. On your toes.
4. Land lightly with bent knees.
5. Jump up and try to touch the ceiling.

FIGURE 15.2 Jumping.

Directives for Suggested Movement Patterns

1. Jump up and down, trying for height. Try small and high jumps. Mix in patterns.
2. Choose a spot on the floor. Jump forward over the spot. Now backward and then sideward.
3. Jump with your body stiff and arms held at your sides. Jump like a pogo stick.
4. Practice jump turns in place—quarter, half, three-quarter, and full.
5. Increase and decrease your jumping speed. Increase and decrease the height of the jump.
6. Land with the feet apart and then together. Alternate with one foot forward and one backward.
7. Jump and land quietly. How is this done?
8. Jump, crossing and uncrossing the feet.
9. See how far you can go in two, three, and four consecutive jumps. Run lightly back to place.
10. Pretend that you are a bouncing ball.
11. Clap the hands or slap the thighs while in the air. Try different arm positions.
12. Begin a jump with your hands contacting the floor.
13. Jump in various patterns on the floor.
14. Pretend that you are a basketball center jumping at a jump ball. Jump as high as you can. Jump from a crouched position.
15. Combine a jump for distance with one for height.
16. Jump and click the heels in the air. Can you do two clicks?
17. Jump like a kangaroo. A rabbit. A frog.
18. Combine contrasting jumps: forward and backward. Big and little. Right and left. Light and heavy.
19. Explore different ways a Jumping Jack can be performed.
20. Jump and clap hands in front. Behind you. Overhead.
21. Give three preliminary swings of arms and then jump forward.
22. Jump. While in the air, touch your heels. Touch both knees. Touch both toes in front.
23. One half of the class is on the floor in selected positions. The other half jumps over those on the floor. Exchange position.

Rhythmic Activities

Most of the activities suggested for hopping to rhythm are suitable for jumping. Other suggestions follow.

1. Begin jumping slowly to the drumbeat and then accelerate. Begin jumping fast and decelerate to the beat.
2. Toss a ball upward and jump in time to the bounce. (The ball must be a lively one.)
3. Do varieties of the Jumping Jack. First, move your feet without any arm movement. Now add an arm lift to shoulder height, then lift the arm to a full overhead position. Finally, add body turns and different foot patterns.
4. Take a forward stride position. Change the feet back and forth to the rhythm.

Sliding

Sliding is done to the side. It is a onc-count movement, with the leading foot stepping to the side and the other foot following quickly. Since the same foot always leads, practice the movement in both directions. Sliding is done on the balls of the feet with the weight shifted from the leading foot to the trailing foot. Body bounce during the slide should be minimal.

Stress Points

1. Emphasize the sideways movement. Often, students move forward or backward, which is actually galloping.
2. Both directions should be used, so that each leg has a chance to lead as well as to trail.
3. The slide is a smooth, graceful, and controlled movement.

Instructional Cues

1. Move sideways.
2. Do not bounce.
3. Slide your feet.

Directives for Suggested Movement Patterns

1. Lead in one direction with a definite number of slides, do a half turn in the air, and continue the slide leading with the other leg in the same direction. (A four-plus-four combination is excellent.)
2. Begin with short slides and increase length. Reverse.
3. Slide in a figure-eight pattern.
4. Change levels while sliding. Slide so that the hands can touch the floor with each slide.
5. Slide quietly and smoothly.
6. Pretend to be a basketball defensive player and slide with good basketball position.
7. Slide with a partner.
8. Try sliding individually in a circle.
9. Do three slides and a pause. Change the leading foot and repeat.
10. In circle formation, facing in, the whole class does ten slides one way followed by a pause. Repeat going in the other direction.

Rhythmic Activities

With appropriate music, many of the above movement patterns can be set to rhythm. Use music phrases to signal a change of direction or to insert another challenge.

Galloping

Galloping is similar to sliding, but progress is in a forward direction. One foot leads and the other is brought rapidly forward to it. There is more upward motion of the body than in sliding. A way to teach the gallop is to have children hold hands and slide in a circle, either to verbal cues or to a drumbeat. Gradually ask the class to face the direction the circle is moving. This takes them naturally from a slide into a gallop. Finally, drop hands and permit free movement in general space.

Stress Points

1. The movement should be smooth and graceful.
2. Each foot should have a chance to lead.

Instructional Cues

1. Keep one foot in front of the other.
2. Now lead with the other foot.
3. Make high gallops.

Directives for Suggested Movement Patterns

1. Do a series of eight gallops with the same foot leading, then change to the other foot. Change after four gallops. Change after two gallops. (Later in the rhythmic program, the gallop is used to teach the polka, so it is important for children to learn to change the leading foot.)
2. Change the size of the gallops.
3. Gallop in a circle with a small group.
4. Pretend to hold reins and use a riding crop.
5. Gallop backward.
6. Gallop like a spirited pony. Like a heavy draft horse.

Rhythmic Activities

Because galloping is essentially a rhythmic movement, many of the patterns described above should be done to rhythm. Use music phrases to signal a change in the lead foot. Check previous sections on locomotor movements for other rhythmic movement suggestions.

Leaping

Leaping is an elongated step designed to cover distance or move over a low obstacle. It is usually combined with running, since a series of leaps is difficult to maintain alone (Figure 15.3). The suggested movement patterns use combinations of running and leaping.

Stress Points

1. Height and graceful flight are goals for which to strive.
2. Landing should be light and relaxed.

Instructional Cues

1. Push off and reach.
2. Up and over, land lightly.
3. Use your arms to help you gain height.

Directives for Suggested Movement Patterns

1. Leap in different directions.
2. See how high you can leap.
3. Leap and land softly.
4. Vary your arm position when you leap. Clap your hands as you leap.
5. Leap with the same arm and leg forward. Try the other way.
6. Show a leap in slow motion.
7. Leap and turn backward.
8. Leap over objects or across a specified space.
9. Practice by playing *Leap the Brook* (page 549).
10. Leap and move into a balanced position.

Rhythmic Activities

Because a leap is essentially an explosive movement through space, it is difficult to apply rhythm to the movement. Children must gather themselves in preparation for the leap, which makes the movement nonrhythmic in nature.

FIGURE 15.3 Leaping.

Skipping

Skipping is a series of step-hops done with alternate feet. To teach skipping, first teach youngsters to do a step and small hop on the same foot. A step followed by a hop is then performed on the other foot. Skipping is done on the balls of the feet with the arms swinging to shoulder height in opposition with the feet. Another way to teach skipping is to have youngsters hold a large ball (9 inches or more) in front at waist height. A step is taken with one foot followed by raising the other knee to touch the ball. This stimulates the hop. Repeat with the other foot and the opposite knee.

Stress Points

1. Smoothness and rhythm are goals in skipping. Speed and distance are not.
2. The weight must be transferred from one foot to the other on the hop.
3. The arms swing in opposition to the legs.

Instructional Cues

1. "Step-hop"
2. Swing your arms.
3. Skip smoothly.
4. On your toes.

Directives for Suggested Movement Patterns

Many of the suggested movement patterns for walking and running can be applied to skipping, particularly those that refer to changing direction, stopping, making floor patterns, and moving at different speeds.

1. Skip with exaggerated arm action and lifted knees.
2. Skip backward.
3. Clap as you skip.
4. Skip with a side-to-side motion.
5. Skip twice on one side (double skip).
6. Skip as slowly as possible. Skip as fast as possible.
7. Skip so lightly that the movement cannot be heard by your partner.
8. Take as few skips as you can to get to a selected spot.

Rhythmic Activities

Almost all the combinations suggested for walking and running are useful for skipping movements, and many combinations of skipping, walking, and running can be devised. The piece "Pop Goes the Weasel" is excellent music for skipping. On the "Pop," some movement challenge can be specified.

NONLOCOMOTOR SKILLS

Nonlocomotor skills include bending, twisting, turning (in place), moving toward and away from the center of the body, raising and lowering the parts of the body, and other body movements done in place. Body control, flexibility, balance, and a variety of movements that lead to effective body management are important goals.

Bending

Bending is movement at a joint. Teach how the body bends, why it needs to bend, and how bends are combined in various movements (Figure 15.4).

Stress Points

1. Bending as far as possible to increase flexibility and range of movement is a key goal.
2. The bending possibilities of many joints should be explored.
3. Time factors can be introduced in slow and rapid bending.

Instructional Cues

1. Bend as far as possible.
2. Bend one part while holding others steady.

Directives for Suggested Movement Patterns

1. Bend your body down and up.
2. Bend forward and backward, left and right, north and south.
3. Bend as many ways as possible.
4. Bend as many body parts as you can below your waist. Above your waist. Bend with your whole body.
5. Sit down and see whether you can bend differently from the ways you bent in a standing position.
6. Try to bend one body part quickly while you bend another part slowly.
7. Lie down and bend six body parts. Can you bend more than six? Now bend fewer.
8. Make a familiar shape by bending two body parts. Add two more parts.
9. Think of a toy that bends; see whether you can bend in a similar fashion.
10. Find a partner and bend together. Have your partner make big bends while you make tiny bends.
11. Show how you would bend to look funny. To look happy or sad. Bend slowly or quickly.
12. Bend your largest part. Your smallest part.
13. Begin by bending one body part. As you return this part to its original position, bend another part.
14. Bend your fingers. Bend all ten of them.
15. Bend your knees in standing position. In sitting position. In lying position. What other joint must be bent in standing position?

FIGURE 15.4 Bending movements.

Rocking and Swaying

Rocking occurs when the center of gravity is fluidly transferred from one body part to another. In rocking, the body is in a rounded position where it touches the floor. The term *swaying* implies a slower movement than rocking and is somewhat more controlled than rocking. The base of support is unchanged in swaying movements.

Stress Points

1. Rocking is done best on a body surface that has been rounded. Arm movements and movements of other body parts can facilitate the rocking motion.
2. Rocking should be done smoothly and in a steady rhythm.
3. Rocking can be started with small movements and increased in extent, or vice versa.
4. Rocking and swaying should be done to the full range of movement.
5. Swaying maintains a stable base.

Instructional Cues

1. Rock smoothly.
2. Rock in different directions. At varying speeds.
3. Rock higher (farther).
4. Sway until you almost lose your balance.

Directives for Suggested Movement Patterns

1. Rock in as many different ways as you can (Figure 15.5).
2. Show how you can rock slowly. Quickly. Smoothly.
3. Sit cross-legged with arms outstretched to the sides, palms facing the floor. Rock from side to side until the hands touch the floor.
4. Lie on your back and rock. Now point your arms and legs toward the ceiling as you rock.
5. Lie on your tummy with arms stretched overhead and rock. Hold your ankles and make giant rocks.
6. Try to rock in a standing position.
7. Rock and twist at the same time.
8. Lie on your back with knees up and rock from side to side.
9. Show me two ways to have a partner rock you.
10. From a standing position, sway back and forth. Right and left. Experiment with different foot positions. Sway slowly and rapidly. What effect does rapid swaying have?
11. Repeat swaying movements from a kneeling position.
12. Start with a small rocking motion and make it progressively bigger.
13. Choose three (or more) ways of rocking and see if you can change smoothly from one to the next.
14. Rock like a cradle. A rocking horse.
15. Sway like a tree in a heavy wind.

Swinging

Swinging involves the movement of body parts in a motion that resembles a swinging rope or pendulum of a

FIGURE 15.5 Rocking variations.

clock. Most swinging movements are confined to the arms and legs.

Stress Points

1. Swinging should be a smooth, rhythmic action.
2. The body parts involved in swinging should be relaxed and loose.
3. The extent of the swing movement should be the same on both sides of the swing.
4. Swinging movements should be as full as possible.

Instructional Cues

1. Loosen up; swing easy.
2. Swing fully; make a full movement.
3. Swing in rhythm.

Directives for Suggested Movement Patterns

1. Explore different ways to swing your arms and legs.
2. Work out swinging patterns with the arms. Combine them with a step pattern, forward and back.
3. Swing the arms back and forth, and go into full circles at times.
4. With a partner, work out different swinging movements (Figure 15.6). Add circles.
5. Develop swinging patterns and combinations. Form sequences with swinging and full-circle movements. (This activity is best done to waltz music with a slow or moderate tempo.)
6. Swing like a clock pendulum. A cow's tail.

FIGURE 15.6 Partner swinging.

Turning

Turning is rotation around the long axis of the body. The terms *turning* and *twisting* are sometimes used interchangeably to designate the movements of body parts. However, turning refers to movements of the body as a whole. Most turns are initiated by a twist. In the movement experiences suggested here, action involves movement of the entire body. Movements of body parts are discussed under "Twisting."

Stress Points

1. Maintaining balance and body control is important.
2. Turning should be tried in both directions, right and left.
3. Turns in standing position can be made by jumping, hopping, or shuffling with the feet.
4. Most turns are made in increments or multiples of quarter turns. Multiples should be practiced.
5. Turns should be practiced in body positions other than standing—seated, on the tummy or the back, and so on.

Instructional Cues

1. Keep your balance.
2. In jump turns, land in a relaxed way with the knees relaxed.
3. Be precise in your movement, whether it is a quarter, half, or full turn.

Directives for Suggested Movement Patterns

1. In standing position, turn your body to the left and right, clockwise and counterclockwise.
2. Turn to face north, east, south, and west. (Post directions on the wall.)
3. Stand on one foot and turn around slowly. Now turn around quickly. Now turn with a series of small hops. Try to keep good balance.
4. Show me how you can cross your legs with a turn and sit down. Can you get up again in one movement?
5. Every time you hear the signal, see whether you can turn around once, moving slowly. Can you turn two, three, or four times slowly on signal?
6. Lie on your tummy on the floor and turn your body slowly in an arc. Turn over so that you are on your back. Turn back to your tummy again.

7. Find a friend and see how many different ways you can turn each other. Take turns.
8. Play *Follow the Leader* with your friend. You make a turn and your partner follows.
9. Begin with a short run, jump into the air, and turn to land facing in a new direction. Practice both right and left turns. Can you make a full reverse (180-degree) turn?
10. Lying on your back, turn and rest on your side. Return. Repeat on the other side.
11. Lying on your back, turn so that you are resting on your stomach. Return. Turn over the opposite way.
12. Find a partner and see how many ways you can rotate each other.
13. Walk in general space and turn completely around on signal.
14. With your hands outstretched to the sides, pretend you are a helicopter.

Twisting

Twisting is the rotation of a selected body part around its own long axis (Figure 15.7). The joints of different body parts can be used for twisting: spine, neck, shoulders, hips, ankles, and wrists. *Twisting* involves movement around the body part itself whereas *turning* focuses on the space in which the entire body turns.

Stress Points

1. Twisting should be extended as far as possible with good control.

FIGURE 15.7 Twisting movements.

2. The body parts on which the twist is based should be stabilized.
3. A twist in one direction should be countered by a reverse twist.
4. Some joints are better for twisting than others. (Explain why this is so.)

Instructional Cues

1. Twist far (fully).
2. Twist the other way.
3. Hold the supporting parts firm.

Directives for Suggested Movement Patterns

1. Glue your feet to the floor. Can you twist your body to the left and to the right? Can you twist your body slowly? Quickly? Can you bend and twist at the same time? How far can you turn your hands back and forth?
2. Twist two or more parts of your body at the same time.
3. Twist one body part in one direction and another in the opposite direction.
4. Try twisting the lower half of your body without twisting the upper half.
5. See what parts you can twist while sitting on the floor.
6. Try to twist one body part around another part. Is it possible to twist together even more parts?
7. Balance on one foot and twist your body. Can you bend and twist at the same time?
8. Show me some different shapes that you can make by twisting your body.
9. Try to twist like a spring. Like a cord on a telephone.
10. Try to move and twist at the same time.
11. With the weight on your feet, twist as far as you can in one direction. Now take the weight on your hands and move your feet.
12. Twist like a pretzel. Like a licorice stick.
13. Twist like you are hitting a home run with a baseball bat.
14. Twist like you are hitting a golf ball.

Stretching

Stretching is a movement that moves body parts away from the body center. Stretching sometimes involves moving a joint through the range of movement. Stretching is necessary for maintaining and increasing flexibility.

Stress Points

1. Stretching should be extended to the full range of movement.

2. Stretching exploration should involve many body parts.
3. Stretching should be done in many positions.
4. Stretching can be combined with opposite movements, such as curling.
5. Stretching is done slowly and smoothly.
6. Hold full stretching position for 10 seconds.

Instructional Cues

1. Stretch as far as possible. Make it hurt a little.
2. Find other ways to stretch the body part (joint).
3. Keep it smooth. Do not jerk.

Directives for Suggested Movement Patterns

1. Stretch as many body parts as you can.
2. Stretch your arms, legs, and feet in as many different directions as possible.
3. Try to stretch a body part quickly. Slowly. Smoothly.
4. Bend a body part and say which muscle or muscles are being stretched.
5. See how many ways you can stretch while sitting on the floor.
6. Lie on the floor and see whether you can stretch two, three, four, or five body parts at once.
7. Try to stretch one body part quickly while you stretch another part slowly.
8. From a kneeling position, see whether you can stretch to a mark on the floor without losing your balance.
9. Stretch your right arm while you curl your left arm.
10. Find a friend and show how many ways you can help each other stretch.
11. Try to stretch and become as tall as a giraffe. (Name other animals.)
12. Stretch and make a wide bridge. Find a partner to go under, around, and over your bridge.
13. Bend at the waist and touch your toes with your fingers. See whether you can keep your legs straight while you are stretching to touch the toes.
14. Combine stretching with curling. With bending.
15. Stretch the muscles in your chest, back, tummy, ankles, wrists, and fingers.
16. Make a shape with your body. Now stretch the shape so that it is larger.
17. As you move at a low level, curl and stretch your fingers.
18. Find a position in which you can stretch one side of the body.
19. Find a position in which you can stretch both legs far apart in the air. Now make the legs as narrow as possible.

FIGURE 15.8 Pushing.

20. Stretch like a rubber band. When I say "Snap!" move the part quickly back to original position.

Pushing

Pushing is a controlled and forceful action performed against an object to move the body away from the object or to move the object in a desired direction by applying force to it (Figure 15.8).

Stress Points

1. A forward stride position should be used to broaden the base of support.
2. The body's center of gravity should be lowered.
3. The line of force is directed toward the object.
4. The back is kept in reasonable alignment, and the body forces gathered for a forceful push. Do not bend the waist.
5. The push should be controlled and steady.

Instructional Cues

1. Broaden your foot base.
2. Use all your body forces.
3. Push steadily and evenly.
4. Lower yourself for a better push.

Directives for Suggested Movement Patterns

1. Stand near a wall and push it from an erect position, then push with the knees bent and one foot behind the other. In which position can you push with more force?
2. Push an imaginary object that is very light. Now imagine that you are pushing a heavy object.
3. Try to push a partner who is sitting on a jumping box, then try to push a partner who is sitting on a

scooter. What changes must you make in your body position?

4. Push an object with your feet without using your arms or hands.
5. Sit down and push a heavy object with your feet. Can you put your back against the object and push it?
6. See how many different ways you can find to push the object.
7. Find a friend and try to push each other over a line in turn.
8. Sit back to back with your partner and see whether you can push each other backward in turn.
9. See if it is possible to lie on the floor and push.
10. Lie on the floor and push your body forward, backward, and sideward.
11. Lie on the floor and push yourself with one foot and one arm.
12. Put a beanbag on the floor and push it with your elbow, shoulder, nose, or other body part.
13. Move in crab position and push a beanbag.
14. Show how you can push a ball to a friend.

Pulling

Pulling is a controlled and forceful action that moves an object closer to the body or the body closer to an object. If the body moves and an object is being pulled, pulling causes the object to follow the body.

Stress Points

1. For forceful pulling, the base of support must be broadened and the body's center of gravity must be lowered.
2. The vertical axis of the body should provide a line of force away from the object.
3. Pulling should be a controlled movement with a minimum of jerking and tugging.
4. The hand grips must be comfortable if pulling is to be efficient. Gloves or other padding can help.
5. Pulling movements can be isolated in the body, with one part of the body pulling against the other.

Instructional Cues

1. Get your body in line with the pull. Lower yourself.
2. Widen your base of support.
3. Gather your body forces and pull steadily.

Directives for Suggested Movement Patterns

1. Reach for the ceiling and pull an imaginary object toward you quickly. Slowly and smoothly.
2. Use an individual tug-of-war rope and practice pulling against a partner. Do this with your hands and arms at different levels.
3. From a kneeling position, pull an object.
4. Try to pull with your feet while you sit on the floor.
5. Pretend to pull a heavy object while you are lying on the floor.
6. Clasp your hands together and pull as hard as you can.
7. Try pulling an object while you stand on one foot.
8. Hold hands with a partner, and pull slowly as hard as you can.
9. Have your partner sit down, and then see how slowly you can pull each other. Take turns.
10. With your partner sitting on the floor, see whether you can pull each other to your feet. Take turns.
11. Pull with different body parts.
12. Pull your partner by the feet as your partner sits on a rug square.
13. Reach for the stars with both hands and pull one back to you.
14. Balance on one foot. Try to pull something. What happens?

Pushing and Pulling Combinations

Combinations of pulling and pushing movements should be arranged in sequence. Musical phrases can signal changes from one movement to the other. Balance-beam benches are excellent for practicing pulling and pushing techniques. Partner tug-of-war ropes provide effective pulling experiences. Partner resistance exercises (pages 257–259) are also useful pulling and pushing experiences.

Fleeing, Chasing, and Tagging

Many physical education games involve fleeing, chasing, and tagging. Speed and reaction are essential for dodging by the person being chased and the response of the chaser to the movements of the target child.

Stress Points

1. Run under control.
2. The fleeing child should be in a moderate crouch position with the feet wider than usual. This position enables moving laterally in either direction quickly.
3. The fleeing child should become adept at faking, which means making a preliminary movement in one direction before determining the final path to take.

4. All runners should move on the balls of their feet.
5. The chaser should maneuver the fleeing youngster into a confined area to facilitate tagging.
6. Eyes should be focused on the center of the dodger's body to negate the effectiveness of the fake.
7. The tag should be made between the knees and shoulders in a gentle but firm manner.

Instructional Cues (chaser)

1. Run under control.
2. Move on the balls of the feet and maintain a slightly crouched position when approaching the dodger.
3. Focus on the waistline of the dodger.
4. Tag gently but firmly.

Directives for Suggested Movement Patterns

1. Run in general space with the stipulation to run toward other classmates and dodge at the last moment. Avoid contact. To vary the activity, change direction on signal.
2. In general space, run and stop on signal.
3. In partners, have one person run and the other shadow (follow closely). The runner should change direction often. Change roles.
4. Move into squads, with the leader 10 yards away from and facing the rest of the squad column. All members of the squad take turns running and dodging around a passive captain. Replace the squad captain regularly.
5. Partners mark a small area (12 by 12 feet) with cones. Chase and dodge within this area. Try with two chasers and one dodger.

MANIPULATIVE SKILLS

Manipulative skills are basic to a number of specialized sport skills—catching, throwing, striking, and kicking, among others. These are complex motor patterns, and stages of development have been identified, from initial stages through mature patterns of performance. Most complex skills should be practiced at near-normal speed. Whereas locomotor skills can be dramatically slowed down to promote learning, doing so with throwing, striking, or kicking will destroy the rhythm of the skills. Analysis of the following skills is listed by developmental stages rather than age because of the wide maturity differences among children of similar ages. Suggested activity challenges for developing throwing, catching, striking, and kicking skills are found in Chapter 18.

Throwing

In throwing, an object is thrust into space and is accelerated through the movement of the arm and the total coordination of the body. Young children often go through two preliminary tossing stages before entering the stages of throwing. The first toss is a two-handed underhand throw that involves little foot movement. A large ball, such as a beach ball, is best for teaching this type of throw, which begins with the ball held in front of the body at waist level. The toss is completed using only the arms. Youngsters often have difficulty maintaining balance when encouraged to throw the ball for any distance. The second preliminary toss is a one-handed underhand throw. In this toss, which resembles pitching a softball, body torque is generated and weight shifted from the rear to the front foot. This toss requires a smaller object such as beanbags, fleece balls, and small sponge balls.

The following skill analysis considers overhand throwing only. Teach proper form before concentrating on distance or accuracy. Velocity, not accuracy, is the primary goal when trying to develop mature patterns characterized by a full range of motion and speed. Throwing for accuracy is only practiced after a mature form of the skill is in place.

Stage One

Stage one throwing is generally observed between the ages of 2 and 3 years. This stage is basically restricted to arm movement from the rear toward the front of the body. The feet remain stationary and positioned at shoulder width, with little or no trunk rotation occurring (Figure 15.9). Most of the movement force originates from flexing the hip, moving the shoulder forward, and extending the elbow.

Stage Two

Stage two throwing develops between the ages of 3 and 5 years. Some rotary motion is developed in an attempt to increase the amount of force. This stage is characterized by a lateral fling of the arm, with rotation occurring in the trunk (Figure 15.10). Often, children step in the direction of the throw, although many keep their feet stationary. This throwing style sometimes looks like a discus throw rather than a baseball throw.

Stage Three

Typically, stage three is found among children ages 5 to 6 years. The starting position is similar to that of stages one and two in that the body is facing the target area, the feet are parallel, and the body erect. In this stage, however, a step is made toward the target with the foot on the same side of the body as the throwing arm. This allows rotation of the body and shifting of the body weight forward as the step occurs. The arm action is nearer to the overhand style of throwing than is the fling of stage two, and there is an increase in hip flexion. Un-

FIGURE 15.9 Throwing form, stage one.

FIGURE 15.10 Throwing form, stage two.

fortunately, the throwing pattern of many students never matures beyond this stage.

Stage Four

Stage four is a mature form of throwing, and more force is applied to the object being accelerated. The thrower uses the rule of opposition in this stage, taking a step in the direction of the throw with the leg opposite the throwing arm. This develops maximum body torque. The target is addressed with the nonthrowing side of the body and strides toward the target to shift body weight. Beginning with the weight on the back leg, the movement sequence is as follows: (a) step toward the target, (b) rotate the upper body, and (c) throw with the arm (Figure 15.11). The cue phrase used is, "Step, turn, and throw." The elbow should lead the way in the arm movement, followed by forearm extension, and a final snapping of the wrist. This pattern must be practiced many times to develop total body coordination. Through a combination of sound instruction and practice, the majority of youngsters are able to develop a mature pattern of throwing by age 8 or 9 years.

Stress Points

1. Stand with the nonthrowing side of the body facing the target. The throwing arm side of the body should be away from the target.
2. Step toward the target with the foot opposite the throwing hand.
3. Rotate the hips as the throwing arm moves forward.
4. Bend the arm at the elbow. The elbow should lead the forward movement of the arm.
5. Body weight remains on the rear foot (away from the target) during early phases of the throw. Just prior to the forward motion of the arm, the weight is shifted from the rear foot to the forward foot (nearer the target).

FIGURE 15.11 Throwing pattern, stage four.

TEACHING TIP

1. Offer a variety of projectiles during throwing practice so that youngsters understand how varying the weight and diameter can regulate throwing distance and speed.
2. When youngsters are learning to throw, they should throw for distance and velocity. Throwing for accuracy will discourage the development of a mature throwing form. Youngsters must be encouraged to "throw as hard as possible." Stress distance and velocity before introducing accuracy.
3. It is ineffective to work on throwing and catching at the same time. If learning to throw is the objective, youngsters will throw inaccurately and with velocity. This makes it difficult for a partner to catch the throw. Throwing should be practiced against a wall (velocity) or on a large field (distance).
4. Carpet squares or circles drawn on the floor can be used to teach youngsters proper foot movement (stepping forward).
5. Beanbags and yarnballs are excellent for developing throwing velocity since they do not rebound throughout the area.

Catching

Catching uses the hands to stop and control a moving object. Catching is more difficult to learn than throwing, because the object must be tracked and the body moved into the path of the object simultaneously. Another element that makes catching more difficult to master is fear of being hurt by the oncoming object. When teaching the early stages of catching, use objects that cannot hurt the receiver. Balloons, fleece balls, and beach balls move slowly, make tracking easier, and do not hurt if they hit a child in the face.

Stage One

In stage one of catching, hold the arms in front of the body, with elbows extended and palms up, until the ball makes contact. Then bend the arms at the elbows (Figure 15.12). The catch is actually more of a trapping movement, since the arms press the ball against the chest. Children often turn their heads away or close their eyes because of the fear response. Eliminate the fear of being hurt by a hard object and encourage them to watch the object rather than the person throwing the object.

Stage Two

In stage two, much of the same behavior as in stage one is repeated. Rather than waiting for the ball to contact the arms, however, an anticipatory movement is made and the ball is cradled somewhat.

FIGURE 15.12 Catching form, stage one.

Stage Three

In stage three, the catch is prepared for by lifting the arms and bending them slightly. The chest is used as a backstop for the ball. During this stage, contact is made with the hands first, and then the object is guided to the chest (Figure 15.13).

Stage Four

The fourth and final stage of catching, which occurs at approximately age 9 years, is characterized by catching with the hands. Encourage catching with the hands by decreasing the size of the ball to be caught. Teach giving with the arms (absorbing force) while catching. The legs bend, and the feet are moved in anticipation of the catch.

Stress Points

1. Maintain visual contact with the projectile.
2. Reach for the projectile and absorb its force by bringing the hands into the body. This "giving"

FIGURE 15.13 Catching form, stage three.

makes catching easier by reducing the chance for the object to rebound out of the hands.

3. Place the feet in a stride position rather than a straddle position. A fast-moving object will cause a loss of balance if feet are in the straddle position.
4. Place the body in line with the object rather than reaching to the side of the body to make the catch.

TEACHING TIP

1. Remove the fear factor by using projectiles that will not hurt the youngster. It is a normal reaction to dodge an object when one feels it could cause harm. The use of foam balls, yarnballs, beach balls, and balloons will facilitate learning to "keep your eye on the ball."
2. The size of the projectile should get smaller as youngsters improve their catching skills. Larger objects move more slowly and are easier than smaller projectiles to track visually.
3. Prepare youngsters for a catch by asking them to focus on the ball while it is in the thrower's hand. Use a verbal cue such as "Look (focus), ready (for the throw), catch (toss the ball)."
4. Balls and background colors should strongly contrast to facilitate visual perception.
5. If the trajectory of the projectile is raised, it will offer the youngster more opportunity for successful tracking. Beach balls will move slowly throughout a high trajectory, giving children time to focus and move into the path of the oncoming object.
6. Bounce objects off the floor so that youngsters learn to judge the rebound angle of a projectile.

Kicking

Kicking is a striking action executed with the feet. There are different types of kicking. Punting (in which the ball is dropped from the hands and kicked before it touches the ground), and placekicking (kicking the ball in a stationary position on the ground) are two. A third type is soccer kicking, which is probably the most difficult of all kicking skills because the ball is moving before the kick is executed.

Stage One

In stage one, the body is stationary, and the kicking foot is flexed in preparation for the kick. The kicking motion is carried out with a straight leg and with little or no flexing at the knee. There is minimal movement of the arms and trunk, and concentration is on the ball.

Stage Two

In the second stage of kicking, the kicking foot is lifted backwards by flexing at the knee. Usually, the child displays opposition of the limbs. When the kicking leg goes forward, the opposite arm moves forward. In stage two, the kicking leg moves farther forward in the follow-through motion compared to stage one.

Stage Three

In stage three, movement toward the object to be kicked is added. There is an increase in the distance the leg is moved, coupled with a movement of the upper body to counterbalance the leg movement.

Stage Four

Mature displays of kicking involve a preparatory extension of the hip to increase the range of motion. A run to the ball and a small leap to get the kicking foot in position are made. As the kicking foot is carried forward, the trunk leans backward, and a small step forward is made on the support foot to regain balance (Figure 15.14).

FIGURE 15.14 Kicking a soccer ball, stage four.

Stress Points

1. Youngsters need to step forward with the nonkicking leg. Stand behind and slightly to the side of the ball. Eyes should be kept on the ball (head down) throughout the kick.
2. Practice kicking with both feet.
3. Use objects that will not hurt youngsters. For example, regulation soccer balls hurt young children's feet because they are heavy and hard-covered. Foam balls and beach balls are excellent projectiles that can be used for kicking practice.
4. Encourage kickers to move their leg backward in preparation for the kick. Beginners often fail to move the leg backward, making it difficult for them to generate kicking force.
5. Arms should move in opposition to the legs during the kick.
6. After speed and velocity of the kick have been developed, focus on altering the force of the kick. Many youngsters learn to kick only with velocity; activities like soccer demand both soft "touch" kicks and kicks of maximum velocity.

TEACHING TIP

1. When teaching kicking skills, focus on velocity and distance rather than accuracy. If youngsters are asked to kick accurately, they will poke at the ball rather than develop a full kicking style.
2. Kicking is similar to throwing in that all youngsters should have a ball to kick. Beach balls (for primary grades) and foam balls are excellent as they do not travel a long distance and the youngster can kick and retrieve the ball quickly.
3. Stationary balls are easier to kick than moving balls. Use this progression when teaching beginners to kick.
4. Teach various types of kicks: the toe kick, instep kick, and the side-of-the-foot kick.

Striking

Striking occurs when an object is hit with an implement. The most common forms of striking are hitting a softball with a bat, using a racket for striking in tennis and racquetball, and striking a ball with the hand as in volleyball.

Stage One

In this stage, the feet are stationary and the trunk faces the direction of the tossed ball (or ball on a tee). The elbows are fully flexed, and the force is generated by extending the flexed joints in a downward plane. Little body force is generated because there is no trunk rotation and the motion developed is back to front. The total body does not play a role in generation of forces; rather, it comes from the arms and wrists.

Stage Two

In stage two, the upper body begins to generate force. The trunk is turned to the side in anticipation of the ball. The weight shifts from the rear foot to the forward foot prior to contacting the ball. The trunk and hips are rotated into the ball as the swing takes place. The elbows are less flexed, and force is generated by extending the flexed joints. Trunk rotation and forward movement are in an oblique plane.

Stage Three

When performing mature striking skills, stand sideways to the path of the oncoming object. Shift the weight to the rear foot and rotate the hips, followed by a shift of weight toward the ball as it approaches the hitter. Striking occurs with the arms extended in a long arc. The swing ends with weight on the forward foot. Mature striking is characterized by a swing through the full range of motion and a sequential transfer of weight from the rear to the front plane of the body.

Stress Points

1. Track the ball as soon as possible and keep tracking until it is hit. Even though it is impossible to see the racket hit the ball, it is an excellent teaching hint and encourages tracking the object as long as possible.
2. Grip the bat with the hands together. If batting right handed, the left hand should be on the bottom (near the small end of the bat).
3. Keep the elbows away from the body. Emphasis should be placed on making a large swing with the elbows extended as the ball is hit.
4. Swing the bat in a horizontal (parallel to the ground) plane. Beginners have a tendency to strike downward in a chopping motion.

TEACHING TIP

1. Striking should be done with maximum force and bat velocity when the focus of instruction is on developing a mature striking form.
2. Practice hitting stationary objects before progressing to moving objects. Batting tees and balls suspended on a string are useful for beginners.
3. Use slow-moving objects such as balloons and beach balls in the early stages of striking practice. This helps the child track the moving projectile.
4. As skill in striking increases, the size of the projectile and bat (or racket) can be decreased.
5. Ensure that there is contrast between the ball and the background to enhance visual perception.
6. Use rubber footprints to help children learn to stride (step) into the ball.

FOR MORE INFORMATION

References and Suggested Readings

Gabbard, C. P. (2003). *Lifelong motor development.* 4th ed. San Francisco, CA: Benjamin Cummings.

Gallahue, D. L., & Ozmun, J. C. (1998). *Understanding motor development: Infants, children, adolescents, adults.* New York: Wiley.

Haubenstricker, J. L., & Seefeldt, V. D. (1986). Acquisition of motor skills during childhood. In V. D. Seefeldt (Ed.), *Physical activity and well-being.* Reston, VA: AAHPERD.

Haywood, K. H. (1993). *Lifespan motor development.* 2nd ed. Champaign, IL: Human Kinetics.

Magill, R.A. (2001). *Motor learning: Concepts and applications.* 6th ed. Madison, WI: WCB: McGraw-Hill.

Payne, G. V., & Isaacs, L. D. (1998). *Human motor development: A lifespan approach.* Mountain View, CA: Mayfield.

Wickstrom, R. L. (1983). *Fundamental movement patterns.* Philadelphia: Lea & Febiger.

	ESSENTIAL COMPONENTS
I	Organized around content standards
II	Student-centered and developmentally appropriate
III	**Physical activity and motor skill development form the core of the program**
IV	Teaches management skills and self-discipline
V	**Promotes inclusion of all students**
VI	**Focuses on process over product**
VII	Promotes lifetime personal health and wellness
VIII	Teaches cooperation and responsibility and promotes sensitivity to diversity

	PHYSICAL EDUCATION STANDARDS
1	**Students are able to move competently using a variety of fundamental and specialized motor skills.**
2	Students can monitor and maintain a health-enhancing level of physical fitness.
3	Students are able to apply movement concepts and basic mechanics of skill performance when learning and refining motor skills.
4	Students comprehend the basic principles of wellness and are able to apply concepts that enable them to make meaningful decisions that positively impact their health and wellness.
5	**Students participate in a wide variety of physical activities and learn how to maintain a personalized active lifestyle.**
6	Students demonstrate empathy, understanding, and respect for the numerous differences exhibited by people in an activity setting.
7	Students exhibit responsible and self-directed behaviors that lead to positive social interactions in physical activity.

CHAPTER 16

Introductory Activities: Applying Fundamental Motor Skills

SUMMARY

Introductory activities are vigorous, challenging, unstructured movements designed to provide maximum participation for all children. These activities allow freedom of movement and challenge each child. Introductory activities comprise the initial phase of the lesson and are approximately 2–3 minutes in duration. They are used to warm children up physiologically and to prepare them for the fitness activity that follows. Introductory activities allow an opportunity for practicing management skills and focusing on the objectives of the lesson.

OUTCOMES

- Describe the rationale for including introductory activities in the lesson plan.
- Characterize various features of the introductory phase of the lesson.
- Develop an introductory activity that meets established criteria for preparing children physiologically and psychologically.
- Describe the type of movements that are used in introductory activities.

STARTING THE LESSON

It is a truism in teaching that a lesson that starts well, ends well. Management skills always take precedence over activity skills because students must be attentive if they are going to learn.

Introductory activities represent the first activity youngsters experience when entering the activity area. Vigorous fundamental locomotor movements that require minimal instruction characterize introductory activities. Introductory activities are used during the first 2 or 3 minutes of the lesson. Regardless of the introductory activity used, it is most important to be sure the class is well-managed and attentive. A good "class check" is to ask the class to enter the teaching area on the move and then freeze on signal. Run and freeze the class two more times to check whether they are with you and ready to perform. This is a good time to talk (while they are jogging) to youngsters who are talking and inattentive. Here is a key point: If the class is not with you, don't teach an introductory activity and focus on management activity such as moving and freezing on signal. Introductory activities, by their nature, are upbeat and active. They will overly arouse a poorly managed class. They are meant to reward a class that is well managed.

Introductory activities are used for a number of reasons:

1. To offer youngsters activity when entering the gym. This satisfies the need to move and gives you an opportunity to establish a learning attitude (purposive, under control) for the class.
2. To warm children up physiologically and prepare them for activity to follow.
3. To focus youngsters on the objectives of the lesson. Focus students on learning objectives by telling them the "what and why" of activities in the upcoming lesson.

Perform introductory activities at a slow pace in the initial stages for safety reasons and to warm up students. For example, if using Rhythmic Running as an introductory activity, begin by walking. As the class warms up, pick up the pace to a run. If using Group Over and Around (see page 342), begin by asking students to moderately move over and around each other. After a short period of warming up, do the activity at full speed.

EUROPEAN RHYTHMIC RUNNING

Rhythmic Running is used in many European countries to open the daily lesson. The European style is light, rhythmic running to the accompaniment of some type of percussion, usually a drum or tambourine. Skilled runners do not need accompaniment but merely keep time with a leader. Much of the running follows a circular path, but it can be done in scatter formation (Figure 16.1). To introduce a group of children to Rhythmic Running, have them clap to the beat of the drum. Next, as they clap, have them shuffle their feet in place, keeping time. Following this, have them run in place, omitting the clapping. Finally, the class can run in single-file formation, if desired. The running should be light, bouncy, and rhythmic in time with the beat. When running in single file, youngsters should stay behind the person in front, maintain proper spacing, and lift the knees in a light, prancing step.

FIGURE 16.1 European running.

A number of movement ideas can be combined with the rhythmic running pattern.

1. On signal (a whistle or a double beat on the drum), runners freeze in place. They resume running when the regular beat begins again.
2. On signal, runners make a full turn in four running steps, lifting the knees high while turning.
3. Children clap hands every fourth beat as they run. Instead of clapping, runners sound a brisk "Hey!" on the fourth beat, raising one arm with a fist at the same time.
4. Children run in squad formation, following the path set by the squad leader.
5. On signal, children run in general space, exercising care not to bump into each other. They return to a circular running formation on the next signal.
6. Students alternate between running with high knee action and regular running.
7. Runners change to a light, soundless run and back to a heavier run. The tone of the drum can control the quality of the movement.
8. Students use Rhythmic Running while handling a parachute.
9. On the command "Center," children run four steps toward the center, turn around (four steps), and run outward four steps to resume the original circular running pattern.

10. On signal, runners go backward, changing the direction of the circle.
11. Students carry a beanbag or a ball. Every fourth step, they toss the item up and catch it while running.
12. A leader moves the class through various formations. A task that is enjoyable and challenging is crossing lines of children while they alternate one child from one line in front of one youngster from another line.
13. The class moves into various shapes on signal. Possible shapes might be a square, rectangle, triangle, or pentagon. The Rhythmic Running must be continued while the youngsters move into position.
14. When a signal is given, each class member changes position with another student and then resumes the activity. An example might be to change position with the student opposite in the circle.
15. Because the movement is rhythmic, students can practice certain skills, such as a full turn. The turn can be done to a four-count rhythm and should be more deliberate than a quick turning movement that lacks definition.
16. When the drum stops, children scatter and run in random fashion. When the beat resumes, they return to circular formation and proper rhythm.

GROSS MOTOR MOVEMENTS

Most movements of the gross movement type stress locomotor activities, but some include manipulative and nonlocomotor activities. The movements should involve the body as a whole and provide abrupt change from one movement pattern to another. A routine can begin with running and then change to another movement pattern that is either specified by the teacher or determined by youngsters. Signals for change can be supplied with a voice command, whistle, drumbeat, or handclap. Children enjoy being challenged by having to change with the signal. Each part of a routine should be continued long enough for good body challenge and involvement, but not so long that it becomes wearisome.

Running provides much of the basis for gross movement activities, but other activities of a vigorous nature can be used. The suggested activities are classified roughly according to type and whether they are individual, partner, or group oriented.

Individual Running and Changing Movements

FREE RUNNING

Students run in any direction, changing direction at will.

RUNNING AND CHANGING DIRECTION

Children run in any direction, changing direction on signal. As a progression, specify the type of angle (right, obtuse, 45-degree, or 180-degree). Alternate right and left turns.

RUNNING AND CHANGING LEVEL

Children run high on their toes and change to a lower level on signal. Require runners to touch the floor sometimes when at the lower level.

RUNNING AND CHANGING THE TYPE OF LOCOMOTION

On signal, runners change from running to free choice or to a specified type of locomotion (such as walking, jumping, hopping, skipping, sliding, or galloping).

RUNNING AND STOPPING

Students run in various directions and, on signal, freeze. Stress stopping techniques and an immobilized position.

MOVE AND PERFORM ATHLETIC MOVEMENTS

Students move and stop on signal. They then perform an athletic skill move, such as a basketball jump shot, leaping football pass catch, volleyball spike, or soccer kick. Students should place emphasis on correct form and timing. A variation of the activity is for students to move with a partner and throw a pass on signal, punt a ball, or shoot a basket. The partner catches the ball or rebounds the shot.

RUN AND ASSUME A POSE

Pupils run and, on signal, assume a statue pose. Allow choice or specify a limitation.

TORTOISE AND HARE

When the teacher calls out "Tortoise," the children run slowly in general space. On the command "Hare," they change to a rapid, circular run. During the latter, stress good knee lift.

PONIES IN THE STABLE

Each child has a stable, his or her spot or place on the floor. This can be marked with a beanbag or a hoop. On the initial signal, children gallop lightly (like ponies) in general space. The next signal tells them to trot lightly to their stable and to continue trotting lightly in place.

HIGH FIVES

Students move in different directions throughout the area. On signal, they are challenged to run toward a partner, jump, and give a "high five" (slap hands) while moving. Emphasis should be placed on timing so that the "high five" is given at the top of the jump. Combinations of changing the level as well as changing the speed of the movement can be developed.

ADDING FITNESS CHALLENGES

Running (or other locomotor movements) can be combined with fitness activities. During the signaled stop, exercises such as push-ups and curl-ups can be done.

MOVE AND PERFORM A TASK ON SIGNAL

Youngsters move and perform a task on signal. Tasks can be individual or partner activities. Examples are Seat Circles, Balances, Wring the Dishrag, Partner Hopping, Twister, and Back-to-Back Get-Up (see Chapter 20).

RUN, STOP, AND PIVOT

Students run, stop, and then pivot. This is an excellent activity for game skill development. Youngsters enjoy it especially when they are told to imagine that they are basketball or football players.

TRIPLE S ROUTINE

The triple S's are *speed, style,* and *stop.* Children are in scatter formation throughout the area. On the command "Speed," they run in general space rapidly while avoiding contact with others. On "Style," all run with style (easy, light, loose running) in a large, circular, counterclockwise path. On the command "Stop," all freeze quickly under control. Repeat as necessary.

AGILITY RUN

Pick two lines or markers 5 to 10 yards apart. Students run (or use other locomotor movements) back and forth between the lines for a specified time (10, 15, or 20 seconds). Students can add a personal challenge by seeing how many times they can move back and forth within the given time limit.

Other Individual Movement Combinations

UPRIGHT MOVEMENT TO ALL FOURS

Youngsters begin with a movement in upright position and change to one on all fours.

SECRET MOVEMENT

The teacher has written a number of movements on cards and selects one. Direction is given by saying, "I want you to show me the secret movement." The children select a movement and continue that movement without change until they are signaled to stop, whereupon the teacher identifies those who performed the movement on the card. The movement is then demonstrated by those who chanced upon it, and all perform it together. If no one comes up with the movement pattern on the card, repeat the activity by asking the children to change their responses.

AIRPLANES

Children pretend to be airplanes. When told to take off, they zoom with arms out, swooping, turning, and gliding (Figure 16.2, page 340). When they are commanded to land, they drop to the floor in prone position, simulating a plane at rest. To start their engines and take off, they can perform a series of push-ups and move up and down while simulating engine noise.

COMBINATION MOVEMENT

Directives for combination movement can establish specified movements or allow some choice. The limitation might be to run, skip, and roll, or to jump, twist, and shake. Another approach is to set a number for the sequence and let the children select the activities. Say, "Put three different kinds of movement together in a smooth pattern."

COUNTDOWN

The teacher begins a countdown for blastoff: "Ten, nine, eight, seven, six, five, four, three, two, one—blastoff!" The children are scattered, and each makes an abrupt, jerky movement on each count. On the word blastoff, they jump up in the air and run in different directions until the stop signal is given.

MAGIC-NUMBER CHALLENGES

A challenge can be issued like this: "Ten, ten, and ten." Children then put together three movements, doing ten repetitions of each. Or the teacher could say, "Today we are going to play our version of Twenty-One." Twenty-one becomes the magic number that is to be fulfilled with three movements, each of which is done seven times.

CROSSING THE RIVER

A river can be set up as the space between two parallel lines about 40 feet apart, or it can be the crosswise area in a gymnasium. Each time the children cross the river, they use a different type of locomotor movement. Children should be encouraged not to repeat a movement. Play is continuous over a minute or so.

FIGURE 16.2 Performing airplanes.

FOUR-CORNERS MOVEMENT

Lay out a square with a cone at each corner. As the student passes each corner, he or she changes to a different locomotor movement with an agility emphasis. Challenge students with some of the following sport agility movements: backward running, leaps, grapevine step, front crossover, back crossover, high knees, and slide steps. Add variation by changing the qualities of movement (i.e., soft, heavy, slow, fast, etc.). Students can pass to the outside of the area if they are doing a faster-moving movement.

JUMPING AND HOPPING PATTERNS

Each child has a home spot. The teacher provides jumping and hopping sequences to take children away from and back to their spot. The teacher could say, "Move with three jumps, two hops, and a half turn. Return to place the same way." The teacher should have on hand a number of sequences. Action can extend beyond simply jumping and hopping.

LEADING WITH BODY PARTS

Students move throughout the area with some body part leading. Try using various body parts, such as elbow, fingers, head, shoulder, knees, and toes. Try the same exercise with different body parts trailing. Try moving and leading with two different body parts. Try with three. Try also with combinations of body parts trailing the body. Children can jog with some body part leading or trailing. On signal, tell them to make a different body part lead or trail the body.

MOVE, ROCK, AND ROLL

Each youngster procures an individual mat and places it on the floor. Students are challenged to move around, over, and on the mats. When a signal is given, children move to a mat and try different ways of rocking and rolling. Rocking on different parts of the body can be specified, and different body rolls can be suggested. As another challenge, tell the children to do a rock or a roll or both on a mat, get up and run to another mat, and repeat the sequence. Older children enjoy seeing how many mats they can move to within a certain amount of time.

Individual Rhythmic Movements

MUSICAL RELAXATION

Musical relaxation can be conducted with a drum or appropriate recorded music. Children run in time to the rhythm. When the rhythm stops, each child reclines on the back, closes the eyes, and remains relaxed until the music begins again.

MOVING TO RHYTHM

The possibilities with rhythm are many. Rhythm can guide locomotor movements, with changes in tempo being part of the activity. The intensity of the sound can be translated into light or heavy movements.

MOVING TO MUSIC

Pieces such as the Bleking song (page 432) and "Pop Goes the Weasel" (pages 436–437) can provide a basis for creative movement. These are two-part pieces, so a nonlocomotor movement can be done to the first part and a locomotor movement to the second.

FOLK DANCE MOVEMENT

Use a CD or tape recording to stimulate different types of rhythmic movement such as polka, schottische, and two-step. Youngsters can move around the room practicing the steps dictated by the music.

Individual Movements with Manipulation

INDIVIDUAL ROPE JUMPING

Each child runs with rope in hand. On the signal to change, the child stops and begins to jump rope.

HOOP ACTIVITIES

Each child runs holding a hoop. When the signal is given to stop, the child either does hula-hooping or lays the hoop on the floor and uses it for hopping and jumping patterns.

WAND ACTIVITIES

Movements similar to those done with jump ropes and hoops can be performed with wands. After they run and stop, the children do wand stunts.

MILK CARTON FUN

Each child has a milk carton stuffed with crumpled newspapers and secured with cellophane tape. The children kick the cartons in different directions for 1 minute.

BALL ACTIVITIES

Youngsters dribble balls as in basketball or (outside) as in soccer. When a change is signaled, they stop, balance on one leg, and pass the ball under the other leg, around the back, and overhead, keeping both control and balance. Other challenges can be supplied that involve both movement with the ball and manipulative actions performed in place.

BEANBAG TOUCH AND GO

Beanbags are spread throughout the area. On signal, youngsters move and touch as many different beanbags as possible with their hands. Different body parts can be specified for children to use for touching. Different colors of beanbags can be selected, and the command might be "Touch as many blue beanbags as possible with your elbow."

Children can also move to and around a beanbag. The type of movement can be varied; for example, they might skip around the yellow beanbags with the left side leading. Change the movement as well as the direction and leading side of the body. Another enjoyable activity for youngsters is to trace out a shape (e.g., triangle, circle, square) as they move from beanbag to beanbag.

TEACHING TIP

Variation: *Vanishing Beanbags.* Students move around the beanbags as described above. While they are moving, the teacher or a designated student picks up one or two of the bags. On signal, students move to a beanbag and sit on it. The goal is not to be left out. The activity is repeated with all students participating each time.

LONG-ROPE ROUTINE

Students begin in a loose column composed of four people holding a long jump rope in their right hands at waist level. A series of four signals is given. On the first signal, youngsters jog lightly in a column. On the second signal, the group shifts the rope overhead from the right side to the left side of the body while jogging. At the third signal, the two inside students release the rope and begin jumping as soon as the two students at the end of the rope start turning the rope. On the fourth signal, the turners become jumpers and vice versa. The sequence is repeated a number of times.

DISAPPEARING HOOPS

Each child gets a hoop and places it somewhere on the floor. Offer challenges such as "Move through five blue hoops, jump over four yellow hoops, and skip around six green hoops." On signal, the children move to find a hoop and balance inside it. As youngsters are moving, take away two or three hoops. At the signal, some students will not find a hoop. Those left out then offer the class the next movement challenge. Different challenges and stunts inside the hoops can be specified.

Partner and Group Activities

MARKING

Each child has a partner who is somewhat equal in ability. Under control, one partner runs, dodges, and tries to lose the other, who must stay within 3 feet of the runner. On signal, both stop. Chasers must be able to touch their partners to say that they have marked them. Partners then change roles.

FOLLOWING ACTIVITY

One partner leads and performs various kinds of movements. The other partner must move in the same fashion. This idea can be extended to squad organization.

FASTEST TAG IN THE WEST

Every player is a tagger. The object is to tag other players without being tagged. Players who are tagged must sit or kneel and await the next game. (Start new games frequently.) If two or more players tag each other simultaneously, they are both (all) "out."

MEDIC TAG

Three or four students are designated as "taggers." They try to tag other students; when tagged, a student kneels as if injured. Another student (not one of the taggers) can "rehabilitate" the injured player with a touch, enabling the student to resume play.

HOSPITAL TAG

Every player is a tagger. Any player who is tagged must cover with one hand the body area that was touched. Students may be tagged twice but must be able to hold both tagged spots and keep moving. A student who is tagged three times must freeze. Restart the game when most of the students have been frozen.

GROUP OVER AND AROUND

Half of the children are scattered. Each is in a curled position, face down. The other children leap or jump over the curled children (Figure 16.3). On signal, reverse the groups quickly. Instead of being curled, the children form arches or bridges, and the moving children go around these. A further extension is to have the children on the floor alternate between curled and bridge positions. If a moving child goes over the curled position, the floor child changes immediately to a bridge. The moving children react accordingly.

LIVING OBSTACLES

This activity is similar to Group Over and Around except that the youngsters on the floor are in a bridged position and moving. The children moving over and around must move quickly, as the obstacles are moving. Change positions after a designated amount of time.

POPCORN

Half the class is scattered throughout the area and assume the push-up position. The other half of the class will move and "pop the popcorn." This is done by moving over and around the students who are in push-up position. When a student moves around a student, that youngster lowers to the floor. When a student moves over a student lying on the floor, that student raises to the push-up position. Moving students should exchange places with those on the floor after a designated time.

PYRAMID POWER

Students move throughout the area. On signal, they find a partner and build a simple pyramid or partner stand. Examples are the hip-shoulder stand, double-crab stand, double-dog stand, and shoulder stand. Students should be cautioned to select a partner of similar size and to stand on the proper points of support.

FIGURE 16.3 Group over and around.

BRIDGES BY THREES

Three children in a group can set up an interesting movement sequence using bridges. Two of the children make bridges, and the third child goes under both bridges and sets up a bridge. Each child in turn goes under the bridges of the other two. Different kinds of bridges can be specified, and the bridges can be arranged so that a change in direction is made. An over-and-under sequence also provides interest. The child vaults or jumps over the first bridge and then goes under the next bridge before setting up the third bridge.

RUBBER BAND

Students gather around the teacher in the center of the area. On signal, students move away from the teacher with a designated movement such as run, hop sideways, skip backward, double-lame dog, or grapevine step. On signal, they sprint back to the central point, jump, and give a shout.

NEW LEADER MOVEMENTS

Squads or small groups run around the area, following a leader. When the change is signaled, the last person goes to the head of the line to lead. Groups of three are ideal for this activity.

MANIPULATIVE ACTIVITIES

Each child has a beanbag. The children move around the area, tossing the bags upward and catching them as they move. On signal, they drop the bags to the floor and jump, hop, or leap over as many bags as possible. On the next signal, they pick up any convenient bag and resume tossing to themselves. Having one fewer beanbag than children adds to the fun. Hoops can also be used in this manner. Children begin by using hoops in rope-jumping style or for hula-hooping. On signal, the hoops are placed on the floor, and the children jump in and out of as many hoops as they can. Next, they pick up a nearby hoop and resume the original movement pattern. The activity also can be done with jump ropes.

BODY PART IDENTIFICATION

Enough beanbags for the whole class are scattered on the floor. The children either run between or jump over the beanbags. When a body part is called out, the children place that body part on the nearest beanbag.

LEAPFROG

Two, three, or four children can make up this sequence. The children form a straight or curved column, with all except the last child in line taking the leapfrog position. The last child leaps over the other children in turn, and after going over all, assumes the leapfrog position at the head of the column. Lines should be scattered to avoid running into other jumpers.

DRILL SERGEANT

The drill sergeant leads the squad marching and in line. When desired, the drill sergeant gives these kinds of commands for the movement sequence to be performed: "Walk, jump twice, land, and roll." "Run, jump-turn, and freeze (pose)." "Shake, jump-turn, land, and roll." "Seal Walk, Log Roll, and jump." The squad leader can be given cards with suggested patterns written on them. To add a realistic flavor, the sergeant can call the squad members to attention, give them the directions, and then call, "March!"

CREATIVE AND EXPLORATORY OPPORTUNITIES

Another approach of interest to children is providing creative and exploratory opportunities at the beginning of a lesson. Some examples follow.

1. Put out enough equipment of one type (hoops, balls, wands, beanbags) so that all children have a piece of equipment with which to explore. This can be open exploration, or the movement can follow the trend of a prior lesson, thus supplying extension to the progression.
2. Have available a number of manipulative items. The children select any item they wish and decide whether to play alone, with a partner, or as a member of a small group.
3. Make available a range of apparatus, such as climbing ropes, climbing apparatus, mats, boxes, balance beams, balance boards, and similar items. Manipulative items also can be a part of the package. The children choose the area in which they want to participate.

TAMBOURINE-DIRECTED ACTIVITIES

The tambourine can signal changes of movement, because it can produce two different kinds of sound: the tinny noise made by vigorous shaking and the percussive sound made by striking the instrument. Movement changes are signaled by changing from one sound to the other.

SHAKING SOUND

1. The children remain in one spot but shake all over. These should be gross movements.
2. The children shake and gradually drop to the floor.

3. The children scurry in every direction.
4. The children run lightly with tiny steps.

DRUM SOUND

1. Students make jerky movements to the percussive beat.
2. They jump in place or through space.
3. Youngsters do locomotor movements in keeping with the beat.
4. Responding to three beats, the children collapse on the first beat, roll on the second, and form a shape on the third.

COMBINATIONS

To form a combination of movements, select one from each category (shaking or percussive). When the shaking sound is made, the children perform that movement. When the sound is changed to the drum sound, the children react accordingly.

GAMES AND MISCELLANEOUS ACTIVITIES

Selected games are quite suitable for introductory activities, provided that they keep all children active, are simple, and require little teaching. Usually, a familiar game is used so that little organizational time is needed. Some appropriate games are listed.

Addition Tag (page 556)
Back to Back (page 555)
Barker's Hoopla (page 567)
Circle Touch (page 568)
Couple Tag (page 560)
Loose Caboose (page 563)
One, Two, Button My Shoe (page 551)
Squad Tag (page 565)
Touchdown (page 570)
Whistle Mixer (page 567)
European Running (pages 337–338)
Performing Airplanes (page 339)
Group Over and Around (page 342)

	ESSENTIAL COMPONENTS
I	Organized around content standards
II	Student-centered and developmentally appropriate
III	**Physical activity and motor skill development form the core of the program**
IV	Teaches management skills and self-discipline
V	**Promotes inclusion of all students**
VI	**Focuses on process over product**
VII	**Promotes lifetime personal health and wellness**
VIII	Teaches cooperation and responsibility and promotes sensitivity to diversity

	PHYSICAL EDUCATION STANDARDS
1	**Students are able to move competently using a variety of fundamental and specialized motor skills.**
2	Students can monitor and maintain a health-enhancing level of physical fitness.
3	**Students are able to apply movement concepts and basic mechanics of skill performance when learning and refining motor skills.**
4	Students comprehend the basic principles of wellness and are able to apply concepts that enable them to make meaningful decisions that positively impact their health and wellness.
5	**Students participate in a wide variety of physical activities and learn how to maintain a personalized active lifestyle.**
6	Students demonstrate empathy, understanding, and respect for the numerous differences exhibited by people in an activity setting.
7	Students exhibit responsible and self-directed behaviors that lead to positive social interactions in physical activity.

CHAPTER 17

Manipulative Skills

SUMMARY

Activities in this chapter develop manipulative skills. A manipulative skill is one in which a child handles an object with the hands, feet, or other body parts. Development of sport skills results from practicing and learning advanced activities in this chapter. Jump rope activities develop specialized motor skills, particularly visual-tactile coordination. Rope-jumping activities in this chapter progress from individual movements using rope patterns, to long-rope jumping with turners, to individual rope-jumping challenges. Rhythmic gymnastic activities combine rhythmic and manipulative skills using a particular piece of manipulative equipment while moving to accompaniment.

OUTCOMES

- Incorporate creative opportunities in teaching manipulative skills.
- Identify instructional procedures related to different types of manipulative skills.
- Outline skill progressions, activities, and instructional hints associated with using balloons, beanbags, balls, paddles, frisbees, hoops, jump ropes, parachutes, and other objects to teach manipulative skills.
- Identify beginning, intermediate, and advanced rope-jumping skills and routines using individual and long ropes.
- List progressions to use when teaching rope-jumping.
- Describe the various criteria used in selecting and evaluating jump ropes.

Manipulative activities are characterized by the use of some type of implement, usually with the hands but possibly with the feet or other body parts. Manipulative activities invite application of educational movement methodology, adding an important dimension to movement experiences. Manipulative activities develop both hand-eye and foot-eye coordination as well as dexterity. Activities with balloons, hoops, wands, beanbags, balls of various types, tug-of-war ropes, Lummi sticks, Frisbees, and scoops round out a basic program. Activities with jump ropes are important in the program because they offer multiple possibilities: manipulative activity, rhythmic activity, and fundamental movement.

Balloons, beanbags, and yarn balls provide early throwing and catching activities for younger children. A soft object reduces the fear younger children have of being hurt while catching an object. After the introductory skills are mastered, other types of balls and more demanding skills can be initiated.

The start-and-expand approach is sound for teaching manipulative activities. Start children with a challenge that allows all to achieve success, and then expand the skills and experiences from that base. Concern for progression usually dictates that most activities begin with the individual approach and move later to partner activity.

PROGRESSION AND MOVEMENT THEMES

Activities within each unit in this chapter are presented in progression and take the form of movement themes or movement tasks and challenges. Movement themes, as opposed to simply listing a series of activities in progression, help teachers instruct toward desired objectives. For example, the first movement theme in beanbag activities is titled *Tossing to Self in Place.* Suggestions for the development of this theme follow. Teachers can take either of two approaches. They can develop one or two themes in depth, exhausting all of the possibilities, or they can select a few activities from a number of themes, moving from one to the other with more dispatch. In the latter case, when the lesson is repeated the following day, the teacher can use the same themes but pose different challenges.

Opportunity for creative expression should be offered on a planned basis. This gives youngsters a chance to practice their favorite skills, work on learning new skills, or invent different ways of performing. The lesson plan should allow time for creative activity in the progressions.

Reinforcing Skills with Creative Games

Skills can be reinforced and enhanced through creative games. Children can be given a brief outline of a game situation on which they can structure a game applying the skills just learned. Specification of the game situation can range from open choice to creativity within guidelines. In either case, the focus is on using the skills just learned. As an example, the teacher might tell youngsters to create a game embodying a certain skill in which they are to select the equipment needed, outline the game space, specify number of participants, and set the rules, including scoring. More specifically, the teacher might outline certain conditions, such as use of two hoops and two bowling pins, space limitations of two lines 20 to 30 feet apart, and competing sides of two against two. Within those parameters, students would then create a game.

Creative games can be oriented toward individuals, partners, or small groups. Groups should be kept small, or individual input becomes minimal. Different kinds of equipment can be specified (such as mats, wands, goals, or benches). After a period of time, different games can be demonstrated. While the creative process certainly has excellent value, the focus on the skill to be practiced must not be lost.

ACTIVITIES WITH BALLOONS AND BEACH BALLS

Balloons provide interesting movement experiences and emphasize hand-eye coordination. Success can be achieved with balloons when students are not ready for faster-moving ball skills. Keeping a balloon afloat is within the capability of young children and special education students. Beach balls are larger, move slowly, and are more predictable in movement. Both objects are harmless and allow youngsters to learn to catch without fear of being hurt by the projectile. Emphasis should be placed on proper footwork. Because these objects move slowly, there is ample time for students to learn proper footwork—preparing for a volley, catching, and striking, for example.

Balloons are inexpensive and readily available. Extras are needed, as there is always breakage. The balloons should be of good quality and spherical in shape. At times, however, oddly shaped balloons can provide a change of pace. Balloons should be inflated only moderately, because high inflation increases the chance of breakage. Beach balls should be inflated with a ball pump. When they are no longer needed for instruction, they can be deflated and stored.

Instructional Procedures

1. Use the following instructional cues when teaching balloon and beach ball skills:
   a. Catch and control with the fingertips.
   b. Keep your eyes on the object.

c. Move your body into the path of the oncoming object.

d. Reach, catch, and move the object to the body (giving).

2. After blowing up each balloon, twist the neck and fix it with a twist tie of the type used to close plastic bags. This permits the balloon to be deflated easily and reused. Tying a knot in the neck makes deflating difficult.
3. Beach balls should not be overinflated. They will last longer and be easier to control if they are a bit underinflated. Sixteen- to 20-inch diameter beach balls are best for most youngsters and can also be used with older students for lead-up games in volleyball and soccer.

Recommended Activities

1. Begin with free exploration, having children play under control with their balloon (Figure 17.1). The objective is to have the children gain a sense of the balloon's flight.
2. Introduce specific hand, finger, and arm contacts. Include using alternate hands; contacting at different levels (low, high, in between); jumping and making high contact; using different hand contacts (palm, back, side, and different fist positions); using different finger combinations (two fingers, index finger, thumb only, others); and using arms, elbows, and shoulders.
3. Expand the activity to use other body parts. Establish contact sequences with three or four body parts. Use various levels and body shapes. Make some visual cards with names of body parts. Students must take their eye off the balloon to see the named body part. This is an excellent challenge to help young children learn to track a moving object.
4. Bat from various body positions—kneeling, sitting, lying.
5. Use an object to control the balloon (a lummi stick, a ball, a stocking paddle).
6. Restrict movement. Keep one foot in place. Keep one or both feet within a hoop or on a mat or carpet square.
7. Work with a partner by alternating turns, batting the beach ball back and forth, employing follow-the-leader patterns, and so on.
8. Introduce some aspects of volleyball technique, including the overhand pass, the underhand pass, and the dig pass. Begin with a volleyball serve. Make this informal and on a "let's pretend" basis. Check the volleyball unit (Chapter 29) for technique suggestions.
9. Propel a balloon upward. Pick up a hoop from the floor, pass it around the balloon, replace the hoop on the floor, and keep the balloon from touching the ground.
10. Have four to six children seated on the floor in a small circle. Each circle gets two balloons to be kept in the air. Children's seats are "glued" to the floor. Once a balloon hits the floor, it is out of play. Play for a specified time (30 to 60 seconds). Increase the challenge by using beach balls.

FIGURE 17.1 Batting balloons from different body positions.

ACTIVITIES WITH BEANBAGS

Activities with beanbags provide valuable learning experiences for elementary school children at all levels. All parts of the body can be brought into play. For tossing and catching, though, the beanbag encourages manipulation with the hands; playground balls lead to arm and body catching. Beanbag activities can be used with older youngsters provided that the activities are carefully selected to challenge students. The more challenging partner activities—juggling, different and unique methods of propulsion, and the Split-Vision Drill (page 350)—are examples of suitable activities.

Instructional Procedures

1. Use the following instructional cues when teaching beanbag activities:

a. Stress a soft receipt of the beanbag by giving with the hands, arms, and legs. "Giving" involves the hands going out toward the incoming beanbag and bringing it in for a soft landing.

   b. Keep your eyes on the beanbag when catching.
   c. When tossing and catching, toss slightly above eye level.

2. Make sure that beanbags are at least 6 inches square. This size balances well and can be controlled on various parts of the body, thus offering greater challenge to intermediate-level children.
3. Throwing and catching skills involve many intricate elements. Emphasize the principles of opposition, eye focus, weight transfer, and follow-through. It is important that children track the object being caught and focus on the target when throwing.
4. Stress laterality and directionality when teaching throwing and catching skills. Children should be taught to throw, catch, and balance beanbags with both the left and right sides of their body. They should learn to catch and throw at different levels.
5. Children should throw at chest height to a partner, unless a different type of throw is specified. Teach all types of return: low, medium, high, left, and right.
6. In partner work, keep distances between partners reasonable, especially in introductory phases. Fifteen feet or so is a reasonable starting distance.
7. In partner work, emphasize skillful and varied throwing, catching, and handling of the beanbag. Throwing too hard or out of range, to cause the partner to miss, should be avoided.

Most activities are classified as individual or partner activities. A few activities are for groups of three or more.

Individual Activities

Tossing to Self in Place

1. Toss with both hands, with right hand only, and with left hand only. Catch the same way. Catch with the back of the hands.
2. Toss the beanbag progressively higher, then progressively lower.
3. Hold the beanbag in one hand and make large arm circles (imitating a windmill). Release the bag so that it flies upward, and then catch it.
4. Toss from side to side, right to left (reverse), front to back (reverse), and around various body parts in different combinations.
5. Toss upward and catch with hands behind the back. Toss upward from behind the body and catch in front. Toss upward and catch on the back, on the knees, on the toes, and on other body parts.
6. Hold the bag at arm's length in front of the body, with palms up. Withdraw hands quickly from under the bag, and catch it from on top in a palms-down stroke before it falls to the floor.
7. Toss upward and catch as high as possible. As low as possible. Work out a sequence of high, low, and in between.
8. Toss upward and catch with the body off the floor. Try tossing as well as catching with the body off the ground.
9. Toss in various fashions while seated and while lying.
10. Toss two beanbags upward and catch a bag in each hand.

Adding Stunts in Place

1. Toss overhead to the rear, turn around, and catch. Toss, do a full turn, and catch.
2. Toss, clap the hands, and catch. Clap the hands more than once. Clap the hands around different body parts.
3. Toss, do pretend activities (e.g., comb hair, wash face, brush teeth, shine shoes), and catch.
4. Toss, touch different body parts with both hands, and catch. Touch two different body parts, calling out the name of the parts. Touch two body parts, clap hands, and catch.
5. Toss, kneel on one knee, and catch. Try this going to a sitting or lying position. Reverse the position order, coming from a lying or sitting position to a standing position to catch.
6. Toss, touch the floor, and catch. Explore with other challenges. Use heel clicks or balance positions.
7. Bend forward, reach between the legs, and toss the bag onto the back or shoulders.
8. Reach one hand over the shoulder, drop the beanbag, and catch it with the other hand behind the back. Reverse the hands. Drop the beanbag from one hand behind the back and catch it with the other hand between the legs. Put the beanbag on the head, lean back, and catch it with both hands behind the back. Catch it with one hand.

Locomotor Movements

1. Toss to self, moving to another spot to catch. Toss forward, run, and catch. Move from side to side. Toss overhead to the rear, run back, and catch.
2. Add various stunts and challenges described previously. Vary with different locomotor movements.

Balancing the Beanbag on Various Body Parts

1. Balance the beanbag on the head. Move around, keeping the beanbag in place. Sit down, lie down, turn around, and so on.
2. Balance the beanbag on other parts of the body and move around. Balance on top of the instep, between the knees, on the shoulders, on the elbows, under the chin. Use more than one beanbag.

Propelling with Various Body Parts

1. Toss to self from various parts of the body: the elbow, the instep, the knees, the shoulders, between the feet, between the heels.
2. Sit and toss the bag from the feet to the hands. Practice tossing in a supine position. From a supine position, pick up the bag between the toes and place it behind the head, using a full curl position. Go back and pick it up, returning it to place.

Juggling

1. Begin with two bags and juggle them in the air. (See pages 354–358 for instructions on juggling.)
2. Juggle three bags.

Other Activities

1. From a standing wide-straddle position, place the beanbag on the floor and push it between the legs as far back as possible. Jump in place with a half turn and repeat.
2. Take the same position as above. Push the bag back as far as possible between the legs, bending the knees. Without moving the legs, turn to the right and pick up the bag. Repeat to the left.
3. Stand with feet apart and hold the beanbag with both hands. Reach as high as possible (with both hands), bend backward, and drop the bag. Reach between the legs, and pick up the bag.
4. On all fours, put the bag in the small of the back. Wiggle and force the bag off the back without moving the hands or knees from place.
5. In crab position, place the beanbag on the stomach, and try to shake it off. On all fours, put it on the back and do a Mule Kick (Figure 20.45 on page 488).
6. Push the beanbag across the floor with different body parts, such as the nose, shoulder, or knee.
7. Each student drops a beanbag on the floor. See how many different ways students can move over, around, and between the beanbags. As an example, jump three bags, crab-walk around two others, and cartwheel over one more.
8. Spread the legs about shoulder width. Bend over and throw the beanbag between the legs and onto the back. Next, throw the beanbag all the way over the head, and catch it.

Partner Activities

Tossing Back and Forth

1. Begin with various kinds of two-handed throws: underhand, overhead, side, and over the shoulder. Change to one-handed tossing and throwing.
2. Throw at different levels, at different targets, right and left.
3. Throw under the leg, around the body. Center as in football. Try imitating the shot put and the discus throw. Try the softball (full arc) throw.
4. Have partners sit cross-legged about 10 feet apart. Throw and catch in various styles.
5. Use follow activities, in which one partner leads with a throw and the other follows with the same kind of throw.
6. Jump, turn in the air, and pass to partner.
7. Toss to partner from unexpected positions and from around and under different body parts.
8. Stand back to back and pass the bag around both partners from hand to hand as quickly as possible. Also try moving the bag around and through various body parts.
9. Toss in various directions to make partner move and catch.
10. Run around partner in a circle, tossing the bag back and forth.
11. Propel two beanbags back and forth. Each partner has a bag, and the bags go in opposite directions at the same time. Try having one partner toss both bags at once in the same direction, using various types of throws. Try to keep three bags going at once.

Propelling Back and Forth with Different Body Parts

1. From a sitting position, toss the bag to partner with foot or toes, from on top of the feet, and from between the feet, with elbow, shoulder, head, and any other body part.
2. With back to partner, take a bunny-jump position. With the bag held between the feet, kick the bag back to partner. Try kicking with both feet from a standing position.

3. Partners lie supine on the floor with heads pointing toward each other, about 6 inches apart. One partner has a beanbag between the feet and deposits it in between their heads. The other partner picks up the bag with the feet (reaching over the head) and places it on the floor by the feet after returning to a lying position. With both partners in backward curl position, try to transfer the bag directly from one partner to the other with the feet.

Group Activities and Games

SPLIT-VISION DRILL

A split-vision drill from basketball can be adapted to beanbags. An active player faces two partners about 15 feet away. They are standing side by side, a short distance apart. Two beanbags, one in the hands of the active player and the other with one of the partners, are needed for the drill. The active player tosses to the open partner and at the same time receives the bag from the other partner. The two bags move back and forth between the active player and the other two, alternately (Figure 17.2). After a period of time, change positions.

TARGET GAMES

Wastebaskets, hoops, circles drawn on the floor, and other objects can be used as targets for beanbag tossing. Target boards with holes cut out are available from commercial sources. Holes can be triangles, circles, squares, and rectangles, thus stressing form concepts.

BEANBAG QUOITS

The game is played in the same way as horseshoes. A court is drawn with two spots on the floor about 20 feet apart. Spots can be made with masking tape and should be 1 inch in diameter. Each competitor has two bags, a different color for each player. Tosses are made from behind one spot to the other spot. The object is to get one or both bags closer to the mark than the opponents do. If a bag completely blocks out the spot, as viewed from directly overhead, the player scores 3 points. Otherwise, the bag nearest the spot scores 1 point. Games are played to 11, 15, or 21 points. In each round, the player winning the previous point tosses first.

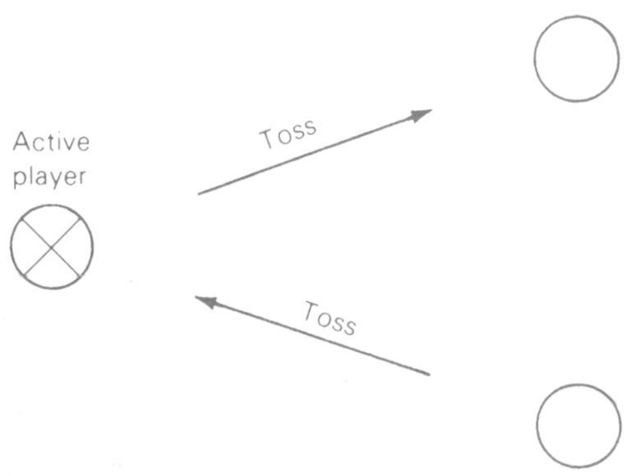

FIGURE 17.2 Split-vision drill for beanbags.

OTHER GAMES

TEACHING TIP

Children enjoy playing One Step (page 564). Teacher Ball (page 555) is also readily adaptable to beanbags.

ACTIVITIES WITH BALLS

Included in this section are the ball skills in which the child handles balls without the aid of other equipment, such as a bat or paddle. Ball skills are mostly of two types: (a) hand-eye skills, including throwing, catching, bouncing, dribbling (as in basketball), batting (as in volleyball), and rolling (as in bowling); and (b) foot-eye skills, including kicking, trapping, and dribbling (as in soccer).

Types of Balls

For younger children, sponge rubber, yarn, and fleece balls are all excellent for introductory throwing and catching, because they help overcome the fear factor. (See Chapter 10 for instructions on how to make balls from yarn.) The innovative teacher can probably develop other suitable objects, such as crumpled-up newspaper balls wrapped with cellophane tape, papier-mâché balls, stitched rolls of socks, and stuffed balloons.

The whiffle ball, a hollow plastic ball with holes cut in the surface, is also useful. Scoops, either commercial or home constructed, provide an extension of whiffle ball activities. Another type of ball that has value is a soft softball, a much softer version of the regular softball. It is suitable for catching and throwing but does not hold up well if batted.

The inflated rubber playground ball (8½-inch size) should be the ball used for most ball-handling experiences. Balls should be inflated moderately so that they bounce well, but not overinflated, which makes them difficult to catch. Overinflation can also distort the ball's spherical shape.

Balls that last longer and have more utility for youngsters are the 8-inch foam balls. The foam balls are easier to catch and pass and will not hurt if youngsters are accidentally hit by one. There are many different types of foam used to make these balls and it is important to make sure that the balls are dense and that they have adequate bounce. Many of the cheaper styles are extremely light and will not bounce. An even better (but more expensive) alternative are the foam "tough-skin" balls. These are foam balls that are covered with a tough plastic coating. This skin causes the balls to bounce better and to resist damage to the soft foam. In the long run, these "tough-skin" balls may be the most economical as they will not leak or develop punctures like the standard playground ball.

Some attention should be given to the color of the balls. In a study comparing blue, yellow, and white balls against a black background and a white background, "blue and yellow balls produced significantly higher catching scores than did a white ball" (Morris, 1976). However, no data were provided for the common playground balls of red color.

Types of Organization

Instruction with younger children should begin with individual work and progress to partner and group activities. After the children have acquired some skill, a lesson can include both individual and partner activities. In propelling the ball back and forth between partners, the children can progress from rolling the ball, to throwing with one bounce, to throwing on the fly. Be sure that a disparity in skill level between partners does not cause a problem for either.

Distance between partners should be short at first and then lengthened gradually. The concept of targets is introduced by directing the children to throw the ball to specified points. Later, a change from a stationary target to a moving target maintains progression. Relays are useful for reinforcing learning, but the skills should be learned reasonably well before application in a relay.

Group work should be confined to small groups (of three to six), so that each child can be active, and should include activities not possible in individual or partner activity.

Instructional Procedures

1. Use the following instructional cues when teaching ball skills.
   a. Keep your eyes on the ball.
   b. Catch and dribble the ball with the pads of the fingers.
   c. Use opposition and weight transfer when passing the ball.
2. In catching, soft receipt of the ball is achieved by "giving" with the hands and arms. The hands should reach out somewhat to receive the ball and then cushion the impact by bringing the ball in toward the body in a relaxed way.
3. To catch a throw above the waist, the hands should be positioned so that the thumbs are together. To receive a throw below the waist, the little fingers should be kept toward each other and the thumbs kept out.
4. In throwing to a partner, unless otherwise specified, the throw should reach the partner at about chest height. At times, different target points should be specified—high, low, right, left, at the knee, and so on.
5. A lesson should begin with basic skills within the reach of all and progress to more challenging activities.
6. Laterality is an important consideration. Right and left members of the body should be given practice in turn.
7. Split-vision should be incorporated in bouncing and dribbling. Children should learn to look forward, rather than at the ball, when bouncing and dribbling.
8. Tactile senses can be enhanced by having children dribble or bounce the ball with eyes closed.
9. Rhythmic accompaniment, particularly for bouncing and dribbling activities, adds another dimension to ball skills.
10. Enough balls should be available so that each child has one.
11. The problem of uncontrolled balls can be solved by telling children to ignore stray balls, as someone is sure to be coming after them.

Activities with balls are presented with an 8½-inch ball in mind. Some modification is needed if the balls used are smaller or are of the type that does not bounce.

Individual Activities

Each child has a ball and practices alone. In the first group of individual activities, the child remains in the same spot. Next, the child rebounds the ball against a wall. (The wall should be reasonably free of projections and irregular surfaces so that the ball can return directly to the student.) In the third group of activities, the child performs alone while on the move.

CONTROLLED ROLLING AND HANDLING IN PLACE

1. In a wide straddle position (other possible positions are seated with legs crossed or outstretched, and push-up position), place the ball on the floor, and roll it with constant finger guidance between and around the legs.
2. Roll the ball in a figure-eight path in and out of the legs.

3. Reach as far to the left as possible with the ball and roll it in front of you to the other side. Catch it as far to the right of the body as possible.
4. Turn in place and roll the ball around with one hand in a large circle.
5. Roll the ball around while lying on top of it. Roll the ball around the floor while on all fours, guiding it with the nose and forehead.
6. With the back moderately bent, release the ball behind the head, let it roll down the back, and catch it with both hands.
7. Make different kinds of bridges over the ball while using the ball as partial support for the bridge.
8. Starting with one arm above the head, roll the ball down that arm, behind the back, and down the other arm, and then catch it.

BOUNCING AND CATCHING IN PLACE

1. Beginning with two hands, bounce and catch the ball. Bounce a given number of times. Bounce at different levels. Bounce one-handed in a variety of ways. Bounce under the legs. Close the eyes and bounce and catch.
2. Bounce, perform various stunts (a heel click, body turn, or handclap), and catch.
3. Bounce the ball around, under, and over the body.
4. Practice various kinds of bounces, catching all with the eyes closed.
5. Bounce the ball with various body parts, such as the head, elbow, or knee.
6. Bounce the ball, using consecutive body parts (such as the elbow and then the knee), and catch.

TOSSING AND CATCHING IN PLACE

1. Toss and catch, increasing height gradually. Toss from side to side. Toss underneath the legs, around the body, and from behind. Add challenges while tossing and catching. Clap the hands one or more times, make body turns (quarter, half, or full), touch the floor, click the heels, sit down, lie down, and so on.
2. To enhance body part identification, toss and perform some of the following challenges: Touch the back with both hands, touch the back with both hands by reaching over both shoulders, touch both elbows, touch both knees with crossed hands, touch both heels with a heel slap, and touch the toes. Be sure to catch the ball after completing each challenge. The teacher or a leader can quickly call out the body part, and the class must respond with a toss, touch, and catch.
3. Toss upward and catch the descending ball as high as possible. As low as possible. Work out other levels and create combinations. Catch with crossed arms.
4. From a seated position, toss the ball to self from various directions. Lie down and do the same. Toss with the feet.
5. Practice catching by looking away after the ball is tossed upward. Experiment with different ways of catching with the eyes closed.

BATTING TO SELF IN PLACE

1. Bat the ball as in volleyball by using the fist, an open hand, or the side of the hand.
2. Bat and let the ball bounce. Catch in different ways.
3. Rebound the ball upward, using different parts of the body. Let it bounce. Practice serving to self.
4. Bat and rebound the ball so that it does not touch the ground. Change position while doing this.
5. Bat the ball, perform a stunt, and bat again.

FOOT SKILLS IN PLACE

1. Put the toes on top of the ball. Roll the ball in different directions, keeping the other foot in place but retaining control.
2. Use a two-foot pickup, front and back. This is done by putting the ball between the feet and hoisting it to the hands.
3. From a seated position with legs extended, toss the ball with the feet to the hands.
4. Try doing a full curl with the ball between the feet, retaining control until the ball is again placed on the floor. Try bringing the ball between the feet to a point directly over the body. With the arms outstretched for support, lower the feet with the ball to the right and left.
5. In a supine position, hold the ball on the floor above the head. Do a curl-up, bring the ball forward, touch the toes with it, and return to supine position.
6. Drop the ball, and immediately trap it against the floor with one foot. Try to bounce it with one foot.

DRIBBLING SKILLS IN PLACE

1. Dribble the ball first with both hands and then with the right and the left. (Emphasize that the dribble is a push with good wrist action. Children should not bat the ball downward.) Use various number combinations with the right and left hands. Dribble under the legs in turn and back around the body. Kneel and dribble. Go from standing to lying, maintaining a dribble. Return to standing position. Dribble the ball at different levels and at various tempos.

2. Dribble without looking at the ball. Dribble and change hands without stopping the dribble. Dribble with the eyes closed. Dribble the way the Harlem Globetrotters do.

THROWING AGAINST A WALL (CATCHING ON THE FIRST BOUNCE)

1. Throw the ball against the wall, and catch the return after one bounce. Practice various kinds of throws: two-handed, one-handed, overhead, side, baseball, chest pass.
2. Throw at a target mounted on the wall.

THROWING AGAINST A WALL (CATCHING ON THE FLY)

Repeat the throws used in the previous activity, but catch the return on the fly. It may be necessary to move closer and to have the ball contact the wall higher.

BATTING AGAINST A WALL (HANDBALL SKILLS)

1. Drop the ball, and bat it after it bounces. Keep the ball going as in handball.
2. Serve the ball against the wall as in volleyball. Experiment with different ways to serve.

KICKING AGAINST A WALL AND TRAPPING (FOOT-EYE SKILLS)

1. Practice different ways to control kicking against the wall and stopping (trapping) the ball on the return. Try using the foot to keep returning the ball against the wall on the bounce.
2. Put some targets on the wall and kick the ball at a target. See how many points are scored after ten kicks.

ROLLING ON THE MOVE

1. Roll the ball, run alongside it, and guide it with the hands in different directions.
2. Roll the ball forward, then run and catch up with it.

TOSSING AND CATCHING ON THE MOVE

1. Toss the ball upward and forward. Run forward and catch it after one bounce. Toss the ball upward in various directions (forward, sideward, backward), run under it, turn, and catch it on the fly.
2. Add various stunts and challenges, such as touching the floor, clicking the heels, or turning around.

BATTING ON THE MOVE

With first the right and then the left hand, bat the ball upward in different directions, and catch it on the first bounce or on the fly.

PRACTICING FOOT SKILLS ON THE MOVE

Dribble the ball (soccer style) forward and in other directions. Dribble around an imaginary point. Make various patterns while dribbling, such as a circle, square, triangle, or figure eight.

DRIBBLING ON THE MOVE

1. Dribble (basketball style) forward using one hand, and dribble back to place with the other. Change direction on a signal. Dribble in various directions, describing different pathways. Dribble around cones, milk cartons, or chairs.
2. Place a hoop on the floor. Dribble inside the hoop until a signal is sounded, then dribble to another hoop and continue the dribble inside that hoop. Avoid dribbling on the hoop itself.

PRACTICING LOCOMOTOR MOVEMENTS WHILE HOLDING THE BALL

1. Hold the ball between the legs and perform various locomotor movements.
2. Try holding the ball in various positions with different body parts.

Partner Activities

ROLLING IN PLACE

Roll the ball back and forth to partner. Begin with two-handed rolls and proceed to one-handed rolls. When partner rolls the ball, pick it up with the toes and snap it up into the hands.

THROWING AND CATCHING IN PLACE

1. Toss the ball to partner with one bounce, using various kinds of tosses. Practice various kinds of throws and passes to partner.
2. Throw to specific levels and points: high, low, right, left, at the knee, and so on. Try various throws: from under the leg, around the body, backward tosses, and centering as in football.
3. Throw and catch over a volleyball net.
4. Work in a threesome, with one person holding a hoop between the two partners playing catch. Throw the ball through the hoop held at various levels. Try throwing through a moving hoop.

BATTING IN PLACE (VOLLEYBALL SKILLS)

1. Toss the ball upward to self, bat it two-handed to partner, who catches and returns it in the same manner. Serve as in volleyball to partner. Partner

makes a return serve. Toss the ball to partner, who makes a volleyball return. Keep distances short and keep the ball under control. Try to keep the ball going back and forth as in volleyball.

2. Bat the ball back and forth on one bounce. Bat it back and forth over a line, wand, jump rope, or bench.

KICKING IN PLACE

1. Practice different ways of controlled kicking between partners and different ways of stopping the ball (trapping).
2. Practice a controlled punt, preceding the kick with a step on the nonkicking foot. Place the ball between the feet and propel it forward or backward to partner.
3. Practice foot pickups. One partner rolls the ball, and the other hoists it to self with extended toes.

THROWING FROM VARIOUS POSITIONS IN PLACE

Practice different throws from a kneeling, sitting, or lying position. (Allow the children to be creative in selecting positions.)

TWO-BALL ACTIVITIES IN PLACE

Using two balls, pass back and forth, with balls going in opposite directions.

FOLLOW ACTIVITIES IN PLACE

Throw or propel the ball in any manner desired. Partner returns the ball in the same fashion.

THROWING AND CATCHING AGAINST A WALL

Alternate throwing and catching against a wall. Alternate returning the ball after a bounce, as in handball.

THROWING ON THE MOVE

1. One child remains in place and tosses to the other child, who is moving. The moving child can trace different patterns, such as back and forth between two spots or in a circle around the stationary child. (Spatial judgments must be good to anticipate where the moving child should be to receive the ball. Moderate distances should be maintained between children.)
2. Practice different kinds of throws and passes as both children move in different patterns. (Considerable space is needed for this type of work.) Practice foot skills of dribbling and passing.
3. Partners hold the ball between their bodies without using the hands or arms. Experiment with different ways to move together.
4. Carrying a ball, run in different directions while partner follows. On signal, toss the ball upward so that the child following can catch it. Now change places and repeat the activity.

JUGGLING

Juggling is a novel task that is exciting to elementary school youngsters. It is a challenging task that demands practice and repetition to learn.

An excellent medium for teaching beginners is sheer, lightweight scarves that measure 18 to 24 inches square. These move slowly, allowing children to track them visually. Juggling with scarves teaches children correct patterns of object movement; however, it does not transfer easily to juggling with faster-moving objects such as fleece balls, tennis balls, rings, and hoops. Therefore, two distinct sections for juggling are offered: a section dealing with learning to juggle with scarves and a second discussion explaining juggling with balls. Juggling with scarves will bring success to a majority of the class. Youngsters who have mastered the scarves can move to balls and other objects.

Juggling lessons should allow opportunity for children to move, at will, between scarves and faster-moving objects. This will allow them to find an acceptable balance between success and frustration. Much practice is necessary to learn to juggle, and there will be a lot of misses during the acquisition of this skill. Because youngsters tire quickly if they are not having success, it may be desirable to play a game and then return to juggling practice.

Juggling with Scarves

Scarves are held by the fingertips near the center. To throw the scarf, it should be lifted and pulled into the air above eye level. Scarves are caught by clawing, a downward motion of the hand, and grabbing the scarf from above as it is falling. Scarf juggling should teach proper habits (for example, tossing the scarves straight up in line with the body rather than forward or backward). Many instructors remind children to imagine that they are in a phone booth or large refrigerator box—to emphasize tossing and catching without moving.

CASCADING

Cascading is the easiest pattern for juggling three objects. The following sequence can be used to learn this basic technique.

1. *One scarf.* Hold the scarf in the center. Quickly move the arm across the chest and toss the scarf with the palm out. Reach out with the other hand

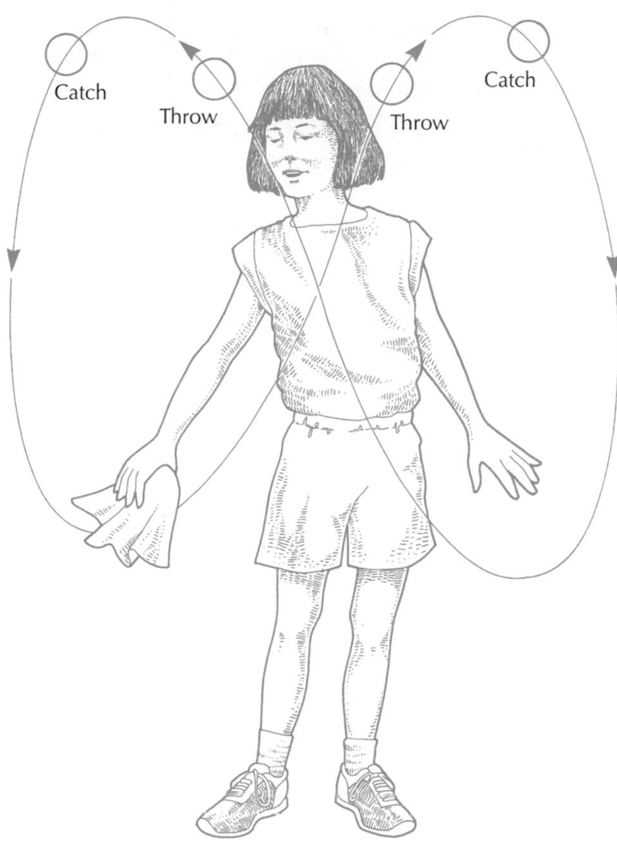

FIGURE 17.3 Clawing a scarf.

FIGURE 17.4 Tossing and clawing with two scarves.

and catch the scarf in a straight-down motion (clawing). Toss the scarf with this hand using the motion and claw it with the opposite hand. Continue the tossing and clawing sequence over and over. The scarf should move in a figure-eight pattern as shown in Figure 17.3.

2. *Two scarves—two hands.* Hold a scarf with the fingertips in each hand. Toss the first one across the body as described in step 1. When it reaches its peak, look at it, and toss the second scarf across the body in the opposite direction. The first scarf thrown is caught (clawed) by the hand throwing the second scarf and vice versa (Figure 17.4). Verbal cues such as "Toss, claw, toss, claw" are helpful.
3. *Two scarves—one hand.* This sequence is a requisite if youngsters are going to juggle three scarves. Start with both scarves in one hand (hold them as described below in three-scarf cascading). The important skill to learn is to toss the first scarf, then the second scarf, and then catch the first and the second. Verbal cues to use are toss, toss, catch, catch. If youngsters cannot toss two scarves before catching one, they will not be able to master juggling with three scarves. Practice tossing skills with both hands.
4. *Three-scarf cascading.* A scarf is held in each hand by the fingertips as described in step 2. The third scarf is held with the ring and little fingers against the palm of one hand. The first scarf to be thrown will be from the hand that is holding two scarves. Toss this scarf from the fingertips across the chest as learned earlier. When scarf one reaches its peak, scarf two from the other hand is thrown across the body. As this hand starts to come down, it catches scarf one. When scarf two reaches its peak, scarf three is thrown in the same path as that of scarf one. To complete the cycle, as the hand comes down from throwing scarf three, it catches scarf two. The cycle is started over by throwing scarf one with the opposite hand. Figure 17.5 (on page 356) illustrates the figure-eight motion that is used in cascading. Tosses are always alternated between left and right hands with a smooth, even rhythm.

REVERSE CASCADING

Reverse cascading involves tossing the scarves from waist level to the outside of the body and allowing the scarves to drop down the midline of the body (Figure 17.6 on page 356).

1. *One scarf.* Begin by holding the scarf as described previously. The throw goes away from the midline of the body over the top, releasing the scarf so that it falls down the center of the body. Catch it with the opposite hand and toss it in similar fashion on the opposite side of the body.
2. *Two scarves.* Begin with a scarf in each hand. Toss the first as described in step 1. When it begins its

FIGURE 17.5 Three-scarf cascading.

descent, toss the second scarf. Catch the first scarf, then the second, and repeat the pattern in a toss, toss, catch, catch manner.

3. *Reverse cascading with three scarves.* Think of a large funnel fixed at eye level directly in front of the juggler. The goal is to drop all scarves through this funnel so that they drop straight down the center of the body. Begin with three scarves as described previously for three-scarf cascading. Toss the first scarf from the hand holding two scarves.

COLUMN JUGGLING

Column juggling is so named because the scarves move straight up and down as though they were inside a large pipe or column and do not cross the body. To perform three-scarf column juggling, begin with two scarves in one hand and one in the other hand. Begin with a scarf from the hand that has two scarves, and toss it straight up the midline of the body overhead. When this scarf reaches its peak, toss the other two scarves upward along the sides of the body (Figure 17.7). Catch the first scarf with either hand and toss it upward again. Catch the other two scarves and toss them upward continuing the pattern.

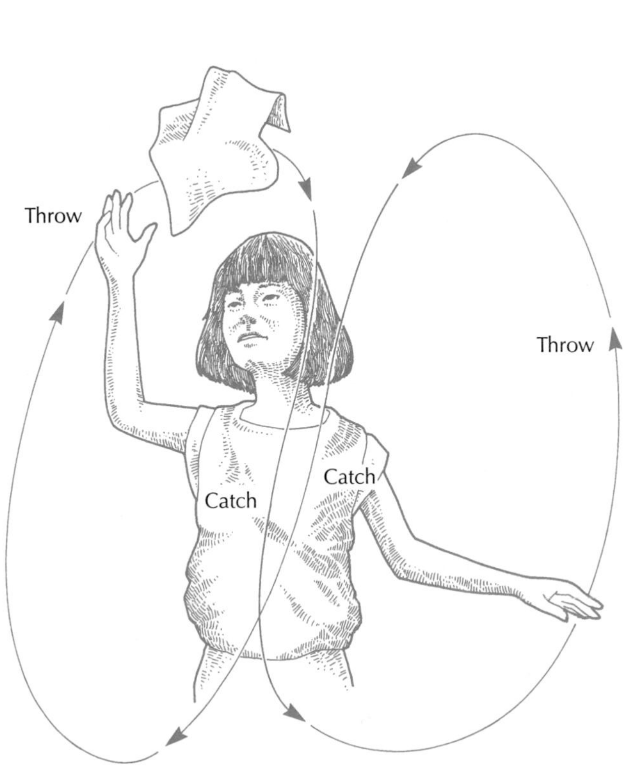

FIGURE 17.6 Reverse cascading.

FIGURE 17.7 Column juggling.

SHOWERING

Showering is more difficult than cascading because of the rapid movement of the hands. There is less time allowed for catching and tossing. The scarves move in a circle following each other. It should be practiced in both directions for maximum challenge.

Start with two scarves in the right hand and one in the left. Begin by throwing the first two scarves from the right hand. Toss the scarves in a large circle away from the midline of the body and overhead as high as possible. As soon as the second scarf is released, toss the scarf across from the left hand to the right and then toss the scarf in the opposite hand and catch the first scarf with this hand also. Finish by tossing the last scarf (Figure 17.8). All scarves are caught with the left hand and passed to the right hand.

JUGGLING CHALLENGES

TEACHING TIP

1. While cascading, toss a scarf under one leg.
2. While cascading, toss a scarf from behind the back.
3. Instead of catching one of the scarves, blow it upward with a strong breath of air.
4. Begin cascading by tossing the first scarf into the air with a foot. Lay the scarf across the foot and kick it into the air.
5. Try juggling three scarves with one hand. Do not worry about establishing a pattern, just catch the lowest scarf each time. Try both regular and reverse cascading as well as column juggling.
6. While doing column juggling, toss up one scarf, hold the other two, and make a full turn. Resume juggling.
7. Juggle three scarves while standing alongside a partner with inside arms around each other. This is actually easy to do, because it is regular three-scarf cascading.
8. Try juggling more than three scarves (up to six) with a partner.

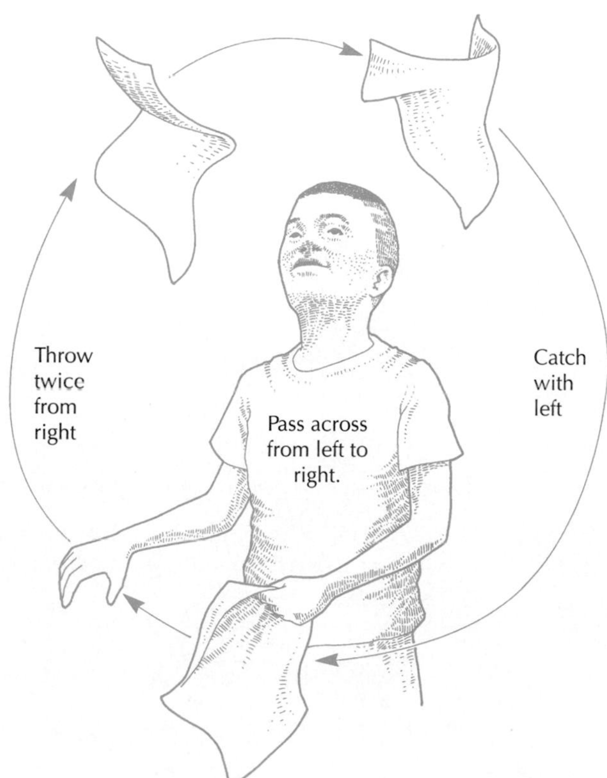

FIGURE 17.8 Showering with scarves.

Juggling with Balls

Two balls can be juggled with one hand, and three balls can be juggled with two hands. Juggling can be done in a crisscross fashion, which is called *cascading,* or it can be done in a circular fashion, called *showering.* Cascading is considered the easier of the two styles and should be the first one attempted.

Instructional Procedures

1. Juggling requires accurate, consistent tossing, and this should be the first emphasis. The tosses should be thrown to the same height on both sides of the body, about 2 to 2½ feet upward and across the body, since the ball is tossed from one hand to the other. Practice tossing the ball parallel to the body; the most common problem in juggling is that the balls are tossed forward and the juggler has to move forward to catch them.
2. The fingers, not the palms, should be used in tossing and catching. Stress relaxed wrist action.
3. The student should look upward to watch the balls at the peak of their flight, rather than watching the hands. Focus on where the ball peaks, not on the hands.
4. The balls should be caught about waist height and released a little above this level.
5. Two balls must be carried in the starting hand, and the art of releasing only one must be mastered.
6. Progression should be working successively with first one ball, then two balls, and finally three balls (Figure 17.9 on page 358).

Recommended Progression for Cascading

1. Using one ball and one hand only, toss the ball upward (2 to 2½ feet), and catch it with the same hand.

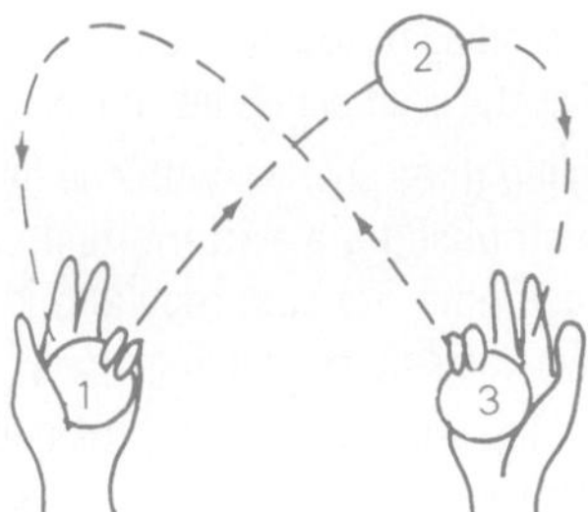

FIGURE 17.9 Cascading with three balls.

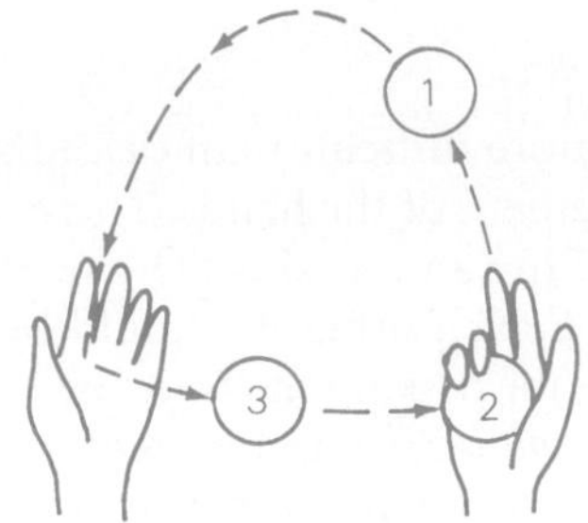

FIGURE 17.10 Showering with three balls.

Begin with the dominant hand, and later practice with the other. Toss quickly, with wrist action. Then handle the ball alternately with right and left hands, tossing from one hand to the other.

2. Now, with one ball in each hand, alternate tossing a ball upward and catching it in the same hand so that one ball is always in the air. Begin again with a ball in each hand. Toss across the body to the other hand. To keep the balls from colliding, toss under the incoming ball. After some expertise has been acquired, alternate the two kinds of tosses by doing a set number (four to six) of each before shifting to the other.
3. Hold two balls in the starting hand and one in the other. Toss one of the balls in the starting hand, toss the ball from the other hand, and then toss the third ball.

Recommended Progression for Showering

1. The showering motion is usually counterclockwise. Hold one ball in each hand. Begin by tossing with the right hand on an inward path and then immediately toss the other ball from the left directly across the body to the right hand. Continue this until the action is smooth.
2. Now, hold two balls in the right hand and one in the left. Toss the first ball from the right hand on an inward path and immediately toss the second on the same path. At about the same time, toss the ball from the left hand directly across the body to the right hand (Figure 17.10).
3. A few children may be able to change from cascading to showering and vice versa. This is a skill of considerable challenge.

ACTIVITIES WITH SCOOPS AND BALLS

Scoops can be purchased (Figure 17.11) or made with bleach bottles or similar containers (see Chapter 10). They are excellent for practicing catching and tossing skills using an implement rather than the hands. The following activities are recommended.

Individual Activities

1. Put the ball on the floor and pick it up with the scoop. Toss the ball upward and catch it with the scoop. Throw the ball against a wall and catch it in the scoop. Put the ball in the scoop, throw it in the air, and catch it. Throw the ball against a wall with the scoop and catch it with the scoop.
2. Throw the ball, switch the scoop to the opposite hand, and catch in the scoop. Toss the ball upward from the scoop, perform a stunt, such as a heel click or a body turn, and catch the ball in the scoop.
3. Toss the ball upward and catch it as low as possible. As high as possible. Toss it a little higher each time,

FIGURE 17.11 Catching a whiffle ball with a scoop.

and catch it in the scoop. Tell students to toss the ball so that they have to stretch to catch it. (Most activities should begin with a toss from the free hand and later employ a toss from the scoop.)

Partner Activities

1. One partner rolls the ball on the floor, and the other catches it in the scoop. Partners throw the ball back and forth and catch it in the scoop. Play One Step (page 564) while playing catch to add some challenge to the activity.
2. One partner tosses the ball from the scoop and the other partner catches. Throw the ball from the scoop at different levels and catch it at different levels. Throw and catch from various positions, such as sitting, back to back, prone, and kneeling.
3. Work with more than one partner, with more than one ball, and with a scoop in each hand.

Games and Relays

Many games and relays can be played using scoops. Modified lacrosse can be played using the scoops and a whiffle ball. Set up a lesson in which children devise games for themselves that use the scoop and a ball.

BOWLING ACTIVITIES

Younger children should practice informal rolling. As they mature, the emphasis should change from informal rolling to bowling skills. Bowling skills begin with a two-handed roll and progress to one-handed rolls, alternating between the right and left hand. Various targets can be used, including bowling pins, milk cartons, small cones, blocks, and even people.

The 8½-inch foam or playground ball is excellent for teaching bowling skills. Volleyballs and soccer balls also can be used. Stress moderate speed in the motion of the ball. The ball should roll off the tips of the fingers with good follow-through action.

The four-step approach is the accepted form for tenpin bowling, and its basis can be set in class work. The technique, in brief form, for a right-handed bowler follows:

Starting position: Stand with the feet together and the ball held comfortably in both hands in front of the body.

Step one: Step forward with the right foot, pushing the ball forward with both hands and a little to the right.

Step two: Step with the left foot, allowing the ball to swing down alongside the leg on its way into the backswing.

Step three: Step with the right foot. The ball reaches the height of the backswing with this step.

Step four: Step with the left foot and bowl the ball forward.

For instructional cues, the teacher can call out the following sequence for the four steps: "Out," "Down," "Back," and "Roll."

Bowling activities are organized mostly as partner or group work. When targets are being used, having two children on the target end is desirable. One child resets the target, while the other recovers the ball. The following are partner activities unless otherwise noted. A fine game for rounding off the activities is Bowling One Step (page 565).

RECOMMENDED ACTIVITIES

1. Use a wide straddle stance, and begin with two-handed rolls from between the legs.
2. Roll the ball first with the right and then with the left hand. The receiver can use the foot pickup, done by hoisting the ball to the hands with the extended toes.
3. Practice putting different kinds of spin (English) on the ball. (For a right-handed bowler, a curve to the left is called a hook ball, and a curve to the right is a backup ball.)
4. Get into groups of three (Figure 17.12 on page 360) and use human straddle targets. Using a stick 2 feet long, make marks on the floor for the target child, who is in the middle between the two bowlers. The target child stands so that the inside edges of the shoes are on the marks, thus standardizing the target spread. (Targets must keep their legs straight and motionless during the bowling. Otherwise, they can make or avoid contact with the ball and upset the scoring system.) Start from a moderate distance (15 to 20 feet) at first, and adjust as proficiency increases. Scoring can be 2 points for a ball that goes through the legs without touching and 1 point for a ball that goes through but touches the leg.
5. Use milk cartons or bowling pins as targets. Begin with one and progress to two or three. (Plastic bowling pins are available. Other targets might be a wastebasket lying on its side—the ball is rolled into it—or a 3-lb. coffee can for a smaller ball.)

ACTIVITIES WITH PADDLES AND BALLS

The present popularity of racquet sports makes it imperative that the schools give attention to racquet skills. For primary-level children, the nylon-stocking paddle (see Chapter 10 for its construction) can be used to introduce the racquet sports. Much of this early activity is

FIGURE 17.12 Bowling through a human straddle target.

devoted to informal, exploratory play. Different types of objects can be batted: table tennis balls, newspaper balls, shuttlecocks, and tennis balls. Plastic or wooden paddles (see Chapter 10) and appropriate balls can be used to establish a basis for future play in racquetball, table tennis, squash, and regular tennis. These activities, particularly paddle tennis, take considerable space, so emphasis must be placed on controlled stroking rather than wild swinging.

Instructional Procedures for Wooden or Plastic Paddles

1. Use the following instructional cues:
   a. Hold the wrist reasonably stiff.
   b. Use a smooth arm action.
   c. Stroke through the ball and follow through.
   d. Watch the ball strike the paddle.
2. All paddles should have leather wrist thongs. The hand goes through the leather loop before grasping the paddle. No play should be permitted without this safety precaution.
3. Proper grip must be emphasized, and seeing that children maintain this is a constant battle. The easiest method to teach the proper grip is to have the student hold the paddle perpendicular to the floor and shake hands with it (Figure 17.13). Young people tend to revert to the inefficient hammer grip, so named because it is similar to the grip used on a hammer.
4. Accuracy and control should be the primary goals. The children should not be concerned with force or distance.
5. Early activities can be attempted with both the right and the left hand, but the dominant hand should be developed in critical skills.
6. During a lesson, related information about racquet sports may be quite relevant.
7. Practice in racquet work should move from individual to partner work as quickly as is feasible, because partner work is basic to racquet sports.
8. For the forehand stroke, the body is turned sideways; for a right-handed player, the left side points in the direction of the hit.
9. For the backhand stroke, the thumb is placed against the handle of the racquet for added support and force, and the body is turned sideways so the shoulder on the side of the racquet hand points in the direction of the stroke.
10. During either type of stroke, a step is made with the foot that is forward with respect to the direction of the stroke.
11. A volley is made with a sort of punch stroke. The hitter faces in the direction of the hit, and the rac-

FIGURE 17.13 Handshake grip.

quet is pushed forward rather than being stroked. To practice volleys, students need a firm surface from which the ball can rebound.

INDIVIDUAL ACTIVITIES

1. Place a ball on the paddle and attempt to keep it from falling off. As skill increases, attempt to roll the ball around the edges of the paddle.
2. Using the paddle, rebound the ball upward. Bounce it on the paddle without letting it touch the floor. Bounce it off the paddle upward, and catch it with the other hand. Increase the height of the bounce.
3. Dribble the ball with the paddle, first while stationary and then while moving. Change the paddle from hand to hand while the ball is bouncing off the floor.
4. Alternate bouncing the ball in the air and on the floor.
5. Bounce the ball off the paddle upward and catch it with the paddle. This requires giving with the paddle to create a soft home for the ball.
6. Put the ball on the floor and scoop it up with the paddle. Start dribbling the ball without touching it with the hands. Put a reverse spin on the ball and scoop it up into the air.
7. Bounce the ball off the paddle into the air and turn the paddle to the other side as you bounce the ball.
8. Bat the ball into the air and perform the following stunts while the ball is in the air: Touch the floor, do a heel click (single and double), clap hands, turn around. Do various combinations of these activities.

PARTNER ACTIVITIES

Beginning partner activity should involve feeding (controlled throwing) by one partner and the designated stroke return by the other. In this way, the child can concentrate on the stroke without worrying about the competitive aspects of the activity.

1. Return partner's feed with a forehand stroke. Return backhand. Switch roles.
2. Stroke back and forth with partner, first forehand and then backhand.
3. Play back and forth over a net. The "net" can be a jump rope lying on the floor crosswise to the field of play, a wand supported on blocks or cones, or a bench. (See Chapter 10 for a diagram of a home-constructed net.)
4. Volley partner's feed. Volley back and forth with partner. (In the volley, the ball does not touch the floor.)
5. Play doubles. Partners on each side alternate turns returning the ball.
6. Volley using a whiffle ball. (A whiffle ball moves slowly and allows children time to position their feet properly.) Play with a partner. Allow the ball to bounce before returning it. Perform stunts while the ball is in the air.
7. Dribble the ball with your paddle and try to pull a flag from an opponent's pocket without losing control of the ball.
8. While moving with a partner, keep the ball in the air by alternating bounces.
9. Develop a cooperative score by developing a routine with five individual tasks in sequence.

ACTIVITIES WITH FRISBEES (FLYING DISKS)

Frisbee activities are popular with children of all ages, but younger children may need considerable guidance to develop skills. The following are the basic skills that should be taught before a variety of activities are presented.

Throwing the Disk

Backhand Throw

The backhand grip (Figure 17.14 on page 362) is used most often. The thumb is on top of the disk, the index finger along the rim, and the other fingers underneath. To throw the Frisbee with the right hand, stand in a sideways position with the right foot toward the target. Step toward the target and throw the Frisbee in a sideways motion across the body, snapping the wrist and trying to keep the disk flat on release.

FIGURE 17.14 Gripping the Frisbee for backhand throw.

Underhand Throw

The underhand throw uses the same grip as in the backhand throw, but the thrower faces the target and holds the disk at the side of the body. Step forward with the leg opposite the throwing arm while bringing the Frisbee forward. When the throwing arm is out in the front of the body, release the Frisbee. The trick to this throw is learning to release the disk so that it is parallel to the ground.

Catching the Disk

Thumb-Down Catch

The thumb-down catch is used for catching when the disk is received at waist level or above. The thumb is pointing toward the ground. The Frisbee should be tracked from the thrower's hand. This clues the catcher about any tilt on the disk that may cause it to curve.

Thumb-Up Catch

The thumb-up catch is used when the Frisbee is received below waist level. The thumb points up, and the fingers are spread.

Trick Catches

The disk can be caught in different positions. The two most popular trick-catch positions are behind the back and between the legs. In the behind-the-back catch, the thumb-up technique is used, and the disk is caught with the arm that is farthest away from the thrower. For the between-the-legs catch, the thumb-up catch is also used, and one leg can be lifted to facilitate the catch.

Instructional Procedures

1. Use the following instructional cues:
   a. Release the disk parallel to the ground. If it is tilted, a curved throw results.
   b. Step toward the target and follow through on release of the disk.
   c. Snap open the wrist and make the Frisbee spin.
2. If space is limited, all Frisbees should be thrown in the same direction. Students can line up on either side of the area and throw across to each other.
3. Each child should have a disk so that practice time can be maximized. However, most activities are best practiced by pairs of students using one disk.
4. Youngsters can develop both sides of the body by learning to throw and catch the disk with either hand. The teacher should design the activities so that youngsters get both right-hand and left-hand practice.
5. Because a Frisbee is somewhat different from the other implements that children usually throw, devote some time to teaching form and style in throwing and catching. Avoid drills that reward speed in throwing and catching.

RECOMMENDED ACTIVITIES

1. Throw the Frisbee at different levels to a partner.
2. Catch the Frisbee, using various catching styles and hand positions.
3. Throw a curve by tilting the disk. Try curving it to the left, the right, and upward. Throw a slow curve and then a fast slider.
4. Throw a bounce pass to partner. Throw a low, fast bounce. Throw a high, slow bounce.
5. As the catcher, do various stunts after the disk has left partner's hand. Examples are a full turn, heel click, handclap, or touching the ground.
6. Throw the disk with the nondominant hand. Try to throw for accuracy first, and then strive for distance.
7. Make the disk respond like a boomerang. Throw into the wind at a steep angle and see whether it comes back to you.

8. Throw the Frisbee into the air, run, and catch it. Try to increase the throwing distance and still make the catch before the disk touches the ground.
9. Have partner hold a hoop as a target. See how many times you can throw the Frisbee through the hoop. Play a game of *One Step* in which you move back a step each time you throw the disk through the hoop. When you make two misses in a row, your partner gets a chance to try.
10. Place a series of hoops on the ground. Different colored hoops can signify different point values. Have a contest with your partner to see who can earn more points in five throws.
11. Play catch while both partners are moving. Try to throw the disk so that your partner does not have to break stride to catch it.
12. Throw for distance. Try to throw farther than your partner by using a series of four throws.
13. Throw for both distance and accuracy. Using a series of four or more throws, try to reach a goal that is a specified distance away. Many different objects can be used as goals, such as basket standards, fence posts, and trees. (This could be the start of playing Frisbee Golf, which is becoming a popular recreational sport.)
14. Set a time limit of 30 seconds. Within this time, see how many successful throws and catches can be made. A certain distance apart must be set for all pairs, and missed catches do not count as throws.
15. Working in groups of three, try to keep the disk away from the person in the middle. The children can establish their own rules as to when someone else must move to the middle.
16. In groups of three, with one person in the middle, try to throw the Frisbee through the middle person's legs. A point is scored each time the disk is thrown through the legs without touching. Legs must be spread to shoulder width.

ACTIVITIES WITH WANDS

Wands have been used in physical education programs for many years, but only recently have a wide variety of interesting and challenging activities been developed. Wands can be made from ¾-inch maple dowels or from a variety of broom and mop handles. If two lengths are chosen, make them 36 and 42 inches. If only one size is to be used, a length of 1 meter is recommended. Wands are more interesting when they are painted with imaginative designs, a chore that can be a class project. Wands are noisy when they hit the floor. Putting rubber crutch tips on the ends of a wand alleviates most of the noise and makes it easier to pick up. The tips should be put on with mucilage.

The year's supply of wands should include five or six extras beyond the number of children. There will be some breakage. Wands serve the physical education program in four ways: challenge activities, stunts, exercises, and personal challenge activities. Challenge activities, stunts, and exercises are presented here, and personal challenge activities are presented in Chapter 21.

Instructional Procedures

1. Because wands are noisy when dropped, the children should hold their wands with both hands or put them on the floor during instruction.
2. Many wand activities require great flexibility, which means that not all children are able to do them. Girls usually perform better than boys at flexibility stunts.
3. An adequate amount of space is needed for each individual, because wand stunts demand room.
4. Wands are not to be used as fencing foils. Children may easily be injured using wands improperly. Teach children proper use of wands. Emphasize the need to use care when handling wands to avoid injury to self and others. Do not allow any improper use of wands (or other potentially dangerous equipment).

RECOMMENDED ACTIVITIES

Wands can be used for challenge activities that offer a relatively unstructured approach. The following are some of the many possible challenges.

1. Can you reach down and pick up your wand without bending your knees?
2. Try to balance your wand on different body parts. Watch the top of the wand to get cues on how to retain the balance.
3. Can you hold your stick against the wall and move over and under it?
4. Let's see whether you can hold the stick at both ends and move through the gap.
5. Can you spin the wand and keep it going like a windmill?
6. Let's see how many different ways you can move over and around your wand when it is on the floor.
7. Put one end of the wand on the floor and hold the other end. How many times can you run around your wand without getting dizzy?
8. Place one end of the wand against a wall. Holding the other end and keeping the wand against the wall, duck underneath. Place the wand lower and lower on the wall and go under.

9. Place the wand between your feet and hop around as though you are on a pogo stick.
10. Throw your wand into the air and catch it.
11. Hold the wand vertically near the middle. Can you release your grip and catch the wand before it falls to the floor?
12. Have a partner hold a wand horizontally above the floor. Jump, leap, and hop over the wand. Gradually raise the height of the wand.
13. Put your wand on the floor and try making different kinds of bridges over it.
14. Place the wand on the floor. Curl alongside it, just touching it. Curl at one end of the wand.
15. Balance the wand vertically on the floor. Release the wand and try to complete different stunts—clapping the hands, doing a heel click, touching different body parts—before the wand falls to the floor.
16. Put the wand on the floor and see how many ways you can push it, using different body parts.

Individual Wand Stunts

WAND CATCH

Stand a wand on one end and hold it in place with the fingers on the tip. Loop the foot quickly over the stick, letting go of the wand briefly but catching it with the fingers before it falls. Do this right and left for a complete set. Try to catch the wand with just the index finger.

THREAD THE NEEDLE (V-SEAT)

Maintaining a V-seat position, with the wand held in front of the body with both hands, bend the knees between the arms and pass the wand over them and return, without touching the wand to the legs. Try with the ankles crossed.

THREAD THE NEEDLE (STANDING)

Holding the wand in both hands, step through the space, one leg at a time, and return without touching. Step through again, but this time bring the wand up behind the back, over the head, and down in front. Reverse. Try from side to side with the stick held front and back.

GRAPEVINE

Holding the wand near the ends, step with the right foot around the right arm and over the wand inward, toward the body (Figure 17.15). Pass the wand backward over the head and right shoulder (Figure 17.16), and continue sliding the wand down the body until you are standing erect with the wand between the legs. Reverse the process back to original position. Try with the left foot leading.

FIGURE 17.15 Beginning the Grapevine.

FIGURE 17.16 Grapevine, second stage (head ducks under, and wand is pressed down the back).

BACK SCRATCHER

Hold the wand with an underhand grip (palms up), arms crossed in front of the body (Figure 17.17). Bend the elbows so that the wand can go over and behind the head. Attempt to pass the wand down the length of the body from the back of the shoulders to the heels. Do not release the grip on the wand. The wand is worked down behind the back while the arms stay in front of the body.

WAND WHIRL

Stand the wand upright in front of the body. Turn around quickly and grasp the wand before it falls. Do the movement both right and left. Try making two full turns and still catching the wand before it falls.

TWIST UNDER

Grasp the upright wand with the right hand. Twist around under the right arm without letting go of the wand, taking it off the floor, or touching the knee to the floor. Repeat, using the left arm.

FIGURE 17.17 Back Scratcher (wand has been passed overhead and is now being forced down the back).

JUMP WAND

Holding the wand in front with the fingertips of both hands, jump over it. Jumping back is not recommended, because the wand can hit the heels and cause an awkward fall. (A rope or a towel can be substituted for the wand if children are having difficulty.)

BALANCING THE WAND

Balance the wand vertically with one hand. Experiment with different hand and finger positions. Walk forward, backward, and sideward. Sit down, lie down, and move into other positions while keeping the wand balanced. Keep the eyes on the top of the wand. Balance the wand horizontally on the hands, arms, feet, and thighs. Balance it across the back of the neck. In crab position, balance it across the tummy.

THE SPRINTER

Get into a sprinter's position, with the wand on the floor, between the feet, and perpendicular to the direction of the sprint. Change the feet rapidly, alternating over the wand. Try moving both feet together forward and backward over the wand.

CRAB LEAP

Place the wand on the floor. Get into crab position and attempt to move the feet back and forth over the wand without touching it. Try this with alternating feet.

LONG REACH

Stand with legs extended and feet spread about 12 inches apart. Hold a wand in the left hand, and use it like a third limb. With a piece of chalk in the right hand, reach forward as far as possible and make a mark. Use the wand as a support and see whether the mark can be bettered.

WAND BRIDGE

On a mat, start in a straddle stance with legs straight. Hold a wand near one end, with the other end above the head and pointed toward the ceiling. Bend backward, place the wand on the mat behind you, and walk the hands down the wand. Return to standing position.

WAND TWIRL

Children in the class who have baton-twirling experience can show the class some points of technique.

Partner Wand Stunts

PARTNER CATCH

Partners face each other a short distance (5 feet) apart, each holding a wand in the right hand. On signal, each throws the wand to the partner with the right hand and catches the incoming wand with the left. Distances can be increased somewhat.

PARTNER CHANGE

Partners face each other a short distance (5 feet) apart. Each has a wand standing upright, held on top by the right hand. On signal, each runs to the other's wand and tries to catch it before it falls. This can also be done in the same way as the Wand Whirl, with each whirling to the other's wand. Try with a small group of five or six. On signal, all move to the next wand.

TURN THE DISHRAG

Partners face each other and grasp a wand. When ready, they perform a dishrag turn (Figure 20.38).

JUMP THE WAND

One partner moves the wand back and forth along the floor, while the other partner jumps over it. To add challenge, partners should change the tempo of movement and raise the level of the wand.

WAND REACTION

One partner holds the wand horizontally. The other partner places one hand directly above the wand, palm down. When the first partner drops the wand, the second partner tries to catch it before it strikes the floor.

COOPERATIVE MOVEMENTS

Holding a wand between them, partners stand toe to toe and circle either way with light foot movements. Together, partners squat down and stand up. Sit down and come up. Kneel and hold the wand overhead as they face each other. Bend sideways and touch the wand to the floor.

Isometric Exercises with Wands

The isometric exercises with wands presented here are mainly grip exercises. A variety of grips should be used. With the wand horizontal, use either the overhand or underhand grip. With the wand in vertical position, grip with the thumbs pointed up, down, or toward each other. Repeat each exercise with a different grip. Exercises can also be repeated with the wand in different positions: in front of the body (either horizontal or vertical), overhead, or behind the back. Hold each exercise for 8 to 12 seconds.

PULL THE WAND APART

Place the hands 6 inches apart near the center of the wand. With a tight grip to prevent slippage and with arms extended, pull the hands apart. Change grip and position.

PUSH THE WAND TOGETHER

Hold the wand as previously, except push the hands together.

WAND TWIST

Hold the wand with both hands about 6 inches apart. Twist the hands in opposite directions.

BICYCLE

Holding the wand horizontally using an overhand grip, extend the wand outward and downward. Bring it upward near the body, completing a circular movement. On the downward movement, push the wand together, and on the upward movement, pull the wand apart.

ARM SPREADER

Hold the wand overhead with hands spread wide. Attempt to compress the stick. Reverse force, and attempt to pull the stick apart.

DEAD LIFT

Partially squat and place the wand under the thighs. Place the hands between the legs and try to lift. Try also with hands on the outside of the legs.

ABDOMINAL TIGHTENER

From a standing position, place the wand behind the buttocks. With hands on the ends of the wand, pull forward and resist with the abdominal muscles.

Stretching Exercises with Wands

Wands are useful for stretching, bending, and twisting movements.

SIDE BENDER

Grip the wand and extend the arms overhead with feet apart. Bend sideways as far as possible, maintaining straight arms and legs. Recover, and bend to the other side.

BODY TWIST

Place the wand behind the neck, with arms draped over the wand from behind. Rotate the upper body first to the right as far as possible and then to the left. The feet and hips should remain in position. The twist is at the waist.

BODY TWIST TO KNEE

Assume body twist position. Bend the trunk forward and twist so that the right end of the wand touches the left knee (Figure 17.18). Recover, and touch the left end to the right knee.

SHOULDER STRETCHER

Grip the wand at the ends in a regular grip. Extend the arms overhead and rotate the wand, arms, and shoulders backward until the stick touches the back of the legs. The arms should be kept straight. Those who find the stretch too easy should move their hands closer to the center of the wand.

TOE TOUCH

Grip the wand with the hands about shoulder width apart. Bend forward, reaching down as far as possible without bending the knees. The movement should be slow and controlled. Try the same activity from a sitting position.

FIGURE 17.18 Body twist to knee.

OVER THE TOES

Sit down, flex the knees, pass the wand over the toes, and rest it against the middle of the arch on the bottoms of the feet. Grip the stick with the fingers at the outside edge of the feet. Slowly extend the legs forward, pushing against the stick and trying for a full extension of the legs.

ACTIVITIES WITH HOOPS

Most hoops manufactured in the United States are plastic, but Europeans sometimes use wooden ones. The plastic variety is less durable but more versatile. Extra hoops are needed because some breakage will occur. The standard hoop is 42 inches in diameter, but it is desirable to have smaller hoops (36 inches) for primary-grade children.

Instructional Procedures

1. Hoops produce noisy activity. The teacher may find it helpful to have the children lay their hoops on the floor when they are to listen.
2. Hoops can be a creative medium for children. Allow them free time to explore their own ideas.
3. Give the children an adequate amount of space in which to perform, for hoops require much movement.
4. In activities that require children to jump through hoops, instruct the holder to grasp the hoop lightly, so as not to cause an awkward fall if a performer hits it.
5. Hoops can serve as a "home" for various activities. For instance, the children might leave their hoops to gallop in all directions and then return quickly to the hoop on command.
6. Hoops are good targets. A hoop can be made to stand by placing an individual mat over its base.
7. When teaching the reverse spin with hoops, have the students throw the hoop up, in place, rather than forward along the floor. After they learn the upward throw, they can progress to the forward throw for distance.

Recommended Activities

HOOPS AS FLOOR TARGETS

Each child has a hoop, which is placed on the floor. A number of movement challenges can give direction to the activity.

1. Show the different patterns you can make by jumping or hopping in and out of the hoop.

2. Do a Bunny Jump and a Frog Jump into the center and out the other side.
3. Show the ways you can cross from one side of the hoop to the other by taking the weight on your hands inside the hoop.
4. What kinds of animal walks can you do around your hoop?
5. On all fours, show the kinds of movements you can do, with your feet inside the hoop and your hands outside. With your hands inside the hoop and your feet outside. With one foot and one hand inside, and one foot and one hand outside.
6. (Set a time limit of 15 to 30 seconds.) See how many times you can jump in and out of your hoop during this time. Now try hopping.
7. Balance on and walk around the hoop. Try to keep your feet from touching the floor.
8. Curl your body inside the hoop. Bridge over your hoop. Stretch across your hoop. See how many different ways you can move around the hoop.
9. Pick up your hoop and see how many different machines you can invent. Let your hoop be the steering wheel of a car. What could it be on a train or a boat?
10. Jump in and out of the hoop, using the alphabet. Jump in on the vowels and out on the consonants. Use odd and even numbers in the same way. Vary the locomotor movements.
11. Get into the hoop by using two different body parts. Move out by using three parts. Vary the number of body parts used.
12. Get organized in squads or comparable groups, and divide the hoops. Arrange the hoops in various formations, and try different locomotor movements, animal walks, and other ways of maneuvering through the maze. (After the children have gained some experience, this can become a follow-the-leader activity.)

HOOP HANDLING

1. Spin the hoop like a top. See how long you can make it spin. Spin it again, and see how many times you can run around it before it falls to the floor.
2. Hula-hoop using various body parts such as the waist, legs, arms, and fingers. While hula-hooping on the arms, try to change the hoop from one arm to the other. Lie on the back with one or both legs pointed toward the ceiling and explore different ways the legs can twirl the hula hoop. Hula-hoop with two or more hoops.
3. Jump or hop through a hoop held by a partner. Further challenge can be added by varying the height and angle of the hoop.
4. Roll the hoop and run alongside it. Change direction when a command is given.
5. Hula-hoop on one arm. Throw the hoop in the air and catch it on the other arm.
6. Hold the hoop and swing it like a pendulum. Jump and hop in and out of the hoop.
7. Use the hoop like a jump rope. Jump forward, backward, and sideward. Do a crossover with the hands.
8. Roll the hoop with a reverse spin to make it return to you. The key to the reverse spin is to pull down (toward the floor) on the hoop as it is released. Roll the hoop with a reverse spin, jump over it, and catch it as it returns. Roll the hoop with a reverse spin, and as it returns, hoist it with the foot and catch it. Roll the hoop with a reverse spin, kick it up with the toe, and go through the hoop. Roll the hoop with a reverse spin, run around it, and catch it. Roll the hoop with a reverse spin, pick it up, and begin hooping on the arm—all in one motion.
9. Play catch with a partner. Try with two or more hoops.
10. Hula-hoop. Attempt to change hoops with a partner.
11. Have one partner roll the hoop with a reverse spin and the other attempt to crawl through the hoop. (This is done most easily just after the hoop reverses direction and begins to return to the spinner. Some children can go in and out of the hoop twice.)
12. Tell partners to spin the hoops like tops and see who can keep theirs spinning longer.

Games with Hoops

COOPERATIVE MUSICAL HOOPS

Hoops, one per student, are placed on the floor. Players are given a locomotor movement to do. On signal, they cease the movement, find a hoop, and sit cross-legged in the center of it. Music can be used, with the children moving to the music and seeking a hoop when the music stops. Hoops can be removed by the teacher, challenging students to share hoops with each other. This can continue until all students are in three or four hoops.

AROUND THE HOOP

The class is divided into groups of three, with children in each group numbered 1, 2, and 3. Each threesome sits back to back inside a hoop. Their heels may need to be outside the hoop. The leader calls out a direction (right or left) and names one of the numbers. The child with that number immediately gets up, runs in the stipulated direction around the hoop, then runs back to place and sits down. The winner is the first group sitting in good position after the child returns to place.

HULA-HOOP CIRCLE

Four to six children hold hands in a circle, facing in, with a hoop dangling on one pair of joined hands. They move the hoop around the circle and back to the starting point. This requires all bodies to go through the hoop. Hands can help the hoop move, but grips cannot be released.

HULA-HOOP RELAY

Relay teams of four to six players, each with a hoop, are placed in line or circle formation. The hoop must be held upright with the bottom of the hoop touching the floor. On signal, designated starters drop their hoops and move through the hoops held by squad members. The sequence repeats until every player has moved through the hoops.

BUMPER CAR TAG

The class is divided into partners. The partners stand inside a hoop held at waist level. Three or more sets of partners are declared to be it. The object is to tag other partners, who are also moving inside a "bumper car." The game can also be played with three players in a hoop. This is challenging, as players will want to move in different directions.

HOOP ADDITION RELAY

Divide the class into relay teams of four. On signal, the first person moves to the end marker (a hoop), returns, and takes the next person to the marker and so on, until all four players are in the hoop. Players must sit down in the hoop when the relay is completed.

ACTIVITIES WITH JUMP ROPES

Rope jumping is an excellent activity for conditioning all parts of the body. It increases coordination, rhythm, and timing, while offering a wide range of challenges. Rope jumping is regarded as an excellent medium for fitness development. It can be designed to suit the activity needs of all individuals regardless of age or condition. Workloads can easily be measured and modified by changing the amount of time jumped or the number of turns. It is a useful activity to teach children, because it offers carryover value for activity in later life.

Rope jumping has increased in popularity during the past decade, with the Jump Rope for Heart program offering national leadership. The program is sponsored by the American Alliance for Health, Physical Education, Recreation, and Dance as a fund-raising activity for the American Heart Association (Jump Rope for Heart materials can be obtained by contacting your local affiliate of the American Heart Association or by calling AAHPERD at 800-213-7193, x429). This nationwide movement has spawned school teams, exhibitions, and competition in the form of state and national tournaments. It is a creative medium with an incredible number of variations possible. Rope-jumping skills presented in this chapter are those deemed suitable for inclusion in an elementary school physical education program. Not included are highly advanced and complex activities that are often used in competitive settings. The difficulty of advanced activities makes them less suitable for bringing success to all youngsters in physical education programs. For more information about advanced activities, review the references at the end of the chapter. Rope-jumping activities in this chapter are grouped into three categories: (a) movements guided by rope patterns, (b) long-rope jumping, and (c) individual rope jumping.

MOVEMENTS GUIDED BY ROPE PATTERNS

Ropes can be placed on the floor in various fashions to serve as stimuli for different locomotor and nonlocomotor movements. The activities should stress creative responses within the limits of the challenge. The educational movement factors of space, time, force, and flow can be interwoven in the activity. The key is teacher ingenuity in providing direction for the movement patterns. The child can move as an individual, with a partner, or as a member of a small group. Generally, a rope is placed in a straight line or in a circle. Geometric figures can also be formed and numbers or letters of the alphabet featured. The discussions are organized around these patterns.

Rope Forming a Straight Line

When the rope is placed in a straight line, one approach is for children to begin at one end and to perform activities as they move down the line. Much of the movement can be based on hopping or jumping. The children then return, back up the line, to the starting point. Movement suggestions follow.

1. Jog around the rope forward and backward. Try other locomotor skills such as hopping, jumping, skipping, and sliding. Crab Walk down and back. Use various animal walks such as Bear Walk or Lame Dog Walk.
2. Hop back and forth across the rope, moving down the line. Return, using the other foot.

3. Jump lightly back and forth down the line. Return.
4. Hop slowly, under control, down the line. Hop rapidly back.
5. Jump so that the rope is between the feet each time, alternately crossing and uncrossing the feet.
6. Move on all fours, leading with different body parts.
7. Do Crouch Jumps back and forth across the rope. Vary with three points and then two points of contact.
8. Jump as high as possible going down the line and as low as possible coming back.
9. Hop with a narrow shape down and a different shape back.
10. Walk the rope like a tightrope.
11. Begin with a bridge and move the bridge down the line. Return with a different bridge.
12. Lie across the rope, holding one end. Roll down the line, causing the rope to roll around the body. Unroll the rope back to position.
13. Do a movement with the rhythm slow-slow, fast-fast-fast, going down the line, and repeat coming back.
14. "Pull" yourself down the line and "push" yourself back.

For the following movements, the child is positioned close to the center of the line and simply moves back and forth across it without materially changing the relative position.

1. Hop back and forth across the line. Jump back and forth.
2. Go over with a high movement. Come back with a low one.
3. Do a Bunny Jump across and back. A Frog Jump. A Crouch Jump.
4. Lead with different parts of the body back and forth. Propel with different parts.
5. Get into a moderately crouched position over the rope. Jump the feet back and forth over the rope.
6. Take a sprinter's position with the rope between the feet. Alternate the feet back and forth over the rope.
7. Jump back and forth lightly on the tiptoes.
8. Go back and forth, using different shapes.
9. With toes touching the rope, drop the body forward across the rope, taking the weight on both hands. Walk the hands forward, out to the limit.
10. Pretend that the rope is a river. Show different kinds of bridges that you can make over the river.
11. Stand straddling the rope. Jump up, perform a heel click (or two), and return to original position.

Rope Forming a Circle

With the rope in a circle, children can do movements around the outside clockwise and counterclockwise—walking, skipping, hopping, sliding (facing toward and away from the circle), jumping, running, and galloping. The following activities can be done with hoops also.

1. Hop in and out of the circle, moving around. Jump.
2. Jump directly in and then across. Jump backward.
3. Jump in, collapse, and jump out, without touching the rope.
4. Begin in the center of the circle. Jump forward, backward, and sideward, each time returning to the center.
5. Place the feet in the circle and walk the hands all around the outside of the circle. Place the hands inside and the feet outside. Face the floor, the ceiling, and to the side.
6. Inside the circle, make a small shape. Make a large shape so that you are touching all sides of the circle.
7. Try different balance stunts inside the circle. Close your eyes and balance.
8. Make a bridge over the circle. How many types of bridges can you make?
9. Do a Pogo Stick Jump in and out of the rope circle.
10. Do a Tightrope Walk clockwise and counterclockwise.
11. Jump and click the heels, landing inside the circle. Repeat, going out.
12. Do jump turns inside the circle without touching the rope: quarter turns, half turns, and full turns.
13. Jump in with a Bunny Jump. Jump out. Try with a Frog Jump.
14. Take the weight on the hands inside the circle so that the feet land on the other side. Try a cartwheel.

Rope Forming Various Figures

Have the rope form different figures, such as geometric shapes, letters, and numbers. In addition to the following challenges, many of the previous ones can be applied here, too.

1. With the rope and your body, form a triangle, a square, a rectangle, a diamond shape, and a figure eight.
2. With the rope and your body, form a two-letter word. Form other words.
3. Get a second rope and make your own patterns for hopping and jumping.
4. Toss the rope in the air and let it fall to the floor. Try to shape your body into the same figure that the rope made on the floor.

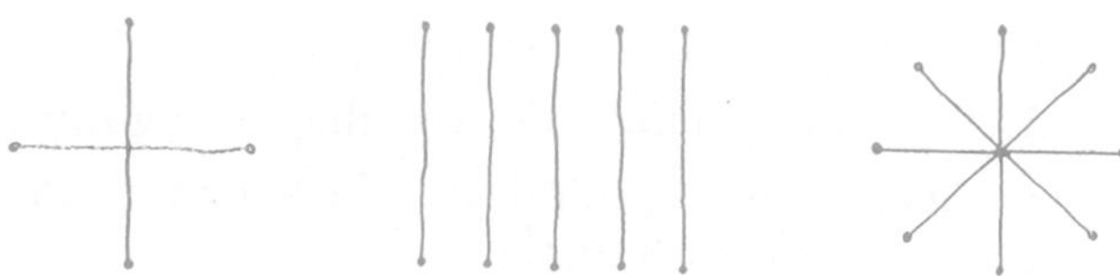

FIGURE 17.19 Suggested rope forms.

Partner Activity

Partner activity with ropes is excellent. Partners can work with one or two ropes, and can do matching, following, or contrasting movements. Add-On is an interesting game: One partner does an activity and the other adds on an activity to form a sequence. Using the suggested rope forms (multiple ropes) in Figure 17.19, one partner makes a series of movements. The other partner has to try to duplicate the movements.

Group Activity

Group activity with jump ropes also has good possibilities. Each child brings a rope to the group. Patterns for hopping, jumping, and other locomotor movements can be arranged with the ropes. An achievement demonstration after a period of practice allows each group to show the patterns that they have arranged and the movements that can be done in the patterns. A further extension is to leave the patterns where they are and to rotate the groups to different locations.

LONG-ROPE JUMPING

Long-rope jumping is an excellent activity for beginning jumpers. Youngsters can concentrate on jumping the rope without learning the skill of turning. Many activities with two or more long ropes add a great deal of variety to long-rope jumping and can make it challenging for the most skilled jumpers. Long jump ropes should be 9 to 14 feet in length, with 12 to 14 feet the most commonly used. The exact length depends on the age and skill of the children; the longer the rope, the more difficult it is to turn. For primary-grade children, individual jump ropes can be used to teach beginning skills as they are shorter, making it easier for young children to turn. Another alternative is to fasten one end of the rope with a snap to an eye bolt fixed on a post or to the side of a wall. This eases the task of turning and allows more children to be actively jumping.

Chants are suggested for many of the jumping sequences. Rope-jumping chants represent a cultural heritage. In many cases, children have their own favorites. Traditionally, many chants used girls' names, because rope jumping was considered a feminine activity. Today, however, this has changed, and both sexes participate in rope-jumping activities with equal vigor and success. Several of the chants included have been modified to reflect this change.

Instructional Procedures

1. Four or five children is an appropriate group size for practicing long-rope skills. Two members of the group turn the rope while the others practice jumping. A plan for rotating turners is important so that all children receive similar amounts of practice jumping.
2. Turning the rope is a difficult skill for young children. It must be practiced regularly until children can maintain an even, steady rhythm. Effective turning is one key to successful jumping. If turning is not rhythmic, even skilled jumpers will have problems. Youngsters must be taught: Learn to turn first, then learn to jump.
3. When learning to turn the rope, incorporate the following points:
   a. Keep the elbow close to the body and concentrate on turning the rope with the forearm.
   b. The thumb should stay up during the turning motion of the hands. This will emphasize turning with the forearm.
   c. Hold the rope in front of the body at waist level. Keep the body perpendicular to the rope.
4. To practice turning, youngsters are motivated by turning the rope under a lively bouncing ball. Turners stand ready, and a third child tosses a ball upward so that it will remain in one spot while bouncing. Turners adjust the speed of the turning as the bounces become smaller and more rapid. A count can be kept of the number of successful turns before the ball ceases bouncing.
5. Children of all ages can perform long-rope jumping. To check the readiness of the children, see if they are capable of jumping in place with both feet leaving the ground simultaneously. They should be able to jump at least 2 to 3 inches off the ground, be well balanced, and land lightly with reasonably straight knees.
6. Children should understand the terms used to describe entry into the long jump rope. *Front door* means entering from the side where the rope is turning forward and toward the jumper after it reaches its peak. *Back door* means entering from the side where the rope is turning backward and away from the jumper. To enter front door, the jumper follows the rope in and jumps when it completes the

turn. To enter back door, the jumper waits until the rope reaches its peak and moves in as the rope moves downward. Learning to enter at an angle is usually easier, but any path that is comfortable is acceptable.

7. Introducing and teaching youngsters long-rope jumping skills can be accomplished with the following steps:
   a. Use a shorter long rope (8 to 12 foot). Lay the rope on the floor and have youngsters jump back and forth across the rope. Emphasis should be on small, continuous jumps and learning how to jump back and forth continuously without stopping. Jumps should not be high, just enough to clear the rope.
   b. Turners slowly move the rope back and forth along the floor while the jumper moves over the rope each time it moves near. The speed of the rope moving along the floor should be increased gradually. The jumper should be encouraged to jump up and down with as little forward-backward-sideways movement as possible. If necessary, use white shoe polish to mark an "X" on the floor and encourage the child to stay on target.
   c. The jumper stands near the center of the rope. The rope is now moved in pendulum fashion back and forth while the jumper clears the rope each time it hits the floor. Typically, this activity is called *Blue Bells.*
   d. The jumper starts by facing the center of the stationary rope. Use three pendulum swings followed by a full turn of the rope rotating from the jumper's back to the front. Continue jumping until a miss occurs. Verbal cueing helps most beginners find success; each time the rope hits the floor, say "Jump." If youngsters are having difficulty, have them stand behind a turner and jump (without the rope) each time the rope hits the floor.
   e. When jumpers have difficulty with the rhythm, they can practice off to one side without actually jumping over the rope. A drumbeat can reinforce the rhythm with alternating heavy (jump) and light (rebound) beats.
   f. Teach front-door and back-door entry, making sure that the jumper enters at an angle rather than perpendicular to the rope.
8. Instructional cues to teach long-rope jumping skills are:
   a. Turn the rope with the forearm.
   b. Lock the wrist and keep the thumb up while turning.
   c. Stand perpendicular to the rope.
   d. Barely touch the floor with the turning rope.
   e. Don't cross the midline of the body with the forearm while turning the rope.
   f. Jump on the balls of the feet.
   g. To enter, stand near the turner and move to the center of the rope.

Introductory Skills

Some introductory skills and routines follow.

1. Holders hold the rope in a stationary position 6 inches above the ground. Jumpers jump over, back and forth. Raise the rope a little each time. Be sure to hold the rope loosely in the hands. This is called *Building a House.*
2. Ocean Wave is another stationary jumping activity. Turners make waves in the rope by moving the arms up and down. Jumpers try to time it so that they jump over a low part of the wave.
3. Holders stoop down and wiggle the rope back and forth on the floor. Jumpers try to jump over the rope and not touch it as it moves. This activity is called *Snake in the Grass.*
4. The jumper stands in the center between the turners, who carefully turn the rope in a complete arc over the jumper's head. As the rope completes the turn, the jumper jumps over it and exits immediately in the direction in which the rope is turned.
5. Children run through the turning rope (front door) without jumping, following the rope through.
6. While the rope is being turned, the jumper runs in (front door), jumps once, and runs out immediately.
7. Children can play school and go through the following sequence, trying to pass to the sixth grade. To pass kindergarten, run through the turning rope. To pass first grade, run in, take one jump, and run out. For the second through sixth grades, increase the number of jumps by one for each grade. A jumper who misses becomes a turner.
8. When children can jump a number of times consecutively, add motivation by using some of the chants that follow.

Intermediate Skills, Routines, and Chants

Intermediate routines require the jumper to be able to go in front door, jump, and exit front door, and to do the same sequence back door. Enough practice in the simple jumping skills and exits should be held so that confidence is fortified; students then can turn to more intricate routines. Entries and exits should be varied in the following routines.

1. Jumpers run in, jump a specified number of times, and exit.
2. Children can add chants that dictate the number of jumps, which are followed by an exit. Here are some examples.

   Tick tock, tick tock,
   What's the time by the clock?
   It's one, two, [up to midnight].

   I like coffee, I like tea,
   How many people can jump like me?
   One, two, three, [up to a certain number].

   Hippity hop to the butcher shop,
   How many times before I stop?
   One, two, three, [and so on].

   Bulldog, poodle, bow wow wow,
   How many doggies have we now?
   One, two, three, [and so on].

   Michael, Michael (student's name) at the gate,
   Eating cherries from a plate.
   How many cherries did he (she) eat?
   One, two, three, [and so on].
3. Children can label their first jump "kindergarten" and exit at any "grade." To graduate from high school, the exit would be at the twelfth grade. Each grade should be sounded crisply in succession.
4. Kangaroo (or White Horse) gets its name from the jump required for back-door entry, in which the jumper resembles a kangaroo or a leaping horse. The jumper calls out "Kangaroo!" takes the entry jump through the back door, and exits. Next time, the same jumper calls out "Kangaroo one!" and adds a jump. Successive jumps are called and added until a designated number is reached.
5. An interesting challenge is to turn the rope over a line parallel to it and have the jumper jump back and forth over the line. The jumper can vary foot position: feet together, feet apart, stride forward and back.
6. Jumpers can vary the pattern with turns. Make four quarter turns until facing the original direction. Reverse the direction of the turns.
7. Youngsters can add stunts as directed by selected chants.

   Teddy Bear, Teddy Bear, turn around.
   Teddy Bear, Teddy Bear, touch the ground.
   Teddy Bear, Teddy Bear, show your shoe.
   Teddy Bear, Teddy Bear, you better skidoo.
   Teddy Bear, Teddy Bear, go upstairs.
   Teddy Bear, Teddy Bear, say your prayers.
   Teddy Bear, Teddy Bear, turn out the light.
   Teddy Bear, Teddy Bear, say good night.

   Daddy, daddy (mommy, mommy), I am sick.
   Get the doctor quick, quick, quick.
   Daddy, daddy, turn around.
   Daddy, daddy, touch the ground.
   Daddy, daddy, are you through?
   Daddy, daddy, spell your name.
8. In Hot Pepper, turners turn the rope faster and faster, while the jumper tries to keep up with the increased speed. The following chants are good for Hot Pepper.

   Charlie, Charlie (student's name), set the table.
   Bring the plates if you are able.
   Don't forget the salt and
   Red hot pepper!

   (On the words "Red hot pepper," the rope is turned as fast as possible until the jumper misses.)

   Pease porridge hot, pease porridge cold,
   Pease porridge in a pot, nine days old.
   Some like it hot, hot, hot!

   Ice cream, ginger ale, soda water, pop.
   You get ready 'cause we're gonna turn hot!
9. In Calling In, the first player enters the rope and calls in a second player by name. Both jump three times holding hands, and then the first runs out. The second player then calls in a third player by name. Both jump three times holding hands, and the second player exits. Players should be in an informal line, since the fun comes from not knowing when one is to enter.
10. Children can enter and exit according to the call in the following chants.

    In the shade and under a tree,
    I'd like ____________ to come in with me.
    She's (he's) too fast and I'm too slow.
    He stays in and I must go.

    Calling in and calling out,
    I call (student's name) in and I'm getting out.

    House for rent,
    Inquire within.
    When I move out,
    Let (student's name) move in.
11. In High Water, the rope is turned so that it becomes gradually higher and higher off the ground.

    At the beach, at the sea,
    The waves come almost to the knee.
    Higher, higher, [and so forth].
12. In Stopping the Rope, the jumper (a) stops and lets the rope hit the feet, (b) stops the rope by straddling it, (c) stops with the legs crossed and the rope between the feet, or (d) stops the rope by stamping on it. The following chant works well, with accompanying action as indicated.

Junior, Junior, climb the tree.
Junior, Junior, slap your knee.
Junior, Junior, throw a kiss.
Junior, Junior, time to miss.

13. Two, three, or four children can jump at a time. After some skill has been achieved, children in combination can run in, jump a specified number of times, and run out, keeping hands joined all the time.
14. Two, three, or four children can start as a small moving circle. They run in and jump in a circle, keeping the circle moving in one direction. They run out as a circle.
15. The jumper takes in a ball or other object. Bounce the ball while jumping. Try balancing a beanbag on a body part while jumping.
16. A partner stands ready with a ball and tosses it back and forth to the jumper.
17. For Chase the Rabbit, four or five jumpers are in single file with a leader, the Rabbit, at the head. The Rabbit jumps in any manner he or she may wish, and all of the others must match the movements. Anyone who misses must go to the end of the line. A Rabbit who misses or stops the rope, goes to the end of the line, and the next child becomes the new Rabbit. Set a limit on how long a Rabbit can stay at the head of the line.
18. In On Four Cylinders, the challenge is to do activities in a series of fours—four of one kind of jump, four of another, and so on. The number of series can be specified, and the children may choose what they wish to include. (Tell the children that their "engines are running on four cylinders.")
19. In Begging, a jumper runs in and works his way up the rope toward one of the turners. As he jumps, he says, "Father, Father, give me a dollar." The turner replies, "Go see your mother." The jumper works his way toward the other turner and says, "Mother, Mother, give me a dollar." The turner replies, "Go to your father." This continues until a miss occurs or until one of the turners says in reply, "Get out" or "Get lost," at which time the jumper exits.
20. In Setting the Table, a jumper enters and starts jumping. A partner stands ready with at least four beanbags. While the following verse is recited, the partner tosses in the beanbags one at a time, and the jumper catches and places them in a row on the side (with the upward swing of the rope) and then exits.

    Debbie, Debbie (student's name), set the table (toss in one bag),
    Bring the plates if you are able (toss in another bag),
    Don't forget the bread and butter (toss in the other two bags).

21. Partners can go in and perform a number of stunts, such as Wring the Dishrag (Figure 20.38), Partner Hopping (Figure 20.81), or Bouncing Ball (Figure 20.37). Examine the partner stunts for other selections.
22. Children can enter and begin with a hop (one foot), then make a jump (two feet), add a hand touch next (two feet, one hand), and then jump with both hands and feet (two feet, two hands). Selected movements on hands and feet, such as Rabbit Jumps or Push-Ups, can be executed.
23. For jumping with the eyes closed, single or multiple jumpers enter and begin jumping to this chant.

    Peanuts, popcorn, soda pop,
    How many jumps before you stop?
    Close your eyes and you will see
    How many jumps that this will be!

    The eyes remain closed during the jumping, which continues to a target number or a miss.
24. One or both holders can go inside and jump, turning with their outside hands. First attempts should begin with a pendulum swing and proceed to a full turn.

DOUBLE DUTCH (TWO-ROPE) JUMPING

Double Dutch rope jumping (Figure 17.20) is popular on playgrounds and in gymnasiums across the country. This type of jumping requires two rope turners using two long ropes that are turned in opposite directions. Turning two ropes simultaneously requires practice, and time must be allotted for this. Handling two ropes is tiring, so turners should be rotated frequently.

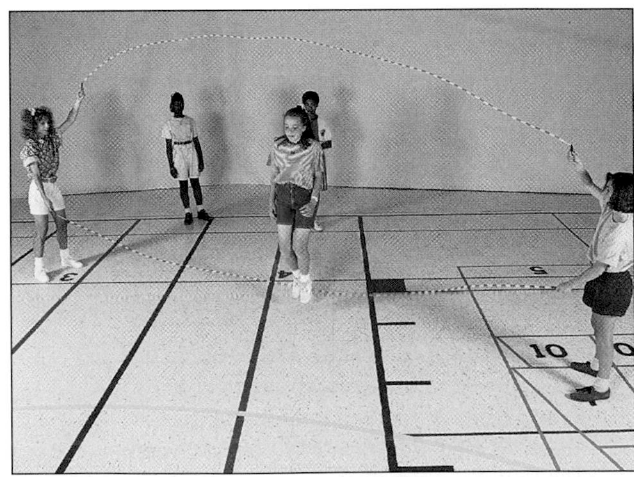

FIGURE 17.20 Double Dutch rope jumping.

Instructional Procedures

1. Arm positions and turning motions are similar to turning a single long rope. In short, keep the upper arm stationary, rotate at the elbow with locked wrist, and keep the thumb up. Avoid crossing the midline of the body, and establish an even cadence. Rotate the hands inward toward the midline of the body (right forearm counterclockwise and left forearm clockwise). Students should concentrate on the sound of the ropes hitting the floor so that they make an even and rhythmic beat.
2. Double Dutch turning takes considerable practice. Take time to teach it as a skill that is necessary for successful jumping experiences.
3. When entering, stand beside a turner and run into the ropes when the back rope (farther from the jumper) touches the floor. Turners should be taught to say "Go" each time the back rope touches the floor.
4. Concentrate on jumping in the center of the ropes facing a turner. Use white shoe polish to mark a jumping target.
5. Exit the ropes by facing and jumping toward one turner and exiting immediately after jumping. The exit should be made as close to the turner's shoulder as possible.
6. Practice many of the skills listed in the long-rope jumping section (pages 371–374). Many of the chants and stunts provide challenge and variety to the unit.

DOUBLE DUTCH SKILLS

1. *Basic jump on both feet.* Land on the balls of the feet, keeping ankles and knees together with hands across the stomach.
2. *Turnaround.* Circle left or right using the basic jump. Begin circling slowly at first and then increase speed. To increase the challenge, try the turnaround on one foot.
3. *Straddle Jump.* Jump to the straddle position and return to closed position. Try a *Straddle Cross Jump* by crossing the legs on return to the closed position. The straddle jumps should be performed facing away from the turners.
4. *Scissors Jump.* Jump to a stride position with the left foot forward and the right foot back about 8 inches apart. Each jump requires reversing the position of the feet.
5. *Jogging Step.* Run in place with a jogging step. Increase the challenge by circling while jogging.
6. *Hot Peppers.* Use the Jogging Step and gradually increase the speed of the ropes.
7. *Half turn.* Perform a half turn with each jump. Remember to lead the turn with the head and shoulders.
8. *Ball tossing.* Toss and catch a beanbag or playground ball while jumping.
9. *Individual rope jumping.* Enter double dutch with an individual rope and jump. Face the turner and decrease the length of the individual jump rope.
10. The following activities are interesting variations for reviving motivation:
    a. *Double Irish.* Two ropes are turned in the reverse directions used in Double Dutch. The left hand turns counterclockwise and the right hand clockwise. Entry is made when the near rope hits the floor. Jumpers should time their entry by following the near rope on its downward swing.
    b. *Egg Beater.* Two long ropes are turned at right angles simultaneously by four turners (Figure 17.21 on page 376). Entry is made at the quadrant where both ropes are turning front doors. The number of ropes being turned can be increased to three or four. This activity is easier than jumping Double Dutch since the jumping action is similar to single-rope jumping. It is an excellent activity for building confidence in jumping more than one long rope.

Formation Jumping

For formation jumping, four to six long ropes with turners can be placed in various patterns, with tasks specified for each rope. Ropes can be turned in the same direction, or the turning directions can be mixed. Several formations are illustrated in Figure 17.22 (on page 376).

INDIVIDUAL ROPE JUMPING

Individual rope jumping should place emphasis on establishing basic turning skills and letting children create personal routines. Individual rope jumping is particularly valuable as part of the conditioning process for certain sports. It lends itself to prescribed doses based on number of turns, length of participation, speed of the turning rope, and various steps. Because rope jumping is of a rhythmic nature, the addition of music is a natural progression. Music adds much to the activity and enables the jumper to create and organize routines to be performed to the musical pieces. The most effective approach is probably a combination of experiences with and without music.

There are a number of types of jump ropes on the market, all of which are satisfactory, depending on the likes and dislikes of the instructor. The most popular ap-

FIGURE 17.21 Egg Beater.

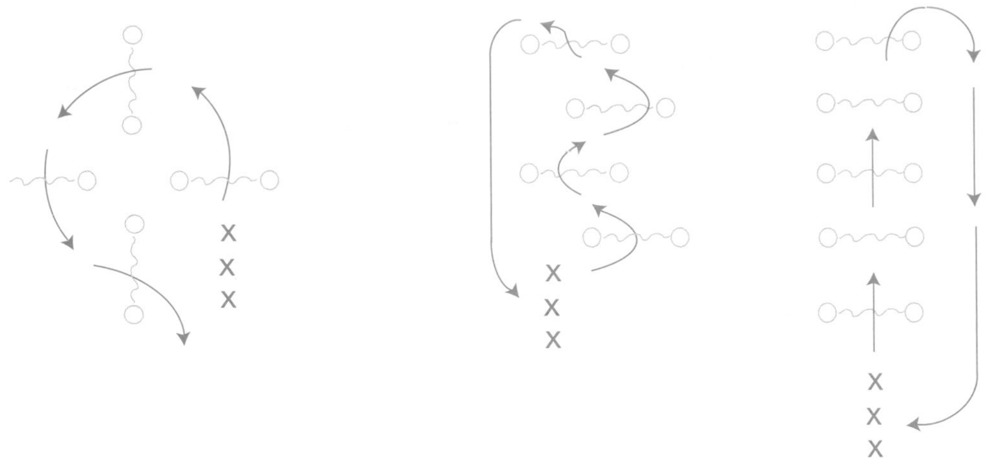

FIGURE 17.22 Formations for jumping rope.

pear to be the solid plastic speed (often called licorice) ropes and the beaded or segmented ropes. The speed rope is excellent for rapid turning and doing tricks. It does not maintain momentum as well as the segmented ropes, which can be important for beginners. Sash cord is economical but doesn't wear well on blacktop or cement. In addition, without handles, it is a second-rate jump rope.

Instructional Procedures

1. The length of the rope is dependent on the height of the jumper. It should be long enough so that the ends reach to the armpits (Figure 17.23 on page 377) or slightly higher when the child stands on its center. Preschool children generally use 6-foot ropes, and the primary-level group needs mostly 7-foot ropes, with a few 6- and 8-foot lengths. Grades three through six need a mixture of 7-, 8-, and 9-foot ropes. A 9- or 10-foot rope serves well for tall students and most instructors. Ropes or handles can be color-coded for length.

   Two types of ropes are available—the beaded (plastic segment) and the plastic (licorice) rope. The beaded ropes are heavier and seem easier to

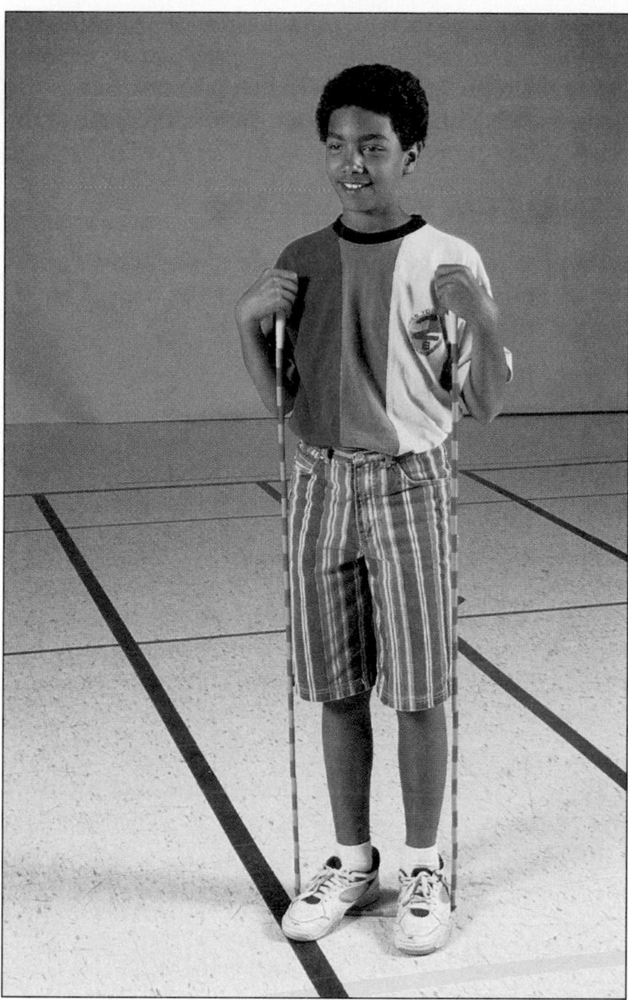

FIGURE 17.23 Correct jump rope length.

turn for beginning jumpers. The drawback to the beaded ropes is that they hurt when they hit another student. Also, if the segments are made round, the rope will roll easily on the floor and cause children to fall when they step on it. The plastic licorice ropes are lighter and give less wind resistance. For experienced jumpers more speed and control can be gained with this type of rope. An ideal situation would be to have a set of each type.

2. Posture is an important consideration in rope jumping. The body should be in good alignment, with the head up and the eyes looking straight ahead. The jump is made with the body in an erect position. A slight straightening of the knees provides the lift for the jump, which should be of minimal height (about 1 inch). The wrists supply the force to turn the rope, with the elbows kept close to the body and extended at a 90-degree angle. A pumping action and lifting of the arms is unnecessary. The landing should be made on the balls of the feet, with the knees bent slightly to cushion the shock. Usually, the feet, ankles, and legs are kept together, except when a specific step calls for a different position.
3. The rope should be held by the index finger and thumb on each side with the hands making a small circle. The elbows should be held near the sides to avoid making large arm circles with the rope.
4. Introducing and teaching youngsters individual rope jumping skills can be accomplished with the following steps:
   a. Students should first jump without the rope until they learn the correct rhythm and footwork. For slow time, this would be a jump and then a rebound step. Children can pretend that they are turning the rope. Remember that rope jumping involves learning two separate skills: jumping a rope and turning a rope. Youngsters who have a problem need to practice the parts separately before they are put together as a whole.
   b. Turn the rope over the head of the jumper and catch it with the toes.
   c. The jumper holds the rope stationary in front of the body. Jump forward and backward over the rope. To increase the challenge, swing the rope slightly. Gradually increase the swing until a full turn of the rope is made.
   d. Hold the rope to one side with both hands, swing the rope forward and jump each time the rope hits the floor. If swinging the rope is a problem, practice without jumping first.
5. Music can be added when jumpers have learned the first stages of jumping. Music provides a challenge for continued jumping.
6. In the primary-level group, some children cannot jump, but by the third grade, all children who have had some experience should be able to jump. Children who cannot jump may be helped by the pendulum swing of the long rope, or another student jumping with the child inside an individual rope. Cues such as "Jump" or "Ready-jump" should be used.
7. Most steps can be done with either rhythm: slow time or fast time. In slow-time rhythm, the performer jumps over the rope, rebounds, and then executes the second step (or repeats the original step) on the second jump. The rebound is simply a hop in place as the rope passes over the head. Better jumpers bend the knees only slightly, without actually leaving the floor on rebound. The object of the rebound is to carry the rhythm between steps. The rope is rotating slowly, passing under the feet on

every other beat, and the feet also move slowly, since there is rebound between each jump.

In fast-time rhythm, the rope rotates in time with the music, one turn per beat (120 to 180 turns per minute, depending on the tune's tempo), and the performer executes a step only when the rope is passing under the feet.

8. Instructional cues to use for improving jumping technique are as follows:
   a. Keep the arms at the side of the body while turning. (Many children lift the arms to shoulder level trying to move the rope overhead. This makes it impossible for the youngster to jump over the elevated rope.)
   b. Turn the rope by making small circles with the wrists.
   c. Jump on the balls of the feet.
   d. Bend the knees slightly to absorb the force of the jump.
   e. Make a small jump over the rope.
9. To collect ropes at the completion of a rope-jumping activity, have two or three children act as monitors. They put both arms out to the front or to the side at shoulder level. The other children then drape the ropes over their arms (Figure 17.24). The monitors return the ropes to the correct storage area.

Basic Steps

The basic steps presented here can be done in slow or fast time. After youngsters have mastered the first six steps in slow time, fast time can be introduced. The Alternate-Foot Basic Step and Spread Legs Forward and Backward are two steps that work well for introducing fast-time jumping.

FIGURE 17.24 Collecting the ropes.

SIDE SWING

Swing the rope, held with both hands to one side of the body. Switch and swing the rope on the other side of the body.

DOUBLE SIDE SWING AND JUMP

Swing the rope once on each side of the body. Follow the second swing with a jump over the rope. The sequence should be swing, swing, jump.

TWO-FOOT BASIC STEP

In the Two-Foot Basic Step, jump over the rope with feet together as it passes under the feet, then take a preparatory rebound while the rope is over the head.

ALTERNATE-FOOT BASIC STEP

In the Alternate-Foot Basic Step, as the rope passes under the feet, the weight is shifted alternately from one foot to the other, raising the unweighted foot in a running position.

BIRD JUMPS

Jump with the toes pointed in (pigeon walk) and with the toes pointed out (duck walk). Alternate toes in and toes out.

SWING-STEP FORWARD

The Swing-Step Forward is the same as the Alternate-Foot Basic Step, except that the free leg swings forward. The knee is kept loose, and the foot swings naturally.

SWING-STEP SIDEWARD

The Swing-Step Sideward is the same as the Swing-Step Forward, except that the free leg is swung to the side. The knee should be kept stiff. The sideward swing is about 12 inches.

ROCKER STEP

In executing the Rocker Step, one leg is always forward in a walking-stride position. As the rope passes under the feet, the weight is shifted from the back foot to the forward foot. The rebound is taken on the forward foot while the rope is above the head. On the next turn of the rope, the weight is shifted from the forward foot to the back foot, repeating the rebound on the back foot.

SPREAD LEGS FORWARD AND BACKWARD

For Spread Legs Forward and Backward, start in a stride position (as in the Rocker) with weight equally distributed on both feet. As the rope passes under the feet, jump into the air and reverse the position of the feet.

STRADDLE JUMP

Alternate a regular jump with a straddle jump. The straddle jump is performed with the feet spread to shoulder width.

CROSS LEGS SIDEWARD

In Cross Legs Sideward, as the rope passes under the feet, spread the legs in a straddle position (sideward) to take the rebound. As the rope passes under the feet on the next turn, jump into the air and cross the feet with the right foot forward. Then repeat with the left foot forward and continue this alternation.

TOE-TOUCH FORWARD

To do the Toe-Touch Forward, swing the right foot forward as the rope passes under the feet and touch the right toes on the next count. Then alternate, landing on the right foot and touching the left toes forward.

TOE-TOUCH BACKWARD

The Toe-Touch Backward is similar to the Swing-Step Sideward, except that the toes of the free foot touch to the back at the end of the swing.

SHUFFLE STEP

The Shuffle Step involves pushing off with the right foot and sidestepping to the left as the rope passes under the feet. Land with the weight on the left foot and touch the right toes beside the left heel. Repeat the step in the opposite direction.

SKIER

The Skier is a double-foot jump similar to a technique used by skiers. A chalked or painted line is needed. The jumper stands on both feet to one side of the line. Jumping is done sideways back and forth over the line. Children should try it in a forward and backward direction also.

HEEL-TOE

In the Heel-Toe, as the rope passes under the feet, jump with the weight landing on the right foot while touching the left heel forward. On the next turn of the rope, jump, land on the same foot, and touch the left toes beside the right heel. This pattern is then repeated with the opposite foot bearing the weight.

LEG FLING

On the first jump, bring the right leg up so that it is parallel to the floor with the knee bent. On the second jump, kick the same leg out and up as high as possible. Try with the other leg.

HEEL CLICK

Do two or three Swing-Steps Sideward, in slow time, in preparation for the Heel Click. When the right foot swings sideward, instead of a hop or rebound when the rope is above the head, raise the left foot to click the heel of the right foot. Repeat on the left side.

STEP-TAP

In the *Step-Tap,* as the rope passes under the feet, push off with the right foot and land on the left. While the rope is turning above the head, brush the sole of the right foot forward and then backward. As the rope passes under the feet for the second turn, push off with the left foot, land on the right, and repeat.

SKIPPING

Do a step-hop (skip) over the rope. Start slowly and gradually increase the speed of the rope.

SCHOTTISCHE STEP

The Schottische Step can be done to double-time rhythm, or it can be done with a varied rhythm. The pattern is step, step, step, hop (repeat), followed by four step-hops. In varied rhythm, three quick turns in fast time are made for the first three steps and then double-time rhythm prevails. The step should be practiced first in place and then in general space. Schottische music should be introduced.

BLEKING STEP

The Bleking Step has the pattern slow-slow, fast-fast-fast. The rope should turn to conform to this pattern. The step begins with a hop on the left foot with the right heel forward, followed by a hop on the right with the left heel forward. This action is repeated with three quick changes: right, left, right. The whole pattern is then repeated, beginning with a hop on the right foot with the left heel extended. If done to the music for the bleking dance (page 432), four bleking steps of slow-slow, fast-fast-fast are done. The second part of the music (the chorus) allows the children to organize a routine of their own. They must listen for changes in the music.

Crossing Arms

Once the basic steps are mastered, crossing the arms while turning the rope provides an interesting variation. Crossing the arms during forward turning is easier than crossing behind the back during backward turning. During crossing, the hands exchange places. This means that for forward crossing, the elbows are close to each other. This is not possible during backward crossing.

Crossing and uncrossing can be done at predetermined points after a stipulated number of turns. Crossing can be accomplished during any of the routines.

Double Turning

The double turn of the rope is also interesting. The jumper does a few basic steps in preparation for the double turn. As the rope approaches the feet, the child gives an extremely hard flip of the rope from the wrists, jumps from 6 to 8 inches in height, and allows the rope to pass under the feet twice before landing. The jumper must bend forward at the waist somewhat, which increases the speed of the turn. A substantial challenge for advanced rope jumpers is to see how many consecutive double-turn jumps they can do.

Shifting from Forward to Backward Jumping

To switch from forward to backward jumping without stopping the rope, any of the following techniques can be used.

1. As the rope starts downward in forward jumping, rather than allowing it to pass under the feet, the performer swings both arms to the left (or right) and makes a half turn of the body in that direction (i.e., facing the rope). On the next downward swing, the jumper spreads the arms and starts turning in the opposite direction. This method also works for shifting from backward to forward jumping.
2. When the rope is directly above the head, the performer extends both arms, causing the rope to hesitate momentarily, at the same time making a half-turn in either direction and continuing to skip with the rope turning in the opposite direction.
3. From a crossed-arm position, as the rope is going above the performer's head, the jumper may uncross the arms and turn simultaneously. This starts the rope turning and the performer jumping in the opposite direction.

Sideways Skipping

In sideways skipping, the rope is turned laterally with one hand held high and the other extended downward. The rope is swung around the body sideways. To accomplish this, the jumper starts with the right hand held high overhead and the left hand extended down the center of the body. Swing the rope to the left, at the same time raising the left leg sideways. Usually the speed is slow time, with the rebound taken on each leg in turn. Later, better jumpers may progress to fast-time speed. The rope passes under the left leg, and the jumper then is straddling the rope as it moves around his body behind him. Take the weight on the left foot, raising the right foot sideways. A rebound step on the left as the rope moves to the front brings the jumper back to the original position.

Combination Possibilities

Numerous combinations of steps and rope tricks are possible in rope jumping. Some ideas are:

1. Changes in the speed of the turn—slow time and fast time—can be made. Children should be able to shift from one speed to another, particularly when the music changes.
2. Developing expertise in various foot patterns and steps is important. Children should practice changing from one foot pattern to another.
3. The crossed-hands position should be tried both forward and backward. Many of the basic steps can be combined with crossed-hands position to add challenge.
4. Moving from a forward to a backward turn and returning should be practiced. Perform the turn while doing a number of different basic steps.
5. Double turns combined with basic steps look impressive and are challenging. A few children may be able to do a triple turn.
6. Children should try to move forward, backward, and sideward, employing a variety of the basic steps.
7. Backward jumping is exciting as it is a different skill than forward jumping. Most basic steps can be done backward or modified for the backward turn.
8. Speedy turns (*Hot Peppers*) can be practiced. Have children see how fast they can turn the rope for 15 or 30 seconds.

Individual Rope Jumping with Partners

Many interesting combinations are possible when one child turns the individual rope and one or more children jump it. For those routines in which the directions call for a child to run into a jumping pattern, it may be more effective to begin with the child already in position, before proceeding to the run-in stage.

1. The first child turns the rope and the other stands in front, ready to enter.
   a. Run in and face partner, and both jump (Figure 17.25).
   b. Run in and turn back to partner, and both jump.
   c. Decide which steps are to be done; then run in and match steps.

FIGURE 17.25 Rope jumping with a partner.

   d. Repeat with the rope turning backward.
   e. Run in with a ball and bounce it during the jumping.
2. Partners stand side by side, clasp inside hands, and turn the rope with outside hands.
   a. Face the same direction and turn the rope.
   b. Face opposite directions, clasp left hands, and turn the rope.
   c. Face opposite directions, clasp right hands, and turn the rope.
   d. Repeat routines with inside knees raised.
   e. Repeat routines with elbows locked. Try other arm positions.
3. The first child turns the rope while the second is to the rear ready to run in. The second child runs in and grasps the first child's waist or shoulders, and they jump together (engine and caboose).
4. The children stand back to back, holding a single rope in the right hand.
   a. Turn in one direction—forward for one and backward for the other.
   b. Reverse direction.
   c. Change to left hands, and repeat.
5. Three children jump. One turns the rope forward; one runs in, in front; and one runs in behind. All three jump. Try with the rope turning backward.
6. Two jumpers, each with a rope, face each other and turn both ropes together, forward for one and backward for the other, jumping over both ropes at once. Turn the ropes alternately, jumping each rope in turn.
7. One partner jumps in a usual individual rope pattern. The other is positioned to the side. The turning partner hands over one end of the rope, and the other maintains the turning rhythm and then hands the rope back.
   a. Try from the other side.
   b. Turn the rope backward.
8. Using a single rope held in the right hand, partners face each other and turn the rope in slow time. With the rope overhead, one partner makes a turn to the left (turning in) and jumps inside the rope, exiting by turning either way. See if both can turn inside.

Movement Sequences to Music

The opportunities for creative movement sequences performed to music are unlimited. Music must have a definite beat and a bouncy quality. Pieces with a two-part format, usually labeled the verse and the chorus, are excellent. The change from the verse to the chorus signals changes in rope-jumping pattern. Many of the recordings listed in Chapter 19 can be used quite successfully for rope jumping to music. Schottisches, marches, and polkas provide good background. Popular rock music can be used to motivate youngsters if it has a strong and even rhythm. In addition, special selections for rope jumping are available from commercial sources. Suggested recordings include:

The Muffin Man (page 428)
Looby Loo (page 425)
Bleking (page 432)
Pop Goes the Weasel (pages 436–437)
Schottische (page 458)
Polka (pages 453–454)

Devising Sequences to Music

Devising jumping sequences is a good opportunity for children to create their own routines to selected music. Simple changes from slow time to fast time can introduce this activity. Later, different steps can be incorporated, crossing and uncrossing arms can be included, and then the turning direction can be varied. Partner rope-jumping stunts can also be adapted to music. Suggestions for incorporating different steps in the sequences follow.

1. "Pop Goes the Weasel" has a definite verse and chorus change. The children can switch from slow-time jumping to fast-time jumping on the chorus.
2. Bleking offers an interesting change in rope speed. The rhythm is slow-slow, fast-fast-fast (four times).

The rope should be turned in keeping with the beat. Later, the bleking step can be added.

3. Using schottische music, children can do the schottische step in place twice and four moving step-hops in different directions during the chorus.
4. To "Little Brown Jug," a four-part routine can be done to four rounds of the music.

   First verse: Two-Foot Basic Step (slow time)
   Chorus: Two-Foot Basic Step (fast time)
   Second verse: Alternate-Foot Basic Step (slow time)
   Chorus: Alternate-Foot Basic Step (fast time)
   Third verse: Swing-Step Forward (slow time)
   Chorus: Swing-Step Forward (fast time)
   Fourth verse: Swing-Step Sideward (slow time)
   Chorus: Swing-Step Sideward (fast time)

Assessment of Individual Rope Jumping

Individual rope-jumping stunts, because of their specificity and individuality, can be adapted easily to learning packages and contract teaching. Skill assessment can be based on the accomplishment of a stated maneuver in so many turns of the rope. The assessment can be organized progressively, or can be grouped by beginning, intermediate, and advanced tests. An example of a beginning test follows. All test items are done first in slow time and then in fast time.

1. *Two-Foot Basic Step:* 10 turns
2. *Alternate-Foot Basic Step:* 10 turns
3. *Turning rope backward:* 10 turns
4. *Alternate crossing arms:* 10 turns
5. *Running forward:* 20 turns

Intermediate and advanced tests can be organized similarly.

FOOTBAG ACTIVITIES

A footbag is a specific object used for footbag skills and games. The construction varies with the manufacturer, although most footbags are spheres constructed of leather and are stitched internally for durability. Normal size is about 2 inches in diameter, and the weight is a little over 1 ounce. The object of the activities is to keep the bag in the air by means of foot contact.

The kicking motion used for footbag activities is new to most participants because of the lift, which is performed by lifting the foot upward, not away from the body. The lifting motion enables the footbag flight to be directed upward for controlled consecutive kicks and passes. The ball is soft and flexible, with no bounce. It must be designed specifically as a footbag.

Several points contribute to successful footbag work. The basic athletic stance (ready position) is used with the feet at approximately shoulder width and pointed straight ahead. Knees are bent slightly, with the weight lowered.

There should be equal use of both feet for lifting and kicking. The support (nonkicking) foot is important for maintaining balance and keeping the body in a crouched position. Eye focus on the footbag is essential. Kicking speed should be slow; most beginners tend to kick too quickly. The kicking speed should be about that of the descending footbag. "Slow" and "low" are the key words in kicking.

The arms and upper body are used for balance and control. For the outside and back kicks, an outstretched arm, opposite to the kicking foot and in line with it, aids in maintaining balance. The near arm is carried behind the body so as not to restrict the player's vision. For inside kicks, the arms are relaxed and in balanced position.

To begin, start with a hand toss to self or with a courtesy toss from another player. A restriction is made that touching the footbag with any part of the body above the waist is a foul and interrupts any sequence of kicks. Three basic kicks are recommended.

1. *Inside kick.* This kick is used when the footbag falls low and directly in front of both shoulders. Use the inside of the foot for contact by turning the instep and the ankle upward to create a flat striking surface. Curling the toes under aids in creating a flat striking surface. Contact with the footbag is made at about knee level.
2. *Outside kick.* This kick is used when the footbag falls outside of either shoulder. The outside of the foot is used by turning the ankle and knee in to create a flat striking surface. With the kicking foot now parallel to the playing surface, use a smooth lifting motion, striking the footbag at approximately knee level. Pointing the toes up aids in creating a flat surface.
3. *Back kick.* This kick is somewhat similar to the outside kick and serves when the footbag goes directly overhead or is approaching the upper body directly. The hips and body must rotate parallel to the flight direction to enable the footbag to pass while still maintaining constant eye contact. Lean forward in the direction of the footbag's flight and allow it to pass by before executing the kick.

Play can take different forms.

1. *Individual play.* Individuals attempt to see how many consecutive times they can keep the footbag in play. One point is scored for each kick.
2. *Partner play.* Partners alternate kicking the footbag. Score 1 point for each alternate successful kick.

3. *Group play.* A circle of four or five individuals is the basic formation. Rules governing consecutive kicks are (a) all members of the circle must have kicked the footbag for a consecutive run to count, and (b) return kicks are prohibited; that is, kickers may not receive return kicks from the person to whom they kicked the footbag.

Footbag play is an enjoyable activity, but the skills are not easily learned. Persistence and patience are needed. There will be many misses before students slowly gain control. Many physical education suppliers carry footbags, but if sources are needed and information is desired, write to: World Footbag Association, P.O. Box 775208, Steamboat Springs, CO 80477; 1-800-878-8797, http://worldfootbag.com.

RHYTHMIC GYMNASTICS

Rhythmic gymnastics became popular in the United States during the 1970s and was then accepted as an official sport competition in the 1984 Olympic Games. The activities are broad in scope and merit much more explanation than can be presented in this context. Essentially, activities in rhythmic gymnastics are routines done to music by a performer using a particular type of manipulative equipment. The routine can be either individual, partner, or team competition. Equipment used are balls, jump ropes, hoops, ribbons, and clubs. Wands, flags, and scarves are sometimes included, but not in national or international competition. The elements of competition will not be discussed in this presentation.

Many movement qualities, such as balance, poise, grace, flow of body movement, coordination, rhythm, and kinesthetic sense, grow out of serious participation in rhythmic gymnastics. Fitness qualities of agility, flexibility, and proper posture are also developed. Furthermore, skill in handling the various pieces of manipulative equipment is enhanced, because these skills must be mastered before they can be organized into a routine set to music.

Participants, after initial practice in skill development, should work with music. In competitive situations the music is restricted to one instrument. In the school setting the music should be instrumental, light, lively, and enjoyable to the gymnast. Most companies dealing in music for physical education stock specialized recordings for gymnastic movement, with different selections specified for various pieces of equipment. Most of these contain directions for suggested routines. There is no substitute, however, for teacher ingenuity in helping children expand and create their routines.

This is an excellent unit for developing group routines in which a class works together. Routines can be used for physical education demonstrations, back-to-school presentations, and at halftimes of athletic events. The routines are impressive and do not require a high level of skill. All youngsters are capable of participating and will enjoy the opportunity to be involved in a "team" event.

Organizing the Program

The activities presented here focus on balls, jump ropes, hoops, and ribbons, all of which ordinarily are covered in the elementary program. The club is one of the most difficult of the hand apparatus to use and is therefore not an item for instruction in elementary school programs.

The goal of rhythmic gymnastics is continuous body movement with the selected piece of equipment. Composition goals are originality, variety of movement, use of the performing area, performance presentation, and smoothness of transition. Harmony of movement with the music, the apparatus, and execution factors are also important. The length of an individual competitive routine is 1 minute to 1 minute and 30 seconds, but performing time should be shortened for youngsters. Group routines last 2 to 3 minutes and may involve one or two types of equipment. The primary goal is the personal satisfaction that students receive from participating in the program. Offering students an introduction to these activities is more important than the competitive aspect.

Probably the most practical way to include rhythmic gymnastics in the curriculum is a dual approach. The basic skills are taught to all children in physical education classes, allowing opportunity for expression through the composition of creative routines. More refined work can take place through the intramural program or a sport club. Students can choose on an elective basis to participate in competition. Instructors often lack background in these activities. This problem may be solved by bringing in dance instructors from private clubs to introduce the activities.

Developing Routines

Routines for the elementary level should be uncomplicated and based on learned skills. Aesthetics, although important as skill develops, should be of secondary emphasis. Ballet, jazz, and modern dance movements, along with basic dance steps, are normally included in high-level competition.

In developing routines to music, children need to remember that most music is based on units of 8 or 16 counts. Movements are performed in the sagittal, frontal, and horizontal planes. This is the terminology used when developing routines and should be learned by youngsters. The *sagittal* plane is an imaginary division of the body into right and left halves. Movements "in the sagittal" are performed parallel to this plane on either side of the body. The *horizontal* plane involves movements that are parallel to the floor. The *frontal* plane divides the body into front and rear halves. Movements in this plane are performed parallel to this plane either in front of or in back of the body.

An effective way to form a routine is to teach the beginning of a routine and then let youngsters create the remainder. For example, perform the following movements using ribbons. End each series with the hands in front of the waist.

Sagittal forward circles on the right side (6 counts)
Sagittal forward circles on the left side (6 counts)
Elevator (page 483) (4 counts)

In this fashion the routine could consist of a number of 16-count units, each of which is concluded with the Elevator (4 counts). Students could develop additional units. For any one piece of apparatus, certain skill areas can be specified. It is then up to the participant to include these at some point in the routine.

RHYTHMIC GYMNASTIC BALL SKILLS

The ball should be of sufficient size that it cannot be grasped by the hand but must rest in the hand and be controlled by balance. For elementary school children, use either a 6-inch or an 8½-inch ball. Balls should be moderately inflated.

In handling the ball, the fingers should be closed and slightly bent, with the ball resting in the palm. In throwing, the ball can roll from the fingertips. After catching, the ball returns immediately to the palm.

The following ball skills are representative of activities that can be combined to develop a routine:

1. Rolling. In a sitting position, try the following activities: Roll under the legs and around the back; around the body; down the legs; down the arms; down the legs, lift legs and toss the ball off the toes into the air and catch.
2. Bouncing. Combine basketball dribbling drills with graceful body movements; execute locomotor dance-type movements while bouncing.
3. Toss and catch the ball employing different body positions.
4. Add locomotor movements to tosses and catches.
5. Perform body waves with the ball.
6. Throw and/or bounce the ball in a variety of ways.
7. Execute swinging movements (also circular movements). Swinging movements are more difficult than they first appear. The ball must be retained in the palm while the movements are performed.

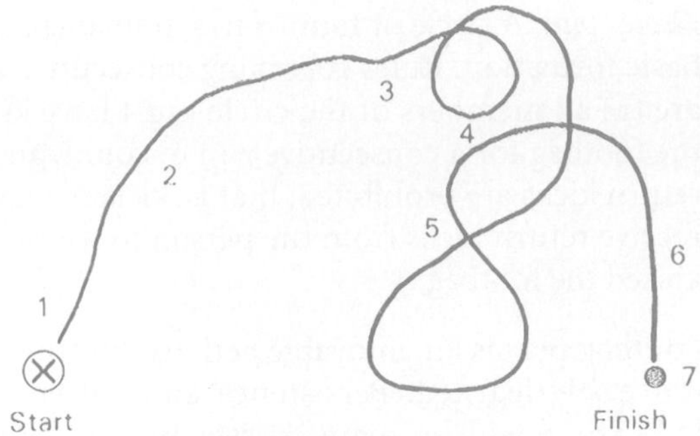

FIGURE 17.26 Floor pattern for routine using balls.

8. Try different balancing movements. These are spirals, curls, and other balances that are inherent to rhythmic gymnastics.
9. Allow opportunity for student exploration combining a number of these activities.

Figure 17.26 is an example of a simple routine using balls. The numbers refer to the floor area in the figure where each activity should be performed.

1. Bounce the ball in place.
2. Bounce the ball while moving forward slowly.
3. Run forward while making swing tosses from side to side.
4. Bounce the ball and make a full turn.
5. Run in a figure-eight pattern.
6. Toss the ball up and catch it with one hand.
7. Finish with a toss and catch behind the back.

RHYTHMIC GYMNASTIC ROPE ROUTINES

As with ball routines, jump rope routines can be categorized in a number of areas. Most important is that the participant be able to do the basic jumps with consummate skill. Ropes can be used full length, folded in half, or folded in fourths. Knotting the end of the rope makes it easier to handle. Proper length is determined by standing on the center of the rope with one foot and extending the rope ends to the outstretched hands at shoulder level. Handles are not appropriate. Most rope jumping is done with the hands far apart. The rope should not touch the floor, but should pass slightly above it. The jumping techniques used for rhythmic gymnastics obviously differ from those taught in the physical education class. The following are examples of movements that can be performed using jump ropes.

1. Try single and double jumps forward and backward.
2. Circle the rope on each side of the body holding both ends of the rope.

3. Make figure-eight swings: Holding both ends of the rope; or, holding the center of the rope and swinging the ends.
4. Swing the rope in pendulum fashion and jump it.
5. Run or skip over a turning rope. Try forward and backward.
6. Do a schottische step over a turning rope.
7. Holding the ends and center of the rope, kneel and horizontally circle the rope close to the floor. Stand and circle the rope overhead.
8. Perform a body wrap with the rope. (Hold one end on the hip, wrap the rope around the body with the other hand.)
9. Upon completion of a jump over a backward-turning rope, toss the rope with both ends into the air and catch.
10. Run while holding both ends of the rope in one hand and circling the rope sagittally backward at the side of the body. Toss the rope and catch it while running.
11. While performing a dance step, toss and catch the rope.
12. Hold both ends of the rope and swing it around the body like a cape.
13. Perform leaps while circling the rope sagittally at one side of the body.
14. Try different balance movements. Balance movements add variety and permit the performer to catch his breath. These involve held body positions, with the rope underneath the foot or hooked around a foot.
15. Hold the rope around the foot and make shapes with the body and foot-rope connection.
16. Explore and combine a number of the activities described.

RHYTHMIC GYMNASTIC HOOP MOVEMENTS

The basic hoop stunts and challenges (pages 367–369) should first be mastered. The same hoop used in physical education classes is suitable for these routines. The hoop may be held, tossed, or caught in one or both hands and with a variety of different grips (Figure 17.27). Hoops may turn forward or backward. Some suggested rhythmic movements with hoops follow.

1. *Swinging movements.* A variety of swinging movements are possible. The swinging movement should be very large. Good alignment between body and hoop is important. Hoops can be swung in a frontal, sagittal, or horizontal plane. The movements can be done in place or involve locomotion. Examples are the following:

FIGURE 17.27 Rhythmic gymnastic movements using hoops.

   a. across the body
   b. with body lean
   c. around the body, changing hands
   d. across the body, changing hands
   e. overhead, changing hands, and swinging downward
   f. swinging in a figure-eight pattern
2. *Spinning movements.* This movement entails turning the hoop, usually with both hands but sometimes with one. The hoop also can be spun on the ground. Examples are the following:
   a. Spin in front of the body.
   b. Spin on the floor.
   c. Spin and kick one leg over the hoop. Add a full body turn after the kickover.
3. *Circling movements.* These are the movements most characteristic of hoop activities. Hoops can be twirled by the hand, wrist, arm, leg, or body (hula-hooping). Changes are made from one hand or wrist to the other. Examples of possible activities are the following:
   a. Extend the arm in front of the body. Circle on the hand between the thumb and first finger in the frontal plane.
   b. Circle the hoop while swaying from side to side.
   c. Circle the hoop horizontally overhead.
   d. Hold both sides of the hoop and circle it in front of the body.
   e. Circle the hoop around different parts of the body.
4. *Tossing and catching movements.* The hoop can be tossed high in the air with one or both hands. The

catch should be one-handed, between the thumb and index finger. Most tosses grow out of swinging or circling movements. Examples are the following:

a. Try with one- and two-handed catches.
b. Toss the hoop in different directions.
c. Toss overhead from hand to hand.
d. Circle the hoop on the hand, toss into the air, and catch.

5. *Rolling movements.* The hoop can be rolled on the floor—either forward or reverse (return) rolling—or can be rolled on the body in diverse ways. If rolled along the floor, various jumps can be executed over the rolling hoop. The hoop can be rolled along one arm to the other, on the front or the back of the body. Specific rolling activities are the following:
   a. Roll the hoop and run alongside it.
   b. Roll the hoop and move through it.
   c. Roll the hoop and jump over it.
6. *Jumping movements.* The hoop, turned forward or backward, can be used in a manner similar to a jump rope.

RHYTHMIC GYMNASTIC RIBBON MOVEMENTS

Ribbon movements are spectacular and make effective demonstrations. Official ribbon length is around 21 feet with the first 3 feet doubled, but for practical purposes, shorter lengths are used at the elementary school level.

Ribbons can be made easily in a variety of colors. A rhythmic flow of movement is desired, featuring circular, oval, spiral, and wavelike shapes. A light flowing movement is the goal, with total body involvement. The dowel or wand to which the ribbon is attached should be an extension of the hand and arm. Laterality is also a consideration. The following are basic ribbon movements.

1. *Swinging movements.* The entire body should coordinate with these large, swinging motions:
   a. Swing the ribbon forward and backward in the sagittal plane.
   b. Swing the ribbon across and in front of the body in the frontal plane.
   c. Swing the ribbon overhead from side to side.
   d. Swing the ribbon upward and catch the end of it.
   e. While holding both ends of the ribbon, swing it upward, around, and over the body.
2. *Circling movements.* Large circles should involve the whole arm; smaller circles involve the wrist. Circles are made in different planes: frontal, sagittal, and horizontal.
   a. Circle the ribbon at different levels.
   b. Circle the ribbon horizontally, vertically, or diagonally.
   c. Circle the ribbon in front of the body, around the body, and behind the body.
   d. Run while circling the ribbon overhead; leap as the ribbon is circled downward and under the legs.
   e. Add dance steps and turns while circling the ribbon.
3. *Figure-eight movements.* Figure eights are also made in the three planes. The two halves of the figure eight should be the same size and on the same plane level. The figure can be made with long arm movements or with movements of the lower arm or wrist. While performing a figure eight, hop through the loop when the ribbon passes the side of the body.
4. *Zigzag movements.* Zigzag movements can be made in the air or on the floor. These are done with continuous up-and-down hand movements, using primarily wrist action. The following are suggested:
   a. Execute the zigzag in the air in front, around, and behind the body.
   b. Run backward while zigzagging the ribbon in front of the body. Perform at different levels.
   c. Run forward while zigzagging behind the body at different levels.
5. *Spiral movements.* The circles in the spiral can be of the same size or of an increasing or decreasing progression. Spirals can be made from left to right or the reverse.
   a. Execute spirals around, in front of, or beside the body while performing locomotor dance steps.
   b. Execute spirals while performing forward and backward rolls.
6. *Throwing and catching movements.* These skills are usually combined with swinging, circling, or figure-eight movements. The ribbon is tossed with one hand and is caught with the same hand or with the other hand. Throwing and catching is a difficult maneuver.
7. *Exchanges.* During group routines, the ribbon is handed or tossed to a partner.

FOR MORE INFORMATION

References and Suggested Readings

Fujimoto, M. (1996). *Rhythmic gymnastics.* Los Angeles: Price Stern Sloan.

Hackett, P., & Owen, P. (1997). *The juggling book.* New York: Lyons & Burford.

Loredo, E. (1996). *The jump rope book.* New York: Workman Publishers.

Marrott, B. (1997). *Getting a jump on fitness.* New York: Barricade Books.

Mauer, T. (1997). *Rhythmic gymnastics.* Vero Beach, FL: Rourke Press.

Mitchelson, M. (1997). *The most excellent book of how to be a juggler.* Brookfield, CT: Copper Beech Books.

Morris, G. S. (1976). Effects ball and background color have upon the catching performance of elementary school children. *Research Quarterly,* 47, 409–415.

Poppen, J. D. (1989). *Action packet on jumping rope.* Puyallup, WA: Action Productions.

Robertson-Williams, J. (1994). *So, you want to learn how to double dutch?* Pittsburgh: Dorrance Publishers.

Websites

Concise Teaching Cues
http://www.pecentral.org/lessonideas/cues/archive9798/cues119798.html
http://www.pecentral.org/lessonideas/cues/archive9798/cues149798.html
http://www.pecentral.org/lessonideas/cues/tennisgrip.html

Footbag
http://www.worldfootbag.org/

Frisbees
http://www.afda.com/trashtalk/showarticle.php?articleid=30
http://www.halcyon.com/richardc/ultimate.htm

Jump Rope
http://family.go.com/yourtime/fitness/feature/dony0601bwks_jump/dony0601bwks_jump2.html

SECTION 6

Specialized Motor Skills

CHAPTER 18

Body Management Skills

ESSENTIAL COMPONENTS

I	Organized around content standards
II	**Student-centered and developmentally appropriate**
III	**Physical activity and motor skill development form the core of the program**
IV	Teaches management skills and self-discipline
V	**Promotes inclusion of all students**
VI	**Focuses on process over product**
VII	Promotes lifetime personal health and wellness
VIII	Teaches cooperation and responsibility and promotes sensitivity to diversity

PHYSICAL EDUCATION STANDARDS

1	**Students are able to move competently using a variety of fundamental and specialized motor skills.**
2	Students can monitor and maintain a health-enhancing level of physical fitness.
3	Students are able to apply movement concepts and basic mechanics of skill performance when learning and refining motor skills.
4	Students comprehend the basic principles of wellness and are able to apply concepts that enable them to make meaningful decisions that positively impact their health and wellness.
5	**Students participate in a wide variety of physical activities and learn how to maintain a personalized active lifestyle.**
6	Students demonstrate empathy, understanding, and respect for the numerous differences exhibited by people in an activity setting.
7	Students exhibit responsible and self-directed behaviors that lead to positive social interactions in physical activity.

SUMMARY

Body management skills are required for control of the body in a variety of situations. Body management skills require an integration of agility, coordination, balance, and flexibility. Activities in this chapter help students learn to control their bodies using a wide variety of apparatus. This chapter offers organizational hints, instructional strategies, and activities for helping youngsters develop body management skills.

OUTCOMES

- Know how to help students develop body management skills using large and small apparatus.
- Apply proper instructional procedures to a wide variety of apparatus activities.
- Design a safe environment when teaching large apparatus activities.
- Teach a variety of activities on large apparatus, including climbing ropes, benches, balance beams, horizontal ladders, exercise bars, jumping boxes, and parachutes.
- Teach activities using small apparatus, including magic ropes, individual mats, tug-of-war ropes, and gym scooters.

Body management skills are an important component of movement competency. Efficient movement demands integration of a number of physical traits, including agility, balance, flexibility, and coordination. In addition, youngsters must develop an understanding of how to control their bodies while on large apparatus, such as beams, benches, and jumping boxes. A basic understanding of movement concepts and mechanical principles used in skill performance is necessary for quality movement.

The focus of this chapter is on developing body management skills using large and small apparatus. Children have an innate desire to run, jump, swing, and climb. The first half of this chapter includes large apparatus activities, including climbing ropes, benches, balance beams, horizontal ladders, exercise bars, jumping boxes, and parachutes. Large apparatus activities offer an opportunity to learn body management skills while free of ground support. The second half of the chapter contains small apparatus activities, including magic ropes, individual mats, and gym scooters. Small apparatus activities help develop body control in space and on the ground.

RETURN ACTIVITIES

The use of return activities increases the movement potential of apparatus. Return activity requires children to perform a movement task (jumping, hopping, skipping, animal walks, etc.) after they have performed on the apparatus. This reduces the time children stand in line waiting for another turn after completion of their task on the apparatus. To increase the amount of time youngsters are actively engaged, increase the distance children have to travel. Return activities demand little supervision. An example of a return activity to use when teaching balance beam activities would be the following: Walk across the beam, do a straddle dismount, and crab walk to a cone and back to place.

SAFE USE OF APPARATUS

Apparatus often has to be placed in position before a class arrives. Youngsters should understand they are not to use the equipment until instructor approval has been given. Establish instructional procedures for setup, storage, and safe use of apparatus and mats. The following are examples of safety guidelines that can be applied to appropriate situations.

1. Placement of tumbling mats for shock absorption is critical. Tumbling mats should be positioned for safety in dismounting and where falls are possible. Tumbling mats should be placed directly under all climbing ropes.
2. Apparatus should be carried, not dragged, across the floor. For particular pieces that need cooperation among the children, designate the number of children and the means of carrying. Teach children how to lift and carry the apparatus properly. Proper setup and storage of apparatus should be discussed and practiced by students.
3. Activity on apparatus should occur only when it is directed by teachers. Youngsters should be instructed to stay away from all apparatus in the area that has been prearranged for later use.
4. Because improper use of apparatus can result in injury, instruction should precede apparatus activity. Signs emphasizing proper use of apparatus can be placed on cones near individual pieces of equipment.

ACTIVITIES WITH CLIMBING ROPES

Climbing ropes offer high-level developmental possibilities for the upper trunk and arms as well as training in coordination of different body parts (Figure 18.1 on page 392). Adequate grip and arm strength are prerequisites for climbing. Becoming accustomed to the rope and gaining confidence are important early goals. Climbing rope sets can be purchased from Gopher Sport, 220 24th Avenue NW, P.O. Box 998, Owatonna, MN 55060-0998 (1-800-533-0446 or www.gophersport.com).

Instructional Procedures

1. Mats should be placed under all ropes.
2. The hand-over-hand method should be used for climbing and the hand-under-hand method for descending.
3. Caution the children not to slide; sliding can cause rope burns on the hands and legs.
4. A climber who becomes tired should stop and rest. Proper rest stops should be taught as part of the climbing procedure.
5. Children also should be taught to leave enough margin for a safe descent. No children should go higher than their strength allows.
6. Spotters should be used initially for activities in which the body is inverted.
7. Rosin in powdered form and magnesium chalk aid in gripping. It is particularly important that they be used when the rope becomes slippery.
8. Children swinging on the ropes should be instructed to make sure that other children are out of the way.

FIGURE 18.1 Rope-climbing on an eight-rope set.

9. Marks to limit the climb can be put on the rope with adhesive tape. A height of 8 to 10 feet above the floor is reasonable until a child demonstrates proficiency.
10. If the ceiling is higher than 15 or 16 feet, a wooden stop (circle) positioned on the rope to limit climbing beyond that height is suggested.

Preliminary Activities

Progression is important in rope climbing, and the fundamental skill progressions should be followed.

SUPPORTED PULL-UPS

In supported Pull-Up activities, a part of the body remains in contact with the floor. The Pull-Up is hand-over-hand and the return is hand-under-hand.

1. Kneel directly under the rope. Pull up to the tiptoes and return to kneeling position.
2. Start in sitting position under the rope. Pull up; legs are supported on the heels. Return to sitting position.
3. Start in a standing position. Grasp the rope, rock back on the heels, and lower the body to the floor. Keep a straight body. Return to standing position.

HANGS

In a hang, the body is pulled up in one motion and held up for a length of time (5, 10, or 20 seconds). Progression is important.

1. From a seated position, reach up as high as possible and pull the body from the floor, except for the heels. Hold.
2. Same as the previous stunt, but pull the body completely free of the floor. Hold.
3. From a standing position, jump up, grasp the rope, and hang. This should be a Bent-Arm Hang, with the hands about even with the mouth. Hold.
4. Repeat the previous stunt, but add leg movements—one or both knees up, bicycling movement, Half Lever (one or both legs up, parallel to the floor), Full Lever (feet up to the face).

PULL-UPS

In the Pull-Up, the body is raised and lowered repeatedly. The initial challenge should be to accomplish one Pull-Up in the defined position. The number of repetitions should be increased with care. All of the activities described for hangs are adaptable to Pull-Ups. The chin should touch the hands on each Pull-Up.

INVERTED HANG

For the Inverted Hang, both hands reach up high. The rope is kept to one side. The performer jumps to a bent-arm position, and at the same time brings the knees up to the nose to invert the body, which is now in a curled position. In a continuation of the motion, the feet are brought up higher than the hands, and the legs are locked around the rope. The body should now be straight and upside down. In the learning phase, teachers should spot.

SWINGING AND JUMPING

For swinging and jumping, a bench, box, or stool can serve as a takeoff point. To take off, the child reaches high and jumps to a bent-arm position. Landing should be with bent knees.

1. Swing and jump. Add half turns and full turns.
2. Swing and return to the perch. Add single- and double-knee bends.
3. Jump for distance, over a high-jump bar or through a hoop.
4. Swing and pick up a bowling pin and return to the perch.
5. Carry objects (beanbags, balls, or deck tennis rings). A partner, standing to the side away from the take-

off bench, can put articles to be carried back on the takeoff perch by placing each article between the knees or feet.

6. Not using a takeoff device, run toward a swinging rope, grasp it, and gain momentum for swinging.

Climbing the Rope

SCISSORS GRIP

For the Scissors Grip, approach the rope and reach as high as possible, standing with the right leg forward of the left. Raise the back leg, bend at the knee, and place the rope inside the knee and outside the foot. Cross the forward leg over the back leg, and straighten the legs with the toes pointed down (Figure 18.2). This should give a secure hold. The teacher can check the position.

To climb using the Scissors Grip, raise the knees up close to the chest, the rope sliding between them, while supporting the body with the hand grip. Lock the rope between the legs and climb up, using the hand-over-hand method and stretching as high as the hands can reach. Bring the knees up to the chest and repeat the process until you have climbed halfway. Later, strive for a higher climb.

LEG-AROUND REST

To do the Leg-Around Rest (Figure 18.3), wrap the left leg completely around the rope, keeping the rope between the thighs. The bottom of the rope then crosses over the instep of the left foot from the outside. The right foot stands on the rope as it crosses over the instep, providing pressure to prevent slippage. To provide additional pressure, release the hands and wrap the arms around the rope, leaning away from the rope at the same time.

To climb using the Leg-Around Rest, proceed as in climbing with the Scissors Grip, but loosen the grip each time and re-form higher up on the rope.

Descending the Rope

There are four methods to descend the rope. The only differences are in the use of the leg locks, as the hand-under-hand is used for all descents.

SCISSORS GRIP DESCENT

From an extended scissors grip position, lock the legs and lower the body with the hands until the knees are

FIGURE 18.2 Scissors Grip.

FIGURE 18.3 Leg-Around Rest.

against the chest. Hold with the hands, and lower the legs to a new position.

LEG-AROUND REST DESCENT

From the leg-around rest position, lower the body until the knees are against the chest. Lift the top foot, and let the feet slide to a lower position (Figure 18.3). Secure with the top foot and repeat.

INSTEP SQUEEZE DESCENT

Squeeze the rope between the insteps by keeping the heels together. Lower the body while the rope slides against the instep.

STIRRUP DESCENT

Have the rope on the outside of the right foot and carry it over the instep of the left. Pressure from the left foot holds the position. To get into position, let the rope trail along the right leg, reach under, and hook it with the left instep. When the pressure from the left leg is reduced, the rope slides smoothly while the descent is made with the hands.

Other Climbing Activities

CLIMBING FOR TIME

To climb for time, a stopwatch and a definite mark on the rope are needed. The height of the mark depends on the children's skill and capacity. Each child should have three trials (not in succession, however), with the best time recorded. Children should start from a standing position with hands reaching as high as desired. The descent should not be included in the timing, because too much emphasis on speed in descent may incite the children to drop or may promote rope burns.

CLIMBING WITHOUT USING THE FEET

The strenuous activity of climbing without using the feet should be attempted only by the more skilled. During early sessions, the mark should not be set too high. Climbers start from a sitting position. The activity can be timed.

ORGANIZING A TARZAN CLUB

The teacher can put a marker at the top limit of the rope. Each child who climbs to and touches the marker becomes a member of the Tarzan Club. A Super-Tarzan Club can be formed for those who can climb to the marker without using their feet. The climber must start from a sitting position on the floor.

Stunts Using Two Ropes

Two ropes hanging close together are needed for the following activities.

STRAIGHT-ARM HANG

To do the Straight-Arm Hang, jump up, grasp one rope with each hand, and hang with the arms straight.

BENT-ARM HANG

Perform as for the Straight-Arm Hang, but bend the arms at the elbows.

ARM HANGS WITH DIFFERENT LEG POSITIONS

1. Do single- and double-knee lifts.
2. Do a Half Lever. Bring the legs up parallel to the floor and point the toes.
3. Do a Full Lever. Bring the feet up to the face and keep the knees straight.
4. Do a Bicycle. Pedal as on a bicycle.

PULL-UPS

The Pull-Up is the same as on a single rope, except that each hand grasps a rope.

INVERTED HANGS

1. Hang with the feet wrapped around the ropes.
2. Hang with the feet against the inside of the ropes.
3. Hang with the toes pointed and the feet not touching the ropes (Figure 18.4).

SKIN THE CAT

From a bent-arm position, kick the feet overhead and continue the roll until the feet touch the mat. Return to the starting position. A more difficult stunt is to start from a higher position so that the feet do not touch the mat. Reverse to original position.

CLIMBING

1. Climb up one rope, transfer to another, and descend.
2. Climb halfway up one rope, cross over to another rope, and continue to climb to the top.
3. Climb both ropes together without using the legs. This is difficult and requires the climber to slide one hand at a time up the ropes without completely releasing the grip.
4. Climb as on a single rope, with hands on one rope and feet on the other rope.

FIGURE 18.4 Spotting an Inverted Hang on two ropes. (Holding the performer's hands ensures confidence and safety.)

Activity Sequences

Rope-climbing activities are conducive to forming sequences through which the child can progress. The following sequence represents the kind of progressive challenges that can be met.

1. Jump and hang (10 seconds).
2. Pull up and hold (10 seconds).
3. Scissors climb to blue mark (10 feet).
4. Scissors climb to top (15 feet).
5. Demonstrate Leg-Around Rest (10 feet).
6. Do an Inverted Hang, with body straight (5 seconds).

Teachers can structure three achievement levels from the activities included in this chapter. Each level could be given a characteristic name and organized as a task card or a contract project.

ACTIVITIES ON THE BALANCE BEAMS

Balance-beam activities contribute to control in both static and dynamic balance situations (Figure 18.5). The

FIGURE 18.5 Walking on a balance beam bench.

balance-beam side of a balance beam bench is ideal for such activities, with its 2-inch-wide and 12-foot-long beam. Balance-beam benches can be purchased from Gopher Sport, 220 24th Avenue NW, P.O. Box 998, Owatonna, MN 55060-0998 (1-800-533-0446 or www.gophersport.com). Balance beams come in many other sizes, however, and can be constructed from common lumber materials (see Chapter 10). Some teachers prefer a wider beam for kindergarten and first-grade children and, in particular, for special education children. Students should graduate to the narrower beam as soon as the activities on the wider beam no longer seem to challenge them.

Other ideas for balance equipment are also interesting. A pole with ends shaped to fit the supports can be substituted for the flat balance beam. The pole is more challenging. Another idea is constructing a beam that begins with a 2-inch width and narrows to a 1-inch width at the other end. Beams of varying widths (from 1 to 4 inches) can also be used. Children progress from the wider to the narrower beams. A variety of widths is preferable for children with disabilities.

Instructional Procedures

1. Children should move with controlled, deliberate movements. Speed is not a goal. The teacher should advise performers to recover their balance before taking another step or making another movement.
2. In keeping with the principle of control, children should step slowly on the beam, pause momentarily in good balance at the end of the activity, and dismount with a small, controlled jump from the end of the beam when the routine is completed.
3. Mats can be placed at the end of the bench to cushion the dismount and to allow for rolls and stunts after the dismount.

4. Visual fixation is important. Children should look straight ahead rather than down at the feet. Eye targets can be marked on or attached to walls to assist in visual fixation. This fixation allows balance controls other than vision to function more effectively. From time to time, movements can be done with the eyes closed, entirely eliminating visual control of balance.
5. Children should be told to step off the beam when they lose their balance, rather than teetering and falling off awkwardly. Allow the performer to step back on the beam and to continue the routine.
6. Success in a balance-beam activity can be based on two levels. The lower level allows the performer to step off the beam once during the routine. The higher level demands that the student remain on the beam throughout. For both levels, the children should pause in good balance at the end of the beam before dismounting.
7. Both laterality and directionality are important. Right and left feet should be given reasonably equal treatment. For example, if a performer does steps leading with the right foot, the next effort should be made leading with the left foot. Directions right and left should be given equal weight. A child naturally uses the dominant side and direction but must be encouraged to perform with both sides.
8. The child next in line should begin when the performer ahead is about three-quarters of the distance across the beam.
9. Return activities (see page 391) are a consideration for enhancing the breadth of activity.
10. A child or the teacher can assist the performer. The assistant holds the hand palm up, ready to help the performer if and when help is needed.

Activity Sequences

Activities for the balance beam are presented as a progression of movement themes. The teacher can develop fully all of the activities and possibilities within a theme before proceeding to the next theme, or can take a few activities from each theme and cover more territory.

ACTIVITIES ON PARALLEL BEAMS

Activities on two parallel beams are presented first as lead-up practice for the single-beam tasks. The beams should be placed about 10 to 30 inches apart. The parallel-beam activities can be done alone or with a partner when more security is desired.

1. With a partner, join inside hands and walk forward, backward, and sideward. Walk sideward, using a grapevine step. Hold a beanbag in the free hand.
2. Without a partner, perform various animal walks, such as the Crab Walk, Bear Walk, Measuring Worm, and Elephant Walk.
3. With one foot on each beam, walk forward, backward, and sideward.
4. Step to the opposite beam with each step taken.
5. Progress the length of the beams with hands on one beam and feet on the other.
6. Progress to the middle of the beams and perform various turns and stunts, such as picking up a beanbag, moving through a hoop, and stepping over a wand.

MOVEMENTS ACROSS THE FULL LENGTH OF A SINGLE BEAM

1. Perform various locomotor tasks, such as walking, follow steps, heel-and-toe steps, side steps, tiptoe steps, the grapevine step (step behind, step across), and so on.
2. Follow different directions—forward, backward, sideward.
3. Use different arm and hand positions—on the hips, on the head, behind the back, out to the sides, pointing to the ceiling, folded across the chest.
4. Move across the beam as you assume different shapes.
5. Balance an object (beanbag or eraser) on various body parts—on the head, on the back of the hands, on the shoulders. Try balancing two or three objects at once.

HALF-AND-HALF MOVEMENTS

Half-and-half movements repeat the movements, arm positions, and balancing stunts described previously, except that the performer goes halfway across the beam using a selected movement and then changes to another type of movement on the second half of the beam.

CHALLENGE TASKS OR STUNTS

For challenge tasks, the performer moves halfway across the beam with a selected movement, performs a particular challenge or stunt at the center, and finishes the movements on the second half of the beam. Examples of challenges or stunts that can be performed at the center of the beam are the following:

1. Balances: Forward Balance (pages 481–482), Backward Balance (page 482), Stork Stand (page 481), Seat Balance (page 495).
2. Stunts: Leg Dip (page 495), Finger Touch (pages 495–496).

3. Challenges: Make a full turn, pick up a beanbag at the center, pick up some paper at the center with the teeth, do a Push-Up.

MORE DIFFICULT MOVEMENTS ACROSS THE BEAM

1. Hop the length of the beam—forward, sideward, and backward.
2. Do the Cat Walk (page 472), Rabbit Jump (page 476), Lame Dog Walk (page 477), Seal Crawl (page 488) or Crab Walk (page 477).
3. Do various locomotor movements with the eyes closed.
4. Walk to the center of the beam and do a Side-Leaning Rest. Try on the other side as well.
5. Walk to the center and do a complete body turn on one foot only.

ACTIVITIES WITH WANDS AND HOOPS

1. Carry a wand or hoop. Step over the wand or through the hoop in various fashions.
2. Step over or go under wands or hoops held by a partner.
3. Twirl a hula-hoop on the arms or around the body while moving across the beam.
4. Balance a wand on various body parts while moving across the beam.
5. Balance a wand in one hand and twirl a hoop on the other hand and proceed across the beam.

MANIPULATIVE ACTIVITIES WITH SELF

1. Using one or two beanbags, toss to self in various fashions—over the head, around the body, under the legs.
2. Using a ball, toss to self. Circle the ball around the body, under the legs.
3. Bounce a ball on the floor. On the beam. Dribble on the floor.
4. Roll a ball along the beam.

MANIPULATIVE ACTIVITIES WITH A PARTNER

With a partner standing beyond the far end of the beam, throw a beanbag or ball back and forth. Have partner toss for a volleyball return. Bat the ball (as in a volleyball serve) to partner.

STUNTS WITH A PARTNER

1. Do a Wheelbarrow (page 502) with the supporting performer keeping the feet on the floor.
2. Partners start on opposite ends of the beam and move toward each other with the same kind of movement, do a balance pose together in the center, and return to their respective ends of the beam.
3. Partners start on opposite ends of the beam and attempt to pass each other without losing their balance and without touching the floor. Find different ways to pass.

ACTIVITIES ON BENCHES

The balance-beam bench is effective in developing strength and balance. Bench activities are challenging to children and offer a variety of movement possibilities.

Instructional Procedures

1. All activities on the benches should be broken down into three distinct parts: the approach to and mounting of the bench, the actual activity on the bench, and the dismount from the bench.
2. Mats should be placed at the ends of the bench to facilitate the dismount and various rolls and stunts executed after the dismount.
3. Benches can be positioned horizontally or inclined. They can also be combined with other equipment for variation and greater challenge.
4. Four to five children is the maximum number that should be assigned to one bench.
5. The child next in turn should begin when the performer ahead is about three-quarters of the way across the bench.
6. Return activities add to the activity potential.
7. Speed is not a goal in bench activities. Movements should be done deliberately and carefully, with attention given to body control and body management.
8. Attention also should be paid to laterality and directionality. For example, if a child hops on the right foot, the next effort should be made on the left foot. In jump turns, both right and left movements should be used.

Activity Sequences

ANIMAL WALKS

Perform various animal walks on the bench, such as the Seal Crawl (page 488), Cat Walk (page 472), Lame Dog Walk (page 477), and Rabbit Jump (page 476).

LOCOMOTOR MOVEMENTS

Perform various locomotor movements along the length of the bench, such as stepping or jumping on and off the side of the bench, hopping on and off the side of the bench, or skipping and galloping on the bench.

PULLS

Pull the body along the bench, using different combinations of body parts. Use the arms only, the legs only, the right leg and the left arm, or the left leg and the right arm. Pull along the bench, using the following positions.

1. Prone position (head first and feet first) (Figure 18.6)
2. Supine position (head first and feet first) (Figure 18.7)
3. Side position (head first and feet first)

Various leg positions (such as legs up in a half-lever position, knees bent, and so on) should be used in performing pulls and pushes. Those body parts not being used to pull can be used to carry a piece of manipulative equipment, such as a beanbag, ball, or wand. Employ different body shapes. Try the Submarine (one foot in the air like a periscope).

PUSHES

Push the body along the bench, using different parts of the body as discussed for pulls. Push the body, using the following positions.

1. Prone position (head first and feet first)
2. Supine position (head first and feet first)
3. Side position (head first and feet first)

MOVEMENTS ALONG THE SIDE OF THE BENCH

Proceed alongside the bench in the following positions with the hands on the bench and the feet on the floor as far from the bench as possible.

1. Prone position
2. Supine position
3. Turn-over (Proceed along the bench, changing from prone to supine position.)

FIGURE 18.6 Prone movements, head first.

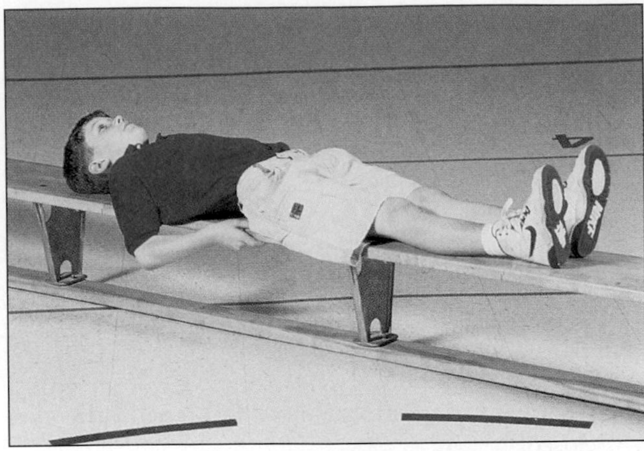

FIGURE 18.7 Supine movements, feet first.

Repeat these positions with the feet on the bench and the hands on the floor as far from the bench as possible.

SCOOTER MOVEMENTS

Sit on the bench and proceed along it without using the hands in the following ways.

1. Do a Scooter. Proceed with the feet leading the body. Try to pull the body along with the feet.
2. Do a Reverse Scooter. Proceed as for the Scooter but with the legs trailing and pushing the body along the bench.
3. Do a Seat Walk. Proceed forward by walking on the buttocks. Use the legs as little as possible.

CROUCH JUMPS

Place both hands on the bench and jump back and forth over it. Progress the length of the bench by moving the hands forward a few inches after each jump.

1. Do a regular Crouch Jump (Figure 18.8). Use both hands and both feet. Jump as high as possible.
2. Do a Straddle Jump. Straddle the bench with the legs, take the weight on the hands, and jump with the legs as high as possible.
3. Use one hand and two feet. Do a Crouch Jump, but eliminate the use of one hand.
4. Use one hand and one foot. Perform the Crouch Jump, using only one hand and one foot.
5. Stand to one side, facing the bench, with both hands on it. With stiff arms, try to send the seat as high as possible into the air. Add the Mule Kick (page 488) before coming down.

BASIC TUMBLING STUNTS

Basic tumbling stunts can be incorporated into bench activities: the Back Roller (page 478), Backward Curl

FIGURE 18.8 Crouch jumping.

(page 479), Forward Roll (page 478) (Figure 18.9), Backward Roll (page 479), and Cartwheel (page 492).

DISMOUNTS

All bench activities in which the child moves from one end of the bench to the other should end with a dis-

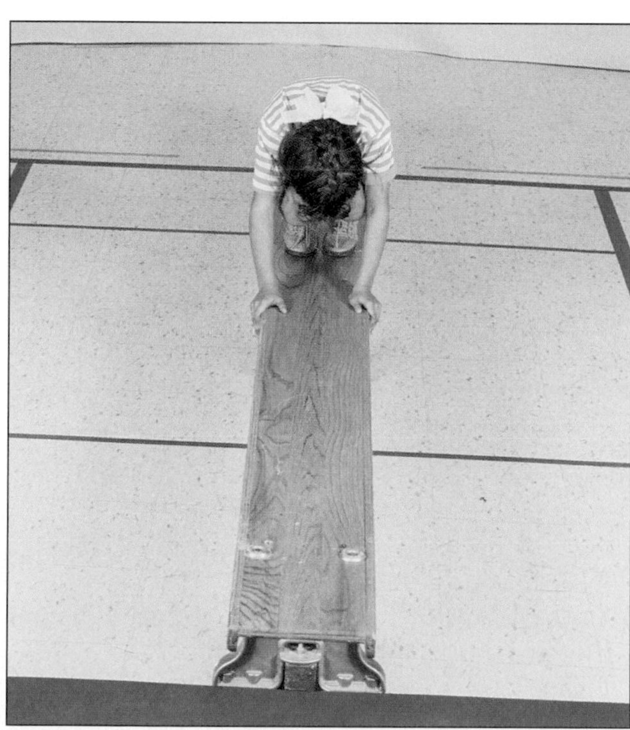

FIGURE 18.9 Preparing to do a Forward Roll on the bench.

FIGURE 18.10 Dismounting from a bench.

mount. The following dismounts are suggested. Many other stunts can be used.

1. Single jump (forward or backward) (Figure 18.10).
2. Jump with turns (half turn, three-quarter turn, or full turn).
3. Jackknife. Jump, kick the legs up, and touch the toes with the fingertips. Keep the feet together.
4. Jackknife Split. Same as the Jackknife, but spread the legs as far as possible.
5. Jump to a Forward Roll.
6. Backward jump to a Backward Roll.
7. Side jump to a Side Roll (page 478).
8. Judo Roll.
9. Jump with combinations of the stunts noted in this list.

Additional Experiences on Benches

1. The range of activities can be extended with the addition of balls, beanbags, hoops, and wands. Wands and hoops can be used as obstacles to go over, under, around, or through. Basic balance and manipulative skills can be incorporated into the activity with balls and beanbags.
2. Two can perform at one time, each child near an opposite end of the bench, doing different balance positions on the bench.
3. Children like to go over and under a row of benches arranged in a kind of obstacle course. Some of the benches can be supported by jumping boxes, making them excellent for vaulting activities.
4. A bench can be supported by two jumping boxes and used as a vaulting box. Each bench is long enough to accommodate three children. They can jump off it, Mule Kick on it, and vault over it.

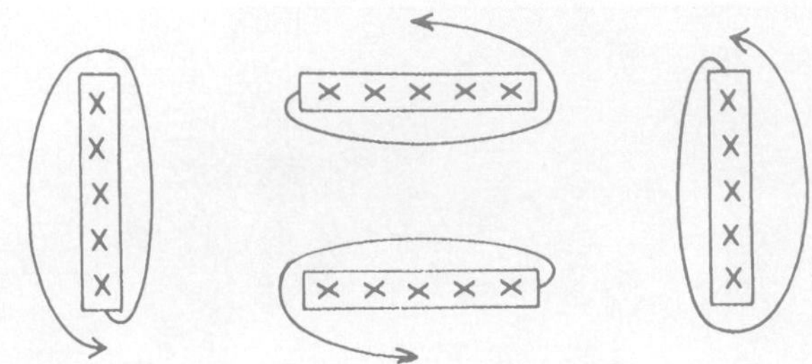

FIGURE 18.11 Rectangular bench activities.

5. Four benches can be placed in a large rectangle (Figure 18.11), with a squad standing at attention on top of each bench. On signal, each squad gets off its bench, runs around the outside of the other three benches, and then runs back to its own bench. The first squad back and at attention on the bench is the winner.
6. Benches can be placed in a square formation, with children moving around the square and doing a different movement on each bench.
7. One end of the bench can be placed on a jumping box or on another bench. Children receive jumping practice by running up the incline and striving for jump height at the end of the bench.
8. Benches are appropriate for some partner activities. Partners can start on each end and pass through or around each other, reversing original positions. Wheelbarrow Walks are also suitable.
9. Another enjoyable activity is arranging the benches in a course as illustrated in Figure 18.12. A student is chosen to lead the squad or class through the challenge course. A different activity must be performed at each bench.

ACTIVITIES WITH JUMPING BOXES

Jumping boxes can be constructed or purchased. They provide opportunities for children to jump from a height and propel the body through space. Activities with jumping boxes are generally confined to the primary grades. Boxes can be of varying heights; 8 inches and 16 inches are suggested. A rubber floor pad can be placed under the box to protect the floor and to prevent sliding. Plans for constructing boxes are given in Chapter 10.

Instructional Procedures

1. Attention should be given to landing in proper form. Lightness, bent-knee action, balance, and body control should be stressed.
2. Mats should be used to cushion the landing.
3. The exploratory and creative approach is important; there are few standard stunts in jumping box activities.
4. No more than four or five children should be assigned to each series of boxes.
5. Additional challenges can be incorporated by the use of hoops, wands, balls, and the like. Rolling stunts after the dismount extend the movement possibilities.
6. Return activities work well with boxes.
7. Children should strive for height and learn to relax as they go through space.

Activity Sequences

The activities that follow can be augmented easily. Let the children help expand the activity.

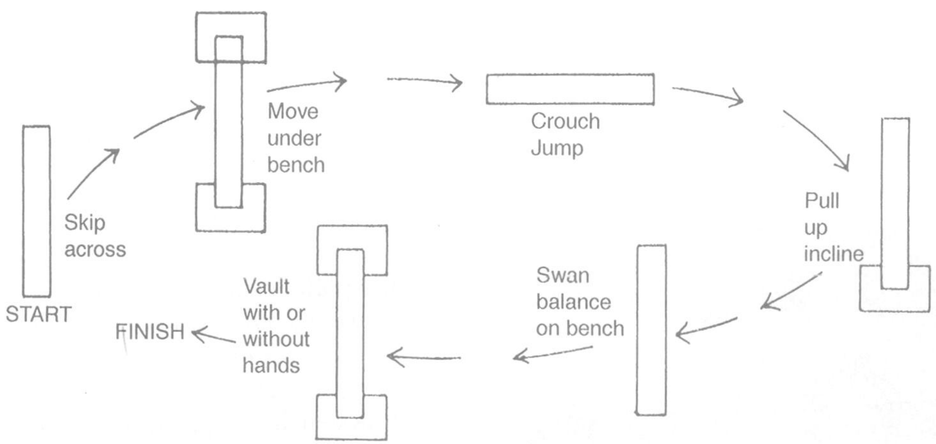

FIGURE 18.12 Challenge course using benches.

VARIOUS APPROACHES TO THE BOXES

The approach to the boxes can be varied by performing movements such as these.

1. Fundamental locomotor movements: Run, gallop, skip, and hop
2. Animal walks: Bear Walk, Crab Walk, and so on
3. Moving over and under various obstacles: jumping over a bench, moving through a hoop held upright by a mat, doing a Backward Roll on the mat
4. Rope jumping to the box: students try to continue jumping while mounting and dismounting the box

MOUNTING THE BOX

Many different combinations can be used to get onto the box.

1. Practice stepping onto the box (mounting) by taking the full weight on the stepping foot and holding it for a few seconds. This develops a sense of balance and tends to stabilize the support foot.
2. Mount the box, using locomotor movements such as a step, jump, leap, or hop. Perform various turns—quarter, half, three-quarter, and full—while jumping onto the box.
3. Use a Crouch Jump to get onto the box.
4. Back up to the box and mount it without looking at it.
5. Mount the box while a partner tosses you a beanbag.
6. Make various targets on top of the box with a piece of chalk, and try to land on the spot when mounting.

DISMOUNTING THE BOX

The following dismounts can be used to develop body control.

1. Jump off with a quarter turn, half turn, or full turn.
2. Jump off with different body shapes: stretching, curling up in a ball, jackknifing.
3. Jump over a wand or through a hoop.
4. Jump off, and do a Forward Roll or a Backward Roll.
5. Change the foregoing dismounts by substituting a hop or a leap in place of the jump.
6. Increase the height and distance of the dismount.
7. Dismount in various directions, such as forward (Figure 18.13), backward, sideward, northward, and southward.
8. Jump off using a jackknife or wide straddle dismount.
9. Perform a balance stunt on the box and then dismount.

FIGURE 18.13 Jump dismounting.

After the class has learned the basic movements used with jumping boxes, continuous squad motion can be incorporated. The squad captain is responsible for leading the group through different approaches, mounts, and dismounts. The same activity cannot be used twice in succession.

ADDITION OF EQUIPMENT

Various pieces of equipment enhance box activities. Some suggestions follow.

1. Toss beanbags up while dismounting, or try to keep one on your head while mounting or dismounting the box.
2. Try to dribble a playground ball while performing the box routine.
3. Jump through a stationary hoop held by a partner while dismounting, or use the hoop as a jump rope and see how many times you can jump through it while dismounting.
4. Jump over or go under a wand.

BOX COMBINATIONS

Boxes can be arranged in a straight line and in other patterns. Children do a different movement over each box as though running a challenge course.

ACTIVITIES WITH HORIZONTAL LADDERS

Horizontal ladders are manufactured in a variety of models. The most usable ladder is one that can be stored against the wall out of the way. If the ladder can be inclined, the movement possibilities are extended. Horizontal ladders provide a good lead-up activity for rope climbing, because their rigidity makes them easier to climb. Grip strength and arm-shoulder girdle development are enhanced by the suspension of body weight. This development can help improve posture.

Instructional Procedures

1. The opposed-thumb grip, in which the thumb goes around the bar, is important. In most activities, the back of the hands should face the child. (This is the upper grip.) The grip should be varied occasionally, making use of the lower grip (palms toward the face) and the mixed grip (one hand facing one way and one the other).
2. Whenever the child is doing an Inverted Hang, spotters should be present.
3. Speed is not a goal of climbing activity. In fact, the longer the child hangs from the ladder, the more beneficial the activity is. There is value in simply hanging.
4. In activities involving movement across the ladder, all children should travel in the same direction.
5. Mats must be placed under the apparatus when it is in use.
6. Children should be instructed in the dismount. They should land in a bent-leg position, on the balls of the feet.

Activity Sequences

HANGS

Hangs should be performed with the opposed-thumb grip and usually with straight arms. Encourage children to hang in a bent-arm position, however, to involve more muscles in the upper arm. The following variations of the hang are suggested.

1. Keep the legs straight and point the toes toward the ground.
2. Lift the knees as high as possible toward the chest.
3. Lift the knees and pedal a bicycle.
4. Bring the legs up parallel to the ground, with the knees straight and the toes pointed.
5. Touch the toes of one or both feet to a rung or to the side of the ladder.
6. Bring the feet up and over one rung and hook the toes under a second rung. Release the hand grip and hang in an inverted position.
7. Stand on a box if necessary to get into position for a Flexed-Arm Hang. Hang as long as possible with the chin even with the hands.
8. Swing the body back and forth.
9. Swing back and forth and jump as far as possible. Vary with turns.
10. Hang from the ladder, first with one hand and then with the other.

TRAVELING ACTIVITIES

Throughout the suggested traveling activities, have the children use different body shapes.

1. Travel the length of the ladder, using the rungs. Start by traveling one rung at a time, and then skip one or more rungs to add challenge.
2. Travel the length of the ladder, using both side rails. Now use one rail only to travel the ladder.
3. Hang with both hands on the side rails. Progress the length of the ladder by jumping both hands forward at once.
4. Hang with both hands on the same rung. Progress by jumping both hands forward simultaneously.
5. Travel underneath the ladder in monkey fashion, with both hands and feet on the rungs. Try with the feet on the side rails.
6. Travel the length of the ladder carrying a beanbag, a ball, or any similar object.
7. Travel the length of the ladder sideways and backward.
8. Travel the length of the ladder, doing a half turn each time a move is made to a new rung.
9. Get a partner. The children start at opposite ends of the ladder, and they pass each other along the way.

ACTIVITIES ON THE EXERCISE BAR (LOW HORIZONTAL BAR)

Horizontal bars should be installed on the playground in a series of at least three at different heights. Indoor bars can be freestanding and have adjustable heights. Care must be taken that they are secured properly. The primary program should be limited to hangs, travels, and simple stunts. To perform many of the more complicated stunts on the bar, sufficient arm strength is necessary to pull the body up and over the bar. Some of the youngsters in the third grade will begin to have this capacity, but the emphasis in the primary grades should be on the more limited program. In the intermediate program, attention should turn to gymnastic stunts. The advanced skills are, however, difficult and the teacher should not be discouraged by the children's apparent lack of progress.

Instructional Procedures

1. Only one child should be on a bar at one time.
2. The bar should not be used when it is wet.
3. The basic grip is the opposed-thumb grip, facing away.

Activity Sequences

HANGS

To hang from the bar, point the feet, one or both knees up, in a Half or Full Lever. Bring the toes up to touch the bar inside the hands. Outside the hands. Use different body shapes.

SWINGS

Swing back and forth, release the grip, and propel the body forward. Land in a standing position.

MOVING ALONG THE BAR

Begin at one side and move hand against hand to the other end of the bar. Move with crossed hands. Travel with different body shapes.

SLOTH TRAVEL

Face the end of the bar, standing underneath. Grasp the bar with both hands and hook the legs over the bar at the knees like a sloth. In this position, move along the bar to the other end. Return by reversing the movement.

ARM AND LEG HANG

Grasp the bar with an upper grip. Bring one of the legs up between the arms and hook the knee over the bar.

DOUBLE-LEG HANG

Perform as in the preceding stunt, but bring both legs between the hands and hook the knees over the bar. Release the hands and hang in the inverted position. If the hands touch or are near the ground, a dismount can be made by releasing the legs and dropping to a crouched position on the ground.

SKIN THE CAT

Bring both knees up between the arms as in the previous stunt, but continue the direction of the knees until the body is turned over backward. Release the grip and drop to the ground.

SKIN THE CAT RETURN

Perform as in preceding stunt, but don't release the hands. Bring the legs back through the hands to original position.

FRONT SUPPORT

Grasp the bar with an upper grip, and jump to a straight-arm support on the bar. Jump down.

FRONT SUPPORT PUSH-OFF

Mount the bar in the same way as for a Front Support. In returning to the ground, push off straight with the arms and jump as far back as possible.

TUMMY BALANCE

Jump to the bar as in preceding stunt. Position the body so you can balance on the tummy with hands released.

SITTING BALANCE

Jump to the bar as for a Front Support. Work the legs across the bar so that a sitting balance can be maintained. If you lose your balance backward, grasp the bar quickly and bend the knees.

TUMBLE OVER

Jump to a Front-Support position. Change the grip to a lower grip. Bend forward and roll over to a standing position under the bar.

SINGLE-KNEE SWING

Using the upper grip, swing one leg forward to hang by the knee. Using the free leg to gain momentum, swing back and forth.

SIDE ARC

Sit on the bar with one leg on each side, both hands gripping the bar in front of the body. Lock the legs and fall sideways. Try to make a complete circle back to position. Good momentum is needed.

SINGLE-LEG RISE

Using the position of the Single-Knee Swing, on the backswing and upswing, rise to the top of the bar. The down leg must be kept straight. Swing forward (down) first, and on the backswing, push down hard with straight arms. A spotter can assist by pushing down on the straight leg with one hand and lifting on the back with the other.

KNEE CIRCLES

Sit on top of the bar, with one leg over and one under the bar. Lock the feet. With the hands in an upper grip, shift the weight backward so that the body describes a circle under the bar and returns to place. Try this with a forward circle, with hands in a lower grip. Note that considerable initial momentum must be developed for the circle to be completed.

ACTIVITIES WITH PARACHUTES

Parachute play can be enjoyed by children of all ages. Activities must be selected carefully for younger children, since some of the skills presented would be difficult for them. One parachute is generally sufficient for a class of 30 children. Parachutes come in different sizes, but those with diameters ranging from 24 to 32 feet are suitable for a regular class. The size with most utility is the 28-foot parachute. Each parachute has an opening near the top to allow trapped air to escape and to keep the parachute shaped properly. Most parachutes are constructed of nylon. A parachute should stretch tight and not sag in the middle when it is pulled on by children spaced around it. One that does not do so has limited usefulness.

Values of Parachute Play

Parachutes provide an interesting means of accomplishing physical fitness goals: a good development of strength, agility, coordination, and endurance. Strength development is focused especially on the arms, hands, and shoulder girdle. At times, however, strength demands are made on the entire body. A variety of movement possibilities, some of which are rhythmic, can be used in parachute play. Locomotor skills can be practiced while manipulating the parachute. Rhythmic beats of the tom-tom or appropriate music can guide locomotor movements. Parachute play provides many excellent cooperative group learning experiences.

Grips

The grips used in handling the parachute are comparable to those employed in hanging activities on an apparatus. Grips can be with one or two hands, overhand (palms facing away), underhand (palms facing toward), or mixed (one hand underhand and the other overhand). The grips should be varied.

Instructional Procedures

1. Certain terms peculiar to parachute activity must be explained carefully. Terms such as *inflate, deflate, float, dome,* and *mushroom* need to be clarified when they are introduced.
2. For preliminary explanations, the parachute can be stretched out on the ground in its circular pattern, with the children seated just far enough away so that they cannot touch the parachute during instructions. When the children hold the parachute during later explanations, they should retain their hold lightly, letting the center of the parachute drop to the ground. Children must be taught to exercise control and not to manipulate the parachute while explanations are in progress.
3. The teacher explains the activity, demonstrating as needed. If there are no questions, the activity is initiated with a command such as "Ready—begin!"
4. Squads can be used to form the parachute circle, with each squad occupying a quarter of the chute's circumference. Squads are useful for competitive units in game activity.
5. The teacher must watch for fatigue, particularly with younger children.

Activities are presented according to type, with variations and suggestions for supplementary activities included. Unless otherwise specified, activities begin and halt on signal. Pupils' suggestions can broaden the scope of activity.

Exercise Activities

Exercises should be done vigorously and with enough repetitions to challenge the children. In addition to the exercises presented, others can be adapted to parachute play.

TOE TOUCHER

Sit with feet extended under the parachute and hold the chute taut with a two-hand grip, drawing it up to the chin. Bend forward and touch the grip to the toes. Return parachute to stretched position.

CURL-UP

Extend the body under the parachute in curl-up position, so that the chute comes up to the chin when held taut. Do Curl-Ups, returning each time to the stretched chute position.

DORSAL LIFT

Lie prone, with head toward the parachute and feet pointed back, away from it. Grip the chute and slide toward the feet until there is some tension on it. Raise the chute off the ground with a vigorous lift of the arms, until head and chest rise off the ground. Return.

V-SIT

Lie supine, with head toward the chute. Do V-Sits by raising the upper and lower parts of the body simultaneously into a V-shaped position. The knees should be kept straight.

BACKWARD PULL

Face the parachute and pull back, away from its center. Pulls can be made from a sitting, kneeling, or standing position.

OTHER PULLS

With arm flexed, do Side Pulls with either arm. Other variations of pulling can be devised.

HIP WALK AND SCOOTER

Begin with the parachute taut. Move forward with the Scooter (page 398) or Hip Walk (page 496). Move back to place with the same movement until the chute is taut again.

ELEVATOR

Begin with the chute taut and at ground level. On the command "Elevator up," lift the chute overhead while keeping it stretched tight. On the command "Elevator down," lower the chute to starting position. Lowering and raising can be done quickly or in increments. Levels can also bring in body part identification, with children holding the chute even with their head, nose, chin, shoulders, chest, waist, thighs, knees, ankles, and toes.

RUNNING IN PLACE

Run in place while holding the chute at different levels.

ISOMETRICS

Hold the chute taut at shoulder level and try to stretch it for 10 seconds. Many other isometric exercises can be performed with the parachute to develop all body parts.

Dome Activities

To make a dome, children begin with the parachute on the floor, holding with two hands and kneeling on one knee. To trap air under the chute, children stand up quickly, thrusting their arms above the head (Figure 18.14), and then return to starting position (Figure 18.15, page 406). Some or all of the children can change to the inside of the chute on the down movement. Domes can also be made while moving in a circle.

STUDENTS UNDER THE CHUTE

Tasks for under the chute can be specified, such as turning a certain number of turns with a jump rope, throwing and catching a beanbag, or bouncing a ball a number of times. The needed objects should be under the chute before the dome is made.

FIGURE 18.14 Making a dome.

FIGURE 18.15 Holding the air inside a dome.

NUMBER EXCHANGE

Children are numbered from one to four. The teacher calls a number as the dome is made, and those with the number called must change position to be under the dome before the chute comes down. Locomotor movements can be varied.

PUNCHING BAG

Children make a dome and stand on the edges. They then punch at the chute while slowly and gently walking the edges of the chute toward the center.

BLOOMING FLOWER

Children make a dome and kneel with both knees on the edge of the chute. Youngsters hold hands around the chute and lean in and out to represent a blooming flower opening.

LIGHTS OUT

While making a dome, the children take two steps toward the center and sit inside the chute. The chute can be held with the hands at the side or by sitting on it.

MUSHROOM ACTIVITIES

To form a mushroom, students begin with the chute on the ground, kneeling on one knee and holding with two hands. They stand up quickly, thrusting the arms overhead. Keeping the arms overhead, each walks forward three or four steps toward the center. The arms are held overhead until the chute is deflated.

MUSHROOM RELEASE

All children release at the peak of inflation and either run out from under the chute or move to the center and sit down, with the chute descending on top of them.

MUSHROOM RUN

Children make a mushroom. As soon as they move into the center, they release holds and run once around the inside of the chute, counterclockwise, back to place.

Activities with Equipment

BALL CIRCLE

Place a basketball or a cageball on the raised chute. Make the ball roll around the chute in a large circle, controlling it by raising or lowering the chute. Try the same with two balls. A beach ball is also excellent.

POPCORN

Place a number of beanbags (from six to ten) on the chute. Shake the chute to make them rise like corn popping (Figure 18.16).

CAGEBALL ELEVATOR

A 2-foot cageball is placed on the chute. On signal, he class elevates the chute and allows it to make a mushroom. Just before the chute with the ball on it reaches its apex, youngsters snap the chute to the floor. Done correctly, the cageball should be elevated to the ceiling.

TEAM BALL

Divide the class in half, each team defending half of the chute. Using from two to six balls of any variety, try to bounce the balls off the opponents' side, scoring 1 point for each ball.

POISON SNAKE

Divide into teams. Place from 6 to 10 jump ropes on the chute. Shake the chute and try to make the ropes hit players on the other side. For each rope that touches one team member, that team has a point scored against it. The team with the lower score is the winner.

CIRCULAR DRIBBLE

Each child has a ball suitable for dribbling. The object is to run in circular fashion counterclockwise, holding onto the chute with the left hand and dribbling with the right hand, retaining control of the ball. As an equalizer for left-handers, try the dribbling clockwise. The dribble should be started first, and then, on signal, children start to run. A child who loses a ball must recover it and try to hook on at his or her original place.

HOLE IN ONE

Use four or more plastic whiffle balls the size of golf balls. The balls should be of two different colors. The class is divided into two teams on opposite sides of the chute. The object is to shake the other team's balls into the hole in the center of the chute.

Other Activities

MERRY-GO-ROUND MOVEMENTS

Merry-go-round movements, in which children rotate the chute while keeping the center hole over the same spot, offer many opportunities for locomotor movements,

FIGURE 18.16 Popping popcorn.

either free or to the beat of a tom-tom. European Rhythmic Running is particularly appropriate. Also appropriate are fundamental movements, such as walking, running, hopping, skipping, galloping, sliding, draw steps, and grapevine steps. The parachute can be held at different levels. Holds can be one- or two-handed.

SHAKING THE RUG AND MAKING WAVES

Shaking the Rug involves rapid movements of the parachute, either light or heavy. Making Waves involves large movements to send billows of cloth up and down. Waves can be small, medium, or high. Different types of waves can be made by having children alternate their up-and-down motions, or by having the class work in small groups around the chute. These small groups take turns showing what they can do. For a more demanding activity, children can perform locomotor movements while they shake the rug.

CHUTE CRAWL

Half the class, either standing or kneeling, stretches the chute at waist level parallel to the ground. The remaining children crawl under the chute to the opposite side from their starting position.

KITE RUN

The class holds the chute on one side with one hand. The leader points in the direction they are to run while holding the chute aloft like a kite.

RUNNING NUMBER GAME

The children around the chute count off by fours; then they run lightly, holding the chute in one hand. The teacher calls out one of the numbers. Children with that number immediately release their grip on the chute and run forward to the next place vacated. They must put on a burst of speed to move ahead.

ROUTINES TO MUSIC

Like other routines, parachute activities can be adapted to music. A sequence should be based on eight counts, with the routine composed of an appropriate number of sequences.

TUG-OF-WAR

For team tug-of-war, divide the class in halves. On signal, teams pull against each other and try to reach a line located behind them (Figure 18.17). Another approach that is often more enjoyable for primary-age children is an individual tug, in which all children pull in any direction they desire.

ACTION SONGS AND DANCES

A number of action songs, games, and dances can be performed while children hold on to a parachute. The following are suggested: Carousel (page 432), Bingo (pages 438–439), and Seven Jumps (page 429).

FIGURE 18.17 Parachute Tug-of-War.

ACTIVITIES WITH INDIVIDUAL MATS

Individual mats have an English origin and are the basis for many exploratory and creative movements. Essentially, the mat serves as a base of operation or as an obstacle to go over or around. Mats vary in size, with the most popular being 24 by 48 inches. Standard thickness is 0.75 inch, but this also varies. The mat should have rubber backing to prevent slipping. Rubber-backed indoor-outdoor carpeting makes excellent mats; however commercial models are available.

Instructional Procedures

1. Educational movement techniques are very important in mat work.
2. Body management and basic skills of locomotor and nonlocomotor movement should be emphasized.
3. Mats should be far enough apart to allow free movement around them.
4. Each child should have a mat.

Activity Sequences

Rigid adherence to the sequence presented below is not necessary. The activities are quite flexible and require only fundamental skills.

Command Movements

In command movements, children change movement on command. The commands used are the following:

Stretch: Stretch your body out in all directions as wide as possible.

Curl: Curl into a tight little ball (Figure 18.18).

Balance: Form some kind of balanced position.

Bridge: Make a bridge over the mat.

Reach: Keeping the toes of one foot on the mat, reach out as far as possible across the floor in a chosen direction.

Rock: Rock on any part of the body.

Roll: Do some kind of roll on the mat.

Twist: Make a shape with a part of the body twisted.

Prone: Lie prone on the mat.

Melt: Sink down slowly into a little puddle of water on the mat.

Shake: Shake all over, or shake whatever parts of the body are designated.

Fall: Fall to the mat.

Collapse: The movement is similar to a fall but follows nicely after a bridge.

Sequencing can be established in several ways. The children can emphasize flow factors by moving at will from one movement to another, or changes can be made on a verbal signal or on the beat of a drum. Magic number challenges can be used, too.

Another means of exploration is selecting one of the movement challenges—say, Stretch—and changing from one type of stretch position to another. If Balance is selected, the movement sequence can begin with a balance on six body parts; then the number can be reduced by one on each signal until the child is balancing on one body part. Different kinds of shapes can be explored.

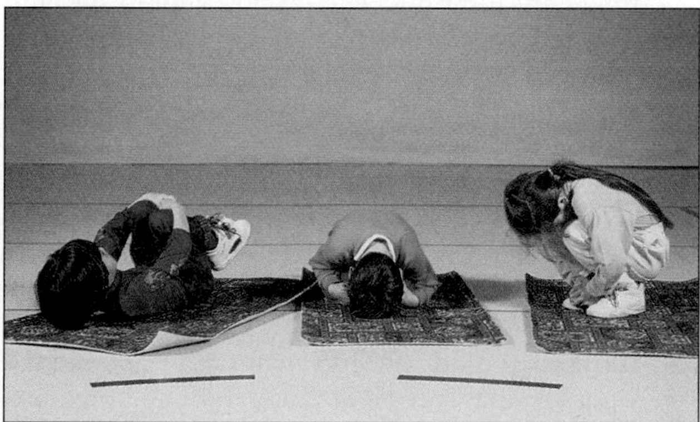

FIGURE 18.18 Curl activities on individual mats.

MOVEMENTS ON AND OFF THE MAT

Children do different locomotor movements on and off the mat in different directions. Turns and shapes can be added (Figure 18.19).

1. Take the weight on the hands as you go across the mat.

FIGURE 18.19 Movements on and off the mat.

2. Lead with different body parts as you go on and off the mat. Move on and off the mat with a specified number of body parts (one, two, three, four, five) used for landing.
3. Jump backward, forward, sideward. Make up a rhythmic sequence. Move around the area, jumping from mat to mat.

MOVEMENTS OVER THE MAT

Movements over the mat are similar to the preceding movements, but the child goes completely over the mat each time.

MOVEMENTS AROUND THE MAT

Locomotor movements around the mat are done both clockwise and counterclockwise.

1. Do movements around the mat, keeping the hands on the mat. Now do movements around, keeping the feet on the mat.
2. Change to one foot and one hand on the mat. Vary with the Crab position.
3. Work out combinations of stunt movements and locomotor activities, going around the mats. Reverse direction often.
4. Move throughout the area, running between the mats, and on signal jump over a specified number of mats.

ACTIVITIES USING MATS AS A BASE

1. Stretch and reach in different directions to show how big the space is.
2. Do combination movements away from and back to the mat. For example, do two jumps and two hops or six steps and two jumps.
3. Use the magic-number concept.
4. See how many letters you can make. Find a partner, put your mats together, and make your bodies into different letters and numbers.

MAT GAMES

Each child is seated on a mat. On signal, each rises and jumps over as many different mats as possible. On the next signal, each child takes a seat on the nearest mat. The last child to be seated can pay a penalty. The game can also be played by eliminating one or two mats so that one or two children are left without a home base. The teacher can stand on a mat or turn over mats to put them out of the game. To control roughness, the rule should be that the first child to touch a mat gets to sit on it.

A variation of this game is to have each child touch at least ten mats and then sit cross-legged on the eleventh, or a child can be required to alternate touching a mat and jumping over the next mat until a total of ten is reached. "See how many mats you can cartwheel or jump over in 10 seconds." Change the challenge and try again.

DEVELOPMENTAL CHALLENGES

1. Experiment with Curl-Ups (partial or full). (This can be done informally and on a challenge basis.)
2. From a sitting position on the mat, pick up the short sides of the mat and raise the feet and upper body off the floor. Try variations of the V-Up (page 508).

MANIPULATIVE ACTIVITIES

Keeping one foot on the mat, maintain control of a balloon in the air, either with a hand, a nylon-stocking paddle, or a lummi stick. Try the same activity with a stocking paddle and a paper ball. The number of touches, or strokes, can be counted. Try with both feet on the mat.

ACTIVITIES WITH MAGIC ROPES

Magic rope activities originated in Germany. Each rope is similar to a long rubber band. Magic ropes can be made by knitting wide rubber bands together, or they can be constructed from ordinary ¾-inch elastic tape available in most clothing stores. Children place their hands through loops on each end and grasp the rope. Ropes should be long enough to stretch to between 30 and 40 feet (see Chapter 10). A major advantage of the magic rope is its flexibility; children have no fear of hitting it or tripping on it while performing. Ropes should be stretched tight, with little slack.

Instructional Procedures

1. Two or more children are rope holders while the others are jumping. The teacher should develop some type of rotation plan so that all children participate as holders.
2. Many variations can be achieved with the magic ropes by changing the height or by raising and lowering opposite ends of the ropes.
3. The jumping activities are strenuous and should be alternated with activities that involve crawling under the ropes.
4. The class should concentrate on not touching the rope. The magic rope can help develop body perception in space if the rope is regarded as an obstacle to be avoided.

5. Better use can be made of the rope by using an angled approach, which involves starting at one end of the rope and progressing to the other end by using jumping and hopping activities. In comparison, the straight-on approach allows the child to jump the rope only once.
6. A total of 8 to 12 ropes is needed for a class, 2 for each squad. Squads are excellent groups for this activity, because the leader can control the rotation of the rope holders.
7. The child next in turn begins when the child ahead is almost to the end of the rope.

Activity Sequences

ACTIVITIES WITH SINGLE ROPES

Start the ropes at a 6-inch height and raise them progressively to add challenge.

1. Jump over the rope (Figure 18.20).
2. Hop over the rope.
3. Jump and perform various body turns while jumping.
4. Make different body shapes and change body size while jumping.
5. Crawl or slide under the rope.
6. Crouch-jump over the rope.
7. Hold the rope overhead and have others jump up and touch it with their foreheads.
8. Gradually lower the rope, and do the limbo under it without touching the floor with the hands.
9. Jump over the rope backward without looking at it.
10. Perform a Scissors Jump over the rope.

ACTIVITIES WITH DOUBLE ROPES

Vary the height and spread of the ropes.

1. Do these activities with the ropes parallel to each other.
   a. Jump in one side and out the other (Figure 18.21).
   b. Hop in one side and out the other.
   Crouch-jump in and out.
   d. Perform various animal walks in and out of the ropes.
   e. Do a long jump over both of the ropes.
   f. Perform a stunt while jumping in between the two ropes. Possible stunts are the Heel Click, body turn, handclap, and Straddle Jump.
   g. Jump or leap over one rope and land on the other rope.
2. With the ropes crossed at right angles to each other, do these activities:
   a. Perform various movements from one area to the next.
   b. Jump into one area and crawl out of that area into another.
3. With one rope above the other to effect a barbed-wire fence, do these activities. Vary the height of the ropes and their distance apart. This adds much excitement to the activity because the children are challenged not to touch the ropes.
   a. Step through the ropes without touching.
   b. Crouch-jump through.

FIGURE 18.20 Jumping over a single magic rope.

FIGURE 18.21 Jumping in and out of two magic ropes.

MISCELLANEOUS ACTIVITIES WITH MAGIC ROPES

These miscellaneous activities are useful, too. The class should be given time to create their own ideas with the ropes and other pieces of equipment.

1. Perform the various activities with a beanbag balanced on the head. Perform while bouncing a ball.
2. Use four or more ropes to create various floor patterns.
3. Use a follow-the-leader plan to add variety to the activity.
4. Create a Challenge Course with many ropes for a relay.

ACTIVITIES WITH PARTNER TUG-OF-WAR ROPES

A partner tug-of-war rope is about 6 feet long with a loop on each end. (See Chapter 10 for instructions on making partner tug-of-war ropes.) Tug-of-war ropes help in the development of strength, because contestants must use maximum or near-maximum strength in the contests. These strength demands may continue over a short period of time. Because considerable effort is demanded in some cases, force concepts are concomitant learnings.

Instructional Procedures

1. Contests should be between opponents of comparable ability. Each child should have a chance to win.
2. Plan a system of rotation so that children meet different opponents.
3. Caution students to not let go of the rope. If the grip is slipping, they should inform the other student, renew the grip, and start over.
4. Individual ropes are excellent for partner resistance activities. A few of these activities should be practiced each time the children use the ropes.
5. Make the starting routine clear so that each contestant understands. Make definite rules about what constitutes a win and how long a contest must endure to be called a tie.
6. A line on the floor perpendicular to the direction of the rope makes a satisfactory goal for determining a win. One child pulls the other forward until the second child is over the line. Another criterion for a win could be for children to pick up objects placed behind them.

Partner Activities

Children should try the following ways of pulling. The tug-of-war rope offers good possibilities in movement exploration. Let students try to devise ways other than those mentioned by which they can pull against each other.

1. Pull with the right hand only, the left hand only, both hands.
2. Grasp with the right hand, with the body supported on three points (the left hand and the feet). Change hands.
3. Pull with backs toward each other, with the rope between the legs, holding with one hand only.
4. Opponents get down on all fours, with feet toward each other. Hook the loops around one foot of each opponent. For each contestant, the force is provided by both hands and the foot that remains on the floor.
5. Opponents get into Crab position and pull the rope by hooking a foot through the loop (Figure 18.22).
6. Opponents face each other and stand on one foot only. Contestants try to pull each other off balance without losing their own balance. If the raised foot touches the floor, the other person is declared the winner.
7. Contestants stand with opposite sides toward each other. They hold a tug-of-war rope with opposite hands and move apart until the rope is taut. The goal is to make the other person move the feet by pulling and giving on the rope. The legs must be kept straight, and only the arms can be used in the contest.
8. Students stand 10 feet away from the rope, which is on the floor. On signal, they run to the rope, pick it up, and have a tug-of-war. Contestants can start from different positions, such as push-up, curl-up, or Crab.

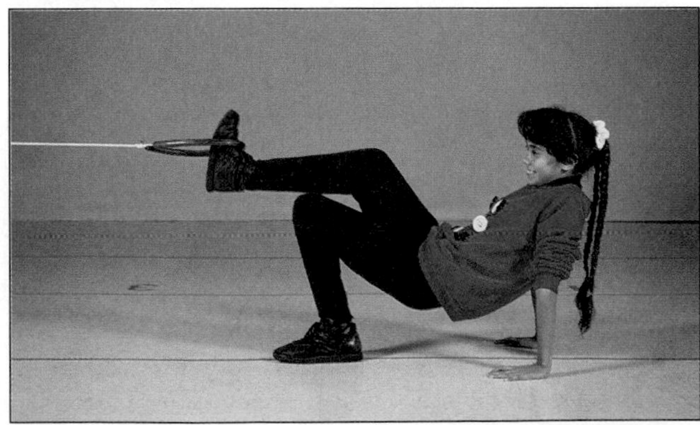

FIGURE 18.22 Pulling in Crab position.

9. Instead of opponents pulling each other across a line, each tries to pull the other toward a peg or bowling pin placed behind them so that they can pick up the objects.
10. Two individual ropes are tied together at the center so that four loops are available for pulling. Four cones form a square, and four children compete to see who can pick up a cone first.
11. Two children pull against two others. The rope loops should be made big enough so that both can secure handholds on each end. They can use right hands only or left hands only.
12. For Frozen Tug-of-War, two children take hold of a rope, each with both hands on a loop. The children are positioned close enough together so that there is some slack in the rope. A third child grasps the rope to make a 6-inch bend at the center, and the contestants then pull the rope taut so that there is no slack (Figure 18.23). On the signal "Go," the third child drops the loop, and the opponents try to pull each other off balance. The feet are "frozen" to the floor; if the position of either foot is moved, that player loses.
13. Hawaiian Tug-of-War is an exciting game activity for youngsters. Two parallel lines are drawn about 20 feet apart. The game is between two people, but as many pairs as are in a class can play. A partner tug-of-war rope is laid on the floor at right angles to, and midway between, the two parallel lines. The players position themselves so that each is standing about 1 foot from one of the loops of the rope. They are in position to pick up the rope and pull against each other on signal. The object of the game is to pull the other child far enough to be able to touch the line behind. The magic word is "Hula." This is the signal to pick up the rope and begin to pull. Children must not reach down and pick up the rope until "Hula" is called. The teacher can use other commands, such as "Go" and "Begin," to deceive the children.

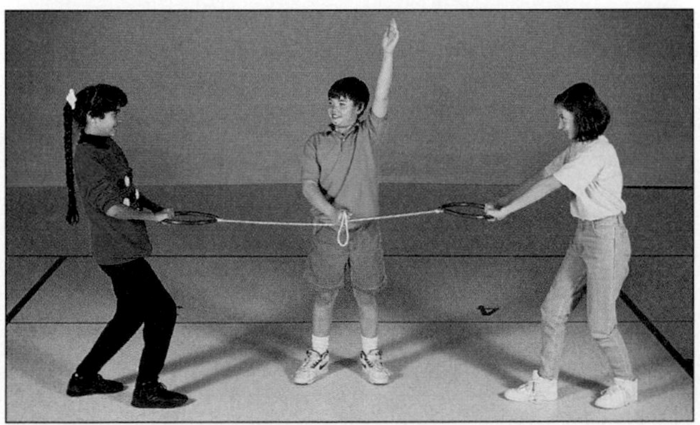

FIGURE 18.23 Frozen Tug-of-War.

14. Group contests are possible. (See Figure 10.18 for a diagram of rope arrangements suitable for groups.)

Partner Resistance Activities

Children should follow exercise principles, exerting sufficient force (near maximum), maintaining resistance through the full range of motion for 8 to 10 seconds, and stabilizing the base so that the selected part of the body can be exercised. The force is a controlled pull, not a tug. The partner should not be compelled to move out of position. Much of the exercise centers on the hands and arms, but other parts of the body come into play as braces. Partners work together, both in the same position.

As in other activities, grip can be varied. The upper grip (palms away from performer) and the lower grip (palms toward performer) are usually used. Occasionally, a mixed grip, with one hand in upper position and one hand in lower position, can be used. Laterality must be kept in mind so that the right and left sides of the body receive equal treatment.

PARTNERS STANDING WITH SIDES TOWARD EACH OTHER

1. Use a lower grip. Do a flexed-arm pull, with elbows at right angles.
2. Use an upper grip. Extend the arm from the side at a 45-degree angle. Pull toward the side.
3. Use a lower grip. Extend the arm completely overhead. Pull overhead.
4. Loop the rope around one ankle. Stand with feet apart. Pull with the closer foot.

PARTNERS STANDING, FACING EACH OTHER

1. Use a lower grip. Do a flexed-arm pull, with one and then both hands.
2. Use an upper grip. Extend the arms at the side or down. Pull toward the rear.
3. Use an upper grip. Pull both hands straight toward chest.
4. Use an upper grip. Extend the arms overhead. Pull backward.

PARTNERS SITTING, FACING EACH OTHER

1. Repeat the activities described for standing position (Figure 18.24 on page 414).
2. Hook the rope with both feet. Pull.

PARTNERS PRONE, FACING EACH OTHER

1. Use an upper grip. Pull directly toward the chest.
2. Use a lower grip. Do a flexed-arm pull.

FIGURE 18.24 Partner resistance activity in sitting position.

PARTNERS PRONE, FEET TOWARD EACH OTHER

1. Hook the rope around one ankle. With knee joint at a right angle, pull.
2. Try with both feet together.

Pulling Resistance Activities

Using mostly the standing positions, work out resistance exercises such as the following: One child pulls and makes progress with eight steps. The other child then pulls the first back for eight counts. The addition of music makes this an interesting activity. The child being pulled must provide enough resistance to make the puller work reasonably hard.

ACTIVITIES WITH GYM SCOOTERS

Gym scooters make excellent devices for developmental activity when used properly. The minimum number is one scooter for two children, unless the scooters are used for relays only. In that case, four or six scooters will suffice for an average-sized class. Two rules are important in the use of scooters. First, children are not to stand on scooters as they would on skateboards. Second, scooters, with or without passengers, must not be used as missiles.

Children can work individually or in pairs. A child working alone can do many different combinations by varying the method of propulsion and the method of supporting the body. Children can propel the scooter with their feet, their hands, or both. The body position can be kneeling, sitting, prone, supine, or even sideways. The body weight can be wholly or partially supported on the scooter. The variation of space factors, particularly direction, adds interest.

When children work in pairs, one child rides and the other pushes or pulls. The rider's weight may be wholly supported by the scooter or partially supported by the scooter and partially supported by the partner. Educational movement methodology is applicable to scooter work, but care should be exercised so that the scooter activities are developmental and not just a free play session. Scooters are excellent for relays, and many games can be adapted for their use.

CHAPTER 19

Rhythmic Movement Skills

	ESSENTIAL COMPONENTS
I	Organized around content standards
II	**Student-centered and developmentally appropriate**
III	**Physical activity and motor skill development form the core of the program**
IV	Teaches management skills and self-discipline
V	Promotes inclusion of all students
VI	**Focuses on process over product**
VII	Promotes lifetime personal health and wellness
VIII	**Teaches cooperation and responsibility and promotes sensitivity to diversity**

	PHYSICAL EDUCATION STANDARDS
1	**Students are able to move competently using a variety of fundamental and specialized motor skills.**
2	Students can monitor and maintain a health-enhancing level of physical fitness.
3	Students are able to apply movement concepts and basic mechanics of skill performance when learning and refining motor skills.
4	Students comprehend the basic principles of wellness and are able to apply concepts that enable them to make meaningful decisions that positively impact their health and wellness.
5	**Students participate in a wide variety of physical activities and learn how to maintain a personalized active lifestyle.**
6	**Students demonstrate empathy, understanding, and respect for the numerous differences exhibited by people in an activity setting.**
7	**Students exhibit responsible and self-directed behaviors that lead to positive social interactions in physical activity.**

SUMMARY

Activities in this chapter are selected for the purpose of developing rhythmic movement skills. The activities are listed in progression of easy to more complex and by developmental level. The development of social skills and a positive self-concept occur when rhythmic activities are taught in a sensitive and educational manner. Rhythmic activities should be scheduled in the same manner as other phases of the yearly physical education program. Most dances use skills and steps that are learned in a sequential manner.

OUTCOMES

- Know where to find sources of rhythmic accompaniment.
- Understand the inherent rhythmic nature of all physical activity.
- Outline components of the yearly rhythmic movement program and identify accompanying activities and skill progressions.
- Describe instructional procedures and ideas to facilitate implementation of rhythmic movements into the yearly program.
- Cite creative rhythms, movement songs, folk dances, and other dance activities that are used as learning experiences in physical education.
- Describe dance progressions that are appropriate for the various levels of development that children exhibit.

Rhythm is the basis of music and dance. Rhythm in dance is simply expressive movement made with or without music. All body movements tend to be rhythmic—the beating of the heart, swinging a tennis racket, wielding a hammer, throwing a ball. Most movements that take place in physical education class contain elements of rhythm. Movement to rhythm begins early in the child's school career and continues throughout. Rhythmic activities are particularly appropriate for younger children. A sizable portion of the developmental level I program is devoted to such activities. One problem in incorporating rhythmic activities in the program is the vast amount of material available, which requires judicious selection to present a broad, progressive program. Another problem is that many teachers are hesitant about the subject area. If you prepare properly, you will become comfortable with rhythms and find that these activities are a favorite of children.

Early experiences center on functional and creative movement forms. Locomotor skills are inherently rhythmic in execution, and the addition of rhythm can enhance development of these skills. An important component of children's dance is fundamental rhythms. Instruction begins with and capitalizes on locomotor skills that children already possess—walking, running, hopping, and jumping. Rhythmic activities provide a vehicle for expressive movement. These activities offer opportunity for broad participation and personal satisfaction for all, as children personalize their responses within the framework of the idea. Youngsters have a chance to create unique rhythmic responses within action songs and dances.

TABLE 19.1 Types of rhythmic activity

Activity	Developmental Level I	II	III
Fundamental rhythms	X	X	S
Creative rhythms	X		
Singing movement songs	X		
Folk dances	X	X	X
Line dances		X	X
Mixers	X	X	X
Aerobic dancing		X	X
Square dancing			X
Rope jumping to music	S	X	X
Musical games	S	S	S
Rhythmic gymnastics (refer to Chapter 17)			

Note: X means that the activity is an integral part of the program. S means that the activity is given only minor emphasis.

IMPLEMENTING THE RHYTHMIC MOVEMENT PROGRAM

The rhythmic program should be balanced and should include activities from each of the categories of rhythmic movement. Table 19.1 shows recommended types of rhythmic activities for each developmental level.

Skill Progressions

Another factor in program construction is the progression of basic and specific dance steps. Dances employing the following skills and steps appear in each of the respective developmental level programs.

Developmental Level I

In the early primary grades, fundamental locomotor skills are stressed. (Skipping and sliding are taught and practiced, but students are not expected to master them.) Combinations of two or more fundamental movements are presented; for example, the Bleking Step.

Developmental Level II

At this level, rhythmic activities should include fundamental locomotor skills, more combinations of locomotor skills, the step-hop, and the grand right and left. Marching, basic tinikling steps, and introductory square dancing steps are taught as skill improves.

Developmental Level III

By Level III, students are able to master the grapevine step, schottische, polka, intermediate tinikling steps, two-step, advanced tinikling step, square dancing, and all steps introduced at earlier levels.

Understanding Rhythmic Accompaniment

Music has essential characteristics that children should recognize, understand, and appreciate. These characteristics are also present to varying degrees in other purely percussive accompaniment.

Tempo is the speed of the music. It can be constant or show a gradual increase (acceleration) or decrease (deceleration).

Beat is the underlying rhythm of the music. Some musicians refer to the beat as the pulse of the music. The beat can be even or uneven. Music with a pronounced beat is easier to follow.

Meter refers to the manner in which the beats are put together to form a measure of music. Common meters used in rhythmics are 2/4, 3/4, 4/4, and 6/8.

Certain notes or beats in a rhythmic pattern receive more force than others, and this defines *accent*. Usually, accent is applied to the first beat of a measure and generally is expressed by a more forceful movement in a sequence of movements.

The *intensity* of music can be loud, soft, light, or heavy. *Mood* is related to intensity but carries the concept deeper into human feelings. Music can reflect many moods—happiness, sadness, gaiety, fear, or stateliness, for example.

A *phrase* is a natural grouping of measures. In most cases, a phrase consists of eight underlying beats. Phrases of music are put together into rhythmic *patterns.* Children should learn to recognize when the pattern repeats or changes.

Sources of Rhythmic Accompaniment

Essential to any rhythmic program is accompaniment that encourages desired motor patterns and expressive movement. If children are to move to a rhythm, it must be stimulating, appropriate for the expected responses, and appealing to the learners. Skillful use of a drum or tambourine adds much to rhythmic experiences. A major use of the drumbeat is to guide the movement from one pattern to another by signaling tiny increments of change with light beats that control the flow. The motion in striking is essentially a wrist action, not an arm movement.

Each school and teacher should build a collection of recorded music. Sets created especially for physical education movement patterns and dance are available from a number of sources. Physical education CDs or tapes should be stored in the physical education facility rather than in the school library. Storage should be arranged so that each recording has its assigned place and is readily available. Keeping extra copies of the more frequently used pieces in reserve is an excellent practice, especially in centralized equipment distribution centers for larger school systems.

FUNDAMENTAL RHYTHMS

Fundamental rhythms are an outgrowth of the movement activities with which the children are already familiar, such as walking (stepping), running, jumping, and hopping. To these acquired skills, rhythm is added. Fundamental rhythms are emphasized in the primary grades and are extended to the intermediate level on a smaller scale. The general purpose of a fundamental rhythms program is to provide a variety of fundamental movement experiences so the child can learn to move effectively and efficiently and can develop a sense of rhythm. Although the creative aspect of fundamental rhythms is important, even more important is first establishing a vocabulary of movement competencies for each child. The skills in a fundamental rhythm program are important as the background for creative dance and also as the basis for the more precise dance skills of folk, social, and square dance, which follow later in school programs. (Fundamental skills are described, together with teaching hints and stress points, in Chapter 15.)

Locomotor Skills

Even rhythm locomotor skills are walking, running, hopping, leaping, jumping, draw steps, and such variations as marching, trotting, stamping, and twirling. Uneven movements are skipping, galloping, and sliding.

Nonlocomotor Skills

Simple nonlocomotor skills are bending, swaying, twisting, swinging, raising, lowering, circling, and rotating various parts of the body. Mimetic movements include striking, lifting, throwing, pushing, pulling, hammering, and other common tasks.

Manipulative Skills

Manipulative skills involve object handling, such as ball skills. Other objects such as hoops, wands, and even chairs can be used.

Instructional Procedures

1. Success depends on initiating and guiding simple patterns. Of prime importance is the class atmosphere, which should be one of enjoyment. Furthermore, the accompaniment must be suitable for the movements to be experienced.
2. The element of creativity should not be stifled in a program of fundamental rhythms. The instruction can be directed toward a specific movement (such as walking), and a reasonable range of acceptable performance, which permits individual creativity, can be established.
3. If you feel awkward or insecure about developing rhythmic programs with a strong creative approach, fundamental rhythms are a good starting point. Combining rhythmic movement with movements students enjoy can be the beginning of a refreshing and stimulating experience for both you and your students.
4. The approach to fundamental rhythms should be a mixture of direct and indirect teaching. Many of the movements do have standard or preferred techniques. For example, there is a correct way to walk. Children should recognize and learn such fundamentals. Within the framework of good technique, however, a variety of movement experiences can be elicited.

Suggestions for Teaching Fundamental Rhythmic Movements

Children enjoy change and the challenge of reacting to change. They can be encouraged to change the movement pattern or some aspect of it (direction, level, body leads, and so on) at the end of a musical phrase. Changes can be signaled by variations in the drumbeat. A heavy, accented beat, for example, can signal a change in direction or type of movement. Stops and starts, changes to different rhythms, and other innovations are within the scope of this process. The intensity of the drumbeat can call for light or heavy movements or for different levels of movement: high, middle, or low. As an example of how to do this, picture a class of children walking heavily in general space to a heavy, even beat. The teacher sounds one extra-heavy beat, whereupon students change direction abruptly, now moving very lightly on the toes to a light, even beat. This sequence finishes with another heavy beat, which signals the children again to change direction and their movement as indicated by the next sequence of beats. The opportunities for movement combinations are many.

The use of different parts of the body, singly and in various combinations, is important in establishing movement variety. Different positions of the arms and legs can vary the ways of moving. Children can perform high on the toes, with toes in or out; on the heels, with stiff knees; kicking high in front or to the rear, with knees brought up high; in a crouch or any number of different positions. The arms can swing at the sides or be held stiff, be held out in front, or held overhead. The arms can move in circles or in different patterns. The body can bend forward, backward, or sideward, and it can twist and turn. By combining different arm, leg, and body positions, the children can assume many interesting position variations. Changes in body level and patterns of movement for outlining circles, squares, triangles, and other shapes also add interest. Ideas and suggestions for using fundamental skills with rhythm are found in Chapter 15.

CREATIVE RHYTHMS

Creativity should be part of all dance and rhythmic activities, with the scope of the activity determining the degree of freedom. Creative rhythms, however, provide a special program area in which creativity is the goal and functional movement is secondary. The emphasis is on the process and not on the movement outcomes.

Creativity manifests itself in the opportunity for each child to respond expressively within the scope of the movement idea, which can range from total freedom to stated limits. The child's judgment should be respected, and the teacher should look for original interpretations. Stimulation should be positive in nature, guiding the movement patterns by suggestions, questions, encouragement, and challenges that help children structure their ideas and add variety. Careful guidance is necessary to fan the spark of self-direction, because freedom in itself does not automatically develop creativity.

Instructional Procedures

1. Appropriate music or rhythmic background is important; otherwise, movement can become stilted. An atmosphere of creative freedom must be established. The class should be comfortable and relaxed.
2. When analyzing the setting, ask, What is the basic idea? What expressive movements can be expected? What are the guidelines or boundaries of movement? What space are the children to use?
3. Listening is an important element, because children must understand the mood or sense of the rhythmic background. Some questions that can be posed to children are, "What does the music make us think of?" and "What does the music tell us to do?" If the movement or interpretation is preselected, little time need be wasted in getting under way. Provide enough music so children can grasp the impact. Have them clap the beat if necessary and then move into action.
4. Use action-directing statements such as, "Let's pretend we are . . . ," "Let's try being like . . . ," "Try to feel like a . . . ," and "Make believe you are. . . ."
5. In some lessons, the initial focus may be on the selection of appropriate rhythmic background. In this instance children formulate a creative rhythm of the dramatic type and then seek suitable music for their dance.
6. Give children time to develop and try their ideas. This is an open-ended process that has a variety of solutions. Coaching and guidance are important aspects at this stage. Application of time, space, force, flow, and body factors is essential. Encourage large, free movement of all body parts. Use the entire area and fill in the empty places in general space. Allow time for exploration.

Suggestions for Teaching Creative Rhythms

The following suggestions can be used for development of creative rhythmic activities.

Understanding and Relating to Rhythm

Teachers can bring in the idea of meter ($^2/_4$, $^3/_4$, $^4/_4$, and $^6/_8$ time) and have children move in time to the meter. Other movements can illustrate even and uneven time, accents, phrasing, and other elements of rhythmic structure.

Fundamental Motor Rhythms

Creativity can be developed through various locomotor movements. The use of the drum is recommended for varying the tempo and signaling movement changes. Some suggested ideas are:

1. On a single loud beat, each student changes direction abruptly, turns around, or jumps or leaps in the air.
2. A quick, heavy, double beat signals children to stop in place without any further movement or to fall to the floor.
3. Various changes in beat and accent pattern can be given, with children instructed to follow the pattern with movement.

CDs and tapes designed for fundamental movements are excellent teaching aids. Selected music sources should have sections featuring separate skills and sections to guide movement combinations. These can be used for both instruction and creative activities. As an example, children who are seated in a circle tap out a rhythm with lummi sticks. After the rhythm is sufficiently established, half of the class moves in general space to the rhythm, which is continued by those who remain seated.

Expressive Movement

Children can express moods and feelings and show reactions to colors and sounds by improvising dances or movements that demonstrate different aspects of force, or gestures that depict different feelings. A piece of music is played and is followed by a discussion of its qualities and how it makes the children feel. Children may interpret the music differently. Moods can be described as happy, lighthearted, sad, brave, fearful, cheerful, angry, solemn, silly, stately, sleepy, funny, cautious, bold, or nonchalant.

Identification

There are endless subject sources for identification and interpretation. Children can take on the identity of a familiar character, creature, or object. The following ideas should be useful.

1. Animals—elephants, ducks, seals, chickens, dogs, rabbits, lions, and others
2. People—soldiers, firefighters, sailors, nurses, various kinds of workers, forest rangers, teachers, cowboys and cowgirls, and so on
3. Play objects—seesaws, swings, rowboats, balls, various toys, and many other common articles with which children play
4. Make-believe creatures—giants, dwarfs, gnomes, witches, trolls, dragons, pixies, fairies, and so on
5. Machines—trains, planes, jets, rockets, automobiles, bicycles, motorcycles, tractors, elevators, and the like
6. Circus characters—clowns, various trained animals, trapeze artists, tightrope performers, jugglers, acrobats, and bands
7. Natural phenomena—fluttering leaves, grain, flowers, rain, snow, clouds, wind, tornadoes, hurricanes, volcanoes, and others

Dramatization

Dramatization and rhythm are useful vehicles for group activity. Suitable background music or rhythmic accompaniment is a necessary ingredient. Excellent recordings are available, from short numbers lasting a minute or two to more elaborate productions such as those found in the Dance-a-Story series (RCA Victor).

Here are some useful ideas for dramatic rhythms.

1. Building a house, garage, or other building project.
2. Making a snowman, throwing snowballs, going skiing.
3. Flying a kite, going hunting or fishing, going camping.
4. Acting out stories about astronauts, cowboys and cowgirls, firefighters, explorers.
5. Interpreting familiar stories, such as "Sleeping Beauty," "The Three Bears," or "Little Red Riding Hood."
6. Doing household tasks such as chopping wood, picking fruit, mowing the lawn, cleaning the yard, washing dishes, and vacuuming.
7. Celebrating holidays such as Halloween, the Fourth of July, Thanksgiving, or Christmas, or dramatizing the seasons.
8. Playing sports such as football, basketball, baseball, track and field, swimming, tennis, and golf.
9. Divide the class in groups of three or four, and assign each group a sport other than one of the major sports. Have them develop a series of movements dramatizing that sport to the class. Have the remaining groups guess which sport is being presented. Slow-motion movements add to this activity.
10. Plan a trip through a haunted house. A recording by Hap Palmer ("Movin'," Kimbo EA 546) has an excellent sequence about being in a haunted house.
11. Have the children make a motor. One student starts by getting into a position of choice in the middle of the floor and by putting one body part in motion. The motion should be a steady, rhythmic movement.

The remaining students, one at a time, attach onto the first person, and each person puts one body part in motion. After all are attached, a machine with many moving parts is the result.

12. Act out the children's favorite parts in popular movies. Having the children perform to the original sound track brings more realism to the performance.
13. Select a favorite poem ("Old Mother Hubbard," "Pat-a-Cake," "The Giant") and design a sequence of activities to fit the meaning of the poem. Stories have excellent appeal.

An example that shows how an idea can be exploited for a lesson on creative rhythm is called "The Wind and the Leaves." One or more children are chosen to be the wind, and the remaining children are the leaves. Two kinds of rhythm are needed; a tambourine can be used. The first rhythm should be high, fast, and shrill, indicating the blowing of the wind. The intensity and tempo should illustrate the speed and force of the wind. The second rhythm should be slow, measured, and light, to represent the leaves fluttering in the still air and finally coming to rest at various positions on the ground. During the first rhythm, children representing the wind act out a heavy gust. While this is going on, the leaves show what it is like to be blown about. During the second rhythm, the wind is still and the leaves flutter to the ground. Other characterizations can be added. For example, street sweepers can come along and sweep up the leaves.

Another lesson strategy is to divide the class into groups and to give each group the task of acting out an idea with percussive accompaniment. Each group puts on a performance for the others. At completion, the other groups guess what the interpretation was. In this game, the interpretations should not last too long.

Creating Dances

A wide range of creative endeavor is possible in making up dances. Efforts can vary from construction of simple routines to formulation of a complete dance to a new or familiar piece of music. Students need to analyze the characteristics of the piece, determine the kinds of movement best suited to the musical elements, and design an appropriate movement routine or dance. This works best with small groups.

FOLK DANCES

A *folk dance* is defined as a traditional dance of a particular culture. In this concept, a definite pattern or dance routine is usually specified and followed. Folk dancing is one phase of a child's education that can assist in bringing about international understanding. A country's way of life and many other habits are often reflected in its folk music. From these dances, children gain an understanding of why people from certain countries act and live as they do, even though modern times may have changed their lifestyle from that of days gone by.

Folk dances in developmental level I consist of simple fundamental locomotor skills, either singly or in combination. Dances such as the two-step, polka, and schottische, with more specialized steps, are found in developmental levels II and III. The first consideration when teaching folk dance is to determine whether children know the basic skills required for the dance. If a skill needs to be taught, it can be handled in one of two ways. The first way is to teach the skill separately, before teaching the dance. The second is to teach the dance in its normal sequence, giving specific instruction at the time when the skill appears. The first method is often best, because children can concentrate solely on learning the skill.

Teaching New Dances Successfully

The underlying goal of folk dancing is to learn to move rhythmically. Unfortunately, many students (often boys) develop negative attitudes and feelings of failure about rhythmic activities. Effective teachers have long recognized the need to modify sport activities to ensure that students learn skills correctly and experience success. Modifications such as using smaller balls, lower baskets, slower-moving objects, etc. are now commonplacc in most elementary school physical education activities. Interestingly, when teaching rhythmic activities the same approach is often discarded. Dances are taught with precision and emphasis on "doing it right," instead of making modifications so they are appealing and easier to learn. The following steps offer guidelines for modifying rhythmic activities to increase the probability of success.

1. *Slow down the music.* The first contact with the activity must be a successful one. No student wants to be embarrassed because he or she is out of step. If it appears that students are still not doing well, stop the music and walk them through it. If there is difficult footwork, repeat the sequence a number of times. Start from the beginning each time so students who are lost can begin anew.
2. *As a general rule, if the dance is short, use the whole-teaching approach.* If it is a longer dance with several different parts, use the part–whole method and teach one part at a time. For example, have children learn half of a two-part dance or one-third of a three-part dance and then put that part to music. After all the parts are learned, put them together in a complete dance.
3. *Introduce a new dance with students placed in scattered formation.* Circles and formations cause some

students to feel others are looking directly at them. If they are self-conscious about their ability, a circle formation may be intimidating. A scattered formation allows them to move near the rear of the area where fewer peers can see them perform.

4. *Avoid the use of partners when teaching a new activity.* Partners add a degree of complexity to many dances and should be added only after the basic steps have been mastered. In addition, avoid forcing intermediate grade students to pair up with a partner of the opposite sex unless they choose to do so. Students who do not want to dance with a partner should be allowed to perform the steps without one.
5. *Avoid the left-right and clockwise-counterclockwise orientation when introducing a new dance.* Anytime students are asked to move in a specified direction, it increases the possibility of error. Allow students to choose the direction they would like to move when learning new steps. Later, after the steps have been mastered, left-right and clockwise-counterclockwise orientations and formations can be added.
6. *To avoid stressing students, perform a dance once or twice in a daily lesson.* Presenting a number of dances, rather than one or two in depth, gives students who are having difficulty a chance to start with a clean slate on a new dance. Come back to a difficult dance and practice it in a later lesson. Some students panic when they experience difficulty and the increased stress limits their ability to learn. Not staying on any one dance for too long keeps students from becoming frustrated.
7. *Teach rhythmic activities in the same way sport skills are taught.* Teachers expect that students will make mistakes regardless of their ability level; baskets are missed and passes are dropped. Treat rhythmic activities like sport skills and expect that perfection is virtually impossible to reach. The purpose of teaching rhythmic activities is to learn to move rhythmically, not to showcase one or two dances learned perfectly. If student errors are accepted, students soon learn that rhythms are fun and worth trying.
8. *Dances that emphasize strong movements such as hand clapping and foot stomping appeal to boys.* Since boys are often "hard to sell" on rhythmic activities, it makes sense to introduce them to some activities that include strong and bold physical movements.

Modifying Rhythmic Activities

Folk dances are traditional rhythmic activities that have been done for generations. However, the traditional music and style may not appeal to some youngsters in a school setting. With a few modifications, the dances can become easier to learn. Table 19.2 shows how some common folk dances can be modified to increase student interest and increase the ease of learning.

Another way to motivate students is to use current music and change traditional dances into line dances. Line dances can motivate students to learn new steps without worrying about a partner. The following are examples of folk and popular dances that can be done as line dances.

Popcorn, page 445
Alley Cat, page 454
Cotton-Eyed Joe, page 453
Jessie Polka, page 455
Jiffy Mixer, page 455
Teton Mountain Stomp, page 453

Arranging for Partners

Arranging for partners can be a source of deep hurt or embarrassment for some children. To be acceptable, a method of arranging for partners must avoid the situation in which children are looked over and overlooked. Some suggestions follow.

1. Dancing boy-girl fashion in the traditional mode is not necessary. When starting a dance program with students who are uncomfortable with each other, allow students to dance with a partner of their choice. If this places boys with boys and girls with girls, allow that arrangement. Partners can be referred to as number 1 and number 2 or colored pinnies can be placed on one of the partners. Instead of giving directions for the girl's part, call it out as "The people in red on the outside of the circle do. . . ." Be careful not to label one group as playing the role of boys or girls. Change partners frequently; sooner or later the members of both sexes will dance with members of the opposite sex. In this chapter we use the designations "partner A" and "partner B" for the leading and following positions respectively. Gender references, where they appear, will alternate by example.
2. In a follow-the-leader approach, put on some brisk marching music and begin walking among the students, who are scattered in general space. As you pass students, tap them on the shoulder, and ask them to "fall in" behind you. Subsequent students go to the end of the line when tagged until all students are chosen. This allows you to arrange students as desired—boy-girl, or just to separate children who do not work well together.
3. Boys join hands in a circle formation, and each girl steps behind a boy. Reverse the procedure, and have girls make the circle, or have half of the class wear red pinnies and form the circle.

TABLE 19.2 Examples of dance modifications

Dance	Skills	Modifications	Formation
The Bird Dance	Skipping or walking, elbow swing or star	Good introductory dance for all levels	Scattered
Shortnin' Bread	Sliding, turning with a partner, clapping	Slow music Practice without partner	Scattered first, then with partner
Jump Jim Jo	Jumping, running, draw step	No partner Move in any direction	Scattered
Eins Zwie Drie	Walking, heel-toe step, sliding	No partner, no numbering Slide any direction Play giant cymbals	Scattered, then facing center of area
Wild Turkey Mixer	Walking, elbow swing	Groups of three—scattered Center person with pinnie Don't mix when learning	Scattered first, then circle formation
Irish Washerwoman	Walking, swinging, promenade position	No partners Swing and promenade the closest partner or move to the center for a partner Emphasize clapping and stomping	Facing center
Oh Susanna	Walking, promenade, grand right and left	Half of class with pinnies Use a wild grand right and left Go to center and find partner if left without one	Facing center
Jessie Polka	Step and touch, two-step or polka	Slow down music No partners Practice step and touch first	Scattered, students can hook on if they desire
Limbo Rock	Touch step, swivel step, jump clap clap	Slow down music Teach steps and add together	Scattered
Inside Out Mixer	Wring the Dishrag, walk, change partners	Practice without music No mixing until learned	Groups of three
Teton Mountain Stomp	Walking, two step	Do individually Emphasize clapping Move in any direction No side car or banjo position	Scattered

4. Boys stand in a circle facing counterclockwise, while girls form a circle around them facing clockwise. Both circles move in the direction in which they are facing and stop on signal. The boy takes the girl nearest him as his partner.
5. For square dances, take the first four couples from any of the previous formations to form a set. Continue until all sets are formed.

CDs and Cassette Tapes for Folk Dances

Quality recordings are difficult to find. Wagon Wheel Records is a reliable source for obtaining music accompaniment for all the dances included in this chapter. You can order compact discs (CDs), cassette tapes, and a catalog from the following address:

Wagon Wheel Records
16812 Pembrook Lane
Huntington Beach, CA 92649
(714) 846-8169

In this chapter, a code is listed for each dance that identifies whether it is in CD or cassette format and a catalog number to identify the source for ordering. **WWCD** indicates it is available in CD format while **WWC** signifies cassette tape format.

Formations for Folk Dances

Figure 19.1 illustrates the formations that are used with folk dances that follow in this chapter. Each folk dance description begins with a listing of records, skills, and the formation to be used. If teachers are unsure about

SINGLE–CIRCLE FORMATIONS

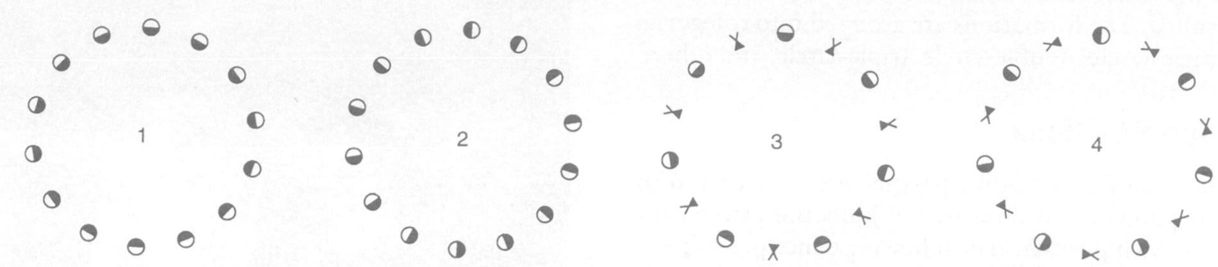

1. All facing center, no partners
2. All facing counterclockwise

3. By partners, all facing center
4. By partners, with partners facing

DOUBLE–CIRCLE FORMATIONS

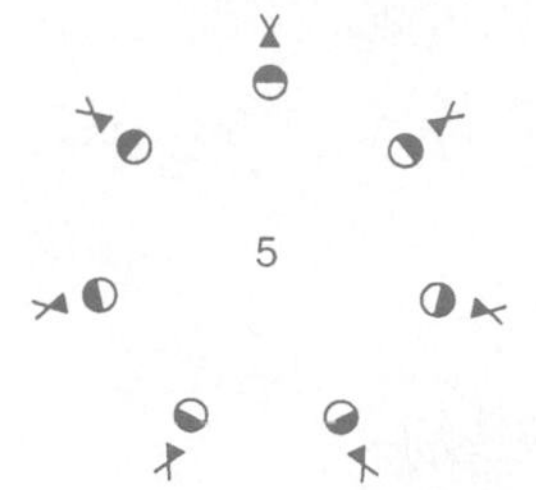

5. Partners facing each other

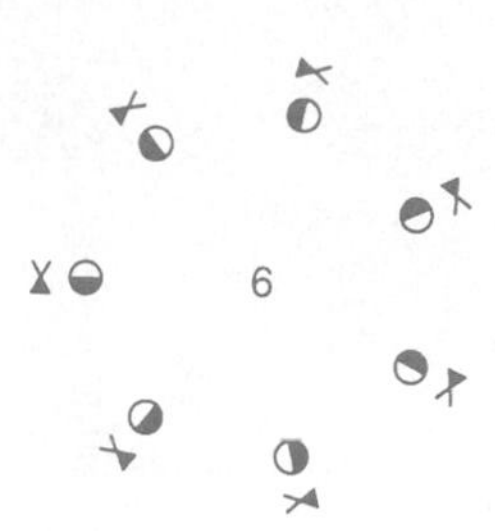

6. Partners side by side, facing counterclockwise

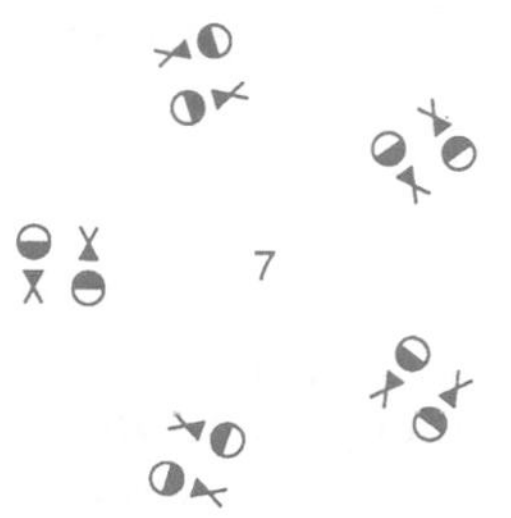

7. Sets of four, couples facing with girl on partner's right

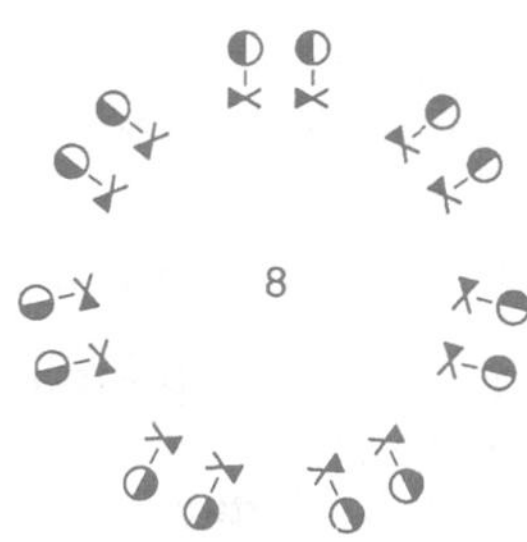

8. Sets of four, all facing counterclockwise

TRIPLE–CIRCLE FORMATIONS

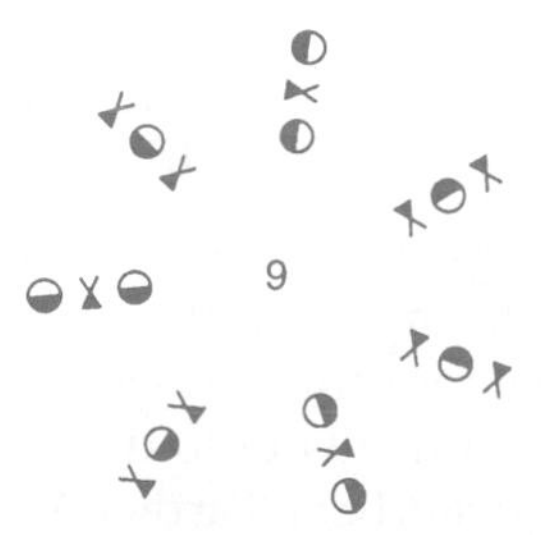

9. Standing side by side

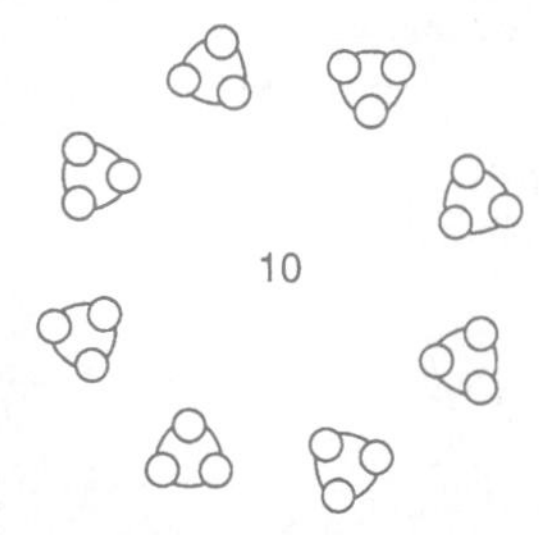

10. In small circles

OTHER FORMATIONS

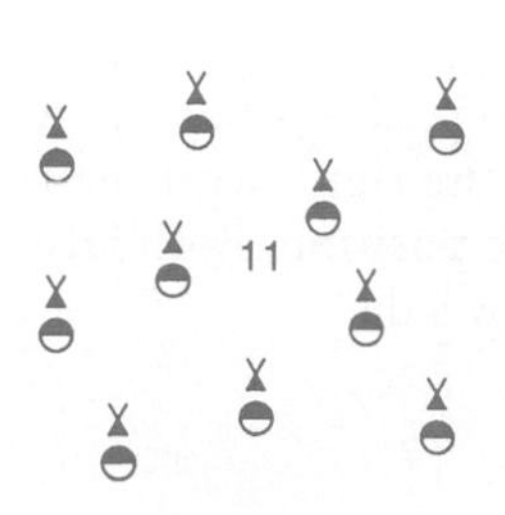

11. Partners in scattered formation

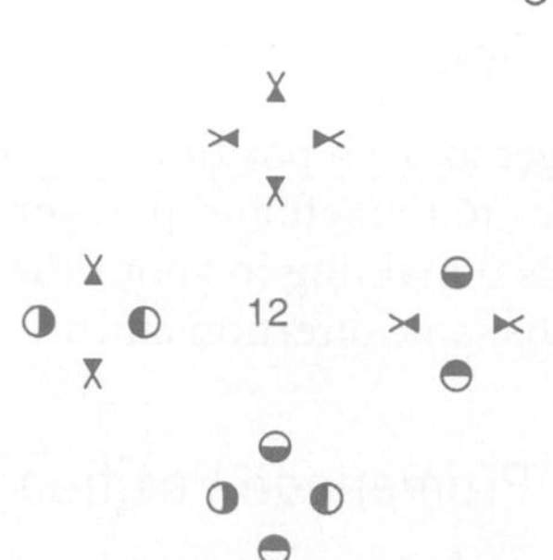

12. Groups of four, partners facing each other

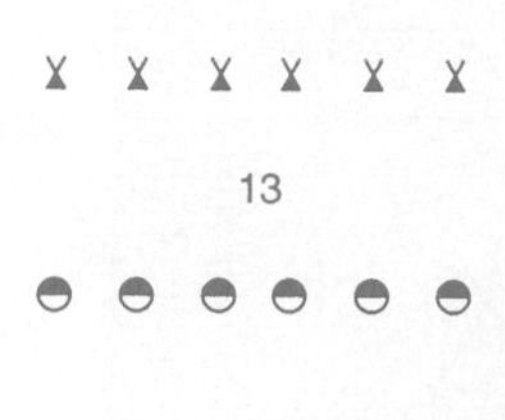

13. Longways set

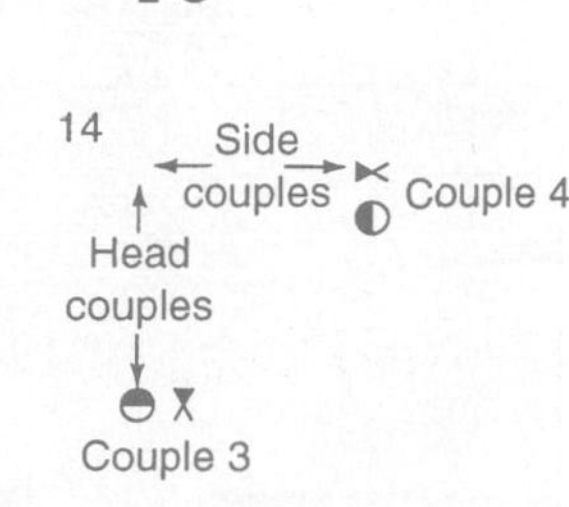

14. Square dance formation

FIGURE 19.1 Dance formations.

how the class should be arranged, the figure should be consulted. The formations are grouped into categories of single-circle, double-circle, triple-circle, and others.

Dance Positions

In most dance positions, partner A holds a hand or hands palms up and partner B joins the grip with a palms-down position. The following dance positions or partner positions are common to many dances.

Partners Facing Position

In partners facing position, as the name suggests, the partners are facing. Partner A extends hands forward with palms up and elbows slightly bent. Partner B places hands in A's hands.

Side-by-Side Position

In side-by-side position (Figure 19.2), partner A always has partner B to the right. Partner A offers the right hand, held above the waist, palm up. B places the left hand in A's raised hand.

FIGURE 19.2 Side-by-side position.

FIGURE 19.3 Promenade position.

Closed Position

Closed position is the social dance position. Partners stand facing each other, shoulders parallel, and toes pointed forward. Partner A holds partner B's right hand in A's left hand out to the side, at about shoulder level, with elbows bent. Partner A places the right hand on B's back, just below the left shoulder blade. B's left arm rests on A's upper arm, and B's left hand is on A's right shoulder.

Open Position

To get to open position from closed position, partner A turns to the left and partner B to the right, with their arms remaining in about the same position. Both face in the same direction and are side by side.

Promenade Position

Promenade position (Figure 19.3) is the crossed-arm position in which dancers stand side by side, facing the same direction, with the right hand held by partner's right and the left by partner's left.

Varsouvienne Position

Partners stand side by side and face the same direction. Partner B is slightly in front and to the right of Partner A. A holds B's left hand in his or her left hand in front and at about shoulder height. B brings the right hand directly back over the right shoulder, and A reaches behind B at shoulder height and grasps that hand with his or her right hand.

PROGRESSION OF FOLK DANCES

The dances in this section are listed in progression beginning with the easiest and progressing to the most difficult dance. Three developmental levels are listed to give you the widest possible latitude in selecting dances that fit the maturity and skill of the youngsters. Table 19.3 (pages 426–427) lists all dances in alphabetical order by developmental level and lists skills required for the dance. Dances throughout the chapter can be found easily by referring to the page number in the table. This table gives instructors a quick and clear overview of the total dance program.

Regarding level of difficulty, teachers must keep in mind that if a group of students is lacking in rhythmic background, the dances in the progression may be too difficult. A sixth-grade class, for example, lacking in dance skills, may need to begin with developmental level II dances. On the other hand, avoid boring a class by starting children on material below their maturity level.

DEVELOPMENTAL LEVEL I DANCES

Dances in this section contain movement songs and folk dances that are introductory in nature and involve simple formations and uncomplicated changes. The movements are primarily basic locomotor skills and hand gestures or clapping sequences. There are dances both with and without partners. As the difficulty of the dances increases, patterns become more definite, and more folk dances are included. The movements are still primarily of the simple locomotor type, with additional and varied emphasis on more complicated movement patterns.

MOVIN' MADNESS (AMERICAN)

Music Source: WWCD-1044

Skills: Keeping time, creativity

Formation: Scattered

Directions: The music is in two parts.

Part I: The tempo is slow, slow, fast-fast-fast. The children do any series of movements of their choice to fit this pattern, repeated four times. The movements should be large, gross motor movements.

Part II: During the second part (chorus) of the music, the children do any locomotor movement in keeping with the tempo. The step-hop or a light run can be used with the tempo of Part II.

TEACHING TIP

Have the youngsters clap the rhythm. They should pay particular attention to the tempo in Part I. The music is Bleking, a dance presented later. The music for "I See You" is also suitable, but note that the movements in Part I are repeated twice instead of four times. The Part II music is suitable for skipping, sliding, or galloping.

DID YOU EVER SEE A LASSIE? (SCOTTISH)

Music Source: WWCD-7054; WWC-7054

Skills: Walking at ¾ time, creativity

Formation: Single circle, facing halfway left, with hands joined; one child in the center

Directions:

Measures	***Action***
1–8	All walk (one step per measure) to the left in a circle with hands joined. (Walk, 2, 3, 4, 5, 6, 7, 8) The child in the center gets ready to demonstrate some type of movement.
9–16	All stop and copy the movement suggested by the child in the center.

As the verse starts over, the center child selects another to do some action in the center and changes places with him or her.

LOOBY LOO (ENGLISH)

Music Source: WWCD-7054; WWC-7054

Skills: Skipping or running, body identification

Formation: Single circle, facing center, hands joined

Directions: The chorus is repeated before each verse. During the chorus, all children skip around the circle to the right. On the verse part of the dance, the children stand still, face the center, and follow the directions of the words. On the words "and turn myself about," they make a complete turn in place and get ready to skip around the circle again. The movements should be definite and vigorous. On the last verse, they jump forward and then backward, shake vigorously, and then turn about.

The dance can be made more fun and more vigorous by changing the tasks in the song. Try these tasks: Right side or hip, left side or hip, big belly, backside.

TABLE 19.3 Alphabetical listing of folk dances by developmental level

Dance	Skills	Page
	Developmental Level I	
Ach Ja	Walking, sliding	428
Bleking	Bleking step, step-hop	432
Bombay Bounce	Hesitation step, side step	432
Carousel	Draw step, sliding	432
Children's Polka	Step-draw	430
Chimes of Dunkirk (Var. 1)	Turning in a small circle with a partner, changing partners	429
Chimes of Dunkirk (Var. 2)	Turning with a partner, skipping	431
Circassian Circle	Walking, skipping, promenade	434
Danish Dance of Greeting	Running or sliding, bowing	428
Did You Ever See a Lassie?	Walking at ¾ time, creativity	425
Eins Zwei Drei	Walking, sliding	431
Hokey Pokey	Body identification, nonlocomotor movements	428
How D'Ye Do, My Partner?	Bowing, curtsying, skipping	428
Hitch Hiker, The	Chug step, skipping	434
Jingle Bells (Var. 1)	Elbow swing, skipping, sliding	434
Jolly Is the Miller	Marching	432
Jump Jim Jo	Jumping, running, draw step	430
Looby Loo	Skipping or running, body identification	425
Movin' Madness	Keeping time, creativity	425
Muffin Man, The	Jumping, skipping	428
Nixie Polka	Bleking step	433
Rhythm Sticks (It's a Small, Small World)	Rhythmic tapping and manipulation of sticks	435
Seven Jumps	Step-hop, balance, control	429
Seven Steps	Running, hopping	435
Shoemaker's Dance	Skipping, heel and toe	430
Shortnin' Bread	Sliding, turning with a partner	430
Skip to My Lou	Skipping, changing partners	428
Turn the Glasses Over	Walking, wring the dishrag	433
Yankee Doodle	Walking, galloping, sliding, bowing	431
	Developmental Level II	
Apat Apat	Walking, star hold	444
Bingo	Walking, right-and-left grand	438
Bird Dance, The (Chicken Dance)	Skipping or walking, elbow swing or star	436
Crested Hen	Step-hop, turning under	442
Csebogar (Csehbogar)	Skipping, sliding, draw step, elbow swing	436
E-Z Mixer	Walking, elbow swing, or swing in closed position	441
Grand March	Controlled walking, marching, grand march figures	439
Green Sleeves	Walking, star formation, over and under	440
Gustaf's Skoal	Walking (stately), skipping, turning	443
Irish Washerwoman	Walking, elbow swing, promenade	442

TABLE 19.3 Alphabetical listing of folk dances by developmental level (continued)

Dance	Skills	Page
	Developmental Level II	
Jingle Bells (Var. 2)	Skipping, promenade position, sliding, elbow swing	440
La Raspa	Bleking step, running, elbow swing	437
Lummi Sticks	Rhythmic movements	446
Oh, Susanna	Walking, promenade position, grand right and left	442
Pata Pata	Toe touches, knee lifts, quarter turns	444
Patty Cake (Heel and Toe) Polka	Heel and toe polka step, sliding, elbow swing, skipping	438
Polly Wolly Doodle	Sliding, turning, walking	438
Pop Goes the Weasel	Walking, skipping, turning under	436
Popcorn	Toe touches, knee lifts, jumps	445
Red River Valley	Walk, buzz swing	446
Savila Se Bela Loza	Running step, crossover step, hop	445
Shoo Fly	Walking	444
Sicilian Circle	Walking, two-hand swing, wheel turn	446
Tinikling	Tinikling steps	447
Troika	Running step, turning under	443
Ve David	Walking, pivoting, buzz-step turn	441
Wild Turkey Mixer	Walking, elbow swing, partner change	437
	Developmental Level III	
Alley Cat	Grapevine step, touch step, knee lifts	454
Alunelul	Step behind step, grapevine step, stomping	458
Big Sombrero Circle Mixer	Circling, do-si-do, swing	460
Circle Virginia Reel	Star, swing, do-si-do, promenade	460
Cotton-Eyed Joe	Heel-toe, two-step	453
D'Hammerschmiedsgselln	Clapping routine, step-hops	456
Doudlebska Polka	Polka step, walking, clapping pattern	457
Hora	Stepping sideward, step-swing	451
Horse and Buggy Schottische	Schottische step	458
Inside-Out Mixer	Wring the dishrag, walking, changing partners	456
Jessie Polka	Step and touch, two-step or polka step	455
Jiffy Mixer	Heel-and-toe step, chug step	455
Jugglehead Mixer	Two-step, elbow turn (forearm grasp)	452
Kalvelis	Polka step, swing, clapping pattern, grand right and left	457
Klumpakojis	Walking, starts, polka step	454
Korobushka	Schottische step, balance step, cross-out-together step, walking step	459
Limbo Rock	Touch step, swivel step, jump clap step	455
Oh Johnny	Shuffle step, swing, allemande left, do-si-do, promenade	459
Shindig in the Barn	Walking, do-si-do, swinging, sliding	459
Ten Pretty Girls	Walking, grapevine	455
Teton Mountain Stomp	Walking, banjo position, sidecar position, two-step	453
Trio Fun Mixer	Walking, do-si-do, star	460
Virginia Reel	Skipping, arm turn, do-si-do, sliding (sashay), reeling	451

HOKEY POKEY (AMERICAN)

Music Source: WWCD-4903; WWC-9126

Skills: Body identification, nonlocomotor movements

Formation: Single circle, facing center

Directions: During the first four lines, the children act out the words. During lines 5 and 6, they hold their hands overhead with palms forward and do a kind of hula while turning around in place. During line 7, they stand in place and clap their hands three times.

The basic verse is repeated by substituting, successively, the left foot, right arm, left arm, right elbow, left elbow, head, right hip, left hip, whole self, and backside.

TEACHING TIP

Encourage the youngsters to make large and vigorous motions during the hokey pokey portions and during the turn around. This adds to the fun. The children should sing lightly as they follow the directions given in the song.

THE MUFFIN MAN (AMERICAN)

Music Source: WWCD-YR002; WWC-YR002

Skills: Jumping, skipping

Formation: Single circle, facing center, hands at sides. One child, the Muffin Man, stands in front of another child of the opposite gender.

Directions:

Verse 1: The children stand still and clap their hands lightly, with the exception of the Muffin Man and his partner. These two join hands and jump lightly in place while keeping time to the music. On the first beat of each measure, a normal jump is taken, followed by a bounce in place (rebound) on the second beat.

Verse 2: The Muffin Man and his partner then skip around the inside of the circle individually and, near the end of the verse, each stands in front of a child, thus choosing a new partner.

Verse 1 is then repeated, with two sets of partners doing the jumping. During the repetition of verse 2, four children skip around the inside of the circle and choose partners. This procedure continues until all children have been chosen.

The children choose the name of a street to put in the verses.

SKIP TO MY LOU (AMERICAN)

Music Source: WWCD-7054; WWC-7054

Skills: Skipping, changing partners

Formation: Scattered with a partner

Directions: During the chorus, partners skip around the area. At the verse, everyone finds a new partner and continues skipping.

HOW D'YE DO, MY PARTNER? (SWEDISH)

Music Source: WWCD-1041; WWC-07042

Skills: Bowing, curtsying, skipping

Formation: Double circle, partners facing, partner A on inside

Directions:

Measures	*Action*
1–2	Partners A bow to their partner. (Bow)
3–4	Partners B bow. (Bow)
5–6	A offers the right hand to B, who takes it with the right hand. (Join right hands) Both turn to face counterclockwise. (Face counterclockwise)
7–8	Couples join left hands in promenade position in preparation to skip when the music changes. (Join left hands)
9–16	Partners skip counterclockwise in the circle, slowing down on measure 15. (Skip) On measure 16, Bs stop and As move ahead to secure a new partner. (New partner)

DANISH DANCE OF GREETING (DANISH)

Music Source: WWCD-1041; WWC-07042

Skills: Running or sliding, bowing

Formation: Single circle, all face center. Partner A stands to the left of partner B.

Directions:

Measures	*Action*
1	All clap twice and bow to partner. (Clap, clap, bow)
2	Repeat but turn back to the partner and bow to the neighbor. (Clap, clap, bow)
3	Stamp right, stamp left. (Stamp, stamp)
4	Turn around in four running steps. (Turn, 2, 3, 4)
5–8	Repeat the action of measures 1–4.
9–12	All join hands and run to the left for four measures. (Run, 2, 3, 4, . . . 16)
13–16	Repeat the action of measures 9–12, taking light running steps in the opposite direction. (Run, 2, 3, 4, . . . 16)

TEACHING TIP

Variation: Instead of a running step, use a light slide.

ACH JA (GERMAN)

Music Source: WWCD-0860; WWC-0860

Skills: Walking, sliding

Formation: Double circle, partners facing counterclockwise, partners A on the inside, inside hands joined

Directions: Explain that "Ach Ja" means "Oh yes."

Measures	*Action*
1–2	Partners walk eight steps in the line of direction. (Walk, 2, 3, 4, 5, 6, 7, 8)
3	Partners drop hands and bow to each other. (Bow)
4	Each A then bows to the B on the left, who returns the bow. (Bow)
5–8	Measures 1–4 are repeated.
9–10	Partners face each other, join hands, and take four slides in the line of direction. (Slide, 2, 3, 4)
11–12	Four slides are taken clockwise. (Slide, 2, 3, 4)
13	Partners bow to each other. (Bow)
14	A bows to the B on the left, who returns the bow. (Bow) To start the next dance, A moves quickly toward this B, who is the next partner.

SEVEN JUMPS (DANISH)

Music Source: WWCD-1043; WWC-3528

Skills: Step-hop, balance, control

Formation: Single circle, hands joined

Directions: There are seven jumps to the dance. Each jump is preceded by the following action.

Measures	*Action*
1–8	The circle moves to the right with seven step-hops, one to each measure. On the eighth measure, all jump high in the air and reverse direction. (Step-hop, 2-hop, 3-hop, . . . 7-hop, change direction)
9–16	Circle to the left with seven step-hops. Stop on measure 16 and face the center. (Step-hop, 2-hop, 3-hop, . . . 7-hop, face center)
17	All drop hands, place their hands on hips, and lift the right knee upward with the toes pointed downward. (Knee up)
18	All stamp the right foot to the ground on the signal note, then join hands on the next note. (Stamp)
1–18	Repeat measures 1–18, but do not join hands.
19	Lift the left knee, stamp, and join hands.
1–19	Repeat measures 1–19, but do not join hands.
20	Put the right toe backward and kneel on the right knee. Stand and join hands.
1–20	Repeat measures 1–20; do not join hands.
21	Kneel on the left knee. Stand and join hands.
1–21	Repeat measures 1–21; do not join hands.
22	Put the right elbow to the floor with the cheek on the fist. Stand and join hands.
1–22	Repeat measures 1–22; do not join hands.
23	Put the left elbow to the floor with the cheek on the fist. Stand and join hands.
1–23	Repeat measures 1–23; do not join hands.
24	Put forehead on the floor. Stand, join hands.
1–16	Repeat measures 1–16.

TEACHING TIP

This dance was performed originally in Denmark by men as a control-elimination competition. Those who made unnecessary movements or mistakes were eliminated.

Variation: To increase motivation, the dance can be done with a parachute. The dancers hold the parachute taut with one hand during the step-hops. The chute is kept taut with both hands for all jumps except the last, during which the forehead touches the chute on the floor.

CHIMES OF DUNKIRK, VAR. 1 (FRENCH-BELGIAN)

Music Source: WWCD-1042; WWC-07042

Skills: Turning in a small circle with a partner, changing partners

Formation: Double circle, partners facing

Directions:

Measures	*Action*
1–2	Stamp three times in place, right-left-right. (Stamp, 2, 3)
3–4	Clap hands three times above the head (chimes in the steeple). (Clap, 2, 3)
5–8	Partner A places both hands on partner B's hips; B places both hands on A's shoulders. Taking four steps, they turn around in place. (Turn, 2, 3, 4) On the next four counts, partner B (on the outside) moves one person to the left with four steps. (Change, 2, 3, 4) Repeat the sequence from the beginning.

TEACHING TIP

An alternative to the turn described is to do an elbow turn by linking right elbows.

SHORTNIN' BREAD (AMERICAN)

Music Source: WWCD-7050; WWC-7050

Skills: Sliding, turning with a partner

Formation: Scattered with partner

Directions:

Measures	*Action*
1–2	Clap own hands
3–4	Slap partner's hands, palms together
5–6	Clap own hands
7–8	Slap own thighs
9–16	Repeat measures 1–8
17–20	Couples slide to the right holding hands.
21–24	Circle holding hands.
25–32	Repeat measures 17–24 moving to the left.

CHILDREN'S POLKA (GERMAN)

Music Source: WWCD-07042; WWC-07042

Formation: Single circle of couples, partners facing

Skills: Step-draw

Directions:

Measures	*Action*
1–2	Take two step-draw steps toward the center of the circle, ending with three steps in place. (Draw, draw, step, 2, 3)
3–4	Take two step-draw steps away from the center, ending with three steps in place. (Draw, draw, step, 2, 3)
5–8	Repeat the pattern of measures 1–4.
9	Slap own knees once with both hands; clap own hands once. (Slap, clap)
10	Clap both hands with partner three times. (Clap, 2, 3)
11–12	Repeat the pattern of measures 9 and 10.
13	Hop, placing one heel forward, and shake the forefinger at partner three times. (Scold, 2, 3)
14	Repeat the "scolding" pattern with the other foot and hand. (Scold, 2, 3)
15–16	Turn once around in place with four running steps and stamp three times in place. (Turn, 2, 3, 4; Stamp, 2, 3)

SHOEMAKER'S DANCE (DANISH)

Music Source: WWCD-1042; WWC-07042

Skills: Skipping, heel and toe

Formation: Double circle, partners facing, with partner A's back to the center of the circle

Directions:

Measures	*Part I Action*
1	With arms bent and at shoulder height, and with hands clenched to form fists, circle one fist over the other in front of the chest. (Wind the thread)
2	Reverse the circular motion and wind the thread in the opposite direction. (Reverse direction)
3	Pull the elbows back vigorously twice. (Pull and tighten the thread)
4	Clap own hands three times. (Clap, 2, 3)
5–7	Repeat the pattern of measures 1–3.
8	Tap own fists together three times to drive the nails. (Tap, 2, 3)
	Part II Action
9–16	Partners face counterclockwise, inside hands joined. Skip counterclockwise, ending with a bow. (Skip, 2, 3, . . . 15, bow)

TEACHING TIP

Variation of Part II Action

9	Place the heel of the outside foot forward (counts 1 and), and point the toe of the outside foot in back (2 and).
10	Take three running steps forward, starting with the outside foot and pausing on the last count.
11–12	Repeat the pattern of measures 9–10, starting with the inside foot.
13–16	Repeat the pattern of measures 9–12, entire "heel and toe and run, run, run" pattern dance, four times singing Part II verse.

JUMP JIM JO (AMERICAN)

Music Source: WWCD-1041

Skills: Jumping, running, draw step

Formation: Double circle, partners facing, both hands joined

Directions:

Measures	*Action*
1–2	Do two jumps sideward, progressing counterclockwise, followed by three quick jumps in place. (Slow, slow, fast, fast, fast)
3–4	Release hands and turn once around in place with four jumps (two jumps per measure). Finish facing partner and rejoin hands. (Jump, turn, 3, 4)

5	Take two sliding steps sideward, progressing counterclockwise. (Slide, slide)
6	Partners face counterclockwise with inside hands joined and tap three times with the toe of the outside foot. (Tap, tap, tap)
7–8	Take four running steps forward, then face partner, join both hands, and end with three jumps in place. (Run, 2, 3, 4; Jump, 2, 3)

YANKEE DOODLE (AMERICAN)

Music Source: WWCD-FDN

Skills: Walking, galloping, sliding, bowing

Formation: Scattered or open circle facing counterclockwise

Directions:

Measures	*Action*
1–4	All gallop 8 steps (Gallop, 2, . . . 8)
5–8	All stop, face center, point to cap and bow on word "macaroni." (Stop, point, bow)
9–12	All join hands and take six slides to the right and stamp feet two times on word "dandy." (Slide, 2, 3, . . . 6; Stamp, stamp)
13–16	All slide six times to the left and clap hands two times on the word "candy." (Slide, 2, 3, . . . 6; Clap clap)

TEACHING TIP

Variation: Change the locomotor movements to fit the age and interest of the group. Have the class create new movement patterns.

EINS ZWEI DREI (GERMAN)

Music Source: WWCD-1042

Skills: Walking, sliding

Formation: Single circle of couples (partner B to partner A's right) facing the center and numbered alternately couple 1, 2, 1, 2

Directions: Explain that "Eins, Zwei, Drei" means "one, two, three" in German.

Measures	*Part I Action*
1–2	Couples 1 take three steps toward the center of the circle as they clap their hands by brushing them vertically like cymbals. (Forward, 2, 3, pause)
3–4	Couples 1 repeat measures 1–2, walking backward to place. (Back, 2, 3, pause)
5–8	Couples 1 face, join both hands, and take four slides toward the center of the circle and four slides back to place. Partner A starts with the left foot, partner B with the right. (Slide, 2, 3, 4)
9–16	Couples 2 repeat measures 1–8.
	Part II Action
17	Partner A turns and touches the right heel sideward while shaking the right index finger at partner. Partner B does the same with the left heel and left index finger. (Scold, 2, 3)
18	Repeat measure 17 with the corner, reversing footwork and hands. (Scold, 2, 3)
19–20	Repeat measures 17 and 18.
21–24	All join hands and circle left with eight slides. (Slide, 2, 3, . . . 8)
25–32	Repeat measures 17–24, reversing the direction of the slides. (Slide, 2, 3, . . . 8)

TEACHING TIP

Variation: To facilitate learning, practice all steps individually in a scattered formation.

CHIMES OF DUNKIRK, VAR. 2 (FRENCH-BELGIAN)

Music Source: WWCD-1042

Skills: Turning with a partner, skipping

Formation: Single circle of couples, partners facing

Directions:

Measures	*Action*
1–2	Stamp three times in place. (Stamp, 2, 3)
3–4	Clap own hands three times. (Clap, 2, 3)
5–8	Do a two-hand swing with partner. Join both hands with partner and turn once clockwise with eight running or skipping steps. (Swing, 2, 3, . . . 8)
Chorus Action	
1–8	Circle left, singing, "Tra, la, la, la, la, . . ." All join hands and circle left with 16 running or skipping steps, ending with a bow. (Run, 2, 3, . . . 15, bow)

TEACHING TIP

The dance can also be used as a mixer by partner B's advancing one partner to the left. Also, instead of a two-hand swing with partner, substitute the shoulder-waist position. A places a hand on B's waist, and B places both hands on A's shoulders.

To facilitate forming the circle for the chorus, make a four-step turn instead of an eight-step turn on measures 5–8. This gives the children four counts to get ready for the circle formation and four counts to make the circle.

BOMBAY BOUNCE

Music Source: Any music with a definite and moderately fast beat

Skills: Hesitation step, side step

Formation: Scattered, all facing forward

Part I (16 counts): A hesitation step to the left is performed by taking a short step to the left followed by touching the right foot near the left while the weight remains on the left foot. A hesitation step to the right is similar except it begins with a step to the right. To begin the dance, eight hesitation steps are performed in place with a hand clap on each touch. (Left, touch and clap; right, touch and clap) Repeat 4 times.

Part II (16 counts): Take two side steps to the left, then two to the right. Clap on counts 4 and 8. (Left, close; Left, close and clap; Right, close; Right, close and clap). Repeat the pattern.

Part III (16 counts): Take four side steps left and four side steps right. Clap only on count 8. (Left, close, left, close, left, close, left, close and clap). Repeat to the right.

Part IV (16 counts): Take four steps forward and four steps backward, four steps forward and four steps backward. Clap on counts 4, 8, 12, and 16. (Forward, 2, 3, 4 and clap; Backward, 2, 3, 4 and clap; Forward, 2, 3, 4 and clap; Backward 2, 3, 4 and clap)

TEACHING TIP

Variations are possible (e.g., in Part IV, instead of four steps, use three steps and a kick [swing].)

CAROUSEL (SWEDISH)

Music Source: WWCD-1041

Skills: Draw step, sliding

Formation: Double circle, facing center. The inner circle, representing a merry-go-round, joins hands. The outer players, representing the riders, place their hands on the hips of the partner in front.

Directions:

Measures	***Verse Action***
1–16	Moving to the left, children take 12 slow draw steps and stamp on the last three steps. (Step, together, 2, 3, . . . 12, stamp, stamp, stamp, rest)

Measures	***Chorus Action***
17–24	Moving left, speed up the draw step until it becomes a slide or gallop. Sing the chorus. (Slide, 2, 3, . . . 8)
25–32	Repeat measures 17–24 while moving to the right. (Slide, 2, 3, . . . 8)

During the chorus, the tempo is increased, and the movement is changed to a slide. Children should take short, light slides to prevent the circle from moving out of control.

TEACHING TIP

Variation: The dance can also be done with youngsters holding the perimeter of a parachute.

JOLLY IS THE MILLER (AMERICAN)

Music Source: WWC-317

Skills: Marching

Formation: Double circle, partners facing counterclockwise, the A partners on the inside, with inside hands joined. A "miller" is in the center of the circle.

Directions: All sing. Youngsters march counterclockwise, with inside hands joined. During the second line when "the wheel goes round," the dancers turn their outside arm in a circle to form a wheel. Children change partners at the words "right steps forward and the left steps back." The miller then has a chance to get a partner. The child left without a partner becomes the next miller.

BLEKING (SWEDISH)

Music Source: WWCD-1044; WWC-07042

Skills: Bleking step, step-hop

Formation: Single circle, partners facing, both hands joined. Partners A face counterclockwise and partners B clockwise.

Directions:

Part I—The Bleking Step: Cue by calling "Slow-slow, fast-fast-fast."

Measures	***Action***
1	Hop on the left foot and extend the right heel forward with the right leg straight. At the same time, thrust the right hand forward. Hop on the right foot, reversing the arm action and extending the left foot to rest on the heel. (Slow, slow)
2	Repeat the action with three quick changes—left, right, left. (Fast, fast, fast)
3–4	Beginning on the right foot, repeat the movements of measures 1 and 2. (Slow, slow, fast, fast, fast)
5–8	Repeat measures 1–4.

Part II—The Windmills: Partners extend their joined hands sideways at shoulder height.

Measures	***Action***
9–16	Partners turn in place with a repeated step-hop. At the same time, the arms move

up and down like a windmill. The turning is done clockwise, with A starting on the right foot and B on the left. At the completion of the step-hops (16), the partners should be in their original places ready for Part I again. (Step-hop, 2-hop, 3-hop, . . . 16-hop)

TEACHING TIP

Variations:

1. Change from original positions to a double circle, partners facing, A partners with back to the center. Part I is as described. For Part II, all face counterclockwise, and partners join inside hands. Partners do the basic schottische of "step, step, step, hop" throughout Part II (page 458).
2. Another excellent variation is to do the dance with partners scattered in general space. Part I is as described. For Part II, the children leave their partners and step-hop in various directions around the dancing area. When the music is about to change back to Part I, performers find a partner wherever they can, and the dance is repeated.
3. Bleking is excellent music for creative dance, with the stipulation that the children maintain individually the bleking rhythm of "slow-slow, fast-fast-fast" during Part I and do any kind of movement in place that they wish. During Part II, they may do any locomotor or other movement that they choose.

NIXIE POLKA (NIGAREPOLSKA) (SWEDISH)

Music Source: WWCD-1041; WWC-572

Skills: Bleking step

Formation: Single circle, all facing center, with one or more children scattered inside the circle

Measures	***Part I Action***
1–4	With hands joined, all spring lightly onto the left foot and extend the right foot forward, heel to ground, toe up. Next, spring lightly onto the right foot and extend the left foot forward. Repeat this action until four slow bleking steps are completed. (Slow, slow, slow, slow)
5–8	All clap hands once and shout "Hey!" The center child then runs around the inside of the circle, looking for a partner, finally selecting one. They join both hands and run lightly in place until the music is finished. This refrain is repeated, so the children have time to get back to the center of the circle. (Clap, run)
	Part II Action
1–4	The center dancer and partner, with both hands joined, repeat the action of measures 1–4. All dancers in the circle also repeat the action of measures 1–4. (Slow, slow, slow, slow)
5–8	On the first count, all clap hands, shouting "Hey!" The center dancer then about-faces and places both hands on the shoulders of partner, who now becomes the new leader. In this position, both shuffle around the inside of the circle, looking for a third person to dance with. The music is repeated again to allow ample time to return to the center. (Clap, run)
	Part III Action
1–4	The action of measures 1–4 is repeated, with the new dancer facing the circle and the two others facing the new dancer. (Slow, slow, slow, slow)
5–8	On the first count, all clap hands, shouting "Hey!" The two people in the center then about-face. All three now face the center to form a line of three dancers with a new leader, who looks for a fourth dancer. The music is repeated. (Clap, run)

The entire dance is thus repeated, accumulating dancers with each repetition. There should be one center dancer for each dozen dancers in the circle.

TURN THE GLASSES OVER (AMERICAN-ENGLISH)

Music Source: WWCD-W0F1

Skills: Walking, wring the dishrag

Formation: Single circle of couples in promenade position. Extra students are in the center.

Directions:

Measures	***Verse Action***
1–16	The couples walk forward singing the verse. At the words "turn the glasses over," they raise their arms, keeping the hands joined, and turn under the raised arms, making one complete outward "dishrag" turn. Youngsters must anticipate the turn and be prepared to start in time to complete the movement by the end of the phrase.
Measures	***Chorus Action***
1–16	Youngsters in the outer circle continue walking while those in the inner circle turn and walk in the opposite direction. An extra player(s) joins one of the circles and

continues with the group. At the words "girl in the ocean," youngsters take the nearest person for a new partner. Those without a partner move to the center.

JINGLE BELLS, VAR. 1 (DUTCH)

Music Source: Any version of Jingle Bells

Skills: Elbow swing, skipping, sliding

Formation: Double circle, partners facing, with both hands joined

Directions:

Measures	*Action*
1–2	Partners take eight slides counterclockwise. (Slide, 2, 3, . . . 8)
3–4	Partners turn so they are standing back to back, and take eight more slides in the line of direction. This move is best made by dropping the front hands and swinging the back hands forward until the dancers are standing back to back. They rejoin the hands that are now in back. Make this move with no loss of rhythm. (Slide, 2, 3, . . . 8)
5–6	Repeat the action of measures 1 and 2. To get back to the face-to-face position, let go of the back hands and swing the front hands backward, allowing the bodies to pivot and face again. (Slide, 2, 3, . . . 8)
7–8	Repeat measures 3 and 4. (Slide, 2, 3, . . . 8)
	Chorus Action
1	Clap own hands three times. (Clap own, 2, 3)
2	Clap both hands with partner three times. (Clap both, 2, 3)
3	Clap own hands four times. (Clap own, 2, 3, 4)
4	Clap both hands with partner once. (Clap both)
5–8	Right elbow swing with partner. Partners hook right elbows and swing clockwise with eight skips. (Swing, 2, 3, 4, 5, 6, 7, 8)
9–12	Repeat clapping sequence of measures 1–4.
13–16	Left elbow swing with partner for eight skips, finishing in the original starting position, ready to repeat the entire dance with the same partner; or do a left elbow swing with partner for four skips, which is once around, then all children in the inner circle skip forward to the outer dancer ahead and repeat the entire dance from the beginning with a new partner. (Swing, 2, 3, 4, 5, 6, 7, 8)

THE HITCH HIKER (AMERICAN)

Music Source: WWCD-FDN

Skills: Chug step (a short backward jump with the feet together on the floor), skipping

Formation: Double circle, partners facing each other with boys inside facing out

Directions:

Measures	*Action*
2	Introduction
1–2	Take two chugs away from partner and clap hands on each step. Jerk right thumb over right shoulder while twisting right foot with heel on the floor. Repeat. (Chug chug, right, right)
3–4	Same as measures 1–2 except use left thumb and foot. (Chug, chug, left, left)
5–6	Same as measures 1–2 except use both thumbs and feet. (Chug, chug, both, both)
7–8	Skip diagonally forward and to the right toward a new partner with four skips; continue with four more skips around your new partner with right hands joined and get ready to repeat the dance. (Skip, 2, 3, 4, around, 2, 3, 4)

The sequence repeats eight times.

CIRCASSIAN CIRCLE (ENGLISH)

Music Source: WWCD-FDN

Skills: Walking, skipping, promenade

Formation: Large single circle of couples facing center with all hands joined

Directions:

Measures	*Action*
2	Introduction
1–2	All walk four steps toward center and back four steps to place (Walk 2, 3, 4; back, 2, 3, 4)
3–4	Repeat measures 1 and 2 (Walk 2, 3, 4; back, 2, 3, 4)
5–6	Girls walk four steps toward center and back four steps (Girls, 2, 3, 4; back, 2, 3, 4)
7–8	Boys walk four steps toward center, then turn a half-turn left and walk diagonally clockwise four steps to a new partner. (Boys, 2, 3, 4; move to new partner)

9–10	Using a cross-arm grip, new partners lean away from each other and skip eight steps clockwise once around each other. (Skip, 2, 3, 4, 5, 6, 7, 8)
11–12	Without dropping hands, couples promenade counterclockwise for eight steps. Take the last two steps to stop and face the center to do the dance again. (Promenade, 2, 3, 4, 5, 6, face center)

The dance is performed four times.

SEVEN STEPS (AUSTRIAN)

Music Source: WWCD-FDN

Skills: Running, hopping

Formation: Double circle with couples facing counterclockwise with inside hands joined

Directions:

Measures	*Action*
2	Introduction
1–2	Start with outside foot and run seven steps forward counterclockwise, and then pause with weight on outside foot on eighth count. (Run, 2, 3, 4, 5, 6, 7, pause)
3–4	Start with inside foot and run seven steps backward (clockwise), and then pause with weight on inside foot on eighth count. (Run, back, 3, 4, 5, 6, 7, pause)
5	Release hands, turn away from partner and starting with the outside foot, run three steps away from partner and hop on the outside foot on the fourth count. (Away, 2, 3, hop)
6	Turn and face partner and starting with the inside foot, run three steps toward partner and then hop on the inside foot on the fourth count. (Back, 2, 3, hop)
7–8	Partners with right hands joined run once around each other with eight running steps clockwise to the right. (Swing, 2, 3, 4, 5, 6, 7, 8)
9	Release hands, turn away from partner and starting with the outside foot, run three steps away from partner; on the fourth count hop and turn on the outside foot to face diagonally toward new partner. (Apart, 2, 3, hop)
10	Take three running steps to a new partner (inside partner moves counterclockwise forward diagonally toward new partner and outside partner moves clockwise backward diagonally to next partner). Then hop on the fourth count.
11–12	New partners run once around each other with eight running steps counterclockwise with left hands joined. Finish in starting position with inside hands joined.

Perform the dance a total of five times.

RHYTHM STICKS – IT'S A SMALL, SMALL WORLD (AMERICAN)

Music Source: WWCD-2015; WWC-2015

Skills: Rhythmic tapping and manipulation of sticks

Formation: Children sitting cross-legged individually scattered around the area

Rhythm sticks or lummi sticks are 12 to 15 inches in length. Activities may be done individually or in partners. This routine is done individually. The sticks are held in the thumb and the forefinger at about the bottom third of the stick.

Measures	*Call*	*Action*
1–2	Down, cross, down, cross	Tap ends of both sticks on the floor, and then cross the arms over, tapping the sticks on the floor again.
3–4	Down, cross, down, cross	Repeat
5–6	Down, cross, down, cross	Repeat
7–8	Chorus: It's a small, small world.	Lean forward touching head to knees (curl forward).
9–10	Tap, tap, knees, knees	Tap sticks two times in front of the chest, and then lightly tap the knees twice.
11–12	Tap, tap, knees, knees	Repeat
13–14	Tap, tap, knees, knees	Repeat
15–16	Chorus: It's a small, small world.	Lean forward touching head to knees (curl forward).

The sequence above repeats a number of times with touches to the toes, shoulders, head, and nose. As a variation, youngsters can face a partner and tap both of their sticks to their partner's sticks.

DEVELOPMENTAL LEVEL II DANCES

Developmental level II activities focus clearly on folk dance. Locomotor skills are still the basis of the movement patterns, but in most of the dances, the patterns are more difficult than those in developmental level I. At this level, each dance always has at least two parts and may have three or more. Because the movement patterns are longer, the part-whole teaching method is used more often with this age group. These dances are vigorous and fast moving, which makes them exciting for youngsters to perform.

Tinikling and lummi sticks are introduced at this level, which lend challenge and novelty to the progression. Emphasis should be on participation and enjoyment without excessive concern for perfection. Normal progress through the rhythms program will assure that adequate quality will result.

THE BIRD DANCE (CHICKEN DANCE)

Music Source: WWCD-4903; WWC-9126

Skills: Skipping or walking, elbow swing or star

Formation: Circle or scatter formation, partners facing

Directions:

Measures	***Part I Action***
1	Four snaps—thumb and fingers, hands up
2	Four flaps—arms up and down, elbows bent
3	Four wiggles—hips, knees bent low
4	Four claps
5–16	Repeat action of measures 1–4 three times
	Part II Action
1–8	With a partner, either do a right-hand star with 16 skips or 16 walking steps, or do an elbow swing. (Skip, 2, 3, . . . 15, change hands)
9–16	Repeat with the left hand. On the last four counts of the last swing, everyone changes partners. If dancing in a circle formation, partners B advance forward counterclockwise to the next partner A. If dancing in a scattered formation, everyone scrambles to find a new partner. (Skip, 2, 3, . . . 12, change partners)

TEACHING TIP

Perform the dance individually, with everyone moving to find a new partner on the skipping sequence. The locomotor movements can be varied to include sliding or galloping.

CSEBOGAR (HUNGARIAN)

Music Source: WWCD-1042

Skills: Skipping, sliding, draw step, elbow swing

Formation: Single circle, partners facing center, hands joined with partners B on the right

Directions:

Part I:

Measures	***Action***
1–4	Take seven slides to the left. (Slide, 2, 3, 4, 5, 6, 7, change)
5–8	Take seven slides to the right. (Back, 2, 3, 4, 5, 6, 7, stop)
9–12	Take three skips to the center and stamp on the fourth beat. Take three skips backward to place and stamp on the eighth beat. (Forward, 2, 3, stamp; Backward, 2, 3, stamp)
13–16	Hook right elbows with partner and turn around twice in place, skipping. (Swing, 2, 3, 4, 5, 6, 7, 8)

Part II: Partners face each other in a single circle with hands joined.

Measures	***Action***
17–20	Holding both of partner's hands, take four draw steps (step, close) toward the center of the circle. (Step-close, 2-close, 3-close, 4-close)
21–24	Take four draw steps back to place. (Step-close, 2-close, 3-close, 4-close)
25–26	Go toward the center of the circle with two draw steps. (In-close, 2-close)
27–28	Take two draw steps back to place. (Out-close, 2-close)
29–32	Hook elbows and repeat the elbow swing, finishing with a shout and facing the center of the circle in the original formation. (Swing, 2, 3, 4, 5, "Csebogar")

TEACHING TIP

Instead of an elbow swing, partners can use the Hungarian turn. Partners stand side by side, put the right arm around the partner's waist, and lean away from partner. The left arm is held out to the side, with the elbow bent, the hand pointing up, and the palm facing the dancer.

POP GOES THE WEASEL (AMERICAN)

Music Source: WWCD-1043; WWCD-FDN

Skills: Walking, skipping, turning under

Formation: Double circle of sets of four; couples facing with partner B on partner A's right. Couples facing clockwise are number 1 couples; couples facing counterclockwise are number 2 couples.

Directions:

Measures	*Action*
1–4	Join hands in a circle of four and circle left, once around, with eight skipping or sliding steps. (Circle, 2, 3, 4, 5, 6, 7, 8)
5–6	Take two steps forward, raising the joined hands, and two steps backward, lowering the hands. (Forward, 2; Back, 2)
7–8	"Ones" pop the "Twos" under (i.e., couples number 1 raise their joined hands to form an arch and pass the number 2 couples under). All walk ahead to meet a new couple. (Forward, and pop through)

Repeat as desired.

TEACHING TIP

Variations:

1. Dancers are in sets of three, all facing counterclockwise. Each forms a triangle with one child in front and the other two with joined hands forming the base. The front dancer reaches back and holds the outside hands of the other two dancers. The groups of three are in a large circle formation.

Measures	***Action***
1–2	Sets of three dancers skip forward four times. (Forward, 2, 3, 4)
3–4	Sets of three skip backward four times. (Backward, 2, 3, 4)
5–6	Sets of three skip forward four times. (Forward, 2, 3, 4)
7–8	On "Pop goes the weasel," the two back dancers raise their joined hands, and the front dancer backs up underneath to the next set. This set, in the meantime, has "popped" its front dancer back to the set behind it. (Raise and pop under)

2. "Pop Goes the Weasel" is excellent for stimulating creative movement. The music actually consists of a verse and a chorus part. During the verse part, the children can slide, gallop, or skip until the "Pop" line, at which time they make a half or full turn in the air. During the chorus, they can do jerky nonlocomotor movements. Other options include ball routines, in which the children dribble in time to the music during the verse and pass the ball around various parts of the body during the chorus. Another variation involves ropes. The children carry a jump rope while skipping, sliding, or galloping. During the chorus, they jump in time to the music, and on the word "Pop," they try to do a double jump.

WILD TURKEY MIXER

Music Source: WWC-FFD or any music with a definite rhythm

Skills: Walking, elbow swing, partner change

Formation: Trios abreast facing counterclockwise around the circle

Directions:

Measures	*Action*
1–8	In lines of three, with the right and left person holding the near hand of the center person, all walk 16 steps forward. (Walk, 2, 3, . . . 16)
9–12	The center person (Wild Turkey) turns the right-hand person once around with the right elbow. (Turn, 2, 3, 4, 5, 6, 7, 8)
13–16	The Wild Turkey turns the left-hand person with the left elbow, and then moves forward to repeat the dance with the two new people ahead. (Turn, 2, 3, 4; Forward, 2, 3, 4)

The same dance can be adapted to other pieces of music. With a faster tempo, the elbow swings are done with a skip instead of a walk.

LA RASPA (MEXICAN)

Music Source: WWCD-05117

Skills: Bleking step, running, elbow swing

Formation: Partners facing, couples scattered around room

Directions: La raspa means "the rasp" or "the file," and the dance movements are supposed to represent a rasp or file in action. Directions are the same for both partners.

Part I: To begin, the partners face each other, partner B with hands at sides and partner A with hands behind the back.

Measures	*Action*
1–4	Beginning right, take one Bleking step (page 432). (Slow, slow, fast, fast, fast)
5–8	Turn slightly counterclockwise away from partner (right shoulder to right shoulder) and, beginning with a jump on the left foot, repeat measures 1–4. (Slow, slow, fast, fast, fast)
9–12	Repeat action of measures 1–4, facing opposite direction (left shoulder to left shoulder). (Slow, slow, fast, fast, fast)
13–16	Repeat action of measures 1–4, facing partner. (Slow, slow, fast, fast, fast)

Part II: Partners hook right elbows; left elbows are bent and left hands are pointed toward the ceiling.

Measures	***Action***
1–4	Do a right elbow swing, using eight running or skipping steps. Release and clap the hands on the eighth count. (Swing, 2, 3, 4, 5, 6, 7, clap)
5–8	Do a left elbow swing, using eight running or skipping steps. Release and clap the hands on the eighth count. (Swing, 2, 3, 4, 5, 6, 7, clap)
9–16	Repeat the actions of measures 1–8.

TEACHING TIP

Variations:

1. Face partner (all should be in a single-circle formation for this version) and do a grand right and left around the circle. Repeat Part I with a new partner.
2. All face center or face a partner and do the Bleking or raspa step. On each pause, clap own hands twice.

PATTY CAKE (HEEL AND TOE) POLKA (INTERNATIONAL)

Music Source: WWCD-FDN

Skills: Heel and toe polka step, sliding, elbow swing, skipping

Formation: Double circle, partners facing, A in the inner circle with back to the center. Both hands are joined with partner. A's left and B's right foot are free.

Directions:

Measures	***Part I Action***
1–2	Heel-toe twice with A's left and B's right foot. (Heel, toe, heel, toe)
3–4	Take four slides sideward to A's left, progressing counterclockwise. Do not transfer the weight on the last count. Finish with A's right and B's left foot free. (Slide, 2, 3, 4)
5–8	Repeat the pattern of measures 1–4, starting with A's right and B's left foot, progressing clockwise. Finish with the partners separated and facing. (Heel, toe, heel, toe; Slide, 2, 3, 4)

Measures	***Part II Action***
9	Clap right hands with partner three times. (Right, 2, 3)
10	Clap left hands with partner three times. (Left, 2, 3)
11	Clap both hands with partner three times. (Both, 2, 3)
12	Slap own knees three times. (Knees, 2, 3)
13–14	Right elbow swing with partner. Partners hook right elbows and swing once around with four walking steps, finishing with A's back to center. (Swing, 2, 3, 4)
15–16	Progress left to a new partner with four walking steps. (Left, 2, 3, 4)

Repeat the entire dance with the new partner.

POLLY WOLLY DOODLE (AMERICAN)

Music Source: WWCD-1041

Skills: Sliding, turning, walking

Formation: Double circle of dancers, partners facing with both hands joined, partner A with back to the center of the circle

Directions:

Measures	***Part I Action***
1–4	All slide four steps—A partners to left, Bs to right, counterclockwise. (Slide, 2, 3, 4)
5–8	Drop hands and all turn solo circle, A partners to left, Bs to right, with five stamps in this rhythm: 1-2-1, 2, 3. (Stamp on the word "polly," stamp on the other foot on the word "doodle," and take three quick stamps on the word "day.") (Turn, 2, stamp, 2, 3)
9–16	Repeat measures 1–8, but in the opposite direction, A partners moving to right and Bs to left. (Slide, 2, 3, 4; Turn, 2, stamp 2, 3)
	Part II Action
1–4	Both bow to each other, A partners with hands on hips, Bs with hands at sides. (A bows; B bows)
5–8	With four walking steps (or skipping steps), both move backward, away from each other. (Back, 2, 3, 4)
9–12	Both move diagonally forward to own left to meet a new partner. (Diagonal, 2, 3, 4)
13–16	With the new partner, elbow swing in place using a skipping step. (Swing, 2, 3, 4) Repeat the dance from the beginning with the new partner.

BINGO (AMERICAN)

Music Source: WWCD-FDN

Skills: Walking, right-and-left grand

Formation: Double circle, partners side by side and facing counterclockwise, partners A on the inside and inside hands joined.

Note: "Bingo" is a favorite of young people. The singing must be brisk and loud. The dance is in three parts.

Directions:

Part I: Partners walk counterclockwise around the circle, singing the refrain. (Walk, 2, 3, . . . 15, face center)

Part II: All join hands to form a single circle, partner B on partner A's right. They sing (spelling out) with these actions.

Action

All take four steps into the center.

All take four steps backward.

All take four steps forward again.

Take four steps backward, drop hands, and face partner.

Part III: Shake right hands with the partner, calling out B on the first heavy note. All walk forward, passing their partner, to meet the oncoming person with a left handshake, calling out I on the next chord. Continue to the third person with a right handshake, sounding out the N. Pass on to the fourth person, giving a left handshake and a G. Instead of a handshake with the fifth person, face each other, raise the arms high above the head, shake all over, and sound out a long, drawn-out O. The fifth person becomes the new partner, and the dance is repeated.

TEACHING TIP

The dance can be adapted to the use of a parachute. At the end of Part II (the end of the line "And Bingo was his name") partners A face the chute and hold it with both hands, lifting it to shoulder level. Partners B drop their hands from the parachute and get ready to move clockwise. On each of the letters B-I-N-G-O, they move inside the first A, outside the next, and so on, for five changes. They then take a new place as indicated and get ready to repeat the dance. The next sequence can have partners B remaining in place, holding the chute, while partners A move counterclockwise.

GRAND MARCH (AMERICAN)

Music Source: WWCD-W0F-2 or any good march or square dance music

Skills: Controlled walking, marching, grand march figures

Formation: Partners B are on the left side of the room, facing the end, and partners A are on the right side, facing the same end. This is the foot of the hall. The teacher or caller stands at the other end of the room, the head of the hall. An alternative formation is to put half of the class on each side of the room and to designate each half with different colored pinnies.

Directions:

Call	***Action***
Down the center by twos.	The lines march forward to the foot of the hall, turn the corner, meet at the center of the foot of the hall, and march in couples toward the caller (Figure 19.4), with inside hands joined. The Bs' line should be on the proper side so that, when the couples come down the center, A is on B's left. Odd couples are numbered 1, 3, 5, and so on. Even couples are numbered 2, 4, 6, and so on.
Twos left and right.	The odd couples go left and the even couples go right around the room and meet at the foot of the hall.
Down the center by fours.	The couples walk down the center, four abreast.
Separate by twos.	When they approach the caller, odd couples go left and even couples right. They meet again at the foot of the hall.
Form arches.	Instead of coming down the center, odd couples form

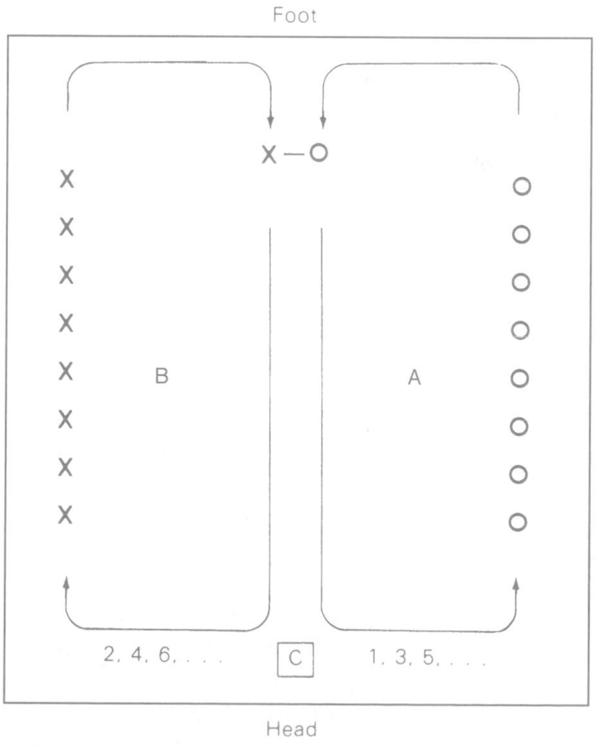

FIGURE 19.4 Formation and action for grand march.

	arches and even couples tunnel under. Each continues around the sides of the hall to meet at the head.
Other couples arch.	Even couples arch, and odd couples tunnel under. Each continues around the sides of the room to the foot.
Over and under.	The first odd couple arches over the first even couple, then ducks under the second even couple's arch. Each couple goes over the first couple and under the next. Continue around to the head of the hall.
Pass right through.	As the lines come toward each other, they mesh and pass through each other in the following fashion: All drop handholds. Each B walks between the A and B of the opposite couple and continues walking to the foot of the hall.
Down the center by fours.	Go down the center four abreast.
Fours left and right.	The first four go left around the room, and the second four go right. The fours meet at the foot of the hall.
Down the center by eights.	Go eight abreast down the center.
Grapevine.	All persons in each line join hands and keep them joined. The leader takes either end of the first line and starts around the room with the line trailing. The other lines hook on to form one long line.
Wind it up.	The leader winds up the group in a spiral formation, like a clock spring. The leader makes the circles smaller and smaller until he or she is in the center.
Reverse (unwind).	The leader turns and faces in the opposite direction and walks between the lines of winding dancers. The leader unwinds the line and leads it around the room.
Everybody swing.	After the line is unwound, everybody does a square dance swing.

TEACHING TIP

The leaders (couples 1 and 2) should maintain an even, steady pace and not hurry, or the march becomes a race. When one set of couples forms arches (as in movements 5 and 6) for the other set of couples to tunnel under, the arches should be made with the inside arms, and the couples should continue marching while they form the arches.

GREEN SLEEVES (ENGLISH)

Music Source: WWCD-1042

Skills: Walking, star formation, over and under

Formation: Double circle with couples in sets of four, facing counterclockwise. Two couples form a set and are numbered 1 and 2. Inside hands of each couple are joined.

Directions:

Measures	***Call***	***Action***
1–8	*Walk*	Walk forward 16 steps.
9–12	*Right-hand star*	Each member of couple 1 turns individually to face the couple behind. All join right hands and circle clockwise (star) for eight steps.
13–16	*Left-hand star*	Reverse direction and form a left-hand star. This should bring couple 1 back to place facing in the original direction.
17–20	*Over and under*	Couple 2 arches and couple 1 backs under four steps while couple 2 moves forward four steps. Couple 1 then arches and couple 2 backs under (four steps for each).
21–24	*Over and under*	Repeat the action of measures 17–20.

JINGLE BELLS, VAR. 2 (DUTCH)

Music Source: Any version of Jingle Bells

Skills: Skipping, promenade position, sliding, elbow swing

Formation: Circle of couples facing counterclockwise, partner B on partner A's right. Promenade position, hands crossed in front, right hands joined over left, right foot free.

Directions:

Measures	*Part I Action*
1–2	Take four skips forward and four skips backward, starting with the right foot free. (Forward, 2, 3, 4; Back, 2, 3, 4)
3–4	Repeat the pattern of measures 1 and 2. (Forward 2, 3, 4; Back, 2, 3, 4)
5	Do four slides to the right, away from the center of the circle. (Out, 2, 3, 4)
6	Now do four slides left, toward the center. (In, 2, 3, 4)
7–8	Execute eight skips, making one turn counterclockwise, with partner A pivoting backward and partner B moving forward. Finish in a double circle, partners facing, with A's back to the center. (Skip, 2, 3, 4, 5, 6, 7, 8)

	Part II Action
1	Clap own hands three times. (Clap, 2, 3)
2	Clap both hands with partner three times. (Both, 2, 3)
3	Clap own hands four times. (Clap, 2, 3, 4)
4	Clap both hands with partner once. (Both)
5–8	Right elbow swing with partner. Partners hook right elbows and swing clockwise for eight skips. (Swing, 2, 3, 4, 5, 6, 7, 8)
9–12	Repeat clapping pattern of measures 1–4.
13–16	Left elbow swing with partner using eight skips and finishing in the original starting position to repeat the entire dance with the same partner; or left elbow swing with partner once around, then all of the children in the inner circle skip forward to the outer dancer ahead and repeat the entire dance with a new partner. (Swing, 2, 3, 4, 5, 6, 7, 8)

E-Z MIXER

Music Source: WWC-FFD or any music with a definite rhythm

Skills: Walking, elbow swing or swing in closed position

Formation: Circle formation with couples in promenade position, inside hands joined, facing counterclockwise

Directions:

Measures	*Action*
1–2	With partner B on the right, walk forward four steps. (Forward, 2, 3, 4) Back out to face center in a single circle. (Circle, 2, 3, 4)
3–4	Partners B walk to the center. (In, 2, 3, 4) Back out of the center. (Out, 2, 3, 4)
5–6	Partners A take four steps to the center, turning one half left face on the fourth step. (In, 2, 3, turn left face) They take four steps toward the corner. (Out, 2, 3, 4)
7–8	A partners swing the corner B twice around, opening up to face counterclockwise, back in starting position, to begin the dance again. (Swing, 2, 3, open)

Any piece of music with a moderate $\frac{4}{4}$ rhythm is appropriate for this basic mixer.

VE DAVID (ISRAELI)

Music Source: WWCD-RM3; WWC-RM3

Skills: Walking, pivoting, buzz-step turn

Formation: Double circle, couples facing counterclockwise, partner B on partner A's right. Inside hands joined, right foot free.

Directions:

Measures	*Part I Action*
1–2	All walk forward and form a ring. Take four walking steps forward, starting with the right foot and progressing counterclockwise, then back out, taking four walking steps to form a single circle, facing center, with all hands joined. (Walk, 2, 3, 4; Single, circle, 3, 4)
3–4	All forward and back. Four steps forward to center and four steps backward, starting with the right foot. (Forward, 2, 3, 4; Back, 2, 3, 4)
	Part II Action
1–2	Bs forward and back; A partners clap. Partners B, starting with the right foot, walk four steps forward to the center and four steps backward to place while partners A clap. (Bs in, 2, 3, 4; Out 2, 3, 4)
	Part III Action
1–2	Partners A forward, circle to the right, and progress to a new partner; all clap. A partners, clapping hands, walk four steps forward to the center, starting with the right foot. They turn right about on the last "and" count and walk forward four steps, passing their original partner and progressing ahead to the next. (A partners in, 2, 3, 4; Turn to new partner)
3–4	Swing the new partner. The A and the new partner B swing clockwise with right

shoulders adjacent, right arms around each other across in front, and left arms raised—pivoting with right foot for an eight count "buzz-step" swing. (Swing, 2, 3, 4, 5, 6, 7, 8)

Repeat the entire dance.

IRISH WASHERWOMAN (IRISH)

Music Source: WWCD-1043

Skills: Walking, elbow swing, promenade

Formation: Single circle, couples facing center, partner B to the right, hands joined

Directions: Dancers follow the call.

Action

Beginning left, take four steps to the center. (Center, 2, 3, 4)

Stamp four times in place (Stamp, 2, 3, 4)

Take four steps backward to place (Back, 2, 3, 4)

Swing the corner and promenade in the line of direction. (Swing, 2, 3, promenade)

Dancers keep promenading until they hear the call again to repeat the pattern.

OH, SUSANNA (AMERICAN)

Music Source: WWCD-1043

Skills: Walking, promenade position, grand right and left

Formation: Single circle, all facing center, partner B on the right

Directions:

Measures	***Part I Action***
1–4	Partners B walk forward four steps and back four, as partners A clap hands. (Forward, 2, 3, 4; Back, 2, 3, 4)
5–8	Reverse, with A walking forward and back, and B clapping time. (Forward, 2, 3, 4; Back, 2, 3, 4)
	Part II Action
1–8	Partners face each other, and all do a grand right and left by grasping the partner's right hand, then passing to the next person with a left-hand hold. Continue until reaching the seventh person, who becomes the new partner. (Face, 2, 3, 4, 5, 6, 7, 8)
	Chorus
1–16	All join hands in promenade position with the new partner and walk counterclockwise around the circle for two full choruses. (Promenade, 2, 3, . . . 16)

Repeat the dance from the beginning, each time with a new partner. For variety in the chorus, skip instead of walk, or walk during the first chorus and swing one's partner in place during the second chorus.

CRESTED HEN (DANISH)

Music Source: WWCD-1042

Skills: Step-hop, turning under

Formation: Sets of three. One child is designated the center child.

Directions:

Part I:

Measures	***Action***
1–4	Dancers in each set form a circle. Starting with a stamp with the left foot, each set circles to the left, using step-hops. (Stamp and, 2 and, 3 and, 4 and, 5 and, 6 and, 7 and, stop)
5–8	The figure is repeated. Dancers reverse direction, beginning again with a stamp with the left foot and following with step-hops. The change of direction should be vigorous and definite, with the left foot crossing over the right. At the end of the sequence, two dancers release each other's hands to break the circle and stand on either side of the center person, forming a line of three while retaining joined hands with the center dancer. (Stamp and, 2 and, 3 and, 4 and, 5 and, 6 and, 7 and, line)

Part II: During this part, the dancers use the step-hop continuously while making the pattern figures.

Measures	***Action***
9–10	The dancer on the right moves forward in an arc to the left and dances under the arch formed by the other two. (Under and, 2 and, 3 and, 4 and)
11–12	After the right dancer has gone through, the two forming the arch turn under (dishrag), to form once again a line of three. (Turn and, 2 and, 3 and, 4 and)
13–16	The dancer on the left then repeats the pattern, moving forward in an arc under the arch formed by the other two, who turn under to unravel the line. (Under and, 2 and, 3 and, 4 and; Turn and, 2 and, 3 and, circle)

As soon as Part II is completed, dancers again join hands in a small circle. The entire dance is repeated. Another of the three can be designated the center dancer.

TROIKA (RUSSIAN)

Music Source: WWCD-3528; WWC-3528

Skills: Running step, turning under

Formation: Trios face counterclockwise. Start with hands joined in a line of three. The body weight is on the left foot; the right foot is free.

Directions:

Measures	***Part I Action***
1	Take four running steps diagonally forward right, starting with the right foot. (Forward, 2, 3, 4)
2	Take four running steps diagonally forward left, starting with the right foot. (Diagonal, 2, 3, 4)
3–4	Take eight running steps in a forward direction, starting with the right foot. (Forward, 2, 3, 4, 5, 6, 7, 8)
5–6	The center dancer and the left-hand partner raise joined hands to form an arch and run in place. Meanwhile, the right-hand partner moves counterclockwise around the center dancer with eight running steps, goes under the arch, and back to place. The center dancer unwinds by turning under the arch. (Under, 2, 3, 4; Turn, 2, 3, 4)
7–8	Repeat the pattern of measures 5 and 6, with the left-hand partner running under the arch formed by the center dancer and the right-hand partner. (Under, 2, 3, 4; Turn, 2, 3, circle)
	Part II Action
9–11	The trio joins hands and circles left with 12 running steps. (Run, 2, 3, 4, 5, 6, 7, 8, 9, 10, 11, 12)
12	Three stamps in place (counts 1–3), pause (count 4). (Stamp, 2, 3, pause)
13–15	The trio circles right with 12 running steps, opening out at the end to re-form in lines of three facing counterclockwise. (Run, 2, 3, 4, 5, 6, 7, 8, open, 10, 11, 12)
16	The center dancer releases each partner's hand and runs under the opposite arch of joined hands to advance to a new pair ahead. Right- and left-hand partners run in place while waiting for a new center dancer to join them in a new trio. (Stamp, 2, line, pause)

TEACHING TIP

Practice the running steps in groups of three. Then introduce turning under the arch and finish by practicing the running circle with accent stamps.

GUSTAF'S SKOAL (SWEDISH)

Music Source: WWCD-1044CD; WWCD-FDN

Skills: Walking (stately), skipping, turning

Formation: The formation is similar to a square dance set of four couples, each facing center. Partner A is to the left of partner B. Couples join inside hands; the outside hand is on the hip. Two of the couples facing each other are designated the head couples. The other two couples, also facing each other, are the side couples.

Directions: The dance is in two parts. In Part I, the music is slow and stately. The dancers perform with great dignity. The music for Part II is light and represents fun.

Measures	***Part I Action***
1–2	The head couples, inside hands joined, walk forward three steps and bow to the opposite couple. (Forward, 2, 3, bow)
3–4	The head couples take three steps backward to place and bow to each other. (The side couples hold their places during this action.) (Back, 2, 3, bow)
5–8	The side couples repeat action of measures 1–4 while the head couples hold their places. (Forward, 2, 3, bow; Back, 2, 3, bow)
9–16	The dancers repeat measures 1–8.
	Part II Action
17–22	The side couples raise joined hands to form an arch. Head couples skip forward four steps, release partners' hands, join inside hands with opposite person, and skip under the nearest arch with new partner. After going under the arch, they drop hands and head back home to their original partner. (Head couples: Skip, 2, 3, 4; Under, 2, 3, 4; Around, 2, 3, 4)
23–24	All couples join both hands with partners and swing once around with four skipping steps. (Swing, 2, 3, 4)
25–30	Head couples form arches while side couples repeat the action of measures 17–22. (Side couples: Skip, 2, 3, 4; Under, 2, 3, 4; Around, 2, 3, 4)
31–32	All couples then repeat the movements in measures 23–24. (Swing, 2, 3, 4)

TEACHING TIP

During the first action sequence of Part I (in which the dancers take three steps and bow), a shout of "Skoal" and raising the right fist high above the head as a salute can be substituted for the bow. The word *skoal* is a toast. (Note that the dancers' hands are not joined.)

SHOO FLY (AMERICAN)

Music Source: WWCD-FDN

Skills: Walking

Formation: Single circle of couples facing the center with all hands joined; approximately six couples to a circle

Directions:

Measures	***Part I Action***
4	Introduction
1–4	All walk four steps to the center and four steps back to place. (Center, 2, 3, 4; back, 2, 3, 4)
5–8	Repeat action of measures 1–4. (Center, 2, 3, 4; back, 2, 3, 4)
9–12	Partners turn each other clockwise with a right forearm grasp using eight walking steps. (Turn, partner, 3, 4, 5, 6, 7, 8)
13–16	Partners turn each other counterclockwise with a left forearm grasp using eight walking steps. (Turn, partner, 3, 4, 5, 6, 7, 8)
	Part II Action
1–8	Repeat action of measures 1–8 in Part I.
9–12	Keep hands joined. The leading couple (must be designated) forms an arch by lifting inside joined hands and moves toward the center of the circle. The couple opposite the leading couple pulls the continuous circle through the arch using eight steps. (Through, arch, 3, 4, 5, 6, 7, 8)
13–16	When all have passed through the arch and are facing out, the leading couple turns under their joined arms turning the circle inside-out. (Inside, out, 3, 4, 5, 6, 7, 8)
	Part III Action
1–8	Repeat the action of measures 1–8 in Part I except that all walk backward four steps to the center and then forward four steps back to place. Repeat. (Backward, 2, 3, 4, forward, 6, 7 8; repeat)
9–12	Leading couple release joined hands (others keep joined hands) and separate pulling dancers attached to them by joined hands around the circle with eight walking steps. (Release, 2, 3, 4, 5, 6, 7, 8)
13–16	Continue following leaders with 8 walking steps until in original places facing the center. Lead couple joins hands to form a circle again. (Circle, 2, 3, 4, 5, 6, 7, 8)

Perform the dance twice.

APAT APAT (PHILIPPINES)

Music Source: WWCD-RM4; WWC-572

Skills: Walking; star hold

Formation: Double circle of partners facing counterclockwise with inside hands joined

Directions:

Measures	***Action***
	Introduction
1	All face counterclockwise with inside hands joined and walk forward four steps. On count four, release hands and execute a half turn right to face clockwise. (Walk, 2, 3, turn)
2	Take four walking steps forward clockwise. Release hands on the fourth step and face partner. (Walk, 2, 3, face)
3	Walk four steps backward away from partner. (Away, 2, 3, 4)
4	Walk four steps forward toward partner with each partner taking a quarter turn to the right on the fourth count. Partners will be facing in opposite directions. (Forward, 2, 3, right turn)
5	Walk forward four steps with partners moving in opposite directions. (Forward, 2, 3, 4)
6	Walk backward four steps to meet partner. (Backward, 2, 3, 4)
7	Face partner. With right hand star (join right hands with elbows bent) walk clockwise around partner four steps in place. (Star, 2, 3, 4)
8	Release hands, inside circle youngsters walk forward four steps counterclockwise to meet next partner. Outside circle youngsters turn a half turn in place to wait for new partner.

Repeat the dance.

PATA PATA (AFRICAN)

Music Source: WWCD-3528; WWC-3528

Skills: Toe touches, knee lift, quarter turns

Formation: Single lines facing in one direction

Directions:

Measures	***Action***
1–2	Start with feet together; touch right foot sideward right and return next to left foot. (Right touch, together)
3–4	Same as above with left foot. (Left touch, together)
5	With feet together, move toes out keeping heels on the ground. (Toes out)
6	Turn heels out keeping toes on the ground. (Heels out)
7	Turn heels in keeping toes on the ground. (Heels in)
8	Turn toes in keeping heels on the ground. The feet should now be together. (Toes in)
9–12	Raise right knee diagonally in front of the body and then touch right foot next to left foot. Repeat for counts 11–12. (Lift, touch, lift, touch)
13–16	Kick left foot forward while turning a quarter turn to the right with weight on the right foot. Step backward left, right, left. Feet should be together at the end of count 16. (Kick, left, right, left)

Repeat the dance.

TEACHING TIP

When youngsters learn the footwork, it is enjoyable to add some arm movements to the dance. At count 5, with elbows close to the body, raise hands up and straight out palms up. Count 6 turn palms down with elbows out. Count 7, turn palms up. Count 8, turn palms down.

SAVILA SE BELA LOZA (SERBIAN)

Music Source: WWCD-572; WWC-572

Skills: Running step, crossover step, hop

Formation: Broken circle or line; joined hands held down

Directions: Explain Savila Se Bela Loza (pronounced SAH-vee-lah say BAY-lah LOH-zah) means a "grapevine entwined in itself."

Measures	***Part I Action***
	Introduction
1–20	Face slightly to right, move right starting with the right foot taking 18 small running steps forward. Do a step-hop on steps 19 and 20. (Run, 2, 3, . . . 18, step, hop)
21–40	Face slightly left and repeat above action starting with the left foot. Finish with a step hop on the left foot. (Run, 2, 3, . . . 18, step, hop)
	Part II Action
41–44	Beginning with right, take one schottische step moving right. Translated, this is a step to the right sideward on the right foot, a step with the left foot behind the right followed by a step-hop on the right foot. (Right, left, right, hop)
45–48	Beginning with left, take one schottische step moving left. This is done with a step to the left sideward on left foot, a step with the right foot behind the left followed by a step-hop on the left foot. (Left, right left, hop)
49–64	Repeat the action of counts 41–48 two more times.

Repeat the dance. During the music for Part I, the leaders on the ends of the lines may lead the line anywhere, winding or coiling the line like a grapevine.

POPCORN (AMERICAN)

Music Source: WWCD-RM7; WWC-RM7

Skills: Toe touches, knee lifts, jumps, quarter turns

Formation: Single lines of students; no partners

Directions:

Counts	***Measures***
24	Wait 24 counts; gently bounce up and down by bending the knees during the introduction
1–4	Touch right toe in front and return; repeat. (Right, together, right, together)
5–8	Touch left toe in front and return; repeat. (Left, together, left, together)
9–12	Touch right toe in back and return; repeat. (Back, together, back, together)
13–16	Touch left toe in front and return; repeat. (Back, together, back, together)
17–20	Lift right knee up in front of left knee and return; repeat. (Knee up, return, knee up, return)
21–24	Lift left knee up in front of right knee and return; repeat. (Knee up, return, knee up, return)
25–26	Lift right knee up in front of left knee and return. (Knee up, return)
27–28	Lift left knee up in front of right knee and return. (Knee up, return)
29–30	Clap both hands together once. (clap)
31–32	Jump and turn a quarter turn to the right. (Jump and turn)

Repeat entire dance to the end of the music.

RED RIVER VALLEY (AMERICAN)

Music Source: WWCD-FDN

Skills: Walk, buzz swing

Formation: Triple circle with three dancers side by side in sets of six dancers—two trios facing each other. Half the trios face counterclockwise and half face clockwise.

Directions:

Measures	***Part I Action***
4	Introduction
1–4	Middle person of each trio leads partners forward to right to meet oncoming trio using eight walking steps. (Walk, 2, 3, . . . 8)
5–8	Join hands with oncoming trio and circle to the left (clockwise) four walking steps; reverse direction and circle right using four walking steps. (Circle, left, 3, 4; circle, right, 3, 4)
9–12	Middle person swings around with person on left using eight buzz (shuffling) steps. (Swing, 2, 3, . . . 8)
13–16	Middle person swings around with person on right using eight buzz (shuffling) steps. (Swing, 2, 3, . . . 8)
	Part II Action
1–8	Repeat action of measures 1–8 in Part I. (Walk, 2, 3, . . . 8)
9–12	The four outside youngsters form a right hand star in the center of the set and walk around once to starting point using eight walking steps. (Star, 2, 3, . . . 8)
13–16	The two middle youngsters "do-si-do" around each other, returning to own place using eight walking steps. (Do-si-do, 2, 3, . . . 8)
	Part III Action
1–8	Repeat action of measures 1–8 in Part I. (Walk, 2, 3, . . . 8)
9–12	The two left-hand outside youngsters change places diagonally across using eight walking steps. (Left, diagonal, 3, . . . 8)
13–16	The two right-hand outside youngsters change places diagonally across using eight walking steps. The middle person now has different partners. (Right, diagonal, 3, . . . 8)

The entire dance is repeated twice.

SICILIAN CIRCLE (AMERICAN)

Music Source: WWCD-FDN

Skills: Walking, two-hand swing (either walking or buzz turn), wheel turn

Formation: Double circle composed of groups of two couples facing each other with partners side by side. Couples are numbered 1 and 2 with #1 couples moving counterclockwise and #2 couples clockwise.

Directions:

Measures	***Part I Action***
4	Introduction
1–4	The sets of two couples join hands and walk eight steps to the left, ending where they started, and drop hands. (Circle, left, 2, 3, 4, . . . 8)
5–8	Partners join both hands and swing once around to the left using eight walking or buzz steps. (Swing, left, 2, 3, 4, . . . 8)
9–12	Couples advance toward each other and pass right shoulders through to opposite's place using four walking steps. As soon as they are across, couples do a wheel-turn around with partner on the left walking backward four steps and moving into place on partner's left who turns in place using four steps. If desired, left partner can hold left hand with partner's left hand and right hand around back of partner's waist. Hands are dropped. (Pass, through, 3, 4; Wheel, turn, 3, 4)
13–16	Couples pass through again as described in measures 9–12. (Back, through, 3, 4; Wheel, turn, 3, 4)
17–20	Right hand partners advance toward each other, join right hands briefly, pass each other by right shoulders, drop hands, and join left hand with opposite left partner using four steps. The opposite left partner does a wheel turn as described in measures 9–12 using four steps. (Right partner, chain, 3, 4; Wheel, turn, 3, 4)
21–24	Right hand partners chain back again and turn as in measures 17–20 using eight steps and end with left hands joined with partner. (Chain, back, 3, 4; Wheel, turn, 3, 4)
25–28	Partners join hands in promenade position and advance four steps toward opposite and four steps backward to place. (Forward, 2, 3, 4; Back, 2, 3, 4)
29–32	Each couple with hands in promenade position advance to the left of the opposite couple to the next couple using eight steps. (New couple, 2, 3, . . . 8)

Dance is repeated three times.

LUMMI STICKS

Music Source: WWCD-2015 or 2014; WWC-2000

Skills: Rhythmic tapping, flipping, and catching of sticks

Formation: Couples scattered throughout the area

Lummi sticks are smaller versions of wands; they are 12 to 15 inches long. Some believe that lummi sticks were a part of the culture of the Lummi Indians in northwest Washington. Others give credit to South Pacific cultures for the origin of the sticks. Their actual origin remains obscure.

Most lummi stick activities are done by partners, although some can be done individually. Each child sits cross-legged, facing a partner at a distance of 18 to 20 inches. Children adjust this distance as the activities demand. The sticks are held in the thumb and fingers (not the fist) at about the bottom third of the stick.

Routines are based on sets of six movements; each movement is completed in one count. Many different routines are possible. Only the basic ones are presented here. The following one-count movements are used to make up routines.

Vertical tap: Tap both sticks upright on the floor.

Partner tap: Tap partner's stick (right stick to right stick, or left to left).

End tap: Tilt the sticks forward or sideward and tap the ends on the floor.

Cross-tap: Cross hands and tap the upper ends to the floor.

Side tap: Tap the upper ends to the side.

Flip: Toss the stick in air, giving it a half turn, and catch other end.

Tap together: Hold the sticks parallel and tap them together.

Toss right (or left): Toss the right-hand stick to partner's right hand, at the same time receiving partner's right-hand stick.

Pass: Lay the stick on the floor and pick up partner's stick.

Toss right and left: Toss quickly right to right and left to left, all in the time of one count.

A number of routines, incorporating the movements described, are presented here in sequence of difficulty. Each routine is to be done four times to complete the 24 beats of the chant.

1. Vertical tap, tap together, partner tap right, vertical tap, tap together, partner tap left.
2. Vertical tap, tap together, pass right stick, vertical tap, tap together, pass left stick.
3. Vertical tap, tap together, toss right stick, vertical tap, tap together, toss left stick.
4. Repeat numbers 1, 2, and 3, but substitute an end tap and flip for the vertical tap and tap together. Perform the stated third movement (that is, end tap, flip, partner tap right, end tap, flip, partner tap left).
5. Vertical tap, tap together, toss right and left quickly, end tap, flip, toss right and left quickly.
6. Cross-tap, cross-flip, vertical tap (uncross arms), cross-tap, cross-flip, vertical tap (uncross arms).
7. Right flip side—left flip in front, vertical tap in place, partner tap right. Left flip side—right flip in front, vertical tap in place, partner tap left.
8. End tap in front, flip, vertical tap, tap together, toss right, toss left.
9. Vertical tap, tap together, right stick to partner's left hand, toss own left stick to own right hand. Repeat. This is the circle throw.
10. Same as in number 9, but reverse the circle.

The activity can be done by four children with a change in the timing. One set of partners begins at the start, and the other two start on the third beat. All sing together. In this way, the sticks are flying alternately.

TINIKLING (PHILIPPINE ISLANDS)

Music Source: WWC/CD-8095; WWC/CD-9015

Skills: Tinikling steps

Formation: Sets of fours scattered around the room. Each set has two strikers and two dancers (Figure 19.5 on page 448).

Note: The dance represents a rice bird as it steps, with its long legs, from one rice paddy to another. The dance is popular in many countries in Southeast Asia, where different versions have arisen.

Directions: Two 8-foot bamboo poles and two crossbars on which the poles rest are needed for the dance. A striker kneels at each end of the poles; both strikers hold the end of a pole in each hand. The music is in waltz meter, $\frac{3}{4}$ time, with an accent on the first beat. The strikers slide and strike the poles together on count 1. On the other two beats of the waltz measure, the poles are opened about 15 inches apart, lifted an inch or so, and tapped twice on the crossbars in time to counts 2 and 3. The rhythm "close, tap, tap" is continued throughout the dance, each sequence constituting a measure.

Basically, the dance requires that a step be done outside the poles on the close (count 1) and that two steps be done inside the poles (counts 2 and 3) when the poles are tapped on the crossbars. Many step combinations have been devised.

The basic tinikling step should be practiced until it is mastered. The step is done singly, although two dancers are performing. Each dancer takes a position at an opposite end and on the opposite side so that the dancer's right side is to the bamboo poles.

Count 1: Step slightly forward with the left foot.

Count 2: Step with the right foot between the poles.

FIGURE 19.5 Tinikling set.

Count 3: Step with the left foot between the poles.

Count 4: Step with the right outside to dancer's own right.

Count 5: Step with the left between the poles.

Count 6: Step with the right between the poles.

Count 7: Step with the left outside to the original position.

The initial step (count 1) is used only to get the dance under way. The last step (count 7) to original position is actually the beginning of a new series (7, 8, 9–10, 11, 12).

Some tinikling dances and records guide the dancers with a different type of rhythm (tap, tap, close), necessitating adjustment of the steps and patterns in these descriptions.

Tinikling steps also can be adjusted to $\frac{4}{4}$ rhythm (close, close, tap, tap), which requires the poles to be closed on two counts and open on the other two. The basic foot pattern is two steps outside the poles and two inside. For the sake of conformity, we present all routines in the original $\frac{3}{4}$ time (close, tap, tap). If other rhythms are used, adjust accordingly.

Dancers can go from side to side, or can return to the side from which they entered. The dance can be done singly, with the two dancers moving in opposite directions from side to side, or the dancers can enter from and leave toward the same side. Dancers can do the same step patterns or do different movements. They can dance as partners, moving side by side with inside hands joined, or facing each other with both hands joined.

TEACHING TIP

Steps should be practiced first with stationary poles or with lines drawn on the floor. Jump ropes can be used as stationary objects over which to practice. Students handling the poles should concentrate on watching each other rather than the dancer to avoid becoming confused by the dancer's feet.

To gain a sense of the movement pattern for $\frac{3}{4}$ time, slap both thighs with the hands on the "close," and clap the hands twice for movements inside the poles. For $\frac{4}{4}$ time, slap the right thigh with the right hand, then the left thigh with the left hand, followed by two claps. This routine should be done to music, with the poles closing and opening as indicated. Getting the feel of the rhythm is important.

OTHER TINIKLING STEPS AND ROUTINES

Straddle step: Dancers do a straddle jump outside the poles on count 1 and execute two movements inside the poles on counts 2 and 3. Let the dancers explore the different combinations. Jump turns are possible.

Jump step: Dancers begin the side jump with their side toward the poles. They can execute the jump from either side.

Measure 1:

Count 1: Jump lightly in place.

Counts 2 and 3: Jump twice between the poles.

Measure 2:

Count 1: Jump lightly in place (other side).

Counts 2 and 3: Jump twice between the poles.

The feet should be kept close together to fit between the poles. Dancers can exit to the same side from which they entered, or can alternate sides. Another way to enter and exit is by facing the poles and jumping forward and backward rather than sideward. When jumping sideward, one foot can be kept ahead of the other in a stride position. This position can be reversed on the second jump inside the poles.

Rocker step: For the rocker step, dancers face the poles and begin with either foot. As they step in and out (forward and backward), they make a rocking motion with the body.

Crossover step: The crossover step is similar to the basic tinikling step, except that the dancer begins with the right foot (forward step) and steps inside the poles with the left foot, using a cross-foot step. Each time, the dancer must step in or out using a cross-step.

Circling poles: For circling the poles, dancers position themselves as in the basic tinikling step (Figure 19.6) and execute the following movements:

Measure 1:

Count 1: Step slightly forward with the left foot.

Count 2: Step with the right foot between the poles.

Count 3: Step with the left foot between the poles.

Measure 2:

Count 1: Step with the right foot outside the poles to the right.

Counts 2 and 3: With light running steps, make a half circle to a position for the return movement.

Measures 3 and 4: Dancers return to their original position using the same movements as in measures 1 and 2.

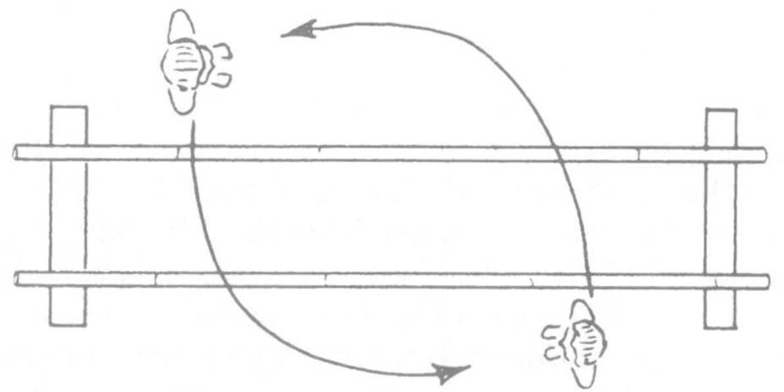

FIGURE 19.6 Circling poles for tinikling.

Fast tinikling trot: The fast tinikling trot is similar to circling the poles, except that the step goes twice as fast and thus requires only two sets of three counts. Instead of having the side of the body to the poles, as in the basic tinikling step, the dancers face the poles. The following steps are taken:

Measure 1:

Count 1: Shift the weight to the left foot and raise the right foot.

Count 2: Step with the right foot between the poles.

Count 3: Step with the left foot outside the poles and begin turning to the left.

Measure 2:

Count 1: Step with the right foot outside the poles, completing the left turn to face the poles again.

Count 2: Step with the left foot inside the poles.

Count 3: Step outside with the right foot.

The next step is done with the left foot to begin a new cycle. The movement is a light trot with quick turns. Note that the step outside the poles on count 3 in each measure is made with the poles apart.

Cross-step: To do the cross-step, the dancer begins with the basic tinikling position, and uses the following sequence:

Measure 1:

Count 1: Cross-step across both poles with the left foot, hopping on the right side.

Counts 2 and 3: Hop twice on the right foot between the poles.

Measure 2:

Count 1: Hop on the left foot outside the poles to the left.

Counts 2 and 3: Hop twice again on the right foot between the poles.

Line of poles: Three or more sets of poles are about 6 feet apart. The object is to dance down the sets, make a circling movement (as in Circling Poles), and return down the line in the opposite direction (Figure 19.7 on page 450). The dancer keeps his right side toward the poles throughout.

During measure 1 (three counts), the dancer does a basic tinikling step, finishing on the right side of the first set of poles. During measure 2 (three counts), he uses three light running steps to position himself for the tinikling step at the next set of poles. When he gets to the end, he circles with three steps to get in position for the return journey.

Square Formation: Four sets of poles can be placed in a square formation for an interesting dance sequence (Figure 19.8 on page 450). Four dancers are positioned

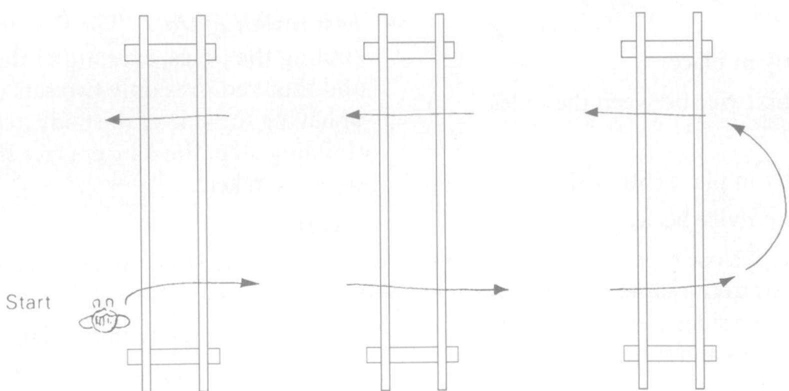

FIGURE 19.7 Movement through line of poles for tinikling.

as shown. The movements are as follows: During measure 1, each dancer does a tinikling step, crossing to the outside of the square. On measure 2, the dancers circle to position for a return tinikling step. During measure 3, the dancers do a tinikling step, returning to the inside of the square. On measure 4, they rotate counterclockwise to the next set of poles with three running steps.

The basic tinikling step must be mastered if children are to enjoy the activity. Tell them to look ahead (not at the poles), so they learn by thinking and doing and not by gauging the pole distances visually.

Four pole set: This arrangement features two longer crossbars, on which two sets of poles rest, leaving a small space between the poles when the sets are open. Four clappers control the poles. Two dancers begin by each straddling a set of poles on opposite ends, so the dancers face each other. Changes in foot pattern should be made every 16 measures, which for most selections is a full pattern of music. The following steps and routines are suggested.

1. Straddle, jump, jump, exiting on measure 16 to the left.
2. Do the basic tinikling step, exiting on the left foot.
3. Do the basic tinikling step, first on one's own set of poles and then on the other set of poles. As the dancer comes out of the first set of poles with the right foot, she makes a half turn to do the tinikling step through the other poles. On the return, she makes another half turn in the middle to face and return to her original position. Repeat the sequence twice.
4. Do the same routine as in number 3, but move diagonally, passing the oncoming dancer with right shoulder to right shoulder, in effect changing places. (Do not use half turns.) Turn around in six steps and return to position. Repeat.
5. Jump to a straddle position with one foot in each of the pole openings. On "close," jump to the space between the sets. On measure 16, the dancer jumps out to the left on both feet.
6. Two-footed step: Jump twice with both feet inside the first set of poles, to the space between, twice inside the second set, and out. Return. Repeat twice.

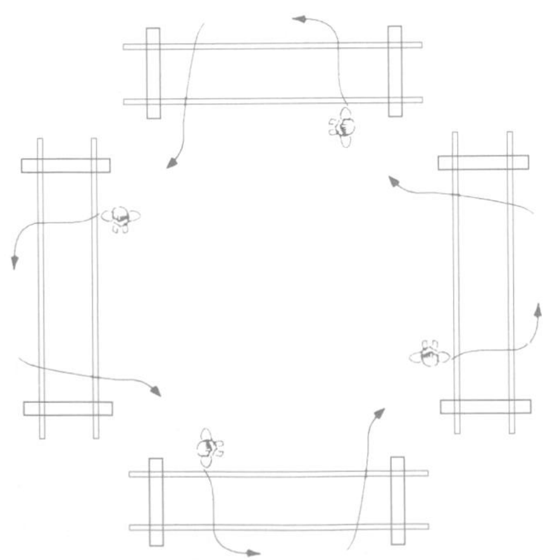

FIGURE 19.8 Square formation for tinikling.

DEVELOPMENTAL LEVEL III DANCES

At this level, children should be adept dancers, especially if they have participated in rhythmic activities for several years. If students do not have a well-developed dance background, it is recommended that they first learn dances from developmental levels I and II. Developmental level III dances include dance patterns that must be performed with skill and finesse. At this level, patterns become longer, requiring more concentration and memorization. The schottische, polka, and two-step make their first appearance in these dances. The progression ranges from a dance that is performed in a circle and introduces square dance moves, to dances that feature the two-step, polka step, and schottische.

HORA (HAVA NAGILA) (ISRAELI)

Music Source: WWCD-3528; WWC-3528

Skills: Stepping sideward, step-swing

Formation: Single circle, facing center, hands joined. The circle can be partial.

Note: The hora is regarded as the national dance of Israel. It is a simple dance that expresses joy. The traditional hora is done in circle formation, with the arms extended sideward and the hands on the neighbors' shoulders. It is easiest to introduce the dance step individually. Once the step is learned, youngsters can join hands and practice the circle formation counterclockwise or clockwise. The clockwise version is presented here.

There are an old and a new hora, as done in Israel. The new hora is more energetic, with the dancers springing high in the air and whirling around with shouts of ecstasy. The hora can be done to many tunes, but the melody of "Hava Nagila" is the favorite.

Directions—Old Hora:

Measures	*Action*
1–3	Step left on the left foot. Cross the right foot in back of the left, with the weight on the right. Step left on the left foot and hop on it, swinging the right foot forward. Step-hop on the right foot and swing the left foot forward. The same step is repeated over and over. (Side, behind, side, swing; Side, swing)

The circle may move to the right also, in which case the same step is used, but the dancers begin with the right foot.

Directions—New Hora:

Measures	*Action*
1–3	Face left and run two steps. Jump in place. Hop on the left foot, swinging the right foot forward. Take three quick steps in place. Continue in the same manner, moving to the left. (Run, run, jump, hop-swing, step, step, step)

The hora often begins with the dancers swaying in place from left to right as the music builds. Gradually, the dance increases in pace and intensity. Shouts accompany the dance as the participants call to each other across the circle. The words *Hava Nagila* mean "Come, let us be happy!"

VIRGINIA REEL (AMERICAN)

Music Source: WWCD-05114

Skills: Skipping, arm turn, do-si-do, sliding (sashay), reeling

Formation: Six couples in a longways set of two lines facing. Partners on one end of the set are designated the head couple.

Directions:

Measures	*Call*	*Action*
1–4	*All go forward and back.*	Take three steps forward, curtsy or bow. Take three steps back and close.
5–8	*Right hands around.*	Move forward to partner, turn once in place using a right forearm grasp and return to position.
9–12	*Left hands around.*	Repeat measures 5–8 with a left forearm grasp.
13–16	*Both hands around.*	Partners join both hands, turn once in a clockwise direction, and move backward to place.
17–20	*Do-si-do your partner.*	Partners pass each other right shoulder to right shoulder and then back to back and move backward to place.
21–24	*All go forward and back.*	Repeat the action of measures 1–4.
25–32	*Head couple sashay.*	The head couple, with hands joined, takes eight slides down to the foot of the set and eight slides back to place.
33–64	*Head couple reel.*	The head couple begins the reel with linked right elbows and turns one and one-half times to face the next couple in line. Each member in the head couple then links left elbows with the person facing and turns once in place. The head couple meets again in the center and turns once with a right elbow swing. The next dancers down the line are turned with a left elbow swing and then the head couple returns to the center for another right elbow turn. The head couple thus progresses down the line, turning each dancer in order. After the head couple has turned

		the last dancers, they meet with a right elbow swing, turn halfway around, and sashay (slide) back to the head of the set.
65–96	*Everybody march.*	All couples face toward the head of the set with the head couple in front. The person on the right turns to the right while the person on the left turns to the left and goes behind the line followed by the other dancers. When the head couple reaches the foot of the set, they join hands and make an arch, under which all other couples pass. The head couple is now at the foot of the set and the dance is repeated with a new head couple.

The dance is repeated until each couple has had a chance to be the head couple.

TEACHING TIP

Versions of this dance vary. Some allow time at the beginning for a do-si-do after the "both hands around" (measures 13–16) while others do not. Check the music for phrasing before presenting the dance to the class.

Technically, the dance is written for eight couples in each set. For the head couple to reel all couples in the set, they must not miss one beat of the music or they will be behind the phrasing for the reel section. When introducing the dance to a class for the first time, having only six couples in each set is helpful. Then, if a couple gets behind the music for the reeling section, they still can stay in time to the music and finish before the "casting off" section begins.

Teaching the Two-Step

Children can be taught the forward two-step simply by moving forward on the cue "Step, close, step," starting on the left foot and alternating thereafter. The close-step is made by bringing the toe of the closing foot to a point even with the instep of the other foot. All steps are almost slides, a kind of shuffle step.

The two-step just described is nothing more than a slow gallop, alternating the lead foot. One way to help students learn the step-close-step pattern is to put them in a single circle and have them gallop forward. They should all start on the left foot and move forward eight slow gallops. Stop the class and have them put their right foot forward and repeat the gallops. Continue this pattern, and have the students make the change from galloping with their left foot forward to galloping with their right foot forward without stopping. When they make this transition, they should bring the right foot forward in a walking step—the weight being on the left foot. Reverse the procedure when moving the left foot forward. The movement should be very smooth. When the students master this pattern, repeat the sequence, but do four gallops with each foot forward. After this pattern is mastered, repeat the pattern with two gallops on each foot. When students can do this, they are performing the forward two-step.

Next, arrange the children by couples in a circle formation, partners A on the inside, all facing counterclockwise. Repeat the instruction, with both partners beginning on the left foot. Practice the two-step with a partner, with partner A beginning on the left foot and partner B starting on the right. In the next progression, the children move face to face and back to back.

JUGGLEHEAD MIXER (AMERICAN)

Music Source: Any music with a definite and steady beat

Skills: Two-step, elbow turn (forearm grasp)

Formation: Double circle facing counterclockwise in promenade position

Directions: Actions described are for the inside partner; directions are opposite for the partner on the outside of the circle.

Measures	***Call***	***Action***
1–4	*Two-step left and two-step right, walk-2-3-4.*	Do a two-step left and two-step right and take four walking steps forward.
5–8	*Two-step left and two-step right, walk-2-3-4.*	Repeat measures 1–4.
9–10	*Turn your partner with the right.*	Inside partner takes the outside partner's right hand and walks around to face the person behind.
11–12	*Now your corner with your left.*	Inside partner turns the person behind with the left hand.
13–14	*Turn your partner all the way around.*	Inside partner turns partner with the right hand going all the way around.

15–16	*And pick up the forward lady.*	Inside partner steps up one place to the outside person ahead, who becomes the new partner.

TETON MOUNTAIN STOMP (AMERICAN)

Music Source: WWCD-FDN

Skills: Walking, banjo position, sidecar position, two-step

Formation: Form single circle of partners in closed dance position, partners A facing counterclockwise, partners B facing clockwise.

Directions:

Measures	*Action*
1–4	Step to the left toward the center of the circle on the left foot, close right foot to the left, step again to the left on the left foot, stomp right foot beside the left but leave the weight on the left foot. Repeat this action, but start on the right foot and move away from the center. (Side, close; Side, stomp; Side, close; Side, stomp)
5–8	Step to the left toward the center on the left foot; stomp the right foot beside the left. Step to the right away from the center on the right foot, and stomp the left foot beside the right. In "banjo" position (modified closed position with right hips adjacent), partner A takes four walking steps forward while partner B takes four steps backward, starting on the right foot. (Side, stomp, side, stomp; Walk, 2, 3, 4)
9–12	Partners change to sidecar position (modified closed position with left hips adjacent) by each making a one half turn to the right in place, A remaining on the inside and B on the outside. A walks backward while B walks four steps forward. Partners change back to banjo position with right hips adjacent by each making a left-face one half turn; then they immediately release from each other. A walks forward four steps to meet the second B approaching, while B walks forward four steps to meet the second A approaching. (Change, 2, 3, 4; New partner, 2, 3, 4)
13–16	New partners join inside hands and do four two-steps forward, beginning with A's right foot and B's left. (Step, close, step; Repeat four times)

TEACHING TIP

If the dancers are skillful enough, use the following action for measures 13–16: New partners take the closed dance position and do four turning two-steps, starting on A's left (B's right) and make one complete right-face turn while progressing in the line of direction.

COTTON-EYED JOE (AMERICAN)

Music Source: WWCD-FDN

Skills: Heel-toe, two-step

Formation: Double circle of couples with partner B on the right, holding inside hands and facing counterclockwise. Varsouvienne position can also be used.

Directions:

Measures	*Action*
1–2	Starting with the left foot, cross the left foot in front of the right foot, kick the left foot forward. (Cross, kick)
3–4	Take one two-step backward. (Left, close, left)
5–6	Cross the right foot in front of the left foot; kick the right foot forward. (Cross, kick)
7–8	Do one two-step backward. (Right, close, right)
9–16	Repeat measures 1–8.
17–32	Perform eight two-steps counterclockwise beginning with the left foot. (Step, close, step; Repeat eight times)

TEACHING TIP

During measures 17–32, the last four two-steps may be done in a circle.

Teaching the Polka Step

The polka and the two-step are much alike. They both have a step-close-step pattern. The two-step is simply step-close-step, but the polka is step-close-step-hop. Technically, the polka is usually described as hop-step-close-step (or hop-step-together-step). However, the first description is probably more helpful when working with beginning students.

The polka step can be broken down into four movements: (1) step forward left, (2) close the right foot to the left, bringing the toe up and even with the left instep, (3) step forward left, and (4) hop on the left foot. The series begins with the weight on the right foot.

Several methods can be used to teach the polka:

1. *Step-by-step rhythm approach.* Analyzing the dance slowly, have the class walk through the steps together in even rhythm. The cue is "Step, close, step, hop." Accelerate the tempo to normal polka time and add the music.
2. *Gallop approach.* A method preferred by many elementary instructors is the gallop approach. (Review the previous section on teaching the two-step, which uses the gallop.) The approach is the same, but add the polka hop and speed up the tempo. When moving the right foot forward, a hop must be taken on the left foot. When moving the left foot forward, the hop is on the right foot.
3. *Two-step approach.* Beginning with the left foot, two-step with the music, moving forward in the line of direction in a single circle. Accelerate the tempo gradually to a fast two-step and take smaller steps. Without stopping, change to a polka rhythm by following each two-step with a hop. Use polka music for the two-step, but slow it down considerably to start.
4. *Partner approach.* After the polka step has been learned individually by one of the three methods, the step can be practiced with partners in a double-circle formation, partners A on the inside and all facing counterclockwise, with inside hands joined. Partners A begin with the left foot and partners B with the right.

KLUMPAKOJIS (SWEDISH)

Music Source: WWCD-1042

Skills: Walking, stars, polka step

Formation: Couples in a circle, side by side, all facing counterclockwise, with partner B to the right

Directions:

Measures	***Part I Action***
1–4	With inside hands joined, free hand on hip, all walk briskly around the circle for eight steps counterclockwise. (Walk, 2, 3, 4, 5, 6, 7, turn)
5–8	Turn individually to the left, reverse direction, change hands, and walk eight steps clockwise. (Walk, 2, 3, 4, 5, 6, 7, turn)
	Part II Action
9–12	Face partner and make a star by joining right hands (making certain that the right elbow is bent). The left hand is on the hip. With partner, walk around clockwise for eight walking steps. Change hands and repeat the eight steps, reversing direction. (Star, 2, 3, 4, 5, 6, 7, 8; Reverse, 2, 3, 4, 5, 6, 7, 8)
	Part III Action
13–16	Listen to the musical phrase, then stamp three times on the last two counts. Listen to the phrase again, then clap own hands three times. (Listen, listen, stamp, 2, 3; Listen, listen, clap, 2, 3)
17–20	Shake the right finger in a scolding motion at partner. (Scold, 2, 3) Shake the left finger. (Scold, 2, 3)
21–24	Turn solo to the left, clapping partner's right hand once during the turn. Use two walking steps to make the turn, and finish facing partner. (Turn, 2, stamp, 2, 3)
25–32	Repeat the action of measures 13–24.
	Part IV Action
33–40	With inside hands joined, do 16 polka steps (or two-steps) forward, moving counterclockwise. (Later, as the dance is learned, change to the promenade position.) On polka steps 15 and 16, partner A moves forward to take a new partner B while handing the original partner B to the A in back. New couple joins inside hands. (Step, close, step, hop; Step, close, step, hop; Repeat for a total of 16 polka steps)

ALLEY CAT (AMERICAN)

Music Source: WWCD-4903; WWC-RM3

Skills: Grapevine step, touch step, knee lifts

Formation: None, although all should face the same direction during instruction

Directions:

Measures	***Action***
1–2	Do a grapevine left and kick: Step sideward left, step right behind left, step left again, and kick. Repeat to the right. (Left, behind, left, kick; Right, behind, right, kick)
3–4	Touch the left toe backward, bring the left foot to the right, touch the left toe backward again, bring the left foot to the right, taking the weight. Repeat, beginning with the right toe. (Left and, left and; Right and, right and)
5–6	Raise the left knee up in front of the right knee and repeat. Raise the right knee up twice, similarly. (Left and, left and; Right and, right and)
7–8	Raise the left knee and then the right knee. Clap the hands once and make a jump

quarter turn to the left. (Left and, right and, clap and, jump)

After the routine is repeated three times, the dancer should be facing in the original direction.

TEN PRETTY GIRLS (AMERICAN)

Music Source: WWCD-1042

Skills: Walking, grapevine

Formation: Circle of groups of any number, with arms linked or hands joined, all facing counterclockwise

Directions:

Measures	*Action*
1–2	Starting with the weight on the right foot, touch the left foot in front, swing the left foot to the left and touch, swing the left foot behind the right foot and put the weight on the left foot, step to the right, close the left foot to the right. (Front, side, back-side, together)
3–4	Repeat, starting with the weight on the left foot and moving to the right. (Front, side, back-side, together)
5–6	Take four walking or strutting steps forward, starting on the left foot. (Walk, 2, 3, 4)
7–8	Swing the left foot forward with a kicking motion; swing the left foot backward with a kicking motion; stamp left, right, left, in place. (Swing, swing, stamp, stamp, stamp)

Repeat the entire dance 11 times, starting each time with the alternate foot. The dance can be used as a mixer when performed in a circle by groups of three. On measures 7–8, have the middle person move forward to the next group during the three stamps.

LIMBO ROCK

Music Source: WWCD-4903

Skills: Touch step, swivel step, jump clap step

Formation: Single circle or scattered

Directions:

Measures	*Part I Action*
1–2	Touch left foot in. Touch left foot out. Three steps in place. (In, out, left, right, left)
3–4	Repeat measures 1 and 2 beginning with opposite foot. (In, out, right, left, right)
5–8	Repeat measures 1–4.
	Part II Action
9–10	Swivel toes right, swivel heels right. Repeat and straighten feet. (Swivel, 2, 3, straighten)
11–12	Repeat beats 1 and 2 beginning with swivel toes left.
13–14	Jump in, clap; jump out, clap. (Jump, clap, jump, clap)
15–16	Repeat measures 13 and 14.

TEACHING TIP

An easier version involves walking eight steps right during measures 9–16.

JESSIE POLKA (AMERICAN)

Music Source: WWCD-RM8

Skills: Step and touch, two-step, or polka step

Formation: Circle, couples facing counterclockwise with inside arms around each other's waist

Directions:

Measures	*Part I Action*
1	Beginning left, touch the heel in front, then step left in place. (Left heel, together)
2	Touch the right toe behind. Then touch the right toe in place, or swing it forward, keeping the weight on the left foot. (Right toe, touch)
3	Touch the right heel in front, then step right in place. (Right heel, together)
4	Touch the left heel to the left side, sweep the left foot across in front of the right. Keep the weight on the right. (Left heel, crossover)
	Part II Action
5–8	Take four two-steps or polka steps forward in the line of direction. (Step, close, step; Step, close, step; Step, close, step; Step, close, step)

TEACHING TIP

The dance may be done as a mixer by having partner B turn out to the right on the last two two-steps and come back to the A behind her. Partners A continue to move forward on the last two two-steps, to make it easier to meet the B coming toward them. Another variation is to perform this activity as a line dance. Youngsters place the hands on the waist or shoulders of the dancer in front of them.

JIFFY MIXER

Music Source: WWCD-FDN

Skills: Heel-and-toe step, chug step

Formation: Double circle, partners facing

Directions: The music includes an introduction. Directions are for partners A; B's actions are opposite.

Measures	*Introduction*
1–4	Wait, wait, balance apart (push away on the left foot and touch the right). Balance together (forward on the right and touch the left).
	Action
1–4	Strike the left heel diagonally out and return to touch the toe near the right foot. Repeat. Do a side step left with a touch. (Heel, toe; Heel, toe; Side, close; Side, touch)
5–8	Repeat while moving in the opposite direction, beginning with the right foot. (Heel, toe; Heel, toe; Side, close; Side, touch)
9–12	Take four chug steps backward clapping on the up beat. (Chug, clap, chug, clap, chug, clap, chug, clap)
13–16	Starting with the left foot, take four slow, swaggering steps diagonally to the right, progressing to a new partner. (Walk, 2, 3, 4)

The chug step is done by jumping and dragging both feet backward. The body is bent slightly forward.

TEACHING TIP

The dance can be introduced by having all join hands in a single circle, facing inward. There are no partners and no progressions to new partners.

INSIDE-OUT MIXER

Music Source: Any music with a pronounced beat suitable for walking at a moderate speed

Skills: Walking, wring the dishrag, change partners

Formation: Triple circle (three children standing side by side), facing counterclockwise, inside hands joined. A piney can be worn by the center person for identification.

Directions:

Measures	*Action*
1–4	Take eight walking steps forward. (Forward, 2, 3, 4, 5, 6, 7, 8)
5–8	Form a small circle and circle left in eight steps back to place. (Circle, 2, 3, 4, 5, 6, 7, 8)
9–12	The center person walks forward under the raised arms opposite, pulling the other two under to turn the circle inside out. (Inside-out, 2, 3, 4, 5, 6, 7, 8)
13–16	The trio circles left in eight steps, returning to place. When almost back to place, drop hands. The center person walks forward counterclockwise, and the other two walk clockwise (the way they are facing) to the nearest trio for a change of partners. (Circle, 2, 3, 4, mix, 6, 7, 8)

D'HAMMERSCHMIEDSGSELLN (BAVARIAN)

Music Source: WWCD-TC1; WWC-TC1

Skills: Clapping routine, step-hops

Formation: Circle of four

Directions: Translated, the title of the dance means "The Journey Blacksmith."

Measures	*Action*
1–16	First opposites do a clapping pattern beginning on the first count of measure 1, while the other pair does a clapping pattern beginning on the first count of measure 2. The six-count pattern is performed as follows: With both hands, slap own thighs (count 1), slap own chest (count 2), clap own hands (count 3), clap right hands (count 4), clap left hands (count 5), and clap opposite's hands (count 6). (Thighs, chest, together, right, left, both) Repeat the six-count pattern seven additional times.
	Part I
17–24	Join hands and circle left with eight step-hops. (Step-hop, 2-hop, ... 8-hop)
25–32	Circle right in the same manner. (Step-hop, 2-hop, ... 8-hop)
33–48	Repeat the chorus action.
	Part II—Star
49–56	Right-hand star with eight step-hops. (Step-hop, 2-hop, . . . 8-hop)
57–64	Left-hand star in the same manner. (Step-hop, 2-hop, . . . 8-hop)
65–80	Repeat the chorus action.
	Part III—Big Circle
81–88	Circles of four open to form one large circle, and circle left with eight step-hops. (Step-hop, 2-hop, . . . 8-hop)
89–96	Reverse direction, continuing with eight step-hops. (Step-hop, 2-hop, . . . 8-hop)

TEACHING TIP

As a mixer, try the following sequence.

Measures	***Action***
1–16	Use the chorus clapping pattern described.
17–24	As in Part I or II, circle left, or do a right-hand star with step-hops (or simple walking steps).

25–32	Do eight step-hops with the corner in general space or in any comfortable position, progressing anywhere.

Repeat the entire sequence with a new foursome.

KALVELIS (LITTLE BLACKSMITH) (LITHUANIAN)

Music Source: WWCD-WOF3

Skills: Polka step, swing, clapping pattern, grand right and left

Formation: Single circle of couples facing center, partner B on partner A's right, all hands joined in a single circle with the right foot free

Directions:

Measures	*Part I Action*
1–8	Circle right with seven polka steps, ending with three stamps. (Circle and, 2 and, 3 and, 4 and, 5 and, 6 and, 7 and, stamp, stamp, stamp)
9–16	Circle left with seven polka steps, ending with three stamps. (Circle and, 2 and, 3 and, 4 and, 5 and, 6 and, 7 and, stamp, stamp, stamp)
	Chorus
1–2	Clap own hands four times, alternating, left hand onto own right, then right hand onto own left. (Clap, 2, 3, 4)
3–4	Right elbow swing with four skips. (Swing, 2, 3, 4)
5–6	Repeat the clapping pattern of measures 1 and 2. (Clap, 2, 3, 4)
7–8	Left elbow swing with four skips. (Swing, 2, 3, 4)
9–16	Repeat the pattern of measures 1–8.
	Part II Action
1–8	Partners B dance three polka steps forward toward the center, ending with three stamps. They then turn to face their partner and return to place with three polka steps forward, ending with three stamps, facing center again. (Step-close-step-hop; Step-close-step-hop; Step-close-step-hop; Stamp, stamp, stamp)
9–16	Partners A repeat the pattern of measures 1–8, but dance more vigorously, stamping on the first beat of each measure. (Step-close-step-hop; Step-close-step-hop; Step-close-step-hop; Stamp, stamp, stamp)
	Chorus
1–16	As described above.
	Part III Action
1–16	Grand right and left around the circle with 16 polka steps, meeting a new partner on the last measure. (Step-close-step-hop; Repeat 16 times)
	Chorus
1–16	As described, but with a new partner.

DOUDLEBSKA POLKA (CZECHOSLOVAKIAN)

Music Source: WWCD-572; WWC-572

Skills: Polka step, walking, clapping pattern

Formation: Make either one large circle or several smaller circles scattered around the floor. The following description is for one large circle.

Directions:

Measures	*Part I Action*
1–16	Partners assume the varsouvienne position and do 16 polka steps around the circle, one couple following another. (Polka, 2, 3, . . . 16)
	Part II Action
17–32	Partner A puts the right arm around partner B's waist as they stand side by side, while B puts the left hand on A's right shoulder. A puts the left hand on the shoulder of the A in front. This closes the circle. Partners A move sideward to the center to catch up with the A ahead. In this position, all march forward counterclockwise and sing loudly, "La, la, la," and so forth. This takes 32 walking steps. (Walk, 2, 3, . . . 32)
	Part III Action
33–48	Partners A face the center, and partners B drop behind their partner. Bs turn to face the other way, clockwise, and polka around the circle (around the A partners) with their hands on hips. At the same time, A partners, who face center, clap a rhythm as follows: Clap hands twice, then extend both hands, palms outward, toward the neighbor on each side, and clap hands once with the neighbor. Repeat this pattern over and over. For variation, A partners may slap a thigh occasionally, or duck down, or cross their arms when clapping the neighbor's hand. (A: Clap, clap, out; Repeat 16 times) (B: Polka, 2, 3, . . . 16)

At the end of Part III, partners A turn around, take whichever partner B is behind them, and resume the dance from the beginning. If some children are without a partner, they move to the center and thus find a partner.

Extra children can enter the dance during the clapping part for partners A, and some can join the ring to polka around the outside. Those left without a partner wait for the next turn. When the group is large, several circles can be made, and it is perfectly proper for unpartnered children to steal into another circle. The polka in this case is done anywhere around the room. During the march, make circles of any number of people.

Teaching the Schottische Step

The schottische is actually a light run, but when students are learning, it should be practiced as a walking step. (This is also true in polka instruction.) Lively music will quicken the step later. The cue is "Step, step, step, hop; step, step, step, hop; step-hop, step-hop, step-hop, step-hop." A full pattern of the schottische, then, is three steps and a hop, repeated once, followed by four step-hops. Partner A starts on the left foot and partner B on the right. The step can be learned first in scattered formation, then a single circle, and practiced later by couples in a double circle. An effective way to introduce the schottische is with the "Horse and Buggy Schottische."

HORSE AND BUGGY SCHOTTISCHE (AMERICAN)

Music Source: WWCD-1046

Skills: Schottische step

Formation: Couples in sets of four in a double circle, facing counterclockwise. Couples join inside hands and give outside hands to the other couple (Figure 19.9).

Directions:

Measures	*Action*
1–2	Moving forward, perform two schottische steps. (Step, step, step, hop; Step, step, step, hop)
3–4	Progress in line of direction performing four step-hops. (Step-hop, 2-hop, 3-hop, 4-hop)

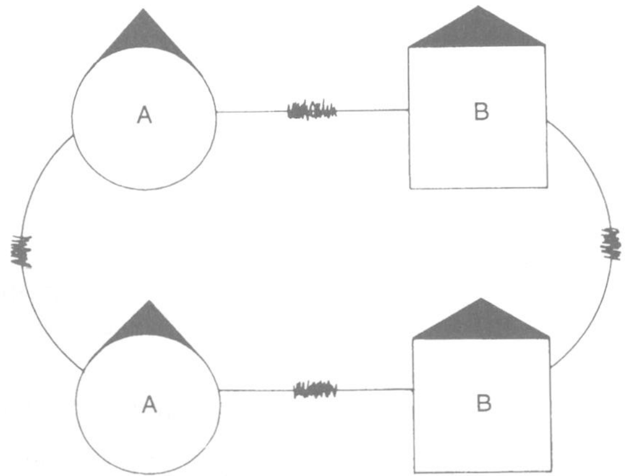

FIGURE 19.9 Horse and Buggy Schottische formation.

During the four step-hops, one of three movement patterns can be done.

1. The lead couple drops inside hands and step-hops around the outside of the back couple, who move forward during the step-hops. The lead couple then joins hands behind the other couple, and the positions are reversed.
2. The lead couple continues to hold hands and move backward under the upraised hands of the back couple, who untwist by turning away from each other.
3. Alternate 1 and 2.

ALUNELUL (ROMANIAN)

Music Source: WWCD-TC1; WWC-TC1

Skills: Step behind step, grapevine step, stomping

Formation: Single circle, hands on shoulders to both sides, arms straight ("T" position)

Directions: The Romanians are famous for rugged dances. This dance is called "Little Hazelnut." The stomping action represents the breaking of the hazelnuts. The title is pronounced "ah-loo-NAY-loo."

Measures	*Part I Action*
1–2	Sidestep right, step left behind right, sidestep right, step left behind right, sidestep right, stomp left foot twice. (Side, back, side, back, side, stomp, stomp)
3–4	Beginning with the left foot, repeat the action but with reverse footwork. (Side, back, side, back, side, stomp, stomp)
5–8	Repeat the action of measures 1–4.
	Part II Action
9–10	Sidestep right, left behind right, sidestep right, stomp. (Side, back, side, stomp)
11–12	Sidestep left, right behind left, sidestep left, stomp. (Side, back, side, stomp)
13–16	Repeat the action of measures 9–12.
	Part III Action
17–18	In place, step right, stomp left; step left, stomp right; step right, stomp left twice. (Side, stomp, side, stomp, side, stomp, stomp)
19–20	In place, step left, stomp right; step right, stomp left; step left, stomp right twice. (Side, stomp, side, stomp, side, stomp, stomp)
21–24	Repeat action of measures 17–20.

TEACHING TIP

The stomps should be made close to the supporting foot. In teaching the dance, scatter the dancers in general space so they can move individually.

KOROBUSHKA (RUSSIAN)

Music Source: WWCD-572; WWC-572

Skills: Schottische step, balance step, cross-out-together step, walking step

Formation: Double circle, partner A's back to the center, with partners facing and both hands joined. A's left and B's right foot are free.

Directions:

Measures	***Part I Action***
1–2	Take one schottische step away from the center (partner A moving forward, partner B backward) starting with A's left and B's right foot. (Out, 2, 3, hop)
3–4	Repeat the pattern of measures 1 and 2, reversing direction and footwork. (In, 2, 3, hop)
5–6	Repeat the pattern of measures 1 and 2, ending on the last count with a jump on both feet in place. (Out, 2, 3, jump)
7–8	Hop on the left foot, touching the right toes across in front of the left foot (count 1). Hop on the left foot, touching the right toes diagonally forward to the right (count 2). Jump on both feet in place, clicking the heels together (count 1), pause, and release the hands (count 2). (Across, apart, together)
	Part II Action
9–10	Facing partner and beginning with the right foot, take one schottische step right, moving sideways away from partner. (Side, back, side, hop)
11–12	Facing partner and beginning with the left foot, take one schottische step left, returning to partner. (Side, back, side, hop)
13–14	Joining right hands with partner, balance forward and back: Step forward on the right foot (count 1), pause (count 2), rock back on the left foot in place (count 3), pause (count 4). (Forward, hop, back, hop)
15–16	Take four walking steps forward, starting with the right foot, and change places with partner. (Walk, 2, 3, 4)
17–24	Repeat the pattern of measures 9–16, returning to place.

TEACHING TIP

To use the dance as a mixer, during measures 19 and 20, move left to the person just before partner and continue with this new partner.

Practice the schottische steps in different directions prior to introducing the dance as a whole.

OH JOHNNY (AMERICAN)

Music Source: WWCD-05114; WWC-57

Skills: Shuffle step, swing, allemande left, do-si-do, promenade

Formation: Single circle of couples facing inward with partner B on the right

Directions: A shuffle step is used throughout this dance.

Action

All join hands and circle for eight steps.

All stop and swing with partner.

A partners turn to their left and swing the corner B.

Swing with partner again.

A partners turn to their left and do an allemande left with their corner.

A partners turn to their right and do a do-si-do with their partner.

A partners promenade with the corner B, who becomes the new partner for the next repetition.

TEACHING TIP

To simplify the dance, begin in scattered formation and teach each call with students changing from partner to corner using any nearby person. Since this is a fast-moving dance, the music should be slowed down until students can successfully complete the dance.

SHINDIG IN THE BARN (AMERICAN)

Music Source: WWC-FFD

Skills: Walking, do-si-do, swinging, sliding

Formation: Contra Style (two lines with partners facing each other). Seven couples will fit the music

Directions:

Measures	***Action***
2 (8 counts total)	Introduction
1–2	Everybody walk forward four steps and back four steps. (Forward, 2, 3, 4; Back, 2, 3, 4)
3–4	All pass through to the other side by walking forward four steps toward partner, do

	a half turn while passing right shoulder of partner, and walk four steps backward. (Walk, 2, 3, 4, turn, 6, 7, 8)
5–6	Everybody forward and back—repeat measures 1–2 above. (Forward, 2, 3, 4; Back, 2, 3, 4)
7–8	Everybody pass through to the other side with eight steps—repeat measures 3–4 above. (Walk, 2, 3, 4, turn, 6, 7, 8)
9–10	All couples do-si-do by passing right shoulders and back. (Do-si-do, 2, 3, . . . 8)
11–12	All couples do a two-hand swing one time around to the left using eight steps. After the swing, all couples except the head couple go back to their original position. The head couples remain in the middle with their hands joined facing each other. (Swing, 2, 3, . . . 8)
13–14	The head couple takes eight sliding (sashay) or skipping steps to the foot of the line. All the other couples clap to the beat and watch. (Slide, 2, 3, . . . 8)
15–16	Head couple does a right elbow swing at the foot of the line for eight counts and remains at the foot of the line creating a new head couple. (Swing, 2, 3, . . . 8)

Repeat dance to the end of the music.

BIG SOMBRERO CIRCLE MIXER (AMERICAN)

Music Source: WWC-FFD

Skills: Circling, do-si-do, star, swing

Formation: Sicilian Circle. Couples facing couples clockwise and counterclockwise around the circle

Directions:

Measures	***Action***
2 (8 counts total)	Introduction
1–2	Join hands with the facing couple and circle left using eight walking steps. (Circle, 2, 3, . . . 8)
3–4	Keeping hands joined, circle right using eight walking steps. (Circle right, 2, 3, . . . 8)
5–6	Face partner and do-si-do using eight walking steps. (Do-si-do, 2, 3, . . . 8)
7–8	Face opposite and do-si-do using eight walking steps. (Opposite, 2, 3, . . . 8)
9–10	All four circle while doing a right hand star using eight walking steps. (Star, 2, 3, . . . 8)
11–12	All four circle while doing a left hand star using eight walking steps. (Star, 2, 3, . . . 8)
13–14	Swing partner by linking right elbows and swinging once or twice. (Swing, 2, 3, . . . 8)
15–16	Pass through the opposite couple passing right shoulders and walk to the next couple using eight steps. (Pass, through, 3, 4, . . . 8)

Repeat the dance to the end of the music. Youngsters should always return back to their starting position after every eight count movement.

TRIO FUN MIXER (AMERICAN)

Music Source: WWC-FFD

Skills: Walking, do-si-do, star

Formation: Lines of three facing lines of three in a large circle

Directions:

Measures	***Action***
1–4	Facing threesomes (six dancers) join hands and circle left one time around back to place. (Circle, 2, 3, . . . 16)
5–6	Center student in each threesome does a do-si-do with each other. (Do-si-do, 2, 3, . . . 8)
7–8	Right youngsters in each threesome move diagonally to do-si-do with each other. (Do-si-do, 2, 3, . . . 8)
9–10	Left youngsters in each threesome move diagonally to do-si-do with each other. (Do-si-do, 2, 3, . . . 8)
11–12	Center person in each threesome faces the person on the right and turns that person with a right hand star and then turns the person on the left with a left hand star and goes back to place. (Star, 2, 3, 4; Left, 2, 3, 4)
13–14	Lines of three go forward four counts and back four counts. (Forward, 2, 3, 4; Back, 2, 3, 4)
15–16	Lines of three walk forward passing right shoulders and move forward to the next group of three. (Forward pass, 2, 3, . . . 8)

Repeat to the end of the music.

CIRCLE VIRGINIA REEL (AMERICAN)

Music Source: WWCD-57; WWC-57

Skills: Star, swing, do-si-do, swing, promenade

Formation: Couples facing in a double circle with dancers about 4 feet apart

Directions:

Measures	***Action***
1–4	Partners walk forward four and backward four steps; repeat. (Forward, 2, 3, 4; Back, 2, 3, 4; Forward, 2, 3, 4; Back, 2, 3, 4)
5–8	Partners make a start by joining right hands (with bent elbows) and circling around once clockwise in eight steps. Reverse direction and star with left hands back to place in eight steps. (Right star, 2, 3, . . . 8; Left star, 2, 3, . . . 8)
9–10	Partners join hands with bent elbows held chest high and circle clockwise back to place in eight steps. (Circle, 2, 3, . . . 8)
11–12	Partners walk forward and do-si-do passing right shoulders and stepping to the right when passing back to back. After passing, each partner moves diagonally (veers) to the right to end in front of a new partner. (Do-si-do, 2, 3, 4; Veer, 2, 3, 4)
13–16	Facing a new partner and joining hands, inside circle partner begins with left foot and outside circle begins with right foot doing two heel-toe steps and four slide steps counterclockwise. Repeat to the other side sliding clockwise. (Heel, toe, heel toe, slide, slide, slide, slide; Heel, toe, heel, toe, slide, slide, slide, slide)
17–20	Partners do a right elbow swing in place for 12 counts using a walking step and use four counts to end in promenade position. (Swing, 2, 3, . . . 12; Promenade position 15, 16)
21–24	In promenade position, partners walk forward counterclockwise 16 steps and end facing each other. (Promenade, 2, 3, . . . 16)

INTRODUCTORY SQUARE DANCE

Introductory square dance should be just that—introductory. In no case should the goal be finished, accomplished square dancing. The emphases should be on enjoyment and learning the basics within the maturity capabilities of elementary school children. This can involve, however, considerable skill and polish. Square dancing is a broad and colorful activity with numerous figures, patterns, and dances. The large quantity of materials (introductory, intermediate, and advanced) poses a selection problem given the limited amount of program time that can be allocated to the activity.

Square dance fun begins with an effective caller, and calling takes practice. In a few instances, youngsters can develop into satisfactory callers. One solution is to select square dance music that includes some selections with calls and some with the music only. Directions are usually supplied with the CDs. Singing calls should be used that can be done by one individual, by a group, or by the entire class. Singing calls are fun to dance to, because youngsters know what is coming next.

Square dance instruction should begin modestly in the fourth grade, with the impetus increasing in the fifth and sixth grades. This does not rule out the use of square dance–related figures in folk dances taught earlier. Square dance as a specialized dance activity requires the application of appropriate methodology. Some teaching suggestions follow.

1. In early figure practice or patter calls, pairing off by gender is not important. Let boys dance with boys and girls with girls if necessary. Avoid labeling one position for boys and one for girls. In a couple, one partner becomes the left partner and the other the right. The goal is, however, to have boys dance with girls, and vice versa. In the following section, calls will be given in their traditional forms, and gender references, where they appear, will correspond with the traditional calls.
2. The shuffle step should be used, rather than the skipping or running step that beginners usually tend to use. The shuffle step makes a smoother and more graceful dance, has better carryover to other dancing, and conserves energy. It is a quick walk, almost a half glide, in time to the music and is done by reaching out with the toes in a gliding motion. The body should be in good posture position and should not bounce up and down on each step.
3. Teach the children to listen to the call. Equally important is that they know what the call means. They should have fun, but they must be quiet enough to hear the call.
4. It is important to follow the caller's directions and not move too soon. The children should be ready for the call and then move at the proper time.
5. Generally, the caller explains the figures, has the children walk through the patterns, and then calls the figures.
6. The teacher should remember that there are many different ways to do different turns, swings, hand positions, and so on, and as many opinions on how these should be done. Settle on good principles and stick with them.
7. When a set becomes confused, each couple should return to its home position and try to pick up from that point. Otherwise, the choice is to wait until the dance is over or a new sequence has started.

8. Change partners at different times during the dancing. Have each partner A move one place to the right and take a new partner, or have all of the A partners (or Bs) keep their positions and have their partners change to another set.

The Movement Approach to Square Dance

Many square dance terms can be taught using a movement approach. The students are scattered in general space. A piece of country and western music with a strong beat is played. Anytime students hear the call, they perform the same task with the person nearest to them. Note that there are no boy or girl roles. The two-handed swing is to be used instead of the regular buzz-step swing.

Two calls are basic. "Hit the lonesome trail" directs students to promenade individually in general space in diverse directions. This call can be inserted at any time to move the students in new directions. The other basic call is "Stop where you are and keep time to the music." Students stop and beat time to the music with light claps. Other calls can be selected from the following list.

1. *Right (or left) arm round.* With a forearm grasp, turn your partner once around and return to place.
2. *Honor your partner, honor your corner.* Bow to one person, then bow to another.
3. *Do-si-do your partner, do-si-do your corner.* Pass around one person, right shoulder to right shoulder, and back to place. Repeat with another person.
4. *Right- (or left-) hand star.* Place indicated hands (palm to palm with fingers pointed upward) about shoulder height with elbow somewhat bent. The next call will indicate how far to turn the star.
5. *Two-hand swing.* Partners grasp both hands, lean away from each other, and circle clockwise once around.
6. *Go forward and back.* Move forward with three steps and a touch toward another person, who is moving similarly toward you. Move back to place with three steps and a touch.

The next teaching strategy is to divide the class into groups of four. Use a call such as, "Circle up, four hands round." Groups of four circle clockwise. There usually will be extras. If there are three extras, one person can pretend to have a partner. Rotate the extras in and out.

Circle fours until all groups are formed. With the call, "Break and swing," the fours separate into pairs within the foursome. Position the pairs so they face each other. Use the terms "left partner" and "right partner" instead of boy and girl. If convenient, when there are mixed pairs put the girl on the right.

The following figures can be practiced in fours.

1. *Circle to the left (or right).* Join hands and circle once around as indicated.
2. *Form a right- (or left-) hand star.* Hold right hands at about shoulder height and turn clockwise. A left-hand star reverses the direction.
3. *Swing your opposite and swing your partner.* Left partners walk toward their right partner opposite and swing. They walk back to their own partner and swing. The call can be reversed.
4. *Birdie in the cage and three hands round.* One child (the birdie) goes to the center, while the other three join hands and circle left once around.
5. *The birdie hops out and the crow hops in.* The birdie joins the circle and another child goes in the center.
6. *Go into the middle and come back out; go into the middle and give a little shout.* This is done from a circle-right or circle-left formation. The dancers face center and come together. Repeat again, but with a light shout.
7. *Round and round in a single file; round and round in frontier style.* Circle left (or right), drop hands and move into a single file.
8. *Dive for the oyster—dig for the clam.* Usually after circling left once around, one couple goes partially under the raised joined hands of the other couple. The other couple repeats the same maneuver. Stepping should be: In, 2, 3, touch; Out, 2, 3, touch.

The caller can use the "Hit the lonesome trail" call at any time to break up the makeup of the fours, and then reorganize later with different combinations of students.

Square Dance Formation

Each couple is numbered around the set in a counterclockwise direction. It is important that the couples know their position. The couple with their backs to the music is generally couple 1, or the head couple. The couple to the right of them is number 2, and so on. While the head couple is number 1, the term *head couples* includes both couples 1 and 3; couples 2 and 4 are the *side couples.*

With respect to any one left-hand partner (gent), the following terms are used in traditional calls (adjust references to gender as necessary):

Partner: The other (right-hand) dancer of the couple

Corner or corner lady: The right-hand partner on the left

Right-hand lady: The right-hand partner in the couple to the right

Opposite or opposite lady: The right-hand partner directly across the set

Other terms that are used include these:

Home: The couple's original or starting position

Active or leading couple: The couple leading or visiting the other couples for different figures

Once the square dance formation has been introduced, the figures and patter calls discussed previously should be practiced in the full formation of four couples. Although there is some repetition of material already presented in the movement approach section, the following figures merit discussion with the square dance formation as the background.

American Square Dance Figures

Some common square dance figures are the following:

1. *Honor your partner.* Partners bow to each other.
2. *Honor your corner.* Left-hand dancer bows to corner, who returns the bow.
3. *Shuffle step.* A light walking step on the ball of the foot. The body is upright and movement is in time with the music.
4. *Do-si-do your partner (or corner).* Partners face and pass each other right shoulder to right shoulder, move around each other back to back, and return to the original position facing their partner.
5. *Promenade.* The couple walks side by side, right hand joined to right hand and left to left in a crossed-arm promenade position. They walk around the square once and return to home position.
6. *Circle right (or left).* All eight dancers join hands and circle. The caller can add "Into the center with a great big yell." The circle can be broken with a swing at home place.
7. *Right-and-left grand.* All face their partner, join right hands, walk past the partner, and join left hands with the next person in the ring, and so on down the line. This causes left-hand partners to go in one direction (counterclockwise) around the circle and right-hand partners to go in the other direction, alternately touching right and left hands until partners meet again. Right-and-left grand starts with your partner and ends with your partner, at which time another call is needed.
8. *Allemande left.* Left-hand dancer faces corner, grasps corner with a left-forearm grip, walks around corner, and returns to partner.
9. *Arm swing.* Left-hand dancer turns partner with a right-arm swing, using a forearm grasp.
10. *Swing your partner (or corner).* Partners stand side by side with right hip against right hip. The dancers are almost in social dance position, except that the left-hand partner's right arm is more around to the side than back at the shoulder blade. The dancers walk around each other with a slight lean away from each other until they reach their starting position.
11. *Do paso.* Starting position is a circle of two or more couples. Partners face, take a left forearm grasp, and turn each other counterclockwise until facing the corner. Turn corner with right forearm grasp until facing partner. Take partner with the left hand; left-hand partner turns the other with a courtesy turn.
12. *All around your left-hand lady, seesaw your pretty little taw.* Corners move one time around each other in a loop pattern, left-hand dancer starting behind the corner, on around corner and back to place, right-hand dancer starting in front of corner and around back to place. Repeat with partner to complete the other half of the loop.
13. *Ladies chain.* From a position with two couples facing each other, the girls cross over to the opposite boy, touching right hands as they pass each other. When they reach the opposite boy, they join left hands with him. At the same time, each boy places his right arm around the girl's waist and turns her once around to face the other couple. On "Chain right back," the girls cross back to their partner in a similar figure.
14. *Right-and-left through (and back).* Two couples face each other. Dancers join right hands and pull past opposite, passing right shoulder to right shoulder. Couples have backs to each other. Courtesy turn to face again and repeat to original place.

Selecting Square Dances and Music

In past years, the types of square dances suggested for elementary students were traditional square dances using a patter call. Today, square dancing is a popular form of adult recreation. The singing call and use of modern music has helped in adult popularity, but more important is the difference in traditional calls versus modern calls. In traditional square dancing everyone knew what call was coming next. In modern square dancing nobody knows what the next call will be and nobody wants to know.

Two popular series of albums with different developmental levels and proper progression are the *Wagon Wheel Fundamentals of Square Dancing, Levels 1, 2, & 3,* and *Square Dance Party for the New Dancer, No. 1 & No. 2.* Both series feature the calling of Bob Ruff. They can be ordered from the following source:

Wagon Wheel Records and Books
16812 Pembrook Lane
Huntington Beach, CA 92649
(714) 846-8169

CULMINATING EVENTS FOR THE RHYTHMS UNIT

Country-Western Day

After all of the grade levels have reached a specified performance level in square dancing, a country-western day can be sponsored by the school. Teachers and students should be encouraged to wear country-western-style clothing all day, and then during the last hour of the school day, the student body can have a square dance. It is important to include activities that everyone, from third-grade students to sixth graders, can do together. The movement approach presented previously can help achieve this goal.

May Festival

In the spring when the rhythm program is drawing to a close, it is exciting to feature in a May festival all of the dances learned. To have this activity include everyone, each class or grade level should make a dance presentation. The announcer should describe the history and background of each dance (consult specialty dance books for a description of the various dances), and the festival should end with the entire school performing the Maypole Dance.

FOR MORE INFORMATION

Websites

Dance Ideas
http://pecentral.org/lessonideas/dance/danceindex.asp

Dances of Mexico
http://www.alegria.org/rgndance.html

Levels of Rhythmic Skills
http://www.edb.utexas.edu/coe/depts/kin/Faculty/slacks/crpac/rhythms_levels.html

Multicultural Dances
http://grassroots.brunnet.net/marshviewms/multiculturalweek/multicultural_dances.htm

Square Dancing
http://www.dosado.com/articles/hist-sd.html

CHAPTER 20

Gymnastic Skills

ESSENTIAL COMPONENTS

I	Organized around content standards
II	**Student-centered and developmentally appropriate**
III	**Physical activity and motor skill development form the core of the program**
IV	Teaches management skills and self-discipline
V	**Promotes inclusion of all students**
VI	**Focuses on process over product**
VII	Promotes lifetime personal health and wellness
VIII	Teaches cooperation and responsibility and promotes sensitivity to diversity

PHYSICAL EDUCATION STANDARDS

1	**Students are able to move competently using a variety of fundamental and specialized motor skills.**
2	Students can monitor and maintain a health-enhancing level of physical fitness.
3	**Students are able to apply movement concepts and basic mechanics of skill performance when learning and refining motor skills.**
4	Students comprehend the basic principles of wellness and are able to apply concepts that enable them to make meaningful decisions that positively impact their health and wellness.
5	**Students participate in a wide variety of physical activities and learn how to maintain a personalized active lifestyle.**
6	**Students demonstrate empathy, understanding, and respect for the numerous differences exhibited by people in an activity setting.**
7	Students exhibit responsible and self-directed behaviors that lead to positive social interactions in physical activity.

SUMMARY

Gymnastic activities make a significant contribution to the overall physical education experience for children in elementary schools. Gymnastic activities develop body management skills without the need for equipment and apparatus. Flexibility, agility, balance, strength, and body control are outcomes that are enhanced through participation in gymnastics. Specialized motor skills such as body rolling, balance skills, inverted balances, and tumbling skills are learned through these activities. Various partner and group activities offer opportunity for social interaction and cooperation. Positive learning experiences in gymnastic activities are dependent on progression. When teaching activities, developing a positive attitude and overcoming students' personal limitations are more important than stressing performance with perfect technique. Safety is foremost in the gymnastic program.

OUTCOMES

- List progressions and developmental level placements for gymnastic activities.
- Understand the techniques of spotting when teaching gymnastic activities.
- Organize a comprehensive lesson of gymnastic activities that includes the six basic groups: (a) animal movements; (b) tumbling and inverted balances; (c) balance stunts; (d) individual stunts; (e) partner and group stunts; and (f) partner support activities.
- Identify effective management techniques when teaching gymnastic activities.
- Cite safety considerations essential to the gymnastic program.
- Describe tumbling activities that are appropriate for elementary school children.

Gymnastic activities are an important part of every child's overall experience in physical education, and they can make a significant contribution to the goals of physical education. Through the gymnastics program, such personal characteristics as dedication and perseverance can be furthered, for stunts are seldom mastered quickly. Because much of the work is individual, children face challenges and have the opportunity to develop resourcefulness, self-confidence, and courage. When a challenging stunt is mastered, satisfaction, pride of achievement, and a sense of accomplishment contribute to improved self-esteem. Social interplay is provided through various partner and group stunts requiring cooperative effort. The social attributes of tolerance, helpfulness, courtesy, and appreciation for the ability of others grow out of the lessons when the methodology is educationally sound.

Important physical values emerge from a gymnastics program. Body management opportunities are presented, and coordination, flexibility, and agility are enhanced. The opportunity to practice balance is present in many activities. The demands of holding positions and executing stunts contribute to the development of strength and power in diverse parts of the body. Many stunts demand support, wholly or in part, by the arms, thus providing development of the often weak musculature of the arm-shoulder girdle.

PROGRESSION AND DEVELOPMENTAL LEVEL PLACEMENT

Progression is important in the gymnastics program. In this book, activities are listed in progression within the three developmental levels. To avoid safety problems, the order of these activities should be reasonably maintained. Adherence to developmental level is secondary to the principle of progression. If children have little or no experience in these activities, start them on activities specified in a lower developmental level.

Activities in this chapter are divided into six basic groups: (1) animal movements; (2) tumbling and inverted balances; (3) balance stunts; (4) individual stunts; (5) partner and group stunts; and (6) partner support activities. This arrangement allows the individual to pick activities from each group for a well-balanced lesson. Often, too much time is spent on tumbling activities, causing children to become bored and fatigued. In addition, for children who do not like tumbling activities, choosing activities from all the categories will help them find something they enjoy. At the heart of a gymnastic program are the standard tumbling activities, such as rolls, stands, springs, and related stunts. In performing the activities, emphasis should be placed on exposure and overcoming fear. Perfect technique is less important than developing positive approach behaviors. The suggested progression of the basic activities for each development level is presented in the following lists.

Developmental Level I

Rolling Log
Side Roll
Forward Roll (Tuck Position)
Back Roller
Forward Roll (Straddle Position)
Backward Curl
Backward Roll (Handclasp Position)
Climb-Up
Three-Point Tip-Up
Mountain Climber—Handstand Lead-Up Activity
Switcheroo—Handstand Lead-Up Activity

Developmental Level II

Forward Roll (Pike Position)
Backward Roll (Inclined)
Backward Roll (Regular)
Frog Handstand (Tip-Up)
Half Teeter-Totter—Handstand Lead-Up Activity
Cartwheel
Forward Roll to a Walkout
Forward Roll Combinations
Backward Roll Combinations
Headstand Practice and Variations
Teeter-Totter—Handstand Lead-Up Activity
Handstand

Developmental Level III

Forward and Backward Roll Combinations
Back Extension
Headstand Variations
Handstand against a Wall
Freestanding Handstand
Cartwheel and Round-Off
Judo Roll
Forward and Backward Roll Combinations
Developing Gymnastic Routines
Straddle Press to Headstand
Headspring
Walking on the Hands
Walk-Over

The developmental level I program relies on simple stunts, with a gradual introduction to tumbling stunts classified as lead-ups or preliminaries to more advanced stunts. Stunts requiring exceptional body control, critical balancing, or substantial strength should be left for higher levels of development. The developmental level II and III programs are built on activities and progressions developed earlier. Emphasis is placed on learning more standard gymnastic activities. Most stunts at developmental level I can be performed with a certain degree of choice, whereas at developmental levels II and III more conformance to correct technique is desirable. In general, the upper developmental level activities place higher demands on strength, control, form, agility, balance, and flexibility.

Most activities at developmental level I can be done—at least in some fashion—by most students; but certain activities at levels II and III may be too challenging for some students. Arrange lessons that include a variety of activities: stunts that everyone can do, stunts that are moderately challenging, and stunts that are more challenging.

INSTRUCTIONAL METHODOLOGY FOR GYMNASTICS

Warm-Up and Flexibility Activity

Normal introductory activity and fitness development activity usually supply sufficient warm-up for the gymnastics lesson. If additional stretching seems warranted, take a wide straddle position with the feet about 3 feet apart and the toes pointed ahead. With arms out to the sides, bend, twist, and generally stretch in all directions. Next, touch the floor with the hands to the front, sides, and back, with some bending of the knees.

Extra flexibility may be required in the wrists, ankles, and neck. The following activities can be used prior to participating in the gymnastic activities.

WRISTS

1. Extend one arm forward. With the other hand, push the extended hand down, thus stretching the top of the wrist and forearm muscles. Hold the position for eight counts. Next, pull the hand backward and hold for eight counts to stretch the wrist flexor muscles.
2. Clasp the fingers of both hands in front of the chest. Make circles with both hands and stretch the wrists.

ANKLES AND QUADRICEPS

1. Kneel and sit on both feet. Smoothly and gently lean backward over the feet, using the arms to support the body.
2. In a sitting position, cross one leg over the other. Use the hands to help rotate each foot through its full range of motion. Reverse legs and repeat.

NECK

1. In a sitting position, slowly circle the head in both directions through the full range of motion.
2. In the same position, hold the chin against the chest for eight counts. Repeat with the head looking backward as far as possible. Look to each side and hold for eight counts.

LOWER BACK AND SHOULDERS

Begin in a supine position. Place the hands back over the head on the mat so that the fingers point toward the toes. Bridge up by extending the arms and legs. While in the bridge position, slowly rock back and forth.

Effective Class Management

A commonly heard criticism of gymnastics lessons is that children must wait in line for turns on the mat. Waiting can be controlled so that everyone is reasonably active. How children are arranged depends on the activities selected and whether mats are required. The following ideas help establish priorities.

1. Whenever possible, all children should be active and performing. When mats are not required for the activities, there is little problem. Individual mats can be used for many of the simple balances and rolling stunts, particularly at developmental level I. When larger mats are required, be more ingenious. Ideally, each group of three students should have a mat. When return activities are used in conjunction with groups as small as three, there is little standing around. Small groups also work well when spotting and other types of cooperation are needed.
2. When the number of mats is limited, perform across the mats sideways. On a 6-foot-long mat, two children can tumble sideways. An 8-foot-long mat can be used by three performers at the same time. With this arrangement, the focus is on single rolls, but an occasional series of rolls lengthwise on the mat is not ruled out. The ends of the mats can be used for various stands, as long as children do not fall toward each other.
3. Consider station teaching if equipment is limited. Make plans that ensure the experience stresses progress and diligence. A few tumbling and inverted balance stations can be included, with other stations featuring less demanding activities. The arrangement might include Forward and Backward Rolls at the first station, Headstands at the second, Cartwheels at

the third, and partner stunts at the fourth. Wall charts listing the activities in progression provide excellent guidance. A chart illustrated with stick figures can be made as a class project.

Formations for Teaching

Squad formation. Mats are placed in a line, with squads lined up behind the mats. Each child takes a turn and then goes to the end of the squad line, with the others moving up. An alternative method is for each child to perform and then return to a seated position.

Semicircular formation. Students are positioned in a semicircular arrangement. This formation directs attention toward the teacher, who stands in the center.

U-shaped formation. The mats are placed in the shape of a large U. This formation offers an excellent view for the teacher, and children are able to see what their classmates are doing.

Demonstration mat. One mat is placed in a central position and is used exclusively for demonstrations. Little movement is necessary to see demonstrations.

Description and Demonstration of New Gymnastic Activities

To enhance student learning when presenting an activity, the following sequence may be helpful.

1. *Significance of the name.* Most activities have a characteristic name which should be learned. If the stunt is of an imitative type, the animal or character represented should be described and discussed.
2. *Description of the activity.* Stunts can be approached in terms of three parts: starting position, execution, and finishing position. Most stunts have a defined starting position which must be performed properly. Explain the position to assume as the first step. Next, key movements for proper execution of the activity are presented. Such factors as how far to travel, how long to balance, and how many times a movement should be done can be clarified. In some gymnastic activities, a definite finishing position or action is part of the stunt. In balancing stunts try to return to a standing (or some other) position without losing balance and moving the feet.
3. *Demonstration of the activity.* Three levels of demonstration are recognized: (a) minimal demonstration in the form of the starting position; (b) slow, step-by-step demonstration of the entire stunt, with an explanation of what is involved; and (c) execution of the stunt as it is normally done. Keep in mind that children need to analyze and solve problems. Too much demonstration defeats this goal. Explanation and demonstration should cover only one or two points. Show points necessary to get the activity under way. Add further details and refinements as the instruction progresses. Demonstrations at the end of a unit can show what has been achieved. Allow each squad or group to demonstrate its achievements in turn.

Opportunities for Practice and Improvement

The character of each stunt determines the amount of practice needed and the number of times the stunt should be performed. Analyze the stunt thoroughly enough so you can verbalize the points necessary for proper performance. Practice and repetition are essential in establishing effective movement patterns. To maximize activity and minimize standing in line, allow the class to practice the activity a desired number of times. On the command or whistle to "freeze," the class stops whatever they are doing without returning to formation. Directions are given for the next activity, and the class resumes practicing. This method decreases the amount of management time spent waiting for each squad to finish and return to formation.

SAFETY CONSIDERATIONS

Safety is a foremost consideration in the gymnastic program. The inherent hazards of an activity and how to avoid them must be included in the instructional procedures.

Spotting

The purpose of spotting is twofold. First and most important are the performer's safety and the prevention of injury. Of secondary importance is guiding the performer through the stunt to help develop proper body awareness. When spotting for safety, the goals are to assist the performer, help support the body weight, and prevent a hazardous fall. A particularly difficult problem is working with obese children in tumbling activities.

Two major questions are related to spotting. Should you spot youngsters? Can other students spot their peers? The answer is grounded in your expertise and experience. Many teachers have little, if any, gymnastics background. This makes spotting correctly a difficult task. In addition, obese youngsters may actually weigh more than you, making spotting next to impossible. If this is the case, it is probably best to avoid activities that involve spotting. The issue of peer spotting is also a sensitive one. In many situations, it is difficult to get all students to take spotting responsibilities seriously. Additionally, if many students are spotting in the class, how do you assure quality control? If an accident were to occur while a student was spotting, who would be liable? Legal authorities might try to show that you were not supervising the spotting carefully or that students are too young and are not responsible enough to fulfill the duties of correct spotting.

You will have to decide whether to teach activities that require spotting. If you lack confidence in this area or lack adequate knowledge about proper presentation of the activities, it is probably best to avoid tumbling and inverted balance activities. Because tumbling and inverted balance activities make up only about 20 percent of the activities in this chapter, there are many other stunts and balance activities that can be offered to teach youngsters body management skills. Above all, do not force youngsters to participate in tumbling and inverted balance activities. Specific spotting techniques are offered in this chapter with activities that demand spotting.

INSTRUCTIONAL PROCEDURES

1. Although mats are not necessary for some stunts, it is wise to include stunts requiring mats in every lesson. Children like to perform on mats, and rolling stunts using mats are vital to the gymnastic program.
2. Many partner stunts work well only when partners are about the same size. If the stunt requires partner support, the support child should be strong enough to hold the weight of the other.
3. No two children are alike. Respect individual differences, and allow for different levels of success.
4. Relating new activities to those learned previously is important. An effective approach is to review the lead-up stunt for an activity.
5. When a stunt calls for a position to be held for a number of counts, use a standard counting system (e.g., "One thousand one, one thousand two, . . ." or "Monkey one, monkey two, . . .").
6. When appropriate, have children work in pairs, with one child performing and the second providing a critique.
7. Shifting of mats should not be necessary during the course of instruction. When arranging a gymnastic routine for a day's lesson, group the mat stunts. The tumbling mats should be bordered with Velcro so that, once fastened, they stay fastened together.

Start-and-Expand Technique

The start-and-expand technique should be applied to stunts when feasible. Consider someone teaching a simple Heel Click (page 483). The instructor begins by saying, "Let's see all of you jump high in the air and click your heels together before you come down." (This is the start.) "Now, to do the stunt properly, you should jump into the air, click your heels, and land with your feet apart with a nice bent-knee action to absorb the shock." (This is the expansion.) Further expansion could be adding a quarter or half turn before landing, clapping the hands overhead while clicking the heels, or clicking the heels twice before landing. In general, the start is made simple, so that all children can experience a measure of success. The instruction then expands to other elements of the stunt, with variations and movement factors added and refined as indicated.

Basic Mechanical Principles

Certain mechanical principles should be established as the foundation of an effective gymnastic program. If children can build on these basic principles, instruction is facilitated.

1. Momentum needs to be developed and applied, particularly for rolls. Tucking, starting from a higher point, and preliminary raising of the arms are examples of ways to increase momentum.
2. The center of weight must be positioned over the center of support in balance stunts, particularly in the inverted stands.
3. In certain stunts, such as the Headspring, the hips should be projected upward and forward to raise the center of gravity for better execution.
4. In stunts in which the body is wholly or partially supported by the hands, proper positioning of the hands is essential for effective performance. The hands should be approximately shoulder width apart, and the fingers should be spread and pointed forward.

Basic Gymnastic Positions

Students should be able to recognize and demonstrate basic positions that are unique to gymnastics. Emphasis at the elementary level should be placed on a rough estimation of how the positions are performed, rather than on pure technique.

Tuck Position

The tuck position is performed with the legs bent and the chin tucked to the chest. Students can be cued to "curl up like a ball." There are three different tuck positions, and students should know all of them: the Sitting Tuck (Figure 20.1 on page 470), the Standing Tuck, and the Lying Tuck.

Pike Position

The pike position is performed by bending forward at the hips and keeping the legs straight. The three basic

FIGURE 20.1 Tuck position.

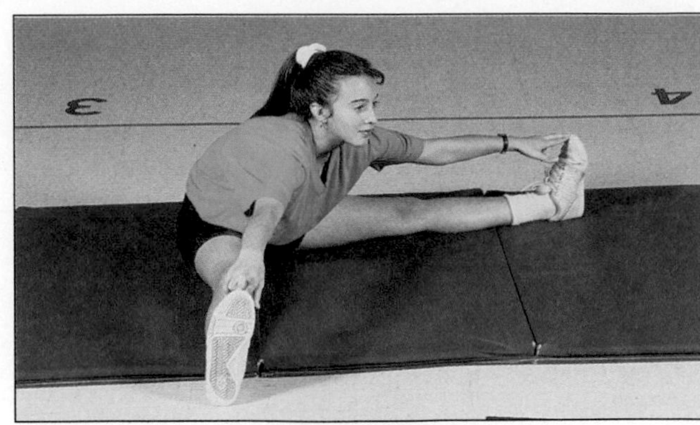

FIGURE 20.3 Straddle position.

pike positions are the Sitting Pike (Figure 20.2), the Standing Pike, and the Lying Pike.

Straddle Position

The straddle position is accomplished by bending forward at the hips and spreading the legs apart to the sides as far as possible. The legs should be kept straight. Variations of the straddle position are the Sitting Piked Straddle (Figure 20.3), the Standing Piked Straddle, and the Lying Piked Straddle.

FIGURE 20.4 Front-support position.

Front-Support Position

This position is similar to the push-up position. The body is straight with the head up (Figure 20.4).

Back-Support Position

The back-support position is an inverted push-up position. The body is kept as straight as possible (Figure 20.5).

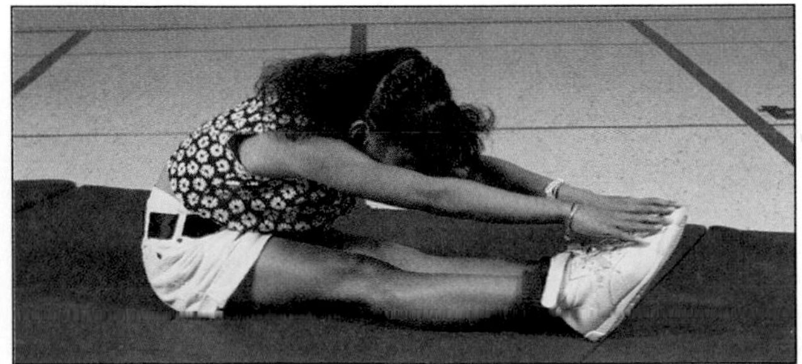

FIGURE 20.2 Pike position.

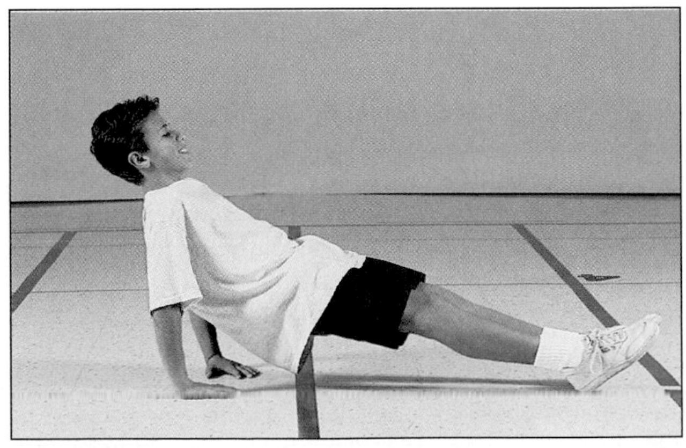

FIGURE 20.5 Back-support position.

Gymnastic Dance Positions

Attitude

An attitude is a position in which the body weight is supported on one leg while the other leg is lifted and bent at the knee. The arm on the side of the lifted leg is usually bent over the head, and the other arm is extended at the side (Figure 20.6).

Lunge Position

In lunge position, the nonsupporting rear leg is straight while the forward, supporting leg is bent at the hip and knee. Most of the weight is placed on the forward leg. The arms are extended, and the head is up with the eyes forward (Figure 20.7).

Plié

A plié is the bending of the knees. Both knees are bent, the arms are extended at right angles to the sides, and the seat is tucked to maintain a flat abdominal wall. The plié teaches children how to absorb the force of the landing. There are different plié positions, but the basic purpose of the plié in gymnastic instruction is to teach landing with grace and control.

FIGURE 20.7 Lunge position.

FIGURE 20.6 Attitude.

Relevé

The relevé is an extension movement from the plié position. The movement goes from the plié (knees bent) position to the extended position. Extension should be complete through all of the joints, stretching upward from the balls of the feet.

Arabesque

In the arabesque position, the weight is supported on one leg while the other leg is extended to the rear. The extended leg is kept straight with the toe pointed, and the chest is kept erect (Figure 20.8 on page 472). The Back Extension and the Cartwheel are often brought to completion with an Arabesque.

Jumps

Three jump variations are used commonly in gymnastic dance. They are the Tuck Jump, the Pike Jump, and the Straddle Jump. These jumps are simply a jump with the prescribed position added. The arms are raised in a lifting motion to increase the height of the jump and to enhance

FIGURE 20.8 Arabesque.

balance. The impact of the landing is absorbed at the ankles and knee joints.

Chassé

The Chassé is a slide. This basic locomotor movement involves one leg chasing the other out of position. It is done close to the floor with a light spring in the step.

Stunts and Tumbling Activities

The stunts and tumbling activities are organized in order of difficulty into three developmental levels. Table 20.1 (pages 473–475) lists all the activities in each of the levels and offers a page reference for rapid access to descriptions of each activity. A brief discussion of each of the developmental levels follows.

DEVELOPMENTAL LEVEL I ACTIVITIES

Developmental level I consists primarily of imitative walks and movements, plus selected balance stunts and rolls. The Forward Roll is practiced, but its refinement is left to later levels. The Back Roller is practiced as a prelude to the Backward Roll.

Emphasis should be placed on the creative aspects of the activities as well as on performance standards. Children at this level tend to do stunts in different ways because of their different interpretations of what is required. Directional concepts and a basic understanding of common movement terminology should have a prominent place in the instruction. The "why" of an activity should be explained to children.

Animal Movements

ALLIGATOR CRAWL

Lie facedown on the floor with elbows bent. Move along the floor in alligator fashion, keeping the hands close to the body and the feet pointed out (Figure 20.9). First, use unilateral movements—that is, right arm and leg moving together—then change to cross-lateral movements.

KANGAROO JUMP

Carry the arms close to the chest with the palms facing forward. Place a beanbag or ball between the knees. Move in different directions by taking small jumps without dropping the object.

PUPPY DOG RUN

Place the hands on the floor, bending the arms and legs slightly. Walk and run like a happy puppy. Look straight ahead. Keeping the head up, in good position, strengthens the neck muscles (Figure 20.10 on page 476). Go sideward, backward, and so on. Turn around in place.

TEACHING TIP

Variations:

1. *Cat Walk.* Use the same position to imitate a cat. Walk softly. Stretch at times like a cat. Be smooth and deliberate.
2. *Monkey Run.* Turn the hands and feet so that the fingers and toes point in (toward each other).

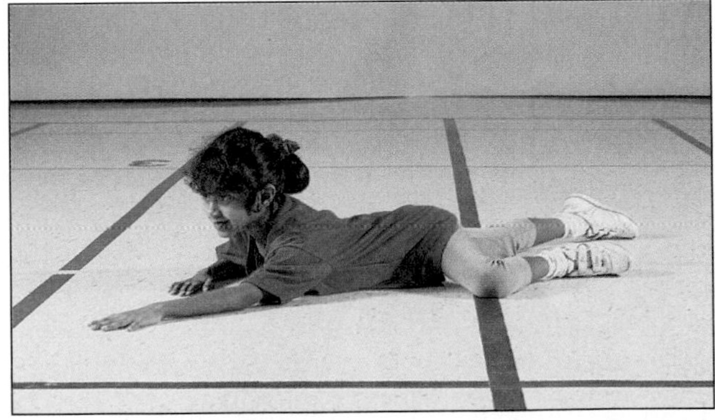

FIGURE 20.9 Alligator Crawl.

TABLE 20.1 Stunts and tumbling activities

Developmental Level I									
Animal Movements		**Tumbling and Inverted Balances**		**Balance Stunts**		**Individual Stunts**		**Partner and Group Stunts**	
Alligator Crawl	472	Rolling Log	477	One-Leg Balance	480	Directional Walk	482	Bouncing Ball	486
Kangaroo Jump	472	Side Roll	478	Double-Knee Balance	480	Line Walking	482	Seesaw	486
Puppy Dog Run	472	Forward Roll	478	Head Touch	480	Fluttering Leaf	482	Wring the Dishrag	486
Cat Walk	472	Back Roller	478	Head Balance	480	Elevator	483	Partner Toe Toucher	486
Monkey Run	472	Forward Roll—Straddle Position	478	One-Leg Balance Stunts	480	Cross-Legged Stand	483	Double Top	487
Bear Walk	476	Backward Curl	479	Kimbo Stand	481	Walking in Place	483	Roly Poly	487
Gorilla Walk	476	Backward Roll—Handclasp Position	479	Knee-Lift Stand	481	Jump Turns	483		
Rabbit Jump	476	Climb-Up	479	Stork Stand	481	Rubber Band	483		
Elephant Walk	476	Three Point Tip-Up	480	Balance Touch	481	Pumping Up the Balloon	483		
Siamese Twin Walk	477	Mountain Climber	480	Single-Leg Balance	481	Rising Sun	483		
Tightrope Walk	477	Switcheroo	480	Forward Balance	481	Heel Click	483		
Lame Dog Walk	477			Backward Balance	482	Lowering the Boom	484		
Crab Walk	477			Side Balance	482	Turn-Over	484		
				Hand-and-Knee Balance	482	Thread the Needle	484		
				Single-Knee Balance	482	Heel Slap	484		
						Pogo Stick	484		
						Top	485		
						Sitting Stand	485		
						Push-Up	485		
						Crazy Walk	485		
						Seat Circle	486		

(continued)

TABLE 20.1 Stunts and tumbling activities (continued)

Developmental Level II											
Aminal Movements		**Tumbling and Inverted Balances**		**Balance Stunts**		**Individual Stunts**		**Partner and Group Stunts**		**Partner Support Stunts**	
Cricket Walk	487	Forward Roll to a Walkout	490	One-Leg Balance Reverse	493	Reach-Under	496	Partner Hopping	500	Double Bear	504
Frog Jump	487	Backward Roll	490	Tummy Balance	494	Stiff Person Bend	496	Partner Twister	501	Table	504
Seal Crawl	488	Backward Roll—Inclined	490	Leg Dip	495	Coffee Grinder	496	Partner Pull-Up	501	Statue	504
Reverse Seal Crawl	488	Headstand	491	Balance Jump	495	Scooter	496	Back-to-Back Get-Up	501	Lighthouse	504
Elbow Crawl	488	Climb-Up	491	Seat Balance	495	Hip Walk	496	Rowboat	501	Hip-Shoulder Stand	505
Measuring Worm	488	Kick-Up	491	Face-to-Knee Touch	495	Long Bridge	497	Leapfrog	502		
Mule Kick	488	Frog Handstand (Tip-Up)	492	Finger Touch	495	Heelstand	497	Wheelbarrow	502		
Walrus Walk	489	Half Teeter-Totter	492			Wicket Walk	497	Wheelbarrow Lifting	502		
Double-Lame Dog	489	Cartwheel	492			Knee Jump to Standing	498	Camel Lift and Walk	503		
Turtle	489	Forward Roll—Pike Position	493			Knee Drop	498	Dump the Wheelbarrow	503		
Walrus Slap	490	Forward Roll Combinations	493			Forward Drop	498	Dromedary Walk	503		
Reverse Walrus Slap	490	Backward Roll Combinations	493			Dead Body Fall	498	Centipede	503		
		Headstand Variations	491			Stoop and Stretch	499	Double Wheelbarrow	503		
		Teeter-Totter	493			Tanglefoot	499				
		Handstand	493			Egg Roll	499				
						Toe Touch Nose	499				
						Toe Tug Walk	500				

TABLE 20.1 Stunts and tumbling activities (continued)

Developmental Level III									
Tumbling and Inverted Balances		**Balance Stunts**		**Individual Stunts**		**Partner and Group Stunts**		**Partner Support Stunts**	
Forward and Backward Roll Combinations	506	V-Up	508	Wall Walk-Up	510	Double Scooter	513	Merry-Go-Round	515
Back Extension	506	Push-Up Variations	509	Skier's Sit	510	Double Roll	513	Gymnastics Routines	516
Headstand Variations	506	Flip-Flop	509	Rocking Horse	510	Tandem Bicycle	513	Back Layout	517
Handstand Against a Wall	506	Long Reach	509	Heel Click (Side)	510	Circle High Jump	513	Front Sit	517
Freestanding Handstand	506	Toe Jump	509	Walk-Through	511	Stick Carries	513	Flying Dutchman	517
Cartwheel and Round-Off	506	Handstand Stunts	510	Jump-Through	511	Two-Way Wheelbarrow	514	Knee-and-Shoulder Balance	518
Judo Roll	506	Front Seat Support	510	Circular Rope Jump	511	Partner Rising Sun	514	Press	518
Advanced Forward and Backward Roll Combinations	507	Elbow Balance	510	Bouncer	511	Triple Roll	515	All-Fours Support	518
Straddle Press to Headstand	507			Pretzel	512	Quintuplet Roll	515	Angel	518
Handstand Variations	507			Jackknife	512	Dead Person Lift	515	Side Stand	519
Headspring	508			Heel-and-Toe Spring	512	Injured Person Carry	515	Pyramids	519
Walking on the Hands	508			Single-Leg Circle (Pinwheel)	512				
Walk-Over	508								

FIGURE 20.10 Puppy Dog Run.

BEAR WALK

Bend forward and touch the ground with both hands. Travel forward slowly by moving the hand and foot on the same side together (that is, first the right hand and foot, then the left hand and foot) (Figure 20.11). Make deliberate movements.

TEACHING TIP

Variation: Lift the free foot and arm high while the support is on the other side.

GORILLA WALK

Bend the knees and carry the trunk forward. Let the arms hang at the sides. Touch the fingers to the ground while walking.

TEACHING TIP

Variation: Stop and beat on the chest like a gorilla. Bounce up and down on all fours with hands and feet touching the floor simultaneously.

FIGURE 20.11 Bear Walk.

RABBIT JUMP

Crouch with knees apart and hands placed on the floor. Move forward by reaching out with both hands and then bringing both feet up to the hands. The eyes look ahead.

The teacher should emphasize that this is a jump rather than a hop because both feet move at once. Note that the jump is a bilateral movement.

TEACHING TIP

Variations:

1. Try with knees together and arms on the outside. Try alternating with knees together and apart on successive jumps. Go over a low hurdle or through a hoop.
2. Experiment with taking considerable weight on the hands before the feet move forward. To do this, raise the seat higher in the air when the hands move forward.

ELEPHANT WALK

Bend well forward, clasping the hands together to form a trunk. The end of the trunk should swing close to the ground. Walk in a slow, deliberate, dignified manner, keeping the legs straight and swinging the trunk from side to side (Figure 20.12). Stop and throw water over the back with the trunk. Recite the following verse while walking, and move the trunk appropriately.

The elephant's walk is steady and slow,
His trunk like a pendulum swings to and fro.
But when there are children with peanuts around
He swings it up and he swings it down.

FIGURE 20.12 Elephant Walk.

TEACHING TIP

Variation: With a partner, decide who will be the mahout (the elephant keeper) and who will be the elephant. The mahout walks to the side and a little in front of the elephant, with one hand touching the elephant's shoulder. Lead the elephant around during the first two lines of the poem, and then during the last two lines release the touch, walk to a spot in front of the elephant, and toss the elephant a peanut when the trunk is swept up. Return to the elephant's side and repeat the action.

SIAMESE TWIN WALK

Stand back to back with a partner. Lock elbows (Figure 20.13). Walk forward, backward, and sideward in unison.

TIGHTROPE WALK

Select a line, board, or chalked line on the floor as the high wire. Pretend to be on the high wire and do various tasks with exaggerated loss and control of balance. Add tasks such as jumping rope, juggling balls, and riding a bicycle. Pretend to hold a parasol or a balancing pole while performing.

FIGURE 20.13 Siamese Twin Walk.

Children should give good play to the imagination. The teacher can set the stage by discussing what a circus performer on the high wire might do.

LAME DOG WALK

Walk on both hands and one foot. Hold the other foot in the air as if injured. Walk a distance and change feet. The eyes should look forward. Move backward also and in other combinations. Try to move with an injured front leg.

CRAB WALK

Squat down and reach back, putting both hands on the floor without sitting down. With head, neck, and body level, walk forward, backward, and sideward (Figure 20.14).

Children have a tendency to lower the hips. The teacher should emphasize that the body is kept in a straight line.

TEACHING TIP

Variations:

1. As each step is taken with one hand, slap the chest or seat with the other.
2. Move the hand and foot on the same side simultaneously.
3. Try balancing on one leg and the opposite hand for 5 seconds.

Tumbling and Inverted Balances

ROLLING LOG

Lie on the back with arms stretched overhead (Figure 20.15 on page 478). Roll sideways the length of the mat. The next time, roll with the hands pointed toward the

FIGURE 20.14 Crab Walk.

FIGURE 20.15 Rolling Log.

other side of the mat. To roll in a straight line, keep the feet slightly apart.

TEACHING TIP

Variation: Alternately curl and stretch while rolling.

SIDE ROLL

Start on the hands and knees, with one side toward the direction of the roll. Drop the shoulder, tuck both the elbow and the knee under, and roll over completely, returning to the hands-and-knees position. Momentum is needed to return to the original position. Practice rolling back and forth from one hand-and-knee position to another.

FORWARD ROLL

Stand facing forward, with the feet apart. Squat and place the hands on the mat, shoulder width apart, with elbows against the insides of the thighs. Tuck the chin to the chest and make a rounded back. A push-off with the hands and feet provides the force for the roll (Figure 20.16). Carry the weight on the hands, with the elbows bearing the weight of the thighs. If the elbows are kept against the thighs and the weight is assumed there, the force of the roll is transferred easily to the rounded back. Try to

FIGURE 20.16 Forward Roll.

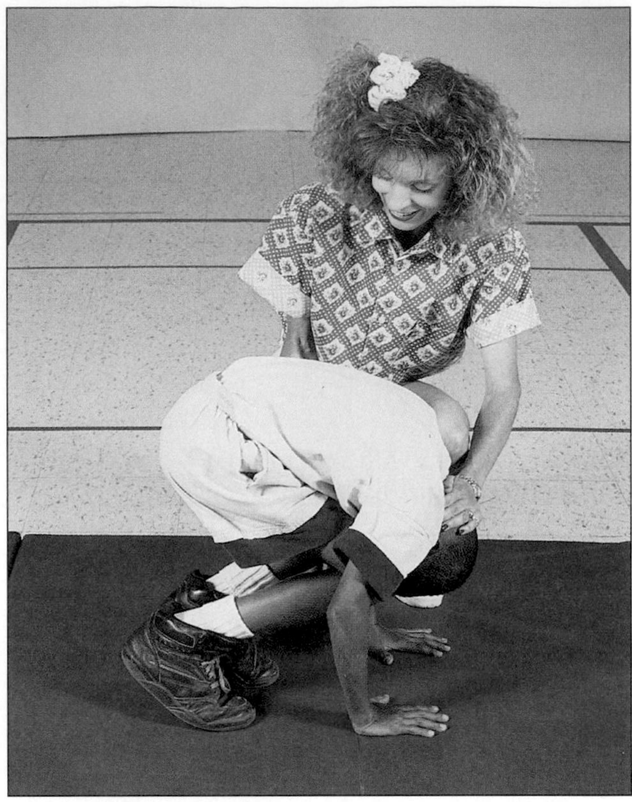

FIGURE 20.17 Spotting the Forward Roll. (One hand is on the back of the head and one is under the thigh.)

roll forward to the feet. Later, try with the knees together and no weight on the elbows.

Spotting: The spotter should kneel alongside the child and place one hand on the back of the child's head and the other under the thigh (Figure 20.17). As the child moves through the roll, give an upward lift on the back of the neck to assure the neck does not absorb the weight of the body. This technique should be used for all forward roll variations.

BACK ROLLER

Begin in a crouched position with knees together and hands resting lightly on the floor. Roll backward, securing momentum by bringing the knees to the chest and clasping them with the arms (Figure 20.18). Roll back and forth rhythmically. On the backward movement, go well back on the neck and head. Try to roll forward to original position. If you have difficulty rolling back to original position, cross the legs and roll to a crossed-leg standing position. (This stunt is a lead-up to the Backward Roll.)

FORWARD ROLL (STRADDLE POSITION)

Start with the legs spread in the straddle position. Bend forward at the hips, tuck the head, place the hands on

FIGURE 20.18 Back Roller.

the mat, and roll forward. A strong push with the hands at the end of the roll is necessary to return to the standing position.

FORWARD ROLL PRACTICE

Review the Forward Roll (tucked), with spotting and assistance as necessary. Work on coming out of the roll to the feet. Grasping the knees at the end of the roll will help.

TEACHING TIP

Variations:

1. Roll to the feet with ankles crossed.
2. Try to roll with knees together.

BACKWARD CURL

Approach this activity in three stages. For the first stage, begin in a sitting position, with the knees drawn up to the chest and the chin tucked. The hands are clasped and placed behind the head with the elbows held out as far as possible. Gently roll backward until the weight is on the elbows (Figure 20.19). Roll back to starting position.

In stage two, perform the same action as before, but place the hands alongside the head on the mat while rolling back. The fingers are pointed in the direction of the roll, with palms down on the mat. (A good cue is, "Point your thumbs toward your ears and keep your elbows close to your body.")

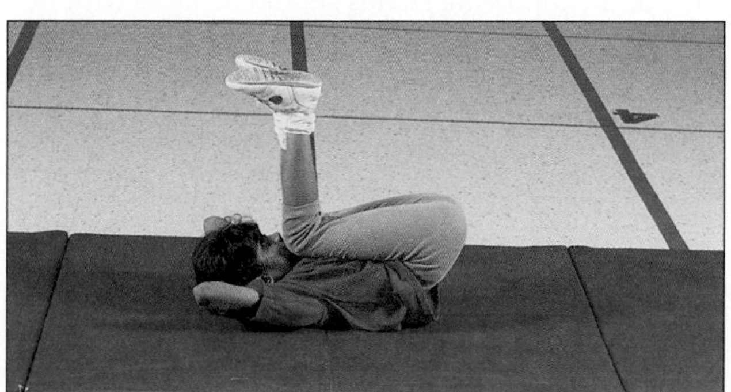

FIGURE 20.19 Backward Curl (handclasp position).

FIGURE 20.20 Handclasp Position.

For stage three, perform the same action as in stage two, but start in a crouched position on the feet with the back facing the direction of the roll. Momentum is secured by sitting down quickly and bringing the knees to the chest. This, like the Back Roller, is a lead-up to the Backward Roll. Teach children to push against the floor to take pressure off the back of the neck.

BACKWARD ROLL (HANDCLASP POSITION)

Clasp the fingers behind the neck, with elbows held out to the sides (Figure 20.20). From a crouched position, sit down rapidly, bringing the knees to the chest for a tuck to secure momentum. Roll completely over backward, taking much of the weight on the forearms (Figure 20.21). With this method, the neck is protected.

Spotting: Spotting is not necessary for this lead-up activity. Youngsters can have early success in learning the backward roll by using this approach. Children should be reminded to keep their elbows back and out to the sides to ensure maximum support and minimal neck pressure. This is a lead-up activity to the regular backward roll. If youngsters cannot roll over, allow them to practice rocking back and forth with the elbows out. In no case should force be applied to the hips by another individual in an attempt to force the child over.

CLIMB-UP

Begin on a mat in a kneeling position, with hands placed about shoulder width apart and the fingers spread and pointed forward. Place the head forward of the hands,

FIGURE 20.21 Backward Roll.

so that the head and hands form a triangle on the mat. Walk the body weight forward so that most of it rests on the hands and head. Climb the knees to the top of the elbows. (This stunt is a lead-up to the Headstand.)

Spotting: In the Climb-Up as well as in the Three-Point Tip-Up, overweight or weak children may need spotting. This is done by placing one hand on the child's shoulder and the other on the back of the thigh.

TEACHING TIP

Variation: Raise the knees off the elbows.

THREE-POINT TIP-UP

Squat down on the mat, placing the hands flat with fingers pointing forward. The elbows should be inside and pressed against the inner part of the lower thighs. Lean forward, slowly transferring body weight to the bent elbows and hands until the forehead touches the mat (Figure 20.22). Return to starting position.

The Three-Point Tip-Up ends in the same general position as the Climb-Up, but with the elbows on the inside of the thighs. Some children may have better success by turning the fingers in slightly, thus causing the elbows to point outward more and offering better support at the thigh contact point. This stunt is a lead-up to the Headstand and the Handstand done at later levels.

Spotting: Same as for the Climb-Up.

TEACHING TIP

Variation: Tuck the head and do a Forward Roll as an alternative finishing act.

MOUNTAIN CLIMBER

This activity is similar to the exercise known as the Treadmill. The weight is taken on the hands with one foot forward and one foot extended back, similar to a sprinter's start. When ready, the performer switches foot position with both feet moving simultaneously. This activity is a lead-up to the Handstand and teaches children to support the body weight briefly with the arms.

SWITCHEROO

This Handstand lead-up activity begins in the front lunge position with the arms overhead. In one continuous movement, bend forward at the hips, place the hands on the mat, and invert the legs over the head. Scissor the legs in the air, and then reverse the position of the feet on the mat. Repeat in a smooth and continuous motion.

Balance Stunts

ONE-LEG BALANCE

Lift one leg from the floor. Later, bring the knee up. The arms should be free at first and then assume specified positions: folded across the chest, on the hips, on the head, or behind the back.

DOUBLE-KNEE BALANCE

Kneel on both knees, with the feet pointed to the rear. Lift the feet from the ground and balance on the knees. Vary the position of the arms. Experiment with different arm positions.

HEAD TOUCH

On a mat, kneel on both knees, with feet pointed backward and arms outstretched backward for balance. Lean forward slowly and touch the forehead to the mat. Recover to position (Figure 20.23). Vary the arm position.

HEAD BALANCE

Place a beanbag, block, or book on the head (Figure 20.24). Walk, stoop, turn around, sit down, get up, and so on. The object should be balanced so that the upper body is in good posture. Keep the hands out to the sides for balance. Later, vary the position of the arms—folded across the chest or placed behind the back or down the sides. Link together a series of movements.

ONE-LEG BALANCE STUNTS

Each of the following stands should be done with different arm positions, starting with the arms out to the

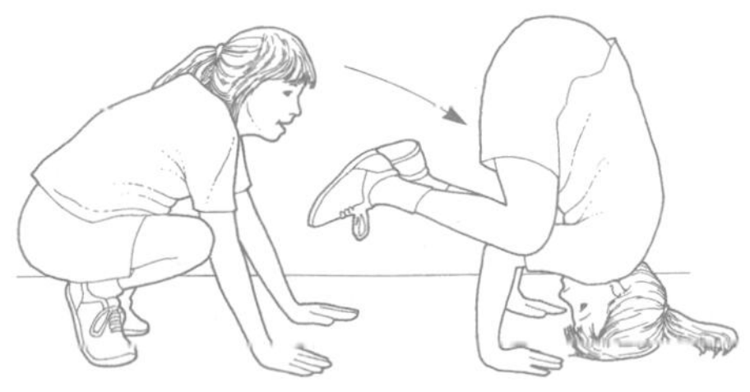

FIGURE 20.22 Three Point Tip-Up.

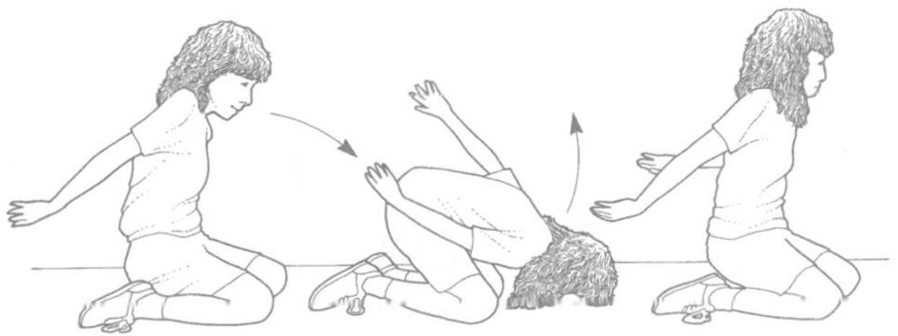

FIGURE 20.23 Head Touch.

FIGURE 20.24 Head Balance.

sides and then folded across the chest. Have children devise other arm positions.

Each stunt can be held first for 3 seconds and then for 5 seconds. Later, the eyes can be closed during the count. The child should recover to original position without loss of balance or excessive movement. Stunts should be repeated, using the other leg.

1. *Kimbo Stand.* With the left foot kept flat on the ground, cross the right leg over the left to a position in which the right foot is pointed partially down and the toe is touching the ground.
2. *Knee-Lift Stand.* From a standing position, lift one knee up so that the thigh is parallel to the ground and the toe is pointed down. Hold. Return to starting position.
3. *Stork Stand.* From a standing position, shift all of the weight to one foot. Place the other foot so that the sole is against the inside of the knee and thigh of the standing leg (Figure 20.25). Hold. Recover to standing position.

BALANCE TOUCH

Place an object (eraser, block, or beanbag) a yard away from a line. Balancing on the line on one foot, reach out with the other foot, touch the object (no weight should be placed on it) (Figure 20.26), and recover to the starting position. Reach sideward, backward.

FIGURE 20.25 Stork Stand.

TEACHING TIP

Variation: Try placing the object at various distances. On a gymnasium floor, count the number of boards to establish the distance for the touch.

SINGLE-LEG BALANCES

1. *Forward Balance.* Extend one leg backward until it is parallel to the floor. Keeping the eyes forward and the arms out to the sides, bend forward, balancing

FIGURE 20.26 Balance Touch.

FIGURE 20.27 Forward Balance.

on the other leg (Figure 20.27). Hold for 5 seconds without moving. Reverse legs. (This is also called a Forward Scale.)

2. *Backward Balance.* With knee straight, extend one leg forward, with toes pointed. Keep the arms out to the sides for balance. Lean back as far as possible. The bend should be far enough back so that the eyes are looking at the ceiling.
3. *Side Balance.* Stand on the left foot with enough side bend to the left so that the right (top) side of the body is parallel to the floor. Put the right arm alongside the head and in line with the rest of the body. Reverse, using the right leg for support. (Support may be needed momentarily to get into position.)

HAND-AND-KNEE BALANCE

Get down on all fours, taking the weight on the hands, knees, and feet, with toes pointed backward. Lift one hand and the opposite knee (Figure 20.28). Keep the free foot and hand from touching during the hold. Reverse hand and knee positions.

FIGURE 20.28 Hand-and-Knee Balance.

SINGLE-KNEE BALANCE

Perform the same action as in the previous stunt, but balance on one knee (and leg), with both arms outstretched to the sides (Figure 20.29). Use the other knee.

Individual Stunts

DIRECTIONAL WALK

For a left movement, begin in standing position. Do all of the following simultaneously: Take a step to the left, raise the left arm and point left, turn the head to the left, and state crisply "Left." Close with the right foot back to standing position. Take several steps left and then reverse.

The Directional Walk is designed to aid in establishing right-left concepts. Definite and forceful simultaneous movements of the arm, head (turn), and leg (step) coupled with a crisp enunciation of the direction are the ingredients of this stunt.

LINE WALKING

Use a line on the floor, a chalked line, or a board. Walk forward and backward on the line as follows. First, take regular steps. Next, try follow steps—the front foot moving forward and the back foot moving up. The same foot always leads. Then do heel-and-toe steps, bringing the back toe up against the front heel on each step. Finally, hop along the line on one foot. Change to the other foot. The eyes should be focused ahead.

FLUTTERING LEAF

Keeping the feet in place and the body relaxed, flutter to the ground slowly, just as a leaf would do in autumn.

FIGURE 20.29 Single-Knee Balance.

Swing the arms back and forth loosely to accentuate the fluttering.

ELEVATOR

With the arms out level at the sides, pretend to be an elevator going down. Lower the body a little at a time by bending the knees, but keep the upper body erect and the eyes forward. Return to position. Add a body twist to the downward movement. (A drum can be used.)

CROSS-LEGGED STAND

Sit with the legs crossed and the body bent partially forward. Respond appropriately to these six commands.

"Touch the right foot with the right hand."

"Touch the left foot with the right hand."

"Touch the right foot with the left hand."

"Touch the left foot with the left hand."

"Touch both feet with the hands."

"Touch the feet with crossed hands."

The commands should be given in varied sequences. The child must interpret that his right foot is on the left side, and vice versa. If this seems too difficult, have children start with the feet in normal position (uncrossed).

TEACHING TIP

Variation: Do the stunt with a partner, one child giving the commands and the other responding as directed.

WALKING IN PLACE

Pretend to walk vigorously by using the same movements as in walking but without making any progress. This is done by sliding the feet back and forth. Exaggerated arm movement should be made. (Children can gain or lose a little ground. Two children can walk alongside each other, with first one and then the other going ahead.)

JUMP TURNS

Do jump turns (use quarter turns and half turns) right and left, as directed. The arms should be kept outstretched to the sides. Land lightly without a second movement.

Jump turns reinforce directional concepts. Number concepts can also be developed with jump turns. The teacher calls out the number as a preparatory command and then says, "Move." Number signals are: "One" for a left quarter turn, "Two" for a right quarter turn, "Three" for a left half turn, and "Four" for a right half turn. Give children a moment after the number is called and before the "Move" command.

RUBBER BAND

Get down in a squat position with the hands and arms clasped around the knees. On the command "Stretch, stretch, stretch," stretch as tall and as wide as possible. On the command "Snap," snap back to original position.

TEACHING TIP

Variation: *Pumping Up the Balloon.* One child, the pumper, is in front of the other children, who are the balloons. The pumper pretends to use a bicycle pump to inflate the balloons. The balloons get larger and larger until the pumper shouts, "Bang," whereupon the balloons collapse to the floor. The pumper should give a "shoosh" sound every time a pumping motion is made.

RISING SUN

Lie on the back. Using the arms for balance only, rise to a standing position.

TEACHING TIP

Variation: Fold the arms over the chest. Experiment with different positions of the feet. The feet can be crossed, spread wide, both to one side, and so on.

HEEL CLICK

Stand with the feet slightly apart, jump up, and click the heels, coming down with the feet apart (Figure 20.30). Try with a quarter turn right and left.

TEACHING TIP

Variations:

1. Clap the hands overhead as the heels are clicked.
2. Join hands with one or more children. Count, "One, two, THREE," jumping on the third count.

FIGURE 20.30 Heel Click.

3. Begin with a cross-step to the side, then click the heels. Try both right and left.
4. Try to click the heels twice before landing. Land with the feet apart.

LOWERING THE BOOM

Start in push-up (front-leaning rest) position. Lower the body slowly to the floor. The movement should be controlled so that the body remains rigid.

TEACHING TIP

Variations:

1. Pause halfway down.
2. Go down in stages, inch by inch. (Be sure that children understand the concept of an inch as a measure of distance.)
3. Go down slowly to the accompaniment of noise simulating air escaping from a punctured tire. Try representing a blowout, initiated by an appropriate noise.
4. Go down in stages by alternating lowering movements of the right and left arms.
5. Vary the stunt with different hand-base positions, such as fingers pointed in, thumbs touching, and others.

TURN-OVER

From a front-leaning rest position, turn over so that the back is to the floor. The body should not touch the floor. Continue the turn until the original position is reassumed. Reverse the direction. Turn back and forth several times. The body should be kept as rigid as possible throughout the turn.

THREAD THE NEEDLE

Touch the fingertips together in front of the body. Step through with one foot at a time while keeping the tips in contact (Figure 20.31). Step back to the original position. Next, lock the fingers in front of the body, and repeat the stunt. Finally, step through the clasped hands without touching the hands.

HEEL SLAP

From an erect position with hands at the sides, jump upward and slap both heels with the hands (Figure 20.32).

TEACHING TIP

Variation: Use a one-two-three rhythm with small preliminary jumps on the first and second counts. Make a quarter or half turn in the air. During a jump, slap the heels twice before landing.

FIGURE 20.31 Thread the Needle.

POGO STICK

Pretend to be on a pogo stick by keeping a stiff body and jumping on the toes. Hold the hands in front as if grasping the stick (Figure 20.33). Progress in various directions. (The teacher should stress upward propelling action by the ankles and toes, with the body kept stiff, particularly at the knee joints.)

FIGURE 20.32 Heel Slap.

FIGURE 20.33 Pogo Stick.

TOP

From a standing position with arms at the sides, try jumping and turning to face the opposite direction, turning three-quarters of the way around, or making a full turn to face the original direction. Land in good balance with hands near the sides. No movement of the feet should occur after landing. Turn both right and left. (Number concepts can be stressed in having children do half turns, three-quarter turns, and full turns.)

TEACHING TIP

Variation: Fold the arms across the chest.

SITTING STAND

Stand with feet apart and arms folded in front. Pivot on the balls of both feet, and face the opposite direction. The legs are now crossed. Sit down in this position. Reverse the process. Get up without using the hands for aid, and uncross the legs with a pivot to face in the original direction. Little change should occur in foot position (Figure 20.34).

PUSH-UP

From a front-leaning rest position, lower the body and push up, back to original position. Be sure that the only movement is in the arms, with the body kept rigid. (Because the Push-Up is used in many exercises and testing programs, it is important for children to learn proper execution early.)

FIGURE 20.34 Sitting Stand.

TEACHING TIP

Variation: Stop halfway down and halfway up. Go up and down by inches.

CRAZY WALK

Progress forward in an erect position by bringing one foot behind and around the other to gain a little ground each time (Figure 20.35). (The teacher can set a specified distance and see which children cover the distance in the fewest steps.)

FIGURE 20.35 Crazy Walk.

TEACHING TIP

Variation: Reverse the movements and go backward. This means bringing the foot in front and around to gain distance in back.

SEAT CIRCLE

Sit on the floor, with knees bent and hands braced behind. Lift the feet off the floor and push with the hands, so that the body spins in a circle with the seat as a pivot (Figure 20.36). Spin right and left.

TEACHING TIP

Variation: Place a beanbag between the knees or on the toes and spin without dropping it.

Partner and Group Stunts

BOUNCING BALL

Toss a lively utility ball into the air and watch how it bounces lower and lower until it finally comes to rest on the floor. From a bent-knee position with the upper body erect, imitate the ball by beginning with a high bounce and gradually lowering the height of the jump to simulate the ball coming to rest. Children should push off from the floor with the hands to gain additional height and should absorb part of the body weight with their hands as well. Toss a real ball into the air and move with the ball.

TEACHING TIP

Variation: Try this with a partner, one partner serving as the bouncer and the other as the ball (Figure 20.37). Reverse positions. Try having one partner dribble the ball in various positions.

SEESAW

Face and join hands with a partner. Move the seesaw up and down, one child stooping while the other rises. Recite the words to this version of "Seesaw, Margery Daw."

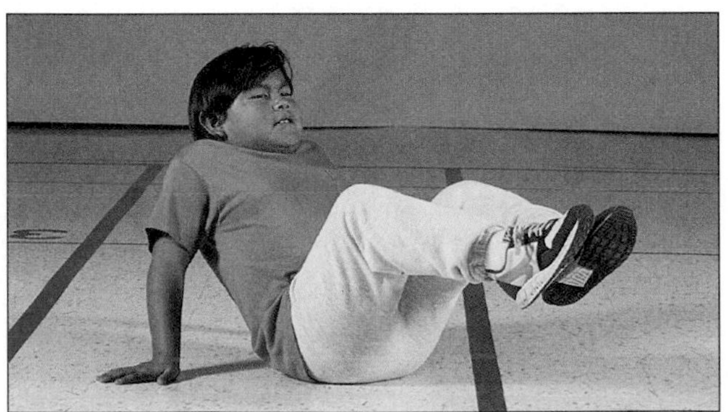

FIGURE 20.36 Seat Circle.

FIGURE 20.37 Bouncing Ball.

Seesaw, Margery Daw,
Maw and Paw, like a saw,
Seesaw, Margery Daw.

TEACHING TIP

Variation: Jump upward at the end of the rise each time.

WRING THE DISHRAG

Face and join hands with a partner. Raise one pair of arms (right for one and left for the other) and turn under, continuing a full turn until back to original position (Figure 20.38). Take care not to bump heads. Reverse.

TEACHING TIP

Variation: Try the stunt at a lower level, using a crouched position.

PARTNER TOE TOUCHER

Partners lie on their backs with heads near each other and feet in opposite directions. Join arms with partner using a hand-wrist grip, and bring the legs up so that the toes touch partner's toes. Keep high on the shoulders and touch the feet high (Figure 20.39). Strive to attain the high shoulder position, as this is the point of most difficulty. (Partners should be of about the same height.)

TEACHING TIP

Variation: One child carries a beanbag, a ball, or some other article between the feet, and transfers the object to the partner, who lowers it to the floor.

FIGURE 20.38 Wring the Dishrag.

DOUBLE TOP

Face partner and join hands. Experiment to see which type of grip works best. With straight arms, lean away from each other and at the same time move the toes close to partner's (Figure 20.40). Spin around slowly in either direction, taking tiny steps. Increase speed.

TEACHING TIP

Variations:

1. Use a stooped position.
2. Instead of holding hands, hold a wand and increase the body lean backward. Try the stunt standing right side to right side.

FIGURE 20.39 Partner Toe Toucher.

FIGURE 20.40 Double Top.

ROLY POLY

Review the Rolling Log. Four or five children lie face-down on the floor, side by side. The last child does a Rolling Log over the others and then takes a place at the end. Continue until all have rolled twice.

DEVELOPMENTAL LEVEL II ACTIVITIES

In developmental level II, more emphasis is placed on form and quality of performance than at the previous level. Stunts such as the Frog Handstand, Mule Kick, Teeter-Totter, and Handstand give children experience in taking the weight totally on the hands. Partner support stunts are introduced. Flops or falls are another addition.

Animal Movements

CRICKET WALK

Squat. Spread the knees. Put the arms between the knees and grasp the outside of the ankles with the hands. Walk forward or backward. Chirp like a cricket. Turn around right and left. See what happens when both feet are moved at once!

FROG JUMP

From a squatting position, with hands on the floor slightly in front of the feet, jump forward a short distance, landing on the hands and feet simultaneously

FIGURE 20.41 Frog Jump.

(Figure 20.41). Note the difference between this stunt and the Rabbit Jump. Emphasis eventually should be on both height and distance. The hands and arms absorb part of the landing impact to prevent excessive strain on the knees.

SEAL CRAWL

Start in the front-leaning rest position, the weight supported on straightened arms and toes. Keeping the body straight, walk forward, using the hands for propelling force and dragging the feet (Figure 20.42). Keep the body straight and the head up.

FIGURE 20.42 Seal Crawl.

TEACHING TIP

Variations:

1. Crawl forward a short distance and then roll over on the back, clapping the hands like a seal, with appropriate seal barks.

FIGURE 20.43 Elbow Crawl.

2. Crawl with the fingers pointed in different directions, out and in.
3. *Reverse Seal Crawl.* Turn over and attempt the crawl, dragging the heels.
4. *Elbow Crawl.* Assume the original position but with weight on the elbows. Crawl forward on the elbows (Figure 20.43).
5. Use the crossed-arm position for a more challenging stunt.

MEASURING WORM

From a front-leaning rest position, keeping the knees stiff, inch the feet up as close as possible to the hands. Regain position by inching forward with the hands. Keep the knees straight, with the necessary bending occurring at the hips (Figure 20.44).

MULE KICK

Stoop down and place the hands on the floor in front of the feet. The arms are the front legs of the mule. Kick out with the legs while the weight is supported momentarily on the arms (Figure 20.45). Taking the weight on the hands is important. The stunt can be learned in two stages. First, practice taking the weight momentarily on the hands. Next, add the kick.

TEACHING TIP

Variation: Make two kicks before the feet return to the ground.

FIGURE 20.44 Measuring Worm.

FIGURE 20.45 Mule Kick.

WALRUS WALK

Begin in a front-leaning rest position, with fingers pointed outward. Make progress by moving both hands forward at the same time (Figure 20.46). Try to clap the hands with each step. (Before doing this stunt, review the similar Seal Crawl (Figure 20.42) and its variations.)

TEACHING TIP

Variation: Move sideways so that the upper part of the body describes an arc while the feet hold position.

DOUBLE-LAME DOG

Support the body on one hand and one leg (Figure 20.47). Move forward in this position, maintaining balance. The distance should be short (5 to 10 feet), as this stunt is strenuous. Different leg-arm combinations should be employed such as cross-lateral movements (right arm with left leg and left arm with right leg).

TEACHING TIP

Variation: Keep the free arm on the hip.

FIGURE 20.46 Walrus Walk.

FIGURE 20.47 Double-Lame Dog.

TURTLE

Hold the body in a wide push-up position with the feet apart and the hands widely spread (Figure 20.48). From this position, move in various directions, keeping the plane of the body always about the same distance from the floor. Movements of the hands and feet should occur in small increments only.

FIGURE 20.48 Turtle.

WALRUS SLAP

From the front-leaning rest position, push the body up in the air quickly by force of the arms, clap the hands together, and recover to position. Before doing this stunt, review the Seal Crawl and the Walrus Walk.

TEACHING TIP

Variations:

1. Try clapping the hands more than once.
2. Move forward while clapping the hands.
3. *Reverse Walrus Slap.* Turn over and do a Walrus Walk while facing the ceiling. Clapping the hands is quite difficult in this position and should be attempted only by the more skilled. Work on a mat.

Tumbling and Inverted Balances

FORWARD ROLL TO A WALKOUT

Perform the Forward Roll as described previously, except walk out to a standing position. The key to the Walkout is to develop enough momentum to allow a return to the feet. The leg that first absorbs the weight is bent while the other leg is kept straight.

Spotting: Same as the Forward Roll (Figure 20.16).

BACKWARD ROLL (REGULAR)

In the same squat position as for the Forward Roll, but with the back to the direction of the roll, push off quickly with the hands, sit down, and start rolling over onto the back. The knees are brought to the chest, so that the body is tucked and momentum is increased. Quickly bring the hands up over the shoulders, with palms up and fingers pointed backward. Continue rolling backward with knees close to the chest. The hands touch the mat at about the same time as the head. It is necessary at this point to push hard with the hands to release pressure on the neck. Continue to roll over and to push off the mat until the roll is completed (Figure 20.49). Emphasize proper hand position by telling children to point their thumbs toward their ears and spread their fingers for better push-off control.

FIGURE 20.49 Regular Backward Roll.

Spotting: In spotting, care must be taken never to push a child from the hip, thus forcing the roll. This puts undue pressure on the back of the neck. The proper way to aid the child who has difficulty with the stunt is as follows: The spotter stands in a straddle position, with the near foot alongside the spot where the performer's hands and head will make contact with the mat (Figure 20.50). The other foot is one stride in the direction of the roll. The critical point is for the spotter to lift the hips just as the head and hands of the performer make contact with the mat. This is accomplished by taking the back hand and reaching across to the far hip of the performer, getting under the other hip with the near hand. The lift is applied on the front of the hips just below the beltline. The object is to relieve the pressure on the neck.

Rather than spotting the youngster who is having trouble doing the Backward Roll, it may be wise to substitute the Handclasp Backward Roll (Figure 20.19) and practice on an inclined mat (see the following activity).

BACKWARD ROLL (INCLINED)

If possible, the Handclasp Backward Roll should be practiced on an inclined mat. The gentle incline allows the youngster to learn to develop momentum in a nonthreatening manner. An inclined mat can be made by leaving one mat folded and laying a crash pad or another mat over it.

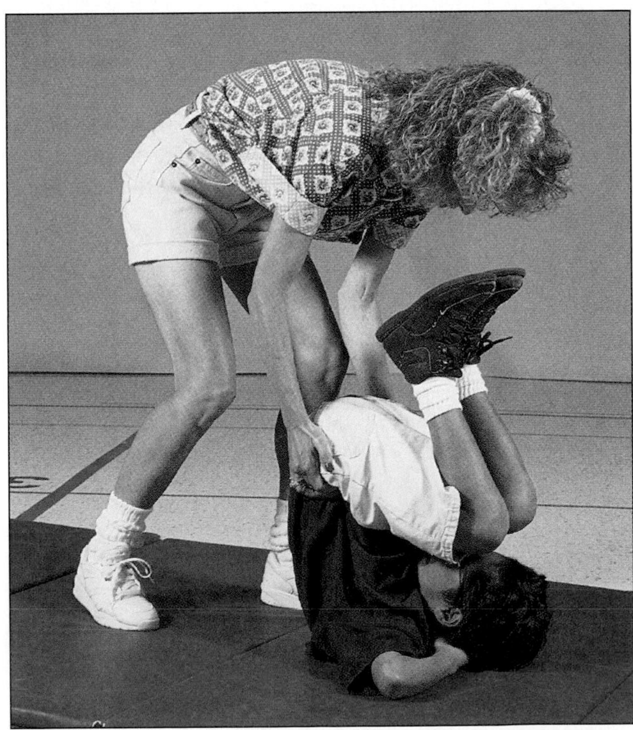

FIGURE 20.50 Spotting the Backward Roll. (The lift is at the hips of the roller. The performer should be lifted, not forced, over.)

HEADSTAND

Two approaches are suggested for the Headstand. The first is to relate the Headstand to the Climb-Up, and the second is to go directly into a Headstand, using a kick-up to achieve the inverted position. With either method, maintaining the triangle position of the hands and the head is essential.

In the final inverted position, the feet should be together, with legs straight and toes pointed. The weight is evenly distributed among the three points—the two hands and the forward part of the head. The body should be aligned as straight as possible.

The safest way to come down from the inverted position is to return to the mat in the direction that was used in going up. Recovery is helped by bending at both the waist and the knees. The child should be instructed, in the case of overbalancing, to tuck the head under and go into a Forward Roll. Both methods of recovery from the inverted position should be included in the instructional sequences early in the presentation.

HEADSTAND CLIMB-UP

Take the inverted position of the Climb Up (page 479) and move the feet slowly upward to the headstand position (Figure 20.51), steadied by a spotter only as needed.

Spotting: The spotter is stationed directly in front of the performer and steadies as needed. The spotter can first apply support to the hips and then transfer to the ankles as the climb-up position is lengthened into a Headstand. If unable to control the performer, the spotter must be alert to moving out of the way when the performer goes into a Forward Roll to come out of the inverted position.

HEADSTAND KICK-UP

Keeping the weight on the forward part of the head and maintaining the triangle base, walk the feet forward until the hips are high over the body, somewhat similar to the Climb-Up position. Keep one foot on the mat, with the knee of that leg bent, and the other leg extended somewhat backward. Kick the back leg up to the inverted position, following quickly with a push by the other leg, thus bringing the two legs together in the inverted position (Figure 20.52). The timing is a quick one-two movement.

FIGURE 20.51 Headstand based on the Climb-Up.

FIGURE 20.52 Headstand based on the Kick-Up.

The teacher should emphasize the importance of the triangle formed by the hands and the head and the importance of having the weight centered on the forward part of the head. Most problems that occur during performance of the Headstand come from an incorrect head-hand relationship. The correct positioning has the head placed the length of the performer's forearm from the knees and the hands placed at the knees. A useful technique to aid children in finding the proper triangle is to mark the three spots on the mat with chalk. (More lasting spots can be made with paint.)

Spotting: When learning, youngsters can attempt the stunt with a spotter on each side. Each spotter kneels, placing the near hand under the shoulder of the performer. The performer then walks the weight above the head and kicks up to position. The spotter on each side supports by grasping a leg (Figure 20.53 on page 492).

It is not desirable to let children stay too long in the inverted position or to hold contests to see who can remain in the Headstand longest. Most of the responsibility for getting into the inverted position should rest with the performer. Spotters may help some, but they should avoid wrestling the performer up. The goal of the kick-up method is to establish a pattern that can be used in other inverted stunts.

HEADSTAND PRACTICE AND VARIATIONS

Continue work on the Headstand. Try the following variations. (Spot as needed.)

1. Clap the hands and recover. The weight must be shifted momentarily to the head for the clap. (Some

FIGURE 20.53 Spotting the Headstand.

children will be able to clap the hands twice before recovery.)

2. Use different leg positions (Figure 20.54)—legs split sideward, legs split forward and backward, and knees bent.
3. Holding a utility ball or a beanbag between the legs, go into the Headstand, retaining control of the ball.

FROG HANDSTAND (TIP-UP)

Squat down on the mat, placing the hands flat, with fingers pointing forward and elbows inside and pressed against the inner part of the knees. Lean forward, using the leverage of the elbows against the knees, and balance on the hands (Figure 20.55). Hold for 5 seconds. Return to position. The head does not touch the mat at any time. The hands may be turned in slightly if this makes better contact between the elbows and the insides of the thighs. (This stunt follows from the Three-Point Tip-Up.)

FIGURE 20.54 Headstand Variation.

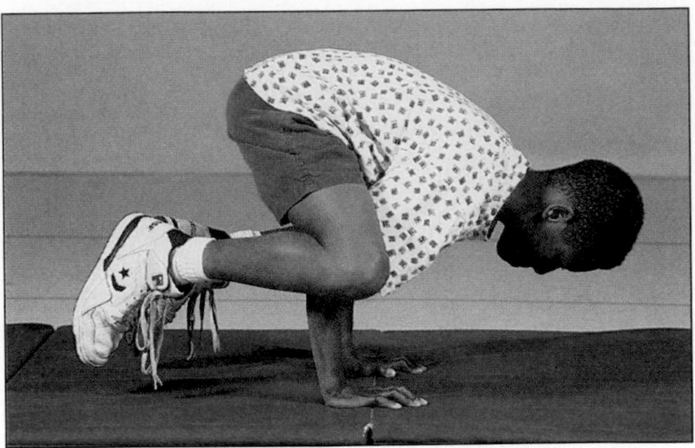

FIGURE 20.55 Frog Handstand.

HALF TEETER-TOTTER

This comprises continued lead-up activity for the Handstand. Begin in the lunge position and shift the weight to the hands. Kick the legs up in the air to a 135-degree angle, then return to the feet. This activity is similar to the Switcheroo, except that the feet are kicked higher without switching foot position.

CARTWHEEL

Start with the body in an erect position, arms outspread and legs shoulder width apart. Bend the body to the right and place the right hand on the floor. Follow this, in sequence, by the left hand, the left foot, and the right foot (Figure 20.56). Perform with a steady rhythm. Each body part should touch the floor at evenly spaced intervals. The body should be straight and extended when in the inverted position. The entire body must be in the same plane throughout the stunt, and the feet must pass directly over the head.

Children who have difficulty with the Cartwheel should be instructed to concentrate on taking the weight of the body on the hands in succession. They need to get the feel of the weight support and later can concentrate on getting the body into proper position. After the class has had some practice in doing Cartwheels, a running approach with a skip can be added before takeoff.

Spotting: In spotting, the spotter stands behind and moves with the performer. To assist, the spotter assumes a crossed-arm position and grasps the performer at the waist. The spotter's arms uncross as the performer wheels.

FIGURE 20.56 Cartwheel.

FORWARD ROLL (PIKE POSITION)

Begin the piked Forward Roll in a standing pike position. Keep the legs straight and bend forward at the hips. Place the hands on the mat, bend the elbows, and lower the head to the mat. Keep the legs straight until nearing the end of the roll. Bend at the knees to facilitate returning to the feet.

FORWARD ROLL COMBINATIONS

Review the Forward Roll, with increased emphasis on proper form. Combinations such as the following can be introduced.

1. Do a Forward Roll preceded by a short run.
2. Do two Forward Rolls in succession.
3. Do a Leapfrog (page 502) plus a Forward Roll.
4. Do a Forward Roll to a vertical jump in the air, and repeat.
5. Do a Rabbit Jump plus a Forward Roll.
6. Hold the toes while doing a Forward Roll.

BACKWARD ROLL COMBINATIONS

Review the Backward Roll. Continue emphasis on the Push-Off with the hands. Combinations to be taught are these:

1. Do a Backward Roll to a standing position. A strong push by the hands is necessary to provide enough momentum to land on the feet.
2. Do two Backward Rolls in succession.
3. Do a Crab Walk into a Backward Roll.
4. Add a jump in the air at the completion of a Backward Roll.

TEETER-TOTTER

The Teeter-Totter is the final lead-up activity for the Handstand. It is performed in a manner similar to the Half Teeter-Totter, except that the feet are held together for a moment in the handstand position before returning to the standing position.

HANDSTAND

Start in the lunge position. Do a Teeter-Totter to the inverted position. The body, which is extended in a line from the shoulders through the feet, should be kept straight with the head down. It is helpful to teach the correct position first in a standing position with the arms overhead and the ears between the arms.

Spotting: The Handstand can be done with double or single spotting. In double spotting, the spotters are stationed on both sides of the performer. Each spotter should have a firm grip with one hand beneath the performer's shoulder. The other hand can assist the lift by upward pressure on the thigh (Figure 20.57). The performer walks the hips forward until they are over the hands and then kicks up with one foot, pushing off with the other and raising that leg to join the first in the inverted position (Figure 20.58 on page 494). The rhythm is a one-two count.

In single spotting, the spotter takes a stride position, with the forward knee bent somewhat (Figure 20.59 on page 494). The performer's weight is transferred over the hands, and the body goes into the handstand position with a one-two kick-up. The spotter catches the legs and holds the performer in an inverted position (Figure 20.60 on page 494).

Balance Stunts

ONE-LEG BALANCE REVERSE

Assume a forward balance position (pages 481–482). In a quick movement, to give momentum, swing the free

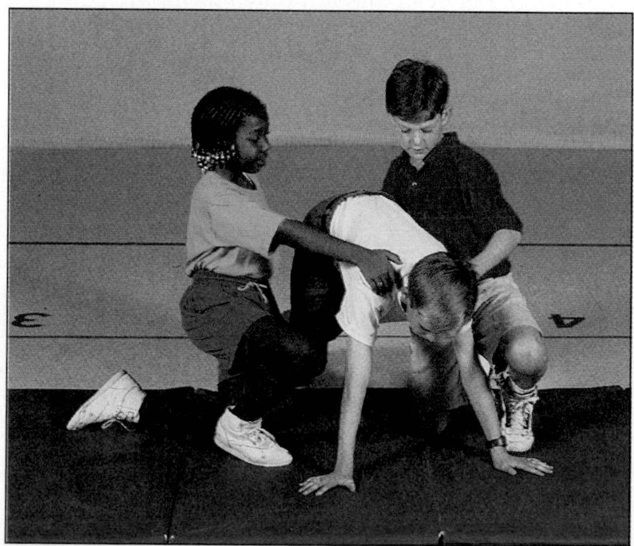

FIGURE 20.57 Double Spotting for the Handstand, first stage. (Note the hand support under the shoulders.)

FIGURE 20.58 Double spotting for the Handstand, second stage.

leg down and change to the same forward balance position facing in the opposite direction (a 180-degree turn) (Figure 20.61). No unnecessary movement of the supporting foot should be made after the turn is completed. The swinging foot should not touch the floor.

FIGURE 20.59 Single Spotting for the Handstand, first stage. (The performer's shoulder is against the spotter's leg.)

FIGURE 20.60 Single spotting for the Handstand, second stage. (Note knee pressure against performer's shoulder.)

TUMMY BALANCE

Lie prone on the floor with arms outstretched forward or to the sides, with palms down. Raise the arms, head, chest, and legs from the floor and balance on the tummy (Figure 20.62). The knees should be kept straight.

FIGURE 20.61 One-Leg Balance Reverse.

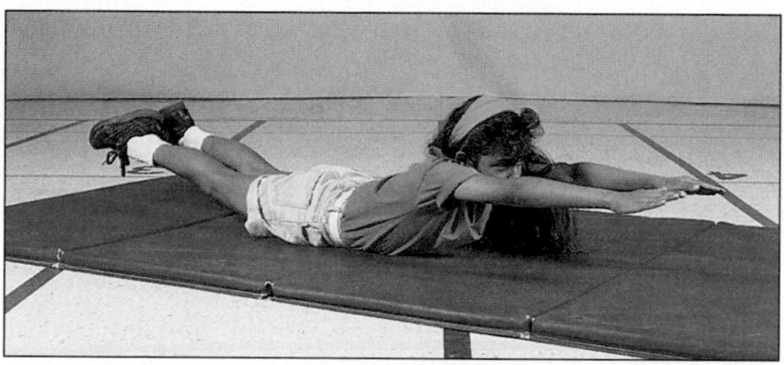

FIGURE 20.62 Tummy Balance.

LEG DIP

Extend both hands and one leg forward, balancing on the other leg. Lower the body to sit on the heel and return without losing the balance or touching the floor with any part of the body. Try with the other foot. (Another child can assist from the back by applying upward pressure to the elbows.)

BALANCE JUMP

With hands and arms out to the sides and body parallel to the ground, extend one leg back and balance the weight on the other leg (Figure 20.63). Quickly change balance to the other foot, maintaining the initial position but with the feet exchanged (Figure 20.64). Keep the body parallel to the ground during the change of legs. Try with arms outstretched forward. Working in pairs might be helpful. One student critiques the other's performance to make sure that the arms and body are straight and parallel to the floor.

FIGURE 20.63 Balance Jump, starting position.

FIGURE 20.64 Balance Jump.

SEAT BALANCE

Sit on the floor, holding the ankles in front, with elbows inside the knees. The feet are flat on the floor, and the knees are bent at approximately a right angle. Raise the legs (toes pointed) so that the knees are straight (Figure 20.65), and balance on the seat for 5 seconds.

FACE-TO-KNEE TOUCH

Begin in a standing position with feet together. Placing the hands on the hips, balance on one foot, with the other leg extended backward. Bend the trunk forward and touch the knee of the supporting leg with the forehead (Figure 20.66 on page 496). Recover to original position.

Teachers can have children begin by keeping the arms away from the sides for balance and then stipulate the hands-on-hips position later. In the learning stages, assistance can be given from behind by supporting the leg extended backward, or the child can place one hand against a wall.

FINGER TOUCH

Put the right hand behind the back with the index finger straight and pointed down. Grasp the right wrist with the left hand. From an erect position with the feet about 6 inches apart, squat down and touch the floor with the

FIGURE 20.65 Seat Balance.

FIGURE 20.66 Face-to-Knee Touch.

index finger (Figure 20.67). Regain the erect position without losing balance. Reverse hands. (In the learning stages, the teacher can use a book or the corner of a mat to decrease the distance and make the touch easier.)

Individual Stunts

REACH-UNDER

Take a position with the feet pointed ahead (spaced about 2 feet apart) and toes against a line or a floor board. Place a beanbag two boards in front of, and midway between, the feet. Without changing the position of the feet, reach one hand behind and between the legs to pick up the beanbag. Now pick up with the other hand. Repeat, moving the beanbag a board farther away each time.

TEACHING TIP

Variation: Allow the heels to lift off the floor. Use the other hand.

STIFF PERSON BEND

Place the feet about shoulder width apart and pointed forward. Place a beanbag a few inches behind the right heel. Grasp the left toes with the left hand, thumb on top. Without bending the knees, reach the right hand outside the right leg and pick up the beanbag without releasing the hold on the left toes. Gradually increase the distance of the reach. Reverse sides (Figure 20.68).

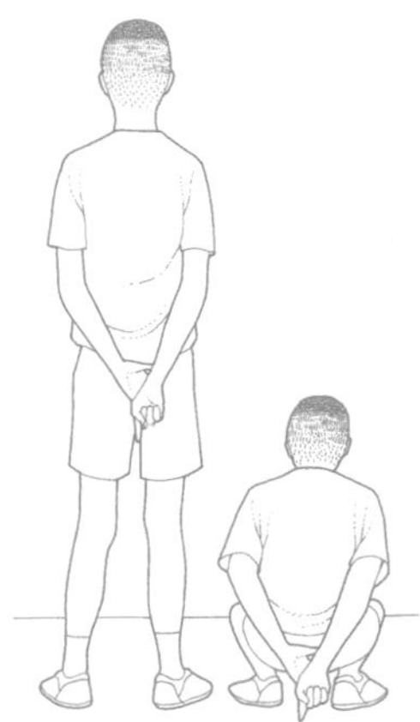

FIGURE 20.67 Finger Touch.

COFFEE GRINDER

Put one hand on the floor and extend the body to the floor on that side in a side-leaning rest position. Walk around the hand, making a complete circle and keeping the body straight (Figure 20.69). The stunt should be done slowly, with controlled movements. The body should remain straight throughout the circle movement.

SCOOTER

Sit on the floor with legs extended, arms folded in front of the chest, and chin held high. To scoot, pull the seat toward the heels, using heel pressure and lifting the seat slightly (Figure 20.70). Extend the legs forward again and repeat the process. (This is an excellent activity for abdominal development.)

HIP WALK

Sit in the same position as for the Scooter, but with arms in thrust position and hands making a partial fist.

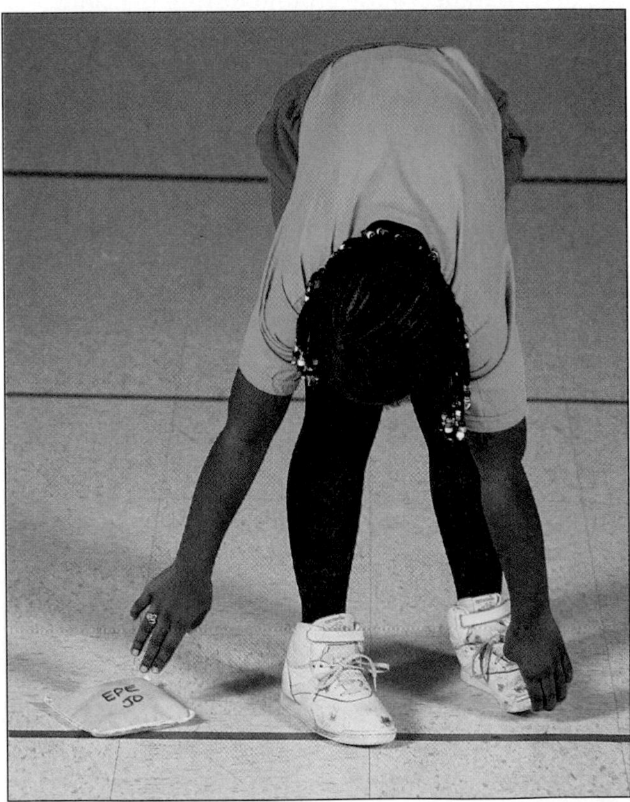

FIGURE 20.68 Stiff Person Bend.

FIGURE 20.69 Coffee Grinder.

Progress forward by alternate leg-seat movements. The arm-leg coordination is unilateral.

LONG BRIDGE

Begin in a crouched position with hands on the floor and knees between the arms. Push the hands forward a little at a time until an extended push-up position is reached (Figure 20.71). Return to original position. (The teacher should challenge children to extend as far forward as they can and still retain the support.)

TEACHING TIP

Variations:

1. Begin with a forward movement, then change to a sideward movement, establishing as wide a spread as possible.
2. Work from a crossed-hands position.

HEELSTAND

Begin in a full-squat position with the arms dangling at the sides. Jump upward to full leg extension with the weight on both heels and fling the arms out diagonally. Hold momentarily, then return to position (Figure 20.72 on page 498). Several movements can be done rhythmically in succession.

WICKET WALK

Bend over and touch the floor with the weight evenly distributed on the hands and feet, thus forming a wicket. Walk the wicket forward, backward, and sideward. Keep the arms and legs as nearly vertical as possible (Figure 20.73 on page 498). Be sure that the knees are reasonably straight, for the stunt loses much of its flexibility value if the knees are bent too much. A common error in the execution of this stunt is to keep the hands positioned too far forward of the feet. (The stunt gets its name from the child's position, which resembles a wicket in a croquet game.)

FIGURE 20.70 Scooter.

FIGURE 20.71 Long Bridge.

FIGURE 20.72 Heelstand.

FIGURE 20.74 Knee Jump to Standing.

KNEE JUMP TO STANDING

Kneel, with seat touching the heels and toes pointing backward (shoelaces against the floor). Jump to a standing position with a vigorous upward swing of the arms (Figure 20.74). It is easier to jump from a smooth floor than from a mat, because the toes slide more readily on the floor.

TEACHING TIP

Variation: Jump to a standing position, doing a quarter turn in the air in one quick motion. Try a half turn.

INDIVIDUAL DROPS OR FALLS

Drops, or falls, can challenge children to achieve good body control. Mats should be used. The impact of a forward fall is absorbed by the hands and arms. During the fall, the body should maintain a straight-line position. Make sure that little change in body angles occurs, particularly at the knees and waist.

FIGURE 20.73 Wicket Walk.

KNEE DROP

Kneel on a mat, with the body upright. Raise the feet up, off the floor, and fall forward, breaking the fall with the hands and arms (Figure 20.75).

FORWARD DROP

From a forward balance position on one leg with the other leg extended backward and the arms extended forward and up, lean forward slowly, bringing the arms toward the floor. Continue to drop forward slowly until overbalanced, then let the hands and arms break the fall (Figure 20.76). The head is up and the extended leg is raised high, with knee joints kept reasonably straight. Repeat, changing position of the legs.

DEAD BODY FALL

Fall forward from an erect position to a down push-up position (Figure 20.77). A slight bend at the waist is per-

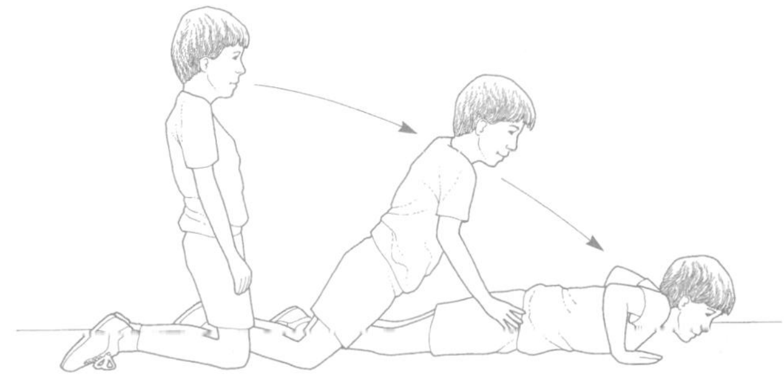

FIGURE 20.75 Knee Drop.

FIGURE 20.76 Forward Drop.

missible, but the knees should be kept straight, and there should be no forward movement of the feet.

STOOP AND STRETCH

Hold a beanbag with both hands. Stand with heels against a line and feet about shoulder width apart. Keeping the knees straight, reach between the legs with the beanbag and place it as far back as possible. Reach back and pick it up with both hands.

TEACHING TIP

Variations:

1. Bend at the knees, using more of a squatting position during the reach.
2. Use a piece of chalk instead of a beanbag. Reach back and make a mark on the floor. Try writing a number or drawing a small circle or some other figure.

TANGLEFOOT

Stand with heels together and toes pointed out. Bend the trunk forward and extend both arms down between the knees and around behind the ankles. Bring the hands around the outside of the ankles from behind and touch the fingers to each other (Figure 20.78). Hold for a 5-second count.

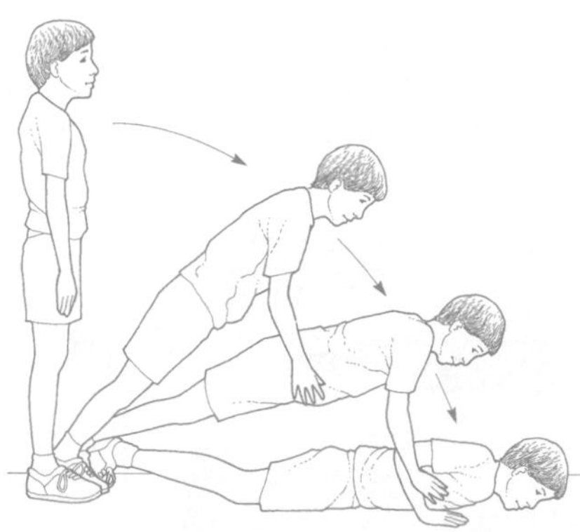

FIGURE 20.77 Dead Body Fall.

FIGURE 20.78 Tanglefoot.

TEACHING TIP

Variation: Instead of touching, clasp the fingers in front of the ankles. Hold this position in good balance for 5 seconds without releasing the handclasp.

EGG ROLL

In a sitting position, assume the same clasped-hands position as for Tanglefoot. Roll sideways over one shoulder, then to the back, then to the other shoulder, and finally back up to the sitting position (Figure 20.79 on page 500). The movements are repeated in turn to make a full circle back to place. The secret is a vigorous sideward movement to secure initial momentum. If mats are used, two should be placed side by side to cover the extent of the roll. (Some children can do this stunt better from a crossed-ankle position.)

TOE TOUCH NOSE

From a sitting position on the floor, touch the toes of either foot to the nose with the help of both hands. Do first one foot and then the other. More flexible youngsters will be able to place the foot on top of the head or even behind the neck. Although this is a flexibility

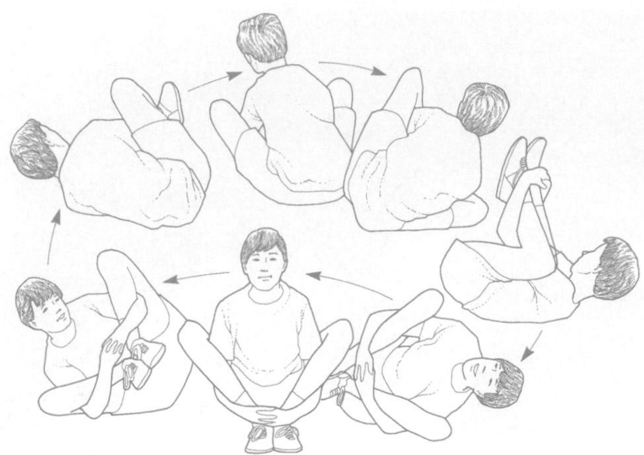

FIGURE 20.79 Egg Roll.

exercise, caution should be used; the leg can be forced too far.

TEACHING TIP

Variation: Perform from a standing position. Touch the toes to the nose and return the foot to original position without losing balance. Try the standing version with eyes closed.

TOE TUG WALK

Bend over and grasp the toes with thumbs on top (Figure 20.80). Keep the knees bent slightly and the eyes forward. Walk forward without losing the grip on the toes. Walk backward and sideward to provide more challenge. Walk in various geometric patterns, such as a circle, triangle, or square. (This stunt can be introduced in an easier version by having children grasp the ankles, thumbs on the insides, and perform the desired movements.)

TEACHING TIP

Variation: Try doing the walk with the right hand grasping the left foot, and vice versa.

Partner and Group Stunts

PARTNER HOPPING

Partners coordinate hopping movements for short distances and in different directions and turns. Three combinations are suggested.

1. Stand facing each other. Extend the right leg forward to be grasped at the ankle by partner's left hand. Hold right hands and hop on the left leg (Figure 20.81).
2. Stand back to back. Lift the leg backward, bending the knee, and have partner grasp the ankle. Hop as before.

FIGURE 20.80 Toe Tug Walk.

FIGURE 20.81 Partner Hopping.

3. Stand side by side with inside arms around each other's waist. Lift the inside foot from the floor and make progress by hopping on the outside foot.

If either partner begins to fall, the other should release the leg immediately. Reverse foot positions.

PARTNER TWISTER

Partners face and grasp right hands as if shaking hands. One partner swings the left leg over the head of the other and turns around, taking a straddle position over partner's arm (Figure 20.82). The other swings the right leg over the first partner, who has bent over, and the partners are now back to back. First partner continues with the right leg and faces in the original direction. Second partner swings the left leg over the partner's back to return to the original face-to-face position. Partners need to duck to avoid being kicked by each other's feet as the legs are swung over.

TEACHING TIP

Variation: The stunt can be introduced by grasping a wand instead of holding hands.

PARTNER PULL-UP

Partners sit facing each other in a bent-knee position, with heels on the floor and toes touching. Pulling cooperatively, they come to a standing position (Figure 20.83).

TEACHING TIP

Variation: Try with feet flat on the floor.

BACK-TO-BACK GET-UP

Partners sit back to back and lock arms. From this position, they try to stand by pushing against each other's back (Figure 20.84). Sit down again. If the feet are sliding, do the stunt on a mat.

FIGURE 20.82 Partner Twister.

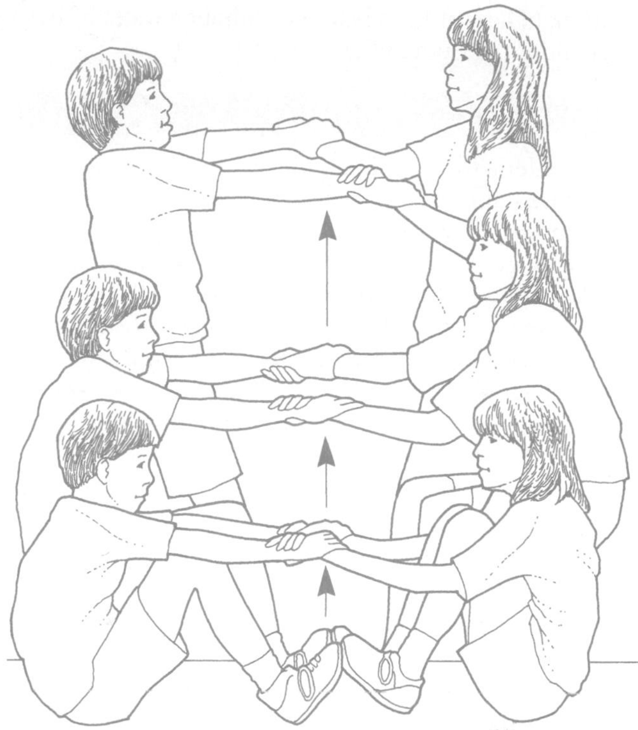

FIGURE 20.83 Partner Pull-Up.

TEACHING TIP

Variations:

1. Try with three or four children.
2. Try from a halfway-down position, and move like a spider.

ROWBOAT

Partners sit on the floor or on a mat, facing each other with legs apart and feet touching. Both grasp a wand with both hands. Pretend to row a boat. Seek a wide range of movement in the forward-backward rowing

FIGURE 20.84 Back-to-Back Get-Up.

motion. (The stunt can be done without a wand by having children grasp hands.)

LEAPFROG

One student forms a back. A leaper takes a running start, lays hands flat on the back at the shoulders, and vaults over the low student. Backs are formed at various heights (Figure 20.85). To form a low back, crouch down on the knees, curling into a tight ball with the head tucked well down. To form a medium back, reach down the outside of the legs from a standing position and grasp the ankles. The feet should be reasonably spread and the knees straight. The position must be stable in order to absorb the shock of the leaper. To form a high back, stand stiff-legged, bend over, and brace arms against the knees. The feet should be spread, the head down, and the body braced to absorb the vault.

Leapfrog is a traditional physical education activity, but the movement is actually a jump-and-vault pattern. The takeoff must be made with both feet. At the height of the jump, the chest and head must be held erect to avoid a forward fall. The teacher should emphasize a forceful jump to achieve height, coordinated with light hand pressure to vault over the back. Landing should be done lightly and under good control, with a bent-knee action.

TEACHING TIP

Variations:

1. Work in pairs. Alternate leaping and forming the back while progressing around the room.
2. Have more than one back for a series of jumps.
3. Using the medium back, vault from the side rather than from the front. The vaulter's legs must be well spread, and the back must keep the head well tucked down.
4. Following the Leapfrog, do a Forward Roll on a mat.

WHEELBARROW

One partner gets down on the hands with feet extended to the rear and legs apart. The other partner (the pusher) grasps partner's legs about halfway between the ankles and the knees. The wheelbarrow walks forward on the hands, supported by the pusher (Figure 20.86). Movements should be under good control.

FIGURE 20.85 High, medium, and low Leapfrog positions.

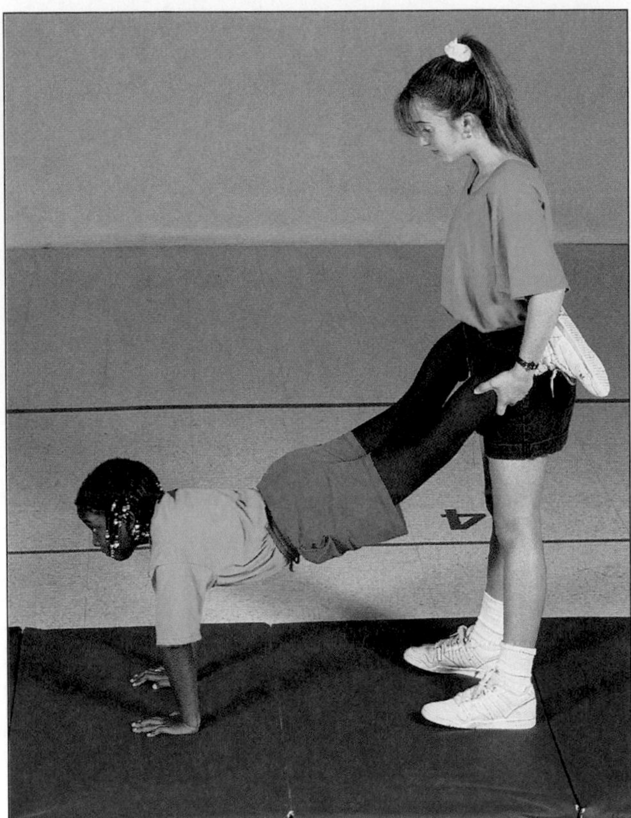

FIGURE 20.86 Wheelbarrow.

Children have a tendency to grasp the legs too near the feet. The pusher must not push too fast. The wheelbarrow should have the head up and look forward. Fingers should be pointed forward and well spread, with the pads of the fingers supporting much of the weight. The pusher should carry the legs low and keep the arms extended.

WHEELBARROW LIFTING

Partners assume the wheelbarrow position. The pusher lifts partner's legs as high as possible without changing the hand position. The pusher should be able to lift the legs enough so that the lower child's body is at an angle of about 45 degrees to the floor.

TEACHING TIP

Variation: The pusher brings the legs up to the level described, changes the handgrip to a pushing one, and continues to raise the lower child toward a handstand position. The lower child keeps arms and body straight.

FIGURE 20.87 Dromedary Walk.

CAMEL LIFT AND WALK

In the wheelbarrow position, the wheelbarrow raises the seat as high as possible, forming a camel. Camels can lower themselves or walk in the raised position.

DUMP THE WHEELBARROW

Get into the wheelbarrow position. Walk the wheelbarrow over to a mat. The lower child ducks the head (chin to waist), raises the seat (bending at the waist), and exits from the stunt with a Forward Roll. The pusher gives a little push and a lift of the feet to help supply momentum.

DROMEDARY WALK

One child (the support) gets down on the hands and knees. The other child sits on the support, facing the rear, and fixes the legs around the support's chest. The top child leans forward, to grasp the back of the support's ankles. The top child's arms are reasonably extended (Figure 20.87). The support takes the weight off the knees and walks forward with the top child's help.

CENTIPEDE

One child, the stronger and larger individual, gets down on the hands and knees. The other child faces the same direction, places the hands about 2 feet in front of the support's, then places the legs and body on top of the support. The knees should be spread apart and the heels locked together. The centipede walks with the top child using hands only and the supporting child using both hands and feet. The support should gather the legs well under while walking and not be on the knees.

TEACHING TIP

Variation: More than two can do this stunt (Figure 20.88). After getting into position, the players should keep step by calling "Right" and "Left" out loud.

DOUBLE WHEELBARROW

Two children assume the same position as for the Centipede, except that the under child has the legs extended to the rear and the feet apart. A third child stands between the legs of the under child, reaches down, and picks up the legs of the lower child (Figure 20.89 on page 504). The Double Wheelbarrow moves forward with right and left arms moving together.

An easy way to get into position for this activity is to form the front of the wheelbarrow first and then to pick up the legs of the second child. This stunt usually is done by three children but can be done by more.

Partner Support Stunts

Several considerations are important in the conducting of partner support stunts at this level. The lower child (the support) should keep the body as level as possible. This means widening the hand base so that the shoulders are more nearly level with the hips. The support performer must be strong enough to handle the support chores. Spotters are needed, particularly when the top position involves a final erect or inverted pose. The top child should avoid stepping on the small of the lower child's back. In the Lighthouse and the Hip-Shoulder Stand, the top performer can remove the shoes, making the standing position more comfortable for the support.

FIGURE 20.88 Centipede.

FIGURE 20.89 Double Wheelbarrow.

When holding the final pose, the top child should fix the gaze forward and relax as much as possible while maintaining the position.

DOUBLE BEAR

The bottom child gets down on the hands and knees. The top child assumes the same position directly above the support, with hands on the shoulders and knees on the hips of the support (Figure 20.90). Touch up the final position by holding heads up and backs straight.

FIGURE 20.90 Double Bear.

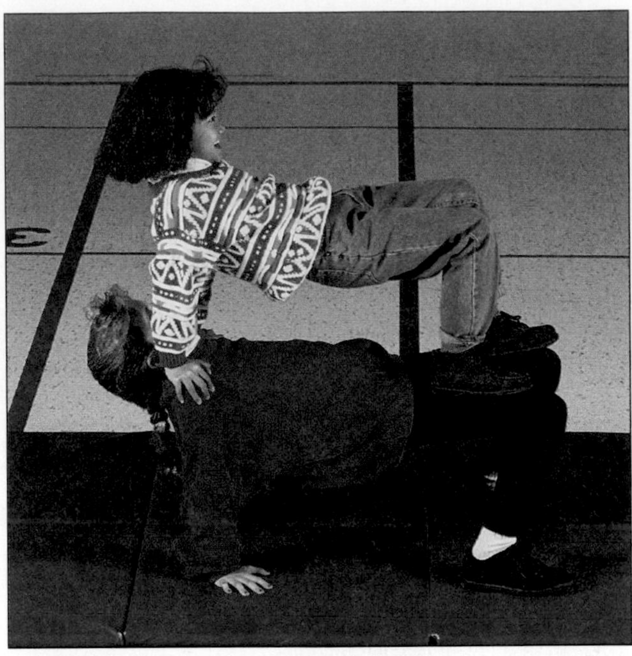

FIGURE 20.91 Table.

TABLE

The bottom performer assumes a crab position. The top performer straddles this base, facing the rear, and positions the hands on the base's shoulders, fingers pointing toward the ground. The top child then places the feet on top of base's knees, forming one crab position on top of another (Figure 20.91). As a final touch, the heads are positioned so that the eyes look up toward the ceiling, and the seats are lifted so that the backs are straight.

STATUE

The first child gets down in crab position. The second child straddles either foot, facing the child in crab position. With the help of a third person, the second child mounts each knee of the base child so that the statue is standing erect (Figure 20.92). Hold the position for a few seconds. Partners should be facing each other. The top child should not mount with back toward the base child. (Spotters are important and must not be eliminated until the stunt is mastered.)

LIGHTHOUSE

The support gets down on the hands and knees. The top child completes the figure by standing on the support's shoulders and facing in the same direction. The lighthouse stands erect with hands out to the sides (Figure 20.93).

FIGURE 20.92 Statue.

TEACHING TIP

Variation: The support turns around in a small circle, while the partner keeps the standing balance.

FIGURE 20.93 Lighthouse.

HIP-SHOULDER STAND

The support is on the hands and knees, with hands positioned out somewhat so that the back is level. The top child faces to the side and steps up, first with one foot on support's hips and then with the other on the shoulders (Figure 20.94).

A spotter should stand on the opposite side and aid in the mounting. Care must be taken to avoid stepping on the small of the support's back.

DEVELOPMENTAL LEVEL III ACTIVITIES

Children at this level should be skillful in both the Forward and the Backward Roll. Routines involving these rolls can also be expanded. The Judo Roll, Cartwheel with Round-Off, and Double Roll continue the mat-type activities. Improvement in the Headstand is expected. Such stunts as the Headspring, Front Seat Support, Elbow Balance, Straddle Press to Headstand, and Walk-Over provide sufficient breadth for even the most skilled. It is unrealistic to expect all children to accomplish the entire list of stunts at this level.

Particular attention should be paid to the gymnastic-type stunts. Although there is still opportunity at this level for exploration and individual expression, more emphasis is placed on execution, conformity, and form.

FIGURE 20.94 Hip-Shoulder Stand.

Tumbling and Inverted Balances

FORWARD AND BACKWARD ROLL COMBINATIONS

Combinations from developmental level II should be reviewed. The following routines can be added.

1. Begin with a Forward Roll, coming to a standing position with feet crossed. Pivot the body to uncross the feet and to bring the back in the line of direction for a Backward Roll (Figure 20.95).
2. Hold the toes, heels, ankles, or a wand while rolling. Use different arm positions, such as out to the sides or folded across the chest. Use a wide straddle position for both the Forward Roll and the Backward Roll.

BACK EXTENSION

Carry the Backward Roll to the point where the feet are above and over the head. Push off vigorously with the hands, shoot the feet into the air, and land on the feet.

HEADSTAND VARIATIONS

Review the various aspects of the Headstand, using the single-spotter technique as needed. Vary with different leg positions. Add the two-foot recovery. After the stand has been held, recover by bending at the waist and knees, pushing off with the hands, and landing on the feet back in the original position.

HANDSTAND AGAINST A WALL

Using a wall as support, do a Handstand. The arms must be kept straight, with the head between the arms (Figure 20.96). Some performers like to bend the knees so that the soles of the feet are against the wall.

A critical point in the Handstand against a Wall is to position the hands the correct distance from the wall. It is better to be too close than too far. Being too far can cause the performer to collapse before the feet gain the support of the wall. A mat should be used in the preliminary stages.

FREESTANDING HANDSTAND

Perform a Handstand without support. Students must learn to turn the body when a fall is imminent, so that they land on the feet. (Spotters can be used to prevent an awkward fall.) Move the hands to help control the balance.

CARTWHEEL AND ROUND-OFF

Practice the Cartwheel, adding a light run with a skip for a takeoff. To change to a Round-Off, place the hands somewhat closer together during the early Cartwheel action. Bring the feet together and make a quarter turn to land on both feet, with the body facing the starting point. The Round-Off can be followed by a Backward Roll.

JUDO ROLL

For a left Judo Roll, stand facing the mat with the feet well apart and the left arm extended at shoulder height. Bring the arm down and throw the left shoulder toward the mat in a rolling motion, with the roll made on the shoulder and the upper part of the back (Figure 20.97). Reverse for a right Judo Roll. Both right and left Judo Rolls should be practiced. Later, a short run and a double-foot takeoff should precede the roll. The Judo Roll is a basic safety device to prevent injury from tripping and falling. Rolling and taking the fall lessen the chances of injury. The Judo Roll is essentially a Forward Roll with the head turned to one side. The point of impact is the back of one shoulder and the finish is a return to the standing position.

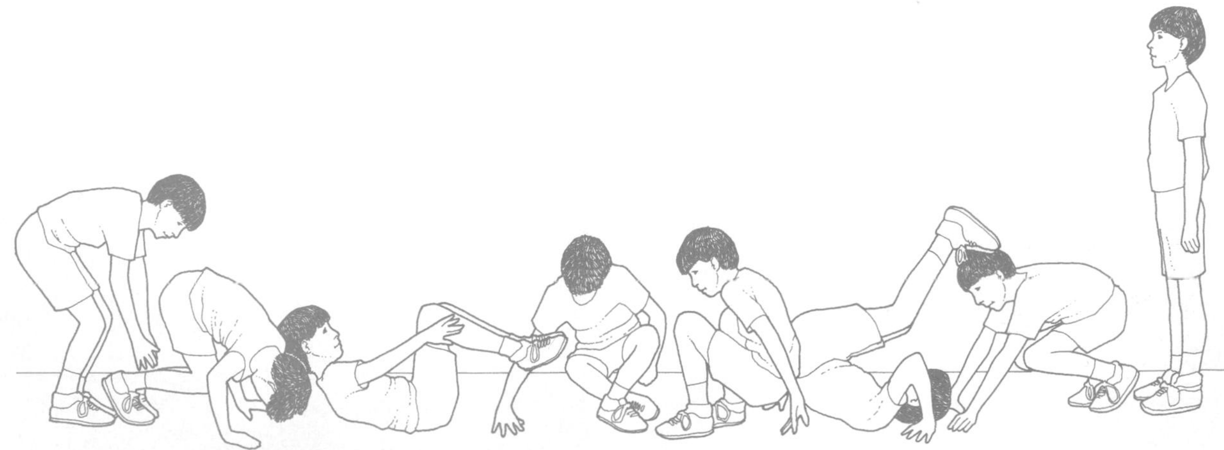

FIGURE 20.95 Alternating Forward and Backward Rolls.

FIGURE 20.96 Handstand against a wall.

TEACHING TIP

Variations:

1. Roll to the feet and to a ready position.
2. Place a beanbag about 3 feet in front of the toes and go beyond the bag to start the roll.

FIGURE 20.97 Judo Roll.

ADVANCED FORWARD AND BACKWARD ROLL COMBINATIONS

Put together different combinations of Forward Rolls and Backward Rolls. The emphasis should be on choice, exploration, and self-discovery. Variations can involve different approaches, execution acts, and finishes. Try the following variations of the Forward Roll.

1. Roll while holding the toes, heels, ankles, or a wand.
2. As above, but cross the hands.
3. Roll with hands on the knees or with a ball between the knees.
4. Roll with arms at the sides, folded across the chest, or on the back of the thighs.
5. Press forward from a front-leaning rest position and go into the roll.

Try the following suggestions with the Backward Roll.

1. Begin with a Stiff-Legged Sitdown and go into the roll.
2. Push off into a Back Extension, landing on the feet.
3. Roll to a finish on one foot only.
4. Roll with hands clasped behind the neck.
5. Roll with a ball between the knees.
6. Walk backward using a Crab Walk and then roll.

In addition to these, combine Forward Rolls with Backward Rolls in various ways.

STRADDLE PRESS TO HEADSTAND

Begin by placing the hands and head in the Triangular Headstand position. The feet are in a wide straddle position and the hips are up. Raise the hips slowly by pressing to a point over the base of support. Slowly raise the legs to a straddle position and finish with the legs brought together in regular Headstand position. All movement is done as a slow, controlled action. (This is a more difficult stunt than the regular Headstand.)

HANDSTAND VARIATIONS

The first two stages of the Handstand, done with double spotting and then single spotting with knee support (pages 493–494), should be reviewed. Progression can then follow this order.

1. Single spotting, without knee support
2. Handstand against a Wall
3. Freestanding Handstand
4. Walking on the Hands
5. Stunts against a wall

Spotting: For single spotting without knee support, the performer and the spotter face each other 4 or 5 feet apart. The performer lifts both arms and the left leg upward as a preliminary move, with the weight shifted to the right leg. The lifted arms and forward leg come down forcefully to the ground, with the weight shifted in succession to the left leg and then to the arms. The right leg is kicked backward and upward for initial momentum and is followed quickly by the left leg. The downward thrust of the arms, coupled with the upward thrust of the legs, inverts the body to the handstand position. The placement of the hands should be about 2 feet in front of the spotter, who reaches forward and catches the performer between the knees and the ankles (Figure 20.98).

HEADSPRING

With forehead and hands on the mat and knees bent, lean forward until almost overbalanced. As the weight begins to overbalance, raise the feet sharply and snap forward, pushing with the hands. As the feet begin to touch the ground, snap the body to a bent-knee position (Figure 20.99). Keep control of balance and rise to a standing position.

Spotting: Two spotters should be used, one on each side of the performer. Each spotter places one hand under the performer's back and the other hand under a shoulder. The spotters should give the performer a lift under the shoulders to help in snapping to the standing position.

FIGURE 20.98 Single spotting for the Handstand.

FIGURE 20.99 Headspring.

Some instructors like to introduce this stunt by performing it over a rolled-up mat, which provides more height for the turn. A slight run may be needed to get the proper momentum.

WALKING ON THE HANDS

Walk on the hands in a forward direction, bending the knees slightly, if desired, for balance. (Walking can be done first with a spotter supporting, but this support should be minimal.)

TEACHING TIP

Variation: Walk on the hands, using a partner. The performer does a Handstand and the partner catches the feet. The performer then walks the hands forward until they are on the partner's feet. The two walk cooperatively.

WALK-OVER

Do preliminary movements as if for the Handstand. Let the legs continue beyond the handstand position and contact the floor with a one-two rhythm. The body must be well arched as the leading foot touches the floor. Push off with the hands and walk out.

Spotting: The spotter gives support under the small of the back.

Balance Stunts

V-UP

Lie on the back, with arms overhead and extended. Keeping the knees straight and the feet pointed, bring the legs and the upper body up at the same time to form a V shape. The entire weight is balanced on the seat (Figure 20.100). Hold the position for 5 seconds.

This exercise, like the Curl-Up, is excellent for development of the abdominal muscles. It is quite similar to the Seat Balance except for the starting position.

TEACHING TIP

Variation: Place the hands on the floor in back for support. (This makes the stunt easier for those students having trouble.)

FIGURE 20.100 V-Up.

PUSH-UP VARIATIONS

Begin the development of Push-Up variations by reviewing proper Push-Up techniques. The only movement is in the arms. The body should come close to, but not touch, the floor. Explore the following variations.

Monkey Push-Up Point the fingers toward each other. Next, bring the hands close enough for the fingertips to touch.

Circle-O Push-Up Form a circle with each thumb and forefinger.

Fingertip Push-Up Get up high on the fingertips.

Different Finger Combinations Do a Push-Up using the thumb and three or two fingers only.

Extended Push-Up Extend the position of the hands progressively forward or to the sides.

Crossed Push-Up Cross the arms. Cross the legs. Cross both.

One-Legged Push-Up Lift one leg from the floor.

One-Handed Push-Up Use only one hand, with the other outstretched or on the hip.

Exploratory Approach See what other types of Push Ups or combinations can be created.

FLIP-FLOP

From a push-up position, propel the body upward with the hands and feet, doing a Turn-Over (Figure 20.101).

FIGURE 20.101 Flip-Flop.

FIGURE 20.102 Long Reach.

Flip back. The stunt should be done on a mat. (Review the Turn-Over [page 484] before having students try this stunt.)

LONG REACH

Place a beanbag about 3 feet in front of a line. Keeping the toes behind the line, lean forward on one hand and reach out with the other hand to touch the beanbag (Figure 20.102). Recover in one clean, quick movement to the original position, lifting the supporting hand off the floor. Increase the distance of the bag from the line.

TOE JUMP

Hold the left toes with the right hand (Figure 20.103). Jump the right foot through without losing the grip on the toes. Try with the other foot. (Teachers should not

FIGURE 20.103 Toe Jump.

be discouraged if only a few can do this stunt; it is quite difficult.)

HANDSTAND STUNTS

Try these challenging activities from the handstand position against a wall.

1. Turn the body in a complete circle, maintaining foot contact with the wall throughout.
2. Shift the support to one hand and hold for a moment.
3. Do an Inverted Push-Up, lowering the body by bending the elbows and then returning to handstand position by straightening the elbows.

FRONT SEAT SUPPORT

Sit on the floor, with the legs together and forward. Place the hands flat on the floor, somewhat between the hips and the knees, with fingers pointed forward. Push down so the hips come off the floor, with the weight supported on the hands and heels. Next, lift the heels and support the entire weight of the body on the hands for 3 to 5 seconds. (Someone can help the performer get into position by giving slight support under the heels.)

ELBOW BALANCE

Balance the body facedown horizontally on two hands, with elbows supporting the body in the hip area. To get into position, support the arched body with the toes and forehead. Work the forearms underneath the body for support, with fingers spread and pointed to the back. Try to support the body completely on the hands for 3 seconds, with elbows providing the leverage under the body (Figure 20.104). (Slight support under the toes can be provided.)

The Elbow Balance presents a considerable challenge. The teacher should take time to discuss the location of the center of gravity. The elbow support point should divide the upper and lower body mass.

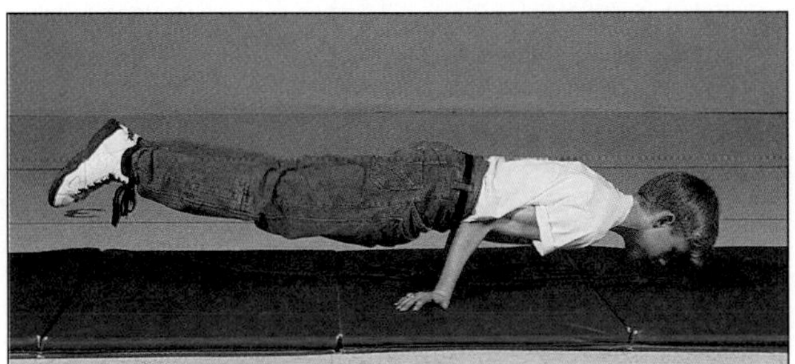

FIGURE 20.104 Elbow Balance.

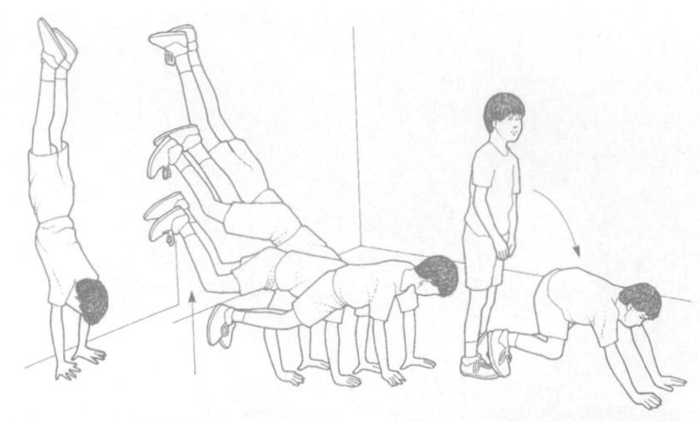

FIGURE 20.105 Wall Walk-Up.

Individual Stunts

WALL WALK-UP

From a push-up position with feet against a wall, walk up the wall backward to a handstand position (Figure 20.105). Walk down again.

SKIER'S SIT

Assume a sitting position against a wall with the thighs parallel to the floor and the knee joints at right angles. (The position is the same as if sitting in a chair, but, of course, there is no chair.) The hands are placed on the thighs with the feet flat on the floor and the lower legs straight up and down (see Figure 20.106, page 511). Try to sit for 30 seconds, 45 seconds, and 1 minute.

The Skier's Sit is an isometric type of activity and is excellent for developing the knee extensor muscles. It is done by skiers to develop the muscles used in skiing.

TEACHING TIP

Variation: Support the body with crossed legs. A more difficult stunt is to support the body on one leg, with the other leg extended forward.

ROCKING HORSE

Lie facedown on a mat with arms extended overhead, palms down. With back arched, rock back and forth (Figure 20.107). (Some children may need to have someone start them rocking.)

TEACHING TIP

Variation: Reach back and grasp the insteps with the hands. (The body arch is more difficult to maintain in this position.) Also try rocking from a side position.

HEEL CLICK (SIDE)

Balance on one foot, with the other out to the side. Hop on the supporting foot, click the heels, and return to balance. Try with the other foot.

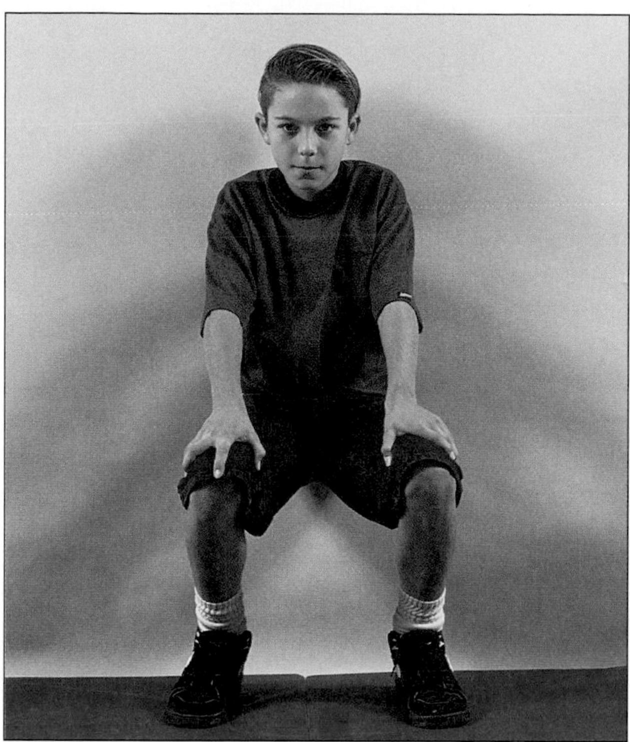

FIGURE 20.106 Skier's Sit.

The child should recover to the one-foot balance position without excessive foot movement. The teacher should insist on good balance.

TEACHING TIP

Variations:

1. Take a short step with the right foot leading. Follow with a cross-step with the left and then a hop on the left foot. During the hop, click the heels together. To hop on the right foot, reverse these directions.
2. Jump as high as possible before clicking the heels.
3. Combine right and left clicks.

WALK-THROUGH

From a front-leaning rest position, walk the feet through the hands, using tiny steps, until the body is fully ex-

FIGURE 20.107 Rocking Horse.

FIGURE 20.108 Walk-Through.

tended with the back to the floor (Figure 20.108). Reverse the body to original position. The hands stay in contact with the floor throughout.

JUMP-THROUGH

Starting in a front-leaning rest position, jump the feet through the arms in one motion. Reverse with another jump and return to original position. The hands must push off sharply from the floor, so the body is high enough off the floor to allow the legs to jump under. (The child may find it easier to swing a little to the side with one leg, going under the lifted hand, as indicated in Figure 20.109).

CIRCULAR ROPE JUMP

Crouch down in a three-quarter knee bend, holding a folded jump rope in one hand. Swing the rope under the feet in a circular fashion, jumping it each time (Figure 20.110 on page 512). Reverse the direction of the rope. Work from both right and left sides with either a counterclockwise or clockwise turn of the rope.

TEACHING TIP

Variations:

1. Perform the rope jump with a partner.
2. Jump using different foot patterns (one foot or alternate feet) and using slow and fast time.
3. Establish standards for declaring a class champion in different areas. Some categories could be maximum number of turns in 30 seconds, most unique routine, and most jumps without a miss.

BOUNCER

Start in a push-up position. Bounce up and down with the hands and feet leaving the ground at the same time.

FIGURE 20.109 Jump-Through.

FIGURE 20.110 Circular Rope Jump.

Try clapping while doing this. Move in various directions. Turn around.

PRETZEL

Touch the back of the head with the toes by raising the head and trunk and bringing the feet to the back of the head. Try first to bring the toes close enough to the head so the head-to-toe distance can be measured by another child with a handspan (the distance between the thumb and little finger when spread) (Figure 20.111). If this distance is met, then try touching one or both feet to the back of the head.

JACKKNIFE

Stand erect with hands out level to the front and a little to the side. Jump up and bring the feet up quickly to touch the hands. Vary by starting with a short run. Be sure the feet come up to the hands, rather than the hands moving down to the feet (Figure 20.112). Do several Jackknives in succession. The takeoff must be with both feet, and good height must be achieved.

HEEL-AND-TOE SPRING

Place the heels against a line. Jump backward over the line while bent over and grasping the toes. (Lean forward slightly to allow for impetus and then jump backward over the line.) Try jumping forward to original

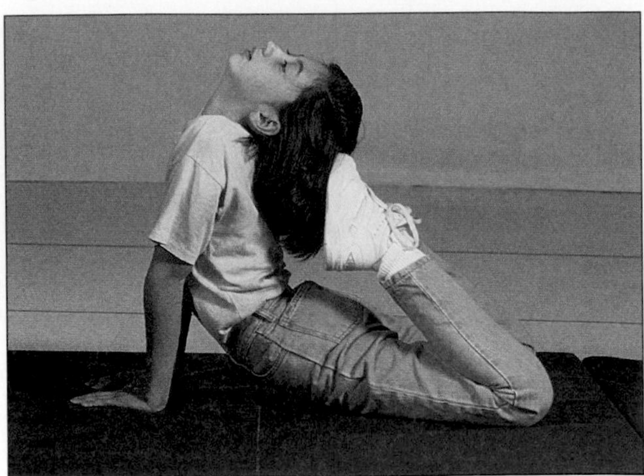

FIGURE 20.111 Pretzel.

position. To be successful, the child should retain the grasp on the toes. The teacher can introduce the stunt by first having children grasp their ankles when making the jumps. This is less difficult.

SINGLE-LEG CIRCLE (PINWHEEL)

Assume a squatting position, with both hands on the floor, left knee between the arms and right leg extended to the side. Swing the right leg forward and under the lifted right arm, under the left leg and arm, and back to starting posi-

FIGURE 20.112 Jackknife.

FIGURE 20.113 Single-Leg Circle.

tion (Figure 20.113). Several circles should be made in succession. Reverse position and try with the left leg.

Partner and Group Stunts

DOUBLE SCOOTER

Two children about the same size face each other, sitting on each other's feet (Figure 20.114). With arms joined, scoot forward or backward with cooperative movements. When one child moves the seat, the other child should help by lifting with the feet. Progress is made by alternately flexing and extending the knees and hips. (Review the Scooter [Figure 20.70] before doing this stunt.)

DOUBLE ROLL

One child lies on a mat with his feet in the direction of the roll. The other takes a position with feet on either side of the first child's head. The first child reaches back and grasps the other's ankles with thumbs on the inside and then raises his own feet, so that the other child can similarly grasp his ankles. The second child propels her hunched body forward, while the first sits up and takes the position originally held by the other (Figure 20.115). Positions are then reversed and the roll continues.

FIGURE 20.114 Double Scooter.

Be sure that the top child hunches well and ducks the head to cushion the roll on the back of the neck and shoulders. Also, when the top child propels herself forward, bent arms should momentarily take the weight. It is important that the underneath child keep the knees bent.

TANDEM BICYCLE

One child forms a bicycle position, with back against a wall and knees bent, as if sitting. The feet should be placed under the body. The second child backs up and sits down lightly on the first child's knees. Other children may be added in the same fashion, their hands around the waist of the player immediately in front for support (Figure 20.116 on page 514). Forward progress is made by moving the feet on the same side together.

CIRCLE HIGH JUMP

Stand in circles of three, each circle having children of somewhat equal height. Join hands. One child tries to jump over the opposite pair of joined hands (Figure 20.117 on page 514). To be completely successful, each circle must have each child jump forward in turn over the opposite pair of joined hands. (Jumping backward is not recommended.) To reach good height, an upward lift is necessary. Try two small preliminary jumps before exploding into the jump over the joined hands.

TEACHING TIP

Variation: Precede the jump with a short run by the group. A signal can be sounded so that all know when the jump is to occur during the run.

STICK CARRIES

Children of similar weight stand in groups of three, each group having a sturdy broom handle about 4 feet long.

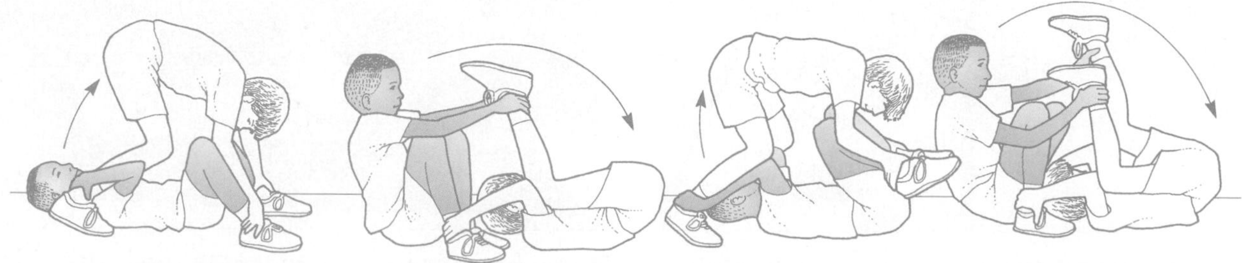

FIGURE 20.115 Double Roll.

FIGURE 20.116 Tandem Bicycle.

Using movement exploration techniques, two of the children carry the third with the broom handle (Figure 20.118). The child who is carried may be partially or wholly supported by the handle. Exchange positions. (It is better to use special sticks for this purpose because ordinary wands may break.)

TWO-WAY WHEELBARROW

One child holds two wheelbarrows, but with one in front and one behind. The child secures the front wheelbarrow first in a normal wheelbarrow position. The back wheelbarrow assumes position by placing the ankles over the already established hand position of the holder (Figure 20.119). (Review the various wheelbarrow activities [pages 502–503] before doing this stunt.)

FIGURE 20.117 Circle High Jump.

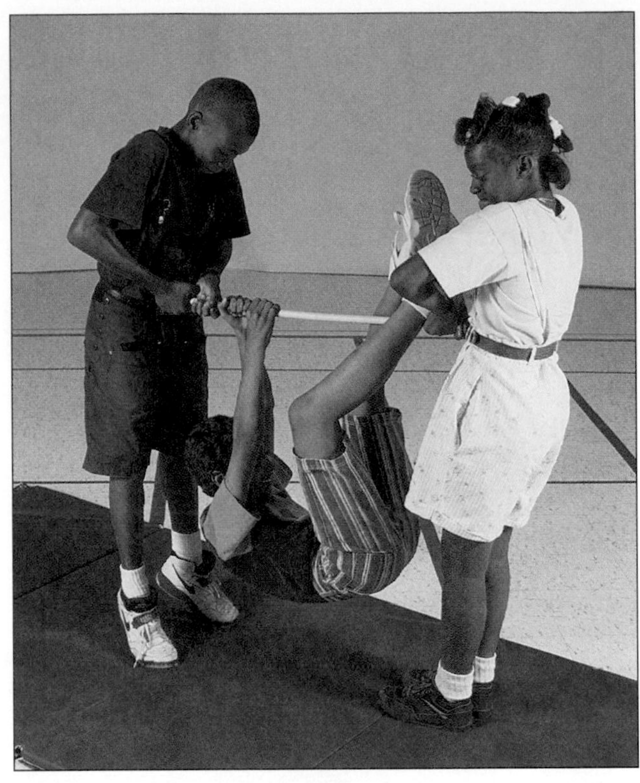

FIGURE 20.118 Stick Carry.

PARTNER RISING SUN

Partners lie facedown on the floor, with heads together and feet in opposite directions. They hold a volleyball or a basketball (or a ball of similar size) between their heads (Figure 20.120). Working together, they stand up

FIGURE 20.119 Two-Way Wheelbarrow.

FIGURE 20.120 Partner Rising Sun.

and return to position while retaining control of the ball. Do not touch the ball with the hands.

A slightly deflated ball works best. Some caution is necessary to prevent bumping heads if the ball is suddenly squeezed out.

TRIPLE ROLL

Three children get down on their hands and knees on a mat, with heads all in the same direction to one of the sides. The performers are about 4 feet apart. Each is numbered—1, 2, or 3—with the number 1 child in the center. Number 2 is on the right and number 3 is on the left. Number 1 starts rolling toward and under number 2, who projects upward and over number 1. Number 2 is then in the center and rolls toward number 3, who projects upward and over number 2. Number 3, in the center, rolls toward and under number 1, who, after clearing number 3, is back in the center. Each performer in the center thus rolls toward and under the outside performer (Figure 20.121). (Review the Side Roll [page 478] before doing this stunt.)

FIGURE 20.121 Triple Roll.

FIGURE 20.122 Quintuplet Roll.

Children should be taught that as soon as they roll to the outside, they must get ready to go over the oncoming child from the center. There is no time for delay. The upward projection of the body to allow the rolling child to go under is important.

QUINTUPLET ROLL

Five children can make up a roll series. They are numbered 1 through 5, as shown in Figure 20.122. Numbers 3 and 5 begin by going over numbers 2 and 4, respectively, who roll under. Number 1 goes over number 3 as soon as possible. Each then continues to go alternately over and under.

DEAD PERSON LIFT

One child lies facing the ceiling, with body stiff and arms at the sides. Two helpers stand, one on each side of the "dead" person, with hands at the back of the neck and fingers touching. Working together, they lift the child, who remains rigid, to a standing position (Figure 20.123 on page 516). From this position, the child is released and falls forward in a Dead Body Fall.

INJURED PERSON CARRY

The "injured" child lies on the back. Six children, three on each side, kneel down to do the carry. The lifters work their hands, palms upward, under the person to form a human stretcher, then lift up (Figure 20.124 on page 516). (The "injured" child must maintain a stiff position.) They walk a short distance and set the person down carefully.

MERRY-GO-ROUND

From 8 to 12 children are needed. Half of the children form a circle with joined hands, using a wrist grip. The remaining children, the riders, stand within the circle and each one leans back against a pair of joined hands. The riders stretch out their bodies, faces up, toward the center of the circle, with the weight on the heels. Each rider then connects hands, behind the circle of standing children, with the riders on either side. There are two sets of joined hands—the first circle, or merry-go-round, and the riders (Figure 20.125, page 516). The movement of the Merry-Go-Round is counterclockwise. The circle children, who provide the support, use sidesteps. The riders keep pace, taking small steps with their heels.

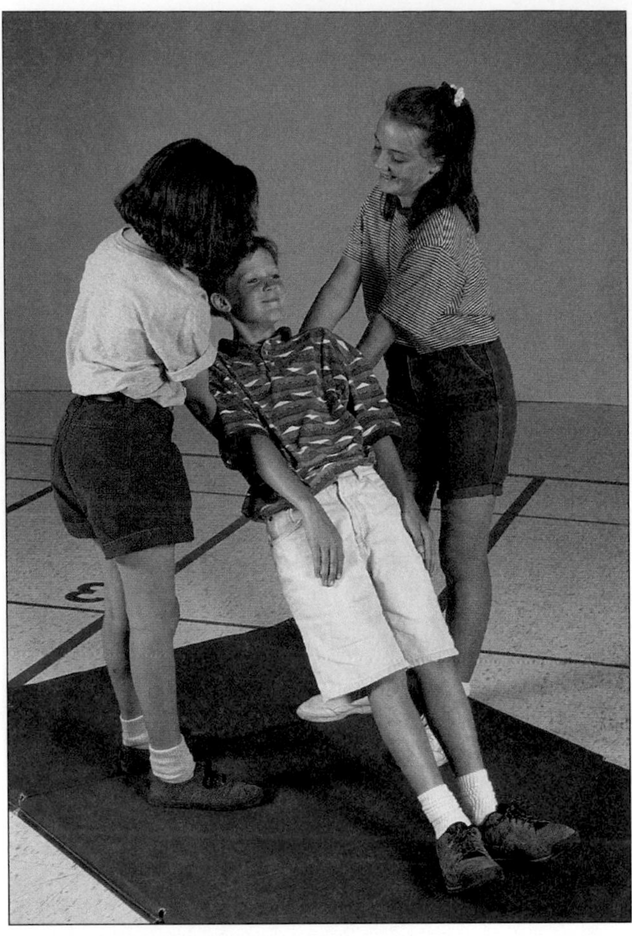

FIGURE 20.123 Dead Person Lift.

FIGURE 20.124 Injured Person Carry.

Developing Gymnastic Routines

The teacher can put together in sequence various stunts and other movements. The problems might be structured like the following.

1. Specify the number and kind of stunts and movements to be done and the sequence to be followed. For example, tell the child to do a balance stunt, a locomotor movement, and a rolling stunt.
2. Arrange the mats in some prescribed order so that they become the key to the movement problems. Two or three might be placed in succession, three or four in a U shape, or four in a hollow-square formation. There should be some space between mats, depending on the conditions stated in the problem. The problem could be presented like this: "On the first mat, do a Forward Roll variation and then a movement to the next mat on all fours. On the second mat, do some kind of balance stunt, and then proceed to the next mat with a jumping or hopping movement. On the third mat, you have a choice of activity." The problem can also be stated in more general terms, and children can do a different stunt or variation on each mat and a different movement between mats.
3. Have partners work out a series of stunts. The paired children should be of equal size and strength, so that

FIGURE 20.125 Merry-Go-Round.

they can alternate as the support. If children are of different sizes, the larger child can provide support for the smaller, and a third child may act as a spotter to take care of safety factors. After children have practiced for a period of time, each partnership can demonstrate the routines they have developed.

Partner Support Stunts

The basic instructions for partner support stunts (pages 503–504) should be reviewed.

BACK LAYOUT

The under, or support, partner lies on the back, with arms outstretched and palms down for support. The legs are raised, and the feet are positioned as if pushing up the ceiling. The support bends the knees and the partner lies back, resting the small of the back on support's soles. The top partner balances in a layout position with arms out to the sides for balance and body in a slight curve. The bottom partner reaches up and gives support to the top child's arms to provide stability (Figure 20.126). (A spotter can help position the top partner.)

FRONT SIT

The support gets down in the same position as for the Back Layout. The top partner straddles the support so that the support and the top partner are looking at each other. The top partner backs up to sit on the support's feet. As the support raises the top partner into a seated position, the top partner extends the legs forward so that the support can reach up and grasp them to stabilize the seated position (Figure 20.127). (Spotting should be done from behind.)

FLYING DUTCHMAN

The support takes a position as for the Back Layout. The top child takes a position facing the support, grasping support's hands and at the same time bending over support's feet. The support then raises the top partner from the floor by extending the knees. The top child arches the back and can then release the grip and put the arms out level to the sides in a flying position (Figure 20.128). A little experimentation determines the best place for the foot support. (Spotting should be available for getting into position and for safety.)

FIGURE 20.127 Front Sit.

FIGURE 20.126 Back Layout.

FIGURE 20.128 Flying Dutchman.

KNEE-AND-SHOULDER BALANCE

The support partner is lying supine, knees well up and feet flat on the floor. Support puts the hands out, ready to brace the shoulders of the top child. The top child takes a position in front of the support's knees, placing the hands on them. The top performer leans forward so that the shoulders are supported by the hands of the bottom partner, and kicks up (Figure 20.129).

Spotters are needed on both sides of the pair. If the top child begins to fall, the support partner should maintain the support under the shoulders so that the top child will land on the feet. Key points for the top partner are to keep the arms straight and the head up, and to look directly into the support partner's eyes.

PRESS

The bottom partner lies on the back, with knees bent and feet flat on the floor. The top partner takes a straddle position over the bottom partner, facing the support's feet. Performers then join hands with each other. The top partner sits on the joined hands, supported by the bottom partner, and rests the legs across the bottom partner's knees (Figure 20.130). Both performers should keep the elbows quite straight. Hold for a specified time.

FIGURE 20.129 Knee-and-Shoulder Balance.

FIGURE 20.130 Press.

ALL-FOURS SUPPORT

The bottom performer lies on the back with legs apart and knees up. The hands are positioned close to the shoulders with palms up. The top performer stands on the partner's palms and leans forward, placing the hands on the support performer's knees. The support raises the top performer by lifting with the arms. The top performer is then in an all-fours position, with feet supported by the bottom performer's extended arms and hands supported by the bottom performer's knees (Figure 20.131).

ANGEL

The top performer stands in front of the support partner. Both face the same direction. The support squats

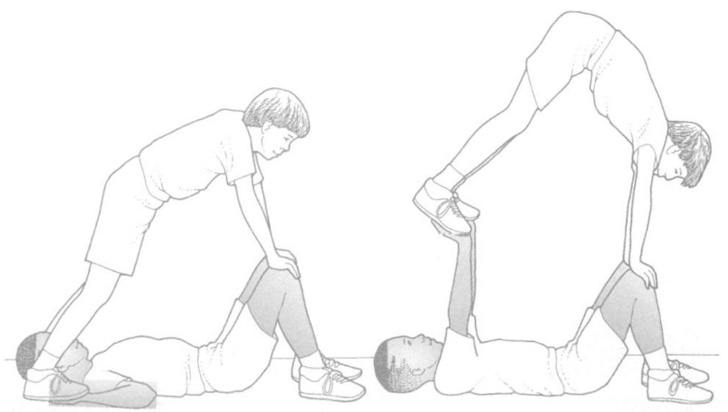

FIGURE 20.131 All-Fours Support.

down, placing the head between the legs of the top performer. Support rises, so that the top partner is sitting on support's shoulders. The top performer then proceeds to take a position on support's knees. Support must lean well back for balance, removing the head from between the top performer's legs. The top performer stands erect on support's knees, with arms held level out to the side. The bottom performer takes hold of the top's thighs and leans back to place the pose in balance (Figure 20.132). Hold for 5 seconds. (Children need to experiment to determine the best way to achieve the final position.)

SIDE STAND

The support partner gets down on the hands and knees to form a rigid base. The top performer stands to the side, bends over the support's back, and hooks the hands, palms up, well underneath the support's chest and waist. The top child leans across, steadying with the hands, and kicks up to an inverted stand (Figure 20.133). (Spotters are needed on the far side.)

FIGURE 20.132 Angel.

FIGURE 20.133 Side Stand.

TEACHING TIP

Variation: The top performer, instead of hooking hands underneath, grasps the bottom performer's arm and leg.

PYRAMIDS

Making pyramids is a pleasurable activity for children and uses skills learned in the gymnastics program. Emphasis in this section is on smaller pyramid groups. Pyramids provide an opportunity for creativity, since a variety of figures can be made. Stunts using only one performer or pair should be practiced as a preliminary to pyramid building with three students. The examples presented in Figure 20.134 on page 520 are composed of three performers; groups larger than this are not recommended as they increase the potential for accidents.

FIGURE 20.134 Pyramid Formations.

FOR MORE INFORMATION

References and Suggested Readings

Bizley, K. (1999). *Gymnastics.* Des Plaines, IL: Heineman Library.

Feeney, R. (1992). *Gymnastics: A guide for parents and athletes.* Indianapolis, IN: Masters Press.

Mattern, J. (1999). *Gymnastics.* Vero Beach, FL: Rourke Corporation.

Readhead, L. (1997). *The fantastic book of gymnastics.* Brookfield, CT: Copper Beech Books.

Werner, P. H. (1992). *Teaching children gymnastics: Becoming a master teacher.* Champaign, IL: Human Kinetics Publishers.

C H A P T E R 21

Cooperative and Personal Challenge Skills

ESSENTIAL COMPONENTS	
I	Organized around content standards
II	Student-centered and developmentally appropriate
III	**Physical activity and motor skill development form the core of the program**
IV	**Teaches management skills and self-discipline**
V	**Promotes inclusion of all students**
VI	**Focuses on process over product**
VII	Promotes lifetime personal health and wellness
VIII	**Teaches cooperation and responsibility and promotes sensitivity to diversity**

PHYSICAL EDUCATION STANDARDS	
1	**Students are able to move competently using a variety of fundamental and specialized motor skills.**
2	Students can monitor and maintain a health-enhancing level of physical fitness.
3	**Students are able to apply movement concepts and basic mechanics of skill performance when learning and refining motor skills.**
4	Students comprehend the basic principles of wellness and are able to apply concepts that enable them to make meaningful decisions that positively impact their health and wellness.
5	**Students participate in a wide variety of physical activities and learn how to maintain a personalized active lifestyle.**
6	**Students demonstrate empathy, understanding, and respect for the numerous differences exhibited by people in an activity setting.**
7	**Students exhibit responsible and self-directed behaviors that lead to positive social interactions in physical activity.**

SUMMARY

Cooperative activities teach youngsters to work together for the common good of other players. Activities teach cooperative skills when all students must follow specific rules and reach common goals. Although relays are a poor activity for teaching motor skills because they focus on competition rather than on proper skill performance, relays do present opportunities for teaching social skills such as cooperation, competition, and sportsmanship. All relays in this chapter require fundamental skills (running, jumping, and so on). Because students have overlearned these skills, all can complete the relays in this chapter successfully. Personal challenge skills give students an opportunity to test their strength, quickness, and balance. Cooperative challenge activities help youngsters work together in an effort to complete the group task.

OUTCOMES

- Understand that relays should not be used for teaching physical skills.
- Realize that an inherent problem associated with relays is that most children are inactive, standing in line waiting their turn.
- Describe different types of relay activities.
- List instructional procedures used to teach relays.
- Know how to present personal challenge skills so all students learn about their physical traits.

RELAYS

Relays offer children opportunities to learn cooperative skills because they must follow rules and directions to complete the activity successfully. Because one component of a relay is to complete an activity quickly, they are not good tools for teaching new skills. Youngsters usually concentrate on the outcome of the relay rather than performing skills correctly and learning is negated. Relays are appropriate when they feature skills children have overlearned. Examples of skills that can be effectively used in relays are basic locomotor skills such as running, skipping, sliding, and jumping.

Not all children are motivated by competitive activities. Some youngsters dislike having to perform competitively in front of others. Another inherent problem with relays is that the majority of children are inactive—standing in line waiting for their turn. Try to find ways to modify relays so activity is increased. An example is to have team members run in place and cheer for their teammate who is moving. Use relays judiciously at opportune times. The following procedures should be followed when setting up relays.

1. Restrict teams to four or five players. Too many on a team increases the amount of time spent waiting for a turn.
2. Change teams regularly so all youngsters have a chance to be on a winning team. You have the right to change team makeup and the order in which the students are placed on individual teams to create a better learning environment. Teams should not have to lose more than twice in a row. Try changing teams after each new relay.
3. Placing less skilled or slower players in the first or last position of the relay team often creates an embarrassing situation. If a slower student is placed at the start of the line, it is obvious that he is slower than others. If placed at the end of the line, the slower student will lose the lead his team had and be subject to ridicule. Therefore, place less skilled students in the middle of the team. Use discretion when moving players to avoid labeling them as unskilled performers.
4. Infractions of rules should be briefly discussed. Relays are a social learning experience. Children are in a situation where they have to conform to rules if the experience is to be enjoyable for all. Discuss how cooperation precedes competition; it is impossible to compete if players choose not to cooperate.
5. Designate a deceleration zone with cones or spots to prevent students from running into the wall. Place the markers at least 10 feet from the wall.
6. Too much emphasis on winning makes the skilled resent losing and intimidates those of lesser ability. Concentrate on the process of children participating rather than identifying a winner each time. Add other incentives to the relay so the focus isn't only on speed. For example, the winning team must have all players sitting and in a straight line to be eligible for a win. Another way to increase the excitement is to have a number for each team written on small individual pieces of paper. A number is pulled and the team that finishes in that order is the winner. For example, if the number 4 is pulled, the 4th place team is declared the winner. Since teams have no way of knowing what number will pulled by the teacher, the winner is randomly selected. This also can take the emphasis off winning at all costs.
7. Always conduct a trial run so each team clearly understands the procedures. If a new relay does not start properly, stop the activity and review the instructions. The trial run assures that all students understand how to perform. Sometimes, youngsters do not understand the task, creating an embarrassing situation for them.
8. Clarify traffic rules. In most cases, the way to the right governs. When runners go around the turning point, they do it from the right (counterclockwise), returning past the finish line on the right side. Procedures to ensure a fair tagging with the next runner assure students don't start too early. Runners may not leave the restraining line before being tagged. Exchanging a baton or a beanbag can also be used to restrain runners from leaving too early.

RELAYS FOR DEVELOPMENTAL LEVELS II AND III

Most of the relays presented here can be used successfully with children in developmental levels II and III. The relays incorporate learned motor skills and are arranged in order of increasing difficulty. If youngsters have not learned the skill required for the relay, the relay should not be used until proper learning occurs.

Beanbag Relays

Beanbag relays make a good starting point for younger children, because beanbags can be handled more easily than balls.

BEANBAG PASS RELAY

Players are in a line, standing side by side. The player on the right starts the beanbag, which is passed from one player to the next down the line. When it gets to the end of the line, the relay is over. The teacher should be sure that each player handles the bag. Children should rotate positions in line.

In the next stage, a revolving relay can be developed in which each member of the team rotates from the right of the squad to the left. When each child has had an opportunity to be the lead member of the group, the relay is finished. This relay can be varied with an underleg pass. The child passes the beanbag underneath one leg to the next player.

CIRCLE BEANBAG PASS RELAY

Players stand in a circle, facing out, but close enough so that the beanbag can be handed from player to player. One circuit begins and ends with the same player. The underleg pass can be used in this formation also.

CARRY-AND-FETCH RELAY

Players are in closed squad formation, with a hoop or circle positioned up to 30 feet in front of each team. The first runner on each team has a beanbag. On the command "Go," this player carries the beanbag forward and puts it inside the hoop, then returns and tags off the next runner. The second runner goes forward, picks up the beanbag, and hands it off to the third runner. One runner carries the beanbag forward and the next runner fetches it back. Different locomotor movements can be specified.

BEANBAG CIRCLE CHANGE RELAY

Players are in lane formation. Two hoops or circles are about 15 and 30 feet in front of each team. A beanbag is in the far hoop (Figure 21.1). The first runner runs forward, picks up the beanbag, and moves it to the inner hoop. The next player picks it up and takes it back to the other hoop. The beanbag must rest inside the hoop.

THE FARMER AND THE CROW RELAY

Runners are in lane formation. A line is drawn about 20 feet in front of the teams. The first runner of each team is the farmer, the second runner the crow, and so on. The farmer has five beanbags. On the signal "Go," the farmer hops forward and drops the five beanbags in a reasonably spaced fashion, with the last beanbag placed beyond the drawn line. The farmer then runs back and tags the next player, the crow. The crow runs to the farthest beanbag, and begins hopping, picking up the beanbags. The crow hands the five beanbags to the third runner, another farmer, who puts the objects out again.

Whenever players have a beanbag, they hop; when they have no beanbags, they run. The last beanbag should be placed beyond the far line, because this determines how far each player has to move. The relay can be done with only hopping allowed.

FIGURE 21.1 Formation for Beanbag Circle Change Relay

Lane Relays without Equipment

In lane relays, each runner runs in turn. The race is over when the last runner finishes. Lane relays are usually regular relays. Different types of movements can be used to challenge the runners.

1. Locomotor movements: Walking, running, skipping, hopping, galloping, sliding, jumping
2. Stunt and animal movements: Puppy Dog Run (page 472), Seal Crawl (page 488), Bear Walk (page 476), Rabbit Jump (page 476), Frog Jump (page 487), Crab Walk (page 477)
3. Restricted movements: Heel-and-toe walk, sore toe walk (hold the left foot with the right hand), walking on the heels, Crazy Walk (page 485), Toe Tug Walk (page 500)

Partner relays are also challenging and fun.

1. Children run (walk, skip, gallop, hop) with partners (inside hands joined) just as a single runner would.
2. Children face each other with hands joined (as partners), slide one way to a turning point, and slide back to the starting point—leading with the other side.
3. *Wheelbarrow Relay.* One person walks on her hands while the partner holds her by the lower legs, wheeling her down to a mark. Positions are switched for the return. Distances should not be too long.

Lane Relays with Equipment

EQUIPMENT AND BASIC LANE RELAYS

1. *All Up, All Down Relay.* Three bowling pins are set in a small circle about 20 feet in front of each team. The first player runs forward and sets up the pins one at a time, using only one hand. The pins must stand. The next player puts them down again, and so on.
2. A short line (24 inches) is drawn about 20 feet in front of each team. A bowling pin stands on one side of the line. Each player must run forward and stand the pin on the other side of the line, using one hand only.
3. Two adjacent circles are drawn about 20 feet in front of each team. Three bowling pins stand in one of the circles. A player runs forward and moves the pins, one at a time, standing each pin in the other

circle. The next player moves the pins back, one at a time, to the original circle, and so forth.

4. *Roll-and-Set Relay.* Each team has a mat and a bowling pin. The mat is placed lengthwise in front of the team (40 to 60 feet away), and the pin is between the team and the mat. The first player runs toward the mat, picking up the pin. Carrying the pin in one hand, he does a Forward Roll, sets the pin beyond the far edge of the mat, and runs back and tags off the next player. This player runs to the pin, picks it up, does a Forward Roll on the way back, and sets the pin in the original spot. The players alternate in this fashion until all have run. The pin must stand each time, or the player must return and make it stand.

THREE-SPOT RELAY

Three parallel lines are drawn in front of the teams to provide three spots for each team (Figure 21.2). Each player is given three tasks to perform, one at each spot. The player then runs back and tags off the next player, who repeats the performance. Suggestions for the tasks are:

1. Lie prone.
2. Lie supine.
3. Do an obeisance (touch the forehead to the floor).
4. Do a nose-and-toe (touch the toe to the nose from a sitting position).
5. Do a specified number of hops, jumps, push-ups, or curl-ups.
6. Perform a designated stunt, such as the Coffee Grinder or Knee Dip.
7. Jump rope for a specified number of turns.

The runner must perform according to the directions at each spot, completing the performance before moving to the next spot. Other task ideas can be used. The winning team selects the requirements for the next race.

FIGURE 21.2 Formation for Three-Spot Relay.

GYM SCOOTER RELAYS

Each team has a gym scooter. Scooters lend themselves to a variety of movements, both with individuals and with partners. Scooters should not, however, be used as skateboards. Some suggestions for individual movements follow:

1. Sit on the scooter and propel with the hands or feet.
2. Kneel and propel with the hands.
3. Lie facedown and move in alligator or swimming fashion.

Partner activity can feature any of several approaches. Partners can operate as a single unit, doing the task and passing the scooter to the next pair, or one partner can push or pull the other to the turning point, where they exchange roles and return to the starting line. A third approach is for the pusher to become the rider on the next turn. Some partner actions follow.

1. Rider kneels, and partner pushes or pulls.
2. Rider sits in a Seat Balance, and partner pushes or pulls on the rider's feet.
3. Rider does a Tummy Balance, and partner pushes on his feet.

A wheelbarrow race also can be done with the down person supporting the hands on the scooter.

POTATO RELAY

A small box about a foot square is placed 5 feet in front of each lane. Four 12-inch circles are drawn at 5-foot intervals beyond the box (Figure 21.3). This makes the last circle 25 feet from the starting point. Four blocks or beanbags are needed for each team.

To start, the blocks are placed in the box in front of each team. The first runner goes to the box, takes a single block, and puts it into one of the circles. She repeats this performance until there is a block in each circle; then she tags off the second runner. This runner brings the blocks back to the box, one at a time, and tags off the third runner, who returns the blocks to the circles, and so on.

Using a box to receive the blocks makes a definite target. When the blocks are taken to the circles, some rules must be made regarding placement. The blocks should be considered placed only when they are inside or touching a line. Blocks outside need to be replaced before the runner can continue. Paper plates or pie plates can be used instead of circles drawn on the floor.

TEACHING TIP

The race can also be done with bowling pins. Instead of being placed in a box, they are in a large circle at the start.

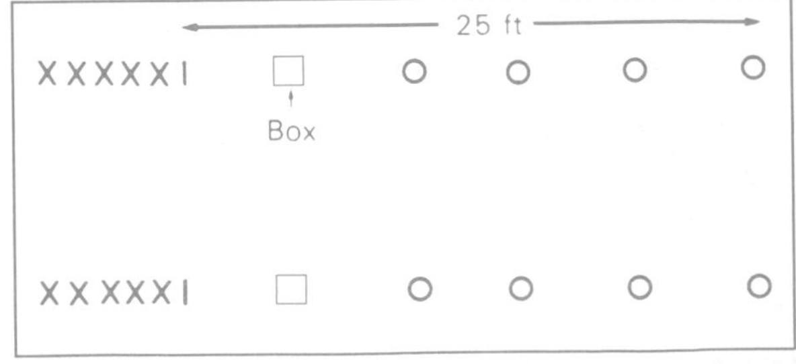

FIGURE 21.3 Formation for Potato Relay.

Lane Relays with Balls

A number of interesting lane relays (some regular and some revolving) feature ball-handling skills. The balls should be handled crisply and cleanly. A mishandled ball must reenter the race at the point of error. (See Chapters 23 and 26 for some suggested basketball and soccer ball dribbling relays.)

BOUNCE BALL RELAY

A circle is drawn 10 to 15 feet in front of each team. The first player runs to the circle, bounces the ball once, runs back to the team, and gives the ball to the second player, who repeats the routine. Each player has a turn, and the team whose last child carries the ball over the finish line first wins. To vary the relay, players can bounce the ball more than once.

KANGAROO RELAY

The first player in each lane holds a ball between the knees. He jumps forward, retaining control of the ball, rounds the turning point, jumps back to the head of the file, and hands the ball to the next player. If a player loses the ball from between the knees, she must stop and replace it. Slightly deflated balls are easier to retain.

BOWLING RELAY

The player at the head of each team has a ball. A line is drawn 15 to 20 feet in front of each team. The first player runs to the line, turns, and rolls the ball back to the second player. The second player must wait behind the starting line to catch the ball and then repeats the pattern. The race is over when the last player has received the ball and carries it over the forward line.

CROSSOVER RELAY

The Crossover Relay is similar to the Bowling Relay, except that the ball is thrown instead of rolled.

OBSTACLE RELAYS

Obstacle relays involve some kind of task that the runners must do.

OVER-AND-UNDER RELAY

A magic rope is stretched about 18 inches above the floor to serve as the turning point. Each runner jumps over the rope and starts back immediately by going under the rope.

FIGURE-EIGHT RELAY

Three or four cones are spaced evenly in front of each team. Players weave in and out in figure-eight fashion.

BENCH RELAYS

Several interesting races can be run using benches. A balance-beam bench or an ordinary bench stands in front of each of two teams in lane formation. The following races are suggested.

1. Run forward, jump over the bench, jump back again, return, and tag off.
2. Run to the bench, pass a beanbag underneath it, run around the bench, pick up the beanbag, and return to the team. Give the beanbag to the next player.
3. Place a beanbag about 3 feet in front of the bench. The first player runs forward, picks up the beanbag, and jumps over the bench while carrying the bag. The child then drops the bag on the far side of the bench, jumps back over the bench, returns to the line, and tags off. The next runner jumps over the bench, picks up the bag, jumps back over the bench with it, and places it on the floor near original position. The pattern is alternately carrying the bag over and bringing it back to the near side.

ICEBERG RELAY

Teams are in lane formation, with each team having two rubber marking spots (small rubber mats). The mats represent icebergs, and the task is to use the spots as stepping-stones. Each player moves their own icebergs by placing one in front, jumping on it, and reaching back to pick up the one from which they jumped. The floor cannot be touched (a fall in the ocean) or the player must go back to the previous spot and try again. As soon as the player reaches the opposite end, they can pick up their spots and run them back to the next competitor.

JACK RABBIT RELAY (JUMP STICK RELAY)

The relay starts with the first player in line running forward around the turning point and back to the head of the line (Figure 21.4). In the meantime, the next person in line holds a 36-inch wand. The runner returns and grabs one end of the wand from the player at the front of the line. These two runners then move the stick under the rest of the team members in line who jump it. When the stick has passed under all players, the previous stick holder hands the stick to the next person in line and runs around the turning point and returns. He then helps the next player in line hold the stick who becomes the next runner, and so on. When the stick is being jumped, it should be held close to the ground.

HULA-HOOP RELAY

Each team consists of a file of five or six children who join hands. The leader, in front, holds a hoop in the free hand. The object is to pass the hoop down the line so

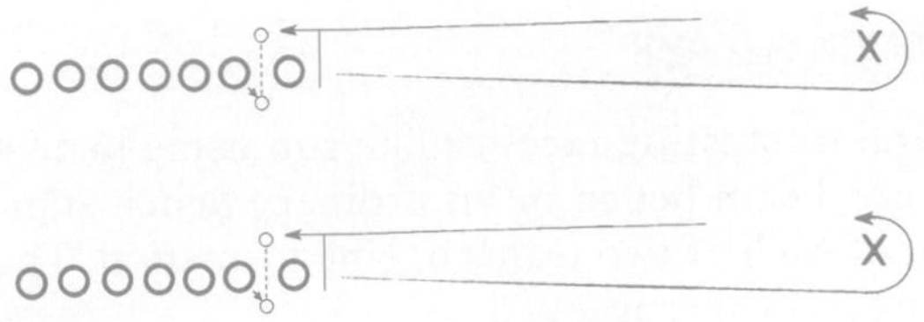

FIGURE 21.4 Formation for Jack Rabbit Relay.

that all bodies go through it, until the last person holds the hoop. The last person takes the hoop to the head of the line, and the process is repeated until the original leader is again at the head. Children may manipulate the hoop with their hands as long as they keep their hands joined. They should lock little fingers if necessary. All team members must pass through the hoop, including the last person.

The hoop can be moved around a circle of children with hands joined. The hoop starts on a pair of joined hands. When it has gone around the circle, over all of the bodies, and returned to the same spot, the race is over.

Revolving Team Ball Relays

ARCH BALL RELAY

Each team is in lane formation. Each player, using both hands, passes a ball overhead to the next person, and so on to the back player. The last player, on receiving the ball, runs to the head of the column, and the activity is repeated. The race is over when the original front player comes back to his spot at the head of the line. Each player must clearly handle the ball.

RIGHT AND LEFT RELAY

The action is the same as for Arch Ball, except that the ball is handed to the person behind with a side turn. The first turn is to the right, and the next person turns to the left.

STRADDLE BALL RELAY

Players are in lane formation. Each player takes a wide straddle stance, forming an alley with the legs. The ball is rolled down the alley to the back person, who runs to the front with it and repeats the activity. Players may handle the ball to help it down the alley, but it is not required that each person do so.

OVER AND UNDER RELAY

Players take a straddle position in lane formation. The first player hands the ball overhead with both hands to the player behind, who in turn hands the ball between her legs to the next player. The ball goes over and under down the line.

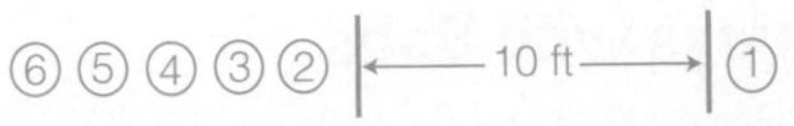

⑥⑤④③② |←10 ft→| ①

FIGURE 21.5 Formation for Pass and Squat Relay.

PASS AND SQUAT RELAY

One player (number 1) with a ball stands behind a line 10 feet in front of his teammates, who are in lane formation (Figure 21.5). Number 1 passes the ball to number 2, who returns the ball to number 1. As soon as he has returned the ball to number 1, number 2 squats down so that the throw can be made to number 3, and so on, down the file. When the last person in line receives the ball, she does not return it but carries it forward, straddling the members of her team, including number 1, who has taken a place at the head of the file. The player carrying the ball forward then acts as the passer. The race is over when the original number 1 player receives the ball in the back position and straddles the players to return to his original position.

Some care must be taken that the front player in the file is behind the team line as the passing starts. After the straddling, repositioning the file is necessary. Each player should form a compact ball during the straddling activity. This is an interesting relay, but some practice is needed for it to function properly.

Circle Pass Relays

Circle Pass relays involve ball handling in a circular formation.

SIMPLE CIRCLE RELAY

Each team forms a separate circle of the same size. At first, the circle should be small enough so that players can hand the ball to each other. The leader of each group starts the ball around the circle by handing it to the player on her right. As soon as the ball gets back to the leader, the entire team sits down. The first team to be seated in good formation wins.

Later, the circle can be enlarged so that the ball must be passed from player to player. More than one circuit of the circle can be specified. The leader can hold the ball aloft to signal completion.

CIRCLE-AND-LEADER RELAY

A circle 15 to 20 feet in diameter is formed. One player is in the center with a ball. The ball is passed in succession to each of the players. The race is over when the ball is returned to the center player by the last circle player. Different passes can be specified.

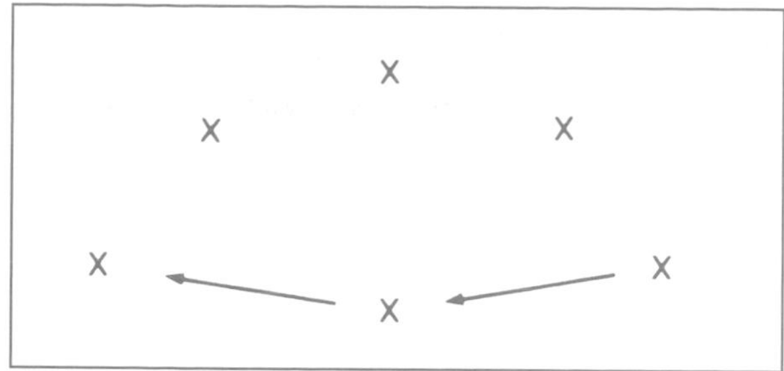

FIGURE 21.6 Formation for Corner Fly Relay.

CORNER FLY RELAY

The players are in a line or semicircle facing the leader (Figure 21.6), who has a ball. The ball is passed to and received from each player, beginning with the player on the left. When the last player receives the ball, he calls out "Corner fly" and takes the position of the leader. The leader takes a position in the line to the left. In the meantime, all players adjust positions to fill the spot vacated by the new leader. The relay continues, with each player becoming the leader in turn. When the original leader returns to the spot in front of the team, the relay is over.

A marker can be placed behind the leader so that the last player in line, when she receives the ball, runs around the marker to the leader's spot. This gives a little more time for the team to shift places and get ready for the new leader.

If a team is one person short of the number of players on the other teams, two consecutive passes could be made by the leader to the first person. Alternatively, the initial leader might take two turns (first and last), which means that another person comes forward after the second turn to provide the finish.

TADPOLE RELAY

One team forms a circle, facing in, and has a ball. Another team is in lane formation about 10 feet behind the circle (Figure 21.7). The object of the game is to see how many times the ball can be passed completely around the circle while the other team completes a relay. Each player from the team in lane formation runs in turn around the outside of the circle and tags off the next runner until all have run. In the meantime, the ball is being passed around the circle on the inside. Each time the ball makes a complete circuit, the circle players count the number loudly. After the relay is completed and the count established, teams trade places and the relay is repeated. The team making the higher number of circuits by passing the ball is the winner. The relay gets its name from the shape of the formation, which resembles a tadpole.

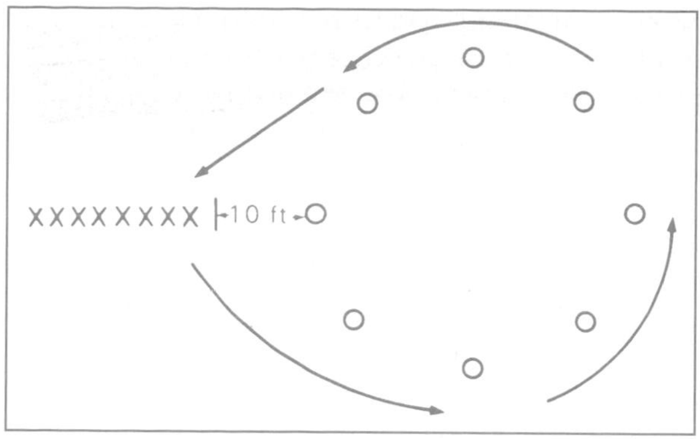

FIGURE 21.7 Formation for Tadpole Relay.

TEACHING TIP

Different types of passes and different methods of locomotion provide variation.

Miscellaneous Relays

The following relays are interesting.

PASS THE BUCK RELAY

Players are facing sideways, with teams about 5 feet apart. All players of a team are linked by joined hands. The leader is on the right of each team. On signal, the leader "passes the buck" to the next player by squeezing his hand. This player in turn passes the squeeze to the next, and so on down the line. The end player, when she receives the buck, runs across the front of the team and becomes the new leader. She starts the squeeze, and it is passed down the line. Each player in turn comes to the front of the line, with the original leader finally returning to the head position.

RESCUE RELAY

Lane formation is used, with the first runner behind a line about 30 feet in front of the team (Figure 21.8). The first runner runs back to the team, takes the first player

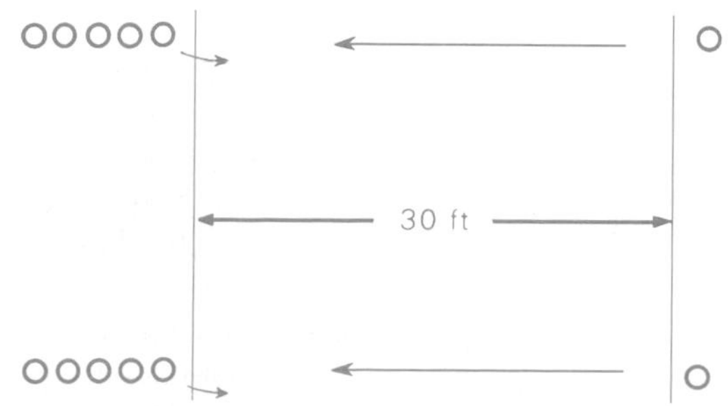

FIGURE 21.8 Formation for Rescue Relay.

in line by the hand, and "rescues" him by leading him back to the 30-foot line. The player who has just been rescued then runs back to the team and gets the next player, and so on, until the last player has been conducted to the line.

AROUND-THE-BASES RELAY

Four bases are laid out as in a baseball diamond. Two teams, lined up at opposite bases on the inside of the diamond (Figure 21.9), compete at the same time. The lead-off player for each team makes one complete circuit of the bases and is followed by each player in turn.

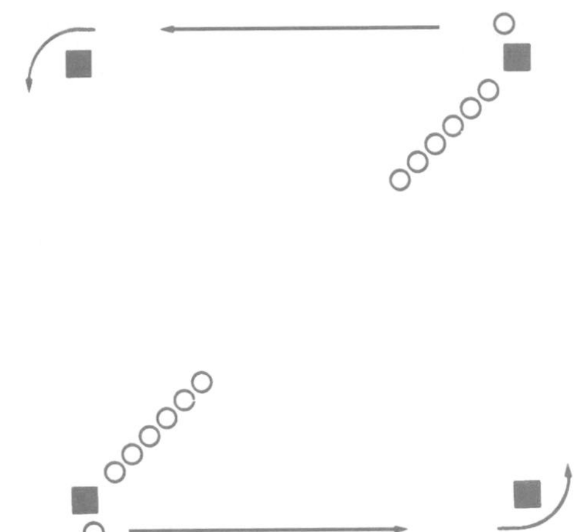

FIGURE 21.9 Formation for Around-the-Bases Relay.

TEACHING TIP

The same type of relay can be run indoors by using chairs or bowling pins at the four corners. Further variations can require children to run more than one lap or circuit on a turn.

Modified Relays

In modified relays, players are numbered and run as individuals. These are not relays in the true sense of the term.

ATTENTION RELAY

The players on each team are facing forward in lane formation with team members about arms' distance apart. The distance between the teams should be about 10 feet. Two turning points are established for each team—one 10 feet in front of the team and the other 10 feet behind (Figure 21.10). Players are numbered consecutively from front to rear. The teacher calls, "Attention." All come to the attention position. The teacher calls out a number. (The route of player number 2 is shown in Figure 21.10.) The player on each team holding that number steps to the right, runs around the front and the back markers, and returns to place. The rest of the team runs in place. The first team to have all members at attention, including the returned runner, wins a point.

FIGURE 21.10 Formation for Attention Relay.

The numbers should not be called in consecutive order, but all numbers should be called. There must be enough distance between teams so that runners do not collide.

TEACHING TIP

Variations:

1. Different means of locomotion can be used.
2. The teams can be organized by pairs, and two can run at one time, holding inside hands.
3. *Under the Arch.* The leader calls two consecutive numbers, say, numbers 3 and 4. Immediately, numbers 3 and 4 on each team face each other and form an arch by raising both hands. The players in front of the arch (numbers 1 and 2) run forward around the front marker, around the back marker, and then back to place, passing under the arch. The players behind the arch run under the arch first, around the front marker, around the back marker, and back to place. When all have returned to place, the arch players drop hands and resume position. The first team to be at attention is the winner. The running is always forward at the start. Each player follows the person ahead, keeping in numbered order. Each goes around the front marker, around the back marker, and back to place after passing under the arch.
4. Each team stands on a bench. With the teams standing at attention, a number is called, and that team member jumps down from the bench, runs completely around it, and runs back to place on top of the bench.

CIRCULAR ATTENTION RELAY

Two teams form a circle, with players facing counterclockwise and each team occupying half of the circle. The players of each team are numbered consecutively (Figure 21.11). The teacher calls the group to attention and then calls a number. Children with that number (one on each team) immediately run counterclockwise around the circle and back to place, and stand at attention. The first to get back to place scores a point for the team. All numbers should be called.

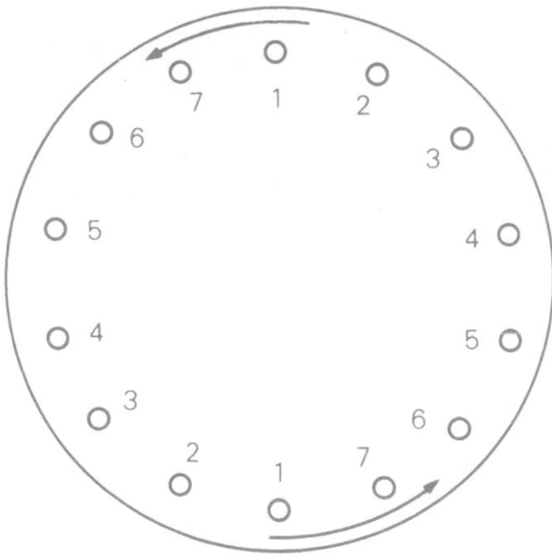

FIGURE 21.11 Formation for Circular Attention Relay.

TEACHING TIP

Variation: *Circle Leapfrog.* All players crouch on their knees, facing counterclockwise, with the forehead supported in cupped hands on the floor. When a number is called, the runner straddles or leapfrogs all children around the circle, returns to place, and resumes the original position. Scoring is the same as in Circular Attention

SUPINE RELAY

Players lie supine on the floor, in a circle, with their heads toward the center of the circle and hands joined. The members of each team are numbered consecutively. When a number is called, the player with that number runs around or over the players on her team, and then returns to her place, assuming the supine position with hands rejoined. The first player back scores a point for the team. The game can continue to a definite score or until all numbers are called.

TEACHING TIP

The following are exciting variations for children.

1. *Human Hurdle.* Each team forms a small circle and sits with backs to the center. The action is the same as for the Supine Relay.
2. *Cyclone.* This is a team race, with the team getting back to original place first declared the winner. At the signal, the first player gets up and starts around the group. Immediately after the first player passes him, the second player follows. The third player follows as soon as the first two have passed. The remaining players follow in the same manner. When the first player gets back to place, she takes her original seated position. Each player in turn goes around until she is back to her original place. The last player cannot move until all the other players have gone by. When she gets back to place, the race is over.

PERSONAL CHALLENGE ACTIVITIES

Personal challenge activities offer students an opportunity to match strength and wits with others. When teaching personal challenge activities, be sensitive to the feelings of participants, as the appeal of such activities is not universal among children. Children who are quick and strong perform well in personal challenge activities. However, youngsters who are less aggressive may not enjoy extensive participation in such activities. Proper perspective is important when using personal challenge activities. The goal is to give students an opportunity to test themselves. Trying to determine a class champion or placing youngsters in situations in which they continually lose is detrimental to class morale. Short bouts of activity (5 to 10 seconds is plenty) and a new partner each time decreases the competitive nature of the activity and helps make it a social experience. Restrict personal challenge activities to children in developmental levels II and III. Such activities are most often presented as a change of pace activity to rekindle motivation. Using one of the activities to pick up the energy level of the class is effective. After a minute or two, resume the lesson focus. Use the following procedures when setting up a personal challenge activity.

1. Emphasize safety factors. Match youngsters for size; a common method is to ask students to pair up with someone who is similar in height. Make the length of bouts short—usually 5 to 10 seconds of performance is adequate. Have the class practice freezing immediately when the whistle is blown.
2. Make instructions as explicit as necessary. Starting positions should be defined so that both contestants begin in an equal and neutral position. What constitutes a win and the number of trials permitted should be clearly defined.
3. Some of the activities should be done on tumbling mats. Combining some of the personal challenge activities with gymnastics activities adds excitement to the lesson.
4. You start the contests or teach youngsters to start contests. If children lack self-discipline, it is best for you to start and stop all contests.
5. To add variety, contests should be done with the right side (arm or leg), the left side, and both sides. Body position can be varied. Children can stand, crouch, sit, or lie for the same contest.
6. Develop a system of rotation, so that youngsters have more than one opponent. Rotating assures that one child will not continually dominate another.

HAND WRESTLE

Starting Position: Contestants place right foot against right foot and grasp right hands in a handshake grip. The left foot is planted firmly to the rear for support.

Action: Try to force the other, by hand and arm pressure, to move either foot. Any movement by either foot means a loss.

TEACHING TIP

Variations:

1. Stand left foot against left foot and wrestle with left hands.
2. Stand balanced on the right foot and clasp right hands. A player loses if the right foot is moved or if the back foot touches the ground. Try with the left foot and left hand. The foot off the ground can be held with the free hand.

FINGER FENCING

Starting Position: Contestants stand on the right foot (Figure 21.12).

Action: Hook index fingers of the right hands and try to push the opponent off balance. Change feet and hands. Any movement of the supporting foot means a loss.

TOUCH KNEES

Starting Position: Contestants stand on both feet and face each other.

Action: Touch one of the opponent's knees without letting the opponent touch yours. Five touches determine the victor.

FIGURE 21.12 Finger Fencing.

TEACHING TIP

Variations:

1. Grasp left hands and try to touch the knees with the right hand. The first one to touch wins that bout.
2. Either with hands free or with left hands grasped, try to step lightly on the other's toes.

GRAB THE FLAG

Starting Position: Opponents are on their knees, facing each other on a tumbling mat. Each has a flag tucked in the belt near the middle of the back.

Action: Remain on the knees at all times. Try to grab the flag from the other.

TEACHING TIP

Variation: Try this as a group contest in which contestants pull flags until a champion is established.

ROOSTER FIGHT

Starting Position: Players stoop down and clasp hands behind the knees.

Action: Try to upset the other player or cause the handhold to be released.

TEACHING TIP

Variations:

1. Squat down and hold the heels with the hands. A player loses when she is upset or when her hands come loose from her heels.
2. Try this as a group contest. Children stand around the edges of an area large enough to contain the group. On signal, they come forward and compete team against team or as individuals. A child who is pushed out of the area is eliminated. The last one left is the winner.

PALM PUSH

Starting Position: Contestants face each other, standing 12 inches apart. They place the palms of their hands together and must keep them together throughout the contest.

Action: Try to push the opponent off balance.

TEACHING TIP

Use a wand instead of pushing the palms together.

BULLDOZER

Starting Position: Opponents are on their hands and feet (not knees), facing each other, with right shoulders touching.

Action: Try to push (not bump) each other backward. Pushing across the mat or across a restraining line determines the winner. Change shoulders and repeat.

BREAKDOWN

Starting Position: Opponents are in a front-leaning rest (push-up) position, facing each other.

Action: Using one hand, try to break down the other's position by pushing or dislodging his support while maintaining your own position.

TEACHING TIP

Variation: Try the contest with each contestant in wheelbarrow position with the legs held by a partner.

ELBOW WRESTLE

Starting Position: Contestants lie on the floor or sit at a table and face each other. Their right hands are clasped, with right elbows bent and resting on the surface, and right forearms pressed against each other.

Action: Force the other's arm down while keeping the elbows together. Raising the elbow from the original position is a loss.

TEACHING TIP

Variation: Change to a position using the left arm.

LEG WRESTLE

Starting Position: Opponents lie on their backs on the floor or on a mat, with heads in opposite directions, trunks close, and near arms locked at the elbow.

Action: Three counts are given. On each of the first two counts, lift the leg nearer to the opponent to a vertical position. On the third count, hook legs with the opponent near the foot. Try to roll the opponent over backward.

TEACHING TIP

Variation: Use the right and left legs in turn.

CATCH-AND-PULL TUG-OF-WAR

Starting Position: Two teams face each other across a line.

Action: Try to catch hold of and pull any opponent across the line. A player pulled across the line waits in back of the opposing team until time is called. The team capturing the most players wins.

TEACHING TIP

Pulling by catching hold of clothing or hair is not permitted. The penalty is disqualification. Players may cross the line to pull if they are securely held by a teammate or by a chain of players.

Variation: Have those pulled across the line join the other team. This keeps all children in the game.

STICK TWIST

Starting Position: Contestants face each other with their feet approximately 12 inches apart. They hold a wand above their heads with both hands, the arms completely extended.

Action: On signal, try to bring the wand down slowly without changing the grip. The object is to maintain the original grip and not to let the wand twist in the hands. The wand does not have to be forced down, but rather should be moved down by mutual agreement. It can be moved down completely only if one player allows it to slip.

TOE TOUCH

Starting Position: Contestants form a large circle.

Action: On signal, players try to step lightly on the opponent's toes (those on the player's left and right) while not allowing the opponent to step on your toes. Keep score by counting the number of touches made.

TEACHING TIP

Variation: Try in push-up position. The goal is to touch the opponent's hand.

CRAB CONTEST

Starting Position: Both contestants are in crab position with seats held high.

Action: On signal, try, by jostling and pushing, to force the other's seat to touch the mat.

TEACHING TIP

Variation: Place a beanbag on the tummy. Try to knock the opponent's beanbag to the floor.

SHOULDER SHOVE

Starting Position: Each contestant raises the left leg, holding the ankle with the right hand and holding the right elbow with the left hand.

Action: Try to bump the other person off balance with the left shoulder so that one hand releases its position.

TEACHING TIP

The teacher or a referee should call a loss when the left hand releases the right elbow, because this is difficult for the opponent to see. Dropping the hold on the ankle is definite and visible.

Variations:

1. Stand on one foot and fold the arms. Try to knock the other player off balance so that the uplifted foot touches the ground.
2. Using a 6- or 8-foot circle, try to force the opponent out of the circle.
3. Use a kangaroo theme. Carry a volleyball between the legs at the knees. Try to maintain control of the ball while shoving the opponent with the shoulder.

WAND WRESTLE

Starting Position: Players face each other, grasping a wand between them. The grips must be fair, with each child having an outside hand.

Action: By twisting and applying pressure on the wand, try to get the opponent to relinquish her grip.

TEACHING TIP

Variations:

1. *Basketball Wrestle.* Use a basketball instead of a wand. Each should have the same grasp advantage at the start.
2. Squat down while maintaining a grip on the wand. Attempt to take away the wand or to upset the opponent.

PARTNER PULL-UP

Starting Position: Two students sit on the floor and face each other, with knees straight and soles of the feet against the opponent's. Each bends forward, and they grasp a wand between them.

Action: Pull the other player forward to cause him to release the grip. Only straight pulling is allowed.

TEACHING TIP

To provide a straight pull, one player should have both hands on the inside and the other both hands on the outside, rather than having alternate grip positions.

WAND LIFT

Starting Position: Two contestants stand facing each other and hold a 3-foot-long stick or wand between them. Each holds one end of the stick with the right hand, using an underhand grip. Each places the left hand, in an overhand grip, next to and touching the opponent's right-hand grip. The elbows are bent at approximately a right angle.

Action: Press down with the left hand and lift with the right to bring the stick up to a vertical position. The body can be braced for action, but body motion should be minimal. This contest is meant to be a test of pure strength.

TEACHING TIP

Try with a left-hand lift.

SITTING ELBOW WRESTLE

Starting Position: Contestants sit on a mat, back to back, with elbows locked. The legs are spread wide.

Action: Pull to the left in an attempt to tip the opponent.

TEACHING TIP

Variations:

1. Reverse direction.
2. Position the legs so the knees are bent and the soles of the feet are flat on the mat.

POWER PULL

Starting Position: One contestant stands with fingers touching in front of and close to chest. The other person stands facing the opponent and grasps opponent's wrists.

Action: On signal, the contestant holding the wrists attempts to pull the opponent's fingers apart. A straight pull (no jerking) is the action.

ROPE TUG-OF-WAR

Starting Position: Two equal teams face each other on opposite ends of a rope. A piece of tape marks the center of the rope. Two parallel lines are drawn about 10 feet apart. At the start, the center marker on the rope is midway between the lines.

Action: Try to pull the center marker over your team's near line.

TEACHING TIP

The rope should be long enough to accommodate the children without crowding. It should be at least an inch in diameter. Children should never wrap the rope around the hands, arms, or body in any manner.

Variation: Use different positions for pulling—with the rope overhead (teams have their backs toward each other), with one hand on the ground, or from a seated position (with feet braced on the floor).

FOUR-TEAM TUG-OF-WAR

Starting Position: Four teams line up as shown in Figure 21.13. A special rope is needed, the size and extent of which depend on the number of children. A cone, a bowling pin, or a beanbag is placed an equal distance behind each team.

Action: Pull, on signal, in the direction of your team's cone. A team wins when the player on the end of the rope can knock over the cone, or pick up the club or beanbag, without losing contact with the rope.

TEACHING TIP

An automobile tire can be substituted for the center rope square. Simply tie four tug-of-war ropes to the tire.

Variation: Try this as a three-team contest, with the center figure a rope triangle.

COOPERATIVE CHALLENGES

Cooperative challenges teach students how to work together as a team to solve a group challenge. Students learn to be both leaders and followers and to accept primary and secondary roles. Students have to communicate with each other and all players must participate and succeed if the team is going to succeed. Success comes in many forms and if players can contribute to team goals they will feel as though they are needed by other members. Team building challenges such as those that follow will add positive feelings to the group at large.

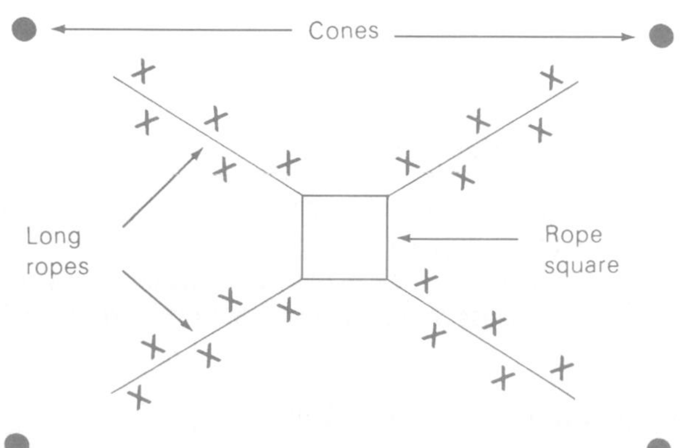

FIGURE 21.13 Formation for Four-Team Tug-of-War.

LIFEBOATS

Formation: 4 squads of equal number

Supplies: 8 to 12 individual mats or hoops, 4 scooters, and 4 long jump ropes.

The entire class is divided into 4 squads of equal number and positioned on one side of the gym. Each squad is given a scooter (lifeboat) and a long jump rope. The objective is to get the entire class across the ocean to the mainland (the other side of the gym) using only their lifeboats. Spaced randomly between the starting and stopping points are 3 individual mats, which are islands in the ocean. Any students that touch the gym floor (water) must return to the starting point or island they were on. Thus, all students must remain on a mat at all times unless they are traveling across the ocean in a lifeboat (scooter). Students may be pulled with the jump rope but may not be pushed. Students who are transported across the ocean must remain on the mainland and cannot return to the island or lifeboats; however, if they step into the "water" trying to rescue a teammate, they must return to the island.

MAT FOLDING

Formation: Squads of 4 to 5 students

Supplies: One tumbling mat for each squad of 4–5 students

Groups of 4–5 students are each assigned a tumbling mat. While keeping their feet on the mat at all times, teams are given the following challenges:

1. Rotate the mat 360 degrees.
2. Move the mat 15 feet.
3. Without using any hands, fold the mat into fourths.
4. Unfold the mat without using any hands.

TEACHING TIP

This is an enjoyable activity to use at the end of a gymnastics unit.

ATTACHED AT THE . . .

Formation: All players along one sideline

Supplies: One beanbag or ball for each set of partners

Partners stand on one side of the activity area. The challenge is to get to the other sideline or end line while attached at the hip, head, back, ankle, elbow, hamstring, etc. Locomotor movements can be specified for moving across the area. For a more difficult activity, provide a beanbag or ball for the students to put between the "attached" body parts.

MOVING TOGETHER

Formation: Groups of 4 students

Supplies: none

Groups of 4 students form teams on the sidelines of the teaching area. The objective is for the team to move to the other sideline with the following stipulations:

1. Six feet touching the floor and all team members touching an ankle.
2. Eight body parts (not heads) touching the ground at all times.
3. Half of the team at a high level and half the team at a low level.
4. Every foot touching one other foot.
5. Only four feet can touch the ground.
6. Four feet and 1 hand must be on the ground.
7. Move with the fewest number of feet as possible touching the floor.
8. Move with the most hands and fewest feet touching the floor.

TEACHING TIP

Additional challenges can be made by providing the teams with different pieces of equipment to carry while attempting the challenges.

BALANCE BEAM MIXER

Formation: Small groups of 8

Supplies: One low balance beam or bench for every 8 students

Students stand shoulder to shoulder on a low balance beam or bench (for younger students) with mats alongside the beam for safety. While remaining on the balance beam or bench, students are challenged to get in order based on the following criteria:

1. Alphabetical order by first name from left to right.
2. Alphabetical order by first name from right to left.
3. Tallest to shortest.
4. Month of birth date (January to December or vice versa).

QUIET COOPERATION

Formation: 4 equal size squads

Supplies: 1 marking spot for each student

Students stand in a line shoulder to shoulder with a marking spot under their feet. Without talking, making any noise, or touching the gym floor, students get in order using these criteria:

1. Number of pets (fewest to most).
2. Alphabetical by first name (father's, mother's, or pet name can also be used).
3. Alphabetical by last name.
4. Month of birthday (January to December or vice versa).
5. Shortest to tallest.

ALL ABOARD

Formation: Scattered with hoops spread through area

Supplies: 15 hoops

Students are challenged to get as many students as possible into one hoop placed on the ground. In order for a person to be considered "on board," 1 foot must be touching the ground inside of the hoop and no body parts touching the floor outside the hoop. One technique to lead up to this activity is to play **Musical Hoops.** Hoops are scattered throughout the gym and music is playing. When the music stops students move to a hoop placing at least 1 foot inside the hoop. More than 1 student can be in a hoop. Each time the music plays the teacher removes 1 or 2 hoops until only enough hoops remain for all students to be aboard.

HUMAN SPELLING BEE

Formation: Squads of 5 to 6 players

Supplies: none

Groups of 5–6 students are challenged with spelling out words, letter by letter, with their bodies while lying on the floor. All team members must be in the letter and the team must identify the bottom of the letter. Physical education terms or spelling words may be used. Also, students can spell out answers to questions asked by the teacher. Mathematic equations could also be written (i.e., $7 \times 7 = 49$) 1 number and symbol at a time.

MOVING THE WORLD

Formation: Entire class scattered throughout area

Supplies: One large cageball

Using a cageball or other large ball as the world, the world is transported to different locations in the gym. Unless instructed the ball may not be kicked, thrown, or struck and all class members must be involved:

1. No hands can touch the world.
2. Only feet can touch the ball.
3. Half of the team must be lying on their back.
4. Only backs can touch the ball.

5. Only elbows can touch the ball and no talking is allowed.
6. Students must crabwalk.

TEACHING TIP

Directions such as "move the ball 30 feet northwest" or "move the world 25 feet in the same direction you would travel from Dayton to Columbus" can be used.

GROUP JUGGLING

Formation: Squads of 5 to 6 students

Supplies: 1 ball or beanbag for each student

Teams of 5–6 students are formed and each student has a ball or beanbag. A variety of types of balls will add to the excitement of this activity. On signal (e.g. "1, 2, ready, toss"), each team member tosses his ball to another teammate and then catches a ball tossed to him. The objective is to see how many successful tosses can be made in unison. Typically students will toss to the same person each time. A successful toss occurs when all team members catch the ball tossed to them. After several tosses, the teacher gives each group the responsibility of selecting one team to give the signal for their group.

STRANDED

Formation: Squads of 5 to 6 students

Supplies: 1 tumbling mat, 3 hoops (or volleyball standards), 2 scooters, and 1 long jump rope per team

The objective of this challenge is to get all team members from a capsized, but floating, boat (represented by a tumbling mat), across the river via 3 islands in the river, to the shore. Each island (represented by a hoop) is approximately 15 feet apart from the others and has two team members on it. The remainder of the team is positioned on a boat, or mat. The students on the boat have 2 scooters and a 16 to 20 ft. long jump rope. *While on the scooters students may not be **pushed** by other students or **pulled** using the rope; they must find a way to move without touching the "water."* Any student touching the water must return to the boat.

SCOOP BALL

Formation: Squads of 6 to 8 students

Supplies: 4 basketballs, 1 hoop, 4 tinikling poles (or 10–15 ft PVC pipe), and 2 scoops for every team

Teams of 6–8 students attempt to move 4 basketballs approximately 50 feet, without touching the basketballs with any body parts, and place the balls into a hoop. Four tinikling poles and 2 scoops are provided. The following rules apply:

1. If a ball touches the floor or a student it must be retuned to the starting point.
2. Players may not walk with the balls.
3. The balls may not be thrown, kicked, or passed.
4. Balls that roll or bounce out of the hoop must be returned to the starting point.
5. Students are only permitted to hold one scoop at a time.

CENTIPEDE

Formation: Entire class shoulder to shoulder

Supplies: None

All students stand shoulder to shoulder on a sideline, facing the same direction, and feet touching the person next to them. The entire class must move to the other sideline without breaking the chain of touching feet. If the chain breaks, the group must take 3 steps back. Students may put their arms around each other if desired.

TEACHING TIP

Some classes may require a progression starting with partners, then small groups, and finally the entire class.

FLIPPERS

Formation: Entire class divided into 2 teams

Supplies: 30–40 flying disks

30–40 flying disks are spread throughout the teaching area and two teams formed. One team is charged with flipping the disks so they are face up, while the other team attempts to flip the disks to a face down position. After a practice game, the following stipulations can be used.

1. No hands.
2. Feet only.
3. Students must crab walk or bear crawl.
4. Feet only, and only one foot can touch the disk at a time.
5. Knees only.
6. Heel only.

C H A P T E R 22

Game Skills

ESSENTIAL COMPONENTS	
I	**Organized around content standards**
II	**Student-centered and developmentally appropriate**
III	**Physical activity and motor skill development form the core of the program**
IV	**Teaches management skills and self-discipline**
V	**Promotes inclusion of all students**
VI	**Focuses on process over product**
VII	Promotes lifetime personal health and wellness
VIII	**Teaches cooperation and responsibility and promotes sensitivity to diversity**

PHYSICAL EDUCATION STANDARDS	
1	**Students are able to move competently using a variety of fundamental and specialized motor skills.**
2	Students can monitor and maintain a health-enhancing level of physical fitness.
3	**Students are able to apply movement concepts and basic mechanics of skill performance when learning and refining motor skills.**
4	Students comprehend the basic principles of wellness and are able to apply concepts that enable them to make meaningful decisions that positively impact their health and wellness.
5	**Students participate in a wide variety of physical activities and learn how to maintain a personalized active lifestyle.**
6	**Students demonstrate empathy, understanding, and respect for the numerous differences exhibited by people in an activity setting.**
7	**Students exhibit responsible and self-directed behaviors that lead to positive social interactions in physical activity.**

SUMMARY

Games are excellent activities for developing social skills. Students can be taught to display appropriate interactive skills, such as leading, following, and making decisions. Cooperative skills that include following directions, accepting individual differences, and participating in a teamwork situation are necessary for reaching common goals. Game situations offer many scenarios for teaching sportsmanship behavior. Games that involve only a few children, allow some children to dominate, or offer little opportunity for skill development should not be part of the program. Children should be allowed the opportunity to create and modify games to meet their needs. Safety is a primary concern in the selection and presentation of game activities.

OUTCOMES

- Explain various ways in which games can be created or modified.
- Understand safety precautions associated with the teaching of games.
- Cite various ways to teach games effectively.
- Identify games that provide maximum participation and afford an opportunity for skill development.
- List games that can be explained quickly and can be implemented quickly.
- Classify various games according to developmental levels.

Games make a valuable contribution to the growth and development of youngsters. Through games, children receive an opportunity to experience success and accomplishment. Some social objectives that can be accomplished through games are the development of interpersonal skills, understanding rules and limitations, and learning how to behave in a variety of competitive and cooperative situations. Games are a laboratory where children can apply physical skills in a game-like setting. Many games help develop large-muscle groups and enhance the child's ability to run, dodge, start, and stop under control while sharing space with others. By applying strategy in games, children learn the importance of alertness and the mental aspect of participation.

As an important part of the physical education program, games should be scrutinized and evaluated in terms of what they offer children. Many traditional games can be modified so they make a meaningful contribution to the program. Offering youngsters a chance to create and modify games fosters an understanding that game components can be changed to make the play experience beneficial for all.

EVALUATING GAMES

A number of factors impact the worth of games including the physical skills required, the number of participants, the complexity of rules, and the amount of strategy involved. Successful participation demands that youngsters have learned requisite skills in a practice setting. If skills are not learned, it will be difficult for players to apply the skills in a game setting. For example, children may be able to throw with proper form, but unable to throw accurately in a game setting. They may be able to hit a stationary object but not a moving target.

Youngsters also have to learn how to cooperate with teammates and compete against peers. The greater the number of teammates and competitors, the more difficult the game becomes. Cooperating with teammates is just as difficult as competing in a meaningful fashion. Moving from partner, to small-group, to team games is a natural progression and a formula for success. A number of games are more effective when played in small groups, because the participants handle objects more often and have more chances to be an active contributor.

The number of rules and the amount of strategy required increase the difficulty of a game. Developmental level I children find it difficult (and uninteresting) to play a game that has many rules. If cognitive strategy is required, requisite physical skills should be learned previously (overlearned) so concentration can be applied to the mental aspect of the game rather than the skill. Most elementary school children are not able to concentrate on skill performance and strategy simultaneously. Complex games require team members to play specific roles, and some of these roles (such as goalkeeper or line positions) may not appeal to many youngsters. In contrast, many of the more popular games are spontaneous in nature and demand little concentration on strategy.

Be sure that children receive positive feedback from game experiences. The younger children are, the less willing they are to wait for the outcome; feedback must be immediate. Children become bored and tire of playing long games. Fatigue is also a factor in the interest level of children; watch carefully for such signs.

Games require a combination of skills. A game in which children must sequence many skills may result in failure or frustration for many. Lead-up games are developed for the express purpose of limiting the number of skills needed for successful participation. Evaluate the number of skills required and build a progression of games that gradually increases the use of skill combinations.

CREATING OR MODIFYING GAMES

Games can be modified and new variations created by you or students or by both together. For example, you may observe that a specific game is not meeting the desired objectives and may decide to modify or change the game to facilitate skill development. Stop the class and ask them to think of a way to make the game better. Alternatives can be implemented and the newly created activity tested to see whether it is indeed more effective. With developmental level II and III students, you can offer some parameters for developing a game and then allow time for the class to create and to implement the activity. Establish ground rules that facilitate group dynamics. For example, suggest voting on a rule change or specify a maximum number of changes allowed per period.

If students and teachers are to make meaningful modifications, they must understand how to analyze a game. The most recognized elements of game structure are desired outcomes, skills, equipment, rules or restrictions, number of players, and scheme of organization. Morris and Stiehl (1999) provide an approach to game analysis that may be helpful if you are interested in game modification. Youngsters need to learn how and what to modify and they need to practice the process. Some suggestions to start youngsters thinking include the following:

1. Change the distance to be run by decreasing or increasing it. For example, in Star Wars, go around once instead of twice.
2. Change the means of locomotion. Use hopping, walking, skipping, or galloping instead of running.
3. Play the game with one or more partners. The partners can move and act as if they were a single person.

4. Change the method of tagging in simple tag games. Call out "Reverse" to signal that the chaser is to become the tagger and vice versa.
5. Make goals or restricted areas larger or smaller. In Over the Wall, the restraining area can be made larger or smaller or its shape can be changed.
6. Vary the boundaries of the game by making them larger or smaller, as dictated by the number of players.
7. Change the formation in which the game is played. For example, Circle Kickball could be played in a square or triangular shape.
8. Change the requirements necessary for scoring. In Hand Hockey, players might be required to make four passes before a shot is taken.
9. Increase the number of players, taggers, or runners. The amount of equipment used can also be increased. For example, in Nine Lives, the more fleece balls used, the more practice youngsters get in throwing at a moving target.
10. Change the rules or penalties of the game. For example, allow players a maximum of three dribbles or to hold the ball for no more than 3 seconds.

COOPERATION AND COMPETITION

Without cooperation there would be no game activities. If participants chose not to follow the rules and play with teammates, it would be impossible to structure games. Clearly, games require cooperation before competition can be an outgrowth of an activity. *Cooperation* involves two or more children working together to achieve a common goal. *Competition* is characterized by opponents working against each other as each tries to reach a goal or reward. Since cooperation precedes competition and is more difficult for youngsters to learn, emphasis should be placed on this phase of game activity. Through games, players can develop a spirit of working together, a concern for teammates, and an appreciation for the collective skills of the group.

Achieving a balance between offense and defense helps participants understand that both phases are important. In tag and capture games, offer opportunities to remain safe as well as a challenge to be at risk and elude capture. Evaluate game components continually and modify them in the interest of retaining an enjoyable environment. Teams should be somewhat equal so all participants have an opportunity to find success. There is little motivation when there is no opportunity to win. Emphasizing cooperation reinforces the need to play with all classmates regardless of ability level. It is the teacher's responsibility to assure that teams offer youngsters a chance to be successful. Rotate students regularly so they have a chance to play with different classmates and to play on a winning team. Include youngsters with disabilities in all rotation plans.

SAFETY

Safety is a primary consideration in game situations. Check the play area for dangerous objects and hazards. Tables, chairs, equipment, and apparatus can become dangerous when a high-speed game is under way. Teach children to move in a controlled fashion and to use the entire playing area to avoid collisions. Learning to stop play immediately when a signal is given conditions youngsters to games with referees and assures safety. This is an important prerequisite for later sports experiences.

TEACHING GAMES EFFECTIVELY

1. *Put youngsters in the formation they are going to use prior to presenting a new game to a class.* If they can sit in game formation, that will make it easier to understand instructions. Make directions as brief as possible and implement the game quickly. Get the game under way with minimal instruction and gradually implement more subtle rules. Try the game first before answering any questions students may have. This ensures they have some perception of the game and how it is to proceed, so many questions are answered without using additional time and boring students who already understand.
2. *Use a trial period (no scoring) during the first stages of learning a game.* This avoids the possibility of children feeling resentful about losing a point or being caught off guard because they did not understand the activity.
3. *Do not use games that isolate one child.* This may create a negative experience for youngsters who have low self-esteem. Instead, place two to four youngsters in isolated position so the team can share the credit and blame. An example of a common game where this happens is "Birdie in the Cage." This sport lead-up game traditionally puts one youngster in the center of the circle to try and intercept or touch passes made by circle players. A youngster who doesn't have quick reactions or is overweight may never be successful and might bear the brunt of failure. Placing a couple of other students in the center makes it a team game and passes the responsibility to all center players.
4. *Develop a rotation plan that allows all children to play for an equal amount of time.* Avoid a situation where winners stay on the court and losers sit out,

receiving much less practice than the better players. By the same token, do not play elimination games until one or two children remain. The least skilled youngsters will be eliminated early and have to sit the most. Keep in mind that the purpose of games is to keep youngsters involved in physical activity. Sitting out does not contribute to the goals of physical education.

5. *Assure that all children have an equal chance to participate in games that require taking turns.* When using games where numbers are called, write the numbers on a card so no one is left out. Use caution with games that eliminate children. If children are eliminated, do so for one or two turns only, and allow them back in the game quickly.
6. *Do some careful planning before attempting to teach a new game.* Identify safety hazards, anticipate difficult concepts, and adapt the game to the class and the situation. Make physical preparations prior to teaching. Establish boundaries and have equipment ready for distribution. The size of the playing area is usually dictated by thc skill and age of the participants. If you plan to do some instruction during a game, decrease the size of the playing area so students are closer to you.
7. *When playing low-organized and sport lead-up games, try to avoid using the out-of-bounds rule.* Instead, make a rule that whoever gets to the ball first gains possession. This speeds up the pace of the game and offers a strong incentive for quickly getting the ball back into play. If playing a game that uses a goal line or running to a line, establish a *safety zone.* Instead of using the wall or a line near the wall as the goal, draw safety lines 10 feet from the wall to allow for deceleration. Cones or spots can be used to mark the deceleration zone. Try to play as many games as possible
8. *Change the makeup of the teams often and play relatively short games.* Nobody likes to lose all the time. Playing games for short periods of time means more games can be played, so more winners can be identified. If a team wins twice in a row, that is usually a signal to scramble the students into new teams. This gives everybody a fresh start and keeps a greater number of students motivated.
9. *To identify teams, use pinnies, crepe paper armbands, colored shoulder loops, or team belts worn around the waist.* Have a standing rule that the team that puts on the pinnies gets to have the ball out of bounds first. Youngsters usually don't like to wear pinnies and this gives them some incentive.
10. *Games are an excellent platform for learning social skills.* Encourage children to call infractions or penalties on each other and on themselves. Teach youngsters to accept calls made by officials as an integral part of any game situation. When disagreements occur, adopt the role of arbitrator, rather than taking one side or the other. Encourage players to learn negotiation skills and to resolve differences among themselves rather than having a teacher decide each issue.
11. *Help youngsters understand that learning to perform skills correctly is more important than the outcome of the game.* Continue instruction throughout the early phases of a game. Look for opportunities to stop the game briefly and offer instruction or correction. Offer coaching hints to improve skill techniques.
12. *Use the "rule of three" as a way of simplifying rules.* For example, the "rule of three" means you can only hold the ball for three seconds, take three steps, or miss three catches, etc. This reduces the number of rules youngsters have to remember and makes games easier to play. It also seems to diminish the disagreements youngsters have about rules.

SELECTION OF GAMES

Games in this chapter were selected because they require minimal skill and offer activity for all children. Analyze the skills children must practice before playing. Drills and skill practice become more meaningful when children comprehend that the skill will be used in a game situation. Games have been sorted by difficulty and placed into three developmental levels. Table 22.1 (pages 540–542) lists each of the games alphabetically by developmental level. Also listed in Table 22.1 are the skills required for successful play and the page in the text where the description of the game is listed. Games in developmental level I do not require competency in sport skills. Most use basic locomotor skills and offer an environment in which children can practice and participate successfully. These games can be modified easily to allow all children to have enjoyable experiences.

Specialized sport skills are required in many of the games in developmental levels II and III. Ball-handling and movement skills, with emphasis on agility, are important for success in many of these games. Offer opportunities for children to practice requisite game skills prior to being placed in a competitive situation.

SPORT LEAD-UP GAMES

Games in developmental levels II and III fall into two categories: sport lead-up games and low-organization games. This chapter includes low-organization games

TABLE 22.1 Alphabetical listing of games by developmental level

Developmental Level I Games

Games	Skills	Page
Animal Tag	Imagery, running, dodging	543
Aviator	Running, locomotor movements, stopping	543
Ball Passing	Object handling	543
Blindfolded Duck	Fundamental locomotor movements	545
Bottle Bat Ball	Batting, retrieving balls	545
Bottle Kick Ball	Kicking, trapping	545
Cat and Mice	Running, dodging	546
Change Sides	Body management	546
Charlie over the Water	Skipping, running, stopping, bowling (rolling)	546
Circle Stoop	Moving to rhythm	546
Circle Straddle Ball	Ball rolling, catching	547
Colors	Color or other perceptual concepts, running	547
Corner Spry	Light, silent walking	547
Firefighter	Running	547
Flowers and Wind	Running	548
Forest Ranger	Running	548
Freeze	Locomotor movements to rhythm	548
Hill Dill	Running, dodging	549
Hot Potatoes	Object handling	549
Jack Frost and Jane Thaw	Running, dodging, holding position	549
Leap the Brook	Leaping, jumping, hopping, turning	549
Marching Ponies	Marching, running	549
May I Chase You?	Running, dodging	550
Midnight (Lame Wolf)	Running, dodging	550
Mix and Match	Fundamental locomotor movements	550
Mousetrap	Skipping, running, dodging	551
Musical Ball Pass	Passing and handling	551
One, Two, Button My Shoe	Running	551
Popcorn	Curling, stretching, jumping	551
Red Light	Fundamental locomotor movements, stopping	552
Right Angle	Rhythmic movement, body management	552
Rollee Pollee	Ball rolling, dodging	552
Scarecrow and the Crows, The	Dodging, running	553
Sneak Attack	Marching, running	553
Soap Bubbles	Body management	553
Squirrel in the Trees	Fundamental locomotor movements	553
Statues	Body management, applying force, balance	554
Stop Ball	Tossing, catching	554
Tag Games (Simple) Back-to-Back Bowing Frozen	Fundamental locomotor movements, dodging	554

TABLE 22.1 Alphabetical listing of games by developmental level *(continued)*

Games	Skills	Page
Developmental Level I Games		
Tag Games (Simple) *(continued)* Locomotor Nose-and-Toe Skunk Stoop Stork Turtle		554
Teacher Ball (Leader Ball)	Throwing, catching	555
Toe to Toe	Fundamental locomotor movements	555
Tommy Tucker's Land	Dodging, running	555
Twins (Triplets)	Body management	555
Up Periscope	Fundamental locomotor movements	556
Where's My Partner?	Fundamental locomotor movements	556
Developmental Level II Games		
Addition Tag	Running, dodging	556
Alaska Baseball	Kicking, batting, running, ball handling	556
Arches	Moving rhythmically	557
Bat Ball	Batting, running, catching, throwing	557
Beach Ball Bat Ball	Batting, tactile handling	558
Bird Catcher	Chasing, fleeing, dodging	558
Bounce Ball	Throwing, ball rolling	558
Box Ball	Running, ball handling	558
Busy Bee	Fundamental locomotor movements	559
Cageball Kick-Over	Kicking	559
Club Guard	Throwing	559
Competitive Circle Contests Circle Club Guard Touch Ball	Throwing, catching	560
Couple Tag	Running, dodging	560
Crows and Cranes	Running, dodging	560
Fly Trap	Fundamental locomotor movements	561
Follow Me	All locomotor movements, stopping	561
Fox Hunt	Running, dodging	561
Galloping Lizzie	Throwing, dodging, running	562
Hand Hockey	Striking, volleying	562
Home Base	Reaction time, locomotor movements, body management	562
Indianapolis 500	Running, tagging	562
Jump the Shot	Rope jumping	563
Keep 'em Movin'	Body management, cooperation	563
Loose Caboose	Running, dodging	563
Nine Lives	Throwing, dodging	564
Nonda's Car Lot	Running, dodging	564
One Behind	All locomotor and non-locomotor movements	564

(continued)

TABLE 22.1 Alphabetical listing of games by developmental level *(continued)*

Games	Skills	Page
	Developmental Level II Games	
One Step	Throwing, catching	564
Partner Stoop	Marching rhythmically	565
Ricochet	Rolling	565
Squad Tag	Running, dodging	565
Steal the Treasure	Dodging	565
Trades	Imagery, running, dodging	566
Trees	Running, dodging	566
Whistle March	Moving rhythmically	566
Whistle Mixer	All basic locomotor movements	567
Wolfe's Beanbag Exchange	Running, dodging, tossing, catching	567
	Developmental Level III Games	
Air Raid	Throwing	567
Barker's Hoopla	Running	567
Cageball Target Throw	Throwing	568
Chain Tag	Running, dodging	568
Circle Touch	Dodging, body management	568
Clean-Up	Throwing	569
Fast Pass	Passing, catching, moving to an open area	569
Flag Chase	Running, dodging	569
Four Square	Batting a ball	575
Frisbee Bowling	Frisbee throwing	569
Frisbee Golf	Frisbee throwing for accuracy	569
Galactic Empire and Rebels	Chasing, fleeing, dodging	569
Guess the Leader	Body management	570
Jolly Ball	Kicking	570
Jump-the-Shot Variations	Rope jumping	570
Mushrooms	Rolling and throwing	570
Octopus	Maneuvering, problem solving	571
One-Base Tagball	Running, dodging, throwing	571
Over the Wall	Running, dodging	571
Pacman	Fleeing, reaction time	572
Partner Dog and Cat	Chasing, fleeing, dodging	572
Pin Knockout	Rolling, dodging	572
Right Face, Left Face (Streets and Alleys)	Running, dodging	572
Scooter Kickball	Striking with various body parts	573
Star Wars	Running	573
Strike the Pins	Throwing	573
Sunday	Running, dodging	574
Team Handball	Running, dribbling, passing, throwing, catching	576
Tetherball	Batting a ball	577
Touchdown	Running, dodging	570
Triplet Stoop	Moving rhythmically	571
Two Square	Batting a ball	578
Volley Tennis	Most volleyball skills	578
Whistle Ball	Passing, catching	571

only; however, sport lead-up games can also be integrated into the games program. Sport lead-up games limit the number of skills required for successful participation in order to help children experience success in a sport setting. For example, Five Passes is a game designed to develop passing skills. Children do not have to perform other skills (such as dribbling or shooting) required by the regulation sport to achieve success. Table 22.2 (pages 544–545) lists all sport-related lead-up games presented in Chapters 23 to 29. If you are teaching soccer skills and want to finish the lesson with a lead-up game, consult this chart to find an appropriate activity. Many of the lead-up games are excellent choices for skill development, particularly with developmental level III youngsters.

DEVELOPMENTAL LEVEL I

Games in the early part of developmental level I feature individual games and creative play. Little emphasis is placed on team play or on games that have a scoring system. The games are simple, easily taught, and not demanding of skills. Dramatic elements are present in many of the games, and others help establish number concepts and symbol recognition. As children mature, they enjoy participation in running, tag, and ball games. Few team activities are included, and the ball games require the skills of throwing and catching.

ANIMAL TAG

Supplies: None

Skills: Imagery, running, dodging

Formation:

```
X|          |O
X|          |O
X|          |O
X|          |O
X|          |O
X|          |O
X|          |O
X|          |O
X|          |O
X|          |O
X|          |O
```

Two parallel lines are drawn about 40 feet apart. Children are divided into two groups, each of which takes a position on one of the lines. Children in one group get together with their leader and decide what animal they wish to imitate. Having selected the animal, they move over to within 5 feet or so of the other line. There they imitate the animal, and the other group tries to guess the animal correctly. If the guess is correct, they chase the first group back to its line, trying to tag as many as possible. Those caught must go over to the other team. The second group then selects an animal, and the roles are reversed. If the guessing team cannot guess the animal, however, the performing team gets another try. To avoid confusion, children must raise their hands to take turns at naming the animal. Otherwise, many false chases will occur. If children have trouble guessing, the leader of the performing team can give the initial of the animal.

AVIATOR

Supplies: None

Skills: Running, locomotor movements, stopping

Formation:

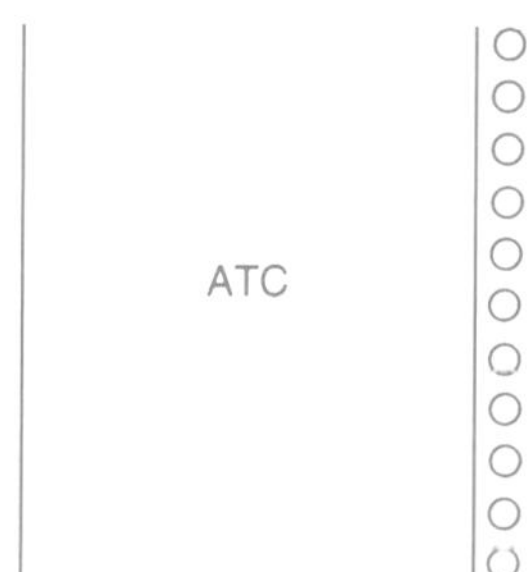

Players are parked (in push-up position) at one end of the playing area. The air traffic controller (ATC) is in front of the players and calls out, "Aviators aviators, take off!" Youngsters take off and move like airplanes to the opposite side of the area. The first person to move to the other side and land the plane (get into push-up position facing the ATC) is declared the new ATC.

If the ATC yells out some type of stormy weather, all planes must return to the starting line and resume the parked position. Examples of stormy weather commands are lightning, thunder, hurricane, and tornado. Each ATC is allowed to give stormy weather warnings once.

BALL PASSING

Supplies: Five or six different kinds of balls for each circle

Skill: Object handling

Formation: Circles with 15 or fewer in each circle

The class is divided into two or more circles, with no more than 15 children in any one circle. Each circle consists of two or more squads, but squad members need not stand together.

The teacher starts a ball around the circle; it is passed from player to player in the same direction. The teacher introduces more balls until five or six are moving around the circle at the same time and in the same direction. If a child drops a ball, he must retrieve it, and a point is

TABLE 22.2 Lead-up games from sport Chapters 23 to 29*

Basketball (Chapter 23)

Developmental Level II	*Page*
Circle Guard and Pass	594
Basketball Tag	594
Birdie in the Cage	595
Captain Ball	595
Dribblerama	594
Around the Key	596
Five Passes	596

Developmental Level III	*Page*
Captain Basketball	596
Quadrant Basketball	597
Sideline Basketball	597
Twenty-One	597
Lane Basketball	598
Freeze Out	598
Flag Dribble	598
One-Goal Basketball	599
Basketball Snatch Ball	599
Three-on-Three	600
Basketrama	600

Football (Chapter 24)

Developmental Level II	*Page*
Football End Ball	609
Five Passes	610
Speed Football	610

Developmental Level III	*Page*
Kick-Over	610
Fourth Down	611
Football Box Ball	611
Flag Football	612
Pass Ball	613

Hockey (Chapter 25)

Developmental Level II	*Page*
Circle Keep-Away	622
Star Wars Hockey	622
Lane Hockey	622
Modified Hockey	622

Hockey (Chapter 25)

Developmental Level III	*Page*
Goalkeeper Hockey	623
Sideline Hockey	623
Regulation Elementary Hockey	623

Soccer (Chapter 26)

Developmental Level II	*Page*
Circle Kickball	638
Soccer Touch Ball	638
Diagonal Soccer	638
Dribblerama	639
Bull's-Eye	639
Pin Kickball	639
Sideline Soccer	640

Developmental Level III	*Page*
Manyball Soccer	640
Addition Soccer	641
Over the Top	641
Lane Soccer	641
Line Soccer	642
Mini-Soccer	642
Six-Spot Keepaway	643
Regulation Soccer	643

Softball (Chapter 27)

Developmental Level II	*Page*
Throw-It-and-Run Softball	658
Two-Pitch Softball	659
Hit and Run	659
Kick Softball	660
In a Pickle	660
Beat Ball	660
Steal a Base	660

Developmental Level III	*Page*
Five Hundred	660
Batter Ball	661
Home Run	662
Tee Ball	662
Scrub (Work-Up)	662
Slow-Pitch Softball	663
Babe Ruth Ball	663
Hurry Baseball (One Pitch)	664

TABLE 22.2 Lead-up games from sport Chapters 23 to 29* *(continued)*

Volleyball (Chapter 29)			
Developmental Level II	**Page**	***Developmental Level III***	**Page**
Beach Ball Volleyball	685	Pass and Dig	686
Informal Volleyball	685	Mini-Volleyball	686
Shower Service Ball	686	Rotation Mini-Volleyball	687
		Regulation Volleyball	687
		Three-and-Over Volleyball	687
		Rotation Volleyball	687
		Four-Square Volleyball	688
		Wheelchair Volleyball	688

*Many of these games are used as culminating activities with sport lesson plans.

scored against his squad. After a period of time, a whistle is blown, and the points against each squad are totaled. The squad with the lowest score wins. Beanbags, large blocks, or softballs can be substituted for balls.

BLINDFOLDED DUCK

Supplies: A wand, broomstick, cane, or yardstick

Skills: Fundamental locomotor movements

Formation:

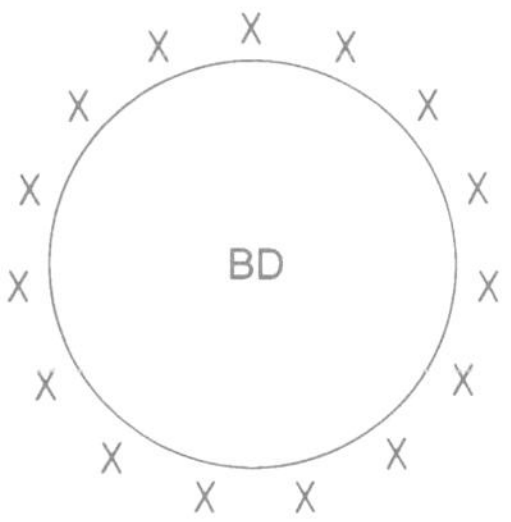

One child, designated the duck (Daisy if a girl, Donald if a boy), stands blindfolded in the center of a circle and holds a wand or similar article. She taps on the floor and tells children to hop (or perform some other locomotor movement). Children in the circle act accordingly, all moving in the same direction. Daisy then taps the wand twice on the floor, which signals all children to stop. Daisy moves forward with her wand, still blindfolded, to find a child in the circle. She asks, "Who are you?" The child responds, "Quack, quack." Daisy tries to identify this person. If the guess is correct, the identified child becomes the new duck. If the guess is wrong, Daisy must take another turn. After two unsuccessful turns, another child is chosen to be the duck.

BOTTLE BAT BALL

Supplies: A plastic bottle bat, whiffle ball, batting tee (optional), home plate, base marker

Skills: Batting, retrieving balls

Formation: Scattered

Batters get three pitches (or swings if a batting tee is used) to hit a fair ball, or they are out. The pitches are easy (as in slow-pitch softball), so that the batter has a chance to hit the ball. The batter hits the ball and runs around the base marker and back to home. If the ball is returned to the pitcher's mound before the batter reaches home, the batter is out. (A marker should designate the pitcher's mound.) Otherwise, the batter has a home run and bats again. One fielder other than the pitcher is needed, but another can be used. The running distance to first base is critical. It can remain fixed or can be made progressively (one step) longer, until it reaches such a point that the fielders are heavily favored.

TEACHING TIP

Use a plastic bottle bat and whiffle ball. A rotation system should be established when an out is made. Limit the number of home runs per at bat to three.

BOTTLE KICK BALL

Supplies: Plastic gallon jugs (bleach or milk containers) and 8-inch foam balls

Skills: Kicking, trapping

Formation:

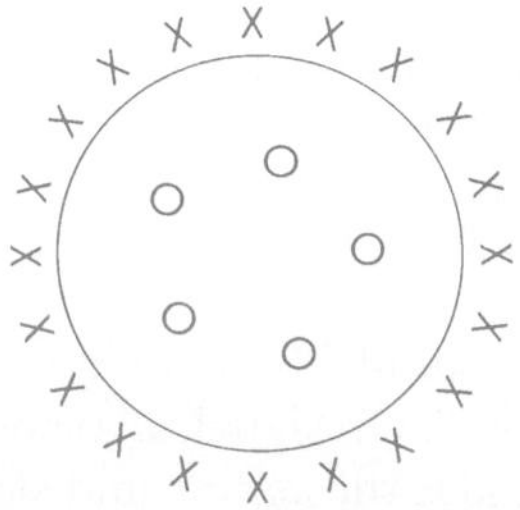

Players form a large circle around 10 to 12 plastic gallon jugs (bowling pins) standing in the middle of the circle. Students kick the balls and try to knock over the bottles. Use as many foam balls as necessary to keep all children active. If the group is large, make more than one circle of players.

CAT AND MICE

Supplies: None

Skills: Running, dodging

Formation:

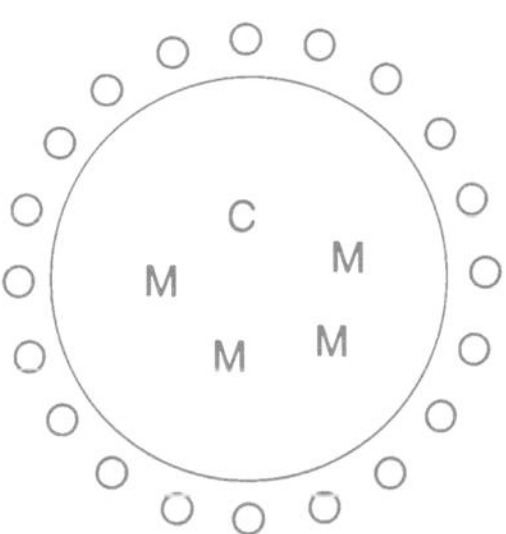

Form a large circle. Two or three children are the cats and four others are the mice. The cats and mice cannot leave the circle. On signal, the cats chase the mice inside the circle. As they are caught, the mice join the circle. The last three mice caught become the cats for the next round. Start at one point in the circle and go around the circle selecting mice so that each child gets a chance to be in the center.

Sometimes, children have difficulty catching the last mouse or any of the mice. If this is the case, children forming the circle can take a step toward the center, thus constricting the running area. Regardless, cut off any prolonged chase sequence.

CHANGE SIDES

Supplies: None

Skill: Body management

Formation:

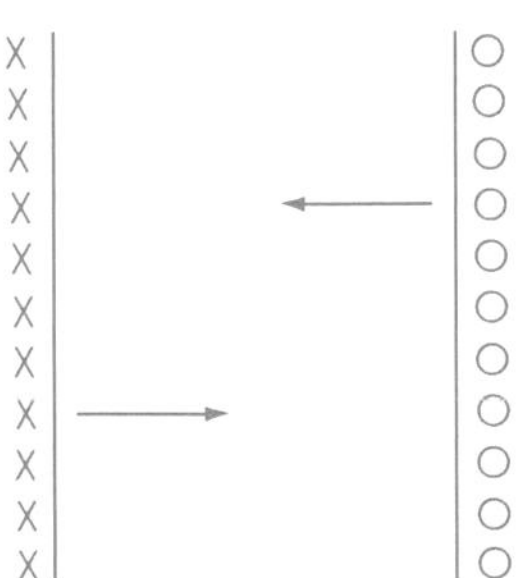

Establish two parallel lines 30 feet apart with half of the class on each line. On signal, all players cross through to the other line, face the center, and stand at attention. The first group to do all three things correctly wins a point. Children must be cautioned to use care when passing through the opposite group. They should be spaced well along each line; this allows room for them to move through each group. Vary the locomotor movements used by specifying skipping, hopping, long steps, sliding, and other varieties of movement. The position to be assumed at the finish can be varied also.

CHARLIE OVER THE WATER

Supplies: A volleyball or playground ball

Skills: Skipping, running, stopping, bowling (rolling)

Formation: Scattered

Place the class in circle formation. Two or more children are placed in the center of the circle, holding a ball. One of the center players is designated as Charlie (or Sally). The class skips around the circle to the following chant.

Charlie over the water,
Charlie over the sea,
Charlie caught a bluebird,
But can't catch me!

On the word *me,* the center players toss their balls in the air while the rest of the class runs and scatters throughout the area. When Charlie catches his ball, he shouts, "Stop!" All of the children stop immediately and must not move their feet. All of the center players roll their ball in an attempt to hit one of their scattered classmates. If a ball is rolled into a scattered player, that child becomes a new Charlie. If center players miss, they remain in the center, and the game is repeated. If a center player misses twice, however, he or she joins the circle and picks another person as a replacement.

CIRCLE STOOP

Supplies: Music or tom-tom

Skills: Moving to rhythm

Formation:

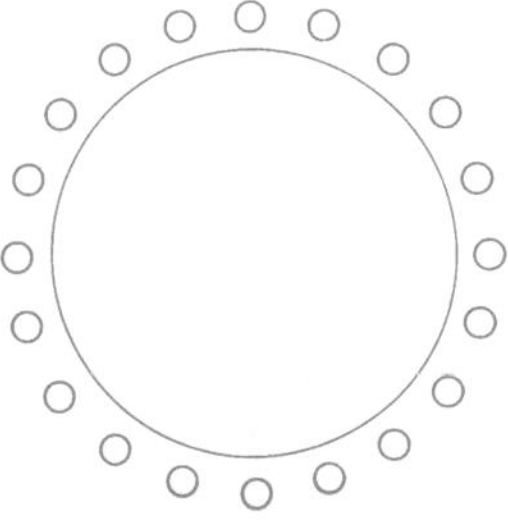

Children are in a single circle, facing counterclockwise. A march or similar music, or a tom-tom beat, can be used to signal movement. The class marches until the music stops, at which point they stoop and touch both hands to the ground without losing balance. The last child to touch both hands to the ground and those children who lost balance pay a penalty by going into the mush pot (the center of the circle) for one turn. The duration of the music should be varied so youngsters don't anticipate the signal.

TEACHING TIP

Variations:

1. Using suitable music, have children employ different locomotor movements, such as skipping, hopping, or galloping.
2. Vary the stopping position. Instead of stooping, use positions such as the push-up, Crab, or Lame Dog, balancing on one foot, or touching with one hand and one foot.

CIRCLE STRADDLE BALL

Supplies: Two or more 8-inch foam balls

Skills: Ball rolling, catching

Formation: Circles of 10–15 students

Children are in circle formation, facing in. Each player stands in a wide straddle stance with the side of each foot against their neighbors'. Their hands are on the knees. Two or more balls are used. The object of the game is to roll a ball between the legs of another player before that player can get hands down to stop the ball. Keep the circles small so students have more opportunities to handle the ball. Players must catch and roll the ball, rather than batting it. Children must keep their hands on their knees until a ball is rolled at them. After some practice, the following variation can be played.

TEACHING TIP

Variation: Two or more children are in the center, each with a ball. The other children are in the same formation as before. The center players try to roll the ball through the legs of any child, masking intent by using feints and changes of direction. Any child allowing the ball to go through becomes it.

COLORS

Supplies: Colored paper (construction paper) cut in circles, squares, or triangles for markers

Skills: Color or other perceptual concepts, running

Formation:

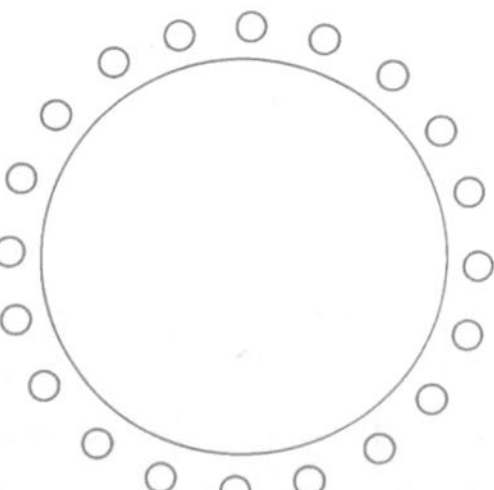

Use five or six different-colored markers, with a number of children having the same color. Children are standing or seated in a circle with a marker in front of each child. The teacher (or another player) calls out a color. Everyone having that color runs counterclockwise around the circle and back to place. The first player seated upright and motionless is declared the winner. Different kinds of locomotor movement can be specified, such as skipping, galloping, walking, and so on. After a period of play, the children leave the markers on the floor and move one place to the left.

TEACHING TIP

Variation: Shapes (circles, triangles, squares, rectangles, stars, and diamonds) can be used instead of colors, as can numbers or other articles or categories, such as animals, birds, or fish.

CORNER SPRY

Supplies: Blindfold

Skills: Light, silent walking

Formation:

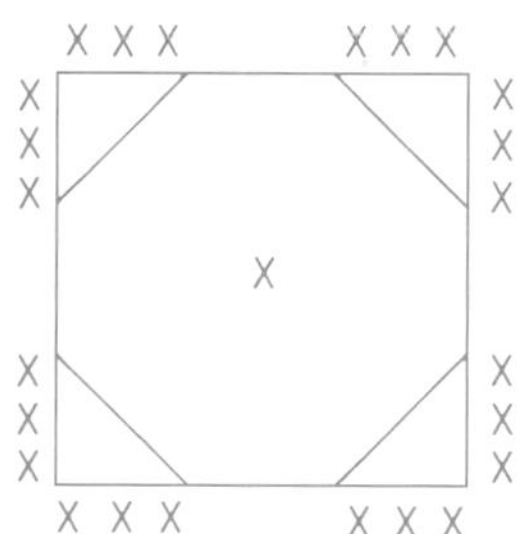

One person is blindfolded and stands in the center of the square. The other players are scattered in the corner areas. On signal they travel as quietly as possible from corner area to corner area. The blindfolded person, when ready (less than 20 seconds), calls out "Corner Spry!" All players finish their trips to the corner nearest them. The blindfolded person then picks (by pointing) a corner, trying to select the one with the most players. A new player is then selected to be blindfolded.

TEACHING TIP

Variation: The corners can be numbered 1, 2, 3, 4 and the blinfolded person can call out the corner number. The leader can also start class movement by naming the locomotor movement to be used.

FIREFIGHTER

Supplies: None

Skill: Running

Formation:

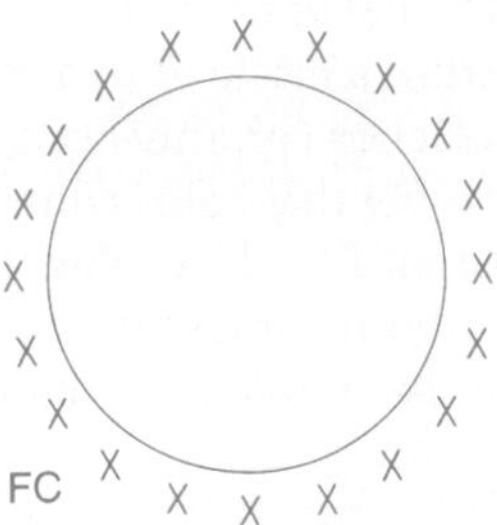

A fire chief runs around the outside of a circle of children and taps a number of them on the back, saying "Firefighter" each time. After making the round of the circle, the chief goes to the center. When the chief says "Fire," the firefighters run counterclockwise around the circle and back to place. The one who returns first and is able to stand in place motionless is declared the winner and the new chief.

The chief can use other words to fool children, but they run only on the word *Fire*. This merely provides some fun, since there is no penalty for a false start. The circle children can sound the siren as the firefighters run.

TEACHING TIP

Have children stand while the chief is circling. All children not tapped drop to their knees as they would if there was a fire.

FLOWERS AND WIND

Supplies: None

Skill: Running

Formation:

Two parallel lines long enough to accommodate the children are drawn about 30 feet apart. Children are divided into two groups. One is the flowers and the other the wind. Each of the teams takes a position on one of the lines and faces the other team. The flowers secretly select the name of a common flower. When ready, they walk over to the other line and stand about 3 feet away from the wind. The players on the wind team begin to call out flower names—trying to guess the flower chosen. When the flower has been guessed, the flowers run to their goal line, chased by the players of the other team. Any player caught must join the other side. The roles are reversed and the game is repeated. If one side has trouble guessing, a clue can be given to the color or size of the flower or the first letter of its name.

TEACHING TIP

Change the object that students choose to integrate other academic areas, i.e., trees, spelling words, math functions.

FOREST RANGER

Supplies: None

Skill: Running

Formation:

Half of the class forms a circle and faces the center. These are the trees. The other half of the class stands behind the trees as forest rangers. An extra child, the forest lookout, is in the center. The forest lookout starts the game by calling, "Fire in the forest. Run, run, run!" Immediately, the forest rangers run around the outside of the circle to the right. After a few moments, the lookout steps in front of one of the trees. This is the signal for each of the rangers to step in front of a tree. One player is left out, who then becomes the new forest lookout. The trees become rangers and the rangers become trees. Each time the game is played, the circle must be moved out somewhat, because the formation narrows when the rangers step in front of the trees.

FREEZE

Supplies: Music or tom-tom

Skills: Locomotor movements to rhythm

Formation: Scattered

Scatter the class throughout the room. When the music starts, players move throughout the area, guided by the music. They walk, run, jump, or use other locomotor movements, depending on the selected music or beat. When the music is stopped, they freeze and do not move. Any child caught moving after the cessation of the rhythm receives a point. The object is to not accumulate points. A tom-tom or a piano is a fine accompaniment for this game, because the rhythmic beat can be varied easily and the rhythm can be stopped at any time.

This game is useful for practicing management skills because it reinforces freezing on a stop signal.

TEACHING TIP

Variations:

1. Specify the level at which children must freeze.
2. Have children fall to the ground or balance or go into a different position, such as the push-up, Crab, Lame Dog, or some other defined position.

HILL DILL

Supplies: None

Skills: Running, dodging

Formation:

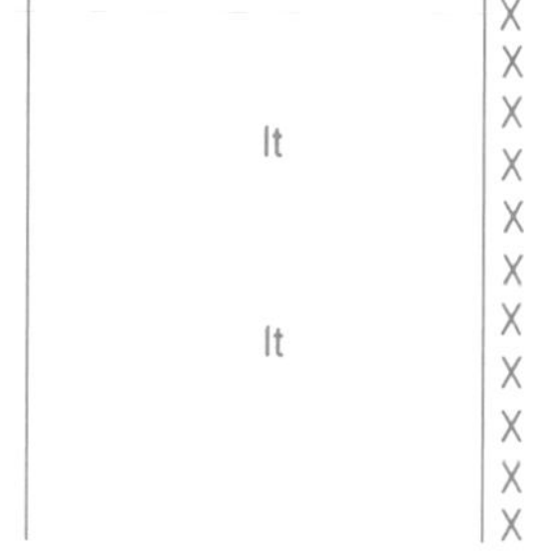

Two parallel lines are established 50 feet apart. Two or more players are chosen to be it and stand in the center between the lines. The other children stand on one of the parallel lines. One of the center players calls,

> Hill Dill! Come over the hill,
> Or else I'll catch you standing still!

Children run across the open space to the other line, while the one in the center tries to tag them. Anyone caught helps the tagger in the center. When children cross over to the other line, they must await the next call. Start a new game when a majority of youngsters have been tagged.

HOT POTATOES

Supplies: One to three balls or beanbags for each group

Skill: Object handling

Formation: Circles with 8–12 players

Group players in small circles (8 to 12 per circle) so objects can be passed from one to another around the circle. Balls or beanbags or both are passed around the circle. The teacher or a selected student, who is standing with his or her back to the class, randomly shouts, "Stop!" The point of the game is to avoid being the person who passes the object to the person who caught it when the signal occurs. If this happens, the player(s) who passed the object gets up and moves to the next circle. Begin the game with one object and gradually add objects if the class is capable. Call out "Reverse" to signal a change in the direction the object is passed.

JACK FROST AND JANE THAW

Supplies: Blue streamers or pinnies for Jack Frosts and red ones for Jane Thaws

Skills: Running, dodging, holding position

Formation: Scattered

The class is scattered and moves to avoid being frozen (tagged) by two or three Jack Frosts, who carry a blue pinnie or streamer in one hand. Frozen children remain immobile until touched (thawed) by the Jane Thaws who are identified by a red streamer or pinnie.

LEAP THE BROOK

Supplies: None

Skills: Leaping, jumping, hopping, turning

Formation:

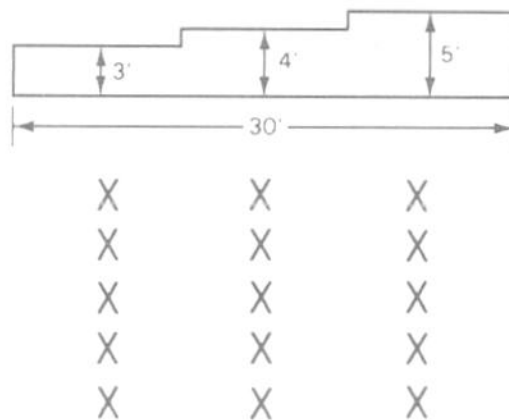

Mark off a brook across the floor. For the first third of the brook, it is about 3 feet wide; for the next third, about 4 feet wide; and for the last third, it is 5 feet wide. Youngsters line up on one side of the area. On the signal, "Cross the Brook!" players pick a challenge and try to jump across the brook. The wider the brook, the greater the challenge. Use different styles of locomotor movements such as hopping, jumping, and leaping over the brook. The selection of the distances is arbitrary and can be changed if they seem unsuitable for any particular group of children.

TEACHING TIP

Variation: Use different types of turns while jumping the brook, such as right or left; quarter, half, three-quarter, or full. Use different body shapes, different arm positions, and so on.

MARCHING PONIES

Supplies: None

Skills: Marching, running

Formation:

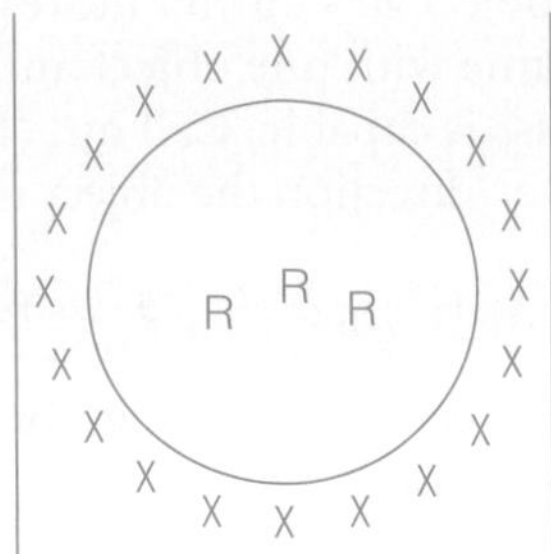

Two or three children are ringmasters and crouch in the center of a circle of ponies formed by the rest of the class. Two goal lines on opposite sides of the circle are established as safe areas. The ponies march around the circle in step, counting as they do so. At a predetermined number (whispered to the ringmasters by the teacher), the ringmasters jump up and attempt to tag the others before they can reach the safety lines. Anyone tagged joins the ringmasters in the center and helps catch others. Reorganize the game after six to eight children have been caught. Try other characterizations, such as lumbering elephants, jumping kangaroos, and the like.

MAY I CHASE YOU?

Supplies: None

Skills: Running, dodging

Formation:

The class stands behind a line long enough to accommodate all. Two or three runners stand about 5 feet in front of the line. The class asks, "May I chase you?" One of the runners (designated by teacher) replies, "Yes, if you are wearing . . ." and names a color, an article of clothing, or a combination of the two. All who qualify immediately chase the runners until one is tagged. New runners are chosen and the game is repeated. Encourage players to think of other ways to identify those who run.

MIDNIGHT

Supplies: None

Skills: Running, dodging

Formation:

A safety line is established about 40 feet from a den in which two or three players, the foxes, are standing. The others stand behind the safety line and ask, "What time is it, Mr. Fox?" One of the foxes is designated to answer in various fashions, such as "one o' clock," "four o' clock," etc. When the fox says a certain time, the class walks forward that number of steps. For example, if the fox says, "six o'clock" the class has to move forward six steps. The fox continues to draw the players toward him. At some point, the fox answers the question by saying "Midnight," and chases the others back to the safety line. Any player who is caught becomes a fox in the den and helps to catch others.

TEACHING TIP

Variation: *Lame Wolf.* The wolf is lame and advances in a series of three running steps and a hop. Other children taunt, "Lame Wolf, can't catch me!" or "Lame Wolf, tame wolf, can't catch me!" The wolf may give chase at any time. Children who are caught join the wolf and must also move as if lame.

MIX AND MATCH

Supplies: None

Skills: Fundamental locomotor movements

Formation:

A line is established through the middle of the area. Half of the children are on one side and half are on the other. Two or three extra persons are on one side of the area. The teacher gives a signal for children to move as directed on their side of the line. They can be told to run, hop, skip, or make some other movement. On signal, players run to the dividing line and reach across to join hands with a player on the opposite side. The goal is to find a partner and not be left out. Children may reach over but may not cross the line. The players left out move to the opposite side so that players left out come from alternating sides of the area.

TEACHING TIP

Variation: The game also can be done with music or a drumbeat, with the players rushing to the centerline to find partners when the rhythm stops.

MOUSETRAP

Supplies: None

Skills: Skipping, running, dodging

Formation:

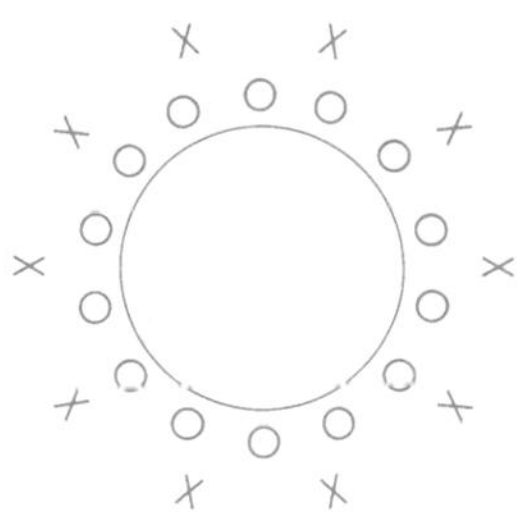

Half of the class forms a circle with hands joined and face the center. This is the trap. The other children are on the outside of the circle. These are the mice. Three signals are given for the game. These can be word cues or other signals. On the first signal, the mice skip around, outside the circle, playing happily. On the second signal, the trap is opened. (The circle players raise their joined hands to form arches.) The mice run in and out of the trap. On the third signal, the trap snaps shut. (The arms come down.) All mice caught inside join the circle. The game is repeated until most of the mice are caught. The players then exchange places, and the game begins anew.

MUSICAL BALL PASS

Supplies: One or two playground balls per group, music

Skills: Passing and handling

Formation:

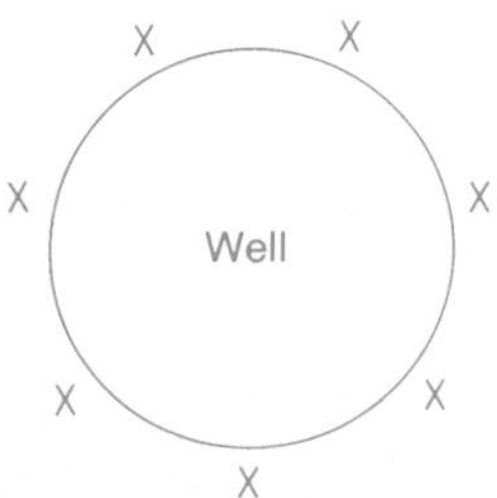

Break the class into a number of small groups (6–7 players) in circle formation facing the center. One ball is given to a player in each circle and is passed around the circle when the music starts. When the music stops, the player with the ball (or the last player to touch the ball) takes the ball and moves to another circle. To avoid arguments, a player must move to the next circle if the ball is in her hands or on the way to her. More than one ball may be used.

ONE, TWO, BUTTON MY SHOE

Supplies: None

Skill: Running

Formation:

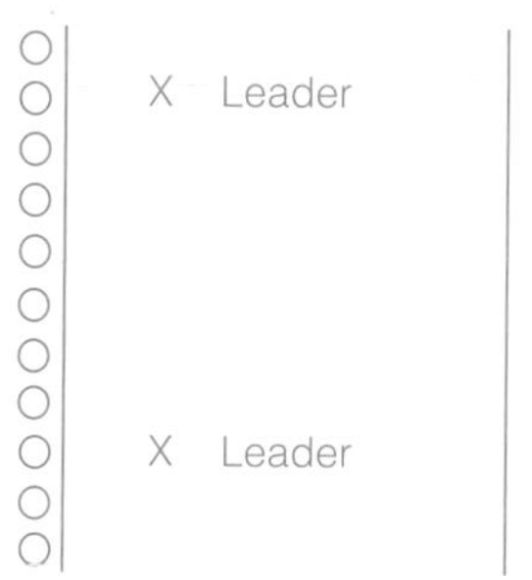

Two parallel lines are drawn on opposite sides of the playing area. Two or three players are selected as leaders and stand in front of the class. The rest of the class is behind one of the lines. The leaders say "Ready." The following dialogue takes place between the leaders and the children.

CHILDREN: One, two.

LEADER: button my shoe.

CHILDREN: three, four.

LEADER: close the door.

CHILDREN: five, six.

LEADER: pick up sticks.

CHILDREN: seven, eight.

LEADER: run, or you'll be late!

As children carry on the conversation with the leaders, they toe the line, ready to run. When the leaders say the word *late*, players run to the other line and return. New leaders are chosen after each run. The leaders can give the last response ("Run, or you'll be late!") in any timing desired—pausing or dragging out the words. No player can leave before the word *late* is uttered.

POPCORN

Supplies: None

Skills: Curling, stretching, jumping

Formation:

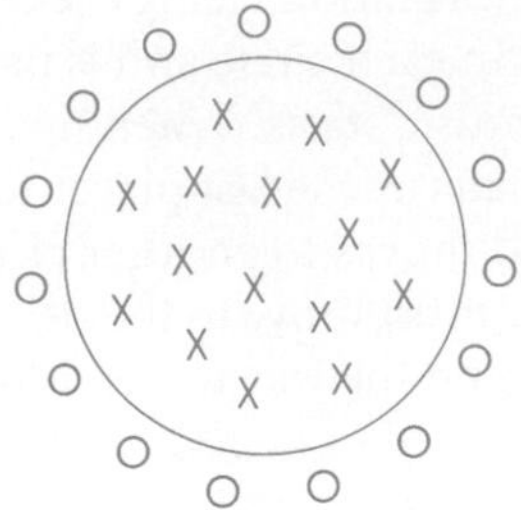

Half of the class is designated as popcorn; they crouch down in the center of the circle formed by the rest of the class. The circle children, also crouching, represent the heat. One of them is designated the leader whose actions serve as a guide to the other children. The circle children gradually rise to a standing position, extend their arms overhead, and shake them vigorously to indicate the intensifying heat. In the meantime, the popcorn in the center starts to pop. This should begin at a slow pace and increase in speed and height as the heat is applied. In the final stages, children are popping up rapidly. After a time, the groups change places and the action is repeated.

RED LIGHT

Supplies: None

Skills: Fundamental locomotor movements, stopping

Formation:

A goal line is established at one end of the area. The object of the game is to move across the area successfully without getting caught. Two or three players are leaders and stand on the goal line. The leaders turn away from the players. One of the leaders claps five times. All leaders turn around on the fifth clap. In the meantime, the players move toward the goal line, timing their movements to end on the fifth clap. If any of the leaders catch any movement by any person, that person is required to return to the starting line and begin anew. After the clapper turns away, she can turn back immediately to catch any movement. Once she begins clapping, however, five claps must be completed before she turns around. The first child to reach the goal line successfully without being caught in an illegal movement is the winner. New leaders are chosen for the next game.

TEACHING TIP

Variations:

1. An excellent variation of the game is to have the leaders face the oncoming players. The designated leader calls out "Green light" for them to move and "Red light" for them to stop. When the leader calls other colors, the players should not move.
2. Different types of locomotion can be explored. The leader names the type of movement (e.g., hop, crawl, skip) before turning her back to the group.
3. The leader can specify how those caught must go back to place—walk, hop, skip, slide, crawl.
4. Divide the area into quadrants and have four games with one or two leaders.

TEACHING TIP

In the original game of Red Light, the leader counts rapidly, "One, two, three, four, five, six, seven, eight, nine, ten—red light," instead of clapping five times. This has proved impractical in most gymnasiums, however, because children moving forward cannot hear the counting. Clapping, which provides both a visual and an auditory signal, is preferable.

RIGHT ANGLE

Supplies: Music

Skills: Rhythmic movement, body management

Formation: Scattered

A tom-tom can be used to provide the rhythm for this activity. Children quickly change direction at right angles on each heavy beat or change of music. The object of the game is to make the right-angle change on signal and not to bump into other players.

ROLLEE POLLEE

Supplies: Many 8-inch foam balls

Skills: Ball rolling, dodging

Formation:

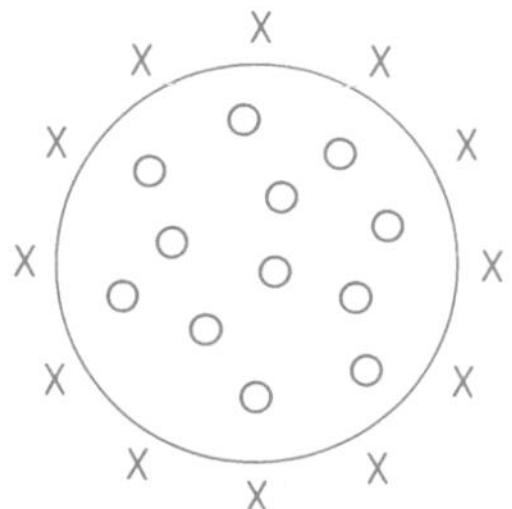

Half of the class forms a circle; the other half is in the center. Balls are given to the circle players. The circle players roll the balls at the feet and shoes of the center players, trying to touch them with a ball. The center players move around to avoid the balls. A center player who is touched leaves the center and joins the circle. After a period of time or when all of the children have been touched, the teams trade places.

TEACHING TIP

The instructor can have the children practice rolling a ball first. Balls that stop in the center are dead and must be taken back to the circle before being put into play again. The preferable procedure is to have players who recover balls roll them to a teammate rather than return to place with the ball.

THE SCARECROW AND THE CROWS

Supplies: None

Skills: Dodging, running

Formation:

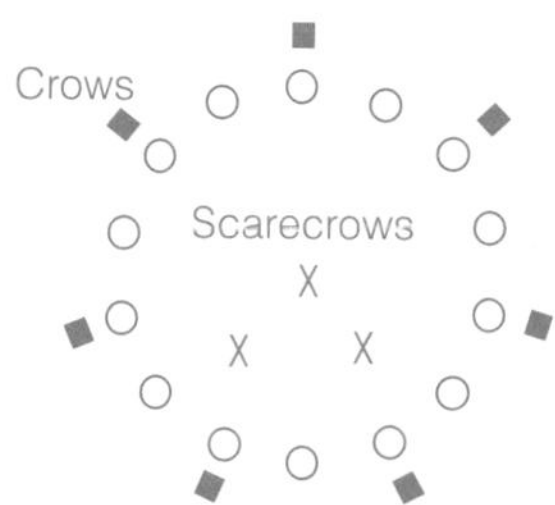

Children form a large circle representing the garden that is guarded by two or three players who are designated as scarecrows. Six to eight crows scatter on the outside of the circle, and the scarecrows assume a characteristic pose inside the circle. Players in the the circle raise their joined hands and let the crows run through, into the garden, where they pretend to eat. The scarecrows try to tag the crows. The circle children help the crows by raising their joined hands and allowing them to leave the circle, but they try to hinder the scarecrows. If the scarecrows run out of the circle, all the crows immediately run into the garden and start to nibble at the vegetables while the circle children hinder the scarecrows' reentry.

When the scarecrows have caught one or two crows, new players are selected. If, after a reasonable period of time, the scarecrows have failed to catch any crows, change players.

SNEAK ATTACK

Supplies: None

Skills: Running

Formation:

Two parallel lines are drawn about 60 feet apart. The class is divided into two teams. One team takes a position on one of the lines, with their backs to the area. These are the chasers. The other team is on the other line, facing the area. This is the sneak team. The sneak team moves forward on signal, moving toward the chasers. When they get reasonably close, a signal is given, and the sneak team turns and runs back to their line, chased by the other team. Anyone tagged before reaching the line changes to the chase team. The game is then repeated, with the roles exchanged.

SOAP BUBBLES

Supplies: Cones to delineate space, music

Skills: Body management

Formation: Scattered

Four cones are used to delineate the movement area. Each player is a soap bubble floating throughout the area. A locomotor movement is called out and youngsters perform it, moving within the four cones. As the game progresses, the cones are moved toward the center of the area to decrease the size of the area. The object of the game is not to touch or collide with another bubble. When this occurs, both bubbles burst and sink to the floor, making themselves as small as possible. The space is made smaller until only a few have not been touched. Players who are broken bubbles can go to the area outside of the cones and move. This game teaches the concept of moving in general space without touching.

SQUIRREL IN THE TREES

Supplies: None

Skills: Fundamental locomotor movements

Formation:

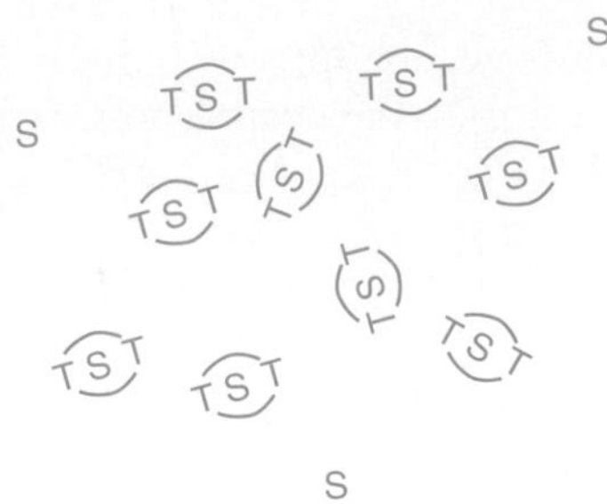

A number of trees are formed by two players facing each other and holding hands or putting hands on each other's shoulders. A squirrel is in the center of each tree, and one or two extra squirrels are outside. On signal, the trees open up and let the squirrels move around the area. The trees also stay together and move throughout the area. On signal, the trees freeze in place and the squirrels find any available tree. Only one squirrel is allowed in a tree. Quickly begin another game to avoid drawing attention to those who did not find a tree.

TEACHING TIP

Rotation is necessary so all students get to be a squirrel. Once the squirrels are in a tree, ask them to face one of the tree players. The person they are facing becomes their partner for a tree and the other person becomes a new squirrel.

STATUES

Supplies: None

Skills: Body management, applying force, balance

Formation: Scattered in pairs

Children are scattered in pairs around the area. One partner is the swinger and the other the statue. The teacher voices a directive, such as "Pretty," "Funny," "Happy," "Angry," or "Ugly." The swinger takes the statue by one or both hands, swings it around in a small circle two or three times (the teacher should specify), and releases it. The statue then takes a pose in keeping with the directive, and the swinger sits down on the floor.

A committee of children can determine which children are the best statues. The statue must hold the position without moving or be disqualified. After the winners are announced, the partners reverse positions. Children should be cautioned that the swinging must be controlled.

TEACHING TIP

Variation: In the original game, the swinging is done until the directive is called. The swinger then immediately releases the statue, who takes the pose as called. This gives little time for the statue to react. More creative statues are possible if the directive is given earlier.

STOP BALL

Supplies: A ball

Skills: Tossing, catching

Formation:

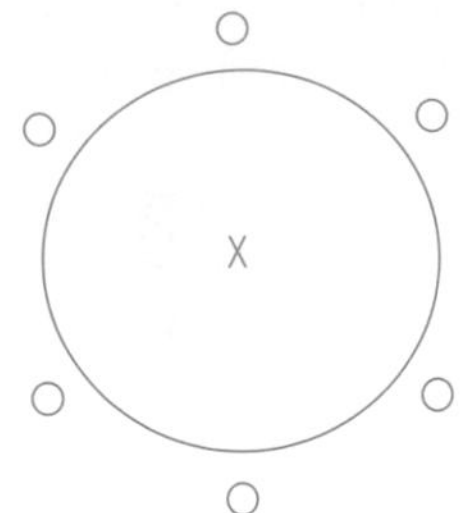

Divide the class into small circles of 5 to 7 players. One player, with hands over the eyes, stands in the center of each circle. A ball is tossed clockwise or counterclockwise from player to player around the circle. At a time of her own selection, the center player calls, "Stop." The player caught with the ball (or the ball coming to her) takes the ball to the next circle and plays with a new team. The center player should be allowed three or four turns and then be changed.

TAG GAMES (SIMPLE)

Supplies: None

Skills: Fundamental locomotor movements, dodging

Formation: Scattered

Tag has many variations. The following are "give up the tag" games because a player is no longer it when they tag another person, who then becomes *it*. Children are scattered throughout the area. A number of players are designated as *it*. When a tag is made, that player states, "You're *it*." The new *it* can chase any player other than the person who tagged them (no tagbacks).

TEACHING TIP

Variations:

1. Touching a specified type of object (such as wood or iron) or the floor or an object of a specified color can make a runner safe.
2. Children can be safe by doing a particular action or by striking a certain pose.
   a. *Stoop Tag.* Players touch both hands to the ground.
   b. *Stork Tag.* Players stand on one foot. (The other cannot touch.)
   c. *Turtle Tag.* Players get on their backs, feet pointed toward the ceiling.
   d. *Bowing Tag.* Players make an obeisance with forehead to the ground.

e. *Nose-and-Toe Tag.* Players touch the nose to the toe.

f. *Back-to-Back Tag.* Players stand back to back with any other child.

g. *Skunk Tag.* Players reach an arm under one knee and hold the nose.

3. *Locomotor Tag.* The child who is it specifies how the others should move—skipping, hopping, jumping. The tagger must use the same kind of movement.

4. *Frozen Tag.* Two children are *it*. The rest are scattered over the area. When caught, they are "frozen" and must keep both feet in place. Any free player can tag a frozen player and thus release her. The goal of the tagger is to freeze all players. Frozen players can be required to hop in place until released.

TEACHER BALL (LEADER BALL)

Supplies: A volleyball or rubber playground ball

Skills: Throwing, catching

Formation:

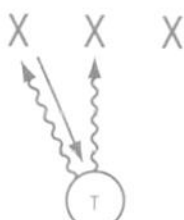

One child is the leader and stands about 10 feet in front of three other students, who are lined up facing the leader. The object of the game is to move up to the teacher's spot by avoiding making bad throws or missing catches. The leader throws to each child in turn, beginning with the child on the left, who must catch and return the ball. Any child making a throwing or catching error goes to the end of the line, on the leader's right. Those in the line move up, filling the vacated space.

A leader who makes a mistake must go to the end of the line and the child at the head of the line becomes the new leader. The leader scores a point by remaining in position for three rounds (three throws to each child). After scoring a point, the leader takes a position at the end of the line, and another child becomes the leader.

TEACHING TIP

Variation: The leader can suggest specific methods of throwing and catching, such as "Catch with the right hand only" or "Catch with one hand and don't let the ball touch your body."

TOE TO TOE

Supplies: None

Skills: Fundamental locomotor movements

Formation: Scattered

Youngsters perform a locomotor movement around the area. On signal, each child must find a partner and stand toe to toe (one foot only) with that person. An important skill is to take the nearest person for a partner instead of searching for a particular friend. Youngsters who can't find a partner within their immediate area must run quickly to the center of the area (use a marking spot or cone) to find a partner. The goal is to find a nearby partner as quickly as possible and avoid being the last pair formed. If the number of youngsters playing is uneven, the teacher can join in and play. Change locomotor movements often.

TOMMY TUCKER'S LAND

Supplies: About ten beanbags for each game

Skills: Dodging, running

Formation:

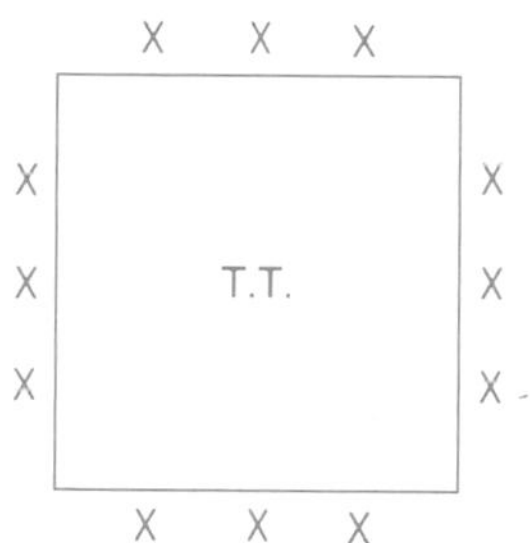

Two or three youngsters, Tommy and Tammy Tucker, stand in the center of a 15-foot square, within which the beanbags are scattered. The Tuckers are guarding their land and treasure. The other children chant,

I'm on Tommy Tucker's land,
Picking up gold and silver.

Children attempt to pick up as much of the treasure as they can while avoiding being tagged by the Tuckers. Any child who is tagged must return the treasure and retire from the game. The game is over when only one child is left or when all of the beanbags have been successfully filched. The teacher may wish to call a halt to the game earlier if a stalemate is reached. In this case, new Tuckers are selected.

TWINS (TRIPLETS)

Supplies: None

Skills: Body management, running

Formation: Scattered with partner

Youngsters are scattered throughout the area with a partner (twin). The teacher gives commands such as "Take three hops and two leaps" or "Walk backward four steps and three skips." When the pairs are separated, the teacher says, "Find your twin!" Players find their twin and stand frozen toe to toe. The goal is to not be the last pair to find each other and assume the frozen position. Make sure students move away from each other during the movements. One alternative is to find a new twin each time. Another variation is to separate twins in opposite ends of the playing area.

TEACHING TIP

Variation: The game becomes more challenging when played in groups of three (triplets). When using this variation, new partners should be selected each time.

UP PERISCOPE

Supplies: None

Skills: Fundamental locomotor movements

Formation: Scattered

While in scattered formation, children move around the area pretending to be ships. Remind the ships to not contact another ship and to keep as much space as possible. When the teacher says "Submarines," players quickly lower their bodies and move at a low level. When the teacher says "Up periscope," students move to their backs and put one leg in the air to imitate a periscope. On "Double periscope," both legs are raised to imitate two periscopes. While the students are in Double periscope position, the teacher can quickly give the previous commands to keep students moving. When the teacher says "Surface," the students resume moving through the area as ships.

WHERE'S MY PARTNER?

Supplies: None

Skills: Fundamental locomotor movements

Formation:

Children are in a double circle by couples, with partners facing. The inside circle has two or three more players than the outside. When the signal is given, the circles skip (or walk, run, hop, or gallop) to the right. This means that they are skipping in opposite directions. On the command "Halt," the circles face each other to find partners. The players left without a partner go to the mush pot (the center area of the circle) for one turn. The circles should be reversed after a time.

TEACHING TIP

Variation: The game can also be played with music or a drumbeat. When the music stops, the players seek partners.

DEVELOPMENTAL LEVEL II

Compared with the games in developmental level I, the games program undergoes a definite change. Chase and tag games become more complex and demand more maneuvering. Introductory lead-up games make an appearance. The interests of children turn to games that have a sport slant, and kicking, throwing, catching, batting, and other sport skills are beginning to mature.

ADDITION TAG

Supplies: None

Skills: Running, dodging

Formation:

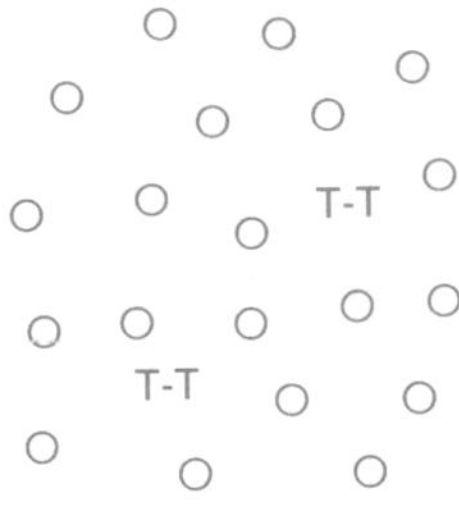

Two or more couples are it, and each stands with inside hands joined. These are the taggers. The other children run individually. The couples move around the area, trying to tag with the free hands. The first person tagged joins the couple, making a trio. The three then chase until they catch a fourth. Once a fourth person is caught, the four divide and form two couples, adding another set of taggers to the game. This continues until the majority of players are tagged.

TEACHING TIP

Some area restrictions can be established if couples are having problems catching the runners. The game moves faster if started with more couples. A tag is legal only when the couple or group of three keeps their hands joined.

ALASKA BASEBALL

Supplies: A volleyball or soccer ball

Skills: Kicking, batting, running, ball handling

Formation:

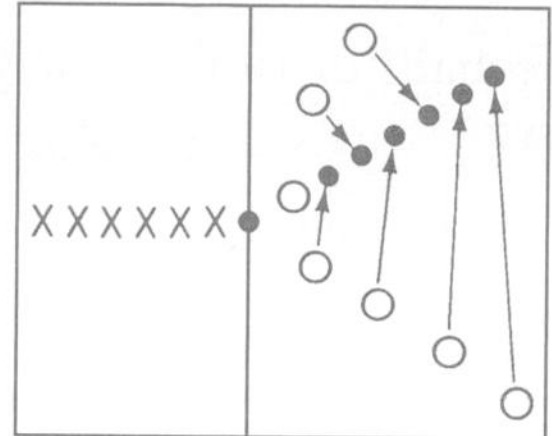

Players are organized in two teams; one is at bat while the other is in the field. A straight line provides the only out-of-bounds line, and the team at bat is behind this line at about the middle. The other team is scattered around the fair territory.

One player propels the ball, either batting a volleyball or kicking a stationary soccer ball. Teammates are in a close file behind the batter. As soon as the batter sends the ball into the playing area, he or she starts to run around the line of teammates. Each time the runner passes the head of the file, the team gives a loud count.

There are no outs. The first fielder to get the ball stands still and starts to pass the ball back overhead to the nearest teammate, who moves directly behind to receive it. The remainder of the team in the field must run to the ball and form a file behind it. The ball is passed back overhead, with each player handling the ball. When the last field player in line has a firm grip on it, she shouts "Stop." At this signal, a count is made of the number of times the batter ran around her own team. To score more sharply, half rounds should be counted.

Five batters or half of the team should bat; then the teams should change places. This is better than allowing an entire team to bat before changing to the field, because players in the field tire from many consecutive runs.

TEACHING TIP

Variation: Regular bases can be set up, and the batter can run the bases. Scoring can be in terms of a home run made or not; or the batter can continue around the bases, getting a point for each base.

ARCHES

Supplies: Music

Skills: Moving rhythmically

Formation:

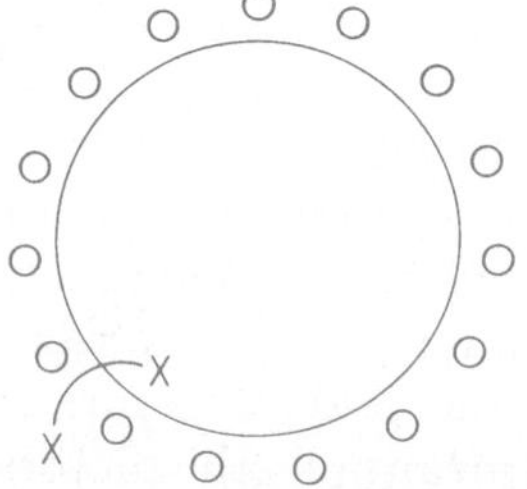

The game is similar to London Bridge. An arch is placed in the playing area. (To form an arch, two players stand facing one another with hands joined and arms raised.) When the music starts, the other players move in a circle, passing under the arch. Suddenly, the music stops, and the arch is brought down by dropping the hands. All players caught in an arch immediately pair off to form other arches, keeping in a general circle formation. If a caught player does not have a partner, he waits in the center of the circle until one is available. The last players caught (or left) form arches for the next game.

The arches should be warned not to bring down their hands and arms so forcefully that children passing under are pummeled.

TEACHING TIP

Variation: Different types of music can be used, and children can move according to the pattern of the music.

BAT BALL

Supplies: An 8-inch foam ball

Skills: Batting, running, catching, throwing

Formation:

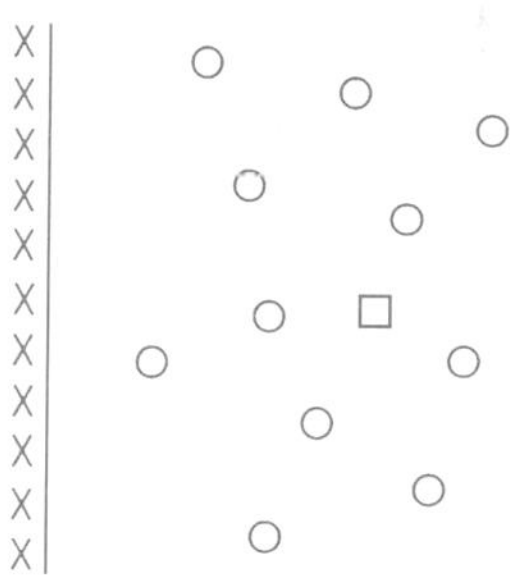

A serving line is drawn across one end of the field, and a 3-by-3-foot base is established about 50 feet from the serving line. Children are divided into two teams. One team is scattered over the playing area. The other team is behind the serving line, with one player at bat. The batter puts the ball into play by batting it with a hand into the playing area. To be counted as a fair ball, the ball must land in the playing area or be touched by a member of the fielding team. As soon as the ball is hit, the batter runs to the base and back across the serving line. In the meantime, the fielding team fields the ball and attempts to complete 5 passes before the runner gets back across the line.

Fielders may not run with the ball. It must be passed from fielder to fielder. A pass may not be returned to the fielder from whom it was received. Violation of any of these rules constitutes a foul.

A run is scored each time the batter hits a fair ball, touches the base, and gets back to the serving line. A run is also scored if the fielding team commits a foul.

The batter is out when the ball is caught on the fly. Two consecutive foul balls also put the batter out. The batter is out when hit by a thrown ball in the field of play. Sides change when three outs are made.

BEACH BALL BAT BALL

Supplies: Four to six beach balls

Skills: Batting, tactile handling

Formation:

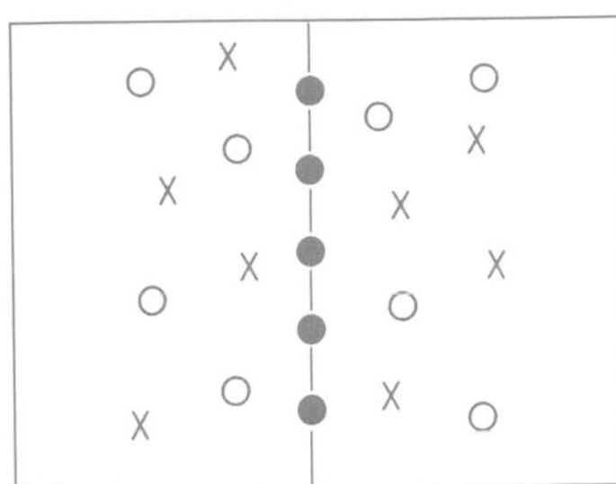

To begin the game, the balls are placed on the centerline dividing the court area. Four to six beach balls are in play at the same time. A score occurs when the beach ball is batted over the end line. Once the ball moves across the end line it is dead. Players concentrate on the remaining balls in play. If a ball is on the floor, it is picked up and batted into play. At no time may a ball be carried. After all four balls are scored, the game ends. A new game is started after teams switch goals.

BIRD CATCHER

Supplies: Hoops or cones

Skills: Chasing, Fleeing, Dodging

Formation: Class in line formation with 2–4 players in the bird nest

Two to four players are designated bird catchers and stand in the center of the teaching area. One child is chosen as the mother/father bird and stands on an end line or other predetermined line. An area around the mother/father bird can be established with cones and called a nest. The remainder of the class stands on the other end line. Students on the end line quickly choose the type of bird they will be for the game On signal, the mother/father bird commands a specific type of bird to fly, for example, "Cardinals fly." All students that chose to be cardinals then attempt to get to the mother/father birds nest without being tagged by the bird catchers. If tagged by the bird catchers, students begin helping the bird catcher until a new game is started.

TEACHING TIP

Specific types of birds may need to be given to expedite the game.

BOUNCE BALL

Supplies: Volleyballs or rubber playground balls of about the same size

Skills: Throwing, ball rolling

Formation:

The court is divided into halves. Children form two teams. Each team occupies one half of the court and is given a number of balls. Two players from each team are assigned to retrieve balls behind their own end lines. The object of the game is to bounce or roll the ball over the opponents' end line. A ball thrown across the line on a fly does not count. Two scorers are needed, one at each end line. Players can move wherever they wish in their own area but cannot cross the centerline. After the starting signal, the balls are thrown back and forth at will.

BOX BALL

Supplies: A sturdy box, 2 feet square and about 12 inches deep; four volleyballs (or similar balls)

Skills: Running, ball handling

Formation:

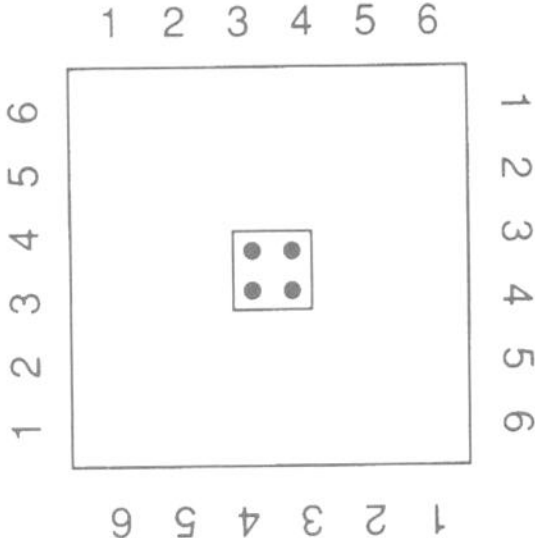

The class is divided into four even teams, with 6 to 10 players per team. Each team occupies one side of a hollow square at an equal distance from the center. Players face inward and each team numbers off consecutively from right to left.

A box containing four balls is put in the center. The instructor calls a number, and the player from each team who has that number runs forward to the box, takes a ball, and runs to the head of her line, taking the place of player 1. In the meantime, the players in the line have moved to the left just enough to fill in the space left by the runner. On reaching the head of the line, the runner passes the ball to the next person and so on down the line to the end child. The last child runs forward and returns the ball to the box. The first team to return the ball to the box scores a point.

The runner must not pass the ball down the line until she is in place at the head of the line. The ball must be caught and passed by each child. Failure to conform to these rules results in team disqualification. Runners stay at the head of the line, retaining their original number. The lines are not kept in consecutive number sequence.

BUSY BEE

Supplies: None

Skills: Fundamental locomotor movements

Formation:

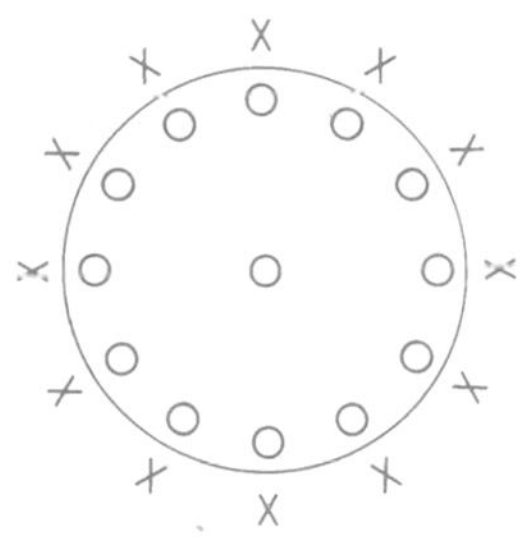

Half of the class forms a large circle, facing in, and is designated the stationary players. The other players seek partners from this group, and stand in front of the stationary players. An extra child in the center is the busy bee. The bee calls out directions such as "Toe to toe," "Face to face," "Shake hands," "Kneel on one knee [or both]," and "Hop on one foot." The other children follow these directions. The center child then calls out, "Busy bee." Stationary players stand still, and their partners seek new partners while the center player also tries to get a partner. The child without a partner becomes the new busy bee.

TEACHING TIP

Teach youngsters a variety of movements they can do if they become the busy bee. When changing partners, children must select a partner other than the stationary player next to them. After a period of time, the active and stationary players are rotated.

CAGEBALL KICK-OVER

Supplies: A cageball, 18-, 24-, or 30-inch size

Skill: Kicking

Formation:

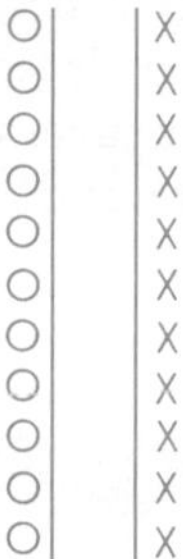

Players are divided into two teams and sit facing each other, with legs outstretched and soles of the feet about 6 to 12 feet apart. While maintaining the sitting position, each player supports his weight on the hands, which are placed slightly to the rear.

The teacher rolls the cageball between the two teams. The object of the game is to kick the ball over the other team, thereby scoring a point. After a point is scored, the teacher rolls the ball into play again. Rotate players by having a player on the left side of the line take a place on the right side after a point is scored, thus moving all the players one position to the left. When the ball is kicked out at either end, no score results, and the ball is put into play again by the teacher.

TEACHING TIP

Children can be allowed to use their hands to stop the ball from going over them.

CLUB GUARD

Supplies: A juggling club or bowling pin and foam-rubber ball

Skill: Throwing

Formation:

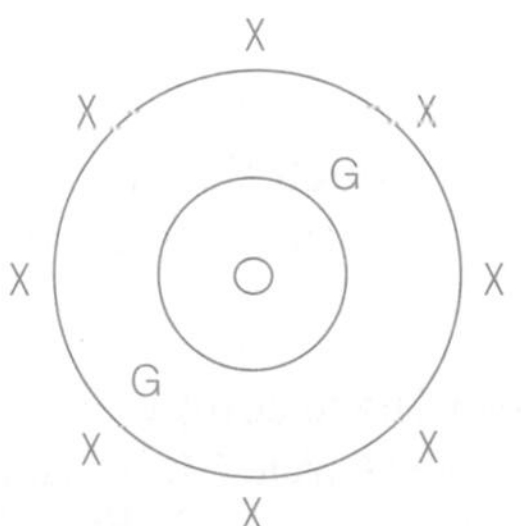

A circle about 15 feet in diameter is drawn. Inside the circle at the center, an 18-inch circle is drawn. The club is put in the center of the small circle. Two or three youngsters guard the club. The other players stand outside the large circle, which is the restraining line for them.

The circle players throw the ball at the club and try to knock it down. The guards try to block the throws with the legs and body but must stay out of the small inner circle. The outer circle players pass the ball around rapidly so that one of the players can get an opening to throw as the guards maneuver to protect the club. Rotate in new guards after a short period of time (15–20 seconds). The guards are disqualified if they step into the small circle.

TEACHING TIP

Variations: More than one club can be placed in the center.

Play multiple games to increase the activity level for all players.

COMPETITIVE CIRCLE CONTESTS

Supplies: Volleyballs or 8-inch foam rubber balls, two bowling pins

Skills: Throwing, catching

Formation: Two circles with the same number of students in each

Two teams arranged in independent circles compete against each other. The circles should be of the same diameter; lines can be drawn on the floor to ensure this. The players of each team are numbered consecutively so that each player in one circle corresponds to a player in the other circle. Two numbered players, in sequence, go to the center of the opponents' circle to compete for their team in either of the following activities.

1. *Circle Club Guard.* The two center players guard a bowling pin. The circle that knocks down the club first wins a point. The ball should be rolled at the club.
2. *Touch Ball.* The circle players pass the ball from one to another while the two center players try to touch it. The center player who touches the ball first wins a point for the respective team. In case neither player is able to touch the ball in a reasonable period of time, the action should be cut off without awarding a point.

After all players have competed, the team with the most points wins. For Circle Club Guard, there must be three passes to different people before the ball can be rolled at the club. Establishing circle lines may be necessary to regulate throwing distance.

COUPLE TAG

Supplies: None

Skills: Running, dodging

Formation:

It couples

Two goal lines are established on opposite sides of an area. Players run in pairs, with inside hands joined. All pairs, except two, line up on one of the goal lines. The pairs in the center are *it.* They call "Come," and the children, keeping hands joined, run to the other goal line. The pairs in the center, also retaining joined hands, try to tag any other pair. As soon as a couple is caught, they help the center couples. The game continues until all are caught. The last two couples caught are *it* for the next game.

TEACHING TIP

Variation: *Triplet Tag.* The game can be played with sets of threes. Tagging is done with any pair of joined hands. If a triplet breaks joined hands, it is considered caught.

CROWS AND CRANES

Supplies: None

Skills: Running, dodging

Formation:

Establish two goal lines on opposite sides of an area. The class is divided into two groups—the crows and the cranes. The groups face each other at the center of the area, about 5 feet apart. The leader calls out either "Crows" or "Cranes," using a cr-r-r-r-r-r sound at the start of either word to mask the result. If "Crows" is the call, the crows chase the cranes to the goal line. If "Cranes" is the call, then the cranes chase. Any player caught goes over to the other side and becomes a member of that group. The team that has the most players when the game ends is the winner.

TEACHING TIP

Variations:

1. *Toe to Toe.* Instead of facing each other, children stand back to back, about a foot apart, in the center.
2. *Red and Blue.* A piece of cardboard painted red on one side and blue on the other can be thrown into the air between the teams, instead of having someone give calls. If red comes up, the red team chases, and vice versa.
3. *Nouns and Verbs.* When the leader calls out any verb, the nouns team chases and vice versa.
4. *Odd and Even.* Large foam rubber dice can be thrown in the air. If they come up even, the even team chases. If they come up odd, the odd team chases.
5. *Blue, black, and baloney.* On the command "Blue" or "Black," the game proceeds as described. On the command "Baloney," no one is to move. The caller should draw out the bl-l-l-l sound before ending with one of the three commands.
6. Have a leader tell a story using as many words beginning with cr- as possible. Words that can be incorporated into a story might be *crazy, crunch, crust, crown, crude, crowd, crouch, cross, croak, critter.* Each time one of these words is spoken, the beginning of the word is lengthened with a drawn out *cr-r-r-r* sound. No one may move on any of the words except *crows* or *cranes.*

FLY TRAP

Supplies: None

Skills: Fundamental locomotor movements

Formation:

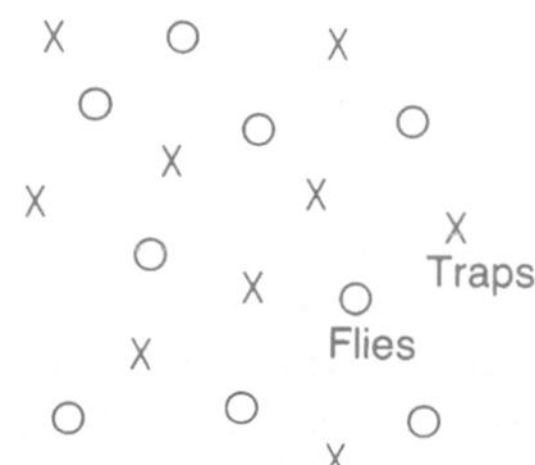

Half of the class is scattered around the playing area, sitting on the floor in cross-legged fashion. These children form the trap. The rest of the players are the flies, and they buzz around the seated children. When a whistle is blown, the flies must freeze where they are. If any of the trappers can touch a fly, that fly sits down at that spot and becomes a trapper. The trappers must keep their seats glued to the floor. The game continues until all of the flies are caught. Some realism is given to the game if the flies make buzzing sounds and move their arms as wings.

TEACHING TIP

Variation: Some experience with the game enables the teacher to determine how far apart to place the seated children. After most of the flies have been caught, the groups trade places. The method of locomotion should be changed occasionally.

FOLLOW ME

Supplies: A marker for each child (squares of cardboard or plywood can be used; individual mats or beanbags work well)

Skills: All locomotor movements, stopping

Formation:

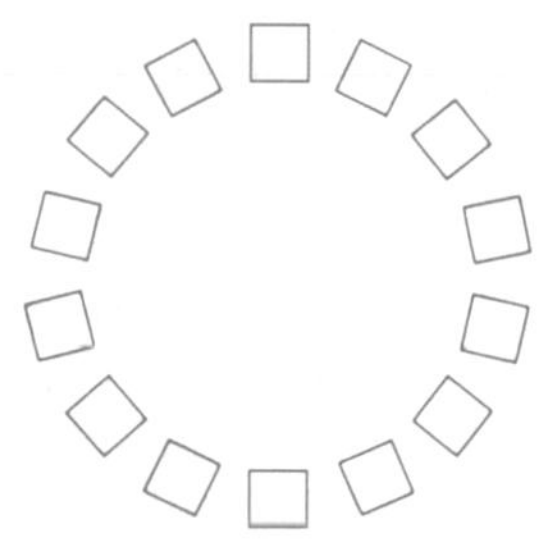

The class is arranged in a rough circle, each youngster standing or sitting with one foot on a marker. Two extra players are guides. They move around the circle, pointing at different players and asking them to follow until all players are selected. Each player chosen falls in behind the guide that pointed at him or her. The guides then take the groups on a tour, and the members of each group perform just as the guide does. The guide may hop, skip, do stunts, or execute other movements, and children following must do likewise. At the signal "Home," all run for places with a marker. Two players will be left without a marker. They can become guides or choose other guides.

FOX HUNT

Supplies: None

Skills: Running, dodging

Formation:

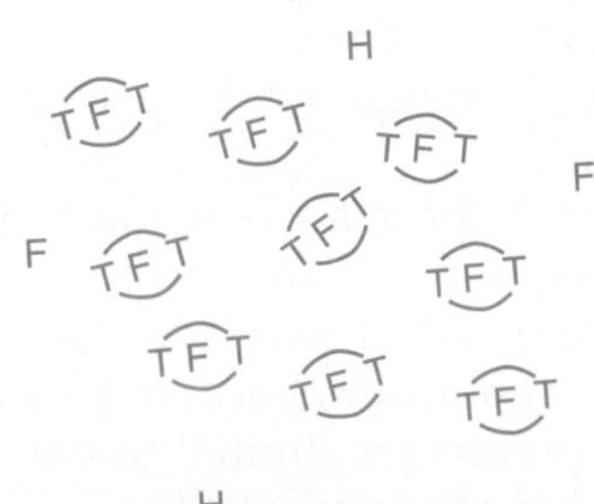

Pairs of players form trees by facing each other and holding hands. A third member of each group is a fox and stands between the hands of the trees. Three players are identified as foxes without trees and three players are designated as hounds. The hounds try to tag foxes who are not in trees. The extra foxes may move to a tree and displace the fox who is standing in the tree. In addition, the foxes in trees may leave the safety of their trees at any time. If the hound tags a fox, their roles are reversed immediately, the fox becoming the hound.

The game should be stopped at regular intervals to allow the players who are trees to change places with the foxes and hounds. Different locomotor movements can be specified to add variety to the game.

GALLOPING LIZZIE

Supplies: A beanbag or fleece ball

Skills: Throwing, dodging, running

Formation: Scattered

Two or more players are *it* and have fleece balls. The other players are scattered around the playground. The players with the balls run after the others and attempt to hit other players below the waist with the fleeceball. The person hit becomes *it,* and the game continues. The tagger must throw the ball, not merely touch another person with it.

HAND HOCKEY

Supplies: 8-inch gray foam balls

Skills: Striking, volleying

Formation:

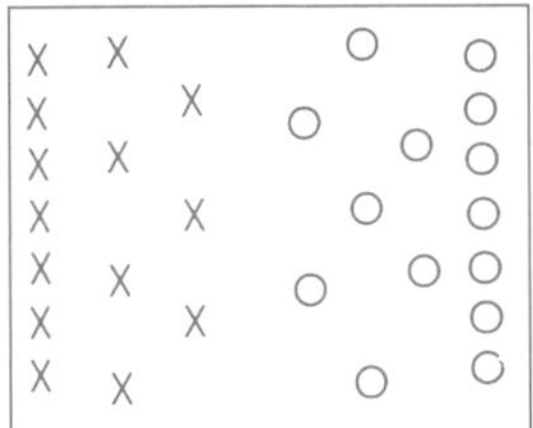

Players are divided into two teams. Half of the players on each team are guards and are stationed on the goal line as defenders. The other half are active players and are scattered throughout the playing area in front of their goal line.

The object of the game is to bat or push the ball with either hand so that it crosses the goal line that the other team is defending. Players may move the ball as in hockey but may not throw, hoist, or kick it. The defensive goal line players are limited to one step into the playing field when playing the ball.

The ball is put into play by being rolled into the center of the field. After a goal has been scored or after a specified period, guards become active players, and vice versa. An out-of-bounds ball goes to the opposite team and is put into play by being rolled from the sidelines into the playing area. If the ball becomes entrapped among players, play is stopped, and the ball is put into play again by a roll from the referee.

Players must play the ball and not resort to rough tactics. A player who is called for unnecessary roughness or for illegally handling the ball must go to the sidelines (as in hockey) and remain in the penalty area until the players change positions. Players should scatter and attempt to pass to each other rather than bunch around the ball.

Once youngsters learn the game, introduce more than one ball to increase the amount of activity.

TEACHING TIP

Variation: *Scooter Hockey.* The active center players from each team are on gym scooters. The position that each child takes on the gym scooter can be specified or can be a free choice. Possible positions are kneeling, sitting, or balancing on the tummy. A hard surface is needed. This game version is usually played indoors on a basketball court.

HOME BASE

Supplies: Cones to delineate the area, four pinnies

Skills: Reaction time, locomotor movements, body management

Place a number of marking spots on the floor throughout the area. Divide the class into groups of 5 or 6. Ask each group to quickly line up with one person on a marking spot and the rest of the players behind in single file. The person on the spot is designated as the team captain. A locomotor movement is called and all players do this movement throughout the area. When "Home base" is called, the captains quickly find the closest spot and their respective squad members line up behind them. The first team to return to proper position (standing in a straight line) is declared the winner.

TEACHING TIP

Avoid calling "Home base" until the students are thoroughly mixed. A number of different formations can be specified that students must assume upon return to their home base.

INDIANAPOLIS 500

Supplies: None

Skills: Running, tagging

Formation:

Children start in a large circle and are numbered off in threes or fours. A race starter says "Start your engines," and then calls out a number. Those children with the corresponding number run the same way around the circle and try to tag players in front of them. If the leader yells "Pit stop," all runners have to stop and return to their original position. If "Car Wreck" is called by the leader, all runners change direction and continue running until "Pit Stop" is called. Change the starter often.

JUMP THE SHOT

Supplies: 5 Jump-the-shot ropes

Skill: Rope jumping

Formation:

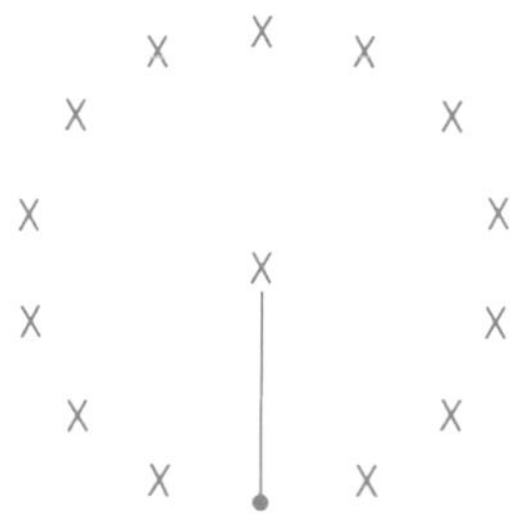

Divide the class into 4 or 5 small circles. One player with a long rope stands in the center. A soft object is tied to the free end of the rope to give it some weight. An old, deflated ball or beanbag makes a good weight (tie the rope to it and use duct tape to keep it from becoming untied). The center player turns the rope under the feet of the circle players, who must jump over it. A player who touches the rope with the feet must move up to the next group.

TEACHING TIP

Variations:

1. Change the center player after one or two misses. The center player should be cautioned to keep the rope along the ground. The rope speed can be varied. A good way to turn the rope is to sit cross-legged and turn it over the head. Different tasks can be performed such as hopping, jumping and turning, or jumping and clapping.
2. Squads line up in spoke formation. Each member does a specified number of jumps (from three to five) and then exits. The next squad member in line must come in immediately without missing a turn of the rope. A player scores a point for the squad by coming in on time, jumping the prescribed number of turns, and exiting successfully. The squad with the most points wins.
3. Couples line up in the same formation. They join inside hands and stand side by side when jumping.

KEEP 'EM MOVIN'

Supplies: Tennis balls, whiffle balls, foam balls

Skills: Body management

Formation: Scattered throughout the teaching area

Numerous tennis balls and/or whiffle balls (10–15 more than there are students) are scattered throughout the teaching area. Students are in scattered formation. On signal, students begin tapping the tennis balls with their feet or hands to get them moving or "alive." Balls may not be picked up or kicked. While the students try to keep all balls moving, the teacher looks for balls that are stationary. Once three different balls are seen not moving the teacher yells, "Dead Bugs," and all students move to their backs with their arms and legs up and moving like a bug. After several seconds, the teacher gives the start signal and the game begins again.

LOOSE CABOOSE

Supplies: None

Skills: Running, dodging

Formation:

Two or three children are designated as loose cabooses that try to hook onto a train. Trains are formed by three or four children standing in column formation with their hands placed on the shoulders of the child immediately in front. The trains, by twisting and turning, endeavor to keep the caboose form hooking onto the back. Should the caboose manage to hook on, the front child in the train becomes the new caboose. Each train should attempt to keep together. If a train breaks while being chased, they go to the side and count to 25 before reentering.

NINE LIVES

Supplies: Fleece balls

Skills: Throwing, dodging

Formation: Scattered

Any number of fleece balls can be used—the more the better. At a signal, players get a ball and hit as many people below waist level as possible. When a player counts that she has been hit nine times, she leaves the game and stands out of bounds until she has counted to 25. A player may run anywhere with a ball or to get a ball, but may possess only one ball at a time. Players must not be hit in the head. This puts the thrower out.

TEACHING TIP

Children often cheat about the number of times they have been hit. A few words about fair play may be necessary, but a high degree of activity is the important game element.

Variations:

1. For a ball caught on the fly, a designated number of hits may be taken away.
2. Either left- or right-hand throwing can be specified.

NONDA'S CAR LOT

Supplies: None

Skills: Running, dodging

Formation:

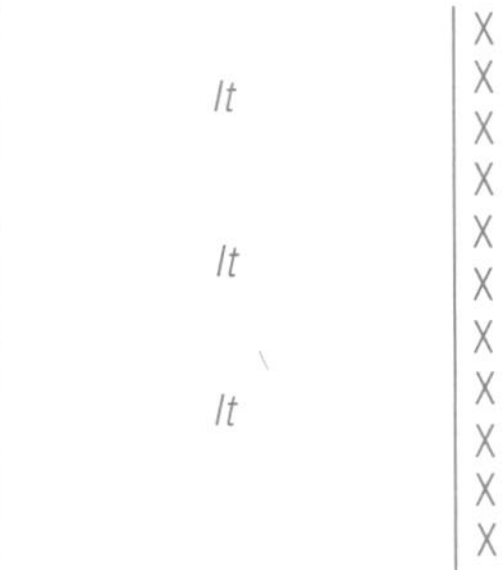

Two or three players are *it* and stand in the center of the area between two lines established at opposite ends of the playing area. The class selects four brands of cars (e.g., Honda, Corvette, Toyota, Cadillac). Each student then selects a car from the four but does not tell anyone what it is.

One of the taggers calls out a car name. All students who selected that name attempt to run to the other line without getting tagged. The tagger calls out the cars until all students have run. When a child (car) gets tagged, he must sit down at the spot of the tag. He cannot move but may tag other students who run too near. When the one who is *it* calls out "Car lot," all of the cars must go. Change taggers often.

ONE BEHIND

Supplies: None

Skills: All locomotor and nonlocomotor movements

Formation: Scattered formation

Students are instructed to watch the leader's activities and stay 1 move behind. As the leader begins an activity, the children watch. After 10–15 seconds the leader changes movements and the students begin the first leader movement. Each time the leader changes movements, the students stay "1 behind." The leader can attempt to trick students by doing an activity with her eyes closed. Thus, when the students begin this activity, they have no way of knowing when to change activities or what the preceding leader activity was.

TEACHING TIP

This activity can be done for any skills or with any piece of equipment.

ONE STEP

Supplies: A ball or beanbag for each pair of children

Skills: Throwing, catching

Formation:

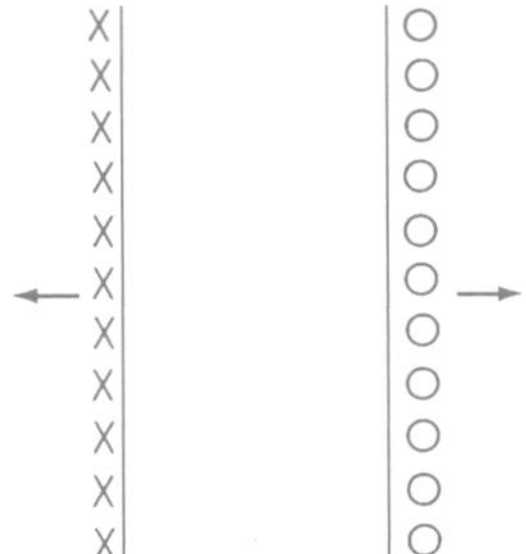

Two children stand facing each other about 3 feet apart. One has a ball or a beanbag. The object of the game is to throw or toss the item in the stipulated manner so that the partner can catch it without moving the feet on or from the ground. When the throw is completed successfully, the thrower takes one step backward and waits for the throw from her partner. Children can try to increase their distance to an established line, or the two children who move the greatest distance apart can be declared the winners. When either child misses, moves the feet, or fails to follow directions, the partners move forward and start over. Variables to provide interest and challenge are type of throw, type of catch, and kind of step. Throwing can be underhand, overhand, two-handed, under one leg, around the back, and so on. Catching can be two-handed, left-handed, right-handed, to the side, and so on. The step can be a giant step, a tiny step, a hop, a jump, or a similar movement.

TEACHING TIP

Variation: *Bowling One Step.* In groups of 4 to 6, each of the players in turn gets a chance to roll the ball at a bowling pin. A minimal distance (5 to 10 feet) is established, so that most bowlers can hit the pin on the first try. The player takes a step backward each time the pin is knocked down, and keeps rolling until he misses. The winner is the child who has moved the farthest from the pin.

PARTNER STOOP

Supplies: Music

Skills: Marching rhythmically

Formation:

The game follows the same basic principle of stooping as in Circle Stoop, but is played with partners. The group forms a double circle, with partners facing counterclockwise; one partner is on the inside, and one is on the outside. When the music begins, all march in the line of direction. After a short period of marching, a signal (whistle) is sounded, and the inside circle reverses direction and marches the other way—clockwise. The partners are thus separated. When the music stops, the outer circle stands still, and the partners making up the inner circle walk to rejoin their respective outer circle partners. As soon as children reach their partner, they join inside hands and stoop without losing balance. The last couple to stoop and those who have lost balance go to the center of the circle and wait out the next round.

Start the game walking and gradually increase the speed of movements when the class moves under control.

RICOCHET

Supplies: Foam balls, fleece balls

Skills: Ball rolling

Formation: Circle

Several foam balls are placed in the center of a large circle of students. The class is also given a number of fleece balls. On signal, the class begins rolling the fleece balls in an attempt to hit the foam balls and move them out of the circle. Children may move outside of the circle to retrieve fleece balls, but may not enter the circle. The game is over when all or most of the foam balls are out of the circle.

TEACHING TIP

1. Time the students and challenge them to beat their best class time.
2. Have several games at one time.
3. Use beach balls rather than foam balls.

SQUAD TAG

Supplies: Pinnies or markers for one squad, stopwatch

Skills: Running, dodging

Formation:

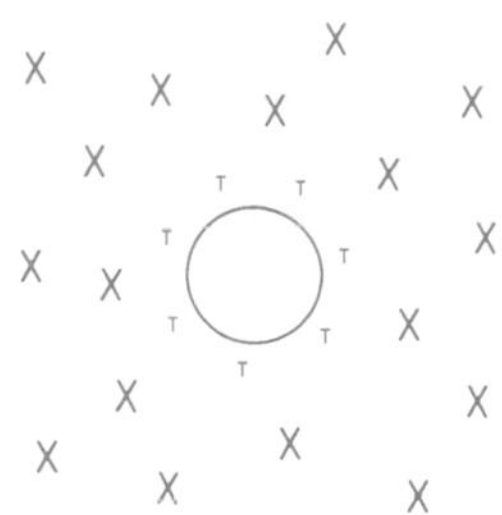

Delineate the running area with cones. An entire squad acts as taggers. The object is to see which squad can tag the remaining class members in the shorter time. The tagging squad should be marked. They stand in a football huddle formation in the center of the area with their heads down. The remainder of the class scatters as they wish throughout the area. On signal, the tagging squad scatters and tags the other class members. A class member who is tagged stops in place and remains there. Time is recorded when the last person is tagged. Each squad gets a turn at tagging.

TEACHING TIP

Children should be cautioned to move under control, because there is much chasing and dodging in different directions. Definite boundaries are needed.

STEAL THE TREASURE

Supplies: A bowling pin

Skill: Dodging

Formation:

A playing area about 20 feet square is outlined, with a small circle in the center. A bowling pin placed in the small circle (hula hoop) is the treasure. Two or more guards are selected to protect the treasure. The guards can move as far from the treasure as they like to tag a player. Anyone tagged must retire and wait for the next game. To successfully steal the treasure, a player must pick it up cleanly without getting tagged. The guards tag them when they come too near. If the treasure is knocked over by a player trying to steal it, that player must also wait out a turn. There is a delicate balance for the guards between being too far from the treasure and staying too near the treasure and never tagging anyone. If the guards tag all players, they are declared billionaires.

TEACHING TIP

Variation: *Bear and Keeper.* Instead of a treasure, a bear (seated cross-legged on the ground) is protected by two keepers. Anyone who touches the bear without being tagged becomes the new keeper.

TRADES

Supplies: None

Skills: Imagery, running, dodging

Formation:

The class is divided into two teams of equal number, each of which has a goal line on opposite sides of the area. One team, the chasers, remains behind its goal line. The other team, the runners, approaches from its goal line, marching to the following dialogue:

RUNNERS: Here we come.

CHASERS: Where from?

RUNNERS: New Orleans.

CHASERS: What's your trade?

RUNNERS: Lemonade.

CHASERS: Show us some.

Runners move up close to the other team's goal line and proceed to act out an occupation or a specific task that they have chosen previously. The opponents try to guess what the pantomime represents. On a correct guess, the running team must run back to its goal line chased by the others. Any runner tagged must join the chasers. The game is repeated with roles reversed. The team ending with the greater number of players is the winner.

TEACHING TIP

If a team has trouble guessing the pantomime, the other team should provide hints. Teams also should be encouraged to have a number of activities selected so that little time is consumed in choosing the next activity to be pantomimed.

TREES

Supplies: None

Skills: Running, dodging

Formation:

Two parallel lines are drawn at opposite ends of the playing area. All players, except 2 or 3 taggers, are on one side of the area. On the signal "Trees," the players run to the other side of the court. The taggers try to tag as many as possible. Any player tagged becomes a tree, stopping where tagged and keeping both feet in place. Trees cannot move their feet but can tag any runners who come close enough. The taggers continue to chase the players as they cross on signal until a few are left. New players are selected to be taggers.

WHISTLE MARCH

Supplies: Music

Skill: Moving rhythmically

Formation: Scattered

Brisk marching music is used with this game. Children are scattered around the room, walking in various directions and keeping time to the music. A whistle is blown a number of times. At this signal, lines are formed of that precise number of children, no more and no fewer. To form the lines, children stand side by side with locked elbows. As soon as a line of the proper number is formed, it begins to march to the music counterclockwise around the room. Any children left over go to the center of the room and remain there until the next signal. On the next whistle signal (a single blast), the lines break up, and all walk individually around the room in various directions.

When forming a new line, stipulate that children may not form the same combinations as in the previous line.

WHISTLE MIXER

Supplies: A whistle

Skills: All basic locomotor movements

Formation: Scattered

Children are scattered throughout the area. To begin, they walk around in any direction they wish. The teacher blows a whistle a number of times in succession with short, sharp blasts. Children then form small circles with the number in the circles equal to the number of whistle blasts. If there are four blasts, children form circles of four—no more, no less. The goal is not to be left out or caught in a circle with the incorrect number of students. Encourage players to move to the center of the area and raise their hands to facilitate finding others without a group. After the circles are formed, the teacher calls "Walk," and the game continues.

TEACHING TIP

Variation: Another version of this game is done with the aid of a tom-tom. Different beats indicate different locomotor movements—skipping, galloping, slow walking, normal walking, running. The whistle is still used to set the number for each circle.

WOLFE'S BEANBAG EXCHANGE

Supplies: One beanbag per child

Skills: Running, dodging, tossing, catching

Formation: Scattered

Five or six children are identified as taggers. The remaining children start scattered throughout the area, each with a beanbag in hand. The taggers chase the players with beanbags. When a tag is made, the tagged player must freeze, keeping her feet still and beanbag in hand. To unfreeze a player, a nonfrozen player can exchange his beanbag for a beanbag held by a frozen player. If two frozen players are within tossing distance, they can thaw each other by exchanging their beanbags through the air using a toss and catch. Both tosses have to be caught or the beanbags must be retrieved and tried again.

TEACHING TIP

Variation: After students have learned the game, tell the taggers that they may interfere with the tossing of beanbags between two frozen players by batting them to the floor. This forces the toss to be tried again and the players remain frozen until successful catches are made by both players.

DEVELOPMENTAL LEVEL III

Games at this level become more complex and organized. A great deal more cooperation is needed to make the activities enjoyable. In addition, an opportunity to use strategy exists, thus encouraging cognitive development. Strategy is important for successful play at this level.

AIR RAID

Supplies: 4–8 tumbling mats, fleece balls, foam balls

Skills: Throwing

Formation: Class divided into 2 teams

Two teams are placed on opposite halves of the teaching area. Each team is given 2 tumbling mats that are fastened together and set on end to form an upright cylinder or target. The target is then placed near the back wall in the center of the gym (if baskets are obstructing the flight of balls the cylinder may need to be moved). Teams are also given fleece balls and foam balls to throw. On signal, teams attempt to throw as many balls into the target as possible. The team with the most balls in at the end of the game wins.

TEACHING TIP

Variations:

1. Use two targets for each side
2. Place the target in a corner and have balls that ricochet in count a two points.
3. Allow the students to decide where to place the target.
4. Allow students to guard their target. This may require cones around the target to keep guards from colliding with the target.

BARKER'S HOOPLA

Supplies: Hoops, beanbags

Skill: Running

Formation:

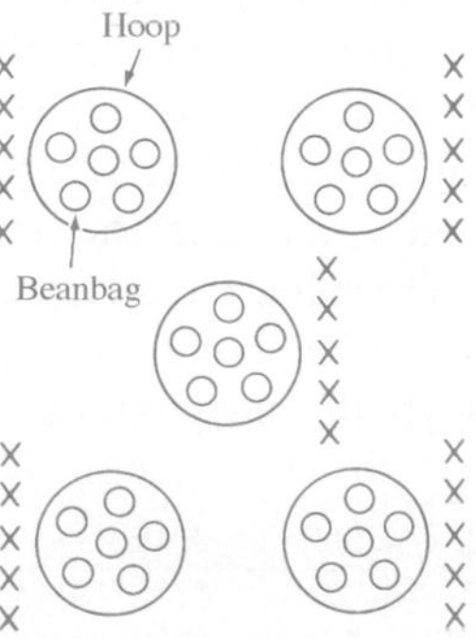

Five hoops are arranged with one in each corner and the other in the center of the playing area. Any distance between hoops can be used, but 25 to 30 feet is a challenging distance. Five to six beanbags are placed in each hoop. The class is divided into five equal teams, one group near each hoop. This is their home base. The object of the game is to steal beanbags from other hoops and return them to the hoop that is home base for each respective team. The following rules are in effect:

1. A player can take only one beanbag at a time. That player must take the beanbag to the home base before returning for another one.
2. Beanbags cannot be thrown or tossed to the home base, but must be placed on the floor in the hoop before being released.
3. No player can protect the home base or its beanbags with any defensive maneuver.
4. Beanbags may be taken from any hoop.
5. When the stop signal is given, every player must freeze immediately and release any beanbags in possession. Any follow-through of activities to get a better score is penalized.

The team with the most beanbags in their home-base hoop is declared the winner.

CAGEBALL TARGET THROW

Supplies: A cageball (18- to 30-inch), 12 to 15 smaller balls of various sizes

Skill: Throwing

Formation:

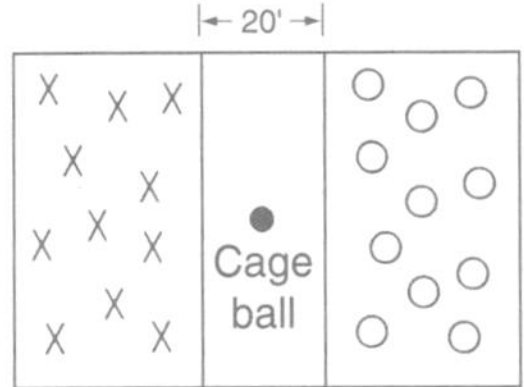

An area about 20 feet wide is marked across the center of the playing area, with a cageball in the center. The object of the game is to throw the smaller balls against the cageball, thus forcing it across the line in front of the other team. Players may come up to the line to throw, but they may not throw while inside the cageball area. A player may enter the area, however, to recover a ball. No one is to touch the cageball at any time, nor may the cageball be pushed by a ball in the hands of a player. If the cageball seems to roll too easily, it should be deflated slightly. The throwing balls can be of almost any size—soccer balls, volleyballs, playground balls, for example.

CHAIN TAG

Supplies: None

Skills: Running, dodging

Formation:

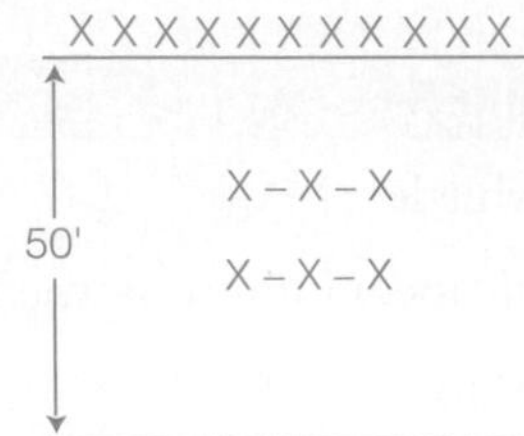

Two parallel lines are established at opposite ends of the playing area. Two groups of three players form a chain with joined hands and occupy the center. The players with free hands on either end of the chain do the tagging. All other players line up on one of the parallel lines. The players in the center call "Come on over," and children cross from one line to the other. The chains try to tag the runners. Anyone caught joins the chain. When the chain grows to six players, it divides into two groups of three players.

TEACHING TIP

Variation: *Catch of Fish.* The chain catches runners by surrounding them like a fishing net. The runners cannot run under or through the links of the net.

CIRCLE TOUCH

Supplies: Yarnballs

Skills: Dodging, body management

Formation:

One child plays against three others, who form a small circle with joined hands. The object of the game is for the lone child to touch a designated child (on the shoulders) in the circle with a yarnball. The other two children in the circle, by dodging and maneuvering, attempt to keep the tagger away from the third member of the circle. The circle players may maneuver and circle in any direction but must not release hand grips. The tagger, in attempting to touch the protected circle player, must go around the outside of the circle. He is not permitted to go underneath or through the joined hands of the circle players. To avoid roughness, the game should be played in short, 10-second bouts and then rotate in a new tagger.

TEACHING TIP

Variation: *Grab the Flag.* A piece of cloth, a handkerchief, or a flag is tucked into the belt in back of the protected child. The fourth child, the tagger, tries to pull the flag from the belt.

CLEAN-UP

Supplies: Volleyball net or magic rope, fleece balls, and/or foam balls

Skill: Throwing

Formation: Scatter formation with the class in two large groups

The gym is divided in half by a volleyball net with 1 team placed on each side of the net. Numerous fleece balls are scattered around each side of the gym (the more balls the better). On signal, students begin throwing balls over the net 1 at a time. After throwing 1 ball, students quickly find another ball and throw it over the net. This process continues until the game is stopped. The team with the fewest number of balls on their side of the gym is declared the winner.

TEACHING TIP

Variation: Scoring can be tracked individually, with children getting 1 point for each ball thrown over the net. Balls that hit the back wall are worth 2 points.

FAST PASS

Supplies: One 8-inch foam rubber ball, pinnies

Skills: Passing, catching, moving to an open area

Formation: Scattered

One team begins with the ball. The object is to complete five consecutive passes without the ball touching the floor. The team without the ball attempts to intercept the ball or recover an incomplete pass. Each time a pass is caught, the team shouts the number of consecutive passes completed. Each time a ball touches the floor or is intercepted, the count starts over.

Players may not contact each other. Emphasis should be placed on spreading out and using the entire court area. If players do not spread out, the area can be broken into quadrants and players restricted to one quadrant.

FLAG CHASE

Supplies: Flags, stopwatch

Skills: Running, dodging

Formation: Scattered

One team wears flags positioned in the back of the belt. The flag team scatters throughout the area. On signal, the object is for the chasing team to capture as many flags as possible in a designated amount of time. The flags are brought to the teacher or placed in a box. Players cannot use their hands to ward off a chaser. Roles are reversed. The team pulling the most flags is declared the winner.

FRISBEE BOWLING

Supplies: Frisbees, bowling pins

Skills: Frisbee throwing

Formation: Teams of 4

This game is played exactly like bowling with the exception that a Frisbee, rather than a bowling ball, is used. Depending on the skill level of students, the distance of the lane may also be altered.

GALACTIC EMPIRE AND REBELS

Supplies: None

Skills: Chasing, fleeing, dodging

Court markings:

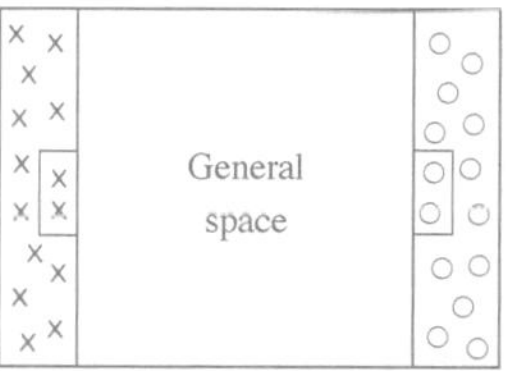

This game can be played indoors or outdoors in a square that is approximately 100 feet on each side. Each team's spaceport is behind the end line, where the single space fighters are stationed, waiting to issue against the enemy. To begin, one or more space fighters from either team move from their spaceport to entice enemy fliers for possible capture. A flyer leaving the spaceport may capture only opposing flyers who previously have left their respective spaceport. This is the basic rule of the game. A flyer may go back to her spaceport and be eligible immediately to issue again to capture an opponent who was already in general space. The technique of the game is to entice enemy flyers close to the spaceport so that fellow flyers can issue and capture (tag) an opposing flyer.

As an illustration of how the game proceeds: Rebel flyer 1 moves into general space to entice Empire flyer 1 so that he can be captured. Rebel flyer 1 turns back and heads for her spaceport, chased by Empire flyer 1. Rebel flyer 2 now leaves her spaceport and tags Empire flyer 1 before the Empire flyer can tag Rebel flyer 1. The Empire flyer is now a prisoner.

A player captured by an opposing flyer is taken to the tagger's prison—both captor and captive are given free passage to the prison. In prison, the captives form a chain gang, holding hands and extending the prisoners' line toward their own spaceport. The last captive is always at the end of the prisoners' line with one foot in the prison. Captives can be released if a teammate can get to them without being tagged. The released prisoner (only the end one) is escorted back to her own spaceport, and both players are given free passage.

The game becomes one of capturing opposing flyers and securing the release of captured teammates. Flyers stepping over the sideline automatically become prisoners. One or two players in the spaceport should be assigned to guard the prison.

Set a time limit of 10 minutes, and declare the team with the most prisoners the winner.

GUESS THE LEADER

Supplies: None

Skills: Body management

Formation:

The class forms a large circle and 2–3 people, the guessers, are chosen to be in the middle. While the guessers have their eyes closed, a leader in the circle is chosen. This person leads the class in an exercise and the guessers open their eyes and attempt to guess who the leader is. As the guessers watch the class, the leader continues to lead the class in various exercises. The guessers are watching for the student that changes first (the leader). The guessers are allowed three guesses before the leader is identified. A new leader is then identified.

JOLLY BALL

Supplies: A cageball 24 inches or larger (or a 36- to 48-inch pushball)

Skill: Kicking

Formation:

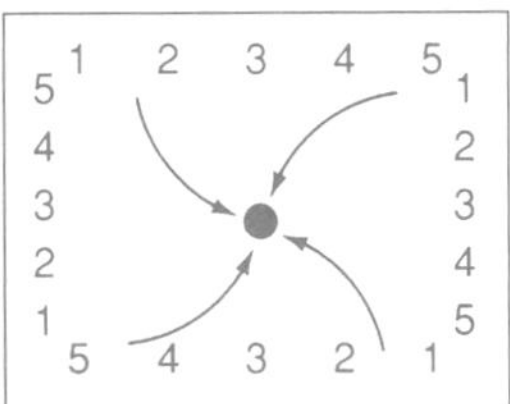

Four teams are organized, each of which forms one side of a hollow square. Children sit down, facing in, with hands braced behind them (crab position). The members of each team are numbered consecutively. Children wait until their number is called. Four active players (one from each team) move in crab position and try to kick the cageball over any one of the three opposing teams. The sideline players can also kick the ball. Ordinarily, the hands are not used, but this could be allowed in the learning stages of the game.

A point is scored against a team that allows the ball to go over its line. A ball that goes out at the corner between teams is dead and must be replayed. When a point is scored, the active children retire to their teams and another number is called. The team with the fewest points wins the game. This game is quite strenuous for the active players, so they should be rotated after a reasonable length of time when there is no score.

TEACHING TIP

Variation: Two children from each team can be active at once.

JUMP-THE-SHOT VARIATIONS

Supplies: A jump-the-shot rope

Skill: Rope jumping

Formation:

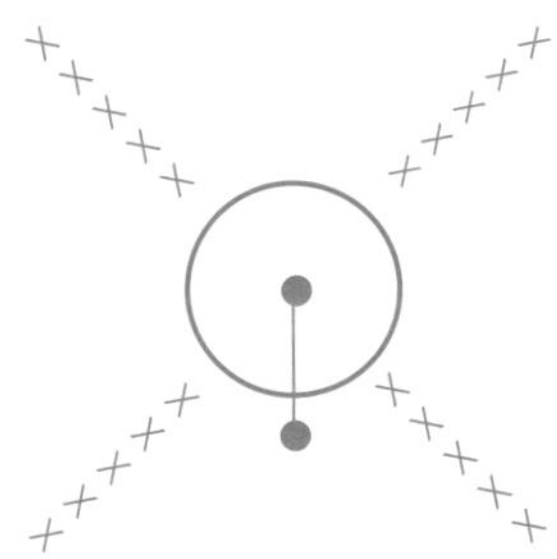

Before the following variations are tried, the jump-the-shot routines and variations listed previously (page 563) should be reviewed.

1. Two or more squads are in file formation facing the rope turner. Each player runs clockwise (against the turn of the rope), jumping the rope as often as necessary to return to the squad.
2. Each player runs counterclockwise and tries to run around the circle before the rope can catch up with him. If this happens, he must jump to allow the rope to go under him. The best time for a player to start his run is just after the rope has passed.
3. Players can try some of the stunts in which the hands and feet are on the ground, to see whether they can have the rope pass under them. The Rabbit Jump, push-up position, Lame Dog, and others are possibilities.

MUSHROOMS

Supplies: 10–16 cones, 10–16 Frisbees, fleece balls (or foam balls)

Skill: Rolling, throwing

Formation: Class divided into 2 equal teams; scattered formation

Two teams are formed with each occupying 1 half of the gym. On the end line of each half are 5–8 cones with a Frisbee balanced on top of the cone (these resemble mushrooms). Each team is also given enough foam balls for each child to have 1. On signal, team members try to roll (or throw) their balls and knock off the Frisbees. Students may not guard the cones and any Frisbee knocked off has to stay off, even if touched by a team's member. When all Frisbees have been knocked off, the game is over.

OCTOPUS

Supplies: None

Skills: Maneuvering, problem solving

Formation: Groups of six to nine, holding hands, tangled

Octopus is a game that gets its name from the many hands joined together in the activity. Children stand shoulder to shoulder in a tight circle. Everyone thrusts the hands forward and reaches through the group of hands to grasp the hands across the circle. Players must make sure that they do not hold both hands of the same player. Players also may not hold the hand of an adjacent player. The object is to untangle the mess created by the joined hands by going under, over, or through fellow players. No one is permitted to release a hand grip during the unraveling. What is the end result? Perhaps one large circle or two smaller connected circles.

TEACHING TIP

If, after a period of time, the knotted hands do not seem to unravel, call a halt and administer first aid. The teacher and group can decide where the difficulty is and allow a change in position of those hands until the knot is dissolved. This is a cooperative game that demands teamwork.

ONE-BASE TAGBALL

Supplies: A base (or standard), a volleyball (8-inch foamball for younger children)

Skills: Running, dodging, throwing

Formation:

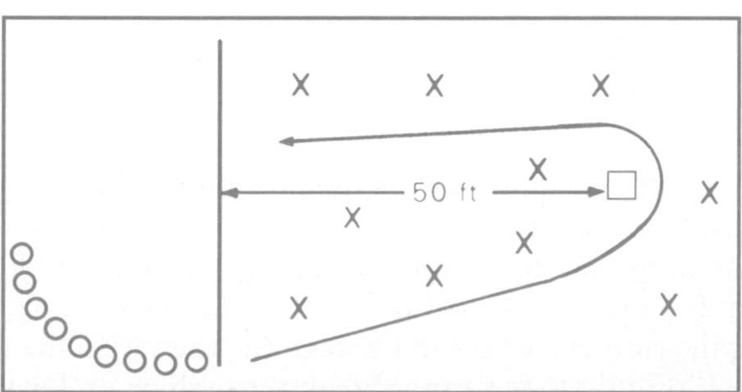

A home line is drawn at one end of the playing space. A base or standard is placed about 50 feet in front of the home line. Two teams are formed. One team is scattered around the fielding area, the boundaries of which are determined by the number of children. The other team is lined up in single file behind the home line.

The object of the game is for the fielding team to tag the runners with the ball. Two runners at a time try to round the base and head back for the home line without being tagged. The game is continuous, meaning that as soon as a running team player is tagged or crosses the home line, another player starts immediately.

The fielding team may run with the ball and pass it from player to player, trying to tag one of the runners. The running team scores a point for each player who runs successfully around the base and back to the home line.

At the start of the game, the running team has two players ready at the right side of the home line. The others on the team are in line, waiting for a turn. The teacher throws the ball anywhere in the field, and the first two runners start toward the base. They must run around the base from the right side. After all of the players have run, the teams exchange places. The team scoring the most points wins.

TEACHING TIP

To facilitate tagging a runner, players on the fielding team should make passes to a person close to the runner. They must be alert, because two children at a time are running. The next player on the running team must watch carefully in order to start the instant one of the two preceding runners is back safely behind the line or has been hit.

OVER THE WALL

Supplies: None

Skills: Running, dodging

Formation:

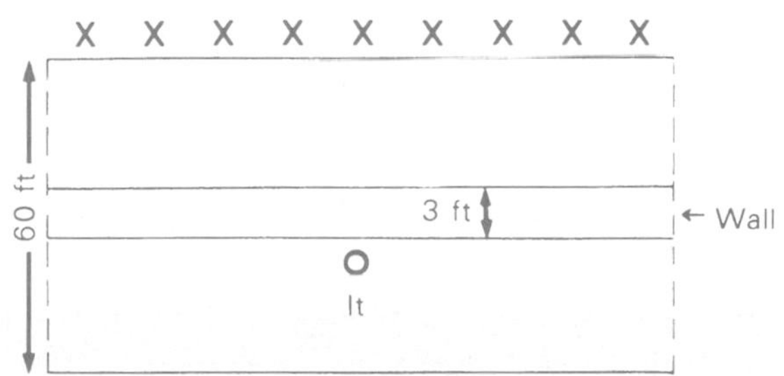

Two parallel goal lines are drawn about 60 feet apart. Two additional parallel lines about 3 feet apart are laid out parallel to the goal lines in the middle of the game area. This is the wall. Two or three players are *it* and stand on, or behind, the wall. All of the other players are behind one of the goal lines. One of the taggers calls "Over the wall." All of the players must then run across the wall to the other goal line. The taggers try to tag any crossing players. Anyone caught helps catch the others. Players also are considered caught when they step on the wall. They must clear it with a leap or a jump and cannot step on it anywhere, including on the lines. After crossing over to the other side safely, players wait for the next call. The game can be made more difficult by increasing the width of the wall. Taggers can step on or run through the wall at will.

PACMAN

Supplies: Markers in the shape of Pacman

Skills: Fleeing, reaction time

Formation:

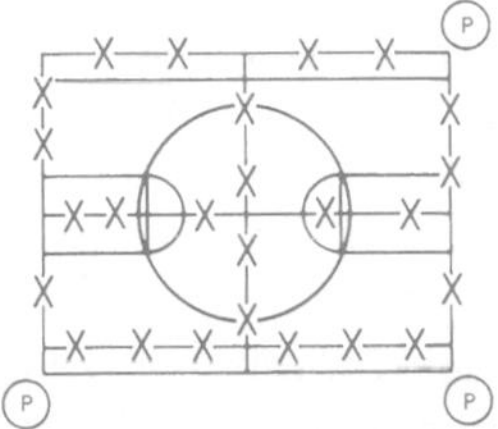

Three students are *it* and carry the Pacman marker. The remainder of the class is scattered throughout the area, standing on a floor line. Movement can only be made on a line. Begin the game by placing the three taggers at the corners of the perimeter lines. Play is continuous; a player who is tagged takes the marker and becomes a new tagger. If a player leaves a line to escape being tagged, that player must secure a marker and become an additional tagger. Tagbacks are not allowed; that is, players may not tag the person who tagged them.

PARTNER DOG AND CAT

Supplies: None

Skill: Chasing, fleeing, dodging

Formation: Partners

Partners stand toe to toe on a line in the center of the gym. Partner A begins the game by saying "Dog." Partner B can then say "Dog" or "Cat." If partner B says "Cat," she is chased to a designated line by Partner A. If partner A tags partner B, partner A gets a point and the game starts over.

TEACHING TIP

Try varying the number of "dogs" that must be said before "cat" can be called out. Usually 4 or 5 "dogs" will make the game more enjoyable for partners.

PIN KNOCKOUT

Supplies: Many playground balls, 12 bowling pins

Skills: Rolling, dodging

Formation:

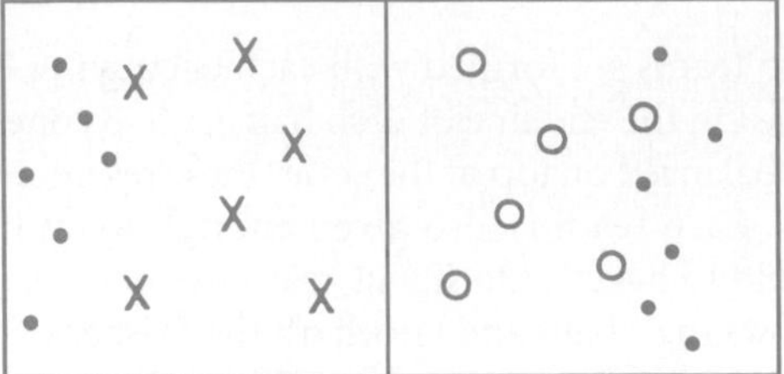

Two teams of equal number play the game. Each team is given many playground balls and six bowling pins. A court 30 by 60 feet or larger with a centerline is needed. The size of the court depends on the number of children in the game. The object of the game is to knock down all of the opponents' bowling pins. The balls are used for rolling at the opposing team's pins. Each team stays in its half of the court.

A player is eliminated if any of the following occurs:

1. He is touched by any ball at any time, regardless of the situation (other than picking up a ball).
2. She steps over the centerline to roll or retrieve a ball. (Any opposing team member hit as a result of such a roll is not eliminated.)
3. He attempts to block a rolling ball with a ball in his hands and the rolling ball touches him in any manner.

A foul is called when a player holds a ball longer than 10 seconds without rolling at the opposing team. Play stops, and the ball is given to the opposing team.

The bowling pins are put anywhere in the team's area. Players may guard the pins, but must not touch them. When a pin is down, even though it might have been knocked over unintentionally by a member of the defending team, it is removed immediately from the game. The game is over when all pins on one side have been knocked down.

RIGHT FACE, LEFT FACE (STREETS AND ALLEYS)

Supplies: None

Skills: Running, dodging

Formation:

X X X X
X X X X
X X X X
X X X X

Children stand in rows that are aligned both from front to rear and from side to side. Two runners and two chasers are chosen. Players all face the same way and join hands with the players on each side. The chasers try to tag the runners, who run between the rows with the restriction that they cannot break through or under the arms. The teacher can help the runners by calling "Right face" or "Left face" at the proper time. On command, the children drop hands, face the new direction, and grasp hands with those who are then on each side, thus making new passages available. When the runner is caught or when children become tired, new runners and chasers are chosen.

TEACHING TIP

Variations:

1. Directions (north, south, east, west) can be used instead of the facing commands.
2. *Streets and Alleys.* The teacher calls, "Streets," and the children face in one direction. The call "Alleys" causes them to face at right angles.
3. The command "Air raid" can be given, and children drop to their knees and make themselves into small balls, tucking their heads and seats down. This allows unlimited movement by the taggers and runners.

SCOOTER KICKBALL

Supplies: A cageball, gym scooters for active players

Skill: Striking with various body parts

Formation:

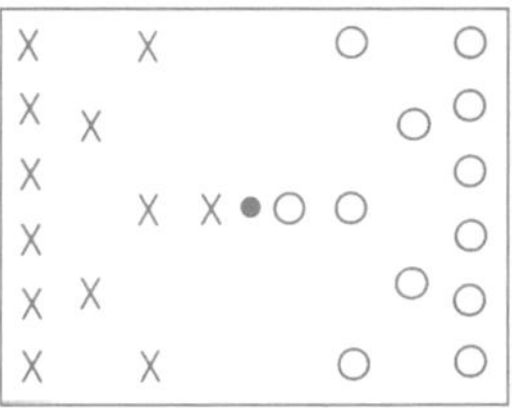

Divide each team into active players (on scooters) and goal defenders. The active players are seated on the scooters, and the goal defenders are seated on the goal line, with feet extended. The object of the game is to kick the cageball over the goal line defended by the opposite team. The players are positioned as shown above.

The game starts with a face-off of two opposing players on scooters at the center of the court. The face-off is also used after a goal is scored. The active players on scooters propel the ball mainly with their feet. Touching the ball with the hands is a foul and results in a free kick by the opposition at the spot of the foul. A player also may use the head and body to stop and propel the ball.

The players defending the goal are seated on the goal line. They may not use their hands either, but use of the feet, body, and head is permitted. (If scoring seems too easy, then the defenders can be allowed to use their hands.) Defenders should be restricted to the seated position at the goal line and are not permitted to enter the field of play to propel or stop the ball.

TEACHING TIP

The number of scooters determines the number of active players. The game works well if half of the players from each team are in the center on scooters and the other half are goal defenders. After a goal or after a stipulated time period, active players and goal defenders exchange places. Any active player who falls off a scooter should be required to sit again on the scooter before becoming eligible to propel the ball.

TEACHING TIP

Variation: If there are enough scooters for everyone, the game can be played with rules similar to soccer. A more restricted goal (perhaps half of the end line) can be marked with standards. A goalie defends this area. All other players are active and can move to any spot on the floor. The floor space should be large enough to allow some freedom of play.

STAR WARS

Supplies: Four bowling pins

Skill: Running

Formation:

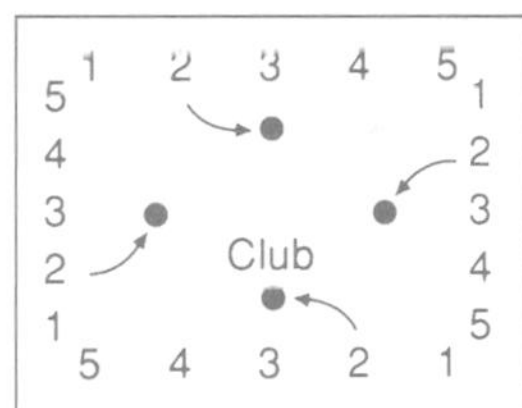

Four teams, each of which occupies one side facing in, form a hollow square, about 10 yards on each side. Members of each team are numbered consecutively from right to left. This means that one person on each team has the same number as one player on each of the other three teams. At the center of the square, place four bowling pins, one in front of each team and placed apart so as to avoid collisions of players.

When a number is called, the four children with that number run to the right, around the square, and through their own vacated space to the center of the square. The first child to lay the team bowling pin down on the floor is the winner.

Scoring is kept by letters in the words *Star Wars.* The player who puts the pin down first receives two letters while the second player gets one letter. The first team to spell *Star Wars* is the winner and a new game begins. Since numbers are not called in order, keep a tally to make sure every number is called.

STRIKE THE PINS

Supplies: 8 to 12 bowling pins per team, 15 to 20 foam-rubber balls

Skill: Throwing

Formation:

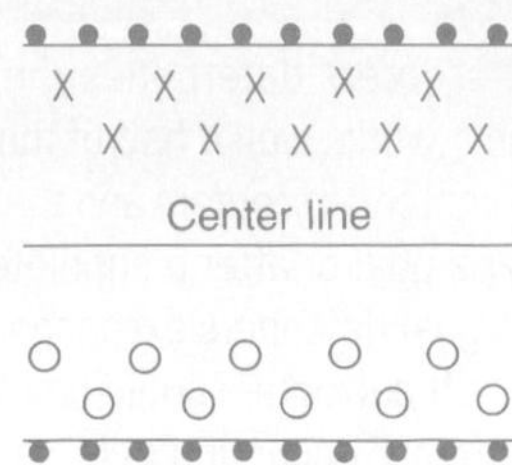

A line is drawn across the center of the floor wall to wall. This divides the floor into two courts, each of which is occupied by one team. Another line is drawn 25 feet from the centerline in each court. This is the line where each team spaces its bowling pins. Each team has at least five balls. The object of the game is to knock over the other team's pins by rolling the balls. Players roll the balls back and forth, but cannot cross the centerline. Whenever a pin is knocked over by a ball or player (accidentally or not), that pin is removed. The team with the most pins standing at the end of the game is declared the winner. Out-of-bounds balls can be recovered but must be rolled from inside the court.

TEACHING TIP

Variation: Pins can be reset instead of removed. Two scorers, one for each pin line, are needed.

SUNDAY

Supplies: None

Skills: Running, dodging

Formation:

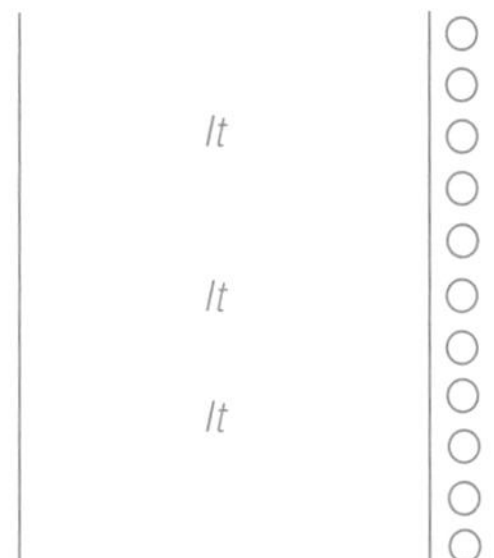

Two parallel lines are drawn at each end of the playing area. Three or more players are *it* and stand in the center of the area between the two lines. The rest of the class is on one of the two lines. The object is to cross to the other line without being tagged or making a false start.

All line players stand with their front foot on the line. The line players must run across the line immediately when the tagger calls "Sunday." Anyone who does not run immediately is considered caught. The tagger can call other days of the week to confuse the runners. No player may make a start if another day of the week is called.

TEACHING TIP

"Making a start" must be defined clearly. To begin, it can be defined as a player moving either foot. Later, when children get better at the game, any forward movement of the body can constitute a start.

TOUCHDOWN

Supplies: A small object (coin, thimble) that can be concealed in the hand

Skills: Running, dodging

Formation:

Two parallel lines are placed at each end of the playing area. Two teams face each other, each standing on one of the parallel lines. One team (offensive) huddles and the members decide which player is to carry an object to the opponents' goal line. The offensive team moves out of the huddle and spreads out along the line. On the signal "Hike," the offensive players move toward the opponents' goal line, each player holding the hands closed as if carrying the object. On the charge signal, the opponents (defense) also run forward and try to tag the players. On being tagged, players must stop immediately and open both hands to show whether or not they have the object. If the player carrying the object reaches the goal line without being tagged, that player calls "Touchdown," and scores 6 points. The defensive team now goes on the offense.

TRIPLET STOOP

Supplies: Music

Skill: Moving rhythmically

Formation:

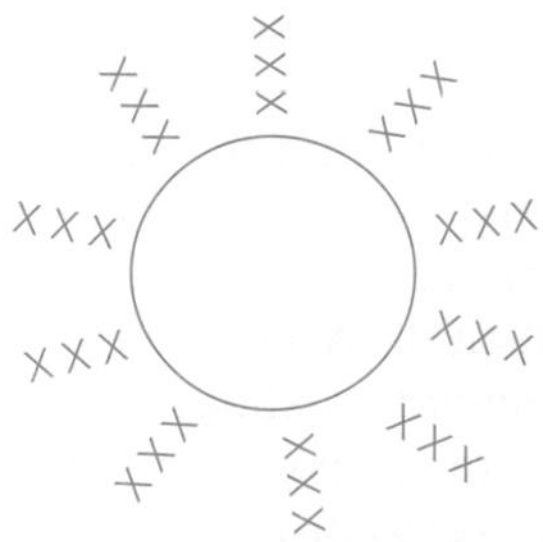

The game is played in groups of three with the three youngsters marching abreast in the same direction. On signal, the outside player of the three continues marching in the same direction. The middle player stops and marches in place. The inside player reverses direction. When the music stops, the groups of three attempt to reunite at the spot where the middle player stopped. The last three to join hands and stoop move to the center to wait out one turn.

WHISTLE BALL

Supplies: A ball for each group of six to eight players

Skills: Passing, catching

Formation: Circles of six to eight

Eight or fewer children stand in circle formation. A ball is passed rapidly back and forth among them in any order. The object is to stay in the game as long as possible. A player sits down in place after making any of the following errors:

1. A player has the ball or the ball is on the way when the signal occurs. (Time intervals can be signaled with music on—music off, taped in segments of 5 to 15 seconds.)
2. A poor throw is made or a catch is not made after a catchable throw.
3. A pass is made back to the person from whom it was received.

TEACHING TIP

Another way to control the time periods is to appoint a child as timer and to give her a list of the time periods, a whistle, and a stopwatch. The timer should be cautioned not to give any advance indication of when the stop signal will be blown. Restart the game when there are four or five players left standing so no one sits out for too long.

MISCELLANEOUS PLAYGROUND GAMES

The following games are useful only for small groups, but children do enjoy playing them on the playground.

Suggested Games

Four Square
Frisbee Golf (disk golf)
Team Handball
Tetherball
Two Square
Volley Tennis

FOUR SQUARE

(Developmental Levels II and III)

Supplies: 8-inch playground ball or volleyball

Skill: Batting a ball

Court markings:

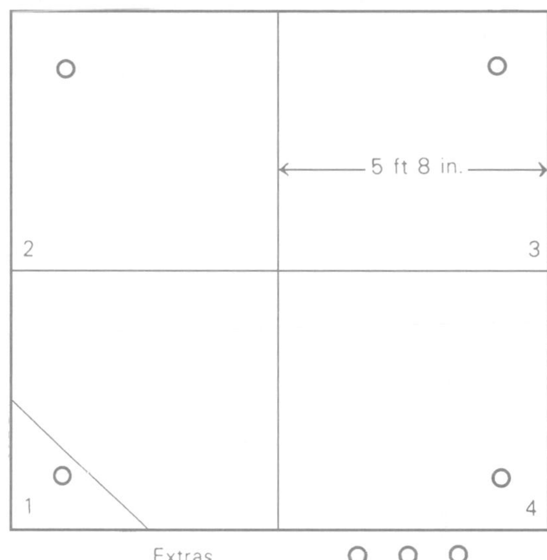

Lines are drawn as shown above. The squares should be numbered 1, 2, 3, and 4. A service line is drawn diagonally across the far corner of square 1. The player in this square always serves and must stay behind the line when serving.

The ball is served by dropping and serving it underhanded from the bounce. If the serve hits a line, the server is out. The server can hit the ball after it has bounced once in his square. The receiver directs it to any other square with an underhand hit. Play continues until one player fails to return the ball or commits a fault. Any of the following constitutes a fault:

1. hitting the ball sidearm or overhand
2. landing a ball on a line between the squares (A ball landing on an outer boundary is considered good.)
3. stepping into another square to play the ball
4. catching or carrying a return volley
5. allowing the ball to touch any part of the body except the hands

A player who misses or commits a fault goes to the end of the waiting line and all players move up. The player at the head of the waiting line moves into square 4.

TEACHING TIP

Variations:

1. A 2-foot circle can be drawn at the center of the area. Hitting the ball into the circle constitutes a fault.

2. The game can be changed by varying the method of propelling the ball. The server sets the method. The ball can be hit with a partially closed fist, the back of the hand, or the elbow. A foot or knee also can be used to return the ball. The server calls "Fisties," "Elbows," "Footsies," or "Kneesies" to set the pattern.
3. *Chain Spelling.* The server names a word, and each player returning the ball must add the next letter in the sequence.
4. Hula Hoops can be used so that all students can play at one time.
5. Cooperative scoring can be used with Level I students to see how many consecutive hits they can make without missing.

FRISBEE GOLF

Supplies: One Frisbee per person, hoops for hole markers, cones

Skills: Frisbee throwing for accuracy

Suggested golf course design:

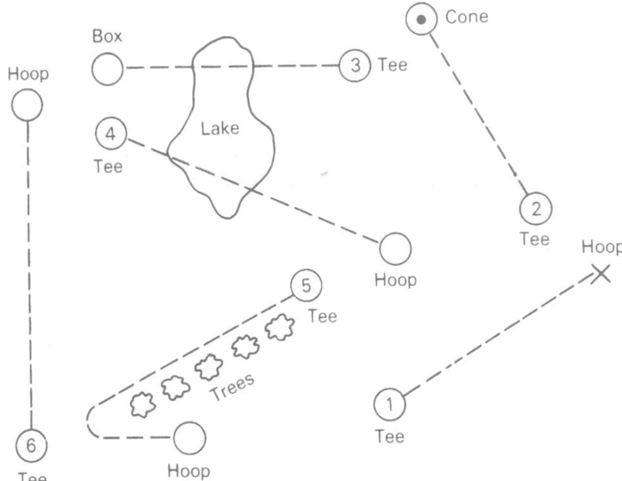

Frisbee Golf or disk golf is a favorite game of many students. Boundary cones with numbers can be used for tees, and holes can be boxes, hula hoops, trees, tires, garbage cans, or any other available equipment on the school grounds. Draw a course on a map for students and start them at different holes to decrease the time spent waiting to tee off. Regulation golf rules apply. The students can jog between throws for increased activity.

Disk golf is played like regular golf. One stroke is counted for each time the disk is thrown and when a penalty is incurred. The object is to acquire the lowest score. The following rules dictate play:

Tee-throws: Tee-throws must be completed within or behind the designated tee area.

Lie: The lie is the spot on or directly underneath the spot where the previous throw landed.

Throwing order: The player whose disk is the farthest from the hole throws first. The player with the least number of throws on the previous hole tees off first.

Fairway throws: Fairway throws must be made with the foot closest to the hole on the lie. A run-up is allowed.

Dog leg: A dog leg is one or more designated trees or poles in the fairway that must be passed on the outside when approaching the hole. There is a two-stroke penalty for missing a dog leg.

Putt throw: A putt throw is any throw within 10 feet of the hole. A player may not move past the point of the lie in making the putt throw. Falling or jumping putts are not allowed.

Unplayable lies: Any disk that comes to rest 6 feet or more above the ground is unplayable. The next throw must be played from a new lie directly underneath the unplayable lie (one-stroke penalty).

Out-of-bounds: A throw that lands out-of-bounds must be played from the point at which the disk went out (one-stroke penalty).

Course courtesy: Do not throw until the players ahead are out of range.

Completion of hole: A disk that comes to rest in the hole (box or hoop) or strikes the designated hole (tree or pole) constitutes successful completion of that hole.

TEAM HANDBALL

Supplies: Team handball, foam rubber ball, or volleyball; cones; pinnies

Skills: Running, dribbling, passing, throwing, catching

Court markings:

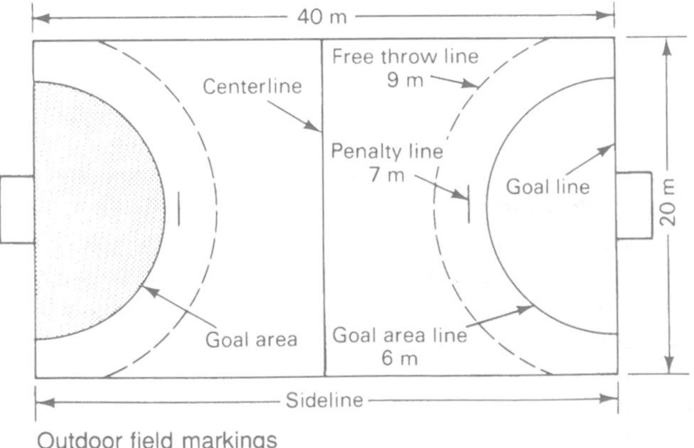

Outdoor field markings

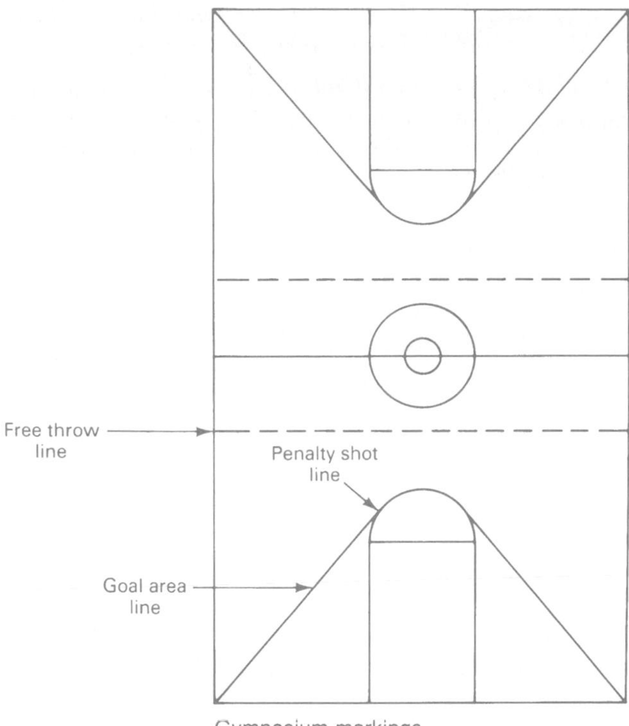

Gymnasium markings

The court is marked with a 6-meter goal area, a 7-meter penalty line, and a 9-meter free-throw line. The goal is 2 by 3 meters. The goal area inside the 6-meter line is only for the goalie. Other players are not allowed in this area. The 7-meter line is used for a major penalty shot, and the 9-meter line is used for a minor penalty shot. A regulation court is 20 by 40 meters. Boundary cones, tape on the wall, rope through a chain-link fence, soccer goals, or field hockey goals can be substituted for actual team handball goals. For indoor play, a basketball court can be modified for team handball by running a line from the corners of the court to top of the key.

The object of the game is to move a small soccer ball down the field by passing and dribbling and then to throw the ball into a goal area that is 3 meters wide and 2 meters high. In regulation play, each team has six court players and one goalie. The six court players cover the entire court. A player is allowed three steps before and after dribbling the ball. There is no limit on the number of dribbles. Dribbling is, however, discouraged because passing is more effective. A double dribble is a violation. A player can hold the ball for 3 seconds only before passing, dribbling, or shooting. Players cannot kick the ball in any way, except the goalie.

One point is awarded for a goal. Violations and penalties are similar to basketball. A free throw is taken from the point of the violation, and defense must remain 3 meters away while protecting the goal. A penalty throw is awarded from the 7-meter line for a major violation. A major violation occurs when an offensive player who is inside the 9-meter line in a good shooting position is fouled. During a penalty throw, all players must be behind the 9-meter line.

For more in-depth coverage of rules, a rulebook can be secured from the United States Team Handball Federation, 1750 E. Boulder, Colorado Springs, CO 80909.

The offensive team starts the game with a throw-on from the center line. A throw-on also initiates play after each goal. All six offensive players line up at the centerline, and a teammate throws the ball to a teammate. The defense is in position, using either a zone or person-to-person defense. Offensive strategy is similar to basketball with picks, screens, rolls, and movement to open up shots on the goal. With a zone defense, short, quick passes are made in an overloaded portion of the zone.

The defensive strategy is similar to basketball, with person-to-person and zone defense being popular. Beginning players should start with the person-to-person defense and learn how to stay with an offensive player. The back players in the zone are back against the goal line, while the front players are just inside the 9-meter line. The zone rotates with the ball as passes are made around the court.

TEACHING TIP

Learning stations can be set up for passing, shooting, goal tending, dribbling, and defensive work. Performance objectives are useful for structuring practice time at each station. Students can play with nerf balls, playground balls, and volleyballs to get more practice attempts and to help beginning goalies perfect their skills. Group drills from basketball are applicable to team handball defense, offense, passing, and dribbling. Various instructional devices can be included for targets in passing, timing for dribbling through cones, or narrowing the goal area for shots to the corners. Penalty shots should be practiced. Competitive-type drills are enjoyable and motivating for most students.

Variation: *Sideline Team Handball.* This game can be played when space is limited and too many students are in a class. Extra team members spread out along each sideline. These sideline players can receive passes from teammates and can help pass the ball down the court. Sideline members can only pass the ball, however, and the 3-second rule applies to them. One sideline can be one team, and the other sideline the other team. A challenging variation might have different team members on each sideline. This distribution forces the active players to sharpen their passing skills.

TETHERBALL

(Developmental Levels II and III)

Supplies: A tetherball assembly (pole, rope, and ball)

Skill: Batting a ball

Court markings:

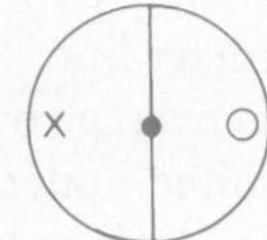

The first server is picked by lot. One player stands on each side of the pole. The server puts the ball into play by tossing it into the air and hitting in the direction he chooses. The opponent must not strike the ball on the first swing around the pole. On its second swing around the pole, she hits the ball back in the opposite direction. As the ball is hit back and forth, each player tries to hit it so that the rope winds completely around the pole in the direction in which he is hitting the ball. The game is won by the player who succeeds in doing this or whose opponent forfeits the game by making a foul. A foul is any of the following:

1. hitting the ball with any part of the body other than the hands or forearms
2. catching or holding the ball during play
3. touching the pole
4. hitting the rope with the forearms or hands
5. throwing the ball
6. winding the ball around the pole below the 5-foot mark

After the opening game, the winner of the preceding game serves. Winning four games wins the set.

TWO SQUARE

(Developmental Levels II and III)

Supplies: A playground ball or volleyball

Skill: Batting a ball

The basic rules and lines are the same as for Four Square, except that only two squares are used. If there are players waiting for a turn, the active player who misses or fouls can be eliminated as in Four Square. If only two players wish to play, score can be kept. The ball must be served from behind the baseline.

VOLLEY TENNIS

Supplies: A volleyball

Skills: Most volleyball skills

Formation: Scattered

The game can be played as a combination of volleyball and tennis. The net is put on the ground, as in tennis, and the ball is put into play with a serve. It may bounce once or can be passed directly to a teammate. The ball must be hit three times before going over the net. Spiking is common because of the low net. A point is scored when the ball cannot be returned over the net to the opposing team.

FOR MORE INFORMATION

References and Suggested Readings

Morris, G. S. D., & Stiel, J. (1999). *Changing kids' games* (2nd ed.). Champaign, IL: Human Kinetics.

SECTION 7

Sport Skills

CHAPTER 23

Basketball

ESSENTIAL COMPONENTS

I	**Organized around content standards**
II	**Student-centered and developmentally appropriate**
III	**Physical activity and motor skill development form the core of the program**
IV	**Teaches management skills and self-discipline**
V	**Promotes inclusion of all students**
VI	**Focuses on process over product**
VII	Promotes lifetime personal health and wellness
VIII	**Teaches cooperation and responsibility and promotes sensitivity to diversity**

PHYSICAL EDUCATION STANDARDS

1	**Students are able to move competently using a variety of fundamental and specialized motor skills.**
2	Students can monitor and maintain a health-enhancing level of physical fitness.
3	**Students are able to apply movement concepts and basic mechanics of skill performance when learning and refining motor skills.**
4	Students comprehend the basic principles of wellness and are able to apply concepts that enable them to make meaningful decisions that positively impact their health and wellness.
5	**Students participate in a wide variety of physical activities and learn how to maintain a personalized active lifestyle.**
6	**Students demonstrate empathy, understanding, and respect for the numerous differences exhibited by people in an activity setting.**
7	**Students exhibit responsible and self-directed behaviors that lead to positive social interactions in physical activity.**

SUMMARY

Skills instruction for basketball is introduced primarily during the intermediate grades after youngsters have mastered the basic prerequisite skills. The teaching of rules and strategies for basketball should be an integral part of the instructional process. Using proper progression is a key to success when teaching fundamental skills and lead-up games associated with basketball. Lead-up games provide an opportunity to emphasize development of selected basketball skills in a setting that is compatible with the ability of participants.

OUTCOMES

- Structure learning experiences efficiently with respect to appropriate formations, progressions, and coaching techniques.
- Know the basic rules of basketball.
- Develop a unit plan and lesson focus for basketball.
- Identify safety precautions associated with teaching basketball.
- Describe essential elements for a successful lead-up game.
- Cite assessment procedures for evaluating basketball skills.

Basketball is an activity enjoyed by many American boys and girls. The reinforcement offered when a basket is made renders it an attractive game, and this, when coupled with the impact that basketball has on the participants' cardiorespiratory system, makes it a strong contributor to the total curriculum. Basketball instruction in the elementary school focuses on developing skills and competence so students can participate later in life. Often, elementary basketball programs have sought to develop future high school stars with little concern for less talented youngsters. Place emphasis on lead-up games that allow all students to experience success and enjoyment.

With emphasis on instruction and skill development in the physical education setting, little time is available for regulation basketball during school hours. More skilled and interested students should be given additional opportunities through intramural programs, recreational leagues (such as the Youth Basketball Association), or an educationally sound interschool competitive league.

Modifying equipment used by elementary school children is important. Smaller balls and lower baskets help develop technically correct patterns, increase the success of the participants, and maintain motivation. It is impossible for youngsters to practice the ball control drills if the ball is too large for their hands.

INSTRUCTIONAL EMPHASIS AND SEQUENCE

Table 23.1 (page 582) shows the sequence of basketball activities divided into two developmental levels. In most cases, youngsters are not ready to participate in the activities in this chapter until the age of 8.

Developmental Level II

Little emphasis is placed on regulation basketball at this level. Concentration is placed on the fundamental skills of passing, catching, shooting, and dribbling. Lead-up games such as Birdies in the Cage, Circle Guard and Pass, and Basketball Tag allow participants to learn skills in a setting that offers both enjoyment and success. Movement of players is somewhat limited, which increases the opportunity for a positive experience. As children mature at this level, a goal should be to develop a range of skills, including passing, catching, dribbling, and shooting. The lay-up shot and the one-hand push shot should receive instructional attention. Captain Ball adds elements of simple defense, jump balls, and accurate passing.

Developmental Level III

A number of lead-up activities are introduced at this level. Shooting games, such as Twenty-One and Freeze Out, become favorites. Sideline Basketball and Captain Basketball offer meaningful competition. Continued practice on fundamental skills is necessary to ensure a good base of motor development. Drills to enhance skill performance are used, and rules for regulation basketball are presented. Teach officiating so youngsters can learn to appreciate the importance and difficulty of refereeing. Allow players to conduct some games through self-officiating.

BASKETBALL SKILLS

Basketball skills at the elementary level are divided into the following categories: passing, catching, dribbling, shooting, defending, stopping, and pivoting. Feinting should be taught as part of the passing, dribbling, and offensive maneuvers.

Passing

Certain factors are common to all passes regardless of which pass is used. For firm control, the ball should be handled with the thumb and finger pads, not with the palms of the hands. The passer should step forward in the direction of the receiver. Passes should be made with a quick arm extension and a snap of the wrists, with thumbs and fingers providing momentum. After the pass is released, the palms should be facing the floor. Passers should avoid telegraphing the direction of the pass. They should learn to use peripheral vision and keep their eyes moving from place to place to develop an awareness of their teammates' positions. At the same time, they should anticipate the spot toward which a teammate will be moving to receive the pass.

The following are instructional cues that can be used to help students focus on proper performance of passing.

1. Fingers spread with thumbs behind the ball.
2. Elbows in; extend through the ball.
3. Step forward, extend arms, and rotate hands slightly inward.
4. Throw at chest level to the receiver.
5. For bounce passes, bounce the ball past the halfway point nearer the receiver.

Chest (or Two-Hand) Pass

For the chest, or two-hand, pass, one foot is ahead of the other, with the knees flexed slightly. The ball is released at chest level, with the fingers spread on each side of the ball (Figure 23.1 on page 583). Pass the ball by extending the arms and snapping the wrists as one foot moves toward the receiver (Figure 23.2 on page 583).

TABLE 23.1 Suggested basketball program

Developmental Level II	Developmental Level III
Skills	
Passing	
Chest pass	All passes to moving targets
Baseball pass	Two-hand overhead pass
One-hand push pass	Long passes
Bounce pass	Three-player weave
Underhand pass	
Two-hand overhead pass	
Catching	
Above the waist	While moving
Below the waist	
Dribbling	
Standing and moving	Figure eight
Down and back	Pivoting
Right and left hands	Individual dribbling skills
Shooting	
One-hand (set) push shot	Free-throw shot
Lay-up, right and left	Jump shot
Defending and stopping	
Pivoting	Parallel stop
Feinting	Stride stop

Developmental Level II	Developmental Level III
Knowledge	
Dribbling	Held ball
Violations	Personal fouls
Traveling	Holding
Out-of-bounds	Hacking
Double dribbling	Charging
	Blocking
	Pushing
	Conducting the game
	Officiating
Activities	
Circle Guard and Pass	Quadrant Basketball
Basketball Tag	Sideline Basketball
Dribblerama	Twenty-One
Birdies in the Cage	Lane Basketball
Captain Ball	Freeze Out
Around the Key	Flag Dribble
Five Passes	Through the Maze
Captain Basketball	One-Goal Basketball
	Basketball Snatch Ball
	Three-on-Three
	Basketrama
	Paper Clip Basketball
Skill Tests	
Dribble	Figure-eight dribble
	Wall pass test
	Baskets per minute
	Free throws

Baseball (or One-Hand) Pass

For the baseball, or one-hand, pass, the passer imitates the action of a baseball catcher throwing the ball to second base. The body weight shifts from the back to the front foot. Sidearm motion should be avoided, because it puts an improper spin on the ball. Figure 23.3 shows a left-hander throwing the pass.

One-Hand Push Pass

For a one-hand push pass, the passer holds the ball with both hands but supports the ball more with the left than with the right, which is a little back of the ball. The ball is pushed forward, with a quick wrist snap, by the right hand.

Bounce Passes

Any of the preceding passes can be adapted to a bounce pass. The object is to get the pass to the receiver on the first bounce, with the ball coming to the receiver's outstretched hands at about waist height. Some experimentation determines the distance. The ball should be bounced a little more than halfway between the two players to make it come efficiently to the receiver.

Underhand Pass

For a two-hand underhand pass, the ball should be held to one side in both hands, with the foot on the opposite side toward the receiver. The ball is "shoveled" toward the receiver and a step is made with the leading foot

FIGURE 23.1 Ready for a chest push pass.

(Figure 23.4). The one-hand underhand pass is made like an underhand toss in baseball.

Two-Hand Overhead Pass

The two-hand overhead pass is effective against a shorter opponent. The passer is in a short stride posi-

FIGURE 23.2 Chest push pass.

FIGURE 23.3 Baseball pass.

tion, with the ball held overhead (Figure 23.5, page 584). The momentum of the pass comes from a forceful wrist and finger snap. The pass should take a slightly downward path.

Catching

Receiving the ball is a most important fundamental skill. Many turnovers involve failure to handle a pass properly. The receiver should move toward the pass with the fingers spread and relaxed, reaching for the ball with elbows bent and wrists relaxed. The hands should give as the ball comes in.

Instructional cues for catching include the following:

1. Move to the ball.
2. Spread the fingers and catch with the fingertips.
3. Reach for the ball.
4. Give with the ball (absorb the force of the ball by reaching and bringing the ball to the chest).

FIGURE 23.4 Underhand pass.

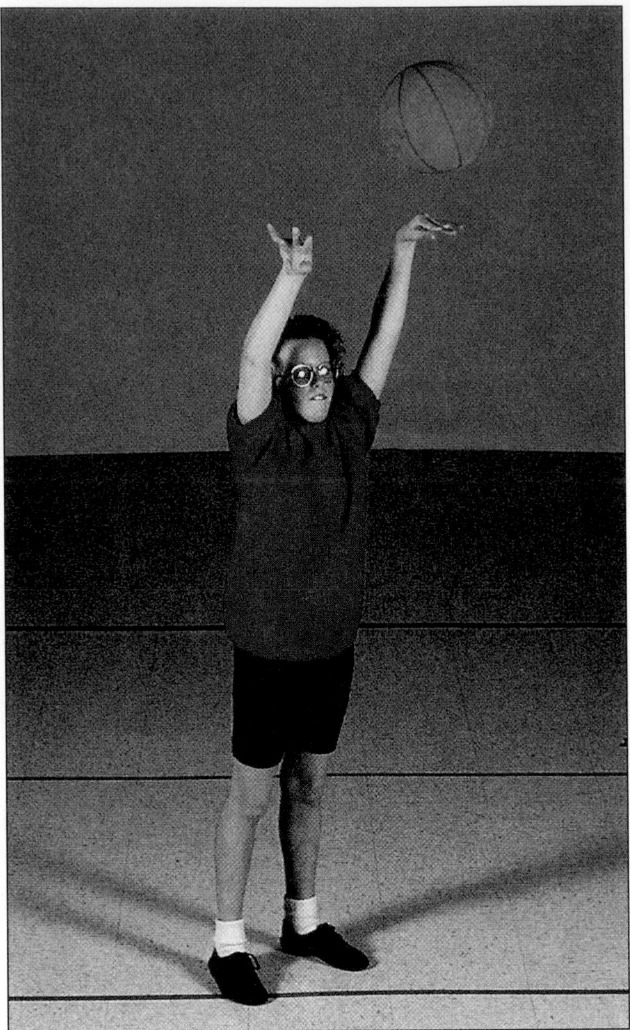

FIGURE 23.5 Releasing the two-handed overhead pass.

Dribbling

Dribbling is used to advance the ball, break for a basket, or maneuver out of a difficult situation. The dribbler's knees and trunk should be slightly flexed (Figure 23.6), with hands and eyes forward. Peripheral vision is important. The dribbler should look beyond the ball and see it in the lower part of the visual area. The ball is propelled by the fingertips with the hand cupped and relaxed. There is little arm motion. Younger children tend to slap at the ball rather than push it. The dribbling hand should be alternated, and practice in changing hands is essential.

FIGURE 23.6 Dribbling.

Instructional cues for dribbling include the following:

1. Push the ball to the floor. Don't slap it.
2. Push the ball forward when moving.
3. Eyes forward and head up.

Shooting

Shooting is an intricate skill, and students need to develop consistent and proper technique rather than be satisfied when the ball happens to drop into the basket.

1. Good body position is important. Both the toes and the shoulders should face the basket. The weight should be evenly distributed on both feet. In preliminary phases, the ball should be held between shoulder and eye level.
2. A comfortable grip, with fingers well spread and the ball resting on the pads of the fingers, is essential. One should be able to see daylight between the palm of the hand and the ball. For one-hand shots, the shooting elbow is directly below the ball.
3. As soon as the decision is made to shoot, the eye is fixed on the target (the rim or the backboard) for the rest of the shot.
4. As the shot starts, the wrist is cocked.
5. The follow-through imparts a slight backspin to the ball. The arms are fully extended, the wrist is completely flexed, and the hand drops down toward the floor. The arc should be 45 degrees or a little higher.

The following instructional cues aid skill development:

1. Use the pads of the fingers. Keep the fingers spread.
2. Keep the shooting elbow near the body.
3. Extend through the ball.
4. Bend the knees and use the legs.
5. Release the ball off the fingertips.

One-Hand (set) Push Shot

The one-hand push shot is usually a jump shot at short distances and a set shot at longer distances. The ball is held at shoulder-eye level with both hands; the body is erect, and the knees are flexed slightly in preparation for a jump. For a jump shot, the shooter executes a vertical

FIGURE 23.7 One-hand push shot.

jump, leaving the floor slightly (Figure 23.7). (In a set shot, the shooter rises on the toes.) The supporting (nonshooting) hand remains in contact with the ball until the top of the jump is reached. The shooting hand then takes over with fingertip control, and the ball rolls off the center three fingers. The hand and wrist follow through. Visual concentration on the target is maintained throughout. Proper technique should be emphasized rather than accuracy.

Lay-Up Shot

The lay-up is a short shot taken when going in toward the basket either after receiving a pass or at the end of a dribble. In a shot from the right side, the takeoff is with the left foot, and vice versa. The ball is carried with both hands early in the shot and then shifted to one hand for the final push. The ball, guided by the fingertips, should be laid against the backboard with a minimum of spin.

Free-Throw Shot

Free-throw shooting can be performed successfully with different types of shots. The one-hand foul shot is most popular. Complete concentration, relaxation, and a rhythmic, consistent delivery are needed. Some players find it helpful to bounce the ball several times before shooting. Others like to take a deep breath and exhale completely just before shooting. The mechanics of the shot do not differ materially from those of any shot at a comparable distance. Smoothness and consistency are most important.

Jump Shot

The jump shot has the same upper-body mechanics as the one-hand push shot already described. The primary difference is the height of the jump. The jump should be straight up, rather than at a forward or backward angle. The ball should be released at the height of the jump (Figure 23.8). Because the legs cannot be used to increase the force applied to the ball, the jump shot is difficult for the majority of elementary school youngsters. It may be best to avoid teaching the shot to youngsters who lack enough strength to shoot the ball correctly and resort to throwing it. If the jump shot is presented, the basket should be at the lowest level available and a junior-sized basketball used to develop proper shooting habits.

Another way to practice proper form with the jump shot is to use gray foam balls. They are light and can be shot easily by children. Concentrate on proper form rather than on making baskets. Reinforce students who use good technique.

Defending

Defending involves a characteristic stance. The defender, with knees bent slightly and feet comfortably

FIGURE 23.8 One-handed jump shot.

FIGURE 23.9 The defensive position.

spread (Figure 23.9), faces the opponent at a distance of about 3 feet. The weight should be distributed evenly on both feet to allow for movement in any direction. Sideward movement is done with a sliding motion. The defender should wave one hand to distract the opponent and to block passes and shots. A defensive player needs to learn to move quickly and not be caught flatfooted.

Instructional cues for proper defending are as follows.

1. Keep the knees bent.
2. Keep the hands up.
3. Don't cross the feet when moving.

Stopping

To stop quickly, the weight of the body is dropped to lower the center of gravity and the feet are applied as brakes (Figure 23.10). In the parallel stop, the body turns sideward and both feet brake simultaneously. The stride stop comes from a forward movement and is done in a one-two count. On the first count, one foot hits the ground with a braking action; the other foot is planted firmly ahead on the second count. The knees are bent, and the center of gravity is lowered. From a stride stop, the player can move into a pivot by picking up the front foot and carrying it to the rear and, at the same time, fading to the rear.

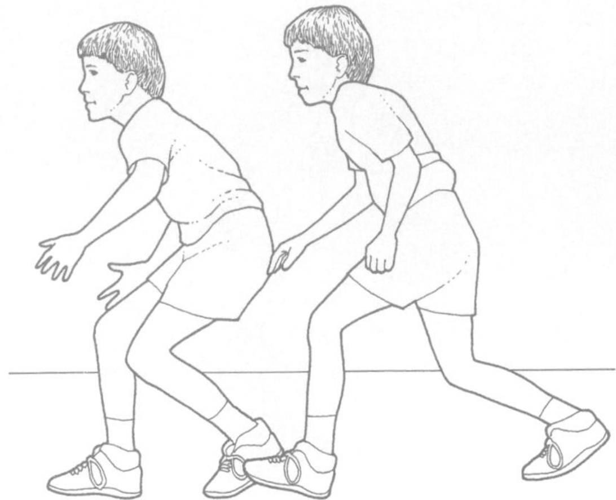

FIGURE 23.10 Stopping.

Pivoting

Pivoting is a maneuver that protects the ball by keeping the body between the ball and the defensive player. The ball is held firmly in both hands, with elbows out to protect it. One foot, the pivot foot, must always be in contact with the floor. Turning on that foot is permitted, but it must not be dragged away from the pivot spot. The lead foot may, however, step in any direction (Figure 23.11).

If a player has received the ball in a stationary position or during a jump in which both feet hit the ground simultaneously, either foot may become the pivot foot. If a player stops after a dribble on a one-two count, the pivot foot is the foot that made contact on the first count.

Feinting

Feinting (faking) masks the intent of a maneuver or pass and is essential to basketball. Feinting is a deceptive mo-

FIGURE 23.11 Pivoting.

tion in one direction when the intent is to move in another direction. It can be done with the eyes, the head, a foot, or the whole body. In passing, feinting means faking a pass in one manner or direction and then passing in another.

INSTRUCTIONAL PROCEDURES

1. Many basketball skills do not require the use of basketballs. Other balls, such as volleyballs or rubber balls, can be used successfully.
2. Many skills can be practiced individually or in pairs with playground balls. This allows all children to develop at their own pace, regardless of skill level. Dribbling, passing, and catching skills receive more practice when many balls are used.
3. Baskets should be lowered to 7, 8, or 9 feet, depending on the size of the youngsters. If the facility is also used for community purposes, adjustable baskets—preferably power-driven—are the key. Baskets of 5- or 6-foot height are good for children in wheelchairs. This height also allows for experimentation by younger children. These lower baskets can be mounted directly on a wall and set up and removed as needed. No backboard is necessary. When the baskets are mounted to one side, children with disabilities can shoot baskets even though they may not be able to participate in other basketball activities.
4. The program should concentrate on skills and include many drills. Basketball offers endless possibilities, and using many drills gives variety and breadth to the instructional program. Each child should have an opportunity to practice all skills. This is not possible when a considerable portion of class time is devoted to playing regulation basketball on a full-length court.

BASIC BASKETBALL RULES

The game of basketball played at the elementary school level is similar to the official game played in the junior and senior high schools, but is modified to assure the opportunity for success and for proper skill development. A team is made up of five players, including two guards, one center, and two forwards. The game is divided into four quarters, each 6 minutes in length. The game is under the control of a referee and an umpire, both of whom have an equal right to call violations and fouls. They work on opposite sides of the floor and are assisted by a timer and a scorer. The following rules apply to the game for elementary school children.

Putting the Ball into Play

Each quarter is started with a jump ball at the center circle. Throughout the game, the jump ball is used when the ball is tied up between two players or when it is uncertain which team caused the ball to go out-of-bounds. After each successful basket or free throw, the ball is put into play at the end of the court under the basket by the team against whom the score was made.

Violations

The penalty for a violation is to award the ball to the opponents near the out-of-bounds point. The following are violations.

1. Traveling, that is, taking more than one step with the ball without passing, dribbling, or shooting (sometimes called *walking* or *steps*).
2. Stepping out-of-bounds with the ball or causing the ball to go out-of-bounds.
3. Taking more than 10 seconds to cross the centerline from the back to the front court. (Once in the forward court, the ball may not be returned to the back court by the team in control.)
4. Double dribbling, which is taking a second series of dribbles without another player's having handled the ball; palming (not clearly batting) the ball; or dribbling the ball with both hands at once.
5. Stepping on or over a restraining line during a jump ball or free throw.
6. Kicking the ball intentionally.
7. Remaining more than 3 seconds in the area under the offensive basket, which is bounded by the two sides of the free-throw lane, the free-throw line, and the end of the court.
8. To equalize scoring opportunities, a time limit (30 seconds) may be established during which the offensive team must score or give up the ball.

Fouls

Personal fouls are holding, pushing, hacking (striking), tripping, charging, blocking, and unnecessary roughness. When a foul is called, the person who was fouled receives one free throw. If fouled in the act of shooting and the basket was missed, the child receives two shots. If, despite the foul, the basket was made, the score counts and one free throw is awarded. A player who has five personal fouls is out of the game and must go to the sidelines.

Scoring

A basket from the field scores 2 points and a free throw 1 point. In most cases, the 3-point goal is not a consideration due to the distance of the shot. If desired, teachers could create a 3-point line to simulate the game played by older students. The team that is ahead at the end of the game is declared the winner. If the score is tied, an overtime period of 2 minutes is played. If the score is still tied after this period, the next team to score (1 or 2 points) is declared the winner.

Substitutes

Substitutes must report to the official scorer and await a signal from the referee or umpire before entering the game. The scorer will sound the signal at a time when the ball is not in play so that the official on the floor can signal for the player to enter the game.

BASKETBALL DRILLS

Drills should emulate actual game situations. Youngsters should understand that practice is ineffective unless it is purposeful and correct. When using drills, instructors should use the technique suggestions for the skill being practiced and apply movement principles. The drills presented here cover both single skills and combinations of skills.

Ball-Handling Drills

These drills are practiced continuously for about 30 seconds. The ball is handled with the pads of the fingers. The drills are listed in order of difficulty.

AROUND THE BODY DRILLS

1. *Around the waist.* Hold the ball in the right hand, circle it behind the back, and transfer to the left hand. The left hand carries it to the front of the body for a transfer to the right hand. Start with the left hand and move the ball in the opposite direction.
2. *Around the head.* With shoulders back, send the ball around the head in much the same manner described above. Perform in both directions.
3. *Triple play.* Begin by circling around the head; move to waist level and follow by knee level circles. Move the ball in the opposite direction.

FIGURE EIGHT

1. Begin in a squatting position with the ball in the right hand. Move the ball around the leg to the right and bounce the ball between the legs to the left hand. Circle the ball around the left leg, through the legs to the right hand.
2. Bounce the ball through the legs front to back followed by the figure-eight motion.

FIGURE 23.12 Speed drill.

SPEED DRILL

Feet are placed shoulder width apart. The ball is held between the legs with one hand in front and the other behind the back in contact with the ball. In a quick motion, flip the ball slightly upward and reverse the hand positions. Using a quick exchange of the hands, make a series of rapid exchanges. The ball will appear to be suspended between the legs (Figure 23.12).

DOUBLE CIRCLE DRILL

Beginning with the ball in the right hand, go around both legs, with an assist from the left hand. When the ball returns to the right hand, move the left foot away from the right foot. With the ball moving in the same direction, circle the right leg. Move the leg back to the starting position and circle both legs followed by moving the legs apart and circling the left leg (Figure 23.13). In short, circle both legs, circle the right leg, circle both legs, circle the left leg. Try moving the ball in the opposite direction.

TWO-HAND CONTROL DRILL

Start from a semicrouched position with the feet shoulder width apart. The ball is held with both hands between the legs in front of the body (Figure 23.14). Let go of the ball, move the hands behind the body, and catch it before the ball hits the floor. It may be helpful to give the ball a slight upward flip to facilitate the catch. Reverse the action moving the hands to the front of the body. Perform continuously.

CHANGING HANDS CONTROL DRILL

Begin with the ball in the right hand; move it around the back of the right leg and catch with both hands. The right hand should be in front and the left hand behind. Drop the ball and quickly change position of the hands on the ball after it has bounced once (Figure 23.15). Immediately after the catch, bring the ball to the front of the body with the left hand and switch the ball to the right hand. Repeat continuously. Try moving the ball in the opposite direction.

FIGURE 23.13 Double circle drill.

FIGURE 23.14 Two-hand control drill.

Individual Dribbling Drills

HOOP DRIBBLING DRILL

Each youngster has a ball and hula hoop. Place the hoop on the floor and practice dribbling the ball inside the hoop while walking outside the hoop. Dribble counterclockwise using the left hand and clockwise using the right hand. Repeat with the dribbler inside the hoop and the ball dribbled outside the hoop.

RANDOM DRIBBLING

Each child has a ball. Dribbling is done in place, varied by using left and right hands. Develop a sequence of body positions (standing, kneeling, lying on the side, on two feet and one hand). Encourage players to develop a sequence by dribbling a certain number of times in each selected position. Dribble with each hand.

ONE-HAND CONTROL DRILL

Begin with the right hand holding the ball. Make a half circle around the right leg to the back. Bounce the ball between the legs (back to front) and catch it with the right hand and move it around the body again (Figure 23.16 on page 590). After continuing for a short time, switch to the left hand.

FIGURE-EIGHT DRIBBLING DRILL (SPEED)

Start with the right or left hand. Dribble outside the respective leg, between the feet, and continue in front with the opposite hand in figure-eight fashion. Begin slowly and gradually increase the speed of the dribble.

FIGURE-EIGHT DRIBBLING DRILL (ONE BOUNCE)

Assume a semicrouched position with the feet shoulder width apart. Start with the ball in the right hand and bounce it from the front of the body between the legs. Catch it with the left hand behind the legs (Figure 23.17 on page 590). Bring the ball to the front of the body with the left hand and start the sequence over with that hand.

FIGURE 23.15 Changing hands control drill.

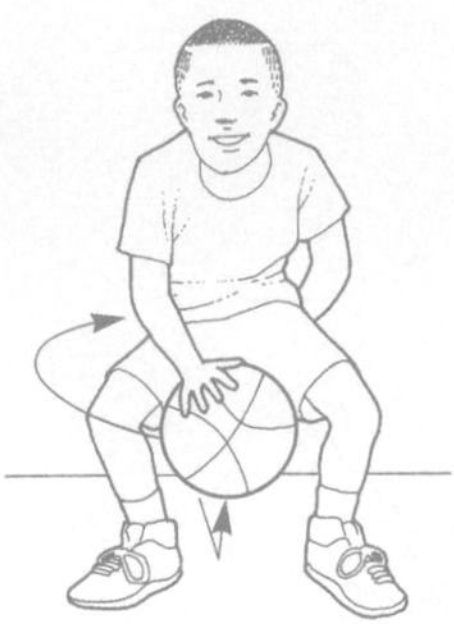

FIGURE 23.16 One-hand control drill.

FIGURE 23.17 Figure-eight dribbling drill (one bounce).

FIGURE-EIGHT DRIBBLING DRILL (TWO BOUNCES)

Begin in the same position as described in the preceding drill. Using the right hand, take one dribble outside the right leg (angled toward the back) and a second dribble between the legs to the left hand in front of the body (Figure 23.18). Repeat, starting with the left hand.

Group Dribbling Drills

Dribbling can be practiced as a single skill or in combination with others.

FIGURE 23.18 Figure-eight dribbling drill (two bounces).

FILE DRIBBLING

In file dribbling, players dribble forward around an obstacle (such as a bowling pin, a cone, or a chair) and back to the line, where the next player repeats (Figure 23.19). A variation has each player dribbling down with one hand and back with the other.

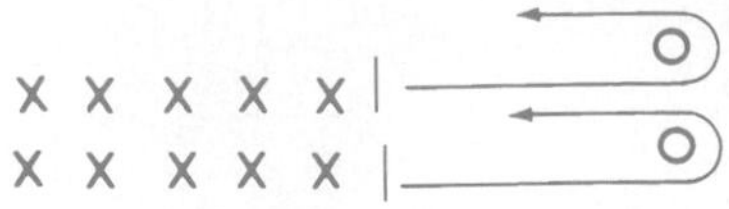

FIGURE 23.19 File dribbling.

SHUTTLE DRIBBLING

Shuttle dribbling begins at the head of a file. The head player dribbles across to another file and hands the ball off to the player at the head of the second file. The first player then takes a place at the end of that file (Figure 23.20). The player receiving the ball dribbles back to the first file. A number of shuttles can be arranged for dribbling crossways over a basketball court.

FIGURE 23.20 Shuttle dribbling.

OBSTACLE, OR FIGURE-EIGHT, DRIBBLING

For obstacle, or figure-eight, dribbling, three or more obstacles are positioned about 5 feet apart. The first player at the head of each file dribbles in and around each obstacle, changing hands so that the hand opposite the obstacle is the one always used (Figure 23.21).

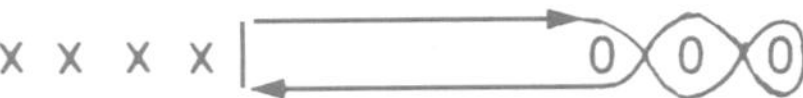

FIGURE 23.21 Obstacle, or figure-eight, dribbling.

Dribbling and Pivoting Drills

In dribbling and pivoting drills, the emphases are on stopping and pivoting.

FILE DRILL

For the file drill, each player in turn dribbles forward to a designated line, stops, pivots, faces the file, passes back to the next player, and runs to a place at the end of the line (Figure 23.22). The next player repeats the pattern.

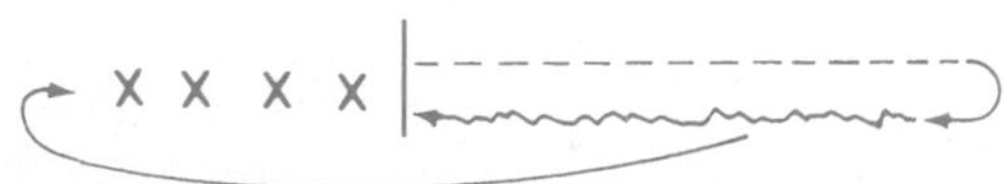

FIGURE 23.22 File drill.

DRIBBLE-AND-PIVOT DRILL

For the dribble-and-pivot drill, players are scattered by pairs around the floor (Figure 23.23). One ball is required for each pair. On the first whistle, the front player of the pair dribbles in any direction and fashion on the court. On the second whistle, the player stops and pivots back and forth, and on the third whistle, dribbles back and passes to the partner, who immediately dribbles forward, repeating the routine.

FIGURE 23.23 Dribble-and-pivot drill.

Passing Drills

In passing practice, regular use should be made of the various movement formations (Chapter 3), including two-line, circle, circle-and-leader, line-and-leader, shuttle turn-back, and regular shuttle formations. A number of other drills should be considered.

SLIDE CIRCLE DRILL

In the slide circle drill, a circle of four to six players slides around a person in the center. The center person passes to and receives from the sliding players. After the ball has gone around the circle twice, another player takes the center position.

CIRCLE-STAR DRILL

With only five players, a circle-star drill is particularly effective. Players pass to every other player, and the path of the ball forms a star (Figure 23.24). The star drill works well as a relay. Any odd number of players will cause the ball to go to all participants, assuring that all receive equal practice.

TRIANGLE DRILL

Four to eight players can participate in the triangle drill. The ball begins at the head of a line and is passed forward to a player away from the line. This player then passes to a teammate out at a corner, who then passes back to the head of the line (Figure 23.25). Each player passes and then moves to the spot to which he passed the ball, thus making a continual change of positions.

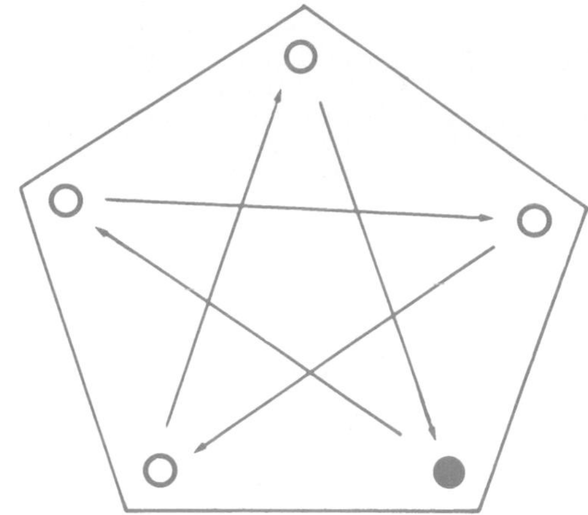

FIGURE 23.24 Circle-star drill formation.

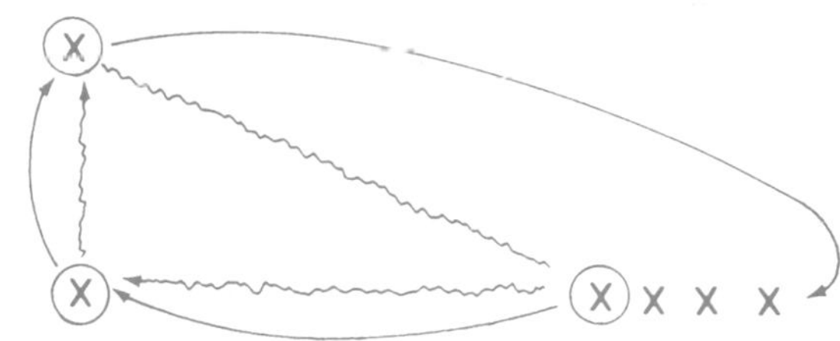

FIGURE 23.25 Triangle drill formation.

SQUAD SPLIT-VISION DRILL

This drill requires two basketballs. The center player holds one ball, while player 1 (see Figure 23.26 on page 592) has the other. The center player passes the ball to player 2, while receiving the other ball from player 1. The center player now passes to player 3 and receives the other ball from player 2 until the balls move completely around the semicircle. To rotate to a new center player, the center player becomes player 1 while player 6 (with the ball) moves to the center spot. All players adjust one space to the right.

THREE-LANE RUSH

This is a lead-up to the three-player weave, which is difficult for elementary school youngsters to learn. Youngsters are in three lines across one end of the area. The first three players move parallel down the court while passing the ball back and forth to each other. A lay-up shot can be taken as players near the basket.

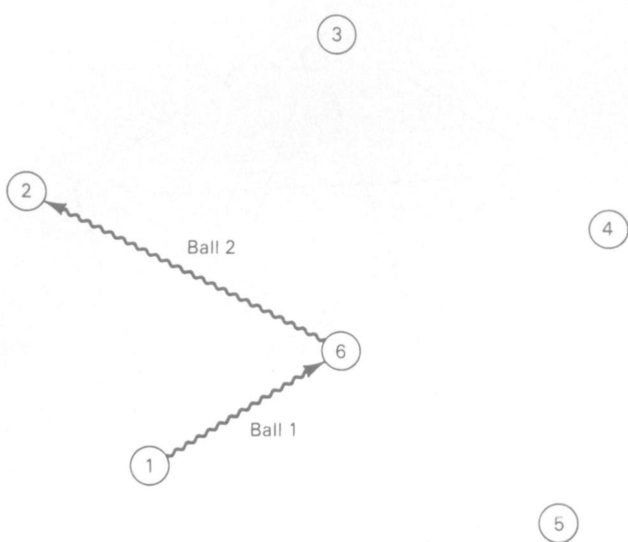

FIGURE 23.26 Squad split-vision drill.

THREE-PLAYER WEAVE

This drill requires practice and should be learned at slow speed. Walking students through the drill can sometimes help. If it is too difficult for a class, it should be avoided. The player in the center always starts the drill. She passes to another player coming across in front and then goes behind that player. Just as soon as she goes behind and around the player, she heads diagonally across the floor until she receives the ball again. The pass from the center player can start to either side.

Shooting Drills

Shooting drills may involve just shooting or a combination of shooting and other skills.

SIMPLE SHOOTING DRILL

In one simple shooting drill, players form files of no more than four people, and take turns shooting a long and then a short shot or some other prescribed series of shots.

FILE-AND-LEADER DRILL

For a file-and-leader drill, the first player in each file has a ball and is the shooter. He passes the ball to the leader, who returns the ball to the spot that the shooter has selected for the shot (Figure 23.27).

DRIBBLE-AND-SHOOT DRILL

For the dribble-and-shoot drill, two files are established on one end of the floor. One file has a ball. The first player dribbles in and shoots a lay-up. A member of the

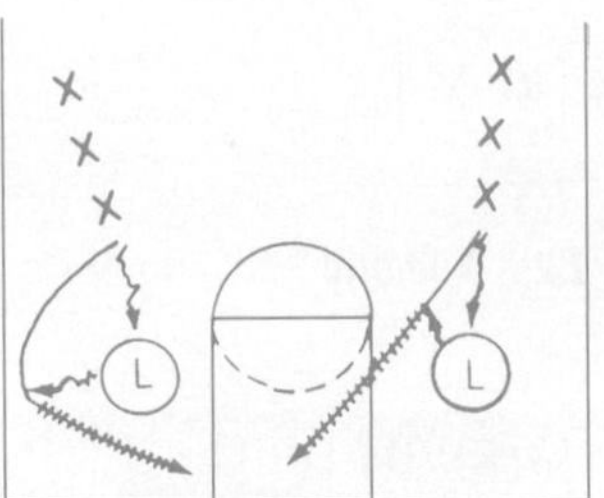

FIGURE 23.27 File-and-leader drill.

other file recovers the ball and passes it to the next player (Figure 23.28). As each person in turn either shoots or retrieves, she goes to the rear of the other file. After some proficiency in the drill has been developed, two balls can be used, allowing for more shooting opportunities.

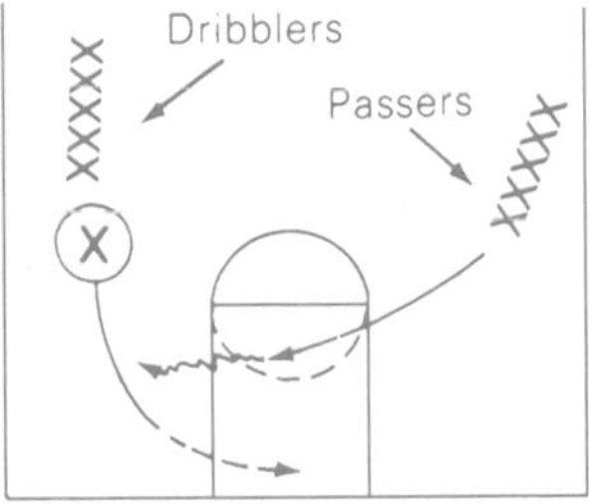

FIGURE 23.28 Dribble-and-shoot drill.

SET-SHOT DRILL

In the set-shot drill, players are scattered around a basket in a semicircle, with a leader in charge (Figure 23.29). Players should be close enough to the basket so that they can shoot accurately. The leader passes to each in turn to take a shot. The leader chases the ball after the shot. A bit of competition can be injected by allowing a successful shooter to take one step back for the next shot, or a player can shoot until he misses.

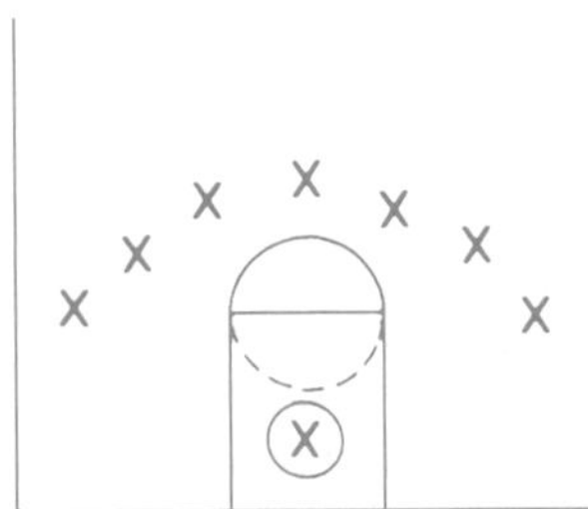

FIGURE 23.29 Set-shot drill formation.

LAY-UP DRILL

The lay-up drill is a favorite. One line passes to the other line for lay-up shots (Figure 23.30). Shooters come in

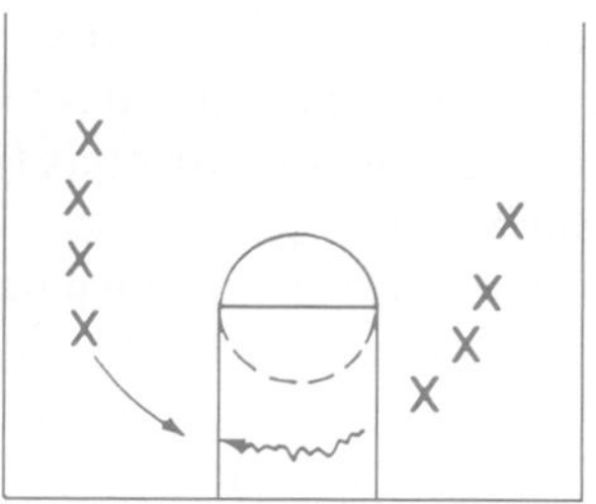

FIGURE 23.30 Lay-up drill.

from the right side first (this is easier), then from the left, and finally from the center. Each player goes to the end of the other line.

JUMP-SHOT DRILL

The jump-shot drill is similar to the lay-up drill, except that the incoming shooter receives the ball, stops, and takes a jump shot. The line of shooters should move back so that there is room for forward movement to the shooting spot. As soon as the passer releases the ball to the shooter, he moves to the end of the shooter's line. The shooter goes to the passer's line after shooting (Figure 23.31).

One extension of this drill is to allow a second jump shot when the shooter makes the first. In this case, the incoming passer passes to the shooter taking a second shot as well as to the next shooter. Another extension, which creates a gamelike situation, is having both the shooter and the incoming passer follow up the shot when the basket has not been made. As soon as the follow-up shot is made or there are three misses by the followers, the passer passes the ball to the new shooter. The avenues by which the shooters approach should be varied, so that children practice shooting from different spots.

Offensive and Defensive Drills

GROUP DEFENSIVE DRILL

For the group defensive drill, the entire class is scattered on a basketball floor, facing one of the sides (Figure 23.32). The instructor or the student leader stands on the side, near the center. The drill can be done in a number of ways.

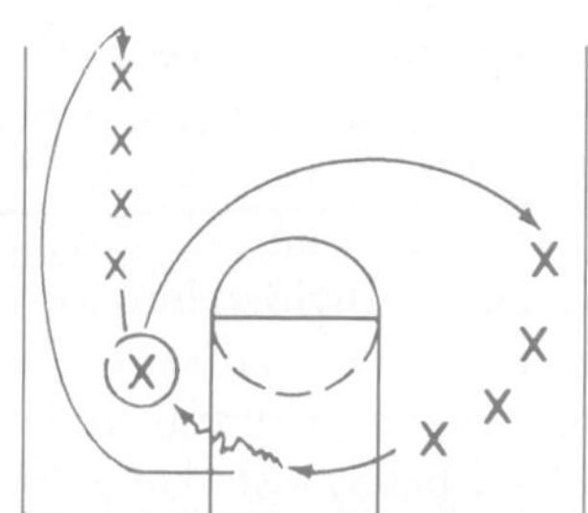

FIGURE 23.31 Jump-shot drill.

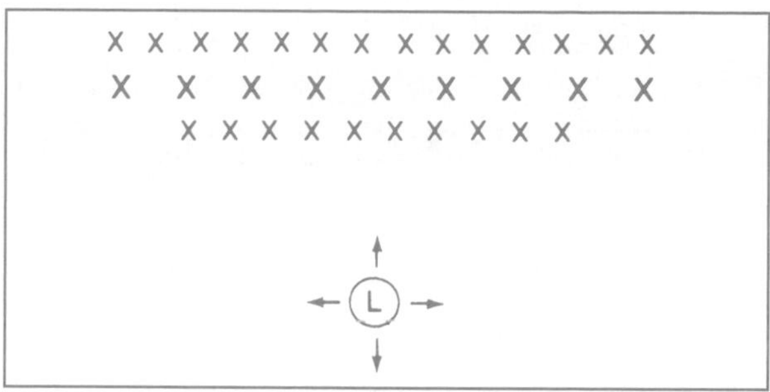

FIGURE 23.32 Group defensive drill.

1. The leader points in one direction (forward, backward, or to one side) and gives the command "Move." When the students have moved a short distance, the leader commands, "Stop." Players keep good defensive position throughout.
2. Commands can be changed so that movement is continuous. Commands are "Right," "Left," "Forward," "Backward," and "Stop." The leader must watch that movement is not so far in any one direction that it causes players to run into obstructions. Commands can be given in order, and pointing can accompany commands.
3. The leader is a dribbler with a ball, who moves forward, backward, or to either side, with the defensive players reacting accordingly.

It is important to stress good defensive position and movement. Movement from side to side should be a slide. Movement forward and backward is a two-step, with one foot always leading.

OFFENSIVE-DEFENSIVE DRILL WITH A POST

The offensive-defensive drill with a post consists of an offensive player, a defensive player, and another player who acts as a passing post. The post player generally remains stationary and receives the ball from and passes to the offensive player. The player on offense tries to maneuver around or past the defensive player to secure a good shot (Figure 23.33 on page 594). Plays can be confined to one side of an offensive basket area, thus allowing two drills to go on at the same time on one end of the basketball floor. If there are side baskets, many drills can be operated at the same time. After a basket has been attempted, a rotation of players, including any waiting player, is made.

The defensive player's job is to cover well enough to prevent shots in front of her. Some matching of ability must occur or the drill is nonproductive.

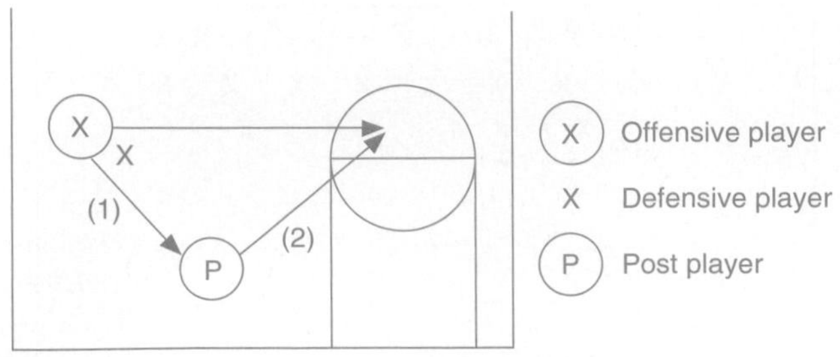

FIGURE 23.33 Offensive-defensive drill with post.

BASKETBALL ACTIVITIES

Developmental Level II

CIRCLE GUARD AND PASS

Playing Area: Any smooth surface with circle markings

Players: Eight to ten per team

Supplies: A basketball or playground ball

Skills: Passing, catching, guarding

The offensive team is placed in formation around a large (30-foot diameter) circle. Two or more offensive players move into the center. The defensive team is in position around a smaller (20-foot) circle inside the larger circle. On signal, the offensive team tries to pass the ball to the center players. They may pass the ball around the circle to each other before making an attempt to the center. The defensive team tries to bat the ball away but cannot catch it. After a stipulated time (1 minute), offensive and defensive teams trade positions. If score is kept, 2 points are awarded for each successful pass.

TEACHING TIP

Variation: More than one ball can be used, and different types of passes can be stipulated. The defensive team also can earn points for each time a team member touches the ball.

BASKETBALL TAG

Playing Area: Gymnasium or playground area, 30 by 50 feet

Players: 8 to 10 per team

Supplies: A foam rubber basketball, pinnies

Skills: Catching, passing, dribbling, guarding

There are two versions of this game. The simpler version is to designate 3 to 5 students to be *it* and wear a pinnie. The rest of the class may only pass the ball and tries to tag one of the students who is *it* with the ball. Players may move wherever they desire when they don't have the ball. However, when they have the ball in their control they may not move or dribble. If desired, more than one ball can be used.

A more difficult version of the game allows dribbling and tagging with the hands. Two or more players from each team are designated to be "*its*" and they wear pinnies. The object of the game is to tag the "*its*" with a hand when they have the ball. The players who are *it* may move only by walking. The rest of the players can only move when they are dribbling or do not have the ball. The players who are *it* try to avoid moving near the ball, while other players try to pass and dribble in an attempt to get close enough to tag the roving "*its*."

TEACHING TIP

1. Play 2 or more games simultaneously so students get more opportunity to handle the ball.
2. Designate two teams to play each other. Both teams have "its" who wear different colored pinnies. They are it when their team does not have the ball. When their team has the ball, they play offense with their teammates.

DRIBBLERAMA

Playing Area: Any smooth surface with a large circle or square, clearly outlined

Players: Entire class

Supplies: 1 basketball for each player

Skills: Dribbling and protecting the ball

The playing area is a large circle or square. Dribblerama can be played at three levels of difficulty.

Level 1: All players dribble throughout the area, controlling their ball so that it does not touch another ball. If a touch occurs, both players go outside the area and dribble around the area. Once youngsters have completed dribbling around the area, they reenter the game.

Level 2: The area is divided in half and all players move to one of the halves. While dribbling and controlling a ball, each player attempts to cause another player to lose control of his ball. When control is lost, that player takes his/her ball and moves to the opposite half of the area. Play continues against other players who have lost control. When 5 or 6 players remain, bring all players back into the game and start over.

Level 3: The class is divided into four teams and the area is divided into equal quadrants. Each of the four teams goes to one of the quadrants in the teaching area. When control of the ball is lost, that player moves to the next quadrant and begins play. This variation is more controlled and keeps youngsters involved continuously.

BIRDIES IN THE CAGE

Playing Area: Any smooth surface with circle marking

Players: 8 to 15 per team

Supplies: A soccer ball, basketball, or volleyball

Skills: Passing, catching, intercepting

Players are placed in circle formation with two or more children in the center of the circle. The object of the game is for the center players to try to touch the ball while circle players are passing it. After a brief time (15–20 seconds) choose new players to enter the circle. If scoring is desired, center players can count the number of touches they made. The ball should move rapidly. Passing to a neighboring player is not allowed. Play can be limited to a specific type of pass (bounce, two-hand, push).

CAPTAIN BALL

Playing Area: Playground or gymnasium area, about 30 by 40 feet

Players: 7 or more on each team

Supplies: A basketball, pinnies, mats or spots

Skills: Passing, catching, guarding

Two games can be played crosswise on a basketball court. A centerline is needed (Figure 23.34); otherwise, normal boundary lines are used. Marking spots delineate where forwards and the captains must stay. A team is composed of a captain, 3 or more forwards, and 3 or more guards. The guards are free to move in their half of the playing area and try to keep the ball from being thrown to the opposing captain. The captain and forwards are each assigned to their respective spots and must always keep one foot on their assigned marking spot.

The game is started by a jump at the centerline with two guards from opposing teams. The guards can rove in their half of the court but may not touch the opposing forwards. Once points are scored by getting the ball to the captain, an opposing guard immediately puts the ball into play with an inbounds throw. Guards try to throw the ball to their forwards, who maneuver to be open while keeping a foot on their spot. The forwards can throw the ball to their guards and forwards or to the captain. Three points are scored when 2 forwards handle the ball and it is passed to the captain. Two points are scored when the ball is passed to the captain but has not been handled by two forwards. No points are scored when a guard throws the ball to the captain.

Stepping over the centerline is a foul. It is also a foul if a guard steps on a forward's marking spot or makes personal contact with a player on a spot. The penalty for a foul is a free throw. For a free throw, the ball is given to an unguarded forward, who has 5 seconds to get the ball successfully to the guarded captain. If the throw is successful, one point is scored. If it is not successful, the ball is in play. Rotate free-throw shooting among all the forwards.

As in basketball, when the ball goes out of bounds, it is awarded to the team that did not cause it to go out. If a forward or a captain catches a ball without a foot touching their spot, the ball is taken out of bounds by the opposing guard. For violations such as traveling or kicking the ball, the ball is awarded to an opposing guard out of bounds. No score may be made from a ball that is thrown in directly from out of bounds.

TEACHING TIP

An effective offensive formation places guards spaced along the centerline (Figure 23.35—only the offensive team is diagrammed). By passing the ball back and forth among the guards, the forwards have more opportunity to be open, since the passing makes the guards shift position. The guards may dribble, but are restricted to 3 dribbles for the purpose of advancing the ball. The forwards and captain should shift back and forth to become open for passes. They must keep 1 foot on the spot. Short and accurate passing uses both chest and bounce passes. Forwards and centers may jump for the ball but must come down with 1 foot on their spot.

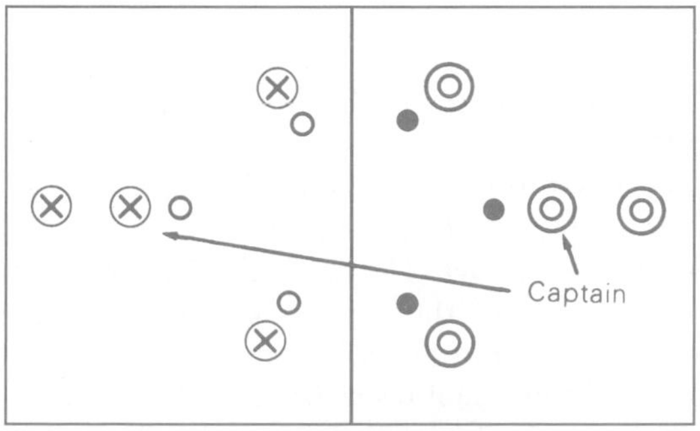

Captain

FIGURE 23.34 Formation for Captain Ball.

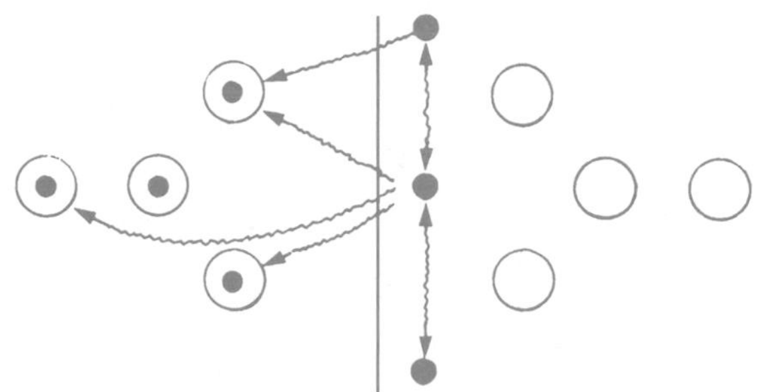

FIGURE 23.35 An effective offensive formation in Captain Ball.

Variations:

1. A 5-spot formation like that on a die can be used. Nine players are needed on each team: 4 forwards, 4 guards, and 1 captain. Depending on space and the size of the courts, even more players can be utilized.
2. Use more than 1 captain on each side to make scoring easier.

AROUND THE KEY

Playing Area: One end of a basketball floor

Players: Three to eight

Supplies: A basketball

Skills: Shooting

Spots are arranged for shooting as indicated in Figure 23.36. A player begins at the first spot and continues around the key, shooting from each spot. When a miss occurs, the player can stop and wait for the next opportunity and begin from the point at which the miss occurred. The alternative to waiting is to "risk it" and try another shot immediately from the point at which the first try was missed. If the shot is made, the player continues. If the shot is missed, the player must start over from the beginning spot on the next turn. The winner is the player who completes the key first or who makes the most progress.

TEACHING TIP

Variations:

1. Each child shoots from each spot until a basket is made. A limit of three shots from any one spot should be set. The child finishing the round of eight spots with the lowest number of shots taken is the winner.
2. The order of the spots can be changed. A player can start on one side of the key and continue back along the line, around the free-throw circle, and back down the other side of the key.

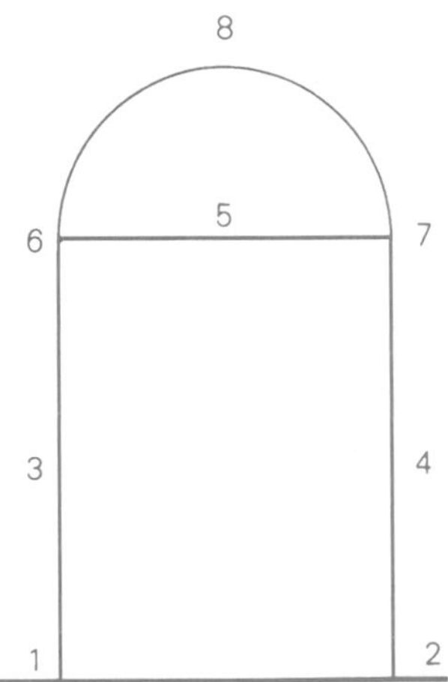

FIGURE 23.36 Shooting positions for Around the Key.

FIVE PASSES

Playing Area: Half of a basketball floor

Players: Five or more on each team

Supplies: A basketball, pinnies

Skills: Passing, guarding

Two teams play. Divide the area into smaller areas so many teams can play simultaneously. The object of the game is to complete five consecutive passes, which scores a point. The game is started with a jump ball at the free-throw line. The teams observe regular basketball rules in ball handling and with regard to traveling and fouling. The team with the ball counts out loud as a pass is completed.

The ball may not be passed back to the person from whom it was received. No dribbling is allowed. If for any reason the ball is fumbled and recovered or improperly passed, a new count is started. After a successful score, the ball is immediately turned over to the other team. A foul draws a free throw, which can score a point. Teams should be well marked to avoid confusion.

TEACHING TIP

Variations:

1. After each successful point (five passes), the team is awarded a free throw, which can score an additional point.
2. After a team has scored a point, the ball can be given to the other team out of bounds to start play again.

CAPTAIN BASKETBALL

Playing Area: A basketball court with centerline

Players: Six or more on each team

Supplies: Basketballs, pinnies

Skills: All basketball skills except shooting

A captain's area is laid out by drawing a line (or placing a tumbling mat) between the two foul restraining lines 4 feet out from the end line. The captain must keep one foot in this area. Captain Basketball is more like regulation basketball than Captain Ball. Captain Ball limits the movements of the forwards. Captain Basketball brings in more natural passing and guarding situations without the movement restrictions on the forwards.

A team typically is composed of three forwards, one captain, and four guards. The captain must keep one foot in the area under the basket. The game is started with a jump ball, after which the players advance the ball as in basketball. No player may cross the centerline, however. The guards must bring the ball up to the centerline and throw it to one of their forwards. The forwards maneuver and attempt to pass successfully to the captain. A throw by one of the forwards to the captain scores 2 points; a free throw scores 1 point.

Fouls are the same as in basketball. In addition, stepping over the centerline or a guard stepping into the captain's area draws a foul. In the case of a foul, the ball is given to a forward at the free-throw line. The player is unguarded and has 5 seconds to pass successfully to the captain, who is guarded by one player. The ball is in play if the free throw is unsuccessful.

TEACHING TIP

Using a folding tumbling mat to designate the captain's area at each end of the court discourages intrusion by guards. Even though players are required to remain in their own half of the court, they should be taught to move freely within that area. Short, quick passes should be stressed, because long passes are often ineffective. Captain Basketball offers the chance for practicing proper guarding techniques.

Developmental Level III

QUADRANT BASKETBALL

Playing Area: Basketball court divided into four equal areas

Players: At least eight per team with a minimum of two placed in each area

Supplies: Basketball, pinnies

Skills: Passing, catching, dribbling, guarding, shooting

Divide the court by its length and width into four equal areas with markers. Play can be started with a jump ball or by giving the ball to one team. Two offensive and two defensive players are placed in each quadrant. Players may not leave the quadrant during the course of play. Normal rules of basketball are used, with the exception of limiting the number of dribbles to three. The purpose of this game is to teach youngsters to remain spaced throughout the area. Rotate players to different quadrants so that they have the opportunity to play offense and defense.

TEACHING TIP

Variation: Limit the number of passes that may be made consecutively in one quadrant to encourage passing to other areas. Reduce amount of time a player may hold the ball to 5 seconds to encourage passing.

SIDELINE BASKETBALL

Playing Area: Basketball court

Players: Entire class

Supplies: A basketball, pinnies

Skills: All basketball skills

Divide the class into 2 teams, each lined up along 1 side of the court, facing the other. Three or 4 active players from each team enter the floor to play regulation basketball. The remainder of the players, who stand on the sideline, can catch and pass the ball to the active players. Sideline players may not shoot, nor may they enter the playing floor. They must keep 1 foot completely out of bounds at all times.

The active players play regulation basketball, with the additional rule that they must pass and receive the ball 3 times from sideline players before they can attempt a goal. Sideline players may pass to each other but must pass back to an active player after 3 sideline passes. The game starts with active players occupying their half of the court. The ball is taken out of bounds under its own basket by the team that was scored on. Play continues until a period of time (i.e., 30 seconds to 1 minute) elapses. **Teams do not change after a score; only after the time has elapsed.** The active players then go to the end of their line and 3 new active players come out from the right. All other players move down and adjust to fill the space left by the new players.

No official out of bounds on the sides is called. The players on that side of the floor simply recover the ball and put it into play with a pass to an active player without delay. Out of bounds on the ends is the same as in regular basketball. If 1 of the sideline players enters the court and touches the ball, it is a violation, and the ball is awarded out of bounds on the other side to a sideline player of the other team. Free throws are awarded when a player is fouled.

TEACHING TIP

A modified scoring system is an excellent idea that allows all students to contribute to the game. Hitting the backboard is 1 point, hitting the rim is 2 points, and making a basket is worth 3 points.

TWENTY-ONE

Playing Area: One end of a basketball court

Players: Three to eight in each game

Supplies: A basketball

Skills: Shooting

Players are in file formation by teams. Each player is permitted a long shot (from a specified distance) and a follow-up shot. The long shot, if made, counts 2 points and the short shot counts 1 point. The follow-up shot must be made from the spot where the ball was recovered from the first shot. The normal 1-2-step rhythm is permitted on the short shot from the place where the ball was recovered. The first player scoring a total of 21 points is the winner. If the ball misses the backboard and basket altogether on the first shot, the second shot must be taken from the corner.

TEACHING TIP

The rules above are for regulation Twenty-One. A modified version is an excellent idea that allows for more activity time and practice on rebounding skills. The scoring modification gives 1 point for hitting the backboard, 2 points for hitting the rim, and 3 points for a made basket. If a player makes the basket or hits the rim he or she gets a free long shot that must be go through the basket to count. If the long shot is missed, the player that gets the rebound attempts to score. If the shot is not made but hits the backboard or rim, the shooter gets 1 point or 2 points, respectively, and play continues. Because players are learning these skills, standing and waiting for long shots will not occur often.

TEACHING TIP

Variations:

1. Start with a simpler game that allows dribbling before the second shot.
2. Allow players to shoot as long as every shot is made. This means that if both the long and the short shot are made, the player goes back to the original position for a third shot. All shots made count and the shooter can continue until a miss.
3. Use various combinations and types of shots.

LANE BASKETBALL

Playing Area: Basketball court divided into six or more lanes

Players: Five per team

Supplies: Basketball, pinnies, cones to mark zones

Skills: All basketball skills

The court is divided into six lanes as shown in Figure 23.37. Players must stay in their lane and cannot cross the midcourt line. Regular basketball rules prevail, with the exception that players cannot dribble more than three times. Play is started with a jump ball. At regular intervals, youngsters rotate to the next lane to assure they get to play offense and defense.

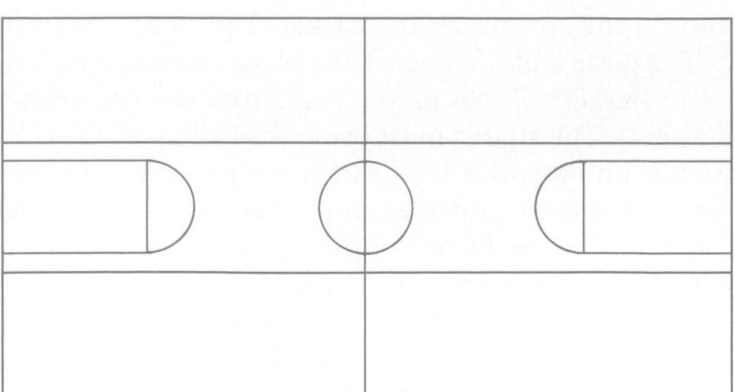

FIGURE 23.37 Court markings for Lane Basketball.

A number of rule changes can be implemented to change the focus of the game. For example, three passes may be required before shooting may occur. Also, to increase the amount of activity, youngsters can move the entire length of the floor within their lane.

FREEZE OUT

Playing Area: One end of the basketball court

Players: Four to eight

Supplies: A basketball

Skills: Shooting under pressure

There are many types of freeze-out shooting games. This version is an interesting shooting game that culminates quickly and allows players back into the game with minimal wait time. Each player can have three misses before being out. After the first miss, the player gets an *O;* after the second, a *U;* and after the third, a *T.* This spells *OUT* and puts the player out. The last player remaining is the winner.

The first player shoots a basket from any spot desired. If the basket is missed, there is no penalty and the next player shoots. If the basket is made, the following player must make a basket from the same spot or it is scored as a miss (and a letter). If the player ahead of them misses, they may shoot from any spot they choose without penalty.

FLAG DRIBBLE

Playing Area: One end of a basketball floor or a hard-surfaced area outside with boundaries

Players: 10 to 20

Supplies: A basketball and a flag for each player

Skills: Dribbling

The object is to eliminate other players and avoid being eliminated. Players are eliminated if they lose control of the ball, if their flag is pulled, or if they go out of bounds. Keeping control of the ball by dribbling is interpreted to mean continuous dribbling without missing a bounce. A double dribble (both hands) is regarded as a loss of control.

Start the game with players scattered around the area near the sidelines. Each has a ball, and all have flags tucked in the back of their belts. On signal, all players begin to dribble in the area. While keeping control of the dribble and staying in bounds, they attempt to pull a flag from any other player's back. When players lose control, they move to the perimeter of the area and practice their dribbling skills. As soon as the game is down to a few players, start the game over. Sometimes two players lose control of their basketball at about the same time. In this case, both are eliminated.

TEACHING TIP

Variations:

1. If using flags is impractical, the game can be played without this feature. The objective then becomes to knock aside or deflect the other basketballs while retaining control of one's own ball.
2. Flag Dribble can be played with teams or squads. In this case, each squad or team is clearly marked.

THROUGH THE MAZE

Playing Area: Basketball court

Players: Two teams of 5 to 7

Supplies: Each player on offense has a ball

Skills: Dribbling, ball control, guarding, tackling

One team is on offense and one on defense, placed according to Figure 23.38. Defensive players stay in their assigned areas. On signal, all offensive players try to dribble through the 3 areas without losing their ball. A player is eliminated if her ball is recovered by a defensive player or goes out of bounds. The offensive team scores 1 point for each ball dribbled across the opposite end line. Reverse roles and give the other team a chance to score. Use a number of marking spots to identify the areas where the defensive players must stay. A variation is to put neutral zones between the active zones.

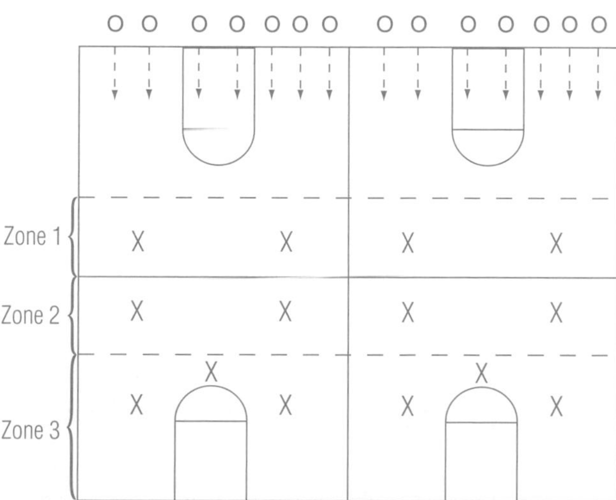

FIGURE 23.38 Through the Maze.

ONE-GOAL BASKETBALL

Playing Area: An area with one basketball goal

Players: Two to four on each team

Supplies: A basketball, pinnies (optional)

Skills: All basketball skills

This is an excellent class activity if four or more baskets are available. The game is played by two teams according to the rules of basketball but with the following exceptions.

1. When a defensive player recovers the ball, either from the backboard or on an interception, the ball must be taken out beyond the foul-line circle before offensive play is started and an attempt at a goal is made.
2. After a basket is made, the ball is taken in the same fashion away from the basket to the center of the floor, where the other team starts offensive play.
3. Regular free-throw shooting can be observed after a foul, or some use can be made of the rule whereby the offended team takes the ball out-of-bounds.
4. An offensive player who is tied up in a jump ball loses the ball to the other team.
5. Individuals are responsible for calling fouls on themselves.

BASKETBALL SNATCH BALL

Playing Area: Basketball court

Players: 6 to 20 on each team

Supplies: Two basketballs, two hoops

Skills: Passing, dribbling, shooting

Each of two teams occupies one side of a basketball floor. The players on each team are numbered consecutively from the right-hand end of the line. Two balls are placed inside two hoops, one hoop on each side of the centerline. When the teacher calls three or more numbers, players from each team whose numbers were called run to the ball assigned to them. These players pass and dribble to the basket on their right and try to make a basket. Three passes must be made and all players must handle the ball before a basket can be shot. As soon as a basket is made, the players pass and dribble back and place the ball in the hoop. The first team to return the ball after making a basket scores a point for that team. Use a system to keep track of the numbers so that all children have a turn. Numbers are called in any order.

THREE-ON-THREE

Playing Area: Half of a basketball court

Players: Many teams of three players each

Supplies: Basketballs

Skills: All basketball skills

Three teams of three are assigned to a basket. The offensive team stands at the top of the key facing the basket. The defensive team starts at the free throw line. The remaining team waits for their turn beyond the end line. Regular basketball rules are used. The offensive team tries to score. The offensive team plays until they score or the ball is stolen by the defense. In either case, the defensive team moves to the center of the floor and becomes the offensive unit. The waiting team moves onto the floor and plays defense. The previous offensive team goes to the rear of the line of waiting players. Each of the teams keeps its own score. Many games can be carried on at the same time depending on the number of available baskets. A team wins when they score three points. Winning teams can be rotated to games at other baskets.

BASKETRAMA

Playing Area: Area around one basket

Players: Usually two

Supplies: A basketball for each player

Skills: Shooting under pressure

On signal, two players, each with a basketball, begin to shoot individually as rapidly as possible, taking any kind of shots they wish, until one scores 10 baskets to become the winner. Each player must handle her own basketball and must not impede or interfere with the other's ball. Naturally, the balls do collide at times, but deliberate interference by knocking the other ball out of the way or kicking it means disqualification.

Balls should be marked so that there is no argument as to ownership. This can be done by using different types of basketballs or by marking with chalk or tape. Each player can count out loud each basket he makes, or another student can keep score for each contestant.

PAPER CLIP BASKETBALL

Playing Area: Basketball court

Players: Entire class

Supplies: Basketballs, hoops, paper clips, Frisbees

Skills: Shooting, passing, dribbling

Four equal teams are formed and each team stands on the sideline of 1 quadrant of the basketball floor (see Figure 23.39). Each team has a basketball and a hoop that has been placed near the center of the gym. Allow enough room between the hoops so players do not collide. On signal, the first 3 players for each team must hustle for their ball, then pass and dribble toward 1 basket. Each team member must receive the ball before a shot can be attempted. Once a shot is made or after 3 shots, the players return the ball to their team's hoop and return to their team and give a "high five" to the next 3 players. These 3 players repeat the process toward the other basket. On the sideline each team also has a Frisbee and several paper clips. If any of the 3 players makes a basket the team places 1 paper clip into the Frisbee upon returning to the sideline. The game continues or several minutes and the team with the most paper clips in their Frisbee at the conclusion is declared the winner. In order to have different combinations of players working together, it is best if the team number is not divisible by 3.

BASKETBALL SKILL TESTS

Tests in basketball cover dribbling, passing, shooting, and making free throws. For each of the first four tests presented here, a stopwatch is needed.

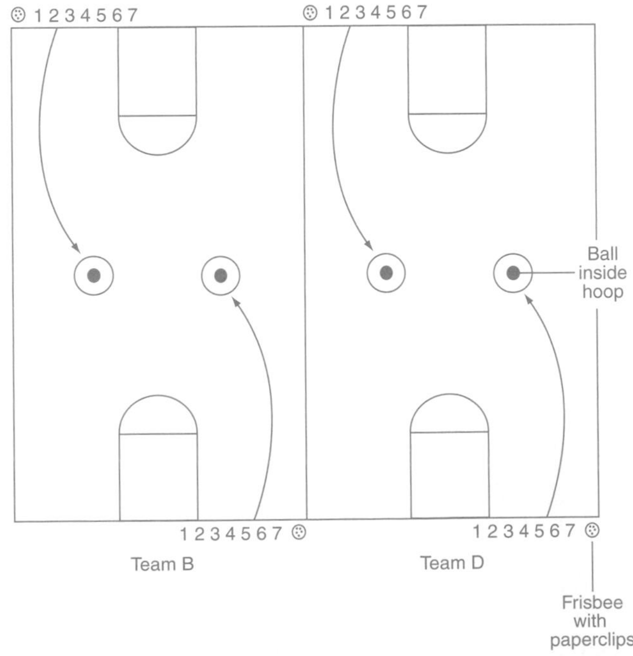

FIGURE 23.39 Paper Clip Basketball.

Straight Dribble

A marker is placed 15 yards down the floor from the starting point. The dribbler must dribble around the marker and back to the starting position, where he finishes by crossing the starting line. The marker must remain standing or disqualification results. The teacher should allow two or three trials and take the best time.

Figure-Eight Dribble

Four obstacles (bowling pins, bases, or cones) are placed 5 feet apart in a straight line beginning 5 feet from the starting line. The player must dribble in and out of the markers in the path of a figure eight, finishing at the point where she started. The teacher can allow two or three trials and take the best time.

Wall Pass Test

A player stands 5 feet from a smooth wall. He is given 30 seconds to make as many catches as he can from throws or passes against the wall. The two-hand or chest pass is generally used. Balls must be caught on the fly to count. Another student should do the counting. Only one trial is allowed. A board or mat provides a definite restraining line.

Baskets Made in Thirty Seconds

A player stands near the basket in any position she wishes. On signal, she shoots and continues shooting for a period of 30 seconds. Her score is the number of baskets she makes during the time period. Another student should do the counting. Only one trial is allowed.

Free Throws

Score is kept of the number of free throws made out of ten attempts. The player should get three or four warm-up trials and announce when he is ready. Score should be kept by another student with pencil and paper. An X is marked for a basket made, and an O for a miss.

FOR MORE INFORMATION

References and Suggested Readings

American Sport Education Program. (2001). *Coaching youth basketball,* 3rd ed. Champaign, IL: Human Kinetics.

Head-Summitt, P. H., & Jennings, D. (1996). *Basketball,* 2nd ed. Dubuque, IA: McGraw-Hill.

Krause, J. (2000). *Basketball skills and drills,* 2nd ed. Champaign, IL: Human Kinetics.

Mood, D. P., Musker, F. F., & Rink, J. E. (1991). *Sports and recreational activities for men and women.* 10th ed. St. Louis: Mosby.

Moore, B., & White, J. (1980). *Basketball: Theory and practice.* Dubuque, IA: Wm. C. Brown Group.

Nix, C. (2000). *Skills, drills and strategies for basketball.* Scottsdale, AZ: Holcomb Hathaway Publishers.

Paye, B. (2001). *Youth basketball drills.* Champaign, IL: Human Kinetics.

Wilkes, G. (1998). *Basketball.* 7th ed. Dubuque, IA: McGraw-Hill.

Wissel, H. (1994). *Basketball: Steps to success.* Champaign, IL: Human Kinetics.

Websites

American Basketball Consulting Services
http://sites.tier.net/americanbball

American Youth Basketball Tour
www.aybtour.com

Basketball Congress International
www.bcibasketball.org

Youth Basketball of America
www.yboa.org

CHAPTER 24

Football

ESSENTIAL COMPONENTS	
I	**Organized around content standards**
II	**Student-centered and developmentally appropriate**
III	**Physical activity and motor skill development form the core of the program**
IV	**Teaches management skills and self-discipline**
V	**Promotes inclusion of all students**
VI	**Focuses on process over product**
VII	Promotes lifetime personal health and wellness
VIII	**Teaches cooperation and responsibility and promotes sensitivity to diversity**

PHYSICAL EDUCATION STANDARDS	
1	**Students are able to move competently using a variety of fundamental and specialized motor skills.**
2	Students can monitor and maintain a health-enhancing level of physical fitness.
3	**Students are able to apply movement concepts and basic mechanics of skill performance when learning and refining motor skills.**
4	Students comprehend the basic principles of wellness and are able to apply concepts that enable them to make meaningful decisions that positively impact their health and wellness.
5	**Students participate in a wide variety of physical activities and learn how to maintain a personalized active lifestyle.**
6	**Students demonstrate empathy, understanding, and respect for the numerous differences exhibited by people in an activity setting.**
7	**Students exhibit responsible and self-directed behaviors that lead to positive social interactions in physical activity.**

SUMMARY

Skills instruction for football is introduced during the intermediate grades after youngsters have mastered the basic prerequisite skills. The teaching of rules and strategies for football is an integral part of the instructional process. Using proper progression is a key to success when teaching fundamental skills and lead-up games associated with football. Lead-up games provide an opportunity to emphasize development of selected football skills in a setting that is compatible with the abilities of participants.

OUTCOMES

- Structure learning experiences efficiently with respect to appropriate formations, progressions, and coaching techniques.
- Develop a unit plan and lesson focus for football.
- Identify safety precautions associated with teaching football.
- Describe instructional procedures for implementing a successful lead-up game.
- Cite assessment procedures for evaluating football skills.

The shape of the football makes throwing and catching more difficult than with a round ball. Specialized skills are needed, which means that time must be spent on football skills if children are to enjoy participating. Touch and Flag Football are modifications of the game of American football. A ball carrier usually is considered down in Touch Football when touched by one hand. In Flag Football, a player wears one or two flags, which opponents must seize to down the ball carrier; hence the name Flag Football. Flag Football has advantages over Touch Football in that there is more twisting and dodging, which makes the game more interesting and challenging. In addition, in Flag Football, argument over whether the ball carrier was downed is less likely.

INSTRUCTIONAL EMPHASIS AND SEQUENCE

Table 24.1 shows the sequence of football activities divided into two developmental levels. Regular and junior-sized footballs are difficult to throw and catch. The ends of the football are hard and can hurt children who haven't mastered catching skills. For this reason, the use of foam footballs is encouraged. A number of companies manufacture the balls in a size that is suitable for youngsters. Youngsters will show a greater tendency to participate when they know the projectile is harmless.

Developmental Level II

Passing, centering, and catching receive the majority of focus at this level. Most of the instructional time should be spent on skills. The lead-up games of Five Passes and Football End Ball make use of the skills listed.

Developmental Level III

At this level, emphasis shifts to passing skills, with moving receivers in football drills. Punting and kicking games are introduced. More specialized skills, such as blocking, carrying the ball, exchanging the ball, and football agility skills, provide lead-up work for the game of Flag Football.

TABLE 24.1 Suggested football program

Developmental Level II	Developmental Level III
Skills	
Forward pass	Stance
Centering	Pass receiving
Catching	Punting
	Blocking
	Carrying the ball
	Running and dodging
	Handing off the ball
	Lateral pass
Knowledge	
Football rules	Plays and formations
Activities	
Football End Ball	Kick-Over
Five Passes	Fourth Down
Speed Football	Football Box Ball
	Flag Football
	Pass Ball
Skill Tests	
Passing for distance	Kicking for distance
Centering	Passing for distance
	Passing for accuracy

FOOTBALL SKILLS

Forward Pass

Skillful forward passing is needed in Flag Football and in the lead-up games; passing is a potent weapon. The ball should be gripped lightly behind the middle with the fingers on the lace. The thumbs and fingers should be relaxed (Figure 24.1, page 604).

In throwing, the opposing foot should point in the direction of the pass, with the body turned sideways. In preparation for the pass, the ball is raised up and held over the shoulders. The ball is delivered directly forward with an overhand movement of the arm and with the index finger pointing toward the line of flight. A left-hander is illustrated in Figure 24.2 (page 604).

The following instructional cues will help students improve their throwing technique:

1. Turn the nonthrowing side toward the direction of the throw.
2. Grasp the ball with the pads of the fingers.
3. Throw the ball with an overhand motion.
4. Step toward the pass receiver.
5. Follow through with the arm after releasing the ball.

Lateral Pass

Lateral passing is a simple underhand toss of the ball to a teammate (Figure 24.3 on page 604). The ball must be

FIGURE 24.1 Preparing to pass.

FIGURE 24.3 Preparing for a lateral pass.

FIGURE 24.2 Passing (left-handed thrower).

tossed sideward or backward to qualify as a lateral. It should be tossed with an easy motion, and no attempt should be made to make it spiral like a forward pass.

Catching

In catching, the receiver should keep both eyes on the ball and catch it in the hands with a slight give (Figure 24.4). As soon as the ball is caught, it should be tucked into the carrying position. The little fingers are together for most catches.

The following instructional cues will help students focus on catching technique:

1. Keep eyes on the ball.
2. Thumbs together for a high pass (above shoulder level).
3. Thumbs apart for a low pass (below shoulder level).
4. Reach for the ball, give, and bring the ball to the body.

FIGURE 24.4 Catching a pass.

Handing Off the Ball

Children enjoy working plays in which the ball is exchanged from one player to another, as for a reverse. In a reverse, the object is to start the play in one direction and then give the ball to another player heading in the opposite direction. The ball can be handed backward or forward. The player with the ball always makes the exchange with the inside hand, the one near the receiving player. The ball is held with both hands until the receiver is about 6 feet away. The ball then is shifted to the hand on that side, with the elbow bent partially away from the body. The receiver comes toward the exchange player with the near arm bent and carried in front of the chest, the palm down. The other arm is carried about waist height, with the palm up (Figure 24.5). As the ball is handed off (not tossed), the receiver clamps down on the ball to secure it. As quickly as possible, the receiver then changes to a normal carrying position.

FIGURE 24.5 Handing off the ball.

A fake reverse, sometimes called a *bootleg,* is made when the ball carrier pretends to make the exchange but keeps the ball instead and hides it momentarily behind one leg.

Carrying the Ball

The ball should be carried with the arm on the outside and the end of the ball tucked into the notch formed by the elbow and arm. The fingers add support for the carry (Figure 24.6, page 606).

Centering

Centering involves transferring the ball, on a signal, to the quarterback. In elementary school, the shotgun formation is most often used. This requires snapping the ball a few yards backward to the quarterback. A direct snap involves placing the hands under the buttocks of the center. The ball is then lifted, rotated a quarter turn, and snapped into the hands of the quarterback.

The centering player takes a position with the feet well spread and toes pointed straight ahead. Knees are

FIGURE 24.6 Carrying the ball securely.

bent and close enough to the ball to reach it with a slight stretch. The right hand takes about the same grip as is used in passing. The other hand is on the side near the back of the ball and merely acts as a guide (Figure 24.7). On signal from the quarterback, the center extends the arms backward through the legs and centers the ball to the quarterback.

Instructional cues for centering include the following:

1. Keep legs spread and toes straight ahead.
2. Reach forward for the ball.
3. Snap the ball with the dominant hand.
4. Guide the ball with the nondominant hand.

Stance

The three-point stance is the offensive stance most generally used in Flag Football. The feet are about shoulder width apart and the toes point straight ahead, with the toes of one foot even with the heel of the other. The hand on the side of the foot that is back is used for support; the knuckles rest on the ground. The player should look straight ahead and always take the same stance (Figure 24.8).

FIGURE 24.7 Centering (note the hand and finger positions).

Some players prefer the parallel stance, in which the feet, instead of being in the heel-and-toe position, are lined up evenly. In this case, either hand can be placed down for support. Some defensive players like to use a four-point stance, as shown. Both hands are in contact with the ground (Figure 24.9).

The following instructional cues will help students learn proper stance:

1. Bend the knees; keep the back parallel to the ground.
2. Keep the majority of the weight on the legs.
3. Don't lean forward or backward.

FIGURE 24.8 Offensive three-point stance.

FIGURE 24.9 Defensive four-point stance.

Blocking

When blocking, the blocker must maintain balance and not fall to the knees. The elbows are out, and the hands are held near the chest. The block should be more of an obstruction than a takeout and should be set with the shoulder against the opponent's shoulder or upper body (Figure 24.10). Making contact from the rear in any direction not only is a penalty but also could cause injury.

Instructional cues for blocking technique are the following:

1. Keep feet spread and knees bent.
2. Keep head up.
3. Stay in front of the defensive player.
4. Move your feet; stay on the balls of the feet.

FIGURE 24.10 Blocking position.

FIGURE 24.11 Punting.

Punting

The kicker stands with the kicking foot slightly forward. The fingers are extended in the direction of the center. The eyes should be on the ball from the time it is centered until it is kicked, and the kicker should actually see the foot kick the ball. After receiving the ball, the kicker takes a short step with the kicking foot and then a second step with the other foot. The kicking leg is swung forward and, at impact, the leg is straightened to provide maximum force. The toes are pointed, and the long axis of the ball makes contact on the top of the instep. The leg should follow through well after the kick (Figure 24.11). Emphasis should be placed on dropping the ball properly. Beginners have a tendency to throw it in the air, making the punt more difficult.

Instructional cues for teaching punting are the following:

1. Drop the football; don't toss it upward.
2. Keep the eyes focused on the ball.
3. Kick upward and through the ball.
4. Contact the ball on the outer side of the instep.

INSTRUCTIONAL PROCEDURES

1. All children need the opportunity to practice all skills, and a system of rotation should be set up to ensure this.
2. Drills should be performed with attention to proper form, and they should approximate game conditions. For example, when going out for passes is being practiced, start the pattern using the proper stance.
3. Junior-sized or foam footballs should be used. At least six to eight footballs should be available for football drills. The best teaching situation is to have one football for each pair of children.
4. Roughness and unfair play must be controlled by supervision and strict enforcement of the rules.

FOOTBALL DRILLS

BALL CARRYING

Formation: Scattered

Players: Four to six

Supplies: A football, a flag for each player, cones to mark the zones

The ball carrier stands on the goal line ready to run. Three defensive players wait at 20-yard intervals, each one stationed on a zone line of a regular Flag Football field, facing the ball carrier (Figure 24.12). Each defender is assigned to the zone that she is facing and must down the ball carrier by pulling a flag while the carrier is still in the zone. The ball carrier runs and dodges, trying to get by each defender in turn without having her flag pulled. If the flag is pulled, the runner continues, and the last defender uses a two-handed touch to down the ball carrier. After the runner has completed the run, she goes to the end of the defender's line and rotates to a defending position.

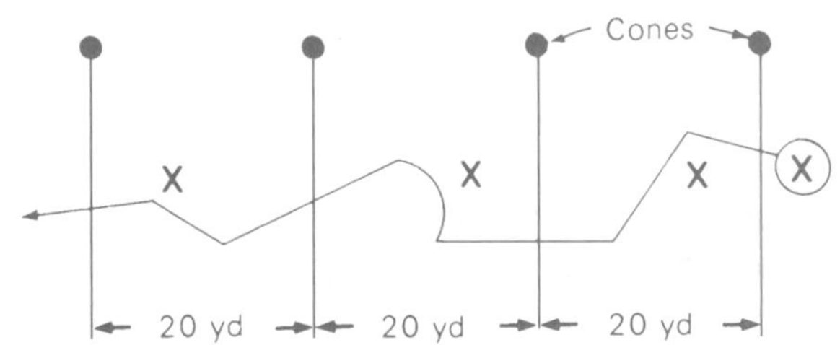

FIGURE 24.12 Ball carrying drill.

BALL EXCHANGE

Formation: Shuttle, with the halves about 15 yards apart

Players: Four to ten

Supplies: A football

The two halves of the shuttle face each other across the 15-yard distance. A player at the head of one of the files has a ball and carries it over to the other file, where he makes an exchange with the player at the front of that file (Figure 24.13). The ball is carried back and forth between the shuttle files. The receiving player should not start until the ball carrier is almost up to him. A player, after handing the ball to the front player of the other file, continues around and joins that file.

FIGURE 24.13 Ball exchange drill.

COMBINATION

Formation: Regular offensive formation with passer, center, end, and ball chaser

Players: Four to eight

Supplies: A football

Passing, centering, and receiving skills are combined in one drill. Each player, after her turn, rotates to the next spot. A minimum of four players is needed. The center player centers the ball to the passer; the passer passes the ball to the end; the end receives the pass; and the ball chaser retrieves the ball if missed by the end, or takes a pass from the end (if she caught the ball) and carries the ball to the center spot, which is her next assignment (Figure 24.14).

The rotation follows the path of the ball. This means that the rotation system moves from center to passer to end to ball chaser to center. Extra players should be stationed behind the passer for their turns.

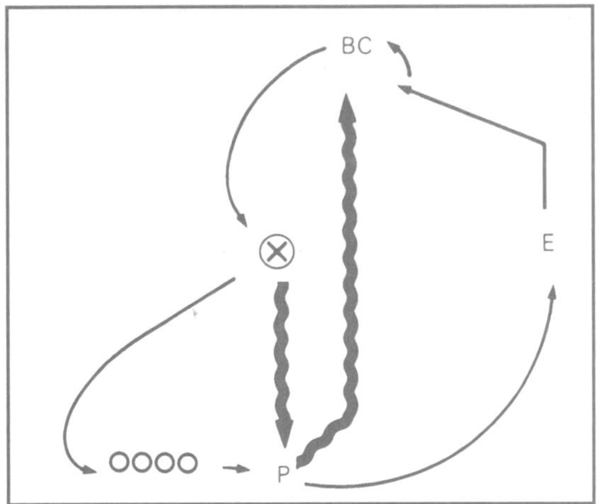

FIGURE 24.14 Combination drill.

ONE-ON-ONE DEFENSIVE DRILL

Formation: Center, passer, end, defender

Players: Eight to ten

Supplies: A football

The one-on-one defensive drill is as old as football itself. A defensive player stands about 8 yards back, waiting for an approaching end. The passer tries to complete the pass to the end while the defender tries to break up the pass or intercept the ball. One defender should practice against all the players and then rotate (Figure 24.15). The passer must be able to pass well or this drill has little value.

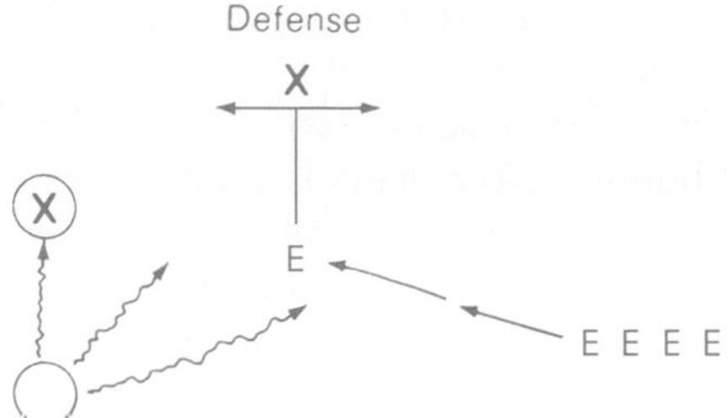

FIGURE 24.15 One-on-one defensive drill.

TEACHING TIP

Variation: The drill can be played with two ends and two defenders. The passer throws to the end who appears to be most unguarded.

PUNT RETURN

Formation: Center, kicker, two lines of ends, receivers

Players: 10 to 20

Supplies: A football, a flag for each player

The object of the drill is for the receiver to catch a punted ball and return it to the line of scrimmage while two ends attempt to pull a flag or make a tag. Two ends are ready to run downfield. The center snaps the ball to the kicker, who punts the ball downfield to the punt receiver. The ends cannot cross the line of scrimmage until the ball has been kicked. Each end makes two trips downfield as a "tackler" before rotating to the punt-receiving position.

TEACHING TIP

An effective punter is necessary for this drill. Only children with the degree of skill required to punt far enough downfield should be permitted to kick. It is also important for the ends to wait until the ball is kicked, or they will be downfield too soon for the receiver to have a fair chance of making a return run.

STANCE

Formation: Squads in extended file formation

Players: Six to eight in each file

Supplies: None

The first person in each file performs and when finished with his chores, goes to the end of his file. On the command "Ready," the first person in each file assumes a football stance. The teacher can correct and make observations. On the command "Hike," the players charge forward for about 5 yards (Figure 24.16). The new player at the head of each line gets ready.

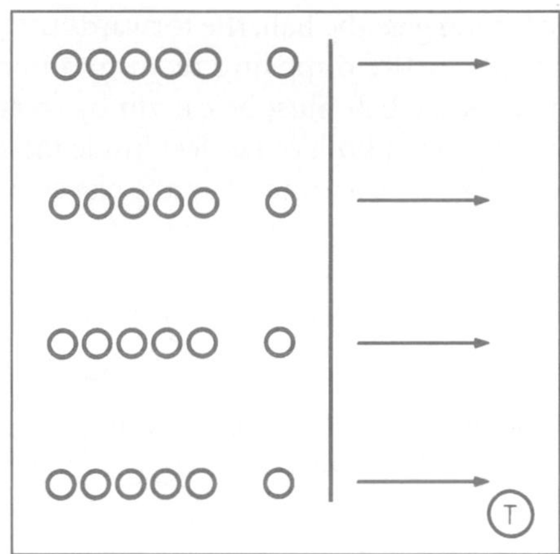

FIGURE 24.16 Stance drill.

FOOTBALL ACTIVITIES

Developmental Level II

FOOTBALL END BALL

Playing Area: A court 20 by 40 feet

Players: 9 to 12 on each team

Supplies: Footballs

Skills: Passing, catching

The court is divided in half by a centerline. End zones are marked 3 feet wide, completely across the court at each end. Players on each team are divided into three groups: forwards, guards, and ends. The object is for a forward to throw successfully to one of the end-zone players. The players from each team are positioned as diagrammed in Figure 24.17. End-zone players take positions in one of the end zones. Their forwards and guards then occupy the half of the court farthest from this end zone. The forwards are near the centerline, and the guards are back near the end zone of their half of the court.

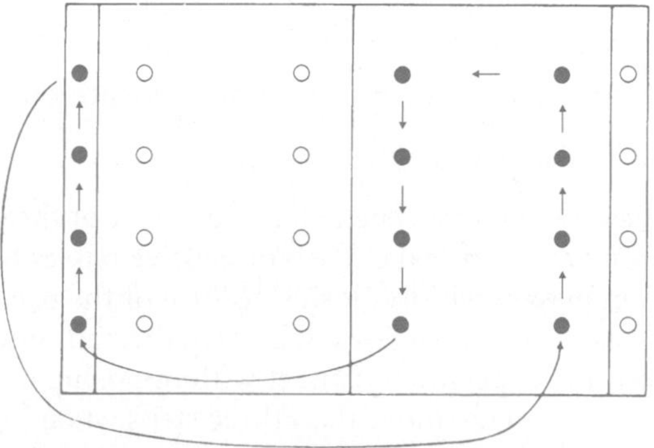

FIGURE 24.17 Player positions for Football End Ball.

When a team gets the ball, the forwards try to throw over the heads of the opposing team to an end-zone player. To score, the ball must be caught by an end-zone player, who must have both of her feet inside the zone. No moving with the ball is permitted by any player. After each score, play is resumed by a jump ball at the centerline.

A penalty results in loss of the ball to the other team. Penalties are assessed for the following.

1. Holding a ball for more than 5 seconds
2. Stepping over the end line or stepping over the centerline into the opponent's territory
3. Pushing or holding another player

In case of an out-of-bounds ball, the ball belongs to the team that did not cause it to go out. The nearest player retrieves the ball at the sideline and returns it to a player of the proper team.

TEACHING TIP

Variation: Using more than 1 ball increases activity and throwing repetitions. However, more than 1 ball requires a different rotation system. When a throw is completed to an end, he or she switches with the forward that threw the ball. Throughout the game, play is stopped, and forwards/ends quickly become guards and guards assume the role of forwards and ends.

Fast, accurate passing is to be encouraged. Players in the end zones must practice jumping high to catch the ball while still landing with both feet inside the end-zone area.

A system of rotation is desirable. Each time a score is made, players on that team can rotate one person (see Figure 24.17 on page 609).

To outline the end zones, some instructors use folding mats (4 by 7 feet or 4 by 8 feet). Three or four mats forming each end zone makes a definite area and eliminates the problem of defensive players (guards) stepping into the end zone.

FIVE PASSES (FOOTBALL)

Playing Area: Football field or other defined area

Players: Six to ten on each team

Supplies: A football, pinnies or other identification

Skills: Passing, catching

Players scatter on the field. The object of the game is for one team to make five consecutive passes to five different players without losing control of the ball. This scores 1 point. The defense may play the ball only and may not make personal contact with opposing players. No player can take more than three steps when in possession of the ball. More than three steps is called traveling, and the ball is awarded to the other team.

The ball is given to the opponents at the nearest out-of-bounds line for traveling, minor contact fouls, after a point has been scored, and for causing the ball to go out of bounds. No penalty is assigned when the ball hits the ground. It remains in play, but the five-pass sequence is interrupted and must start again. Jump balls are called when the ball is tied up or when there is a pileup. Players should call out the pass sequence.

SPEED FOOTBALL

Playing Area: Football field 30 by 60 yards divided into three equal sections

Players: Entire class divided into two teams

Supplies: Football, flag for each player

Skills: Passing, catching, running with ball

The ball is kicked off or started at the 20-yard line. The object is to move the ball across the opponent's goal by running or passing. If the ball drops to the ground or if a player's flag is pulled when carrying the ball, it is a turnover and the ball is set into play at that spot. Interceptions are turnovers and the intercepting team moves on offense. Teams must make at least four complete passes before they are eligible to move across the opponent's goal line. No blocking is allowed. To speed up the game, as soon as a team scores, the team can immediately (without waiting for the opponents to set up) kick or throw off. This provides incentive for all players to hustle after a score.

TEACHING TIP

Variation: Playing more than one game at a time on smaller fields allows more students to be actively involved in the game. This is also an enjoyable game when played with Frisbees.

Developmental Level III

KICK-OVER

Playing Area: Football field with a 10-yard end zone

Players: Six to ten on each team

Supplies: A football

Skills: Kicking, catching

Teams are scattered on opposite ends of the field. The object is to punt the ball over the other team's goal line. If the ball is caught in the end zone, no score results. A ball kicked into the end zone and not caught scores a goal. If the ball is kicked beyond the end zone on the fly, a score is made regardless of whether the ball is caught.

Play is started by one team with a punt from a point 20 to 30 feet in front of its own goal line. On a punt, if the ball is not caught, the team must kick from the spot of recovery. If the ball is caught, three long strides are allowed to advance the ball for a kick.

TEACHING TIP

The player kicking next should move quickly to the area from which the ball is to be kicked. Players are numbered and kick in rotation. If the players do not kick in rotation, one or two aggressive players will dominate the game.

FOURTH DOWN

Playing Area: Half of a football field or equivalent space

Players: Six to eight on each team

Supplies: A football, pinnies

Skills: Most football skills, except kicking and blocking

Every play is a fourth down, which means that the play must score or the team loses the ball. No kicking is permitted, but players may pass at any time from any spot and in any direction. There can be a series of passes on any play, either from behind or beyond the line of scrimmage.

The teams line up in an offensive football formation. To start the game, the ball is placed into the center of the field, and the team that wins the coin toss has the chance to put the ball into play. The ball is put into play by centering. The back receiving the ball runs or passes to any of his teammates. The one receiving the ball has the same privilege. No blocking is permitted. After each touchdown, the ball is brought to the center of the field, and the team against which the score was made puts the ball into play.

To down a runner or pass receiver, a two-handed touch above the waist is made. The back first receiving the ball from the center has immunity from tagging, provided that he does not try to run. All defensive players must stay 10 feet away unless he runs. The referee should wait for a reasonable length of time for the back to pass or run. If the ball is still held beyond that time, the referee should call out, "Ten seconds." The back must then throw or run within 10 seconds or be rushed by the defense.

The defensive players scatter to cover the receivers. They can use a one-on-one defense, with each player covering an offensive player, or a zone defense.

Because the team with the ball loses possession after each play, the following rules are used to determine where the ball should be placed when the other team takes possession.

1. If a ball carrier is tagged with two hands above the waist, the ball goes to the other team at that spot.
2. If an incomplete pass is made from behind the line of scrimmage, the ball is given to the other team at the spot where the ball was put into play.
3. Should an incomplete pass be made by a player beyond the line of scrimmage, the ball is brought to the spot from which it was thrown.

TEACHING TIP

The team in possession must pass by the count of 10, because children tire from running around to become free for a pass. The defensive team can score by intercepting a pass. Because passes can be made at any time, on interception the player should look down the field for a pass to a teammate.

Variation: The game can be called Third Down, with the offensive team having two chances to score.

FOOTBALL BOX BALL

Playing Area: Football field 50 yards long

Players: 8 to 16 on each team

Supplies: A football, pinnies

Skills: Passing, catching

Five yards beyond each goal is a 6-by-6-foot square, which is the box. Teams are marked so they can be distinguished. The game is similar to End Ball in that the teams try to make a successful pass to the captain in the box.

To begin the play, players are onside, which means that they are on opposite ends of the field. One team, losing the toss, kicks off from its own 10-yard line to the other team. The game then becomes a kind of keep-away, with either team trying to secure or retain possession of the ball until a successful pass can be made to the captain in the box. The captain must catch the ball on the fly and still keep both feet in the box. This scores a touchdown.

A player may run sideward or backward when in possession of the ball. Players may not run forward but are allowed momentum (two steps) if receiving or intercepting a ball. The penalty for illegal forward movement while in possession of the ball is loss of the ball to the opponents, who take it and immediately begin play.

The captain is allowed only three attempts to score or one goal. If either occurs, another player is rotated into the box. On any incomplete pass or failed attempt to get the ball to the captain, the team loses the ball. If a touchdown is made, the team brings the ball back to its 10-yard line and kicks off to the other team. If the touchdown attempt is not successful, the ball is given out of bounds on the end line to the other team.

Any out-of-bounds ball is put into play by the team that did not cause the ball to go out of bounds. No team can score from a throw-in from out of bounds.

In case of a tie ball, a jump ball is called at the spot. The players face off as in a jump ball in basketball.

Players must play the ball and not the individual. For unnecessary roughness, the player is sidelined until a pass is thrown to the other team's captain. The ball is awarded to the offended team out of bounds.

On the kickoff, all players must be onside, that is, behind the ball when it is kicked. If the kicking team is called offside, the ball is awarded to the other team out of bounds at the centerline. After the kickoff, players may move to any part of the field. On the kickoff, the ball must travel 10 yards before it can be recovered by either team. A kickoff outside or over the end line is treated as any other out-of-bounds ball.

A ball hitting the ground remains in play as long as it is in bounds. Players may not bat or kick a free ball. The penalty is loss of the ball to the other team out of bounds. Falling on the ball also means loss of the ball to the other team.

TEACHING TIP

A 4-by-7-foot or a 4-by-8-foot folding tumbling mat can be used to define the box in which the captain must stand to catch the ball for a score.

FLAG FOOTBALL

Playing Area: Field 30 by 60 yards

Players: Six to nine on a team

Supplies: A football, two flags per player (about 3 inches wide and 24 inches long), pinnies

Skills: All football skills

The field is divided into three zones by lines marked off at 20-yard intervals. There also should be two end zones, from 5 to 10 yards in width, defining the area behind the goal in which passes may be caught. Flag Football is played with two flags on each player. The flag is a length of cloth that is hung from the side at the waist of each player. To down (stop) a player with the ball, one of the flags must be pulled.

Flag Football should rarely, if ever, be played with 11 players on a side. This results in a crowded field and leaves little room to maneuver. If six or seven are on a team, four players are required to be on the line of scrimmage. For eight or nine players, five offensive players must be on the line.

The game consists of two halves. A total of 25 plays makes up each half. All plays count in the 25, except the try for the point after a touchdown and a kickoff out of bounds.

The game is started with a kickoff. The team winning the coin toss has the option of selecting the goal it wishes to defend or choosing to kick or receive. The loser of the toss takes the option not exercised by the first team. The kickoff is from the goal line, and all players on the kicking team must be onside. The kick must cross the first zone line or it does not count as a play. A kick that is kicked out of bounds (and is not touched by the receiving team) must be kicked again. A second consecutive kick out of bounds gives the ball to the receiving team in the center of the field. The kickoff may not be recovered by the kicking team unless caught and then fumbled by the receivers.

A team has four downs to move the ball into the next zone or they lose the ball. If the ball is legally advanced into the last zone, then the team has four downs to score. A ball on the line between zones is considered in the more forward zone.

Time-outs are permitted only for injuries or when called by the officials. Unlimited substitutions are permitted. Each substitute must report to the official.

The team in possession of the ball usually huddles to make up the play. After any play, the team has 30 seconds to put the ball into play after the referee gives the signal.

Blocking is done with the arms close to the body. Blocking must be done from the front or side, and blockers must stay on their feet.

A player is down if one of her flags has been pulled. The ball carrier must make an attempt to avoid the defensive player and is not permitted to run over or through the defensive player. The tackler must play the flags and not the ball carrier. Good officiating is needed, because defensive players may attempt to hold or grasp the ball carrier until they are able to remove one of her flags.

All forward passes must be thrown from behind the line of scrimmage. All players on the field are eligible to receive and intercept passes.

All fumbles are dead at the spot of the fumble. The first player who touches the ball on the ground is ruled to have recovered the fumble. When the ball is centered to a back, she must gain definite possession of it before a fumble can be called. She is allowed to pick up a bad pass from the center when she does not have possession of the ball.

All punts must be announced. Neither team can cross the line of scrimmage until the ball is kicked. Kick receivers may run or use a lateral pass. They cannot make a forward pass after receiving a kick.

A pass caught in an end zone scores a touchdown. The player must have control of the ball in the end zone. A ball caught beyond the end zone is out of bounds and is considered an incomplete pass.

A touchdown scores 6 points, a completed pass or run after touchdown scores 1 point, and a safety scores 2 points. A point after touchdown is made from a distance of 3 feet from the goal line. One play (pass or run) is allowed for the extra point. Any ball kicked over the goal line is ruled a touchback and is brought out to the 20-yard line to be put into play by the receiving team. A pass intercepted behind the goal line can be a touchback if the player does not run it out, even if she is tagged behind her own goal line.

A penalty of 5 yards is assessed for the following.

1. Being offside
2. Delay of game (too long in huddle)
3. Failure of substitute to report to the official
4. Passing from a spot not behind line of scrimmage (This also results in loss of down.)
5. Stiff-arming by the ball carrier, or not avoiding a defensive player
6. Failure to announce intention to punt
7. Shortening the flag in the belt, or playing without flags in proper position
8. Faking the ball by the center, who must center the pass on the first motion

The following infractions are assessed a 15-yard loss.

1. Holding, illegal tackling
2. Illegal blocking
3. Unsportsmanlike conduct (This also can result in disqualification.)

TEACHING TIP

Specifying 25 plays per half eliminates the need for timing and lessens arguments about a team's taking too much time in the huddle. Using the zone system makes the first-down yardage point definite and eliminates the need for a chain to mark off the 10 yards needed for a first down.

PASS BALL

Playing Area: Field 30 by 60 yards

Players: Six to nine on a team

Supplies: A football, flags (optional), pinnies

Skills: All football skills, especially passing and catching

Pass Ball is a more open game than Flag Football. The game is similar to Flag Football with these differences.

1. The ball may be passed at any time. It can be thrown at any time beyond the line of scrimmage, immediately after an interception, during a kickoff, or during a received kick.
2. Four downs are given to score a touchdown.
3. A two-handed touch on the back is used instead of pulling a flag. Flags can be used, however.
4. If the ball is thrown from behind the line of scrimmage and results in an incomplete pass, the ball is down at the previous spot on the line of scrimmage. If the pass originates otherwise and is incomplete, the ball is placed at the spot from which this pass was thrown.
5. Because the ball can be passed at any time, no downfield blocking is permitted. A player may screen the ball carrier but cannot make a block. Screening is defined as running between the ball carrier and the defense.

FOOTBALL SKILL TESTS

Tests for football skills cover centering, passing, and kicking (punting).

Centering

Each player is given five trials to center at a target. The target should be stationed 6 yards behind the center. Some suggestions for targets follow.

1. An old tire can be suspended so that the bottom of the tire is about 2 feet above the ground. For centering the ball through the tire, 2 points are scored. For hitting the tire but not going through it, 1 point is scored. The possible total is 10 points.
2. A baseball pitching target from the softball program can be used. Scoring is the same as with the tire target.
3. A 2-by-3-foot piece of plywood is held by a player at the target line in front of his body, with the upper edge even with the shoulders. The target is held stationary and is not to be moved during the centering. For hitting the target, 1 point is scored. The possible total is 5 points.

Passing for Accuracy

To test accuracy in passing, each player is given five throws from a minimum distance of 15 yards at a tire suspended at about shoulder height. (To make the tire fairly stable, it can be suspended from goal posts or from volleyball standards.) As skill increases, increase the distance.

For throwing through the tire, 2 points are scored. For hitting the tire but not passing through, 1 point is scored. The possible total for each player is 10 points.

Passing for Distance

Each player is allotted three passes to determine how far she can throw a football. The longest throw is measured to the nearest foot. Reserve the test for a relatively calm day, because the wind can be quite a factor (for or against the player) in this test.

Balanced (tight ends):

E O X O E

Unbalanced right (tight ends):

E X O O E

Line over right (tight end):

X E O O E

Right end out (can be one or both):

E O X O (5 yards) E

Right end wide (can be one or both):

E O X O (15 yards) E

Right end wide, left end out (can be reversed):

E (5 yards) O X O (15 yards) E

Spread (3 to 5 yards between each line position):

E O X O E

FIGURE 24.18 Offensive line formations.

The passes should be made on a field marked off in 5-yard intervals. Use markers made from tongue depressors to indicate the first pass distance. If a later throw is longer, the marker should be moved to that point. When individual markers are used, the members of a squad can complete the passing turns before measuring.

Kicking for Distance

Punting, place kicking, and drop kicking can be measured for distance by using techniques similar to those described for passing for distance.

FLAG FOOTBALL FORMATIONS

A variety of offensive formations are shown in Figures 24.18 and 24.19, including the T-formation. The T-formation has limited use in Flag Football, because the passer (the quarterback) is handicapped by being too close to the center. Emphasis should be on using a variety of formations and on spread formations, with flankers and ends positioned out beyond normal placement.

The following formations are based on a nine-player team, with four in the backfield and five on the line. The formations will vary if the number on each team is decreased. Presenting a variety of formations to

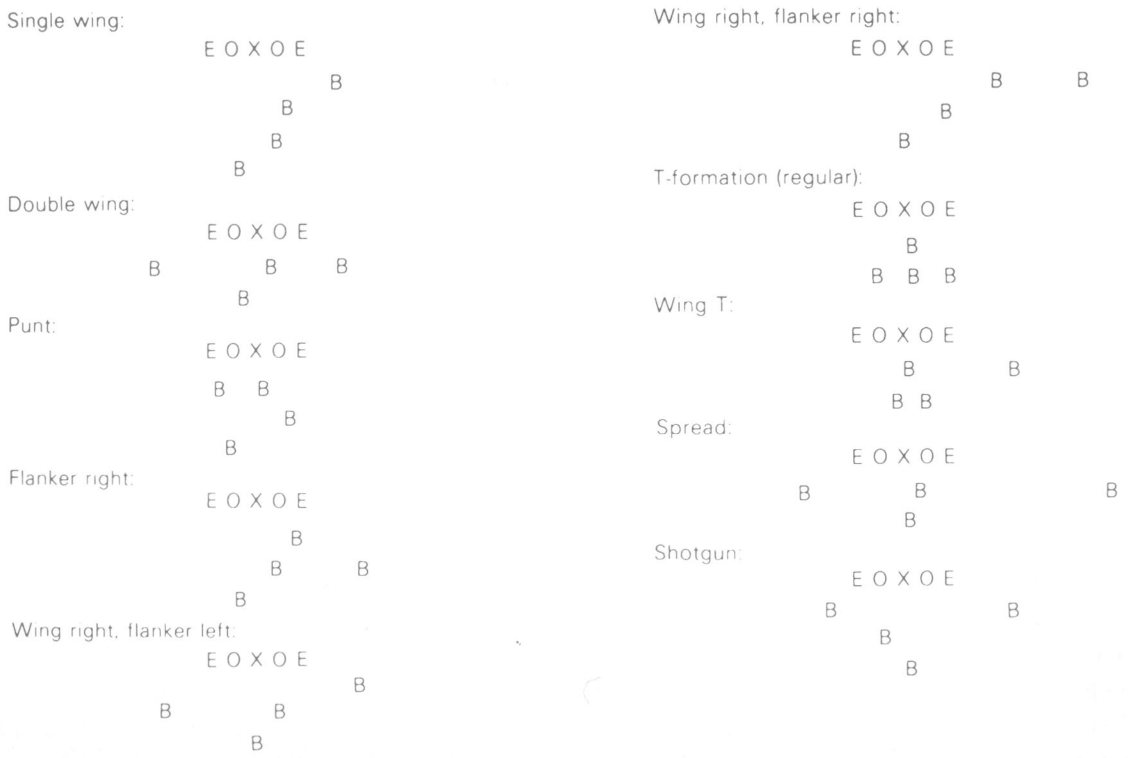

Single wing:

```
EOXOE
          B
      B
     B
 B
```

Double wing:

```
      EOXOE
B         B     B
       B
```

Punt:

```
EOXOE
B  B
     B
 B
```

Flanker right:

```
EOXOE
      B
    B      B
 B
```

Wing right, flanker left:

```
      EOXOE
              B
B         B
       B
```

Wing right, flanker right:

```
EOXOE
          B     B
      B
   B
```

T-formation (regular):

```
EOXOE
   B
B  B  B
```

Wing T:

```
EOXOE
   B       B
  B B
```

Spread:

```
         EOXOE
B          B          B
          B
```

Shotgun:

```
   EOXOE
B           B
  B
    B
```

FIGURE 24.19 Offensive backfield formations.

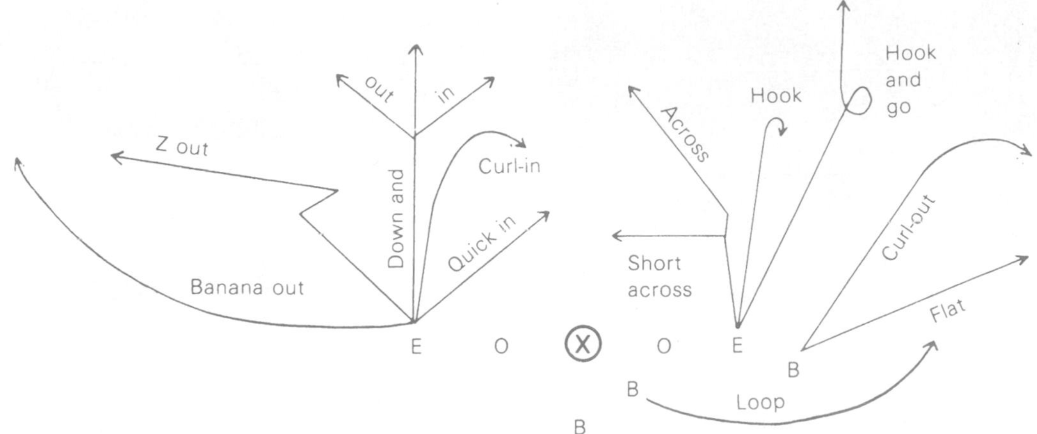

FIGURE 24.20 Pass patterns.

players makes the game more interesting. Backfield formations can be right or left (Figure 24.19).

Offensive Line Formations

Only formations to the right are presented in Figure 24.18. The center is indicated by an X, backs by B, ends by E, and line positions by O.

Offensive Backfield Formations

The formations diagrammed in Figure 24.19 can be combined with any of the offensive line formations. For purposes of clarity, however, the illustrations for all formations show a balanced line with tight ends.

Pass Patterns

The pass patterns illustrated in Figure 24.20 may be run by the individual pass catcher, whether he occupies a line position or is a back. They are particularly valuable in practice, when the pass receiver informs the passer of his pattern.

FOR MORE INFORMATION

References and Suggested Readings

Domitrovitz, M. (1993). *Flagball.* In N. Dougherty (ed.), *Physical activity and sport for the secondary school student.* Reston, VA: NASPE and AAHPERD.

Mood, D. P., Musker, F. F., & Rink, J. E. (2003). *Sports and recreational activities.* 13th ed. New York: McGraw-Hill.

The United States Flag and Touch Football League. Current ed. *The United States flag and touch football rules.* Mentor, OH: USFT Football League. (Available from NIRSA, 850 SW 15th St., Corvallis, OR 97333)

Websites

American Flag and Touch Football League
www.aftfl.com

Flag Football Magazine
www.flagmag.com

National Touch Football League
www.nftl.com

United States Flag Football League
www.c-sports.com

CHAPTER 25

Hockey

ESSENTIAL COMPONENTS

I	**Organized around content standards**
II	**Student-centered and developmentally appropriate**
III	**Physical activity and motor skill development form the core of the program**
IV	**Teaches management skills and self-discipline**
V	**Promotes inclusion of all students**
VI	**Focuses on process over product**
VII	Promotes lifetime personal health and wellness
VIII	**Teaches cooperation and responsibility and promotes sensitivity to diversity**

PHYSICAL EDUCATION STANDARDS

1	**Students are able to move competently using a variety of fundamental and specialized motor skills.**
2	Students can monitor and maintain a health-enhancing level of physical fitness.
3	**Students are able to apply movement concepts and basic mechanics of skill performance when learning and refining motor skills.**
4	Students comprehend the basic principles of wellness and are able to apply concepts that enable them to make meaningful decisions that positively impact their health and wellness.
5	**Students participate in a wide variety of physical activities and learn how to maintain a personalized active lifestyle.**
6	**Students demonstrate empathy, understanding, and respect for the numerous differences exhibited by people in an activity setting.**
7	**Students exhibit responsible and self-directed behaviors that lead to positive social interactions in physical activity.**

SUMMARY

Skills instruction for hockey is introduced during the intermediate grades after youngsters have mastered basic prerequisite skills. Teaching the rules and strategies for hockey is an integral part of the instructional process. Using proper progression is a key to success when teaching fundamental skills and lead-up games associated with hockey. Lead-up games provide an opportunity to emphasize development of selected hockey skills in a setting that is compatible with the abilities of participants.

OUTCOMES

- Structure learning experiences efficiently using appropriate formations, progressions, and coaching techniques.
- Develop a unit plan and lesson focus for hockey.
- Identify safety precautions associated with teaching hockey.
- Describe instructional procedures used for implementing a successful lead-up game.
- Cite assessment procedures used for evaluating hockey skills.

Hockey is a fast-moving game that can be adapted for use in the elementary school. Hockey at the elementary level is a lead-up to ice hockey as well as field hockey. With a plastic puck or yarn ball, hockey can be played indoors (Figure 25.1). Outdoors, a plastic whiffle ball is used. Success at hockey demands much running and team play. Teach fundamental skills and position play rather than the disorganized "everyone chase the puck" style of hockey.

INSTRUCTIONAL EMPHASIS AND SEQUENCE

Table 25.1 shows the sequence of hockey activities divided into two developmental levels. The actual presentation of activities is dictated by the maturity and past experience of participants.

Developmental Level II

At this level, little strategy is introduced. Drills are used to develop fundamental skills. Learning to dribble and carry the ball loosely, fielding the ball, and making short passes should receive the most attention.

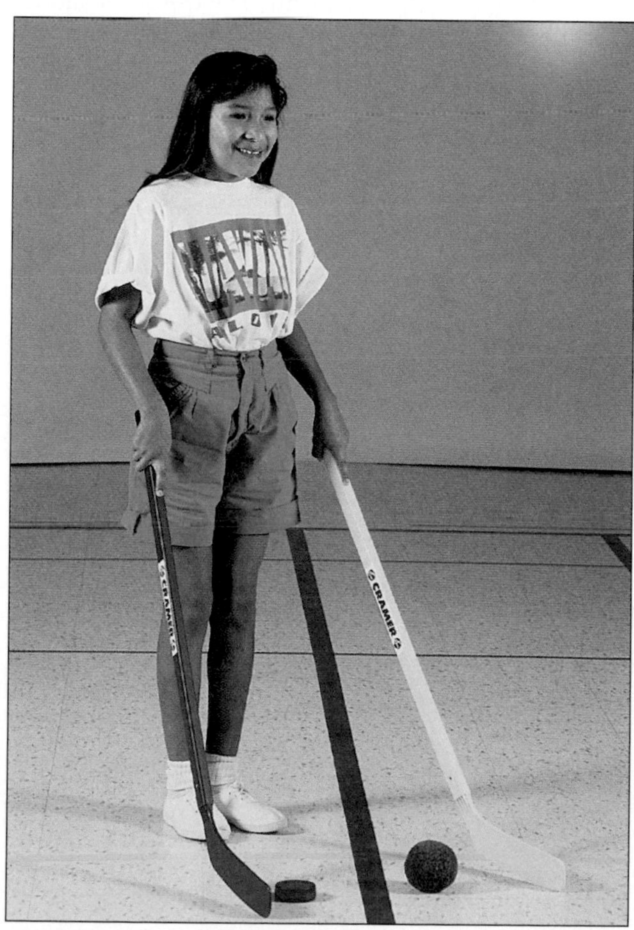

FIGURE 25.1 Hockey equipment.

TABLE 25.1 Suggested hockey program

Developmental Level II	Developmental Level III
Skills	
Gripping and carrying the stick	Controlled dribble
Loose dribble	Side field
Passing	Tackle
Front field	Dodging
Goalkeeping	Face-off
	Driving
	Jab shot
Knowledge	
Hockey rules	Ball handling and passing
	The game of hockey
	Team play and strategy
Activities	
Circle Keep-Away	Goalkeeper Hockey
Star Wars Hockey	Sideline Hockey
Lane Hockey	Regulation Elementary Hockey
Modified Hockey	
Skill Tests	
Passing for accuracy	Dribbling for speed
Fielding	Driving for distance

Developmental Level III

At developmental level III, skill development continues, with more emphasis on ball control and passing accuracy. Lead-up games using skills involved in regulation hockey are played. The drills presented are designed to foster team play. Lead-up games are used to introduce strategy and field positioning. The rules of regulation hockey are introduced, and the actual game is played. Skills should be reviewed and practiced through the use of selected drills and lead-up games.

HOCKEY SKILLS

Gripping and Carrying the Stick

The hockey stick should be held with both hands and carried as low to the ground as possible. The basic grip puts the left hand at the top of the stick and the right

FIGURE 25.2 Gripping and carrying.

hand 6 to 12 inches below the left (Figure 25.2). The player should learn to carry the stick to the right of the body, with the blade close to the ground, while running. To ensure accuracy as well as safety, the stick must not be swung above waist height.

Dribbling and Carrying

Dribbling is used to carry the ball without the aid of teammates. Players should be taught to look for a pass first and then dribble if there is no immediate opportunity to make a pass. The following instructional cues offer points of emphasis for skill performance.

1. Control the puck. It should always be within reach of the stick.
2. Move under control.
3. Hold the stick firmly.
4. Keep the head up.
5. Keep the elbows away from the body.

Loose Dribble

The loose dribble is a form of carrying the ball under control. It demands less skill than controlled dribbling. In loose dribbling, the ball is pushed 10 to 15 feet in front of the player. The player then runs to the ball and gives it another push, repeating the sequence. This type of dribble is used in open-field play when there is little chance that an opponent will intercept the ball. The loose dribble also allows skilled players to run at maximum speed. The ball must be pushed with the flat side of the blade and kept in front of the body.

Controlled Dribble

The controlled dribble consists of a series of short taps in the direction in which the player chooses to move. The hands should be spread 10 to 14 inches apart to gain greater control of the stick. As the player becomes more skilled, the hands can be moved closer together. The stick is turned so that the blade faces the ball. The grip should not be changed, but rather, the hands should be rotated until the back of the left hand and the palm of the right hand face the ball (Figure 25.3). The ball can then be tapped just far enough in front of the player to keep it away from the feet but not more than one full stride away from the stick. The emphasis should be on controlling the ball during heavy traffic so that opposing players cannot easily intercept it.

Passing

The most commonly used passes in floor hockey are the forehand pass and the quick hit. The quick hit should be taught simultaneously with dribbling skills. Emphasis should be on accuracy rather than on swinging wildly. The following instructional cues can be used to help youngsters concentrate on correct technique.

FIGURE 25.3 Starting the dribble.

1. Approach the puck with the side facing the direction of the pass.
2. Keep the head down and eyes on the puck.
3. Keep the stick below waist level at all times.
4. Transfer weight from the rear to the front foot.
5. Drive the stick through the puck.
6. Keep the stick on the floor until the puck is struck.

Forehand Pass

The forehand pass is a short pass that usually occurs from the dribble. It should be taught before driving, because the quick hit requires accuracy rather than distance. The player spreads the feet with toes pointed slightly forward when striking. Approach the ball with the stick held low and bring the stick straight back, in line with the intended direction of the hit. The hands should be the same distance apart as in the carrying position, and the stick should be lifted no higher than waist level. The player's right hand guides the stick down and through the ball. The head should be kept down with the eyes on the ball. A short follow-through occurs after contact.

Driving and Shooting

Driving (Figure 25.4) is used to hit the ball moderate to long distances and to shoot at the goal. It differs from other passes in that the hands are brought together more toward the end of the stick. This gives the leverage necessary to apply greater force to the ball and results in more speed and greater distance. The swing and hit are similar to the quick hit. Stick control should be stressed so that wild swinging does not occur.

Fielding

The term *fielding* refers to stopping the ball and controlling it. Fielding the ball in hockey is as important as catching the ball in basketball. As a skill, it requires much practice. Emphasize the following instructional cues:

FIGURE 25.4 Driving.

1. Field with a "soft stick." This means holding the stick with relaxed hands.
2. Allow the puck to hit the stick and then "give" to make a soft reception.
3. Keep the hands apart on the stick.

Front Field

For the front field, the student must keep an eye on the ball, move to a point in line with its path, and extend the flat side of the blade forward to meet the ball (Figure 25.5). The faster the ball approaches, the more the player must learn to give with the stick to absorb the momentum of the ball. The player should field the ball in front of the body and not permit it to get too close.

Side Field

A ball approaching from the left or right side is more difficult to field than one approaching from the front. When the ball is approaching from the left, the player must allow the ball to travel in front of the body before fielding it. If the ball is approaching from the right, it must be intercepted *before* it crosses in front of the body (Figure 25.6 on page 620). The player's feet should be pointed in the direction in which he plans to move after controlling the ball. Regardless of the direction of the ball, the side of the blade must always be used to field it.

FIGURE 25.5 Front field position.

FIGURE 25.6 Side field position.

Tackling

The tackle is a means of taking the ball away from an opponent. The tackler moves toward the opponent with the stick held low. The tackle is timed so that the blade of the stick is placed against the ball when the ball is off the opponent's stick (Figure 25.7). The tackler then quickly dribbles or passes in the direction of the goal. Throwing the stick or striking carelessly at the ball should be discouraged. Players need to remember that a successful tackle is not always possible.

Jab Shot

The jab shot is used only when a tackle is not possible. It is a one-handed, poking shot that attempts to knock the ball away from an opponent.

FIGURE 25.7 Tackling.

Dodging

Dodging is a means of evading a tackler and maintaining control of the ball. The player dribbles the ball directly at the opponent. At the last instant, the ball is pushed to one side of the tackler, depending on the direction the player is planning to dodge. If the ball is pushed to the left, the player should move around the right side of the opponent to regain control of the ball, and vice versa. Selecting the proper instant to push the ball is the key to successful dodging. Dodging should not be attempted if a pass would be more effective.

Face-Off

The face-off is used at the start of the game, after a goal, or when the ball is stopped from further play by opposing players. The face-off is taken by two players, each facing a sideline, with their right sides facing the goal that their team is defending. Each player hits the ground on her side of the ball and the opponent's stick over the ball, alternately, three times. After the third hit the ball is played, and each player attempts to control the ball or to pass it to a teammate. The right hand can be moved down the stick to facilitate a quick, powerful movement. An alternate means of starting action is for a referee to drop the ball between the players' sticks.

Goalkeeping

The goalie may kick the ball, stop it with any part of the body, or allow it to rebound off the body or hand. He may not, however, hold the ball or throw it toward the other end of the playing area. The goalkeeper is positioned in front of the goal line and moves between the goal posts. When a ball is hit toward the goal, the goalie should attempt to move in front of the ball and to keep the feet together. This allows the body to block the ball should the stick miss it. After the block, the ball is passed immediately to a teammate.

INSTRUCTIONAL PROCEDURES

1. For many children, hockey is a new experience. Few have played the game, and many may never have seen a game. Showing a film of a hockey game as an introduction may be helpful.
2. Since few children have had the opportunity to develop skills elsewhere, it is necessary to teach the basic skills in a sequential manner and to allow ample time in practice sessions for development.
3. Hockey is a rough game if children are not taught the proper methods of stick handling. They need to

be reminded often to use caution and good judgment when handling hockey sticks.

4. Ample equipment increases individual practice time and facilitates skill development. A stick and a ball or puck for each child are desirable.
5. If hockey is played on a gym floor, a plastic puck or yarn ball should be used. If played on a carpeted area or outdoors, a whiffle ball is used. An 8-foot folding mat set on end makes a satisfactory goal.
6. Hockey is a team game that is more enjoyable for all when the players pass to open teammates. Excessive control of the ball by one person should be discouraged.
7. An individual who is restricted to limited activity can be designated as a goalie. This is an opportunity for children with disabilities to participate and receive reinforcement from peers. An asthmatic child, for example, might serve as a goalkeeper.
8. Fatigue may be a problem, for hockey is a running game that demands agility and endurance. Children should be in reasonably good physical condition to participate. Frequent rotation and rest periods help prevent fatigue.

HOCKEY DRILLS

DRIBBLING AND CARRYING DRILLS

1. Successful hockey play demands good footwork and proper stick handling. To develop these skills, spread players on the field, carrying the stick in proper position, in a group mimetic drill. On command, players move forward, backward, and to either side. Quick reactions and footwork are the focus.
2. Each player with a ball practices dribbling and carrying individually. Dribbling should be practiced first at controlled speeds and then at faster speeds as skill develops.
3. Players can practice in pairs, with partners standing about 20 feet apart. One player carries the ball toward a partner, goes around the partner, and returns to the starting spot (Figure 25.8). The ball is then passed to the partner, who moves in a similar manner. A shuttle type of formation can be used with three players.

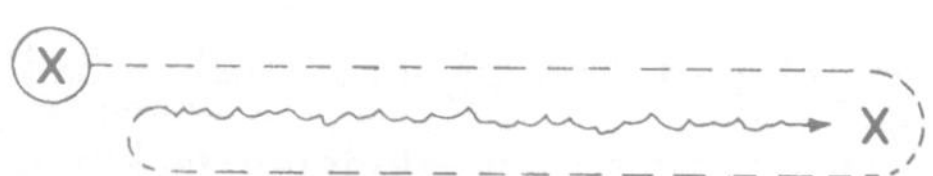

FIGURE 25.8 Dribbling drill.

PASSING AND FIELDING DRILLS

1. In pairs, about 20 feet apart, players pass the ball quickly back and forth. Emphasis should be on passing immediately after fielding the ball. The cue phrase might be "Field, pass."
2. One player passes the ball to a partner, who fields the ball, dribbles twice, and passes back to the other. Passes should be fielded from various angles and from the right and left sides.
3. Use the shuttle turn-back formation, where two files of four or five players face each other. The first person in the file passes to the first person in the other file, who in turn fields the ball and returns the pass. Each player, when finished, goes to the end of the file.
4. The downfield drill is useful for polishing passing and fielding skills while moving. Three files of players start at one end of the field. One player from each file proceeds downfield, passing to and fielding from the others until the other end of the field is reached. A goal shot can be made at this point. The players should remain close together for short passes until a high level of skill is reached.
5. Practice driving for distance and accuracy with a partner.

DODGING AND TACKLING DRILLS

1. Players are spread out on the field, each with a ball. On command, they dribble left, right, forward, and backward. On the command "Dodge," the players dodge an imaginary tackler. Players should concentrate on ball control and dodging in all directions.
2. Three players form the drill configuration as diagrammed in Figure 25.9. Player 1 has the ball in front, approaches the cone (which represents a defensive player), dodges around the cone, and passes to player 2, who repeats the dodging maneuver in the opposite direction. Player 2 passes to player 3, and the drill continues in that manner.
3. Players work in pairs. One partner dribbles toward the other, who attempts to make a tackle. If the tackle is successful, roles are reversed. This drill should be practiced at moderate speeds in the early stages of skill development.
4. A three-on-three drill affords practice in many skill areas. Three players are on offense and three are on

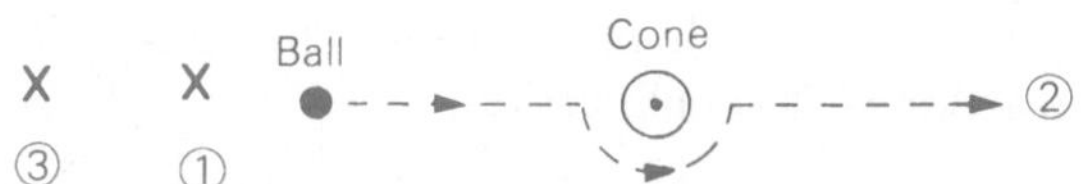

FIGURE 25.9 Shuttle-type drill.

defense. The offense can concentrate on passing, dribbling, and dodging, while the defense concentrates on tackling. A point is given to the offense when they reach the opposite side of the field. The defensive team becomes the offensive team after a score.

HOCKEY ACTIVITIES

Developmental Level II

CIRCLE KEEP-AWAY

Playing Area: A 20- to 25-foot circle

Players: Eight to ten

Supplies: One stick per person, a puck or ball

Skills: Passing, fielding

Players are spaced evenly around the circle, with two or more players in the center. The object of the game is to keep the players in the center from touching the puck. The puck is passed back and forth, with emphasis on accurate passing and fielding. Center players see how many touches they can make during their turn. Change the center players after a time limit so all youngsters have an opportunity to be center players.

STAR WARS HOCKEY

Playing Area: Playground or gymnasium

Players: Four teams of equal size

Supplies: One stick per player, four pucks or balls

Skills: Dribbling

Each team forms one side of a square formation. The game is similar to Star Wars (page 573), with the following exceptions:

1. Four pucks (or balls) are used. When a number is called, each player with that number goes to a puck and dribbles it out of the square through the spot previously occupied, around the square counterclockwise, and back to the original spot. Circles 12 inches in diameter are drawn on the floor to provide a definite place to which the puck must be returned. If the game is played outdoors, hoops can mark the spot to which the puck must be returned.
2. No player is permitted to use anything other than the stick in making the circuit and returning the puck to the inside of the hoop. The penalty for infractions is disqualification.

LANE HOCKEY

Playing Area: Hockey field or gymnasium, 60 by 100 feet

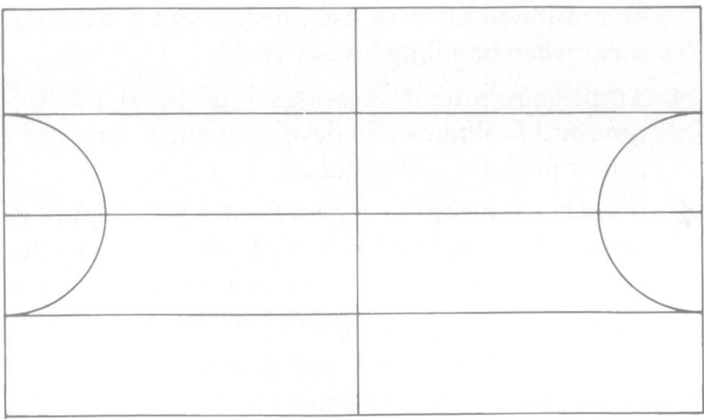

FIGURE 25.10 Field markings for Lane Hockey.

Players: Nine per team

Supplies: Hockey stick per player, puck, two goals

Skills: All hockey skills

The field is divided into eight lanes as illustrated in Figure 25.10. A defensive and an offensive player are placed in each of the eight lanes. A goalkeeper for each team is also positioned in front of the goal area. Players may not leave their lane during play. A shot on goal may not be taken until a minimum of two passes have been completed. This rule encourages looking for teammates and passing to someone in a better position before taking a shot on goal.

Players should be encouraged to maintain their spacing during play. The purpose of the lanes is to force them to play within a zone rather than rushing to the puck. Rules used for regulation hockey enforce situations not described here. A free shot (unguarded) is awarded a team if a foul occurs. Players should be rotated after a goal is scored or at regular time intervals.

TEACHING TIP

To add more activity to Lane Hockey, use more than one puck or add one or two more goals and goalies.

Variation: Increase the number of lanes to five or six. This involves a larger number of players. On a large playing area, the lanes may be broken into thirds rather than halves. Increase the number of passes that should be made prior to a shot on goal.

MODIFIED HOCKEY

Playing Area: Hockey field or gymnasium

Players: 7 to 11 on each team

Supplies: One stick per person, a puck or ball

Skills: Dribbling, passing, dodging, tackling, face-off

The teams may take any position on the field as long as they remain inside the boundaries. The object of the game is to hit the puck through the opponent's goal. No goalies are used. At the start of the game and after each score, play begins with a face-off. Each goal is worth one point.

TEACHING TIP

The distance between goal lines is flexible but should be on the long side. If making goals is too easy or too difficult, the width of the goals can be adjusted accordingly.

Developmental Level III

GOALKEEPER HOCKEY

Playing Area: A square about 40 by 40 feet

Players: Two teams of equal size

Supplies: One stick per player, a puck or ball

Skills: Passing, fielding, goalkeeping

Each team occupies two adjacent sides of the square (Figure 25.11). Team members are numbered consecutively from left to right. Two or three numbers are called by the instructor. These players enter the playing area and attempt to capture the ball, which is placed in the center of the square, and to pass it through the opposing team. A point is scored when the ball goes through the opponent's side. Sideline players are goalies and should concentrate on goalkeeping skills. After a short period of time (1 minute), the active players return to their positions, and new players are called.

TEACHING TIP

Keep track of the numbers called so that all players have an equal opportunity to play. Different combinations can be called.

SIDELINE HOCKEY

Playing Area: Hockey field or gymnasium area, 60 by 100 feet

Players: 6 to 12 players on each team

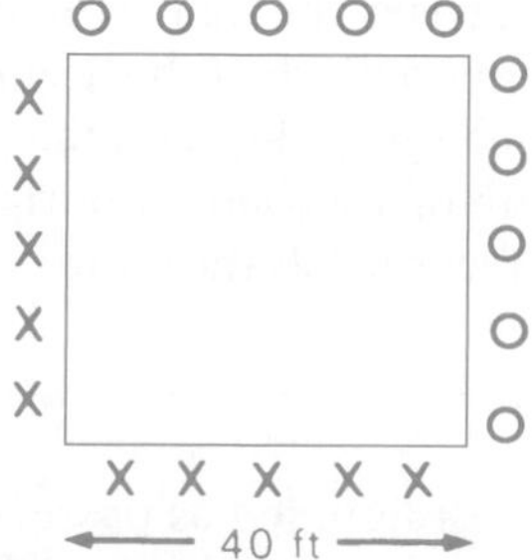

FIGURE 25.11 Team positions for Goalkeeper Hockey.

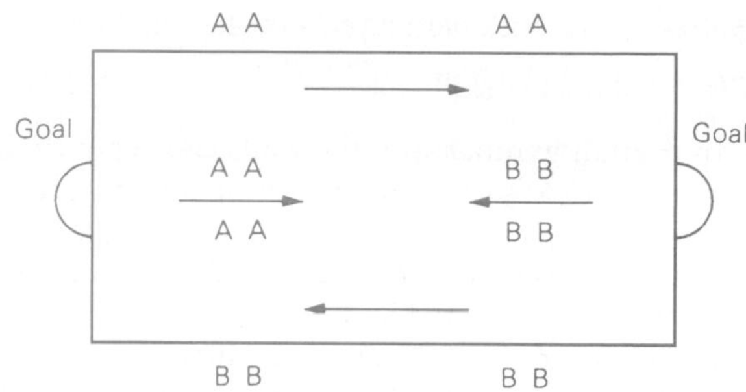

FIGURE 25.12 Team positions for Sideline Hockey.

Supplies: One hockey stick per player, a puck or ball, two 4-by-8-foot folding tumbling mats

Skills: Most hockey skills, except goaltending

Each team is divided into two groups. They are positioned as indicated in Figure 25.12, which shows eight players on each team. Three to six players from each team move onto the court; these are the active players. The others will actively participate on the sidelines. No goalkeeper is used. A face-off at the center starts the game and puts the ball into play after each score. Each team on the field, aided by the sideline players, attempts to score a goal. The sideline players help keep the ball in bounds and can pass it onto the court to the active players. Sideline players may pass to an active player or to each other.

Any out-of-bounds play on a sideline belongs to the team guarding that sideline and is immediately put into play with a pass. An out-of-bounds shot over the end line that does not score a goal is put into play by the team defending the goal. The group of players on the field changes places with the sideline players on their team as soon as a goal is scored or after a specified time period.

Illegal touching, sideline violations, and other minor fouls result in loss of the ball to the opposition. Roughing fouls and illegal striking should result in banishment to the sideline for the remainder of the competitive period.

TEACHING TIP

Try to encourage team play and passing strategies rather than having all players charge and swarm the puck. An effective rule is to require active players to make three passes to their teammates before taking a shot on goal. This makes all players an important part of the game.

REGULATION ELEMENTARY HOCKEY

Playing Area: Hockey field or gymnasium area, approximately 40 to 50 feet by 75 to 90 feet

Players: Six or more on each team

Supplies: One stick per player, a puck or ball

Skills: All hockey skills

In a small gymnasium, the walls can serve as the boundaries. In a large gymnasium or on an outdoor field, the playing area should be delineated with traffic cones. The area should be divided in half, with a 12-foot restraining circle centered on the midline. This is where play begins at the start of the periods, after goals, or after foul shots. The official goal is 2 feet high by 6 feet wide, with a restraining area 4 by 8 feet around the goal to protect the goalie (Figure 25.13). Each team has a goalkeeper, who stops shots with her hands, feet, or stick; a center, who is the only player allowed to move full court and who leads offensive play (the center has her stick striped with black tape); two guards, who cannot go beyond the centerline into the offensive area and who are responsible for keeping the puck out of their defensive half of the field; and two forwards, who work with the center on offensive play and who cannot go back over the centerline into the defensive area.

A game consists of three periods of 8 minutes each, with a 3-minute rest between periods. Play is started with a face-off by the centers at midcourt. Other players cannot enter the restraining circle until the ball has been hit by the centers. The clock starts when the puck is put into play and runs continuously until a goal is scored or a foul is called. Substitutions can be made only when the clock is stopped. If the ball goes out of bounds, it is put back into play by the team that did not hit it last.

Whenever the ball passes through the goal on the ground, 1 point is scored. If, however, the ball crosses the goal line while in the air, it must strike against the mat or back wall to count for a score. Under no circumstances can a goal be scored on a foul. The puck can deflect off a player or equipment to score, but it cannot be kicked into the goal.

The goalkeeper may use her hands to clear the puck away from the goal, but she may not hold it or throw it toward the other end of the playing area. She is charged with a foul for holding the puck. The goalkeeper may be pulled from the goal area but cannot go beyond the centerline. No other player may enter the restraining area without being charged with a foul.

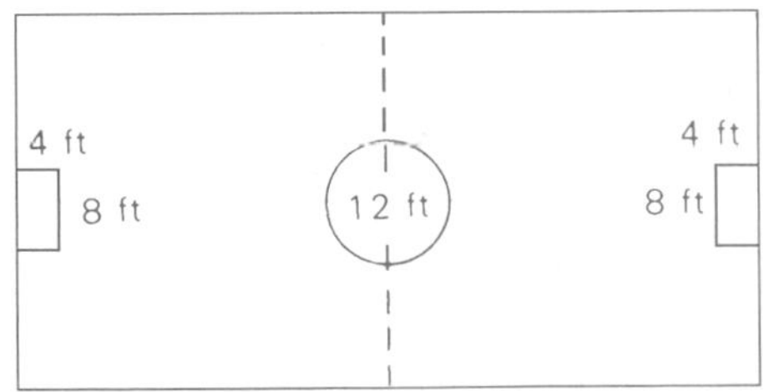

FIGURE 25.13 Regulation elementary hockey playing field.

The following are fouls and are penalized by loss of the puck at the spot of the foul.

1. Illegally touching the puck with the hands
2. Swinging the stick above waist height (called sticking)
3. Guards or forwards moving across the centerline
4. Player other than the goalie entering the restraining area
5. Goalie throwing the puck
6. Holding, stepping on, or lying on the puck

Defenders must be 5 yards back when the puck is put into play after a foul. If the spot where the foul occurred is closer than 5 yards to the goal, only the goalkeeper may defend. The puck is then put into play 5 yards directly out from the goal.

Personal fouls include any action or rough play that endangers other players. A player committing a personal foul must retire to the sidelines for 2 minutes. The following are personal fouls.

1. Hacking or striking with a stick
2. Tripping with either the foot or the stick
3. Pushing, blocking

HOCKEY SKILL TESTS

Passing for Accuracy

In passing for accuracy, the player has five attempts to pass the puck or ball into a 3-by-3-foot target. The target can be drawn or taped on the wall, or a 3-foot square of cardboard can be used. The player must pass from a distance of 30 feet. He can approach the 30-foot restraining line in whatever fashion he chooses. Two points are awarded for each successful pass.

Carrying for Speed

To test carrying for speed, three cones are placed in line 8 feet apart. The first cone is 16 feet from the starting line. The player carries the ball around the cones in a figure-eight fashion to finish at the original starting line. A stopwatch is used for timing, and the score is recorded to the nearest tenth of a second. Two trials are given, and the faster trial is recorded as the score.

Fielding

Three players are designated as passers and pass from different angles to a person being tested in fielding. The ball must be definitely stopped and controlled. The instructor can judge whether the pass was a good opportunity for the player to field. Six passes, two from each angle, are given, and one point is awarded for each successful field.

Driving for Distance

Driving for distance should be tested outdoors only. A restraining line can be used as a starting point. Each player is given five trials, and the longest two attempts are recorded as the player's score. Distance is measured to the nearest foot. Players can be lined up in four or five squads behind the restraining line. At any one time, one-third of the class can measure distances and return the balls. After players have taken their five trials, they can exchange places with someone who is measuring or returning balls. The test should be done on grass, because solid ground permits the ball to roll unimpeded.

FOR MORE INFORMATION

References and Suggested Readings

Anders, E. (1999). *Field hockey: Steps to success.* Champaign, IL: Human Kinetics.

Mood, D. P., Musker, F. F., & Rink, J. E. (2003). *Sports and recreational activities.* 13th ed. New York: McGraw-Hill.

Rulebook for outdoor and indoor hockey. (Current edition). Colorado Springs: United States Field Hockey Association.

Trimble, R. M. (1997). *The ultimate hockey drill book.* Indianapolis: Masters Press.

Whitney, M. G. (Ed.). *Eagle, Official Publication of the United States Field Hockey Association Inc.* USFHA: Colorado Springs, CO (periodical).

Websites

Field hockey information
www.fieldhockey.com

United States Field Hockey Association
www.usfieldhockey.com

CHAPTER 26

Soccer

ESSENTIAL COMPONENTS

I	**Organized around content standards**
II	**Student-centered and developmentally appropriate**
III	**Physical activity and motor skill development form the core of the program**
IV	**Teaches management skills and self-discipline**
V	**Promotes inclusion of all students**
VI	**Focuses on process over product**
VII	Promotes lifetime personal health and wellness
VIII	**Teaches cooperation and responsibility and promotes sensitivity to diversity**

PHYSICAL EDUCATION STANDARDS

1	**Students are able to move competently using a variety of fundamental and specialized motor skills.**
2	Students can monitor and maintain a health-enhancing level of physical fitness.
3	**Students are able to apply movement concepts and basic mechanics of skill performance when learning and refining motor skills.**
4	Students comprehend the basic principles of wellness and are able to apply concepts that enable them to make meaningful decisions that positively impact their health and wellness.
5	**Students participate in a wide variety of physical activities and learn how to maintain a personalized active lifestyle.**
6	**Students demonstrate empathy, understanding, and respect for the numerous differences exhibited by people in an activity setting.**
7	**Students exhibit responsible and self-directed behaviors that lead to positive social interactions in physical activity.**

SUMMARY

Skills instruction for soccer is introduced during the intermediate grades after youngsters have mastered basic prerequisite skills. Teaching the rules and strategies for soccer is an integral part of the instructional process. Using proper progression is a key to success when teaching fundamental skills and lead-up games associated with soccer. Lead-up games provide an opportunity to emphasize development of selected soccer skills in a setting that is compatible with the abilities of participants.

OUTCOMES

- Structure learning experiences efficiently using appropriate formations, progressions, and coaching techniques.
- Develop a unit plan and lesson focus for soccer.
- Identify safety precautions associated with teaching soccer.
- Describe instructional procedures used for implementing a successful lead-up game.
- Cite assessment procedures used for evaluating soccer skills.

Soccer is the most popular sport in America for youth, with a tremendous growth rate among girls. Effective soccer stresses position play, in contrast to a group of children chasing the ball. If players are to improve their playing ability, organized practice that emphasizes handling the ball as often as possible is essential. Offer students frequent opportunities on offense to kick, control, dribble, volley, and shoot and frequent opportunities on defense to mark, guard, tackle, and recover the ball. Success in soccer depends on how well individual skills are coordinated in team play.

MODIFICATIONS OF SOCCER FOR CHILDREN

A regulation soccer ball is oversized and too heavy for young soccer players who want to learn the sport. Many youngsters avoid contact with the regulation ball for fear of getting hurt. There are a number of manufacturers producing junior-sized soccer balls that move and rebound in a manner identical to regulation balls. Foam balls that are covered with a tough plastic skin to simulate the appearance of a soccer ball can negate the fear of being hurt. Beach balls are excellent for teaching beginning skills because they move slowly and don't hurt when one is struck. If heading skills are taught, a beach ball should be the only type of ball used.

Decrease the number of players in games to ensure that there is more opportunity to practice skills. When learning soccer, the 11-person team is not suitable. Mini-Soccer is an excellent game with six or seven players on a side. Two games can be played crosswise on a regulation soccer field. With the exception of a penalty area and the out-of-bounds lines, the field does not have to be marked. The official regulation soccer goal, 24 feet wide and 8 feet high, is too large for elementary school play. The size should be such that teams have a reasonable chance of scoring as well as preventing a score. The suggested size is from 18 to 21 feet in width and 6 to 7 feet in height. The size can be further scaled down as determined by the character of the game.

INSTRUCTIONAL EMPHASIS AND SEQUENCE

Table 26.1 shows the sequence of soccer activities divided into developmental levels. Depending on the amount of experience children have received through community sports programs, the actual sequence may differ in certain areas and communities.

TABLE 26.1 Suggested soccer program

Developmental Level II	Developmental Level III
Skills	
Dribbling	Dribbling
Inside-of-the-foot pass	Outside-of-the-foot pass
Long pass	Ball control (trapping)
Foot trap	Passing
Passing	Tackling
Goalkeeping	Kicking goals
Defensive maneuvers	Kickoff (placekicking)
	Punting
	Volleying
	Heading
Knowledge	
Soccer rules	Ball control and passing
	The game of soccer
	Team play and strategy
Activities	
Circle Kickball	Manyball Soccer
Soccer Touch Ball	Addition Soccer
Diagonal Soccer	Over the Top
Dribblerama	Lane Soccer
Bull's-Eye	Line Soccer
Pin Kickball	Mini-Soccer
Sideline Soccer	Six-Spot Keepaway
Kick Bowling	Regulation Soccer
Soccer Golf	
Skill Tests	
Controlled passing	Figure-eight dribbling
Kicking for accuracy	Controlling (three types)
Placekicking	Punting for distance
	Penalty kicking

Developmental Level II

The two basic skills in soccer are (1) controlling or stopping the ball with the foot so that the ball is in a position to be kicked and (2) passing the ball with the foot to another player or to a target. Activities at this level should stress games and drills that facilitate practice and use of fundamental skills. To maximize involvement, one ball for every two players should be available.

Developmental Level III

To enhance control of the ball, dribbling skills are introduced and students are taught to control the ball with other parts of the body, such as the thigh and chest. Passing continues to receive major emphasis so that small-side games or Mini-Soccer, with two to five players per team, can be introduced. The basic goalkeeping skills of catching low and high balls are taught. Further development of basic skills is recommended, along with the introduction of shooting, tackling, heading, jockeying, and the concept of two-touch soccer for more advanced players. Fundamentals of team and positional play are taught, along with the rules of the regular game. A unit of study focusing on soccer as an international game is of value because few children in the United States realize how important this game is in other countries.

SOCCER SKILLS

Offensive skills taught in the elementary grades are passing, kicking, controlling, dribbling, volleying (including heading), and shooting. *Shooting* is defined as taking a shot at the goal with the intent to score. Defensive skills include marking, guarding, jockeying, tackling, and recovering the ball.

Dribbling

Dribbling is moving the ball with a series of taps or pushes to cover ground and still retain control. It allows a player to change direction quickly and to avoid opponents. The best contact point is the inside of the foot, but the outside of the foot will be used at faster running speeds. The ball should be kept close to the player to maintain control. The following instructional cues can be used to emphasize proper form:

1. Keep the head up in order to see the field.
2. Move on the balls of the feet.
3. Contact the ball with the inside, outside, or instep of the foot.
4. Keep the ball near the body so it can be controlled. (Don't kick it too far in front of the body.)
5. Dribble the ball with a controlled tap.

Passing

Balance and timing provide the keys to accurate passing. The basic purposes of passing are to advance the ball to a teammate and to shoot on goal. Occasionally, a pass is used to send the ball downfield so that a team has a chance to regroup, with their opponents having an equal chance to recover the ball.

The following are instructional cues to enhance accurate passing:

1. Place the nonkicking foot alongside the ball.
2. Keep the head down and the eyes focused on the ball during contact.
3. Spread the arms for balance.
4. Follow through with the kicking leg in the intended direction of the ball.
5. Make contact with the outside or inside of the foot rather than with the toe.
6. Practice kicking with both the left and right foot.

Inside-of-the-Foot Pass (Push Pass)

The inside-of-the-foot pass is used for accurate passing over distances of up to 15 yards. Because of the technique used, this pass is sometimes referred to as the *push pass*. The nonkicking foot is placed well up, alongside the ball. As the kicking foot is drawn back, the toe is turned out. During the kick, the toe remains turned out so that the inside of the foot is perpendicular to the line of flight. The sole is kept parallel to the ground. At contact, the knee of the kicking leg should be well forward, over the ball, and both knees should be slightly bent (Figure 26.1).

Outside-of-the-Foot Pass (Flick Pass)

The nonkicking foot is placed more to the side of the ball than for the inside-of-the-foot kick, and the approach of the kicking leg is from directly behind the ball. The kicking foot is fully extended and contact with the ball is on the outside of the foot between laces and sole-line. This pass can be used effectively while running, without breaking stride, or for flicking the ball to the side.

The Long Pass (Shoelace Kick)

The long pass is the power pass in soccer. It is used for kicking for distance or for power to kick the ball past a goalie. Beginners often use the toes instead of the top of the foot (shoelace) area, which can result in injury or an inaccurate kick. The ball is approached at an angle to the line of flight in a full running stride. The nonkicking foot is placed alongside the ball, with the kicking leg cocked in the backswing. Just before contact, the ankle of the kicking foot is fixed with the toes pointed down. As with all passes, the head is kept down with the eyes focused on the ball. Contact is made with the top of the foot on the shoelaces. The passer gives the lower leg a good forward snap at the knee. A normal follow-through in the intended direction of the pass completes the action. To lift the ball, contact is made below the

FIGURE 26.1 An inside-foot pass.

midline of the ball, close to the ground, with the body leaning slightly backward. The nonkicking leg is placed to the side and slightly behind the ball so that the kicking foot makes contact just on the start of the upswing of the leg. The lofted pass is made over the heads of opposing players.

Ball Control (Trapping)

Learning to receive a ball and how to place it into the ideal position for making a pass or shot is vital. In fact, one of the best measures of skilled players is how quickly they can bring the ball under control with either the feet, legs, or torso. Advanced players are able to achieve this in one smooth movement, with one touch of the ball. The second touch occurs when the pass is made.

For efficient control, a large surface should be presented to the ball. On contact, the surface should be momentarily withdrawn to produce a spongelike or shock-absorbing action, which decelerates the ball and allows it to drop in an ideal position about a yard in front of the body. The pass or shot can then be made. The following instructional cues will help students develop ball control skills:

1. Move in line with the path of the ball.
2. Reach to meet the ball and give with the contact.
3. Stay on the balls of the feet.
4. Keep the eyes on the ball.

Inside-of-the-Foot Trap

This is the most common method of control; it is used when the ball is either rolling along the ground or bouncing up to knee height. The full surface of the foot, from heel to toe, should be presented alongside the ball (Figure 26.2).

Chest and Thigh Traps

The inside of the thigh and the chest also are used to deflect the ball downward when it is bouncing high. The chest trap requires that the chest be lined up squarely with the direction from which the ball is traveling (Figure 26.3 on page 630). On contact, the chest and waist are drawn back, causing a forward body lean. This will cause the ball to drop directly to the ground in front of the player. The thigh trap demands that the player turn the body sideways to the flight of the ball. The ball is contacted with the inside of the thigh. Upon contact

FIGURE 26.2 Controlling with the inside of the foot.

FIGURE 26.3 Chest trap.

with the ball, the thigh is relaxed and drawn backwards. This action absorbs the force of the ball and causes it to drop to the ground ready to be played.

Sole-of-the-Foot Trap

This method of control, sometimes called trapping the ball, is used occasionally to stop the ball. With beginners, it is not as successful a method as the inside-of-the-foot control, because the ball can roll easily under the foot. The sole is also used to roll the ball from side to side in dribbling and to adjust for a better passing position.

Heading

Heading is a special kind of volleying in which the direction of flight of the ball is changed through an impact with the head. Recent research has shown that heading might cause some brain damage. With this in mind, if heading skills are going to be practiced, beach balls should be used in place of soccer balls. Since beach balls move slowly, they offer beginners time to get in proper position. *Heading with a regulation ball should be avoided with elementary school youngsters.*

In heading, the neck muscles are used to aid in the blow. The eye must be kept on the ball until the moment of impact. The point of contact is the top of the forehead at the hairline. In preparation for contacting the ball with the head, the player stands in stride position, with knees relaxed and trunk bent backward at the hips. At the moment of contact, the trunk moves forward abruptly, driving the forehead into the ball. Advanced heading is achieved in midair, and is especially useful in beating other players to the ball. Midair heading can be done by a running one-footed takeoff or a standing two-footed jump.

Defensive Maneuvers

Tackling is a move by a player to take possession of the ball away from an opponent who is dribbling. The most common tackle is the front block, which involves contacting the ball with the inside of the foot just as the opponent touches it. The tackler presents a firm instep to the ball, with weight behind it. The stronger the contact with the ball, the greater the chance of controlling it. Body contact should be avoided, as this may constitute a foul. Other tackles may be made when running alongside the player with the ball.

How much tackling to teach in elementary school programs is a question of concern. In most cases, it is probably best to teach tackling skills that involve the defensive player remaining upright. Methods like the hook slide and split slide are of little value in elementary school instructional programs.

Jockeying

Knowing when to make a tackle, and when not to, is one of the most difficult skills to learn. A failed tackle may mean that an attacker breaks through with a free shot on goal. Often, defenders should jockey until defensive support arrives. This means backing off while staying close enough to pressure the advancing player. The defender should stay on the toes, watch the ball rather than the opponent's feet, and keep within 1 to 2 yards of the ball.

Throw-Ins

The throw-in is the only time the ball can be handled by field players with their hands. The throw-in is guided by rules that must be followed closely or the result is a turnover to the other team. The rules are as follows:

1. Both hands must be on the ball.
2. The ball must be released from over the thrower's head.
3. The thrower must face the field.
4. The thrower may not step onto the field until the throw is released.
5. Both feet must remain in contact with the ground until the ball is released.
6. The thrower cannot play the ball until it has been touched by another player on the field.

The throw-in from out of bounds (see Figure 26.20) may be executed from a standing or running position. Beginning players should learn the throw without a running start. The feet often are placed one behind the other, with the rear toe trailing along the ground. Delivery of the ball should be from behind the head, using both arms equally. Release should be from in front of the forehead with arms outstretched. Instructional cues to help students perform correctly are "drag your back foot" and "follow through with both hands pointing toward the target."

Shooting

Scoring is the purpose of the game, and shooting skills should be practiced both while stationary and while on the run. As with passing, the inside, outside, and top of the foot can be used.

Goalkeeping

Goalkeeping involves stopping shots by catching, stopping, or otherwise deflecting the ball. Goalkeepers should become adept at catching low rolling balls, diving on rolling balls, catching airborne balls at waist level and below (Figure 26.4), and catching airborne balls at waist height and above.

Youngsters should practice catching low rolling balls in much the same manner as a baseball outfielder does. The goalie gets down on one knee, with her body behind the ball to act as a backstop, and catches the ball with both hands, fingers pointing toward the ground.

If the goalie must dive for the ball, he should throw his body behind it and cradle it with his hands. A goalie should always try to get his body behind the ball.

When catching a ball below the waist, the thumbs should point outward and the arms reach for the ball, with body and arms giving and bringing the ball into the abdomen. For balls above waist level, the thumbs should be turned inward, arms reaching to meet the ball and giving to guide it to the midsection.

Drills for goalies should offer opportunities to catch the different shots described. All students should receive goaltending practice.

FIGURE 26.4 Goalie catching a ball below waist level.

Punting

Used by the goalkeeper only, the punt can be stationary or can be done on the run. The ball is held in both hands at waist height in front of the body and directly over the kicking leg. For the stationary punt, the kicking foot is forward. A short step is taken with the kicking foot, followed by a full step on the other foot. With the knee bent and the toe extended, the kicking foot swings forward and upward. As contact is made with the ball at the instep, the knee straightens, and additional power is secured from the other leg through a coordinated rising on the toes or a hop (Figure 26.5).

The goalkeeper who can develop a strong placekick has an advantage. Distance and accuracy are important in setting up the next attack. Over shorter distances, throwing underhand or overhand can be more accurate than kicking. A straight arm should be used for rolling or throwing the ball to players.

Instructional Procedures

1. Soccer skills must be practiced if children are to participate successfully in the sport. Controlling the ball and passing predominate in practices. Organize drills and activities to maximize the involvement of all children. One ball is needed per two children.
2. Many combination drills featuring both offense and defense should be included. Enjoyment is the key to continued learning. Drills and lead-up activities can be used to make the skills challenging, but all activities should be appropriate to the developmental level of players.
3. Use small-group games (with two to five players per team) to ensure maximum activity. The number of team members can be increased as skill improves.

FIGURE 26.5 Punt.

4. Lead-up games are designed to encourage the use of the skills practiced in drills. For example, if long passing is the skill of the day, lead-up games requiring and rewarding long passing should be played. In the early stages of learning soccer, it may be best not to allow tackling.
5. The grid system is useful when organizing drills, activities, and small-sized games. Using cones or chalk, mark a grid system of 10-yard squares on the playing field. The number of squares needed depends on the size of the class, but at least one square for every three students is recommended. Possible layouts are shown in Figure 26.6. The squares are used as boundaries for tackling, keeping possession, and passing diagonally or sideways. Drill and game areas can be defined easily, so that a number of small-sized games can be played simultaneously.
6. Balls smaller and lighter than the regulation soccer ball should be used. Partially deflated 8-inch rubber playground balls can be used, provided their quality is good enough to withstand the kicking. A better alternative for novices is the toughskin foam-rubber training ball. It withstands heavy usage and does not hurt youngsters on impact. Another alternative is a beach ball. They are light and move slowly, making them an excellent choice for unskilled players. The key to soccer practice is to have plenty of balls available. Rubber balls mean more fun, because they can be kicked far, controlled easily, and even headed without discomfort. Junior-sized soccer balls (No. 4) are also excellent but are more expensive.
7. Soccer, with its attack and defense, can be a rough game. Rough play such as pushing, shoving, kicking, and tripping must be controlled. Rules need to be strictly enforced.
8. Modified scoring can be used to make the activity more enjoyable for more children. To score must be a challenge—neither too easy nor too difficult. To avoid arguments in situations in which the ball is to be kicked through a line of children, limit the height of the kick to shoulder level or below. Cones and spots can be used to mark goal outlines. Regulation soccer goals are not necessary for the elementary school program.

SOCCER DRILLS

In soccer drills, two approaches are most often used. The first is to practice technique with no opposition from any defense. The second is the skill approach, which involves both offensive and defensive players and perhaps a target. In drills using the skill approach, the goal is to outmaneuver the opponent. Some drills begin with the technique approach and then move to the skill approach. Individual practice is excellent, particularly with dribbling techniques, but most practice is best accomplished with combinations of two or three students and small groups.

The type of surface has a marked effect on the quality of soccer practice. Grass is the most desirable practice surface, but some schools have only hard-top surfaces. In

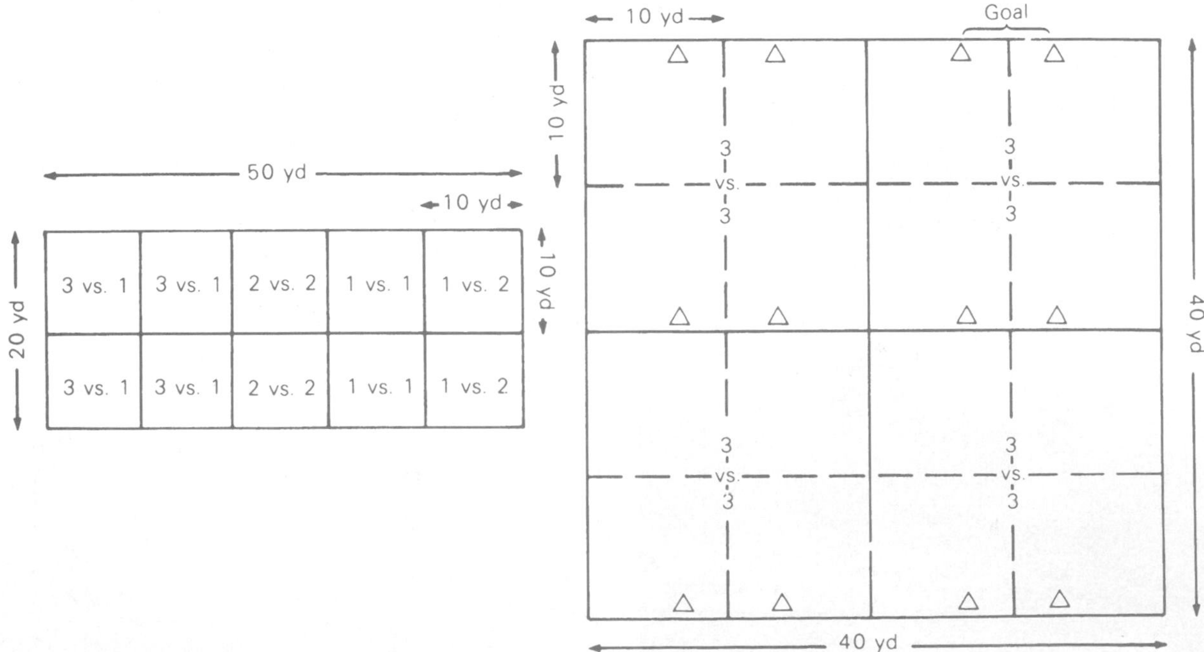

FIGURE 26.6 Examples of grid layouts and usage.

this case, balls should be deflated slightly to approximate how they travel on grass. When space is restricted, outline areas with cones, beanbags, jugs, or boundary boards.

INDIVIDUAL WORK

Dribbling practice is best done individually. Activity can begin by having youngsters dribble in various directions and signaling them to make right and left turns. As a variation, children can react to signals: One whistle means turn left, two means turn right, and three means reverse direction. A number of cones can be scattered around the area. Players then dribble around one cone clockwise and around the next cone counterclockwise.

Have youngsters practice heading skills by tossing a beach ball overhead and heading it. Alternate heading with a short period of dribbling practice. To teach trapping skills, drop a ball and show students how to smother it with a foot. Another drill is to have youngsters toss the ball in the air, let it bounce and then kick it to themselves with an instep kick. Yet another trick is to toss the ball high and use the instep kick to control the ball.

Rebounding to oneself continuously, although not actually used in the game of soccer, is an excellent way to learn ball control. (This is sometimes called foot juggling.) Students begin by dropping the ball so that it bounces at waist height, and then practice the following skills:

1. Rebound the ball with alternating feet, letting it bounce between contacts.
2. Play the ball twice with one foot, let it bounce, and then play it twice with the other foot.
3. Toss the ball so it can be handled with the thigh and then catch. Add successive rebounds with the thigh.
4. Play ball with the foot, thigh, head, thigh, foot, and catch.

The foot pickup is another skill that can be taught in two ways. The first is to have students put the ball between the feet, jump up, and hoist the ball so it can be caught. The second is the toe pickup. Students put the toe on top of the ball and pull the toe back and down so that the ball spins up the instep, from which it can be hoisted to the hands. Another bit of individual work is toe changing on top of the ball. Students put the ball of the foot on top of the ball. On signal, they change feet.

DRILLS FOR TWO PLAYERS

Many introductory drills can be practiced best with a partner. One of the best ways to organize partner drills is to use the grid system mentioned earlier in this chapter. The distance between the grid lines depends on the skills to be practiced. Partners position themselves opposite each other so that two lines of players are formed, which gives the teacher a clear view of the class in action (Figure 26.7). This approach is recommended for introducing all new skills, such as passing with both sides of the foot, and ball control. Skill combinations can be used, such as throw-ins by one partner and control-and-pass by the other. Within the grids, partners can work on passing, dribbling, keepaway, and one-on-one games.

The following are examples of drills that can be used in partner formation.

1. *Dribbling, marking, and ball recovery.* Pairs are scattered, with one player in each pair having a soccer ball. That player dribbles in various directions, and the second player attempts to stay close to the first (marking). As skill improves, the defensive player attempts to recover the ball from the dribbler. If successful, roles are reversed.
2. *Dribbling.* One player of the pair has a ball and dribbles in different directions. On signal, she passes to her partner, who repeats the dribbling, continuing until another signal is given.
3. *Dribbling, moving, and passing.* Two lines of paired children face each other across a 40-to-60-foot distance, as illustrated in the diagram (Figure 26.8, page 634). Each child in one of the lines has a ball and works with a partner directly across from him. A player with a ball from line A moves forward according to the challenges listed below. When he moves near his partner, he passes to him, and the

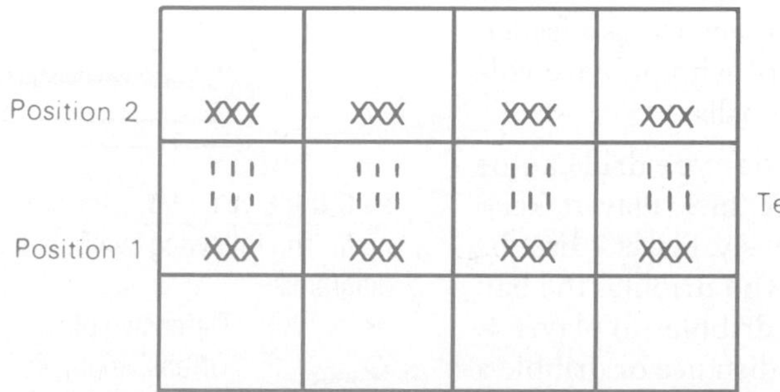

FIGURE 26.7 Class organized along grid lines.

FIGURE 26.8 Dribbling, moving, and passing.

partner (line B) repeats the same maneuver back to line A. Repeating the maneuver immediately results in both players returning to their starting place.

a. Dribble across to partner. Dribble using the outside of either foot.
b. Gallop across, handling the ball with the front foot only. On return, lead with the other foot.
c. Skip across, dribbling at the same time.
d. Slide across, handling the ball with the back foot. On return, lead with the other foot.
e. Hop across, using the lifted foot to handle the ball. Be sure to change feet halfway across.
f. Dribble the ball to a point halfway across. Stop the ball with the sole of the foot and leave it there. Continue to the other line. In the meantime, the partner from line B moves forward to dribble the ball back to line A.
g. Player A dribbles to the center and passes to player B. Player A now returns to line A. Player B repeats and returns to line B.

4. *Volleying and controlling.* Pairs of players are scattered. One player in each pair has a ball and acts as a feeder, tossing the ball for various receptive skills including different volleys and controlling balls in flight. Controlled tossing is essential to this drill.

DRILLS FOR THREE PLAYERS

With one ball for three players, many of the possibilities suggested for pair practice are still possible. An advantage of drills for three players is that fewer balls are needed.

1. *Passing and controlling.* The trio of players set up a triangle with players about 10 yards apart. Controlled passing and practice in ball control should occur.
2. *Volleying and controlling.* One player acts as a feeder, tossing to the other two players, who practice volleying and controlling air flight balls.
3. *Dribbling and passing.* A shuttle-type drill can be structured as shown in Figure 26.9. Players keep going back and forth continuously. Player 1 has the ball and dribbles to player 2, who dribbles the ball back to player 3, who in turn dribbles to player 1. Players can dribble the entire distance or dribble a portion of the distance and then pass the ball to the end player. Obstacles can be set up to challenge players to dribble through or around each obstacle.

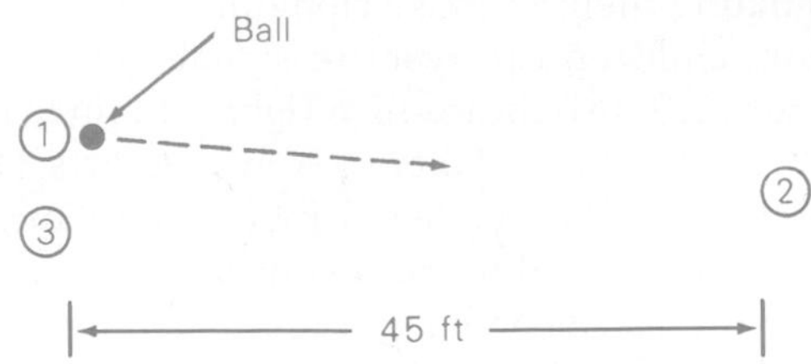

FIGURE 26.9 Shuttle-type dribbling drill.

4. *Dribbling and stopping the ball.* Three dribblers are in line, each with a ball. The leader moves in various directions, followed by the other two players. On signal, each player controls her ball. The leader circles around to the back ball, and the other two move one ball forward. The dribbling continues for another stop. A third stop puts the players back in their original positions.
5. *Passing.* Players stand in three corners of a 10-yard square. After a player passes, he must move to the empty corner of the square, which is sometimes a diagonal movement (Figure 26.10).

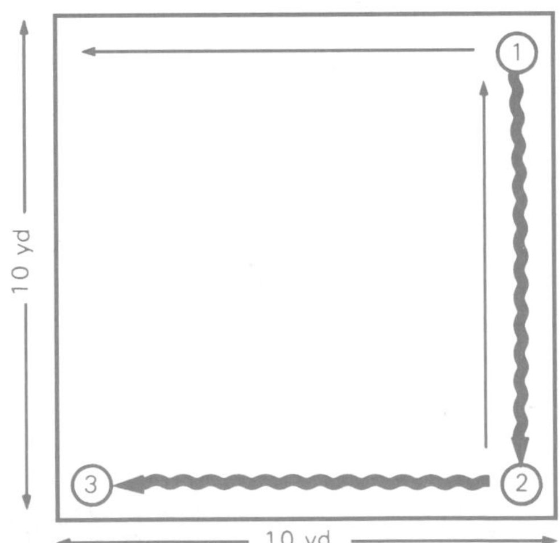

FIGURE 26.10 Passing drill.

Note: The following symbols are used in soccer game formation diagrams:

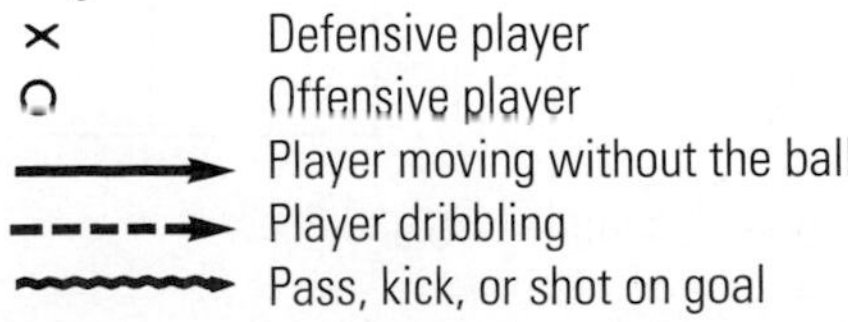

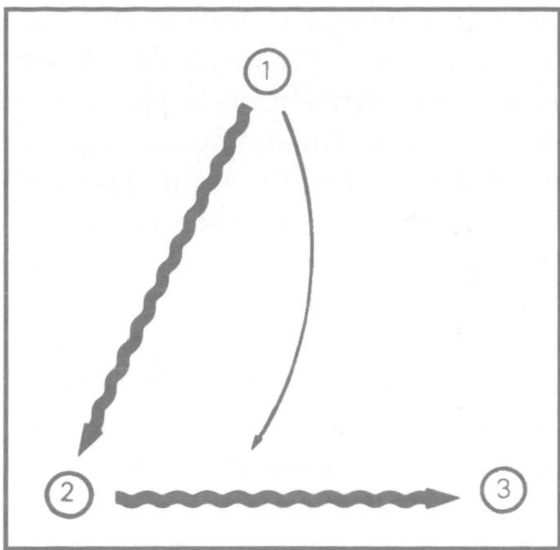

FIGURE 26.11 Passing and defense drill.

6. *Passing and defense.* One player is the feeder and rolls the ball to either player. As soon as she rolls the ball, she attempts to block or tackle the player receiving the ball to prevent a pass to the third player, who, if the pass is completed, attempts to pass back (Figure 26.11).

DRILLS FOR FOUR OR MORE PLAYERS

Drills for four or more players should be organized so that a rotation gives all players an equal opportunity to practice skills.

1. *Dribbling.* Four players are in line as diagrammed in Figure 26.12. Each player in front has a ball. Both front players dribble to the center, where they exchange balls and continue dribbling to the other side. The next players perform similarly. A variation is to have the two players meet at the center, exchange balls, and dribble back to their starting point. Action should be continuous.
2. *Passing, guarding, and tackling.* Four players occupy the four corners of a square respectively (Figure 26.13). One player has a ball. Practice begins with one player rolling the ball to the player in the opposite corner, who, in turn, passes to either of the other two players. There should be two attempts each round so that kicks are possible both ways. The next progression calls for the player who rolled the ball to move forward rapidly to block the pass to either side. Several tries should occur before another player takes over the rolling duties.

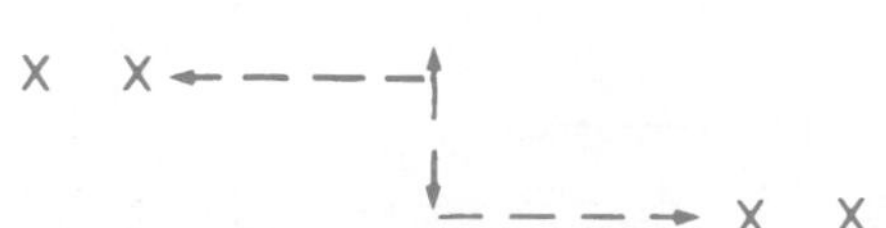

FIGURE 26.12 Dribble exchange drill.

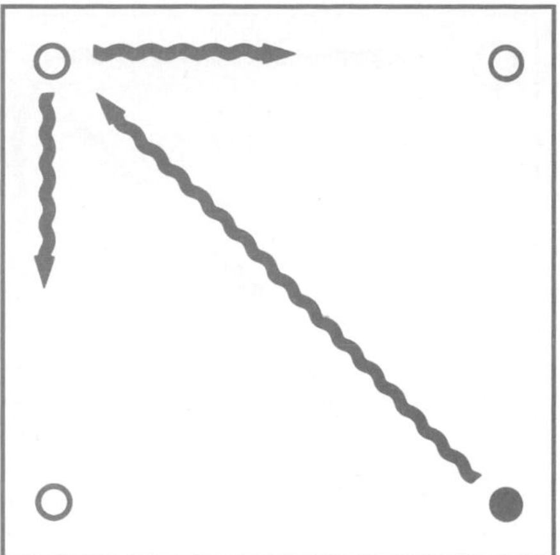

FIGURE 26.13 Passing, guarding, and tackling drill.

3. *Shooting, goalkeeping, and defense.* A shooting drill against defense can be run with four players and a 15-foot goal set off with cones or other markers (Figure 26.14). One player has the ball. He advances and attempts to maneuver around a second player so that he can shoot past the goalkeeper guarding a goal. A fourth player acts as the retriever. Rotate positions.
4. *Dribbling.* Four or five players, each with a ball, form a line. A "coach" stands about 15 yards in front of the line. Each player, in turn, dribbles up to the coach, who indicates with a thumb in which direction the player should dribble past. The coach should give the direction at the last possible moment.
5. *Passing, controlling, and defense.* Four players stand in the four corners of a square, 10 yards on a side. Two defensive players are inside the square. The corner players stay in place within the square and attempt to pass the ball among themselves, while the two defenders attempt to recover the ball (Figure 26.15 on page 636). After a period of time, another two players take over as defenders.
6. *Shooting.* For two-way goal practice, two to six players are divided, half on each side of the goal. The width of the goal can vary, depending on the skill of the players. Two types of shooting should be practiced: (a) kicking a stationary ball from 10 to 20 yards out and (b) preceding a kick with a dribble. In the second type, a restraining line 12 to 15 yards out is needed. This line can be marked by cones, as

FIGURE 26.14 Shooting, goalkeeping, and defense.

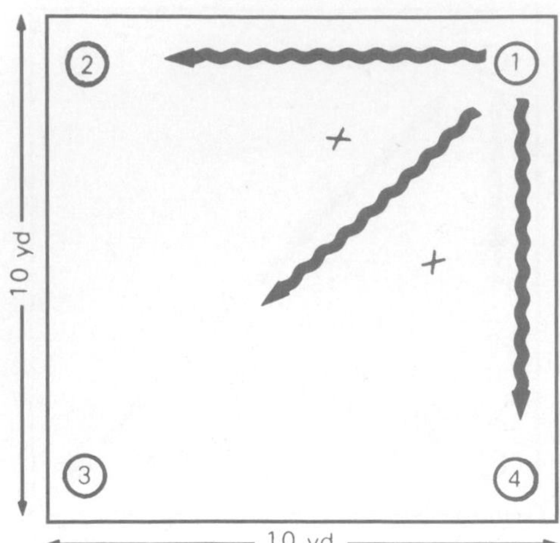

FIGURE 26.15 Passing, controlling, and defense.

illustrated (Figure 26.16). Use at least four balls for this two-way drill. After a period of kicking, the groups should change sides. Ball chasers are the players at the end of each line.

7. *Shooting and goalkeeping.* Scoring can also be practiced with a goalkeeper (Figure 26.17). Practice should be done with a stationary ball from 12 yards out (penalty distance) and with kicks preceded by a dribble. The goalie and the chaser should remain for one complete round and then rotate. Having a second ball to play with saves time because play can continue while the chaser is recovering the previous ball.
8. *Kicking and trapping.* This is an excellent squad drill. Approximately eight players form a circle 15 yards in diameter. Two balls are passed back and forth independently. Passes should be kept low, using primarily the side-of-the-foot kick. Using three balls can be tried also.
9. *Passing and shooting.* The drill can be done with four to six players. Two balls are needed. A passer is stationed about 15 yards from the goal, and a retriever is behind the goal. The shooters are in line, 20 yards from the goal and to the right. The first shooter passes to the passer, and then runs forward. The passer returns the ball to the shooter. The shooter tries to time her run forward so that she successfully shoots the pass through the goal. Both the passer and the retriever should stay in position for several rounds of shooting and then rotate to become shooters. The first pass can be from a stationary ball. Later, however, the kicker can be allowed to dribble forward a short distance before making the first pass. Reverse the field and practice from the left, shooting with the nondominant leg (Figure 26.18).
10. *Tackling and ball handling.* A defender is restricted to tackling in the area between two parallel lines, which are 1 yard apart. The field is 20 by 40 yards (Figure 26.19). Four to six players can practice this drill. Player 1 advances the ball by dribbling and attempts to maneuver past the defender. After he has evaded the defender, he passes to player 2 and takes his place at the other side of the field. Player 2 repeats the routine, passing the ball off to the next player in the line. If the ball goes out of control or is stopped by the defender, it is rolled to the player whose turn is next. Play is continuous, with the defender maintaining his position for several rounds.

BASIC SOCCER RULES FOR LEAD-UP GAMES

The ball may not be played deliberately with the hands or arms, but incidental or unintentional handling of the

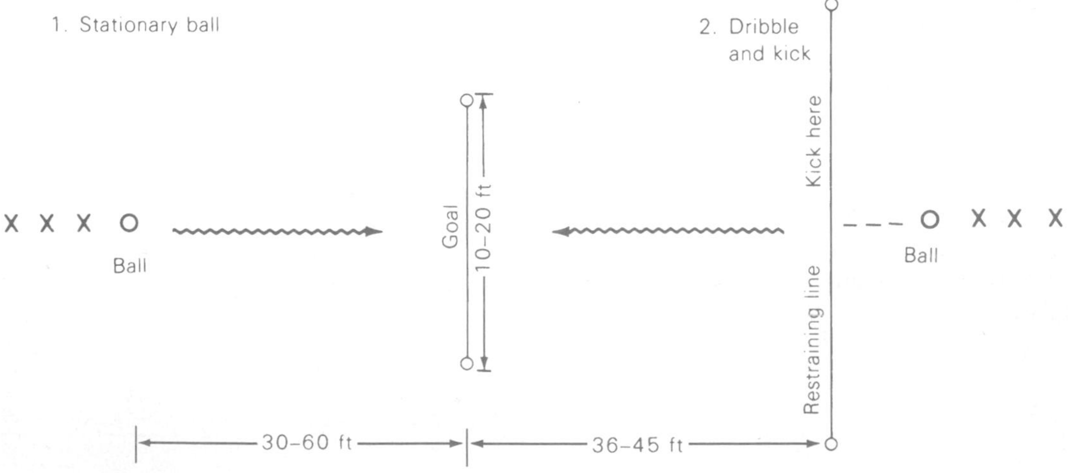

FIGURE 26.16 Shooting drill.

FIGURE 26.17 Shooting and goalkeeping.

ball should be disregarded in the early stages. Eventually, a violation leads to a direct free kick in which the ball is placed on the ground with the opposition a specified distance away (10 yards on a full-sized field). A goal can be scored directly from this type of kick.

The goalkeeper is allowed to handle the ball within her area by catching, batting, or deflecting with the hands. If the goalie has caught the ball, she may not be charged by the opponents. While the goalie is holding the ball, official rules limit her to four steps. In elementary school play, the teacher should insist on the goalkeeper's getting rid of the ball immediately by throwing or kicking. This removes the temptation to rough up the goalie. In some lead-up games, a number of students may have the same ball-handling privileges as the goalie. The rules need to be clear, and ball handling should be done within a specified area.

All serious fouls, such as tripping, kicking a player, holding, or pushing, result in a direct free kick. If a defender commits one of these fouls or a handball in his own penalty area, a penalty kick is awarded. Only the goalkeeper may defend against this kick, which is shot from 12 yards out. All other players must be outside the penalty area until the ball is kicked. In lead-up games, consideration should be given to penalty fouls committed in a limited area near the goal by the defensive team.

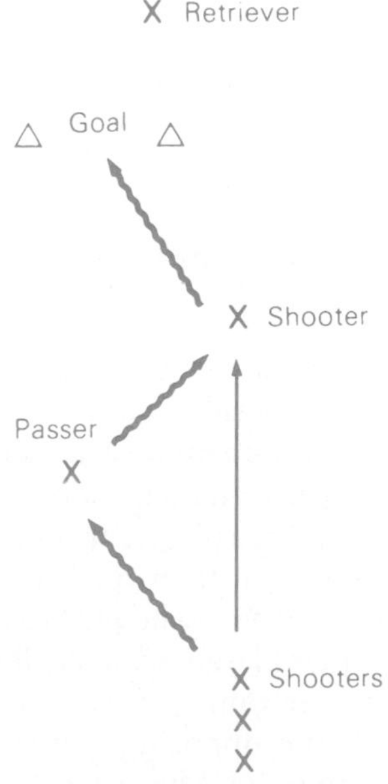

FIGURE 26.18 Passing and shooting.

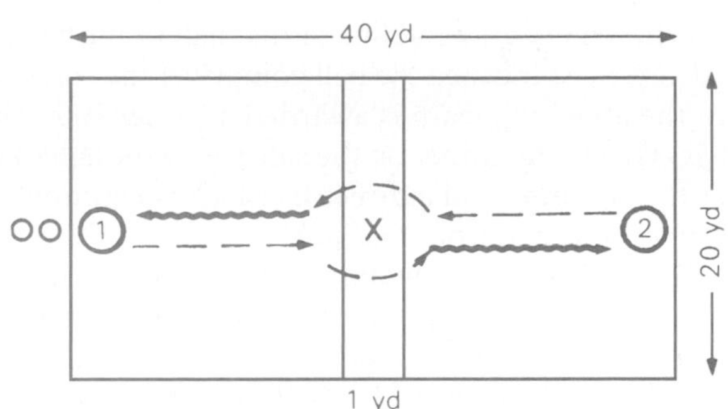

FIGURE 26.19 Tackling and ball-handling drill.

A kick can be awarded or an automatic goal can be scored for the attacking team.

The ball is out of play and the whistle blown when the ball crosses any of the boundaries, when a goal is scored, or when a foul is called. The team that last touched the ball or caused it to go out of bounds on the side of the field loses possession. The ball is put into play with an overhead throw-in using both hands (Figure 26.20).

If the attacking team causes the ball to go over the end line, the defending team is awarded a kick from any

FIGURE 26.20 Throwing in, from out of bounds.

point chosen near the end line of that half of the field. If the defense last touched the ball going over the end line, then the attacking team is awarded a *corner kick*. The ball is taken to the corner on the side where the ball went over the end line, and a direct free kick is executed. A goal may be scored from this kick.

The game is normally started by a kickoff with both teams onside. In lead-up games, the ball can be dropped for a free ball. In some games, the teacher may find it advisable simply to award the ball for a free kick in the backcourt to the team not making the score.

Lead-up games can continue for a set length of time (by halves) or until a predetermined score is attained. In a regular soccer game, the play is timed.

When the ball is ensnarled among a number of players or when someone has fallen, a quick whistle is needed. The ball can be put into play by dropping it between players of the opposing teams.

Even though implementation of the offside rule is of little value in elementary school play, children should understand the rule and the reasons for it. Its purpose is to prevent the "cheap" goal (i.e., a player on offense waits near the goal to take a pass behind the defenders and to score easily against the goalkeeper). Although the concept of *offsides* involves a number of details, it essentially means that a player on offense who is ahead of the ball must have two defensive players between her and the goal when the ball is kicked forward. One of these players is, of course, the goalie. The offside rule does not apply when the player receives the ball directly from an attempted goal kick, from an opponent, on a throw-in or corner kick, or when the player is in her own half.

Players should not raise their feet high or show the soles or cleats when other players are in the vicinity. This constitutes dangerous play, and an *indirect free kick* is awarded.

SOCCER ACTIVITIES

Developmental Level II

CIRCLE KICKBALL

Playing Area: Playground or gymnasium

Players: 10 to 20

Supplies: Two beachballs or 8-inch foam rubber balls

Skills: Blocking (goalie skills) and kicking

Players are in circle formation. Using the side of the foot, players kick the balls back and forth inside the circle. The object is to kick a ball from going out of the circle beneath the shoulder level of the circle players. Circle players can use their hands and feet to block the ball since they are goalies. A point is scored against each of the players if a ball leaves the circle between them. If, however, a lost ball is clearly the fault of a single player, then the point is scored against that player only. Any player who kicks a ball higher than the shoulders of the circle players has a point scored against her. Players with the fewest points scored against them win. A player is not penalized if she leaves the circle to recover a ball and the second ball goes through the vacated spot.

TEACHING TIP

Specify the types of kicks players can use.

SOCCER TOUCH BALL

Playing Area: Playground or gymnasium

Players: Eight to ten

Supplies: Soccer balls, beach balls or 8-inch foam-rubber balls

Skills: Kicking, controlling

Players are spaced around a circle 10 yards in diameter with two players in the center. The object of the game is to keep the players in the center from touching the ball. The ball is passed back and forth as in soccer. If a center player touches the ball with a foot, they are awarded a point. Implement a rule that no player may contain or hold the ball longer than 3 seconds to keep the game moving. Rotate two new players into the center after 15 to 30 seconds.

DIAGONAL SOCCER

Playing Area: A square about 60 by 60 feet

Players: 20 to 30

Supplies: Soccer ball, beach ball or 8-inch foam-rubber ball, pinnies (optional)

Skills: Kicking, passing, dribbling, some controlling, defending, blocking shots

Two corners are marked off with cones 5 feet from the corners on both the sides, outlining triangular dead areas. Each team lines up as illustrated in Figure 26.21 and tries to protect two adjacent sides of the square. To begin competition, three players from each team move into the playing area in their own half of the space. These are the active players who may roam anywhere in the square. The other players act as goalkeepers.

The object of the game is for active players to kick the ball through the opposing team's line (beneath shoulder height) to score. After 30 to 45 seconds, active players rotate to the sidelines and new players take their

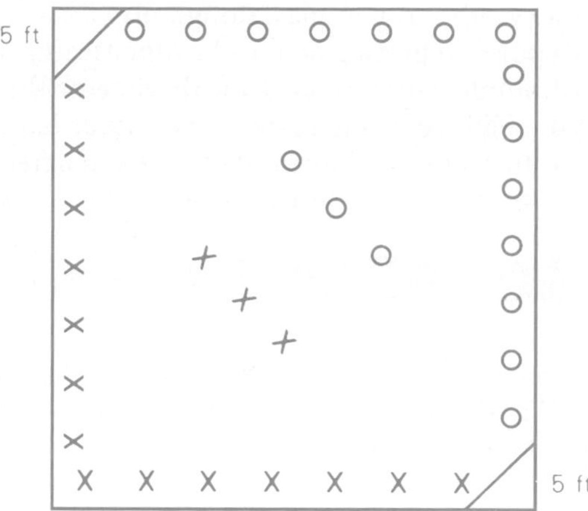

FIGURE 26.21 Formation for diagonal soccer.

place. Players on the sidelines may block the ball with their bodies and use their hands. The team against whom the point was scored starts the ball for the next point. Only active players may score. Scoring is much the same as in Circle Kickball in that a point is awarded for the opponents when any of the following occur:

1. A team allows the ball to go through its line below the shoulders.
2. A team touches the ball illegally.
3. A team kicks the ball over the other team above shoulder height.

DRIBBLERAMA

Playing Area: Playground

Players: 10 to 20

Supplies: Soccer ball or 8-inch foam-rubber ball for each player

Skills: Dribbling, protecting the ball

The playing area is a large circle or square, clearly outlined. All players dribble within the area. The game is played on two levels.

Level 1: Each player dribbles throughout the area, controlling the ball so it does not touch another ball. If a touch occurs, both players go outside the area and dribble around the area. Once youngsters have completed dribbling one lap, they may reenter the game.

Level 2: Two equal playing areas are delineated. All players start in one of the areas. While dribbling and controlling the ball, each player attempts to kick any other ball out of the area. When a ball is kicked out, the player owning that ball takes it to the other area and dribbles. As more players move to the second area, a second game ensues. Players in this area move back to the opposite side. This keeps all players actively involved in the games.

Level 3: Start with one game on each half of the teaching area. When a person is out, they move to the other game. Or they take one lap dribbling and then join the other game. Also, the area can be divided into quadrants and four games played with players choosing another game to move to when ousted form a game.

BULL'S-EYE

Playing Area: Playground

Players: Six to ten

Supplies: Soccer ball or 8-inch foam rubber ball for each player

Skills: Dribbling, protecting the ball

The playing area is a large outlined area—circle, square, or rectangle. One player holds a ball in her hands, which serves as the bull's-eye. The other players dribble within the area. The player with the bull's-eye attempts to throw her ball (basketball push shot) at any other ball. The player whose ball is hit now becomes the new bull's-eye player. The old bull's-eye becomes one of the dribblers. A new bull's-eye cannot hit back immediately at the old bull's-eye. If the group is large, have two bull's-eyes. No score is kept and no one is eliminated.

TEACHING TIP

Specify that the bull's-eye must keep one foot on a marking spot.

PIN KICKBALL

Playing Area: Playground or gymnasium

Players: Seven to ten on each team

Supplies: Ten or more pins (cones or bowling pins), many soccer or foam-rubber balls

Skills: Kicking, controlling

Two teams start about 20 yards apart, facing each other. At least ten pins are placed between the two lines of players. A number of balls are given to each team at the start of the kicking (Figure 26.22 on page 639). Kicks must be made from the line behind which the team is standing. Each pin knocked down scores a point for that team. After all of the pins have been knocked down, they are reset, and the game resumes.

TEACHING TIP

This is a flexible game; the number of pins, balls, and players can be varied easily. The type of kick can be specified, or it can be left up to the player to choose. As accuracy improves, the distance between the teams can be increased.

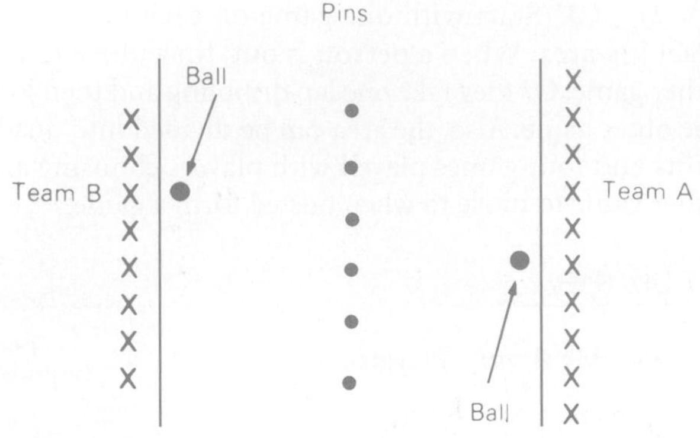

FIGURE 26.22 Formation for Pin Kickball.

SIDELINE SOCCER

Playing Area: Rectangle about 60 by 100 feet

Players: 10 to 12 on each team

Supplies: A soccer or foam-rubber ball, four cones, pinnies (optional)

Skills: Most soccer skills, competitive play

Teams line up on the sidelines of the rectangle. Three or four active players from each team are called from the end of the team line (Figure 26.23). These players remain active until a point is scored; then they rotate to the other end of the line. The object is to kick the ball between cones (goals) that define the scoring area. The active players on each team compete against each other, aided by their teammates on the sidelines.

To start play, the ball can be given to one team or dropped between two opposing players at the center of the field. To score, the ball must be kicked last by an active player and must go through the goal at or below shoulder height. A goal counts one point. Sideline players can pass to other sideline players or an active teammate, but a sideline kick cannot score a goal.

Regular soccer rules generally prevail, with special attention to the restrictions of no pushing, holding, tripping, or other rough play. Rough play is a foul and causes a point to be awarded to the other team. For an out-of-bounds ball, the team on the side of the field where the ball went out-of-bounds is awarded a free kick near that spot. No score can result from a free kick. Violation of the touch rule also results in a free kick.

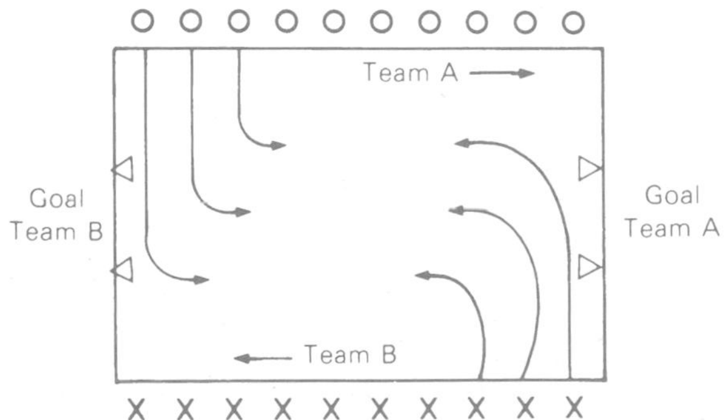

FIGURE 26.23 Formation for Sideline Soccer.

TEACHING TIP

Rotate in a new set of players after 30 to 45 seconds. More active players can be added when the class is large. A number of passes to sideline players can be mandated before a shot on goal can be taken. After some expertise is acquired, the cones should be moved in to narrow the goal area. If the ball goes over the end line but not through the goal area, the ball is put into play by a defender with a kick.

KICK BOWLING

Playing Area: Playground or soccer field

Players: Groups of four

Supplies: Soccer balls or 8-inch foam-rubber balls, bowling pins

Skills: Kicking

Kick bowling is played similar to bowling with the exception that students kick the ball at pins rather than roll the ball. Place students in groups of four. One student is the kicker, one the pinsetter, and the other two are ball retrievers.

SOCCER GOLF

Playing Area: Playground or soccer field

Players: Groups of three to four

Supplies: One soccer ball per student, hoops to mark each hole and cones to mark tees

Skills: Kicking, knowledge of golf rules

This game is played like golf, with the only exception that students kick the soccer ball rather than hitting a golf ball. A course similar to a Frisbee golf course (page 576) can be set up prior to the lesson with trees, boxes, and other equipment as obstacles.

Developmental Level III

MANYBALL SOCCER

Playing Area: Soccer field

Players: Entire class

Supplies: Six foam or soccer balls, cones, pinnies

Skills: All soccer skills

Players are divided into two teams and begin in their defensive half of the field. Players are free to roam the entire field with the exception of the goalie boxes, which are delineated with cones. Only the goalie is allowed in the goalie box. Goalies are the only players who can touch the ball with their hands. The goalie tries to keep the balls from going between the cones. The goalie can return the ball to play by punting or throwing. More than one goalie can be used to increase the difficulty of scoring.

The object is to kick one of the six balls through the goal. If a ball goes through the goal, the player who scored (not the goalie) retrieves the ball and returns it to the midline for play. All balls are in play simultaneously except when being returned after a goal. Basic soccer rules (pages 636–638) are used to control the game.

ADDITION SOCCER

Playing Area: Playground

Players: 10 to 15

Supplies: One soccer ball per player

Skills: Dribbling, ball control

Five or more players are designated to defend against the other players. The remainder of the players dribble throughout the area, trying to keep the defenders from touching any ball with their feet. When a ball is touched, that player rolls the ball to the side of the playing area and joins hands with the defender to become his partner. They operate as a twosome and must keep hands joined as they try to touch other balls. When another ball is touched, that player takes his ball to the side and joins hands with one of the other defenders. This twosome becomes defenders also, adding their efforts to those of the first twosome. Play continues until all the defenders have touched a ball and have a partner or for one minute, which ever occurs first. The game then starts over. If partners break joined hands in touching a ball, the touch does not count. The game is similar to Addition Tag (page 556).

OVER THE TOP

Playing Area: Playground

Players: Two teams of five to seven

Supplies: Each player on offense has a ball

Skills: Dribbling, ball control, guarding, tackling

One team is on offense and one on defense, placed according to Figure 26.24. Defensive players stay in their respective areas. On signal, all offensive players dribble through the three areas. A player is eliminated if her ball is recovered by a defensive player or goes out of bounds.

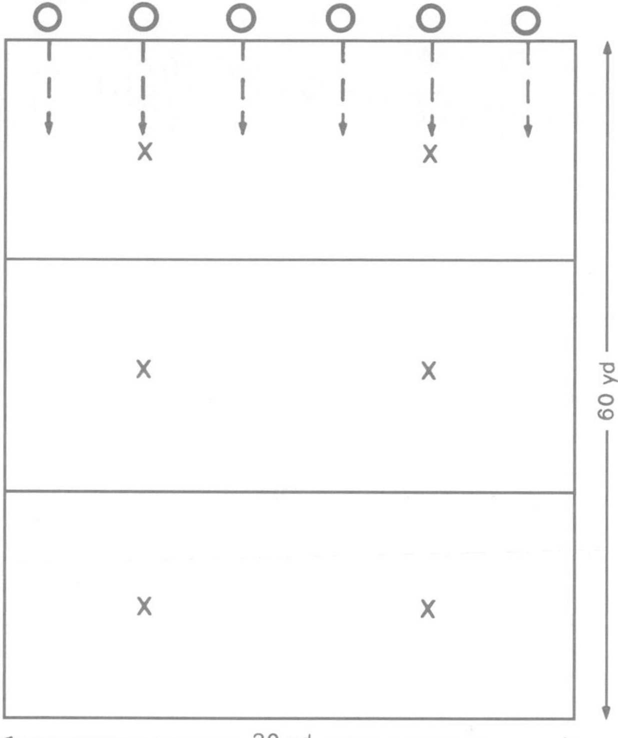

FIGURE 26.24 Over the Top.

The offensive team scores 1 point for each ball dribbled across the far end line. Reverse roles and give the other team a chance to score. Field markings need to be definite to keep the defensive players in their respective zones. A variation is to put neutral zones between the active zones.

LANE SOCCER

Playing Area: Soccer field

Players: Nine per team

Supplies: Soccer, foam-rubber, or beach balls; pinnies

Skills: All soccer skills

The field is divided into four lanes (eight equal sections) as illustrated in Figure 26.25 on page 642. A defensive and an offensive player are placed in each of the eight areas. A goalkeeper guards each goal per regulation soccer goals. At least two passes must be made before a shot on goal can be taken. Basic soccer rules guide play. The goalie is the only player who can handle the ball with the hands. A free kick is given to a player who has been fouled by an opponent. Failing to stay within a lane also results in a free kick. Players must be rotated after a goal is scored or a specified amount of time has elapsed. This rotation will enable all students to play four positions; defense, midfield defense, midfield offense, and offense.

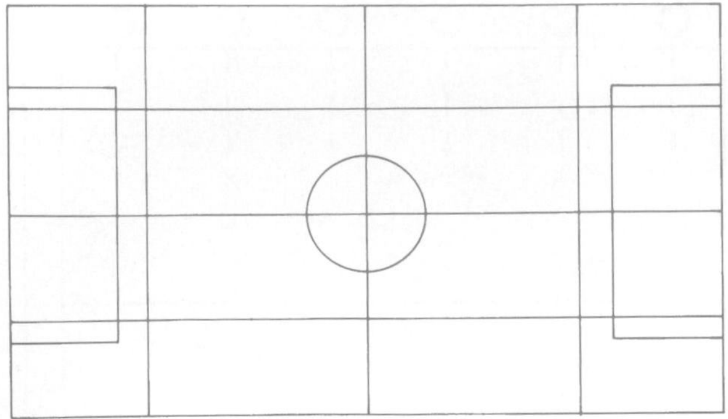

FIGURE 26.25 Field markings for Lane Soccer.

TEACHING TIP

The number of lanes can be varied depending on the number of players and the size of the field. Allow players to choose an opponent for their lane. Usually, they will choose an opponent of equal ability.

Increase the number of balls, goals, and goalies.

LINE SOCCER

Playing Area: Soccer field

Players: Eight to ten players on each team

Supplies: A soccer, foam-rubber, or beach ball; four cones; pinnies

Skills: Most soccer skills, competitive play

Two goal lines are drawn 80 to 120 feet apart. A restraining line is drawn 15 feet in front of and parallel to each goal line. Field width can vary from 50 to 80 feet. Each team stands on one goal line, which it defends. The referee stands in the center of the field and holds a ball (Figure 26.26). At the whistle, three players (more if the teams are large) run from the right side of each line to the center of the field and become the six active players. The referee drops the ball to the ground, and the players try to kick it through the other team defending the goal line. The players in the field may advance by kicking only.

A score is made when an active player kicks the ball through the opposing team and over the end line (provided that the kick was made from outside the restraining line). Cones should be put on field corners to define the goal line. One point is scored when the ball is kicked over the opponent's goal line below shoulder level. One point is also scored in case of a personal foul involving pushing, kicking, tripping, and the like.

Line players act as goalies and are permitted to catch the ball. Once caught, however, the ball must be laid down immediately and either rolled or kicked. It cannot be punted or drop-kicked.

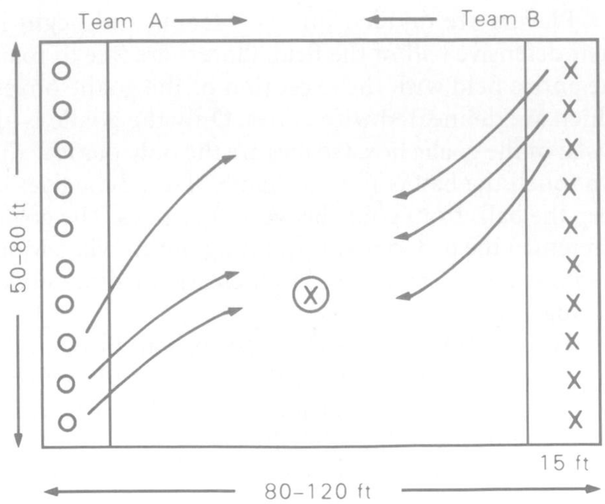

FIGURE 26.26 Line Soccer.

For illegal touching by the active players, a direct free kick from a point 12 yards in front of the penalized team's goal line is given. All active players on the defending team must stand to one side until the ball is kicked. Only goalies defend. An out-of-bounds ball is awarded to the opponents of the team last touching it. The regular soccer throw-in from out of bounds should be used. If the ball goes over the shoulders of the defenders at the end line, any end-line player may retrieve the ball and put it into play with a throw or kick.

A time limit of 1 minute is set for any group of active players. After time is up, play is halted and the players are changed. Use a system of player rotation so all participants get to play.

MINI-SOCCER

Playing Area: Any large area 100 by 150 feet, with goals

Players: Seven on each team

Supplies: A soccer ball, pinnies or colors to mark teams, four cones for the corners

Skills: All soccer skills

Each end of the field has a 21-foot-wide goal marked by jumping standards. A 12-yard semicircle on each end outlines the penalty area. The center of the semicircle is at the center of the goal (Figure 26.27).

The game follows the general rules of soccer, with one goalie for each side. One new feature, the corner kick, is incorporated in this game. This kick is used when the ball, last touched by the defense, goes over the end line but not through the goal. The ball is taken to the nearest corner for a direct free kick, and a goal can be scored from the kick. In a similar situation, if the attacking team last touched the ball, the goalkeeper kick is

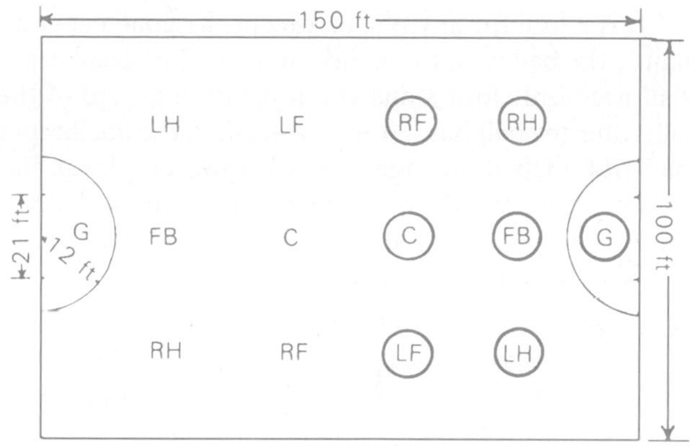

FIGURE 26.27 Formation for Mini-Soccer.

awarded. The goalie puts the ball down and placekicks it forward.

The players are designated as center forward, outside right, outside left, right halfback, left halfback, fullback, and goalie. Players should rotate positions. The forwards play in the front half of the field, and the guards in the back half. Neither position, however, is restricted to these areas entirely, and all may cross the centerline without penalty.

A foul by the defense within its penalty area (semicircle) results in a penalty kick, taken from a point 12 yards distant, directly in front of the goal. Only the goalie is allowed to defend. The ball is in play, with others waiting outside the penalty area.

TEACHING TIP

Position play should be emphasized. The lines of three should be encouraged to spread out and stay in their area. The number of players can vary, with some games using as few as three on a side in a more restricted area.

SIX-SPOT KEEPAWAY

Playing Area: Playground, gymnasium

Players: Two teams, six offensive and three defensive

Supplies: One soccer ball, stopwatch

Skills: Passing, ball control, guarding

There are six offensive and three defensive players in this activity. Five offensive players are arranged in a pentagon formation, with one player in the center (Figure 26.28). The pentagon is about 20 yards across. Three defenders from the other team enter the pentagon and attempt to interrupt the passing of the offensive team from one to another. A player may not pass the ball back to the person from whom it was received. The game begins with the ball in possession of the center player.

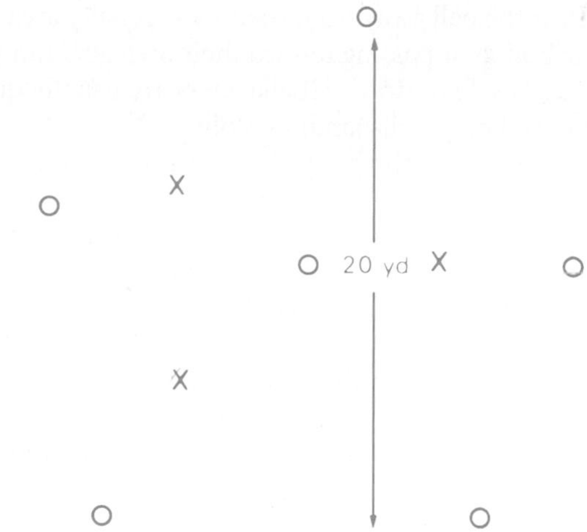

FIGURE 26.28 Six Spot Keepaway.

The object of the game is to make as many good passes as possible against three defenders. After one minute, three offensive players become defensive players and repeat the activity. One more rotation occurs so that all players have been on defense. The threesome scoring the most points is the winner. Offensive players should stay reasonably in position.

REGULATION SOCCER

Playing Area: Soccer field (Figure 26.29)

Players: 11 on each team

Supplies: A soccer ball, pinnies

Skills: All soccer skills

A team usually consists of three forwards, three midfield players, four backline defenders, and one goalkeeper. More can be placed on a team depending on class size. Forwards are the main line of attack and focus primarily on scoring. Midfield players need good passing and tackling skills as well as a high level of cardiovascular fitness. Defenders work to keep the opponent from scoring. They

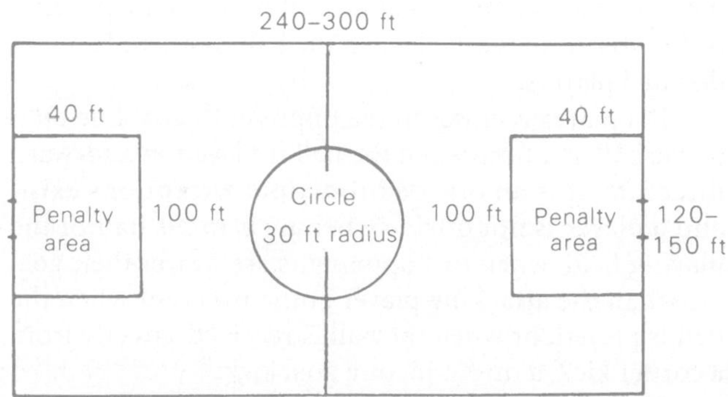

FIGURE 26.29 Regulation soccer field.

try to clear the ball away from their own penalty area and avoid dribbling or passing toward their own goal unless it is absolutely safe to do so. Goalkeepers are usually quick and agile and have ball-handling skills.

On the toss of the coin, the winning team gets its choice of kicking off or selecting which goal to defend. The loser exercises the option not selected by the winner.

On the kickoff, the ball must travel forward at least about 1 yard, and the kicker cannot touch it again until another player has kicked it. The defensive team must be 10 yards away from the kicker. After each score, the team not winning the point gets to kick off. Both teams must be onside at the kickoff. The defensive team must stay onside and out of the center circle until the ball is kicked. Regular soccer rules call for scoring by counting the number of goals made.

Elementary school children usually play 6-minute quarters; however, this can be adjusted depending on the development of the players. There should be a rest period of 1 minute between quarters and 10 minutes between halves.

When the ball goes out of bounds on the sideline, it is put into play with a throw-in from the spot where it crossed the line. A goal may not be scored nor may the thrower play the ball a second time until another player has touched it. All opponents are to be 10 yards back at the time of the throw.

If the ball is caused to go out of bounds on the end line by the attacking team, a goal kick is awarded. The ball is placed in the goal area and kicked beyond the penalty area by a defending player, who may not touch the ball twice in succession. If a player touches the ball before it goes out of the penalty area, it is not yet in play and should be kicked again.

If the defensive team causes the ball to go out of bounds over the end line, a corner kick is awarded. The ball is placed 1 yard from the corner of the field and kicked into the field of play by an attacking player. The 10-yard restriction also applies to defensive players.

If the ball is touched by two opponents at the same time and caused to go out of bounds, a drop ball is called. The referee drops the ball between two opposing players, who cannot kick it until it touches the ground. A drop ball also is called when the ball is trapped among downed players.

If a player is closer to the opponent's goal line than to the ball at a time when the ball is played in a forward direction, it is an offside infraction. Exceptions exist, and a player is not offside when he is in his half of the playing field, when two opponents are nearer their goal line than the attacking player at the moment when the ball is played, or when the ball is received directly from a corner kick, a throw-in, or a goal kick.

Personal fouls involving unnecessary roughness are penalized. Tripping, striking, charging, holding, pushing, and jumping an opponent intentionally are forbidden.

It is a foul for any player, except the goalkeeper, to handle the ball with the hands or arms. The goalkeeper is allowed only four steps and must then get rid of the ball. After the ball has left his possession, the goalkeeper may not pick it up again until another player has touched it. Players are not allowed to screen or obstruct opponents, unless they are in control of the ball.

Penalties are as follows:

1. A direct kick is awarded for all personal fouls and handballs. A goal can be scored from a direct free kick. Examples of infringements are pushing, tripping, kicking a player, and holding.
2. A penalty kick is awarded if a defender in his penalty area commits direct free-kick infringements.
3. An indirect free kick is awarded for offsides, obstruction, dangerous play such as high kicking, a goalkeeper's taking more than four steps or repossessing the ball before another player has touched it, and playing the ball twice after a dead-ball situation. A second player must touch the ball before a goal can be scored. A referee signals if the kick is indirect by pointing one arm upward vertically.

TEACHING TIP

Players should be encouraged to use the space on the field to the best advantage. When a team is in possession of the ball, players should attempt to find a position where they can pass either behind the player with the ball to give support, or toward the goal to be in a better position to shoot. When a team is forced into defense, the defenders should get "goalside" of attackers (between the attackers and their own goal) to prevent them from gaining an advantage.

From an early stage, players should be taught to give information to each other during the game, especially when they have possession of the ball. Valuable help can be given by shouting instructions such as "Man on," "You have time," or "Player behind," and also by calling for the ball when in position to receive a pass.

SOCCER SKILL TESTS

The tests for soccer skills cover various kinds of kicks, dribbling, and controlling. An excellent use of the skill tests is to set up self-testing stations. Signs will tell students how to test themselves. If desired, the teacher can formally test at one of the stations. Students rotate from station to station after a designated amount of time.

Passing against a Wall

Players pass the ball from behind a line between 5 and 10 yards away from a wall. The student should be encouraged to control the ball before kicking. The score is the number of passes made from behind the line in 1 or 2 minutes. This is an excellent test of general ball control and short passing skill.

Figure-Eight Dribbling

For a figure-eight dribbling test, three obstacles or markers are arranged in a line, 4 yards apart, with the first marker positioned 4 yards from the starting line. The finish line is 4 yards wide. A stopwatch is used, and the timing is done to the nearest tenth of a second.

Each player gets three trials, with the fastest trial taken as the score. On each trial, the player dribbles over the figure-eight course and finishes by kicking or dribbling the ball over the 4-yard finish line, at which time the watch is stopped. The test is best done on a grass surface, but if a hard surface must be used, the ball should be deflated somewhat so that it can be controlled.

Controlling

For the controlling test, the formation is a file plus one. A thrower stands 15 to 20 feet in front of the file and rolls or bounces the ball to the player at the head of the file. Three trials each are given for the sole-of-the-foot control, the foot control, and body control. The ball must be definitely stopped and controlled. A score of 9 points, one for each successful control, is possible.

The thrower should adopt one type of throw for all controls and for all players. If the scorer judges that the roll was not a good opportunity, the trial is taken over. Five trials can be allowed.

Placekicking and Punting for Distance and Accuracy

To test punting for distance, a football field or any other field marked in gridiron fashion at 5- or 10-yard intervals is needed. One soccer ball is required, but when three are used, considerable time is saved. A measuring tape (25 or 50 feet) plus individual markers complete the supply list.

Each player is given three kicks from behind a restraining line. One child marks the kick for distance, while one or two others act as ball chasers. After three kicks, the player's marker is left at the spot of the longest kick. This is determined by marking the point at which the ball first touched after the kick. Measurement is taken to the nearest foot.

Every student in the squad or small group should kick before the measurements are taken. The punt must be from a standing, not a running, start. If a child crosses the line during the kick, it counts as a trial and no measurement is taken.

Placekicking for distance is tested in the same way as punting for distance, with two exceptions. The ball is kicked from a stationary position. It must be laid on a flat surface and not elevated by dirt, grass, or other means. The child is given credit for the entire distance of the kick, including the roll. The kicking should be done on a grassy surface, because the ball will roll indefinitely on a smooth, hard surface. If the surface presents a problem, the test can be limited to the distance the ball has traveled in flight.

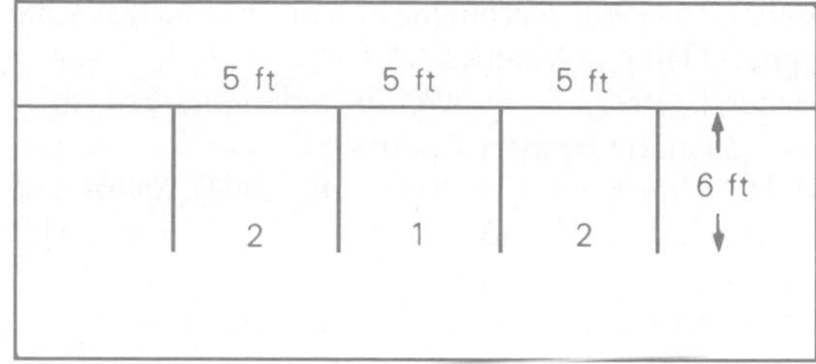

FIGURE 26.30 Penalty-kicking target area.

Penalty Kicking and Short Passing Accuracy

In the penalty-kicking test, the kicker faces a target area from a point 12 yards out, where the ball has been placed. The target area is formed by a rope stretched tight 6 feet above the ground. Four ropes, at distances 5 feet apart, are dropped from the stretched rope. This outlines three target areas 6 feet high and 5 feet wide. The center target area scores 1 point and the side areas 2 points (Figure 26.30). (This reflects the principle that a penalty kick should be directed away from a goalkeeper toward either corner of the goal.) Each child is allotted five kicks at the target. A score of 10 points is possible.

The same target is used for kicking for accuracy, but the center area scores 2 points and the side areas 1 point each. A chalk line is drawn about 20 feet from the target. The child is back another 20 feet for the start. The player dribbles the ball forward and must kick the ball as it is moving and before it crosses the balk line. Five trials are given, and a score of 10 points is possible.

FOR MORE INFORMATION

References and Suggested Readings

Beswick, B. (2001). *Focused for soccer.* Champaign, IL: Human Kinetics.

Bungsbo, J., & Peitersen, B. (2000). *Soccer systems and strategies.* Champaign, IL: Human Kinetics

Fellenbaum, J. E. (1993). Soccer. In N. Dougherty (Ed.), *Physical activity and sport for the secondary school student.* Reston, VA: NASPE and AAHPERD.

Luxbacher, J. (1995). *Soccer practice games.* 2nd ed. Champaign, IL: Human Kinetics.

Luxbacher, J. (1996). *Teaching soccer: Steps to success.* Champaign, IL: Human Kinetics.

Luxbacher, J. (1999). *Soccer winning techniques.* 3rd ed. Champaign, IL: Human Kinetics.

Mood, D. P., Musker, F. F., & Rink, J. E. (2003). *Sports and recreational activities.* 13th ed. New York: McGraw-Hill.

National Soccer Coaches Association of America. T. Schum (Ed.). (1996). *Coaching soccer.* Indianapolis: Masters Press.

Negroesco, S. (1993). *Soccer.* Dubuque, IA: Brown & Benchmark.

U.S. Soccer Federation. (1998). *FIFA laws of the game: A guide for referees.* Hitzigweg, Switzerland: FIFA.

Wein, H. (2000). *Developing youth soccer players.* Champaign, IL: Human Kinetics.

Wein, H. (2000). *105 practical soccer drills.* Orange, CA: Oceanprises Publications.

Websites

Soccer America Magazine
www.socceramerica.com

Soccer Coaching.net Interactive Coaching
www.soccercoaching.net

U.S. Youth Soccer Association
www.usysa.org

CHAPTER 27

Softball

ESSENTIAL COMPONENTS

I	**Organized around content standards**
II	**Student-centered and developmentally appropriate**
III	**Physical activity and motor skill development form the core of the program**
IV	**Teaches management skills and self-discipline**
V	**Promotes inclusion of all students**
VI	**Focuses on process over product**
VII	Promotes lifetime personal health and wellness
VIII	**Teaches cooperation and responsibility and promotes sensitivity to diversity**

PHYSICAL EDUCATION STANDARDS

1	**Students are able to move competently using a variety of fundamental and specialized motor skills.**
2	Students can monitor and maintain a health-enhancing level of physical fitness.
3	**Students are able to apply movement concepts and basic mechanics of skill performance when learning and refining motor skills.**
4	Students comprehend the basic principles of wellness and are able to apply concepts that enable them to make meaningful decisions that positively impact their health and wellness.
5	**Students participate in a wide variety of physical activities and learn how to maintain a personalized active lifestyle.**
6	**Students demonstrate empathy, understanding, and respect for the numerous differences exhibited by people in an activity setting.**
7	**Students exhibit responsible and self-directed behaviors that lead to positive social interactions in physical activity.**

SUMMARY

Skills instruction for softball is introduced during the intermediate grades after youngsters have mastered basic prerequisite skills. Teaching the rules and strategies for softball is an integral part of the instructional process. Using proper progression is a key to success when teaching fundamental skills and lead-up games associated with softball. Lead-up games provide an opportunity to emphasize development of selected softball skills in a setting that is compatible with the abilities of participants.

OUTCOMES

- Structure learning experiences efficiently using appropriate formations, progressions, and coaching techniques.
- Develop a unit plan and lesson focus for softball.
- Identify safety precautions associated with teaching softball.
- Describe instructional procedures used for implementing a successful lead-up game.
- Cite assessment procedures used for evaluating softball skills.

Youngsters enjoy softball, and a good program should make use of this drive. The emphases in softball should be on instruction and lead-up games. Children have adequate opportunity during recess, at the noon hour, and at other times to play the regulation game.

INSTRUCTIONAL EMPHASIS AND SEQUENCE

Table 27.1 shows the sequence of softball activities divided into two developmental levels. The activities are listed in progression. Youngsters can practice many of the skills of softball but may not be ready to participate in the activities in this chapter until the age of 8 years.

Developmental Levels I and II

The fundamental skills of batting, throwing, and catching are emphasized at these levels. Batting receives attention, for softball is little fun unless children can hit. Proper form and technique in all three fundamental skills are parts of the instruction, with attention paid not only to the how but also to the why. Lead-up games provide an introduction to the basic rules of the game. As youngsters mature, specific skills for pitching, infield play, base running, and batting make up the instructional material.

Developmental Level III

Youngsters at this level develop the background to play the game of regulation softball. Tee Ball provides an opportunity for developing all softball skills except pitching and catching. Home Run and the ever-popular Scrub (Work-Up) provide a variety of experiences, and Batter Ball stresses hitting skills. Experiences with batting, throwing, catching, and infield play are practiced. New pitching techniques, situation play, and double-play work is added. Slow-Pitch provides lots of action. Babe Ruth Ball emphasizes selective hitting.

SOFTBALL SKILLS

Children can find many ways to execute softball skills effectively by trial and error and through instruction. Do not attempt to mold every child into a prescribed form. Work toward making the most of each child's movement patterns.

Gripping the Ball

The standard softball grip, difficult for elementary school children, calls for the thumb to be on one side, the index and middle fingers on top, and the other fingers supporting along the other side (Figure 27.1). Younger children with small hands will find it best to use a full-hand grip, in which the thumb and fingers are spaced rather evenly (Figure 27.2). Regardless of the grip used, the pads of the fingers should control the ball.

FIGURE 27.1 Gripping the ball, two-finger grip.

Throwing (Right-Handed)

Softball requires accurate throwing. Players must practice proper throwing technique if they are going to be able to perform well in softball. Of all the team sports, softball is probably the most difficult for youngsters because of the fine motor coordination required. The following instructional cues can be used to help students develop proper throwing technique:

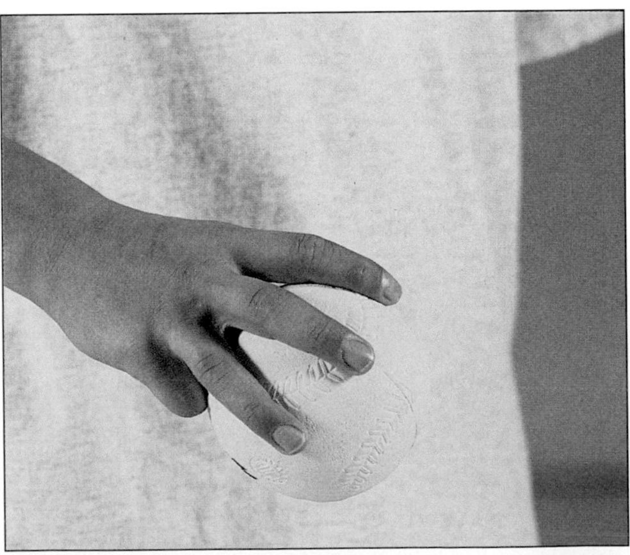

FIGURE 27.2 Gripping the ball, full grip. The little finger supports on the side.

TABLE 27.1 Suggested softball program

Developmental Level II	Developmental Level III
Skills	
Throwing	
Gripping the ball	Throw-in from outfield
Overhand throw	Sidearm throw
Underhand toss	
Around the bases	
Catching and Fielding	
Catching thrown balls	Catching flies from fungo bat
Catching fly balls	Infield practice
Grounders	
Fielding grounders in infield	
Sure stop for outfield	
Batting	
Simple skills	Different positions at plate
Tee batting	Bunting
Fungo hitting	
Fielding Positions	
Infield practice	Backing up other players
How to catch	Double play
Base Running	
To first base and turn	Fast start off base
Circling the bases	Tagging up on fly ball
	Sacrifice
Pitching	
Simple underhand	Target pitching
Application of pitching rule	Slow pitches

Developmental Level II	Developmental Level III
Knowledge, Rules	
Strike zone	Pitching rule Position Illegal pitches
Foul and fair ball	Infield fly
Safe and out	Keeping score
Foul tip	Base running
Bunt rule	Situation quiz
When batter safe or out	
Activities	
Throw-It-and-Run Softball	Five Hundred
Two-Pitch Softball	Batter Ball
Hit and Run	Home Run
Kick Softball	Tee Ball
In a Pickle	Scrub (Work-Up)
Beat Ball	Slow-Pitch Softball
	Babe Ruth Ball
	Hurry Baseball (One-Pitch)
	Three-Team Softball
Skill Tests	
Throwing for distance	Pitching
Throwing for accuracy	Circling the bases
	Fielding grounders

1. Place the throwing arm side of the body away from the target.
2. Step toward the target with the foot opposite the throwing hand.
3. Rotate the hips as the throwing arm moves forward.
4. Bend and raise the arm at the elbow. Lead with the elbow.
5. Prior to the forward motion of the arm, shift the weight from the rear foot to the forward foot (nearest the target).

Overhand Throw

In preparation for throwing, the child secures a firm grip on the ball, raises the throwing arm to shoulder height, and brings the elbow back. For the overhand throw, the hand with the ball is then brought back over the head so that it is well behind the shoulder at about shoulder height. The left side of the body is turned in the direction of the throw, and the left arm is raised in front of the body. The weight is on the back (right) foot, with the left foot advanced and the toe touching the ground. The arm comes forward with the elbow leading, and the ball is thrown with a downward snap of the wrist (Figure 27.3 on page 650). The body weight is brought forward into the throw, shifting to the front foot. Follow through so that the palm of the throwing hand faces the ground at completion of the throw. The eyes should be on the target throughout, and the arm should be kept free and loose during the throw.

Sidearm Throw

The sidearm throw is much the same as the overhand throw, except that the entire motion is kept near a

FIGURE 27.3 Throwing overhand.

FIGURE 27.4 Pitching.

horizontal plane. The sidearm throw is used for shorter, quicker throws than the overhand and employs a quick, whiplike action. On a long throw, the sidearm throw curves more than the overhand, because a side-spinning action is usually imparted to the ball on release. There is generally some body lean toward the side of the throwing arm.

Underhand Throw

For the underhand throw, the throwing hand and arm are brought back, with palm facing forward, in a pendulum swing. The elbow is bent slightly. The weight is mostly on the back foot. The arm comes forward, almost in a bowling motion, and the ball is tossed. The weight shifts to the front foot during the toss. The flight of the ball should remain low and arrive at about waist height.

Pitching

Official rules call for the pitcher to have both feet in contact with the pitcher's rubber, but few elementary schools possess a rubber. Instead, the pitcher can stand with both feet about even, facing the batter, and holding the ball momentarily in front with both hands. The pitcher takes one hand from the ball, extends the right arm forward, and brings it back in a pendulum swing, positioning the ball well behind the body. A normal stride taken toward the batter with the left foot begins the throwing sequence for a right-handed pitcher. The arm is brought forward with an underhanded slingshot motion, and the weight is transferred to the leading foot. Only one step is permitted. The follow-through motion is important (Figure 27.4).

The windmill is an alternate pitching motion in which the arm describes a full arc overhead, moving behind the body and then forward toward the batter. The arm goes into full extension on the downward swing in the back, gathering momentum as the forward motion begins. The pitch is otherwise the same as the normal motion. The windmill is generally a difficult style for youngsters to master. Instructional cues for pitching are as follows:

1. Face the plate.
2. Keep your eyes on the target.
3. Swing the pitching arm backward and step forward.
4. Keep the pitching arm extended.

Fielding

Infielders should assume the ready position—a semicrouch, with legs spread shoulder width apart, knees bent slightly, and hands on or in front of the knees (Figure 27.5). As the ball is delivered, the weight is shifted to the balls of the feet. The outfielder's position is a slightly more erect semicrouch. Instructional cues for fielding are the following:

1. Move into line with the path of the ball.
2. Give when catching the ball.

FIGURE 27.5 Ready position for the infielder.

3. Use the glove to absorb the force of the ball.
4. For grounders, keep the head down and watch the ball move into the glove.

Fly Balls

There are two ways to catch a fly ball. For a low ball, the fielder keeps the fingers together and forms a basket with the hands (Figure 27.6). For a higher ball, the thumbs are together, and the ball is caught in front of the chin (Figure 27.7). The fielder should give with the hands, and care must be taken with a spinning ball to squeeze the hands sufficiently to stop the spinning. The eye is on the ball continually until it hits the glove or hands. The knees are flexed slightly when receiving and aid in giving when the ball is caught.

Grounders

To field a grounder, the fielder should move as quickly as possible into the path of the ball (Figure 27.8) and then move forward and play the ball on a good hop. The eyes must be kept on the ball, following it into the hands or glove. The feet are spread, the seat is kept down, and the hands are carried low and in front (Figure 27.9 on page 652). The weight is on the balls of the feet or on the toes, and the knees are bent to lower the body. As the ball is caught, the fielder straightens up, takes a step in the direction of the throw, and makes the throw.

FIGURE 27.6 Catching a low fly ball.

FIGURE 27.7 Catching a high fly ball.

Sure Stop for Outfield Balls

To keep the ball from going through the hands and thus allowing extra bases, the outfielder can use the body as a

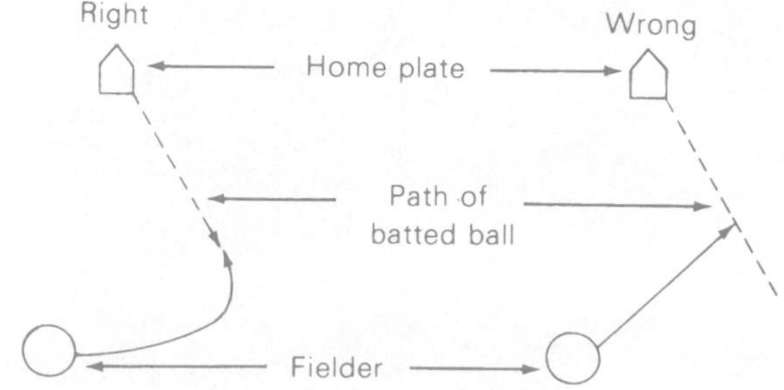

FIGURE 27.8 Fielding a grounder correctly.

FIGURE 27.9 Fielding a grounder.

barrier. The fielder turns half right and lowers one knee to the ground at the point toward which the ball is traveling (Figure 27.10). The hands catch the rolling ball, but if it is missed, the body will generally stop the ball.

First-Base Positioning

When a ball is hit to the infield, the first-base player moves to the base until the foot is touching it. The player then judges the path of the ball, stepping toward it with one foot and stretching forward. The other foot remains in contact with the base (Figure 27.11).

Catcher's Position

The catcher assumes a crouched position with the feet about shoulder width apart and the left foot slightly ahead of the right. The catcher should use a glove and wear a mask. A body protector is desirable. The catcher is positioned just beyond the range of the swing of the bat (Figure 27.12).

Batting (Right-Handed)

The batter stands with the left side of the body toward the pitcher. The feet are spread and the weight is on both feet. The body should be facing the plate. The bat is held with the trademark up, and the left hand grasps the bat lower than the right. The bat is held over the right shoulder, pointing both back and up. The elbows are away from the body (Figure 27.13). The swing begins

FIGURE 27.10 Sure stop.

FIGURE 27.11 First-base player stretching for a catch.

FIGURE 27.12 Catcher's position.

FIGURE 27.13 Batter's position.

with a hip roll and a short step forward in the direction of the pitcher. The bat is then swung level with the ground at the height of the pitch. The eyes are kept on the ball until it is hit. After the hit, there must be good follow-through.

The batter should avoid the following: lifting the front foot high off the ground, stepping back with the rear foot, dropping the rear shoulder, chopping down on the ball, golfing, dropping the elbows, or crouching or bending forward. Failure to keep the eyes on the ball is a serious error. Youngsters should get experience with the choke grip (Figure 27.14 on page 654), the long grip (Figure 27.15 on page 654), and the middle grip (Figure 27.16 on page 655). Beginning batters can start with the choke grip. In any case, the grip should not be too tight. The following are instructional cues for batting:

1. Keep the hands together.
2. Swing the bat horizontally.
3. Swing through the ball.
4. Hold the bat off the shoulder.
5. Watch the ball hit the bat.

Bunting (Right-Handed)

To bunt, the batter turns to face the pitcher, the right foot alongside home plate. As the pitcher releases the ball, the upper hand is run about halfway up the bat. The bunter holds the bat loosely in front of the body and parallel to the ground to meet the ball (Figure 27.17). The ball can be directed down the first- or third-base line.

The surprise, or drag, bunt is done without squaring around to face the pitcher. The batter holds the bat in a choke grip. When the pitcher lets go of the ball, the batter runs the right hand up the bat and directs the ball down either foul line, keeping it as close as possible to the line in fair territory.

Base Running

A batter who hits the ball should run hard and purposefully toward first base, no matter what kind of hit it is. The runner should run past the bag, tagging it in the process, and should step on the foul-line side of the base to avoid a collision with the first-base player.

Because a runner on base must hold the base position until the pitcher releases the ball, securing a fast start away from the base is essential. With either toe in

FIGURE 27.14 Choke grip.

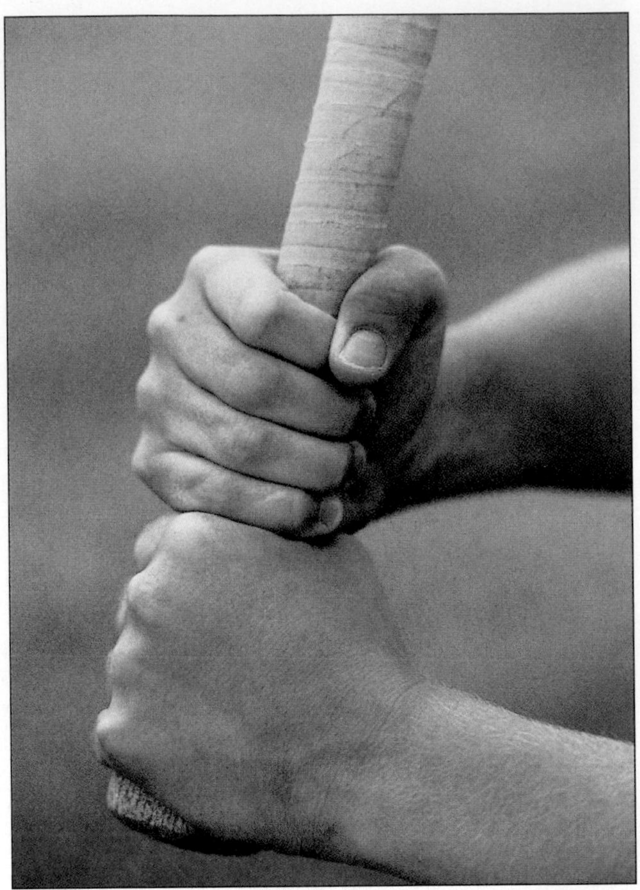

FIGURE 27.15 Long grip.

contact with the base, the runner assumes a body lean, the weight on the ball of the leading foot and the eyes on the pitcher. After the pitch is made, the runner takes a few steps away from the base in the direction of the next base.

Instructional Procedures

1. Safety is of the utmost importance. The following precautions should be observed.
   a. Throwing the bat is a constant danger. Members of the batting team should stand well back from the baseline, preferably behind a fence or in a dugout if available.
   b. The following are techniques that can teach the batter not to throw the bat.
      - Have the batter touch the bat to the ground before dropping it.
      - Call the batter out if the bat is thrown.
      - Have the batter carry the bat to first base.
      - Have the batter change ends of the bat before dropping it.
      - Have the batter place the bat in a 3-foot circle before running.
   c. Sliding can lead to injury and destruction of clothing. With unskilled players, it is best not to permit sliding.
   d. A catcher who stands close behind the plate while catching must wear a mask. A body protector is also recommended.
   e. Colliding while running for a fly ball can be avoided by teaching players to call for the ball and to stay out of another player's area.
   f. When changing fields at the beginning of an inning, the batting team stays on the first-base side of the infield. The fielding team goes to bat via the third-base side of the infield.
   g. Soft softballs should be used, particularly in the early stages of development. Fleece balls are excellent for introductory fielding skills. Many youngsters fear batted balls, which necessitates using balls that will not hurt them.
2. Batting skills must be stressed. There is no more ego-shattering experience for a youngster than to stand at the plate and demonstrate an ineptness that draws scorn and ridicule from peers. Make sure that youngsters know the correct stance and proper me-

FIGURE 27.16 Middle grip.

FIGURE 27.17 Regular bunt position.

chanics of batting. Improved hitting will come with practice.

3. The spoiler of many softball games is the pitcher-batter duel. If this becomes prolonged, the other players become justifiably bored from standing around. Having a member of the batting team pitch or allowing two or three swings per batter are ways to eliminate the problem.
4. Players should rotate positions often. In physical education classes, everyone, including the pitcher, should rotate to another position at the start of each inning.
5. The distance between the bases greatly affects the game. The distance should be lessened or increased according to the game and the capacities of players.
6. Umpires can be appointed, or the team at bat can umpire. A convenient rule to follow is that the person who made the last out of the previous inning will be the umpire for the next inning. Teach all students how to umpire.
7. Encourage players to recognize and give approval and support to those who are less skillful. Because there will be many differences in ability, the opportunity is present for a lesson in tolerance. It is important not to let an error become a tragedy to a player.
8. Each player should run out a hit, no matter how hopeless it seems.
9. Analyze the purpose of lead-up games. The needed skills should be practiced before inclusion in the game.
10. Teach respect for officials and acceptance of the umpire's judgment. The disreputable practice of baiting the umpire should not be a part of the child's softball experiences.

ORGANIZING FOR INSTRUCTION

It is essential that students develop skills in softball and acquire knowledge about the various phases of the game. The amount of field space and the equipment available determine the instructional organization. To cover the various phases of the game, a multiple-activity or station pattern is effective. The following guidelines offer suggestions for instruction.

1. Assure children many opportunities to practice different skills. Even with rotation, there should be as many small groups as possible. For example, throwing and fielding grounders can be practiced between two children.
2. Ability differences need to be addressed at times. Since some players have practiced more, they often have skill levels higher than those of others in the class. Skillful youngsters can be used in various phases of instruction, provided that sufficient direction for these efforts is given.
3. Activities and procedures to be stressed at each station should be carefully planned and communicated to all participants. Prior meetings with captains and other helpers are valuable. Appropriate softball rules should be covered.
4. Complete rotation of stations is not necessary at each class session. During a class session, teams may practice at one station for part of the time and then use the remainder of the time to participate in an appropriate lead-up game.
5. There must be directions listed at each station so students can make the most of the skill development opportunities. Place signs that offer instructional strategies on cones at each station.
6. The use of the rotational station system does not rule out activities involving the class as a whole. Mimetic drills (drills without equipment) are valuable for establishing fundamental movement patterns for most skills. Have students practice such techniques as batting, pitching, throwing, and fielding without worrying about results.
7. Station teaching provides an excellent opportunity for older students to provide assistance. In some school systems, high school students visit elementary schools on a regular basis for observation and educational experiences.
8. Move from one station to another in order to provide encouragement, correction, coaching, and motivation for learning.
9. A motivational factor can be introduced through comparisons of the rotational system with varsity or major league practices. This gives the activity an adult flavor.
10. Selection can be made from the list of lead-up games, particularly for activities that are suitable for squads or smaller groups.

BASIC SOFTBALL RULES

Most sporting goods establishments have copies of the official rules for softball. Although an official rule guide should be used by students when they are studying rules, a general idea of the basic rules of the game can be obtained from the following discussion.

The official diamond has 60-foot baselines and a pitching distance of 46 feet. In elementary school it is recommended that youngsters use a diamond with baselines no longer than 45 feet and a pitching distance of 35 feet or less. The nine players on a softball team are the catcher, pitcher, first-, second-, and third-base players, shortstop, and left, center, and right fielders. The right fielder is the outfielder nearest first base.

Batting Order

Players may bat in any order, although having them bat according to their positions in the field is at times convenient in class. Once the batting order has been established, it may not be changed, even if the player changes to another position in the field.

Pitching

The pitcher must face the batter with both feet on the pitching rubber and with the ball held in front with both hands. The pitcher is allowed one step toward the batter and must deliver the ball while taking that step. The ball must be pitched underhanded. The pitcher cannot fake a pitch or make any motion toward the plate without delivering the ball. It is illegal to roll or bounce the ball to the batter. No quick return is allowed before the batter is ready. To be called a *strike*, a pitch must be over the plate and between the knees and shoulders of the batter. A *ball* is a pitch that does not go through this area.

Batting

The bat must be a softball bat. The batter cannot cross to the other side of the plate when the pitcher is ready to pitch. If a player bats out of turn, she is out. A bunt that goes foul on the third strike is an out. A pitched ball that touches or hits the batter entitles the batter to first base, provided she does not strike or bunt at the ball.

Striking Out

A batter is out who misses the ball on the third strike. This is called striking out.

Batter Safe

The batter who reaches first base before the fielding team can field the ball and throw it to first is safe.

Fair Ball

A fair ball is any batted ball that settles on fair territory between home and first base and home and third base.

A ball that rolls over a base or through the field into fair territory is a fair ball. Fly balls (including line drives) that drop into fair territory beyond the infield are fair balls. Foul lines are in fair territory.

Foul Ball

A foul ball is a batted ball that settles outside the foul lines between home and first or between home and third. A fly ball that drops into foul territory beyond the bases is a foul.

Fly Ball

Any fly ball (foul or fair), if caught, is an out. A foul fly, however, must rise over the head of the batter or it is ruled a foul tip. A foul tip caught on the third strike, then, puts the batter out.

Base Running

In base running, no leadoff is permitted. On penalty of being called out, the runner must stay on base until the ball leaves the pitcher's hand. On an overthrow when the ball goes into foul territory and out of play, runners advance one base beyond the base to which they were headed at the time of the overthrow. On an overthrow at second base by the catcher with the ball rolling into center field, the runners may advance as far as they can. The runner may try to avoid being tagged on a baseline but is limited to a 3-foot distance on each side of a direct line from base to base. A runner hit by a batted ball while off the base is out. The batter, however, is entitled to first base. Base runners must touch all bases. If a runner fails to touch a base, it is an *appeal play*, which means that the fielding team must call the oversight to the attention of the umpire before he will rule on the play.

Runners may overrun first base without penalty. On all other bases, the runner must maintain contact with the base or be tagged out. To score, the runner must make contact with home plate.

Scoring

A run is scored when the base runner makes the circuit of the bases (i.e., first, second, third, and home) before the batting team has three outs. If the third out is a force out, no run is scored, even if the runner crossed home plate before the out was actually made.

The situation needing the most clarification occurs when a runner is on base with one out and the batter hits a fly ball that is caught, making the second out. The runner is forced to return to the base previously occupied before the ball reaches that base, or she, too, is out. If she makes the third out as a result of her failure to return to the base in time, no run is scored.

SOFTBALL DRILLS

Softball drills lend themselves to a station setup. For a regular class of 30 students, four squads with 7 or 8 students each is suggested. Activities at each station can emphasize a single skill or a combination of skills. Situational drills can also be incorporated. Children should realize that constant repetition is necessary to develop, maintain, and sharpen softball skills.

The multitude of softball skills to be practiced allows for many different combinations and organizations. The following are examples of combinations and organizations that can be used in station teaching.

1. Batting can be organized in many ways. One key to an effective program is to ensure that each child has many opportunities to hit the ball successfully. Sufficient area is needed.
   a. Use a batting tee. For each station, two tees are needed, with a bat and at least two balls for each tee. Three to five children are assigned to each tee. There should be a batter, a catcher to handle incoming balls, and fielders. When only three children are in a unit, the catcher should be eliminated. Each batter is allowed a certain number of swings before rotating to the field. The catcher becomes the next batter, and a fielder moves up to catcher.
   b. Organize informal hitting practice. A batter, a pitcher, and fielders are needed. Two batting groups should be organized at each station. A catcher is optional.
   c. Practice hitting a foam rubber ball thrown underhanded. The larger ball is easier to hit.
   d. Practice bunting with groups of three: a pitcher, batter, and fielder.
2. To practice throwing and catching, do the following drills.
   a. Throw back and forth, practicing various throws.
   b. Throw ground balls back and forth for fielding practice.
   c. One player acts as a first-base player, throwing grounders to the other infielders and receiving the put-out throw.
   d. Throw flies back and forth.
   e. Hit flies, with two or three fielders catching.
   f. Establish four bases and throw from base to base.
3. Proper pitching and catching form should be used for pitching practice.
   a. Pitch to another player over a plate.
   b. Call balls and strikes. One player is the pitcher, the second is the catcher, and the third is the

umpire. A fourth player can be a stationary batter to provide a more realistic pitching target.

c. Pitch toward pitching targets—either a wooden target (see page 665) or a similar area outlined on a wall.

4. For infield drill, children are placed in the normal infield positions: behind the plate; at first, second, and third base; and at shortstop. One child acts as the batter and gives directions. The play should begin with practice in throwing around the bases either way. After this, the batter can roll the ball to the different infielders, beginning at third base and continuing in turn around the infield, with each player throwing to first to retire an imaginary runner. Various play situations can be developed. A batter who is skillful enough can hit the ball to infielders instead of rolling it, thus making the drill more realistic. Using a second softball saves time when the ball is thrown or batted past an infielder, because players do not have to wait for the ball to be retrieved before proceeding with the next play. After the ball has been thrown to first base, other throws around the infield can take place. The drill can also be done with only a partial infield.

5. Various situations can be arranged for practicing base running.
   a. Bunt and run to first. A pitcher, a batter, an infielder, and a first-base player are needed. The pitcher serves the ball up for a bunt, and the batter, after bunting, takes off for first base. A fielding play can be made on the runner.
   b. Bunt and run to second base. The batter bunts the ball and runs to first base and then on to second, making a proper turn at first.

6. Play Pepper. (This is one of the older skill games in baseball.) A line of three or four players is about 10 yards in front of and facing a batter. The players toss the ball to the batter, who attempts to hit controlled grounders back to them (Figure 27.18). The batter stays at bat for a period of time and then rotates to the field.

7. Some of the game-type activities, such as Batter Ball, In a Pickle, Five Hundred, and Scrub, can be scheduled at stations. Stations might be organized as follows. (Numbers and letters refer to the drills just listed. Page number refers to activities not yet discussed.)

   Station 1: Batting (see 1a)
   Station 2: Throwing, fielding grounders (see 2c)
   Station 3: Base running—In a Pickle (see page 660)
   Station 4: Bunting and base running (see 5a)

   Another example of station arrangement is the following.

   Station 1: Batting and fielding—Pepper (see 6)
   Station 2: Pitching and umpiring (see 3b)
   Station 3: Infield practice (see 4)
   Station 4: Batting (see 1b)

   Stations might also be arranged as follows.

   Station 1: Fly ball hitting, fielding, throwing (see 2e)
   Station 2: Bunting and fielding (see 1d)
   Station 3: Pitching to targets (see 3c)
   Station 4: Batting (see 1a and 1b)

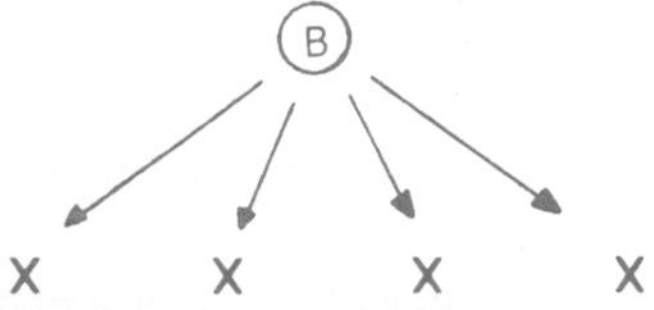

FIGURE 27.18 Play Pepper.

SOFTBALL ACTIVITIES

Developmental Level II

THROW-IT-AND-RUN SOFTBALL

Playing Area: Softball diamond reduced in size

Players: 7 to 11 (usually 9) on each team

Supplies: A softball or similar ball

Skills: Throwing, catching, fielding, base running

Throw-It-and-Run Softball is played like regular softball with the following exception. With one team in the field at regular positions, the pitcher throws the ball to the batter, who, instead of batting the ball, catches it and immediately throws it into the field. The ball is then treated as a batted ball, and regular softball rules prevail. No stealing is permitted, however, and runners must hold bases until the batter throws the ball. A foul ball is an out.

TEACHING TIP

Variations:

1. *Under-Leg Throw.* Instead of throwing directly, the batter can turn to the right, lift the left leg, and throw the ball under the leg into the playing field.
2. *Beat-Ball Throw.* The fielders, instead of playing regular softball rules, throw the ball directly home to the

catcher. The batter, in the meantime, runs around the bases. A point is scored for each base the batter touches before the catcher receives the ball. A ball caught on the fly would mean no score. Similarly, a foul ball would not score points but would count as a turn at bat.

TWO-PITCH SOFTBALL

Playing Area: Softball diamond

Players: 7 to 11 on each team

Supplies: A softball, a bat

Skills: Most softball skills, except regular pitching

Two-Pitch Softball is played like regular softball with the following changes.

1. A member of the team at bat pitches. A system of rotation should be set up so that every child takes a turn as pitcher.
2. The batter has only two pitches in which to hit the ball, and must hit a fair ball on one of these pitches or is out. The batter can foul the first ball, but if the second is fouled, the batter is out. There is no need to call balls or strikes.
3. The pitcher does not field the ball. A member of the team in the field acts as the fielding pitcher.
4. If the batter hits the ball, regular softball rules are followed. No stealing is permitted, however.

TEACHING TIP

Since the pitcher is responsible for pitching a ball that can be hit, the pitching distance can be shortened to give the batter ample opportunity to hit the ball. The instructor can act as the pitcher.

Variation: *Three Strikes:* In this game, the batter is allowed three pitches (strikes) to hit the ball. Otherwise, the game proceeds as in Two-Pitch Softball.

HIT AND RUN

Playing Area: Softball field or gymnasium

Players: 6 to 15 players on each team

Supplies: A volleyball or soccer ball or playground ball, home plate, base markers

Skills: Catching, throwing, running, dodging

One team is at bat, and the other is scattered in the field. Boundaries must be established, but the area does not have to be shaped like a baseball diamond. The batter stands at home plate with the ball. In front of the batter, 12 feet away, is a short line over which the ball must be hit to be in play. In the center of the field, about 40 feet away, is the base marker.

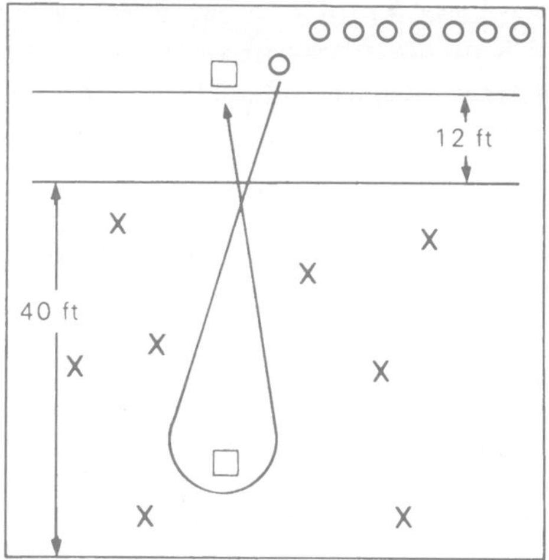

FIGURE 27.19 Hit and Run.

The batter bats the ball with the hands or fists so that it crosses the short line and lands inside the area, then attempts to run down the field, around the base marker, and back to home plate without being hit by the ball (Figure 27.19). The members of the other team field the ball and try to tag the runner. The fielders may not run or walk with the ball but may throw to teammates who are closer to the runner.

A run is scored each time a batter runs around the marker and back to home plate without getting tagged by the ball. A run also is scored if a foul is called on the fielding team for walking or running with the ball.

The batter is out in any of the following circumstances.

1. A fly ball is caught.
2. The ball is not hit beyond the short line.
3. The team touches home plate with the ball before the runner returns. (This out is used only when the runner stops in the field and does not continue.)

The game can be played in innings of three outs each, or a change of team positions can be made after all members of one team have batted.

TEACHING TIP

The distance the batter runs around the base marker may have to be shortened or lengthened, depending on players' abilities.

Variation: *Five Passes:* The batter is out when a fly ball is caught or when the ball is passed among five different players of the team in the field, with the last pass to a player at home plate beating the runner to the plate. The passes must not touch the ground.

KICK SOFTBALL

Playing Area: Regular softball field with a home base 3 feet square

Players: 7 to 11 on each team

Supplies: A soccer ball or another ball to be kicked

Skills: Kicking a rolling ball, throwing, catching, running bases

The batter stands in the kicking area, a 3-foot-square home plate. The batter kicks the ball rolled on the ground by the pitcher. The ball should be rolled at moderate speed. An umpire calls balls and strikes. A strike is a ball that rolls over the 3-foot square. A ball rolls outside this area. Strikeouts and walks are called the same as in regular softball. The number of foul balls allowed should be limited. No base stealing is permitted. Otherwise, the game is played like softball.

TEACHING TIP

Variations:

1. The batter kicks a stationary ball. This saves time, as there is no pitching.
2. *Punch Ball.* The batter can hit a volleyball as in a volleyball serve or punch a ball pitched by the pitcher.

IN A PICKLE

Playing Area: Any flat surface with 60 square feet of room

Players: Three or more

Supplies: A softball, two bases 45 to 55 feet apart

Skills: Throwing, catching, running down a base runner, tagging

A base runner who gets caught between two bases and is in danger of being run down and tagged is "in a pickle." To begin, both fielders are on bases, one with a ball. The runner is positioned in the base path 10 to 15 feet away from the fielder with the ball. The two fielders throw the ball back and forth in an attempt to run down and tag the runner between the bases. A runner who escapes and secures a base gets to try again. Otherwise, a system of rotation is established, including any sideline (waiting) players. No sliding is permitted.

BEAT BALL

Playing Area: Softball diamond, bases approximately 30 feet apart

Players: Two teams of 5 to 12

Supplies: Soft softball, bat, batting tee (optional)

Skills: All softball skills

One team is at bat, and the other team in the field. The object of the game is to hit the ball and run around the bases before the fielding team can catch the ball, throw it to first base, and then throw it to the catcher at home plate. If the ball beats the hitter home or a fly ball is caught, it is an out. If the hitter beats the ball to home plate, a run is scored. All players on a team bat once before switching positions with the fielding team. The ball must be hit into fair territory before the hitter can run. Only three pitches are allowed each hitter.

TEACHING TIP

Variations:

1. Depending on the maturity of the players, a batting tee may be used. The hitter can be allowed the option of using the batting tee or hitting a pitched ball.
2. The pitcher can be selected from the batting team. This assures that an attempt will be made to make pitches that can be hit.
3. Vary the distance so that hitters have a fair opportunity to score. If hitters score too easily, another base can be added.

STEAL A BASE

Playing Area: Any 40 × 20 feet flat area or larger with more skilled students

Players: 6 to 10

Supplies: Hoops, softball, and gloves (optional)

Skills: Throwing, catching, tagging, running

The hoops are spaced approximately 20 feet apart in a rectangular fashion. Hoops are used as bases to prevent collisions. One player, serving as a fielder, is stationed by each hoop to begin the game. All other players are on a base; more than one runner is permitted on a base. On signal, runners begin accumulating runs by running to another base without being tagged. Fielders attempt to work together to tag as many runners as possible. Fielders may leave their base and chase runners if necessary. If a fielder leaves her base, other fielders may rotate to the vacant bag. Fielders and runners change positions every 2–3 minutes.

TEACHING TIP

Variations: Runners may not move to an adjacent base.

Developmental Level III

FIVE HUNDRED

Playing Area: Field big enough for fungo hitting

Players: 3 to 12 (or more)

Supplies: A softball, a bat

Skills: Fungo batting, catching flies, fielding grounders

There are many versions of the old game of Five Hundred. A batter stands on one side of the field and bats the ball to a number of fielders, who are scattered. The fielders attempt to become the batter by reaching a score of 500. Fielders earn 200 points for catching a ball on the fly, 100 points for catching a ball on the first bounce, and 50 points for fielding a grounder cleanly. Whenever a change of batters is made, all fielders lose their points and must start over.

TEACHING TIP

The ball can be hit off a batting tee if fungo hitting is too difficult.

Variations:

1. The fielder's points must total exactly 500.
2. Points are subtracted from the fielder's score if a ball is mishandled. If a fly ball is dropped, for example, 200 points are lost.

BATTER BALL

Playing Area: Softball diamond

Players: 8 to 12 on each team

Supplies: A softball, a bat, a mask

Skills: Slow pitching, hitting, fielding, catching flies

Batter Ball involves batting and fielding but no base running. It is much like batting practice but adds the element of competition. A line is drawn directly from first to third base. This is the balk line over which a batted ball must travel to be fielded. Another line is drawn from a point on the foul line 3 feet behind third base to a point 5 feet behind second base and in line with home plate. Another line connects this point with a point on the other baseline 3 feet behind first base. The shaded area in the diagram is the infield (Figure 27.20).

Each batter is given three pitches by a member of his own team to hit the ball into fair territory across the balk line. The pitcher may stop any ground ball before it crosses the balk line. The batter then gets another turn at bat.

Scoring is as follows:

1. A successful grounder scores 1 point. A grounder is successful when an infielder fails to handle it cleanly within the infield area. Only one player may field the ball. If the ball is fielded properly, the batter is out.
2. A line drive in the infield area is worth 1 point if not caught. It can be handled for an out on any bounce. Any line drive caught on the fly is also an out.

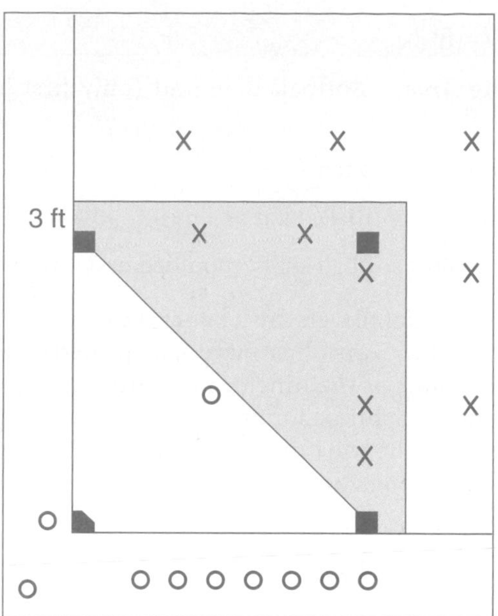

FIGURE 27.20 Field for Batter Ball.

3. A fly ball in the infield area scores 1 point if not caught. For an out, the ball must be caught legally by the first person touching it.
4. A two-bagger scores 2 points. Any fly ball, line drive or not, that lands fairly in the outfield area without being caught scores 2 points. If it is caught, the batter is out.
5. A home run scores 3 points. Any fly ball driven over the head of the farthest outfielder in that area scores a home run.

Three outs can constitute an inning, or all batters can be allowed one turn at bat and then the team changes to the field. A new set of infielders should be in place for each inning. The old set goes to the outfield. Pitchers should be limited to one inning. They also take a turn at bat.

TEACHING TIP

Many games of this type require special fields, either rectangular or narrowly angled. This game was selected because it uses a regular softball field with the added lines. The lines can be drawn with a stick or can be marked using regular marking methods.

The pitcher has to decide whether to stop the ball. If the ball goes beyond the restraining line, it is in play even if the pitcher touched it.

Variations: Batter Ball can be modified for use as a station in rotational teaching, with the emphasis on individual batting and squad organization. One member of the squad would be at bat and would get a definite number of chances (e.g., five) to score. She keeps her own point total. The other squad members occupy the necessary game positions.

HOME RUN

Playing Area: Softball diamond (only first base is used)

Players: Four to ten

Supplies: A softball, a bat

Skills: Most softball skills, modified base running

The crucial players are a batter, a catcher, a pitcher, and one fielder. Any other players are fielders; some can take positions in the infield. The batter hits a regular pitch and on a fair ball must run to first base and back home before the ball can be returned to the catcher.

The batter is out whenever any of the following occurs:

1. A fly ball (fair or foul) is caught.
2. The batter strikes out.
3. On a fair ball, the ball beats the batter back to home plate.

TEACHING TIP

To keep skillful players from staying too long at bat, a rule can be made that, after a certain number of home runs, the batter automatically must take a place in the field. A rotation (work-up) system should be established. The batter should go to right field, move to center, and then go to left field. The rotation continues through third base, shortstop, second base, first base, pitcher, and catcher. The catcher is the next batter. Naturally, the number of positions depends on the number of players in the game. If there are enough players, an additional batter can be waiting to take a turn.

The game can be played with only three youngsters, eliminating the catcher. With only one fielder, the pitcher covers home plate. The first-base distance should be far enough away to be a challenge but close enough so that a well-hit ball scores a home run. The distance depends on the number playing and the capacities of players.

Variations:

1. This game can be played like softball—allowing the batter to stop at first base if another batter is up.
2. A fly ball caught by a fielder puts that player directly to bat. The batter then takes a place at the end of the rotation, and the other players rotate up to the position of the fielder who caught the ball. This rule has one drawback. It may cause children to scramble and fight for fly balls, which is not desirable in softball. The ball belongs to the player in whose territory it falls.
3. *Triangle Ball.* First and third bases are brought in toward each other, thus narrowing the playing field. Second base is not used. The game gets its name from the triangle formed by home plate and the two bases. The batter must circle first and third bases and return home before the ball reaches home plate. This game can also be played with as few as three players, with the pitcher covering home plate.

TEE BALL

Playing Area: Softball field

Players: 7 to 11 on each team

Supplies: A softball, a bat, a batting tee

Skills: Most softball skills (except pitching and stealing bases), hitting a ball from a tee

This game is an excellent variation of softball and is played under softball rules with the following exceptions.

1. Instead of hitting a pitched ball, the batter hits the ball from a tee. The catcher places the ball on the tee. After the batter hits the ball, the play is the same as in regular softball. With no pitching, there is no stealing. A runner stays on the base until the ball is hit by the batter.
2. A fielder occupies the position normally held by the pitcher. The primary duties of this fielder are to field bunts and ground balls and to back up the infielders on throws.

Teams can play regular innings for three outs or change to the field after each player on the batting team has had a turn at bat.

TEACHING TIP

A tee can be purchased or made from a radiator hose. An improvised batting tee is shown in Figure 27.21. (For another type of tee, see page 195.) If the tee is not adjustable, three different sizes should be available. The batter should take a position far enough behind the tee so that, in stepping forward to swing, the ball will be slightly in front of the midpoint of the swing.

Tee Ball has many advantages. There are no strikeouts, every child hits the ball, there is no dueling between pitcher and batter, and fielding opportunities abound.

SCRUB (WORK-UP)

Playing Area: Softball field

Players: 7 to 15

Supplies: A softball, a bat

Skills: Most softball skills

The predominant feature of Scrub is the rotation of the players. The game is played with regular softball rules, with individuals more or less playing for themselves. There are at least two batters, generally three. A catcher,

FIGURE 27.21 Improvised batting tee.

pitcher, and first-base player are essential. The remaining players assume the other positions. A batter who is out goes to a position in right field. All other players move up one position, with the catcher becoming the batter. The first-base player becomes the pitcher, the pitcher moves to catcher, and all others move up one place.

TEACHING TIP

If a fly ball is caught, the fielder and batter exchange positions.

SLOW-PITCH SOFTBALL

Playing Area: Softball diamond

Players: Ten on each team

Supplies: A softball, a bat

Skills: Most softball skills

The major difference between regular softball and Slow-Pitch Softball is in the pitching, but there are other modifications to the game as well. With slower pitching, there is more hitting and thus more action on the bases and in the field. Outfielders are an important part of the game, because many long drives are hit. Rule changes from the game of official softball are as follows.

1. The pitch must be a slow pitch. Any other pitch is illegal and is called a ball. The pitch must be slow, with an arc of 1 foot. It must not rise over 10 feet from the ground, however. Its legality depends on the umpire's call.
2. There are ten players instead of nine. The extra one, called the *roving fielder,* plays in the outfield and handles line drives hit just over the infielders.
3. The batter must take a full swing at the ball and is out if he chops at the ball or bunts.
4. If the batter is hit by a pitched ball, she is not entitled to first base. The pitch is merely called a ball. Otherwise, balls and strikes are called as in softball.
5. The runner must hold base until the pitch has reached or passed home plate. No stealing is permitted.

TEACHING TIP

Shortening the pitching distance somewhat may be desirable. Much of the success of the game depends on the pitcher's ability to get the ball over the plate.

BABE RUTH BALL

Playing Area: Softball diamond

Players: Five

Supplies: A bat, a ball, four cones or other markers

Skills: Batting, pitching, fielding

The three outfield zones—left, center, and right field—are separated by four cones. It is helpful if foul lines have been drawn, but cones can define them (Figure 27.22). The batter calls the field to which he intends to hit. The pitcher throws controlled pitches so that the batter can hit easily. The batter remains in position as long as he hits to the designated field. Field choices must be rotated. The batter gets only one swing to make

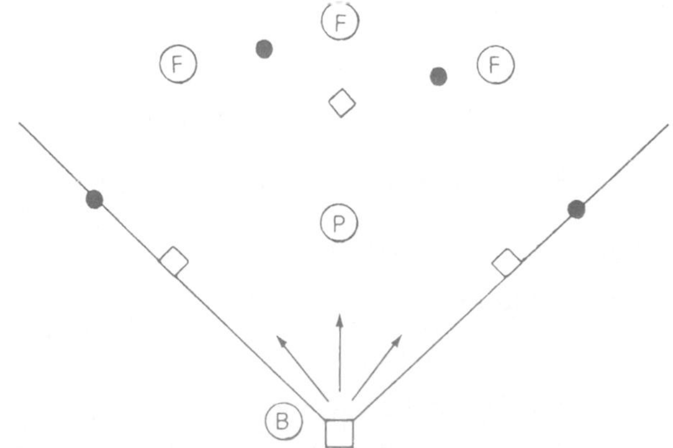

FIGURE 27.22 Babe Ruth Ball.

a successful hit. He may allow a ball to go by, but if he swings, it counts as a try. There is no base running. Players rotate.

TEACHING TIP

Children play this game informally on sandlots with a variety of rules. Some possibilities to consider are these: What happens when a fly ball is caught? What limitations should be made on hitting easy grounders? Let the players decide about these points and others not covered by the stated rules.

HURRY BASEBALL (ONE-PITCH SOFTBALL)

Playing Area: Softball diamond

Players: 8 to 12 on each team

Supplies: A softball, a bat

Skills: Slow pitching, most softball skills except stealing bases and bunting

Hurry Baseball demands rapid changes from batting to fielding, and vice versa. The game is like regular softball, with the following exceptions.

1. The pitcher is from the team at bat and must not interfere with, or touch, a batted ball on penalty of the batter's being called out.
2. The team coming to bat does not wait for the fielding team to get set. Because it has its own pitcher, the pitcher gets the ball to the batter just as quickly as the batter can grab a bat and get ready. The fielding team has to hustle to get out to their places.
3. Only one pitch is allowed to a batter. The batter must hit a fair ball or she is out. The pitch is made from about two-thirds of the normal pitching distance.
4. No stealing is permitted.
5. No bunting is permitted.

The batter must take a full swing. The game provides much activity in the fast place changes that must be made after the third out. Teams in the field learn to put the next hitter as catcher, so that she can bat immediately when the third out is made. Batters must bat in order. Scoring follows regular softball rules.

THREE-TEAM SOFTBALL

Playing Area: Softball diamond

Players: 12 to 15

Supplies: A mask, a ball, a bat

Skills: All softball skills

Three-Team Softball works well with 12 players, a number considered too few to divide into two effective fielding teams. The players are instead divided into three teams. The rules of softball apply, with the following exceptions.

1. One team is at bat, one team covers the infield (including the catcher), and the third team provides the outfielders and the pitcher.
2. The team at bat must bat in a definite order. This means that because of the small number of batters on each side, instances can occur when the person due to bat is on base. To take a turn at bat, the runner must be replaced by a player not on base.
3. After three outs, the teams rotate, with the outfield moving to the infield, the infield taking a turn at bat, and the batters going to the outfield.
4. An inning is over when all three teams have batted.
5. The pitcher should be limited to pitching one inning only. A player may repeat as pitcher only after all members of that team have had a chance to pitch.

SOFTBALL SKILL TESTS

Throwing for Accuracy

To test accuracy in throwing, a target with three concentric circles of 54, 36, and 18 inches is drawn on a wall. Scoring is 1, 2, and 3 points, respectively, for the circles. Five trials are allowed, for a possible score of 15. Balls hitting a line score the higher number.

Instead of the suggested target, a tire can be hung. Scoring allows 2 points for a throw through the tire and 1 point for simply hitting the tire. A maximum of 10 points is possible with this system.

Throwing for Distance

In the test of throwing for distance, each child is allowed three throws, and the longest throw on the fly is recorded.

Fielding Grounders

A file of players is stationed behind a restraining line. A thrower is about 30 feet in front of this line. Each player in turn attempts to field five ground balls. The score is the number of balls fielded cleanly. It is recognized that inconsistencies will occur in the throw and bounce of the ground balls served up for fielding. If the opportunity was obviously not a fair one, the child should get another chance.

Circling the Bases

Runners are timed as they circle the bases. A diamond with four bases is needed, plus a stopwatch for timing.

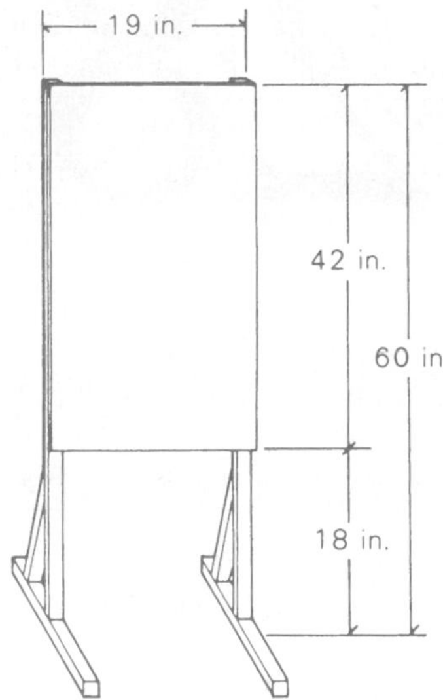

FIGURE 27.23 Old Woody pitching target.

Two runners can run at one time by starting from opposite corners of the diamond. Two watches are needed with this system. The batter can bunt a pitched ball and run around the bases. The timing starts with the bunt and finishes when the batter touches home plate.

Pitching

Pitching is one of the easier skills to test in softball and is certainly one of the most popular with children. Two basic methods are used for testing. In the first, each child takes a certain number of pitches at a target. Scoring is on the basis of the number of strikes that can be thrown. In the second, each child pitches regularly, as if to a batter, with balls and strikes being counted. Batters are either struck out or walked. The test score is the number of batters the child is able to strike out from a given number at bat. This score is expressed as a percentage.

In either method, a target is needed. It should be 19 inches wide and 42 inches high. It can be outlined temporarily on a wall with chalk or paint. The lower portion of the target should be about 18 inches above the ground or floor. If the target is constructed from plywood or wood, some means of support or of hanging the target will be needed. The boundaries of the target should be counted as good. The pitching distance should be normal (35 feet), and regular pitching rules should be observed.

Old Woody is the name of a pitching target in the form of a stand that can be moved from school to school. The target size is shown in Figure 27.23. A sturdy frame holds the target and allows it to be used in almost any spot.

FOR MORE INFORMATION

References and Suggested Readings

American Sport Education Program. (1996). *Coaching youth softball.* Champaign, IL: Human Kinetics.

Garman, J. (2001). *Softball skills and drills.* Champaign, IL: Human Kinetics.

Kneer, M., & McCord, C. (1995). *Softball: Slow and fast pitch.* 6th ed. Dubuque, IA: Brown & Benchmark.

Mood, D. P., Musker, F. F., & Rink, J. E. (2003). *Sports and recreational activities.* 13th ed. New York: McGraw-Hill.

Potter, D. L. & Brockmeyer, G. (1999). *Softball: Steps to success.* Champaign, IL: Human Kinetics.

The Amateur Softball Association of America. (2001). *Official rules of softball.* Oklahoma City, OK.

U.S. Olympic Committee Sport Series. (2001). *A basic guide to softball.* Torrance, CA: Griffen Publishing Group.

Websites

Jim's Slow Pitch Softball
www.staff.uiuc.edu/~j-danner/

Softball Manitoba
www.softball.mb.ca/

USA Softball
www.usasoftball.org

C H A P T E R 28

Track, Field, and Cross-Country Running

	ESSENTIAL COMPONENTS
I	**Organized around content standards**
II	**Student-centered and developmentally appropriate**
III	**Physical activity and motor skill development form the core of the program**
IV	**Teaches management skills and self-discipline**
V	**Promotes inclusion of all students**
VI	**Focuses on process over product**
VII	Promotes lifetime personal health and wellness
VIII	**Teaches cooperation and responsibility and promotes sensitivity to diversity**

	PHYSICAL EDUCATION STANDARDS
1	**Students are able to move competently using a variety of fundamental and specialized motor skills.**
2	Students can monitor and maintain a health-enhancing level of physical fitness.
3	**Students are able to apply movement concepts and basic mechanics of skill performance when learning and refining motor skills.**
4	Students comprehend the basic principles of wellness and are able to apply concepts that enable them to make meaningful decisions that positively impact their health and wellness.
5	**Students participate in a wide variety of physical activities and learn how to maintain a personalized active lifestyle.**
6	**Students demonstrate empathy, understanding, and respect for the numerous differences exhibited by people in an activity setting.**
7	**Students exhibit responsible and self-directed behaviors that lead to positive social interactions in physical activity.**

SUMMARY

Skills instruction for track, field, and cross-country running is introduced during the intermediate grades after youngsters have mastered basic prerequisite skills. Teaching the rules and strategies for track, field, and cross-country running is an integral part of the instructional process. Using proper progression is a key to success when teaching fundamental skills and lead-up games associated with track, field, and cross-country running. Lead-up games provide an opportunity to emphasize development of selected track, field, and cross-country running skills in a setting that is compatible with the abilities of participants.

OUTCOMES

- Structure learning experiences efficiently using appropriate formations, progressions, and coaching techniques.
- Develop a unit plan and lesson focus for track, field, and cross-country running.
- Identify safety precautions associated with teaching track, field, and cross-country running.
- Describe instructional procedures used for implementing a successful lead-up game.
- Cite assessment procedures used for evaluating track, field, and cross-country running skills.

The elementary program in track and field consists of short sprints (40 to 100 yards), running and standing long jumps, high jumps, hop-step-and-jumps, and relays. Jogging and distance running are encouraged throughout the program. The primary emphases are on practice and personal accomplishment, but modified competition in cross-country running is acceptable. Hurdling can be included when the equipment is available.

Children should experience the differences between walking, sprinting, running, striding (for pace), and jogging. Sprinting techniques are particularly important, with instruction centering on correct form for starting, accelerating, and sprinting. Speed and quickness are important attributes that govern the degree of success in many play and sport activities. Teach the rules for different events. Because few elementary schools have a permanent track, laying out and lining the track (see page 674) each year are valuable educational experiences.

INSTRUCTIONAL EMPHASIS AND SEQUENCE

Table 28.1 divides track and field activities into two developmental levels. The activities are listed in progression. Because many track and field skills involve locomotor movements, youngsters of all ages can enjoy and participate in these activities.

Developmental Levels I and II

Running and jumping skills are easily mastered by children, so they are introduced in developmental level I. Early experiences at this level stress running short distances, learning different starting positions, and participating in the two types of long jump. Some running for distance is included, and cross-country meets are introduced. Relays offer exciting experiences and involve a large number of youngsters in a quasi-team activity.

Developmental Level III

More serious efforts to achieve proper form begin at this level. The scissors style can be introduced in high jumping, and experimentation with other styles can be encouraged. Students should begin to use check marks with the running long jump. Running for distance and cross-country activities are emphasized. Hurdling using modified hurdles is an exciting event. In the high jump, critical points of the Straddle Roll and the Western Roll are explained. Developing pace in distance running without strong elements of competition is taught. The hop-step-and-jump extends the range of jumping activities. Relays and baton passing are given increased coverage at this level.

TABLE 28.1 Suggested track, field, and cross-country program

Developmental Levels I and II	Developmental Level III
Track and Cross-Country Skills	
40- to 60-yd sprints	50- to 100-yd sprints
Standing start	Distance running
Sprinter's start	Relays
Jogging and cross-country running	Hurdling
	Baton passing
Field Skills	
Standing long jump	High jump
Long jump	Hop-step-and-jump

TRACK AND FIELD SKILLS

Starting

Standing Start

The standing start should be practiced, because this type of start has a variety of uses in physical education activities. Many children find it more comfortable than the sprinter's start. As soon as is practical, however, children should accept the sprinter's start for track work.

In the standing start, the feet should be in a comfortable half-stride position. An extremely long stride is to be avoided. The body leans forward so that the center of gravity is forward. The weight is on the toes, and the knees are flexed slightly. The arms can be down or hanging slightly back (Figure 28.1).

Norwegian Start

The Norwegians use the standing start in a novel way. On the command "On your mark," the runner takes a position at the starting line with the right foot forward. On "Get set," the left hand is placed on the right knee and the right hand is carried back for a thrust (Figure 28.2). On "Go," the right hand comes forward, coupled with a drive by the right foot. The advantage claimed for this start is that it forces the body to lean and makes use of the forward thrust of the arm coordinated with the step off on the opposite foot.

FIGURE 28.1 Standing start.

FIGURE 28.2 Norwegian start.

Sprinter's Start

There are several kinds of sprinter's starts, but teachers are advised to concentrate on a single one. The "On your mark" position places the toe of the front foot from 4 to 12 inches behind the starting line. The thumb and first finger are just behind the line, with other fingers adding support. The knee of the rear leg is placed just opposite the front foot or ankle (Figure 28.3).

For the "Get set" position, the seat is raised so that it is nearly parallel to the ground. The knee of the rear leg is raised off the ground, and the shoulders are moved forward over the hands. The weight is evenly distributed over the hands and feet (Figure 28.4). The head is not raised, as the runner should be looking at a spot a few feet in front of the starting line.

On the "Go" signal, the runner pushes off sharply with both feet, with the front leg straightening as the back leg comes forward for a step. The body should rise gradually rather than pop up suddenly. The instructor should watch for a stumbling action on the first few steps. This results from too much weight resting on the hands in the "Get set" position.

FIGURE 28.3 Sprinter's start—"On your mark."

FIGURE 28.4 Sprinter's start—"Get Set!"

RUNNING

Sprinting

In proper sprinting form, the body leans forward, with the arms swinging in opposition to the legs. The arms are bent at the elbows and swing from the shoulders in a forward and backward plane, not across the body (Figure 28.5). Forceful arm action aids sprinting. The knees are lifted sharply forward and upward and are brought down with a vigorous motion, followed by a forceful push from the toes. Sprinting is a driving and striding motion, as opposed to the inefficient pulling action displayed by some runners.

Distance Running

In distance running, as compared with sprinting, the body is more erect and the motion of the arms is less pronounced. Pace is an important consideration. Runners should try to concentrate on the qualities of lightness, ease, relaxation, and looseness. Good striding action, a slight body lean, and good head position are also important. Runners should be encouraged to strike the ground with the heel first and then push off with the toes (Figure 28.6).

Relays

Two types of relay are generally included in a program of track and field for children. Instruction in baton passing should be incorporated into relay activity. Running on the track is always done in a counterclockwise direction.

Circular (Pursuit) Relays

Circular relays make use of the regular circular track. The baton exchange technique is important, and practice is needed. On a 220-yard or 200-meter track, relays can be organized in a number of ways, depending on how many runners are spaced for one lap. Four runners can do a lap, each running one quarter of the way; two can do a lap, each running one half of the distance; or each runner can complete a whole lap. In these races, each member of the relay team runs the same distance. Relays can also be organized so that members run different distances.

Shuttle Relays

Because children are running toward each other, one great difficulty in running shuttle relays is control of the exchange. In the excitement, the next runner may leave too early, and the tag or exchange is then made ahead of the restraining line. A high-jump standard or cone can be used to prevent early exchanges. The next runner

FIGURE 28.5 Proper sprinting form.

FIGURE 28.6 Proper running form.

awaits the tag with an arm around the standard or a hand on a cone.

Baton Passing

Two methods of baton passing are commonly used. The first method is the right hand to left hand method and is used in longer distance relays. It is the best choice for elementary school children as it is easy and offers a consistent method for passes. This pass allows the receiver to face the inside of the track while waiting to receive the baton in the left hand. The oncoming runner holds the baton in the right hand like a candle when passing it to a teammate. The receiver reaches back with the left hand, fingers pointing down and thumb to the inside, and begins to run as the runner advances to within 3 to 5 yards. The receiver grasps the baton and shifts it from the left to the right hand while moving. If the baton is dropped, it must be picked up, or the team is disqualified. An alternative way to receive the baton is to reach back with the hand facing up; however, the fingers-down method is considered more suitable for sprint relays.

The second style of passing, the alternating handoff, is usually used in the 400- and 800-meter relays. The first exchange is right to left, the second exchange is left to right, and the third exchange is right to left. This method prevents the runner from having to switch the baton from hand to hand while sprinting. This method is used in high-level competition in short distances, but probably is less useful with elementary-age youngsters.

Receivers can look over their shoulders to see the oncoming runner or can look forward in the direction of the run. Looking backward is called a *visual pass* and is slower than passing while looking forward (called a *blind pass*). However, there is a greater chance for error when the receiver is not looking backward and at the baton during the pass. The visual pass is recommended for elementary school children.

Horizontal Jumping

In both the standing and the running long jump, the measurement is made from the takeoff board or line to the nearest point on the ground touched by the jumper. It is therefore important for children not to fall or step backward after making the jump.

Standing Long Jump

In the standing long jump, the child toes the line with feet flat on the ground and fairly close together. The arms are brought forward in a preliminary swing and are then swung down and back (Figure 28.7). The jump is made with both feet as the arms are swung forcibly forward to assist in lifting the body upward and forward. In the air, the knees should be brought upward and forward, with the arms held forward to sustain balance.

FIGURE 28.7 Standing long jump. (Note position of hands and arms.)

Long Jump

For the running long jump, a short run is needed. The run should be executed so that the toes of the jumping foot contact the board in a natural stride. The jumper takes off from one foot and strives for height. The landing is made on both feet after the knees have been brought forward. The landing should be in a forward direction, not sideward.

More efficient jumping is achieved when a checkpoint is used. The checkpoint can be established about halfway down the run. Competitors can help each other mark checkpoints. Each jumper should know how many steps back from the takeoff board the checkpoint is located. On the run for the jump, the student hits the mark with the appropriate foot (right or left) so as to reach the board with the correct foot in a normal stride for the jump.

The jumper should arrive at the checkpoint at full speed. The last four strides taken before the board should be relaxed in readiness for the takeoff. The last stride can be shortened somewhat (Figure 28.8).

A fair jump takes off behind the scratch line. A foul (scratch) jump is called if the jumper steps beyond the

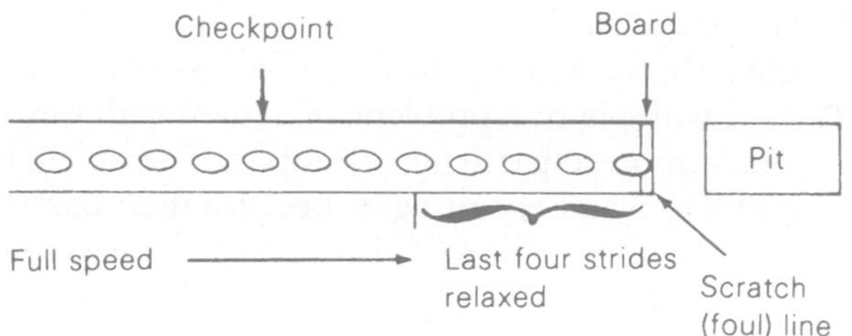

FIGURE 28.8 Long jump.

scratch line or runs into or through the pit. Each contestant is given a certain number of trials (jumps). A scratch jump counts as a trial. Measurement is from the scratch line to the nearest point of touch.

Hop-Step-and-Jump

The hop-step-and-jump event is increasing in popularity, particularly because it is now included in Olympic competition. A takeoff board and a jumping pit are needed. The distance from the takeoff board to the pit should be one that even less skilled jumpers can make. The event begins with a run similar to that for the running long jump. The takeoff is with one foot, and the jumper must land on the same foot to complete the hop. He then takes a step followed by a jump. The event finishes like the long jump, with a landing on both feet (Figure 28.9). The pattern can be changed to begin with the left foot. A checkpoint should be used, as for the running long jump.

The jumper must not step over the takeoff board in the first hop, under penalty of fouling. Distance is measured from the front of the takeoff board to the closest place the body touches. This is usually a mark made by one of the heels, but it could be a mark made by an arm or another part of the body if the jumper landed poorly and fell backward.

High Jumping

High-jump techniques are developed by practice. The bar should be at a height that offers challenge but allows concentration on technique rather than on height. Too much emphasis on competition for height quickly eliminates the poorer jumpers, who need the most practice. Safety is of utmost importance. Using a flexible elastic rope as a crossbar and avoiding any type of flop will prevent injury. Youngsters often want to emulate the Fosbury Flop, but this technique can result in a neck or back injury if not performed correctly. It should not be used in the elementary school program. A crash pad should be used to absorb the force of the landing for Straddle Roll and Western Roll techniques.

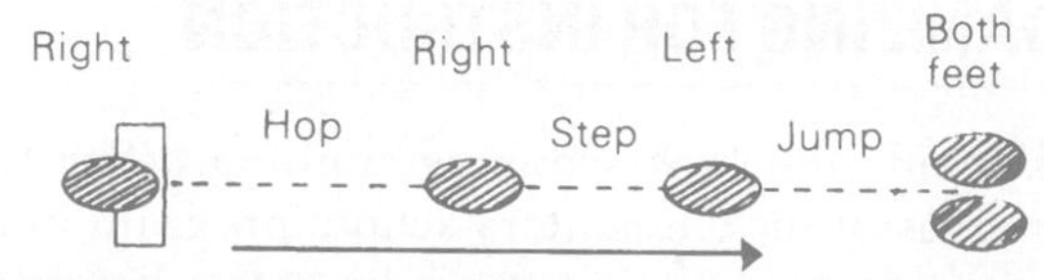

FIGURE 28.9 Hop-step-and-jump.

Scissors Jump

For the Scissors Jump, the high-jump bar is approached from a slight angle. The takeoff is by the leg that is farther from the bar. The near leg is lifted and goes over, followed quickly by a looping movement by the rear leg. Focus on an upward kick with the front leg and an upward thrust of the arms. The knees should be straightened at the highest point of the jump. The landing is made on the lead foot followed by the rear foot.

Straddle Roll

For the Straddle Roll (Figure 28.10), the approach is made from the left side at an angle of no more than 45 degrees. There are four key parts to the jump with respect to coaching:

1. *Gather.* The last three steps are fast and vigorous, with the body leaning back a bit. The takeoff is on the left foot.
2. *Kick.* The right leg is kicked vigorously as the jumping foot is planted.
3. *Arm movement.* An abrupt lift with both arms is made, with the left arm reaching over the bar and the right arm moving straight up. This puts the jumper in a straddle position while going over.
4. *Back leg clearance.* Clearance is accomplished by straightening the body, rolling the hips to the right (over the bar), or dropping the right shoulder.

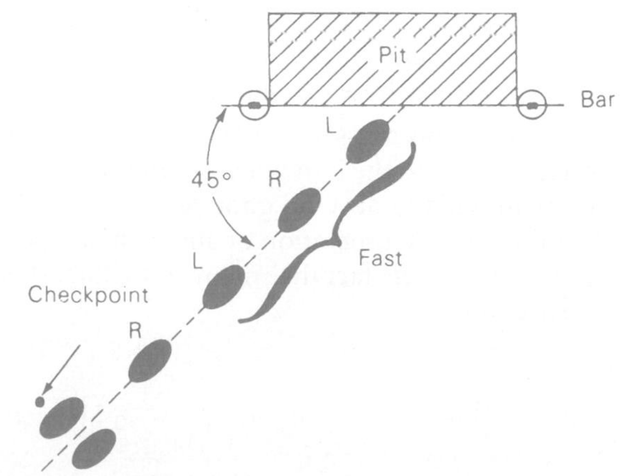

FIGURE 28.10 Straddle Roll.

Western Roll

For the Western Roll, the approach, gather, and kick are the same as for the Straddle Roll, but instead of being facedown, the jumper clears the bar by lying parallel to it on her side. The left arm is pointed down at the legs while crossing the bar and then is lowered. The head is turned toward the pit after clearance, and the landing is made on both hands and the left (takeoff) foot.

Hurdling

For safety, youngsters should use hurdles that are designed specifically for elementary schools. The hurdles should tip over easily when struck by runners. Youngsters have a tendency to want to jump hurdles in the wrong direction. This can cause a serious fall since the hurdles do not give when crossed from the wrong side. Hurdles can be made from electrical conduit pipe. (See page 196 for a diagram.) Wands supported on blocks or cones can also be used as hurdles. Hurdling should begin with hurdles set at 12 inches in height and increase to 18 inches. They should be placed about 25 feet apart. Using six hurdles, a 60-yard (180-foot) course can be established as diagrammed in Figure 28.11.

Several key points govern good hurdling technique. The runner should adjust his stepping pattern so the takeoff foot is planted 3 to 5 feet from the hurdle. The lead foot is extended straight forward over the hurdle; the rear (trailing) leg is bent, with the knee to the side. The lead foot reaches for the ground, quickly followed by the trailing leg. A hurdler may lead with the same foot over consecutive hurdles or may alternate the leading foot. Some hurdlers like to thrust both arms forward instead of a single arm. A consistent step pattern should be developed.

INSTRUCTIONAL PROCEDURES

1. Spiked running shoes are not permitted. They create a safety problem and also give an unfair advantage to children whose parents can afford them.
2. Form should be stressed at all times, but it should be appropriate to the individual. Youngsters should be encouraged to develop good technique within their own style. Observation of any event at a track meet bears out the fact that many individual styles are successful.
3. The program should offer something for all boys and girls, the highly skilled and the less skilled, and those with physical problems. Children with weight problems need particular attention. They must be stimulated and encouraged, because their participation will be minimal if little attention is paid to them. Special goals can be set for overweight children, and special events and goals can also be established for children with disabilities.
4. The amount of activity, particularly distance work, should be increased progressively. A period of conditioning should precede any competition or all-out performance. If this procedure is followed, children will show few adverse effects.
5. Warm-up activity should precede track and field work and should include jogging as well as bending and stretching exercises.
6. Pits for the long jump and the high jump must be maintained properly. They should be filled with fresh sand of a coarse variety. For high jumping, commercial impact landing pads are necessary though expensive. If they are not available, high jumping should be restricted to the scissors style, with tumbling mats used for the landing area.
7. The metal high-jump crossbar is economical in the long run, although it will bend. A satisfactory crossbar can be made of nylon cord with a weight on each end to keep it taut while still allowing it to be displaced. Magic ropes (rubberized stretch ropes) can be adapted for low-level jumping practice.
8. The use of a track starter signal is recommended. The clapboard track starter approximates the sound of the usual starter's gun and does not have the drawback of requiring expensive ammunition. (See page 202 for a diagram showing how to construct this starting device.)
9. The goal of the program should be to allow students to develop at their own rate. Instructional sessions should be strenuous enough to ensure some overload but not so strenuous that students become discouraged or physically ill. The instructor needs to be perceptive enough to determine whether students are working too hard or too little. Special attention must be given to students who appear disinterested, dejected, emotionally upset, or withdrawn.

Start X | 25 ft | 25 ft | 25 ft | 25 ft | 25 ft | 25 ft | 30 ft | Finish
← 180 ft →

FIGURE 28.11 Hurdling course.

ORGANIZING FOR INSTRUCTION

Track, field, and cross-country running differ from other areas of the elementary school program in that considerable preparation must be made before the classes begin.

1. A track or a cross-country course must be laid out when there are no permanent courses. This can be done with marking lime. Lanes for sprinting are of value but are not an absolute requirement.
2. A hurdling area should be similarly outlined in an appropriate location.
3. Separate pits should be placed for the running long jump, the high jump, and the hop-step-and-jump. These pits should be spaced well apart to minimize interference.
4. High-jump equipment should be checked. Standards with pins, crossbars (or cord substitutes), and cushioned landing pads are needed.
5. Takeoff boards for the long jump and hop-step-and-jump should be in place. Jumping without the use of a takeoff board is not a satisfying experience.
6. Accessory materials should be gathered, including batons, starter clapboards, watches, hurdles, and yarn for the finish line.
7. The value of starting blocks is debatable. Doubtless, they add interest to the program, but their use and adjustment are sometimes difficult for the elementary school student to master.

The organization of students is as important as the organization of equipment. Height and weight are factors affecting the degree of physical performance in track, field, and cross-country activities. More efficient instruction is possible when children are grouped by height and weight. They also can be arranged by gender. The following groups may serve as a basis for instruction: (1) heavier and taller boys, (2) shorter and lighter boys, (3) heavier and taller girls, and (4) shorter and lighter girls. A simple way to form groups is to rank boys and girls separately according to the following formula, which yields a standard number: Score = 10 × age (to the nearest half-year) + weight (in pounds).

After the boys have been ranked, the upper 50 percent are assigned to group 1 and the remainder to group 2. A similar division is made with the girls. Some decisions regarding borderline cases must be made.

Some track and field skills can be practiced with a single-activity organization. Starting skills can be practiced with perhaps one-fourth of the children at one time. Four groups can practice baton-passing skills at one time. Striding for distance can be practiced with each group running as a unit.

Station Teaching

The predominant plan of organization should be one of multiple activity. Four stations can make use of the selected group organization, but more stations are desirable. If eight stations are used, two stations can be assigned to each group. Stations can be selected from the following skill areas: (1) starting and sprinting, (2) baton passing, (3) standing and running long jump, (4) hop-step-and-jump, (5) high jump, (6) hurdles, (7) striding for distance and pace judgment, and (8) the Potato Shuttle Race. (See the following section.)

It is generally not sound to have children practice at all stations in any one class session. The entire circuit can be completed during additional sessions. Putting written directions at each station is helpful. The directions can state what is to be accomplished as well as offering points of technique.

In later instruction, students can select the skills that they want to practice. With guidance, the choice system could embrace the entire program, with children determining at each session those areas on which they would like to concentrate. This choice approach can be related to individualized or contract instruction.

TRACK AND FIELD DRILLS AND ACTIVITIES

Potato Shuttle Race

The Potato Shuttle Race is an adaptation of an old U.S. custom during frontier harvest celebrations. For each competitor, a number of potatoes were placed in a line at various distances. The winner was the one who brought in his potatoes first, one at a time. He won a sack of potatoes for the best effort.

The modern version of this race uses blocks instead of potatoes, and each runner runs the following course. A box is placed 15 feet in front of the starting line, with four blocks in individual circles, which are the same distance (15 feet) apart (Figure 28.12). The runner begins behind the starting line and brings the blocks, one at a time, back to the box. She can bring the blocks back in any order desired, but all blocks must be put inside the box. The box should be 12 by 12 inches, with a depth of 3 to 6 inches. Blocks must be placed or dropped, not thrown, into the box.

The most practical way to organize competition in this race is to time each individual and then award places on the basis of elapsed time, for the race is physically challenging. The competitors must understand that each person is running individually and that they

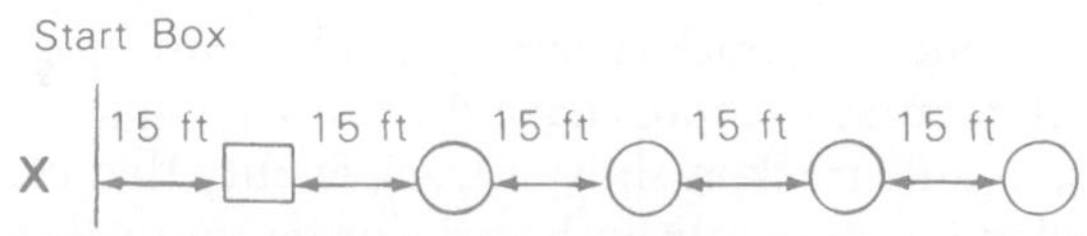

FIGURE 28.12 Potato Shuttle Race.

should strive for their best time, regardless of position or place of finish in the race.

Timers can act as judges to see that the blocks are not thrown into the box. A block that lands outside the box must be placed inside before the student goes after another. Blocks should be about 2 inches square, but this can vary.

The race can be run as a relay. The first runner brings all of the blocks in, one at a time, and then tags off the second member of the team, who returns the blocks, one at a time, to the respective spots. The third relay member brings the blocks in again, and the fourth puts them out again. For this race, it is necessary to have pie tins, floor tiles (9 by 9 inches), or some other items in addition to the box so that when the blocks are put out by the second and fourth runners, it can be determined definitely that they rest in the proper spot. A block must be on its spot in the proper fashion before the runner delivers the next one.

Running for Pace

Children should have some experience in running for moderate distances to acquire an understanding of pace. The running should be loose and relaxed. Distances up to 1600 meters may be part of the work. To check his time, each runner needs a partner. Someone with a stopwatch loudly counts the elapsed time second by second, and the partner notes the runner's time as he crosses the finish line.

Allowing children to estimate their pace and time can be motivating. On a circular track, at a set distance, let each runner stipulate a target time and see how close she can come to it.

Interval Training

Children should know the technique of interval training, which consists of running at a set speed for a specified distance and then walking back to the starting point. On the ⅛-mile track, children can run for 110 yards and then walk to the starting point, repeating this procedure a number of times. They can also run the entire 220 yards, take a timed rest, and then repeat. Breathing should return to near normal before the next 220-yard interval is attempted.

SUGGESTED TRACK FACILITY

The presence of a track facility is a boon to any program. Few elementary schools have the funds or space for a quarter-mile track. A shorter track facility that can be installed permanently with curbs or temporarily with marking lime is suggested. Discarded fire hoses can be

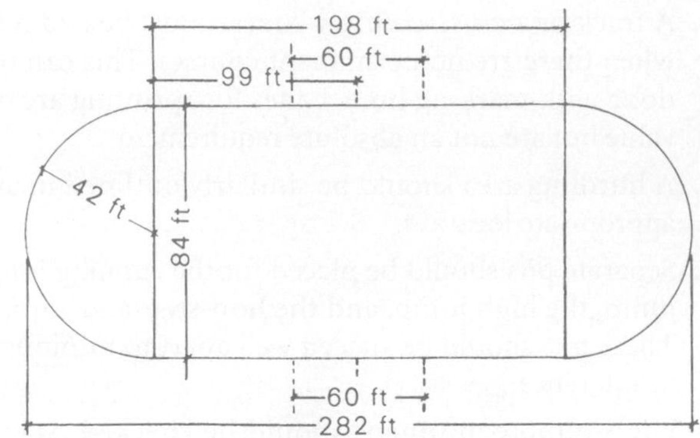

FIGURE 28.13 One-eighth-mile (220-yd) track.

used to mark curbs and can be installed each spring with spikes.

The short facility is ⅛ mile (220 yards) in length and has a straightaway of 66 yards, which is ample for the 60-yard dash (Figure 28.13). It allows flexibility in relays, since relay legs of 55, 110, and 220 yards are possible. In keeping with international practice, a 200-meter track may be preferable (Figure 28.14). Running on a track is always done in a counterclockwise direction.

CONDUCTING TRACK AND FIELD DAYS

Track and field days can range in organization from competition within a single classroom to competition among selected classes, from an all-school playday meet to a meet between neighboring schools or an areawide or all-city meet. In informal meets within a class or between a few classes, all children should participate in one or more events. Each student can be limited to two individual events plus one relay event, with no substitutions permitted. An additional condition could be imposed that competitors for individual events enter only one track event and one field event.

For larger meets, two means of qualification are suggested.

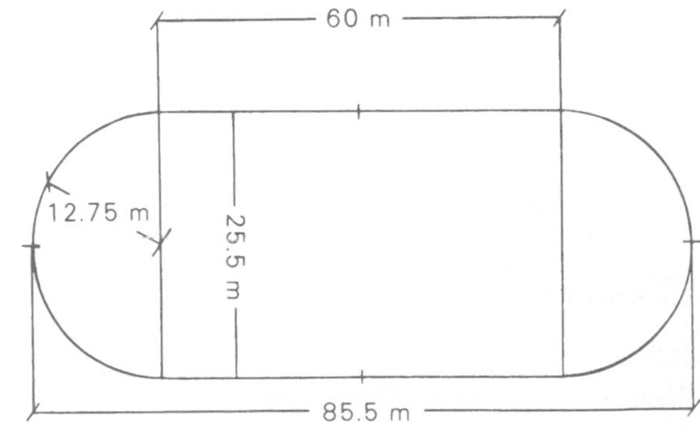

FIGURE 28.14 200-m track.

1. Qualifying times and performance standards can be set at the start of the season. Any student meeting or bettering these times or performances is qualified to compete.
2. In an all-school meet, first- and second-place winners in each class competition qualify for entry. For a district or all-city meet, first- and second-place winners from each all-school meet become eligible.

Generally, competition is organized for each event by sex and grade or age. This does not preclude mixed teams competing against mixed teams in relays. Height and weight classifications can be used to equalize competition.

Planning the Meet

The order of events should be determined by the type of competition. Relays are usually last on the program. If preliminary heats are necessary, these relays are run off first. Color-coded cards should be given to the heat qualifiers. This helps get them into the correct final race.

The local track coach can give advice about details of organizing the meet. Helpers can be secured from among school patrons, secondary students, teacher-training students, and service clubs. Adequate and properly instructed help is essential. A list of key officials and their duties follows.

1. *Meet director.* The meet director should be positioned at a convenient point near the finish line, with a table on which all official papers are kept.
2. *Announcer.* The announcer can be in charge of the public address system. Much of the success of the meet depends on the announcer's abilities.
3. *Clerk of the course.* The clerk of the course has charge of all entries and places the competitors in their proper starting slots.
4. *Starter.* The starter works closely with the clerk of the course.
5. *Head and finish judges.* There should be one finish judge for each place awarded, plus one extra. The first competitor "out of the money" is identified in case there is a disqualification. The head judge can cast the deciding vote if there is doubt about the first- and second-place winners.
6. *Timers.* Three timers should time first place, although fewer can be used. Another timer, if available, can time second place. Timers report their times to the head timer, who determines the correct winning time. Accurate timing is important if records are a factor.
7. *Messenger.* A messenger takes the entry card from the clerk of the course to the finish judge, who records the correct finish places and the winner's time after the race is completed. The messenger then takes the final record of the race to the meet director's table.
8. *Field judges and officials.* Each field event should be managed by a sufficient crew, headed by a designated individual. Each crew head should be given a clipboard with the rules of the particular event fully explained.
9. *Marshals.* Several marshals should be appointed to keep general order. They are responsible for keeping noncompetitors from interfering with the events. Competitors can be kept under better control if each unit has an assigned place, either in the infield or in the stands.

Only the assigned officials and competitors should be present at the scenes of competition.

In smaller meets, first, second, and third places are usually awarded, with scoring on a 5-, 3-, and 1-point basis, respectively. Relays, because of multiple participation, should count double in the place point score. For larger meets, more places can be awarded, and the individual point scores can be adjusted.

Ribbons can be awarded to winners but need not be elaborate. The name of the meet should be printed on the ribbon, with the individual event and the place designated. Blue ribbons are given for first place, red for second, and white for third. They are usually awarded after each event. Awarding ribbons at the conclusion of a large interschool meet is anticlimactic, because many spectators will have left.

An opening ceremony, including a salute to the flag, is desirable for larger meets. Competitors from each unit can be introduced as a group, with announcements and instructions emphasized or clarified at this time. Holding the event on a school morning or afternoon gives status to the affair and allows all children to participate.

It is helpful if the competitors wear numbers. Safety pins, rather than straight pins, should be used to keep the numbers in place. Numbers can be made at the individual schools prior to the meet when well-defined instructions pertaining to the materials, colors, and sizes have been given.

Organizing the Competition

The overriding goal of elementary school competition is to have many children take part and experience a measure of success. The determination of individual champions and of meet winners is lower in priority. Track and field competition can take many forms.

In informal competition, competitors are assigned to different races and compete only in those races. There are no heats as such, nor is there advancement to a final race. Races are chosen so that individuals on the same team usually do not run against each other. Points may or may not be given toward an overall meet score. The informal meet is more like a playday and can include nontrack events also, such as the softball throw, the football kick, and the Frisbee throw.

Track and field competition can be focused on individuals or teams. In individual competition, there is no team scoring and only individuals are declared winners. When team competition is incorporated, both individual winners and team winners are determined. Points scored by individual winners, such as 5 points for first place, or 3 points for second place, are credited to respective teams. The team with the highest score wins. Different team winners can be determined for different grades and/or levels.

Relay competition is a carnival in which a number of relays make up the program. Performances can be combined for several individuals if field events are to be included. Few, if any, uncombined scores are taken into consideration. A number of relays should be part of track and field days under any plan. Relays increase student participation. Mixed relays are a possibility.

CROSS-COUNTRY RUNNING

Many youngsters are motivated by running laps around a track. Others soon tire of these circular efforts, however, and can be motivated by cross-country running. Students can run marked or unmarked courses for enjoyment of the competition. Emphasis is on improving one's personal time rather than on winning. This enables all students to have personalized goals and an ongoing incentive for running.

Cross-country courses can be marked with a chalk line and cones so that runners follow the course as outlined. Checkpoints every 220 yards offer runners a convenient reference point so that they can gauge accurately how far they have run. Three courses of differing lengths and difficulty can be laid out. The beginning course can be 1 mile in length, the intermediate 1.25 mile, and the advanced 1.5 mile. Including sandy or hilly areas in the course increases the challenge. When students run cross country, they can select the course that challenges them appropriately.

It is important for students to learn the concept of pace when running long distances. One technique for teaching students how to pace themselves is to place cones at similar intervals and to challenge students to run from cone to cone at a specified rate. A student or the instructor can call out the time at each cone, and students can adjust their running to the desired pace. Another method is to break down long-distance runs into smaller segments and times, which enables youngsters to get a feel for how fast they must run the shorter distances to attain a certain cumulative time over the longer distance. Table 28.2 gives times for the 40- and 100-yard dashes.

CROSS-COUNTRY MEETS

Cross-country meets provide a culminating activity for youngsters involved in distance running. The attractiveness of cross-country competition lies in the fact that it is a team activity and all members of the team are crucial to its success. Youngsters should learn how to score a meet. Probably the easiest way to keep team scores is to assign seven (depending on class size) members to each team. Points are assigned to finishers based on their placement in the race. For example, the first-place runner receives 1 point, the tenth-place runner 10 points, and so on. The points for all team members are totaled, and the team with the lowest score is declared the winner.

Teams can be equalized by having youngsters run the course ahead of the meet and recording their times. Teams can then be organized by the teacher so that members are somewhat matched. As a guideline, Table 28.3 offers suggested competitive divisions and distances to be run. Divisions 5 and 6 are classed as open divisions, which any child in the elementary school may enter, even if below the age of 12. Ages are defined by birthdays; that is, a child is classified as being a certain age until the next birthday.

TABLE 28.2 Times for 40- and 100-yard dashes

To run a mile in:	Runner has to run 40-yd dash 44 times—each dash run in:	Runner has to run 100-yd dash 17.6 times—each dash run in:
3:44 minutes (world record time)	5.18 seconds	12.95 seconds
5:00 minutes	6.81 seconds	17.04 seconds
6:00 minutes	8.18 seconds	20.45 seconds
7:00 minutes	9.55 seconds	23.87 seconds
8:00 minutes	10.90 seconds	27.25 seconds
10:00 minutes	13.62 seconds	34.08 seconds

TABLE 28.3 Suggested divisions for cross-country meets

Division	Age	Sex	Distance (in miles)
1	8–9	M	1
2	8–9	F	1
3	10–11	M	1.25
4	10–11	F	1.25
5	12–13	M	1.5
6	12–13	F	1.5

A primary concern is that children gauge their running pace so that they are able to finish the race. Improvement of previous times should be the focus of the activity, with place at the finish of the race a secondary goal. The timekeeper can voice the time as each runner finishes to help children evaluate their performance.

A funnel made of cones at the finish line prevents tying times (Figure 28.15). As runners go through the funnel, the meet judges and helpers can hand each one a marker with the place of finish on it. This practice simplifies scoring at the end of the meet. Each team captain can total the scores and report the result.

Cross-country runners should learn to cool down on completion of a race. Youngsters have a tendency to fall down rather than to move. They should jog gently until they are somewhat rested. Because runners do not all finish at the same time, it is sometimes helpful to have some recreational activities set out near the track so that the youngsters can stay involved in activity.

FIGURE 28.15 Funneling runners at the finish line.

FOR MORE INFORMATION

References and Suggested Readings

Carr, G. (1999). *Fundamentals of track and field.* 2nd ed. Champaign, IL: Human Kinetics.

Jackson, C. (1996). *Young track and field athlete.* New York: DK Publishing.

Mood, D. P., Musker, F. F., & Rink, J. E. (2003). *Sports and recreational activities.* 13th ed. New York: McGraw-Hill.

NASPE and Hershey Corporation. (2002). *Hershey's Track & Field Official Rule Book and Manual.* Hershey, PA: Hershey.

Websites

Hershey Youth Track and Field Program
www.hersheytrackandfield.com

National Recreation and Park Association
http://www.nrpa.org/archives.cfm

USA Track & Field
www.usatf.org

CHAPTER 29

Volleyball

ESSENTIAL COMPONENTS

I	**Organized around content standards**
II	**Student-centered and developmentally appropriate**
III	**Physical activity and motor skill development form the core of the program**
IV	**Teaches management skills and self-discipline**
V	**Promotes inclusion of all students**
VI	**Focuses on process over product**
VII	Promotes lifetime personal health and wellness
VIII	**Teaches cooperation and responsibility and promotes sensitivity to diversity**

PHYSICAL EDUCATION STANDARDS

1	**Students are able to move competently using a variety of fundamental and specialized motor skills.**
2	Students can monitor and maintain a health-enhancing level of physical fitness.
3	**Students are able to apply movement concepts and basic mechanics of skill performance when learning and refining motor skills.**
4	Students comprehend the basic principles of wellness and are able to apply concepts that enable them to make meaningful decisions that positively impact their health and wellness.
5	**Students participate in a wide variety of physical activities and learn how to maintain a personalized active lifestyle.**
6	**Students demonstrate empathy, understanding, and respect for the numerous differences exhibited by people in an activity setting.**
7	**Students exhibit responsible and self-directed behaviors that lead to positive social interactions in physical activity.**

SUMMARY

Skills instruction for volleyball is introduced during the intermediate grades after youngsters have mastered basic prerequisite skills. Teaching the rules and strategies for volleyball is an integral part of the instructional process. Using proper progression is a key to success when teaching fundamental skills and lead-up games associated with volleyball. Lead-up games provide an opportunity to emphasize development of selected volleyball skills in a setting that is compatible with the abilities of participants.

OUTCOMES

- Structure learning experiences efficiently using appropriate formations, progressions, and coaching techniques.
- Develop a unit plan and lesson focus for volleyball.
- Identify safety precautions associated with teaching volleyball.
- Describe instructional procedures used for implementing a successful lead-up game.
- Cite assessment procedures used for evaluating volleyball skills.

To play volleyball successfully on the elementary level, basic skills need to be learned properly. This requires sufficient practice in serving and passing skills and the development of hand-eye and body coordination for effective ball control. Attention to proper technique is essential. Informal practice begins with activities that mimic volleyball skills—passing, serving, and rebounding of all types. Blocking is an important skill that youngsters can perform if they anticipate correctly. Setting and spiking are skills that challenge the most skilled youngsters so little time should be devoted to this phase of the game.

INSTRUCTIONAL EMPHASIS AND SEQUENCE

Indoor facilities sometimes pose a problem for volleyball play. In some gymnasiums, the lack of court space means playing with 12 to 15 children on a side in a single game. This arrangement results in little activity for the majority of participants. A few skilled players on each side dominate the game. A basketball court can be divided into two volleyball courts where players play crosswise. Lowering nets to 6 feet or less assures success. The nets can gradually be raised as children mature. Nets should be attached firmly so that both the upper and lower net cords are tight. A loose net does not allow for ball recovery from the net.

An adequate number of volleyballs are necessary. For individual practice, the number of balls can be supplemented with beach balls and foam balls of comparable size. Few schools have 30 to 35 volleyballs available. In larger school systems, having a rotating schedule of volleyball activities from school to school can solve the problem of volleyball supply. Few practice activities require a net, so outdoor participation is possible.

The overhand serve, setup, and spike are skills that are usually introduced when a competitive situation exists, such as intramurals or an interschool program. Normally, in physical education classes, the program dwells on keeping the ball in play, thereby increasing activity, skill development, and enjoyment. As a matter of game orientation, however, students should learn setup, spike, and blocking techniques.

In the primary grades, children can practice ball-handling activities related to volleyball skills. Rebounding and controlling balloons are excellent related experiences, particularly for younger children. These preliminary experiences in visual tracking are advantageous for volleyball skills learned in the upper grades.

Table 29.1 shows a sequence of volleyball activities divided into two developmental levels. In most cases, youngsters are not ready to participate in the activities in this chapter until the age of 8.

TABLE 29.1 Suggested volleyball program

Developmental Level II	Developmental Level III
Skills	
Underhand serve	Overhand pass
Simple returns	Forearm pass
	Overhand serve
	Setup*
	Spike*
	Blocking*
Knowledge	
Simple rules	Basic game rules
Rotation	Game strategy
Activities	
Beach Ball Volleyball	Pass and Dig
Informal Volleyball	Mini-Volleyball
Shower Service Ball	Rotation Mini-Volleyball
	Regulation Volleyball
	Three-and-Over Volleyball
	Rotation Volleyball
	Four-Square Volleyball
Skill Tests	
Simplified serving	Serving for accuracy
	Wall volleying

*Skilled players only.

Developmental Level II

Experiences at this level are based on the use of the beach ball and culminate in the game of Beach Ball Volleyball. A beach ball is larger and more easily handled than a volleyball and allows a level of success not possible with a smaller and heavier ball. Simple returns and underhand serves can be practiced with beach balls. The games of Informal Volleyball and Shower Service Ball are played with a beach ball or volleyball trainer ball, which moves more slowly and is easier to handle.

Developmental Level III

Beach balls and foam balls can be used at this level of instruction, but a shift to volleyball trainer balls should be made when the maturity of the youngsters dictates. Foam rubber and training volleyballs (8-inch) are excellent substitutes for volleyballs (Figure 29.1). They do

FIGURE 29.1 Different balls for Volleyball.

not hurt youngsters, move slowly, and afford an opportunity for successful play. Students should exhibit basic technique in handling high and low passes. Only the most skilled students are able to learn the overhand serve, setup, spike, and blocking. Instruction focuses on the underhand serve and the overhand and forearm passes. An introduction to elementary strategy is part of the instructional approach.

VOLLEYBALL SKILLS

Serving

The serve is used to start play. The underhand serve is easiest for elementary school children to learn even though the overhand (floater) serve is the most effective. Few youngsters will be capable of mastering the overhand serve. The following instructional cues focus on correct performance of the serve:

1. Use opposition. Place the foot opposite of the serving hand forward.
2. Transfer the weight to the forward foot.
3. Keep the eyes on the ball.
4. Decide prior to the serve where it should be placed.
5. Follow through; don't punch at the ball.

Underhand Serve

Directions are for a right-handed serve. The player stands facing the net with the left foot slightly forward and the weight on the right (rear) foot. The ball is held in the left hand with the left arm across and a little in front of the body. The ball is lined up with a straightforward swing of the right hand. The left-hand fingers are spread, and the ball rests on the pads of these fingers. On the serving motion, the server steps forward with the left foot, transferring the weight to the front foot, and at the same time brings the right arm back in a preparatory motion. The right hand now swings forward and contacts the ball just below center. The ball can be hit with an open hand or with the fist (facing forward or sideward). An effective follow-through with the arm ensures a smooth serve (Figure 29.2). Children should explore the best way to strike the ball, with the flat of the hand or the fist. Each player can select the method that is personally most effective.

Overhand Serve

This serve is seldom mastered by elementary school youngsters. It can be presented as an option for students who have mastered the underhand serve. For the right-handed serve, stand with the left foot in front and the left side of the body turned somewhat toward the net. The weight is on both feet. The server must master two difficult skills: how to toss the ball and how to contact the ball. The ball is held in the left hand directly in front of the face. The ball must be tossed straight up and should come down in front of the right shoulder. As the ball is tossed, the weight shifts to the back foot. The height of the toss is a matter of choice, but from 3 to 5 feet is suggested. As the ball drops, the striking arm comes forward, contacting the ball a foot or so above the shoulder. The weight is shifted to the forward foot, which can take a short step forward. The contact is made with the open palm or with the fist. An effective serve is one that has no spin—a floater.

Passing (or Returning)

The overhand pass is probably the most used skill in elementary school volleyball. Using beach balls and

FIGURE 29.2 Underhand serve.

trainer volleyballs will allow youngsters time to move into the path of the volleyball instead of reaching for the ball. Proper footwork is critical to the success of volleyball; using proper balls will help ensure that youngsters learn correctly. Instructional cues for passing include the following:

1. Move into the path of the ball; don't reach for it.
2. Bend the knees prior to making contact.
3. Contact the ball with the fingertips (overhand pass).
4. Extend the knees upon contact with the ball.
5. Follow through after striking the ball.

Overhand Pass (Setting)

The overhand pass is most often used by young players to return the ball to the other team. As players become more proficient, it is used to set up other teammates. To execute an overhand pass, the player moves underneath the ball and controls it with the fingertips. Feet should be in an easy, comfortable position, with knees bent. The cup of the fingers is made so that the thumbs and forefingers are close together and the other fingers are spread. The hands are held forehead high, with elbows out and level with the floor. The player, when in receiving position, looks ready to shout upward through cupped hands (Figure 29.3).

The player contacts the ball above eye level and propels it with the force of spread fingers, not with the palms. At the moment of contact, the legs are straightened and the hands and arms follow through. The set should be passed high enough to allow a teammate time to move under the ball.

FIGURE 29.3 Completing an overhead pass.

Forearm Pass (Underhand Pass)

The body must be in good position to ensure a proper underhand pass. The player must move rapidly to the spot where the ball is descending to prepare for the pass. Body position is important. The trunk leans forward and the back is straight, with a 90-degree angle between the thighs and the back. The legs are bent, and the body is in a partially crouched position, with the feet shoulder width apart (Figure 29.4). The hands are clasped together so that the forearms are parallel. The clasp should be relaxed, with the type of handclasp a matter of choice. In one method, the thumbs are kept parallel and together, and the fingers of one hand make a partially cupped fist, with the fingers of the other hand overlapping the fist. In another method, both hands are cupped and turned out a little, so that the thumbs are apart. In either case, the wrists are turned downward and the elbow joints are reasonably locked. The forearms are held at the proper angle to rebound the ball, with contact made with the fists or forearms between the knees as the receiver crouches.

Dig Pass

The dig pass is an emergency return when neither the overhand nor the forearm pass is possible. It is a stiffened rebound from one arm, contact being made with the cupped fist (Figure 29.5), the heel of the hand, or the inside or outside of the forearm. The dig pass should not be used as a standard return.

Advanced Volleyball Skills

The setup, the spike, and blocking are skills that are difficult for the majority of youngsters to master. Volleyball lead-up games do not require the use of these skills. Because the majority of children will not be able to master these skills, it is best to introduce them on an individual basis.

FIGURE 29.4 Forearm (underhand) pass position.

FIGURE 29.5 Dig pass.

Setup

The term setup applies to a pass that sets the ball for a possible spike. The object is to raise the ball with a soft, easy pass to a position 1 or 2 feet above the net and about 1 foot away from it. The setup is generally the second pass in a series of three. An overhand pass is used for the setup. It is important for the back line player, who has to tap to the setter, to make an accurate and easily handled pass.

Spike

The spike is the most effective play in volleyball, and when properly done is extremely difficult to return. Its success depends a great deal on the ability of a teammate to set up properly. At the elementary school level, spiking should be done by jumping high in the air and striking the ball above the net, driving it into the opponent's court. Experienced players may back up for a short run, but the jump must be made straight up so that the player does not touch the net and the striking hand does not go over the net.

Blocking

Blocking involves one or more members of the defensive (receiving) team forming a screen of arms and hands near the net to block a spike. At the elementary school level, blocking is usually done by a single individual, and little attention is given to multiple blocking. To block a ball, a player jumps high with arms outstretched overhead, palms facing the net, and fingers spread. The jump must be timed with that of the spiker, and the blocker must avoid touching the net. The ball is not struck but rather rebounds from the blocker's stiffened hands and arms.

INSTRUCTIONAL PROCEDURES

1. Most volleyball-type games begin with a serve, so it becomes critical that this be successful. Regular volleyball rules call for one chance to serve the ball over the net without touching the net. Three modifications can achieve more successful serving. The first is to serve from the center of the playing area instead of the back line. A second is to allow another serve if the first is not good. The third is to allow an assist by a team member to get the ball over the net.
2. To save time, instruct players to roll the ball back to the server. Other players should let the ball roll to its destination without interception.
3. Effective instruction is possible only when the balls can be rebounded from the hands and arms with-

out pain. A heavy or underinflated ball takes much of the enjoyment out of the game. Beach balls are excellent for beginning players.

4. The predominant instructional pattern should be individual or partner work. For individual work, each child needs a ball.
5. An 8-inch foam rubber training ball has much the same feel as a volleyball but does not cause pain. The foam balls should be used early in skill practice. A new ball, the volleyball trainer, most closely resembles a volleyball but is larger in diameter and lighter in weight. The use of either ball helps keep children from developing a fear of the fast-moving object.
6. The use of the fist to hit balls on normal returns causes poor control and interrupts play. Except for dig passes, both hands should be used to return the ball. Teachers should rule hitting with the fist a loss of a point if the practice persists.
7. Rotation should be introduced early and used in lead-up games. Two rotation plans are illustrated in Figure 29.6.

ORGANIZING FOR INSTRUCTION

Practice sessions can be categorized as individual play, partner work, or group work. These tasks can be prefaced by "Can you . . ." or "Let's see if you can. . . ." A skill to learn early is a toss to oneself to initiate a practice routine. This occurs when the practice directions call for a pass from one individual to oneself or to another.

Two lines

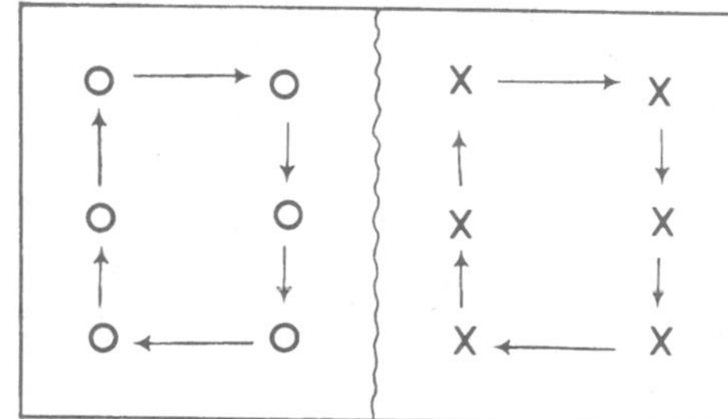

Three lines

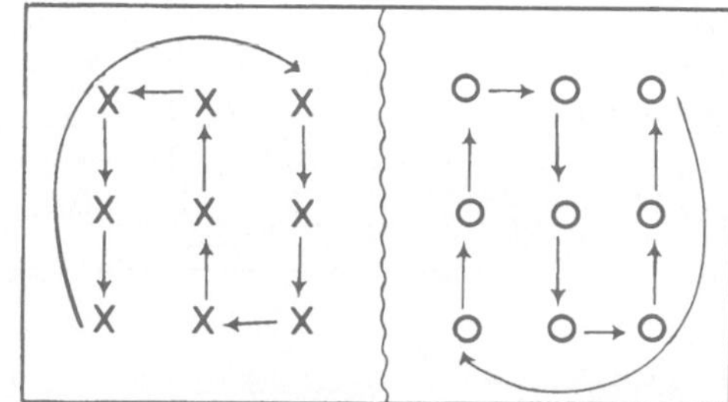

FIGURE 29.6 Rotation plans.

Individual Play

1. For wall rebounding, stand 6 feet away from a wall. Throw the ball against the wall and pass it to the wall. The player then catches and begins again. Allow two passes against the wall before a catch is made. A further extension is to pass the ball against the wall as many times as possible without making a mistake.
2. From a spot 6 feet from the wall, throw the ball against the wall and alternate an overhand pass with a forearm pass. The player then catches the ball.
3. In another wall-rebounding exercise, the player throws the ball to one side (right or left) and then moves to the side to pass the ball to the wall. Catch the rebound.
4. The player passes the ball directly overhead and catches it. Try making two passes before catching the ball. Later, alternate an overhand pass with a forearm pass and catch the ball. A further extension of the drill is to keep the ball going five or six times with one kind of pass or with alternate passes. This is a basic drill and should be mastered before proceeding to others.
5. The player passes the ball 10 feet high and 10 feet forward, moves rapidly under the ball, and catches it. Later, make additional passes without the catch.
6. The player passes the ball 15 feet overhead, makes a full turn, and passes the ball again. Vary with other stunts such as touching the floor, making a half turn, clapping the hands at two different spots, and others. Allow choice in selecting the stunt.
7. Two lines 3 feet apart are needed. The player stands in front of one line, makes a backward pass overhead, moves to the other line, and repeats the procedure.
8. The player passes 3 feet or so to one side, moves under the ball, and passes it back to the original spot. The next pass should be to the other side.
9. The player passes the ball directly overhead. On the return, jump as high as possible to make a second pass. Continue.
10. The player stands with one foot in a hoop. Pass the ball overhead and attempt to continue passing while keeping that foot in the hoop. Try with both feet in the hoop.
11. The player stands about 15 feet away from a basketball goal, either in front or to the side. Pass toward the goal in an attempt to make a basket. Score 3 points if the basket is made, 2 points for no basket but for hitting the rim, and 1 point for hitting the backboard only. A further challenge would be for the player to make a pass to himself first and a second pass toward the goal.

Partner Work (Passing)

1. Players are about 10 feet apart. Player A tosses the ball (controlled toss) to player B, who passes the ball back to A, who catches the ball. Continue for several exchanges and then change throwers. Another option is for player B to make a pass straight overhead, catch the ball, and then toss to player A. Yet another variation is to have one player toss the ball slightly to the side. Player B then makes a pass to player A. Player A can make the toss in such a fashion that player B must use a forearm return.
2. Two players are about 15 feet apart. Player A passes to herself first and then makes a second pass to player B, who catches the ball and repeats. This can be followed with a return by player B.
3. Players A and B try to keep the ball in the air continuously.
4. Players are about 15 feet apart. Player A remains stationary and passes in such a fashion that player B must move from side to side. An option is to have player B move forward and backward.
5. Players are about 10 feet apart. Both have hoops and attempt to keep one foot in the hoop while passing. Try keeping both feet in the hoop.
6. Two players pass back and forth, making contact with the ball while off the ground.
7. Players are about 15 feet apart. Player B is seated. Player A attempts to pass to player B. A second method is for both players to stand. Player A passes to player B and then sits down quickly. Player B attempts to pass the ball back to player A, who catches it in the seated position.
8. Player A passes to player B and does a complete turnaround. Player B passes back to player A and also does a full turn. Other stunts can be used.
9. Player A is stationed near a basketball goal, with player B in the lane. Player A passes to player B in the lane; player B attempts a pass to the basket. Count 3 points for a basket, 2 points for a miss that hits the rim, and 1 point for hitting the backboard only. Any pass from player A that lands outside the center lane is void, and another chance is given.
10. Partners stand on opposite sides of a volleyball net. The object is to keep the ball in the air. The drill can be done by as many as six players.
11. One player stands on a chair in front of the net and holds a ball in such a fashion that spikers can knock the ball over the net. The next progression is to toss the ball about 2 feet above the net for spiking practice.
12. If the net is stretched properly, recovery can be practiced. One player throws the ball against the net, and the active player recovers with a forearm pass.

Partner Work (Serving and Passing)

1. Partners are about 20 feet apart. Partner A serves to partner B, who catches the ball and returns the serve to partner A.
2. Partner A serves to partner B, who makes a pass back to partner A. Switch so Partner B serves.
3. *Service One-Step.* Partners begin about 10 feet apart. Partner A serves to partner B, who returns the serve with partner A catching. If there is no error and if neither receiver moved the feet to catch, both players take one step back. This process is repeated each time no error or foot movement by the receivers occurs. If an error occurs or if appreciable foot movement is evident, the players revert to the original distance of 10 feet and start over.
4. A player stands at the top of the key on a basketball court. The object is to serve the ball into the basket. Scoring can be as in other basket-making drills: 3 points for a basket, 2 points for hitting the rim, and 1 point for hitting the backboard but not the rim. Partner retrieves the ball.

Group Work

1. A leader stands in front of not more than four other players, who are arranged in a semicircle. The leader tosses to each player in sequence around the circle and they return the ball. After a round or two, another player comes forward to replace the leader.
2. For blocking, six players are positioned alongside the net, each with a ball. The players take turns on the other side of the net, practicing blocking skills. Each spiker tosses the ball to himself for spiking. A defensive player moves along the line to block consecutively a total of six spikes. The next step is to have two players move along the line to practice blocking by pairs.
3. Setup and spiking can be practiced according to the drill shown in Figure 29.7. A back player tosses the ball to the setup player, who passes the ball properly

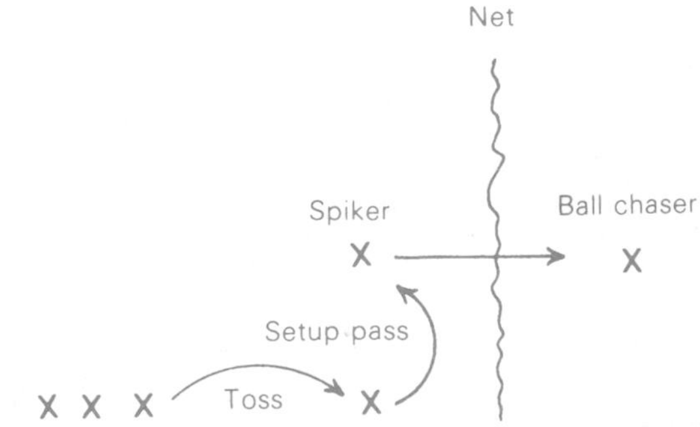

FIGURE 29.7 Setup and spiking drill.

for a spike. The entire group or just the spikers can rotate.

4. Two groups of children stand on opposite sides of a net. Eight to ten balls must be available to make this a worthwhile experience. Players serve from in back of the end line and recover balls coming from the other team. The action should be informal and continuous.

BASIC VOLLEYBALL RULES

Officially, six players make up a team, but any number from six to nine make a suitable team in the elementary school program.

To begin, captains toss a coin for the order of choices. The winner can choose to serve or to select a court. The opposing captain takes the option that the winner of the toss did not select. At the completion of a game, teams change courts, and the losing side serves.

To be in the proper position to serve, a player must have both feet behind the right one-third of the end line and must not step on the end line during the serve. The server covers the right back position. Only the serving team scores. The server retains the serve, scoring consecutive points, until that side loses a point and is put out. Members of each team take turns serving, the sequence being determined by the plan of rotation.

Official rules allow the server only one serve to get the ball completely over the net and into the opponent's court. Even if the ball touches the net (a net ball) and goes into the correct court, the serve is lost. The lines bounding the court are considered to be in bounds; that is, balls landing on the lines are counted as good. Any ball that touches or is touched by a player is considered to be in bounds, even if the player who touched the ball was clearly outside the boundaries at the time. The ball must be returned over the net by the third volley, which means that the team has a maximum of three volleys to make a good return.

The following major violations cause the loss of the point or serve:

1. Touching the net during play.
2. Not clearly batting the ball—sometimes called palming or carrying the ball.
3. Reaching over the net during play.
4. Stepping over the centerline. (Contact with the line is not a violation.)

A ball going into the net may be recovered and played, provided that no player touches the net. The first team to reach a score of 15 points wins the game if the team is at least 2 points ahead. If not, play continues until one team secures a 2-point lead. Only players in the front line may spike, but all players may block. No player may volley the ball twice in succession.

VOLLEYBALL ACTIVITIES

Developmental Level II

BEACH BALL VOLLEYBALL

Playing Area: Volleyball court

Players: Six to nine on each team

Supplies: A beach ball 12 to 16 inches in diameter

Skills: Most passing skills, modified serving

The players of each team are in two lines on their respective sides of the net. Serving is done, as in regulation volleyball, by the player on the right side of the back line. The distance is shortened, however, because serving a beach ball successfully from the normal volleyball serving distance is difficult. The player serves from the normal playing position on the court in the right back position. Scoring is as in regulation volleyball. Play continues until the ball touches the floor.

A team loses a point to the other team when it fails to return the ball over the net by the third volley or when it returns the ball over the net but the ball hits the floor out of bounds without being touched by the opposing team. The server continues serving as long as that team scores. Rotation is as in regulation volleyball.

TEACHING TIP

The server must be positioned as close to the net as possible while still remaining in the right back position on the court. Successful serving is an important component of an enjoyable game.

Variations:

1. In a simplified version of Beach Ball Volleyball, the ball is put into play by one player in the front line, who throws the ball into the air and then passes it over the net. Play continues until the ball touches the floor, but the ball may be volleyed any number of times before crossing the net. When either team has scored 5 points, the front and back lines of the respective teams change. When the score reaches 10 for the leading team, the lines change back. Game is 15.
2. Any player in the back line may catch the ball as it comes initially from the opposing team and may immediately make a little toss and pass the ball to a teammate. The player who catches the ball and bats it cannot send it across the net before a teammate has touched it.

INFORMAL VOLLEYBALL

Playing Area: Volleyball court, 6-foot net

Players: Six to eight on a team

Supplies: A trainer volleyball

Skills: Passing

This game is similar to regulation volleyball, but there is no serving. Each play begins with a student on one side tossing to herself and passing the ball high over the net. Points are scored for every play, as there is no "side out." As soon as a point is scored, the nearest player takes the ball and immediately puts it into play. Otherwise, basic volleyball rules govern the game. Rotation occurs as soon as a team has scored 5 points, with the front and back lines changing place. Action is fast, and the game moves rapidly, as every play scores a point for one team or the other.

SHOWER SERVICE BALL

Playing Area: Volleyball court

Players: 6 to 12 on each team

Supplies: Four to six trainer volleyballs

Skills: Serving, catching

A line parallel to the net is drawn through the middle of each court to define the serving area. Players are scattered in no particular formation (Figure 29.8). The game involves the skills of serving and catching. To start the game, two or three volleyballs are given to each team and are handled by players in the serving area.

Balls may be served at any time and in any order by a server, who must be in the back half of the court. Any ball served across the net is to be caught by any player near the ball. The person catching or retrieving a ball moves quickly to the serving area and serves. A point is scored for a team whenever a served ball hits the floor in the other court or is dropped by a receiver. Two scorers are needed, one for each side.

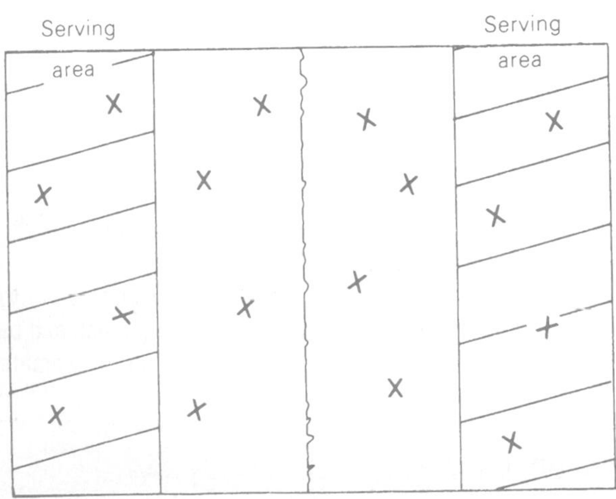

FIGURE 29.8 Formation for Shower Service Ball.

TEACHING TIP

As children improve, all serves should be made from behind the baseline.

Developmental Level III

PASS AND DIG

Playing Area: Playground or gymnasium

Players: Five to eight on each team

Supplies: A trainer volleyball for each team

Skills: Overhand, forearm, and dig passes

Each team forms a small circle of not more than eight players. The object of the game is to see which team can make the greater number of passes in a specified time or which team can keep the ball in the air for the greater number of consecutive passes without error.

On the signal "Go," the game is started with a volley by one of the players. The following rules are in force.

1. Balls are passed back and forth with no specific order of turns, except that the ball cannot be returned to the player from whom it came.
2. A player may not pass a ball twice in succession.
3. Any ball touching the ground does not count and ends the count.

TEACHING TIP

Players should be responsible for calling illegal returns on themselves and thus interrupting the consecutive pass count. The balls used should be of equal quality, so that one team cannot claim a disadvantage. Groups should count the passes out loud, so that their progress is known.

MINI-VOLLEYBALL

Playing Area: Gymnasium or badminton court

Players: Three on each team

Supplies: A volleyball or trainer volleyball

Skills: Most volleyball skills

Mini-Volleyball is a modified activity designed to offer opportunities for successful volleyball experiences to children between the ages of 9 and 12. The playing area is 15 feet wide and 40 feet long. Many gymnasiums are marked for badminton courts that are 20 by 44 feet with a spiking line 6.5 feet from the center. This is an acceptable substitute court.

The modified rules used in Mini-Volleyball are as follows.

1. A team consists of three players. Two substitutions may be made per game.
2. Players are positioned for the serve so that there are two front-line players and one back-line player. After the ball is served, the back-line player may not spike the ball from the attack area or hit the ball into the attack area unless the ball is below the height of the net.
3. The height of the net is 6 feet, 10 inches.
4. Players rotate positions when they receive the ball for serving. The right front-line player becomes the back-line player, and the left front-line player becomes the right front-line player.
5. A team wins a game when it scores 15 points and has a 2-point advantage over the opponent. A team wins the match when it wins two out of three games.

The back-line player cannot spike and thus serves a useful function by allowing the front players to receive the serves while moving to the net to set up for the spikers.

TEACHING TIP

This game can be modified to suit the needs of participants. Sponge training balls work well in the learning stages of Mini-Volleyball.

ROTATION MINI-VOLLEYBALL

Playing Area: Basketball or volleyball court

Players: Three on each team

Supplies: A volleyball or trainer volleyball

Skills: All volleyball skills

Three games, involving 18 active players, can be played at the same time crosswise, on a regular basketball court. The remaining children, organized in teams of three, wait on the sideline with teams designated in a particular order. Whenever a team is guilty of a "side out," it vacates its place on the floor and the next team in line moves in. Each team keeps its own running score. If, during a single side in, 10 points are scored against a team, that team vacates its place. Teams in this arrangement move from one court to another and play different opponents. The one or two extra players left over from team selection by threes can be substitutes and should be rotated into play on a regular basis.

REGULATION VOLLEYBALL

Playing Area: Volleyball court

Players: Six on each team

Supplies: A volleyball or trainer volleyball

Skills: All volleyball skills

Regulation volleyball should be played with one possible rule change: In early experiences, it is suggested that the server be allowed a second chance when failing to get the first attempt over the net and into play. This should apply only to the initial serve. Some instructors like to shorten the serving distance during the introductory phases of the game. It is important for the serving to be done well enough to keep the game moving.

A referee should supervise the game. There are generally three calls.

1. *"Side out."* The serving team fails to serve the ball successfully to the other court, fails to make a good return of a volley, or makes a rule violation.
2. *"Point."* The receiving team fails to make a legal return or is guilty of a rule violation.
3. *"Double foul."* Fouls are made by both teams on the same play, in which case the point is replayed. No score or side out results.

TEACHING TIP

There should be some emphasis on team play. Back court players should be encouraged to pass to front court players rather than merely batting the ball back and forth across the net.

Variation: The receiver in the back court is allowed to catch the serve, toss it, and propel it to a teammate. The catch should be limited to the serve, and the pass must go to a teammate, not over the net. This counteracts the problem of children in the back court being unable to handle the serve to keep the ball in play if the served ball is spinning, curving, or approaching with such force that it is difficult to control.

THREE-AND-OVER VOLLEYBALL

Playing Area: Volleyball court

Players: Six on each team

Supplies: A volleyball or trainer volleyball

Skills: All volleyball skills

The game Three and Over emphasizes the basic offensive strategy of volleyball. The game follows regular volleyball rules with the exception that the ball must be played three times before going over the net. The team loses the serve or the point if the ball is not played three times.

ROTATION VOLLEYBALL

Playing Area: Volleyball court

Players: Variable

Supplies: A volleyball or trainer volleyball

Skills: All volleyball skills

If four teams are playing in two contests at the same time, a system of rotation can be set up during any one class period. Divide the available class time roughly into three parts, less the time allotted for logistics. Each team plays the other three teams on a timed basis. At the end of a predetermined time period, whichever team is ahead wins the game. A team may win, lose, or tie during any time period, with the score determined at the end of the respective time period. The best win-loss record wins the overall contest.

FOUR-SQUARE VOLLEYBALL

Playing Area: Volleyball court

Players: Two to four on each team

Supplies: A volleyball or trainer volleyball

Skills: All volleyball skills

A second net is placed at right angles to the first net, dividing the playing area into four equal courts. The courts are numbered as in Figure 29.9. There are four teams playing, and an extra team can be waiting to rotate to court number 4. The object of the game is to force one of the teams to commit an error. Whenever a team makes an error, it moves down to court 4 or off the courts if a team is waiting. A team errs by not returning the ball to another court within the prescribed three volleys or by causing the ball to go out of bounds.

The ball is always put in play with a serve by a player from team number 1, the serve being made from any point behind the end line of that team. Players must rotate for each serve. The serve is made into court 3 or 4. Play proceeds as in regular volleyball, but the ball may be volleyed into any of the other three courts. No score is kept. The object of the game is for team 1 to retain its position.

TEACHING TIP

The game seems to work best with five or more teams. With four teams, the team occupying court 4 is not penalized for an error, because it is already in the lowest spot.

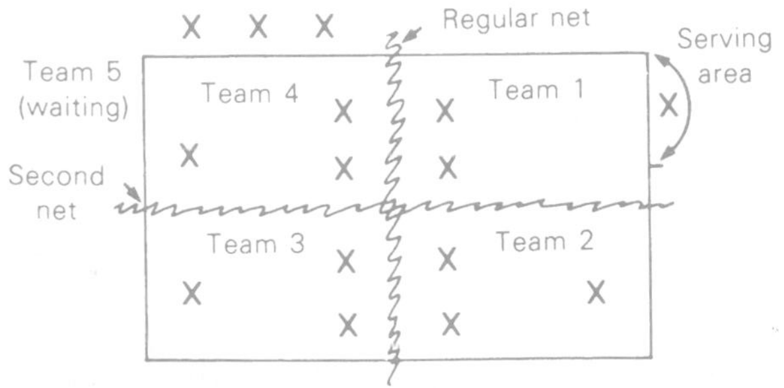

FIGURE 29.9 Four-square volleyball courts.

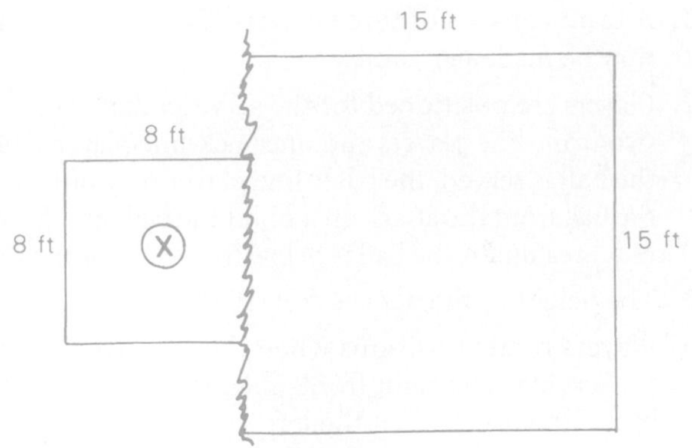

FIGURE 29.10 Court for Wheelchair Volleyball.

WHEELCHAIR VOLLEYBALL

Children in wheelchairs can participate successfully in some phases of volleyball. For example, a child confined to a wheelchair can compete against another student on a one-on-one basis when courts are laid out as illustrated in Figure 29.10. The difference in size of the playing areas equalizes the mobility factor. The net should be about 6 feet in height and a beach ball used. Serving by the able child is done from behind the back line and by the child in a wheelchair with the wheels on the back line. Rules should be adjusted as necessary.

VOLLEYBALL SKILL TESTS

Serving and volleying are the skills to be tested in volleyball. Serving is tested in two ways: (a) with a simple serve and (b) with an accuracy score.

Simplified Serving

In the simplified serving test, the child to be tested stands in normal serving position behind the end line on the right side and is given a specific number of trials in which to serve. The score is the number of successful serves out of ten trials. The serve must clear the net without touching and must land in the opponent's court. A ball touching a boundary line is counted as good.

Serving for Accuracy

To test serving for accuracy, a line is drawn parallel to the net through the middle of one of the courts. Each half is further subdivided into three equal areas by lines drawn parallel to the sidelines. This makes a total of six areas, which correspond to the positions of the members of a volleyball team. The areas are numbered from 1 to 6 (Figure 29.11).

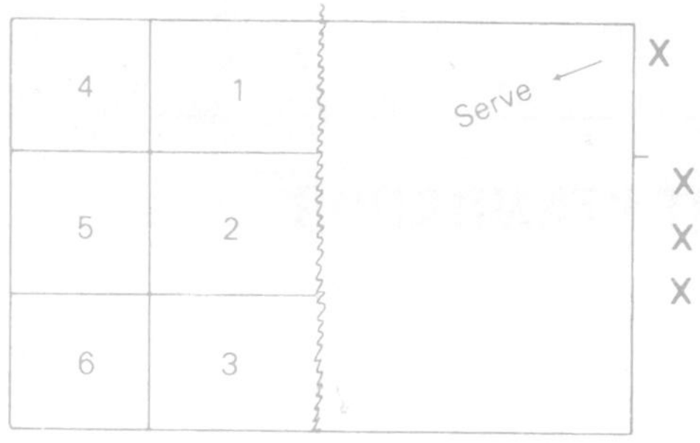

FIGURE 29.11 Layout for court for service testing.

Each child is allowed one attempt to serve the ball into each of the six areas in turn. Two points are scored for serving into the designated court area. One point is scored for missing the designated area but landing in an adjacent area. No points are scored otherwise.

Wall Volleying

For the wall volleying test, the player stands behind a restraining line 4 feet away from a wall. A line, representing the height of the net, is drawn on the wall parallel to the floor and 6.5 feet up. A player is allowed 30 seconds to make as many volleys as possible above the line while staying behind the restraining line. A counter is assigned to each testing station to count the successive volleys. To start, the child makes a short toss to self for the first volley. If time permits, more than one 30-second period can be allowed, with the best count being taken as the score. A mat can mark the restraining line. Stepping on top of the mat makes that volley illegal.

FOR MORE INFORMATION

References and Suggested Readings

American Volleyball Coaches Association, K. S. Asher (Ed.). (1997). *Coaching volleyball.* Indianapolis: Masters Press.

Kluka, D. A., & Dunn, P. J. (2000). *Volleyball.* 4th ed. Dubuque, IA: McGraw-Hill.

Mood, D. P., Musker, F. F., & Rink, J. E. (1991). *Sports and recreational activities for men and women.* 10th ed. St. Louis: Mosby.

Pellet, T. (1999). *Volleyball.* Scottsdale, AZ: Holcomb Hathaway Publishers.

Viera, B. L., & Ferguson, B. J. (1996). *Volleyball: Steps to success.* 2nd ed. Champaign, IL: Human Kinetics.

Wise, M. (1999). *Volleyball drills for champions.* Champaign, IL: Human Kinetics.

Websites

American Volleyball Coaches Association
www.avca.org

Links to national Volleyball Associations
http://dmoz.org/Sports/Volleyball/Organizations/UnitedStates/USAV/

Appendix

OUTCOMES AND THE NATIONAL CONTENT STANDARDS IN PHYSICAL EDUCATION

In 1992, the National Association for Sport and Physical Education (NASPE) took the first steps to address the question "What should Physical Education students know and be able to do?" when they published *Outcomes of Quality Physical Education Programs.* Three years later they followed up this document with *Moving into the Future: National Standards for Physical Education,* which was based upon the earlier Outcomes project. Together they provide physical educators with the guidelines for designing a well-rounded curriculum. This appendix includes a listing of the Outcomes of the physically educated person and the National Content Standards in Physical Education as developed by NASPE.

OUTCOMES OF THE PHYSICALLY EDUCATED PERSON

A Physically Educated Student:

HAS learned skills necessary to perform a variety of physical activities

1. . . . moves using concepts of body awareness, space awareness, effort, and relationships.
2. . . . demonstrates competence in a variety of manipulative, locomotor, and non-locomotor skills.
3. . . . demonstrates competence in combinations of manipulative, locomotor, and non-locomotor skills performed individually and with others.
4. . . . demonstrates competence in many different forms of physical activity.
5. . . . demonstrates proficiency in a few forms of physical activity.
6. . . . has learned how to learn new skills.

IS physically fit

7. . . . assesses, achieves, and maintains physical fitness.
8. . . . designs safe, personal fitness programs in accordance with principles of training and conditioning.

DOES participate regularly in physical activity

9. . . . participates in health-enhancing physical activity at least three times a week.
10. . . . selects and regularly participates in lifetime physical activities.

KNOWS the implications of, and the benefits from, involvement in physical activities

11. . . . identifies the benefits, costs, and obligations associated with regular participation in physical activity.
12. . . . recognizes the risk and safety factors associated with regular participation in physical activity.
13. . . . applies concepts and principles to the development of motor skills.
14. . . . understands that wellness involves more than being physically fit.
15. . . . knows the rules, strategies, and appropriate behaviors for selected physical activities.
16. . . . recognizes that participation in physical activity can lead to multi-cultural and international understanding.
17. . . . understands that physical activity provides the opportunity for enjoyment, self-expression, and communication.

VALUES physical activity and its contributions to a healthful lifestyle

18. . . . appreciates the relationships with others that result from participation in physical activity.
19. . . . respects the role that regular physical activity plays in the pursuit of life-long health and well-being.
20. . . . cherishes the feelings that result from regular participation in physical activity.

THE NATIONAL CONTENT STANDARDS FOR PHYSICAL EDUCATION

A Physically Educated Student:

1. Demonstrates competency in many movement forms and proficiency in a few movement forms.

2. Applies movement concepts and principles to the learning and development of motor skills.
3. Exhibits a physically active lifestyle.
4. Achieves and maintains a health-enhancing level of physical fitness.
5. Demonstrates responsible personal and social behavior in physical activity settings.
6. Demonstrates understanding and respect for differences among people in physical activity settings.
7. Understands that physical activity provides opportunities for enjoyment, challenge, self-expression, and social interaction.

Chapter One speaks of the importance of using content standards when developing a curriculum. The Content Standards identified in *DPE* represent a list developed after reviewing a number of standards documents, including the National Standards from NASPE. While the wording and the order of the standards vary some from the National Standards, the general intent is the same. The following chart indicates how the Content Standards for *DPE* correlate to the National Content Standards for Physical Education.

	Content Standards in DPE						
NASPE National Content Standards	**1**	**2**	**3**	**4**	**5**	**6**	**7**
1. Demonstrates competency in many movement forms and proficiency in a few movement forms.			✓				
2. Applies movement concepts and principles to the learning and development of motor skills.	✓						
3. Exhibits a physically active lifestyle.					✓		
4. Achieves and maintains a health-enhancing level of physical fitness.		✓					
5. Demonstrates responsible personal and social behavior in physical activity settings.							✓
6. Demonstrates understanding and respect for differences among people in physical activity settings.						✓	
7. Understands that physical activity provides opportunities for enjoyment, challenge, self-expression, and social interaction.				✓			

Correlation of Chapters in *Dynamic Physical Education for Elementary School Children* to the National Content Standards for Physical Education

	National Content Standards for Physical Education						
DPE Chapters	**1**	**2**	**3**	**4**	**5**	**6**	**7**
1 Elementary School Physical Education							
2 Teaching Children in the Physical Education Environment							
3 Planning for Quality Instruction			X			X	
4 Improving Instructional Effectiveness						X	X
5 Management and Discipline						X	X
6 Evaluation							
7 Children with Disabilities	X					X	
8 Curriculum Development							
9 Legal Liability, Supervision, and Safety							X
10 Facilities, Equipment, and Supplies							X
11 Interdisciplinary Instruction and Rainy Day Activities						X	
12 Physical Activity and Fitness		X	X	X	X		X
13 Wellness: Developing a Healthy Lifestyle		X		X	X		X
14 Movement Concepts and Themes	X		X		X		
15 Fundamental Motor Skills	X		X		X		
16 Introductory Activities: Applying Fundamental Motor Skills	X				X		
17 Manipulative Skills	X		X		X		
18 Body Management Skills	X				X		
19 Rhythmic Movement Skills	X				X	X	X
20 Gymnastic Skills	X		X		X	X	
21 Cooperative and Personal Challenge Skills	X		X		X	X	X
22 Game Skills	X		X		X	X	X
23 Basketball	X		X		X	X	X
24 Football	X		X		X	X	X
25 Hockey	X		X		X	X	X
26 Soccer	X		X		X	X	X
27 Softball	X		X		X	X	X
28 Track, Field, and Cross-Country Running	X		X		X	X	X
29 Volleyball	X		X		X	X	X

Photo Credits

Section 1

Section 1 opener: Bob Daemmrich/The Image Works; Chapter 1 opener: Bob Daemmrich/The Image Works; Chapter 2 opener: Bob Daemmrich/The Image Works.

Section 2

Section 2 opener: VCG/FPG International; Chapter 3 opener: Elizabeth Crews; Chapter 4 opener: James A. Sugar/Corbis; Chapter 5 opener: Myrleen Ferguson Cate/PhotoEdit; Chapter 6 opener: Will Faller; Chapter 7 opener: Bob Daemmrich/The Image Works.

Section 3

Section 3 opener: Mark Richards/PhotoEdit; Chapter 8 opener: Bob Daemmrich/The Image Works; Chapter 9 opener: David Young-Wolff; Chapter 10 opener: Syracuse Newspapers/Dick Blume/The Image Works; Chapter 11 opener: Bob Daemmrich/The Image Works.

Section 4

Section 4 opener: Ron Chapple/FPG International; Chapter 12 opener: Michael Newman/PhotoEdit; Chapter 13 opener: Stone/Mary Kate Denny.

Section 5

Section 5 opener: Bob Daemmrich/The Image Works; Chapter 14 opener: Bob Daemmrich/The Image Works; Chapter 15 opener: Bob Daemmrich/Stock, Boston; Chapter 16 opener: Bob Daemmrich/The Image Works; Chapter 17 opener: Elizabeth Crews.

Section 6

Section 6 opener: Bob Daemmrich/Stock, Boston; Chapter 18 opener: Bob Daemmrich/The Image Works; Chapter 19 opener: Bob Daemmrich/The Image Works; Chapter 20 opener: Frank Pedrick/The Image Works; Chapter 21 opener: Michelle D. Bridwell/PhotoEdit; Chapter 22 opener: Bob Daemmrich/Stock, Boston.

Section 7

Section 7 opener: Bob Daemmrich/Stock, Boston; Chapter 23 opener: Jeff Kaufman/FPG International; Chapter 24 opener: Ron Chapple/FPG International; Chapter 25 opener: Jim Pickerell/The Image Works; Chapter 26 opener: Nancy Richmond/The Image Works; Chapter 27 opener: David Young-Wolff; Chapter 28 opener: Bob Daemmrich/The Image Works; Chapter 29 opener: Stone/Peter Cade.

General Index

C

J

K

L

T

Activities Index

Gymnastic Activities

Introductory Activities (Applying Fundamental Motor Skills)

Jumping Activities

Personal Challenge Activities

Relays

Rhythmic Activities (Movements)